THE QUEST FOR IDENTITIES

Also by Sabry Hafez at Saqi

The Genesis of Arabic Narrative Discourse: A Study in the Sociology of Modern Arabic Literature

A Reader of Modern Arabic Short Stories (with Catherine Cobham)

Sabry Hafez

THE QUEST FOR IDENTITIES

The Development of the Modern Arabic Short Story

SAQI
London San Francisco Beirut

For Bryony

ISBN: 978–0–86356–363–8

This first edition published by Saqi Books

A full CIP record for this book is available from the British Library.
A full CIP record for this book is available from the Library of Congress.

Manufactured in Lebanon

SAQI

26 Westbourne Grove, London W2 5RH
825 Page Street, Suite 203, Berkeley, California 94710
Tabet Building, Mneimneh Street, Hamra, Beirut
www.saqibooks.com

Contents

A Note on Transliteration

The standard system of transliteration is adopted throughout, albeit with minor modifications. The aim is to produce simple, recognisable and easily pronounced forms of Arabic names and words that can be traced to the original form. Therefore the initial *hamza* is not marked, neither are the final vowels except long vowels and when the word may be misread without the marking, or when it could be easily confused with another word. Because of the occurrence of some colloquial words, both *i* and *y* are used interchangeably for the Arabic letter *yā'*, *i* being generally used in connection with colloquial words or when the sound of the word is of some significance. The final *tā' marbūṭah* is marked as *h* except in an *iḍāfah* construction where it naturally appears as *t*. The final *alif maqṣūrah* is also marked and fully transliterated as *ā*. However, for ease of reading and rendering any Arabic word or name back to its original form, the diacritical marks are fully used in every occurrence. Full references with diacritical marks are also given in the notes and in the bibliography. When Arabic words, whether special terms or titles of works appear in the text, they are fully transliterated and translated in the first instance, but are subsequently used only in their transliterated form.

Foreword

My aim in writing this book is to study the development and different mutations of the modern Arabic short story, and through it Arabic narrative discourse. The genesis of narrative genres in modern Arabic literature is covered in *The Genesis of Arabic Narrative Discourse: A Study in the Sociology of Modern Arabic Literature.*[1] Here, by contrast, the short story is posited as a major literary genre in modern Arabic literature, a narrative genre that played a vital role in changing canons of taste and shaping a new literary sensibility of Arabic culture. The short story is a popular and respectable genre in Arabic literature, through which many an outstanding writer has attained fame and eminence.[2] In the period covered by this study it is rare that a major writer, no matter in any genre has ended his or her literary career without publishing some short stories, even collections of short stories.[3] As argued in *The Genesis*, this was the only literary medium with roots in the Arabic tradition and that could make use of the vast opportunities opened up by the advent of the press and the rapid growth of a new reading public. Although short narrative forms – fabliaux, sketches, yarns, tales, anecdotes, exempla, parables, fables, and so on – have been prominent oral or written genres for centuries,[4] around the turn of the twentieth century the expansion of the reading public gave real impetus to their written replacement in the form of the short story. The new reading public that emerged as a result of radical changes in the educational system, expanding journalism, growing urbanisation and rising national awareness made increasing demands on the literary establishment; yet it had not developed regular reading habits and hence preferred the short story to the novel. Some have even argued that 'short stories can help create an audience, or a larger audience, for novels'.[5]

This situation, elaborated in *The Genesis,* continued to develop, widening the base of the Arab reading public and enhancing the demand for narrative discourse in general and the short story in particular. Another reason for the popularity of the short story was, perhaps, the singularity of its effect, its unity of impression and the fact it was well suited to the conditions and needs of readers emerging from the canons of oral reception: the short story appealed to a restless audience brought up on the theatricality and collectivity of the oral tradition, and especially to the Arab reader whose socially crowded life – a crowdedness that continued to increase during the period covered here – only allowed for short periods of solitude, and whose strict social controls led to an appreciation of the genre's biting criticism. This last feature became increasingly urgent and widely relevant with the decline of free expression and the erosion of liberties, both social and political, in the post-independence Arab world.

This book investigates a number of questions related to the development of the short story, explaining why it followed certain trajectories, the significance of the roads taken or not taken; and what determined its path. How much of its development was intrinsic, related to the inner textual and structural development of the genre, and how much was extrinsic, a product of the context and its socio-cultural forces? How did the impact of decisions taken by writers in one Arab country influence those in other countries? What accounts for the importance of the short story in modern Arabic literature? Is there something inherent in the genre, or in its implied philosophy, that accounts for its wide appeal to both writers and readers of that culture? Can a study of this genre provide us with wider insights into the culture as a whole, or even into the society from which it emerged? Can it provide an insight into the genre as history, or even as ideology, secretly at work in the grain and texture of literary language? These are some of the issues explored here, not merely on the theoretical plain, though some abstract postulations are inevitable, but mainly through detailed investigation and close reading of a large number of authors and texts.

While this book is autonomous, with its own set of hypotheses, it is a sequel to my previous book, *The Genesis*; it has strong links with the themes and assumptions of that first book, and continues the story of Arabic narrative discourse from where its predecessor left off. *The Genesis* ended with the maturation of the short story in 1930; here I examine the development of the genre in the following four decades, from 1930 to 1970. The latter date was selected as a cut-off point because of its historical and literary significance; the succeeding decades constitute a different stage in the development of the genre and in the transformation of the country under study (Egypt), which may be taken up in a third part of this series. Apart from this transparent connection, there is a deeper theoretical link between the present book and its predecessor. Historical perspective in the study of literature makes the investigation of trajectories, maps and development a quintessential part of the genesis; for any genesis that does not lead to rich developments is not worthy of its name. This is particularly relevant to literary genres, which 'may be regarded as institutional imperatives which both coerce and are in turn coerced by the writer'.[6] The institutional imperatives and their coercive dynamics account for the vitality of the genre and its individuality and growth. This makes the development of the genre the necessary proof of its formation or genesis, and the process through which it validates its generic existence. As Wellek and Warren convincingly argue,

> genres should be conceived as a grouping of literary works based, theoretically, upon both outer form (specific meter or structure) and also upon inner form (attitude, tone, purpose – more crudely subject and audience).[7]

If *The Genesis* studied the dynamics of shaping the 'outer form' of narrative discourse in modern Arabic literature, this book, in exploring its development and trajectories, elucidates the genre's 'inner form'.

Ostensibly, this book constitutes a clear departure from the sociology of literature approach of its predecessor, devoting most of its pages to practical criticism and textual analysis and paying little attention to the process of cultural transformation. Its prime concern is to map the texts and develop a schematic configuration that enables the student to navigate his or her way through a rich body of literary texts and appreciate their aesthetic attainments. But despite this apparent difference, there is much in common between the theoretical approaches and implied assumptions of the two books. Though acutely aware of the structuralist legacy of textual analysis, and benefiting from some of their achievements, I have opted for a return to the historical method of literary study, a return to first texts and first questions, as Stephen Greenblatt put it. This is akin to the method of the new historicism, which adopts

> a type of historical inquiry that is simultaneously dialectical (in stressing the interaction of systems of representation

> and practice) and nontotalising (refusing the notion that any given historical field of representation can be made to cohere as some hierarchically stratified totality).[8]

This inquiry provides a satisfactory account of contradictions, distinguishing various discursive practices – even within the realm on the textual – without overlooking the fact that they are dynamically interconnected. This is particularly important in the development and trajectory of the Arabic short story, whose distinct discursive practices are dialectically interconnected. They feed one another and are mutually constitutive, each inflecting the other in a dialectical circularity of text and context, the literary and the social.

Building on the work of Raymond Williams and Lucien Goldmann, Stephen Greenblatt suggests that:

> The work of art is the product of a negotiation between a creator or class of creators, equipped with a complex, communally shared repertoire of conventions and the institutions and practices of society. In order to achieve the negotiation, artists need to create a currency that is valid for a meaningful, mutually profitable exchange. It is important to emphasize that the process involves not simply appropriation, but exchange, since the existence of art always implies a return, a return normally measured in pleasure and interest.[9]

The investigation of this return, its causation, trajectories, scope, transactions and manifestations are the main concern of this book, since this complex process charts the development of narrative genres, a process that is both literary and socio-cultural. Since this study considers a purely textualist position to be somewhat myopic, it roots its investigation in the wider world, believing, with Edward Said, in the worldliness of texts. Said's theory in this respect, inspired by Ibn Hazm and the Zahirites, deals with

> text as significant form, in which worldliness, circumstantiality, the text's status as an event having sensuous particularity as well as historical contingency, are considered as being incorporated in the text, an infrangible part of its capacity for conveying and producing meaning. This means that a text has a specific situation, placing

> restraints upon the interpreter and his interpretation not because the situation is hidden within the text as a mystery, but rather because the situation exists at the same level of surface particularity as the textual object itself.[10]

This study's awareness of the complex position of texts in the world, and that 'the closeness of the world's body to the text's body forces readers to take both of them into consideration',[11] led to the need to draw a map of the world in which these texts exist. This is the main rationale of Chapter One, which will inevitably guide the reading and the interpretation of both the texts studied and their interpretation, and at the same time root this book in the sociology of literature of *The Genesis.*

Like *The Genesis*, this book is primarily interested in Arabic narrative discourse in general and the genre of the short story in particular. The focus on the short story is motivated by a number of factors. First, it has been neglected as a genre, particularly in Western scholarship on Arabic literature.[12] The body of critical work on the Arabic novel, in English and other European languages, has been growing steadily and has been the subject of numerous books;[13] but not that of the short story. The irony is that the genre, which has brilliantly salvaged the marginalised and neglected, has become the victim of its own success and so failed to attract attention to itself. This irony as well as the neglect of the short story seems to be a widely recognised phenomenon. A recent book on the short story, *The Art of the Short Story*, starts thus: 'the short story is probably the most popular literary form among readers, but, strangely, it remains the least discussed among literary critics. This paradox typifies the odd but fascinating history of the form.'[14] The fact that such neglect is much wider than its Arabic dimension lends this study broader relevance and lends validity to the attempt to do justice to a popular and important literary genre.

Second, the widespread practice of short-story writing among most serious writers of Arabic fiction[15] enables the genre to represent the wider cultural and literary scene and present a telling picture of its developments and transformations. Writers from different social backgrounds and even opposite intellectual orientations have produced works in this genre, widening its scope and appeal and incorporating into its fabric an enriching diversity. Further, the sheer number of stories (several thousand in the period studied) has enabled the genre to encompass the different trajectories and various changes of Arabic narrative discourse, and provides the reader with a clear understanding of their cause and effect. The stories cover the major preoccupations of Arabic culture and this makes it, more than any other genre, its literary thermometer. The study of the short story thus offers an answer to the central question of how narrative genres developed in modern Arabic literature, which can be easily applicable to other literary genres. The investigation of the development of the short story sheds some light on the changes of cultural and literary sensibilities that developed coincidentally and often interactively with them. It is well established that 'the materials and their organization in a short story differ from those in a novel in degree and not in kind',[16] and also that 'literary genres are to be understood not as *genera* (classes) in the logical sense, but rather as groups of historical families'.[17] Moreover, the typology offered in this study, though intrinsic to the short story as a genre, may be applicable to other genres. This is so because the short story has been the testing ground for many of the novelists, novella writers and dramatists in the Arab world, whose early works owe a great deal to the technical and stylistic solutions developed and skills mastered during their experimentation with the short story. Furthermore, the poetic nature of the genre makes its development relevant to certain aspects of poetic discourse, particularly poetic drama and lyrical poetry.

Third, among all narrative forms in Arabic, the short story was the first to appear and more importantly, the first to reach maturity. By 1929 there were excellent examples of mature work in the genre, while in other literary genres, works of such maturity and sophistication did not appear for years, or even decades, after this date. This early beginning continued to provide the genre with an edge on other narrative and dramatic genres, for it also ventured into uncharted territories long before any of the other genres attempted to explore them, thus providing the reader with the most detailed and up-to-date map of literary configurations.

It furnishes one, not only with the main roads and approaches that flourished and became widespread and trans-generic, but also with an elaborate web of cul-de-sacs, avoided by other genres, after the short story proved their irrelevance and futility. In addition, its short production cycle, taking only weeks from inception to writing, publication and reading, provides it with the ability to record new textual or structural experimentation and innovation, even short-lived ones, more than any other genre. This also empowers the genre to take risks, whether artistic, social or political, such as the violation of social taboos or censorship codes, hence *inscribing* in its text more than its own theme and technique. The findings and main schematic organisation of a study of the short story can also be applied to the other major narrative genre, the novel. Most of the writers discussed here, with one or two exceptions, also wrote novels, and some, like Idrīs and Qāsim, wrote plays too.

Unlike the *The Genesis*, which investigated narrative discourse across the whole of the Arab world in the nineteenth century and the early decades of the twentieth century, this book focuses its study on one country, Egypt. This shift is necessitated by a radical change in the field of narrative production, which in turn imposed its own limitations. In the half-century covered in *The Genesis*, the production of narrative work was limited statistically and geographically. The short stories published in this period amounted to no more than a few hundred, and they all came from a small number of Arab countries that formed the centre of Arabic cultural activity. These were Egypt, which played the major role in this respect, the countries of the Levant (Lebanon, Palestine and Syria) and Iraq. The role of other Arab countries at the time was negligible, often non-existent, and could easily be overlooked. By contrast, in the period covered in this book, thousands of short stories were produced, from almost every Arab country. To study the entire area in such a way as to provide a useful typology and trace the development of the genre would require several volumes. The enlargement of the field offered only three possibilities for any serious coverage: to reduce the time of the study, to extend the time scale, or to restrict the geographical scope. In the former, the result would have been distorted by the unjustifiable time limits. The second option, to extend the time limit and make a selective study in terms of texts and writers, would have sacrificed comprehensiveness, enfeebling the validity and relevance of the findings.

I therefore decided to limit the geography but not the time covered, and to cover the genre comprehensively in one country, Egypt, the most productive and most outstanding within the wider Arab scene. This choice was not predicated on the fact that, as Erich Auerbach suggested, although the critic's home is the wider culture of all humanity transcending national boundaries, his 'most priceless and indispensable part is his own nation's culture' – I consider the culture of the whole of the Arab world to be my own culture, but

Egypt alone provides a rich enough field for a major study, capable of supplying a complex map of the genre's development. And the map that emerges from this focus is unequal in its detail and scale, and could not have been made by selecting any other country, or even a group of countries. In drawing this map, I hope to achieve a balance between comprehensiveness and in-depth analysis of texts and authors, for without detailed textual analysis the map becomes faceless cartography without colour or soul.

Behind the authors selected for this in-depth analysis, there are other authors, whose work is enumerated and appraised, but who did not receive detailed investigation. This is not because their work does not merit such investigation, but because such a study would not add any further thematic or structural attributes to those already identified. Although I have tried to approach the output of the genre in Egypt comprehensively, mentioning every significant writer, I have also attempted to place the major writers from other Arab countries alongside them, discovering that, with the exception of a one or two writers,[18] who would have merited a focused study alongside those selected here, the contribution of the rest of the most active countries in the genre fitted comfortably within this scheme.

The selection of the short story to illustrate the development of narrative discourse emerged from a long fascination with the genre as an art form – its supreme simplicity, its poetic power, its capacity to portray the innermost depths of the human soul in the most compact manner. This fascination has continued unabated to the present day. Having published a few short stories at the beginning of my literary career, I continue to follow the genre and write about its achievements, including the work of the newest generation of writers in the Arab world.

The cut-off date was dictated by the thesis of this book. The work produced in the last thirty years mostly falls within the boundaries of the last phase of the genre's development, the modernist one. To continue the study to the present would have been to divert it from its main thesis and dilute its findings.

An extension of the time span of the study could only have been achieved at the expense of in-depth analysis of the major writers of the genre, a reduction in the number of writers covered or overlooking major trends in the genre's development. Indeed, the last three decades may require a book of their own, with a different thesis altogether, investigating the cultural rupture in the genre rather than the natural development from the period of genesis and early maturation. Furthermore, the focus on the decades 1930 to 1970 has enabled the development of an ancillary thesis on the interaction between the ideology or philosophy of the form and the socio-cultural reality from which it emanated. This ancillary thesis is deeply grounded in the methodological assumptions of the book, namely that texts are enmeshed in the world from which they emanate. In this respect, the study shares Said's assumption that:

> any occasion involving the aesthetic or literary document and experience, on the one hand and the critic's role and his or her worldliness on the other, cannot be a simple one. ... Once the text goes into more than one copy, the author's work is in the world and beyond authorial control. ... It is not only that any text, if it is immediately not destroyed, is a network of often colliding forces, but also that in its actually being a text is a being in the world.[19]

And as such being, the text, or in a wider perspective the genre, interacts with its readers, with the issues and concerns of that particular world.

The Introduction, 'The Solitary Literary Genre and the Quest for Identities', lays the theoretical foundation for this ancillary thesis and at the same time provides the rationale for its relevance, appeal and popularity. Its treatment of the genre as a kind of formal or generic representation of a state of being or a socio-cultural condition sheds light on why the genre is more popular in some countries than others, and at certain historical moments more than others. If narrative discourse in general translates knowing into telling, the genre in which this discourse is expressed fashions human experience into a form that structures its meaning and gives it a generalised human dimension. The Introduction also makes this book's contribution to the study of the content of form; by opening it to a wider investigation of the content of genre, and particularly its relationship to that of its counter narrative genre, the novel. Thanks to Benedict Anderson, the novel has long been credited with a vital role in the shaping of the 'imagined community',[20] but the role of the short story in articulating other aspects of this 'imagined community' has not been sufficiently studied. The short story's close links to the process of individuation and the articulation of the fragmentary nature of this community and its marginalised voices, suppressed identities and the unsaid is made clear in this chapter. Unlike the novel, with its elaboration of the 'imagined community', the short story is concerned with another imaginary, that of the individual and his or her perception of their multiple identities that in turn influence the 'imagined community'. The Introduction provides the investigation with a theoretical backbone that lends the study wider relevance, beyond the specific case of Arabic literature.

Because culture and society are systems of interlocking representations, the historical and textual mapping of the vast body of work published in this genre[21] requires a wide knowledge of the social, cultural and political background of the period. This is the main aim of Chapter One, 'The Rhythms of Change and Anxiety', which fuses a historical account of the major events of the period with cultural and economic history and delineates the context in which writers worked. It also outlines the main issues that dominated the period, and the various ideologies, discourses and political ideas with which they grappled and which in turn shaped the context in which readers received their work. The chapter elaborates the dialectical interaction between politics, economics and culture in this period and demonstrates how the former influenced the latter and left their indelible marks. This chapter also deals with the important role of literary reviews and journals, book series devoted to narrative fiction, and publishers in the shaping of various trends. These different organs were responsible for the publication of over a thousand short stories, a sizable portion of the total output of the genre in this period. The mapping of this context emerges from a firm belief in the 'worldliness' of the text and the genre, in which the author shares Said's acceptance of Riffaterre's circumstantial fallacy.

Most critics will subscribe to the notion that every literary text is in someway burdened with its occasion, with the plain empirical reality from which it emerged. Pressed too far, such a notion earns the justified criticism of a stylistician like Michael Riffaterre, who in 'The Self Sufficient Text', calls any reduction of a text to its circumstances a fallacy, biographical, genetic, psychological or analogic.[22] Most critics would probably go along with Riffaterre in saying, yes, let us make sure the text does not disappear under the weight of these fallacies.[23]

The study shares Said's criticism of Riffaterre's concept of the 'self-sufficient text', since the idea of a hermitic textual cosmos, whose meaning is, as Riffaterre says, a wholly inward or intellectual one, is in my view another fallacy. Cutting off the literary language from the everyday worldly language overlooks some fundamental aspects of language itself, as well as the various forces at work in the process of writing, reading, interpreting the text and generating its meanings. It is vital

> to deal with a text as significant form in which worldliness, circumstantiality, the text's status as event having sensuous particularity as well as historical contingency, are considered as being incorporated in the text, an infrangible part of its capacity for conveying and producing meaning.[24]

This position is a key thesis in Chapter One, whose leading argument is the formulation of the cultural context – in Raymond Williams's terms – as a 'constitutive human process' inseparable from the totality of social material life. This context embodies not only the issues but also the contradictions through which they have been shaped and emerged. In other words, it sketches what Pierre Bourdieu calls 'the cultural field of production', a field whose picture can only be gleaned in its totality at the end of the book. This is because the context, as new historicism convincingly argued, is 'con' (with) + text, so without the full text in the following chapters, the 'cultural field' cannot be clearly comprehended. Hence this chapter is only the first step in drawing the complex cultural configuration to which the writers studied in the following chapters belonged. For belonging here embodies what constitutes identity and deference. It identifies what Greenblatt calls 'the communally shared repertoire of conventions and the institutions and practices of society' necessary for mapping the different types of negotiations achieved by the writers in the following three chapters.[25]

Chapter Two, 'The Realistic Short Story', is the longest in the book and covers a large body of work, nearly 1,500 stories. It starts with an introductory discussion of classification and the reading public. The former discusses issues of methodological demarcation and the use of critical terminology with Western cultural affiliations in a different culture and distinct literary context. The latter deals with the coexistence of artistic sensibilities and their impact on the perception of the reading public. Unlike the period covered by *The Genesis*, in which the reading public is discussed in general terms, this period is marked by the coexistence of various 'reading publics' demanding different types of stories. The chapter then moves on to investigate the meaning of realism in the modern Arabic short story, emphasising the process of mediation through which the term is subjected when travelling from one culture to another and from one genre to another. Realism for this purpose is neither a period concept not a literary movement, but rather an artistic approach to reality, complex and dynamic, requiring in turn a similar dynamic approach to express its diversity.

The rest of this chapter can be conceived as a cluster of mini chapters, each devoted to the work of a single writer, together forming the vast canvas that makes up this field. The first deals with Maḥmūd Taymūr, whose early and pioneering work was studied in *The Genesis*. Taymūr played a significant role in providing the genre with continuity, constancy, respectability and relevance to the major literary concerns of the day. The dozens of collections studied in this mini chapter, though revisiting the themes and techniques of his earlier collections, solidified his contribution to the genre and established him as one of its most formidable, yet underrated, writers. The second mini chapter deals with one of the greatest writers of this genre, Yaḥyā Ḥaqqī. With Yūsuf Idrīs, Ḥaqqī is the undisputed master of the short story in the Arabic language. His work takes the genre to uncharted territories of complex experience, fine artistic achievement, and rich experimentation in form and technique. This section studies the nature of his narrative and the diverse worlds of experiences he covered as well as his lasting contribution to the development of the genre. The third writer reviewed is Maḥmūd al-Badawī, who is often overlooked or even ignored, despite his great significance as a major short story writer, who has devoted his productive literary career almost solely to this genre, publishing more than a dozen short story collections, some of which reveal unequalled beauty and richness. His narrative world is marked by its sensitive treatment of social polarisation, the physicality of human endurance and the taboo subject of sexuality. His austere style, economic language and direct but poetic description take the genre to new heights of artistic dexterity.

The fourth writer studied in this chapter is Yūsuf Idrīs, the undisputed master of the genre whose meteoric rise to fame (he published five collections before the age of thirty) and charismatic narrative eclipsed two generations of short story writers. Idrīs's wide appeal is the result of his towering talent and mesmerising style of narrative, whose originality is matched by a high degree of poeticality and richness. It is also thanks to his ability to move with great ease between different strata of society, to fathom the inner psyche of his characters, articulate the different agendas of the oppressed and change style and technique to respond to the changing sensibility of the time.

The fifth writer explored here, Muḥammad Shukri 'Ayyād, is the most talented of the generation active before Idrīs's arrival on the scene. 'Ayyād's short stories present some of the genre's most potent explorations of the human psyche, and some of its most biting social criticism – something to be expected from a writer who began his career as a translator of Dostoevsky.

The chapter ends with a study of the work of Abū'l-Ma'āṭī Abū'l-Najā, who represents the closure and almost a culmination of this type of narrative. Abū'l-Najā belongs to the generation known on the Egyptian literary scene as the lost generation, whose work was eclipsed by the charismatic talent of Idrīs and overshadowed by it. His emergence as a major writer marked the triumph of the genre over traditional education: his education was completely Azharite from start to finish. Despite the difficult situation in which the writers of this generation found themselves, Abū'l-Najā distinguished himself by devoting many his stories to the emergence of a new hero, the group. This new hero, together with a sensitive treatment of narrative structure and his considerable attention to the delicate balance between the various elements of narrative, provide the treatment of the conflict between the individual and the group with depth and insight.

Chapter Three, 'Romanticism and the Short Story', begins with a discussion of the complex term 'romanticism' and examines its history, transformation, tenets, and usefulness for the study of the Arabic short story. It traces the long process by which the term was mediated into Arabic and examines some of its salient features and contradictions, pointing out its impact on the style, characterisation, technique and structure of the short story. The second part of the chapter, 'The Shaping and Development of Romantic Sensibility', distinguishes between three categories of romanticism in Arabic literature. The first is a serious literary endeavour to develop romantic sensibility in Arabic literature with its own world and distinguishing features. The second is the more popular and commercial strand, concerned with the popularisation of the genre amongst a wider public, and usually verging on sentimentality; and the third is socialist romanticism, mistakenly known as socialist realism. The chapter goes on to study the work of the first category of romanticism, starting with the work of Maḥmūd Taymūr: the fact that this features both in the previous chapter and again here is a clear indication of the coexistence of the two types of literary sensibility, not only in the period under study but also in the work of a number of the genre's major writers. This is followed by a study of the work of Muḥammad Amīn Ḥassūnah, who was one of the signatories of the important 1930 literary manifesto calling for the establishment of national literature. The emergence of romanticism in Arabic literature was strongly linked to this call for developing national literature, as the work of Ḥassūnah demonstrates. This section culminates in the study of the work of Sa'd Makkāwī, the most accomplished of the writers of this category. Makkāwī's contribution to the genre is remarkable, for it brings the romantic sensibility to its peak and enriches its world by highly memorable stories, beautifully written and dexterously structured.

The third part of this chapter, 'Sentimentality and the Popularisation of the Genre', deals with the second category of romanticism, situating it in its social and cultural context. It opens with a study of the work of Maḥmūd Kāmil whose monthly *al-Jāmi'ah* popularised sentimental romanticism and rooted its conventions in the literary scene. Kāmil's world of middle- and upper-class characters, free of social problems and concerned only with their emotional and moral concerns, appealed to the ever growing middle class and poorly educated reading public. His main theme of lyrical love, strongly associated with sweet dreams and refined thoughts, was equally appealing to them, providing a world made up of their desire for unattainable love and happiness. His lighthearted stories placed few demands on his readers and were thus more popular than his more serious work. He had a significant following amongst writers of his and the succeeding generation, some of whom were very influential on the literary scene, such as Yūsuf al-Sibā'ī, Jādhibiyyah Ṣidqī, and Ibrāhīm al-Wirdānī, and, to a certain extent, Iḥsān 'Abd al-Quddūs.

The last part of the chapter, 'Socialist Realism or Socialist Romanticism?', deals with the third category of romanticism. It begins by examining how the various tenets of socialist realism were introduced into Arabic literature and how they were understood, adapted or mediated into already existing sets of concepts. Then it proceeds to clarify some misconceptions of the term, with its specific applications in Arabic literature, and suggests instead the alternative, socialist romanticism. In order to provide this clarification with a valid example in Arabic, it studies the work of two major writers, 'Abd al-Raḥmān al-Sharqāwī and Muḥammad Ṣidqī, showing how their work reflects strong Romantic features.

Chapter Four, 'Experimentation and Modern Sensibility', charts the dynamics of the changes in literary sensibility and the evolution of modernist narrative. The new literary sensibility, which was heralded by Nadīm at the turn of the twentieth century and was responsible for the genesis of a new narrative discourse that evolved through to the mid-twentieth century, underwent substantial changes. The early phases of these changes, its agenda, and the context in which it emerged and manifested its embryonic features are the subject of the first part of the chapter, 'The Schism in Artistic Sensibility'. This is followed by the study of the work of the pioneers of change in narrative fiction, namely Bishr Fāris, 'Ādil Kāmil and Fatḥī Ghānim. These writers expressed the schism in their work and experimented with new modernist textual strategies, paving the ground for 'The Shaping of Modern Sensibility', which is the subject of the following section of this chapter. Interestingly, the two writers responsible for this stage in the development of modern sensibility are two Copts, Yūsuf al-Shārūnī and Idwār al-Kharrāṭ. This is not a mere coincidence, since the decentred self often experiences change more acutely than, and detects it before, others. This section offers a detailed analysis of their work, showing how changes in literary sensibility pervaded every aspect of their texts, from the nature of the experience tackled to characterisation, narrative conventions, literary language and structure.

The third and last part of the chapter, 'The Triumph of Modern Sensibility', demonstrates the myriad manifestations of modernism in the genre. It starts by locating the triumph of modern sensibility in its cultural and political context, and shows how this triumph influenced the work of well-established writers of realistic sensibility such as Najīb Maḥfūẓ and Yūsuf Idrīs. Then it selects eight writers – Sulaymān Fayyāḍ, Muḥammad Ḥāfiẓ Rajab, Bahā' Ṭāhir, 'Abd al-Ḥakīm Qāsim, Ibrāhīm Aṣlān, Muḥammad al-Bisāṭī, Yaḥyā al-Ṭāhir

'Abd Allah and Jamāl al-Ghīṭānī – and demonstrates the unique contribution of each of them to the genre. They mostly belong to the 1960s generation, and the collective nature of their endeavour lends the triumph of modern sensibility wider relevance. Their early work opened new venues of varied textual approaches and provided the short story with fresh impetus and a new lease of life. Fayyāḍ's fascination with the invincible power of destruction and violence and man's vulnerability vis-à-vis their tyranny provided his narrative with physical vigour and freshness. His lonely, fragile characters seem to be indomitable despite the absolute power of their enemies. Rajab took the genre to the uncharted world of fantasy and surrealism in which the old principles of causality, verisimilitude and symbolic relations start to crumble, thus opening the gates to the nightmarish private hell in which his characters reside. He created a complex purgatory in which taboo relationships often end in patricide or self-destruction. While Ṭāhir's world ostensibly appears as the opposite, his characters are never sure of their innocence or guilt. Under his apt, direct description the false appearance of solidity and cohesion vanishes, and in their place a Kafkaesque new world emerges.

Qāsim developed the fascinating technique of concentric circles resulting from one single event, like throwing a stone in a pool of water, in an episodic structure, which enriches the cognitive process of comprehension. This is in clear contrast to, but subtly complemented by, the narrative approach of Aṣlān's poetic world in which nothing significant happens on the surface. He creates a world of inaction, a world that runs in neutral; yet beneath this ostensible stagnation of the familiar, even hackneyed, reality a rich world of tension and radical human vicissitude is created. Al-Bisati's work's fluctuation between realistic and modernist sensibilities conventionalises the modern. While 'Abd Allah, who is widely considered as the poet of the short story, demonstrates his sensibility by using words to their full poetic value and creating a lyrical atmosphere, he creates an immediacy that is different from the immediacy of narrative action, and provides the closed, austere world of Upper Egypt with a profoundly rich mythic dimension. This contrasts with the return to classical narrative strategies in the work of al-Ghīṭānī, in order to record the devastating shock of the 1967 defeat. The differences between their styles and techniques gave their collective contribution to the genre vitality and richness and brought the process of its development to its remarkable conclusion.

INTRODUCTION

The Solitary Literary Genre and the Quest for Identities

A study of the short story often begins with, or at least contains, a complaint that the genre is insufficiently studied or suffers from neglect.[1] But, attempts in the English language to investigate this genre, define its characteristics, fathom its underlying assumptions, study its unique structure and posit some theoretical postulations about its nature and limits in fact go back a long way. In 1901 Brander Matthews published a small, pioneering study, *The Philosophy of the Short Story*,[2] in which he defined the limits and nature of the genre for the next sixty years or so. His main concern was to identify the short story as a modern literary form distinct from traditional forms of short narrative, and to differentiate it on artistic and formal grounds from the novel and what he called 'novelet'. He states at the outset:

> the difference between the novel and novelet is one of length only, a difference between a novel and a short story is a difference in kind. A true short story is something other and something more than a mere story which is short. A true short story differs from the novel chiefly in its essential unity of impression.[3]

He went on to define this otherness and more elements of the genre, but centred its philosophy on the key concept taken from Edgar Allan Poe, the 'unity of impression'.[4] His identification of the traits of the genre, such as symmetry of design, compression, originality, and now and again a touch of fantasy,[5] are mostly marshalled towards creating this final 'unity of impression'. Matthews followed his study six years later with a much larger endeavour, 400 pages long, *The Short Story: Specimens Illustrating its Development*,[6] which left an indelible mark on future academic books on the genre.

For decades afterwards, particularly in America, the study of the short story had to be 'illustrated' with 'specimens', and confined itself to the genre's formal characteristics. While some authors and academics wrote books about the genre without such 'illustrations', they remained primarily interested in the main issues that Matthews investigated: the distinct nature of the modern form and its dissimilarity with older narrative forms, the difference between the novel and the short story; and the formal and artistic characteristics of the latter.[7] This tradition in the study of the short story reached its acme in England in the work of H. E. Bates,[8] and in America Cleanth Brooks and Robert Penn Warren.[9] In these books, the narrative's structure, its organic relationships, the logic of its unity, its variables and their proportionality, and the nature of its language are clearly elucidated with great attention to exposition, compression, economy, irony and tension. However, rarely does one find here a critical link between all these laudable traits and the nature of the world or the character that the short story creates.

The main break with this tradition came in 1963 with Frank O'Connor's insightful and seminal book *The Lonely Voice*, which I consider to be the first serious investigation of the 'philosophy' of the genre and one of the pioneering studies of the content of form. Like many before him, particularly H.E. Bates, O'Connor attributes the origin of the genre to Gogol's famous short story 'The Overcoat', but unlike them he went beyond the formal aspects of this famous classic and scrutinised its inherent vision and its philosophical ramifications. He posits the genre as the one most suitable for articulating the concerns of the lonely, the forlorn and the marginalised. But, more importantly, he links it to modernity: 'the short story, like the novel, is a modern art form; that is to say, it represents better than poetry or drama, our own attitude to life',[10] and makes the vital distinction between plausibility and verisimilitude. Modern narrative discourse in general would not have been feasible without the establishment of modernity with its different needs, world view and new attitude to life. In this respect O'Connor provides us with the first convincing justification of the genre's distinctiveness from earlier short narratives, through his insight into the dialectical relationship between the genre and modernity, seeing it as 'drastic adaptation of a primitive art form to modern conditions – to printing, science and individual religion'.[11] This in turn is linked in O'Connor's thesis to the fact that the technique of the short story 'was the product of a critical and scientific age',[12] and that its merit is recognisable in terms of plausibility. 'By this I do not mean mere verisimilitude – that we can get from a newspaper report – but an ideal action worked out in terms of verisimilitude,'[13] hence capable of communicating its experience to a new public and satisfying the standards of the individual, solitary, critical reader.

O'Connor starts with Turgenev's famous assertion that 'we all came out from under Gogol's "Overcoat"', and posits Gogol's ability to turn the mock-heroic into 'something that is neither satiric nor heroic, something that perhaps finally transcends both',[14] as providing us with a radical break with traditional narrative, and consequently with the philosophy of this new genre. In Gogol's analysis,

> what [he] has done so boldly and brilliantly is to take the mock-heroic character, the absurd little copying clerk, and impose his image over that of the crucified Jesus, so that even while we laugh we are filled with horror at the resemblance.[15]

Unlike those who studied this beginning before him, who praised Gogol's simple language or his concern for everyday life and uncomplicated experience, O'Connor emphasised his discovery of 'the little man' with his 'lonely voice' as the worthy subject of fiction. The little man is no hero, a character with whom the reader cannot identify, yet he is a character who creates an intense awareness of human loneliness, enables the reader to see things in a different light, to feel the sufferings and aspirations of humanity in the life of the ordinary 'little man'. O'Connor goes on to develop his main thesis of the lonely voice and the submerged population group: the former identifies the nature of the protagonist of the short story as an individual, filled with an intense awareness of human loneliness, incomprehension, ridicule and injustice. He or she is always dreaming of escape, always unsatisfied with his or her condition, or, in O'Connor's words, 'outlawed figures wandering about the fringes of society, superimposed sometimes on symbolic figures whom they caricature and echo – Christ, Socrates, Moses'.[16]

Yet this character is often part of what O'Connor calls a 'submerged population group', which he described as 'a bad phrase which I have had to use for want of a better'.[17] This group changes its nature 'from writer to writer, from generation to generation. It may be Gogol's officials, Turgenev's surfs, Maupassant's prostitutes, Chekhov's doctors and teachers, Sherwood Anderson's provincials, always dreaming of escape.'[18] Although O'Connor's attempt to assemble his lonely voices into 'submerged groups' poses a number of problems, the least of which is the inadequacy of the term, it guided his study of the major authors he selected. The work of many of his authors clearly never gave rise to a neat 'submerged group' or fitted into an easily describable category of the marginalised. But beneath his sensitive analysis of the work of each writer, ostensibly to identify these 'submerged groups', he demonstrated the growing significance of the loneliness of his individual protagonists and their aspiration to escape. The very fact that they are 'submerged' implies that they are under certain pressures which they resent or begrudge; they feel that they have a case, or a grievance, which they need to articulate and draw to the attention of others.

O'Connor suggests that inherent in the genre is 'an attitude of mind that is attracted by submerged population groups, whatever these may be at any given time – tramps, artists, lonely idealists, dreamers and spoiled priests.'[19] Yet these groups are never introduced as a cohesive entity, but as individuals who are concerned only about their own problems yet are unable to speak for themselves. His identification of such an attitude of mind provides further evidence of the difference between the short story and the novel. For him 'the short story remains by its very nature remote from the community – romantic, individualistic and intransigent'.[20] Its remoteness from the community makes it, as I shall demonstrate later, more suited to the elaboration of the agonies of individuation and the quest for identity. O'Connor also noticed the 'peculiar geographical distribution of the novel and the short story', and speculates as to why the short story flourished in some countries but not others, linking this to a vague 'difference in national attitude towards society'.[21] This aspect of the investigation had to wait for the *Kenyon Review*'s 'International Symposium on the Short Story'[22] (ISoSS) in 1968 to receive more thorough investigation. The ISoSS brought together a large number of scholars and writers of the genre to consider its manifestation across a large number of cultures and literatures. The proceedings of ISoSS, which were published in four issues of the *Kenyon Review*, refined O'Connor's rudimentary observations. In dealing with the present state and future of the genre, a number of participants voiced profound doubts about its relevance and survival, and argued that its market was dwindling and that readers, publishers and critics showed little or no interest in it. James T. Farrell (USA) claimed that compared with the novel it is 'generally given second place ... and the short stories can help create an audience, or a larger audience, for novels',[23] while Elizabeth Harrower (Australia) lamented the passing of the glory days of the short story and dated the end of its popularity and appeal in her country to the end of the Second World War.[24] This was echoed by Edward Hyams (England) who observed, 'nobody writes sonnets now, or if they do nobody reads them. Tomorrow nobody will write short stories.'[25] This view was reiterated by David Ballantyne (New Zealand)[26] and Torborg Nedreaas (Norway), who complained about the difficulty of publishing collections of short stories, or even single stories in weekly magazines.[27] George Garrett (USA) added that it was impossible to publish short stories in book form, and prophesied the extinction of the genre,[28] while Elizabeth Taylor (England) regretted the disappearance of journals that published short stories.[29] These views were supported by the literary agent James Oliver Brown, who confirmed that there was no market for collections of short stories in the English language.[30]

However, an equal number of ISoSS participants argued the opposite case. Jack Cope (South Africa) reported that

> in this emergent continent [Africa], the short story is nearly everywhere the most significant literary medium in use, and the debate on its value, health or vitality is here, at least, beside the point.[31]

This was echoed by Erih Kos (Yugoslavia), who stated that 'from the time when our famous national short story first appeared, right up to the present day, in all phases of our literature, the short story has been the most frequently used form of literary expression, and until very recently the most typical form of creative prose writing'.[32] Jun Eto (Japan) considered it a mark of the nation's refinement and quoted Shataro Yasuoka, a distinguished Japanese short story writer, describing the genre as 'a luxurious form of literature that flourished when it was possible for a connoisseur to enjoy an ample taste of a well-written short story over a cup of green tea in his quietly secluded study'.[33] Chanakya Sen (India) attributed the success of the short story to

> its effectiveness as a medium; it suited the limited direct experience and psycho-social awareness of the Indian writer ... its appeal was all the greater because, in general, the writer had also a message to deliver. In most cases, it was a protest against social oppression and a plea for social reform and for greater freedom for the individual.[34]

Another fellow Indian, Khushwant Singh, confirmed that 'there is little doubt that in all of India's fourteen languages the standard of short story writing is uniformly high and their popularity unrivalled'.[35]

Ana Maria Matute (Spain) confessed that 'since I began to write ... I have considered the short story one of the aptest means available to a narrator. The tale captures the fragrance, intensity, and capacity of mystery of poetry, with the clarity, the common language capable of reaching all classes of readers.'[36] Luigi Barzini (Italy) voiced similar views about the genre's suitability for Italian readers: 'I would like to think that the short story will never die in Italy, since it appears to be a form of expression particularly suited to the people's tastes, talents and needs.'[37] Another fellow Italian, Mario Picchi, confirmed the genre's popularity in Italy and suggested that 'the fledging writer often begins, if not with poetry, then with the short story.'[38] In my previous studies and extensive research on the subject of the short story in Arabic culture, I have also argued for the respectability and popularity of the genre and developed similar ideas in demonstrating the importance of the genre and its significant role in Arabic literature, as well as its prestigious position with writers and readers alike.[39]

Before exploring these opposing views, it is important to add another dimension to the geographical distribution of the short story. Hans Bender (Germany) provided us with valuable insights by taking a historical perspective in his discussion of the genre in Germany, observing that it enjoyed a sudden revival there after the Second World War.

> The short story, among other forms, began a new life, so sudden, vigorous, and fresh was its appearance that it

> became the most characteristic genre of the new beginning. Not only did Wolfgang Borchert and Elisabeth Langgässer, Heinrich Böll and Wolfdietrich Schnurre begin with short stories, many other writers of varying talents, even amateurs, produced short stories in those days, as if that genre alone was capable of stimulating them.[40]

Bender linked the resurgence of the genre in Germany to the desire for a new beginning, a clear break with the past, and a need to articulate a different vision and politics. Bender considered the post-war short story as

> the secularised *Kalendergeschichten*[41] of our time. No matter how casual, ironic, churlish or swaggering their stance they have basically the same objective as those pacesetting *Kalendergeschichten* by Johann Peter Hebel, in which both characters and readers were led through error to truth and self-knowledge.[42]

Such an objective is another way of articulating the genre's suitability for a new beginning and the quest for a new identity.

Ezekiel Mphahlele (South Africa) added to this political dimension another spatial slant:

> I have suggested elsewhere that the very physical presence of oppression made the sustained effort required for a novel almost impossible; and that the medium of the short story seemed suited for a fugitive urban culture such as the white society of South Africa had imposed on the non-white.[43]

This link between socio-political conditions and the status of the genre provides us with additional insight into its popularity and relevance. As a black writer in apartheid South Africa Mphahlele found the genre suitable not only because of its brevity and terseness but also because of its ability to articulate his identity and his concerns as an individual in unfavourable social conditions. This seems to be the common denominator among the second group of ISoSS participants. It is noticeable that the short story is popular in India, South Africa, the Arab world, Yugoslavia and Japan, where the processes and articulation of individuation are in progress and clearly needed. At the time of the

ISoSS symposium these cultures were grappling with various aspects of modernity, and particularly its impact on individuals emerging from traditional modes of social interaction. One can even argue that the three European countries, Italy, Spain and Germany, where the short story enjoyed popularity, were also, for different reasons, experiencing similar conditions. This is in clear contrast to the first group of writers – from the USA, England, Norway, Australia and New Zealand – whose societies had reconciled themselves to the demands of modernity and modified their social modes of interaction to cater for the processes of individuation.

In my earlier book, *The Genesis*, I developed a theoretical model for the study of the genesis of modern narrative discourse based on the interaction of a number of deeply structured processes of change. Like modernity itself, the genesis of modern narrative discourse in Arabic culture is seen as the outcome of not one but a series of major historical and cultural transitions that created a new attitude to both life and art. Following on from this theoretical model, the book treats the genre of the short story as a formal or generic representation of a state of being or a socio-cultural condition, for which the artistic rubrics of the genre are highly suited. *The Genesis* demonstrated that, in the early development of a literary genre, the most influential writers are not necessarily those who purposefully develop a new genre, but rather those who are most aware of and sensitive to the needs of the emergent reading public. This is because literary genres emerge as a response to literary, cultural and social exigencies and not as a result of a deliberate attempt to innovate or introduce new cultural products. Those innovative endeavours may widen the scope of an existing genre or at best realise some of its unrealised potential, but they rarely give rise to genres. Since genres are necessary for the process of understanding, their rise is linked to the schism in artistic sensibility which generates, in turn, a new world view and a fresh way of expressing and consequently understanding that view. The relationship between variable and constant structural elements that appeared in the radical change that swept Arabic culture from the turn of the nineteenth century can be established only from a diachronic perspective; and this is the reason for the linear and consecutive arrangement of the content of this study.

Although it is extremely difficult to confine the development of a genre to the evolutionary schema of growth, flowering and decay, this study attempts to demonstrate that it is possible to adhere to the evolutionary schema during the genesis of a new genre but not during its development. It links the subsequent development to the complex processes of socio-cultural change, acculturation, social polarisation and a growing sense of individuation, and roots its texts in the world from which they emerged. This enables close reading to stress the dialectical interaction of systems of representation and practice, and provides critical and artistic insights into the very nature of the genre and its wider significance. If narrative discourse in general translates knowing into telling, the genre in which this discourse is expressed fashions human experience into a form that structures its meaning and gives it a generalised human dimension. Genres have significance and meaning and are enmeshed in their historical context; by taking both into consideration, the study of their development provides us with some insights into the content of form, or rather of genre. This also takes the study beyond the specific world of Arabic literature and gives the genre its special significance and relevance. The content of the form of the short story is one of the main concerns of this study, and particularly its relationship to that of its counter narrative genre, the novel. To provide the development of the genre with such wider significance in a way that sheds light on why it is more popular in some countries than others, and in certain historical periods, it has been important to review some of the major contributions to the theory of the genre.

In his brilliant study of theory of genres and medieval literature[44] Hans Robert Jauss emphasises the importance of the concept of genre for the understanding of literary texts and the aesthetic response to them.

> Just as there is no act of verbal communication that is not related to a general, socially or situationally conditioned norm or convention, it is also unimaginable that a literary work set itself into an informational vacuum, without indicating a specific situation of understanding. To this extent every work belongs to a genre – whereby I mean neither more nor less than that for each work a pre-constituted horizon of expectations must be ready at hand (this can also be understood as a relationship of 'rules of the game' *Zusammenhang von Spielregeln*) to orient the reader's understanding and to enable a qualifying reception.[45]

The concept of genre, whose recognition depends on associating a complex of elements, is a trans-textual one, which is constructed retrospectively. There are a large number of variables operative in the concept, as well as in the relationship between any single manifestation of the concept and the body of work that characterises it. As Jauss points out,

> the relationship between the individual text and the series of texts formative of a genre presents itself as a process of the continual founding and altering of horizon. The new text evokes for the reader the horizon of expectations and 'rules of the game' familiar to him from earlier texts, which as such can be varied, extended, corrected, but also transformed, crossed out, or simply reproduced.[46]

This explains both the dialectics of establishing genres, and breaking with them at the same time. Indeed, the genre as a horizon of communicative expectations is as necessary for understanding a work that is a mere reproduction of the common features of the genre as for comprehending works that attempt to achieve a complete rupture with its canon. In order for rupture to be completely understood as such – as a radical departure from the norm – the norm needs to be firmly established. It is an *a posteriori* classification where familiarity with its conventions is essential to the process of communication and the generation of meaning. The genre involves a formal structure, the traits of which and nets of patterns and internal relations are not necessarily found in one text but can be easily drawn from a body of texts. Hence any theorisation about the significance of the short story genre must take into account this general body of text with its varying schools and trajectories, as a whole.

The novel has long been credited with a vital role in the shaping of the 'imagined community', but the role of the short story in articulating other aspects of this 'imagined community' has not been adequately studied. Benedict Anderson's seminal book *Imagined Communities*[47] constitutes a major break in the theorisation of narrative genres. It drew our attention to the vital role that narrative discourse, and specifically the genre of the novel, played in creating a shared 'imagined community'. Anderson's point of departure, which revitalised the study of the novel, is that the nation 'is an imagined political community – and imagined as both inherently limited and sovereign'.[48] These two aspects of the imagined political community receive detailed attention in his work. 'It is imagined because the members of even the smallest nation will never know most of their fellow-members, meet them or even hear of them, yet in the mind of each lives the image of their communion.'[49] Yet it is not clear from this formulation how 'in the mind of each' the image of this communion lives, and whether some are more comfortable with it than others. What happens to those who do not partake? Do some question its very nature and its internal relations of dominance and subordination? Anderson also states that the nation 'is imagined as a community, because, regardless of the actual inequality and exploitation that may prevail in each, the nation is always conceived as a deep horizontal comradeship'.[50] Similar issues could be raised about how this 'deep horizontal comradeship' lives in harmony or clashes with inequality and exploitation.

Anderson links this 'horizontal comradeship' and the nation as 'imagined community' to the shift, identified by Walter Benjamin, from the simultaneity of traditional 'Messianic time' to a more secular 'homogenous, empty time, in which simultaneity is, as it were, transverse, cross-time, marked not by prefiguring and fulfilment, but by temporal coincidence, and measured by clock and calendar'.[51] This shift is almost a pre-requisite for the birth of the nation as an 'imagined community' because it is at the heart of

> the basic structure of two forms of imagining which first flowered in Europe in the eighteenth century: the novel and the newspaper. For these forms provided the technical means for *re-presenting* the *kind* of imagined community that is the nation.[52]

The novel, thanks to its polyphonic and multilayered narrative structure, is credited with this role because of 'its spectacular possibilities for the representation of simultaneous actions in homogeneous empty time'.[53] It is also vital for the imagining of the nation as a cohesive and homogenous entity, for its ability to fit actions and individuals from different walks of life into the new simultaneity of 'homogeneous empty time' and fashion them into a community, the identification with which generates the sense of 'deep horizontal comradeship'. Unlike short stories, novels aspire to create ideal families or communities and heroes with whom the reader can identify.

What I aim to do here is to extend Anderson's argument, albeit with some modifications, to the genre of the short story. For homogeneous empty time, particularly with its temporal coincidences, is also vital for the imagining of individuals and their perception of, and quest for, their identity. It is also relevant to the emergence of the short story as a modern narrative genre. As we have seen, the theorists of the genre linked the form to modernity and were at pains to deny any genealogical link between the modern short story and its many ancestries in short narrative forms. At the heart of the severance of the genre from its traditional narrative ancestries is the acute awareness of the problem of time inherent in these older forms, with its simultaneity and divine providence, and a desire to break with its assumptions. In Arabic culture, the tension between the old 'Messianic time' and the new 'homogeneous empty time' and their coexistence in the contemporary Arab world complicates the situation further, and this has left its mark on the structure and texture of recent short stories, discussed in the last chapter of this book. There is equally an awareness of the dependence of the new genre on the new 'homogeneous empty time', but in a radically different way from the novel. Its concern is the inscription of the personal, which is largely omitted from the communal narrative of the nation.

If the novel gives a voice to the need of a shiftless and arbitrary (human) being, a promise of immortality, the short story articulates an equally pressing need of being apart, a unique and special individual, with a certain fascination with his own mortality, his constant toying with death. Indeed, it is the medium that articulates the concept of identity and narrates the pains of individuation and the fragmentation of the individual's living experience. Here I would like to recall O'Connor's concept of the genre's ability to superimpose the marginalised 'on symbolic figures whom they caricature and echo', for this sharpens the genre's ability to individuate its protagonists and frame their sense of identity. This is because the short story is the solitary genre, the genre most concerned with the trials and tribulations of forlorn individuals and marginalised groups. Its link to the process of individuation and the articulation of the fragmentary nature of this community and its marginalised voices and the unsaid is one of the issues that this study investigates in its close reading of a number of authors'. The quest for 'identity' that the short story articulates is not for the 'identity' that one inherits but for an 'identity' that one chooses, one that is free from essentialist teleological discourse, and more concerned with the process of individuation and the contextualisation of 'identity' rather than its fixed origin.

The novel's construction of the nation as 'inherently limited' usually privileges certain groups and histories over others to the effect of excluding or marginalising them, or, in O'Connor's words, turning them into submerged groups. But the quest for identity elaborated by the short story is more keenly aware of the multiplicity of identities that populate the 'imagined community' and continually need to be reinvented. The mosaic of identities that makes the large fresco of the nation is the concern of the short story and not its 'deep horizontal comradeship'. Its compact structure enables it to concentrate on the specificity of a tiny fragment of the numerous pieces that make up the large fresco. Unlike the novel, which is mainly concerned with the larger picture, the short story zooms in on the minute details of each fragment. It is particularly fond of those that are overlooked for the sake of the larger picture and of the cracks which run through the fragments. The very concept of the nation as a 'deep horizontal comradeship' requires a disregard for the individual citizen, and citizens' clashes with other individuals who occupy different positions because of temporal coincidences in the homogeneously 'imagined community'. But the short story unpicks this 'deep horizontal comradeship' even when it deals with those who die for the nation, as we shall see in some of the stories discussed in Chapter Two. It shows that the imagination of the homogeneous community is often achieved at the expense of certain groups and individuals.

If the imagination of communities can be seen as a diachronic process, that of identities is perceived synchronically where the contending identities coexist within the shared communal space, which is often fraught with rivalry and tension, and ironically different trajectories of aspiration. The short story gives voice to the tension that is subtly at work within the complex process of imagining the nation in a homogeneous empty time, by bringing the community back from this time to the mundane diachronic time. It articulates conflicting agendas by unpicking what the novel glosses over, for its point of departure is that the experience is not quite shared, or is not evenly shared to the same degree, and that some members or groups of the 'community' are more fortunate than others. Unlike the novel, where the tension and acrimony between kinsmen are assumed to be transient and resolvable, where close ties that motivate the 'imagined community' are re-knit once the acrimony is addressed, the short story is more concerned with the grievance itself and not with its resolution. This does not mean that I am positing the short story as the enemy of the idea of nationalism, for the world of the short story largely builds its world on nationalist assumptions, but as playing a different role from that of the novel. Its undermining of the harmony of the imagination that goes into the communal imagining of the 'nation' provides this imagination with a critical and sophisticated edge.

Unlike the novel, which relies on the process of identification between reader and character, a process that invariably leads to some concept of normality in relation to society as a whole, the short story is free from this reliance. The novel's encoding power helps the reader to identify with and partake in an 'imagined community', while the short story, which remains by its very nature remote from the community, is more concerned with the decoding of this national imaginary. It is the genre in which individuals express their innermost feelings and thoughts and shape their sense of individual identity. Its focus is on the overlooked individuals, the small fragments of the large fresco. Such fragments are overlooked, perhaps because of their lack of colour or lustre, or because of their marginal position in the fresco; but the genre is acutely aware that the full picture cannot be complete without them. The short story is the voice of those individuals, of the oppressed, and it writes against the attempt to transmogrify all members of the community into one homogeneous 'imagined community'. In addition, while the novel appeals to imaginary locations and an imagined past, the short story is more concerned with the present in the wider sense, both temporal and psychological. It rejects the allurements of history in a process of differentiation and individuation. As such, it expresses the necessity of standing simultaneously inside and outside the 'nation' and, occasionally, the culture itself. It is the genre that responds to the desire of the individual for coherence. This is perhaps what O'Connor meant when he stated that the difference between the two genres 'is not so much formal, though there are plenty of formal differences, as ideological'.[54] In structural linguistic terms, if the novel draws the reader's attention to the *langue*, the grammar of the community or the nation, the short story is interested in the polyphony of *parole* and the hidden injustices that the overwhelming tendency to impose the rules of the *langue* does to the *parole*; and this makes it in a certain sense a poetic rather than a prosaic genre.

Indeed, the short story's neatness of construction and polish of execution are the manifestation of a solitary self, poised to bestow harmony and elegance on a world that lacks such qualities. The more polished the product the more it hides the inadequacy of the individual, or rather the more it subtly reveals the cracks in the social fabric. This has been pointed out by early theorists of the genre; Matthews suggests 'whatever its form, it should have symmetry of design. If it has also wit or humour, pathos or poetry, and specially a distinct and unmistakable flavour of individuality, so much the better.'[55] Symmetry of design provides the genre with its inherent tension, a source of richness, while the distinct flavour of individuality enhances its ability to shape the complex process of individuation. This is mainly because the short story is the literary genre most suited for the elaboration of the reflexive projection of the individual self. As Ernst Cassirer notes in his description of the singleness of effect of mythical thinking: 'it is as though the isolated occurrence of an impression, its separation from the totality of ordinary, commonplace experience produced not only a tremendous intensification, but also the highest degree of condensation'.[56]

The preoccupation with epistemological themes of most of the authors studied in this book is a clear manifestation of the quest for objective knowledge of the 'self', or, more precisely, the individual self. This quest is paradoxical since the individual's only means of gaining this objective knowledge is his own subjectivity. When all the individual has in the world is his or her own experience of it, all received knowledge becomes suspect and the very nature of knowledge becomes problematic. Once knowledge is problematised, a shared collective imaginary, let alone a national one, becomes impossible. This study demonstrates that the popularity, versatility, vitality and relevance of the short story to the major social and literary issues of contemporary Arab society speak eloquently of the trials and tribulations of its individual characters. If, as Hegel remarks, periods of human happiness and security are blank pages in history, the overabundance of short stories in Arabic, with their stock of marginal and forlorn characters and their narratives of unhappy histories and suffering, may be taken as an indication of the absence of happiness and security, of a problematic time. In other words, the popularity of the short story precludes or undercuts any false assumption of social or historical harmony, and indicates that the quest for identities in the Arab world is as acute and relevant as it has ever been.

CHAPTER ONE

The Rhythms of Change and Anxiety

The Social and Cultural Scene (1930–70)

The first three decades of the twentieth century witnessed the genesis of the Arabic short story in Egypt;[1] the following four decades (1931–70) shaped its journey towards development and maturity. Those four decades proved to be a critical period in the history of modern Egypt. They began with a severe economic crisis and ended with the prospect of an even more serious one, and in the interim Egypt passed through years of fluctuating hope and frustration. During this period, the country provided the stage for certain Second World War operations and fought and lost three wars of its own. The British occupation ended in 1956, but Egypt was re-occupied and humiliated, this time by an enemy seeking to annex a precious part of its territory. It witnessed the unseating of the old ruling class and the emergence of a new one, which lacked many of the positive facets of its predecessor yet preserved all its flaws. Cairo was devastated by fire in these years, and a new entity arose from the ashes. The base of education became wide but shallow; the numbers of the literate increased enormously but their percentage remained relatively constant. The scope of cultural activities enlarged yet the arts were gripped in the iron fist of censorship. Conservative ideas survived alongside progressive notions. There were ebbs and flows at all levels, and all aspects of Egyptian life experienced radical political, social and cultural change. It was very difficult, if not impossible at this time, for anyone involved in public activity (including the writing of short stories) not to engage with the changes. A brief account of Egypt's political, social and cultural life during these four decades is thus needed in order to understand the context of the evolution of the Egyptian short story and the relationship between its development and the reading public.

These four decades started with an international economic crisis whose repercussions in Egypt[2] brought about the fall of the elected Wafdist government, the dissolution of parliamentary life and the abrogation of the 1923 Constitution. They were replaced by a disreputable constitution, unrepresentative parliament and an autocratic government headed by Ismāʿīl Ṣidqī, who formed the ironically named Ḥizb al-Shaʿb (the People's Party). This party managed to win most of the new parliament's seats in the rigged election conducted by Ṣidqī's appointed government. The Ḥizb al-Shaʿb government reigned for three notorious years (1930–3), characterised by hardship, oppression, persecution and terror. The conditions provoked more than ten attempts on the lives of the king, Ṣidqī, the British representative, and leading members of Ḥizb al-Shaʿb.[3] Terror produced counter-terror and the economic crisis made the whole situation worse. The king and the British occupying forces looked for a scapegoat and Ṣidqī's government was the obvious choice. It was replaced in 1933 with a replica, headed by ʿAbd al-Fattāḥ Yaḥyā, which failed to appease the nation's anger or satisfy the British. It was consequently defeated and offered its resignation in November 1934. Tawfīq Nasīm formed the next government, which declared the offending 1930 Constitution null and void yet refused to reinstate the universally desired 1923 Constitution.

After a year of continuous popular pressure and against the will of both the dying king Fu'ād and the British,[4] the 1923 Constitution was reinstated. A new caretaker government, headed by ʿAlī Māhir, was formed to conduct free elections, the results of which brought back a Wafdist government, headed by Muṣṭafā al-Naḥḥās, in May 1935. The following August, Naḥḥās, in cooperation with the major nationalist leaders, concluded the famous treaty of 1936 with the British. Although the treaty recognised the complete independence of Egypt, it did not change the de facto situation of the occupation, and most of the promises it had elicited seemed illusory. The new king, Farūq, seized the opportunity to incite the public to demonstrate against the Wafdist 'sellout' and strip it of its traditional role as the representative of popular aspirations, a role it had enjoyed since 1919.

By the end of 1937, the young and inexperienced king had managed to remove the shrewd politician Naḥḥās and his elected government from office, and asked Muḥammad Maḥmūd, the leader of the Liberal Constitutional Party, to form a new government. In January 1938, Maḥmūd formed his new government, dissolved parliament, which was controlled by a Wafdist majority, and held a fixed election, which granted his party an absolute majority. Māhmud, known as 'Iron-fist', was weakened by old age; his government disintegrated and finally collapsed in August 1939, but not before passing a law establishing a new university in Alexandria. In August 1939, 'Alī Māhir formed a coalition government, which carried out some measure of social reform and founded the first Ministry of Social Affairs. A month later, the Second World War broke out and the country witnessed the influx of more British and Allied soldiers, instead of the evacuation of those already in the country. By 1940 the war had reached the western gate of Egypt with the Italians and Germans in Libya and the western desert, and Māhir's government declared martial law. The Axis powers scored some early victories on the African Front, which encouraged the pro-Axis organisations in Egypt (such as the Muslim Brethren and the Young Egypt Movement) to demonstrate, spread rumours, and agitate against the Allies. There were public disturbances, severe shortages of basic commodities, and serious hampering of the British military efforts to halt the Italian advance. Māhir himself was accused of having Axis leanings and the king was obliged to accept his resignation. The economic situation continued to decline under Ḥussain Sirri's government until it reached its lowest ebb in the second half of 1941, which coincided with Rommel's arrival on the African Front and his quick advance towards the Egyptian western desert. His air raid on Alexandria[5] aggravated the situation and created a period of instability and anger against the British, during which basic commodities disappeared from the market. In January 1942, after a new attack by Rommel's forces, demonstrators in Cairo shouted 'Forward Rommel!' and the economic crisis reached an intolerable level. The British were preparing for their major counter-offensive and needed to stabilise the internal situation to secure their supply lines. Despite their dislike of the Wafd, they felt it was the only power capable of controlling the situation, and therefore asked the king to call upon Naḥḥās to form a new government. The king complied, but Naḥḥās insisted on forming a purely Wafdist administration, rather than a government of national unity, on the grounds that the critical nature of the situation could not tolerate the inevitable compromises of coalition government. The British agreed with Naḥḥās's views but the king dismissed them, leading to what became known as 'The Fourth of February Incident',[6] when the king received a British ultimatum to call upon Naḥḥās to form a government before 6 p.m. or to bear the consequences. The king, on the advice of all leading politicians, including Naḥḥās himself, refused the ultimatum. At 9 p.m. on the same day, the palace was encircled by British tanks. The British Ambassador asked the king to abdicate but he capitulated instead and persuaded Naḥḥās to form a Wafdist government.

Whatever the interpretation of this event,[7] its effect on the political and social life of the country was far-reaching. At one blow, the romantic dreams of Egypt's independence and future evaporated. Frustration and despair reigned at many levels in the country and the people's confidence in themselves and their national leaders was shattered. Cracks soon appeared in the Wafd Party. The palace conspiracy against the party began to bear fruit,[8] and in 1943 the king explored the possibility of dismissing Naḥḥās's government; the British, however, were firmly against any such move. On the battlefield the tide was turning, gradually but consistently, in favour of the British and their Allies. Towards the end of 1944 it became evident that the war was coming to an end and that Naḥḥās would be asking the British to fulfil their promise to evacuate the country completely. The British thus turned a blind eye to the king's attempt to dismiss Naḥḥās in October 1944. Despite the war and palace plotting, the short-lived Wafdist government managed to alleviate the economic crisis, make primary education both compulsory and free, and promote Arabic as the official language in all the dealings of foreign companies. They also undermined the autocracy of the palace, completed and opened Alexandria University, and undertook some measures of social reform concerning both peasants and workers.

In October 1944, Aḥmad Māhir was asked to form a coalition government. On 24 February 1945 he declared war on the Axis powers and was assassinated the same day. His deputy, Maḥmūd Fahmī al-Nuqrāshī, became head of government. Within a few months the war was over and martial law was lifted. Naḥḥās, the leader of the Wafd Party, sent a memorandum to the British Ambassador requesting the immediate evacuation of British troops and the unification of Egypt and Sudan. Massive demonstrations flowed through the streets, the people chanting for evacuation and unification. Nuqrāshī's government was compelled to send a similar memorandum to the British in December 1945, which was rejected. When both the government's note and the British reply were published in January 1946, the meekness of the government's memorandum and the arrogance of the British answer prompted outrage. In February, the streets were awash with demonstrations and riots and the situation reached crisis levels.[9] Many were killed, injured and imprisoned, but this nourished popular anger instead of placating it. To understand the ramifications of the events of 1946, it is necessary to bear in mind the major social and cultural changes that Egypt had undergone during the Second World War,[10] including the development of the bourgeoisie, the growth of the working class, class polarisation in the countryside, the emergence of a communist movement and new schools of political thought,[11] and the coalition between the student movement and workers.

Following the student massacre of 9 February and the assassination attempt on the monarch on 11 February, Nuqrāshī's administration resigned and Ismā'īl Ṣidqī was asked to form a new government. This added fuel to the already inflamed situation, and Ṣidqī had to employ all his experience and skill to calm the situation by way of deception and severe oppression. Most of the cultural associations and publishing houses that had fostered the new trends of political thought were closed, many papers and periodicals censored,[12] and writers and intellectuals arrested. But despite these measures, Ṣidqī failed either to gain the confidence of the British or to calm the explosive internal situation. In November 1946 another wave of demonstrations and violence broke out, protesting against Ṣidqī's attitude to the national question in his negotiations with Bevan, and in December the king asked Nuqrāshī to form a new cabinet. Nuqrāshī's return to office after the student massacre in February was a step backwards and was accompanied by a natural disaster – the cholera epidemic that swept through Egypt in the summer of 1947.[13] The year ended with Nuqrāshī's assassination in the midst of his police apparatus.[14]

The political, social and cultural atmosphere that prevailed during the latter years of the forties had a strong impact on the creative arts. Terror, upheaval and violence had a snowball effect during the latter half of this decade, and the defeat of the Arab army in Palestine shattered the nation's confidence in itself and its institutions. The progressive wing that appeared in Egyptian politics in the aftermath of the Second World War, with its different tendencies and groupings,[15] used demonstrations, pamphlet journalism and the book[16] as its major weapons in the political battle, but the extreme right and its organisations,[17] which had flourished under martial law, resorted to political assassination and violence. Ironically, these two contradictory means of struggle developed side by side,[18] and, along with government intimidation, left their undeniable imprint on all cultural activity. This was the period in which experimental, symbolic and nightmarish writings emerged.

The terror and violence reached their climax in December 1948 when Ibrāhīm 'Abd al-Hādī was asked to form a coalition government and chose to follow in Nuqrāshī's footsteps with a widespread campaign of arrest and torture. Popular and violent reaction spread throughout the country and for the first time reached the villages,[19] and succeeded in deterring the government from pursuing its campaign of terror. But the government looked for a saviour and scapegoat, finding the first in its traditional enemy, the Wafd, and the second in 'Abd al-Hādī's government, which was humiliatingly dismissed from office in July 1949.[20] However, the Wafd refused either to head or to participate in any coalition government and asked for a caretaker government to release political detainees, to prepare for free elections and to abolish martial law. By the end of the transitional period these steps were accomplished. Amid the preparations for the coming elections came horrific revelations of what had occurred in the bowels of 'Abd al-Hādī's government's terror machine.[21] Many of the revelations were inhuman beyond comprehension and their impact upon the reading public was far-reaching. The complete loss of confidence in the system demonstrated itself clearly during the elections when, for the first time in a free election, one-third of the voters did not bother to go to the polls.[22] However, the Wafd won by a convincing majority and formed their last government in January 1950. 'The Wafd carried on in 1950–1951 with more legislations affecting socio-economic problems. But this time it dealt more directly with the welfare of the working and rural classes.'[23] With the late Ṭāhā Ḥusayn as its Minister of

Education, it paid considerable attention to educational and cultural matters. It established a new university, the University of 'Ayn Shams, declared secondary education free and subsidised serious publications and unprofitable translation projects. It also tried to solve the perennial national question by resuming the fruitless negotiations with the British, against a background of continuous rioting and increasing violence in town and village. The tension at the negotiating table and in the street culminated in the repeal of the 1936 treaty and in October 1951 the annulment of the Sudan Agreement. The event marked the climax of the Wafd's political history: it opened the door for popular armed struggle and stripped both the occupation and the constitutional establishment of their legitimacy. Towards the end of 1951 and the beginning of 1952, the Egyptian partisans accelerated their armed struggle against the British troops in the Suez Canal zone and the situation reached crisis level. The urgent need to introduce martial law was felt both by the palace and by the occupation forces. The premeditated burning of the shopping and entertainment centre in Cairo on 26 January 1952 provided the pretext to re-enforce martial law.[24] This curbed the widespread dissemination of news about corruption and muzzled press accounts of the self-indulgent and decadent king in an attempt to restore people's faith in the traditional political powers. During the unstable first half of 1952[25] the ground was thus prepared for a military take-over.

Army officers seized power on 23 July 1952 and before the end of the year they had managed to force the king to abdicate. They crushed the workers' demonstrations, passed a concessionary land reform law and tried to ease the economic situation. They purged the governmental machine, abrogated the 1923 Constitution and disbanded all political parties and groups except the Muslim Brethren. In January 1953, they announced a transitional period of three years during which the military junta was to hold supreme power, and started to militarise the civilian government and form a loose political organisation, the Liberation Rally, which they intended to use to manipulate public opinion. In June 1953, they declared Egypt a republic and appointed Muḥammad Najīb as its first president. In September 1953, the junta turned a blind eye to the Zionist occupation of al-'Uja demilitarised zone, but when students demonstrated in January 1954 they suppressed the movement firmly and violently and seized the opportunity to dissolve the Muslim Brethren. Two months later, in what is known as the Crisis of March 1954,[26] there was a massive round-up of all those who challenged or even questioned the absolute power of the junta, that is, the Communists, Muslim Brethren, Socialists, Wafdists and other independent liberals. The arrests continued throughout 1954 and 1955. In October 1954, the new regime concluded an agreement with the British for the evacuation of the Suez Canal zone in twenty months, but, alongside other minor provisos, the British reserved the right to return in the case of aggression against any Arab country and/or Turkey. The unfair nature of the agreement angered the population at large and was criticised by almost every political group. The immediate consequence was more oppression and detention. During the same month, there was an abortive attempt on the life of Nasser, by that time the clear leader of the junta; this provided an excuse to indulge in intimidation.

In January 1956, the three transitional years came to an end. By this time the officers had succeeded in eliminating most political opposition. They issued a new constitution and in June, after the completion of the British evacuation, Nasser was chosen by an official referendum as the first constitutional President of Egypt. The officers also replaced the Liberation Rally with a similar organisation, the National Union. Throughout the first half of this year, the regime was engaged in negotiations with the United States and Europe to finance the High Dam Project,[27] but in July the negotiations collapsed. Looking for an alternative source of finance for this vital project, Nasser proclaimed the nationalisation of the Suez Canal Company, a long-standing national demand, on 26 July. Three months later, the notorious Suez War began. The complete defeat of the Egyptian army was not revealed to the people; the war was misrepresented, the losses and the territorial concessions concealed, and the political success very much exaggerated. The deception mollified the people; the disastrous results would not become apparent until 1967. The regime derived some strength from standing up to imperialism and Nasser became a popular leader in the Arab world. His stand against the so-called 'Eisenhower Doctrine' of 8 January 1957 confirmed his anti-imperialist credentials, rendered the doctrine useless and exerted genuine pressure on right-wing regimes. From then on, Nasser's regime began to identify with Afro-Asian liberation movements, with all that that entailed, including constant confrontation with Western imperialist policies. In 1958, the country became entangled in a hasty union with Syria and started its war of words against the reactionary Arab regimes. Before the end of the year, Nasser's prestige as the only spokesman for the Arab cause was challenged by Qāsim and his newly emerging revolutionary regime in Iraq. Ironically, the rivalry between the two regimes proved negative for both leaders, and the Ba'thists fanned its fires. The Egyptian domestic scene would pay for the rivalry; because of Qāsim's clear leftist sympathies, the Egyptian Left fell into disfavour, not only for its sympathy with the Iraqis, but also for its opposition to the union with Syria; at the beginning of 1959 all Egyptian Communist and left-wing intellectuals were arrested.

Although the pace of change did not live up to either the stated targets[28] or people's aspirations, the new regime did make substantial strides in the area of education and health reforms. However justified the criticism of Nasser's policies, his measures in these two fields gained him a great deal of popularity and respect. Yet by 1960 the regime had realised that its reforming policies were not sufficient, so it began tightening its grip on the economy by Egyptianising some foreign firms and nationalising a number of large local ones. It also prepared the blue-print for a five-year plan (1960–5) to step up both productivity and gross national income. The plan required tighter control over the economy, and so July 1961 saw a great deal of nationalisation,[29] the introduction of new progressive taxes and land reforms. This alarmed the right wing in Syria, which in September 1961 organised a *coup d'état* and renounced union with Egypt – a shattering blow to Nasser's regime and ambitions. Just as the Egyptian Left paid the price for Nasser's quarrel with the Iraqi leftist regime, the Right would suffer as a result of the secession. The Egyptian regime feared that the success of the right-wing Syrian capitalists would encourage the semi-feudal and semi-capitalist classes in Egypt to follow their example, so it placed over 1,000 of their most respected members under governmental sequestration. It also turned attention to the heart of traditional, religious and conservative culture – al-Azhar – revolutionising its curricula and modernising its institutions: the reform of the Azhar brought new disciplines into its educational system and undermined its archaic methodology. The Syrian secessionist regime waged a war of words against the terror and police rule of the Union era, which

Egypt was obliged to counter. It responded to the instability caused by the event with a wave of re-evaluation and open discussion, which took the form of a national conference to draw up the blue-print for the country's political future. The result was the Charter of May 1962, the replacement of the National Union by the Arab Socialist Union as the only political party, and the introduction of some socialist economic measures. The overall message was that the country's efforts should be concentrated on internal development.

But in September 1962, with the first anniversary of the secession, the army officers in Yemen overthrew the Imam, who managed to escape and, with the support of the Saudi monarchy, manipulated a number of tribes to begin waging a war of attrition from the mountains against the new military regime. The junta sought Nasser's help and, as a true pan-Arab nationalist, he entered the quick-sands of the Yemen war. By the end of 1962 there were about 13,000 Egyptians in the Yemen; the number increased annually until by 1965 there were 70,000.[30] However important for the progressive cause, the manner in which Nasser conducted the intervention in Yemen and tackled the national and international issues involved had a negative effect on economic and political life in Egypt. The period witnessed price increases in a number of basic commodities, a flourishing black market, a yielding to the pressures of the new privileged class, and inflation as a result of the funds required to cover the expenses of the Yemen campaign. The period also unveiled the weakness and inefficiency of the Egyptian army and a rise of American hostility towards Egypt.[31] The only positive aspect of the war was the so-called transistor revolution in Egypt's towns and villages. Every soldier and officer who went to Yemen brought home a number of these small wonders of technology and distributed them among relatives. The impact upon public awareness and understanding of cultural and general issues was significant.

Though of huge importance, the Yemen war was not the only crucial issue during this period. By 1963, two fresh *coups d'état* had been staged in Iraq and Syria, and in March of that year the representatives of the two new regimes sought a tripartite union with Egypt. The attempt failed but nonetheless fuelled Nasser's dreams of pan-Arab leadership and involved the regime in a new wave of verbal dissension and dispute with the two countries. In the meantime, the process of putting Egypt on the road to socialism, to use a favourite term from the Charter, *al-Mīthāq* (Nasser's major political document of the period) gained momentum, and nationalisation was stepped up until more than 75 per cent of the economy was controlled by the public sector. In November 1963, arrangements for new parliamentary elections began. A new scheme for rearranging parliamentary constituencies was completed at the beginning of 1963 and the election was held in March, once all possible opposition had been rendered ineffectual. In the same month, a provisional constitution was issued and an unsuccessful attempt was made to abolish political and administrative detention. In 1964, the first stage of the High Dam was ready and the Soviet leader, Khruschev, came to Egypt to celebrate its completion and to sanction Nasser's progressive policies. Nasser, in a gesture of gratitude, cleared his political prisons of Communists and left-wing intellectuals; in fact, he desperately needed their support for his regime was under constant attack from reactionary forces in the Middle East and from the Americans. It was in this year that relations with America reached their lowest ebb: America cut its agricultural aid and applied economic pressure on Egypt.

At the beginning of 1965 a referendum re-elected Nasser as president. This was also the year of a wide-ranging Muslim Brethren conspiracy against the regime and a Saudi-Iranian attempt to isolate Nasser's influence in the area.[32] Nasser arrested Muslim Brethren and right-wing intellectuals en masse, followed by a group of former Wafdists who turned Naḥḥās's funeral into a huge hostile demonstration, and a group of rebellious Communists who, unlike the majority of their comrades, refused to submit to Nasser's policies. The result was that by the end of 1965 tens of thousands of Egyptians had been imprisoned without trial on various political charges. Nasser also revoked the agreement with Saudi Arabia to withdraw his forces from Yemen and, moreover, increased his operations against the Saudi-based royalist forces (especially when Britain declared its intention to evacuate its base in Aden). He announced that he would pursue the royalist forces across the borders, to which the Saudis responded by asking the Americans for a display of force over their territories, which intensified the hostility between the Egyptians and Americans. Despite the American display of force, the Egyptian army pursued the Yemeni royalist forces inside Saudi territory and bombed them. Nasser's forces were now approaching the world's largest known reserves of oil and the core of American interest in the region. Something had to be done to discipline Nasser; and the trap into which he was finally lured in June 1967 began to be set at this time.[33] All this was accompanied on the domestic front by continuous price increases (20 per cent between 1963 and 1966), which led to the first major violent demonstrations by the workers of Port Said in October 1966. In 1967, Egypt was forced, without adequate preparation, into war and lost both its army and a major part of its territory (the Sinai Peninsula). In the aftermath of this catastrophic defeat, Nasser melodramatically offered his resignation, in a successful attempt to outmanoeuvre popular anger. Because of the complete political vacuum he had created, he was able to survive the crisis and find scapegoats whom he could hold responsible for bringing about the disastrous defeat.

Although this calamitous defeat strengthened Nasser's personal authority, it marked the end of his regime. Nevertheless, having eliminated all possible opposition, the final denouement took three more years, ending with the death of Nasser himself in September 1970. The last three years of his era witnessed a strange amalgam of events: on the economic front there were perpetual increases in prices and taxation, the black market flourished, and standards of living steadily deteriorated. On the other hand, the completion of the High Dam and the erection of a steel plant held the promise of an eventual upturn in the economy. On the military front, Egypt was involved in a war of attrition that saw the evacuation of the canal zone and the consequent destruction of the major cities in the region. But neither the war nor the negotiations succeeded in restoring the occupied lands. This period also saw the rebuilding of the Egyptian army. Politically, it was a time of disillusionment and unrest: there were students' and workers' upheavals, and the public lost confidence in almost every institution, which was echoed in the radicalisation of the mass media.

This brief account demonstrates the extent to which political and social issues dominated people's consciousness during this period. The very fact that Egypt was occupied for most of this time (with the exception of 1957–67) made it inevitable that anyone involved in public activities, including writing, would deal directly or indirectly with the various aspects of these burning socio-political issues. It is also important to take into consideration that any endeavour to write in Egypt implies a certain degree of awareness of being a member of an educated minority and that this places a heavy burden of responsibility upon the writer's shoulders. The creative literature of the period cannot be properly understood without some grasp of the interrelationship between the reader, the writer and the authorities, with all its variations, from challenge and rebellion to repression and frustration. An appreciation of this background may help to explain the rise of certain trends or the decline of others during these decades. It also sheds light on any interpretation of the dominant attitudes or phenomena that appear in the development of the Egyptian short story. This is not only because of the deep interaction between modern Egyptian literature and socio-political life, and the direct involvement of many Egyptian writers in the national cause, but also because changes in the scale of social values, with all their political causes and ramifications, affect the very structure of many literary genres.

Nevertheless, Egyptian cultural life during this period was more complex than this simple outline may suggest. Consequently, a few words on the cultural aspects of this period that shaped the interrelationship between the reading public, the writer and the authorities are necessary. The first of these is education, which provides the basis and the prime motivation for most cultural activities. Although the rate of illiteracy was only reduced from 85 per cent in 1930 to 72 per cent in 1970, the number of literate people grew nearly fivefold from two million to more than nine million during the same period.[34] Despite the high rate of illiteracy, the school population numbered more than five million in 1970, including 771,000 at university and secondary level – an approximate indication of the probable reading public. Although the standard of education deteriorated during the last two decades, and the lack of freedom and the suppression of political activity lowered the cultural awareness of students, the spread of education and widening of its base contributed to the growth of the reading public and granted those with talent the opportunity to express themselves. The expansion of schooling during this period brought about the education (for the first time) of the lower strata of society and, thus, broadened the class structure of education.[35] This change consequently affected both the interests and the nature of the reading public and the creative writer. Any study of the class background of the Egyptian writer will show the gradual shift in class structure: for example, from Haykal, Lāshīn, Taymūr, al-Ḥakīm, the offspring of the feudal families and the aristocracy in the early decades of this century, to Najīb Maḥfūẓ, 'Ādil Kāmil, Iḥsān 'Abd al-Quddūs, 'Abd al-Ḥamīd al-Saḥḥār, the sons of the upper middle class in the 1940s, to Yūsuf Idrīs, 'Abd al-Raḥmān al-Khamīsī, Yūsuf al-Shārūnī, the offspring of the *petits bourgeois* in the 1950s, and finally, to people such as Muḥammad Ḥāfiẓ Rajab, Muḥammad Ibrāhīm Mabrūk, Jamāl al-Ghīṭānī and others from poor, working-class origins in the 1960s. This transformation in the class basis of both writers and readers corresponded to, and was the source of, many alterations in the themes, characters and forms of Egyptian literature. The interrelationship between these changes and the socio-political milieu goes without saying, for these four decades witnessed a deep concern with public issues on the part of the intellectuals, as well as major changes in literary and artistic sensibility.[36]

The 1930s saw a desire among the educated youth to participate in the making of their country's future.

> Economic issues were a major concern of educated youth by the 1930s; the world depression sparked off a wave of economically oriented activities by students, and the youth movements of the 1930s and 1940s were acutely sensitive to questions of economic opportunity.[37]

By the 1940s economic injustice had grown in scope to include social and educational dimensions and to spark off a call for reform, or revolution. It became clear in this period that 'an educated younger generation inevitably means a political avant-garde. This mobile community became more and more acutely aware of the misfortune of the time, and of the part it had to play.'[38] In an attempt to fulfil this role, sections of this generation fell prey to Fascism and Nazism,[39] or fell under the spell of religious fanaticism and right-wing political views.[40] Others had adopted, by the end of the Second World War, revolutionary views and Marxist ideas.[41] The cultural effect of the latter was considerable, despite the fact that it was politically the weakest of the three ideologies. Its radical social and cultural views inspired writers to break new frontiers in their work, and contributed greatly to the development of certain literary schools.

Nevertheless, all three political attitudes, as well as the mainstream of Egypt's policies with its liberal and radical leanings, were different means towards the same goal; the liberation of the country from the British occupation and its local agents. For the young of the 1930s, 1940s and early 1950s the national issues were clear-cut, but they were not so for those of the late 1950s and 1960s. The most significant traditional obstacles to Egypt's progress, that is, the British occupation, the monarchy and the semi-feudal system, were eventually removed by 1957, and the road to all national dreams and aspirations was theoretically opened. Yet most did not come to fruition. The scope of these political movements, with all their cultural ramifications, was relatively narrow. Suspicion and fear of dawn visitors lingered in the air because of the sudden disappearance of many dissidents, and the old corrupt establishment was soon replaced by a new, no less corrupt one. The emergence of new masters, given to embezzling public money, nullified the positive effect of undermining the old ruling class and stripping it of power. The jails grew accustomed to accommodating the whole spectrum of political views that constituted the national conscience, and the country paid dearly for empirical policies and random decisions. On the other hand, this period also witnessed a general growth of industry, the construction of a number of large engineering projects, the spread of education among the poorer classes, the popularisation of the concepts of social justice and equal opportunity, an increase in the numbers of educated and working women,[42] and the rise of the country's prestige and role in international politics.

At this point brief mention should be made of certain material factors relating to the social and cultural scene during these four decades, such as rapid urbanisation (the urban population rose from 4,382,083 in 1937 to 12,032,743 in 1966);[43] the increase of paved roads, from 400 kilometres in 1936 to 13,889 kilometres in 1970, and unpaved and dirt tracks, from 7,000 kilometres in 1936 to 12,000 kilometres in 1970;[44] and the extension of the railway until the length of track reached 4,269 kilometres in 1952.[45] Although the latter did not increase again until 1970, the quality of service improved and the rolling-stock and number of passengers grew. This period also saw an enormous growth in the number of machines in use and their introduction into everyday life. Mechanisation, largely the result of a widespread interest in industrialisation, took place in both urban and rural sectors of the country. For example, in rural areas the number of tractors rose from 3,900 in 1945 to 6,500 in 1950. This played a vital role in changing the rhythm of life and modifying social values and cultural concepts. 'This rapid increase affected the training of workers and artisans. In the long run, mechanisation might modify certain features, not only of the landscape, but of the countryman's psychology.'[46] However, in both industry and agriculture the negative effect of mechanisation was more in evidence than the positive, for the machine was not originally introduced to develop the village or modernise the town: it aimed primarily at increasing productivity, and consequently increased the level of human exploitation. In many cases the purchase of machinery was achieved at the expense of wages.[47] At the same time the price of basic commodities increased rapidly during and after the Second World War. In fact, prices trebled between 1939 and 1944 whereas the real value of *per capita* income dropped from $E 12 to $E 9. The result was a widening of the economic gap between the higher and lower strata of society.[48] These economic and social problems were compounded by the absence of any efficient social security system, and led to constantly deteriorating conditions for the working class, inhuman oppression and exploitation of the peasants in feudal estates, all of which culminated in the political and social upheavals of the second half of the 1940s. It is not surprising, therefore, that some historians consider this time

> a dark period, during which Egypt experienced disappointments as great as her hopes, the anger of the under-privileged flared up in violence, and the contrast between the matureness of men's demands and the indefinite postponement of solutions reached its highest pitch.[49]

Town workers rioted, and the peasants abandoned their work, set fire to the feudal landlords' mansions and crops, destroyed the water-wheels and ruined agricultural machines and tractors in several villages.[50] The first action of the military junta after the deposition of the king was the agricultural reform law. This was an attempt to ease the tension and to ensure the flow of agricultural production, which was the backbone of the Egyptian economy. In this respect the measures taken were a mixture of conciliation and intimidation, and their prime aim was to calm the anger of the underprivileged rather than to bring about radical change.

Thus, urbanisation, mechanisation, the polarisation and intensification of class conflict, the continuation of the patriotic struggle against the occupation, the diffusion of education, the acceleration of women's emancipation and their role and involvement in public life, and the consequent social and political upheavals all form part of the background to the cultural scene during these four decades. They played a decisive, though indirect, role in shaping cultural movements. This is not only because cultural activities in developing countries often relate closely to apparently 'non-cultural affairs', but also because of the complex relationship between literature and the reading public in that period. The reader, at the same time generator and product of the phenomena described above, exerted a considerable impact on the cultural scene. His or her encouragement, or discouragement, of certain magazines (which were often the mouthpieces of specific cultural groups) or literary works proved to be a crucial factor in their development and survival. Because journalism had strong affinities with the evolution of the short story[51] and because, at the time, journalism in Egypt was by and large politically oriented, this important facet of the cultural scene must now be considered further.

The 1930s witnessed notable initiatives in journalism in general, and in literary journalism in particular. The governments of the early 1930s had restricted the scope of political journalism, creating a vacuum that literary journalism tried to fill. The growth of literary journalism continued even after the relative improvement in the political atmosphere brought about by the signing of the 1936 Treaty and the return of the Wafd government in the same year. The 1936 Treaty of Independence inaugurated a new era of hope. It gave Egypt an immediate, yet temporary, feeling that the quest for independence had come to an end, and the task of rebuilding and developing the country had commenced.[52] Although the outbreak of the Second World War jeopardised this newborn enthusiasm, there was nevertheless a tremendous increase in both the quantity and quality of journalism.

There were 152 newspapers and periodicals by 1930, a number that rose sharply to 289 in 1940 and to 422 in 1951,[53] but dropped dramatically to 246 in 1960 and to 221 in 1970;[54] yet quality did not decline to the same extent.[55] Of greatest relevance to this study is the fact that the daily papers and weekly reviews of the 1930s developed a considerable interest in literary matters, especially creative fiction. This also holds true for the 1940s, despite the acute shortage of paper during the war. This interest was not purely literary; it was also motivated by the desire to attract a wider reading public. Experience proved that the reader devoured fictional material (translated or original) and preferred it to other forms of journalism. The reader's responsive and demanding attitude to fictional writing forced some of the established conservative monthly reviews – such as *al-Muqtaṭaf* and *al-Hilāl* – to reverse their policy towards fiction.[56] In the early 1930s, they started grudgingly to include fictional works, and by the 1940s *al-Hilāl* in particular had become an ardent advocate of creative fiction and devoted whole issues to short stories and tales.[57]

During the 1930s and 1940s numerous literary reviews sprang up and flourished, dedicating a great deal of space to fictional writing, both translated and original.[58] A number of interesting characteristics are worth noting; first, the words *qiṣṣah* and *riwāyah* became common features in the titles of many of these magazines.[59] Second, some of the general cultural reviews that appeared in this period began without publishing any fictional material, then hesitantly introduced one short story (usually translated) and, following readers' demands, were forced to increase the number of stories until five or six stories were included in one issue, despite the fact that the magazine did not specialise in short stories or even in literature.[60] Thirdly, several magazines conducted short story competitions,[61] which attracted several hundred entries,[62] for first prizes amounted to as much as four times the annual *per capita* income at the time.[63] Fourthly, some of the magazines that paid special attention to fiction were compelled (especially after 1936) to publish a sister magazine devoted entirely to fiction.[64] Although the latter were short-lived, this was not because of the readers' aversion, or to the saturation of the market by these magazines, but rather to the fact that they exceeded the ability of the available writers and translators to supply them with reasonable material. It was unfortunate that two bi-weeklies – *al-Riwāyah* and

Majallat al-'Ishrīn Qiṣṣah – started simultaneously in 1937 and needed more than fifty short stories a month,[65] while at the same time a massive number of short stories was required by the rest of the dailies, weeklies and periodicals of the same period. The logical consequence was a deterioration of the quality of both original and translated short stories.

The picture in the 1950s and the 1960s did not differ dramatically from that of the 1930s and 1940s, although some changes can be observed. New magazines and periodicals continued to appear[66] and they, like the old ones, were much concerned with fiction. But a new trend began in the 1950s and developed further in the 1960s: this was the publication of Egyptian fictional writing in other Arab countries, not least because of publishing difficulties and censorship inside Egypt. Lebanese reviews in particular became vehicles for much experimental writing.[67] This added a new dimension to the relationship between the short story and journalism. Links between certain periodicals and certain literary schools or trends in the Egyptian short story should also be noted. This is particularly true of the left-wing periodicals that emerged during this period. Although most were short-lived, they managed to nurture and promote realistic literature and to encourage attention to social themes in art in general, and in creative fictional writing in particular.[68]

Publication in collections makes for a greater degree of seriousness and durability for the short story. It reveals the artistic range of the author in both technique and subject matter, and discloses how wide or narrow is his world.[69] It also involves a certain degree of selectivity on the part of the writer. While the circulation of a magazine that includes short stories as a regular item gives a rough indication of the size of the reading public of fiction, the circulation of fictional books provides an even more reliable assessment.

The four decades (1930–70) witnessed important developments in both the quantity and quality of publishing, and this was particularly significant in the realm of fiction. The number of books published in Arabic in Egypt rose from thirty-four in 1900 to 546 in 1947, and then to 2,623 in 1969.[70] If specific data about fictional works is examined, it is revealed that whereas the number of collections of original short stories published from the beginning of the century to 1930 amounted to less than twenty in all, the number of collections of short stories published in the period, 1930–1970, has exceeded 500 collections, a twenty-five fold increase. During the same period the increase in the publication of general literature increased only sixteen fold.[71] There are also three more corroborative facts that confirm the reading public's special interest in books of fiction: the first is that the storage period for fictional works is shorter than any other category of book. The average storage period for books in Egypt (until they go out of print) is five to ten years. This period shrinks to only one year for fictional books.[72] The second fact is that the average number of printed copies for a collection of short stories rose from 500 copies in 1922[73] to about 6,000 throughout the 1960s.[74] The third is the appearance of several popular series of fiction that specialise in publishing original novels or collections of short stories. Examples of these include *Qiṣaṣ li'l-Jamī'* (Stories for Everyone), *Kutub li'l-Jamī'* (Books for Everyone), *al-Kitāb al-Dhahabī* (The Golden Book), *al-Kitāb al-Fiḍḍi* (The Silver Book), and *Kitāb al-Yawm* (Book of the Day). A further contributory factor was the role played by left-wing magazines and left-wing publishing houses, such as Dār al-Nadīm, al-Dār al-Miṣriyyah li'l-Nashr and Dār al-Fikr.

Further evidence of the reading public's great interest in fiction can be obtained by considering translated works,[75] for translations provided the alternative to Egyptian writing in the reading public's market. Furthermore, translations had a vital influence on the development of the indigenous Egyptian short story from the very beginning.[76] Like original short stories, translated stories appeared in both periodicals and books. Moreover, they were the first to appear in periodicals, partly because the editors' awareness of the pedagogic role of their journals encouraged them to offer models both to the reader and to the would-be short story writer, and partly because translated short stories were easier to obtain than originals,[77] and often of better quality. Newspapers and magazines avidly sought any translated or summarised European fiction, which had some negative effects. The periodicals' voracity for translation encouraged many unqualified and ill-equipped translators to send in their contributions until the market became inundated with poor translations. Translated stories appeared often without the name of their author or translator, or with large sections omitted. This does not reflect the translator's desire to disown these works or to improve them, rather it indicates a lack of responsibility and discipline. When some translators were short of foreign stories to translate they produced fakes, confident that the market's appetite for translation and the generally low standards would allow them to pass without exposure.[78] One more negative result was the confusion between translation and summary. Summarising fairly long short stories or even novels was extremely common, and for bad translators this was easier than the more tedious work of accurate translation. This created and perpetuated the impression that the most important element in a story is its moral message derived from the crude compression of the plot. The success and popularity of these summaries encouraged many writers to overlook other structural elements and led to didacticism, over-sentimentality, incoherence, and sacrificing the medium for the message in many of the indigenous short stories of that period.

However, the extensive use of translation widened the knowledge of the reading public, increased their numbers and played an invaluable role in familiarising the reader with the conventions of the short story; without it, artistic communication in this form would have been almost impossible. Translations, especially good ones, continued to familiarise the reader with new techniques and conventions throughout these four decades, and to maintain links between the readership and the new accomplishments of this literary genre across the world. The work of all major short story writers was translated into Arabic and many of these authors left their imprint on the development of the Egyptian short story. To cite a few early examples among the 136 short stories published in *al-Riwāyah* in its first year, 1937, 114 were translated works of masters of fiction. They included works of Pushkin, Turgenev, Dostoevsky, Saltykov, Tolstoy, Chekhov, Salogub, Gorky, Kuprin and Andreyev; Balzac, Mérimée, Musset, Daudet, Zola, France and Maupassant; Irving, Poe, Dickens, Hardy, Wilde, O. Henry, K. Mansfield and O'Flaherty; Deledda and Pirandello; and various German, Austrian, Indian, Japanese, Spanish and Swedish writers. *Al-Hilāl* and *al-Majallah al-Jadīdah*[79] published (throughout the 1930s) many Russian short stories in translation and subsequently often stated on the cover that the book contained Russian short stories,[80] which reflects the popularity of such items. This period also witnessed the publication in book form of many translated collections of short stories.[81] Although Russian stories had the lion's share at first, Soviet writers did not enjoy the same status in the 1950s and 1960s. There was a shift towards modern Western writers such as Joyce, Woolf, Kafka and Hemingway. A further positive contribution of the translation is that it served as an apprenticeship for a number of young writers[82] who began their careers as translators of foreign languages.

After dealing with the three factors – journalism, books and translation – that were closely connected with the development of the Egyptian short story, a brief consideration of the major literary questions of these four decades is necessary. Every short story writer was influenced, positively or negatively, by these questions, even if he did not actively participate in shaping them. They thus provide the intellectual context in which the Egyptian short story developed. The first important literary event of the period that was relevant to the short story was the cry for *al-adab al-qawmī* (a national literature, or a literature that reflects the identity of the nation). This was articulated with a literary manifesto signed by six young writers – Muḥammad Zakī ʿAbd al-Qādir, Muḥammad Amīn Ḥassūna, Muḥammad al-Asmar, Zakariyya ʿAbdu, Maḥmūd ʿIzzat Mūsā and Muʿāwiyah Muḥammad Nūr – and was published in *al-Siyāsah al-Usbūʿiyyah* in 1930.[83] The manifesto contained some seminal ideas and provoked stimulating discussion, which stirred the stagnant literary scene. The manifesto's point of departure was its rejection of the state of Egyptian literature at the time, which it regarded as parasitic and entirely dependent upon translation and adaptation from Western writing. It propounded the view that literature was a mirror for reality, and that by relying on foreign literature, not only was that reality distorted, but Egyptian literature itself. Therefore, it urged

> young writers who are filled with the zeal of renaissance and believe in freedom of expression and independent thought, to pay great attention to the question of creating a literature which bears characteristics peculiar to us and has its specific indigenous features as Russian, English and French literature do.[84]

The manifesto was aware that it called for *adab qawmī*, 'national literature', and not *adab maḥallī*, or 'local literature'. Yet it did not forget to stress the importance of understanding and knowledge of foreign literature, despite its vigorous attack on adaptations and translations. The manifesto provoked a widespread and fierce battle between the traditionalists and the modernists, during which the signatories of the manifesto published further statements on their theme.[85] When they were compelled to spell out their stand with regard to the question of Egyptian literature, *adab Miṣrī*, or oriental literature, *adab sharqī*,[86] they stated categorically that they were promoting pure Egyptian literature as distinct from both occidental and oriental literature.[87] This was sufficient to bring the full weight of the conservative schools in literature and thought to bear against them.[88]

This was the first round[89] of an endless battle between the old and the new that continued to erupt at regular intervals throughout these four decades. It took many forms: the traditional versus the modern, Islamic culture versus Western forms, *l'art pour l'art* versus *l'art de l'engagement*, and finally reactionary thought versus left-wing views. Although this battle was fought so often, every round revolved around different subjects and appeared as if it were a completely new conflict. The second round took place when Tawfīq al-Ḥakīm's play *Ahl al-Kahf* was published in 1933, and the third round revolved around Ṭāhā Ḥusayn's views in his controversial book *Mustaqbal al-Thāqafah fī Miṣr* (1938). From round to round an apparent retrogression can be detected on the part of the partisans of old. This is not because of the persuasiveness of the devotees of the new, but rather results from a certain process of accumulation. Between the first and the third rounds, for instance, al-Ḥakīm published *'Awdat al-Rūh* (1933), *Shahrazād* (1934) and *Yawmiyyāt Nā'ib fī'l-Aryāf* (1937). Several collections of short stories appeared, the Egyptian film industry began to exert a considerable impact on the public, Muḥammad Luṭfī Jum'ah popularised his enthusiasm for collecting Egyptian folklore,[90] and Aḥmad Zakī Abū Shādī introduced new views and concepts in his influential literary review, *Apollo*, which ran from 1932 to 1934. A number of enlightened critics emerged and published numerous studies on fiction in general and Egyptian fiction in particular.[91] Thus when the question was reformulated with Ṭāhā Ḥusayn's book, it was tackled in a more reasonable and mature way. Ṭāhā Ḥusayn not only promoted many of the new literature's arguments, but he also struck at the root of many traditional concepts and managed to bring down the edifice of traditional, ossified approaches to literature. This encouraged other writers to boldly confront different aspects of the perplexing question of future cultural orientation. The late 1930s and the 1940s saw the publication of many radical books, which increased awareness of various dimensions of the national question.[92] It is not by mere chance that the publication of these books coincided with the increase in national awareness of the social and economic aspects of the question of independence, and also with the accentuation of social and economic themes in Egyptian creative literature. This awareness reached its acme in the 1950s, and experienced its lowest ebb during the 1960s, when a mood of despair and frustration prevailed.

However, before moving to the 1950s and the 1960s, a few words about literary criticism in the 1930s and 1940s are appropriate. This criticism formed a bridge between the reader and new fictional work, and also inaugurated a stream of ideas and categories, which aided the creative writer in his difficult task. Apart from Ṭāhā Ḥusayn,[93] ʻAbbās M. al-ʻAqqād[94] and I. ʻAbd al-Qādir al-Māzinī,[95] these two decades witnessed the rise of literary critics from the younger generation such as Muāwiyah M. Nʻūr,[96] Fakhrī Abʻū'l-Suʻūd,[97] Ismāʻīl Adham,[98] Muḥammad Mandūr,[99] Sayyid Qutb,[100] Luwīs ʻAwaḍ[101] and Anwar al-Miʻaddāwī.[102] It goes without saying that these critics represented different literary schools and adopted various approaches to literature, which provided the literary scene with vitality and richness.

In the case of theatre, al-Ḥakīm fought the battle for serious drama almost alone (during the 1930s and 1940s). Of course, the supporters of new literature stood by his work, but he was the only major figure actually writing plays. The novel was a different matter, and by the 1940s a new generation of Egyptian novelists had emerged:

From 1944 onwards a stream of heavily documented novels of angry social protest began to pour out, much more detailed and infinitely more concerned with the horror and degradation of Egyptian urban life than anything that had appeared before. Social injustice and class struggle were now added to national independence as political themes.[103]

The emergence of these new themes was not isolated from the new phases of the perpetual struggle between the old and the new. By the 1950s, and because of radical changes in artistic sensibility, the debate was argued in literary and aesthetic terms while political and religious jargon receded into the background. This does not imply that social and political factors were completely ignored, rather it indicates that many of the rudimentary questions regarding the validity of the new literary genres and their adequacy for Egyptian society had already been decided.[104] The new literary forms (drama, novel and short story) had been vindicated and their existence was no longer in question. It was at this point that splits appeared in the victorious front. The 1950s saw the birth of a new polarisation between the Left and the Right.

In the 1950s, the question of the old versus the new took the form of a wide-ranging discussion on the function of art in society[105] and the relationship between form and content in literature. Despite, or perhaps because of, its simplifications, *Fi'l-Thaqāfah al-Miṣriyyah* (1955) by Maḥmūd Amīn al-'Ālim and 'Abd al-'Aẓīm Anīs, was a milestone in the development of this literary debate. Its major significance lies not in its seminal effect on the younger generation of writers, or in its success in popularising the term *iltizām* (commitment, or the Marxist literary outlook), but in manifesting a radical change in artistic sensibility. Although the short story was the first to record this change in sensibility,[106] in the 1950s poetry and drama were associated to a greater degree with this new departure than any other art form. The change in poetic sensibility was heard as clearly as it was because it affected the very structure of Arabic prosody, and consequently the traditional concept of poetry itself.[107] The change in drama was the second to be recognised. In 1956, Nu'mān 'Āshūr's play *al-Nās Illī Taḥt* was performed. It 'made the theatre immediately relevant to contemporary Egypt. Its galvanising effect on Egyptian theatre was similar to that of John Osborne's *Look Back in Anger* in England.'[108] By the mid-1950s, because of the development of a committed literature, the concept of *iltizām* and the importance of social reality in literature became major themes in any literary discussion. The term *al-adab al-multazim* became extremely popular, not only in Egypt but throughout the Arab world (these were the years of pan-Arabism). Ironically, 1959 saw the wholesale arrest of those who had popularised the concept of *iltizām* in literature and of writers who sincerely tried to convey social reality and to speak for the underprivileged in their creative work.

The 1960s, therefore, had a gloomy beginning and followed a

confused course. Although the left-wing intelligentsia was behind bars, the early 1960s witnessed supposed attempts to transform Egyptian society to socialism. This resulted in the enlargement of the public sector, increased industrialisation, the construction of the High Dam, the expansion of free education, the reclamation of thousands of acres of land and, above all, rising hopes for a better future for peasants and workers. Yet, at the same time, there was a pervasive growth of bureaucracy and corruption, the curtailment of freedom, the abolition of almost all political activity, severe censorship, the degradation of many social values, and a growing unease and frustration amongst the younger generation. The older generation, who acquiesced in such an atmosphere and controlled the cultural establishment, did not recognise the intensity of the contradictions of this epoch from which the younger generation suffered.[109] The literary scene in the early 1960s was relatively stagnant, and the younger generation's attempt to enliven it was a mere cry in the wilderness.[110]

But by 1964, with the release of intellectuals, the struggle between the old and the new, which from then onwards took the form of Right and Left, erupted again. The subject was a memorandum published by the Poetry Committee of the High Council of Arts and Letters – the highest authority in the cultural hierarchy. The memorandum called for a crusade against *al-Shi'r al-Jadīd,* the new movement in poetry that had attained popularity amongst the reading public. It used stultified arguments and a pompous tone as if to try to compensate for the absence of the ardent veteran and former Head of the Committee, 'Abbās M. al-'Aqqād, who had died the previous year. The newly released leftists seized the opportunity to question the very foundations of the Poetry Committee and other literary establishments. The next two years witnessed dramatic changes in the literary establishment in the interests of the new trends. 1966 was the year of the leftists' penetration of cultural institutions, and the leading poets of *al-Shi'r al-Jadīd* became members of the very committee that had called for their persecution two years previously. Great hopes emerged and the literary movement gained momentum. But the gloomy atmosphere of frustration that still existed under the surface found expression in the creative work of talented writers. The apparent contradiction between the mood of success that pervaded the literary establishment and the gloom and frustration suggested by the best literary works of the period went unnoticed by all but the younger generation of writers. Apart from conveying an atmosphere of unease, depression and disappointment in their own work, they were the first to sense the new change in artistic sensibility. This new sensibility was baptised by rituals of defeat and destruction.

The catastrophe of 1967 had shaken the whole system to the foundations. A tidal wave of criticism, self-criticism and re-evaluation swept through the country. In 1968 a conference was held to re-evaluate the works and policies of the Ministry of Culture since its foundation. The conference provoked some interesting ideas concerning the role of the state in cultural activity and stimulated discussion on freedom of expression and future cultural policy. During this debate the young writers asked for a place and a role in the determination of cultural policy. Their voice was critical and distinct, and they asked for a cultural magazine of their own.[111] When they failed to obtain official support, they published their avant-garde periodical at their own expense.[112] In the following year, 1969, the government tried to assimilate this young literary movement, organising a conference that provided the young writers with an arena for further criticism but that failed to fulfil its purpose. The authorities resorted to an iron fist policy and heavy censorship. The 1960s, which opened with the ban of *Awlād Ḥāratinā* [113] by the Azhar, ended with the ban of *Tilk al-Rā'iḥah*[114] and *Tha'r Allāh*[115] (the latter was also banned by the Azhar). The decade that began with gloom and frustration ended with severe self-questioning and despair.

CHAPTER TWO

The Realistic Short Story

Introductory Notes

On Classification

The critical treatment of the Egyptian short story throughout the four decades under study here (1930–70) requires particular methodological demarcation and, consequently, will involve the use of certain critical terms with their varying implications and affiliations in different cultures and a variety of critical contexts. It is necessary to define the major critical terms used in the classification of works discussed below, though in so doing one risks producing what may seem more a simplification than a rigorous clarification. The difficulties of dealing with the issue of classification are manifold, not only because of the resistance within the culture to 'borrowed' Western solutions and the ambiguity of many major critical terms, even in their original cultural contexts, but also because of the novelty of the field and scarcity of reliable critical studies on the subject.

Although modern Arabic criticism has not yet arrived at satisfactory answers to the many methodological questions posed by the rich creative yield of the last seven decades, this study must resolve the initial problem of classification and demarcation with either an extrinsic or intrinsic approach. The extrinsic approach is usually governed by historical and political factors often alien to the richness and sophistication of the artistic phenomenon. Recourse to an extrinsic division involves an undercurrent of overrated assumptions which suggest that the role of those extraneous factors is more important than other elements, if not the most important element, in the process of the development of the genre under discussion.

Yet the application of an intrinsic approach to the historical study of the Egyptian short story is equally inadequate. During the formative years of this new literary genre, it was possible to use the intrinsic approach without disturbing the chronological order of presentation since the number and variety of works were limited and they were produced at reasonably wide intervals. However, when this period ended, the vast increase in the number of writers and works that followed invalidated this approach. By 1930 the indigenous Egyptian short story had crystallised, and it became increasingly difficult to consider these four decades as one period, yet the development of the genre and laws of historical perspective dictate that a division of the genre's literary history into distinct eras becomes progressively more unsatisfactory as one approaches the present. It is perhaps excusable, then, to take the forty years of this study as an integral epoch and try to find an alternative classification for this somewhat intractable product.

Such a classification can only emerge from the material and must not be intrusively imposed upon it; it must adopt a form that appreciates both the independence of the work of art and its relevance to the social and cultural scene from which it springs and to which it is directed. After scrutinising various alternatives, I have chosen to divide the data into artistic schools such as realism or romanticism, accepting that in so doing it runs the risk of using critical terms associated with different cultures and coined to suit different developmental processes. The problem with these terms is not only that they are relatively alien to modern Arabic literature, but that they are surrounded by confusion and ambiguity both in their original use and when related to modern Arabic criticism. There is also a complete absence of any attempt to establish an etymology, that is to say, to define or trace the semantic development of such terms as realism, romanticism or symbolism in Arabic. In addition, those who are familiar with the socio-historical background of European realism or romanticism might find it hard to accept the application of the same terms to Arabic literature.

Even if one dispenses with such prejudices or fixed ideas, several obstacles remain. Apart from the lack of a satisfactory definition of these terms in their original culture, let alone in Arabic – for the short definitions are as oblique and confusing as the long ones – it is impossible to apply them to modern Arabic literature as period concepts. One cannot use them as approximate terms that indicate the dominance of certain norms, moods, ideas and conventions during a specific span of time because modern Arabic literature, especially in its newly acquired forms – the short story, novel and drama – has been exposed over the course of its short history to all manner of European cultural influences. It was not influenced by one school at a time but by all of them at the same time. The influence of realism coexisted with that of romanticism, alongside that of naturalism and symbolism. Moreover, most of these influences intermingled with each other over a relatively short period of time. Therefore it is not surprising to find both realistic and romantic short stories in the work of one writer, and often in one collection of short stories. In other words, there was a degree of coexistence between literary schools that was not paralleled in nineteenth-century Europe, a sort of episodic coexistence of several artistic sensibilities within a span of forty years (1930–70).

However, the affiliation of the works of any one writer to several artistic schools and the coexistence of various artistic sensibilities do not cancel out the validity of this type of classification. This study is concerned with the development of the literary genre and its endeavour to capture the anxieties of individuals in search for identity, not the rigid categorisation or pigeon-holing of certain writers. The development of the Egyptian short story during these four decades is certainly relevant to the critical assessment of individual writers, but it is not governed by the fluctuation of any single writer between two or more artistic schools. It must, however, be understood against the historical and cultural background sketched in the previous chapter, for this will furnish an awareness of the complex mechanisms that created the living experiences treated in the majority of Egyptian short stories of the period. This background also provides some explanation for the episodic coexistence of several artistic sensibilities in this relatively short period and some knowledge of its tastes and preferences, which is a *sine qua non* of the interpretation of this literature.

The Reading Publics

This coexistence of artistic sensibilities interacts with yet another phenomenon, the reading public of the Egyptian short story. In my previous book, *The Genesis*, I referred to the 'reading public' and its role in widening interest in the short story as a literary genre. At that stage, and to avoid unnecessary complication, the term 'reading public' was used in a fairly general way, although it would have been more exact to speak of various 'reading publics',[1] for a homogeneous reading public is really a hypothetical concept. Even within the sphere of the reading public of a specific literary genre – in this case the Egyptian short story – there is enormous disparity in taste and numbers.

This is not only because the reading publics of the genre vary in temperament and social, political, educational and cultural background, but also because there are various types of short story. Works of artistic merit acquired a smaller readership than mediocre ones, while experimental works, directed at avant-garde readers, procured the smallest readership of all.[2] In fact, and in the context of the Egyptian short story, there is an inverse ratio between the awareness of technique and artistic virtuosity in a given work and the size of its reading public. In other words, there is a direct ratio between the writer's awareness of his reader, and the reader's response to the writer's work. This does not negate the fact that every writer has a particular reader in mind and is aware to a greater or lesser extent of that reader's existence and needs. But it indicates that various groups of writers were aiming at different reading publics, and that the order of priorities varied from one group to another. For some the focus was the reader's favourable response, and so they deliberately sacrificed artistic values to attain this aim, while others aimed at long-term artistic values rather than eliciting an immediate response from the existing reading public. Needless to say, the Egyptian, or rather Arab, reading public's taste and preferences fluctuate constantly. As far as the Egyptian short story is concerned, works which were welcomed with adulation and which achieved phenomenal circulation in the 1930s and 1940s had slipped into oblivion by the 1950s and were ridiculed by the 1960s.

This is not a phenomenon unique to modern Arabic literature. A scholar of Western literature has argued that

> it can safely be said that, with few exceptions, the significant artists ... encountered hostility, lack of comprehension, or indifference on the part of the public. They achieved general recognition only at the price of violent and prolonged struggles, many of them only posthumously, or, before their deaths, among but a small circle of followers. Inversely, and again with but few exceptions, it is observable that ... those

> artists who quickly and easily achieved general recognition had no real and lasting importance.[3]

As a general platitude, this fact seems hardly worth mentioning; what is interesting is how this phenomenon affected the development of the Egyptian short story. The reader's response to a certain work is not a mere reaction without further consequences; rather, it is an original action that influences the process of development of the whole literary genre and helps certain changes germinate or discourages others. It also plays an important role in directing the attention of publishers and would-be writers towards certain types of writing and in promoting certain artistic sensibilities.

The relationship between the writer and the reader, or more precisely between the writer's product – the creative work – and the reader, is a complex one indeed, without which the creative work remains somehow incomplete. Publishing plays an important role in this relationship, for it is a selective process in which 'the laws about "writing" are in fact closely tied up with those of the market'.[4] Criticism and the general cultural atmosphere also have a role. 'Publishing is selective, but criticism is even more so. A reviewing market, or even what one might call a reviewing lottery, undeniably exists.'[5] Thus the attention of the reading public, which plays an active role in the development of the literary genre, is drawn to a certain work for a host of non-literary reasons. The laws of the reviewing market are even more ambiguous than those of the publishing market. They take into account the social status of the writer, his public activities, intellectual weight, political affiliations and his ability to maintain an amicable, or even useful, relationship with reviewing circles. They also take into account the status and power of the publisher who published the work and his or her ability to manipulate the reviewing market. The literary merit of the work is only one factor among many, and may even come after a rather vague consideration of public taste.

All such considerations, literary and non-literary alike, greatly affect the reader's response, to the extent that 'apart from those who are particularly well-educated and really interested in literature, no one chooses for himself the fiction he is going to read'.[6] Yet the reader still exerts a clear influence on the development of the literary genre under discussion and participates in formulating literary taste and the general cultural milieu. In general, readers have tended to overrate some works and writers while underrating others, particularly works of artistic merit and importance.

A literary study, while it takes into consideration the complexity of this phenomenon, has to correct the picture with a critical evaluation of the situation as a whole. Nevertheless, this book will not exclude the less artistic and more popular works from the discussion. Such works affected literary taste in general and the development of the form in particular. Furthermore, they increased, if not initiated, the general reading public's awareness of the traditions and conventions of the short story as a literary form. They also made many of the new devices and techniques of serious artistic works palatable to a wider public. Serious writers often tend to tread new ground regardless of the ability of the reader to follow their adventures. But less talented writers, who are still able to produce coherent works, have an important role to play in the gradual familiarisation of the reader with new styles and forms. Thus, while this study attaches more weight to the works of genuine artistic merit, it touches upon other works in each section of its classification and dwells on them according to their role in the development of the Egyptian short story as a literary form.

The Meaning of Realism in the Arabic Short Story

Nothing would be easier than to avoid the use of the term 'realism' in this study and resort instead to an evasive definition that seemingly describes the characteristics of the works dealt with in this chapter or a pseudo-definition that uses the term in pairs of opposites, such as realism versus classicism or realism versus romanticism. Many scholars have complained that '[r]ealism is an elusive and ramifying conception'[7] and 'the most independent, most elastic, most prodigious of critical terms'.[8] Yet it is an important artistic perspective, because with it 'it [has] been possible in literature as well as in visual arts to represent the most everyday phenomena of reality in a serious and significant context'.[9] Thus an attempt to define it is essential. Initially this study used the word realism as an approximate term, and

> like an infinite number of other words in current usage, these approximate terms have a value and answer a useful purpose, provided that they are treated at their proper value ... and that what they cannot give – exact and cogent definition of thought – is not demanded of them'.[10]

In other words, it is an approximate term to indicate a group of characteristics and associations; the intention was not for it to become a criterion of artistic value or a definite aesthetic judgement but 'merely to indicate where the accent falls, and acquire[s] its meaning only within the compass of specified historical periods',[11] and within a certain culture. The purpose of using such a term is not so much to classify as to clarify these traditions and affinities, thereby bringing out a large number of literary relationships that would not be noticed if there were no contexts established for them.

Yet this study does not use the term as a period concept, not only because of the coexistence of realism and other trends throughout the four decades under discussion, but also because realism in Egypt is not a school or movement. It knows no theoretical programme or manifesto, for its range is too wide, embracing all the main forms of the short story, from the social and regional to the idyllic, humorous, lyrical and psychological, and because of the absence of common links – philosophical, cultural or even personal – amongst those who produced what this study terms the realistic short story. Not only did those authors lack the bonds that constitute a movement, but they were displaced from the centre of cultural life by successful essayists, political columnists and poets, who became the spiritual and cultural leaders of the country. Yet while displaced, they were rarely pushed out altogether and rarely became outsiders or rebels. Moreover, their lasting cultural contribution was far greater than that of those who appeared to be the cultural and spiritual leaders of their time.

Realism for the purposes of this study is neither a period concept nor a literary movement. It is not the deliberately limited solipsistic realism of Alain Robbe-Grillet's *Le nouveau roman*, or the widened realism of Roger Garaudy's *D'un realisme sans ravages*, which includes Kafka and Saint-John Perse and embraces various stages of Picasso. Nor is it 'the only and ultimate method of art'. It is, argues René Wellek, 'only one method, one great stream which has its marked limitations, shortcomings, and conventions. In spite of its claim to penetrate directly to life and reality, realism, in practice, has its set conventions, devices, and exclusions.'[12] Realism in this study is rather a view of art and reality, an approach, more precisely an artistic approach, to reality that differs from any other conceptual approach to reality.

Because 'art cannot help dealing with reality, however much we narrow down its meaning or emphasise the transforming or creative power of the artist',[13] it is necessary at this point to address briefly the question of art and reality without stepping into the deep waters of the fundamental epistemological problem of the relation of art to reality, which is the domain of philosophy and aesthetics. Flaubert once expressed a desire to write a book that had no reference to reality, '*ce qui me semble beau, ce que je voudrais, c'est un livre sur rien, un livre sans attache extérieure, qui se tiendrait de lui-même par la force interne de son style, comme la terre sans être soutenue se tient en l'air ... si cela se peut*'.[14] The unfeasibility of such a wish makes a complete divorce between art and reality impossible. 'Reality like "truth", "nature", or "life", is in art, in philosophy and in everyday usage a value-charged word.'[15] The application of such a term implies an attempt to explain a complexity in terms of simplicity, and however hard this study tries to avoid simplification, any explanation will entail a certain degree of such.

Reality as perceived in this study is a complex concept. It is not 'nature' as described by Hegel as pure externality, a matter that can only be given interiority by man. It is rather a combination of this neutral outside existence and what man's mind adds to its externality in his cognition of it and interaction with it. It is the output of man's experience of the external world blended with various aspects of his interiority and various superstructures of his milieu. In other words, it is more than the details of external reality and less than the totality of human experience, which includes artistic experience. It includes various conscious and unconscious levels of man's interaction with his world. Hence it is a dynamic, changing concept that embraces the present, extends its roots to the past, and at the same time includes man's aspirations for the future. Therefore, an understanding of the historical, social and cultural aspects of Egypt between 1930 and 1970, as indicated in the previous chapter, will help in assessing the reality of this period, while not constructing a complete picture of it.

However, the dynamic nature of reality demands a similar dynamic approach to express its immense diversity. Realism, with its comprehension of the complexity and dynamism of reality and its artistic approach to reality, tends to supply this dynamic artistic medium in dealing with reality, because it both dispenses with conceptual approaches[16] to reality and combines perceptible cognition with intuitive knowledge in its attempt to fathom reality. Hence

> there has, from the beginning, been a simple technical use of 'realism' to describe the precision and vividness of a rendering in art of some observed details ... But also from the beginning, this technical sense was flanked by a reference to content: certain kinds of subject were seen as realism ... The most ordinary definition was in terms of an ordinary, contemporary, everyday reality, as opposed to traditionally heroic, romantic, or legendary subjects ... The advocacy and support of this 'ordinary, everyday, contemporary reality' have been normally associated with the rising middle class, the bourgeoisie.[17]

In European literature, 'it is almost a commonplace of criticism to attribute the rise of realism to the emergence ... of a pushful, self-confident, literate middle class'.[18] It is sometimes attributed to the rise of rationalism in philosophy and empiricism in science, and in Egyptian literature, to the rise of a literate middle class, the tremendous and ever-increasing expansion of the reading public, the rise of rationalism, and the interest in the daily, the humdrum, and the contemporary in literature. It is also connected with the concomitant coarsening of taste and the attempt of new groups, who were educated outside the old Azharite system, to dictate their own visions and tastes. For long after their decline as a dominant, influential socio-political power, the educated Azharites continued to dictate the canons of taste, which remained predominantly regressive in outlook. In Egyptian literature, realism is also associated with the middle-class attempt to express itself in literature and speak for the lower classes – the peasants and the workers – from a moralistic and humanistic viewpoint at the beginning and from an ideological standpoint later on. This change was linked to the fact that rationalism, which started with al-Ṭahṭāwī and flourished with Luṭfī al-Sayyid, 'Alī 'Abd al-Rāziq, Ṭāhā Ḥusayn and Ismā'īl Maẓhar, soon acquired a strong social tone with Salāmah Mūsā, Shiblī Shumayyil and 'Iṣām Ḥifnī Nāṣif, and then blended with clear Marxist ideas with Muḥammad Mandūr, Luwīs 'Awaḍ and Maḥmūd Amīn al-'Ālim.

In the Egyptian short story, the emergence of realism coincides with the rise of indigenous literary works, such as those published in the collection *Yuḥkā Anna* by Lāshīn. Before that, the pioneers of the Egyptian short story had endeavoured to root this new form in the cultural life of their society by using it as a means of representing external reality, portraying real characters and articulating their identities. They did so against deep-rooted misconceptions, which conceived of creative literature as mere entertainment or saw its function in didactic terms, and worked vehemently to change readers' views of fictional works. They cultivated new ideas concerning the function of literature and developed rudimentary notions in the sphere of aesthetics and the relation of art to reality.

By the early 1930s, this preliminary task was over and a new artistic sensibility had begun to emerge. Its completion highlighted more than ever the shortcomings of the pioneers' representational approaches. The novelty of the form, which had previously served as an excuse or licence for artistic mediocrity, no longer applied by the early 1930s; not only had some pioneers succeeded in attaining certain literary heights in a few works, but the rising popularity of the genre and the accumulation of original and translated short stories had acquainted the reading public with most of the conventions and devices of the short story. Moreover, the artistic sensibility of the second third of the twentieth century became more complex than that of the first, and towards the late 1950s, and throughout the 1960s, tended to be highly sophisticated. These changes were in keeping with Egypt's burning desire for change in every field; the period was full of élan and aspirations, with optimistic hopes of building a new Egypt. Such urges were behind many of the political movements of the 1930s and 1940s, and were also the source of inspiration for many artistic trends. Here one may mention the impact of experimentation in technique, style, and themes, in this literary genre,[19] on the development of artistic awareness. It is ironic that, in modern Egyptian literature, the inclination towards realism in prose coincided with the blossoming of romanticism in poetry.

This is ironical because realism seems to be the complete opposite of romanticism. For unlike the romantic,

> the realist is supposed to deal with contemporary life and commonplace scenes; ... [he] fixes his gaze on the world of men, the streets where they jostle and the rooms where they meet and converse; ... The realist is drawn into the social vortex, charts the cross-currents of ambition and self-interest, is familiar with all the processes of getting and spending; ... the typical realist ... levels passion down to the play of the senses and has no patience with intimation or

> immorality. The romantic exalts the creative spirit and puts his faith in intuition; the realist's approach to his material is detached and analytical.[20]

This is perhaps because, unlike poetry, prose forms – the novel, short story and drama – in Arabic knew no classical tradition, therefore did not proceed chronologically through a natural course of development from classicism to realism via neoclassicism and romanticism. Or perhaps because modern Egyptian literature, like Russian literature and unlike most other European literatures, was not clearly influenced by classical Greek and Latin literature. It might also be explained by the interest of the prose writer in the 'real' rather than the 'ideal' and his keen desire to play an active social role rather than escape to extravagant cultural, spiritual or idealistic havens. It may be also a result of the reading public's temperament, for the readers of fictional works – and most of their writers – were graduates of the new education system whose knowledge of the classical Arabic literary heritage was relatively limited and whose ability to express themselves poetically was feeble or non-existent.

Whatever the case may be, realism existed side by side with romanticism. Although some of these reasons may suggest a certain animosity to poetic elements, realism has its own type of poetry, since the Egyptian realist, like his European counterpart,

> expressed growing awareness of the contradictions of the age, not in radical representations of external reality, but in a *poetic inward* synthesis of the real and the ideal … he does not show the social and historical world as it existed objectively, rather is this world revealed as it was experienced and understood by the individual.[21]

Yet the world revealed through artistic experience is different from lived experience, because literature is neither a mimetic version of reality nor a photographic copy of it. It is a complex artifact that endeavours to give reality form and meaning. This is what makes the relationship between art and reality so rich and complex. 'The writer is not only influenced by society; he influences it. Art not merely reproduces life but also shapes it.'[22] Hence, realism as a literary term is a world away from reality or any attempt to copy or reproduce it. In realism, reality appears in a new and completely different form in which realistic experience is transmuted into artistic experience, and thus into artifice.

Because art must have form, it contains a certain element of imagination – the form-giving power according to Kermode's definition.[23] Thus, some scholars find no contradiction between 'realism' and 'imagination', because 'the illusions of art are made to serve the purpose of a closer and truer relation with reality'.[24] And some regard the two as inseparable, for

> Realism and imagination are two terms, two notions, which are concomitant, that is to say which cannot be conceived or thought of as one separated from the other; or to be precise, it should be said that if one can conceive of Realism without the existence of imagination to express its truth, one cannot, by any means, conceive of imagination except within the background of Realism.[25]

This is because the point of departure of imagination is reality and its texture is made up of realistic data organised and arranged in a new order and according to a different logic. This new order and logic make imagination a form-giving power because it has a unique ability to compress and synthesise various elements in one form, and this necessitates its inseparable relation to realism.

> Realistic art deserves its name not because it has recourse to external reality, but above all because it can order real forms and figures in such a way as to place them in a relationship to man. Real creation is just as opposed to direct, formless expression as to an imitation or copy.[26]

This is what Flaubert emphasised in a letter to Turgenev: 'it isn't enough merely to observe; we must order and shape what we have seen. Reality, in my view, ought to be no more than a springboard.'[27]

Therefore, to deserve the name, 'realism must break the representational barrier, in a dialectical transcendence that reabsorbs real figures and forms to elevate them to a higher synthesis'.[28] For a

> work of art is never a section of an appearance of reality, but always a selection of various aspects of reality, fused together by creative imagination, giving life to a symbolic

> or figurative entity which corresponds, in varying degrees, to a complex of social actions, reactions and of human experiences which pertain to a given society and also, through their core of truth, to mankind.[29]

Hence, the relationship between art and reality is more complex than it appears. It is a rich dialectical relationship between the artist who is endowed with the power of imagination, insight and the ability to grant available realistic data form and shape on the one hand, and various aspects of the exterior continuum of his society on the other. One important aspect is the historical dimension, because 'reality is organically one and it embraces the past and the future, as well as the living and knowing present'.[30] Another important aspect is the unity within the diversity and multiformity of reality, for the artist's sensitive eye is able to discover beneath the multifarious data of reality the unseen thread of uniformity. In realism

> everything is linked up with everything else. Each phenomenon shows the polyphony of many components, the intertwinement of the individual and social, of the physical and the psychical, or private interest and public affairs.[31]

This dynamic uniform reality is richer and deeper than that everyday, random, fragmented reality with which the layman deals. It is enriched by the creative writer who tries to capture in artifice the essence, logic and, if one can possibly use the phrase, the spirit of the common vision with all the ambiguity that surrounds the word 'common' – it may mean common as average, ordinary, normal, or as shared, normative and perhaps even universal. This common vision cannot include all possible varieties or images of reality because it excludes the uncommon and the abstruse, and this very fact limits the scope of realism and leaves other images to fall into different categories. It is neither fixed nor ultimate, rather it is relative and mutable, not only because it is concerned with what prevails in a certain society at a given time, but also because what is a common vision for one society is strange and exotic for another. Even within the one society, what is a common vision for a certain class or at a certain historical moment is not so for another class or in a different historical context. The common vision that realism endeavours to express lies in the realm of experience, which may be verified and which suggests genuine ideas and reflections on the consciousness of historical moment. 'Realism is obviously a kind of art which does deal with experience, even common and shared, not highly personal or esoteric experience.'[32]

The common vision is not something in external reality that art echoes, adopts or treats; it is the undercurrent and unifying logic beneath fragmentary external reality. Common vision is neither synonymous with traditional vision nor with any superficial or flat simplification. It is a deep, comprehensive analytical understanding of what is common in a certain society. It is an understanding that takes into account the complexity of reality and the laws of its development, and employs both cognitive and intuitive knowledge to reach that end. This vision needs to be embodied through selected convincing situations and characters. Because it is primarily an artistic vision, it combines truth with prophecy and avoids the direct and didactic. The art that crystallises this vision is usually closely connected with the culture within which it expresses itself and the age in which it appears. It is also capable of mastering the necessary technical tools to construct a coherent edifice, and controls 'the arts of creating illusions of objectivity and impartiality, abjuring the cult of artistic personality and the temptation to romantic irony'.[33] Without structure and form there is no art, and all the efforts made to capture the rhythm of reality and the common vision are in vain if they are not assimilated into a mature and coherent structure.

> A work of art is therefore realistic, not, alas, as it is so often said, because it reproduces the surface appearance of an aspect of a small slice of life ..., for this is only photographic reproduction of appearances and therefore naturalism, but when it conveys a fully integrated picture of historico-social reality, apprehended from the inside, and organised by imagination, so as to convey a true (however small it may be) image of the whole ... this picture ... can only be a composite and complex picture, in which opposites and conflicting aspects of life have been harmonised into an organic whole, informed with essential truth.[34]

The organisation of this picture and the fusion of all its conflicting elements cannot be obtained without a coherent edifice.

Hitherto, we have attempted to synthesise an outline of realism as an artistic and sincere approach to reality and as an endeavour to express sincerity in terms of a profound comprehension of the common vision that prevails in certain complex situations. It may be useful here to discuss some other definitions of realism in order to clarify our own. In his paper 'Realism in Literary Scholarship',[35] René Wellek defines the concept as 'the objective representation of contemporary social reality'.[36] Representation is used here in a synecdochic sense, not only because true representation is a theoretical impossibility through a medium other than actual life, namely words, but also because 'stress upon synecdochic representation is thus seen to be a necessary ingredient of a truly realistic philosophy'.[37] If one stresses the synecdochic nature of the representation, one must also see, as Wellek rightly urges, the objectivity of this representation in a 'historical context as a polemical weapon against romanticism, as a theory of exclusion as well as inclusion'.[38] Lukács also emphasises this selective element in realism. For him,

> the hallmark of the great realistic masterpiece is precisely that its intensive totality of *essential* social factors does not require, does not even tolerate, a meticulously accurate or pedantically encyclopaedic inclusion of all the threads making up the social tangle.[39]

This was also expressed almost a century earlier in Dostoevsky's letter to Strachov in which he stated his contempt for the arid observation and inclusion of everything.

> What most people regard as fantastic and lacking in universality, I hold to be the inmost essence of truth. Arid observation of everyday trivialities I have long ceased to regard as realism – it is quite the reverse.[40]

In reflecting objective reality, realism involves us in human reality.

> In this way, art as knowledge of reality can show us a portion of reality – not in its objective essence, which is the specific task of science, but in its relationship to human nature. But the knowledge art can give us about people is gained by particular means which do not include the imitation or

> reproduction of concrete reality; art goes from what we will call an objective concreteness to an artistic concreteness.[41]

This artistic concreteness has its own laws and inner logic, which may correspond to those of reality or differ from them but remain in all cases coherent and convincing. Thus it is able to be in harmony with some notions that appear, at first glance, to be in a state of constant dialectic with realism, such as 'the allowance for subjectivity in the act of writing; the belief that art penetrates to a new, transcendental order of reality, or the acceptance of pattern and convention as a technical necessity'.[42] These ideas are not in fact in contradiction with realism; they are rather in a dialectic with the concept of representation in realism and can easily be reconciled with realism in its deeper sense, a sense in which the criterion is not an external mimetic accuracy in the short story's characterisation and depiction of facts and events, but rather an internal verisimilitude through which the story tries to capture the essence and rhythm of reality. This is a trait that makes realism 'nothing more than artistic sincerity in the portrayal of contemporary life'.[43] This sincerity suggests a close relationship with actual reality, but in realism the mimesis must be combined with a power to transcend, to enable the work to offer some embodiment and revelation of the *infinite* which in this context is made to blend and comport with the *finite.* This is so because the realist can transcend reality, not illusions, by exploring and comprehending the various facts of this reality.

The dialectic between the mimetic and transcendental aspects results partly from operating in a medium other than concrete reality, that is, language. The nature of the relationship between language and the world is a purely philosophical question and remains beyond the scope of this study: here it is sufficient to say that one theory sees language as a hostile and alien medium to reality, while another conceives of it as an image of reality.

> A more sophisticated theory sees language not simply as an image of reality but as an instrument in terms of which reality is realised – made real; carrying with its own declarative structure the material of truth, so that there can be no appeal made outside the inclusive conventions of this system to the dumb materiality of the world of things.[44]

In other words, the details of external reality remain oblique, or even beyond human comprehension, as long as they lack a linguistic identity.

> All reality, spiritual as well as sensory, is transformed into language ... What we designate as the reality of perceptions and bodies is, more profoundly understood, nothing other than the sensuous sign language in which an all-embracing, infinite spirit communicates itself to our finite spirit.[45]

This symbolic verbal system is capable in art of creating a new world, which starts to impose its own system; 'causality and concordance, development, character, a past which matters and a future within certain broad limits determined by the project of the author rather than that of the characters.'[46] The determinism here is an artistic one, utterly dissimilar to that inexorable determinism of Zola's *Le roman experimental* wherein, based on a different law,

> a specific principle of aesthetic formation is at work. The synthesis by which the consciousness combines a series of tones into the unity of a melody ... the sensory particulars do not stand by themselves; they are articulated into a conscious *whole*, from which they take their qualitative meaning.[47]

This qualitatively new meaning distinguishes the artistic experience from the lived experience despite their apparent resemblance. It is also what makes a work of art more than the sum of its concrete particular elements. Then there is the role of the subjective element in the creative process.

> The subjective element ... is essentially more than a mere colouring of sentiment. It can imply the whole involvement of the artist in his creation and leads to what Vernon Lee, for one, saw as the heart or ultimate mystery of aesthetics; that 'un-real truthfulness' which subdues our soul, and can only be called the author's *sympathy*, or passionate personal interest.[48]

This subjective element goes far beyond the limits of sympathy and passion, and well to the *terra incognita*, the philosophical vision and ideological outlook on reality; in other words it becomes one of the major components of the ideology of the artistic work, for

> the ideology of the text is not an "expression" of the authorial ideology: it is the product of an aesthetic working of "general" ideology as that ideology is itself worked and produced by an over-determination of authorial-biographical factors.[49]

In this lies the radical difference between the realistic outlook on the subjective element and its romantic counterpart. Realism neither banishes nor overrates its role, yet it unequivocally breaks with the romantic exaltation of the ego. It sees literature as expressing

> in a generalised and abstract way the dynamic relation of ego to the elements of outer reality symbolised by words. This very generalisation is the source of its ability to voice with unique power the instinctive emotional element in man – the physiological component of the social ego.[50]

Thus the ego in its view is ultimately a social entity. Realism goes even further in watering down the subjective element and reducing the individual role of the writer as a creator. In Pierre Macherey's seminal work, *Pour une théorie de la production littéraire*, the idea of the writer as creator is shattered and a new concept of the writer as a producer emerges in its place.

> The author is essentially a producer who works up certain given material into a new product. The author does not make the materials which he works: forms, values, myths, symbols, ideologies come to him already worked-upon ... The artist uses certain means of production – the specialised techniques of his art – to transform the materials of language and experience into a determinate product.[51]

Although Macherey's theory of literary production underrates the role of the author, it explains (within the framework of realism) the sophistication of the artistic process, and the role played in it by many different social agents and institutions.

Realism is essentially an approach to, or an outlook on, both reality and art, and not a particular technique or device. Yet certain technical characteristics emerge from a critical analysis of various realistic short stories and can, thus, be associated with realism. In dealing with these, it is perhaps easier to first exclude features that cannot be associated with realistic works. 'Realism definitely breaks ... with the emphasis on imagination, the symbolic method, the concern for myth, the romantic concept of animated nature',[52] and any attempt to prettify human reality or smooth its edges. Realism also, as conceived in Auerbach's learned study, 'must not be didactic, moralistic, rhetorical, idyllic or comic'.[53] Yet it has its own subtle means of didacticism, its own poetic touches, and often includes comic and sarcastic elements without declining into farce or melodrama. Realism further

> rejects the "ideality" of classicism: it interprets "type" as a social type and not as universally human. Realism rejects the assumption of classicism that there is a scale of dignity in subject matter; it breaks with the levels of style and the social exclusions inherent in classicism.[54]

Realism also rejects the excessive use of chance, which performs the traditional function of *deus ex machina* and introduces an easy exit when the situation becomes critical. When it employs chance, it is as a means to express social, political, psychological or even metaphysical destiny; it is a functional chance, which plays a designated role in the structural and the general meaning of the work.

This technical use of chance is linked to the shift of emphasis from plot to characterisation; mysterious and unusual events are not part of the repertoire of realism partly because dominating action is such a characteristic feature of inferior melodramatic fiction.[55] It is also related to the fact that well-wrought plots are quite alien to ordinary everyday reality. However, inverting the old Aristotelian order of plot before character does not release the writer from his obligation vis-à-vis the plot, which must be composed of convincing, reasonable and justified actions, and this requires proper characterisation. Without three-dimensional or rounded characters interacting with one another the fictional situation becomes flat and incapable of supporting a revealing plot. 'Character is the axis of serious fiction ... character is source and motive and cause of what happens.'[56] Thus, 'In realistic hands, the tools of the novelist would be devoted to the main end of bodying forth characters in their habits as they lived.'[57] This also includes the use of action and events to crystallise various facets of the character. Characters appear, in the early stages of the fictional work, quite oblique, and through the progression of the action and the development of the work their social, cultural, and psychological features take on a palpable shape. In giving body to these features, writers must avoid excessive emotion or sentiment in the artistic structure of the character and in the general literary effect of the work. For in true realistic works 'literary emotional and sentimental heights, what Howells was to call *"effectism"* were cut down',[58] since the ideas of the sublime and the superhuman are out of keeping with a realistic outlook. A corollary to this cool artistic approach to the character with its avoidance of *'effectism'*, is the control of narrative and the creation of an inner logic in the work which dominates the character and action and is derived at the same time from their idiosyncrasies. Without this inner logic neither the character nor the action could attain their independence from the writer's logic and views and, thus, remain incapable of convincing the reader. This inner logic must be self-evident, and not depend slavishly on the logic of external reality or on the author, yet which benefits from both of them. In other words it must acquire its own reasoning and motivation to qualify for the desired independence. This is achieved by resorting to the realists' favourite technique, or 'what they called "dramatic method". It demands the suppression of the "author" from his scene in the novel[59] as the playwright was excluded from drama, except that of "romantic irony" with its deliberately suicidal destruction of illusion. 'It demanded the creation of "transparent" narrators who seemed never to intrude between the reader and his vision of the characters.'[60]

The use of this dramatic method in Egyptian short stories cured the genre of the heavily obtrusive didactic tone of its early beginnings and did away with all non-functional preambles and similar naive devices that aimed to convince readers that what they were reading really happened. It also created a convention of treating the fictional data – characters, action, situation, setting – in a cool and distant perspective, and it resorted to what T. S. Eliot termed 'objective correlatives' when it tried to express emotions. This, fortunately, resulted in a system of imploding symbols; symbols that functioned to intensify inwardly the total effect of the short story and that did not refer to general meaning outside the story. This system of symbols widens the scope and the levels of meaning in the work and tightens its artistic structure. For a coherent and rich artistic edifice is one of the main features and goals of realism, and to attain it, realistic works use all possible techniques and adapt them to their aims. These techniques will be treated accordingly when they appear in the works dealt with below.

From this delineation of realism as an artistic approach to reality one finds that the realistic writer does not attempt to trap the world in words, nor to use his medium to exorcise reality, nor to reproduce its simple sensory material. He tries to create his new reality, art, which may resemble external reality or draw upon some of its aspects, but which remains radically different from it. Art is a qualitatively different, new reality with its own conventions, structures and laws.

The remainder of this chapter deals with this different new reality itself in the Egyptian short story. In the following sections, realism in the short story during the period 1930–70 will be discussed through a critical investigation of the works of Maḥmūd Taymūr, Yaḥyā Ḥaqqī, Maḥmūd al-Badawī, Yūsuf Idrīs, Shukrī 'Ayyād and Abu'l-Ma'ātī Abu'l-Najā. These writers have been selected on the basis that the achievements of other short story writers during this period are by and large overshadowed by those selected, and less innovative. Other writers will be mentioned in the course of the discussion if they have dealt effectively with variations on a theme addressed by one of the six, or tackled similar artistic aspects or questions concerning the content. The limitations of this study, however, mean this can only be dealt with as part of the background of the critical treatment of the works of the selected author. I am acutely aware of the difficulty, and often injustice, of dealing with the rich creative work of these writers in a section of a chapter when a book-length study would be more fitting.[61] But my primary concern here is the development of a specific literary genre, not the achievements of a certain writer, however great he may be. The work of these writers is thus discussed within this particular perspective and according to the writers' participation in the development of this art form.

Maḥmūd Taymūr: Extending the Old World

Taymūr[62] is a prolific short story writer, one of the most productive among his contemporaries. He tried, ironically with limited success, to develop and improve his work over a long period. When many of the writers of his generation, some more talented than himself, such as Maḥmūd Ṭāhir Lāshīn, gave up writing or lost faith, either in the short story as a literary genre or in the reading public, he continued to write new stories and rewrite old ones.[63] He also returned to some of the main themes of his earlier collections and tried to treat them with greater structural coherence and more convincing characterisation. In his rewriting of previous stories and reworking of old themes, Taymūr demonstrates a steadily growing awareness of the form, though no ability for experimentation. Nevertheless, despite his limited talent and restricted world, his diligent attempt to preserve serious fictional writing in the face of the pervasive flood of frivolous writings throughout the 1930s and 1940s makes Taymūr an important figure in the development of the Egyptian, and Arabic, short story.

Although it is evident that Taymūr made great efforts over his long career to develop and mature the technical aspects of his work, the results did not reflect the magnitude of the effort and his numerous collections do not show any radical departure from his earlier methods and approaches. It is true that the scope of his world became a little wider, but this was due more to extending the old world, than to the discovery of new eras of expression and modes of experience. Taymūr found it both safer and easier to produce variations on old themes than attempt new ones. When pondering in retrospect over this feature of his work he admitted that he had not deliberated over it, and offered as justification the argument that amplitude of scope, a wide range of themes, or variety of characterisation can be outweighed by high artistic value within a narrow range.[64] But it would be difficult to maintain that his own achievement is of an especially high order, and much of his work is artistically weak.

However, he is one of the few writers to have dedicated their lives to the cause of serious literary writing and to have resisted the strong temptations of commercialism. He is also one of the few to have realised the importance of constant rewriting, revising and improving the technical side of their work. Although his endeavours to develop his technique are evident, they remain limited. He focuses heavily on Maupassant's short stories and consistently overemphasises the final denouement. In his later works he uses some modern technical devices, but because of his conventional concept of the form and his traditional understanding of the short story as a literary genre, these new devices appear somehow out of step with the work in general, or they acquire a touch of the conventional which, to an extent, obliterates the element of modernity. Taymūr's understanding of the short story depended heavily on the representational approach to reality, rather than on a more complex and artistic approach.

From the appearance of his first collection he believed that 'the closer the short story was to life the more useful and impressive it becomes'.[65] Thus he praised, and attempted to adopt, an artistic approach that saw the story not only as a mimesis of reality but also as a surrogate for it. In later collections and critical writings[66] he reiterates the same concept with some minor modification. An investigation of his later statements will show that he remained faithful to the bulk of his critical dogma until the end of his career. Yet, probably due to the wide spread of new critical ideas in modern Arabic literature, he wavered towards the end of his career between maintaining his lifelong stand of considering life and external reality as the model and the reference and yielding to the requirements of the more sophisticated conception of the superiority of the inner logic and laws of the artistic work, which are independent and different from those of life.[67] The awareness of this inner logic of the artistic edifice, combined with a clear understanding of the importance of connected narrative,[68] careful selection from the mass of available realistic data,[69] and increasing skill in interweaving the realistic with the imaginary[70]and revealing the inmost depths of the character touching upon the essence of the situation with a view to transcending it,[71] give some of Taymūr's later works the identifiable characteristics of realism and require close detailed consideration.

As with many Egyptian writers, Taymūr's voluminous work does not fall into one category. He writes both realistic and romantic short stories and the two kinds share many themes, traits and influences. So the separation between the two attempted here is somewhat arbitrary, although generally valid. As with the romantic stories (to be dealt with in the following chapter), the present discussion will ignore revisions of his early stories considered in *The Genesis* since no radical changes resulted. Although most of his early stories are equally weak, he did not rewrite them all; one can therefore take the rewritten stories as an indication of the themes and characters that attracted Taymūr throughout his literary career. He also wrote numerous new stories centred on some of his earlier themes and reproduced some of his favourite characters.

One of these recurring themes is his condemnation of shaykhs who use their limited and often faulty knowledge in a specious and hypocritical manner and who use religion to achieve irreligious purposes. In his later stories on this theme, Taymūr manages to mask his personal opinions and feelings and leaves the character and action to speak for themselves in a reasonably coherent fashion. In 'Maktūb 'Alā al-Jabīn'[72] one sees how a religious leader of a village commits adultery but hopes that his good deeds will outweigh the bad and in 'Muḥammad Afandī Ṣallī 'alā al-Nabiyy',[73] the religious shaykh who makes a living by reciting the Qur'an is the epitome of evil, using trickery, sorcery and manipulation to strip a man who trusted him of everything he owned. The *awliyā' Allāh* (holy men) in 'Iḥsān li-llāh'[74] appear as swindlers, imposters and tramps, while 'Tadhkarit Dawūd'[75] depicts the erroneous knowledge of the shaykhs when it is put into practice and shows how it results in the death of an innocent man. Even 'Ḥikāyat Abū 'Ūf',[76] the only story to present in its heroine a seriously devout character, is an indictment of exaggerated piety and demonstrates how the heroine, who is completely engrossed in her prayers and glorification of the Lord, neglects her husband and indirectly pushes him towards sin.

The second early theme that reappears in several new stories is the old Nadīmian theme of the repercussions of gambling, drinking and nocturnal pleasures on society in general and family life in particular. 'Thulāthī 'Umar al-Khayyām'[77] declares drinking to be the short and guaranteed way to moral and physical disaster, while in 'Waraqat al-Naṣīb'[78] gambling is responsible for the fall of the protagonist, down the social ladder and into prison. Nightclubs, with their dazzling lights and prostitutes, ruin the promising future of the bright young hero of 'Hadhih al-Ḥaṣāh'[79] and turn him into a worthless creature. In these stories and others, Taymūr abandons the heavily didactic style of his earlier stories and attempts to create a coherent and convincing work of art, dealing with the vicissitudes of man and the pernicious influences of drinking, gambling and lust on his life and fortunes. Man in these stories seems to be portrayed as a victim of his *gharā'iz* (impulses), sensual instincts and physical dispositions, and his inability to control them. This is a part of Taymūr's general view of man, which will be elucidated in more detail below.

The third early theme that recurs in Taymūr's later work is the tragi-comic treatment of those deluded individuals who are stricken by *laṭshat al-fann* (the craze for art), unable to realise the limits of their potential or to cope with external reality. Instead of the early sarcasm, which ridiculed these hopeless dilettanti, his later stories portray the agony of those who once experienced the rapture and ecstasy of creativity then were denied its elation for one reason or another. 'Al-Bārūnah Umm Aḥmad'[80] centres around this theme, as does 'Tamr Ḥinnah 'Ajab',[81] which attempts to illustrate the paradise of creativity through the hell of its absence. The felicity of creativity is expressed in these two stories in glorious fragments of a remote happy past reflected in the mirrors of the gloomy present. When the character loses the last flicker of hope and is confronted with a definitive exclusion from the lost paradise of art, he either dies, as in 'Al-Bārūnah Umm Aḥmad', or kills those who stand between him and the return to his old paradise in an attempt to extricate himself from his appalling present, as in 'Tāj min Waraq'.[82] In 'Sirr al-Amīr al-Hindī',[83] Taymūr changes his technique and presents a reverse picture in which the felicity of creativity prevails in the present while the wretched life of loss and deprivation from the ecstasy of fulfilment in art is part of the remote past. He also links this story with the title story of his earlier collection, *Abū 'Alī 'Āmil Artist.* The link provides him, incidentally, with an opportunity to voice his contempt for journalists and reviewers who lack the ability and qualifications to judge a work of art and who enjoy an overrated cultural status.

Another feature of Taymūr's early stories that persists in his later work is his predilection for exhibiting a wide spectrum of strange or eccentric characters. The miser, who occupies his own particular niche in classical Arabic literature – thanks to the great work of al-Jāḥiẓ – seems to have fascinated Taymūr too. He portrayed the miser in his earlier collections and continued to depict various aspects of his character by rewriting previous stories ('Janāzah Ḥarrah'[84] and 'Ilā al-Sāriq')[85] and creating new ones. The later stories focus on the comic aspect of the miser's eccentric conduct and the effect of his meanness on his own life.[86] Other eccentric and strange characters include the bohemian ('Al-Shaykh 'Ulwān'),[87] the parrot-brained assistant lawyer who leads a vagabond life ('Ta'mīn 'Alā al-Ḥayāh'),[88] the popular artist who transcends his own grief and suffering through his art ('al-Shaykh 'Afallah'),[89] the outlaw who combines extreme cruelty with extreme tenderness and understanding ('al-Ḥanash wa'l-'Aqrab'),[90] and the bookbinder whose strong and tyrannical personality traps his apprentice, who becomes as a helpless insect in a spider's web ('al-Kasīḥ').[91] There are many other examples ('Anā al-Qātil',[92] 'Fal-Nabda' al-Ḥayāh',[93] 'Ḥāmil al-Athqāl',[94] 'Maw'id'[95] and 'al-'Aduww')[96] that, to some extent, represent explorations of eccentric and of strange human behaviour and that are designed to accentuate the peculiar, funny, egregious or weird, rather than to articulate the uniqueness of their identity. It is as though Taymūr peopled his world with many of these characters to substitute for the lack of the heroic and miraculous in works of realism and to infuse his world with humour and a sense of the absurd.

A further early theme that recurs in the later stories is the suffering of destitute children, a subject he inherited from his elder brother, Muḥammad,[97] or possibly the earlier work of al-Manfalūṭī. Although Taymūr treats this theme only in a few stories, he achieves a notably high degree of artistic coherence and precision in 'Al-Zanātī Khalīfah bi-Qirsh wa-Niṣf'.[98] In this story, he devises a rich set of symbols to widen the scope of meaning and enhance the inner logic of the fictional situation. The main theme of the story is adumbrated from the action and characterisation and is divided into sub-themes. Both the setting and the description are highly functional and properly integrated into the main theme. The irony of the situation in which an adult identifies with the image of the epic hero al-Zanātī Khalīfah engraved on a book cover, while the child impersonates him in action, is reflected in the structure of the story. The story is based on irony, parallel characterisation, and a constant exchange of roles and positions, making the artistic structure part and parcel of the texture of the story and its content and, consequently, strengthens the general impact.

The last of the early themes to reappear in later stories is the 'Ubayd brothers' favourite theme of incompatible marriage. In a sense this represents the shift in Taymur's writing insofar as his treatment introduces fresh variations on earlier portrayals rather than a replication with minor modifications. After exhausting the old and didactic aspects of polygamy and incompatible marriage ('Muḥammad Afandī Ṣallī 'Alā al-Nabiyy',[99] 'Shabāb wa-Ghāniyāt',[100] 'Man minna al-Waghd',[101] 'Takfīr'[102] and 'al-Sajīnah'),[103] Taymūr handles the subject from a new standpoint. It is as if he was no longer satisfied with pointing out the features of incompatible marriage but now tried to discover their sources and the reasons why unsuited couples marry in the first place. The story becomes more of a fictional study of the atmosphere in which marriage is arranged, especially among the supposedly educated middle class. The hero of 'Kul 'Ām wa-Antum bi-Khayr'[104] marries out of boredom and slavery to convention, while the couple of "Indamā Taḍḥak al-Aqdār'[105] marries because of a peculiar turn of fate. Another curious reason for marriage is a desire to pre-empt gossip or comply with certain *mores* ('al-Musta'īn bi'l-llāh al-Kabtin Hardy').[106]

Before proceeding to discuss the new themes in Taymūr's realistic works, a brief critical assessment of the works in which he recapitulates old themes is required. Although the rewriting of the early stories brought about minor improvements, the substantial development, in both content and form, is manifested more clearly in new stories that treat old themes. In many of these, Taymūr abandons intrusive pre-textual moral judgements and endeavours to root his assumptions artistically in the situation with only partial success. He also avoids exaggerated sentiments, actions and reactions, and pays more attention to the inner structure of the characters. Despite a clear attempt to integrate the setting and description of detail into the main theme, some of his scenes are only loosely related to the plot and could easily be eliminated. Moreover, his obviously representational approach to reality, which sees art as a mirror of the outside world, diminishes the artistic stature of some of the stories, while at the same time conferring on them an incidental value as records of certain aspects of social life in the 1930s and 1940s.

Moving on to the new themes Taymūr deals with in his numerous collections throughout the four decades under discussion, one finds many of them revolving around one major pivotal idea: the acceptance of the status quo, which involves a glorification of the customary and ordinary and condemnation of any attempt to change the prevailing order. Thus acquiescence is preferable to rebellion and the past is extolled and seen as a vindication of the present state of events. This idea is based on the assumption that there is a static enduring *nāmūs,* a cosmic law or essence of things, which renders any attempt to change it futile and misguided. The action is seen in terms of complete cycles governed by this eternal *nāmūs,* and man is conceived of, not as an open project that is fulfilled through interaction with reality, but as a creature conditioned by *gharā'iz,* his instincts, and other external factors beyond his comprehension. This amalgam of biological and metaphysical elements by its very nature goes against any dynamic view of social reality and implies a certain degree of animosity to rationalism, and consequently to realism as defined at the beginning of this chapter. Nevertheless, Taymūr's work contains realistic elements and in some stories this carries conviction. This is because his works fluctuate between fidelity to this theoretical view and loyalty to an artistic view of reality. His pivotal idea implies a certain obliteration, or at least obfuscation, of class division, yet his works not only show a clear polarisation in class structure but also adopt the ideas and morals of the dominant semi-feudal semi-bourgeois class. He shows some sympathy with the poor and needy, but this is somehow limited and conditioned by the apparent satisfaction of the poor and their unconditional acceptance of their present place in the class system. When some of the poor question the fabric of society, Taymūr wastes no time in attacking them, even directly. In his vigorous onslaught on those who merely believe in social evolution[107] or ask: 'Should the worker's wages correspond to his production or to his needs?'[108] Taymūr overlooks the most basic artistic conventions by resorting to crude statements that do not emerge from the fabric of the story.

But Taymūr's new stories have other subtle means of conveying their disagreement with those who advocate social change. One of the most common among these is the calculated use of the circular form, where the end of the action is similar to its beginning in a way that renders all that takes place between them futile and meaningless. This circular technique is used to reinforce the present situation and prove that any attempt to change it is destined to return to the situation at the point of departure ('Maktūb 'Alā al-Jabīn', 'Majnūn'[109] or 'Tamr Ḥinnah 'Ajab'). Another technical device used to reinforce present reality and frustrate any attempt to change it is what one may call the 'cosy chat preamble' or the 'prologue-epilogue technique'. In many of his stories Taymūr starts with an artistically unfunctional prologue that depicts a group of friends sitting in a café or one of their elegant homes, sipping drinks, with one of them telling a story, often about something that happened to him or to another known friend. The story is always, by the very nature of this technique, placed in the remote past and has no bearing on the present. When the storyteller brings his story within the story to a conclusion the main story does not end; it continues with the comments and participation of the audience who accentuate the fact that the story inside the story is no more than a little tremor, after which everything goes back to its normal, if not eternal, state. Stories of this category are numerous;

in one collection, *Khalf al-Lithām,* there are four stories that use this technique[110] and in the other collections there are many more.[111]

The perpetual nature of the present order and rejection of radical changes are not made manifest through technical means alone, but also become the main theme of some stories. In 'Shaykh al-Khafar'[112] change not only disturbs the flow of life and its familiar order but also brings misery and destruction. The story starts with a tranquil rural situation characterised by simplicity, goodness and love, 'where things happen *bi'l-barakah'* (naturally by grace of God).[113] The *barakah* in the story is more than a mere word or generalisation; it is more or less a complete system of values, laws and conventions. Then, suddenly, the old governor of the estate dies and a new young governor comes from the city to replace him. The new governor is young, strong-minded and full of aspirations for change and modernisation. The changes he brings about stir up wild inclinations and discord in the tranquil estate and lead eventually to civil strife and bloodshed. The governor himself becomes one of the victims of his new order and the new order he creates collapses with him. The story ends with the action turning full circle and the estate waiting for a new governor.

Apart from its stress on the perpetuation of the present order and excoriation of the attempt to change it, 'Shaykh al-Khafar' is redolent of the political atmosphere of the 1940s and could be interpreted as a coherent and effective political allegory. Since, unlike many of Taymūr's stories opposing change, it qualifies its rejection of the changes introduced and presents them in a powerfully ironic tone, as externally forced upon reality without any understanding of the undercurrents or even the mechanisms of this reality, it succeeds in delineating a valid case and becoming a coherently mature realistic story. It also illustrates the inherent weaknesses of the imposed power structure at work and demonstrates the need to root any new ideas in the tradition of the people concerned. In this story, unlike many others, Taymūr emphasises action rather than character, but without sacrificing the latter. This widens the scope of meaning in the story and undermines the authorial presence and the direct comments, which jeopardise the impact of many of his stories. While 'Shaykh al-Khafar' is by no means free from artistic shortcomings, it remains his most successful story on this theme. 'Al-Ṭā'ir al-Ṭalīq',[114] for instance, deals with the same theme but in a rather naive and abstract manner, while 'Bint al-Shayṭān'[1152] endeavours, not very successfully, to create an elaborate fairytale-like action to manifest the absurdity of any attempt to alter an immutable situation.

The action in this group of stories, based on the technique of describing a pattern of events going full circle, is like a stone thrown into stagnant water. It results in a movement on the surface, which fades gradually until the surface regains its stillness. This technique is more effective when the change is relatively positive because it serves to accentuate the temporary nature of the change. Without the use of this device, the positive change in 'Ḥulm wa-Inqaḍā'[116] or 'Fī Ghafwat al-Aqdār'[117] could arouse false expectations in the reader's mind, or create a favourable impression unintended by the author. When change seems to provide a step forward, the writer tends, in some stories, either to shed doubt on it or to belittle and undermine its effect ('Muẓāharah',[118] 'Iḥsan li-llāh',[119] or 'Fal-Nabda' al-Ḥayāh').[120] In 'al-Ṭāqiyyah',[121] where the change is so evidently positive, the writer introduces a tone of wistful nostalgia, which seems to dissipate the positive impression created by his portrayal of the modern in favour of the past, in a manner that suggests a complete dichotomy of heart and reason.

This dichotomy leads on to the second new theme that contributes to Taymūr's static vision of reality, namely the view of human action as a conflict of spirit and body. 'This conflict between spirit and body, between reason and *gharīzah*, culminates in Taymūr's recent works in the decisive triumph of *gharīzah* over reason. This results in a cutting down of description and augmentation of analytical contemplative elements ... and in the view that man is a creature determined by an unseen irrational power.'[122] Another consequence of this dichotomy between the spiritual and lofty and the sensual, vile and earthly is the apparent pessimism that results from the concentration on man's flaws and disregard for his greatness. This perspective is unable to realise either the relativity of things or the constant interaction between the contradictory elements that make up any human action. Nor does it account for the fact that *gharā'iz* (earthly feelings and instincts) have their own reason and logic.

However, some stories undermine Taymūr's fixed idea about this dichotomy of reason and *gharīzah* by giving a coherent and logical analysis of *gharīzah* ('al-Sajīnah').[123] The main field in which the irrational power of *gharīzah* manifests itself is sex, which is in Taymūr's world synonymous with sin and often leads to murder.

Murder seems, in many stories, the logical outcome of the supremacy of *gharīzah* over reason, not only because the absence of reason makes it easy to kill or commit suicide, but also because the combination of thoughtless passion, lust and jealousy upsets the present order of things; and the elimination of the cause – that is, the murder – is seen as a means of correcting the upset balance. The stories ending in murder seen in this perspective are too many to be counted, but they include: 'Man Minnā al-Waghd', 'Jarīmat Ḥubb',[124] "Abīt ... 'Abīṭ',[125] 'Zawj wa-Ḍurratān',[126] 'al-Ḥukm li-llāh',[127] 'al-Shaykh 'Afallah' and 'Takfīr'.[128]

In 'Ṣirā' fi'l-Ẓalām',[129] Taymūr abandons this dichotomy and creates a coherent and mature story. From a traditional situation of a child suffering the cruelty of a stepmother, Taymūr creates a sensitive story rich in texture and poetic suggestion. The desire to retaliate against the stepmother is mingled in the child with a sexual longing for her. It is a story of conflicting reckless desire and the love–hate relationship between a young man, who suffered in his childhood from the spite of his first stepmother, and his second stepmother, young and lecherous, who turns to him after the death of her husband – his father – for protection and tutelage. The conventional role expected of him as the new head of the family enables him to step into his father's shoes in the full Oedipal sense.

In keeping with the cultural background and beliefs of the characters, the action is governed by a curse, which colours it with a tragic hue and taints every shade and detail with a touch of fatalism. This is supplemented by various technical devices, which envelop the action in a hypnotic atmosphere in which the protagonist sleepwalks to his fate and fails to harmonise the dictates of the head with those of the heart. In this atmosphere, the protagonist's indomitable desire for retaliation blinds him to various snares, a great many of which are of his own creation. He shuns all possible ways of retreat open to him and allows himself to be led to the very situation from which he thought he was escaping. When he realises, too late, that his quest for revenge (suggested throughout the story to be synonymous with fulfilment) has failed, an overwhelming desire for self-destruction comes over him. This comes as no surprise, given the many early hints of a suicidal tendency and the deep scars resulting from his miserable and abnormal childhood. Because the plot is well knit and the action carefully developed, the caprices of desire do not appear to be lacking in inner logic or reason. Thus, the fatalistic element in the story has a social and psychological, as well as a metaphysical, dimension. The story uses irony and parallelism in its structure to intensify its effect and to widen the scope of its theme. Although 'Ṣirā' fi'l-Ẓalām' is by far the most coherent and realistic story in its category, many of its features, techniques and sub-themes (such as self-destruction and narrow-mindedness) are common in stories concerned with the supremacy of *gharīzah* over reason. Because of the acts of murder with which many of these stories end, the action is often charged with tragedy, which involves an underlying reference to the struggle between good and evil, for *gharīzah* in Taymūr's works is more than a mere natural drive or instinctive disposition that tightens man's hold on reality and urges him to survive and make the most of life; it is, rather, a diabolical incentive that instils evil in man's mind and prompts him with wicked suggestions. In other words, it is associated with sadistic revenge ('Zawj wa-Ḍurratān'), greed ('Ta'mīn 'Alā al-Ḥayāh'), frustration ('al-Sajīnah'), lust ('Sarāb'),[130] jealousy ('Majnūn'),[131] and idiocy ("Abīt ... 'Abīt').

A corollary to this concept of *gharīzah* is Taymūr's view of sex. Sex in his stories is not a fully developed concept (as is the case with D. H. Lawrence or Tennessee Williams) because he does not treat it as a vital factor in human life but merely as a destructive element, an often bestial feeling, which is always associated with sin and therefore ought to be avoided and rebuffed. Apart from the Oedipal touch in 'Ṣirā' fi'l-Ẓalām' and 'al-'Aduww', mature treatment of sex appears rarely in his work, and only as an inviolable taboo or *ḥarām* (illegal act). In 'Sarāb' sex is presented, in clear contrast with celestial and sublime love, as an earthly and even disgusting action, while in 'al-Sajīna' it is linked with frustration and failure on one hand, and imbecility and idiocy on the other. It is associated in several stories with remorse and a deep sense of guilt resulting from the fact that the awakening of conscience lags behind the materialisation of actions prompted by *gharīzah.* This belated awakening, and the subsequent remorse, is the main theme of 'Najiyyah bint al-Fiqī',[132] 'Takfīr' and 'Ibtisāmah'.[133]

Another corollary to the same concept is Taymūr's attitude to love. Although his works do not offer any comprehensive or philosophical views about the subject, or even present a unified outlook, his realistic short stories portray love differently from his more romantic writing. It is a clandestine activity which must be concealed from the outside world, not only because it has not, as yet, gained the universal approval of society, but also, and especially, because it is conceived of as *ḥarām* and an act that involves the violation of taboos and conventions. It is not a means by which man expresses his longing to communicate fully with another on many levels, but rather an irrational sensual expression of possessiveness and lust. It is, therefore, enveloped in a thick air of secretiveness and suppression, and becomes thereby distorted. This distorted love is a prelude to various evils: sin ('Zāmir al-Ḥayy'), madness ('Majnūn'),[134] or murder ('Jarīmat Ḥubb'). The heroine of 'al-Qublah al-Akhīrah'[135] not only hides her feelings towards her lover until he dies but also expresses her affection for him after his death in a morbid manner, while the heroine of 'Ma'sāt Nafs'[136] flees from her lover when her love becomes known to him. The discovery of love involves an element of shame; it incurs ignominy and leads to misery and destruction. Therefore, the disclosure of a concealed love in 'Khiṣām'[137] signals its termination, for there is no existence for it outside the protective shell of secrecy. The story, like many of Taymūr's others on this theme, also manifests a clear lack of understanding of the inner mechanism of a reciprocal relationship, which involves a complicated mixture of selfishness and self-denial. Its concept of love is too simplistic and, consequently, fails to sustain a coherent work. There are, however, a few stories in which love is treated as a noble feeling; when it is associated with a marriage proposal and, thus, a sentiment worthy of cherishing and respect. Yet the two stories dealing with this type of love – 'Fal-Nabda' al-Ḥayāh' and "Arūs min Quṭn'[138] – are far from happy. They are imbued with an element of tragedy, for fate intervenes to prevent the proposed marriage from coming to fruition. Although the respectability of the relationship entails fidelity, the devotion to the memory of the dead suitor is exaggerated to a ridiculous extent in the first story, while the loyalty to the dead fiancé in the second story is properly covered and kept as a dark secret.

In harmony with the dichotomy of reason and *ghaẓīrah,* good and evil, is Taymūr's vision of class in his society, an outlook that reveals the same dualism in a different perspective, and adopts a double standard of morality, one for the well-to-do and another for the poor. As far as the class structure of his world is concerned, there are two main classes, the 'haves', who are full of grace and kindness, and the 'have-nots', who are vile and evil. It is understandable that the uneducated poor should be ill-mannered and rough, but it is hard to accept that they should also be idiotic ("Abīṭ ... 'Abīṭ'), sinners ('Ṣirā' fi'l-Ẓalām' and 'Man Minnā al-Waghd'), murderers ('al-Ḥukm li-llah' and 'Ilā al-Sāriq'),[139] corrupt ('Hadhih al-Ḥaṣāh' and 'Kabsh al-Fidā")[140] and morally vicious ('Ta'mīn 'Alā al-Ḥayāh'). Moreover, they lead an empty idle life ('al-Wiṭwāṭ')[141] in which they are 'pursued from childhood, by ignominy, humiliation and inferiority ... as if they are insignificant vermin living on the margin of society'.[142] This may suggest a certain sympathy for the poor, as victims of life, but Taymūr often presents them without much sympathy, understanding or compassion.

On the other hand, the rich are unnaturally good and pure, exuding good manners, consideration and kindness to a nauseating degree. They have no worries about their immediate needs since most of them are heirs to large fortunes. They are a privileged group who spend a great deal of their time touring Europe's best summer resorts and trying to be extremely charitable to the poor. They have sentimental natures, which, significantly, manifest themselves particularly in Europe, with which they identify. They may overlook the devastating scenes of poverty in Egypt, but once they cross the Mediterranean, where they aspire to be accepted, they suddenly overflow with emotion and tenderness. They feel pity for the underprivileged in Switzerland and for the innocent European children who stare in frustration at expensive toys in shop windows ('al-Ṭifl wa'l-Muṣawwir').[143] Being soft-hearted, they rush to buy toys for them. When one of the children leaves without taking his toy, they go to look for him and when they fail to find him, their sentimentality overcomes them and they burst into tears. In 'Sitt al-Kull'[144] the rich person's natural aptitude for kindness and charity is depicted as contrasting to the immorality and ingratitude of the poor.

In many of Taymūr's works, morals are not depicted as something that can be acquired or that develop, but as something one is endowed with from birth, as 'al-Shaḥḥādh wa'l-Faṭā'ir al-'Ashr'[145] suggests. The possession of morals is a natural quality, which enables the rich to awaken a human response even in the poor. As a result, it persists even in a life immersed in sin and fornication. The hero of 'Laylat Uns'[146] is a womaniser who knows a 'lady' who provides him with a steady supply of girls and courtesans. When on one occasion she introduces him to a new girl, and as a man of the world he discovers that the new girl has been drawn into this business by the pressure of penury, his kindness and noble manners assert themselves and he invites the girl to live with him as his wife, or, in the first version of the story, as his daughter. Because this sense of morality is instinctive it does not recognise geographical boundaries. This perhaps explains the number of stories dealing with the well-mannered, good natured charitable rich who are solicitous for the poor in Europe ('Ṣuḥbat Ward'[147] and 'Dhāt Masā"),[148] with whom they feel stronger affinities than with their own compatriots.

A consequence of this direct correlation between the distribution of wealth and possession of morality is the recurrence in Taymūr's stories of characters who are either very rich or very poor. The stories dealing with middle-class characters are marked by an avoidance of controversial moral issues and by an attempt to objectively explore some psychological aspects of human questions and feelings. For example, 'Dhikrā'[149] examines the effect of a closed social atmosphere on the behaviour of the central character and illustrates some of the particular features of sexual and romantic love in the 1930s. 'Qalb Kabīr'[150] is a study of domestic interactions and feelings in a middle-class milieu. 'Majnūn'[151] endeavours to portray the complexity of feelings involved in a situation of adultery and jealousy characterised by hesitation and exaggeration of sentiment and fear. 'Al-Lahumma lkhzik yā Shayṭān'[152] is a fascinating study of the inner life and anxieties of a middle-class family, and 'al-Major Savage'[153] presents a realistic picture of the peaceful struggle of a middle-class youth during the events of the 1919 revolution.

However rigid this dichotomy between rich and poor, with its consequent double standards of morality, few stories in Taymūr's many collections manage to transcend it. Most of the stories deserve detailed critical consideration, but within the confines of the present study only one general aspect can be stressed, their structure, features of which serve to show the extent of the technical evolution in Taymūr's work. The first of these stories, 'Abū 'Arab',[154] is a highly coherent well-structured Maupassant-type story with a terse syllogistic development and a powerful denouement. Its economical structure, together with its gradual syllogistic progression, defies many of Taymūr's presuppositions about human behaviour and establishes the supremacy of the logic of reality over them. It is a story of the conflicting emotions and desires of a simple Bedouin, who is unable to articulate his feelings other than through his physical behaviour. The progression of the action is both logical and convincing, and is in harmony with the characterisation and setting. The carefully developed denouement resolves the accumulated tension and infuses the events of the story with meaning.

Despite its slightly sentimental exaggerations and over-simplification, 'al-Kasīḥ'[155] is a sensitively told story that explores a peculiarly strong affinity between a master binder and his apprentice. It is a coherent, condensed study of obsession and the fall of a weak man into the web of a strong character. The development of the action towards the complete domination of the strong character over his victim is set in motion by a fascinating amalgam of virulence and affection and is portrayed in a simple, though skilfully functional, style of writing. This style appears again in 'Qublah',[156] a well-written story with a coherent structure and effective denouement. It is a story of the frustrated passion of a young stable-hand who is completely overwhelmed in his first encounter with the long-desired prostitute of the quarter.

In many of his stories, Taymūr shows a predilection for fantasy, yet one of his best stories is 'Laylat al-'Urs,[157] in which he uses an anticlimax technique to destroy the 'golden' world of Cinderella on the rocks of gloomy reality. It is a de-mythologising of the well-known fairytale, in which the beautiful and persecuted country girl who has suffered from the cruelty of her stepmother does not meet the fairy or fit the glass shoes. She stays at home weaving her misery into a daydream in which she becomes the bride of the village mayor's son and the star of the best wedding the village has ever seen. The daydream is soon dissipated by the noise of the arrival of the stepmother and her two daughters, merry and full of stories about the party to which our Cinderella never went. When they finish, she tries to tell the story of her dream, but she stammers and they laugh at her. She then goes to sleep by the water-buffalo and, overwhelmed by grief and frustration, unable to sleep, she proceeds to tell the buffalo her story. Although the influence of Chekhov's story 'The Misery'[158] is evident, Taymūr creates a powerful and economically written realistic story in which the prosaic details radiate poetic power, and the story elaborates the identity of its heroine. 'Al-Tirām Raqam'[159] is also a carefully written story that reveals a deep understanding of the realistic approach to both character and situation. It not only succeeds in integrating the character and the action into the setting, but also roots the character's actions and responses in their socio-cultural background while taking account of the individual motives of each character. This is also the case in 'al-Lahumma Ikhzik Yā Shayṭān', in which the writer puts his finger on some of the very parochial, yet generally human, traits of his main character. A glimpse of this Egyptianness in behaviour and atmosphere can also be found in "Īd Mīlād Sa'īd'[160] 'Tadhkarat Dāwūd'[161] and 'Mawlānā Abu'l-Barakāt'.[162]

The scarcity of artistically successful stories among the vast number he has written may give a false impression of Taymūr's artistic accomplishments. Apart from his role in preserving the spirit of seriousness in dealing with this literary genre when commercialism and indifference to literary values prevailed, Taymūr popularised many of its major conventions. He paid special attention to characterisation and emphasised the importance of clear and convincing motivation for the characters' actions and responses. But at the same time he adopted a simplistic stand vis-à-vis the question of motivation and his characterisation is based on the assumption that every character has a key to his innermost soul and that once you find this key you can easily unravel his character. The key is always a psychological one, which is a reflection, first of all, of the demand for *al-qiṣṣah al-taḥlīliyyah*,[163] a sort of analytical or psychological story, in the 1930s and 1940s, but it also indicates the cessation of Taymūr's cultural development in any but small ways beyond the early 1940s. This assessment does not ignore the minor improvements of his technique, or the modification of many early notions that produced a certain amelioration in his technical devices, such as his mastery of the denouement that imbues apparently meaningless details with sense and gives them suggestive and indicative power ('Qalb Kabīr', 'Ibnat Īzīs'[164] and 'al-'Aduww'). He also developed the device of creating imploding symbols that widen the scope of the action and enhance the total effect of the story ('al-Zanātī Khalīfah bi-Qirsh wa-Niṣf', 'al-Gentleman'[165] and "Indmā Naḥyā Ma' al-Aṭyāf').[166] These symbols, which do not usually have any separate value outside the context of the story, are different from allegorical symbols, which have a clear reference to external reality. Taymūr uses allegory successfully in some of his stories ('al-Ṭaqiyyah,[167] 'Muẓāharah'[168] and 'Shaykh al-Khafar'), but his use of the imploding symbol is more coherent from an artistic point of view. This is because he achieves the complete integration of the symbol with the action. In addition to these techniques and the circular structure mentioned earlier, Taymūr played a significant role in familiarising the reader with various types of narrative. Apart from the familiar third-person connected narrative, he uses the first-person narrative more in its written or third-person framework. In other words, his first-person narrative lacks a strong oral tone and is rather a form of written personal memoir aimed at rendering events more plausible when they lack credibility for one reason or another ('al-Ṭā'ir al-Ṭalīq', 'al-Ḥukm li-llah' and 'Man Minnā al-Waghd'). In one of his stories, 'al-Būmah Tan'aq',[169] he produces a convincing and even poetic first-person narrative that comes close to stream of consciousness writing.

Despite his prosaic, sometimes clumsy, handling of the first-person narrative, Taymūr uses other narrative devices more successfully, among them epistles, diaries, telegrams and documents, in addition to his use of more than one person in the narrative process. He also gives greater depth to the use of comic elements, already popularised in earlier works of fiction, developing them into a form of comic irony completely integrated into the action ('Kūb Mā' wa-Laymūnah',[170] 'Ḥarb Khaṭifah',[171] 'Laylat al-Hanā''[172] and 'al-Zanātī Khalīfah bi-Qirsh wa-Niṣf'). In this last story, the comic irony becomes a sophisticated structural device, enriching the story and widening its scope. In one of his later stories, 'Ṭayf Zahīrah', he hesitantly introduces, besides comic irony, the technique of alienation and discusses the notion of artistic determinism at some length. But because the theoretical awareness of a certain artistic principle is one thing, and the successful application of it another, many of Taymūr's stories suffer from the absence of artistic determinism, with its corresponding precision and cohesion. This is particularly the case in those stories in which he endeavours to prove certain notions, or to use the story as a vehicle for a didactic or moral message.[173] Artistic inevitability implies a certain dialectical relationship between the medium and the message; Taymūr touches upon this in 'Ṭayf Zahīrah', but fails to achieve it in a great number of his stories, and indeed in 'Ṭayf Zahīrah' itself.

Taymūr's achievements are significant because of his dedication to the short story and his influence on both his contemporaries and successors. Although tracing Taymūr's influences upon others is beyond the scope of this study, it is worth mentioning that many of the features of his work discussed above, whether relating to form or content, can be found in the work of other Egyptian short story writers, with certain differences in emphasis or tone, writers such as Tawfīq al-Ḥakīm,[174a] Fatḥī Raḍwān,[175] Sa'īd 'Abduh[176] and Ibrāhīm al-Miṣrī,[177] whose work is by no means wholly similar to Taymūr's, but who cover similar ground as far as the development of the Egyptian short story is concerned.

Yaḥyā Ḥaqqī: The Harvest of a Quiet Eye

Ḥaqqī, unlike Taymūr, is not a prolific writer. He started writing and publishing short stories as early as 1926[178] and continued to do so until 1968,[179] but only four collections of his stories appeared in the period under discussion. These four collections, however, are of central importance to the artistic development of the genre and have been, and continue to be, a vital influence on other short story writers. Although Ḥaqqī (1905–93) was younger than most writers publishing during this period, he was more aware than many of them of the importance of artistic criteria in creative works. This is not only evident in his early critical writings,[180] but also in his experimentation in form and style from the beginning of his career as a writer. In Ḥaqqī's early stories, an awareness of artistic representation and expression is demonstrated in the wide variety of techniques he employs and his obvious attempts to explore new ground in both theme and form. Any study of these early stories in their historical perspective will show Ḥaqqī experimenting with form more than any other pioneer of the Egyptian short story. In 'al-Sukhriyah',[181] he imitates Edgar Allan Poe in his use of suspense, gloom, fear and heavily analytical elements, while he uses parallel characterisation in 'Muḥammad Bey Yazūr 'Izbatah'[182] and 'Man al-Majnūn',[183] and experiments with stream of consciousness in 'al-Duktūr Shākir Afandī'.[184] In "Abd al-Tawwāb Afandī al-Sajjān'[185] and 'al-Wasā'iṭ Yā Afandim'[186] he employs comic irony to explore character, while in 'Munīrah',[187] despite its rhetoric, accurate and minute description creates a powerful illusion of reality. In 'Ṣuwar min Ḥayāh',[188] 'Ḥayāt Liṣṣ'[189] and 'Qahwat Dīmitrī'[190] he explores the limits of the naturalistic method of portraying reality and its ability to grasp vivid, comic and commonplace situations. In 'Fullah-Mishmish-Lūlū'[191] domestic pets are allegorical figures in a sensitive portrayal of class barriers and distinctions.

All these techniques and devices were experimented with over a two-year period and were considered by Ḥaqqī to be no more than exercises in writing. When many of his contemporaries collected their early works into books, he refrained from doing so, despite the relative maturity of these works when placed in their historical context.[192] However, many of the themes and technical devices of these early stories reappear and are perfected in later works. After those prolific two years, Ḥaqqī wrote less and concentrated upon drawing more from his direct experiences of life in Egypt. He is the youngest of the important pioneers (the two Taymūrs, the two 'Ubayds, and Lāshīn) of the short story in modern Egyptian literature, all of whom, himself included, were descendants of non-Egyptians, the offspring of foreigners and immigrants from Turkey, Albania, the Peloponnese and Greater Syria, who settled in Egypt.

His father was the first of his family to be born in Egypt. Ḥaqqī himself was born in the poor quarter of al-Qal'ah in Cairo and spent his childhood there and in al-Sayyidah Zaynab, another poor quarter of old Cairo. After obtaining a degree in law (Cairo University, 1925), he worked as a solicitor in the Delta for two years, and as *wakīl niyābah*, an assistant prosecutor, in Upper Egypt for another two years before joining the Foreign Office. This provided him with first-hand experience of both urban and rural Egypt, which, combined with a sensitive eye, deep insight, and a strong awareness of literary form, gave Ḥaqqī's work a more complex approach to reality, for example in his descriptive detail, which lends potentially prosaic items a unique and evocative power. The fact that Ḥaqqī practised literary criticism throughout his career made him constantly aware of the mechanisms of his art and, in this respect, placed him ahead of his time. Within his own work, there is evidence to indicate that he was a meticulous and stern critic, and constantly striving to develop his craft and break new ground for the short story. He published his first collection, *Qindīl Umm Hāshim*, in 1944 after almost twenty years of significant work in the field. In 1955, he published both his second collection, *Dimā' wa-Ṭīn*, and a third collection, *Umm al- 'Awājiz.* In 1961 he published his fourth and last collection, *'Anṭar wa-Juliet.* These four collections, together with a few more recent short stories, are the harvest of more than forty years of continuous work. The publication dates of the first three collections are a little misleading, especially with two published in one year, since the stories themselves appeared as early as 1929 and throughout the 1930s and the 1940s .[193] The delay in publication in book form was not because of the author's indolence or loss of interest in publishing his work in book form, but rather because the artistic sensibility of the 1930s and 1940s was unable to accommodate such writings at the centre of the cultural scene; thus the stories remained on the margins. There were always periodicals willing to risk publishing a single avant-garde short story, but when it came to publishing a whole collection, the prevailing artistic sensibility served as an obstruction. This situation suggests a certain schism in the artistic sensibility or at least indicates a significant change. An understanding of these conflicting sensibilities is necessary to comprehend both Ḥaqqī's role in changing the predominant taste and the reasons why many of his talented associates in Jamā'at al-Madrasah al-Ḥadīthah (the New School) abandoned short story writing. Lāshīn, for example, wrote some short stories in the 1930s, which he was unable to publish in a book until 1940,[194] and before the end of the 1930s he gave up writing altogether.

The sparseness of Haqqī's output does not imply any narrowness of his fictional world. Unlike most of his contemporaries, he does not confine himself to the urban middle class or see the world through this class perspective. Besides middle class characters and peasants, his world is peopled with the poor from all walks of urban and rural Egypt: servants, craftsmen, street-traders, beggars, apprentices, dervishes, whores, fumigators with incense, shepherds, stone-cutters, matchmakers and junk-dealers. In order to illustrate the diversity of Egyptian life and society, Haqqi devotes a great deal of his fictional work to the overpopulated quarter of al-Sayyidah Zaynab and the poor villages of Upper Egypt. In this way, he is able to capture the spirit of Egypt and explore the undercurrent of Egyptian social life in both its urban and rural dimensions. Haqqi's depictions of the old quarters of Cairo transcend local setting; they reach beyond the peculiarities of time and place to address universal human characteristics and concerns. It is not mere chance that the writers who succeed in uncovering the inner structure of Cairo are those who deal with the life of its old and crowded quarters. Ḥaqqī is one of those, and his writing about the old quarters of Cairo oversteps the theme of local colour, goes beyond the surface peculiarities of the region, penetrates to the realm of universal human characteristics and fathoms the core of national idiosyncracies.

Unlike some of his contemporaries, Ḥaqqī seems to have been aware from the beginning of his literary career of the need to avoid the stock characters around which the Egyptian short story had revolved for so long. From 'al-Mawt wa'l-Tafkīr' and 'al-Sukhriyah' onwards, he demonstrates how the creation of individual, distinctive characters accentuates the human aspect of a situation. He soon became aware of the importance of selectivity and, unlike Taymūr, did not dwell too long on his early works. Some of his main themes can be found in these works, but only as themes, not as rudimentary versions of later works. With his predilection for conciseness and experimentation, which proved to be a comprehensive, not merely empirical, artistic attitude with him, he was unlikely to be tempted to dilute earlier characters or experiences, or reuse situations he had treated previously in later work.

Ḥaqqī was also aware of the fact that a good short story needs to comprehend not only a reasonable knowledge of the subject and the limits and nature of the character it deals with, but also and especially, a sound experience of all the social rituals, details of life, sets of values and beliefs, traditional legends, tales, songs and proverbs, and pseudo-scientific lore about the weather, plants, and animals the character portrayed ought to possess, or the ramifications of the situation ought to suggest. His self-conscious decision to write Egyptian short stories rooted in Egyptian culture provides his work with competence and power. Ḥaqqī stated that 'a good short story is the one that omits a long preamble: this omission encourages the reader to feel, from the first line, that he is encountering a living piece of work and an integrated atmosphere.'[195] He consistently tries to live up to this ideal, a trait which enables him to achieve a unity of tone in his short stories and to break new ground as far as tempo and rhythm are concerned. Ḥaqqī writes in the belief that a creative writer must be a tireless observer and that he ceases to be an artist when he ceases to perform this function.[196] Sensitive visual observation is vital if the short story is to leave behind the prosaic enumeration of events and create an artistic narrative that vividly gives concrete form to character and action. Ḥaqqī emphasises the role of the eye and visual imagery against the traditional role of the ear, which responds to pun, paronomasia and euphuism. The rudimentary technique by which stories were overloaded with direct information accompanied by moralistic commentaries upon character and action was thus abandoned, and he began to convey information by means of suggestion or implication, which in turn enhanced the poetic content and imaginative power of his stories.

A characteristic of the visual element in Ḥaqqī's writing is the tendency to present action and character by daylight. He sets his world in the bright sun of Egypt, in the common light of day. The moon seldom appears in his world and when it does it is often the subject of gentle irony. By day everything is clear, which suits Ḥaqqī's predilection for clarity, purity and representing visible nature in all its variety and detail. His predilection for depicting nature is not an expression of affection for rustic scenes, but a means of integrating the character into his or her proper setting and demonstrating the dialectical relationship between the poor and nature in general, and the Egyptian poor and their animals, their domestic animals especially, in particular. For centuries, the relationship between the Egyptian peasant and his or her animals has been deeply rooted in the national consciousness. The number of animal pictures or sculptures in Egyptian archaeological remains substantiates this, as does the content of the present rituals of daily village life.

From the very beginning of his career, Ḥaqqī endeavours to illustrate different aspects of this deep-rooted relationship. 'Fullah-Mishmish-Lūlū' uses it to depict the subtle differences in people's attitude to reality, while 'Qiṣṣah fī Sijn'[197] touches upon its fatalistic and superstitious dimension and draws parallels between animals and men confronted with the vicissitudes of life. The descriptions of the herd of sheep[198] or the death of the hero's dog[199] are beautiful pieces of prose in themselves, but their aesthetic effect on the reader is mainly derived from their skilful integration into the story. The harmony in the relationship between the hero of 'Kūkū'[200] and his pets enables the heroine to see her life in a new perspective. It touches her to the quick, and this endows her with an ability to feel her way in life. In "Anṭar wa-Juliet'[201] the relationship between man and animals becomes the main theme of the story and a means of understanding the characters sensitively and effectively. The story uses poetic imagery and rhythm to illustrate various dimensions of the relationship between the two dogs and their owners. This illuminates not only the rhythm and tone of two contradictory attitudes to reality, but also the unseen, yet fundamental, differences between two social strata and their way of life. The ramifications of the same accidental action differ radically in two families in a way that provides the reader with an insight into their situation, fate and values. When night comes, bringing an end to the actions of the day, the rich family reverses the effects of the unfortunate event, while the other has to yield, unfairly, to the pressure.

Day and night are two important contradictory symbols in Ḥaqqī's work. Those who can barely fulfil their lives by day are unable to afford the peace of the night in "Anṭar wa-Juliet'. In other stories, the conflict between day and night is evident at both realistic and symbolic levels. By presenting his world by day, Ḥaqqī illuminates the main daily activity (work and the struggle for a livelihood) and brings it sharply into focus, while nocturnal activities are marginal to his theme. In daytime in Ḥaqqī's stories man is integrated into society and enveloped in a working atmosphere, whereas night attacks him in his most vulnerable state, when he is alone. The night is gloomy, brutal, inhuman and full of fear, a time when crimes are committed and plots fabricated. The description of night in 'al-Būsṭajī'[202] associates night with blindness, constraint, heaviness, chains, shrouds and obscure anxieties,[203] and attributes to it many of the character's fears and misfortunes. In 'Qiṣṣah fī Sijn' night is conceived of as the corpse of the day and is associated with bats, mosquitoes, trickery, grief and death.[204] Unlike night, day is associated with bright colours, unambiguous sentiments and the simple rituals of life. It is the time for the main action to take place in the broad light of the sun. This consequently entails a higher degree of clarity in the wider sense of the word, in language, characterisation and action;[205] Ḥaqqī believes that this clarity is dependent on genuine experience and profound understanding of the subject matter.[206] But clarity in Ḥaqqī's work is in no way synonymous with directness or crudity of expression. Rather, it is an artistic approach to the subject that enables the writer to be precise and poetic at the same time. Clarity and precision of expression demand experience of form and structure, and an awareness of a new aesthetic outlook on style.

Throughout Ḥaqqī's work clarity is closely connected with contemplative elements, to demonstrate the perceptive insight and the quality of creative imagination which our writer possesses to such a supreme degree. Unlike Taymūr, who imitates Maupassant, or Lāshīn, who was clearly influenced by Chekhov, Ḥaqqī does not imitate any specific European writer, despite his wide knowledge of European literature. Although fascinated by the descriptive technique of Thomas Mann and by Dostoevsky's aptitude for analysing inner feelings, it seems his greatest debt is to Egyptian folk tales and oral literature, to their simplicity, depth, vivid imagery and far-reaching effect. He includes folk songs in some of his works and, like the folk tale, his stories focus on character, which he sets in its appropriate social milieu. Conflict in his stories has two main strands: conflict between the protagonist and his inner being, and the struggle between him and outside reality. In most of his stories the two conflicts are thoroughly interrelated to each other, each participating in the development of the other. This is particularly so in his *Ṣa'īdiyyāt* (stories about Upper Egypt), where tragic elements are interwoven with the rituals of everyday life and with the character's attitude towards self and society. In *Ṣa'īdiyyāt* this interaction enables Ḥaqqī to capture, for the first time in the history of the Egyptian short story, the spirit and particularities of life in Upper Egypt. This is not only because of his deep insight and first-hand experience of the characters and situations he is dealing with, but because he conceives of the short story as a mature and coherent artistic form capable of penetrating reality and exploring its undercurrents, as opposed to simply a means of presenting a form of social survey, which was how many of his predecessors and contemporaries viewed it. In 'al-Būsṭajī', the most important story in *Ṣa'īdiyyāt,* the inner conflict that the hero, 'Abbās, wages with himself is as sharp and complex as his conflict with external reality, and beneath the two there is a deeper and more comprehensive conflict between the ethics, values and lifestyle of the city and the ethos of the village.

In the story's first section, 'Iblāgh Warā' Iblāgh',[207] the external conflict between 'Abbās and the village is introduced, and the second section, "Abbās Aṣluh wa-Faṣluh'[208] offers the first glimpses of the protagonist's social formation and cultural background through a restrained third-person narrative, which evokes the life he had lived in Cairo as a student and then as a civil servant. But when he moves to the village both the rhythm of the language and the narrative technique change in order to prepare the reader for an important turn of events and to demonstrate the intensity of his involvement and foreshadow the coming conflict. The narrative transfers to the first person,[209] not in a third-person framework or the style of literary prose, but in the emotionally charged evocative tones of the spoken language. 'The moment I set foot in this village, I couldn't bear it; I felt as if I was in prison,'[210] he says, and his feeling of imprisonment intensifies with the passing of the days. 'Abbās, as an innocent inexperienced young man from the city, fails to mask, much less to overcome, his early sense of shock and disillusionment, thus he makes no effort to understand the village, let alone to enter its world. On the contrary, he unconsciously blocks his way to understanding and the village becomes increasingly closed, mysterious and hateful to him. The eventual confrontation therefore becomes gradually inevitable; at the beginning it takes a trivial form, which serves to intensify his sense of isolation. His quest for salvation from this predicament and his lost harmony with himself and his external reality only perpetuate his isolation and give his behaviour a quixotic touch.

This consequently drives him to commit the unpardonable sin for a postman; he begins opening and intercepting the villagers' letters. The motivation is boredom and loneliness, but also the desire to account for the village's hostile attitude towards him. This turns out to be a terrible mistake, for what commences as a 'harmless peep' at the villagers' life through their letters soon results in an absurd but tragic situation. After a few days 'Abbās's violation of his sacred duties fails to satisfy him and arouses feelings of guilt. His knowledge of the village remains as shallow after reading the letters as it was before. The magic of violating the taboo soon evaporates and is replaced by boredom at the repetitiveness and paltriness of the letters. He is now more alienated from the village than before. Moreover, his transgression entangles him with another couple in conflict with the values and conventions of the village.

The third section of the story, 'Jamīlah wa-Bint Nās',[211] introduces the love story between Jamīlah and Khalīl, which attracts 'Abbās and which in turn entwines their destinies. Like 'Abbās, Jamīlah was educated in the city and has been exposed to many of its values and ideas. The similarity between 'Abbās's situation and Jamīlah's not only makes him identify with her, but also induces him to become more interested and eventually involved in her story. His involvement, on one level, is an indirect means of communicating with the village and overcoming his alienation. However, because of the clandestine nature of his attempt to break the siege imposed on him by the village, his activities complicate life for Jamīlah, the only person in the village with whom he sympathises, and finally delivers the *coup de grâce* to her, ruining her life but 'Abbās's too.

The fourth section, 'Farḥah Mā Tammat',[212] is short and tense in order to convey the brevity and intensity of Khalīl's attempt to save Jamīlah. The attempt fails because of sectarian differences within the Christian religion, which requires an ecclesiastical procedure, a matter of a few weeks, which neither Jamīlah nor Khalīl can afford. This not only tightens the snare around Jamīlah, but underlines the cultural nature of the problem and shows how her ignorance of certain ridiculous conventions plays against her. The irony is that the educated Jamīlah – in this respect 'Abbās's equal – becomes a victim of her ignorance. The knowledge she has gained from the city somehow acts against her. When she came back to the village she brought with her 'hats and books,[213] two wonders in the mud-brick houses'.[214] The village tolerates these, but stands firm against the third and most important of her 'wonders', that is new attitudes, which include a certain disregard for the village's values and conventions. Jamīlah's internal changes are reflected in the growing embryo of her forbidden relationship with Khalīl.

In the fifth and last section, 'Saqṭat al-Būsṭajī',[215] the story reaches its climax when the destinies of the two agents, who are at the same time the victims, of these conflicts ('Abbās and Jamīlah) become closely interwoven. In a moment of rage, which arises from the long, agonising boredom 'Abbās endures as a result of his inability to understand, let alone to adjust to, the village's world, he stamps an important letter from Khalīl to Jamīlah and becomes unable to return it to its envelope and, consequently, to its addressee. This links 'Abbās's destiny with Jamīlah's since the intercepted letter becomes a crucial link in the progression of Jamīlah's affair. The rest of the section portrays two protagonists groping about in snares of their own making on the one hand, and as victims of the closed atmosphere in the village and conflicting cultural values on the other. Jamīlah is finally killed by her father, who complies with the conventional request to avenge his contaminated honour. 'Abbās falls victim to his own self-censure and regret, then suffers a nervous breakdown and leaves the village.

By illustrating how a simple village, Kawm al-Naḥl, subdues or rather crushes two fragile rebellious characters, the story delineates, with subtlety and delicacy, the strength of the village and the weaknesses of the two educated, but not sophisticated, protagonists. Life in the village is portrayed as solid and consistent to the extent of exerting a tangible physical influence on 'Abbās. It has its own logic and code of conduct and its own ways of enforcing them. The details of daily life are presented as if they are ceremonial events or rituals, carried out in a dignified and sedate manner. The battle is fought on village ground, where the village can mobilise all its forces, while its opponents are isolated and more or less inert. They are presented from the very beginning as trapped individuals, fighting unjust battles and struggling against an almost invisible enemy. Their illusions about themselves prevent them from grasping the situation, so they do not realise, until it is too late, that they are fighting their battle unarmed and partly blindfolded. When it comes to the crucial confrontation, they surrender their reason and fight according to the village's rules. They inevitably lose, for they never exploit what advantages they have over the villagers. The actions of the villagers are highly motivated and deeply rooted in tradition, but they are always reactions or outbursts of anger and despair. The stamping of the letter demonstrates this. Moreover, many of the villagers' actions show the tragic effect of the closed world in which they live upon their souls. Their conflict with outside reality mirrors a deeper conflict with the self, and every battle lost against the external world intensifies their inner struggle.

In the rest of the *Ṣa'īdiyyāt,* Ḥaqqī depicts variations on these interrelated conflicts. In 'Qiṣṣah fī Sijn',[216] the story that follows 'al-Būsṭajī' in *Dimā' wa-Ṭīn,* he shows the vulnerability of the village and the fragility of its values when an outsider, al-Ghajariyyah, disrupts the logic of the existing order and finally succeeds in imposing her will. To express the bewilderment of the people in the village in this situation, Ḥaqqī uses comic irony, avoiding melodrama and exaggeration. In 'Abū Fūdah'[217] the characters' relationship with the natural surroundings, in harmony with them, or violently at odds, is powerfully evoked. The Nile and the mountain and the ritualistic life of Upper Egypt, more than the background of the action, are part of its texture and rhythm. 'Ḥaṣīr al-Jāmi''[218] offers a more light-hearted treatment of the theme of 'al-Būstajī', namely, the inability of the townsman to understand the logic by which the village lives, and 'Izāzit Rīḥah' demonstrates that the only possible life for urban people in the village is a marginal one in a ghetto of their own, and that the village's real life is impenetrable.

The *Ṣa'īd* in these stories is not simply a setting for the action; it has a mysterious life of its own. Life in this part of the world has continued almost unchanged for thousands of years, untouched by change in the rest of Egypt, without any real attempt to understand its particular ethos or special characteristics. Ḥaqqī uses his contemplative insight and descriptive skill to explore the material and spiritual components of life in Upper Egypt. In these five stories, he manages to capture the realistic and mysterious aspects of the principal natural features of the *Ṣa'īd*, the powerful docile Nile, the mysterious mountain, the flat but rough valley, the fearful moonless night, the conspiratorial moonlit night, the friendly tamed animals, and the burning sun. He also captures the spirit of everyday life with its rituals and underlying rhythms and employs them in widening the scope of his action, and in rooting the characters in their cultural and social surroundings. By interweaving the elements of nature with the rituals of the village's daily life, Ḥaqqī puts his finger on the real pulse of Egypt, the core of its social and mythical beliefs, the rhythm of its slow, steady movement, the beat of its heart along the Nile valley, the crudeness of its life in the fist of an oppressive destiny, the interaction between the Nile and men and animals in this area. Indeed, life in the Nile Valley and the interdependence (or unique relationship) of Egyptian peasants and their domestic animals has not been accurately or extensively depicted by any Egyptian short story writer other than Ḥaqqī.

In his *Ṣa'īdiyyāt*, Ḥaqqī presents convincing characterisations of individuals deeply rooted in the Nile Valley and thoroughly integrated into its social life. They represent a complete contrast to Maḥmūd Taymūr's villagers, who are, for the most part, flat characters unable to relate to their milieu. Because of the very nature of their beliefs, Ḥaqqī's characters are entangled in the web of irrevocable fate, which gives the simplicity of their lives a philosophical dimension. In this lies one of Ḥaqqī's most important achievements in the field of Egyptian fiction. In his treatment of the spiral of fate – the revolt which interrupts the flow of life and brings revenge, followed by the restoration of the life-flow after punishment, a feature that will be treated in more detail later – Ḥaqqī introduces the role of chance, not as an unexpected incident that interrupts the main action or diverts its direction, but as a functional and integral part of the conflict. For instance, the sudden death of Umm Aḥmad in 'al-Būsṭajī' underlines the eventual significance of 'Abbās's relatively minor digression; the accidental explosion of a faulty charge in 'Abū Fūdah' brings the cycle of crime and punishment to an end, and a casual meeting between the hero and village mayor in 'Izāzit Rīḥah' shatters the former's illusions, opening his blinkered eyes to certain realities, and contributes to the progress of the action.

Ḥaqqī succeeds in integrating these accidental events into his main plot, thanks to his artistic approach to reality and use of irony, both dramatic and cosmic. It is dramatic irony in 'Qiṣṣah fī Sijn', 'Izāzit Rīḥah' and 'Ḥaṣīr al-Jāmi'', where the reader shares with the author knowledge of which the fictional character is ignorant. In 'al-Būsṭajī' and 'Abū Fūdah' it is cosmic irony, in which God, or destiny, or the universal process, acts as though deliberately manipulating events to frustrate and mock the protagonist. The use of irony enables Ḥaqqī to purge his work of intrusive authorial comment and didacticism, and to sustain a vivid and readable narrative. To construct his artistic irony, Ḥaqqī uses two main forms: syllogistic and qualitative narrative progression.[219] The gradual progression of action in his fictional world includes an eclectic choice of evocative scenes and moments in the life of his character, whereby brief snippets speak for the whole – like Blake, he sees 'the universe in a grain of sand'. He picks the moments of peripeteia, of climax and change, in the life of his character and treats them in the most indirect manner possible. He also sustains his irony through

> the use of fallible narrator, in which the teller of the story is himself participant in it but, although he may be neither foolish nor demented, nevertheless manifests a failure of insight, viewing and appraising his own motives, and the motives and actions of other characters, through the distorting perspective of his prejudices and private interests.[220]

Ḥaqqī approaches the question of creating a sense of 'Egyptianness' in modern literature from a new point of view. Unlike his contemporaries, such as Lashīn, who generally try to achieve this by transferring as much reality as possible into their fictional work, Ḥaqqī prefers to address the issue directly, as, for example, in 'Qindil Umm Hashim',[221] where he presents the dilemma of Egypt's conflict of civilisations. After touching upon the problem of conflicting cultural values in 'al-Būsṭajī' in the mid-1930s,[222] Ḥaqqī went on to explore various aspects of the problem in the second half of the decade.[223] The 1920s and 1930s witnessed the emergence of Egyptian nationalism, while the 1940s posed the crucial question of whether or not to accept European civilisation.[224] Ḥaqqī's investigation of the problem rephrases the question more realistically and examines how Egypt should accept and assimilate aspects of European culture without losing its integrity as a nation. He tries also to prescribe a solution, forgetting Chekhov's valuable advice that: 'it is not the task of fiction writers to solve such problems as God, pessimism, etc. The writer's business is to depict only who spoke or thought about God or pessimism, and how and under what circumstances.'[225] His prescribed solution is to a certain extent ambiguous and hence a cause of controversy among critics.[226]

'Qindīl Umm Hāshim' is one of the most demanding and perplexing experiences in Egyptian fiction. It adopts a wholly ironic perspective while telling the story of a real moral dilemma in psychologically realistic terms. As a result, the reader is sympathetic towards the hero, Ismā'īl, but at the same time uncomfortably entertained by the story. Throughout the work, the reader is asked to identify with a protagonist who cannot himself find an identity, and whose quest at a deeper level of the narrative is a quest for identity. His very name calls to mind the Ismā'īl of Islamic mythology (Abraham's son), who was offered as a sacred sacrifice, for the story centres upon a character floundering in an adverse moral climate and surrounded by problems of both a spiritual and ethical nature. In delineating this situation, the account draws upon at least three traditions for its vocabulary and point of view: satire, allegory and the fiction of psychological development. The story begins with an event that evokes the first phase in the country's encounter with modernity, urbanisation, with the family moving from the village to Cairo. The minute description of the family's arrival in the al-Sayyidah Zaynab quarter, when the father pushes his clumsy son as they approach the doorstep of the saint's shrine to kneel down and kiss the threshold, reveals at a stroke all the information needed about the family's social and cultural background, values and the nature of the relationship between its generations. The writer's account of the family's new life in Cairo complements suggestions and predictions about the hero's distinguished position in the family, and suggests throughout his prophet-like childhood the kind of message he will have to proclaim.[227] The second scene of the story takes the reader to the square of the al-Sayyidah Zaynab mosque, where the message is awaited, a world of the poor and unfortunate, the sick and the ignorant, the busy and the idle – a wilderness that greets its appointed prophet with tenderness and affection at the end of his daily contemplative stroll by the Nile.[228]

In the third scene, the hero reaches the age of puberty and adolescent desires begin to stir in him. He discovers the sensual delights of contact with female bodies in the crowd around the shrine and singles out one of the regular visitors, Naʿīmah, a beautiful prostitute, as a subject for his fantasies. He tries to elevate his carnal desires through spiritual meditation; these centre on the lamp, which he gives symbolic meaning. This period of adolescence, of these concurrent sensual and spiritual experiences, coincides with his final year of secondary education. He fails to obtain the required grade for university and a friend suggests to his father that the only solution is to send him abroad. The fourth and fifth scenes are devoted to the hesitation in sending Ismāʿīl to Europe; then comes the decision and subsequent preparations for his departure to England. The hesitation underlines not only deeply rooted fears about the West, but also the religious and economic implications of this action.[229] When, in their attempt to silence their fears, his family declares their intention to marry him to Fāṭimah al-Nabawiyyah[230] and go complacently through the ceremony of engagement, Ismāʿīl acquiesces but inwardly rejects the idea and questions its validity.[231]

Ismāʿīl's European experience lasts seven years – a number with mythical allusions – and is presented in a series of flashbacks after his return. His confrontation with his old world, which he has continued to love, speaks eloquently for the changes he has undergone. The sixth scene, which describes his return, gives the reader the first glimpse of his spiritual adventure in Europe through his relationship with Mary (another name with a religious connotation).

> Mary is obviously a symbol of western civilisation. She [stands] for lust for life, constant activity, freedom from the shackles of tradition, individuality, complete self-confidence, science and humanism, realistic thinking about concrete problems, belief in this world and appreciation of art and the beauty of nature. In short, she [represents] the complete opposite of the values that had been operative in his life.[232]

Ismāʿīl's experience in Europe fulfils the reader's expectations, confirms the protagonist's role as a messenger, and creates new expectations. In his European wilderness, he undergoes a dramatic change in character and attitude. He exchanges one set of divinities for another, and as soon as he returns, there is conflict between the two sets of beliefs. During his absence, he also acquires a new vision of his country, a mythical one, in which he sees Egypt as the Sleeping Beauty awaiting the arrival of a prince to wake her. He perceives himself as the saviour of his country who will liberate her from the forces of evil.[233] The train journey from Alexandria to Cairo disheartens him, and the way he sees external objects foreshadows the nature of the conflict. Ironically, the first confrontation not only takes place in his own house and on the subject of his specialty, but also entangles him with the lamp, around which his old spiritual meditations centred. The following three scenes elaborate on this clash between absolute mythico-religious belief,[234] represented in the quiet patient Fāṭimah, who on one level of interpretation symbolises Egypt, and mythico-scientific belief, embodied in Ismā'īl after his return from Europe.

The mythico-scientific naturally breaks first, for mythical thought can live in harmony with religion, while scientific thought interwoven with mythical elements harbours at the core of its structure the seeds of its own destruction. Ismā'īl's crisis after this first and crucial confrontation undermines the newfound confidence he has gained in Europe. The tenth scene shows how the miracle he hoped would work and become a decisive sign of his prophetic message, instead achieves the opposite, proving the victory of the opposing set of values and demonstrating his own blindness. He leaves the house, sells some of his books and medical instruments, and moves to the *pension* of Madam Iftālyā – a European woman. In this deformed replica of Europe, stripped of charm and enchantment, he lives in self-imposed exile. He becomes isolated from society in an active quest for self and the sources of his being, undergoing a total revision of his beliefs and the values of his life. He begins to know himself not as a rebel or prophet, but as an individual within the frame of his society. Madam Iftālyā's *pension* fails to work as a personal ivory tower and Ismā'īl is forced to abandon his self-imposed exile and return to reality, the only reality he knows after Madam Iftālyā has eliminated the European option for him.

He finds himself in a dilemma, for he realises that the oil and the lamp occupy in the beliefs of his society the status of what Cassirer calls *sondergotter*, but he also realises that he cannot sacrifice his faith in science all at once. He also discovers in a moment of revelation, portrayed in scene twelve, that the lamp as a symbol is the objective parallel to a pattern of experience, and that this forms a special myth in the life of his milieu in general, and his family in particular.

Myth never breaks out of the magic circle of its figurative ideas. It reaches religious and poetic heights; but the gulf between its conceptions and those of science never narrows the least bit. But language, born in that same magic circle, has the power to break its bounds; language takes us from the mythmaking phase of human mentality to the phase of logical thought and the conception of facts.[235]

Therefore, Ismāʿīl weaves a net of verbal traps to hunt down Fāṭimah's fears and reluctance, and to penetrate the magic circle of myth, fallacy and superstition. On the night of his revelation, he sees Naʿīmah, the prostitute he admired in the past, coming to redeem her votive offering to Umm Hāshim. This stimulates his search for a way back to his forsaken society. He leaves the shrine with a new feeling of humility. He goes back to his house with a bottle of the lantern oil and gives Fāṭimah the illusion that he is going to use the sacred oil to cure her eyes. He traps all her suspicions about his strange method in the faded image of a bottle of sacred oil, while in fact he uses his modern medicine as the only remedy. In a verbal compromise, Ismāʿīl uses religious illusion to break the psychological barrier, and thus comes closer to the essence of the scientific approach; the approach that recognises that understanding and appreciating reality is a prerequisite for change. The process of change is not one-dimensional, nor does it move in one direction: it has a reciprocal effect on both its subject and object, for while superstition is regressive, religion has the ability to penetrate social practice and provide respect for positive aspects of tradition and culture.

At another level of interpretation, it seems that Ḥaqqī is suggesting that a character's opposition to social conventions exposes the individual to either social punishment or voluntary self-sacrifice. When one of Ḥaqqī's characters steps beyond his own time or social limits, a clash with a set of social or divine values is usually involved, which interrupts the continuity of what he seems to conceive of as the spiral movement of time. In this way, Ḥaqqī transcends the duality of Taymūr's world and further eliminates the double standard of morality in the characterisation. His sympathy falls on the side of the rebellious character without, however, mocking social conventions or trying to prove certain inevitable conclusions. This theme appears in 'Qindīl Umm Hāshim' and also, in the background, in 'al-Būsṭajī', where the heroine who oversteps the limits of her society's understanding and breaks its taboos suffers the penalty of death; and the hero who wrongly interferes in the life of the village brings elements of irrational destiny and cosmic irony into play, while suffering from his inability to prevent the grave consequences of his own venal error. Both the hero and the heroine are presented in the story as victims of fate and of the poor, gloomy life around them. In 'Sūsū'[236] the promiscuous hero is afflicted with agony and suffering long after renouncing his life of sin and refraining from violating social or ethical conventions. In 'al-Sullam al-Lawlabī'[237] the hero who tries to cross the class barrier and undergoes immediate punishment corresponding to the triviality of his error is humorously portrayed.

Comic presentation is one of the effective devices Ḥaqqī uses to play down exaggeration and sentimental or even tragic elements in his writing. It is one of the characteristics of his dramatic irony, as embodied in 'Qiṣṣah fī Sijn' and 'al-Sullam al-Lawlabī'. But in other stories, such as 'al-Sulḥufāh Taṭīr'[238] 'Kunnā Thalāthat Aytām',[239] 'Iflās Khāṭibah',[240] 'Tanawwaʿat al-Asbāb',[241] 'Mūlid ... Bilā Ḥummuṣ'[242] 'Fi'l-'Iyādah'[243] and 'al-Wada'',[244] it becomes not only a main feature of the structure of the work, but an integral and important part of the theme. In many of these stories, the humour is not farcical but springs from chance incidents, or from ironic observation of ordinary situations made problematic by the attitudes of the protagonists, whose images of themselves differ from the images they project to outsiders.

In 'al-Sulḥafāh Taṭīr', the comic presentation of the action widens its frame of reference and makes the situation plausible. Ḥaqqī does not record the progression of the action syllogistically, but by registering certain images, moods or actions that reveal the irony of the situation and the private thoughts of the characters. In 'Iflās Khāṭibah' the unexpected and unusual development of the relationship between the matchmaker and her client is given depth and becomes a trivial, peculiar event because of the humour in its treatment. 'Tanawwaʿat al-Asbāb' presents in its heroine a contemporary character who could have stepped out of the pages of al-Jāḥiẓ's famous book *al-Bukhalā'*. It draws upon the tradition in classical Arabic literature of comic satire and emphasises the laughable inconsistencies between people's words and actions. In 'Qiṣṣah fī 'Arḍiḥāl'[245] comic representation saves the work from sentimentality and broadens its outlook, while it creates the right mood of expression to suit the theme of 'Mūlid ... Bilā Ḥummuṣ'. In these stories comic treatment conveys some common form of the ludicrous and underlines the vanity and absurdity of certain forms of behaviour, demonstrating that human life is endlessly rich and fertile, inexhaustible in variety and interest, since Ḥaqqī clearly knows that, as Bergson says, only human beings can be ridiculous.

The other major theme in Ḥaqqī's stories is human will and its vital role in life. Indeed, in an interview Ḥaqqī stated that he considers this to be one of the most important themes in his work.[246] He emphasises that willing and wishing are not synonymous; every character wishes to attain a good life, but when he lacks the will the results are usually grave. Here Ḥaqqī's philosophical outlook seems to be individualistic, one that perceives life as a great battle in which the victors are not the most talented or even the strongest, but those who have the motivation and will-power. Will is the *primum mobile.* At a certain level of interpretation 'Qindīl Umm Hāshim' seems to be a story about conflicting wills, or rather of a man exercising his will in order to achieve the necessary rapprochement with the outside world. However, on the whole, Ḥaqqī tends to concentrate on the grave consequences that arise from an absence of human will in a situation.[247] It may be the story of the success of a strongly motivated character in winning his spurs, but most of Ḥaqqī's works dealing with this theme concentrate on the serious consequences of the absence of this crucial agent provocateur of life, the human will.

In 'Umm al-'Awājiz'[248] the hero loosens his grip on reality and, gradually, loses his will to live. As a result he topples down to the bottom rung of society, from street trader to being a fumigator with incense, then a beggar, and still continues to deteriorate until life almost rejects him. His subsequent descent is depicted, in minute detail, in language and imagery that convey the accompanying physical and mental decay. Lack of will-power deprives the heroine of 'Iḥtijāj'[249] of her natural right to a groom and causes her to lose the only man who might have been interested in her. Here we have a different case, for the heroine has the incentive to marry the man and manages to attract his attention and start a relationship with him. But her aimless life hitherto has affected her will, and when she encounters the first obstacle, after an initial protest, she yields to the pressure and cynicism of her masters. Her failure to assert her will is not, however, the only factor here; the decisiveness of the masters, who know where their interests lie and are ready to defend them and crush the heroine's attempt to challenge her subordination, must also be considered. Thus Ḥaqqī demonstrates that will-power can be a negative force in a situation, that human volition is a resource that can be exercised by individuals at any level of the moral spectrum.

'Dhikrāyāt Dukkān'[250] is a sensitive account of an individual who succeeds in fulfilling himself when he had a strong sense of purpose and let his life slip through his fingers after the death of his son. In this story, Ḥaqqī deals with the long-lasting impact of war on a man and touches upon the familiar theme of drugs and their abuse. Although the addiction to opium here is ascribed to the war, it is depicted as symptomatic of fading will-power. In 'Mir'āh bi-Ghayr Zujāj'[251] Ḥaqqī advances his theme to the sphere of mythology. The story presents two characters, who are identical in terms of outward appearance but whose attitude to life is diametrically opposed; one is strong-willed and practical, the other a dreamer. Elements of metamorphosis and metempsychosis, and the notion of mythological death, which leads to resurrection, are subtly conveyed in the structure of the story. Other variations on the same theme appear in 'al-Nisyān',[252] where the psychological investigation of the complex relationship between a character and his double and opposite becomes more realistic and involves more than one layer of meaning. Ḥaqqī develops this special complex relationship between two conflicting wills in his last short story, 'Ka'ann',[253] in which he explores how both the mysterious and realistic elements link one will to the other.

Ḥaqqī treats this theme of will in many other short stories. He shows in some an individual will struggling with social and psychological pressures,[254] and investigates in others further aspects of the fascinating relationship between two conflicting wills,[255] or the mythical elements entangled with this theme.[256] In these stories, the individual is often shown to possess capacities of feeling and perception but is unable to take initiatives and effectively express or act upon his insights. Ḥaqqī's deep understanding of the losers in the battle for fulfilment and the search for an identity ensures that these stories further our knowledge and experience of man and of some aspects of Egyptian life. However, if many of these examples speak for Ḥaqqī's argument in a negative way, that is to say by demonstrating the fatal consequences of the lack of will and a weak hold on life, there are other characters that manifest the same conception in a positive manner. The narrator of 'al-Sulḥafah Taṭīr'[257] has a strange will indeed and a clear sense of purpose; he succeeds in achieving his goal and his triumph gives him deep satisfaction. In 'Ḥaṣīr al-Jāmi'', the mayor's strong sense of purpose is aided by a powerful will that knows how to manipulate the situation to his own advantage. The heroine of 'Abū Fūdah' gives another demonstration of the ability to manipulate the situation without being the strongest among those involved, for when there is a will there is always a way to defy your opponent's physical or even mental strength. In 'al-Sarīr al-Nuḥās',[258] the heroine's strong will is aided by the pressure of superstitious beliefs; she insistently does what she wants regardless of the comfort of her mother. Even in 'Umm al-'Awājiz', there are three characters who succeed because of their vigorous wills in replacing the title character in the three jobs he successively occupies.

In both his negative and positive methods of illustrating the importance of a strong drive and deep appreciation of life as an ultimate, almost sacred, value, Ḥaqqī extols human will. Yet he cherishes and understands the losers, or rather the victims, in the battle of life, for he is aware of the price of success and the moral and ethical compromises involved in attaining it. In one of his last stories, 'Imra'ah Miskīnah',[259] he depicts the subtle destructiveness, even inhumanity, of imposing one's will at any cost. The heroine of the story, a housewife, faces a grave situation when her husband is sent to a mental asylum. She resents society's pity for her difficulty and hates being seen as a woman victim. She defies this traditional image of the *Imra'ah Miskīnah* (poor woman) and becomes the breadwinner of her family. Her newly acquired power enables her to establish her supreme authority at home, especially over her mother-in-law, and to see herself in a new light. Aware of the power and status she has gained from her new job, she does everything possible to establish and further her career, including compromising her morality. When she discovers that her husband has recovered and is going to be released from the mental asylum, she suspects that this might endanger her progress up the administrative scale. In a further brutal compromise of her ethical values, she persuades the psychiatrist to delay, or even to prevent, her husband's release, then she goes off to Europe on a business-pleasure trip with her boss to advance her career. The heroine is thus depicted as somewhat Machiavellian in pursuit of her goal. She may achieve her purpose, but at a high moral cost. Ḥaqqī, in a subtle and highly artistic manner, sides against spiritless characters who are weak and lack the will to live, but he does not side with senseless individuals who achieve their aims by means of deception or at the expense of humanitarian principles. As an artist, however, his sympathy with the victims of life and social change is clear and strong.

Despite its gloomy and morbid atmosphere, 'al-Firāsh al-Shāghir'[260] is a good example of this sympathy and humanitarianism. It is one of Ḥaqqī's finest short stories as far as characterisation, structure and language are concerned, and a milestone in the development of the Egyptian short story.[261] 'Al-Firāsh al-Shāghir' is the story of an abortive quest for the self and realisation of identity, and a gradual descent into obscurity and perversion, in which an individual from the defeated landowning class is struggling to prove himself in a chaotic and hostile milieu. This individual is ironically named 'Najm al-Usrah', 'the star of the family', whose enormous material wealth matches the poverty of its human contacts and social interactions and experience, since it deliberately refrains from entering into any relationship with others and imposes on itself a sort of voluntary self-confinement. The elders of the family believe that dealings with the outside world would expose both the sordid depravity of external reality and the inadequacy of the self. Their way of consolidating themselves is by withdrawing from the world and erecting a high fence – literally and metaphorically – around themselves. Thus the protagonist, Najm al-Usrah, is protected from external reality and has only a shallow knowledge of the world. His general malaise results from both his lack of experience, thanks to his sheltered upbringing, and his own chaotic approach to reality, which combines a desire to prove himself with tendencies towards self-destruction. The world seems meaningless and sterile to him, which cripples his will but does not lessen his drive to prove himself. Susceptible as he is to boredom, he fails to complete his university education in three different faculties, and each failure furthers his dislike of responsibility. He becomes indifferent and insouciant, a state which he can afford since he does not need to earn his living. But he is still looking for a way to prove and fulfil himself and to rescue himself from boredom and general malaise.

He decides to procure a wife and selects a woman from Upper Egypt whom he expects to be compliant by virtue of her class background and position in society as a widow. However, his assessment proves wrong. She becomes the femme fatale of his life, the final straw that forces him to examine himself, and he finds he does not like what he sees. Rather than rescuing him from a living death, she pushes him deeper into the quicksand of doubt and depression. Her appearance in his life is brief, but in rejecting him she shatters his last hope of fulfilment and heightens his suicidal tendencies. Thereafter he progressively deteriorates, never forgetting his experience with the woman, who becomes for him a dramatic embodiment of his problem. Ḥaqqī emphasises the fact that his problem is not a question of sexual impotence but of social and psychological prostration and decrepitude. It becomes natural for him to develop a morbid association with the world of the dead. He enjoys, as never before, his voluntary work with the corpse washer and finds consolation in his friendship with the mortician's apprentice. The apprentice is a pervert, who articulates his perversity for him and pushes him further towards decline, until he can assert his will only over a dead corpse and revenge his experience with the *Ṣa'īdiyyah*.

The story explores the theme of will-power on many levels. It dwells upon certain philosophical aspects of this theme and tries to bridge the gap between the abstract and the perceptible, yet never departs from the concrete and the realistic, dealing with a specific location and identifiable characters. It manages to do so because of its fine use of language, convincing characterisation and coherent structure. Language, in particular, is illuminating in this work not only because of its richness and fine stylistic features, but also and especially because it powerfully creates the narrative mood corresponding to the general atmosphere of the story with its setting, action, characterisation and general impression. Three sets of vocabulary items are skilfully meshed together: a morbid vocabulary relating to death, corpses, perversity, gloom and the like; a moral vocabulary relating to conscience, salvation, spiritual aspiration and agony; and a social category relating to items of external social significance and to the psychological state of the character and his deterioration at many levels. Ḥaqqī often exploits the phonological level of the language and there is always an interrelationship between the rhythm of the sentence and the rhythm of the situation as it develops. Apart from its structural and thematic significance, the story offers valid solutions to certain chronic problems in the language of the Egyptian short story.

From the beginning of his literary career, Ḥaqqī was aware of the importance of balanced structure and convincing characterisation. In his long literary journey from 'Fullah-Mishmish-Lūlū' (1926) to 'Ka'ann' (1968), he advanced the art of the Egyptian short story and brought its form closer to maturity. His artistic virtuosity enabled him to develop a close relationship between description and narrative and to maintain a balance between disclosing and withholding information on the future of the action in order to hint at, and foreshadow, certain vital events. He released the short story completely from the burden of artistically unfunctional preambles, replacing them with striking, abrupt openings that convey vital information obliquely to the imagination, especially in his later works. He developed, in many of his stories, recurrent images and symbols that act as verbal parallels to a pattern of experience, and some of these symbols – like the lamp in 'Qindīl Umm Hāshim' – have a powerful, and perhaps at the time seminal, impact on the reader. Because 'the symbol is perhaps most overwhelming in its effect when the artist's and the reader's patterns of experience closely coincide … The symbol may also serve to force patterns upon the audience',[262] and thereby broaden their comprehension of reality. Many of Ḥaqqī's symbols are so effective because they are deeply integrated into the work, to the extent that they do not strike the reader as symbols. Thus easily, though indirectly, they penetrate his world and experience.

Ḥaqqī's approach to the short story is a serious one, for he believed that despite its brevity, the new literary genre was capable of conveying complex human feelings and presenting an imaginative recreation of society.[263] Instead of touching upon dominant but trivial social issues, or treating the superficial idiosyncrasies of certain characters, as many of his predecessors and contemporaries did, he established the new genre at the centre of Egypt's most vital intellectual debates, ending questions about its relevance and authenticity. In this manner he brings the debate about the relevance of the new literary form and its authenticity to an end, and transforms the question of a new form's identity to a more general one: a national quest for identity in which the short story is one means of search and discovery. Thus, his stories cease to be a mere survey of middle-class characters and issues, and become a deep investigation of the major questions of society at the time of their writing and a skilful and sensitive exploration of what Max Weber calls 'ideal types' of this society. They broaden the base, horizon, domain, and outlook of the Egyptian short story and integrate it deeply into the cultural life of modern Egypt, for they endeavour to penetrate beneath the surface of both urban and rural life and interweave their exploration of major cultural and philosophical issues with the attempt to give these issues a palpable human face and parochial rhythm and flavour. From the beginning of his literary career, Ḥaqqī stands firmly against redundant explanations and didacticism,[264] because for him the stern artistic discipline is inseparable from the profound realistic outlook. His conscious awareness of the artistic edifice leads him to pay considerable attention to style. This means that his stories contribute not only to the development of the language of Egyptian fiction to a remarkable extent, including the poetic use of the vernacular, but also to nullify the traditional criticism against the new form, which was based largely on linguistic grounds. Ḥaqqī also realises that the writer's perception and experience of social reality are as important as his insight into the art form. His stories demonstrate beyond doubt the first-hand experience behind every tiny detail. They are the harvest of the quiet yet compassionate eye, for in them flows a constant stream of authentic experience of both art and reality.

If Lāshīn's work represents the culmination of the achievements of Jamā'at al-Madrasah al-Ḥadīthah (the New School) during the group's prime and until 1930, Ḥaqqī's work is the development and continuation of these accomplishments. As a member of the group he implemented many of their ideals and fulfilled most of their aspirations. His achievements in style and subject matter encompass and go beyond the ground covered by those of the members of the group who continued writing short stories after 1930, for example Ḥasan Maḥmūd,[265] Ibrāhīm Miṣrī[266] and Ibrāhīm 'Abd al-Qādir al-Māzinī.[267] For in Ḥaqqī's work one finds an exploration of new ground and a quiet, objective description of new scenes, which Ḥasan Maḥmūd's short stories introduce more widely,[268] and an insight into man's spiritual agonies and aspirations, which many of Ibrāhīm al-Miṣrī's collections try to offer.[269] One also finds in Ḥaqqī's stories the comic touches that constitute the core of Ibrāhīm 'Abd al-Qādir al-Māzinī's contribution to the Egyptian short story. As for the themes, although Ḥaqqī's stories seek to fathom the subjects and issues which they treated, they certainly do not cover all the thematic ground which those writers introduced. Yet Ḥaqqī's treatment of theme is far superior to that of these three writers and the many others who were overshadowed by them.

Maḥmūd al-Badawī: Social Polarisation and Human Endurance

When Maḥmūd al-Badawī (1908–85) entered Egyptian cultural life at the beginning of the 1930s, it was amid an atmosphere of gloom and hopelessness, not only because Egypt was in the grip of an international economic crisis and the dictatorship of Ismā'īl Ṣidqī, but also because it seemed that the new literature was ebbing away and and the regressive wave, which had won the battle over Taha Husayn's book (*Pre-Islamic Poetry*) a few years before, was in the ascendant.[270] The euphoria of al-Madrasah al-Ḥadīthah (the New School) was over; Lāshīn had stopped writing and Ḥaqqī had joined the diplomatic corps and gone abroad, while other, less important, members of the group had also abandoned writing, turned to journalism, or left the country.[271] The new magazines that appeared after the closure of *al-Fajr*[272] failed to fill the vacuum and were far more cautious and conservative in their outlook in general, and in their approach to new literature in particular. Mahmūd Taymūr was the only short story writer to continue publishing, but he divided his efforts between the short story, essay, play and novel, as if the short story was not sufficient to sustain the devotion of a serious writer.

Despite this discouraging atmosphere, al-Badawī started his literary career in 1933 by translating Chekhov's short stories,[273] and in 1935 he published his first book, *al-Rahīl*. Apart from a descriptive book about a journey to Japan and the Far East (entitled *Madīnat al-Aḥlām*), he subsequently wrote only short stories, of which he published sixteen collections over a period of thirty-three years.[274] This makes him the only Egyptian writer to date to devote his life entirely to this literary genre and to become, through the short story alone, one of Egypt's major writers. He is also the first eminent short story writer of pure Egyptian descent, for the six major writers dealt with in this study so far[275] were the offspring of immigrants. Consequently, al-Badawī was free from the unconscious desire to overplay his sense of Egyptianness, a feature that characterises the pioneers' work. Instead, he tried to maintain a delicate balance between the parochial and the universal in his fictional world. He was also fortunate to start writing after the question of the validity of the new form was resolved, and after the al-Madrasah al-Ḥadīthah group had successfully fought the battle to root the new literary form in Egyptian culture and to gain for it a sizeable reading public. This meant he had no need to compromise or sacrifice any of his artistic convictions to win over the reading public, as most of his predecessors had been obliged to do. Indeed, he refrained from writing introductions or prefatory notes to his collections, and did away with the dysfunctional preamble to the story.

Al-Badawī was also the most important, thematically and artistically, among the new generation of writers whose cultural formation took place towards the end of the 1920s and the beginning of the 1930s and who began to express themselves through literature at the end of the 1930s and who flourished in the following decade. His early short stories were far superior, in both form and substance, to those of his contemporaries such as Najīb Maḥfūẓ,[276] Maḥmūd Kāmil[277], Ṣalāḥ Dhuhnī,[278] Yūsuf Ḥilmī,[279] Yūsuf Jawhar[280] and others.[281] These, writers[282] and critics[283] alike, recognised his skill and talent as early as 1936, some placing his work above Lāshīn's. But the attention of literary circles to his stories gradually faded, and almost disappeared in the 1950s and, with a few exceptions,[284] the 1960s. This change in critical opinion left a clear mark on his development and was at least partially responsible for his artistic decline. Yet this does not diminish, indeed it may rather accentuate, the importance of his powerful beginning.

Like many of his predecessors, al-Badawī was influenced by the work of the Russian masters in general, and Chekhov in particular, but unlike many of them he succeeded in digesting and assimilating their techniques and major accomplishments before starting to write his own stories. His translation of Russian literature at the beginning of his career served as an apprenticeship, and his early works reveal his understanding of the limits and function of the short story, which owed much to his study of Chekhov's technique. In many of his works, and through what seems to be fictionalised personal data, he underlines the importance of Russian literature and prefers it to other literatures. When the heroine asks him if he reads Russian literature, the hero of 'al-Raḥīl' answers, 'I read nothing but Russian literature because it is the closest among human literatures to our temperament and the most relevant to our feelings and aspirations; besides, it is endowed with splendid analysis and insightful detailed description, and I prefer, by nature, deep analytical fiction.'[285] Another hero in the semi-autobiographical story 'al-Lu'lu'ah'[286] praises Chekhov, whose work is also mentioned in 'Nisā' fi'l-Ṭarīq'.[287] Al-Badawī seems to be anxious to refer to works and writers who may have influenced him, or else he is name-dropping to impress his readers and to demonstrate his wide reading. He mentions James Joyce,[288] Dostoevsky,[289] Freud and Adler,[290] Balzac, Flaubert, Prevaux,[291] Maupassant, Maugham, Kuprin, Andreyev[292] and the Egyptian painter Maḥmūd Sa'īd[293] in his works, often without any artistic motive.[294] But the repetition of the names of Chekhov and Freud is significant because his stories are clearly influenced by their work. His debt to the former is demonstrated in the structure and theme of his work, and to the latter in the motivation of the action and in the characterisation. Yet neither influence is crude or superficial, and al-Badawī's work shows a great deal of coherence and originality.

Al-Badawī breaks through the limited circle of location and character type within which Egyptian short stories were confined. Unlike Lāshīn, who presents his Cairene scenes through the eyes of the middle classes, or Haqqī, who concentrates on certain quarters of Cairo, al-Badawī uses a range of urban locations, some of them appearing for the first time in the Egyptian short story. He is particularly fond of Alexandria and the coastal towns as a setting, and the relationship between man and the sea appears to fascinate him.[295] But the life of the small provincial towns of Upper Egypt does not escape his attention; these towns provide the arena for the confrontation between the villagers and the wonders of urban life in his stories.[296] While Ḥaqqī brings his urban characters to endure the claustrophobic life of the village, al-Badawī deals with the villagers' sense of loss and bewilderment in the city.[297]

In these varied urban locations, al-Badawī does not confine himself to the familiar interiors of middle-class homes or to urban street scenes, as his predecessors did, but tries to break new ground by exploring the closed life of the bars ('Laylah fi'l-Ḥān'[298] and 'Ḥānat al-Maḥaṭṭah')[299] and exotic small hotels ('Bansiyūn Munīrva',[300] 'al-A'raj fi'l-Mīnā'[301] and 'Khayṭ min al-Nūr'),[302] the fascinating world of the docks ('al-Zawraq'[303] and 'al-A'raj fi'l-Mīnā'') and the ghettos of various foreign communities in Egypt (in *al-Raḥīl*, 'Imra'at Aḥlāmī'[304] and 'al-Rajul al-Sharīf').[305] He extends his exploration of foreign communities outside

Egypt by taking his characters on trips abroad to Europe[306] and the Far East.[307] The journey abroad in al-Badawī's world differs radically from that of Taymūr's, as it becomes a means of discovery of both the external world and the self. It takes the villager's encounter with the city a step further in an attempt to investigate not only the question of cross-cultural human communication but also the question of man as a stranger in a world peopled with strangers. To accentuate this theme, al-Badawī often locates the action in ships,[308] trains[309] or cars[310] to give a sense of both transience and flux.

Apart from these abundant variations on the local and foreign urban scene, he also explores a wide range of rural locations. The nocturnal setting in a village in Upper Egypt is a recurring and important scene in his world because of its particular relevance to one of his main themes,[311] and it is in complete contrast to Ḥaqqī's evocation, not only because of his different approach to descriptive narrative but also because he introduces most of his scenes either from a neutral perspective or from the viewpoint of insiders, the villagers or other participants in the action. He has no preconceived notion of the *Ṣa'īd*, for he neither adorns nor stultifies his description, but integrates it into the action. His Ṣa'īd is a peculiarly attractive, yet harsh place, a place endowed with its own characteristics, interwoven with the temperament and destiny of its people. The Nile in this setting contributes to the grim environment; it appears as a wild rebellious river before its long peregrination impinges on its powerful flow.[312] The Nile is at its most powerful when it is in flood, and al-Badawī is so enchanted by it in this season that it rarely appears otherwise in his world. However, his rural scenes are not limited to the villages of Upper Egypt; he takes his action to some of the villages in Lower Egypt too. When he does so, he prefers the virgin land of the Barāri,[313] a wild wilderness, where the roughness of nature is comparable to that of his native Upper Egypt.[314] He is also drawn by the space and stillness of the desert[315] and sometimes takes his middle-class townspeople to the vastness of the mysterious and sometimes frightening Egyptian *ṣaḥārā*, where they are inevitably forced into some kind of encounter with their souls.[316]

The variety of settings is not a decorative factor but part of the writer's attempt to represent a wide range of human characters, for in his stories one meets not only characters from almost every shade of the class spectrum of Egyptian society, but also a wide range of those who people its margins and ghettos. There are characters from the various strata of the upper class (in *al-Raḥīl*, 'Funduq al-Dānūb', 'Ḥallāq al-Sayyidāt',[317] 'Darling'[318] and 'al-Layl wa'l-Rajul'),[319] and many others from the middle classes ('al-Zawjah al-Maṣūnah',[320] 'al-Afyāl',[321] 'Tayfūd',[322] 'Durūs fi'l-Falsafah'[323] and 'al-Arqām al-Nāṭiqah').[324] There are also numerous examples of the peasants of Upper Egypt, from the penniless *trāḥīl* workers in 'Fi'l-Qaryah'[325] and 'al-Rimāl'[326] to the relatively comfortable farmers of 'al-Shaykh 'Umrān',[327] 'al-Ghūl'[328] 'al-Zuhūr'[329] and 'Zawjat al-Ṣayyād'.[330] Yet al-Badawī's intention is not to make a social survey, but to dramatise specific characteristics of individuals, such as the proud and dignified fellah of 'al-Thu'bān',[331] or the landowner whose greed and obsession with owning land have blinded him to the elementary facts of life in 'al-Ghūl'.

Al-Badawī is, in fact, the first Egyptian short story writer to pay great attention to the issues of social disparity. In his world there is clear social polarisation, whereby the opposite ends of the social scale are not only remote from one another but also irreconcilable. The social barrier is impenetrable ('al-Ḥājiz'),[332] even when there is a blood bond between those who live on the opposite sides of the class divide (as in 'Da'wah Ilā 'Urs').[333] Naturally, the destitute, who endure the inhumanity of poverty, attract more of his attention than the wealthy, for, unlike Taymūr, he does not allocate all the virtues to the wealthy and all the vices to the poor, nor does he apply a double standard of morality to his characters according to their social status. He is concerned about human destiny and endeavours to reach a comprehensive understanding of mankind, the causes of his suffering and the sources of his strength. He is not a social reformer or moral preacher, although he wrote several stories in which he attacks poverty and draws attention to acute social disparity;[334] yet, he does not tolerate moral injustice ('al-Jawād al-Jarīḥ') or the blind arrogance of the rich ('al-Thu'bān' and 'Da'wah Ilā 'Urs').[335]

Apart from the two extremes of the social structure, al-Badawī's world is peopled with other distinct groups. The gypsies of Egypt, who seldom appear in its literature, materialise in several of his stories with their special way of life and cultural values,[336] as do the outlaws, tramps and footpads of Upper Egypt, who live obscurely according to traditional standards of masculinity and heroism.[337] Nor does al-Badawī neglect the various foreign communities who lived their exotic, eccentric lives in Egypt's major towns.[338] Unlike Taymūr, who introduces foreign characters only when his protagonists go abroad, al-Badawī tries to comprehend the alienation of local foreigners, who are in constant conflict with the cultural values of the society they live in. Unlike Taymūr also, he does not idolise foreigners but pities them and appreciates their difficult situation, conceiving of them at times as abandoned sensitive pioneers of a more humane and civilised style of living,[339] but more often as wretched, forlorn and lonely individuals.[340] He also introduces another group of sensitive, alienated individuals – artists. Most of these are painters struggling with both their medium and a surrounding world that is blind to their talent ('Fi'l-Qiṭār', 'Lā Tubā'',[341] 'al-Ṣūrah al-Nāqiṣah'[342] and 'al-Lawḥah'),[343] but some are writers ('Ḥayāt Rajul',[344] 'al-Mulhimah',[345] 'Rawḥ al-Fannān'[346] and 'al-Lu'lu'ah') or musicians ('al-Māyistrū'[347] and 'al-Fannān').[348] In many of these stories al-Badawī is concerned with the humanity of art and its social function, especially during times of national crises ('Sayyidah wa Fannān'[349] and 'al-Lawḥah').

Through this wide range of characters and locations, al-Badawī creates a fascinating fictional world, rich in substance and form and capable of raising profound questions through its recurring themes. One of these is human suffering and endurance. In his stories about Upper Egypt, he focuses on physical endurance and the relationship between physical and moral courage. Courage for him is synonymous with manhood and masculinity: it is associated with life in the open, outside the protective, feminine shell of the home. It is the life of legendary men such as 'al-Shaykh 'Umrān', al-Shaykh 'Abd al-Muṭṭalib of 'Ḥāris al-Qaryah',[350] Ma'mūn in 'al-Thu'bān', or the peasant of 'Waqfah 'Alā al-Darb',[351] all of them characterised by extreme boldness and dedication to justice. They lead calm and satisfied domestic lives, usually after years of violence during which they proved their power and daring beyond any doubt. This qualifies them to play the role of arbitrators between the sheltered village communities and the outlaws and to become, if necessary, the protector of the apparently helpless ordinary people. Yet they have many characteristics in common with the outlaws despite their steadfast attachment to the cause of justice.

The outlaw in al-Badawī's world is a symbol of physical endurance and recklessness. He is more of a rebel than a criminal and is viewed by the people with a combination of disapprobation and admiration. They understand, even appreciate, his motives but cannot sanction his methods, especially when he breaks the recognised code of conduct for outlaws.[352] His behaviour is marked by the desire to undermine the present order without losing the sympathy of the people, who he identifies with despite having chosen a path that alienates him from society. Thus he often exhibits sagacious and even noble manners and shows gallantry, even audacity, in defending the poor and helpless ('Laylah Rahībah',[353] 'al-Dhi'b'[354] and 'Laylah fi'l-'Arabah').[355] But despite this strong affinity with the people, his life, which reflects many of the qualities of the natural world of Upper Egypt that surrounds him, is marked by loneliness and misery; the misery of being destined to have no home and the vast surrounding realm of emptiness and night, of fear and tension, with only his astuteness and courage to protect him.

He is permanently besieged by fear in this limitless existence, for he must have a constant alibi. He must be ubiquitous and merge with the mystery of the surroundings.[356] He must also come to terms with the fact that the night, that limitless hallucinatory heartland of darkness, is his only home. Night symbolises both endless freedom and never-ending fear; it envelops the outlaw in its protective murkiness and, at the same time, lays him open to perfidy.[357] Yet it has its own nocturnal rituals and means of fulfilment, for only at night can the outlaw contact his beloved, whom he sacrificed, with his home, when he opted for a completely solitary masculine life in the open. This is seen in the stories as a violation of an unwritten agreement whereby the individual chooses between a domestic life or becoming part of the mystery and power of the universe. Both woman and home are somehow inimical to the life of solitary masculinity, and are presented as the outlaw's weakness, indeed the trap of the outlaw, for when his enemy wants to hunt him down, he stalks him near his mistress's house and shoots him ('Ṣawt al-Damm').[358]

In al-Badawī's world, sex is closely associated with death and violence, and is also an integral part of his investigation of the attraction–repulsion nature of the relationship between the two sexes. Since his first collection, *Rajul* (1936), he tried to express the complicated relationship between sex and human destiny through a carefully knitted set of symbols. In 'al-A'mā''[359] the sexual intercourse that takes place in the open field between the blind muezzin and the village belle is clearly, but indirectly, related to the former's mysterious death at the end of the story.[360] The relationship between the two is not merely casual, but involves a complex interweaving of fate and psychological development. This is communicated through a carefully controlled narrative and ostensibly simple symbols, which contain much more than first meets the eye. The muezzin's strong aversion to women is a basic factor in his relationship with Jamīla, in which the water, field, mud, broken jar, the fact that she physically leads him by the hand because he is blind, and the atmosphere of grief signify the multiple layers of the meaning of this brief but highly significant sexual encounter. The nauseous fear, remorse, fever, wounds, the dog's attack, the muezzin's inability to go back to work, and the sub-plots relating to Nā'isah, Mabrūkah, and 'Azīzah, become the portents of his approaching death.

'Fatāt Aḥlāmī'[361] accentuates the fatal element in male–female relationships and develops a remarkable triangulation process in the construction of the stories that deal with this recurring theme. From this time on (1941), all the stories in which al-Badawī explores the complexity of the male–female relationship involve two overlapping, often concentric and sometimes tangential, circles of relationships. In 'Fatāt Aḥlāmī' there are two circles of relationships, each of which has its own triangle, and one naturally casts its shadow over the other. In 'Fi'l-Qaryah',[362] however, there is one triangle, Nu'mān, Nā'isah and 'Abbās, and two overlapping circles of relationships. On the one hand, there is the purely carnal relationship between Nu'mān and Nā'isah, in which the author employs a host of bodily symbols of virility on one side and femininity on the other. Like most sinful relationships in al-Badawī's world it leads to the downfall of the man, and this is embodied in a physical form as bodily as the relationship is carnal.[363] On the other hand, the sensual relationship between Nu'mān and Nā'isah repeats itself, after Nu'mān's sickness, between Nā'isah and 'Abbās, who replaced her lover as the workers' foreman. When Nu'mān recovers he discovers what has been happening in his absence, and decides to retaliate, especially when Nā'isah refuses to come back to him. For she had enjoyed her sensual relationship with him on a purely carnal basis and now that he is no longer the strongest among the workers, there is no point in her resuming the relationship. At this point the two concentric circles come into conflict and in a game of *taḥṭīb* Nu'mān kills his opponent. When the police come to take him to prison Nā'isah appears in the background, a glaring and vivid symbol of life, beautiful and seductive as ever.

Sex for Nā'isah, as in many other stories, is a vital urge for life.

Indeed, it is almost the essence of life in the sense that it is a life-giving power and a means of unfolding the human personality, as well as the starting point for a build-up of tension. The sexual act in this story, as in 'al-Aʿmā'', takes place in the open fields, amid various symbols of fertility. In 'al-Layl wa'l-Rajul',[364] too, a whole set of fertility symbols is called upon throughout the story. The association between sex and nature is clear and pronounced in his work, for sex is presented as a natural and overpowering instinct, as an outburst of emotion and genuine feeling, as an exuberant grand rapture – as life. Through these associations and modes of presentation al-Badawī succeeds in overcoming the taboo that is attached to this subject. He believes, with Lawrence, that 'sex is a creative flow ... is the fountainhead of our energetic life',[365] but he is also the victim of what Lawrence terms 'the growth of "spiritual-mental" consciousness at the expense of the instinctive-intuitive consciousness',[366] which introduces a certain moralistic tone into the narrative.

Thus, on one level, murder comes as a resolution to these conflicting views, underlining the tragic nature of the conflict; on another level, it marks the reassertion of the hero's masculinity. In either case, it is a desperate act of frustration, the physical epitaph of the lost paradise of frenzied sexuality. In 'Rajul ʿAlā al-Ṭarīq'[367] and 'al-ʿArabah al-Akhīrah'[368] sex represents an act of remonstration against the physical starvation that is unfairly imposed upon the characters. In the first of those two stories, al-Badawī intensifies his metaphor, and nature, symbolised by the roaring sea around the lighthouse, becomes an irresistable force. He also brings marriage into the focus of the action, for the triangular relationship involves a married couple and a single man who works with the husband in the lighthouse. When this single man meets his friend's wife on one of his regular leaves, they both realise, in a moment of physical attraction, that before them is nothing but the void and terrifying chasm of loneliness. This discovery sparks the sexual relationship and the circle is soon completed by murder, by a bloody fight between the two men that ends in the husband's death.

None of al-Badawī's stories dealing with sex (which number more than thirty),[369] escapes this association of sex with death. A remarkable feature of this association is its subtlety and richness; on one level, it is closely related to al-Badawī's investigation of the mystery of fate and human destiny; on another level, it has the character of a complex form of requital, which aims at rebalancing the situation and reinforcing certain aspects of it. This is not a direct or divine reprisal, for the castigation often falls on the ostensibly innocent. Rather, it is a physical demonstration of the burden of human endurance on the one hand, and the absurdity of man's attempt to reason with death or overcome danger on the other. Sex is often portrayed as man's last gasp of protest in the face of death and as a physical ritual to ward off danger ('al-Zallah al-Ūlā', 'Imra'ah fi'l-Jānib al-Ākhar',[370] 'Taḥt al-Rīḥ'[371] and 'al-Ghaḍab').[372] Despite, or rather because of, the desperate nature of sex as portrayed in these stories, it fails to provide the desired haven, and leads to killing; the act of procreation inverted. Moreover, the killings are usually violent and ritualistic, and the murder weapon often a phallic symbol such as a knife,[373] a rod,[374] a staff[375] or a dagger.[376]

In several other stories, death comes naturally, as if to make room for the new sexual relationship[377] or to provide the relationship with its fatal, tragic element,[378] for there is always a tragic element even in the healthiest of male–female relationships in al-Badawī's world. For him, that relationship is complex and mysterious ('al-Sījārah'[379] and 'Laylah fī Ḥān')[380] and prone to tragedy. It cannot materialise except at a price; and the price varies from loss of money[381] or freedom,[382] to the loss of the soul,[383] but it always corresponds to the scale of the compromise involved. The author's conception of man is simpler than his conception of woman. He sees men as physically polygamous but emotionally monogamous, whereas his women seem ostensibly to be emotionally polyandrous but physically monogamous, while in fact they are more complex than this categorisation would suggest: they slip easily from the monogamous to the polyandrous and vice versa, a chaotic movement which disturbs the balance of the carefully determined order of virtue and vice in his world.

Any male–female relationship involves a certain degree of disturbance to this order, and this dooms the relationship to a tragic fate. The situation is worsened by two factors: the first is the triangulation process: al-Badawī is fond of the triangular structure and is uninterested in any relationship that does not include a third party in its core. For him, the third character not only enriches the relationship and broadens its scope, but also proves its social plausibility in that the two partners do not exist in a social vacuum. The second factor, which is evident from his first story, 'al-Raḥīl', onwards, is his fascinatation with men's schizophrenic attitude towards women. Men desire women and long to enter a relationship, but under this craving lies a deep longing for freedom from the shackles of that relationship. The two contradicting desires coexist, and the man is torn between them. The triangular process is one of the ramifications of this continuous struggle between detachment and involvement, for his attempt to liberate himself from being trapped by one woman throws him into the lap of another. Thus the relationship becomes an awkward predicament, and one or more of its participants are doomed to death.[384]

Al-Badawī seems to be one of the few writers who has managed to critique women and the female nature without coming across as misogynistic. The role the woman plays in the development of the male–female relationship is as vital and many-sided as the man's. Although various stories, such as 'Tidhkār',[385] 'al-'Awdah Ilā al-Bayt'[386] and 'Fi'l-Manzil al-Muqābil',[387] suggest that a woman's life is incomplete, almost impossible, without a man, al-Badawī's women are not dependent on men and have an equally positive role to play, for if they were not themselves sophisticated characters they could not sustain such rich and complex relationships with men. Indeed, some of al-Badawī's women seem to be more sophisticated, in both temperament and experience, than many of his men. They are as courageous and reckless,[388] and they display a remarkable ability to endure suffering and overcome difficulties.[389] Yet deep down they have an innate feeling of inferiority to men, towards whom they nourish conflicting feelings of attraction and repulsion.

Their contradictory feelings towards men do not, however, signify the kind of irrationality al-Badawī's men display towards women, for these contradictions do not affect their ability to forge and sustain relationships with men. They are always individuals, with their own distinct character traits, but at the same time manifest a wide range of spiritual capacities. They can be a source of compassion and understanding ('al-Ḥubb al-Awwal'[390] and 'Rassāmah') and offer men comfort and peace of mind ('Funduq al-Dānūb'[391] and 'Qalb 'Adhrā'').[392] They can be lustful and capable of sweeping away any resistance ('al-Khinzīrah')[393] or obstacle ('Fi'l-Qafaṣ'),[394] which often brings disaster ('al-Silsilah')[395] though, in other instances they can ward off death ('Zuhūr Dhābilah')[396] and danger ('al-Zallah al-Ūlā' and 'al-Ghaḍab'). They have the ability to revitalise men and boost their morale ('al-Bāb al-Zujājī'),[397] to inspire them ('Fi'l-Qiṭār' and 'al-Māystrū'), and to console them in moments of despair ('Laylah Lan Ansāhā' and 'Ḥadath Dhāt Laylah'), for they can create familiarity in the bleakest surroundings; their touch revivifies objects and injects life into inertia ('al-'Izbah al-Jadīdah').[398] Yet they are vain and can become a source of boredom ('Ba'd al-'Urs'[399] and 'al-Nisā'')[400] or misery and suspicion ('al-Zawjah al-'Aṣriyyah'[401] and 'Jasad wa-Fannān'), and they can be the cause of death and violence ('Fi'l-Qaryah' and 'Nisā' fi'l-Ṭarīq'). They are enigmatic ('al-Bawāb al-A'raj',[402] 'Hājir'[403] and 'al-Sījārah')[404] and leave men confused, unable to understand or adjust to the turmoil they create. Even in stories that illustrate masculine values and the heroism of physical endurance, women appear as man's only oasis in an absurd wilderness.[405] They also often represent pure chastity,[406] eternal love and fidelity,[407] and on such occasions become a man's true equal and confidante.

Another major theme in al-Badawī's work is the interrelationship between man's action and what seems to be universal reason, the mystery of the unknown. He investigates this complex relationship at various levels, the simplest of which demonstrates itself in the stories in which man encounters different forms of superstition. On the one hand is the generally justifiable irrational fear of what is unknown or mysterious,[408] a fear open to exaggeration and pretension. This pretension becomes a target for comic treatment and forms the basis of a rich comic irony,[409] which, in turn, provides the author with an opportunity to undermine superstitious beliefs and to suggest rational explanations for some ostensibly mysterious phenomena.[410] On the other hand, there are certain phenomena that seem to stand beyond man's comprehension and defeat rational arguments.[411] Here man's attempt to overcome his inadequacies when faced with the inexplicable is remarkable and courageous, and escapes despair despite the persistence of the obstacles created by superstition. Although, in an intrusive authorial tone, al-Badawī advises the reader to succumb to his fate,[412] the implicit meaning ('Never trust the artist, trust the tale') suggests the contrary.

However, this is still the simple, though not the crude, level of the question, for the very mention of the superstitious elements undermines their role in and effect on the situation. The impression is greater when the action is not easily explained or rationalised; when these elements are presented as mere coincidences but, with closer examination of the artistic structure of the story, become part of a broader determinism governing the progression of the plot. Fate or destiny interferes in the development of the action not merely as a moral power which implements requital and restores order but often as an irrational power that strikes the most lively and leaves them full of despair.[413] The main instance in which this power seems to have clear reasoning is when it is endowed with a religious colouring, a spiritual insight.[414] Otherwise fate is the agent of requital and the originator of tragedy,[415] and is one of the major components of the human condition in the works of al-Badawī.

In some stories, the social rather than the metaphysical nature of fate is considered, especially when it is associated with external conditions and crucial events, such as war. Al-Badawī is unique in his illustration of the effects on the country and its people of the various wars that Egypt has endured since the 1930s, and the major national events since the 1919 Revolution. Various facets of that revolution feature in 'Ḥadath Dhāt Laylah', 'al-Rajul al-Ashwal'[416] and 'al-Ṭalqah al-Akhīrah', while the impact of the Second World War on the economic and moral aspects of the life of the individual is illustrated in 'Sukūn al-'Āṣifah',[417] 'Sā'āt al-Hawl'[418] 'Laylah Lan Ansāhā', 'Bayt al-Ashjān'[419] and 'al-'Adhrā' wa'l-Layl'.[420] The 1948 war in Palestine appears in 'Risālah Min al-Maydān',[421] the guerilla war in the Canal Zone in 1951 features in 'al-Ramād al-Mushta'il',[422] the great fire of Cairo in 1952 and the subsequent chaos are depicted in 'al-Ghaḍab', and the Suez War of 1956 is a central theme in several stories.[423] In all these stories, and some others,[424] patriotic sentiment is interwoven with the rhythm and events of everyday life.

Al-Badawī uses man at war or in a wartime situation, as many have done before him, to explore his characters' reactions in extreme situations. Similarly, when he portrays human beings and animals, it is to test his characters in the face of danger[425] – unlike Ḥaqqī, who is concerned to portray the sympathies and the harmony existing between mankind and beasts. In the instances where tamed animals appear in al-Badawī's stories, he concentrates on their wild outbursts and on the inverted process of 'de-domesticating' them, as in 'al-Ḍab'.[426] Yet domestic animals appear as an important part of the setting in many stories and play an important part in the story's symbolism.

Another recurring theme in al-Badawī's world is the study of failure and its social and psychological ramifications. Failure is closely linked with human suffering and endurance. It is portrayed as an inverted form of endurance, as the other face of the physical endurance found in the stories of Upper Egypt. It also has a psychological aspect, in keeping with the complicated, indolent and morally lax existence of city dwellers and their mechanised civilisation.[427] In al-Badawī's world, failure is associated with urban life, an association that reveals something of his attitude to both urban and rural life. The former is a realm of frustration and loneliness, where the forlorn character is destined to take to drink,[428] seek the help of another similar character ('Tidhkār', 'Fi'l-Manzil al-Muqābil' and 'al-Badīl'),[429] or leave the country and look for happiness abroad.[430] The latter is also rough and marked by cruelty and misery, but the physical routine it imposes on its inhabitants, though violent and coarse, relieves man's suppressed feelings and tensions. However, happiness seems to be a rare commodity in either city or village.

Through this wide range of themes and characters, al-Badawī broadens the scope of the Egyptian short story and demonstrates its potential to dramatise the major issues of society in a subtle and artistic manner. From the beginning, he paid considerable attention to the artistic construction of his stories and generally succeeded in finding a mode of expression appropriate to the nature of the experience. Behind his ostensible simplicity, even austerity, of style, there is a remarkable union of the naturalistic and the symbolic through which the development of the action is conducted beneath carefully controlled statements.[431] Like Hemingway, his

> short stories are deceptive somewhat in the manner of an iceberg. The visible areas glint with the hard factual lights of the naturalist. The supporting structure, submerged and mostly invisible except to the patient explorer, is built with a different kind of precision – that of the poet-symbolist.[432]

He deliberately minimises the descriptive details of his action and endeavours to make them appear ordinary, to the extent that the reader might easily overlook some of their nuances and, more importantly, miss the way in which they accumulate.

The accumulation of detail, however, if ostensibly random and insignificant, is carefully and rigorously controlled, for beneath the surface of the story the manner in which the detail accumulates implants a set of imploding symbols that have no significance outside the context. Throughout the story such symbols enhance the economic progression of the action and heighten its implications; they present a set of beautiful crystallisations, compact and buoyant enough to carry the meaning to a new and deeper level of interpretation than first meets the eye. Some of these symbols recur often in al-Badawī's writing, such that they become leitmotifs; as soon as they appear, they bring with them certain ideas and shades of meaning relevant to his general outlook. Among these standard symbols, for example, is *al-mi'addiyyah,* the boat which carries people from one bank of the Nile to another, a symbol of transition and transience in many stories.[433] This boat is not an abstract symbol but a realistically viewed object rooted in its surroundings and interlaced with various other realistic details until it becomes radiant with meaning. The emission of a host of meanings does not diminish the realistic images of the object; it rather enhances it. In al-Badawī's work, each major symbol is associated with a galaxy of hints, or sub-symbols, which provide it with a wide range of implications. These sub-symbols can, at different moments, become major symbols themselves, at which point the dominant symbol retreats into the background along with the other minor symbols.

Al-Badawī is aware of the precision and economy needed in the short story form. He knows

> how to get the most from the least, how to prune language and avoid waste motion, how to multiply intensities, and how to tell nothing but the truth in a way that always allows for telling more than the truth.[434]

He also understands the importance of knowing his material thoroughly in order to relay his set of symbols and allusions in a convincing and unintrusive manner. His comprehensive knowledge of his material enables him to develop his distinct method of narrative, of informing by means of direct, quiet syllogistic account. He is the first Egyptian short story writer to use the first-person technique intensively yet avoids the authorial intrusion that this type of narrative easily incurs. His first-person technique is of a special nature, being an amalgam of the spoken and written first-person past tense presented in a third-person framework. Thus it comprises the freshness and lucidity of the first-person with the calmness and subjectivity of the detached third-person in projecting character. It also serves to create the necessary distance between the narrator, and consequently the narrative, and the action, and to control the rhythm of the story.

The carefully controlled rhythm is relevant to the unity of impression in al-Badawī's work, for he is concerned with the ritualisation of simple scenes. He eschews photographic imitations of reality, without sacrificing the realistic effect. The ritualisation of the action, or certain aspects of it, decreases the narrative's dependence on dialogue. His use of dialogue is scarce and he insists on conducting it in a simple *fuṣḥa*, avoiding the vernacular almost completely. Yet he shows remarkable skill in using dialogue for the purpose of exposition and in employing it to reveal the inner depths of the character and, at the same time, develop the action. But dialogue is only one aspect of language in the narrative form and al-Badawī, though not a great stylist like Ḥaqqī, is aware of the many facets of the language of fiction. Like Hemingway, 'his deepest trust is placed in the accumulative effect of ostensibly simple, carefully selective statement, with occasional reiteration of key phrases for thematic emphasis'.[435] The tone of his narrative is quiet, almost prosaic, yet it is capable of developing highly charged situations. This is because it grafts the emotive onto the referential, delights in irony and comic effects, probes deep into the private subjective world of vision and dream, and eschews forcing decorative embellishment upon the subject matter.

In his early collections, the tone of al-Badawī's narrative is in harmony with the characterisation, and this enhances the artistic structure and general impression of the work. After his sixth collection *'Adhārā al-Layl* (1956), however, his writing seems to decline and he pays increasingly less attention to the artistic structure of the story. But since his sixth collection, like Taymūr, he insists on revisiting old scenes and retelling the same stories, which weakens both the texture and structure of his later works. Unlike Ḥaqqī, and like Taymūr, he lacks the ability to judge when to finish with a subject, and his later stories, largely reproductions of his earlier achievements, dilute the general impact of his work and undermine his early, major contribution to the development of the Egyptian short story.

Yūsuf Idrīs: The Return to the Roots

By the early 1940s, the euphoria that followed the 1936 Treaty of Independence had turned into frustration and despair. The Second

World War crushed hopes of independence, and its aftermath saw a wave of popular anger sweep through the country, culminating in the riots and student uprisings of 1946. One of the participants was a medical student who was to choose the short story as a medium through which he was to become one of the most important literary figures in modern Arabic literature. Yūsuf Idrīs (1927–91) was a great writer by temperament and inspiration rather than by training. His childhood in the Delta and his youth in Cairo provided him with a special kind of training, a feel for and an insight into the life of rural and urban Egypt. His early contact with left-wing student groups at the Faculty of Medicine, which harboured the most active leftist circles in the student movement at the time, nurtured his sharp social and political awareness. His political activities meant that by the age of twenty he had direct experience of the tyranny, oppression and political intimidation of the minority governments which ruled Egypt throughout the late 1940s. And his friendship with the sensitive writer Muḥammad Yusrī Aḥmad[436] led him to literature.

Like Aḥmad Khayrī Sa'īd, who inspired the writers of al-Madrasah al-Ḥadīthah and offered them his patronage, Muḥammad Yusrī Aḥmad was one of those indolent but talented writers who have neither the aptitude nor the drive to continue writing, but who successfully spark off talents in others. Before his acquaintanceship with Aḥmad, Idrīs never dreamt of being a writer, but Ahmad somehow discovered that in the science student and ardent political orator and activist were the makings of an ingenious and gifted writer. He persuaded Idrīs to begin reading literature, especially folk tales and Russian fiction, and encouraged him to try his hand at short story writing. In 1950 Idrīs published his first short story in *al-Qiṣṣah*, where Aḥmad was already an established writer.[437]

At that time two other medical students, Muṣṭafā Maḥmūd[438] and Ṣalāḥ Ḥāfiẓ,[439] were beginning to establish themselves as short story writers. Ibrāhīm Nājī (1893–1953), himself a doctor of medicine, a well-known literary figure, and a regular contributor to *al-Qiṣṣah*, encouraged and supported them.[440] Indeed a wave of young writers at the time embraced the short story, either as their favourite medium of discourse or as the training ground and preparatory phase of a broader writing project. Many of these writers continued writing short stories for some time, such as Ṣūfī 'Abd Allāh,[441] 'Abd al-Raḥmān al-Khamīsī[442] and Luṭfī al-Khūlī,[443] but others, such as Aḥmad 'Abbās

Ṣāliḥ,[444] Aḥmad Rushdī Ṣāliḥ,[445] Amīnah al-Sa'īd[446] and others,[447] left the field and preferred to express themselves in another medium. The new wave of short story writing exerted a powerful influence and attracted well-established writers from other media – Salāma Mūsā being an obvious example. The vigour of these years (1949–59) put the short story in a prominent position on the cultural map and silenced speculation about its demise or triviality.

But a few years later, this vigour seemed to have found in the profound and highly productive talent of Yūsuf Idrīs its supreme expression. As if by force of the law of natural selection, Idrīs's towering talent eclipsed that of others, who soon realised that they were unable to keep up with Idrīs and simply left the field. Idrīs, indeed, was capable of filling the stage with wonderful works, for his oeuvre was not only rich in form and in subject matter, but also prolific and constantly developing. After his first story appeared in 1950, Idrīs continued to publish his work in leading periodicals (such as *Rūz al-Yūsuf, al-Miṣrī* and *al-Taḥrīr*) until his first collection, *Arkhaṣ Layālī*, appeared in 1954. This was followed by eight further collections of short stories and several novels and plays .[448] Although Idrīs's contribution to the Egyptian novel and drama is not inconsiderable, it is in the short story that his major achievement resides. Nevertheless, when he first started writing he was not especially aware of his predecessors' accomplishments in the field; his original motivation was a concern to give expression to the current political and social issues that preoccupied him and many of his fellow Egytpians in different ways. In 1952, two years after the start of his career, the hopes of the people rose high when the army seized power. Some of the dreams which, as a student and political activist, Idrīs had fought for, seemed to be approaching fulfilment, and it appeared that they needed further momentum to materialise.

At this early stage, it seems that Idrīs was willing to use his short stories as a means of giving his dreams this necessary push. He conceived of the short story as as an extension of his political activities, as a subsidiary tool to convey, or rather to prove, the correctness of his political or ideological views. But he grew steadily more aware of his role as an artist and moved from this position towards a more subtle and artistic approach to reality. His writing can, therefore, be divided into two main categories: the first includes the work of the first ten years of his career, during which he published five collections of short stories; the second category comprises the four collections he published during the 1960s. The works of the first stage came out in rapid succession, almost at annual intervals, as if to assert his talent and to secure his place on the literary scene. But during the second stage the intervals were longer, and there were four years of silence (1962–6), or rather of a search for new modes of expression to convey the change in artistic sensibility.

He wrote and published his first five collections before reaching the age of thirty, at a time of great social and political aspirations. The issues were clear in this period, or at least appeared so to writers, and equally clear were the goals and the identity of friends and enemies. These years witnessed the dramatic collapse of the old order and the universally unpopular ruling clique, and introduced the possibility of fulfilling dreams of an almost utopian nature. There was a great outflow of radical and progressive ideas, and Idrīs's stories were the literary expression of these, for they tended to give the often ambiguous aspirations a concrete form. They also seemed to articulate the voice of protest of the underprivileged against the stock-in-trade of the sentimental short stories and literature of entertainment and were a counter to those tales that took place in luxurious places, lofty villas, elegant cars and stylish surroundings.[449] They also speak against the fantasies of those who sought salvation through dreams or by winning lotteries.

Idrīs was able to do this because he created in these five collections a profound artistic world, unique in its depth, richness and authenticity. The first characteristic of this world is its breadth. The realm in which his characters move – despite their belonging mostly to the lower strata of society – is very wide indeed. He moves through all walks of town life with the same sure-footedness and ease with which he wanders through the village. Many of his predecessors and most of his contemporaries are by comparison restricted in their range. Although his predecessor, al-Badawī, presents a wide variety of characters and settings, Idrīs's world is still wider in scope and richer in its diversity. Unlike al-Badawī, he refrains from dwelling upon characters or locations he has previously treated, and hence saves his world from repetition and delusion and increases the value of its abundance and diversity. When he does revisit the same area of experience or characterisation, he is keen to modulate the tone and alter the quality until it appears as if he is embarking on a fresh type of discourse.

In these five collections, Idrīs does not confine himself to a limited number of themes or ideas, nor does he bind himself to one forlorn or oppressed group of people. Rather, he moves freely through the whole social spectrum and across a wide range of settings. He presents the normal size village, hamlet (*kafr*) and country estate (*'izbah*), as well as the coastal village and remote and mysterious rural places. His favourite rural location is the normal size village in Lower Egypt and particularly in his native province of al-Sharqiyyah. When he moves to the city, he sets his work in a range of urban locations, from the capital to the small provincial town. However, the important factor in this abundant diversity of locations is his ability to create a strong sense of reality as if he has first-hand experience of each of the locations.

The diversity of human characters is as rich, or even richer, than that of locations. His first collection, *Arkhaṣ Layālī*, for example, encompasses a tremendous variety in terms of human characters and experiences: a peasant oppressed by poverty and his restricted social horizon,[450] a small girl plucked from her calm rural habitat to work as a servant in the town,[451] a teacher burdened with his family duties and the tricks of his mischievous pupils,[452] an insecure, frustrated housewife who is imprisoned by her fears of an unknown future,[453] a solicitor who is offended by someone wanting a free legal consultation but tries himself to obtain free medical treatment,[454] a poor, crippled man from Upper Egypt who becomes entangled in a web of red tape,[455] an outlaw who loves his native villagers and helps them,[456] a hen-pecked old teacher who suffers from the tyrannical behaviour of his trousered wife,[457] a ravenous nomad who disdains to ask for food,[458] a simple peasant whose only wish is to hold the receiver of the village mayor's telephone and speak like those with status and authority,[459] a group of young and inexperienced doctors who are struggling against both the death of their patients and political intimidation,[460] a police sergeant whose only dream in life is to travel to the capital, and who, when the opportunity comes, must accompany a mad woman to Cairo so turning the trip into an ordeal, the dream into a nightmare,[461] the police officer who has just started smoking some hashish when he receives an order to arrest a group of hashish addicts,[462] a group of Egyptians in a nostalgic mood aboard a ship on their return journey to 'Umm al-Dunyā',[463] a carpenter afflicted by bilharziasis[464] who plumbs the depths of fear and social humiliation,[465] a group of tramps and workers who attempt to transcend their gloomy life but fall instead into the quicksand of gambling,[466] and a witty intelligent villager who finds a comic aspect in his tragic life and turns it into a subject for nightly conversations to pass the time and provide entertainment for his companions.[467]

All these various characters and many more are found in the one collection, demonstrating a variety in occupation, age, class, temperament and fictional situation. In the other four collections, Idrīs expands this already wide range, and continues to break new ground in terms of theme and characterisation. Although he focuses chiefly on the lower classes and the various strata of the middle class, he represents the whole spectrum of Egyptian society. In addition, the great variety of his world also extends to time and place. He gives considerable attention to daytime activities and treats them with care and insight, yet it is nocturnal activity that attracts his attention in particular.[468] Unlike Ḥaqqī, who associates night with grief and loneliness, Idrīs perceives night, particularly in the village, as the time that provides an opportunity for intimate contact, casual gatherings, frank conversation, relaxation and contemplation; he is attracted to the nocturnal atmosphere not only because it adorns the action with mysterious and ambiguous elements, but also, and principally, because it is in keeping with the suffering and grief in the lives of his wretched and sensitive characters. In 'Baṣrah', 'Maẓlūm' and 'Fi'l-Layl', night, more than the time of the action, is an integral part of the situation; while it would be almost impossible to set up the same stories in daytime, the nocturnal setting provides insights into the daytime life of the characters.

Unlike many of his contemporaries, Idrīs avoids lachrymose sentimentality and exaggeration in his portrayal of the suffering of the poor. On the contrary, he has a tendency to accentuate the humorous elements in distressing situations. This does not mean that he superimposes a naive optimism onto tragic circumstances; rather it is an attempt to depict the bitter and difficult life of the lower strata of society as, in many ways, beyond endurance. For him, the most important aspect of endurance is the way in which people surmount their difficulties and preserve their humanity, how they cope with oppression and poverty, and how they find, or indeed create, joy in the midst of tragic situations and in the bleakest surroundings. This is closely linked to both his approach to reality and his view of man.

Although Idrīs presents in these five collections a wide variety of characters, one type is dominant: the frustrated man, full of dreams and projects, often larger than life, who is unable for various reasons to fulfil them. His craving for life and sensuous pleasure is as great as the obstacles that stand between him and his aspirations. Even when a flash of joy appears on the horizon of his closed and gloomy life, it is invariably dim, fleeting and evanescent. Indeed, failure is a dominant strain in the lives of Idrīs's characters, albeit never complete failure or total defeat, because at the lowest ebb of defeat there always appears a possibility of advancement, a reason for a special type of triumph. This limited victory, which may itself be no cause for rejoicing, is the most the character can hope to attain in his closed, unjust world, where neither absolute defeat nor ultimate conquest is a possibility. The life of his heroes is an amalgam of small victories and heroic failures, like the indomitable hero of Hemingway's *The Old Man and the Sea,* who conquers the huge fish but returns, at the end of his fabulous adventure, with only its skeleton.

To present this oppressive atmosphere of frustration in which the character's dreams never come to fruition without descending into crude melodrama, Idrīs treats his material as if it were part of a nightmare, dreadful but transient. Familiar details of the setting, situation and action are transformed, as they are discovered by the character and heighten his suffering, into the components of a bad dream. The world is limited to a confined space; and mainly for social and economic reasons most alleviating elements are eliminated. In *Arkhaṣ Layālī*, for example, the nocturnal world of the village becomes progressively narrower before the eyes of its protagonist, who is encumbered by a large, ever-growing family. He is fully aware of the causes of his distress and tries to avoid the vicious circle that aggravates his poverty. But in his attempt to escape, he only entangles himself further. All possible sources of relief are successively excluded, solely because of economic deficiency. With the mentality of a besieged individual, he finally resorts to the very solution from which he had dissuaded everyone at the opening of the story. At another level of interpretation, the hero's recourse to this desperate solution implies a desire to squeeze some little rapture or sensual delight from this narrowing world. The presentation underlines the constant interaction between failure and success in this nightmarish realm.

In 'Jumhūriyyat Faraḥāt',[469] Idrīs describes a police station in a realistic manner, but by the end of the first page the accumulation of the detail has also created an atmosphere of siege; the nocturnal melancholy atmosphere, the room seen as a tunnel existing without past, present or future, the black walls, viscous floor, nauseous smell, the dim light imprisoned in the lamps rather than radiating from them, the shadows and darkness, the people moving about as though hypnotised, the heap of broken boxes and chairs, the exhausted weary suspects, and the policemen in their black uniforms – all these become part of the texture of the nightmare. The tone and the rhythm of the language, combined with the particular arrangement of the detail, transform the components of the scene into highly significant symbols. The police station becomes an enclosed tunnel, yet is still capable of embracing the spacious world outside its walls. The details become signs, each signifying an important aspect of the experience and playing a vital role in creating the sense of siege.

This nightmarish atmosphere is not confined to nocturnal settings; it is a thematic quality that Idrīs introduces to scenes regardless of time and place. In 'Ḥādithat Sharaf'[470] the action takes place in the bright light of forenoon, yet the progression of events and the heavy accumulation of carefully selected and skilfully depicted details envelop the scene in depression and grief, especially when the ordeal of the heroine reaches its climax. In this story, as also in 'Mishwār',[471] 'Ramaḍān',[472] 'al-Ḥālah al-Rābi'ah',[473] 'Dāwūd',[474] 'Abū'l-Hawl',[475] 'al-Jurḥ',[476] 'Shaykhukhah Bidūn Junūn'[477] and 'Ṭabliyyah Min al-Samā'',[478] Idris accentuates the individual's perpetual struggle with his environment, that is man's heroic resistence and never-ending ability to extract small and often significant victories over the destructive and corrosive forces of his dreary surroundings, which constantly seek to defeat him. He also emphasises man's capacity to transcend his failure, either through art, as in 'Mārsh al-Ghurūb',[479] or through hopes and dreams, as in most of these stories. In each case the interrelationship between illusion and reality contributes, on many levels, to the reader's understanding of the story.

In 'Jumhūriyyat Faraḥāt', gloomy humourless reality is shown to contrast with Faraḥāt's utopia, and his realisation of this contrast forms the main part of the story's subject matter. But the return to reality is not as easy as departure from it, for the character slips easily into dream and illusion, but struggles hard, often incurring significant loss, to return, because the dream has become a means of discovering, or rediscovering, reality. In 'Ḥādithat Sharaf' the nightmarish quality seems not to be an inherent feature of the scene, but a miasma bestowed upon it by man, by the inhabitants of the *'izbah* (country estate) in their desire to blacken the beautiful image of their belle. Thus the nightmare is a transient one and appears only in the scene of the ordeal. Yet when the honour of the heroine is vindicated at the end of this ordeal, her victory nevertheless tastes of defeat, especially in the sense that her clash with the *'izbah* shatters her illusions about it, making it impossible for her to restore the harmonious relationship with her neighbours that she enjoyed previously.

The same theme appears again and has its most rigorous expression in 'Laylat Ṣayf',[480] albeit with certain modification. Here the writer juxtaposes the harsh world of manual labour with the vivid sexual extravaganza collectively created by a group of adolescent peasants. The story is one of Idrīs's most effective attempts to portray the frustration that accompanies severe contradictions between illusion and reality. It is the story of a group of young peasants, one of whom, Muḥammad,[481] has visited the provincial capital. For the adolescent villagers, the city is a paradise of sensuality and carnal pleasure, a place where the villager has a chance to prove his virility and realise his dreams. One night, Muḥammad tells them a story about a sexual encounter he has had in the city: the woman was white – village women are dark-skinned and plump, or skinny – and she gave him a luxurious meal as a prelude to further delights. When Muḥammad's story reaches the point at which the woman appears to offer him her favours the audience takes over, inciting him to do in the story (for they already identify themselves with him) what they are unable to do in reality.

By the time the account approaches its climax, the audience is completely absorbed and participating fully in its creation. When it ends, overwhelmed by the colourful extravaganza they have created, the group has reached a point of no return. Muḥammad, having played an active role in confirming their, and indeed his own, dreams, tries to bring them back to reality but instead is forced by the group to take them to the woman's house in the city, not so much to verify the story as to satisfy their carnal appetite and fulfil their unrealised dreams. The ten pages in which Idrīs describes their trip to the city, walking amid the farms at night, are highly significant; they not only show how the nightmarish atmosphere is conjured up, but they also illustrate the power of illusion and consequently the difficulty of the return to reality. This is particularly apparent when the youths realise belatedly that they have gone too far and are forced by the approaching sunrise to return to their village, physically weary and psychologically frustrated, and unable to come to terms with their discovery. Ironically, the nightmare reaches its high point when the sun rises and shatters the dream.

The sense of nightmare pervades many of Idrīs's early stories, but he provides an element of apocalyptic power and vision. In some stories this vision sheds new light on the realistic details and enables the reader to see in the present situation future changes in embryo,[482] but in many others he fails to integrate the nightmarish elements into the story's realism, or to maintain them as parallel strands in a way that enriches the reader's understanding of both story and reality.[483] This duality in artistic approach arises from a certain duality in the author's perception of reality, from the existence of the two different trajectories along which to approach a situation; the rational or intellectual, and the intuitive. In 'al-Nās' for example, the dichotomy of the rational and the instinctive is quite evident.[484] On the one hand, there is the artistic approach to reality, which is embodied in the relationship between the people and the tree and in the conflict between the educated young people and the illiterate elders of the village. Where reality is seen in artistic terms, the intuitive understanding of the people and their conflicts provides the story with an insight into the situation. On the other hand, there is the rational attempt to prove that the majority, even an illiterate majority, cannot unanimously adopt the wrong stance. Thus before the end of the story, the laboratory test must prove that the leaves of the tree, which the villagers use to cure their eyes, contain a sufficient amount of copper sulphate, which is an important component of medically prepared eye drops. This is presented separately from the intrusive end of the story, which concludes that life always changes for the better and never for the worse.

This dichotomy demonstrates the writer's inability to integrate his rational conceptual views with his artistic intuitive understanding of, or feel for, reality at this stage of his literary career. At the time, Idrīs was an ardent exponent of Marxism and tried, with only partial success, to employ his theoretical understanding of socialism in widening the scope of his vision and the meaning of his fictional works. It seems as if the newly acquired philosophical concepts were to a certain extent out of step with the writer's artistic temperament. His attempt to see his fictional material through an undigested theoretical framework occasionally imposes rational views upon situations that cannot accept them.[485] This approach obscures some vital aspects of certain situations, because it appears as if he assumes, falsely, that the fictional action might contradict his pre-supposed theoretical analysis of the situation in which the action takes place; hence he tries deliberately to tip the balance in favour of his presuppositions.[486] However, in some stories he succeeds in achieving complete harmony between his philosophical views and his artistic temperament;[487] here, rational elements become an integral part of the perceptible detail, and this enables the writer both to discover the permanent and essential behind the contingent and incidental and to grasp the qualitative changes that take place beneath overlooked, occasional and quantitative ones.

The frustrated and forlorn character is a recurring theme in his stories, or rather a recurring human type. He is the natural inhabitant of the nightmarish world, where dreams are difficult, or even impossible, to achieve. In the early works, this character is able to extract some pleasure from the oppressive situation. But gradually it becomes increasingly hard for him to extract any rapture from his life. The indomitable loser moves towards the verge of defeat, without being completely vanquished. The characters move towards defeat, but without succumbing completely. Moving beyond this state involves the termination of the oppressive situation and the emergence of a new situation in which the conflict between illusion and reality is brought sharply into focus. In 'al-Maḥfaẓah'[488] the disappointment of the protagonist, a young boy, and the suppression of his modest dream of going with his friends to the cinema, are accompanied by the devastating conflict between the boy's illusion about his father and the reality of the matter. In 'Abū'l-Hawl' the conflict between the protagonist's perception of learned medical men, with their important-sounding jargon, and the reality, in the form of the medical student with whom he comes into contact, completely destroys all his dreams; and when he leaves carrying the corpse of a dead man on his back and treading alone at night on the village's forsaken paths, he tolls the bell of a forlorn and lonely man bearing his heavy cross and ascending to the unknown.

In Idris's earliest stories,[489] the sense of siege arises from relatively simple social pressures, which the character eventually overcomes.[490] In the later stories of this first stage of writing, Idris adds to these social pressures a number of other factors. In 'Ḥādithat Sharaf' the pressure is mainly psychological, but bound up with the ethos of the society and the protection of its taboos. The beautiful, innocent and spontaneous heroine makes those around her feel inadequate and accentuates their collective frustration; therefore they try to deface her image. In 'Ramaḍān'[491] the metaphysical factor and the tension between religious demands and parental compassion play the most significant role in the action, while in 'Khamas Sā'āt' the pressures of political intimidation and fear are apparent. In all these stories, social and economic factors form an important part of the oppressive atmosphere; they can coexist with the others but cannot be eliminated.

Idrīs uses the circular form to structure his stories, with the action ending back at the point of departure. This technique emphasises cyclical continuity and stresses the main action of the story as a temporary move, but at the same time one that can animate and pervade the whole cycle in a way that leaves its mark on the next revolution. Idrīs therefore deliberately avoids sudden endings and denouements. When the progression of action demands one of these Maupassant-like endings ('Arkhaṣ Layālī', 'al-Makanah', 'Abū'l-Hawl', 'Dāwūd' and 'al-Mustaḥīl') he often continues to elaborate on them in an intrusive manner, with an over-insistent authorial presence, which occasionally jeopardises the artistic effect. But when the story contains an element of structural irony, and is by its very structure incompatible with the closed circular form, he succeeds in transforming the circular into a spiral form, where a subsequent cycle of events takes place at another level, but one on which the influence of the previous cycle can still be felt ('al-Ṭābūr', 'Dāwūd' and 'al-Ḥajjānah').

When the story involves more than two cycles of action, the intrinsic effect of the previous ones manifests in the form, nature and qualitative change of the final revolution. In 'al-Ṭābūr', for example, the action is portrayed in three cycles relating to the people's intensifying resistance to a growing obstacle. Although the story ends before the rising tide of resistance becomes full-scale insurrection, the crescendo of the action leaves no room for speculation about the nature of the future qualitative change in the course of events. However, the circular form is not only thematic; it is also structural, for it concerns the rhythm of the action and the nature of the language. The repetition of words and phrases is often used as a device to underline the circularity of the form. 'Al-Kanz'[492] begins and ends with the same sentence and, like 'Alaysa Kadhalik',[493] invites the reader to turn back the pages and re-read the circular, endless story which has acquired through its structure the quality of a continuous life.

In many of Idrīs's stories the action is carefully controlled by a form of determinism or necessity. Social, cultural, economic, psychological and political factors forge an inescapable progression of events and create a kind of artistic inevitability. At this stage of his literary career, however, this artistic necessity operates, for the most part, on a mechanical level; it required some considerable development in technique before he was able to eliminate the intrusive elements which obstruct its complete integration into the narrative. Deficient fictional form, obtrusive intellectual notes and the dichotomy of the rational and the perceptible are among the factors that contribute to the mechanical aspect of Idrīs's artistic determinism. In addition, there is the dominance of the external type of experience and the interest in the external elements of the narrative in a form that often does not allow enough exploration of interior aspects of the character. For it seems that Idrīs at this stage is mainly concerned with the conflict between man and society, a society that appears as an abstract entity. The people who construct the obstacles or form the pressure do not appear as individuals, but as a vague, somewhat abstract, power.[494]

Another feature that coincides with this emphasis on the external aspects of the experience is the concentration on the sensuous aspects of the story. This appears in Idrīs's attempt to discover elements of beauty in the simple daily activities of the poor, where he deals with some external aspects of the experience as if they were fascinating rituals or a form of liturgical activity. It also appears in his hunt for the rare voluptuous moments in this gloomy, harsh and constricted world. He appears to delight in these and dramatises them in such a way as to suggest they contain spiritual or sublime elements. In 'Ramaḍān' the lucid description of the daily rituals of Ramaḍān as they are seen through the eyes of a young boy turns many of the scenes, especially that of the *suḥūr* (the meal before daybreak), into a feast of sensuous delights. In 'Ṭabliyyah Min al-Samā',[495] 'Taḥwīd al- 'Arūsah'[496] and 'Hi ... Hiyya Li'bah'[497] there are different variations on the pleasures of eating, while 'Laylat Ṣayf', 'Fi'l-Layl' and 'Baṣrah' introduce aspects of the second important set of sensations portrayed in these stories, those associated with conversation. Ironically, sex, the one human activity that is clearly associated with voluptuous pleasure, is rarely presented as such in these early stories.

Sex is one of the more complex themes in Idrīs's work. Although sex is clearly associated with rapture and voluptuousness, it is also linked with frustration and a deep sense of guilt. It is code-named *al-'ayb* (shameful act) and *al-ḥarām* (forbidden act),[498] and hence becomes a taboo, a sin. 'Ḥādithat Sharaf' offers a good example of Idrīs's perception of sex at this time. On the one hand, it presents the delightful aspects of sex in the character of Gharīb, a womaniser who is endowed with pleasing physical features and a strong sexual appetite. He is not only a symbol of virility, but also a personification of the vigour and vitality of life, underlining an important aspect of Idrīs's view of sex. On the other hand, the story shows most clearly through the vicissitudes of the life of the heroine, Fāṭimah, the forbidden and sinful nature of sex and its association with man's defeat and frustration; it suggests that the heroine knows sex only after her crushing ordeal to prove her virginity and links her sin to the loss of innocence, spontaneity and even beauty. It is important to note, however, that this position, this disapproving attitude to sex, is part of contemporary social convention, not the personal view of the author.[499]

There are another two significant themes in Idrīs's early work. The first is the importance of the father's role in a strongly patriarchal society. The father in Idrīs' stories represents ultimate authority; he offers protection and tenderness, but also engenders oppression and fear. He is the axis of family life, and so when he disappears, for one reason or another, life loses its enjoyment and vivacity, for the undermining of patriarchal authority disturbs the order of life and upsets its delicate balance: the wife goes astray ('Qā' al-Madīnah'[500] and 'al-Murjayḥah') or loses her sense of purpose ('al-Ḥādith') and the children miss security and love, and moreover lose their sense of harmony with their surroundings ('al-Yadd al-Kabīrah' and 'al-Murjayḥah'). The positive role of the father is also emphasised in these stories and in several others. Idrīs dramatises his fathers through their wives and children, for it is wholly natural that the kind of conservative peasant or working-class woman he portrays, who sees the world through the eyes of her husband, is the first to be radically affected by what happens to him. The children – Idrīs's world, unlike most Eyptian writers,[501] is full of children – are utterly dependent on the father, and his absence or the deterioration of his power deprives them of a potent source of protection, love and authority. His mere presence offers them enormomous satisfaction ('Hi ... Hiyya Li'bah'), even if he is unable to fulfil their needs ('al-Maḥfaẓah').

The second theme is the conflict between the group and the individual, which reaches a high degree of sophistication and richness in some of the stories. The group is presented, for the first time in modern Egyptian literature, not as a faceless crowd or a reckless mob, but as a humane and almost sacred cluster of loveable persons. In these first five collections, the individual comes into conflict with the group for two main reasons: the first is his attempt to exploit them or overcome their will ('al-Ṭābūr'), the second is his lack of understanding of their logic, ethos or culture ('al-Nās' and 'al-Ḥajjānah'). The wrongdoings are always on the side of the individual, never on that of the group. Though oppressed or frustrated, the group is always right, and its members know clearly what they want ('al-Tamrīn al-Awwal'[502] and 'Ṭabliyyah Min al-Samā''). They hate oppression and despotism and valiantly resist all acts of tyranny ('al-Ṭābūr' and 'al-Tamrīn al-Awwal'). They transcend their own failures and grief through a collective dream ('Laylat Ṣayf') or through uplifting conversations ('Fi'l-Layl').

The structure of Idrīs's short stories is highly coherent and functional and succeeds in reinforcing the manifold facets of his theme. In many of his stories he uses a parallel structure, supported by sub-themes, to widen the scope and the implications of the main theme. Although he depends on consecutive narrative and syllogistic progression in developing the action, he relies on irony in its construction. However, this is irony of a simple and often rudimentary nature, as opposed to the sophisticated modern concept of irony as a means of unifying the apparent contradictions of experience while at the same time asserting the world's diversity. Consequently, it is not able to maintain the necessary balance between the various factors contributing to its formation. It does not, unlike its more sophisticated form, convey meanings different from those which are professed or ostensible, and it fails to exploit the distance that lies between the words or events and their context. Thus, in many cases, it appears simply as a technique for explaining a situation through treating it in the presence of its opposite, without succeeding in creating the juxtaposition described, and at the same time deflates the social aspirations of the protagonist; nor does it succeed in bringing the two conflicting and contrasting worlds into sharp focus through the pivotal character.[503]

Nevertheless, Idrīs manages in his first five collections to create a unique fictional world that draws its material and characters mainly from the life of the desolate poor. It is a world in which sordid slums, dingy rooms and other repellent settings shine with beauty and intimacy under the skilful stroke of his pen. The simple shabby peasants sparkle with human qualities and wit, the stagnant life of many obscure areas of Egyptian society reveals richness and vitality and provides profound conflicts, while rebarbative situations provoke stimulating ideas. But Idrīs's major artistic achievement lies in his impressive characterisation and his ability to illustrate complicated issues without perplexing the reader. Although he focuses on workers and peasants, he treats them, contrary to some of his predecessors, with care and respect. His peasants and workers, lively and real, are not recapitulations of the morally impeccable cardboard characters of the social-romantic stories wrongly called works of social realism. The stories of this period also prove that Idrīs is adept at *obiter dicta*, a quality that provides both the narrative and the dialogue in his stories with insight, depth and vitality. His language is extremely varied and chequered, yet he consistently shows skill in both dialogue and description.

The second group of Idrīs's collections of short stories, that is to say the four collections published during the 1960s, show a substantial change in theme and form. By 1959, the euphoria of the early 1950s was over and most of Idrīs's old comrades in the struggle for independence and for a better future were behind bars. Years had gone by and far too few dreams had come to fruition. Then came the 1960s, a decade of mixed feelings and confusion, of contradictions and crises. The mass arrest of intellectuals and progressive politicians created a sense of loss, oppression and fear; and the ironic growth of the ideas and slogans of those who were put in jail for promoting them resulted in apathy and a sense of absurdity. Moreover, the stifling conditions of the early 1960s and their sharp and often ridiculous contradictions acted as an important catalyst in maturing artistic sensibilities[504] and in bringing about radical changes in artistic conventions, especially in the field of the short story.

Idrīs's work of the 1960s is substantially different from his work of the 1950s, despite a certain element of continuity. As his early works brought a breath of fresh air to the realistic short story and restored its respectability as a literary medium, so his writing in the 1960s played an important role in shaping and crystallising the new sensibility. Moreover, just as he returns to the roots of the problems of Egypt's cultural life and expresses some of the country's aspirations in his early collections, so he continues to strike at the core of society in the 1960s. Although his production of short stories diminishes quantitatively in this period,[505] various earlier artistic qualities and thematic features remain intact. His wide range of location and individual characters still prevails, but the experiences of these characters tend to be more concentrated and revolve around fewer pivotal themes.

In his collection *Lughat al-Āy-Āy* (1966), for example, two main themes run through the stories: the first is the central character's discovery of the futility and absurdity of the life he has been leading. This discovery, coming too late, makes the character a victim of self-reproach and exposes him to censure, and consequently fills him with bitterness and despair. Because the character realises that it is beyond his capacity to put the clock back, his tardy discovery shatters his previous contentment.[506] The second pivotal theme is the experience of isolation and insecurity, expressed often in the character's sense of being the quarry in a mysterious pursuit.[507] Unable to define the identity of his pursuer and incapable of rationalising the hunt, he is therefore defenceless.

However, there are other significant changes besides the concentration of human experience around certain pivots. Of these, the elimination or reduction of the element of claustrophobic nightmare is important. A remnant of this survivies in the strand of pessimism that tends to be preserved in his more abstract presentation of subject matter and the use of a dream-like progression of the action, which involves surrealistic images or details and a fondness for maxims. In 'al-Awūrṭī' the point of departure is unreal and abstract, a myth that cannot be vindicated yet is still capable of convincing the reader.[508] The language of narration, with its direct, sharp, rhythmic sentences, plays a vital role in hypnotising the reader and leading him into the inner logic of the story's make-believe world, a world in which a haunted man, the quarry of a mysterious pursuit, is running through the streets with his aorta recently removed. He has been accused without evidence, convicted without trial, and denied the very essence of life, its basic source, his own aorta; yet he is still walking wound in bandages, like an old Egyptian mummy in its papyrus bandages. The description of the chase and the seizure of the central character and the unwrapping of his bandages has the quality of a slow-motion picture, whereby time is decelerated and scenes frozen in order to zoom in and focus on particular aspects of a situation.

In 'al-Lu'bah' the abstraction is presented not by resorting to the surreal but through the dreamlike progression of the action. The dream here is not synonymous with the nightmare of the previous stage, for the latter is associated with the conditions of reality while the former seeks to achieve its effect by complete detachment, indeed withdrawal, from it. Ironically, the action in the dreamlike technique is in itself quite plausible. In the story in question it concerns a man who goes to a party and participates in one of its games. But behind the deceptively simple appearance there are various layers of meaning at work. The quiet, direct, sharp account of the action in its *tout ensemble* and without any attempt to clarify or justify what ostensibly seems improbable, or which deliberately avoids any explanation, widens the scope of the action and lays it open to several interpretations. Under the virtuous description and the slow-motion technique of narrative, the delusive game ceases to be a single game at a party and becomes *the game of life*; the player is never a specific person but a symbol of humanity, and the silent conniving crowd reflect certain facets of social reality.

In 'al-Mārid' Idrīs uses a stream of contemplative narrative in his depiction of a simple realistic incident, a car accident, in order to transform it into a more abstract statement about human experience, and in particular to reveal some of the hidden powers of man.[509] These three techniques, the abstract or surreal presentation of subject matter, the dreamlike progression of action and the use of the realistic to express abstract realities, replace, or rather take over the thematic function of, the nightmare effect that prevailed in many of Idris's early stories. They also succeed in transcending the division between the rational and intuitive identified above as a weakness in his early writing. Nevertheless, there is still fluctuation in the degree of artistic success or failure achieved through these techniques, not only because the writer uses within them various, often discordant, styles, but also because, in some cases, he overloads the story with details, thus dissipating the impression of unity. A few examples, however ('al-Lu'ba' and 'al-Awurti'), escape these problems and forge a fictional realm on the abstract level in a way that fills them with a suggestive poetic power.[510]

The third change in the stories of this second stage is in character: the oppressed character or heroic failure is often abandoned for characters with miraculous powers, and these are not confined to a certain class or group. In his skilful characterisation Idrīs abandons the simple and schematic development of the character and resorts to various techniques of qualitative progression and to repetitive forms based on a succession of images and actions, for the story's departure from the schematic and syllogistic progression reflects the relinquishing of ordinary logic and entry into a unique logic, which requires a distinct modulation. It is natural that the quality of the character dictates the relevant style of characterisation. Although the miraculous character is a common one at this stage, he is not the common type, but the individual who stands alone in confrontation with various obstacles, as is the case with 'Aḥmad al-Majlis al-Baladī'.[511] The miraculous character challenges the collective submissiveness of the group ('Alif al-Aḥrār')[512] and is capable of defeating, in a subtle and unique manner, those who attempt to terrorise him ('Ṣāḥib Miṣr'), for he possesses a great deal of power ('Mu'jizat al-'Aṣr');[513] he is shrewd, inventive and versatile, and able to create life in places where it is lacking or seems impossible ('Ṣāḥib Miṣr'). But at the same time he is discontented and possessed by visions; like a prophet before his time, he is rejected by his immediate milieu and unable to reconcile his prophetic intuition with the prevailing reality. He seeks to reform but his pronouncements fall on deaf ears, which imbues the story with a satirical quality.

Satire, fiercer than comedy in its moral intentions, measures human conduct not against a norm but against an ideal. The intention is reformative. The artist holds up for his readers to see a distorted image, and the reader is to be shocked into a realisation that the image is his own. Exaggeration of the most extreme kind is central to the shock tactics. The reader must see himself as a monster, in order to learn how far he is from being a saint.[514]

In 'Mu'jizat al-'Aṣr', a story of Swiftian quality, Idrīs employs the technique of satire to present the various facets of his enigmatic miraculous character. The hero is as tall as half a finger joint and is endowed with sensitivity, insight and intelligence as yet unknown to man; thus he is both qualified to, and capable of, solving all the chronic and insoluble problems of the world. But at the same time his genius is not recognised and he has no opportunity to prove himself. Exaggeration of the most extreme kind is employed in two directions: minimising the size of the hero and aggrandising his achievements; reducing the people's awareness of the hero's potential and intensifying the effect of their rejection upon him. The hero is deliberately made very small in order to ridicule the norm and to prevent any identification with him, for the reader, to his own shame, is forced to identify with the narrator and those who victimise the hero, and to realise that he too is far from being an ordinary reasonable person.

The story is a parable; on one level it is an allegory of the common man whose potential and talents are always underrated, whose achievements are often overlooked, and whose greatness is too subtle to be seen; on another level, it is a satirical, and somewhat vain, expression of Idrīs's exasperation at his compatriots' failure to recognise his greatness, which had already been praised abroad.[515] It combines Gulliver in Brobdingnag and the fairy tale of Tom Thumb with the tradition of science fiction; it interweaves prophecy with satire, magic with depression, and fantasy with reality in a fascinating amalgam of events and contemplations. As an allegory of the common man, the story touches upon the crudeness of reality and demonstrates how man's action has both social and moral implications, for the 'allegory follows through the ages the imperatives of conflicting ideals rooted in the nature of thought and belief'.[516] Although the moral implications of the allegory are quite evident, even bearing some direct reference to religion, the social dimension of the story is a powerful one. The interrelationship between the enigmatic miraculous character and 'normal' society is an important one in most of these stories.

In terms of situation and action, Idrīs accentuates the enigmatic miraculous aspect in the confrontation between the individual and the group, which now represents the existing order of society. The group is no longer sacred and infallible as was the case in 'al-Ṭābūr' or 'al-Nās', but stupid, hostile, immoral and submissive. It complicitly acknowledges the status quo and suppresses any individual attempt to defy it.[517] A comparison between the behaviour of the group and the individual in 'al-Ṭābūr' and 'al-Lu'bah' or 'Snobism'[518] demonstrates a complete change of roles; the subdued individual becomes a rebel and the defiant group, ready to fight tyranny, becomes submissive. In 'Snobism', which can be seen as a powerful satire of collective passivity, the group becomes the basic tool of oppression and sees in the individual's attempt to challenge the existing corrupt order a great danger to its stability and delicate balance. Even in stories where the group is neither protagonist nor antagonist, it nevertheless plays a negative part, for it is completely assimilated into the surrounding milieu against which the individual character reacts.[519]

The character's reaction frequently takes the form of withdrawal from outside reality. Although this tendency seems to be in apparent contradiction with the new rebellious quality of the individual, it underlines the pervasiveness of corruption from which the individual seeks to escape and imbues his rebellion with tragedy. In the case of those who are not in any sense rebels, withdrawal from outside reality is a result both of the disintegration of reality and of the inability of the individual to put up with its corrupt order. It is an indication that the collective submissiveness and group connivance in the existing order have perpetuated a perverted scale of social and moral values, within which the innocent individual suffers ('Snobism') and from which he seeks to escape ('Qiṣṣat Dhi al-Ṣawt al-Naḥīl' and 'Ḥalat Talabbus'). The escape takes several forms, which fluctuate between daydreams and fantasies ('Mashūq al-Hams')[520] and the intentionally suicidal isolation ('Qiṣṣat Dhi al-Ṣawt al-Naḥīl'). But neither dreams nor the fleeting moments of isolation and fulfilment ('Ḥalat Talabbus') can offer more than a transient comfort, after which grim reality prevails.

Even in stories that convey man's extraordinary characteristics, the tendency to withdraw from reality demonstrates that, while Idrīs is concerned with the potential greatness in human character, he does not neglect the elements of frustration and failure that accompany it. Shawqī, the hero of 'al-'Askarī al-Aswad',[521] although a victim of political error and brutal intimidation, is an example of a character in whom potential greatness is thwarted and eventually submerged. His withdrawal does not signify a victory of political oppression, for those who inflicted it upon him are as damaged by it as he is; rather, it indicates how vision becomes blurred and issues confused; both the protagonist and the antagonist of this story, despite the disparity of their education, lack a clear understanding of external reality and, consequently, are unable to exercise any control over it. They withdraw into themselves and wage an internal war so that they become progressively more isolated, caught in a vicious circle of remorse and withdrawal.

'Ṣāhib Miṣr' gives another example of how human greatness can coexist with suffering and frustration. Through a pair of characters, one, 'Amm Ḥasan, subject to persecution and unjustified oppression, and the other, Ṣimaydah, ostensibly far removed from any danger,[522] Idrīs intensifies the disintegration of reality and his characters' lack of comprehension to the point of absurdity, which in turn affects everyone in the story. Yet he neither undermines the heroic resistance of the protagonist nor overlooks his great talent and his ability to establish life in the most wild and difficult terrain. He demonstrates how the disintegration of reality and the pervasiveness of perverted values affect those who naively think that they can escape their influence. He also accentuates the 'Egyptianness' of his hero's indomitable character, his talent for construction and his subtle way of defeating his opponents while ostensibly avoiding confrontation. The hero's ability to endure persecution and suffering and to start from the beginning again suggest how suffering and endurance can be part of greatness. The juxtaposition of such contrasting elements gives rise to the insistent question posed in most of these stories: how is it that these characters, despite their enormous human potential, fall victim to misery and frustration?

The number of answers to this provocative question almost equals the number of stories in which it appears, but in general it may be said that less attention is now paid to economic factors. In some the answer lies in the irony with which the discrepancy is portrayed between the character's visions of transcending his ugly present and his realisation of his inability to do so.[523] Alternatively, time, which plays an important role at this stage of Idrīs's development, acting very often against the character's craving for self-fulfilment, may provide the answer in some stories.[524] There is also the concatenation of metaphysical curse and social pressure in which fate enhances man's misery ('Intiṣār al-Hazīmah');[525] the collapse of ideals and the loss of incentive in a manner that stultifies life and renders it absurd and meaningless ('Lughat al-Āy-Āy'); the supremacy of illusion over reality ('al-Lu'bah' and 'al-Awūrṭī'); and the spread of fear and suspicion ('Qiṣṣat Dhi al-Ṣawt al-Naḥīl' and 'Li'anna al-Qiyāmah Lā Taqūm').

The nature of these possible answers ties in with other changes in Idris's writing in this period: his diminishing interest in the sensuous rituals of life and the lack of positive aspects in his portrayal of the patriarchal pattern of society. A number of his characters suffer from the absence of the father, which intensifies their sense of loneliness, abandonment and loss. This absence inverts values; it gives rise to adultery,[526] small things become abstract values,[527] and disturbs the social order by permitting greed[528] and idiocy[529] to prevail, thus placing unbearable burdens on the character's shoulders. 'Li'ann al-Qiyāmah Lā Taqūm' is an important story in this respect, for the oppressive and sinful atmosphere, partly caused by the father's absence, is all-pervasive; it does not stop at the doorstep of the protagonist's home, but follows him into the outside world. The importance of the father is illustrated at this stage only through depicting the effect of his absence, but never by showing what his presence can provide.[530] It appears as if the father's image is associated with a normal, relaxed social life, and when this life is deformed it seems impossible to accommodate the father's role in such a corrupt society, or to reconcile the very fact of his existence with things going wrong.

It seems also as if his protagonist, who by now has reached the age of consent and realised how messy the world is, tries to mollify his discontent and find comfort in sex; an act through which he plays the father's role and compensates for his absence. For sex, which becomes one of the major themes here, is no longer *'ayb* or *ḥarām* in spite of being sinful, but an act of fulfilment and of proving the self and confirming its hold on reality. It is also associated with the various facets of the Oedipus complex on the one hand, and clandestine activities on the other; yet it becomes, more or less, a matter of course and an accepted fact of life. In 'Li'ann al-Qiyāmah lā Taqūm' the boy's Oedipal relationship with his mother is the main theme of the story, and the image of him sleeping under the bed of her sins intensifies the love–hate relationship between them. This complex relationship is developed in 'al-Gharīb' to include a father figure and introduce fear and frustration into the already complex nexus.[531] Thus it sinks in his unconsciousness as a desire for incest and a feeling that sex is a major field for fulfilment. It becomes an obsession, a mania, for he, as 'al-Naddāhah' puts it,

> is crazy about all women, and is willing to achieve the

> impossible in order to have one of them ... he is willing to lie, to dissemble, to steal, to kill, or even to use the atomic bomb, if he possesses one, to have a woman, and for him the woman is non-existent after the first night. [532]

In a way, he is a contemporary image of Shahrayār,[533] but for him all women are not the same, only a certain variety of them can provide him with utmost pleasure:

> his happiest adventure is that in which he hurled himself upon a widow during the very night of the death of her ageing husband; or that, at the beginning of his sexual history, when he slept with his friend's mother when he went to study with him in his house,[534]

for only this type of sexual adventure can satisfy, or even avenge, his unconscious Oedipal desire. The woman's desire for a younger man, virtually of her son's age, is also depicted to complete the picture.[535] However, in both cases sex is seen as the gate to heavenly, but transient, pleasure and as a form of carnal fulfilment – as a stolen moment vivid and lively but destined to end and leave man to endure a difficult world. In 'al-Naddāhah' sex is associated with the fall and is seen as an inverted repetition of an original sin in which man plays the seducer, and as an irrevocable fate before which man has to capitulate. But in 'al-'Amaliyyah al-Kubrā' it is seen as man's only way out of frustration and disappointment, something more than a physical act.

With regard to technique, it is clear that many of the stories of this phase have much in common with those of the earlier phase, yet they are more concerned with structure and experimentation.[536] Nevertheless, irony, both structural and cosmic, still constitutes the core of Idrīs work: it is structural irony in 'Lughat al-Āy-Āy',[537] where the author uses a naive character whose simplicity leads him to apply an interpretation to events which the reader is able to correct, thus sustaining a duplicity of meaning which widens the scope of the story and enriches its implication. In 'al-'Askarī al-Aswad' structural irony is coupled with cosmic irony at the end of the story, where destiny comes into play as if deliberately manipulating events to balance the progression of the action, or, as in 'Intiṣār al-Hazīmah', to mock and frustrate the protagonist. The narrative continues to be predominantly linear, usually a third-person connected narrative aimed at shaping the syllogistic progression of the action and creating three-dimensional characters. Idrīs's resort to the first-person singular decreases gradually, and he uses the second-person narrative in a few stories, possibly for the first time in the Egyptian short story.[538] The circular edifice, particularly in its spiral development, remains his preferred form.

Nevertheless, there are a number of significant changes. His previously intrusive authorial presence almost disappears, and he succeeds in omitting all undesirable preamble and concentrating on the basic situation. A particularly significant technique emerges, the use of fictional time with its own autonomous logic; it is time with a unique duration, almost stagnant, and unreal, but possessing supreme authority over its dreamlike world. Within this particular time, Idrīs presents his fictional situation as if seen in slow motion, a method that allows him to account for the most minute detail and to ponder over the slightest movement. As in cinematic technique, he freezes some of his scenes, focuses on its totality at the beginning then zooms in on its tiny details. This acts as a magnifier of certain moments in the life of the action, blowing them up, often out of proportion, and turning them into moments of examination and discovery. Viewed in the context of this fixed form of time, the fictional situation suggests various levels of meaning. Both the richness and the sophistication of this feature may be exemplified by reference to the collection *Lughat al-Āy-Āy*. In some stories this technique becomes a thematic feature:[539] the fixed prolonged moment in time provides a form of escape from reality and offers some of the characters a kind of stolen relief or fulfilment, and sheds a shaft of light on the meaningless life of the others. In other stories it is the instant of discovery that is dissected with all that this entails in both the structure of the story and the life of the fictional character.[540] The flashback technique is brought into play and the moment of discovery becomes a powerful lens through which the protagonist sees his life in a new light.

Idrīs employs these new techniques and others to suspend the fictional situation in a limbo between illusion and reality where dreams and facts intersect and become complementary. He has clearly abandoned mimetic representation and endeavours to create an artistic world, not congruent with the realistic world but parallel to it, a world rich in inner logic and originality and capable of conveying the essence of life without being lifelike.[541] He uses a wide variety of devices in creating this unique artistic world and attempts to explore new possibilities. One finds, for example, interior monologue side by side with conventional third-person narrative and the curious usage of the second-person singular; dreamlike stories are juxtaposed with stories that use realistic detail as a medium to tackle abstract ideas, in addition to those which try to transfer the dramatic technique of alienation to the short story.

The use of various techniques and devices to create a semi-real semi-illusory world is also employed in his characterisation. At both stages of his development, Idrīs's skilful and convincing characterisation draws upon his studied experience of the character, his stature and gesture, his cultural habits and his mannerisms and language. This first-hand experience, and the skilful emulation of the character's language, enables him to integrate the character into the setting and the situation and to use both of them at the same time in the process of characterisation, which he does not achieve through a descriptive account of the character's qualities or development, but by interweaving the character with the setting and seeing him or her in the context of the action.

> In an action ... the hero reacts in terms of his dearest and deepest beliefs; he makes choices which involve the things he holds most important in the world. Such problems encompass the hero and bring him to reactions and discoveries out of which character emerges.[542]

In Idrīs's characterisation, reactions and discoveries are most important in revealing the inner psyche and introducing its fundamental attitudes towards the world.

Although reactions and discoveries are used as a means to spark off emotional or intellectual outbursts and to give the reader a glimpse into the character's major qualities, his moral bent and intellect, they are closely linked to the character's life and motives; for without clear and convincing motivation they may seem meaningless and redundant. Idrīs is clearly aware of the importance of developing the character through his deep participation in the stories' events: deep is a significant adjective here because it underlines the fact that participation in fictional events is normally conducted on more than one level.

The events are by no means latent or implicit in the character:

rather, they evoke character where previously there had been a self-contained or an unthinking man. They are not events which merely test a person; they bring out the human significance of a world, and the person defines himself and discovers himself as he reaches between himself and his world for the answers to his problem.[543]

The clarity of these self-definitions and discoveries corresponds to the depth of the character's participation – by action and reaction – in events, and Idrīs's awareness of this correlation enriches his world with abundant human discoveries.

As far as the language of his fiction is concerned many of the technical features accounted for above are in one way or another achievements within the fictional language; particularly the slow-motion technique and the freezing of time to focus upon certain situations and zoom in on its details. For without a skilful use of language and a careful control of rhythm, it is extremely difficult to attain this effect. Idrīs had little or no literary training before he started writing, and so he relied at first on his instinctive feel for the poetry of the spoken language and his wide knowledge of its metaphor. He juxtaposes colloquial with literary structures and forges a narrative language, which is often poetic and evocative, though at times stilted and awkward. For this juxtaposition can adulterate the language instead of enriching it, especially when it is interlaced with pathos or sentimentality and often contains grammatical mistakes resulting from prioritising spoken over standard Arabic.

But towards the end of the 1960s Idrīs succeeded in overcoming these difficulties and his style becomes generally lucid and original. His use of simple language abounds with powerful perception where the mainly literary language is interspersed with suggestively poetic vernacular and witty remarks. At this stage he endeavours 'to inject words and images with extraneous meaning which in the context of the story they do not automatically possess'.[544] This is a characteristic inherent in his technique of slow motion and freezing, which often enriches the story and widens its implications. It is also connected with his skilful use of imagery. He uses simple and familiar, but still authentic and pertinent, images, some of which are extended or sustained images, fully integrated into the narrative and are capable of adumbrating future events. Much of the information necessary for the understanding of the various layers of meaning in his stories is insinuated and never flatly stated.

Idrīs succeeds in sensitively adumbrating events and insinuating qualities and information because he blends the descriptive with the contemplative in a balanced amalgam of narrative. Idrīs has a strong sense of rhythm and delicate timing. He knows when to introduce an image, how long to sustain it, and when the appropriate time is for a new one to be introduced, even before the first one is completely over. His mastery of the sustained image enables him to know when to elaborate on the details and when it is more effective to touch upon them succinctly.

His sensitivity to the sounds and rhythms of both the written and spoken languages is generally consistent, but more remarkable than this are the changes in his use of language, and the development of his ability to build upon the raw material of speech as it is used in oratory or in conversation, and incorporate it into his own literary style.[545]

Through these changes in language and technique, Idrīs captured the rhythm and essence of two different sensibilities when many of his contemporaries were lagging behind, ruminating on their old material and techniques. His mastery of form and his profound insight into Egyptian life enabled him to express in his prolific writing the essence of the 1950s and then to participate in crystallising the new vision and sensibility of the 1960s. He is responsible for rooting the short story in the cultural consciousness of Egypt more firmly than anyone before him.

Shukrī Muḥammad 'Ayyād: Social Criticism and Exploration of the Psyche

The work of Yūsuf Idrīs was both so powerful and so popular that it not only overshadowed that of many writers of his own group,[546] but also eclipsed the work of two other groups of writers, the first consisting of writers slightly older than Idrīs, the second those who were slightly younger.[547] Many of the first group had started writing and publishing short stories several years before his arrival on the literary scene, but Idrīs was able to publish his first collection before any of them.[548] Idrīs also took most of the limelight because of his prolific output, his dedication to the genre and the favourable critical response that his early works received. Most of the writers of this first group (which consists of Aḥmad al-Māzinī,[549] Shukrī 'Ayyād, 'Abd al-Raḥmān Fahmī,[550] 'Abd al-Ghaffār Makkāwī,[551] Sa'd al-Dīn Wahbah[552] and others)[553] were far less prolific and, moreover, divided their time and energy amongst other literary activities. In fact, many of them put more emphasis on these other activities than on the short story,[554] while Idrīs abandoned his original profession, medicine, altogether to devote himself entirely to the genre.

The most gifted representative of this group is Shukrī Muḥammad 'Ayyād (1921–99). He devoted most of his attention to literary activities other than the short story – to literary studies and literary criticism. Although he first started publishing short stories in *al-Jāmi'ah* and *al-Riwāyah* as early as 1937, his first collection of short stories, *Mīlād Jadīd*, did not appear until 1957, and his second and only other collection, *Ṭarīq al-Jāmi'ah*, appeared in 1963. Like some of his contemporaries – Murād and Makkāwī in particular – he began his literary career with translations, but unlike most of his predecessors who started in translation, he did not confine himself to a specific writer or even to one country's literature. He translated, mainly from English, several works by Rabindranath Tagore,[555] Hans Anderson,[556] John Millington Synge,[557] Alexander Kuprin,[558] Maupassant[559] and Ruben Dario.[560] In the early 1940s he formed with a group of friends[561] Jamā'at Aṣdiqā' al-Adab al-Rūsī, a society concerned with the promotion and translation of Russian literature, and as a contribution to that society's activities in 1945 he translated Dostoevsky's *The Gambler* and in 1948 Turgenev's *Smoke*.

The period of his concern with Russian literature coincided with the serious beginning of his career as a short story writer during the 1940s, for after having written and published a few short stories towards the end of the 1930s,[562] he abandoned writing in this form for almost ten years before returning to it in a more serious manner. His stories of the late 1940s and the early 1950s comprise the bulk of his first collection,[563] yet it is noteworthy that, although very much in love with Russian literature, he did not completely fall under its spell. He clearly benefited from his knowledge of Russian literature and of other European literatures, but tried to create a genuinely Egyptian and indigenous literature. Like most of the writers of his group, and particularly because of his involvement in both academic and scholarly activities and in the critical movement, 'Ayyād combines the sensitivity and spontaneity of the artist with the intellect of the literary critic. He endeavours to maintain that delicate balance necessary to save creative writings from academic dryness without sacrificing intellectual depth and, unlike other members of the group, he generally succeeds.[564]

One of the reasons for this success is that he selects a number of his characters from the educated classes, which justifies the introduction of intellectual and contemplative elements into the story, and he is able to draw on first-hand experience of these characters and the intellectual issues he addresses. Although some of his stories are set in the village,[565] his world is mainly peopled with middle-class urban characters, of whom a small number are intellectuals. It is natural that most of these should be either writers or academics, for ʿAyyād has first-hand knowledge of the problems and aspirations of these two categories.[566] In ʿShabābʾ[567] he focuses on the agony of the creative writer who aspires to perfection yet is filled with discontent. His discontent concerns aesthetic questions arising from the unbridgeable gap between art and reality, and does not spring from, or touch upon, the problems of the social function of his art. Thus somewhat ironically, ʿAyyād, whilst attempting to capture and portray reality in a convincing manner, is preoccupied with idealistic ideas about the ultimate goal of the artist, though tempered by an awareness of the unattainable nature of the goal, the difficulty of transcending the divide between art and life.

Other stories, however, which deal mainly with the frustrated intellectual, escape this idealism and blend their treatment of the problems of the intellectual with two of ʿAyyād's main recurring themes. The first is social disparity: ʿAyyād is particularly adept at bringing to light the intangible elements of social injustice that the ordinary observer can easily overlook; the second is the powerful influence of certain vivid memories on the lives of his characters regardless of whether the effect is positive or negative. ʿGhurūb al-Shamsʾ[568] fuses these three themes together in a form that merits Yeats' description of the irresistible: 'only that which does not teach, which does not cry out, which does not persuade, which does not condescend, which does not explain, is irresistible in art'.[569] The story eschews the didactic, the loud or pretentious voice and any condescension to sentimentality and redundant repetition in its attempt to explore both the value and absurdity of life by shedding a shaft of light on the long and futile rivalry between two colleagues.

ʿAyyād chooses the revealing moment of the termination of this rivalry as the point of departure in this story, and through carefully selected flashbacks gives the reader an insight into the life of its main character. The story begins with the hero reading the news of his rival's death in an air crash in his morning paper, which bring back memories of him accumulated over the years, which come forth in an apparently disordered manner. They concern their secondary school years when they competed with one another every inch of the way, their time at university, where they joined the same faculty and continued their competition, and the years after graduation when they went on to contend for the same position, until his rival was successful. The hero then spent five years in vain litigation, attempting to win the position back, but when he finally lost he changed his role from contender to spectator. This change affected his whole life, as if the termination of the rivalry robbed him of his urge to live. His work deteriorated and his grip on life loosened, until the only thing that kept him alive was his pursuit of news of his rival, who had become a public figure.

The main subject of the story is the defeated party and the reader is given an insight into his domestic life through his memories, dialogue and his wife's commentary, which are brought into focus dramatically with the powerful denouement. The story does not end when the protagonist's reconstruction of the past concludes, but continues to explore his feelings and thoughts after the news of the death of his rival has taken effect. He questions his part in the dead man's life, indeed he sees his own life in a new light and what he sees destroys him, so when his wife comes to call him in she finds him dead. His death, which constitutes the powerful end of the story, gives both his final contemplation about his wasted life and his account of the rivalry new meaning, for one now understands the significance of various references throughout the story, the undercurrent of a subtle, yet effective, tone of social criticism, and the meaning of the game with its changing roles and transposition. The hero, to his surprise, discovers too late that he has suspended his own life and that confining himself to the role of spectator has nourished a destructive illusion, which has enervated his very soul. He has based his life on morbid, self-indulgent illusions and never attempted to see the whole episode of the rivalry in a rational manner.

The writer does not judge his character, but tries to understand the sources of his misfortune and the ways in which he was disoriented by being unjustly treated, for the hero has lost his sense of purpose as a result of a series of misfortunes. The first occurred at university when he was unfairly failed by an English teacher because of his outspoken nationalism, thus giving his rival, who turned a deaf ear to the English teacher's insult of his country, an advantage. The second was his failing to obtain a scholarship abroad because of this unfortunate incident. But the most shattering was the third, when he lost his case against his rival. Although the author does not give any details of the case, the fact that it lasted for five years suggests that it was not clear-cut, and that the hero may have been justified in feeling persecuted. The feeling that, in standing up to defend his country when the other was cowardly and silent,[570] he was wronged while his rival was favoured, had a devastating effect on him. It turned him from being active and full of dreams and aspirations into a morose inactive man living on old memories and feeding on hatred, so that his intellectual powers are dissipated. The story includes a clear strand of social criticism which manifests itself through the contrast between the two radically different social lives the rivals lead, a contrast which is both effective and subtle, yet to the frustrated hero, who nourishes a deep sense of persecution, it is beyond endurance and continues to gnaw at him up to the last minute of his life.

Memories are not always a burden, for they can provide a haven from the tiresome monotony of life. In 'Ṭarīq al-Jāmi'ah'[571] the hero is shown to rejoice at an old memory in a manner that reinforces the impression that the author is preoccupied with the theme of under-achievement of the previous story. It is one of 'Ayyād's recurrent themes and the lasting effect of certain vivid memories is an important technical device and subsidiary theme. In several stories,[572] 'Ayyād demonstrates how his characters' potential is greater than their achievements and how they are unable, for mainly social reasons, to realise it. They manifest tremendous ability to endure poverty,[573] injustice,[574] distress[575] and deprivation[576] without losing their pride and dignity. Although 'Ayyād attributes importance to economic and social factors, he succeeds, with a few exceptions,[577] in controlling or eliminating the sentimental and pedagogic elements that lay emphasis on social themes. This is so not only because of his awareness of the limitation of his art and the demands of coherent structure, but also, and especially, because he gives the understanding through the story of human character and human relationships first priority.

Many of 'Ayyād's stories are elaborate and penetrating studies of various human types and relationships in which he endeavours to examine the effect of a certain character, relationship, or situation on the main character. He is fascinated by the effect of brief human encounters on the views or feelings of a man and tries to explore and understand the mechanism of such encounters. 'Al-Kawālīnī'[578] attempts to demonstrate that man's perception of, and relations with, others are often contingent upon various accidental events. It also suggests, through a study of the effects of a fortuitous event on the hero's experience in general and on his relationship with his sister in particular, that man's experience is always dynamic. The hero, who is full of love and admiration for his sister when he realises her strong resentment at having to stay behind a locked door, soon gets involved in finding a locksmith to open it. The events of the search for the locksmith are carefully orchestrated to disclose both his deep appreciation of the new dimensions in his sister's character that he has discovered and certain aspects of his own character. The search culminates in his finding a locksmith, an aloof reticent old man whose attempt to open the door involves a very dangerous jump to enter the flat and work on the door from there.

The locksmith's action, his attitude to life and to his work, and his explanation of why he risked this perilous jump fascinate the hero. So when, after the locksmith has opened the door and gone, the sister comments on the jump and insinuates perniciously that the old locksmith may be a burglar, the hero is not only shocked by the way she perceives the whole episode but also changes his perception of her. It is as if the contingent encounter with the locksmith's simple, yet deeply rich and humane, attitude to life sheds a new light on the scene so that the hero discovers the situation afresh; what he saw as resentment of confinement appears now to be sheer selfishness and panic. This recognition, in the Aristotelian sense, is carefully worked through a delicately balanced structure. The interaction between the hero and the locksmith is at one level of interpretation an interrelationship between two different character types and two contradictory attitudes to reality. The hero is a shy, hesitant and contemplative intellectual type, while the locksmith represents the spontaneity, simplicity and courage of an illiterate man who expresses his views and feelings through action. Despite the contrast, their feeling for each other is almost identical, for each is clearly aware that the other possesses what he lacks and admires the other's qualities. The relationship between these two contrary types represents a complete contrast to the relationship in 'Ghurūb al-Shams', not only because one is ephemeral and the other is permanent, but also because one has a positive effect on its participants while the other exerts a destructive influence over the hero. Yet both of them are means of exploring various aspects of human characters, and of examining the effect of certain experiences on the views and lives of two people.

The examination of a relationship is one of ʻAyyād's standard devices for exploring the human psyche, which he exploits in a subtle and allusive manner. In many stories it appears as if the relationship is the main theme or focal point of the story while it is, in fact, no more than a means to fathom the innermost depths of the protagonist.[579] 'Mīlād Jadīd'[580] uses the relationship between its hero and the clerk of the registry office to give the reader an insightful account of the hero's life and thought, as does 'al-Tha'r'[581] in its smooth and swift account of the partly imagined, yet absorbing, relationship between the hero and the belle of the beach. 'Al-Kūmīdī'[582] uses two relationships to present its study of a character torn between illusion and reality, while in 'Dostoevsky wa al-Sikkīr'[583] a relationship is invented deliberately, though not convincingly, when the natural course of events fails to provide one. In 'Jamāl'[584] the relationship becomes a manifestation of the heroine's deterioration as well as a means to understand the sources of her failure. In all these stories the relationship appears to be an interesting theme in itself, not only because of its richness and skilful presentation, but also because ʻAyyād conducts his skilful characterisation under the surface of the gradual development of the relationship that ostensibly occupies the centre of attention.

In 'Shakhṣ Wāḥid'[585] the development of the relationship between the hero and his future son-in-law ostensibly overshadows the main themes of the story: a study of the aspirations and anxieties of a self-made man and social criticism. The two themes are compressed beneath the surface events and ceremonies concerning the preparation for the marriage, so one may easily overlook them. ʻAyyād works out his main themes through a cluster of indirect hints, a description of contingent gestures, a casual mention of a certain mannerism, and the selective progression of the action. He eschews direct references to his main theme and often attempts to create a plot interesting enough to divert the attention of a superficial reader from the main theme. 'Shakhṣ Wāḥid' is a fine example of this technique, for it combines a number of Ayyād's recurrent themes with several of his favourite devices. In addition to the use of a developing relationship as a means of exploring the inner psyche, he uses, in parallel to the main characters, two sub-characters who serve to bring out certain qualities in the protagonist. He also focuses on one main character and directs the action and/or the interaction between him and various other sub-characters in such a way as to enrich the reader's understanding of him, and beneath its profound study of the protagonist's psyche it injects a stream of ideas of social criticism.

In this respect, 'Shakhṣ Wāḥid' is not a unique example, for most of 'Ayyād's stories are concerned with ideas of social criticism and demonstrate a certain moral forcefulness. Yet apart from a few works that display a clear concern for problems of poverty and social disparity,[586] his social critiques, though ubiquitous, are always interwoven into, and integral to, both the progression of the action and the characterisation; like most of his main themes, 'Ayyād keeps his social criticism submerged beneath the surface of the story. This is true of the attack on snobbery and bureaucracy in 'Milād Jadīd', the criticism of the double standards of morality that pervade middle-class social conventions in 'Bayt min al-Qashsh',[587] the probing of the roots of oppression and effects of certain norms of upbringing on people's lives and aspirations in 'Laylā',[588] and other social themes in 'al-Ghā'ib',[589] 'al-Nihayah'[590] and 'al-Kūmīdi'.

In most of 'Ayyād's works,[591] there is a dialectical relationship between man and his social surroundings, and the accentuation of this relationship results in the development of subtle social critiques – even in stories where this is not the main theme. His fiction is marked by a deep concern for the rights and freedom of the individual. The theme of freedom and the image of the prison recur in three stories – 'al-Kawālīni', 'Nuqṭat al-Bad''[592] and 'al-Sijn al-Kabīr'.[593] The latter draws on poetic symbolism in its representation of the subject. The story conceives of life as a huge prison with invisible bars made of frustrated hopes, old memories, wasted efforts and miserable conditions. In other words, all the factors that hinder the individual's fulfilment become part of the writer's concept of prison in this story. In all three stories, 'Ayyād's treatment of the theme of freedom mirrors his approach to his main themes and social criticism mentioned above, for he does not place any of his protagonists in prison or any form of intentional confinement, but rather, draws attention to their uneasiness when they are accidentally shut off ('al-Kawālīni') and their discomfort when faced with closed doors ('Nuqṭat al-Bad''), or uses symbolism ('al-Sijn al-Kabīr).

Apart from this rather negative representation of the individual's encounter with 'other people', 'Ayyād develops, in some stories, a unique dialectical relationship between individuals, a relationship that is both intense and idiosyncratic, and that is mysteriously associated with death and, at the same time, the will to live, for life in these stories is largely dependent on the individual's determination to survive. 'Nuqṭat al-Bad'' presents a peculiar relationship between a young reporter and an ageing social reformer. The two characters are complete opposites – in age, appearance, attitudes and temperament – yet they are attached to each other, not only because the losses of one are the gains of the other, but also because 'Ayyād develops between them an ambiguous relationship that mirrors the mutual attraction of hunter and prey; a struggle between the will to live and a suicidal tendency. Ironically, the sick and ageing man is the hunter in this story; it is he who expresses a strong wish to live and, furthermore, the desire to derive his strength from, and flourish at the expense of, the young man. Thus, the recovery of the sick old man corresponds to the suicide of the younger one and, despite the lack of any direct connection between the two events, provides the relationship between the two men with a fatalistic touch. Variations on the theme of death juxtaposed with and developed alongside the will to live are also found in 'Ghurūb al-Shams', 'al-Nihayah' and 'al-Mi'addiyyah'.

'Ayyād's concern for the freedom of the individual manifests itself also in the way he conducts the dialectical relationship between man and his social surroundings and between him and others. Although man in 'Ayyād's world is definitely social, even societal, the relationship between the individual and others is not always a pleasant or positive one. It appears as if 'Ayyād, himself a lone individual, sees the others – the vague mass of others outside one's direct contacts – as hostile to the individual: or, as Jean-Paul Sartre puts it, hell is others, they are the private hell of anyone who wants to enjoy a moment of innocent fulfilment and satisfaction ('al-Tha'ābīn')[594] or to get away with a stolen comfort which he does not deserve ('al-Nihāyah'). They even appear to be one of the sources of the individual's misery, and stand between him and a moment of happiness which he has truly earned ('Ḥafnat Balaḥ').[595] Yet 'Ayyād's treatment and conception of the known others – the others with whom one engages in various forms of relationship – are clearly different. They become not only an essential part of the individual's life, but also the means through which he expresses himself, and manifests his abilities, feelings and thought.

'Ghurūb al-Shams', discussed above, presents another unique relationship between two characters, in which the two themes of death and the will to survive are developed. And 'al-Nihāya' blends the theme of death with that of social criticism in its development of the unique crossed destinies of two remotely linked characters. The story attempts to cover a long stretch of time, starting from the boyhood of one of its two characters to his manhood, in order to present the vicissitudes of the characters and to illustrate how the destinies of the two characters cross at various points, so linking them together despite the lack of any direct connection. The relationship between the two ends with the death of the old man. In 'al-Mi'addiyyah'[596] the destined death is linked to the unconscious urge to live, thus giving the relationship between the villagers a metaphysical dimension. In other stories also, 'Ayyād develops some unique relationships without associating them with physical death, but which are nevertheless associated with a metaphorical form of death: death of hope ('Jamāl'), values ('Aḥlām')[597], memories ('al-Qiṭṭ'[598] and 'al-Tha'r') or illusion ('Ṣadīq Qadīm'[599] and 'al-Mustaḥimmah').

A corollary of these peculiar dialectical relationships is a certain interest in unique and unforgettable memories, or formative events, in the life of the individual. 'Laylā', for example, depicts the moment in which a boy overhears his parents making love in the darkness of the room where he is sleeping, an experience with multiple ramifications for many boys. Similarly, 'Ṣadīq Qadīm' describes the semi-illusory relationship that develops between a pupil and the family in the French textbook he is studying. The memory of this experience remains vivid in the character's mind long after leaving school, in part because it is related to his struggle to learn a foreign language, but also because it draws his attention to the contradiction between his simple, even dull, present and the ideal dreamworld of the extravagantly stylish life of the family in the textbook. To underline the effect of this memory on the hero,[600] the story perpetuates the illusory aspect of the memory and gives it a realistic dimension, so turning the illusion into a cage, and finally, in a startling denouement, locking the hero inside the cage.

'Ayyād's skilful use of the denouement in this story is, indeed, an integral part of his mastery of technique, for he understands not only the importance of a coherent structure but also the dialectical relationship between form and content. So many of the technical devices that he employs are closely linked to his themes and characters. The importance of memories in his world is associated with various technical characteristics, such as the distinct use of the preamble in a manner that integrates it in the overall structure of the story. Rather than prefatory unfunctional introductions, ʿAyyād's preambles constitute a major part of the story's structure and are aimed at creating a degree of distance between the memorable event and the present, so that the past events are not completely isolated from the present but are seen through a new perspective and through their interaction with the present.[601] On some occasions, the preamble necessitates an epilogue, without which it might seem redundant.[602] These epilogues are further evidence of the author's awareness of the importance of integrating the preamble into the story's structure.

ʿAyyād is one of the very few Egyptian short story writers to appreciate, and understand the limits of, the importance of integrating the preamble into the overall structure of the story. Unlike Ḥaqqī and Idrīs, who eliminated it altogether, ʿAyyād uses the preamble to balance the structure of the story and broaden its implications, and also to neutralise the sentimental and exaggerated aspects of an action,[603] to heighten the plausibility of a certain character type,[604] or to create a contrast between the character's intentions and achievements.[605] He also uses it for addressing the reader directly in the second-person narrative, though unlike Lāshīn, who engaged in direct conversation with his reader in order to create an element of humour, ʿAyyād speaks to his reader for two different reasons: to distance the reader from the story,[606] and to involve him in its events.[607] The former is an attempt to alienate the reader from the story, to prevent him from identifying with the characters or action, and to make him respond to it in a cool and detached manner; while the latter aims at engaging the reader in the story, so that his critical faculties are suspended and his reason approached by way of his emotions.

Another technique associated with the theme of memory is the use of the first-person narrative, which is, in many cases, inserted into the familiar third-person framework. ʿAyyād tells many of his stories through a sub-character, rather than the protagonist, as if endeavouring to demonstrate that he is interested in maintaining the objectivity of the story and in adopting the viewpoint of the common man.[608] However, when attempting to accentuate the contradictions between the hero's conception of reality and reality itself, he allows the hero to narrate his own story, though on such occasions he uses the device of the naive narrator whose simplicity leads him to persist in his illusory interpretation of events,[609] or of a structural irony that aims at sustaining duplicity of meaning.[610] In a few cases, he attempts to put the first person narrative in the form of a casual disconnected chain of thought and memories, without stepping into the quicksand of the stream of consciousness technique, as he is ever anxious not to turn inwards, but to involve the reader in the narrative process.[611] This is so not only because he wants to avoid any trace of subjectivity, but also because he is concerned about involving his character in the social scene rather than withdrawing him from it. However, it is noteworthy that the number of stories narrated in the first person was relatively small in his second collection.

The subsequent reduction in his use of this technique may result from his endeavour to affirm his faithfulness to a close relationship with reality in the face of the rise of subjectivity and the withdrawal from reality associated with contemporary changes in artistic sensibility. 'Ayyād is keen to create in his work a powerful illusion of reality, without, of course, descending into a photographic imitation of life, for he is clearly aware of the radical difference between photographic imitation and artistic mimesis.[612] In his attempt to create this illusion of reality, he uses initials of names, streets, cities, institutions,[613] as though unable to disclose the full names of these characters and places because of their realistic implications in the real world, which was a standard device in the early phases of the Egyptian short story.[614] Although he tried to break new ground, both in theme and form, his debt to his predecessors goes beyond the adoption of one technical device. Apart from rewriting one of Maḥmūd Taymūr's early stories[615] in 'al-Ghā'ib', he displays, both in his brief introduction to *Mīlād Jadīd* and in his subtle, yet recurrent, attacks on strident sentimentality, clear awareness of various strands in the Egyptian short story.

However, despite his use of various techniques to create closer ties with reality, 'Ayyād also tries in a few stories to use symbolic techniques and to create modern myths. Yet even in these stories he still accentuates the social implications. Unlike 'al-Nās wa'l-'Uyūn',[616] it would be difficult to appreciate either 'al-Sijn al-Kabīr' or 'al-

Mustaḥimmah' without their social and political allusions. 'Ayyād's symbolic works, and indeed most of his other works, are characterised by a skilful use of language. He understands the nature and limitations of the language of fiction and, particularly in his explicitly symbolic stories, uses words to their full poetic value. This is partly because as a literary critic he is versed in the linguistic dimension, but also because he endeavours to develop an interaction between the rhythm and structure of the sentence and of the story. Although he uses both *fuṣḥā* (classical Arabic) and vernacular in his dialogue, he is aware in both that dialogue as well as narrative is a means of characterisation. And because the exploration of the psyche is one of his main concerns, he pays close attention to characterisation. His works, in many ways, represent a continuation and development of the achievements of his predecessors and, unlike al-Badawī, he sensed the time when his particular artistic talents had become inappropriate. When radical change in artistic sensibility overpowered the views and visions of his generation, he did not persist with old themes and techniques. As a critic he refrained from investigating the new changes, stood aloof from those who expressed the modern sensibility, and withdrew into the ivory tower of academia. This perhaps explains why his fine achievements in the field of the Egyptian short story are often overlooked and his accomplishments consistently underestimated.

Abū'l-Ma'ātī Abū'l-Najā: The Lost Generation and the Emergence of a New Hero

The second group of writers whose work was overshadowed by Idrīs's achievements consists of writers slightly younger than himself. Although a few began publishing at the same time as, or even before, Idrīs, most made their debuts after Idrīs had already established himself as a literary celebrity. So it was natural that many of them began to follow in his footsteps and that some should fall into the trap of slavishly imitating the language, techniques and, more importantly, the views and character types of the master. Ironically, this imitation placed the work of some writers in the limelight for a while, and thus encouraged them to continue with their reproductions of Idrīs's early work, while the writer himself was gradually, but steadily, moving away from this phase and exploring new frontiers. However, their imitation was not completely negative, for it emphasised the nature of Idrīs's achievements and created a fecund and powerful stream of realistic short stories in the field of modern Arabic literature, which was significant not only because it tipped the balance in favour of the realistic trend, once it had gained a momentum of its own, but produced, beside the mediocre works, many original and important short stories.

Although some of these writers were particularly indebted to Idrīs, many drew upon the wider tradition of the Egyptian short story and specifically the realistic trend within it. One can detect in their work a desire to both emulate and build on the accomplishments of their illustrious predecessors. The writers of this group are too numerous to recount here, but a brief list of the most important representatives, especially those who succeeded in collecting their works in book form, would include: ʻAbd Allāh al-Tukhī (1926–2000),[617] Badr Nash'at (b. 1927),[618] Fahmī Ḥusayn (1928–98),[619] Sulaymān Fayyāḍ (b. 1929),[620] Fārūq Munīb (1929–97),[621] Ṣāliḥ Mursī (1929–99),[622] Fatḥī Zakī (b. 1930–89),[623] Aḥmad Nūḥ (1930–2001),[624] Fatḥī Hāshim (b. 1930),[625] Abū'l-Maʻātī Abū'l-Najā (b. 1931), Ṣabrī Mūsā (b. 1932),[626] Maḥfūẓ ʻAbd al-Raḥmān (b. 1933),[627] Sayyid Jād (b. 1934),[628] Raʻfat Salīm (b. 1934)[629] and others.[630]

Most of these writers were born between 1929 and 1934, and so underwent much of their cultural formation after the Second World War and the Palestine disaster of 1948. They shared more experiences and were more conscious of possessing a shared purpose than the groups that preceded them, a fact which gives them a certain coherence – without denying any of the salient traits of each writer. Their large number is in itself evidence that the short story as a literary genre was becoming popular amongst writers and was acquiring a wider base. These five years (1929–34) produced in effect more short story writers than any previous five-year period, and the fact that the literary market was able to assimilate their work, and that the literary movement succeeded in accommodating their activities in the cultural scene, is in itself further proof of at least a quantitative development in the field. The size of the group and the quantity of their output helped both to popularise the short story as a literary genre, amongst writers and readers, and to familiarise the reading public with its conventions and new techniques.

It is noteworthy that, unlike many of their predecessors, who had a reasonable understanding of foreign languages and literatures and even demonstrated this by translating various literary works at the beginning of their careers, this large group of writers is distinguished by its lack of command of any foreign language. Yet this did not stop them from acquiring some knowledge of foreign literature. Their works betray a reasonable degree of familiarity with Western literature, which they read in translation, for by the time of their cultural formation a number of good Egyptian short stories and also adequate translations of European short stories were available. But the body of material available in Arabic alone, no matter how ample, still had obvious limitations, so their complete dependence on it led to a cultural under-nourishment and the mediocrity and repetitiveness that prevailed in the works of some. Although they derived knowledge and understanding of literature from the sources available in Arabic, their literary knowledge and their ability to avail themselves of it varied considerably. Some[631] were widely read, despite the limiting dependence on one language, and digested their reading in a manner that served their creative work well, while others[632] contented themselves with knowledge of the local literature in general, and Idrīs's oeuvre in particular. Although the work of this second category did not contribute to the advancement of the literary genre, it was not to no avail, for it helped to popularise the achievements of the Egyptian short story and accentuate the accomplishments of Idrīs in this field. That such writing should thrive demonstrated the sterility of the dwindling romantic trend, for although many among this group had read a sufficient number of romantic works and were influenced by some of their characteristics, none of them endeavoured to reproduce them. A few of their works may fall into the category of the romantic short story,[633] yet this is not in any way due to a conscious attempt to write romantic works, but to the general misunderstanding that surrounded the definition of the romantic short story.

However, the more talented writers of this group succeeded in not only assimilating the achievements of previous realistic writers, but also advancing and enriching the realistic short story. They learned from Ḥaqqī's contemplative power, al-Badawī's tragic vision and Idrīs's poetic sensitivity to further their predecessors' achievements and to present them to a wider reading public. Although they did not lack originality, none of them became an instant celebrity like Idrīs, and several of them fell victim to the change in artistic sensibility, which was subtly taking place during the period in which they entered into literary life. Yet a few succeeded in capturing the rhythm of this changing sensibility[634] and participated in the shaping of its major characteristics, especially in their later works.

Abū'l-Ma'āṭī Abū'l-Najā is one of the most talented of this group. Unusually, he had a traditional education, obtaining the Azharite Certificate of Secondary Education in 1952. He then went to Dār al-'Ulūm in Cairo University, from which he graduated in 1956. The significance of this educational career is two-fold, for it gives an insight into the author's cultural background and also indicates how the new literary genre, which started as a revolt against tradition, was not only becoming a major part of the literary tradition but was also finding its way into the stronghold of traditionalism. Abū'l-Najā's interest in the short story was not connected to his arrival at Dār al-'Ulūm in Cairo, a faculty which stands at the crossroads of modernity and tradition, for he had published several stories in one of the leading monthly reviews of the time[635] while still a student at the Zaqāzīq Azharite Institute;[636] in other words, his education was exclusively traditional and conservative.[637] Although he did not include any of these early works in his first collection, *Fatāh fī'l-Madīnah* (1960), the fact that he wrote stories acceptable for publication in a leading monthly magazine is significant as it proves that the new sensibility, which since the turn of the century had endeavoured to develop a distinguishable mode of discourse outside and, in some ways in opposition to, traditional literature, had now established its dominance beyond any doubt.

The emergence of Abū'l-Najā, Fayyāḍ (whose education is completely Azharite from start to finish) and others from the heart of the Azhar, and their significant contribution to the development of the short story is culturally indicative of the major shift in education, outlook and 'worldview' among some of the previously traditionalists. Yet Abū'l-Najā's writings are still representative of the significant characteristics and achievements of the group. After his first collection, he published *al-Ibtisāmah al-Ghāmiḍah* (1963), and *al-Nās wa'l-Ḥubb* (1966), in which he continued to develop and mature. For Abū'l-Najā is, indeed, one of the few writers of this group to continue to develop their techniques and to widen their thematic world, and moreover to express some of the burning issues of the late fifties and early sixties. Like many of his predecessors, he divides his interest between villagers and city-dwellers, though the middle-class urban characters have the lion's share of his concern. Yet in both his rural and urban stories he develops new themes, and, in a few stories, approaches many of his predecessors' favourite themes from a new perspective. Like many good writers, Abū'l-Najā's central themes are inseparable from his major techniques. Thus his fascination with the complex relationship between the individual and the group is closely linked to the emergence of a new collective hero and the development of techniques to shape and express the various facets of this hero. While aspects of the relationship between the group and the individual are portrayed by Idris, Abū'l-Najā's intensive and comprehensive investigation of the theme overshadows any other treatment of it, for he deals with it in over half his stories and, despite some common features, endeavours each time to approach it from a fresh perspective.

There is also a distinct difference between Abū'l-Najā's treatment of this complex theme and all prior attempts. With few exceptions, previous investigations conceived of a conflict between the individual and society, or between the individual and a vague group of people representing certain societal characteristics, reactions or attitudes; the conflict, or rather the interaction, in Abū'l-Najā's work is between the individual and the group as a specific collective. The group in his works is not an ambiguous societal entity but a collective hero, a distinct entity with specific social and psychological characteristics and with a collective reason that operates as if it is a singular mind. So the logic and rules of the relationship between the two in Abū'l-Najā's work are little different from those of a relationship between two wills, two individuals. To portray the group operating as a single-minded individual, Abū'l-Najā has to develop a set of technical devices to enable him to illustrate the singular will of the group without obliterating its collectiveness or cancelling its social and political implications. So the group is conceived of artistically, from the viewpoint of the individual concerned, as a second person singular, and, from the author's standpoint, as a collective and definitely societal entity, with which the readers easily identify.

It is indeed rather striking that in most of the stories the reader is invited, even persuaded, to identify with the group and not with the individual, even in cases where the group is clearly lampooned; for disparagement of the group is intended less to eulogise the individual with which it interacts than to give the reader a shock of realisation and an insight into his own conduct or attitudes, whence the relevance of the techniques and devices aimed at portraying the group in this manner. However, Abū'l-Najā's perception of the group undergoes certain changes, for in *Fatāh fi'l-Madīnah* the emphasis is on the portrayal of the group as a major new hero, worthy of being introduced into the realm of fiction. In 'Fi'l-Ṭābūr'[638] he depicts three different queues in an elaborate manner so as to distinguish their social, cultural and psychological characteristics. Apart from minor skirmishes between the major queue and the other two, there is no real interaction between them, yet each queue – that is to say group – emerges with very distinct individual characteristics and with its own logic and perceptions of the other queues. Although the story frequently zooms in on certain individuals, especially in the major queue, it always relates them to the queue, and never fails to return to the totality of the queue before moving to the next individual. Moreover, the glimpses of individuals are not intended to give a full or partial image of them, but to draw a general image of the group into which the individual is integrated.

'Tajribah Ma' al-Mawt'[639] and 'al-Ākharūn'[640] are both concerned with the process of the individual's integration into the group, or rather with how the group assimilates the individual into its all-embracing character. They investigate how the group absorbs the individual as well as how it changes his personality and provides him with a new vision and power. The fact that these stories are infused with patriotic fervour (they take place during the Suez War and ostensibly deal with popular resistance to the tripartite aggression) is subsidiary to the main theme of integration. Or perhaps the two themes interact so that each reinforces the other and widens its implication. Whatever the interpretation may be, the concord between the two themes is a strong one indeed, for one provides the framework in which the other can manifest itself in the most plausible manner. However, the theme of integration is the more prevalent in Abū'l-Najā's work, for it appears in several other stories, both in the first collection and in the two that followed.

At the same time, the first collection also presents, in embryonic form, the conflict between the individual and the group in 'Khurūj 'an al-Mawḍū''.[641] The story can be seen as an investigation into the group's dominance over the individual while, on another level, it explores certain aspects of the complex relationship between them, for it accentuates the elements of similarity between the individual and the group as well as the illusion that alienates him from it and triggers the confrontation between the two. When confrontation becomes the focus of the writer's concern in the second collection, the stories attempt not only to explore various aspects of the encounter but also to present a wide variety of groups, or a group playing various roles. But regardless of the role or the nature of the group, once the confrontation takes place, the situation is conditioned by, or rather moves to, a forgone conclusion – that is, the supremacy of the group's will over that of the individual. Even if the outcome of the situation is, ostensibly, completely dependent on the conduct of the individual,[642] the action is described in a manner that underlines the impact of the group and its role in providing the individual with both the energy and sense of direction to achieve the results it wants.

'Al-Sibāq'[643] uses the typically solitary activity of a swimming race to explore two main themes: the role of the group in individual achievement and the concept of the hero, the winner, the sports celebrity. It suggests that the group is not only the individual's major source of inspiration, without whose vindication and encouragement he will lose both his sense of purpose and his incentive to win, but also an active participant in what appears to be an individual accomplishment. Thus it presents a new vision of individual heroism, a vision that does not deny the significant role of personal achievement, yet attributes the athlete's second wind, which plays the decisive role in his win, completely to the group: the victory at the end of the race is attained by the group through the individual, hence the swimmer passes out at the finishing line, leaving the crowd to celebrate the victory alone, for it is a victory of their own making. The story continues after the victory to explain, redundantly, what has been effectively conveyed through the progression of its action; but regardless of this explanatory tag, the story also touches upon the love–hate relationship between the individual and the group, a theme hinted at in 'Fi'l-Ṭābūr'. This relationship originates in the individual's awareness of the importance of the group and his anguish at the demands and high expectations placed on his shoulders by it. He is both pleased and dejected by these expectations, and so loves and fears testing his ability to accomplish them. Moreover, since the relationship is depicted as a struggle between two separate wills, the victory becomes less a vindication of his own personal ability and more a triumph of the group's will, thus intensifying the relationship.

The love–hate relationship between the individual and the group is the main theme of 'Ḥaqq'[644] and 'Nā'ib al-Ra'īs',[645] where the changing conduct of the individual alters the group's role and standing in a manner that stirs up conflicting feelings between them. In 'Nā'ib al-Ra'īs' the protagonist encourages the group to follow his example and give up smoking. The idea attracts many supporters, who form a society and elect him as chairman. During the early months, the members of the society play the role of disciples, spreading the word and elaborating on the individual's ideas; they become an extension of him, operating outside the realm of his person. Naturally they develop their own logic, impetus and momentum, so that when the chairman first contemplates smoking and proceeds to smoke again, the group becomes an obstacle blocking his way, an alien power imposing its will on him and constantly making sure that he is complying with its dictates. Yet the group subjugates the individual in the most subtle and persuasive manner, not by crudely enjoining him to obey, but by patiently weaving a net into which he is enticed, one whose meshes are made up of moral obligations and high expectations of illusory personal gain. In Abū'l-Najā's world there is no standard net; everyone has his own, suitable for no one else and adjusted to his own past, characteristics, ambitions, mannerisms and aspirations.

Therefore, the individual is not absolved from responsibility; he is clearly responsible for his own fall both as an individual and as the major component of the group. Responsibility in Abū'l-Najā's work is closely linked to freedom, and together they have political implications. 'Al-Ibtisāmah al-Ghāmiḍah'[646] is rich in political allusion, especially in the context of the Egyptian political situation at the time of its publication, 1962/3. It is a story of a confrontation between a conscientious and dedicated teacher and a class of young girls. The teacher runs his class in a prudent and resolute manner but he is too harsh, for he wants from his pupils nothing less than complete obedience and the utmost attention and he imposes extraordinary punishments on those who defy him. The class becomes orderly, but he continues to penalise those who commit the most trivial offences, until his conduct becomes intolerable. The headmistress fails to persuade him to change his stern approach, and so fear reigns in his class; but at the same time, those around begin to feel a sneaking admiration for the hard work and order he achieves.

One day a peculiar phenomenon appears in the class, a vague smile, almost imperceptible, yet highly infectious, which spreads over the silent expressionless young faces. It is not an open smile, which could be readily prohibited, yet its frequent recurrence annoys, even maddens, the teacher. For him it is a mockery of all his efforts to attain ultimate control over the class, to impose his will over the will of the group; it is an expression of rebellion and open defiance. Like any single-minded dictator, he reacts vigorously to this subtle, but effective, challenge to his authority, and attempts to detect its source and punish its perpetrators. The group's resistance intensifies in a crescendo of subtle, yet prudently orchestrated smiles, which appear simultaneously despite the ubiquitous mask of fear. The teacher begins to dismiss the girls who he thinks are responsible for the appearance of this smile. The class shrinks, but the smile remains. So the teacher starts to question his method, without abandoning it, and the next round of confrontation finds him at his weakest, for he has lost faith in his method and his self-confidence has gone and because the class has become too small to dismiss any more pupils without dissolving it completely and ending his role as a teacher – a form of suicide. The story finishes with his utter defeat, a defeat that drives him to the brink of madness. However, when he leaves the class a heavy despondence settles on the victorious group, which neither intended to drive him mad nor contemplated the possibility or the consequences of losing him.

The irony at the end of the story – a device used in several of Abū'l-Najā's stories – springs not only from the considerable discrepancies between intentions and results, but also from the huge misunderstanding, the unbridgeable gap, between the group and the individual. Although the author accentuates the responsibility of the individual in stirring up this conflict, he stops short of addressing the group's role in its development of this misunderstanding. The story contains a strong attack on the idea of the just dictator – a concept that has found some acceptance in modern Arabic thought – who is granted power to achieve the good of the people, while at the same time it calls for collective resistance to dictatorship and commends the common quest for freedom. This is not the only story in which Abū'l-Najā extols the group's search for freedom and its imaginative ability to create new channels for expression and to destroy arbitrary rules; 'al-Aslāk al-Shā'ikah',[647] 'Qaryat Umm Muḥammad'[648] and 'al-Ṣamt'[649] deal with one aspect or another of the theme of freedom, with obvious political implications, especially 'al-Aslāk al-Shā'ikah' and 'al-Ṣamt'.

Although 'Qaryat Umm Muḥammad' is a study of the psychology of the group and its operative inner mechanisms, it develops this study through its treatment of the manner in which the group creates its own heroes, myths and entertainment, and depicts all its events as reflected in the mirror of the most oppressed, though nevertheless important, section of the village – women. Yet, together with its sequel 'Ḥādithat al-Wābūr,'[650] it presents the transition from the glorified and infallible group to a new kind of collective, which is hypocritical, naive and, for the first time, inferior to the individual. The new group not only betrays its hero, but also exhibits certain pragmatic tendencies; it is willing to sacrifice its hero and saviour in order to rid itself of the oppressive *hajjānah* (camel rider) and restore normality to village life. Although the author attributes each shameful act to a named individual, he is keen in each one of these ignominious events not only to present it through the eyes of the group but also to record the group's reaction to and comment on the event. Thus, at the end of the story, the betrayed hero seems superior to the group and, though empowered by it, he becomes, for the first time, removed from the group, a counter centre of power and respect. Ironically, the triumphant group, which creates, and even exaggerates, the heroic qualities of the individual in 'Ḥādithat al-Wābūr' and in many other stories, and feels that this hero, of its own making, is an extension of itself and expression of its dormant characteristics, begins in the sequel 'Qaryat Umm Muḥammad'[651] to exchange roles with the individual and appear as if trapped in a snare of its own making – such a swing in emphasis presents a change from one simplistic political outlook to another or greater artistic objectivity

'Al-'Ankabūt'[652] is another of these stories devoted to the study of Abū'l-Najā's new hero, the group. It combines its study with a sharp attack on the group's mentality and the psychology of the crowd through an investigation of how a corrupt individual reigns over the group, manipulates it, establishes his grip over it and imprisons it in a web of complex lies, subtle blackmail and a general atmosphere of fear and intimidation. The story depicts a successor to the pragmatic group of 'Qaryat Umm Muḥammad', with all its passive characteristics intensified, an urban middle-class group of cowardly, selfish officials who collaborate in perpetuating the status quo. The story employs one of Abū'l-Najā's standard techniques, the gradual exploration of the individual and the group through the development of a conflicting relationship between them. It presents a group of civil servants walking into the web created by the protagonist, who is one of their colleagues. Unlike the teacher in 'al-Ibtisāmah al-Ghāmiḍah', the individual here has abandoned the pretence that he is controlling the group for its own good, and needs no pretext at all; everyone in the group knows their colleague's ill nature and suffers from the atrocities he perpetrates. Deriving his power from their weaknesses, the notorious individual is capable of dominating the group because he succeeds in dismantling it and dealing with each member as an isolated individual who has arrived at the conclusion that it is safer to avoid his evil actions and turn a blind eye than to challenge him.

The political implications of the story are clear, but what is interesting is the change in the author's attitude between 'al-Ibtisāmah al-Ghāmiḍah' and 'al-'Ankabūt' towards both the group and the individual. Abū'l-Najā gradually strips the individual of heroism, respect and even a reasonable justification for his confrontation with the group, so that, vulnerable as he is, it seems inevitable that he will be the loser in his encounter with the group. His subsequent victory therefore says more about the group than anything else. The group, at this stage, stands condemned, for it is unable to face up to the atrocities of a fragile individual and is severely humiliated. Naturally, the change in the nature of the individual and the group's response to his conduct is reflected in the nature of the relationship between them; instead of the conflicting wills and the love–hate relationship, the link between them is now marked with a higher degree of indifference ('al-'Ankabūt') or even by pure hatred ('al-Nās wa'l-Ḥubb'[653] and 'Dhirā'ān').[654] The individual who was full of respect for, and fear of, the group ('al-Sibāq' and 'al-Ākharūn') becomes almost scornful and disparaging ('al-'Awdah min al-Manfā').[655]

The change in the nature of the individual, the group and the relationship between them does not affect the author's artistic presentation of the group as a new hero, though it reflects a clear shift in his perception of the group and marks a further development in his perception of his role as a writer, from expressing reality to being a provocative herald of change. The situation in his later works is portrayed as if it is a part of a transient nightmare (a technique mastered by Idrīs), so unbearable that it makes a radical change seem inevitable. Unlike Idrīs, the change Abū'l-Najā envisages is not so much social as spiritual, for it is aimed at saving not the body but the soul. In all his stories that deal with aspects of the conflict between the individual and the group, the issue is never physical survival but always of great moral importance. Even in the story 'Ḥaqq', where the conflict has a strong economic theme, the author emphasises the moral aspects of the conflict more than its material implications. This does not imply that Abū'l-Najā pays little attention to social issues; questions of social polarisation and disparity are predominant. 'Ḥāris al-Maqbarah'[656] focuses on the problems of poverty in the village and attacks certain unjust social conventions. The story demonstrates the additional difficulties moral obligations inflict on the poor and views one's obligations to the needy as more important than those imposed by taboos and decayed conventions. 'Al-Raḥīl'[657] also centres on social disparity and combines its treatment of the issue with themes of alienation. It shows the connection between poverty and various forms of alienation, loss of security, and the destruction of hope for the future. Unlike 'Ayyād, who is concerned with the effect of social inequality on the human psyche, Abū'l-Najā attempts to show the effect of poverty on the individual's physical existence, his daily conduct, his attitude to taboos and conventions and his perception of the future. The exchange of roles that takes place at the end of 'al-Raḥīl' illustrates not only the gloomy, almost blocked, path into the future, but also shows how poverty penetrates the individual, leaving him alienated from his surroundings and from the real path to salvation.

Abū'l-Najā also treats some of the favourite themes of his predecessors: in 'Ziyārah' he deals with one of Idrīs's recurrent themes; the father's death and its consequences on the son. Like Idrīs, Abū'l-Najā focuses on the tremendous psychological effect the father's absence has on the son, involving not only loss of security and understanding but also the erosion of the son's world and disintegration of his reality. Although the son is capable of developing his own world, the loss of the father narrows it down and cuts him off from the old world of protection and family emotions. This loss is portrayed not only as an emotional blow but also as a hard form of baptism for maturity, since after the loss he is thrown into the midst of a new world. In 'Mamlakat Nabīl'[658] and 'Madd al-Baḥr'[659] he employs another of Idrīs's favourite themes, the world of children, with its unique feelings and dreams. Although Abū'l-Najā attempts in both stories to illustrate the love of a young lad for an older girl through the eyes of the boy, he incorporates in each story various other elements of the unique realm of boyhood. The contradiction between illusion and reality is one of the strong sub-themes in the stories, which widens the implications of the premature love story without shattering the tender atmosphere that envelops both episodes.

The contradiction between illusion and reality is also evident in another theme, inherited this time from al-Badawī: the anxieties and suffering of the artist. With 'al-Ṣadīq alladhi lā Yarḥam'[660] and 'Thalāth Rasā'il min Imra'ah Majhūlah',[661] in which Abū'l-Najā deals with the agony of writing and the suffering and anxieties of the writer, he chooses to end his second and third collections.[662] It is as if he is appealing to both readers and critics to appreciate the stories they have read not only on their own merits but also on the ground of the agony endured in the process of their creation. His keenness to present this plea demonstrates itself in the former story, which is more of a conversation piece than anything else; yet both works involve little more than mere persuasion. The former portrays the writer's search for the unattainable truth or conviction, while the latter, artistically more coherent, presents his struggle to continue writing and the sacrifices involved in this process. Apart from these stories, 'Liqā''[663] also has a writer as a central character, and although its main theme is the perpetual dialectic between illusion and reality and the death of ideals, it also touches upon the agony of creative writing and the problems of the writer.

Abū'l-Najā also draws on the technical advances of his predecessors; in this he is truly the product of the maturity of the Egyptian short story. He is a sensitive observer, who is capable of noticing minute details that escape the eye because of their subtlety or familiarity, and recording them in the most meaningful manner.[664] He succeeds in presenting the complexity of a human situation, not through speculation but by registering its suggestive manifestations. Like Haqqī, he is fond of contemplating certain aspects of character and situation in order to broaden their implications; but he understands that accurate observation may clash with the contemplative element, so he endeavours to maintain a delicate balance between the two. This balance guarantees wider implications without exceeding the limits of realistic representation, and necessitates a careful and skilful use of language. In this respect, Abū'l-Najā's linguistic abilities are beyond reproach, thanks to his years at the Azhar, for he manages to benefit from his traditional literary training without allowing the redundant aspects of convention to jeopardise modern expression in his writing. For an Azharite, his language is remarkably simple and poetic, free from heavy verbal decoration, and discloses an awareness of the limitations of the language of fiction.

Yet when it comes to dialogue, the effect of tradition is evident, especially in the early works in which he used *fuṣḥā* for dialogue.[665] Although he continued to employ both *fuṣḥā* and vernacular in dialogue, his later attempts to incorporate a *faṣīḥ* (literary) dialogue in the structure of the story are more successful and convincing.[666] The use of the *fuṣḥā* in dialogue performs an additional function, for apart from the standard participation in drawing the situation, making the action progress and developing characterisation, the *faṣīḥ* dialogue, especially in the stories relating to the theme of groups,[667] helps to alienate the action and create a nightmarish effect.[668] The slight artificiality of the language is one way in which the individual image, one may even say character, of the group, is created, because the unified language – a language which does not differ with the change in the cultural or social background of the speaker – consolidates the unity of the group's character. Abū'l-Najā is clearly aware of the role of dialogue in the development of convincing characterisation.

Indeed, characterisation is one of his major strengths, not only because he knows that narrative, description, action and dialogue are means of characterisation, but also because he succeeds in creating the unique group character discussed above, a collective character which draws various individuals together and moulds their features into a unique entity. The glimpses he offers of the different members of the group become the various traits and features that accumulate to construct the personality of the group. Thus, in addition to standard characterisation, which aims at creating a comprehensive picture of a certain individual, Abū'l-Najā creates a new form of characterisation that relies upon a cluster of characters, each incomplete in itself but integrated with the others to create a larger entity: this method of characterisation represents a significant contribution to the development of the Egyptian short story.[669]

Abū'l-Najā also has a fine command of structure. He pays close attention to the delicate balance between the various elements of the story. This balance becomes a major contributor to the theme, for he succeeds in integrating his theme in each component part of the overall structure of the story. Consequently, each element in the structure – the action, characters, setting and so on – is a restatement of the theme in a different way. The repetition of the theme in Abū'l-Najā's works is not a form of tautology but an outstanding structural quality aimed at consolidating its various aspects, widening their implications and providing several layers of meaning. As with many of his predecessors, form in Abū'l-Najā's work is intimately connected to the theme, and the relationship between them is a constant source of richness in his work. Indeed, Abū'l-Najā's writing, and that of the group of writers of whom he is representative, is both a product of the development of the Egyptian short story and at the same time a significant contribution to that development. Nevertheless, the work of this generation has been undervalued, both because it has been overshadowed by the works of Idrīs and because they were eclipsed by the works of the younger group of writers who grasped the spirit of change and gave expression to the modern sensibility. Thus Abū'l-Najā's generation is to some extent a lost generation, for it falls between two more powerful groups of writers; but the neglect that this lost generation has suffered as a result should not blind us to the significance and value of its achievements.

CHAPTER THREE

Romanticism and the Short Story

Romanticism, even more than realism, is a complex term, perhaps the most controversial of literary terms. While some scholars deny it any usefulness and argue that 'it has ceased to perform the function of a verbal sign',[1] others devote sizeable books[2] or lengthy papers[3] to demonstrating its importance and value. Many scholars of Arabic literature appear to use the term with no attempt to define its theoretical implications, thereby involving themselves in contradictory statements.[4] The ambiguity of the term, especially in connection with modern Arabic literature, makes a brief discussion of its meaning and the ideas and values associated with it essential if it is to be used as a means of classification in relation to the development of the Egyptian short story.

'Romanticism is not a unitary quality ... nor, of course, merely a verbal label. It is a historical category or, if one prefers the Kantian terms "a regulative idea", or, rather, a whole system of ideas.'[5] It is an approximate term, which does not intend 'to give exact and cogent definition of thought',[6] but confines itself to a more modest task: the attempt to trace the rise, dominance and disintegration of a system of ideas, artistic practices, convictions and norms. As such, it has some of the qualities of a period concept, and 'a period is not an ideal type or an abstract pattern or a series of class concepts, but a time selection, dominated by a whole system of norms, which no work of art will ever realise in its entirety.'[7] As a system of norms, its ideas and values are disseminated over many works and draw upon multiple sources. So, 'in a sense, Romanticism is the revival of something old, but it is a revival with a difference',[8] for its ideas were translated into terms acceptable to the sensibility of the period, and capable of satisfying its major requirements. Hence, it is both a cluster of associated qualities, which prevail in a large body of literary work over a certain period, and a product of objective factors dominant in that period.

The Rise of a Special Form of Romanticism

It is thus no coincidence that the rise and blossoming of romanticism in the Egyptian short story occurred in the 1930s and 1940s. This was the heyday of romanticism in modern Arabic poetry, when Aḥmad Zakī Abū Shādī (1892–1955), Ibrāhīm Nājī (1893–1953), ʻAlī Maḥmūd Taha (1902–49) and others ensured it was the dominant trend for a time.[9] Short story writers were bound to be influenced by the overwhelming current of romantic ideas. Nor is it surprising that romantic views appeared first in the works of Maḥmūd Taymūr and Muḥammad Amīn Ḥassūnah (1908–58), who were close friends of Nājī. Yet, unlike the Egyptian romantic poets, the short story writers were not necessarily conscious that they were producing romantic works. They did not endeavour, at least not knowingly, to publish fragments of romantic theory in their essays. Romanticism in Egyptian fiction knows no celebrant, no decisive landmark like the preface to *Hernani*; its rise was gradual and can be traced back to the early stage of modern narrative prose.[10] In the works of Jibrān, Maḥmūd Taymūr, Jumʻah, al-Manfalūṭī and al-Rāfiʻī the first signs of romanticism are discernible but diluted amid the attempt to reconcile the new with traditional conventions.

The development of these early romantic ideas into full-scale romanticism is the result of various objective factors, distinct from the mere increase of the early allusions to the romantic tradition in other European literatures, for a literary concept of such profound significance is not incorporated into a literature by straightforward importation but manifests itself in a form that fits in and resonates with the particular context. This reflects Wellek's view of romanticism: 'I do not deny differences between the various romantic movements, difference of emphasis and distribution of elements, differences in the pace of development, in the individualities of the great writers.'[11] The individuality of each indigenous romantic movement is clearly linked to the specific objective factors that contributed to its development. Egyptian romanticism is therefore associated with many social and cultural factors dominant throughout the 1930s and 1940s, and also linked to previous historical contexts. The fact that the age of

Enlightenment in Egypt was weak and of short duration, that there was no leading rational bourgeoisie, created a propitious atmosphere for the rise of romanticism. Then came the dark and emotive gloom of the 1930s to provide favourable conditions for its development. The early attempts at industrialisation were too intermittent and did not capture people's imagination or set the tone for a new era. The awakening of a national identity and the consequent spread of patriotic fervour demanded an artistic expression able to gloss over differences and exaggerate the imagined unity of aims and feelings. Further, frustrated patriotism found clear expression in some kind of escapism, idealism and romantic expression in the arts.

On the cultural front, neoclassicism, especially in poetry, had already reached its zenith and in fact begun to decline. Realism seemed unable to catch the attention of the increasingly gloomy and frustrated reading public or to satisfy its thirst for escapist fiction that ends happily and makes no serious demand on the reader.

> Both the derivative, unoriginal Enlightenment, and the peculiarly rigid religious orthodoxies seemed unsatisfactory. Thus social and intellectual causes opened the way for a literature which was created mostly by unattached intellectuals ... who revolt against feudalism and middle-class ideals.[12]

These unattached intellectuals were aware of two contradictory facts: the reading public's need for light fiction, which provides an escape, a refuge, a pastime; and the absence from the Egyptian short story of elevation, mystery, idealism, sublimity and the unusual. They also noted the phenomenal success of al-Manfalūṭī's florid translations of French romantic fiction, and of many other romantic works translated into Arabic at that period.

It would have been ironic to have slavishly borrowed a cultural concept that

> was first and foremost a movement of liberation – liberation from religious tradition, from political absolutism, from a hierarchical social system, and from a universe conceived on the model of the exact sciences.[13]

But although the task of liberation was not accomplished, Egyptian romanticism, in general, played a considerable part. Of all the literary movements, romanticism was ironically the most influenced by its European counterparts; yet it succeeded in both maintaining its individuality and rooting its ideas, values and norms in Egyptian culture. Unlike European romanticism, it remained philosophically shallow, or at least made no philosophical claims or postulations. This lack of a clear philosophical dimension is responsible for, or perhaps the product of, its essentially non-progressive nature, which in turn eliminated the fierce struggle between various literary doctrines and allowed for their peaceful coexistence.

Egyptian, like European, romanticism is first and foremost a conceptual approach to art and reality. This is ironic since romantic theory was responsible for drawing the fine line between 'symbolism' and 'allegory' in the context of differentiating between two forms of a thematically significant imagery.

> The contrast is between a *concrete* approach to symbols which begins with images of actual things and works outward to ideas and propositions, and an *abstract* approach which begins with the idea and then tries to find a concrete image to represent it.[14]

Yet, in practice, many romantic works betray an approach that works from ideas outward, rather than from reality inwards, to ideas, in spite of Wordsworth's strong condemnation of such an approach: 'personification of abstract ideas ... is utterly rejected as ordinary device to elevate the style'.[15] Whatever the strength of the romantics' denial, 'the Romantic notions of spirit, mind and self are closely connected in pointing to the certainty that mere matter and mere physical event are reflections of prior absolute realities'.[16]

The conceptual approach to reality does not necessarily require a philosophical framework, for it can conceive of reality through a certain state of mind, especially when clouded by emotions; and this results in what Ruskin calls 'the pathetic fallacy'. However, Ruskin insists

> upon respecting the pathetic fallacy – that so far it is a fallacy it is always the sign of a morbid state of mind and of a comparatively weak one. Even in the most inspired

> prophet it is a sign of the incapacity of his human sight or thought to bear what has been revealed to it.[17]

Yet he classifies as inferior the writers who succumb to allowing their feelings to obscure their impressions of external things, as the category of 'reflective or perceptive' as against that of 'creative'.[18] In Egyptian romanticism, especially as expressed in the short story, the pathetic fallacy is a dominant feature, not only because of the shallowness of its philosophical background but also because it was in complete harmony with the system of ideas that made up the core of that romanticism.

The fact that Egyptian romanticism did not develop, particularly in its fictional form, out of a fierce and conscious struggle against rigid classical norms enfeebled its revolutionary nature and also its philosophical outlook. It thus lacks a coherent conception of the universe, time, history and man; nevertheless, it was not completely without norms and ideas. The attempt to deduce its system of ideas and to define the individual characteristics of its components is perhaps the most reasonable way to construct a theoretical framework of romanticism in the Egyptian short story, before we move to a practical study. These romantic ideas generally operate as an integral system, in spite of the changes in emphasis and manifestation; the limits and characteristics of each idea are discussed separately only for the sake of clarity and convenience. Moreover, the whole system cannot be found in a single work or even in the works of one writer, only extracted from an overall survey of romantic short stories or ideally from a consideration of romantic literature in general (although this cannot be attempted here). Romanticism in the Egyptian short story exchanged ideas and influences with other literary genres; however, the limitations of the present study dictate its being discussed in isolation from these genres.

The glorification of nature and the animation of its beauty is the first dominant idea in the romantic Egyptian short story, not only because this romantic notion struck a genuine chord in the Egyptian writer, with his deep-rooted affection for the land, but also because it served to strengthen the readers' patriotic fervour in the struggle for independence. The Egyptian romantic idea of nature mirrors the European tradition in this respect, for it attempts 'to draw from nature a continual lesson of life, of joy, of love'.[19] Like European romantics,

Egyptian short story writers endeavour to 'conceive of nature as an organic whole, ... a nature that is not divorced from aesthetic values'.[20] Their conception of nature is also characterised by its inference that the process of seeing and enjoying nature is as significant as the extraneous manifestations of the beauty of nature itself, for

> the capacity in the individual man to discern the beautiful and to introduce the sublime into the idea of nature'[21] is a very important factor – according to Kant, even more important than nature as a symbol of God's capacity.[22]

Moreover, 'nature described as Romantic is seen through a veil of associations and feelings extracted from poetry and literature in general',[23] which often amount to a means of rediscovery. These associations bring the artistic and creative process into play, for only through art is nature rediscovered, and the romantic view of nature is perceived 'as a language, as a concert of harmonies. The whole universe is conceived of as a system of symbols, correspondences, emblems, which at the same time is alive and pulsates rhythmically.'[24] This transcendental perception of nature is associated with two other romantic ideas: the first is the apocalyptic vision and spirituality; the second is the exultation of art in general and the artistic ego in particular. Romantic writers perceive the harmonious beauty of nature as a song of praise to the prime mover and listen to the voice of God in the tranquillity of life on the banks of the Nile. 'Nature is animated, alive, filled with God or the spirit of the world.'[25] The sublimation of nature includes a strong religious tone, which corresponds clearly to the deeply rooted religious sentiments of the Egyptians. In this respect, the Qur'an provides many writers with both the idea and the approach, for its many verses describing the beauty of nature, the harmony of the universe and the many abilities of man as manifestations of God's power are a ready and highly revered source upon which to draw.

The second idea, the exaltation of art and the artist, is both a reaction to the state of art and the status of the artist in Egyptian society and a product of the strong influence of European romanticism. The general perception of fictional writing was low, and to raise it the romantics associated creativity with the divine power, with inspiration and ivory towers. They saw the function of art as exploring those areas of the mind and universe that lie beyond the confines of rational thought and perception of the common man. The hero of romantic writings becomes the artist himself, who is both the explorer of this unknown realm and the priestly mediator between it and the reader. By raising the status of art, they were endeavouring to advance the cause of the artist, for 'art is the transcendent expression of the artist's ego'.[26] The artist's ego 'is distinguished ... by his inheritance of an intense sensibility and susceptibility to passion',[27] for although the artist (the poet) is according to Wordsworth 'a man speaking to men', he is a special calibre of man, a man

> endowed with more lively sensibility, more enthusiasm and tenderness, who has a greater knowledge of human nature, and a more comprehensive soul, than are supposed to be common among mankind'.[28]

The artist's ego is therefore unique but at the same time the Egyptian romantic, like Fichte, 'identifies the creative Ego with All; his pantheism supposes that nature's task is to reveal the potentiality of the ideal in the real'.[29]

Ironically, the attempt to establish stronger bonds between the creative Ego and the All is accompanied by an endeavour to underline the agony of the artist who is vouchsafed the power of penetrating the secrets of the universe but 'has to pay a heavy price in suffering, to risk his immortal soul and to be alone'.[30] This element of isolation clashes with the identification with the All; but the clash is somewhat illusory, for the identification takes place at a deeper level and through the most indirect of means: art. Through art the romantic writer communicates with both the All and external reality because art is 'knowledge of the deepest reality, of nature as a living whole'.[31] And the artist attains this knowledge because he is endowed with the power of imagination, with the ability, as Blake puts it,

> To see the World in a Grain of Sand
> And a Heaven in a Wild Flower,
> Hold Infinity in the palm of your hand
> And Eternity in an hour.

'Imagination is thus an organ of knowledge which transforms objects, sees through them.'[32] It is the power that

> reveals itself in the balance of reconcilement of opposite or discordant qualities: of sameness, with difference, of the general with the concrete; the idea with the image; the individual and the representative; the sense of novelty and freshness with old and familiar objects; a more than usual state of emotion with more than usual order; judgement ever awake and steady self-passion with enthusiasm and feeling profound or vehement; and while it blends and harmonises the natural and the artificial, still subordinates art to nature; the manner to the matter; and our admiration of the poet to our sympathy with the poetry.[33]

When this imaginative power is sparked off by passion 'the flame of the passions, communicated to the imagination, reveals to us, as with a flash of lighting, the inmost recesses of thought, and penetrates our whole being'.[34]

But when the passions overpower the imagination, as is the case with many Egyptian romantics, the imagination loses its reconciling and synthesising quality and becomes mere *fancy.* 'The fancy is indeed no other than a mode of memory emancipated from the order of time and space; ... the fancy must receive all its material ready made from the law of association.'[35] Naturally, fancy is inferior to imagination, not only because in it 'the poet's own psychological processes are often part of the theme',[36] but also because it is the gateway to sentimentality and one-dimensional views. Indeed, sentimentality is the common denominator of most romantic short story writers. Because sincere emotions have instant appeal, it is natural that many mediocre writers exaggerate the sentiments of their characters and situations in order to captivate and influence their readers. In the Egyptian short story, sentimentality mainly results from an inability to assimilate emotional responses and justify them within the internal laws and logic of the creative work.

Sentimentality also implies a disposition to prejudge reality; and the romantic notion of the writer's special power, which is not acquired through learning or experience but by being born an artist, encourages these preconceptions. The romantic writer does not begin with images of reality and work outwards to ideas and propositions, but the inverse: he starts with ideas and then tries to find images to represent them. His own thoughts are a form of revelation and are usually vindicated not by their similarity to external reality, but by their uniqueness and originality. Therefore, he records without distinction his private dreams, associations, ambitions and desires, for the correspondence is not to external reality, since a neutral reality, devoid of the feelings of the beholder, does not exist, but to a reality transcending the world of sense. The romantic writer does not seek to portray reality, but, as Carlyle proclaims, to 'penetrate into the sacred mystery of the universe' revealing the idea beneath appearances and the infinite behind the finite. He is, therefore, concerned with the ideal, the transcendent and the superhuman. This brings in another romantic notion, the concern for the supernatural, magic, myth and the occult. In drawing upon these realms, romantic writers 'dwelt upon uncommon traits, priding themselves on a catholicity of choice which could find heroic prototypes in every age without engaging their beliefs in the values of any one'.[37]

However, the romantic writer does not focus his world on the superhuman and the extraordinary, but uses them only to broaden the scope of one of his main ideas, the accentuation of the individual.

> The focus on the individual leads to speculation about the radical disjunction between the private man and the public society essentially indifferent to the ethical concerns of the individual ... this disjunction does not allow public rewards for virtue or castigation for vice, does not permit the assumption that the nature of the individual is eventually revealed in public or explicit terms.[38]

The realisation of this disjunction often involves an overabundance of fabricated dreams, which bring into the work a great deal of florid and, on rare occasions, apocalyptic elements. It also involves another romantic quality: the underestimation of convention, which 'appears to be the result of, may even be a part of, the tendency ... to think of the individual as ideally prior to his society'.[39] In the Egyptian short story, the romantic hero endeavours to convey his adversity to the present order as exemplified in external reality, for he

> has individual emotions, ideals, aspirations that cannot be adequately satisfied within the society in which he must operate. The character, developed with complexity and sympathy, finds no locus or representation in the larger

> world he seeks ... one in which the author also cannot find a locus for the character's ideals and aspirations.[40]

There is thus a pervasive air of sorrow and grief at the loss of the horizons that closed before the hero; yet in the bleakest moment of despair the romantic hero allows us a glimpse of his dream, with its new ethical scale superior to that of existing morality. The romantic hero, so sensitive to the horror of external reality 'remains true to a central Romantic tradition in abstaining from any attempt to alter the social order'.[41] The abstention from changing the social order is, perhaps, responsible for the fact that 'Romanticism was manifesting itself, intentionally or not, as a literature of escapism.'[42] In this context, the short story is used as a mode of discourse that facilitates departure from reality, yet, in so doing, it often elevates social ethics and introduces moral and spiritual absolutes.

But the romantic hero is no preacher and he prefers his own dreams to reality, achieving his salvation often through love or art, not as two means to a specific end, but as ultimate ends in themselves. Thus fulfilment in love or art is not conditional on the reciprocity of either the beloved or the audience, because the process is complete in itself within the hero. Unrequited love is as good as reciprocated love, if not better, and a rejected piece of art is no less successful than one accepted by the audience.

The lover experiences supreme joy not from what the beloved offers, but from the tranquillity and elevation that emotion so amply bestows. Egyptian romantic writers place the theme of love in the centre of their world for another reason, too: apart from its strong association with romantic moods, love in Egyptian society involves a challenge to the social order and has an undertone of rebellion against corrupt conventions. Like the lover, the artist also has to contend with the taboos of respectability and convention, so he also attains his sense of achievement not from the audience's response, but from the mystical satisfaction of communication with the ultimate spirit behind the visible, and from the feeling that through his art he is revealing the beauty concealed in both the human and the natural worlds. His creative imagination and passions provide him with the unique ability not only to uncover hidden beauty but also to add grace to familiar scenes and matters.

The romantic artist becomes so intoxicated with himself as a seeker of beauty that he can overlook the fact that 'the pursuit of beauty is much more dangerous nonsense than the pursuit of truth or goodness, because it affords a stronger temptation to the ego. Beauty, like truth and goodness, is a quality that may in one sense be predicated of all great art, but the deliberate attempt to beautify can, in itself, only weaken the creative energy.'[43]

In his quest for beauty, the romantic Egyptian short story writer often overlooks design, order and the interrelationship of parts in the structure of his work, but he pays considerable attention to the representation in words of aesthetic qualities and shades of feeling. One can clearly hear in his rejoicing at finding a fine expression, echoes of Keats saying, 'I look upon fine phrases like a lover.' In describing his emotion and feelings, he shows a particular concern for verbal felicity, which can on occasions lead to florid and purely decorative prose.

Such are the most significant ideas that make up Egyptian romanticism as expressed in the short story; a romanticism that is not in any way a unitary quality, nor, of course, merely a verbal label. It is not a practical model with working distinctions that come to be thought of as forms; it is neither a term of praise or denigration, nor an attempt to draw arbitrary lines or to form inflexible moulds according to which works of fiction are to be shaped. All these features, and many other subsidiary ones, may be found in various forms and in varying degrees in the work of one writer, while few of them will appear in the work of another. And in addition to the qualities generally attributed to romanticism by its exponents, there are also other traits and qualities that were scorned by opponents of European romanticism, for it has some elements worthy of Goethe's definition of the romantic as sickly – the *Romantisch das Kranke.* Yet side by side with these elements is much that relates it to the great achievements of European romanticism, and earns for some of the works written in its spirit a place in the history of the Egyptian short story. However, in all its aspects and manifestations romanticism remains a conceptual approach to reality whose development took various forms and evolved along different lines.

The Shaping and Development of Romantic Sensibility

Because romantic qualities are not evenly distributed amongst writers or their works, and because of the abundance of romantic stories, it is possible to discern three categories. The first consists of the more serious romantic works, which endeavoured to shape and develop a romantic sensibility; the second the more commercial works, concerned with the popularisation of the short story amongst a wider reading public; and the third the works of what can be termed 'socialist romanticism', erroneously known as works of socialist 'realism'. In the first category one finds that the development of a romantic system of ideas is somehow inseparable from the development of the Egyptian short story in general, and of the realistic trend in particular, for works of this category belong to the development of both the form and the content of this new literary genre. They also aspire to widen the scope of the form and to root it in Egyptian cultural life. Because the aims of this category of romantic short story appear to be identical to those of the realistic story, it is natural that the two should overlap and that many writers wrote in both indiscriminately.

Maḥmūd Taymūr

It is appropriate to begin the discussion of this category with the stories of Maḥmūd Taymūr, not only because this will provide us with a good example of the overlapping of the two genres but also because his writing demonstrates the existence of romantic trends from the beginnings of the short story. By the early 1930s the faint romantic elements of the short stories of the 1920s became more pronounced, and a new tone gradually started to develop, accompanied by new moods, emphases and conventions. This process, though spread across the works of many writers,[44] is clearly exemplified in the work of Maḥmūd Taymūr, for his works underwent a significant change in the 1930s and 1940s, without completely abandoning the old pattern. In place of his endeavour to root the short story in the cultural and social reality of Egypt of the 1920s, and to use it as a means of depicting and penetrating the reality of the middle and lower strata of society, he turned his attention in the 1930s to refined, educated or eccentric characters. The didactic tone of the 1920s disappeared and the concern with portraying social defects faded. They were replaced by an attempt to indulge the reader with beautiful pastoral scenes, elevated passions and lofty identities. The problems of moral and social corruption, incompatible marriages and social disparity, which occupied a prominent place in the first five collections, vanished in order to make way for the emergence of new themes and, by implication, new techniques.

Although many of Taymūr's new themes and techniques fall into the category of the realistic short story,[45] some had a distinct romantic colouring. The theme of love plays an important role in this respect, for love in the collections of the 1930s and 1940s is the main pivot around which rotate subsidiary themes with strong romantic qualities. Love offers tranquillity, sublimates the soul ('Khalf al-Lithām')[46] and injects a sense of purpose and fulfilment into the character ('Ḥilm wa-Inqaḍā').[47] Hence the loss of love is associated with gloom and despair ('al-Musta'īn bi'l-Lah al-Kabtin Hardy'),[48] and even on occasions sparks off strong suicidal tendencies ('Jarīmat Ḥubb'[49] and 'Takfīr').[50] When committing suicide, the romantic hero seeks for a death that is worthy of both his romantic perception of his identity and his emotional sacrifice, a martyrdom for the cause of love ('al-Musta'īn bi'l-Lah ...').

Therefore love in many of Taymūr's stories is an ultimate aim and an integral part of the universal spirit ('Basmah al-Lubnāniyyah'[51] and 'Fī Khamīlat al-Ḥubb').[52] Music and poetry are related to love and nature rejoices every time new love is born ('Qaṣīdat Gharām'[53] and 'al-Ta'ir al-Ṭalīq').[54] The relationship is not one-directional, for music and poetry can spark off tender emotions and therefore help to create love ('Ibtisāmah'[55] and 'al-'Uyūn al-Khuḍr').[56] Love, which is filled with elevating elements and associated with these refined aspects of life, opens the lover's eyes to the beauty of nature and leads him to appreciate beauty and art. This sublime love, this fine nature of which no language but music is capable of expressing or communicating to the beloved, knows no social boundaries and is seen as superior to all forms of glory and power ('Fī Ẓulmāt al-Layl').[57] Thus the misconception of love as something secondary to authority or social status involves the destruction of love. The lover of 'Fī Ẓulmāt al-Layl' craves for power to attain his beloved princess, and in doing so overlooks an important factor; that love requires no vindication from outside its own sacred domain and that its brilliance outshines all the trappings of authority and social status.

Love in Taymūr's stories is a sublime, spiritual feeling in which lovers do not dare to touch each other, let alone embrace. In all his love stories there is scarcely a touch or a kiss, because as soon as sensual desire appears, the order and harmony of life become unbalanced and disturbed ('Zāmir al-Ḥayy').[58] Taymūr creates a sharp distinction between love as heavenly feelings and love as earthly carnal desires; one is blessed and constructive, the other damned and destructive. While love inspires the hero of 'Khalf al-Lithām' and refines the senses of the protagonists of 'Ḥilm wa-Inqaḍā' and 'al-'Uyūn al-Khuḍr', lust destroys the hero of 'Jarīmat Ḥubb' and the heroine of 'Najiyyah Bint al-Fiqī'[59] and leads the protagonist of 'Zāmir al-Ḥayy' to madness.[60]

The dichotomy between the emotional and sensual, the sublime and the earthly in male–female relationships is the main theme of 'Sarāb',[61] a story of the contradiction between love and lust, in which nature expresses its rapture or anger accordingly. On the one hand, the beloved is associated with light, tender breezes, flowers, mystic poetry, purity, elevation of the soul, beautiful and harmonious scenes of nature and spiritual tranquillity; on the other hand, the lustful rival of the lover is described literally as a wild boar, representing ugliness, cruelty, greed and every diabolical feeling. What outrages and baffles the hero is that the beloved, conceived of as a creature of light and tenderness and a symbol of beauty, actually enjoys giving herself to this loathsome creature. The wording of these scenes in Arabic is unusually coarse and inimical to the nature of artistic language (particularly because it is not internally justified) to a degree that suggests a lack of detachment on the part of the writer, if not his unconscious personal involvement in the scene.

The language of the narrative and the progression of the action have significant romantic implications. From the beginning of the story the author is keen to develop certain associations and to accentuate some fatalistic elements. The hero, the narrator of the story, does not like the suburban town of Ḥilwān, yet he finds himself mysteriously urged to drive there. When he reaches the town he is disoriented and nervous, and this makes him feel thirsty. As if directed, he walks into a shop to buy a drink. On approaching the counter a snoring lump of flesh, described as being 'in the shape of an ugly, diabolical boar',[62] catches his eye and he retreats, but as he turns to leave, a soft voice calls to him in French. The contradiction between the sight of the repulsive man and the beautiful girl emerging from behind him is so sharp, yet the association between them is also obvious. She offers the hero a cool soothing drink and sells him some sweets but, more importantly, she fires his imagination and he begins to construct his own image of her 'imagined identity'. It is purely imagined to the extent that he goes to a friend, who is a poet, and asks him to read him selections of mystic love poetry, which contributes to his idealisation of her.

This image, solely of his own making, becomes an independent factor in the development of the relationship, for once he has set his beloved on a pedestal, the association with her elevates and chastens his soul. Every day he finds himself driving to Ḥilwān, and the journey is described in terms of a pilgrimage.[63] Although the relationship does not advance beyond small talk, he is captivated by her every gesture and ruminates over every word she utters. He sees the time he spends with her as being 'as tranquil as a sweet dream' for, like many romantics, he associates dreams with happiness and prefers them to reality.[64] But one day he receives a devastating shock when, rushing to see her with inflamed passion, he finds her in the arms of the repulsive boar, happily returning his sensual embrace. The impact of the scene is so powerful that it not only shatters him but also destroys the whole town. When he looks behind him as he leaves, he sees Ḥilwān burning and exploding like a volcano.[65] The story is rich in romantic imagery and associations, particularly in its presentation of the radical disturbance of the universal balance, when the earthly unites with the heavenly.

Love in Taymūr's romantic works is ideally a sublime feeling free from any sensual elements, for when a carnal aspect is introduced into the relationship it becomes sinful. The chastity of love is a precondition for any emotional involvement in most of his love stories, for he links sex to sin ('al-Shaykh 'Afallah'), idiocy ("Abīṭ ... 'Abīṭ'),[66] ugliness ('Sarāb') and vulgarity ('al-Sajīnah'[67] and 'Man minnā al-Waghd?').[68] Moreover, when a lover falls into the sinful abyss of sex he is punished severely before the end of the story. The penalty is, in many cases, out of proportion to the error and constitutes an amalgam of divine decree,[69] social condemnation[70] and psychological suffering.[71] The fall of a relationship from the heaven of love into the chasm of sex outrages nature and all divine powers, which react by casting a spell on the sinful lover.

In the aftermath of events, when the hero is burdened with these psychological agonies and a sense of guilt, the recommended remedy, in many of Taymūr's stories, is to transcend suffering through art. According to Taymūr, great suffering is a suitable preparation for artistic creativity and qualifies the character for communion with the spirit of the universe. Creativity is a heavenly gift, and 'it is a common mistake to conceive of it as something which one can acquire like scientific knowledge'.[72] So it is often associated with the heavenly and divine, with the moon, the spaciousness and calmness of the desert and the tranquillity of beautiful gardens. Since creativity is divine, it is naturally linked to religion. In 'Kān fī Ghābir al-Zamān' creative art is seen as the ultimate form of worship.[73] Tāya, the hero of the story, is a great sculptor who provides the temple with magnificent statues, and is seen as the embodiment of the divine spirit, despite his frequent blasphemous remarks. His artistic gift places him above the common man, so that he is allowed many things denied to ordinary mortals. The officiant of the temple tolerates Tāya's heretical remarks because he considers his artistic work a form of worship superior to all the prayers of devout ordinary men or even low-ranking officiants. In 'Tāj min Waraq',[74] Taymūr urges us to believe that the happiness and fulfilment that the creative process offers to the artist outweigh all other pleasures obtained through money or authority, a theme that recurs in 'al-Bārūnah Umm-Aḥmad'[75] and 'Fī Ẓulmāt al-Layl'.

Indeed, Taymūr's treatment of the theme of art and the artist is clearly influenced by romantic concepts, for it not only associates art with worship, but also accentuates the ecstasy of creativity ('Ibnat Īzīs').[76] In 'Zāmir al-Ḥayy' Taymūr further develops the romantic theme of the relationship between art and suffering foreshadowed in the previous theme of art as redemption, for the artist does not acquire his unique power of penetrating the mystery of the universe through learning or experience but through great suffering. Suffering sharpens his sensitivity and deepens his insight, yet at the same time isolates him from his surroundings and alienates him from society. The creative Ego fails to establish strong affinities with the All, and is sometimes denied the simplest forms of gratitude ('Tamr Ḥinnah 'Ajab').[77] The artist is, however, too proud to bother about gratitude, considering himself above all forms of recognition, and he therefore feels contented within himself and does not expect any vindication or denunciation, praise or abjuration. When he does receive approbation and gratitude, he seems somewhat surprised ('al-Jazā'').[78]

The emergence of romantic themes in Taymūr's writing corresponds, as we have seen, to a shift in his social emphasis, in which he replaces the middle and lower classes who people his early works with elements of the aristocracy, a group of artists and intellectuals, and a handful of eccentric characters. The aristocrats who spend their summer in Lebanon or Europe telling interesting stories over their evening drinks provide him with a convenient opportunity to depict a variety of hackneyed romantic types. He associates high-level morality and humanistic tendencies with an upper-class sense of superiority and a desire to occupy the moral high ground, not only because the rich can afford to be kind and charitable, but also because their superiority envelops them in a glamorous romantic atmosphere ('al-Ṭifl wa'l-Muṣawwir',[79] 'al-Yatīmah',[80] 'Ṣuḥbat al-Ward'[81] and 'Dhāt Masā'').[82] They can afford to go to magnificent ('Basmah al-Lubnāniyyah') and exotic ('Ṣuḥbat al-Ward') places, allowing the reader a chance to appreciate the beauty of nature. The flat Nile Valley is beautiful indeed, as is the sunset on the ocean of calm desert at Heliopolis, but who, other than the rich, can take the reader to admire the splendid beauty of the Swiss mountains and lakes and glorious French beaches, or even the mountains of Lebanon? It seems that even the romantic admiration of nature in Taymūr's work is also hierarchical, and does not confine itself to the pastoral mode, which is easily accommodated in the Egyptian countryside.

The beauty of nature is one of the main themes in Taymūr's romantic works, where nature is a symbol of love, freedom and harmony. The story 'Ḥanīn'[83] focuses on the contradiction between the country and the city, a theme with obvious romantic connotations, expressing nostalgia for the past. The protagonist is a farmer who lives in complete accord with nature: animals and birds set the rhythm for life and provide him with a sense of harmony and purpose, but when he falls ill his son, a successful doctor in Cairo, takes him to the city. The association between ailment and the move to the city is both deliberate and revealing, and its meaning is enhanced when the cure for the protagonist's body is linked to the suffering of his soul. His son persuades him to remain in Cairo and abandon work on the farm because he is ageing, but overlooks the fact that the farm is not merely a work place for his father but a haven and a way of life, without which he is completely at a loss. His perception of his own 'imagined identity' is located in the village and housed in its milieu. As a result he fails to adjust to urban life, and his nostalgia for the village, its animals and trees, people and birds, drives him to escape its cage.[84]

Taymūr's glorification of nature manifests itself not only in the sharp contradiction between country and city but also in the animation of nature. The personification of nature provides its inanimate elements with a sublime spirit such that it becomes superior to man. In 'Fī Khamīlat al-Ḥubb' nature is endowed with human qualities and portrayed as full of music, hope and love, while man is blind to its beauty and harmony and, moreover, destroys it through his clumsiness and ruthlessness. The brief encounter between the rose and the breeze, and the love story between the rose and the butterfly, despite their naiveté, are described in a manner that suggests them to be superior to the sensual relationship between the man and his mistress in the same story. Nature is also portrayed as though it is aware of both its power and the contradiction between itself and man, for the story is told to the narrator by a nightingale which is kept in a cage as a pet – an additional indication of man's brutality and insensitivity to nature.

Another romantic feature associated with nature's awesomeness in Taymūr's world is the mystification of its power and beauty. In 'Ḥūriyyat al-Baḥr'[85] and "Indama Naḥya ma'a al-Aṭyāf'[86] nature is mysterious and mythical and man seems helpless before its strangely seductive power. Its call is irresistible and irrevocable and so becomes part of man's inexplicable destiny. In another story, 'Shabaḥ al-Ḥājj 'Alī',[87] the mystery of nature is reduced to mere superstition and the story fails to exploit the allusive potential of the numerous elements of nature touched upon in the narrative. But in general Taymūr is drawn to imaginary worlds and events, as his many mythical tales[88] and predilection for the era of the Pharaohs,[89] his animation and mystification of nature, clearly show. This relates to two other romantic features in his work: his interest in peopling his world with eccentric types and his endeavour to take ideas and concepts as a starting point.[90] The former provides a number of characters who are unique in the genre (such as the bohemian and quixotic heroes of 'al-Shaykh 'Ulwān'[91] and 'Iflās'[92] whose love and enjoyment of the pleasures of life equal their rebellion against it). The latter, on the other hand, impoverishes both the texture and structure of his work, for the conceptual approach to the subject imposes various extraneous elements without integrating them fully into either the form or the content.

In Taymūr's romantic works, the conceptual approach is associated with a lack of interest in characterisation, attributable largely to the author's overreliance on the power of his ideas, which somehow seem to him self-explanatory. His characters tend in consequence to be one-dimensional and incapable of sustaining plausible action. When the author does, occasionally, succeed in providing his work with convincing characterisation and plausible action the conceptual approach may widen the theme of the story, for then the concept becomes a significant part of a coherent structure. However, the integration of preconceived ideas into the narrative of the story is achieved only rarely, while they lack harmony in stories that deal with fixed ideas and the perpetuation of certain feelings or notions.[93] In many other stories, the author attempts to compensate for this lack of cohesion by using a lyrical style and paying greater attention to description, but his poetic language helps little in consolidating the structure or motivating the character.

The lack of character motivation is one of Taymūr's marked shortcomings. Even when the story includes a plausible situational conflict, he seems to perceive it as self-evident, often based on the assumption that innocence and purity are capable of overcoming evil ('al-Tawbah'[94] and 'al-Shaḥḥādh wa'l-Faṭā'ir al-'Ashr'),[95] an idea which he seems to think requires no vindication. Morality in his world is seen as possessing an independent, abstract power, as if the universe is filled with a mysterious force implementing ethical laws. In many of his short stories, an individual of pure heart faces an evil and corrupt world of social conformity, yet he never seeks to reform it, for he is anxious only to ensure his own personal salvation. The character fluctuates between romantic rebellion and mere exasperation and discontent ('Anā al-Sharīd'[96] or 'Iflās'), or prefers illusion and dream to reality ('Qublah'[97] and 'al-Bāb al-Muqfal')[98] and is capable of finding in them more happiness and fulfilment than in real life. Consequently one learns very little about the social and political aspects of these characters, or indeed of most of Taymūr's characters. This is so mainly because Taymūr, who was seen by the standards of his time as enlightened, liberal and humanitarian and dealing explicitly with moral and ethical issues, seems in fact to have a bankrupt moral position, grounded more in an imagined perception of his characters than in reality.

Muḥammad Amīn Ḥassūnah

One romantic short story writer who saw the importance of introducing the patriotic dimension into his characterisation is Muḥammad Amīn Ḥassūnah, one of the six signatories of the important 1930 literary manifesto *al-Da'wah Ilā Khalq al-Adab al-Qawmī.*[99] Like many of his contemporaries and colleagues,[100] such as Maḥmūd 'Izzat Mūsā (1907–89),[101] Muḥammad Zakī 'Abd al-Qādir (1908–80),[102] Ibrāhīm Ḥusayn al-'Aqqād (1911–99)[103] and Yūsuf Jūhar (1913–2001),[104] Ḥassūnah's romanticism is distinguished by patriotism and nationalistic sentiments. Although he started writing later than some of his contemporaries, he was the first to collect his work in book form. In *al-Ward al-Abyaḍ* (1933), which was in fact to be his only collection,[105] he refers several times to the 1919 Revolution and to the repercussions of the First World War in Egypt.[106] He also creates a connection between the beauty of nature and the eternal beauty of ancient Egyptian monuments and tries to relate his romanticism to the local context and give it a pastoral tone.[107]

His writing rotates around some of the same principal themes as Taymūr's, but with a different set of emphases. Unlike Taymūr, he did not depict nature as something idealised or awe-inspiring, but as something that man could aspire to unite with or whose beauty man could become part of. In Ḥassūnah's work nature is associated with a passionate love of beauty, which reaches, in 'Fi'l-Wāḥah',[108] the point of complete communion. When Mary, the heroine of the story, who is ecstatic about the beauty of al-Fayyūm, the splendour of the temples of Luxor and Aswan, the spaciousness of the desert, and the relics of Tutankhamon, is suffocated by the sands of the vast wild desert which she loved, the scene is presented not as a terrible disaster but as the ultimate form of union between two lovers. The wildness of nature is portrayed as an expression of a unique passion that consciously selects its victim, or rather its beloved. The lyrical language of the final scene, and the heroine's call for her lover, which is answered by the sand-storm passionately enveloping her, dissipates any sense of horror, for the whole event is associated not only with passion, beauty and love but also with memories of the glorious past and sweet dreams of the future.

Unlike Taymūr, who relishes the beauty of nature in Europe and the mountains of Lebanon, Ḥassūnah in 'al-Ghurūb'[109] takes delight in describing the bucolic scenes of the Egyptian village and uncovering the charm of its ritualistic life. He gives his glorification of the beauty of rural Egypt a pantheistic intensity, which enables the hero to endure his tragedy, although a sentimental, even melodramatic, atmosphere weighs down on the story. Ḥassūnah wavers between making the beauty and power of nature a central theme, and using it in a merely decorative way to create atmosphere ('Fīfī',[110] 'al-Tā'irah'[111] and 'Anṣāf 'Adhārā').[112] In 'al-Mar'ah al-Jadīdah',[113] he moves to Lebanon, mecca of Arab romanticism, and extols its beautiful European-like scenery, without being aware of the irony of this portrayal, in view of his parochially nationalistic attitude. Another facet of this irony is manifest in the fact that his world is peopled with foreign characters. Mary of 'Fi'l-Wāḥah' is an American doctor, Patra of 'Gharām al-Shā'ir'[114] is a Greek, Alice of the same story is Syrian, the heroine of 'al-Ghamām'[115] is Italian, the dancer Silvie of 'Raqsat al-Rumbā'[116] is probably French, and Eva of 'al-Mar'ah al-Jadīdah' is a Lebanese brought up in America.

Nevertheless, most of his male characters are Egyptian and it is they who are in love with these foreign-educated, often sophisticated, but always charming women. Apart from the two heroes of 'al-Adīb Abū Darsh'[117] and 'Fi'l-Ghurūb', all his characters belong to the aristocracy or the upper middle classes. It is therefore natural to provide these sensitive delicate souls with refined and beautiful foreign girls with whom they can discuss profound issues and fall in love. However, women do not exist simply to complement the picture or decorate the scene, for the female characters, both Egyptian and foreign, possess more romantic qualities than the male in Ḥassūnah's stories. They are sensitive, educated and modern in an archaic, blunt and backward society which still believes in the superiority of man and sees women as a sex object and as an *'awrah* (shameful weakness). Naturally, an educated woman is filled with discontent when confronted by these social conventions. Like many romantic heroes, she is rebellious, but incapable of altering social conditions or revolting against them. So, filled with exasperation, many of these women begin to treat social convention with extreme cynicism ('Ṣāḥib al-Mu'jizah'[118] and 'Anṣāf 'Adhārā'). The inevitable result of this combination of bitter cynicism and frustrated rebellion is self-defeat and depression, which lead often to a tragic surrender to unjust and tyrannical social convention. The heroine of 'al-Mar'ah al-Jadīdah' is not lacking in ability or knowledge but in motivation and self-confidence, so she ends with many half-finished projects, half-fought battles, half-realised dreams and half-victories. Because her romantic nature refuses to compromise, she prefers complete destruction to half-victories and is finally incapable of consolidating her position.

This is also the case of the hero of 'al-Adīb Abū Darsh', whose ambitious dream is presented as an obsession that blinds him to the simplest facts of reality. Like many romantics, he has dreams that are in complete opposition to reality, and that are inevitably dashed with the first confrontation with reality. The destruction of hollow objects makes a louder noise than that of solid ones, so when the fanciful dreams of the hero collapse, a cloud of sentimentality envelops the story. Sentimentality is a symptom of the hero's predisposition to prejudge reality and to establish illusion as its alternative. However, when his dream is frustrated, he transcends his sorrow through art; thus the ecstasy of art represents another means of eschewing reality and sustaining illusion in this story. In another work, 'Gharām al-Shā'ir', Ḥassūnah presents art in a different light, elaborating the romantic perception of the exceptional gift of the artist and emphasising the special role of inspiration. For him, the creative process needs a continuous source of inspiration, which usually acts as a catalyst, as something that removes the lid, allowing the artist's inner spring of creativity to burst forth. When the artist is without a catalyst, when his creative energy is suppressed within him, he suffers deep anxieties, which result in a gradual loosening of his grip on life and leads, eventually, to suicide. In this story, the progression of the action towards this end develops a clear tone of sentimentality, despite the author's awareness that this is a feature from which the Egyptian short story needs to be freed.[119] Even with this sentimentality, however, Ḥassūnah manages to accentuate various romantic qualities in his work and succeeds in developing certain national facets in his romanticism.

Sa'd Makkāwī

The various characteristics of romanticism in the Egyptian short story appear in the works of many writers, but are usually blended with a great deal of sentimentality and melodrama;[120] and romanticism was to await the arrival of Sa'd Makkāwī (1916–89) to reach its acme. Not only was Makkāwī a talented and prolific writer but also a romantic by temperament and cultural formation. He arrived on the scene when the romantic short story was suffocated by sentimentality, and he brought it new life. His work, together with that of his contemporaries, such as Ibrāhīm Nājī,[121] Muḥammad 'Abd al-Ḥalīm 'Abd Allāh (1913–70),[122] Ḥusayn al-Qabbānī (1916–81),[123] Yūsuf al-Sibā'ī

(1917–78),[124] Ismā'īl al-Ḥabrūk (1923–61),[125] Ṣūfī 'Abd Allāh (b. 1925)[126] and others,[127] makes it difficult to overlook the contribution of the romantic genre to the development of the Egyptian short story.

In 'Shahīrah'[128] one finds a coherent characterisation of a romantic hero, an innocent full of dreams and aspirations, who is also a sensitive artist endowed with deep insight and great talent in the face of a macabre atmosphere and a corrupt society. He is socially naive, yet, armed only with his gift and his vulnerability, he has to force his way through a web of intrigue and manipulation. The story opens with his arrival in Cairo, with the values, morals and mentality of a villager. He comes as an *enfant terrible*, full of dreams and ideas, convinced that his poetic talent alone is sufficient to open the doors of literary life to him, or, as he conceives it, the divine temple of art. But instead of his imaginary 'paradise of art and devotees of thought, he [finds] a jungle full of barking dogs, howling wolves and hissing vipers'.[129] His naiveté and innocence enable him to confront, and even to defeat, the intrigues and manipulations of this wild jungle. The originality of his poetry and the novelty of his ideas ensure him artistic success, but the purity of his soul and his strong ethical and moral sense are a hindrance rather than a help in his social intercourse.

A conflict erupts between innocence (which is associated with artistic talent and pure morals) and experience (which is equated with social corruption, intrigue and moral contamination), and inevitably leads to the destruction of the innocent hero. The story endeavours to glorify innocence and associates it with rural values, thus turning the conflict, at another level of interpretation, into a clash between rural and urban values and views. This interpretation is reinforced by the sub-plot concerning the first encounter between the protagonist and the city, an encounter that leaves a permanent scar on his soul. At this level, the story is an illustration of how the city receives a lively country lad, destroys him, and sends him back to his village having reduced him to a vegetable. The values operating in the countryside are presented with a great deal of partiality, as being intrinsically noble and requiring no justification. They are venerated on abstract moral grounds, despite their apparent impracticality in the city, so that their defeat in the confrontation with the values of the urban jungle does not invalidate their morality. They are presented as being implicitly superior to urban values, for although the latter are illustrated in a relatively impartial manner, there is a certain degree of bias conveyed in the tone of description and in the careful selection of the urban aspects introduced. However, this partiality is attenuated by the employment of sub-plots that vindicate the conflict and widen its implication, and by the interaction between various levels of meaning in the work as a whole.

Another significant interaction is that portrayed as existing between art and love, for the story combines the two favourite themes of Egyptian romanticism, and through the use of a well-written and economic structure creates a tragic and moving story. The protagonist is loved because of his poetic talent and creative soul, and he succeeds in proving himself artistically because he is aided by the love of a capable and well-established actress as well as by the support of a leading poet. Both of them see him as a long-awaited fresh breeze bringing new ideas and ideals. The experienced actress is attracted to his innocent soul and fascinated by his poetic talent, and despite the apparent dissimilarity between the two, they fall in love: thus the story of his artistic success becomes tightly interwoven with that of their love affair. The development of the affair introduces a new aspect to the romantic concept of love, for it involves sex but distinguishes clearly between sex as an expression of great affection within the context of an affair and lust: one is the ultimate form of communication, the other a manifestation of extreme loneliness. In this way, the dichotomy between the emotional and the physical in earlier romantic stories is replaced by a contradiction between two types of physical contact: one acceptable, indeed desirable, because of its association with passion and genuine emotion, the other condemned for being carnal and devoid of the elevating feelings of love. Thus love, in both its emotional and physical expression, becomes more than just a relationship, however important, and turns into a life-giving power, a source of being, and moral indicator.

With this concept of love it is natural that the association between love and creativity, and affection and imagination, should become powerful and significant in Makkāwī's work. Like many of the themes in 'Shahīrah', the interaction between love and creativity is revealed in many of his stories. He avoids merely restating his theme, but develops and enriches it, touching upon a different facet each time; for, amongst romantic writers, he is one of the most conscious of his craft. He tries to reinforce his theme, without repeating it, by presenting it as the main theme of some works[130] and as a sub-theme in others[131] and by the use of carefully orchestrated associations; that is, by the creation of imploding symbols or sets of symbols and the development of relationships between them and the theme, or certain aspects of it. Yet in most of the works in which he deals with the interaction between love and creativity he emphasises the importance of love as a major source of inspiration, not only because love is in complete harmony with art,[132] so that their domains overlap,[133] but also because each of them revitalises the other.[134] Love inspires the creative artist, who is in turn the person most capable of cherishing love and developing it.[135]

However, when a conflict between art and love arises, Makkāwī favours art, for art is the supreme romantic quality, and love can be incidental to art while the reverse is not possible.[136] Art is man's only means to communicate with the secrets of the universe,[137] because it deepens his insight and sharpens his perception. It offers the ultimate ecstasy and self-satisfaction and is associated with freedom on a profound level.[138] It transcends suffering[139] and enables man to embrace nature and understand humanity;[140] it also transcends ordinary life, for it forges illusion with reality to create a higher form of existence.[141] Consequently, the artist in most of these stories is perceived as a prophet or a diviner; he is born an artist with a golden head, according to the allegorical story 'al-Masākīn',[142] and is sought after by everyone around him for varying reasons. This golden-headed artist is capable of achieving miracles, but the tedium of his surroundings causes him much suffering.

In some works[143] the indirect condemnation of outside intervention in the creative process touches upon the issue of artistic freedom of expression. "Urūq al-Wujūd',[144] a fantasy about the reception of Sayyid Darwīsh and Bayram al-Tūnisī in paradise while Aḥmad Shawqī is denied right of entry, adds an interesting dimension to Makkāwī's romantic perception of art and suggests that the true artist should not slavishly follow established rules or imitate classical norms. The world of artistic creativity is also perceived as a dreamworld full of promises of satisfaction in 'al-Kambūshah',[145] a story that touches on another prevalent theme in Makkāwī's view of art – the unbridgeable distance between dream and reality, and intentions and actions.[146] Although Makkāwī's stories about art can be seen as complementary to each other, presenting different facets of his view of creativity, they vary greatly in form. Some use an ordinary syllogistic progression of action and connected narrative, others resort to an allegorical structure and abstract language, while a third group employs a succession of images, each of them recreating the same fictional mood under changing situations.

The other major theme in Makkāwī's world is love, which he treats in a different perspective from that of his predecessors. Love in many of his stories is a strongly passionate feeling that possesses the character in an almost irrational manner. It strikes the character suddenly and seizes him almost unconsciously,[147] yet it is a healing power that cures the sick and transforms suffering into happiness.[148] It generates a sense of purpose and links strangers together with strong spiritual bonds,[149] and its transcending power works miracles, making saints out of lustful sinners[150] and talented writers out of nervous wrecks.[151] Thus it is often seen as the peak of human achievement,[152] not only because it enables man to feel and live the real pulse of the universe but also because it is his only means of entry into harmony and communication with nature; for love enables the character to achieve complete communication with the beloved and also to attain a kind of intuitive understanding of the hidden thoughts and feelings of the beloved.[153] This deep level of communication enables lovers to attain a deeper understanding of the hidden truth, of nature, and ultimately of the prime mover behind the multifarious manifestations of love and harmony.

Indeed, in many of Makkāwī's stories, love is strongly associated with mysticism. 'Qiddīsah min Bāb al-Sha'ariyyah' is a clear example of the interaction between the two.[154] In this story, as in a few others,[155] Makkāwī develops the love relationship from an expression of the lover's concern for communication on both the physical and emotional levels to a demonstration of a deep spiritual yearning. The lovers gradually lose interest in, or affection for, each other, and start to communicate with each other and with the world around them on many levels. The elevation of the physical and emotional manifestations of love to the spiritual level involves the transcendence of the carnal aspects of the relationship to mystic or creative activities. It also sharpens the lovers' sense of beauty and nature and deepens their understanding of both life and man. Naturally, this rich and enriching form of love is associated with many aspects of nature and art such as dawn, flowers, beautiful rustic scenes, music and poetry. In 'Naffūsah',[156] it awakens a character near death, opens her eyes to the wonderful aspects of life, and enables her to attain harmony with both nature and society.

However, in some of Makkāwī's works love is amalgamated with yet another romantic theme, nostalgia. Nostalgia in Makkāwī's love stories is a technical device, a viewpoint through which previous love affairs are presented and tenderly cherished. As a technique, nostalgia endeavours to intensify the effect of the love story, associating it with times of happiness, times past yet viewed with longing and adoration. In 'Liqā' Taḥt al-Miṣbāḥ',[157] nostalgia is not only for time past but also for distant and beautiful European places; and love is blended with the fascinating folk tales of the gypsies and with the vivid memories of France. Indeed, Makkāwī's nostalgia for France equals Taymūr's fondness for the beauty of European nature and Ḥassūnah's love for the nature of Egypt. But unlike them he carefully masks his fondness for European life and nature and endeavours to personalise his views and blend them with vivid memories and actions,[158] presenting his nostalgic sentiments of Europe as a part of a general nostalgia for the past: the time of happy childhood,[159] pleasant memories[160] and fascinating events.[161]

Apart from art and love, there are two other recurring themes in 'Shahīrah' somewhat linked to the theme of nostalgia. The first is the conflict between the country and the city, and the second is innocence versus experience. The contradiction between rural and urban values is the main theme of one of his early and most fascinating stories, 'I'tirafāt Fatā al-Nūbah',[162] a story which sees the city's life and values through the eyes of a young inexperienced Nubian, who comes from the seclusion of his community to work in Cairo's upper-class society, whose life and culture are presented through the filter of a contrasting set of values. Although the presentation caricatures the life of urban society in order to underline the contrast between the two, it employs religion as a criterion in judging various events, with the result of favouring the country's norm of life. Here, as in other stories,[163] Makkāwī associates rural life with childhood and happiness, thus viewing it with adoration and nostalgic sentiments.

In 'Bilā Sayf'[164] he develops the conflict between the country and the city into a clash between two opposite cultures, African and European. One is primitive, simple and dignified, the other modern, sophisticated and immoral. The triumph of European culture results in the destruction of numerous victims and the humiliation of many more, and is portrayed using powerful religious imagery, as the triumph of the devil. The employment of such imagery here exemplifies the conflict between innocence and experience, for it widens the urban–rural dichotomy and its implications. The simplicity and innocence of African tribal society are juxtaposed with a subtle and highly experienced, even sophisticated, code of conduct. The dichotomy inevitably injures, even destroys, the innocent but fails to defeat his blazing spirit. Makkāwī presents the destruction of innocence in a manner that attracts the reader's sympathy and implies that it is far from being a complete defeat. On certain occasions, the triumph of experience is presented in a way that suggests that it cannot be sustained for long because it is based on deception and trickery.[165] In "Iṭr fi'l-Ẓalām'[166] the author develops the confrontation between innocence and experience through his sensitive use of the child as a symbol and the child–adult confrontation. The child is pure, innocent and emotionally honest while the adult is corrupted and contaminated by social obligations and hypocrisy. The use of this romantic cliché provides an opportunity to focus on certain social defects and see them in a new perspective.

The conflict between the child's view of the world and that of the conformist adult involves the theme of romantic rebellion. Like his predecessor Ḥassūnah, Makkāwī is attracted to the theme of rebellion against conformity, especially the rebellion of women characters against unjust social conventions. He pays considerable attention to his female characters, many of whom possess the qualities of the romantic rebel, combined with deep insight and a strong, often pragmatic, sense of purpose.[167] Rebellion is associated with the freedom of a life lived outside the shackles of convention, a demonstration of a strong will to live and to be master of one's own destiny.[168] Yet this will seems to evaporate once events develop beyond the rebel's personal interest. Makkāwī's romantic rebels do not seek to change the prevailing order or to reform society, for they have no coherent vision, much less a practical programme for change. Their anger and discontent at the rigid social order are assuaged by the mere act of defiance, so that to challenge the dominant values is in itself a valid goal and a mission, to which they feel it worth dedicating themselves.

The romantic hero does not find his main reward in achievement but in the process, in the journey towards his goal; attainment does not bring pure satisfaction, rather it is tinged with disappointment.[169]

In this respect the romantic hero resembles, in the simplicity of his approach, the innocent child in contrast to the experienced adult, and is lonely like a child in an adult world. In 'Maṣra' Ḥimār' the romantic rebel acquires, besides his sense of superiority, a sad, almost destructive, feeling of alienation.[170] Not a living soul in his village is capable of understanding him, let alone of communicating with him. The only one who does is a stranger passing through the village on his way from the town. This fleeting moment of contact with another human being does not solve his problem, rather it intensifies his feelings of alienation and separateness.

In 'Al-Qamar al-Mashwī'[171] these feelings of alienation and discontent are also accentuated and associated with the hero's sense of superiority – this is achieved by presenting him as a Byronic hero who is constantly oscillating between impossible dreams and an overwhelming craving for destruction, including his own destruction. He has a strong sense of mission and a burning desire to vindicate his social image and revenge his wounded honour. The irony of his situation is manifold, for he is contemptuous of, and rebellious against, conventional morality yet he desires to live up to his social image as dictated by convention. But complying with the dictates of social convention involves a violation of the prevailing social order, which reigns by terror rather than by convention and consent. So he is torn between defiance and conformity, but, at the same time filled with his own visions. His sense of mission soon becomes a fixed idea, a mania that blinds him to the fact that he is playing into his opponent's hands, which brings him only suffering. Yet he is still capable of affection and remains faithful to his vision despite the tragic course of events.[172]

Unlike many of his predecessors, Makkāwī links his adoration for nature with another recurrent theme in his work: the duality of matter, or simply essence and appearance. For him there are two aspects to everything, a permanent essence and multiple adventitious appearances. The oneness of the essence is closely linked to its intrinsicality while the multiplicity of manifestations is a demonstration of extrinsicality. But Makkāwī's perception of duality does not imply a dichotomy between essence and appearance, for the oneness of the essence suggests that it is latent or inherent in the various manifestations. Even when the manifestations seem to contradict the essence or intend to conceal it, the artist's insight is always capable of seeing the essential beneath the accidental.[173] The artist is an explorer whose domain is the human soul and he is, therefore, capable of discovering beauty and goodness in unlikely places.[174]

The theme of nature is linked inversely to the theme of the duality of matter, for it provides the author with a perfect example of the harmony between the two, when surface manifestations match the essence and the otherwise wide gap between the two almost vanishes.[175] This is because the sublime spirit does not hide behind the visible manifestations of nature; rather it expresses itself through the various aspects of its beauty. But in some cases Makkāwī fails to see the sublime spirit, so that its beauty becomes a purely decorative feature.[176] Moreover, like Taymūr, Makkāwī also falls into the dichotomy of soul and body, dream and reality, with the inevitable result of poor representation and incoherence.[177] This is so not only because Makkāwīfails to accept this dichotomy as one of the perennial problems of mankind and probe its consequences for his culture, but also because, being aware of narrative structure, he feels that he has to bring an external element to justify the dichotomy or to balance the situation. This deus ex machina often emphasises the faulty structure instead of curing it,[178] because it attempts to bestow credibility on a situation which often does not accept it.

In many of these cases Makkāwī resorts to the didactic, to stereotypes and clichés. He imposes the triumph of morality over corruption, even when the natural course of events seems to suggest the contrary.[179] The triumph of morality appears to be more plausible when linked to patriotic nationalistic issues.[180] However, the most common device used to promote a particular interpretation of events of a story is the introduction, often the deliberate development, of a sense of fatalism. When Makkāwī succeeds in interweaving this with the story's narrative structure it widens the scope of the story as a whole and enhances its plausibility.[181] It also creates, in some stories,[182] a desirable mystic atmosphere, which often roots the action in a spiritual collective consciousness.[183] Makkāwī is clearly interested in demonstrating the vital role of religion in society,[184] and particularly in the possibility of creating, or rather recreating, in his stories a myth constituted of religious and superstitious elements and following its way of penetrating the dynamics of action or character until it becomes a vital part of a realistic situation.[185] It is as though he wants to illustrate the power of conceptions over reality; in other words, to justify his preconceived, often idealised, approach to reality.

A further instance of the conceptual approach may be found in his use – for the first time in the history of the Egyptian short story – of the genre of science fiction as a vehicle for apocalyptic vision. In 'Ṣadmah Muḥtamalah'[186] science fiction is used to express his views about the present state of the world and to suggest a remedy. Although the story is profoundly imaginative, it is strongly didactic and its allegorical structure lacks subtlety. Yet it remains significant because in it he moves his vision of love from the general emotional level to a coherently 'philosophical' one, in which love is identical with a pervasive universal spirit that guides, corrects and reigns supreme. While Makkāwī's endeavour to 'philosophise' the situation is strikingly simplistic, 'Ṣadmah Muḥtamalah' remains his most successful attempt to graft 'philosophical' views onto his stories and use them as a vehicle for apocalyptic visions.[187] Nevertheless, in these and other stories Makkāwī's conceptual approach impedes the structural balance and affects the plausibility of the story. Although his evident awareness of his craft and his skilful use of language save some of his works, his preconceived conceptions seem ultimately burdensome.[188]

Yet Makkāwī is the only romantic writer whose work shows a constant development towards the consolidation of structure and a coherent expression of romantic vision or way of articulating them. He seems to equate romanticism with artistic immaturity in his theoretical commentary,[189] but he does not deny that a coherent and complex work must include an element of romanticism.[190] This can be interpreted as an attempt on the part of the author to draw a distinction between two kinds of romanticism: the kind that emerges from a serious analysis of his mature works, and the kind associated with what Goethe terms *Romantisch das Kranke* and with the works treated in the following section of this chapter. Indeed, it would be unfair to associate Makkāwī's works too closely with those generally termed romantic in Egyptian criticism, for his work is far more coherent in both form and content. His poetic use of language offers one example of the extent of his artistic evolution. In his early works he was drawn to lyricism but was unable to harness it in a way that enhanced his work,[191] but he gradually succeeded in finding the right linguistic combination, one that balances poetic and fictional elements. His language thus developed to suit the fictional world portrayed in the story; it became a language that reflects the mood, develops the character and conveys the matter without attracting attention to itself;[192] his language became lucid while retaining a poetic quality that is restrained and latent rather than florid and redundant, so that it enriches the work and does not distract the reader's attention as was the case in the early works.

Apart from the fluency of style and the coherence of structure that distinguish Makkāwī's work from that of other romantics, another feature is his cross-referencing between stories, whereby he refers to actions,[193] characters[194] and places[195] that have already appeared elsewhere. By drawing upon a certain parochial area and group of characters, he attempts to create a self-sustained world that acquires its frame of reference not from external reality but from its own internal coherence. The cross-references create an illusion of artistic credibility and propound a cohesive internal logic, which penetrates his stories and links ostensibly unrelated parts in a manner that consolidates his artistic world and strengthens its effect. Indeed, Makkāwī demonstrates a clear awareness of the sophisticated interaction (which supposes a dichotomy yet alludes to a dialectic) between artistic and external reality.[196] He persuades the reader to abandon the laws of reality, at least partly, on entering his world, so as to be able to penetrate beneath the surface of his artistic realm. For him, artistic reality is not only more important that external reality, but also more plausible and logical within itself.

To reinforce the internal logic, Makkāwī consolidates his cross-references by creating a host of imploding symbols and sustaining certain modes of association. The associations are not only of objects and events but also of ideas and moods, so some themes echo others in a succession of ideas and serve to enhance the major theme and widen its implications.[197] These various forms of association, together with the sensitive use of language, create a subtle structure of sub-plots, which enhances the development of the character and roots it deeply in the situation.[198] Yet Makkāwī's eagerness to create a self-sustained artistic reality, together with his conceptual approach to both external and human realities,[199] often hinders the plausibility of his characterisation.[200] This is so not only because of the introduction of intrusive, frequently pretentious elements in the characterisation but also because he often fails to probe the tension between some of his characters' sense of their own, imagined, identity and their reality. However, his awareness of the importance of a balanced inner logic to sustain the plausibility of his plots saves his characterisation from serious flaws. This, together with the clarity of his ideas, lucidity of style and interest in structure, makes him the most stimulating of all the romantics.

Sentimentality and the Popularisation of the Genre

The strong emphasis of writers classified as romantic on certain aspects of human experience leads, in many romantic works, to a pervasive tone of sentimentality. So too does their preconceived approach to reality, which implies a tendency to beautify, perfect, embellish and glorify. The attempt by such writers to discover the exceptional beneath the ordinary, as well as their rejection of conformity, reaction against prevailing taste, and endeavour to establish new codes often leads to exaggerated expression and thereby to sentimentality. Yet while some romantic qualities may breed sentimental elements, sentimentality is not an inherent characteristic of romanticism, for the more closely the work approaches the spirit of romanticism in its true philosophical stance, the less sentimental it becomes. In a great deal of literary criticism in Arabic, however, romanticism has become a pejorative term because of its associations with sentimentality, especially in fiction. The associations are, perhaps, a result of the belief shared by many critics that the conceptual approach to reality inherent in romantic genres accounts for the excess of emotions, which aims at generating an immediacy of response and sacrifices the valuable artistic process of slowly generating more complex emotions.

Many romantic writers did indeed fall easy prey to sentimentality, for with the availability of a reading public nourished on the writings of al-Manfalūṭī, so prone to emotional exaggeration, sentimental expression found a responsive audience. Moreover, the inherited aesthetic criteria of good style encouraged an overindulgence in the arousal of the emotions of pathos and sympathy, naturally at the expense of the painstaking process of the slow generation of pity and terror, which aspires to weaken and dissipate emotions. Sentimentality is therefore in some way antagonistic to an artistic approach that does not accommodate exaggerated and unjustified responses.

> A response is sentimental if it is too great for the occasion

> ... "sentimental" is equivalent to "crude". A crude emotion, as opposed to a refined emotion ... can be set off by all manners of situations ... Neither crudeness nor refinement need imply anything about the intensity of emotion.[201]

Since excess or overindulgence is clearly relative, some elucidation is necessary before the term can be applied to the Egyptian short story.

The relativity of the sentimental calls for careful consideration of the literary atmosphere in which the works under discussion were written, for to understand a literary work, and much more to dismiss it, 'we must first attempt to bring our views of reality into as close an alignment as possible with the prevailing view in the time of the work's composition'.[202] With the work placed in its context, the charge of sentimentality can be even more effective, for then it is based solely on artistic grounds, and mainly on the lack of convincing justification for the extremity of the response. Indeed, sentimentality is not so much associated with intense feelings, which can be true to life, but with the lack of convincing factors to account for their presence in a given work. Intense emotion may be justified as long as it is functionally appropriate within the situation and an integral part of the structure, and not directed at stimulating a crude emotional response in the reader.

The desire to impress the reader or manipulate him emotionally is a common feature of both melodramatic and sentimental writing, and stems from the writer's eagerness to attract a wider reading public; this may be a legitimate goal in itself, but it is often achieved at the expense of artistic coherence and maturity. Furthermore, such success gives lesser writers a stronger influence over the common reader and consequently a larger share in shaping literary taste, for, in the end, it is not only the public that is affected but also would-be writers, mediocre critics and reviewers, and publishers. Hence works unworthy of publication, from a purely artistic point of view, find their way easily into print, and even receive instant acclaim, while some better works are left in the shade or ignored.[203]

Although the success of mediocrity lowers general literary standards and impedes the development of the short story genre, it is not entirely without advantage. Success requires the right combination of certain factors at the right time, and so establishing the reasons for the success of certain works is significant for the study of the time in which they thrived. It also gives an indication as to why more valuable works failed to attain the status that they deserved. The dominance of sentimental works hindered the process of artistic development in the Egyptian short story and encouraged dilettanti writers, but at the same time it helped popularise the genre and familiarise the wider reading public with its conventions, especially during the 1930s, a generally barren time for the publication of fiction in Egypt. Once the pioneers of the Egyptian short story had begun to shape the features of the new literary form, the task of popularising their discoveries and familiarising the reader with the conventions of the short story became a necessary complementary task. It is on this level that the early popular works played an important role in the development of the genre, despite the lack of evident artistic contribution. It was not until much later that the popularity of such mediocre and sentimental works became an obstacle to further progress and overshadowed more important works.

Maḥmūd Kāmil

Maḥmūd Kāmil (1906–87) is an important figure in the history of the Egyptian short story, for it is largely to him that the new literary genre owes its success and popularity throughout the 1930s and the early 1940s, as well as the considerable respectability it earned amongst both readers and writers. The fact that a successful and respectable *avocat* (when successful *avocats* were leaders or ministers in the making) should indulge in writing short stories and, moreover, make it his main business, boosted the new genre. In 1932 he launched *al-Jāmi'ah*, the first popular and successful magazine devoted to, and deriving its success, indeed its *raison d'être*, from fictional writings. The success of *al-Jāmi'ah* and of his own works led Kāmil in 1937 to establish a publishing house[204] and issue a new bi-weekly, *Majallat al-'Ishrīn Qiṣṣah*, to meet the increasing demand for new short stories.

Ironically, Kāmil is now little remembered, and when his works are mentioned serious critics and highbrow intellectuals treat them with disdain. This critical response is, in many ways, the inverse to that evoked by the work of his contemporary Ḥaqqī. At the beginning the critics fêted his works and scarcely mentioned those of Ḥaqqī, but later on the tide turned so that today Kāmil is almost forgotten while Ḥaqqī's literary reputation lives on. The two are opposites in many respects.[205] They were contemporaries in the Faculty of Law (Cairo), but Kāmil, being slightly younger, graduated two years later. They both worked as lawyers and afterwards as assistant public prosecutors in the countryside, Ḥaqqī in Upper Egypt and Kāmil in Lower Egypt. They both started their literary careers when they were students but led two different literary lives.

While Ḥaqqī kept his literary career and his working life separate for many years, Kāmil tried from the very beginning to combine the two.[206] In contrast to Ḥaqqī, whose affiliation to al-Madrasah al-Ḥadīthah increased his awareness of the artistic aspects of his work and who wrote comparatively little, Kāmil paid only scant attention to the artistic development and did all he could to increase his output and attract a wide reading public. He wrote intensively and published extensively. Thus, by the time Ḥaqqī's first collection appeared, Kāmil had published fourteen collections, many of which were reprinted more than once,[207] several plays and a novel.[208] He even used the fact that he was a respectable barrister by adding the title 'al-Muḥāmī' (defence counsel) to his name until it became a more or less inseparable part of it.

As a barrister he had a compelling urge to defend the oppressed, and as a sentimentalist, by temperament as well as by cultural influence,[209] he had a tendency to exaggerate events and feelings. At the same time he endeavoured to play down severe social contradictions and to limit scenes of suffering, not only because he knew that those who emphasised these issues had little success with the wider public but also because he felt instinctively that his readers wanted an escape from reality (he started writing during the economic crisis of the 1930s). Moreover, his experience of the difficulties in the lives of the lower strata of society was dependent on hearsay and derived from hasty observation.

Thus Kāmil peopled his world with middle- and upper-class characters,[210] eschewing their social problems to concentrate on their emotional and moral issues. Love is the major theme in his work, presented in many of the stories as an unattainable dream associated with sweet music,[211] refined thoughts[212] and poetry.[213] The dreamworld of love is not only superior to reality but has all that it lacks.[214] Love is a world that is complete in itself and is presented as a counter to reality,[215] a world of grace,[216] honour[217] and happiness.[218] Love in most of these stories is first love, and

> very few people fall in love for the first time without

> becoming enthralled by their emotions merely as a novel experience. They become absorbed in them often to the exclusion of genuine interest in the loved object.[219]

Kāmil's characters are completely engrossed in their illusion of love, in their discovery of love, not as a mutual relationship in which two individuals communicate with each other on many levels and become more capable of discovering life and enjoying it, but as personal, often unrequited, feelings generated by the mere discovery of the individual's ability to escape emotional starvation,[220] violate conventional taboos[221] and even to establish in his fantasy a real link between himself and the beloved fictional characters of French romantic and sentimental fiction.[222]

Kāmil's characters seem to conceive of love as a unique experience which happens, if it happens, only once in a lifetime. The realisation of this fact intensifies the characters' feelings about love and opens the flood-gates of their emotions. Thus love becomes an extraordinary event, which generates extreme feelings,[223] triggers melodramatic and tragic actions[224] and radically changes the characters' fortunes.[225] The extremity of these feelings and events turns love into an emotional hell which lacks any purgatorial aspects and thus promises no salvation.[226] The suffering seems to the characters to be an expiation for no apparent wrongdoing, an inexplicable fate which they must endure and accept without questioning.[227] The gloom that envelops the passion of love is associated, in many stories,[228] with an overwhelming sense of guilt, for the characters become engrossed in their emotions to the extent of becoming obsessed with fixed ideas of their own creation. The rules of reason submit to the ruses of the heart, which intensifies the melodramatic elements and exaggerates the tragic events of a story.[229]

Kāmil was aware of the need to emphasise various elements of his work in order to make his points clear in the minds of a reading public brought up on a diet of sentimentality and unaccustomed to the subtle conventions of narrative; thus he uses exaggeration, without discrimination, throughout his works for mainly sentimental and didactic purposes. But despite its sentimentality, the treatment of the theme of love is intended, in many stories[230] to demonstrate the constricting and circumscribed atmosphere in which sensitive and educated characters struggle to express themselves against the odds of convention. It shows the wide gap between the thoughts and aspirations of the newly educated class (the base of the new reading public) and prevailing social conventions. It presents an eloquent defence of love as an honourable sentiment and as a right for those whose cultural formation leads them to recognise its importance.[231]

Kāmil combines his attack on decaying social conventions with a call for the emancipation of women. In many stories,[232] he presents women as helpless victims of the closed social atmosphere and, particularly, of man's inability to appreciate their situation or realise the extent of the cultural changes which they have undergone.[2334] Although the slow process of social change and the conflicting values of the dominant order affect both men and women, Kāmil seems to argue that women suffer from them more than men because they additionally suffer men's tyranny. In some stories[234] he links women's suffering to social disparity, so women are doubly victimised, both by social injustice and by male maltreatment.

Social disparity, though it exists,[235] does not constitute a major theme in Kāmil's writing, for he views spiritual poverty as more loathsome than material deprivation.[236] He even suggests that the poor are more courageous, kind and understanding than the rich, that they possess a high degree of morality and commit themselves to a higher standard of values.[237] In certain stories,[238] material poverty humiliates a man and destroys his hopes and dreams, but in others[239] pride and spiritual richness enable him to overcome his economic difficulties. So poverty in itself is not a significant problem, and may even turn out to be an advantage, while wealth can be a serious disadvantage.[240]

The pride and spiritual richness of the characters are manifestations of their rebellious streak, an expression of exasperation at their closed social horizons,[241] at the prevailing moral corruption[242] or at their inability to comprehend reality.[243] Although these qualities lead many characters to reject humiliating situations, they stop short of motivating them to rebel against the social order or instigate even the most trivial action against the establishment. They view the world that they do not experience directly as ceasing to function. This is in keeping with the dominance of feeling, excluding rationality and nourishing extreme emotions; in other words an atmosphere that is hardly conductive to serious revolt.

Although it is easy to accommodate the rebellious streak in some of Kāmil's characters with romantic ideas, his conception of the conflict between the country and the city is in sharp contrast to that of the romantics. For in harmony with his general viewpoint, which associates sensitive refined souls with education, cultural development and the values of modern society, he adopts the reverse of the romantics' standpoint in this respect. He presents the city as a heaven of civility and kindness, and the only place where characters in love, especially women, can find fulfilment.[244] While the village is the domain of gloom and boredom,[245] where educated people commit sins that haunt them for the rest of their lives,[246] there is nothing of the romantic adulation of the simplicity of rural live in Kāmil's world. Indeed, he rarely presents the village from the villagers' viewpoint, but rather from the point of view of an urban visitor ill at ease with the village's closed atmosphere.[247]

A corollary to this theme is the conflict between the European and Egyptian ways of life and their corresponding ideals, which is seen in terms similar to the urban–rural conflict. European, and particularly Parisian, life is presented with much nostalgia and reverence as a paradise of civility, culture and art. Many characters derive pleasure and satisfaction from memories of their visits to Europe[248] and acquire most of their ideals and value judgements from their experiences of European life. Some stories[249] suggest, however, that occidental ideals do not suit oriental life and that the attempt to implant them in Egyptian society is doomed to failure – needless to say here that this ironic, almost orientalising perception of occident and orient is adopted by Kāmil without any awareness of the irony involved, or that he is adopting a category of an 'imagined identity' that interiorises his characters. Kāmil also eulogises the Egyptian nature in a number of stories.[250]

However limited his themes, in number as well as in depth Kāmil succeeded in reproducing them in a great number of stories over a relatively short time span. Yet he failed to develop his craft and his later works are artistically no better or worse than his earlier ones. He continued to rely heavily on chance as a major element in the construction of his plots, and his works abound with unexpected occurrences, which are intended to tighten the plot and enhance the *vraisemblance* of the action but only succeed in weakening their plausibility. In some stories,[251] there are three or four of these coincidences, without which the story would lose a great deal of its coherence; yet this simplistic use of chance as a major structural ploy intensifies the sentimental elements, increasing the likelihood of extreme responses, and makes the stories lack credibility.[252] In several stories,[253] chance plays a vital role in the progression of the action, yet Kāmil still treats it in a facile way and fails to develop any carefully worked out ideas about social or metaphysical fate.

The frequent use of unexpected occurrences in the progression of the action brings a touch of suspense, albeit superficial, which adds to the stories' entertainment value. Kāmil endeavoured to counter the enfeebling effect of chance on the plausibility of his stories by using other narrative techniques. His frequent use of the letter form,[254] in which the story is either in the form of one long letter from the protagonist to the narrator or a group of letters exchanged between the two main characters – often two lovers[255] – is the most common of these devices. In many cases, he enhances the function of the letter as a fictional device by the addition of a preamble in which the narrator explains how he came to possess such revealing personal letters. He also uses the technique of diaries and memoirs to create an illusion of reality,[256] again often reinforced with a preamble to verify its credibility.

Another common make-belief device in Kāmil's works is the intensive use of, and often over-reliance on, dialogue,[257] since the use of direct speech and colloquialism can make a situation spring into life. He does not, however, make full use of dialogue, especially as a means of characterisation, and it is mainly confined to developing the action. Most is written in a language that combines certain features of both the spoken and the written languages. The result is a monochromatic language, which has no regard for the temperament, background or mood of the characters involved. Although Kāmil is aware of some aesthetic aspects of literary style, his appreciation of the special nature and various functions of the language of fiction is very limited. His use of language is intended to influence the reader emotionally and provoke in him excessive sentiments, with the result that he uses emotive language which often cannot be verified semantically.[258] Yet although he often uses superfluous words to create specious effects, in comparison with prevailing linguistic taste, his language is relatively simple and lucid. It may even be argued that he played an important role in developing the language of fiction and freeing it from the shackles of traditional taste. The attractive lyrical quality in his style, which occasionally borders on the poetic, is part of his general attitude that makes him want to add a touch of grandeur and glamour to his works, an attitude that also accounts for the many references to European places, literary works and nostalgic memories of journeys there, for nothing was capable of overwhelming the average reader of the time so much as allusions to the glittering lights of European life, which was so real to him yet quite beyond his reach.

Kāmil's works were highly acclaimed at the time of their publication. They were praised on both artistic and thematic grounds[259] and exonerated from any artistic defects.[260] The author was extolled as a fine observer and sensitive analyst of the human psyche and of the life of modern Egypt, and throughout the 1930s his works were highly commended by leading writers in magazines.[261] In the mid-1940s his fame dwindled, yet he still exerted considerable influence on the emerging younger generation. One writer of this generation called him the legitimate father of journalistic fiction,[262] while another considered his works and the magazine he edited amongst the major features of cultural life in Cairo at that time, and portrays them in one of his novels as playing an important role in the formation of literary taste.[263]

Although Kāmil is the figure who stands out among the writers of sentimental short stories of the 1930s and the greater part of the 1940s, there were other writers who deserve to be mentioned, such as Ḥabīb Tawfīq,[264] Ibrāhīm Ḥusayn al-ʿAqqād[265] and others.[266] By the latter part of the 1940s a group of writers began to publish sentimental works extensively. They survived by availing themselves of the thematic and technical achievements of Kāmil and attempted to continue along the same path and sustain the wider reading public which he had attracted. Instead of developing the reading public, so to speak, vertically, by refining its cultural taste and raising its aesthetic judgement, they attempted to do so horizontally, by widening its base at the expense of artistic criteria.

Some of them, such as Yūsuf al-Sibāʿī,[267] Jādhibiyyah Ṣidqī (b. 1927)[268] and Ibrāhīm al-Wirdānī (1919–88),[269] continued to produce sentimental works, clearly influenced by Kāmil, blending sentimentality with romantic and didactic elements and, on rare occasions, with some realism. Like Kāmil, they paid little attention to the artistic aspects of their work but, unlike him, their works fluctuate widely in quality and they did not know when to stop writing: thus their later work is often weak. Others, such as Amīn Yūsuf Ghurāb

(1911–70),[270] Iḥsān 'Abd al-Quddūs (1919–90)[271] and others,[272] tried to keep Kāmil's sentimentality alive, not only by simply reproducing his themes, techniques and characters but also by developing the escapist elements in his work. In their writing there is a sensual aspect to their characters' exaggerated emotions, which is absent from Kāmil's writing, and their locations are rich and extravagant. They were interested in the artistic aspects of the writing of fiction inasmuch as these would increase the immediate impact of their works with the wider reading public. Ghurāb introduced features of detective novels into his amatory writings and 'Abd al-Quddūs blended his with rudimentary psychoanalysis and crude political allusions.

However, unlike the works of Kāmil and his generation, which tried to sustain the readers' interest in the short story as a new literary genre and to familiarise them with its conventions when serious works were in short supply, the works of all these writers perpetuated sentimentality in the Egyptian short story long after it had lost its positive role. Moreover, they diverted the attention of the wider reading public from the serious writing being produced at the same time, but sustained their interest in the genre. The increase and continuing popularity of these works made the task of serious writers more difficult, for they had to uproot sloppy and false concepts about the short story and establish new and concrete ideas. This two-fold task was singularly laborious, and one that took the compounded effort of many members of two generations of Egyptian writers to accomplish.

Socialist Realism or Socialist Romanticism?

The reaction against the prevalence of middle-class ideals and sentimentality in the short story throughout the 1940s was one of the factors behind the emergence, in the 1950s, of the so-called socialist realist school in modern Egyptian literature. More generally, the particular intellectual climate of the late 1940s and early 1950s generated revolutionary fervour and naive optimism. From the ashes of despair left by the abortive popular uprising of 1946 and the colossal defeat of 1948 appeared a phoenix-like spirit of optimism, which was nourished on spasmodic rioting, a constant flow of left-wing publications, and the activity of small but numerous left-wing intellectual rings. The intensifying struggle against the British occupation and the rising wave of resistance to the pro-British establishment provided an atmosphere favourable to the emergence of such a literary mode.

This mode was popularised by Marxist writers who had come under the spell of Soviet thought and literature. A brief account of the basic ideas of socialist realism as a literary concept may be relevant to the study of its influence on the Egyptian short story. The term itself was introduced into Russia for the first time in 1932 after a long and fierce debate, which lasted fifteen years and involved many prominent members of the Russian revolutionary elite, including Lenin and Trotsky.[273] By 1934, with the dominance of Stalin and the institutionalisation of the revolution, socialist realism became the official policy of the all-powerful Soviet Writers Union. The argument about how much 'true' Marxism and how much heresy or mechanical materialism remained in the final version of the concept is beyond the scope of this study.[274] When the concept reached Egypt in the 1940s it was received not only without question but also with a great deal of comradely respect and adulation.

The relevant part of the struggle for the supremacy of the literary tenets of socialist realism is not how it defeated its opponents and developed its theoretical backbone, but how it finally conceived of its principles. Indeed, the exponents of socialist realism in Egypt were not aware of the details or the nature of the debates that preceded the coinage of the term, nor of the methods used in its consecration. The ability of Egyptian writers and critics to question the revelations of the socialist revolution in literature was not possible at the time, partly because of the blinkers imposed by the party and the official ideological line, which made any criticism of the official line a mortal sin, and partly because of the vagueness of the term and the absence of information. However, the term's very vagueness and the romantic nature of some of its tenets made it appealing to young Egyptian revolutionaries aspiring for change. The Egyptian Marxist writers who came to literature through politics tried to subordinate their ideology to their literary careers and the tenets of socialist realism were particularly suited to both their temperament and their cultural background.

Many of the concepts of socialist realism stem from Marxists' awareness of the powers of persuasion inherent in art and their eagerness to employ this active agent for the good of the cause. They are also associated with various Marxian doctrines (historical necessity, the inevitability of social mobility, men's ability to define, shape and change their lives, class consciousness and class struggle, and other principles of dialectical materialism), and most of all the concept of base and superstructure, in its complex and dynamic form.[275] This concept suggests that art, as a part of the superstructure, is nourished by the social conditions of existence;[276] in other words, art reflects the complexity of social reality without merely illustrating it.[277] Because reality is in itself a dynamic process, 'art, by figurative means, typifies the elements and tendencies of reality that recur according to regular laws, although changing with the changing circumstances'.[278]

From this process of typification emerged the concept of the 'ideal type'; and since Marxism is ideologically concerned with change and the future, this concept was at the heart of socialist realism. It took shape in the 'positive hero' and 'man of the future', for this is the only type capable of realising 'the basic precepts of dialectical materialism that man himself is an active agent and not passive object in the process of social change'.[279] The positive hero is thus very much a feature of socialist realism. Also, because its ideological basis is an understanding of the future, socialist realism is clearly concerned with 'human beings whose energies are devoted to the building of a different future, and whose psychological and moral make-up is determined by this'.[280]

Such positive characters, eager 'to partake with intensity and energy in the process of forming the new man and the new way of life',[281] are not the only means of infusing socialist realist works with revolutionary spirit. The all-important social optimism, an inherent characteristic of Marxist ideology itself, also has a role to play. Because Marxism provides the writer with 'a fuller understanding of the possibilities of human development and of the laws underlying it', Lukács argues that 'socialist realism is in a position both to portray the totality of a society in its immediacy and to reveal its pattern of development'.[282]

The development of society is conceived of in terms of a battle for the future through a revolutionary class struggle, in which the writer, under the guidance of the party, becomes the 'artist in uniform'. He is 'taught to portray what is positive in our life ... [and] to reveal and condemn the imperfections that hinder the forward march of society'.[283] This may explain the abundance of military terminology introduced into literature by socialist realist writers when

> they talked about *assault, siege, offensive, tactical errors* in poetry, of *strategy* and *artillery barrage* in literary criticism, and often called a novel they disliked "a *sortie* of the class enemy" or an "*attack in the rear*" and so on.[284]

The diffusion of military expressions is associated with the strong sense of militancy inherent in socialist realism, and necessary for its didactic purposes.[285]

Indeed, militancy was needed to justify some of the claims of those who prepared the ground for socialist realism to the effect that

> the proper function of art was to organise, not only the ideas of men, their thought and knowledge, but also their feelings and moods. Proletarian art ... is art which organised men's minds towards the ideas of collective labour, solidarity and brotherhood.[286]

Militancy was also socialist realism's interpretation of Lenin's concept of *partiinost* (partymindedness), but linked it with another contradictory concept, that of *narodnost* (folkmindedness), since 'by "partymindedness" Lenin did not mean merely partisanship, but subjugation to the party; it was, therefore, not a question of belief but of obedience',[287] whereas 'folkmindedness' would open the door for individual comprehension of reality and, therefore, for challenging the official line. Militancy was also needed to accomplish the required radical shift in literary attitudes because

> for almost a century and a half Russian literature had been opposed to the established regime and had fought the state and its representatives. Now the Communists wanted a literature that would support the regime, serve the state and be submissive to the government.[288]

However, in the process of this radical change socialist realism reduced art to

> an instrument of mass persuasion and psychological terror, a component of the social system of force, similar to the party and state machinery, the plan bureaucracy, the mass organisations, propaganda, and the secret police.[289]

The overtly close connection between art and politics stripped art of a great deal of its particular and subtle characteristics. Indeed, one cannot deny that art and politics 'can meet, stimulate and inspire one another, as they did in the post-Revolutionary era. But the attempt to make them agree must bring on a collision, and in the case of Stalin ... this ended in the death of art.'[290] The death of art was not merely a bureaucratic act but the result of severe contradictions inherent in the literary doctrine itself.

One major contradiction is conveyed in the actual name of the doctrine, for the word 'socialist' has romantic connotations, not only because socialism was a dream yet to be realised, but also because, with reference to art, it implies that art may be capable of changing human beings and society as a whole. 'That art has this function is, however, a commonplace of the Romantic attitude: the poet as legislator.'[291] It suggests that art 'has human reality as its object, but seeks in it not what it is but what it should be, and transforms things so that they reflect a prettified human reality, with the edges smoothed.'[292] This representation of reality not as it is but as it ought to be, which became the statute adopted by the Soviet Writers Union in 1934 and was reaffirmed in 1959,[293] was later condemned and termed as false, even by ardent Marxists.[294]

The latter part of the name, 'realism', suggests a true representation of reality, thus conflicting with the former. Realism does not take preconceived ideas as its main point of departure, for it adopts an artistic approach to reality that recognises the dialectical interaction between form and content. Yet socialist realism fails to take account of this vital interaction and discerns form and content as completely separate, and gives the latter precedence.[295] It fails also to eschew the pitfalls of resorting to a conceptual approach to reality. Like romanticism, it involves a largely conceptual approach to reality, not only because of being conditioned by Marxian ideology but also because of its stated aim to become 'an active force striving to change the world, purposeful, capable of distinguishing good from evil ... It is realism plus enthusiasm, realism plus a militant mood.'[296]

Indeed, 'socialist realism went beyond mere criticism of decaying capitalism, to portray the rise of the revolutionary proletariat, its struggle and victory: for socialist realism means not only knowing reality as it is, but knowing whether it is moving'.[297] This strong concern for the future is further reinforced by socialist realism's anti-bourgeois ideology, and here again, it resembles 'romanticism, which, though associated with the *bourgeoisie*, was anti-bourgeois in its ideology'.[298] Like romanticism also, socialist realism has a particularly parochial connotation, for it was the literary manifestation of Stalin's nationalistic attitude: 'for Stalin, realism must become patriotic, nationalistic and agitational',[299] three adjectives that might also describe a number of romantic works.

Furthermore, 'the term socialist realism was coined by Gorky, who had in mind a vague combination of realism and socialist romanticism'.[300] Gorky and his annotators 'insisted on identifying socialist realism with revolutionary romanticism, and advised young writers to extol enthusiasm, sacrifice, heroism, and to choose topics of struggle and conflict'.[301] Other expounders went even further and, combining the two opposing terms 'realism' and 'romanticism' in their treatments of socialist realism, urged that 'realism should engage itself and aim at changing reality. And to do this realism must become "romantic realism", and produce a literature flowing with revolutionary ardour and class consciousness'.[302] Needless to say,

> this type of realism falls into the trap of artistic unrealism. For the most part, what was made to pass for socialist realism during the Stalinist period was nothing but its transformation into "socialist" idealism.[303]

This idealistic feature, which was condemned later by subsequent Marxist critics,[304] linked socialist realism further to romanticism. In practice, the link proved to go even deeper than the tenets of any theoretical treatise. Socialist realist writers had, like some romantics, 'an extraordinary relish for the appearances of disaster and misery'.[305] Any critical appraisal of their work would reveal many other qualities associated with romantic literature.

These, then, are the general features and inherent contradictions of socialist realism that seem to have influenced Egyptian literature. When the term came into use in Arabic in the early 1950s, the debate about commitment in literature was in full swing and socialist realist writers were able to argue that their style of writing was synonymous with commitment, or at least an expression of *la littérature engagée.* Historical and political events made Egyptian Marxist writers susceptible to the tenets of socialist realism, which inspired an increasing number of them and opened their eyes to a new mode of discourse.[306] The way they interpreted it, however, makes the coinage of the alternative, 'socialist romantic', particularly apposite in their case.

In Egyptian literature socialist realism was a lax discipline that appealed to many writers in different ways and influenced numerous works. The influence varied considerably, for while writers such as Zakariyyā al-Ḥijjāwī (1914–76),[307] Ibrāhīm 'Abd al-Ḥalīm (1919–98),[308] 'Abd al-Raḥmān al-Sharqāwī (1920–87) and Muḥammad Ṣidqī (1927–2004), fell heavily under its spell, others, like 'Abd al-Raḥmān al-Khamīsī (1919–84?),[309] Aḥmad Rushdī Ṣāliḥ (1921–82)[310] and Maḥmūd al-Sa'danī (b. 1925),[311] were only partially influenced by it. Characteristics of socialist realism, especially those with romantic connotations, can be detected in the work of numerous other writers.[3126] Nevertheless, this influence, whether total or partial, was short-lived, for after sweeping through Egyptian literature in the first half of the 1950s it waned gradually until it died out by the end of the decade – but not before leaving a lasting effect on the development of some literary genres.

'Abd al-Raḥmān al-Sharqāwī

Although al-Sharqāwī is better known for his novels and plays, he was the first of those heavily influenced by Marxian literary doctrine to publish a collection of short stories in which an amalgam of romantic and nascent socialist realist elements is clearly evident. His first collection, *Arḍ al-Ma'rakah* ('The Battlefield'), appeared in 1953 and was shortly followed by his second, *Aḥlām Ṣaghīrah* ('Small Dreams'), in 1956. In these two collections, al-Sharqāwī laid the foundations of Egyptian socialist romanticism in prose fiction and, although he stopped writing short stories after the publication of his second collection, the identifying characteristics of the trend remain apparent in his subsequent writings. Al-Sharqāwī demonstrates a strong sense of history, a sense which he cherished and developed throughout his literary career and which, ironically, makes him prone to embracing the ways of seeing of socialist romantic writers.

Al-Sharqāwī's first collection contains an interesting mixture of intentional conceptualisation and historical material. History provides al-Sharqāwī with the required perspective, in Marxian terms the historical materialist outlook, which vindicates the all-pervasive conceptualisation. The collection appears carefully planned and highly homogenous, and offers, for the first time in Egyptian literature, a new concept of a collection of short stories, not as an accumulative production that derives its *raison d'être* from the mere fact that the writer has amassed, over a period of time, a sufficient number of short stories to publish a book form, but as an integral and homologous work.[313] He creates through the short stories of this collection, and indeed his other collection, a unified and consistent world that centres around one major theme expressed in the title of the collection.

In *Arḍ al-Maʿrakah*, the prevalent theme is the Egyptian people's resistance to all forms of social and political oppression. In order to illustrate the various aspects of this theme, or rather to demonstrate its validity, al-Sharqāwī builds a vast canvas, which covers over a century and a half of Egypt's modern history, stretching from the Mamlūk era and the time of the French expedition, to the violent riots of 1946, and embraces various forms of popular uprisings and mass resistance. It illustrates both passive[314] and active[315] rebellion against the oppressive and corrupt Mamlūks, the tenacity, diversity and vibrancy of Cairo's revolutions against the French,[316] the tragic yet heroic failure of ʿUrābī's revolt,[317] and the many forms of resistance to the British occupation.[318] The modern history of Egypt is thus made to appear as a long and continuous epic of suffering and heroism. On this vast canvas of oppression and resistance, al-Sharqāwī endeavours to portray heroic deeds in the simplest possible manner, integrating them into everyday life and presenting them as part of the normal behaviour of ordinary people. In this way he seems to suggest that if heroic and rebellious deeds were a temporal or even an exceptional phenomenon, they would not have manifested themselves so intensively and frequently throughout a long stretch of modern history.

Ironically, his attempt to simplify heroism and integrate it into Egypt's daily life – an attempt pertaining to the provocative and persuasive function of art – results in the exaggeration of the heroic qualities of ordinary man. Although this is an inherent element in the socialist romantic concept of the positive hero, al-Sharqāwī's exaggeration of these qualities often goes beyond tolerable levels. His ordinary, simple, harmless men are capable not only of challenging and defeating the heavily armed powers that dominate them[319] but also of detecting the germ of a potential unfavourable development and responding accordingly.[320] His exaggeration, which occasionally borders on sentimentality, manifests itself clearly in the polarisation of characteristics in his fictional world. He assigns most benevolent qualities and high moral sense to the poor and underprivileged and presents their oppressors as double-dyed villains. Al-Sharqāwī's poor are courageous, sensitive, moral and wise. They are patient, yet decisive when the need arises,[321] and while they accept fate and endure suffering, they are capable of positive action and resist oppression. The rich, on the other hand, are cruel, corrupt and decadent. The rulers among them are iniquitous and their women are indiscreet, immoral and lacking in charm.

However, this apparent polarisation does not prevent al-Sharqāwī from introducing some convincing human types from various social backgrounds. This is not a consequence of skilful characterisation, for in fact his attempt to integrate his individuals into the masses and to make them indistinguishable from the people whom they represent results in his paying little attention to characterisation; it is rather a product of his attempt to widen the scope and implications of the conflict in his stories, and to explore the complex mechanism of class struggle beneath the patriotic issues. Some of his stories contain insightful Marxian analyses of certain political events,[322] while others reveal social contradictions within certain strata of society.[323] Needless to say, the accuracy of his social analysis is often achieved at the expense of artistic requirements.

Apart from his main theme of struggle and confrontation between the Egyptian people and their oppressors, al-Sharqāwī presents some important sub-themes. One such, which enriches the theme of struggle and confrontation and links al-Sharqāwī's work to the tradition of the Egyptian short story, is the role of religious shaykhs in the vital issues of their societies. His treatment of the subject also stands out from that of other writers on account of its balanced approach. Unlike many of his predecessors, he does not discredit the shaykhs indiscriminately but tries painstakingly to explain their action in class terms[324] and to demonstrate the vital role of religious sentiment in people's lives. He suggests that religion is a double-edged sword; it can (through religious figures) play an effective revolutionary role and it can be used to counter-revolutionary ends.[325] Al-Sharqāwī seems to suggest that the former is closer to the true spirit of religion, and that the betrayal of the revolutionary and patriotic cause equals renunciation of the true faith.[326] Religious leaders in the community who play an active role in fighting for the material cause, and denounce their fellows who prop up the enemy, are common in his work.[327]

Another sub-theme is the attempt to mystify reality and surround the deeds of his positive heroes in legend. He does not achieve this through exaggeration and fantasy but by creating a certain distance between the heroic events and the narrative present. The events are nevertheless relevant to the situation portrayed in the story, which makes them a source of inspiration and legend.[328] Al-Sharqāwī also uses the technique of parallelism, whereby a legendary personality is held up as a mirror to his character, so that the latter's actions are measured against the former's highly revered conduct. To enhance this technique, the comparison is conducted through the opponents of the character, and the character is made to be totally unaware of the magnitude of his predecessor's achievements.[329] Al-Sharqāwī also uses the comparison device to demonstrate the double standard of morality of the occupying forces on the one hand, and to reveal the dissatisfaction and guilt of some of their officers at certain of their outrageous misdemeanours on the other.[330]

Through these recurring themes, al-Sharqāwī tries to rewrite the history of Egypt from the point of view not of the rulers but of the ruled. Although this approach gives him some positive insights, he falls victim to some of the shortcomings of his conceptual approach to reality, for in effect he is substituting one partisan approach to history with another, based on the cult of the masses and often on wishful thinking.[331] He does not portray reality as it is but uses history as a means to reconstruct reality as he thinks it ought to be, especially when historical events run tragically counter to many of his basic assumptions.[332] Moreover, his desire to make his heroes as constructive and progressive and truly 'socialist' as possible results in sentimental inaccuracies and implausible characterisation.

Yet in several works al-Sharqāwī succeeds in turning remote historical events into deeply human and convincing experiences, especially when he illustrates the repercussions of historical events on the lives of Egyptian peasants.[333] His first-hand experience of life in rural Egypt lends credence to his supposedly historical account and enables him to raise the realism in his work from a mere sugar coating of preconceived notions to a genuine component of a convincingly artistic experience.[334] In addition, his awareness of the importance of inner contradictions in both character and situation, and his attempt to demonstrate the Marxian laws of negation and dialectics at work, enhance the plausibility of his work, albeit in few cases.[335] These aspects provide the work not only with a viable plot and multidimensional characterisation but also with a sense of conflict, which widens the implications of the work and substantiates the claim (in theory) of a 'true Marxist' work of art to represent latent developmental tendencies in history.

The representation of developmental tendencies or future potentialities of a given reality is more evident in al-Sharqāwī's second collection, *Aḥlām Ṣaghīrah*. Like the first, this collection presents a homogeneous, integrated world and centres upon one pivotal theme. As its title suggests, the major theme is the hope of the oppressed for a better future. In order to fulfil the demands of socialist realism, the collection endeavours to sketch the means of transforming these impossible, though justifiable, dreams into reality. Indeed, the stories of this collection are evenly divided between the expression of the dreams and aspirations of frustrated characters and the study of the various elements that participate in the creation of the positive hero who is capable of fulfilling such dreams and aspirations.

Despite the lack of any direct connection, *Aḥlām Ṣaghīrah* can be seen in some senses as the sequel of *Arḍ al-Maʿrakah,* not only because it begins, historically speaking, where the first collection leaves off and tackles the realities of the 1940s and 1950s, but also because of the existence of a deeper thematic link. *Arḍ al-Maʿrakah* attempts to rewrite and completely revaluate Egypt's modern history and to reconsider the role of the underprivileged. It is as if *Aḥlām Ṣaghīrah* was written with this historical prelude in mind, and the presentation in *Arḍ al-Maʿrakah* of the heroic resistance of the poor to the various enemies of Egypt throughout its modern history has made debate over their right to a better future unnecessary; so the second collection sets out to portray their dreams and aspirations and delineate the path to fulfilment.

Nevertheless, *Aḥlām Ṣaghīrah* does not rely completely on its precursor and can stand as a separate collection. As well as the dreams, it illustrates the horrors of extreme poverty, where man is denied the bare necessities of life[336] and has to cope with inhumanly humiliating conditions.[337] In such conditions, some characters have to pay dearly to earn a bare living,[338] while others lose their lives in the process.[339] In addition to the crushing poverty, al-Sharqāwī describes the destructive effect of war on the material and moral life of man, particularly the poor,[340] and the corrupting influence of the British occupation on the life of the lower strata of urban society.[341] He also portrays the glaring contradictions perpetuated by the wide and unjust disparities in society, revealing in the process another contradiction between urban and rural ideals,[342] and shows how the presence of certain social conditions can make life seem fatefully predetermined and a curse thwarting the individual's hopes and dreams.[343]

After introducing various facets of the gloomy present that the underprivileged endure, al-Sharqāwī tries to shape and express their hope for a better future – not only because it is the nature of things that people in distress should hope for a better future but mainly because his preconceptions necessitate saturating his world with hopes in order to justify the emergence of the positive hero and motivate him. He describes the euphoria associated with the dream of a poor peasant lad, who hopes to go to school in the town and be saved from labouring on the farm, and elaborates on the ramifications of this in an attempt to give the dream weight and widen its implications. He then illustrates the deep grief and disappointment which befalls the young protagonist when fate turns his simple dream into ashes.[344] In another story,[345] fate becomes instrumental in achieving the hopes of the oppressed, particularly when their failure in fulfilling them intensifies oppression and disillusionment.

He also portrays how dreams of love and happiness fade away in pain and sadness,[346] and how the humblest aspirations for peace and a simple life are extremely difficult to attain.[347] In addition, he illustrates the aspiration of many characters to realise their talents,[348] potential[349] and peace of mind.[350] He also links the dreams of individuals with those of the country as a whole and in so doing he gives their anguish and suffering a wider meaning[351] and lends a touch of patriotism to their folk tales.[352] In a few stories, he succeeds in making the presentation and characterisation suggest the way out from the situation without dwelling upon the thoughts of his characters or obtrusively putting words in their mouths. Yet, even in such stories, he cannot eschew completely the dictates of his preconceptions or the pitfalls of his latent sentimentality.

When some of his characters escape, under the pressure of poverty, from the village to the city, the change of place does not solve their problems. They face new forms of oppression and fail to adjust to the cultural shock of the city and its alternative values,[353] since their past weighs down their attempts at individual salvation. Indeed, al-Sharqāwī's perception of social conditions is static and inflexible, for once the protagonist fails to realise his life in one place, this failure follows him automatically into the new location. This is so neither because of the complete lack of social mobility nor because the character loses stamina and will for living, but mainly because of the author's static preconceptions in which characters are perceived of as social data and not as human beings full of potential. Thus, the failure of the character in the village is conditioned by social realities, and the failure naturally persists despite the new beginning, for the change must start, according to al-Sharqāwī, from within – the fact of moving to the city has no magical power in itself.

Indeed, despite various fundamental differences, the social laws that govern village and city are not dissimilar, yet al-Sharqāwī sees the contradictions between rural and urban communities as two-fold, social and moral. On the one hand, the city is portrayed as an illusory paradise where happiness is easily attainable, but only after sacrificing one's rural values and morals;[354] on the other, the city is not only a dream made of the aspirations of the deprived villagers but mainly a social system in which the class relationships that led the villagers to flee to the city are still prevalent.[355] Furthermore, al-Sharqāwī believes that there are two cities, whose relationship with each other does not radically differ from that between urban and rural societies in either its social or moral dimensions.[356] So the attempt to achieve one's dreams by moving from the poor to the rich city is as futile as the endeavour to change one's social conditions by leaving the village to go to the town.

Al-Sharqāwī suggests that the only way out of the injustice of social disparity is by active alteration of the social order; in other words through the positive hero. In the creation of this positive hero, the city, despite its ineffectuality in providing a haven for the distressed, has a substantial contribution to make, for it is the source of the knowledge and awareness necessary for a positive confrontation with reality. It matures the protagonist's dreams and provides him with understanding and experience, which ensure his success in altering the status quo.[357] It is no coincidence that the only two positive heroes who master the process of changing their reality are armed with both the values of the village and the knowledge and experience acquired in the town.[358] The others, who are lacking in one or other of these, are less successful.[359]

Although al-Sharqāwī portrays the gloomy and inhuman atmosphere in which the poor live and gives expression to their dreams of a better future, he stops short of directing the situation and characterisation to adumbrate future developments. Yet, as a steadfastly committed writer, he has a strong sense of the future, and, when failing to implant it subtly in the narrative, he endeavours to put it across obtrusively. The expectations of his characters are unrealistically high, presumably to make the emergence of the positive hero more credible. He mixes genuine developmental tendencies with unfounded and escapist dreams, and consequently weakens the internal logic of the progression of the action in a number of stories.[360] He also falls victim to what Lukács terms false polarisation and false simplification, when 'on the one hand, theory, from being a guide to practice, becomes a dogma, while, on the other hand, the element of contradiction between the two is eliminated'.[361] Ironically, the theoretical framework, which is meant to enhance the agitational power of literature, produces a literature without conflict and, consequently, enfeebles its ability to inspire the reader or contribute to his experience. The false polarisation and simplification affect not only the characterisation and progression of the action but also the credibility and coherence of the work as a whole. This particular theoretical framework can be extremely valuable, however. The works of Muḥammad Ṣidqī may be cited as an illustration of its usefulness.

Muḥammad Ṣidqī

Unlike all the Egyptian writers before him, Ṣidqī had almost no systematic education, as he was thrown out of school at the age of seven because of his father's inability to pay the fees. So at this early age, as well as experiencing severe poverty, he had to go out to work; he was apprenticed to a carpenter for six years and, at the same time, he had to learn the Qur'an by heart in the evenings to qualify for attendance at the only free educational institutes available at the time, which were those administered by the Azhar. By the time he succeeded in enrolling at the Religious Institute in Alexandria it was only a few years before the Allies reached the town, and he was forced to go back to his native city, Damanhūr. While studying traditional and religious subjects in Alexandria, he had been obliged to work in the textile factory in Karmuz.

During his short period of study at the Azharite institute, Ṣidqī developed a keen interest in literature, and after being forced to leave Alexandria he continued to further his literary reading and knowledge while working as a welder, farm labourer, plumber, mechanic and fitter. He became active in the trade union movement, which gave him a natural introduction to the thriving left-wing politics of the 1940s, and this in turn entailed further study and knowledge. Although he became increasingly involved in politics, he was clearly oriented towards literature and used his political understanding to advantage in his literary studies. His involvement with intellectual and political circles also helped him to publish his work, and it is arguable whether he would have been able to pursue a literary career without the extensive support of left-wing intellectuals and the publications they edited.

Thus by upbringing and cultural formation, as well as by temperament, Ṣidqī was qualified to build upon the socialist romantic qualities in al-Sharqāwī's work. It is no coincidence that his first collection, *al-Anfār* (1956), appeared on the heels of al-Sharqāwī's second and last collection. Nor is it a coincidence that Ṣidqī's first collection was enthusiastically introduced by the ardent advocate of socialist romantic doctrine in Egypt at the time, Maḥmūd Amīn al-ʿĀlim, who hailed the collection in a lengthy adulatory introduction.[362] As a worker and Marxist, Ṣidqī was living proof that socialist romantic literature was not only feasible in Egypt but was thriving.

Ṣidqī's work takes the pioneering achievements of al-Sharqāwī as its departure point, elaborating on his views and discoveries, and widening the applications and implications of his themes and techniques. Socialist romantic writing reached a high point in its development in the 1950s in his work,[363] for he carried both the positive and negative aspects of this literary tendency to their limits. He embarked upon an ambitious course of committed writing, totally dedicated to the cause of the oppressed strata of society. His central characters, almost without exception, are workers and peasants and he devotes many stories to the portrayal of their suffering and crippling problems. He shows, in a palpable and, occasionally, artistically convincing manner, how difficult is the life of the workers. They endure intense insecurity,[364] poverty[365] and injustice,[366] but demonstrate an exceptional ability for survival[367] and struggle constantly merely to subsist. Their intolerable situation is not of their own making, nor is it perceived as an irrevocable fate, but rather as a situation that is imposed upon them by the prevalent mode of production and its values.[368] Most of Ṣidqī's characters are portrayed as intelligent[369] and hard working,[370] cherishing human values and feelings[371] and respecting their work enormously.[372] They are seen to be dignified, honest and proud,[373] therefore they are sensitive to suffering and do their best to assuage it.[374] They are kind-hearted and their sense of responsibility is strong, for they have a code of conduct that is both simple and powerful.[375]

However, these overwhelmingly virtuous characteristics seem to be of no avail in securing a reasonable life. Ṣidqī's protagonists still have no guarantee against misfortune, let alone against unemployment or industrial accidents,[376] and despite all their hard work they cannot provide their children with the simplest pleasures of childhood[377] or an education;[378] the children are therefore compelled to abandon their dreams of a better future.[379] Adults are forced to forsake their lovers and sweethearts and, as a result, their lives are burdened with a deep sense of loss and remorse.[380] They are not even granted the luxury of dwelling upon past love affairs, for they are exhausted by the tiresome quest for subsistence.[381] Moreover, despite their optimism and will to survive, they seem to be permanently enveloped in an air of gloom and sadness, which mocks their optimism and enervates their souls.[382]

The contradiction between their goodness and the prevalent misfortune is not intentional, nor is it a technical device to accentuate the injustice inflicted on them; it is rather a direct product of the author's exaggeration of perspective, which is inseparable from his commitment to the cause of the working class. Like al-Sharqāwī, Ṣidqī emphasises, through his presentation of conceptually controlled reality, the suffering of the underprivileged and the agony of poverty, which he describes in extended scenes. Although the misery of poverty is his main theme, which he sustains throughout almost every story, his conceptual approach to reality dictates the presentation of the workers as being virtuous, intelligent and good-natured. The contradiction poses the question of how such poverty and gloom can produce, and moreover sustain, such qualities of character.

It seems that Ṣidqī sacrifices the Marxian maxim that men are the product of their material circumstances to another Marxian argument, that men are capable of controlling their material existence and hence of changing it. By providing his characters with qualities contrary to those that would be a natural reflection of their surroundings, he qualifies them to change their oppressive reality. In this respect, Ṣidqī excludes the possibility of any other change that would involve escape by social climbing and, at the same time, attempts to illustrate the emergence of a positive hero and link this to various developmental tendencies in the situation portrayed. He also involves his hero with patriotic issues and, on occasions, with revolutionary causes in neighbouring countries.[383]

On the one hand, many of his stories present a rigorous attack on social climbing and demonstrate the futility of the illusion of individual salvation.[384] They advocate the importance of commitment to one's own class and delineate the renunciation of one's class in terms of shame and even treachery.[385] On the other hand, numerous stories hold the protagonists' commitment to their own class in high esteem and present it as the most honourable course of action, particularly when it involves a great deal of sacrifice on the individual's part.[386] A thematic corollary to this is the presentation of the city as a false haven that fails to provide the oppressed villager with the magic solution to his problem; it rather demoralises him and inflicts upon him more pain and suffering.[387] Indeed, the majority of Ṣidqī's stories deal with the urban working-class situation and present the city as an equally oppressive society, thus eliminating a great deal of the grounds for the common romantic theme of the conflict between rural and urban societies.

Ṣidqī's presentation of the benevolent characteristics of the underprivileged acts as a suitable overture for the appearance of the positive hero and his role in changing the prevalent social order, and particularly in the political struggle for a better future. Ṣidqī seems to favour achieving the moral presentation of the militant activist at the expense of the plausibility of the process of characterisation. He is also concerned with the influence of the working-class positive hero on wider national issues.[388] Indeed, it is exceedingly difficult to separate this theme from that of patriotic struggle for independence which, in turn, adumbrates the related theme of political intimidation.[389] It is difficult to avoid, in Ṣidqī's work and indeed in the work of socialist romanticism in general, the clear affinity between the patriotic struggle for independence and Marxian ideas concerning the social content of the nationalistic revolution.[390] The link between these complementary themes is certainly a product of Ṣidqī's involvement in the Egyptian Marxist movement, for the introduction of Marxian and left-wing ideologies into Egyptian cultural and political life in the 1940s was responsible for the emergence of a new approach to the national question – an approach that accentuated its social and class content. It is therefore natural that Ṣidqī should envisage the struggle for independence as being inseparable from the militant attitude of the working class to the prevalent exploitative mode of production and their eagerness to change this.[391] As is also to be expected, he considers his own approach to the national question as the only valid one and treats the workers who follow that path with veneration. Yet he cannot underestimate the difficulties involved in pursuing such a course of action or justify it with anything more than an attitude of blind optimism, often mere wishful thinking.[392] Furthermore, the strong identification between the author's stand and that of his positive hero narrows down the prospect of richness and diversity of characterisation and results in the creation of two-dimensional characters.[393]

However, Ṣidqī succeeds in introducing a considerable number of positive heroes whose attempt to change reality is ironically quixotic rather than Marxist. As a result, their actions only complicate the situation and intensify their agony and suffering.[394] The author is usually quick to introduce a note of historical optimism into these situations but this appears as an extraneous palliative and, unlike al-Sharqāwī, who merely exaggerates, Ṣidqī does not hesitate to impose hopes and optimism on situations that do not accept them.[395] This obtrusiveness is a symptom of his desire to portray an ideal type who is capable of realising the basic precepts of dialectical materialism with a related notion of social optimism, and betrays the weakness of his grasp of artistic structure.

Nevertheless, neither the naiveté of Ṣidqī's imposed social optimism, nor his dogmatic and mechanical understanding of Marxism, prevent him, on some occasions, from presenting a powerful case against political intimidation[396] and, at the same time, developing some convincing positive heroes, especially when he introduces them through the eyes of their antagonists.[397] On these occasions, he avoids exaggeration and stereotypes, emphasises the human dimensions of the complex process of intimidation, and tries to show the brutality of the demoralising forces of coercion at work, uncircumscribed by the dogma of historical necessity, which flattens the presentation of many themes in his work.[398]

Ṣidqī's failure to exclude obtrusive conceptualisation or propaganda is closely connected with his perception of artistic structure as a vehicle separate and less important than content, a dichotomy inherent in Egyptian socialist romanticism. It also seems that although as a Marxist he sees himself as a revolutionary dedicated to changing his society, as an artist he confines himself to preaching and reform, hence the rhetoric and verbosity in his writing, and his lengthy authorial commentary on both events and characters, which are often intended to consolidate the conceptual scheme that controls the progression of the action. This didacticism, which often borders on propaganda and agitation, fails to become a regulative principle of literature.[399]

In many of Ṣidqī's works[400] both characterisation and the progression of the action are governed not by the internal logic of the work but by a conceptual framework that necessitates that the poor should always be in the right while the rich are invariably the wrongdoers. This false polarisation inevitably enfeebles the conflict and flattens the major contradictions that sustain a valid fictional situation. As a result, the action, although it depends on prevailing circumstances and conveys a photographic image of external reality, suffers from incoherence and the characters lack humanity, plausibility and motivation, for they have to submit to the conceptual line and comply with the tenets of the doctrine. In consequence, many of Ṣidqī's stories,[401] despite, or indeed because of, their photographic accuracy, cease, as Lukács says in his analysis on narrative, 'to reflect the dynamic contradictions of social life and become the illustration of an abstract truth'.[402] Whether this 'truth' is in fact true or not, the dominance of the conceptual framework is always achieved at the expense of the inner logic and cohesion of the artistic structure. The dictatorial rule of the conceptual approach to reality, which in this case induces many misrepresented Marxian doctrines, results in what Lukács terms the 'de-poetisation of reality'.

Despite its shortcomings, Ṣidqī's work helped to establish the lives and sufferings of working-class characters as worthy subject matter for the Egyptian short story, and to prove – as al-ʿĀlim rightly suggests[403] – that the new literary genre had penetrated deeply into Egypt's social and cultural life. Both his enthusiasm for the cause of the working class and his artistic defects represent the most significant characteristics of socialist romanticism in Egypt, as his work attracted a relatively wide reading public throughout the 1950s and took socialist romantic writing as far as it could go. When he was imprisoned in 1959 and consequently stopped writing, it appeared to those who did not know much about his imprisonment that the socialist romantic tendency had reached its acme and then died of natural causes, especially as the many younger writers who continued to produce socialist romantic works failed to catch the readers' attention or to attain the minimum level of skill necessary to combine coherent conceptualisation and narrative.

Thus socialist romanticism came to an abrupt end in 1960, not as a result of a calculated decision but, ironically, as the consequence of a political blow: by 1960 most of those who advocated its precepts and those who wrote according to its dictates were imprisoned, and when they were released, after five years, their world was changing. Socialist realism was falling out of favour, even in Russia, and a new artistic sensibility was developing. A few writers continued to tread the old path, while others, including their leading critic al-ʿĀlim, tried to comprehend the new sensibility and adapt to its requirements. But none of the leading writers of socialist romanticism survived the radical changes brought about by the changing, artistically demanding sensibility. As for those who opted to continue writing as if nothing had happened, their voices were incongruous and their works soon overshadowed.

CHAPTER FOUR

Experimentation and Modern Sensibility

The new literary sensibility, which was heralded by Nadīm at the turn of the nineteenth century and was responsible over the following decades for the emergence of the Egyptian short story as a new literary genre, reached its apogee by the middle of the twentieth century, when it began to undergo substantial change. Its early strength and vigour, which had attracted many talents, were dwindling under the influence of sentimentality and socialist romanticism, for neither was responsive to the many cultural shifts and social displacements that were taking place. Many of the gifted writers who had participated in shaping and developing the new sensibility stopped writing or were left dwelling on past discoveries and achievements. The literary style and sensibility of the moment were increasingly unable to come to terms with Egypt's social transformation, a process accelerated by the cultural and political changes that took place between 1940 and 1970, and which resulted in a shift in human relations. 'And when human relations change there is at the same time a change in religion, conduct, politics and literature.'[1]

Although the shift was gradual, it took place with great vigour, for in these three decades the country's population doubled and that of Cairo tripled. The effects of the process of urbanisation, which had taken place in the nineteenth and the first half of the twentieth centuries, were penetrating every aspect of social life. The consequences of one world war and three local wars were also felt throughout this period. Indeed, the period is a testimony to the idea that nothing alters human relations as rapidly and intensely as wars and massive urban population expansion; they destroy the existing order and bring social upheaval, discontent and a sense of loss and estrangement. 'The war itself can be recognised as the apocalyptic moment of transition into the new',[2] not only because it brings about a new reality, but also because it can pose crucial questions that often entail a complete reappraisal of values and culture. Egypt's involvement in the Second World War was tinged with an element of absurdity in the sense that it was forced to provide the stage for a war that did not concern it, suffered its devastating events, and ironically helped its enemy, the British, to win it. This irony sparked off a deep sense of bewilderment, which was soon combined with agony and despair as a result of the failure of the 1946 uprising and the catastrophe of 1948.

Apart from the wars and other social changes, the 1940s witnessed a rise in the political coercion and intimidation that had started in the previous decade, and the introduction of new cultural influences in the form of novel European ideas and modern modes of discourse. The former created a new reality in which the world becomes transferable and arbitrary, or as Walter Benjamin put it, 'exalted and depreciated', and a new kind of human experience, which was characterised by gloom, vagueness and irrationality. The latter deepened writers' perception of this new reality and provided them with both a theoretical background that enabled them to understand and articulate their changing experiences and new techniques capable of assimilating and expressing them. Indeed, some of the new influences (such as certain ideas of Nietzche, Freud, and Frazer) confirmed the irrational trend of argument,[3] while others, such as those of Marx and Darwin, accentuated the rational one. But the greatest stimulus came from the new artistic movements in Europe, which revolutionised painting, music and literature.

In fact, the impact of modern European art on Egyptian cultural life precedes the Second World War and goes back to the early 1930s, when some post-First World War modernist movements, with their 'anti-representationalism in painting, atonalism in music, *vers libre* in poetry, stream-of-consciousness narrative in the novel'[4] reached Egypt. Just as the birth of the modern in Europe 'coincides with the discovery or rediscovery of Japanese graphics, Balinese music, African sculpture, Romanesque painting and the poetry of the troubadours',[5] so the birth of the modern Egypt coincided with the discovery of Freud, Einstein, Kafka, Virginia Woolf and the post-impressionist painters, and the rediscovery of Darwin, Marx, Trotsky and Dostoevsky.[6] The latter half of the 1930s and the 1940s saw the translation of these writers' work and the formation of many literary and artistic coteries to study and elucidate their new ideas and to implement their principles in creative writing.

Painters were the first to respond to anti-representationalism and non-figurative art. Within one decade they moved freely from impressionism and expressionism to cubism, surrealism and the abstract.[7] Nor did they confine themselves to propagating these new concepts in their painting alone; they recognised the importance of promoting their ideas in writing, and tried to express the theoretical background of their impulse towards innovation and change in leaflets and pamphlets, which they distributed at their exhibitions. Ramsīs Yūnān, an able and talented modernist painter, published the most elegant and persuasive defence of new non-figurative art, *Ghāyat al-Rassām al-'Aṣrī* (1938). In this seminal work, Yūnān articulates many of the views and aspirations of his fellow painters, who wished to emphasise the significance of innovation and subjectivity in the creative arts. Although mainly about painting, Yūnān's book was enthusiastically received by many young writers, who saw it as a clear expression of an important phenomenon: the endeavour to re-evaluate the prevalent precepts of art and discover the essential in the accidental.

Yūnān's book delineates the deep concern of many creative minds at the time with making a radical change in artistic perception,

> to objectify the subjective, to make audible or perceptible the mind's inaudible conversations, to halt the flow, to irrationalise the rational, to defamiliarise and dehumanise the expected, to conventionalise the extraordinary and the eccentric, to intellectualise the emotional, to see space as a function of time, mass as a form of energy, and uncertainty as the only certain thing.[8]

This strong drive for change had manifested itself throughout the literary spectrum some years before Yūnān's articulation of the problem, appearing in the early impressionistic paintings of al-Tilmisānī and Fu'ād Kāmil in the mid-1930s, and even in Ṭāhā Ḥusayn's eloquent plea for stronger ties with European culture in his *Mustaqbal al-Thaqāfah fī Miṣr* (1938). It could also be discerned in the allegorical and symbolic elements in some of Tawfīq al-Ḥakīm's plays of the 1930s, especially his so-called rational plays, such as *Ahl al-Kahf* (1934) and *Scheherazade* (1936), and in ʿAlī Aḥmad Bākathīr's introduction to *vers libre* in his translation of *Romeo and Juliet* in 1938, and then in his own play *Akhnātūn wa-Nifirtītī* (1939). The desire for a radical shift in poetry was also expressed in Bishr Fāris's (1907–63) symbolic poems in *al-Muqtaṭaf* in the 1930s and in *Plutoland* by Luwīs ʿAwaḍ (1915–90), which was published in 1947 but written between 1937 and 1940.[9]

The quest for change was expressed most strongly in two important works that played a major role in promoting the spirit of innovation and rebellion against old forms and concepts: *al-Kitāb al-Manbūdh* (1936) by Anwar Kāmil (1912–96) and *Mafriq al-Ṭarīq* (1938) by Bishr Fāris. The first is a scatological work in the form of episodic dialogues between a man and a woman discussing, in shocking and obscene language, their sexual deviations. Despite its episodic structure the work has an inner cohesion, which is based on a symbolic representation inspired by Freud's *The Interpretation of Dreams* and enhanced by Kāmil's use of the full poetic value of words. The second is a symbolic one-act play that endeavours to explore the mysteries of the human psyche through extensive use of theatrical props and poetic language. Its lengthy preface delineates many of the novel ideas contained in Yūnān's seminal work of the same year, especially those concerning the subjectivity of art and its unique logic and harmony.

All these works manifest the beginnings of a radical shift in the artist's attitude towards reality. They are, for the most part, concerned not with reality but with the individual's impression of it. They are interested in reflecting what Edel calls 'the deeper and more searching inwardness',[10] and in discovering new modes of discourse capable of expressing such inwardness. The fact that this shift expressed itself in several artistic and literary media demonstrates the emergence of a schism in artistic sensibility. But what sort of schism was this to be? Generally, the student of cultural seismology – the attempt to record the shifts and displacements of sensibility that regularly occur in the history of art and literature – distinguishes two different kinds of change. On the one hand, are 'those tremors of fashion that seem to come and go in rhythm with the changing generations, the decade being the right unit for measuring the curves that run from first shock to peak activity and on to the dying rumbles of derivative *Epigonentum*'.[11] On the other, are 'those larger displacements whose effects go deeper and last longer, forming those extended periods of style and sensibility'.[12] The following three decades proved that the changes that began to be expressed, almost through every creative medium, in the 1930s were more than tremors of fashion. They continued to affect the arts and even became the prevalent mode in some media in the 1960s, for the early changes of the 1930s soon combined with further innovations in the 1940s and the increasing influence of the literature of ideas of European Modernism. These changes and influences were gradual more than cataclysmic; they continued to ferment in the minds of those who were receptive to the new and free to venture into uncharted ground, and from this gradual process new modes of discourse were working their way into the cultural scene.

Modern sensibility is an expression of the contemporary mind and its multiple achievements. In addition to the factors outlined above, the modern sensibility

> has been intimately associated with the advent of the electronic media – notably, telephone, radio, television, gramophone records and tape-recordings – and the partial suppression of a visual-spatial basis of culture by an oral-aural one.[13]

Indeed, the opening scene of one of the important novels of the 1940s, Najīb Maḥfūẓ's *Zuqāq al-Midaq* (1947), emphasises the drastic impact of the introduction of such media through the replacement of the bard by the radio, then goes on to record the change in values and attitude that accompanied it. Another important novel, *Millīm al-Akbar* (1944) by 'Ādil Kāmil, records the duality of reality and the anxiety of the intellectual confronted with the disintegration of its logic and cohesion. It also portrays one of the major factors behind the dwindling of the artistic sensibility that had prevailed since the turn of the century: the contradictions between the life of the artist and the life of the 'practical' man, and the distinction between the intellectual and the politician.

The rift grew in the 1940s in Egypt and gave birth to a deep sense of frustration among intellectuals, which grew with their increasing awareness of their isolation from the affairs of their country. The more the artist's, or intellectual's,

> knowledge of affairs grows, the less effective the impact of his

> thinking seems to become. Since he grows more frustrated as his knowledge increases, it seems that knowledge leads to powerlessness. He feels helpless in the fundamental sense that he cannot control what he is able to foresee.'[14]

This frustrating contradiction was intensified by the type of politicians who controlled Egyptian life between 1940 and 1970. The more the Egyptian intelligentsia became isolated from the decision-making process, the more frustrated they became. They sought a solution to their problem in culture, but their cultural curiosity served to further their frustration, thus completing the vicious circle.

It is striking that the early 1940s, which saw the emergence of this rift between the intellectual and politician, or to be more precise a strong awareness of its existence and all that it entailed, witnessed the formation of many artistic and literary coteries whose aim was to increase the writer's awareness of his art and surroundings. The most famous of these were Jamā'at al-Fann wa'l-Ḥurriyyah (the Art and Freedom Group) and its faction Jamā'at al-Khubz wa'l-Ḥurriyyah (the Bread and Freedom Group). In January 1940, Anwar Kāmil, author of *al-Kitāb al-Manbūdh*, established his avant-garde magazine *al-Taṭawwur*[15] to express the thoughts and promote the ideas of Jamā'at al-Fann wa'l-Ḥurriyyah, and later in the same year Ramsīs Yūnān, a leading member of the group, took over the editorship of the well-known monthly review *al-Majallah al-Jadīdah* from Salāmah Mūsā. Yūnān was more inclined towards purely artistic subject matter and emphasised the complete separation of art from society, and the shift from external to internal reality, from the outwardness to the hidden world of fantasy and reverie.[16] He was attracted to surrealistic and abstract art, and his extreme doctrine of artistic freedom caused the bifurcation of the group. Kāmil, who led Jamā'at al-Khubz wa'l-Ḥurriyyah after the split, was in favour of a stronger link with society and a deeper interest in its problems, though not, of course, at the expense of artistic freedom and experimentation. In the editorial of the first issue of *al-Taṭawwur* he outlines some of the main ideas behind the drive for change and innovation:

> It is our conviction that Egyptian society in its present state is lacking in equilibrium and harmony: its moral precepts are deficient and erroneous as are its social and economic conditions. The effect of such defectiveness is starkly evident

> in the many symptoms of decay and powerlessness, where the educated youth waste their time day-dreaming as a result of extreme frustration and repression while the majority of the nation lives in destitution, under appalling conditions caused by the apparent lack of justice in the entire system. By issuing this magazine, we hope to prepare the ground for the latent drives and impulses in this generation to express themselves freely and create a new era, a new movement that resists superstition and fights the old values which were formed to drain the physical and spiritual power of the individual. This society urgently needs a new intellectual movement, such as the one we are calling for.[17]

The strong social tone of this editorial is evident, and the need for change is justified in social terms. Yet Kāmil goes on, in the same editorial, as well as in others, to emphasise the importance of spiritual and artistic elements, and particularly the need for a shift towards more internal and subjective concerns.

Although *al-Taṭawwur* was short lived,[18] Yūnān's editorship of *al-Majallah al-Jadīdah* continued until 1944 and provided a platform for the new, the experimental and the surreal. When it ceased publication in 1944, new writing found breathing space for the following four years (1945–8) in Ṭāhā Ḥusayn's leading magazine *al-Kitāb al-Miṣrī*. In this influential, though not experimental, magazine, some of the modernist European writers who had a profound impact on modern Arabic literature in the decades between 1940 and 1970, such as Joyce, Kafka, Eliot, Sartre and Camus, were introduced for the first time. Although *al-Kātib al-Miṣrī* was more concerned with revolutionising the study of literature, popularising the academic, and rationalising the popular, and therefore published only a few creative works, some of the original stories and poems that appeared in this magazine were noted for their innovation and new techniques.[19] By a fortuitous coincidence, the year 1948, which saw the closure of *al-Kātib al-Miṣrī*, witnessed the birth of a new and important magazine, *al-Bashīr,* and the expansion and popularity of another significant but less impressive publication, *al-Fuṣūl*.

In its revolutionary, manifesto-like editorial, written by the talented young poet and critic Maḥmūd Amīn al-'Ālim, *al-Bashīr* presents the most sophisticated formulation of the quest for radical change in literary expression of the young writers of that period. Unlike the preceding experimental coteries, which were largely dominated by painters, *al-Bashīr*'s group was almost exclusively literary,[20] so its manifesto is more explicit and touches upon direct literary questions. It starts with a clear and decisive break with tradition:

> We are roaming sons ... our movement is random for we have lost the way to our mother's breasts ... We walk on water because we are roaming sons. Yet we have a starting point, a way, and an aim. The point is now, the way is action and experiment, and the goal is free and absolute expression. We have no history since we learned that weaning brings responsibility and commitment or even mastership ... We have refused to inhabit the closed verses of Arabic poetry or to feed on a diet of stale stories, essays and philosophical doctrines.
>
> Indeed, we are errant sons, dear reader, for we have declined to bow down in the temple of verbal rhetoric, Aristotelian logic and Euclidian mathematics ... Our rhetoric is an expression of ..., our logic is a contradiction in ..., and our mathematics is based on, chance and probability. We have lost faith in causality, similarity and verbal decorations. We fear not vacuum and nothingness, for nature itself does not fear them. Thus spake the atoms of Buher, the stories of Kafka, the poetry of Eliot, the sculptures of Moore and the music of Schoenberg. And thus started our straying, when space lost its geographical solidity, when figures and equations were filled with emotions and feelings, when Heisenberg formulates the 'Uncertainty principle' ... when Freud turned our mothers into mistresses, and when an ape gave birth to Charles Darwin.[21]

After its eloquent delineation of the need for a complete break with tradition and the cultural factors behind the urgent drive for radical change the editorial goes on to emphasise the importance of experimentation in all literary forms. The experimentation of the *Bashīr* group was one of the most profound in modern Egyptian literature,[22] for it did not confine itself to one form or genre and was receptive to many new ideas and techniques. Even after this group had disappeared, experimentation continued in both Cairo and Alexandria. Although information about experimentation in Alexandria is scarce, enough is known to be fairly certain that around the time of *al-Bashīr*, or a little earlier, a group of young Alexandrian writers were concerned with identical questions of change and innovation.[23] The fact that the need for radical change was pervasive and these two different groups, with almost no contact between them, were attempting the same thing in Cairo and Alexandria, lends weight to the argument that there was a schism in artistic sensibility around this time. Nevertheless, the modern sensibility that emerged from that schism was a complex one and the wider reading public was far from being capable of responding to the host of new techniques and conventions that accompanied it. Thus the works associated with the modern sensibility were easily overshadowed by works of lesser magnitude, and most of them took some time to gain recognition in literary circles, let alone among the wider reading public.

This chapter is devoted to the study of the rise and development of the modern sensibility in the Egyptian short story and the way in which it gradually, but firmly, emerged beneath the dominant sensibility and continued to claim more ground until by the 1960s it had become the prevalent sensibility. Isolating the works of modern sensibility and studying them together is not undertaken here simply because 'it is the privilege of every age to consider its predicament unique, and it is its hope that the predicament may prove the most grave history has known',[24] nor because the isolation of such works helps to present the shift in emphasis more clearly; rather, it is because of methodological considerations, as the works studied here do not fit easily into either the realistic or the romantic category, though they have much in common with the former and their approach to reality is more artistic than conceptual.

It is nevertheless necessary in terms of method to delay the study of the works of modern sensibility until the various romantic contributions have been discussed, not only because 'the modern revolution in the arts was a reaction to decadent Romanticism',[25] but also because 'the Romantic hero began by contemplating his heart; he ended by contemplating his mind. And he discovered that heart, the symbol of feeling and perception, and mind, symbol of thought and reason, could be closely related'.[26] Each outstanding writer emphasises some aspect or another of man's mind or heart, but these remain as adjustments and alterations within a given framework. 'Romanticism, by trying to give full and unfettered expression to the individual, burst this framework and so made it possible for the moderns to step out of the wreckage and discover that the frame only enclosed a small fraction of the universe.'[27] As far as the Egyptian short story is concerned, sentimentality and socialist romanticism helped to reduce the framework of this genre (form and conventions) to ashes, thus preparing the ground for the rise of new modes of discourse and new techniques.

The works of modern sensibility are in some senses complementary to those discussed in Chapter Two and adopt an artistic approach to reality, though their means of realising this approach are different and display a different set of emphases. Many of the realistic works discussed are the forerunners of modern sensibility, for realism is an essentially transmutable concept that can often include many features of the modern;

> the front edge of Realism keeps shifting, so that one generation's Realism is another's Romanticism or high fantasy or escapism, and the definitions are extraordinary multiple, truth or authenticity is, just like reality and history, open to extremes of disputatiousness.[28]

Thus, in one sense, both groups, the realistic and the modern, might be classified as expressions of realism. The former is the realism in which the embodiment of Egyptian life is both inescapable and a condition of personality and growth, while the latter is not so much a substantiation of reality as an exploration of it, an insight into its opaqueness and a realisation of the individual psyche demanding fulfilment and crying out to overcome alienation and apathy.

Indeed, 'it is one of the larger commonplaces of cultural history that we can distinguish a kind of oscillation in style over a period of time, an ebb and flow between a predominantly rational world-view and alternate spasms of irrational or subjective endeavour'.[29] Although the oscillation, in both style and viewpoint, in the Egyptian short story was limited in its scale, it had significant ramifications and played a decisive role in developing and enriching the genre. The shift involved the juxtaposition of contradictions, of intellect and emotions, of lyric imagery and abstract commentary, of apocalyptic vision and blunt and sordid reality, in a manner that enabled the genre to cope artistically with an ever-changing and complex reality. It is, therefore, a radical shift that highlighted the creative command of the modern and integrated it into the cultural life of Egypt. It accentuated

> the significance of de-creating the given surface of reality: intersecting historical time with time according with the movement and rhythm of the subjective mind; the pursuit of the luminous image, or else of fictional order sustained against consecutive story; the belief in perception as plural, life as multiple, reality as insubstantial.[30]

This radical change in outlook is inevitably associated with the development of new technical devices:

> the search for a style and a typology becomes a self-conscious element in the Modernist's literary production; he is perpetually engaged in a profound and ceaseless journey through the means and integrity of art. In this sense, Modernism is less a style than a search for a style in a highly individualistic sense.[31]

Naturally, the techniques developed through this search are fundamentally different from those associated with realism; in the traditional realistic short story the pace is controlled and the transitions and climaxes are organised, while in the stories of modern sensibility the perpetually oscillating pattern of sense-data and memories is aimless and directionless – reflecting the static character of events. There is also another fundamental difference reflected in the techniques and devices associated with the realistic short story and those of the modern sensibility. 'The earlier devices served to draw the attention to the autonomy of the narrator, while the later techniques drew attention to the autonomy of the fictive structure itself.'[32]

The Schism in Artistic Sensibility

The shift from the autonomy of the narrator to that of the fictive structure required a radical change, almost an inversion, of the perception of art itself. This was both analogous and parallel to the change in artistic sensibility and the emergence of the new techniques associated with it. As far as the Egyptian short story is concerned, the process of change was painful and gradual, and was entangled with many other transformations. Isolating the works that reflect and shaped the change enables one to study the various phases of the modern sensibility and to follow the development of its qualities within the prevalent sensibility and, at the same time, against it. These works can be divided into three sections which correspond roughly to the three stages of development and to the three decades between 1940 and 1970, in which the modern visions and techniques evolved and matured.

The early signs of the schism in literary sensibility can be observed in the late 1930s, for these were the years that witnessed dissatisfaction with the cold impersonality and minute description of an objective, external reality, and the resulting early attempts in several genres to turn inwards in order to explore the inner psyche and present the complex world of the subjective. These were also the years that saw the formation of Jamā'at al-Fann wa'l-Ḥurriyyah,[33] the introduction of impressionism, cubism and surrealism in painting, and the interest in symbolism in literature.[34] The late 1930s and early 1940s saw the publication of dozens of articles on the symbolist school and various studies on and translations of Poe, Baudelaire, Rimbaud, Verlaine, Mallarmé and Valery.[35] These articles and translations prepared the ground for original works and heralded their emergence, not only because writers translate what they wish to invent, but also because these studies and translations created a current of ideas and techniques and prompted intellectuals to try their hand at one version or another of these novelties.

The years that saw growing interest in symbolism witnessed the publication of the first self-professed symbolic work of prose, *Mafraq al-Ṭarīq* (1938), by Bishr Fāris. They also witnessed early examples of the works of modern sensibility in the Egyptian short story, for when Kāmil published his magazine, *al-Taṭawwur*, he introduced in its first issue the work of Albert Quṣayrī (b. 1914), a young Egyptian short story writer who wrote in French. As the stories published in *al-Taṭawwur* indicate,[36] Quṣayrī was deeply interested in elevating the world of *al-Ladhin Nasahum al-Lāh* to the realm of poetry. He turns the ostensibly realistic action into a rhythmic and ritualistic world of imagery and symbolism without sacrificing his analytical power or his strong sense of commitment. His analytical approach to characterisation created a bridge between realistic representation and the emphasis on subjectivity and inwardness. Although few of his works were translated and published in Arabic, those that were helped facilitate a smooth transition from realism to symbolism in the Egyptian short story.

Bishr Fāris

Quṣayrī's new works were significant because they were introduced within the framework of the modernist and revolutionary movement. The theoretical ideas of Jamā'at al-Fann wa'l-Ḥurriyyah gave the new techniques of Quṣayrī weight and promoted other techniques associated with symbolism and surrealism. Surrealism was received enthusiastically by painters and poets, but not by prose writers, though they were, nonetheless, influenced by some of its tenets. The prose writers who sensed the need for change did not think that the way to achieve it was by a complete divorce from reality, for the romantic writers had divorced themselves from reality without succeeding in assimilating or expressing the change in artistic sensibility. Instead, many of them directed their attention towards symbolism, whose complexity appealed to the intellectual and élitist attitude of many writers. The success of Fāris's symbolic play created a favourable atmosphere for experimentation with symbolism, and for the popularisation of its philosophical and artistic background.

Although al-Ḥakīm was the first to introduce symbolic and allegorical elements into fiction and drama, Fāris was the first to articulate the relevance of symbolism and to explain its main ideas in a clear and lucid manner. 'Like other Symbolists, Symbolism to Fāris is the discovery of the subconscious, the exposition of hidden feelings and impulses which are revealed when the author turns his back on the actual world.'[37] In his preface to *Mafriq al-Ṭarīq*, Fāris emphasises the importance of a coherent symbolic structure that penetrates beneath the visible world and captures, through its revelations, the inner logic behind accidental appearances.[38] He draws a fine line between metaphor and symbol: the former is an image called on to illuminate certain parts of the work, the latter is the parts themselves, which work along various associational lines, synecdoche, as well as metonymic. For him, the images are associated with the accidental and may become the component parts of the symbol, but not the reverse, for the symbol's domain lies beyond the multiplicity of appearances.[39]

Thus the symbol is the work of the creative insight capable

of unveiling the hidden spirit that looms behind images and metaphors.[40] It has its own unique power of reasoning and has little regard for everyday logic and order, its aim being to capture the vibration of light, colour and sound. Fāris is concerned to stress the uniqueness of the reasoning processes of symbolism and to deny any resemblance between them and anarchy or disorder, for it is not anarchy opposed to order, but creativity versus craft, multiplicity of tone against monotony, and spiritual depth versus artificiality.[41] Thus the symbolic is synonymous with the poetic and inimical to the prosaic with its swollen verbosity, false episodic analysis, literary fabrication and demure creativity.[42] It neither edifies nor stultifies reality; it explores its inmost depths and concerns itself with distilled human experience in its complexity and ambiguity.[43] The importance of visionary and mystic elements is also emphasised, together with the appropriation of the symbolic language of the Sufis, something he initially pioneered.[44]

Fāris's concept of symbolism is tinged with impressionistic qualities, for 'what makes literature to him is the ability to record our own reaction to things, not to describe the logic of the external world'.[45] The subjective impressions of external reality are tempered with an intuitive sense of harmony that give feeling and subjectivity a fine and balanced form. With this amalgam of symbolism, impressionism and intuitive mysticism, Fāris wrote his first play, which was well received by the critics[46] but almost entirely ignored by the general reading public. Like many modern works of art the play has the power to '[shock] us out of our natural sloth and the force of habit, and makes us see for the first time what we had looked at a hundred times but never seen',[47] and its intellectual success encouraged Fāris to apply his symbolic approach to another literary genre in which he had tried his hand a few years earlier without much luck – the short story.[48]

In 1942, he published a collection of short stories, *Sū' Tafāhum*, in which he includes only works of a symbolic nature. Although he had already published many of his stories in leading periodicals, collecting them in book form lent weight to his experiment, and makes it easier to study the many features of his stories. It also accentuates the symbolic nature of some works that otherwise might have escaped attention, for many of Fāris's works are not purely symbolic. Nevertheless, he applies the concept of symbolism outlined in the preface of his play to many of his stories, and considers that 'the story should be poetic in presentation and lyric in description in order to escape the coldness of reality ... and [that it should] eschew logical explanations'.[49] For Fāris, the real creativity of a writer manifests in his ability to engross his reader in the experience narrated rather than relate it to him, which is achieved by moving from the rational to the perceptible.[50]

This brings us to one of the major features of Fāris's work, the constant attempt to philosophise without being analytical, for he rejects the analytical approach, which is based on the inverse movement from the perceptible to the rational. The title of the collection, *Sū' Tafāhum* (Misunderstanding), is a clear indication of this quality, for it is not taken from the title of one of the stories, as is customary, but rather encapsulates an idea that penetrates the collection as a whole. The title is chosen specifically because the idea of contradiction is a major thematic and artistic quality in Fāris's work. This is an idea which, as Luwīs 'Awaḍ rightly suggests, is not simply the misunderstanding between man and others, but 'man's miscomprehension of himself, the contradiction of words and the misconception that lies within the ideas'.[51] In other words, misunderstanding is a philosophical idea that constitutes the core of Fāris's vision and manifests itself in many forms, the essential element with multiple appearances. 'Awaḍ considers it the missing link between the school of realism and that of the absurd, but he fails to substantiate his inference from Fāris's work, and instead tries to prove his point by referring to the details of Fāris's life.[52]

Nevertheless, Fāris's concept of misunderstanding is both philosophical and pervasive and is mainly concerned with the lack of harmony between the various manifestations of a given essence. The manifestations of the relationship between the heroine of 'Qiṣṣah sa-Takmul'[53] and its hero oscillate from one extreme to another, yet the contradictory behaviour reflects one basic idea: the poor understanding that each person has of himself and the futility of self-deception. The heroine becomes trapped in contradictions of her own making, and the author employs the symbols of light and darkness not as an external symbol that reflects or corresponds to a state of mind but as an integral part of the trapping process. If the misunderstanding here is triggered by the extremity of the protagonist's oscillation, in 'Ṭabaq Fūl'[54] it is an external misunderstanding that causes it, so two different forms of understanding are introduced, one external and comic, the other internal and tragic. The two are different in both form and degree; they present two distinct levels of the concept, as well as two different ways of starting its process and developing it. The two levels of the action, operating in the same story, are not isolated from each other; they work upon each other to portray the diversity and richness of the concept, to explain the mechanism of its internal contradiction, and to demonstrate how it has a forcible effect on events as well as on characters.

This is also what happens in 'Yuqāl Qiṣṣah'[55] and 'Nās',[56] where the inner conflict is not between the external and internal nature of misunderstanding within an event, but within two opposite approaches to life and society. These two stories show how this inner conflict, which becomes an integral part of both their narrative details and plot structure, demonstrates itself through the internal and complex mechanism of standard conflicts, for instance between urban and rural values, simplicity and sophistication, wealth and poverty, spontaneity and calculation. For Fāris, the idea of misunderstanding is at the core of every conflict, and the inability to realise its dynamics makes for an ironic element, which naturally contributes to the main concept. In 'Mabrūk'[57] the idea of misunderstanding takes the form of a fixed obsession that turns into a curse in order to shock the protagonist out of his illusion and into painful realisation, while in 'Halak al-Nahār'[58] it takes the form of parallel actions that work upon one another in order to present a strong attack on the corrupt political establishment.

In all these works, and many others,[59] Fāris's point of departure is the rational idea, not the perceptible data. He does not begin with a situation and work inwardly to fathom the idea that forms its core, but with an abstract idea from which he works outwardly towards reality. The final story in the collection, 'al-Mar'ah wa'l-Fannān',[60] which he subtitles 'Māddah li-Qiṣṣah' (The Raw Material for a Story), provides an insight into the mechanics of his creative process. Compared with the rest of the stories, it possesses more than seventy per cent of the actual material usually involved in shaping the story as he perceives it. It appears to be a skeletal framework of theoretical arguments about man and woman, jealousy and creativity, in which the idea of a multi-levelled contradiction, encountered in many of his works, is clearly present. The narrative is not developed beyond its abstract structure, containing no action or characterisation, nor any description or location in the real sense. Yet like many of Fāris's works, it has a theme of contradictory qualities and ideas working at various levels to demonstrate the similarity and dissimilarity between its two main stereotyped characters.

It seems that Fāris depends a great deal on stereotypes. At least, this is the impression created in many of his works, particularly if one fails to appreciate their symbolic qualities as the context was not clearly ready to respond to his symbolism. In this respect, many of his works seem to be marred by what one may call under-characterisation and over-philosophisation – qualities that are both complementary and contradictory. 'Rajul',[61] a story of special significance, since he returned to it later and rewrote it as a play, *Jabhat al-Ghayb* (1960), illustrates this clearly. It is a story of love and great aspirations presented in a semi-mythological and symbolic framework, in a manner that widens the scope and implication of its themes without dissipating the ambiguity that envelops them. Unlike many of Fāris's stories, it pays considerable attention to the location of the action, mainly on account of its typology, as opposed to concern for its topography. The location is a huge mountain that radiates symbolic values, towering over a village and filling its people with awe and hope, fear and confidence. Its might tames their wild desires, yet its heights tempt them, for at the top is a cave in which grows a plant that bestows immortality on him who eats it. As yet, no one has succeeded in conquering this mountain; those who have attempted the ascent have been crippled or gone blind without attaining the eternal life they sought. But one day a young man tries to climb it, in spite of the advice of his fellow villagers, armed only with a clear sense of mission and the love of a devoted girl. Promising to throw a stone every day so that his village will know that he is safe, he disappears into the mountain. The stone is dropped regularly until one day it fails to appear. A deep sense of sadness and disappointment reigns in the village, and the man's beloved falls ill and loses the will to live. One day, he descends the mountain safe and sound. The people crowd around him and ask if he has eaten from the plant of eternity, but he brushes them aside and disregards their questions. When they inquire why he ceased to throw his daily stone, he looks at them in disgust and answers: 'to whom would I throw the stone? ... out of my way you mortals!'[62] He then goes to see his beloved, but to his surprise finds that she has passed away, or as the story puts it, was killed by the stone that failed to come down. He returns to the mountain in fury and makes for the cave in search of an explanation, and a few days later, his dead body rolls down. The closing words of the story confirm the mythological parallel, in case it might have escaped the reader's attention: 'God killed himself, he was put to death by man.'[63]

Fāris's tendency to under-characterisation and over-philosophisation is clearly evident in this story. The Christian imagery behind the carefully planned plot is mixed with various elements from the Mesopotamian epic of Gilgamesh and touches of modern symbolism, and both the symbolic presentation and mythological allusions help to consolidate the artistic edifice of the work. Like many others in this collection, the story has a unique sense of structure, as well as a distinct method of characterisation that does not rely on normal conventions but works out its own technique of developing the character through a group of symbols and associations. Fāris's characters are like abstractions, unlike real characters or even stereotypes, and are sustained largely through their interaction with other abstractions. The difference in nature implies a difference in function, and the emergence of a new process of characterisation.

Fāris's character does not develop, nor is he developed, by an action that progresses, syllogistically or otherwise, throughout the story, but merely reveals various aspects of an essentially static entity. For Fāris, the character is not a means for developing ideas; rather, he is controlled by them and progresses only by discovering this fact. Often the discovery comes too late, which adds a tragic element to the process of recognition, though the tragedy is always individual and has no social bearing. In fact, Fāris plays down any tragic elements in the psychology of the character in order to emphasise rational and symbolic values. He deliberately disregards elements that make characterisation more specific and less abstract (such as details of location, minute description and realistic dialogue) in a manner that differentiates it from both realistic and romantic representation, and prevents any possible identification with the character, other than at the abstract or symbolic level.

Fāris's new form of characterisation required an artistic shift in the perception and employment of other forms of narrative, and the development of poetic and suggestive language. Although the accentuation of abstract and symbolic qualities in characterisation implies a lack of concern for the conventional presentation of location and action, Fāris develops a different form of location that substitutes existence within the specific confines of place and time with an existence in varying shades of light and darkness, fluxion and stillness, transition and permanence, and their various associations. The development of a poetic language and lyrical mode enhances this new form of location where the 'world is but as a poet's vision fashioned as a design'.[64] Within this design, the story 'seeks to combine man and world in a strongly inward, yet aesthetically objective, form'.[65] In the process the action acquires a different function and form, for it ceases to be a descriptive account of a happening in time and space aimed at establishing certain qualities, and becomes a succession of rhythmic movements, which absorb the action altogether and refashion it as a pattern of imagery.

'Ādil Kāmil

Although Fāris developed valuable new techniques of lyrical presentation of action, characterisation and other narrative elements, the transformation of the action to a fine pattern of rich and suggestive imagery reached its apogee in the work of 'Ādil Kāmil (b. 1916). Kāmil had in fact stopped writing by the mid-1940s and is better known for his novels, but he wrote and published a few short stories, some of which are pertinent to the study of the schism in artistic sensibility in the Arabic short story at this time. The publication of his short story 'Ḍabāb wa-Ramād'[66] a few months after Fāris's collection ushers in a more mature form of symbolism, in which the bare abstracts of Fāris's works are enveloped in rich narrative and suggestive poetic allusions. The cohesion of structure in Kāmil's stories and his awareness of the fundamental differences between metaphors and complex symbols enable him to develop many layers of meaning without sacrificing the spontaneity of the work or obliterating its perceptible aspects.

Like Fāris's 'Rajul', Kāmil's 'Ḍabāb wa-Ramād' is a story of a symbolic search for an impossible dream, but unlike 'Rajul' it does not depend on Islamic or ancient mythology for its vision. It is the story of a character of fantasy whose veins are full of pus instead of blood and whose world is made up of fog and ashes; his nights are starless and his days sunless. One murky day, he goes out, wondering whether to adopt the way of Faust or that of Baudelaire, and finally opts for that of the ordinary mortal man despite his overwhelming sense of his own immortality. As a mortal human being, he is torn between an awareness of, and reaching out for, the unknown and an instinctive fear of it. He drifts about the city until he meets an enchanting girl who, though physically, psychologically and spiritually his opposite, shares his interest in poetry.

From the moment of their first encounter, the protagonist becomes bound to the angelically beautiful girl despite, or rather because of, his inability to control her like the rest of those who live in his grey and murky kingdom. At the beginning of their relationship, he enjoys her peculiar domination over him and the degree to which he is enslaved by her, for he feels, ironically, that his relationship with her gives him a strength and power hitherto unknown to him. When he expresses his desire to continue this new relationship and develop it into love, she tells that he is incapable of loving, and that loving her implies appreciating the whole of life, for it is love that provides one with such insights. Because of his compelling desire for her he submits to all her conditions and spends a happy day with her, but as soon as night comes and the forces of darkness get to work, the protagonist rediscovers his instinctive nature; the changes he acquired through love disappear and the relationship disintegrates and ends in the loss of the beloved. The forces of nature, which correspond to the forces of the internal contradictions within the relationship, rejoice at its destruction, and the story ends with their reclaiming the protagonist and enveloping the world in their spirit of doom and misery.

Nature plays an important role in the story. It is used to fuse various aspects of the action in a general pattern of imagery in a manner that enriches the story and widens the scope of its interpretation. The skilful accommodation of detailed natural imagery in a balanced structure charges the imagery and descriptive passages with symbolic and suggestive qualities without turning them into symbolic abstractions, as is the case with many of Fāris's symbols. Kāmil's symbols are distinguished from those of his predecessors by being 'assigned only a quasi-creative status: they are unique halfway points of control between man and his experience, stabilisers and carriers of experience, mediated presentations'.[67] Although their quasi-creative nature limits their horizon and limits the possibilities of interpretation, it saves them from vagueness and obscurity without stripping them of lyricism.

The quasi-creative nature of Kāmil's symbols is one of the facets of his keen interest in structure displayed in this story and others, in particular 'Wayk Tuḥutmus'.[68] Beneath the skilful characterisation that develops through a constant conflict between the author and his rebellious characters, the structure becomes the main theme of the work. The dictates of the inner laws of the artistic edifice prevail over the rules of the author or the ruses of the character to the extent that the whole work becomes too symmetrical. Yet despite his deep interest in structure, or because of it, Kāmil avoids the pitfall common to much symbolist writing of overwriting and, on certain occasions, is able to develop 'antithetic and complementary ranges of meaning inherent in given objects, like life and death in water'.[69] He also envelops the main action in a dream-like atmosphere in which the 'world' becomes

> part of the hero's inner world, the hero, in turn, mirrors the external world and all its multitudinous manifestations. He distorts the universe or dissolves it into hallucination or dream in which its "true" (infinite and organic) nature is revealed.[70]

However, in Kāmil's work, the 'true' nature of the universe is perceived, not in philosophical or realistic terms, but in symbolic and poetic ones, for symbols and poetry are capable of providing the bridge via which one is able to pass from external reality to 'the inner experience that fashions life in a transcendental form'.[71] This is so because

> the logic of images or association is an attempt to show that, so far as the temporal sequences and order of events within the inner world of experience and memory are concerned, we must employ symbols of disorder that violate the strictly "logical" order and progression of events to which we have become accustomed by science and common sense.[72]

So a new 'vision' emerges from the complex process of poetic associations that is capable of removing the film of habit that stands between us and the 'true' nature of the universe. For Kāmil, the balanced, almost symmetric, structure and the quasi-creative symbols are necessary to the exploration of inner experience and the emergence of a new vision that allows us to penetrate the 'true' nature of the universe. 'The inner world of experience exhibits a structure which is causally determined by significant associations rather than by objective causal connections in the outside world.'[73]

The drifting in the city and the love–hate relationship in 'Ḍabāb wa-Ramād', as well as the structural irony of 'Wayk Tuḥutmus', are not determined by the causality of external reality, but by the inner 'logic' of symbolic association in which place and time are constantly modified and reinterpreted in the light of subjective exigencies. The laws of objective reality are rejected, replaced by a form of subjective relativity in which poetic imagery and symbolism persuade us to accept the new order, or rather disorder, that affects time, place, action and characterisation. However, Kāmil only establishes a way forward for this radical change; the brevity of his career and the limited number of his works did not enable him to actually realise it. His works are significant because they advanced the process of change, developed some of the techniques of the symbolic mode and paved the way for the next stage in the change of artistic sensibility.

Fatḥī Ghānim

Unlike Fāris, who was completely isolated, and Kāmil, who was loosely associated with Jamā'at al-Fann wa'l-Ḥurriyyah, Fathi Ghānim (1924–2000) was an active member of the literary coterie that established the experimental magazine *al-Bashīr* in 1948. He was also the most talented of those who published in *al-Bashīr*.[74] In spite of this, when, after almost ten years, he published his first collection, *Tajribat Ḥubb* (1958), he refrained from including his most innovative and experimental works from the *al-Bashīr* period, for these were the years when 'commitment' and socialist romanticism were thriving in the Egyptian short story. Fortunately, this time was coming to an end and the growing awareness of complexity, and the corresponding changes in expression in narrative forms, led him to include his most daring innovative works in his second and last collection, *Sūr Ḥadīd Mudabbab* (1964).

Although his first collection included one significant short story, 'Dunyā',[75] which was published towards the end of the 1940s and reflects the contemporary schism in artistic sensibility, the collection as a whole creates the impression that Ghānim had turned his back on the experiment of the late 1940s in *al-Bashīr* and early 1950s in *al-Fuṣūl*. It also suggests that he was in complete harmony with the prevailing sensibility and that his work expresses its chief preoccupations. However, when he issued his second collection he titled it after one of his most daring and surrealistic experiments and included in it experimental works that had appeared long before the publication of his first collection, for in the 1960s such innovative works were consistent with the literary mood. Nevertheless, their real significance lies in the pioneering role they played in expressing the urgent need for new modes of discourse at an early stage, that is, when they first appeared in periodicals, though their impact on the succeeding generation was not felt until much later, after many had appeared in his second collection.

Ghānim's work represents an important step forward after those of Fāris and Kāmil, not only because it is more experimental and less symmetrical, but also because it introduces a host of novel techniques and devices, and succeeded in making many of them integral to contemporary themes. Even in his least experimental story, 'Dunyā', these techniques are inseparable from the theme of the interaction between the relativity and inevitability of life. To demonstrate his theme, Ghānim tries first to alienate his reader from the story and disrupt any possible identification with either the characters or the action by positing the world as unreal, and deliberately destroying any illusion of reality by the constant use of skilful commentary, generalisation and supposition. He also slows down the rhythm so that it creates the impression of a slow-motion picture. After alienating the reader from the story, he immerses the main strand of the action in numerous secondary ones, which modify our perception of the main strand and help to create, through subtle and complex associations, philosophical layers of meaning expressed through symbolic narrative. So the main action is not only viewed from various perspectives but also compared, directly and indirectly, with other similar or contradictory ones in a manner that enriches the main theme of relativity and inevitability and the sub-theme of the fate-like attraction of opposites.

Nevertheless, Ghānim's experiment in 'Dunyā' is marked by caution and hesitation and, in comparison with many of his other stories, is only the herald of a profound process of innovation in both form and theme. In 'Ghurub al-Shams'[76] all the techniques used in 'Dunyā' are to be found in a more refined and sophisticated form, and the main action, which in 'Dunyā' was immersed in an abundance of detail and secondary action, becomes a condensed and poetic scene which is lively yet has a sense of stillness at its centre. The scene is viewed not only from several perspectives but also from various distances and in terms of differing attitudes: it is seen through the eyes of the simple and the sophisticated, the man who lives in the present and he who lives in the past, the innocent and the corrupt. Furthermore, the change of outlook is accompanied by a change of rhythm, and, on occasions, by a shift from the third- to the first-person narrative, and within the latter from one character to another. These changes in rhythm and narrative type serve to accentuate the shifting angle from which the main scene is viewed and introduce the factors of both time and change within each viewpoint. In this way, the theme of relativity becomes closely interlocked with that of time, and both acquire intensity and philosophical weight because everything in the story takes place in the presence of death.

The theme of relativity acquires a complex nature and is intermingled with various aspects of Heisenberg's 'Uncertainty principle'[77] in 'al-Qizm wa'l-'Imlāq',[78] which employs the technique of stream of consciousness. Yet the *monologue intérieur* is constantly interrupted by realistically portrayed events and details in a manner that forces the intrusion of external reality on the subjective account and allows the two different realities to work upon one another. Nevertheless, the subjective, even fictitious reality, is treated on an equal footing with the external, so the interaction between realistic and spurious details enriches the narrative and envelops it in an air of uncertainty at the same time. This uncertainty acquires a special nature because of its association with the technical device of turning abstract ideas into perceptible data and metaphorical imagery; in the process, Ghānim draws upon the cinematic technique of animation in which the soundtrack is separated from the succession of visual imagery. In addition, he pays special attention to the movement of time and employs the technique of anti-climax to eliminate sentimentality, create a comic effect and emphasise certain parts of the story.

By means of these innovative techniques, the author develops the theme of the failure of people to communicate and understand each other and exploits the notion of absurdity present in the theme alongside his main theme of the relativity of life and events. The two themes are correlated with one another and are enhanced by the presentation of the main action as if shadowing Swift's *Gulliver's Travels* and Camus's *La Peste.* The former gives a startling dimension to relativity while the latter underlines the tragedy of living in a state of permanent siege made worse by the lack of communication. Indeed, the impossibility of any meaningful communication in either of the novels, which the protagonist reads by the sea (with all its diverse symbolism), accentuates both his inability to understand the agony of his friend and the futility of his quest for love. The technique of treating fictitious details on an equal footing with real data enriches the interaction between the main situation and those portrayed in the two novels, while the skilful use of imploding symbols gives the two main themes a poetic and philosophical dimension without, of course, being gratuitous or off the point.

Poetic and philosophical undertones are clearly evident in 'Khuḍrat al-Barsīm'[79] thanks to its fine use of rhythmic language, oxymoron and other juxtapositions of contradictory qualities. The story presents a character who is divided between three worlds: the actual world in which he lives, the realm of dreams and fantasy, and the world that is created and perceived by art. The three worlds interact and are interchanged as the unique love story develops, in which the main character is cleaved into two – a living being and an observer – without any implications of schizophrenia. The cleavage is more a technical device than a symptom of personality disorder, which serves to present the comparative, if not relative, view of things, for it is not confined to the character that affects events, which are divided into real and illusory to the extent of developing an intentional sense of confusion. This is aided by another technical device: the swift change of subject, imagery and mental associations. The unusual nature of these changes, together with the dialogue based on unexpected encounters, gives the whole work a sense of poetic absurdity, which is both poetic and philosophical because of the panoramic image of opposites interacting and the holistic view of the world which it presents.

Ghānim's poetic absurdity is consummated in his fine surrealistic story 'Sūr Ḥadīd Mudabbab'[80] in which every aspect of narrative takes on a new form and function. The description becomes a narrative replica of abstract painting, with its clear interest in line and colour and complete rejection of any photographic or representational illustration. The action consists of inexplicable dream sequences, which are colourful and full of what Breton calls 'concrete intensity', yet seem to be almost motionless and, on occasions, meaningless. Time and location lose their conventional nature, for in surrealistic fiction, 'respect for chronological time and for spatial limitations easily loses its meaning'.[81] Thus, action is deliberately situated 'in a world where time runs in neutral'[82] and space is stripped of its geographical or realistic nature, for the writer's aim

> has ceased to be to persuade his readers that he is transcribing events borrowed from the familiar world of the real or invented according to its laws. On the contrary, the surrealist ... shares with Geracq the wish "to carry conviction away" under the pressure of an anguish.[83]

Indeed, Ghānim's aim to create a propitious atmosphere for surrealistic experience leads him to charge his story, under the pressure of this anguish, with surrealistic imagery of violence and blood together with enviable moments of insight. Such moments are closely associated with his innovative use of linguistic disorder and unique syntax, for 'with the direct aid of beneficent change, exploration of the potentialities of language itself may be made to contribute efficaciously to the liberation of the imaginative process'.[84] Yet in Ghānim's story the linguistic disorder, with its unique logic and syntax, is neither instrumental in liberating the imagination nor a result of it; rather, it is one of the manifestations of profound fantasy. It is also part and parcel of the poetic incoherence of surrealistic vision and of its attempt to dispense with the veil of familiarity which, according to the dogma of surrealism, prevents one from any real exploration of the self and the world.

Both the diversity of Ghānim's technique and the intensity of his narration illustrate clearly the schism in artistic sensibility during the 1940s. He develops Fāris and Kāmil's symbolic presentation into a more poetic and suggestive approach and advances their dissatisfaction with spiritless representational literature and the conceptual approach to reality, bringing about a radical rift in emphasis. Despite this, the modernists of the 1940s, though important, failed to carry out the revolution that many of their works seemed to herald, not only because these were limited but also because various extraneous factors allowed other literary achievements to overshadow such genuinely avant-garde works. Nevertheless, the literary discoveries of these three writers are of great significance, for they present us with the vague intuitive glimmers that were to become the mature visions of the following decade, and they are also an expression of the dramatic fission and fusion that continued to gain momentum and that gave rise to a new mode of discourse, a mode that proved, after a brief period during the 1950s, to be responsive to, and relevant for, the complexity of the modern sensibility.

The importance of these three writers lies not only in their expression of a growing change in artistic sensibility or as harbingers of future developments but also in the fact that they adumbrated the gradual development of

> a model of artistic creation in which art was the product of creative ferment, analogous indeed to rebellion in other spheres, but distinguishable from it, and the artist was an isolated figure in communion not with his gross and material milieu but with an artistic utopia, hints of whose existence lay in aesthetic consonance, the epiphanies of form.[85]

Indeed, it is no coincidence that they were very much lone figures, for the change in the perception of art affects the artist, and pioneering experimentation requires a degree of isolation from, indifference to, or rebellion against prevalent taste and values. Furthermore, experimentation was, indeed still is, unpopular with the wider reading public, and required a measure of dedication, which is often attendant in meditation and isolation. The two writers who developed the discoveries of Fāris, Kāmil and Ghānim throughout the 1950s, and well into the 1960s, were also relatively marginalised within the literary establishment, although not forever.

The Shaping of Modern Sensibility

The modernist works of the 1940s are, in a sense, simply a prelude to the stories of Yūsuf al-Shārūnī (b. 1924) and Idwār al-Kharrāṭ (b. 1926), which constitute the core of modernist writing in the 1950s. Although both started writing in the 1940s, their first collections appeared in the 1950s and their cultural presence was not felt until then. Thus the shaping of the modern sensibility through the works of al-Shārūnī and al-Kharrāṭ took place alongside the triumph of other sensibilities, and in opposition to them. The 1950s in Egypt was a decade that allowed for such diversity, for it started soon after the blow of 1948 with a popular government that raised the hopes of the nation but failed to fulfil them or even to dissipate the gloom and frustration that lingered from the previous decade. Then came the *coup d'état* of the Free Officers led by Nasser, and its aspirations and disillusionments. The political persecution and intimidation of the 1940s soon reappeared, and many intellectuals either withdrew into their shells or disappeared behind bars.

Cultural activity nevertheless flourished in the 1950s. A considerable number of serious writers were officially sanctioned and introduced to the wider reading public and many new ones, including al-Shārūnī himself, had their début on the widest possible platform.[86] The flow of serious works affected literary taste and made an important impact on the reading public who was, by this stage, dissatisfied with the prevalence of mediocrity. The publication of modernist and experimental work became possible, albeit not necessarily easy or popular. The wider reading public discovered, for the first time, works by Ḥaqqī, al-Badawī and Maḥfūẓ that had been published some ten or even twenty years earlier. They delighted in these, as well as the work of a few contemporary writers, such as Idrīs and al-Shārūnī, but the rediscovery of previously published stories that had been little known until the early 1950s was accompanied by inattention to some important pieces that appeared for the first time; the enthusiastic unearthing of the older works was part of the belated triumph of the artistic sensibility that first emerged in the 1920s and matured throughout the 1930s and 1940s, not the result of a more consistent literary awakening that would have scrutinised the literary scene with discipline and vigour. The repetition of the same error by the Egyptian literary movement was not mere obstinacy but a result of the inherent complexity of the phenomenon of culture. The triumph of the realistic sensibility, long overdue, created its own momentum and brought to the fore many works that had been unjustly treated, received less than their rightful dues, or had even failed to appear in book form before.[87] Inevitably this resulted in many works of modern sensibility being overshadowed. However, literary movements, like men, learn from their errors, which is in itself a sign of development and maturity. The Egyptian literary movement was quick to realise its mistake and reconsider the modernist works it had overlooked. There is ample evidence to suggest that a sizeable reading public, and particularly would-be writers, were aware of the significance of such modernist works, and their impact upon them became evident in the following decade. While Ḥaqqī had to wait thirty years to gain public acclaim, al-Shārūnī and al-Kharrāṭ acquired the literary status they deserved in the decade immediately following the publication of their first collections.

Yūsuf al-Shārūnī

Although al-Shārūnī started his literary career in the mid-1940s as a romantic, writing contemplative pieces of lyrical prose,[88] by the late 1940s he was directing his attention to the short story and within a few years had largely purged his style of negative romantic qualities. Unlike most of the writers discussed so far, al-Shārūnī began publishing his short stories in a Lebanese monthly review;[89] almost none of his works were published in Egypt until the 1950s. Nevertheless, he benefited from the upsurge in cultural activity at the beginning of the 1950s and his first collection, *al-'Ushshāq al-Khamsah* (1954), was published and distributed widely, in the same year and the same series as Idrīs's first collection. Yet al-Shārūnī failed to attract the same enthusiastic reception as Idrīs, and his collection did not have such an impact on the cultural scene as Idrīs's *Arkhaṣ Layālī.* Although al-Shārūnī's collection contains works that reflect an amalgam of both the prevailing socialist realist and modernist sensibilities, the modernist elements are the more dominant and may be the reason the book did not meet immediate acclaim. Al-Shārūnī continued to write, but not at a rate comparable, either quantitatively or qualitatively, to Idrīs, and in more than twenty-five years published only two collections, *Risālah Ilā Imra'ah* (1960) and *al-Ziḥām* (1969).[90]

Al-Shārūnī is not, by any standard, a prolific writer, in terms of either quantity or talent and technical resources; rather, he is a writer of limited, but significant, means, who refrains from diluting his discoveries and labours diligently to crystallise them. His work does not depend on richness of feeling and texture, nor does it draw upon a wide variety of profound experience, but it relies on carefully balanced and logically thought-out structure. Al-Shārūnī's study of philosophy[91] may have something to do with this; it certainly has left a clear mark on his themes and on the type of modern sensibility that emerges from his work. As he himself admits,[92] the study of philosophy had a tremendous impact on his perception of man and society and consequently on his literary career, for it enabled him to see universal ideas behind ostensibly insignificant events and to realise that any moment of time embraces eternity and contains profound, yet irreconcilable, contradictions. It also led him to believe that the function of the artist is akin to that of the philosopher: to reveal the richness of ideas behind the apparent trivia of life and the pattern beneath the chaos of accidentals, to raise and regulate man's perception of the world and enable him to reconcile the individual with the social and the parochial with the universal.

Al-Shārūnī's philosophical inclinations manifest themselves in some over-intellectualisation of his themes and an obvious interest in portraying intellectuals who can sustain complex and sometimes obtuse philosophical themes. Apart from his own pronouncements and a few references in his stories,[93] one can infer from al-Shārūnī's work that he was influenced by two major philosophers, Marx and Kierkegaard (two Hegelians despite their apparent contrariety), without being either Marxian or existentialist. Marx's influence is more evident in his early stories, especially his deliberate attempt to link individual events to general, even international, situations and to postulate that single isolated incidents are the direct consequence of wider international developments,[94] and to demonstrate that quantitative accumulations lead to qualitative changes.[95] Marx's influence appears also in al-Shārūnī's attribution of many of the feelings, characteristics and problems of the individual to the conditions of his material existence and to interpret his psychology according to these conditions.

Al-Shārūnī's interest in the psychology of his characters saves him from undermining the richness of the human psyche or relegating man to the status of a reflexive automaton.

> The growth of psychology ... has stressed the fact that to know is to know oneself in the act of knowing, a very difficult task to which physics, with the theory of relativity and the Quantum theory, has added its weight, which has contributed to the final rejection of the notion of objective knowledge and of the exact delineation and separation between matter and energy.[96]

Here one sees the influence of Kierkegaard, whose ideas do not clash, at any level, with modern psychology and, moreover, help to attenuate many of the tenets of the Marxian influence on al-Shārūnī's work. The most obvious of Kierkegaard's ideas to influence al-Shārūnī are the distrust of reason, the importance of individual values, the necessity of the subjectivity of truth, the incommunicability of the individual self, and the belief that to exist is to feel. At the same time, the revulsion against feelings caused by the frustration of ideals is also evident in his work and is responsible for a pervasive fatalism.

Despite his attachment to philosophy and psychology, al-Shārūnī is no philosopher or psychologist, but an artist who tries to express the troubled experience of his generation and chose the short story as his medium. Unlike the previous modernists, who expressed their dissatisfaction with the prevalent sensibility and the dominant social order fairly directly using innovative techniques, al-Shārūnī attempted to introduce to the Egyptian short story an impressive image of the generation that had experienced, and endured, the contradictions that brought about the radical change in artistic sensibility. He therefore portrays sensitive intellectuals who crave communication yet are loath to sacrifice their dignified solitude, and so they do what they can, intentionally or otherwise, to reinforce their isolation.[97] In some stories, [98] the conflict between communication and solitude transforms the pursuit of living into a state of being that is oriented towards nothingness – the sort of nothingness that Sartre regards as a source of knowledge and the basis of freedom, the nothingness that, according to Kierkegaard, gradually becomes an entity, a state of being.

The craving for communication and the cherishing of solitude are both contradictory and complementary, for the conflict between them is an expression of more fundamental conflicts between society and the individual, the objective and the subjective, or the outer and inner realities. It is also a manifestation of wistful anxieties and the failure either to accept or to reject a shifting and rapidly disintegrating, occasionally hostile, external reality, while at the same time demonstrating the lack of a satisfactory surrogate for such a loved/hated reality. In many of al-Shārūnī works, the lack of any acceptable surrogate for the external reality includes an element of existential agony and Kierkegaard's idea of the inevitability of facing a sense of tragedy and dread.[99] Thus the desire to communicate with external reality represents an attempt to overcome this Kierkegaardian inevitability, while the resort to a solitary existence involves both a submission to its dictates and rebellion against its gloom.

Al-Shārūnī's favourite hero, or rather anti-hero, is a man tormented by his vision, a Prometheus-like character whose knowledge and sensitivity put him at a disadvantage, since they fail to either detach him or protect him from a hostile reality. He is aware that he is ordained to live in a world that has closed around and before him, as he has been forced to come to terms with realities that he neither understands nor controls.[100] Yet this tragic awareness does not induce him to try to comprehend the world he inhabits, but instead pushes him in the opposite direction, for despite his knowledge of the impossibility of avoiding such destiny, al-Shārūnī's protagonist rarely tries to improve his hold on and grasp of external reality, but is absorbed in an irrational and all-consuming pursuit of what one might call 'redundant knowledge'. Although redundant knowledge seems a contradiction in terms, it appears that this is the only term that accurately describes the kind of knowledge that al-Shārūnī's protagonist seeks. It is a knowledge that cannot be seen as negative or harmful, yet fails to help the character in any real sense, and often intensifies his dilemma. It provides him with insights that he is incapable of acting upon, and enables him to strip the world of its masks and see clearly through things to the extent of rendering him inactive.

The character continues in his quest for such knowledge and becomes increasingly trapped by his own vision and discoveries, yet he continues the search for salvation in a manner that only enforces his isolation.[101] This self-defeating attitude seems to be an inherent characteristic of many of al-Shārūnī's protagonists,[102] who constantly fail to achieve any kind of rapprochement with the outside world, not because they lack the capacity to feel and perceive but because of a chronic inability to express or act on their insights effectively. The temporary isolation or solitary existence thus becomes a permanent condition and any attempt to ease the situation is doomed to failure and counter-productive.[103] Yet the protagonist does not appear frustrated and accepts his failure gracefully, often with a great deal of propitiation or even satisfaction.

The hero in whom these traits are presented is a character who recurs in a number of al-Shārūnī's stories and is most convincingly and subtly portrayed in one of his later works, 'Lamaḥāt min Ḥayāt Mawjūd'.[104] Although the protagonist of this story encompasses the anxieties and aspirations of many previous characters,[105] it is no coincidence that the most mature version of al-Shārūnī's principal character-type appears towards the end of the 1960s, with the triumph of modern sensibility. The hero who before either was unaware of his tragic existence,[106] was the quarry in a mysterious chase,[107] or was trapped by his own visions, now becomes the hunter and the quarry in a tragic and metaphysical game.[108] He is obsessed by fear and falls into a state of melancholic depression, which makes his existence meaningless.

The biblical phraseology of the opening scene of the story ('In the beginning was the Fear, all things were made by Him and without Him was not anything made that was made'[109]) is followed by a corruption of the Cartesian *cogito, ergo sum* – I fear, therefore I am – [110] that makes the submission to this all-pervasive god of dread a demonstration of existence. The fear is, therefore, of not only an authoritative and supreme being that establishes its will over its subject but also a condition of being that reigns over the whole of the story and turns it into a contemporary nightmare. In the midst of this nightmare lives the protagonist of the story, or more precisely exists, for everything in his life seems unreal: his ironic and illusory name Mawjūd 'Abd al-Mawjūd, his present and his past, and his futile attempt to assert his being in the kingdom of fear. On each page of the story he uses the first person pronoun 'I', and thus the story, written in the first person, is an affirmation of his being; yet he is unaware that his every move and every undertaking negate this being and contribute only to his progressive isolation and advance his march towards nothingness.

His nightmare, and the weak point at which fear tightens its grip over him, is his uncertainty, which is in turn a symptom of submission to fear. He does not know if he is innocent or guilty and has to endure the hell of oscillating between conviction and doubt, between being the victim and the perpetrator of crime. The interaction between these contradictions demonstrates the Hegelian dialectical element that is also suggested by the third part of the opening scene: 'my fear assuages, soothes and protects me'.[111] Indeed, his fear acts as an invincible amulet that wards off dread and protects him from the unknown, for the expectation of the worst of possibilities becomes in itself a talisman that prevents it from happening. But warding off evil in this way is achieved at too high a price, because living in fear erodes the hero's being day after day without saving him from the nightmare of uncertainty. Moreover, fear strips him of his insight and renders his actions useless, so his persistent attempt to defend himself leads only to frustration and despair to the point where he is unable to recognise himself. This in turn alienates him from himself and from reality and exacerbates his uncertainty, especially when external events confirm, by means of fate and chance, some of his worst doubts and suspicions.

At one level of interpretation, the story is an amalgam of social and political criticism, Christian mythology[112] and the psychoanalytical Oedipus complex, where the strong sense of sin is linked to the doctrine of salvation through sacrifice.[113] Like Oedipus, our protagonist's life seems to be controlled by a Delphic oracle from which escape is unthinkable, so he is destined to live out the tragedy. Like Oedipus, too, he feels responsible for the death of his father and develops a sinful relationship with his mother-in-law that results in the traumatic death of her daughter/his wife when she discovers their adultery. The death of the wife becomes equivalent to the curse and famine and brings agony to the adulterous couple: the mother terminates not only the relationship but also any link with the world and escapes into a kind of quasi-insanity and mock-Sufism, while the aberrant protagonist curtails his whole existence by immersing himself in the deep waters of fear and uncertainty.

In the well-wrought structure of the story al-Shārūnī develops a suggestive analogy between Mawjūd and Oedipus without falling into the trap of twisting the progression of the action to accentuate the elements of similarity or distracting attention from the world of events in which the protagonist's agonies are portrayed. Instead, he swiftly draws an analogy, then directs our attention to the hero's hidden terror and guilt, which, for him, absorbs the external world. The hero's vision, which in previous stories was depicted by means of symbolic presentation or shaped through metaphors, is now implied through the enactment of his inner condition in a manner that reveals much insight on the part of the author or his hero about the realities portrayed. The overt symbolism of al-Shārūnī's modernist predecessors is replaced by inconspicuous types of imploding symbols that are capable of enriching the work without obscuring it or impairing its poetic nature.

The presentation of the hero's vision in this story suggests not only a departure from the techniques used by preceding modernists, but also a substantial shift away from those used by al-Shārūnī himself in his first collection, where he uses many of the techniques introduced by Fāris, Kāmil and Ghānim with skill and originality and adds to them his own. While his work at the time cannot be classified as symbolist or purely surrealist, he uses a number of symbolic and surreal devices and imagery to develop a clearly expressionistic mode of discourse in which minute description and illustration of atmospheric effects are as essential to the development of the theme as the action and characterisation. In a few stories,[114] the virtuosity of the description and the subtlety of the imploding symbols succeed in making the atmosphere not only the main theme but also the main character, hence characterisation takes on a new form and nature.

Al-Shārūnī's obvious interest in philosophy and his attempt to treat subjective reality on an equal footing with objective reality in order to integrate the two on a wide expressionistic canvas leads him to develop new techniques that are capable of penetrating beneath the surface of both subjective and objective realities. He uses the technique of interrupting the subjective account with abstract statements and rudimentary fragments of external reality that are usually orchestrated to vindicate the subjective account or to widen its implications.[115] The intention is to present the individual's case in its social and philosophical perspective as both valid and universal, and to link the personal to the national, and often to the international, without impairing its uniqueness.[116] In order to juxtapose perceptible and abstract data without disturbing the unity of impression and the harmony of tone, al-Shārūnī adds a cosmic touch,[117] or uses an extraneous marker of time[118] or location,[119] which helps to develop an internal logic and sense of cohesion.

The laws of development that control the artistic balance and cohesion in al-Shārūnī's work are completely independent from, though often similar to, those of external reality. Both their independence and similarity are maintained through the use of a technique that might be called the 'duality of perspective', for there are in several stories two distinct visions at work: two realities,[120] two different philosophies (those of Marx and Kierkegaard), and two distinct layers of data. A further aspect of this duality of perspective manifests itself in al-Shārūnī's interest in the dialectical interaction between ideas and in his endeavour to detect the elements of similarity and contrast in images, characters and situations. In 'Lamaḥāt min Ḥayāt Mawjūd' the analogous relationship between Mawjūd and Oedipus is based on both the similarity and dissimilarity of the two tragic characters, while in 'Qiddīs fī Ḥāratinā'[121] the duality of perspective is illustrated through the metamorphosis of the hero's image from lunatic outcast to revered saint. In 'Zayṭah Ṣāni' al-'Āhāt'[122] the ironic similarity between the hero and Christ involves a complete inversion of Christ's image without sacrificing the essence of Christ's message, for Zayṭah appears as the complete antithesis of Christ in status and stature, while their roles, in the lives of their people, are almost identical. In 'al-Laḥm wa'l-Sikkīn'[123] the author develops a suggestive parallelism between the events of Christ's crucifixion and the death of the mother in the story and, at the same time, sustains his favourite theme of the interaction between the perceptible and the abstract and between isolation and communication.

The technique of the duality of perspective is also associated with al-Shārūnī's treatment of the relativity of truth, one of the modernists' favourite themes. In many stories[124] it appears not as the main theme but as a latent element in the presentation, appearing through glimmers of commentary. Instead of setting subjective against objective reality in order to accentuate the relativity of truth, al-Shārūnī tries to integrate the two without disregarding their potential incompatibility or reducing the number of ways in which each can be seen. Instead of recording everyday experience, he endeavours to express distilled reality which is, by its nature, a blend of the subjective and objective, expressionistic but not photographic. This is further associated with al-Shārūnī's concern for economy and compression of style, and with his attempt to develop poetic elements in his narrative, for he is aware of the importance of these elements, as expressed in his mode of writing, which tries to reconcile modern with conventional techniques and visions.

The reconciliation of these seeming opposites was necessary to subdue the freakishness and unprecedented usages of modernism and to root it in the literary traditions of the Egyptian short story. It was also relevant to al-Shārūnī's attempt to concentrate on the contemporary nightmare and avoid the use of the stereotype, since some of his works[125] enact a Kafkaesque exploration of the nightmare world of contemporary reality, a theme that recurs from his first collection to his latest works. Although the presentation of this theme in the work of other writers entails the negation of external elements to the point where outer reality is reduced to a nightmare, al-Shārūnī succeeds in maintaining a large section of external reality, and presents it in juxtaposition to the individual's dismay at its disintegration.

Indeed, external elements are crucial for an understanding of the social and political dimensions of the individual's dilemma and alienation, and al-Shārūnī, it would appear, is particularly keen to emphasise the contribution of the political situation in the formation of such a nightmare.

Both the duality of perspective and the reduction of outer reality to a contemporary nightmare demand greater reliance on the technique of the *monologue intérieur*. Although this was by no means new to the Egyptian short story, al-Shārūnī uses it much more than most of his predecessors. However, interior monologue has to be used in a subtle manner to be successful, and al-Shārūnī's monologues are often too organised to be a stream of disorder, for the portrayal of the flux of the mind loses much of its spontaneity when it is subjected to the heavy hand of authorial interference. Instead of being marked by an evident sense of discontinuity that is capable of suggesting spontaneity through a poetic mixture of the irrelevant and the relevant, of furtive thoughts and fleeting impressions, of continuity and constant change, al-Shārūnī's monologues are symmetrical and functional. Their poetry is superficial, their cohesion and internal logic are too dry and rational, and their symmetry is marked by apparent superfluity.

Al-Shārūnī's works are often artificially structured, and some are little more than crude exercises in form and geometrical balance.[126] Every move is calculated, every detail of action or description taken into account, every word over-polished, and every thought or notion investigated and reckoned with, thus the end result is often a somewhat grotesque work, lacking in spirit and forced in its symmetry and balance. In the collection *Risālah Ilā Imra'ah* the over-planning is carried beyond the confines of the individual stories to the link that connects them so that the stories cover the various stages of a man's life and delineate the specific nature, anxieties and aspirations of each phase. The first story is about the problems associated with conceiving a child, being pregnant and giving birth.[127] This is immediately followed by a story that tries to prove that once conception has taken place, the foetus dictates its presence, defies any attempt to abort it, and when born imposes its love and its will on its family[128] and, as the following story tells us, that every adult is no more than a child at heart.[129] These two stories also deal with problems concerning children's activities, their toys, the responsibilities of their upbringing, and the painful process of integrating them into the adult's world, or vice versa.

By the fourth story[130] the child has become a teenager and a well-known soccer player. He falls in love for the first time and starts to bear some of his family's responsibilities. The love experience is so important that two further stories are devoted to it,[131] for the experience of love is part of this hero's quest for identity and involves much self-questioning. Love puts him in direct conflict with social convention, especially when he wants his love to culminate in marriage and he has to confront the practical problems of engagement and marriage-related ceremonies.[132] Even if the initial stages are successfully completed, there are always complications that arise from the complexity of the issue and the elaborate rituals that accompany it.[133] The ceremonies are always fascinating, yet they can be accompanied by a host of unexpected worries.[134] Before reaching the end of the collection, the hero has come full circle, faced the inevitability of death[135] and given birth to a new generation that continues the cycle of life, which goes on for ever.

Although the planning of the collection in this rigid manner grants the work a certain degree of cohesion, the excessive symmetry of each story weakens the work, impairs its plausibility, and decreases its impact on the reader, for it brings an element of shallowness and superficiality to an otherwise impressive work. Al-Shārūnī's method can be seen in part as a reaction to the elevation of content at the expense of form that took hold of the Egyptian short story in the 1950s. It is also an attempt to give logic and shape to a speciously chaotic sequence of events and to balance the disintegration and absurdity of reality with a rigorous and symmetric pattern.

Nevertheless, despite his exaggeration of the formalistic aspects of his work, al-Shārūnī succeeded in putting many of the discoveries of the preceding Egyptian modernists to good use and integrating them into the tradition of the Egyptian short story. In addition, he gave many of the vague innovative gestures of his predecessors a well-wrought form and made a genuine contribution to the modern sensibility, for he developed what proved to be the most influential accomplishment of modern sensibility – the portrayal of the contemporary nightmare. The development of this vision of the world, which al-Shārūnī first dramatised in 'Difāʿ Muntaṣaf al-Layl'[136] and brought to maturity in 'Lamaḥāt min Ḥayāt Mawjūd', is a substantial achievement because it is much more than a discovery of a theme or a technical device; it is the origin of a mode of discourse that answers real needs and opens new horizons.

In the short story al-Shārūnī was the first coherent exponent of the modern sensibility. He succeeded in articulating many of the ambiguous fears and anxieties that had characterised the atmosphere of Egyptian society since the late 1940s and became almost palpable towards the 1960s. He discerned the various furtive neuroses that were produced by the prevalence of such fears and dramatised them in order to portray how this lack of security could impede fulfilment and disturb the individual's expression of his potential and his aspirations. Not unlike the pioneers who tried to root the new literary genre in the social and literary life of Egypt, al-Shārūnī attempts to root it in the spiritual and psychological life of Egypt at a time when a new experience was emerging. As was the case with the writing of many of the pioneers, the advances he made, whether thematic or technical, are significant in themselves regardless of his occasional lack of dexterity or his insensitivity in implementing them, for once made they are part of the tradition and available to be built upon or put into practice more competently by others.

Idwār al-Kharrāṭ

Untangling the pose from the prose is a major problem in any critical assessment of al-Kharrāṭ's work. Sometimes his writing is fine and assiduous, other times it suffers from a chronic syndrome of the swaggering persona. He is an expert at the intrigues of literary politics: when the wind blew in the opposite direction he sheltered behind the institutionally powerful Yūsuf al-Sibā'ī, busying himself with translations and radio programmes until the right moment arrived. Like al-Shārūnī, al-Kharrāṭ started writing his short stories in the seminal years of the late 1940s but his first collection was not published until the 1950s; but unlike him, he did not publish his early works in Lebanon nor did he have the entrée into Egyptian literary circles that he might have enjoyed had he published his collection in a respectable and widely circulated edition. Instead, he had to publish his first collection, *Ḥīṭān 'Āliyah* (1958), at his own expense, and as a result its appearance was delayed and it had nothing of the immediate acclaim afforded al-Shārūnī's first collection. In the event, however, its lasting influence proved to be much greater than that of al-Shārūnī's work, especially on the generation that began writing in the 1960s.

Al-Kharrāṭ's first collection stood as a solitary achievement for some time, as it was fourteen years before he published his second collection, *Sā'āt al-Kibriyā'* (1972),[137] which contains only seven stories.

Although most of the stories in al-Kharrāṭ's first collection were written around the same time as, or even earlier than, those of al-Shārūnī's first collection, they seem to start, both thematically and artistically, from the point at which al-Shārūnī's last collection (which was, of course, not written until the 1960s) ends. In the 1940s and 1950s al-Kharrāṭ explored many of the areas that otherwise remained untouched until the 1960s. When he treats the hackneyed themes of social disparity and injustice, as he does in some of his early stories, he does so from a broader perspective than his contemporaries, taking into account in more poetical language the spiritual dimensions of his character's suffering. Al-Shārūnī categorises his first collection into socialist realist and modernist stories, although his so-called 'modernist' works contain many of the conventions of a more naturalistic narrative form, whereas al-Kharrāṭ continually seeks to recreate the tradition and perceive his subject matter in more revealing ways. In the time span that concerns this study, he went through three distinct phases of development, within a consistent artistic framework. Thus it seems appropriate to delineate this general perspective before identifying the three stages and isolating their traits.

Al-Kharrāṭ's writing is marked by an attempt to posit the individual psyche as the core of being, for without man everything loses not only its value and meaning, but its *raison d'être.* Man, although influenced by social factors, is not perceived of only as a social entity but a complex individual who aspires to assert his will over his surroundings. He is a hyper-sensitive and insightful creature whose constant surprise *vis-à-vis* everyday events strips the ordinary of its familiarity and renders external reality crude and illogical. In al-Kharrāṭ's world man is seen as being detached from outer reality, and this very distance reveals the nakedness and idleness of natural objects and, at the same time, accentuates his ability to give or deny life to location and events; for, in al-Kharrāṭ's world, things do not exist in themselves or for themselves but in, for and by man.

Man is presented as being bored with his own life above anything else, so he naturally looks down upon those who live in harmony with life and immerse themselves in its trivialities. Al-Karrāṭ's hero prefers to adopt a contemplative and critical approach to life, to remove himself a little distance from it in order to readdress it, analyse himself and be consumed by his own visions and aspirations. He prefers solitude to communicating with, or submitting to, the banality of life. To articulate this complex stand, al-Kharrāṭ provides his protagonist with exceptionally sharp insight and a comprehensive awareness of his surroundings. His characters are for the most part intellectuals with a greater or lesser degree of intuitive insight and capacity for rational thought, and it is significant that their intellect does not eliminate either the ironic contradictions between their aspirations and reality, or the conflict between the crudeness of the outside world and the world as perceived or posited by them.

The removal of man from reality and the emphasis given to the contradictions that arise from man's attempts to confront reality are part of a philosophical perspective that does not posit any precepts for man's existence or behaviour, nor assume any preconceived ideas about his stand *vis-à-vis* the world. It sees man as a seeker of meaning, a giver of sense, who is forced to live in an unjustifiable world, whose incomprehensible presence is conveyed through the dextrous use of verbs in the passive form in Arabic, in which, unlike English, the subject of a passive sentence cannot be identified. The use of the passive structure in the narrative implies that many things are taking place despite man (the giver of meaning and value) and beyond his control or comprehension, whence absurdity, meaninglessness and fear creep in, and man loses his centrality and starts to doubt himself. 'The self is not only a passive recipient of stimuli, external or internal, but an active centre controlling, modifying, organizing, and integrating these stimuli.'[138] Once the self loses this controlling and synthesising power, meaninglessness moves from the outer reality to the inner world of man and starts to threaten his sanity.

The transferring of meaninglessness from outer to inner reality disturbs the balance of the world and sends it into a terrible state of flux and makes the character's existence heavy and purposeless. The only way he can terminate this state is by action, by regaining control, and so action in itself acquires a great importance in al-Kharrāṭ's works, even if it results in adverse consequences. What is important in the action is not the results but the very act itself, as a vindication of man's existence and a demonstration of his ability to choose, though it is sometimes perceived as an exercise of his will and at other times as a submission to necessity. Indeed, many of al-Kharrāṭ's characters act for the sake of action, impulsively rather than as a result of awareness or rational consideration, and often with an obvious lack of motivation. The instinctive impulse to act constitutes the unconscious will to live; yet the ostensible lack of a rational explanation becomes a factor in intensifying the character's sense of meaninglessness, especially when the action alters the direction of his life entirely, as it often does. In many stories,[139] the conflict is not simply between the character's visions and his actions, but between two different sensibilities: external and internal, or social and individual. Al-Kharrāṭ's protagonist is a man who is torn between his ideals and accomplishments and whose sensitivity and apocalyptic vision stand between him and adjustment in social terms. The intensity of the conflict and the ever-widening gap between his aspirations and potential blind him to certain aspects of reality, and his actions bring about adverse results and alienate him further from reality. In his powerlessness and isolation, al-Kharrāṭ's character grows bitter, cynical and rebellious as a defence against the meaninglessness that threatens to close in on him. But bitterness and cynicism provide only a momentary haven, and once the effect recedes he is once again the victim of incomprehensible conditions, and gradually loses all interest in controlling his life at all.

To make the absurdity and isolation of his main character's existence more dramatic and poignant, al-Kharrāṭ makes the external world that his character holds back from very much alive, vibrant and even beautiful. Al-Kharrāṭ conveys the world through senses and feelings; it is visualised and made audible, perceived through smells, tastes and touches rather than through rationalised precepts. It is therefore marked by a richness of detail and an abundance of concrete experiences that sweep through the pages in a manner that gives existence precedence over being and avoids any speculative attempt to explore the world before establishing its existence very firmly. This serves to emphasise the heaviness and complexity of the overpowering sense of presence in a given moment, scene or situation. This affects time and location as well as man and the interaction between him and others, and between the set of relationships portrayed.

One way in which the author conveys the power of the momentary existence of perceptible data is by avoiding the frequent use of perfect tenses and concentrating on the imperfect and present tenses,[140] despite the fact that many of his works are told in the third person, which is usually associated, at least in the Egyptian short story, with the use of past tenses. The intensive use of present tenses and the frequent resort to verbal forms V (tafa‘‘al), VI (trfā‘al) and X (istaf‘al), which imply longer duration, are not purely technical devices but an integral part of the vision and perspective. In this way, the meaninglessness of the world and the frustrations and anxieties of the character cease to be speculative moods and become a concrete condition of living and a state of being, their impact and their implications correspondingly greater and more profound.

Al-Kharrāṭ frequently presents his characters in a nocturnal world, where the interests of daytime – work, hot sun, mundane dealings – are minimal or non-existent. When one of these features prominently in a story[141] it often becomes part of a nightmare, or a dream incorporated into night and into the perception of life as a realm of quasi-reality – dark, grey, murky and dimly lit, painted in dark colours and set in an atmosphere of gloom and suspense. The man who lives such a life appears somehow sheltered by an inherent and unconscious yearning to return to the darkness, to the protective existence of the womb, and this is only one of the numerous manifestations of his withdrawal tendencies. Such tendencies to retreat or hide are not seen in any way as an expression of a morbid lack of interest in life, but rather as an indication of a premonition of failure and also an interest in eschewing confrontation with a rejected condition, and directing the attention to a deeper and more searching inwardness. Rather than a disclosure of suicidal tendencies, as it might seem, it is a rejection of reality, a rejection that is both subjective and objective. On the one hand, the character's inability to cope with the ever-increasing demands of the outward world results in his avoidance of certain aspects of reality; on the other, the heavy presence of external reality and the growth of absurdity and meaninglessness affect the character's sense of centrality and banish him from its domain. Moreover, his desire to stand apart is characterised plainly by his rebellion against certain conditions, that qualifies his withdrawal with positive qualities. Even in the most reclusive and sequestered cases, al-Kharrāṭ's characters never completely lose interest in life. From their solitude, they continue to view life with affection and reverence, so that their own lives are impressive in their mingled asceticism and sensuality, which are directed towards life, not away from it. However, the contradictions in his characters' lives between violently opposing values often lead only to apathy, particularly as they are self-absorbed and egocentric. The complexity of such paradoxical elements in al-Kharrāṭ's perspective cannot be explained without a brief assessment of the stages through which his work developed and advanced with the modernist vision and narrative techniques.

The first stage includes his early works, which were originally written in the 1940s.[142] Although some were rewritten later, when preparing the collection for publication, they nevertheless stand out as both artistically and thematically distinct from the rest of the stories of his first collection. The main theme is the overwhelming will to live and to ward off sterility and meaningless at any cost. In 'Fī Ẓuhr Yawm Ḥārr'[143] the longing for life demonstrates itself in every detail and at many levels of the story. The hero, an adolescent student, is annoyed with the repetitiveness of his daily frustrations and anxieties and aspires to find a meaning and justification for his tasteless and trivial life. He is full of sensual desires and simple dreams, of sundry frustrations and grief, and is tormented by his realisation that he is capable neither of holding the interest of the beautiful and haughty daughter of the landlord who has stirred up a host of contradictory feelings in him, nor of retaliating against her dismissive brief encounter with him. The sun, with its hellish heat and blinding brightness outside his room, enflames his desires and ripens his frustrations, as if preparing him for the violent changes that he is about to undergo.

The heroine of the story, a young wife, who is illiterate though not lacking in sensitivity and insight, is also surrounded by trouble and oppressed by the same overpowering sun, which acts as a symbol without losing its objective status. After the collapse of her first marriage, the result of a terrible misunderstanding, failure is now threatening her second marriage. Her anxieties are intensified by her certainty that if it collapses she will be faced with a gloomy future. Her husband starts to hint that he may divorce her for not producing children, and she has a strong conviction that she is not to blame for this, yet realises that she cannot suggest that he is sterile, since this might hasten the divorce. In her seclusion, she continues to ruminate on her fears and longs for an end to her worries and suffering.

The two characters, who are developed along parallel lines, are now ripe for an encounter, for a combined effort to shrug off the pressure that burdens their existence. So when they have a chance to be alone at noon of this hot day, the heat urging them on and numbing their inhibitions, they purify their souls in the heat of the sexual moment, for their intercourse becomes a ritual of purification and fulfilment of the self without the slightest hint of guilt. It is an act that establishes the characters' power over their destiny and the oppressive elements in their present situation and enables them to avenge the injustice that has afflicted both of them. The hero, in his sensuous frenzy, sees not the heroine but the desired daughter of the landlord responding to every sexual move, submissive and subdued. The heroine is no less engrossed in her own world, for despite the passion that envelops her she feels a certain dislike, even disgust, at the encounter, as though she is being raped but partially consenting. When it is over there is no trace of remorse or regret in either of them; rather each feels a little stronger and more capable of coping with their problems. The anxieties and grief begin to evaporate as a result of the human action – a flicker of hope has appeared on the horizon.

In this story, as well as in the rest of the works of this phase, the human action is both spontaneous and inevitable, natural and deliberate, for it is linked to all the pressures and aspirations of the characters and controlled, in this case, by the sun, which, though shut off from the scene behind the shutters of the window, nonetheless demonstrates its compelling presence and is strongly felt amid the dim atmosphere and nerve-racking heat and heaviness of the summer noon. The action is the culmination of a long and painful self-questioning and the characters' answer to the nothingness and meaninglessness that seem to invert the scale of values, erode logic and comprehension, and bring about the disintegration of reality. In 'Ṭalqat Nār'[144] the hero's action is a powerful remonstration against such meaninglessness, and it comes not as a direct and simple objection but as an inexorable mission whose accomplishment is a demonstration of his existence. The hero is possessed by this sense of mission, which operates on much deeper levels and drives him to act against his conscious will. The night and solitude play the role of the compelling sun in the first story and help to justify the patricide.

The same role is played by the deafening silence punctuated by the howling of wolves in 'Abūnā Tūmā'.[145] The monk kills without being aware of his exact action, as if he is driven to act against all his past history, his reason, even his own character. The moment of action itself has a peremptory and hypnotic power, and when it acquires its *raison d'être* it materialises as if it has its own independent mechanism. In 'Abūnā Tūmā' the conflict between the utopian vision of the Revelation of St John and the sensuous life of the cities of Rome, Corinth, Ephesus and Thessalonica as described in the Epistles becomes a catalyst in bringing about the tragic act of murder. However, in both stories the killing is not perceived as an act of destruction, but rather as a manifestation of an overwhelming longing for creation, similar to that which brought about the sexual intercourse in 'Fī Ẓuhr Yawm Ḥārr', for it stems from the urge to eliminate meaninglessness and frustration. It represents the shedding of blood in a complex rite of fertility where the murder is both the opposite of and complementary to the act of creation, for it involves the termination of certain qualities in the character and the resurrection of many facets of the self: the rebirth of whatever has been suffocated by frustration and meaninglessness.

The second phase of al-Kharrāṭ's development includes the stories written in the 1950s and represents, with his previous work, his major contribution to the shaping of modern sensibility in the Egyptian short story, both technically and thematically. After presenting, in the first stage, the alienating power of external reality and the effect of its compulsory presence on the character, al-Kharrāṭ begins to investigate the lasting mark of this disintegrated yet compelling reality on man and to explore the complex mechanism of the movement of meaninglessness from objective to subjective reality. The relationship between the character and the outside world develops from the simple conflict of wills to a dialectical love–hate relationship, in which the character dislikes the outer reality yet desires its continuity in order to sustain his dislike for it. The hate relationship becomes vital for his psychological balance and welfare, an active demonstration of existence and a *raison d'être*.

The change in the nature of the relationship postulates a change in the characterisation, narrative and techniques. In the title story, 'Ḥīṭān 'Āliyah',[146] the nameless protagonist[147] is bored at the repetitiveness of his life, yet he is surprised at how little he knows his wife after five years of cohabitation and how little he can communicate with her at the more important levels. He experiences an acute type of loneliness, which drives him to act purposelessly and even against his best reason. As a result, the conflict with external elements is transformed into one with the self and the division in the protagonist is illustrated as if it is actually happens. This is equalled by the coming together of anxieties into a corporeal existence when his sick child, who is in effect the embodiment of his anxieties, materialises in the café where he is sitting and exposes his vulnerability to the curious and alien eyes. Her materialisation, which cannot be taken at a realistic level, alarms him, accentuates his impotence and creates in him a nagging sense of guilt. Yet this humiliating and demanding presence, showing him his monumental failure and unhappiness, cannot induce an action of the type experienced in the earlier stories. It only intensifies his solitude and pushes him into further withdrawal and inwardness, so that he erects high walls around himself and enters into a world of frustration and absurdity.

The withdrawal into an imposed yet self-made cocoon does not save the character from external reality, however; it is rather a declaration of intent – there would be no more futile attempts to overcome the pervasive sense of absurdity. It is, in a sense, a submission to the meaninglessness and frustration that come as a culmination of so many impossible dreams, unsuccessful endeavours, unfulfilled aspirations and frustrated ambitions. Yet it nevertheless contains an element of protest and a wan faith in life and spontaneity as 'al-Ūrkistrā'[148] suggests, an element that suggests that entry into the chrysalis-like existence is no more than a temporary torpid stage as long as the outbursts of spontaneity occur. Although 'Mughāmarah Gharāmiyyah'[149] suggests that these spontaneous outbursts, no matter how strong they may be, are lacking in reason and logic, and 'Fī Dākhil al-Sūr'[150] almost warns of their fatal consequences, the rest of al-Kharrāṭ's stories in this phase[151] vindicate them and associate them with rejuvenation, the dissipation of old fears and myths,[152] the quest for freedom, and the attempt to liberate the soul from the shackles of the past.[153]

In these stories, the quest for liberty operates on a spiritual level – it represents liberation from the manacles of fear, impotence, deception, frustration, unattainable dreams and, more importantly, from the obligation to act against one's will or conviction. The structure of the stories and the mode of narrative give the character's attempt to rid himself of these burdens a symbolic and philosophical implication without any trace of pretence, and, at the same time, lend the failure to attain such liberty a tragic colouring. In 'Maḥaṭṭat al-Sikkah al-Ḥadīd',[154] al-Kharrāṭ presents a concrete and poetic image of the sense of living a nightmare as a result of failing to obtain such liberty. The tragedy of the situation is heightened by presenting the nightmare in an understated tone and as part of normal everyday reality.

The nameless protagonist of the story seems to be thrown into this nightmare through no fault of his own, for unlike many of al-Kharrāṭ's nameless heroes, this one appears lively, compassionate, understanding and keen to help others. After an ordinary trip on a train, with its small pleasures and minor difficulties, the hero reaches the station without seemingly arriving at his destination, for in the station, instead of the mixed feelings of arrival and fulfilment, he experiences an ambiguous fear in which every ordinary detail is transformed into a nightmare. The spacious station becomes a narrow cell with an oppressive atmosphere, time loses its normal duration, becomes arbitrary and hangs heavily, even ceasing to register the passing of minutes, and the air is still, almost stagnant, charged with inhuman fears. The hero starts to panic, yet continues to resist in a spirit similar to that of the nameless hero of 'Amām al-Baḥr'[155] who plucks out from the overpowering sea a new life.

The significance of this story is two-fold; it perfects the technique of the contemporary nightmare and gives it philosophical and poetic dimensions on the one hand, and it integrates both the nightmare and the protagonist's defiance of its supremacy in everyday reality on the other. Unlike al-Shārūnī's nightmares, which seem superficial and obtrusive, a little illusory and contrived by the characters' exaggeration of certain facets of reality, al-Kharrāṭ's nightmare situation seems more plausible and objectively valid, not made by the character but for him, not created by his fears but sparking off these fears. The nightmare is both metaphorical and real, for although it appears as the private nightmare of a specific individual and is formulated through his *monologue intérieur,* it has its valid presence in the Kafkaesque world of this second stage: a world that seems grotesque and unrealistic because of being painfully real.

Nevertheless, al-Kharrāṭ's technique is far from purely realistic, for while he uses many of the techniques of realistic presentation of action and character, at the same time he makes use of the devices associated with surrealism and expressionism. The virtuosity of his detailed poetic description and the uniqueness of the way in which the action progresses, not in a direct line but in a suggestive, pulsating movement that retains its syllogistic development, give the speciously realistic narrative a new character. The pulsation of the progression of the action is designed to present the interaction of realistic details and the human psyche in a manner that puts subjective data on an equal footing with objective happenings, and provides the reader with an image of the world, not as it appears to a neutral observer, but to a participant who is both involved in and detached from it. The characterisation is thus intermingled with the progression of the action, for when the objective details recede the character surges forward; characterisation retreats to the background when the movement of the action rises again, and this harmonious interplay continues throughout the work.

Apart from the simultaneous development of the action and the character, this interplay emphasises two significant ideas. The first is the sharp contradiction between the internal observing man and the external participant in events, and the opposing directions they take. Hence doubts about the reality of happenings start to emerge and crucial, if not devastating, questions are posed about the collective split personality and the relationship between the public and the private man. The second is the dichotomy and interaction between objective and subjective realities and their adverse nature and logic. Although it is clear that in al-Kharrāṭ's world both subjectivity and objectivity are relative concepts and that one does not exist, function or operate without the other, the alternate presentation of action and character accentuates their conflicting natures without eliminating their interdependence, a feature which al-Kharrāṭ stresses and develops in the third stage of his work.

This third stage consists of the seven short stories of his second collection, *Sā'āt al-Kibriyā'*, which were written and published between 1963[156] and 1970.[157] These seven stories assume the axiomatic nature of the interdependence of characterisation and action, subjectivity and objectivity, without completely eliminating the contradictions that exist between them. The title of the collection, which unusually is not the title of one of the stories, refers to the hours of pride and grandeur in which the characters are portrayed. These are the hours, or rather the moments, of painful confrontation with the self and the world when the character is forced to come out of his shell and give his last testimony. They are tense and rich moments of revelation and insight in which the most crucial issues of the protagonist's life come into focus in a dolorous and, in most of the stories, ultimate self-appraisal. To intensify the situation further, al-Kharrāṭ adds the presence of death, whether literal or metaphoric: death serves to emphasise the finality of the character's testimony and, at the same time, introduces an element of absurdity into the situation.

In 'al-Amīrah wa'l-Ḥiṣān'[158] the whole story is told in the grip of death, as one final gasp in one long paragraph of around 400 lines and a short one of commentary, seven lines long, which presents the external aspects of the event that triggered off the stream of consciousness – the story. The protagonist's life is distilled and condensed in a rich moment of consciousness, in which pure subjectivity reigns without succeeding in eclipsing the objective reality symbolised in the imminent presence of death. The prevalence of subjectivity is further enhanced by a radical change in al-Kharrāṭ's favourite character, that is, the deposition of the intellectual hero in favour of a more practical type who is struck by the shocking imminence of death. Indeed, the presence of death makes the details of things remembered radiate with new meaning, for it cancels out any speculative notions about future potential that may alter the meaning of things remembered and roots everything firmly in the past. The employment of the present tense for relating things past puts the past on an equal footing with the present in an attempt to make the re-enactment of the past a filter through which the tragic implications of the present are realised.

At the same time, the presence of death undermines the effect of self-deception, which is an inherent characteristic of the remembrance of past events at a moment of distress, and enhances the credibility of the story. It also casts a tragic light on the action and affirms that it is too late to do anything about it. Surely this reawakening and recreation of the past is closely linked with Christian concepts of forgiveness and grace, and therefore with the possibility of 'avoiding' the inevitable. Nevertheless, when the death is metaphoric, as in 'Taḥt al-Jāmi''[159] and 'Jurḥ Mafthūḥ',[160] and involves the demise of purity, innocence and peace and the birth of a bitter, lonely and morally contaminated protagonist, the tragic sense is sharp and deep because it emerges from an irreversible situation and is associated with the character's inability to cope with the consequences of such a situation. The situation is both made by and imposed on the character so that it is almost impossible to avoid or even to resist, for it is a situation whose deterministic features are deeply rooted in the character's background and temperament and in the components of the action.

The situation is therefore self-contained and irrevocable, a world of its own that has its structure and laws of inevitability.

Al-Kharrāṭ seems to be gradually aspiring to create a self-contained world that, although alluding to the external world, is completely independent of it: a world that does not derive its credibility from its reflection of reality but from its own internal cohesion, its own ethos, its own laws of probability and its own logic. Although it selects its primary data from external reality, it transforms them with a dexterous, surrealistic touch into components of a dreamlike world, then rearranges and reorganises them in a different form. In 'Fi'l-Shawāri'',[161] one of his richest stories, al-Kharrāṭ succeeds in combining the best characteristics of the two previous stages and retaining the introduction of the situation in the presence of an imminent death. He skilfully combines the presence of the perceptible with a remarkably powerful symbolism and abstraction that create a fine Kafkaesque world and an impressively suggestive nightmare.

The story presents its hero as being incapable of facing himself, for he nourishes an illusory sense of security by being rather removed and insouciant. He pretends to be indifferent to external reality, which is charged with enormous danger, and assumes that by being phlegmatic and asocial he can procure individual safety and salvation for himself. So he continues to play the game according to this golden rule, concealing his feelings, turning a blind eye to what is going on around him and refusing to believe that the monster (the unmentionable) can appear to him and subject him to 'the unnamable', without however being quite able to dismiss a penetrating fear of the very possibility of confrontation. The amalgam of fear and illusory safety disturbs the hero's private and public life, yet there is no easy way out, for it appears that, although the rules of the game imply that he should act as if the monster does not exist, he is incapable of shrugging off the fear and leading a normal life. The fear becomes indispensable, not only because it provides immunity against lapses or mistakes, but also because it offers a proof to the hero of his own existence in his refusal to accept the existence of the monster.

The beast is both a realistic and surrealistic creature, a mixture of intimate and familiar features, monstrous and unrealistic qualities, a curious amalgam of the subjective and the objective, illusion and reality, the mundane and the spiritual, externally hostile elements and intimately internal worries and anxieties. It is also so concrete that it can be seen, heard and touched but, at the same time, so ambiguous and abstract that it is beyond any comprehension or visualisation. Though both a private and public creature, familiar and unknown, it is not like the anxieties of the hero of 'Ḥīṭān 'Āliyah', which become concrete and visible at one stage, for its public nature gives it strong social and political implications. Like fate, political terror, a pervasive intelligence service, the unknown, it stands there and nowhere, sometimes tame, sometimes wild, temperamental, ready to strike when it wants, and peaceful, almost amiable, when it suits it to be so. It becomes a permanent feature of daily life, feared and cherished by everyone, and more importantly, it transforms life into a heavy and surrealistic nightmare.

In the presence of such a monster lives the protagonist of the story, but the very existence of such a creature renders his life meaningless and alienates him even from himself. The protagonist continues to fear confrontation with the beast without realising that constant fear has left a lasting mark on him comparable to that which the dreaded confrontation itself would have created. His position is, in effect, no better or worse than that of those who have returned from a brief encounter with the monster, speechless and spiritless, unable to relate the details of the confrontation or to lead the modest lives they led before. They are the living dead, whose knowledge of the beast has reduced them to vegetables, yet the protagonist's life, regulated and motivated by fear, is no better. The very fact that no one is able to talk about what took place during the confrontation implies it is both a private and public experience, which has an objective existence and validity, and at the same is made up of each individual's own fears and anxieties.

The protagonist is by no means a conscious objector who rejects the existing order, but an ordinary man who wants to lead a peaceful existence as a good citizen, an apolitical creature who cares only for the safety and well-being of his own family. He is a conformist who does not aspire to eminence, yet the growth of fear invades his apathetic conformity and tinges his acquiescence with doubts about his own safety in the absurd and irrational world of the beast. Nevertheless, he continues to conceal his fears and pretends to be oblivious in an attempt to disguise his awareness and ensure his security. Then the confrontation takes place, the dreaded encounter with the monster at midday in the largest and busiest square in Cairo, with everybody watching and pretending, actually believing, that nothing unusual is going on. The implication is that the whole situation, despite its grotesque nature, has become completely natural and is both accepted as normal by the inhabitants of this bizarre world and integrated into their daily lives.

For the individual protagonist, whose name is significantly the same as the author's, that the confrontation with the beast takes places in the midst of the apathetic and acquiescent crowd accentuates his isolation and intensifies the devastating effect of this mute encounter. The name of the protagonist and the dreamlike ending of the story are just two of many devices employed to root the work in external reality without affecting its non-realistic nature. As in many others, the relationship between the action and external reality is complex, for although al-Kharrāṭ's fictional world is deliberately unrealistic, it is almost entirely made up of realistic data, which serve to link the work to outer reality. The realistic detail establishes the concrete nightmare, beyond any doubt, as part of the daily Egyptian life at the time of writing, and delineates the nightmarish aspects of external reality in a provocative and artistic manner. It also integrates the protagonist-author in external reality and brings into focus, in a subtle and suggestive manner, the factors that enable the monster to exist and thrive.

In this story and many others, the author's lack of control over the mass of detail and his inclusion of functionless data mar the artistic edifice by creating an obtrusive authorial presence and dispersing the unity of impression. Such traits are found in various degrees throughout the three stages of his work, despite his efforts to overcome them, and are associated with the contradiction between subjective and objective realities and visions, with its implied dichotomy between the I and the All. In all these stages, al-Kharrāṭ seems to be torn between the relevance of his work to external reality and the desire to create a self-contained and timeless world that transcends the relevance of factual data to the realm of poetry. Although he continues to be undecided and fluctuates between emphasising the relevance of his work to the present and creating timeless works, he fails to combine the two and transcend the dilemma by concentrating on the present scene.

When the emphasis is on transcending realistic detail and atmospheres, al-Kharrāṭ does not attempt to do so through the action or characterisation but by the elaborate use of language. In some of his works, the skilful use of language maintains the story's plausibility in a manner that sustains the two levels of artistic presentation – the realistic and the unrealistic – and lends the work a poetic quality. Al-Kharrāṭ's language contains, on occasions, an unusual infusion of the language of poetry, which refashions action and location as a pattern of imagery and develops a tradition that is neither didactic nor dramatic, although it contains features of both. He aims to create a style in which every word, every nuance, every cadence, every detail should perform a definite function and produce an intense effect.

In the process, he sometimes falls victim to the lure of certain words, syntactical constructions and juxtapositions and produces a string of endless sentences, a stream of language that flows without illuminating the truth, and a useless display of rhetoric and impressively functionless synonyms. The maze of language, which in some works is intended to plaster over serious structural defects, obscures some of al-Kharrāṭ's genuinely profound clusters of images and taints them with deliberation, which, unlike poetic succession, neither illuminates the symbols nor gives them the desired 'timeless' quality. Even some of his best works, such as 'Maḥaṭṭat al-Sikka al-Ḥadīd' and 'Fi'l-Shawāri'', lose a great deal of their potential richness, impact and cohesion if they are taken out of the context of contemporary Egypt, despite their apparent abstraction.

The negative qualities of his language are perhaps responsible for his very limited readership, which came only after the ascendancy of the modern sensibility in the 1960s and thanks to constant reference to his work by young writers and critics. However, despite the fundamental linguistic shortcomings affecting a whole range of artistic and thematic issues, al-Kharrāṭ's work developed certain technical features that contributed to the shaping of the modern sensibility. Apart from the development of the contemporary nightmare and the emphasis on subjective reality with its corollary schizophrenic dichotomy between the I and the All, his work represents the beginning of the shift from the techniques of reporting to those of rendering, a shift which developed later with the 1960s' generation of writers. This shift manifests itself most clearly in the use of the *monologue intérieur*, for although al-Shārūnī had made extensive use of the first person, al-Kharrāṭ introduced new qualities to this technique.

Instead of the author's report of what is occurring in the mind of his character, or the organised soliloquies in which the mind presents reasoned and ordered thoughts, al-Kharrāṭ attempts to present a flowing stream of thought, thought written by the author yet supposedly free from his interference, whether by comment or by angled perspective. The author's withdrawal from the work, or from the monologue, is never complete, for he creeps in again through an obtrusive use of language which, although tolerable in the second stage with the prevalence of the intellectual hero, cannot be accepted in the third stage with the shift to the ordinary character, despite the conscious endeavour to sprinkle it with vernacular words and phrases. In spite of this fundamental stumbling block, al-Kharrāṭ's monologues represent an early example of the shift from reporting to rendering, a shift associated with his attempt to create a self-contained world independent of the laws of verisimilitude.

Like al-Shārūnī, and as a reaction to the prevalent sentimentality, al-Kharrāṭ's words are marred by over-writing, over-rationalising and over-planning. Yet, also like al-Shārūnī, his artistic and thematic discoveries and contributions are important despite a failure to perfect or use many of them effectively. Both he and al-Shārūnī built upon many of the achievements of preceding modernist writers and prepared the ground, particularly throughout the 1950s, for the triumph of the modern sensibility in the 1960s. The fact that both of them belong to the Coptic minority might have helped them to portray in their fiction the experiences of persecuted, solitary, alienated characters, and their experiments in this direction proved invaluable in the 1960s. When the modern sensibility triumphed through the vigorous work of the younger generation, al-Shārūnī and al-Kharrāṭ benefited greatly, as their work was retrieved from oblivion and obscurity and given a new, and to some extent exaggerated, significance.

The Triumph of the Modern Sensibility

The 1960s is an important decade in the history of modern Egyptian literature in general and the Egyptian short story in particular, for it is the decade that witnessed the blossoming of a new generation of Egyptian writers, the triumph of the modern sensibility, and the edification of a new mode of discourse. It is the decade that established new values and new rules of literary presentation, dealt a substantial blow to romantic, sentimental and naturalistic approaches to reality, and rooted the modern sensibility in the literary scene.

After the balmy days of the 1950s, during which cultural activities thrived and socialist realism and realism flourished in the arts, writers like Idrīs and al-Sharqawī were at the centre of public life, and those whose works had been overshadowed by romanticism and sentimental fiction were brought to the attention of the reading public and widely acclaimed (writers such as Ḥaqqī, Maḥfūẓ, and al-Badawī); the 1960s witnessed a cultural blossoming of all that was of value in Egyptian literature and drama.

Despite the sharp contradictions of this decade and the obvious lack of political freedom, men of letters enjoyed relative freedom of expression even if their work contained a constant flow of overt or latent social and political criticism.[162] It was a decade of paradox, for despite the heavy-handed paternalism in the arts, many opponents of the regime became pillars of the literary establishment and enjoyed considerable influence and freedom – some were even sanctioned by the very regime they continued to oppose.[163] The tight control over political activity made the relative freedom in the arts, which was far from being absolute or ideal, more important; it became a valuable outlet which many writers used to voice political opinions, and inevitably it made literature into a more sensitive barometer of subtle changes of awareness than it might have been in a more liberal society.

The apparent liberty in the cultural field was a double-edged phenomenon, for it attracted a vast number of semi-talented politically motivated writers, who tried to use literature as a vehicle for political ends, which inevitably had an impact on literary standards and artistic values. Yet the fact that many of the writers were opposing the regime under which they lived and, ironically, thrived, and that they controlled the literary establishment, edited the state-financed magazines and ran the state-subsidised theatres and publishing houses, called for the development of a more complex and subtle approach to literary expression. The more artistically committed writers wanted to play it safe, if not to play according to the regime's rules, and most were keen to develop a special code that was not so esoteric as to alienate them from their readers but that would imply enough to enable them to divulge their views without making an issue of them. The artistic process, which was marred by the advent of the former group, benefited from the latter, who were obliged to become more sophisticated and accurate in their metaphors, allegories and parables.

However, these young writers, whose cultural roots lay in the 1950s and whose careers began in the paradoxical decade of the 1960s, were faced with a difficult situation. They shared with the 'established' writers the desire to oppose many aspects of the social and political life of the country, even if they did not necessarily have identical convictions. The pillars of the cultural establishment, many of whom had to compromise some of their ideas and past convictions in order to sustain their prominent social positions and mundane privileges, saw in the rising generation, with their radical innocence and vigorously uncompromising approach, a threat to their peace of mind and to the fragile balance they maintained with the authorities. The new generation awakened their uneasy consciences and asked irritating questions about their compromises; and if they succeeded in their art, their very success would cast doubt on their compromises. It seems that most of those who had compromised were not happy with their situation and nursed psychological scars that manifested themselves in their hostility to the new generation of writers. The very appearance of this generation seemed to remind them of how they had sold their souls, and forced them to see themselves in a new light – and they were not pleased with what they saw.

The easy way out was to adopt a firm stand against the new generation, which was, of course, reciprocated. Although the younger generation received some support from the older writers, and notably from Ḥaqqī, this gradually dwindled and the hostility between the two rose steadily until it reached its highest pitch towards the end of the decade. The younger generation, who continued to be disappointed in the older generation, refused, immaturely on occasions, either to accept the guardianship of the former, or to acknowledge any debt to it. Some even went further and insisted that their work was not, in any way, a continuation of literary achievements of preceding generations and denied that they had learned anything from them.[164]

The conflict between the young and the older writers, especially those who controlled the literary establishment, is clearly associated with a significant development in the mode of literary presentation and the code of reference to external reality. Egypt had known censorship for decades and in many forms, and this continued in the 1960s. Yet in spite of, or rather because of, this history, which goes back to the turn of the twentieth century, Egyptian writers had contrived ways and means of defying the censor, who was, as far as literature was concerned, no more than an uncultured automaton. So when the pillars of the literary establishment, who were after all outstanding writers and knew the literary code of reference too well to be fooled by newcomers, started to play the role of censor, often voluntarily, the situation called for serious consideration and radical change.

The new generation was obliged to impose an extra censor upon itself; the censor moved from outside to inside the creative process and became, in a sense, one of its components, for without this self-imposed censorship it was almost impossible to publish. The conflict between young and older writers did not, in fairness, create this situation; it was only one of many objective factors that combined to create an atmosphere of insecurity and fear, for many of the older writers were also subject to this self-imposed censorship, which, sadly, was not completely without merit. It resulted in the abandoning of naive didacticism and sentimentality, and the introduction of new and more sophisticated techniques ceased to be a luxury but an urgent necessity, without which many writers had either to forsake their profession or to expose themselves to danger. The development of a new code and more complex techniques was in fact both a blessing and a curse, for it alienated the work of the new writers from the wider reading public, who were not accustomed to the new code of reference and the new literary conventions that accompanied it but, at the same time, it eliminated the undesirable elements of empty sentimentality and weak allusions.

The 1960s' generation had to tread carefully from the beginning of their literary careers, for they had to prove themselves without the help of the preceding generations. They were keen to identify neither with their predecessors nor with the establishment, but to create their own expression of Egypt in the 1960s and to reveal the innermost spirit of this troubled decade. They aspired to test the possibilities of the society in which they lived, to dramatise its anxieties and perversions, and to capture the rhythm and the undercurrent of its life. They tried to test writing against the life of action and that life against the necessities of the mind and the soul without being caught in their contradictions. Indeed, to be a young writer in Egypt in the 1960s was

> to stagger openly between wisdom and foolishness, lucidity

> and dementia; to risk and to play it safe, to fall and to be resurrected; to be a conscious, exemplary, half-clownish and half-grave and naked public destiny; to throw the ego against the impersonal rubric of the age, to try to move and shake the times while representing an unappeasable nostalgia for the artist's indifference to temporality; to be Narcissus and to be Prometheus; to be a cloud of discontent that bumps the stagnant heaven into motion.[165]

A young Egyptian writer in the 1960s was the mouthpiece of a whole generation that had been prohibited from any genuine political activity and surrounded by deformed values, slanted facts and confused fallacies. This generation had grown up in a paternalistic society, in the fullest and worst sense of the word, where the ruler and the corrupted bureaucratic establishment considered themselves the only possible substitute for all political systems and organisations. Against all odds, these writers survived the crucial test and made a lasting impact on the development of Egyptian literature in general and that of the short story in particular. Indeed, it is denying them their full due to treat their valuable contribution to the Egyptian short story at the end of this study, for it deserves a sizeable book in itself. Their contribution was not confined to their own work, for their ideas, techniques and modes of expression influenced the whole cultural scene, including many established writers.[166] However, in the time scale of this study many of these young writers were at the outset of their careers. It is necessary to consider their early works here, for the selection of 1970 as the limit for this study takes into consideration two principal factors: the first is that 1970 marked the end of an era in the history as well as in the culture of Egypt; the second, and more important, is that the end the 1960s is a natural terminating point when two cycles of development in the history of the Egyptian short story were completed.

The flowering of the modern sensibility, in which many social, cultural and political factors played a decisive role, was not only confined to the works of the younger generation, for the new atmosphere, the shift in sensibility, and the change in artistic emphasis influenced the work of the writers of the preceding generation. An important literary event at the beginning of the 1960s was the publication of Ḥaqqī's 'al-Firāsh al-Shāghir', one of the finest and richest works of modern sensibility and a story that is radically different from Ḥaqqī's previous works, yet akin to them. Before the middle of the decade Idrīs began to publish some modernist works, which appeared in his collection *Lughat al-Āy-Āy* (1965),[167] and after 1967 Najīb Maḥfūẓ (1911–2006), who had firmly established himself as the leading Egyptian novelist, fell under the spell of the modernist short story and produced some significant stories, amongst which *Taḥt al-Miẓallah* (1969) stands as a rich and revealing work. Although it is difficult to argue that writers of Maḥfūẓ's and Idrīs's calibre could have been influenced by younger writers, the idea is not completely invalid. Even if one rejects any direct influence, the mere production of such works by writers who are wellknown for a different kind of writing enhances the validity of the notion of the triumph of modern sensibility and suggests that it was deeply rooted in the literary consciousness of the period.

Before identifying some of the major contributions of the 'generation of the sixties', it is appropriate to mention the remarkable and decisive role of Yaḥyā Ḥaqqī and 'Abd al-Fattāḥ al-Jamal (1923–94) in facilitating its important contribution. By a happy coincidence, the decade had only just begun when Ḥaqqī resumed the editorship of *al-Majallah,* and al-Jamal editorship of the cultural page of *al-Masā'*.[168] Indeed, Ḥaqqī and al-Jamal, men of integrity and insight, are the two shining exceptions among the older generation; they took a sympathetic and encouraging attitude towards the younger generation and as a result they continued to mentor and help young writers until the end of the decade.[169]

Ḥaqqī and al-Jamal opened their journals to the writings of the younger generation and in different ways each provided them with valuable platforms, for while Ḥaqqī was fatherly, cautious and selective, al-Jamal was amiable, completely committed to the younger generation, and never deterred by their excessive experimentation. Al-Jamal also had control of the wider platform, for while Ḥaqqī was in charge of a conventional monthly review, whose motto *'sijill al-thaqāfah al-rafī'ah'*, the record of high culture, had strong conservative connotations, and which had to maintain a delicate balance between the traditional and experimental and could publish no more than one 'modern' short story every month, if not every other month, al-Jamal had a daily page for five or six days a week, so he could publish in a month the same number of 'modern' works that *al-Majallah* could publish in a whole year. In fact, it is possible that without al-Jamal's publishing outlets, some of the young writers who were reluctant to banish their work to Beirut would have found it extremely difficult to publish or to develop and continue as writers.

Their revolt against previous generations was more than simply a reciprocation of hostility; it was a rebellion against the establishment and the authority of diverse father figures in the paternalistic atmosphere of this complex decade. They formed a new generation, in the real sense of the word, in the same way that the American writers of the Lost Generation form a distinct generation in the history of American literature.

A generation, in historical terms, is no more a matter of dates that it is one of ideology. A new generation does not appear every thirty years, as Pio Baroja and other theorists have maintained, or 'about three times in a century' to quote Fizgerald; it appears when writers of the same age join in a common revolt against the fathers and when, in the process of adopting a new life style, they find their own models and spokesmen.[170]

Although the new writers in Egypt were not a self-conscious group and had no leader, no apparent programme, no sense of their own power, and no culture that was exclusively their own, they formed a generation in Cowley's definition. Towards the end of the decade, after the defeat in the Arab-Israeli war of 1967, they launched their own magazine, *Gallery 68*, which was in many ways an inadequate expression of their talents and ambitions, but its appearance was in itself a significant phenomenon.

Although they were not conscious of their own power, but rather of their vulnerability to intimidation by the establishment, the new writers were acutely aware of the defects of their society and they held the previous generation responsible for betraying the national dream. Unfortunately for them, their cultural background coincided with the development of a bizarre reality and the emergence of a deepening distrust of the national state that was once everybody's dream. They were exposed to the resurrection of the debate about national identity in a gloomy atmosphere in which many prophets of doom presented their eloquent visions and revelations[171] to intellectuals who were suffering the repercussions of overwhelming defeat. For the sixties generation, the defeat of 1967 was a vindication of their criticism of the establishment and an eloquent testimony to their claim that the older generation was bankrupt and that their failure was not only political but also social and cultural. The new writers did not question the declared political and social aspirations of the establishment, for they shared these aims and aspirations, but rather quarrelled with the methods of implementing the policies, the approach to problems, the presentation of facts, and the incomprehension of and failure to grasp the underlying spiritual agonies of society.

Naturally, the rejection of the values and viewpoints of the previous generation necessitated the development of alternative values and visions, for without these the new writers could not be distinguished from their predecessors. Whether the rejection of the old brought about these new visions or whether it is an inherent characteristic of the modern to reject the conventional – as Frank Kermode says 'a new modernism prefers and professes to do without the tradition and the illusion'[172] – is a controversial and somewhat polemical question. What concerns this study is that the development of these new qualities and this rebellious vision led the sixties generation to regard themselves, implicitly, as an élite.

> They were an élite not by birth or money or education, not even by acclaim ... but rather by such inner qualities as energy, independence, vision, rigor, an original way of combining words (a style, "voice"), and utter commitment to a dream.[173]

Unlike the lost generation of Abu'l-Najā, they did not fall under the spell of romanticism and sentimentality, and by this time these were distinctly out of favour.

The sixties generation capitalised on a vast intellectual readjustment and radical dissatisfaction with the artistic past, yet their 'disparagement and nihilist rejection of the past are founded partly on ignorance and partly on a development of the earlier modernist doctrine'.[174] Only a few of them were aware of the existence and achievements of romantic and sentimental writers, so they were introduced from the very beginning to the more valuable achievements of the Egyptian short story, and discovered at an early stage of their careers that there were subtler methods and more demanding standards in literature than those of the popular writers. They were widely read in Egyptian, Arabic, European and American literature and seized upon the works of the modernists with joy and insight. They realised that the importance of such works was not simply as examples to be followed but that they contained glimmers of inspiration that could become the mature foundation of a succeeding stage and could help them to shape their own vision, ways of thinking and areas of subject matter.

The affinities between the ways of seeing and the subject matter of the sixties generation and that of the preceding Egyptian modernists are numerous, for the two responded to similar conditions and phenomena and were a product of two phases of modern sensibility, which differ in degree but not in nature. The affinity can be easily established by a study of the new vision of the sixties generation as a collective vision shaped by a whole generation and not by single writers, and by the delineation of the major differences in emphasis within this unified vision, which will entail a brief discussion of the distinct characteristics of those who contributed to this new vision, and these new ideas and values, from an artistic and thematic angle.

As a reaction to the prevalence of sentimental emotions and ideas in the mainstream of Egyptian literature, and in an attempt to portray the disintegration of personality, which reflected a disintegration of external reality, the younger writers paid close attention to sense data and momentary sensory impressions through which persons or events emerge fleetingly from the stream and vanish again. These brief, fleeting appearances indicate much about these writers' perceptions of external reality, and reflect the nature of the chances for contact between people or with surrounding events in the fragmentary world of the 1960s. Without the clear emphasis on sensory data, which is associated with the authors' complete withdrawal from the narrative, it would have been extremely difficult to eliminate the note of exaggeration in describing a world that was rife with frustration and despair – the world of the sixties generation.

The emphasis on sensory data and momentary impressions also has undeniable significance in more general literary terms:

> the feeling of surveying an existence without essence, a continuum without structure, runs deep in the art and gives it a sense of internal strain – a certain terminal quality in the writing which reveals that it is attempting to reach towards the limits of language, the ultimate possibilities of form, the extreme of an aesthetic order beyond time and history.[175]

It is also associated with yet another image common in modernist writing, the perception of the world as a prison. Here it is appropriate to mention that many of the young writers suffered for their defiance of the established order, and those who lived through the experience of political intimidation or endured detention, collected a great deal of nervous energy, enough to carry them through the next frantic years. Even those who did not endure such traumata realised that the contemporary self

> was not only born, like Little Dorrit, in a prison, and has not only made of its prison, like Axel, a fortress and mausoleum. It has also been discovering the strange secrets of all prisons: that though their doors are never locked, no prisoner wishes to escape; that all avenues of escape lead to the same cell; that nothing may really exist beyond prison walls; that every jailer is merely another prisoner in disguise. The contemporary self recoils from the world, against itself. It has discovered absurdity.[176]

Indeed, the withdrawal from the world, which is the most momentous characteristic of the new anti-hero, is a recoiling both *into* and *against* the self. It is a withdrawal into the self inasmuch as it explores the human psyche or, more accurately, the impact of grotesque aspects of reality upon man. As in psychoanalysis, the hero is isolated from outside stimuli so that his mind can play freely over his past and his perception of the present. Therefore a painful, though not often painstaking, process of self-analysis takes place, where the aim, which is occasionally more ambitious than the hero can sustain, is the comprehension of both the self and the world. It is a recoiling into the self because outer reality is cruel and any movement to alter it is futile and doomed to fail, so the hero has no choice but to accept such reality and to become a defeated anti-hero. The writing of the 1960s expresses a firm conviction that a feeling of isolation is by no means a rare condition and is indeed an inescapable fact of human experience.

Nonetheless, the anti-hero accepts his solitude with great reluctance, for he is undoubtedly 'the creator of his world, a passive creator on whom the existence of the world entirely depends. In him sensations and impressions are received, symbolic figures emerge and fall behind as trees pass by a traveller moving along in a very slow cart'.[177] Yet, unlike European modernists, who negate the independent existence of outer reality and emphasise the role of human consciousness, which is constantly building, modifying and rebuilding a new world out of its own creativity, the Egyptian writers of the 1960s were too aware of the external reality to eliminate it from the world. Hence the solitude of their anti-hero is a recoiling both from the self and from outward reality, and is one of the resources of his awareness, what Ihab Hassan calls 'a strategy of the will'.

The anti-hero's withdrawal from outer reality combines a sense of despair with the ability to use this destructive despair constructively by turning it into a gesture of opposition that proclaims involvement in the world it opposes. In other words, the idea of victimisation is combined with a feeling of alienation and an implicit rebellion that involves a sense of revulsion as an attitude towards history. The plight of the displaced person and his isolation becomes a form of rebellion that aims to verify the existence of the anti-hero and that of his compatriots, for it is the kind of rebellion that aspires to merit Camus's existential *cogito*, 'I rebel therefore we exist.' Indeed,

> the problem of the anti-hero is essentially one of identity. His search is for existential fulfilment, that is for freedom and self-definition. What he hopes to find is a position he can take within himself. Society may modulate his awareness of his situation, but only determines his stand.[178]

However, the withdrawal from reality is associated with frustration and despair, often leads to violence and estrangement, augments the anti-hero's sense of guilt and absurdity, and obscures objective standards for evaluating human action. Both subjective and objective criteria become blurred and this

> leads to speculation about the radical disjunction between the private man and the public society essentially indifferent to the ethical concerns of the individual. Handled either comically or tragically, this disjunction does not allow public rewards for virtue or castigations for vice, does not permit the assumption that the nature of the individual is eventually revealed in public or explicit terms.[179]

This, in turn, subjects the anti-hero to abject suffering, to relentless, ironic, introspective questioning of the self and the surrounding reality, which sheds many doubts on the outer reality but fails to release the anti-hero from the grip of absurdity and uncertainty, so he continues to endure his reclusiveness as an asocial being leading a meaningless existence.

Although it is obvious that he resents the complacency of the common folk and tries to prove to them that their petty self-satisfaction is illusory and unfounded, he is unable, for various reasons, to defend the scale of values, whose disintegration, under the constant hammering of the inverted scale of values, infuriates him and alienates him further from reality. The protest expressed by his flight into subjectivity often becomes an abstract gesture whose rejection of reality is too general to be effective, for it does not constitute a rebellion against certain conditions but rather a nihilistic or anarchic refusal of the social order. In this sense, the anti-hero becomes ahistorical, asocial, apolitical, yet this form of existence is not void of historical, social or political significance. It enhances the constructive use of withdrawal as a gesture of opposition, for it had been government policy, by both omission and commission, at different times, to isolate the intellectuals progressively from the people, and at the same time, attempts to transcend the anti-hero's endurance to the realm of abstraction by negating any form of historicity.

> [The] negation of history takes two different forms in modernist literature. First, the hero is strictly confined within the limits of his own experience. There is not for him – and apparently not for his creator – any pre-existent reality beyond his own self, acting upon him or being acted upon by him. Secondly, the hero himself is without personal history. He is 'thrown-into-the-world': meaninglessly, unfathomably. He does not develop through contact with the world; he neither forms nor is formed by it.[180]

These two forms, an amalgam of which appear in many works of the sixties generation, have one implied message: the world is not worth living in, for it fails to provide man with a sense of being and an identity. Yet, the anti-hero has no choice but to continue living in the very world he detests, and as a result he becomes a forlorn character in a forlorn condition, retreating into himself in despair at the hostility of harsh outward reality. This often leads to an image of a man vegetating in a remote inaccessible room whose suffering has no bearing on the world in which he lives, or more precisely from which he withdraws.

Such an image is evidently historically inaccurate, and indeed the location of many of the works deals a blow to their ahistoricity and sets them firmly in the contemporary scene. Most of the writers use Cairo as the locus of their writing, which is marked by an apparent rejection of the village, yet the urban setting is little more than a backcloth or a device for making the character credible. It is true that the large city, with its disintegrating social structure, is well-suited to the conditions of the anti-hero, to his psychology, his state of mind and his fragmentary existence, yet in the work of the sixties generation this is rarely illustrated in a manner that makes it an integral part of the theme or that is at all reminiscent of the realistic tradition. Indeed, the presentation of the location is part and parcel of this generation's perspective and outlook and is tinged with unrealism, even when it appears to be realistic or photographic.

The assumption that the external reality is not only alien and inherently inexplicable but also inimical to the character's peace of mind and aspirations gives rise to a new state of being and necessitates a host of new techniques suited to its presentation. This expresses itself negatively through man's retreat from unpleasant conditions, his avoidance of commitment or action, his endurance, even acceptance, of human degradation, and other features associated with a state of suspension. The literary techniques employed to convey this state of being are not used with a view to exaggerating or belittling the situation, but are based on the fact that

> art does not feed us information and it does not provide us with a passport to some higher realm of existence. What it does is to open our eyes by removing the film of habit which we normally carry around with us.[181]

Without this revelation, this removal of the film of habit, the possibility of understanding the essence of the human psyche and human condition decreases, even disappears.

Apart from their awareness of the elusive nature of man and his conditions, the sixties generation was aware of the double obligation of their art: 'it must know and explore the world outside itself and it must also explore within itself – its language, its structure, its form'.[182]

This led them to pay closer attention to the internal stylisation of the genre,

> the distortion of the familiar surface of observed reality, and the use of what has been called 'spatial form' – a disposition of artistic content according to the logic of metaphor, form, or symbol, rather than to the linear logic of story, psychological progress, or history. The artist is thus radical in a particular sense: he is concerned not so much with revolution in the world as with revolution in the word.[183]

The sixties generation paid great attention to technique and explored the limits and potentials of the short story genre in an unprecedented manner, so that they were able to create through their art a new reality, which was neither identical to external reality nor completely alien to it, a reality made up of, to use Goethe's term, *Dichtung und Wahrheit*, poetry and truth: a subjective pattern of significant associations fused with an objective structure of verifiable data. In many of their works, reality is subjectivised and made to appear arbitrary, for they consistently exhibit an urge to make the unreal into a possibility, then into a probability, then into an irrefutable fact. At the same time, they use techniques that cast substantial doubts on realistic data and make them appear absurd, even unreal. The two complementary processes are sustained by maintaining a suggestive interaction between explicit statements and implicit imagery, and by preferring subjective time to metric time.

The writers of the 1960s were more conscious than their predecessors of the pervasive and precarious nature of time, for

> time, as Kant and others have observed, is the most characteristic mode of our experience. It is more general than space, because it applies to the inner world of impressions, emotions, and ideas for which no spatial order can be given.[184]

Their use of time is related to their approach to reality, in which they are not concerned with reality as such but with the individual's impressions of it – impressions that are free from the sequence imposed by chronological time. The flux of a distorted time becomes an inherent part of the blend of subjectivity and objectivity, for

> the quest for a clarification of the self leads to a *recherche du temps perdu*. And the more seriously human beings become engaged in this quest, the more they become preoccupied and concerned with the consciousness of time and its meaning for human life.[185]

So it is natural that subjective time is preferred to metric objective time, for subjective time has a speed of its own, it can be stretched to ten or fifty times its clock length and can be reduced in the same manner at the rapid summoning of a scene, word or image.

In the works of the sixties generation, the interest in time and the distortion of its logical sequence are linked to the development of the technique of the cluster of images deployed in a certain succession, in a stream of association, which is a carefully plotted sequence gradually piercing to the core of the situation without any detailed illustration of its composition. Indeed, the succession of images and its delicate associations develop an internal logic within the work that cements and consolidates the speciously incoherent flux of images and time. The term logic is, of course, a misnomer, for

> this logic is distinguished by the fact that its causal connections are altogether different – i.e. "illogical" – from those in ordinary logic, by which is meant either the logic of common sense or the logic of inductive, causal inferences defining objective sequences and connections in the external world.[186]

The internal logic of a modernist work of art does not necessarily comply with the strict order of outer reality nor with its metric time. 'The inner world of experience and memory exhibits a structure which is causally determined by significant associations rather than by objective causal connections in the outside world.'[187] Fictional time has a unique duration that permits the fusion of times, of things remembered and those hoped for, desired, or even feared, and allows the constant modification and reinterpretation of the whole fusion in the light of present exigencies, past frustrations and future fantasies. The structure of such complex time

> requires a symbolism or imagery in which the different modalities of time – past, present and future – are not

> serially, progressively and uniformly ordered but are always inextricably and dynamically associated and mixed up with each other.[188]

The mixing of these three times is a mode of experience, for the erosion of time is the medium suited to portray the erosion of existence and the confusion of values and areas of experience.

In the process of incorporating these three kinds of time and fusing them into a new kind of time, the sixties generation make use of what Meyerhoff has defined as the

> six aspects of time characteristic in literature: (1) subjective reality or unequal distribution; (2) continuous flow, or duration; (3) dynamic fusion, or interpenetration, of the casual order in experience and memory; (4) duration and the temporal structure of memory in relation to self-identity; (5) eternity; (6) transitoriness, or the temporal direction towards death.[189]

The use of all these time techniques is closely linked to the departure from the objective approach to reality, which flourished with the realistic short story, in favour of a new amalgam of the subjective and objective. The writers of the 1960s were aware that the rejection of narrative objectivity leads occasionally to a surrender of unverifiable subjectivity and often to a form of existence without quality – a pseudo-realisation of the human psyche. Consequently, they sought to blend subjectivity with objectivity in a balanced mixture to avoid such false realisations in their literature, hence the use of the six techniques of time and even the blending and fusing of some of these techniques.

The balanced mixture of subjectivity and objectivity was intended to reveal the 'otherness' of the world, to emphasise the abhorrent disintegration of reality, and to enable the reader to identify, or at least to sympathise, with the characters and events portrayed. It seems that many of them held that

> the work of art is meaningful precisely because it reveals to us the "otherness" of the world – it shocks us out of our natural sloth and the force of habit, and makes us see for

> the first time what we had looked at a hundred times but never seen.[190]

The achievement of such a sudden shift from the habitual way of seeing requires different emphases which, in turn, give precedence to different priorities, different essential forms of interpretation, different symbolic organisation and, more importantly, a different approach to art and reality. The change in the writers' approach to their material created

> a stylistic milieu in which some practices which had been very close to the centre of fiction as a story-telling art were brought into question; it seemed that certain well-established types of narrative presentation, certain kinds and modes of Realism, certain poised relationships between the story and its teller, certain forms of chronological ordering and particular views of character, even the belief that a form does not need to exceed the working needs immediately occasioning it, were being restructured to fit the form of a new world.[191]

The restructuring of all these vital aspects of the work of art created a new artistic and thematic milieu, which called into question the major issues of art and society, not merely in terms of their interaction or lack of it, but at a more fundamental level. The flux of experience sparked off a new vision of open existence and a more sophisticated form of fiction that did not aspire to reflect or portray reality but to capture its rhythm and recreate the flux of existence without obstructing its flow or delimiting its continuity. In order to achieve this, the sixties generation fused the individual and the prototype with the abstract and used a blend of description and statements to create a sense of openness.

Their experience of life, which they tried to recreate in their art, seems to have been continual and open-ended, a sustained nightmare in which actual happenings were not significant in themselves but only through the reflections of the individual upon them. The interest in these reflections accentuated the role of the *monologue intérieur* and the technique of mirroring,

> since the self is the point at which inner and outer worlds

> are joined, the hero's mental picture reflects the universe of sensible encounters as an image. The "world" is part of the hero's inner world; the hero, in turn mirrors the external world and all its multitudinous manifestations.[192]

These two techniques, the monologue and the mirroring, are marked by their attentive or inattentive selectivity, and enable the author to focus his attention on certain objects and areas of experience and to block out others. They also enable the author, or more precisely, his characters, to 'distort the universe or dissolve it into hallucination or dream in which its "true" (infinite and organic) nature is revealed'.[193]

An interest in external reality was maintained throughout the works of the sixties generation, for it is the world into which the characters' discoveries are projected, and whose exploration is the author's aim. The characters' withdrawal from reality makes the presentation of the external world more of a projection of the psyche than a neutral image of the world of objects and events. This is enhanced by the distrust of most of the rational and scientific means of comprehension, which prevailed in the work of 1960s' writers. Although this attitude may appear to resemble romanticism, their excuse must be that in the 1960s these means were distorted by propaganda; the writers, therefore, tried to establish the supremacy of intuition – of feelings, visions, dreams, imagery, fantasy and other forms of intuitive knowledge. This intuitive perspective is more than a means of discovery; it becomes in many works a synthesising principle, for within it

> every thought necessarily absorbs and subsumes elements, which, looked at and detached from it, may contradict it or seem opposed to it, but which assume different meanings and values once they have been absorbed in the total structure of the final synthesis.[194]

Intuitive knowledge was favoured because of its appropriateness to the prevalent mode of existence, its applicability in understanding the ambiguous nature of their most recurring theme – ubiquitous fear, the overwhelming sense of dread that enervates the soul and erodes human existence. To penetrate the nature of this general fear requires an intuitive insight, for 'it is a fear which leads to self-intimidation and finally becomes so habitual that the scholar is unaware of it'.[195] Only the artist is capable of hunting its intangible details, as his medium is appropriate for discerning the elusive nature of such fear, which despite its ubiquity is concealed under the masks of discretion, good taste or balanced judgement. Fear penetrates every aspect of human existence and becomes the underlying element of many inexplicable phenomena and a force for evasion that induces silence, inaction and conformity. It engenders a mood of grey despair, self-mockery and irony and causes widespread feelings of discontent, a sense of impotence and a general dissatisfaction with society and the self.[196]

In the writing of the 1960s, this ubiquitous fear is a destructive force that accepts nothing less than reducing man to a frustrated being, sulking in silence with his anxieties and suffering a minor sort of hell, of being perpetually in the purgatory between innocence and guilt. It is a state of existence that affects both the authors and their anti-heroes, the form and the content of their fictional work. Nevertheless, ubiquitous fear is only one of several themes through which the younger generation of the 1960s tried, in their various ways, to express the essence of their time and to develop the visions and techniques of modern sensibility. The thematic and artistic qualities discussed above appear in the work of many writers, in different forms and through various individual themes and specific techniques. Discussion of all the significant works that contributed to the triumph of the modern sensibility or of the many talented writers who created them would be both premature and lengthy. However, a brief word on the most outstanding authors is needed in order to substantiate the characteristics discussed above and to demonstrate their rich variety.

Sulaymān Fayyāḍ

Although Sulaymān Fayyāḍ (b. 1929)[197] belongs by age and cultural background to the lost generation of Abu'l-Najā, he is a modernist at heart, both by temperament and in terms of the greater part of his work. In his first collection, *'Aṭshān Yā Ṣabāyā* (1961), both realistic and modernist features coexist, but his second, *Wa-Ba'danā al-Ṭufān* (1968) established him at the centre of the modernist movement, although he never completely abandoned realism. He is concerned with the invincible powers of destruction, whether social or metaphysical, and man's vulnerability and isolation in the face of tyranny. The violence in his work is a result of his pushing the confrontation between these two forces to its ultimate limits.[198] Yet isolated, vulnerable, fragile man proves to be indomitable, for it is possible to destroy him but not to conquer his spirit or will.

In many of Fayyāḍ's works,

> violence assumes a different aesthetic function. The hero finds himself in a predicament such that the only possible exit is through inflicting physical harm on some other human. In the infliction of harm he also finds the way to his own destruction. But still he accepts the way of violence because life, as he sees life, is like that: violence is man's fate.[199]

Violence becomes a means of communication through which man defeats isolation and projects himself as being worthy of the challenge of life and of his manhood, for physical violence and the extreme endurance of pain are the infallible means of defying destruction and meaninglessness.[200] Yet man cannot live by violence alone, nor can he escape the inevitability of death through physical endurance. He is destined to lead a tragic existence punctuated by violence and suffering and controlled by agony and fear,[201] in a manner that permits elements of absurdity and meaninglessness to invade his soul.[202]

In his presentation of such a tragic world, Fayyāḍ treats this and other lesser themes as they operate in people's consciousness in the daily life of rural Egypt. He portrays them as an integral part of this culture and shows how they penetrate its songs, myths and folklore. He is the first writer of modern fiction in Egypt to begin to reveal the richness of this untapped mine of folk-tales, folk medicine and popular mythology, and his use of mythology gives his tragic vision a revelatory poetic power.[203] This is heightened by his economical use of language and ostensibly matter-of-fact description, in which he is influenced by Hemingway's short stories in particular.[204] He avoids the use of emotive language, shuns speculation and sentimentality, and develops what might be called the poetry of unadorned language, symbols and action. Although he abandoned this approach in his third collection, *Ahzan Haziran* (1969), when he developed lucid and lyrical language to suit the mode of experience, he returned to it in his subsequent works.

Muḥammad Ḥāfiẓ Rajab

The controversial and often shocking work of Muḥammad Ḥāfiẓ Rajab (b. 1934) was the first to stimulate wide literary concern for the new generation of Egyptian short story writers.[205] After a short period during which he wrote in conventional style,[206] Rajab developed a unique style that established him as the most talented and the most dedicated surrealist writer in modern Egyptian literature. His surrealist works shocked literary circles into realising that a radical change in artistic sensibility was taking place and sweeping away many of the old conventions and beliefs. Rajab's view of the world does not differ very much from that of Fayyāḍ, for his is a violent world in which man is condemned to solitude, suffering and meaninglessness. Yet his presentation of this world, which in turn entails differences in vision and theme, is radically different not only from Fayyāḍ's but also from any the Egyptian short story had experienced so far.

With Rajab's work the old principles of causality, verisimilitude, psychological analysis and symbolic relations, principles on which the bulk of the Egyptian short story once rested, begin to crumble. Instead a new order, or rather a poetic disorder, begins to take over, opening the gates of imagination and wild fantasy, often onto a private hell of triangular relationships that dislodge man from his sanity and even from his humanity. When the relationship involves man, his son and a woman,[207] whether related to them or not, these gates open wide and a rich and tragic world of agony, poetry and apocalyptic vision appears. In Rajab's stories, hell is neither metaphysical nor rational, it is perceptible, physical and paralysing, a hell that has social, psychological and moral implications.

The father–son relationship, which in some stories[208] ends in patricide, has multiple implications and ramifications, for it involves the complex mixture of feelings suggested by Freud in his analysis of the patricide in Dostoevsky's work on the one hand, and raises crucial issues concerning the relationship of the son to his cultural legacy on the other. In some stories[209] the hostility directed towards the oppressive patriarch is extended to include the pillars of the cultural establishment, while in others the fantasmagoria has political and symbolic connotations.[210] The other central relationship that the author investigates, his anti-hero's relationship with the other sex, develops further the symbolic and political connotations and intensifies the impact of failure and isolation upon the character.

The woman in these stories[211] is elusive, sensuous, lively, selfish, tender, cruel and larger than life; at the physical level it is possible to communicate with her, but at other, deeper levels she seems unattainable. She symbolises the power of nature and fertility, but since the relationship with her is often interwoven with the father–son relationship, it involves an attenuated sense of castration, which sparks off remorse, agony and meaninglessness, and often results in the shedding of blood – a symbol of contraries in Rajab's works, of death and creation.

Around these two central themes, Rajab develops a world that does not comply with the laws of probability and verisimilitude yet is capable of providing us with profound insights into external reality. His nightmares are not made up of contemporary reality but of surrealistic imagery, as if created through a normal or drug-induced state of hallucination, or born out of the conflict between the inexhaustible powers of the mind and the impoverished and appalling conditions of outer reality. They are freed from the mechanisms of scientific rationality and social repression, so that they can constitute a world that transports the reader away from the living world in order to reappraise it. Rajab develops the techniques of association, symbolic presentation and poetic imagery in an unprecedented way and captures the rich and impressive themes of isolation and the accompanying struggle for liberty and fulfilment.

Bahā' Ṭāhir

Bahā' Ṭāhir (b. 1935) is one of the most sophisticated and widely read members of the sixties generation – a writer of profound vision, with a corresponding sense of structure, who stood aloof from the hurly-burly of the young literary movement, yet contributed to and participated in the shaping of its most valuable achievements.[212] Although he published comparatively little, his work made a lasting impact on his contemporaries and on the development of the genre in general, distinguished by its economy of language and delicate narrative structure. His stories are sophisticated and ostensibly conventional; they are not designed to attract attention but to induce a radical change in the literary approach to both art and society.

Ṭāhir does not seek to impress but to shock. His writing does not aim to arouse sentiments or stir up emotions, but to sharpen the reader's insight, and enhance his powers of discernment, to reveal the essence beneath specious appearances. Even more than Fayyāḍ, he eschews speculation and employs the direct line between the eye and the object in a manner that discloses the horrors of everyday reality and shocks both his hero and his reader into anagnoresis. This dramatic recognition, though intentional, does not appear forced, as Ṭāhir plays down his dramatic effects and contrives what might be called poetry in inaction. Although he avoids lyricism and verbal embellishments, he develops new criteria for stylistic aesthetics by his complete shift from 'reporting' to 'rendering' in the narrative and by his exposition of the beauty of simplicity and bareness.

With his aptly direct and precise rendering, specious solidity and cohesion vanish from the world of everyday reality, and the transferability and disintegration portrayed constitute a judgement on a profane world, a world where feelings and aspirations are of small importance. Ṭāhir presents two main character types: one is unreflective and completely instinctive, doomed to apathy, solitude and frustration;[213] the other is intellectual, born to fear and intimidation and subject to the relentless dialectic of innocence and guilt.[214] Yet the two different types seem to live in the same world of disintegrated reality and inverted values – a world of contemporary nightmares. Unlike Rajab, Ṭāhir establishes his nightmare outside the world of fantasy and roots it in familiar everyday reality, for such a nightmare is conceived as a part of the human condition where the absurdity of daily life, of life without essence, obscures events and pushes them beyond the comprehension of the anti-hero, who, in turn, responds instinctively, whence he steps into the quicksand of the contemporary nightmare.

In many stories[215] the contemporary nightmare is not a temporary condition but a permanent state of existence, which defies the individual's attempt to change it. The characters, whether positive or negative, participate, almost unconsciously, in perpetuating the nightmare by transcending their involvement in its stratagems, and raising it to the level of a ritualistic act of self-destruction. This is accompanied by the dependence of the story's structure upon the dialogue and 'upon a kind of thought stream in an indirect discourse couched in the same language the character actually spoke',[216] in a manner that demonstrates that first-person narrative may become a double mirror reflecting infinity. It creates a panoramic or kaleidoscopic image of life as a tormenting and lengthy process of interrogation. The dialogue, which is often based on litotes, also plays a significant part in constructing such an image. The ostensible conventionality of structure attenuates the peculiarity of the contemporary nightmare, confirms its tenacity and invincibility, and presents both the world and the anti-hero in a rational manner, which is not devoid of poetry despite its bareness and directness.

'Abd al-Ḥakīm Qāsim

Although 'Abd al-Ḥakīm Qāsim (1935–90) is best known for his important novel, *Ayyām al-Insān al-Sab'ah* (1968), he published some short stories that made a considerable contribution to the young literary movement of the 1960s despite his failure to publish them in a collection.[217] After a few unremarkable stories,[218] he developed a technique that enabled him to present a comprehensive and revealing vision of reality – a vision that is relative and takes account of the relativity of truth. This was his technique of developing the action and characterisation by dividing the main plot of the story into interdependent fragments, each of which constitutes a complete sub-plot while at the same time complementing the others in forming the major plot and creating various layers of meaning. In this way, Qāsim projects each episodic sub-plot on to a different level of reality in order to demonstrate that what appears on the surface is not the only truth or perhaps not the truth at all, and poses some awkward questions about external reality.

In some of his artistically successful and perceptive stories[219] Qāsim employs this technique, taking into account the view of the relativity of truth, and develops a collective vision of reality that accentuates the role of the All in shaping the individual I and in alienating him at the same time. To create this dialectical relationship between the individual I and the social All, Qāsim selects a rebellious character and sets him not only against the established order, but also in direct confrontation with a taboo, either social, political or metaphysical. The rebellious character is perceived of as a germ of disorder that breeds discontent but casts creative doubt on the status quo and opens the door to a radical evaluation of what has been, hitherto, accepted as axiomatic and factual.

The episodic structure in many of these stories has analogies with symphonic form, for it develops the major theme in separate movements, each of which is complete in itself yet grows out of the previous movement and contains the nucleus of the following. On occasions, the final movement suggests a return to the first, making a circular structure and indicating the continuity of the action. The circular form widens the implications of Qāsim's treatment of the taboos and his exploration of various layers of folkloric mythology.[220] His sensitive use of language and of perceptual, even sensuous, details also widens implications and enables him to contribute to the exploration of the limits of the literary genre and the crucial issues of man and society in the 1960s.

Ibrāhīm Aṣlān

The existence of a writer such as Ibrāhīm Aṣlān (b. 1937) is in itself a sign of the maturity of the short story in Egypt, for without the firm establishment of the conventions of the genre in the literary consciousness it would have been difficult for readers to comprehend, let alone appreciate, Aṣlān's works.[221] Aṣlān creates a complex and poetic world in which nothing significant happens on the surface – a world of inaction, a world that runs in neutral. Yet, beneath this ostensible stagnation of the familiar, even hackneyed reality, a rich world full of tension and change provides the reader with a terrifying, though profound, insight into Egyptian society in the 1960s.

Aṣlān's world is a profound one indeed, for it borders the realistic realm of experience without being real, it verges on the hackneyed without losing its freshness and vivacity, it approaches the boring without abandoning its ability to shock and surprise. It is a world that resembles familiar reality yet remains dissimilar in both nature and rhythm – a world of sordid reality charged with an attenuated surrealistic atmosphere where boredom is the only human condition, reality and logic disintegrate, and apathy dominates the scene. To heighten the peculiar nature of his world, Aṣlān juxtaposes contradictory qualities without the slightest attempt to explain or rationalise them, and the world appears as if seen through the eyes of a child who discerns its contradictions without fully comprehending their implications or their absurdity and cruelty. This reduces the perspective of narrative to the common denominator of the cursory glance of incomprehension, which is ironically able to reveal the contradictions beneath the surface. The world seen from the child's perspective never ceases to surprise, for it is presented as a contemporary nightmare that runs in slow motion and is always indifferent and apathetic to man.[222]

The technique of relying and concentrating on the visual only, of excluding any dramatic events, of developing whimsical stories in which whims become obsessions, and of using irony, quaintness and black humour, heightens the impact of the recognition by character and reader alike that the world is a wasteland, where nothing is of ultimate value. As a result, the anti-hero, a radical innocent who never gets over his constant surprise at the complexity of the world, wallows in misery and sadness and forsakes any hope of communicating with the world.[223] Any attempt by others to relieve the hero of his misery or dissipate his boredom and discontent only serves to intensify his agony and isolation.[224] Another device that the author uses to stress the anti-hero's isolation and misery is the presentation of occasional glimpses of happiness that seem unreal and unattainable, yet are ostensibly within the anti-hero's reach.[225]

In several stories the hero responds to the mounting tension by taking his clothes off as a gesture of forsaking the world of reality and convention. The desire for nakedness is shown in some stories[226] to express an overwhelming longing for the lost paradise of childhood. The resolution of tension through the ritualistic stripping off of clothes involves, at one level of interpretation, a desire for recognition, for the acknowledgement of the anti-hero's existence. At another level, it suggests a complete rejection of the sordid and apathetic world – a rejection that is silent, passive and powerful, without rebellion or action and which often leads to bitterness and solitude. Like Ṭāhir, Aṣlān avoids emotive language and eschews the slightest shade of sentimentality, conducting his narrative in a direct and economical language that is not devoid of poetry. Although he ostensibly reports on factual events, he creates a perplexing duality of time, action and character that blurs the reader's perception of these features, sheds profound doubt on the world, and suggests the futility of life.[227]

Muḥammad al-Bisāṭī

Apart from Fayyāḍ, who belongs to the generation of the sixties by temperament and the content of his output, rather than by age, Muḥammad al-Bisāṭī (b. 1938) was the only one in his generation to have published two collections by 1970.[228] In his first collection, *al-Kibār wa'l-Ṣighār* (1967), only a few works belong to the modern sensibility or contribute to the new vision shaped by the sixties generation;[229] the majority are of a conventional realistic nature. Al-Bisāṭī is not alone in this as many other writers of the same generation wrote largely within the framework of conventional realism, for example, 'Abd al-'Āl al-Ḥamamṣī (b. 1932), 'Abd Allāh Khayrat (1936–2001), Sa'īd Muḥammad Ḥasan (b. 1936), Muḥammad Rūmaysh (1937–91), Diya' al-Sharqawī (1937–1977), Zuhayr al-Shāyib (1938–81), Ḥasan Miḥassib (b. 1938), Muḥammad Mustajāb (1939–2005), 'Izz al-Dīn Najīb (b. 1940), and others.[230] In his second collection, *Ḥadīth min al-Ṭābiq al-Thālith* (1970), al-Bisāṭī continues to oscillate between the two veins but with a clear shift towards the modern.

The fluctuation between the two sensibilities results in a number of al-Bisāṭī's stories[231] in a fine blend of neo-realist and modernist features. In other works, it is evident that he endeavours to conventionalise the modern or modernise the traditional in a manner that establishes the embryos of the modern in the traditional and roots the modern in the conventional at the same time. Unlike many of his *confrères*, he tries to portray the disintegration of reality without forsaking the connected narrative, the syllogistic progression of the action, or the causal and continuous duration of time. In 'Mishwār Qaṣīr',[232] the most coherent and impressive story in his first collection, he succeeds in creating an oppressive nightmare without abandoning realistic narrative form, for the nightmare is not a situation imposed upon man, but an inherent quality in the human predicament portrayed.

In many other works[233] al-Bisāṭī creates what might be termed a stream of trivial experience in which he stresses the important side of inanimate objects and the apparent fragility of human character. His conventional approach leads him to concentrate on forlorn characters living in forlorn conditions, which, coupled with the contradiction between the fragility of man and the solidity of matter, creates a world that fluctuates between melancholy and subjective fancy, especially when he takes dreams or daydreams as a point of departure. Yet fantasy is subjected to the rules and logic of reality, for unlike Rajab, who submits to the ruses of wild imagination, al-Bisāṭī uses dream or fantasy only as a departure point, after which he treats the details of his portrayal realistically. This Kafkaesque technique aims to establish a nightmare that is thoroughly familiar and operates according to the same rules as those pertaining in the real world. Thus his nightmares, instead of being the antithesis of everyday working reality, become reality; next to al-Bisāṭī's dreams, rooted in everyday experience, the bizarre fantasies of De Sade and the surrealists seem to lose some of their poignancy.[234]

Unlike most of his contemporaries, who use Cairo as the locus of their work and use the alienating nature of a large city to accentuate the loneliness of their anti-hero, al-Bisāṭī locates many of his stories in the countryside, which is a further indication of his traditional tendency. For a character to be isolated in Cairo is axiomatic, but the alienation of the character in the warm and friendly atmosphere of the village gives the anti-hero's agony and solitude further weight. It proves that the worm has reached the core of the human condition and that the human predicament has become insoluble, the forces of alienation and destruction having invaded the last shelter of man and deprived him of his final refuge.[235]

Yaḥyā al-Ṭāhir 'Abd Allāh

When in 1964 Yaḥyā al-Ṭāhir 'Abd Allāh (1940–81) came, for the first time, to Cairo from his village in Upper Egypt with a few of his short stories and a desire to succeed in the capital by his talent alone, he shocked his contemporaries as well as writers of the older generation.[236] For here was someone of their own generation who had a degree of self-confidence, amounting to a conviction, that as soon as the literary circles had heard his stories (he knew them by heart and was prepared to recite them), they would place him second only to Yusūf Idrīs among Egyptian short story writers. His arrival in Cairo reveals something about the author, innocent and romantic rather than arrogant, and about his approach to and style of writing the short story, treating it as a poem that can be memorised and recited. Although life in Cairo in the 1960s tempered these two qualities, they remain at the core of his more mature work.

In his early work,[237] 'Abd Allāh demonstrates his poetic sensibility by using words to their full poetic value and grafting a lyrical atmosphere upon the narrative. In his later work,[238] the poetry goes deeper than linguistic embellishment; it is poetry that penetrates the situation, manifests itself in the minutest details, heightens the tension, cements the structure and enhances the organic unity of the whole work. However, in both periods the poetry is associated with the passive protagonist's point of view, which draws the contours of the lyrical form as his perceptions absorb external reality and transform them into images. The anti-hero not only mirrors the world as he sees it, but lends it a specific colour and shape, distorting or even displacing it, for the individual encounters he absorbs seem to be random and meaningless. 'Actually they cohere as a texture, intermingling past and present, occult and real events, mythical and historical figures with persons in the hero's life.'[239]

The texture and structure of the work are designed to create a lyrical immediacy which 'is different from the immediacy of narrative action ... It is an immediacy of portraiture, an availability of themes and motifs to the reader's glance without the interposition of a narrative world'.[240] After attempting to graft this lyrical immediacy on his world, in his early work, through the intensive use of the *monologue intérieur*, the distortion of consecutive time and the suggestive use of poetic language, he tried, in his later work, to create the lyrical immediacy by developing what al-Kharrāṭ terms a meta-realistic dimension,[241] in which myth, ritual, death, life in its very biological and sensual aspects, and the hidden logic or the ultimate will interact and intermingle all at once to alienate the situation from the realistic world and, at the same time, establish it at a deeper level.

'Abd Allāh acquires his unique place amongst the writers of the 1960s because of his ability to express this deep level of reality through a perceptive exploration of the world of Upper Egypt. In this respect, his work represent the most substantial creative contribution to the treatment of the world of the Upper Egypt in the short story since the remarkable works of Ḥaqqī and al-Badawī, for he succeeds in conveying not only the essential features of the culture of rural life in Upper Egypt, but also its rhythm and undercurrents, its vision and basic structures at both the perceptible and philosophical levels. His artistic virtuosity in presenting his unique vision of the ethos of Upper Egypt is displayed through his use of detail impassively recorded, the past tense used within the context of the present, the accentuation of sensuous details and the incantation of myth, and the introduction of a neutral commentary shedding fresh light on routine situations. He also develops the techniques of integrating ancient legend into the web of contemporary reality and of introducing *monologue intérieur* when the narrative is written in the third person, allowing for a profound interaction between external details and internal visions.

Jamāl al-Ghīṭānī

Jamāl al-Ghīṭānī (b. 1945) is the youngest among the writers of the sixties generation and the most prolific, though like most of them he published only one collection, *Awrāq Shābb 'Āsh Mundh Alf 'Ām* (1969), before 1970.[242] Like many of his *confrères*, he started by writing a mixture of conventional and modernist works,[243] but he soon discovered his own world and techniques. In many of his early works it is possible to detect the embryos of his major themes and character types and a deep concern for language, which takes its more individual form of development in his later works. The gloomy present is skilfully portrayed, where communication and fulfilment are different or non-existent, there is no sense of peace or security, and accordingly the characters feel an overwhelming desire to escape from the brutality and injustice of external reality. The major character type of these early works is the frustrated individual who retreats, under the pressure of outward reality, to an internal haven of daydreams or to a depressing isolation.

Al-Ghīṭānī's major contribution to the triumph of modern sensibility in the Egyptian short story lies in the work that he wrote after the devastating shock of 1967. It appears that al-Ghīṭānī was aware that his early works, most of which had been written and published before he came of age, served only as a testing ground; they were not included in his first collection. He excluded them because he wanted to draw attention to the new technique he developed in four of the five stories of his first collection[244] – the technique of mirroring the present in the past or the future, which serves to create a distance between the author and the sensitive issues he wishes to treat, and sets his world apart so that he can reshape, modify or exaggerate certain aspects of reality. This technique aspires not only to distance the situation in order to scrutinise it with objectivity, but also to place it in a wider historical perspective in order to attenuate its harshness, in other words, to suggest that 'disaster comes and goes in cunning rhythms ... that the way down is the way out, and that the end of things heralds a new beginning'.[245]

This technique, which al-Ghīṭānī continued to use in other works,[246] enables him to touch upon some of the taboos of the 1960s: the monopoly of political power, the growth of corruption in the highest quarters, the ubiquity of secret intelligence services, the pervasiveness of political intimidation and the swelling numbers in the detention camps.[247] The assumption of a historical mask is not the same thing as writing historical works that illuminate aspects of the present; al-Ghīṭānī did not write historical works in the strict sense of the term, and most of the speciously historical events, characters, or locations are more or less of his own invention. Rather, he uses the mask of historicity to penetrate present reality more effectively and to distance the situation from the reader so that he can re-think it for himself – not to mention the aim of defeating the censor.

Al-Ghīṭānī does not write within the tradition of historical fiction in Egypt but borrows the archaic style of Ibn Iyās and al-Jabartī to disrupt any identification with the situation and, more significantly, to create a harmonious relationship between the disintegration of reality and the disintegration of the language. The obsolete vocabulary and pallid syntactic structures of these two shrewd chronologists, when used to portray contemporary horrors, acquire in al-Ghīṭānī's work a new character, for the ostensible aridity of the language constitutes a skilful irony with the situation which it tries to portray. In some works[248] both the language and the historical mask tend only to simplify the complex nature of the issues without providing the reader with a profound insight into the situation, while in others[249] they succeed in revealing the intrinsic mechanism of such complex issues and creating plausible characters and an impressive artistic structure.

These eight writers are the most representative of a wide range of authors whose work made a genuine contribution to the development of the Egyptian short story in the 1960s. Important omissions are Ghālib Halasā (1936–89), Ḥusnī 'Abd al-Fādīl (b. 1936), Jamīl 'Aṭiyya Ibrāhīm (b. 1937), Ḍiyā' al-Sharqawī, Majīd Ṭūbya (b. 1939), Aḥmad Hāshim al-Sharīf (b. 1940), 'Izz al-Dīn Najīb, Muḥammad Ibrāhīm Mabrūk (b. 1940) and others whose work constitutes a valuable contribution to the triumph of modern sensibility and many of whom deserve closer consideration. The works of these leading, if diverse, writers of the sixties generation were disparaged at home and adulated abroad at the beginning of the sixties. However, towards the end of the decade they succeeded in gaining the recognition of Egyptian literary circles and are considered increasingly as forming a major part of the Egyptian literary tradition. As Eliot rightly said in his last book:[250]

A new kind of writing appears, to be greeted at first with disdain and derision; we hear that the tradition has been floated, and that chaos has come. After a time it appears that the new way of writing is not destructive but re-creative. It is not that we have repudiated the past, as the obstinate enemies – and also the stupidest supporters – of any new movement like to believe; but that we have enlarged our conception of the past; and that in the light of what is new we see the past in a new pattern.

[illegible] of the Modern Sensibility

The 1960s is an important decade in the history of modern Egyptian literature in general and the Egyptian short story in particular, for it is the decade that witnessed the blossoming of a new generation of Egyptian writers, the triumph of the modern sensibility, and the elaboration of a new mode of discourse. It is the decade that [illegible] a new set of literary presentations [illegible] romanticism and naturalism [illegible] and [illegible] the modern sensibility on the literary scene.

Notes

Foreword

1. Sabry Hafez, *The Genesis of Arabic Narrative Discourse: A Study in the Sociology of Modern Arabic Literature* (London 1993).
2. Such as Maḥmūd Ṭāhir Lāshīn, Yaḥyā Ḥaqqī, Mahmūd al-Badawī, Yūsuf al-Shārūnī in Egypt; 'Abd al-Salām al-'Ujayli, Sa'īd Ḥūrāniyyah and Zakariyyā Tāmir in Syria; Samīrah 'Azzām and Ghassān Kanafāni in Palestine; and Dhū-l-Nūn Ayyūb, Fu'ād al-Takarli and 'Abd al-Malik Nūri in Iraq.
3. Such as Ṭaha Ḥusain, Sahīr al-Qalamŋwi and 'A'isha 'Abd al-Raḥmān who established their reputation as literary scholars, Najīb Maḥfūẓ and 'Abd al-Rahmān al-Sharqāwī , as major novelists, Ibrāhīm Nāji as a poet, and Nu'mān 'Āshūr, Rashād Rushdi and Sa'd al-Dīn Wahbah as dramatists, to mention but a few.
4. Arab culture has its fair share of these genres and other narrative forms, from the epics *'Antrah, al-Zīr Sālim, Sayf ibn Dhi Yazan, al-Hilāliyyah, Sirat Dhāt al-Himmah,* and *'Ali al-Zaibaq* to the elaborate and fascinating narrative *Alf Laylah wa-Laylah* or the stories of the *Qur'ān* and those of *al-Bukhalā'* and others.
5. James T. Farrel, 'The International Symposium on the Short Story', Part IV, *The Kenyon Review,* vol. 32, no. 1, 1970, p. 88.
6. N. H. Pearson, 'Literary Forms and Types', *English Institute Annual,* 1940, p. 59 quoted in René Wellek and Austin Warren, *Theory of Literature* (London 1963), p. 226.
7. Wellek and Warren, *Theory of Literature,* p. 231.
8. Christopher Prendergast, *The Triangle of Representation* (New York 2000), p. 50.
9. Stephen Greenblatt, 'Towards a Poetics of Culture', in *New Historicism,* ed. H. Aram Veseer (London 1989), quoted in Prendergast, *Triangle of Representation,* p. 56.
10. Edward Said, *The World, the Text and the Critic* (Cambridge, MA 1983), p. 39.
11. *Ibid.*
12. There are a few books on the Arabic short story, in Arabic, most of which are listed in the bibliography, and a couple in English which are either outdated, such as Abdel-Aziz Abdel-Meguid, *The Modern Arabic Short Story: Its Emergence Development and Form* (Cairo n.d.), or eccentric, such as Mohammad Shaheen, *The Modern Arabic Short Story: Shahrazad Returns* (London 1989), or limited, such as Jan Beyerl, *The Style of the Modern Arabic Short Story* (Prague 1971).
13. See e.g. Hamdi Sakkut, *The Egyptian Novel and its Main Trends from 1913–1952* (Cairo 1971); Fatma Moussa-Mahmoud, *The Arabic Novel in Egypt* (Cairo 1973); Hilary Kilpatrick, *The Modern Egyptian Novel: A Study in Social Criticism*

(London 1974); Roger Allen, *The Arabic Novel: An Historical Introduction* (Manchester 1982); Francis Raymond, *Taha Hussein Romancier* (n.d.); Ali Jad, *Form and Technique in the Egyptian Novel 1912–1971* (1983); Rasheed El-Enany, *Naguib Mahfouz: The Pursuit of Meaning* (London 1993); Samia Mehrez, *Egyptian Writers between History and Fiction* (Cairo and New York 1994); Ibrahim Taha, *The Palestinian Novel: A Communication Study* (London 2002), to mention but a few.

14. Dana Gioia and R. S. Gwynn, *The Art of the Short Story* (New York 2006), p. 3.
15. I refer here to hundreds of writers, some 700 or so, with more than 2,000 collections of short stories in the first six decades of the twentieth century. The trend continues unabated until today. See for example my brief bibliography of the collections of short stories in this period in M. M. Badawī (ed.), *Cambridge History of Arabic Literature, Modern Arabic Literature* (Cambridge 1992), pp. 514–34.
16. Norman Friedman, *Form and Meaning in Fiction,* (Athens, GA 1975), p. 169.
17. Hans Robert Jauss, *Towards an Aesthetic of Reception,* tr. Timothy Bahti, (Minneapolis, MN 1982), p. 80.
18. Such as Zakariyyā Tāmir or Fu'ād al-Takarli
19. Said, *The World, the Text and the Critic,* p. 32.
20. See Benedict Anderson, *Imagined Communities: Reflections on the Origin of Nationalism* (London 1991).
21. Thousands of short stories.
22. Michael Riffaterre, 'The Self Sufficient Text', *Diacritics,* vol. 3, no. 1, 1973, p. 40.
23. Said, *The World, the Text and the Critic,* p. 35.
24. *Ibid.*, p. 39.
25. See Stephen Greenblatt, *Shakespearean Negotiations: The Circulation of Social Energy in Renaissance England* (Oxford 1990), p. 128.

Introduction

1. To mention only a few recent studies, see Dana Gioia and R. S. Gwynn, *The Art of the Short Story* (New York 2006); Frank Mysznor, *The Modern Short Story* (Cambridge 2001); Dominic Head, *The Modernist Short Story* (Cambridge 1992); Suzan Lohafer and Jo Clarey, *Short Story Theory at a Crossroad* (Baton Rouge, LA 1989); and Ian Reid, *The Short Story* (London 1977).
2. Brander Matthews, *The Philosophy of the Short Story* (New York 1901).
3. *Ibid.*, p. 15.
4. This term comes from his famous article on the work of Hawthorne, 'Review of *Twice Told Tales*' republished in Charles E. May (ed.) *Short Story Theories* (Ohio 1976), pp. 45—51.
5. Matthews, *Philosophy of the Short Story*, p. 72.
6. Brander Matthews (ed.), *The Short Story: Specimens Illustrating its Development* (New York, American Book Co., 1907).
7. See e.g. Barry Pain, *The Short Story* (London 1917) and H. E. Bates, *The Modern Short Story* (London 1941).
8. Bates, *The Modern Short Story.*
9. Cleanth Brooks and Robert Penn Warren, *Understanding Fiction* (New York 1943).
10. Frank O'Connor, *The Lonely Voice: A Study of the Short Story* (Hoboken, NJ 2004), p. 13.
11. *Ibid.*, p. 43.

12. *Ibid.*
13. *Ibid.*
14. *Ibid.*, p. 15.
15. *Ibid.*, p. 16.
16. *Ibid.*, p. 18.
17. *Ibid.*, p. 17.
18. *Ibid.*
19. *Ibid.*, p. 20.
20. *Ibid.*
21. *Ibid.*, p. 19.
22. This was a large international symposium organised by the *Kenyon Review*, and published in four different issues: vol. 30, no. 4 (1968), pp. 443–90; vol. 31, no. 1 (1969), pp. 58–94; vol. 31, no. 4 (1969), pp. 450–502; and vol. 32, no 1 (1970), pp. 78–108.
23. James T. Farrell, *Kenyon Review*, vol. 32, no. 1 (1970), p. 88.
24. Elizabeth Harrower, *Kenyon Review*, vol. 31, no. 4, (1969) p. 479.
25. Edward Hyams, *Kenyon Review*, vol. 32 no. 1 (1970), p. 79.
26. See David Ballentyne, *Kenyon Review*, vol. 32, no. 1 (1970), p. 94.
27. See Torborg Nedreaas, *Kenyon Review*, vol. 31, no. 4 (1969), pp. 455 and 457.
28. See George Garrett, *Kenyon Review*, vol. 31, no. 4 (1969), p. 462.
29. See Elizabeth Taylor, *Kenyon Review*, vol. 31, no. 4 (1969), p. 470.
30. See James Oliver Brown, *Kenyon Review*, vol. 31, no. 1 (1969), pp. 92–4.
31. See Jack Cope, *Kenyon Review*, vol. 32, no. 1 (1970), p. 78.
32. See Erih Kos, *Kenyon Review*, vol. 30, no. 4 (1968), p. 455.
33. See Jun Eto, *Kenyon Review*, vol. 31, no. 1 (1969), p. 63.
34. See Chanakya Sen, *Kenyon Review*, vol. 31, no. 1 (1969), p. 76.
35. See Shushwant Singh, *Kenyon Review*, vol. 31, no. 4 (1969), p. 500.
36. See Ana Maria Matute, *Kenyon Review*, vol. 31, no. 4 (1969), p. 450.
37. See Luigi Barzinin, *Kenyon Review*, vol. 32, no. 1 (1970), p. 95.
38. See Mario Picchi, *Kenyon Review*, vol. 31, no. 4 (1969), p. 487.
39. See e.g. *The Genesis*, pp. 12–15 and Sabry Hafez, 'The Modern Arabic Short Story', in M. M. Badawī (ed.) *Modern Arabic Literature* (Cambridge 1992), pp. 270–328.
40. See Hans Bender, *Kenyon Review*, vol. 31, no. 1 (1969), pp. 85–6.
41. This is a famous German collection by Johann Peter Hebel that influenced many German writers, such as Kafka, Brecht and Böll, who even gave its title to one of his collections.
42. Bender, *Kenyon Review*, vol. 31, no. 1 (1969), p. 92.
43. See Ezekiel Mphahlele, *Kenyon Review*, vol. 31, no. 4 (1969), p. 474.
44. Hans Robert Jauss, *Towards an Aesthetic of Reception*, tr. Timothy Bathi, (Minneapolis 1982), pp. 76–109. A French version of this appeared in *Théorie des genres*, (Paris 1986), pp. 37–76.
45. *Ibid.*, p. 79.
46. *Ibid.*, p. 88.
47. See Benedict Anderson, *Imagined Communities: Reflections on the Origin and Spread of Nationalism* (London 1983). The new (2006) edition is used for quotation in this study.
48. *Ibid.*, p. 6.
49. *Ibid.*
50. *Ibid.*, p. 7.

51. Walter Benjamin, *Illuminations*, p. 263, quoted in Anderson, *Imagined Communities*, p. 24.
52. Anderson, *Imagined Communities*, p. 25.
53. *Ibid.*, p. 194.
54. O'Connor, *The Lonely Voice*, p. 20.
55. Matthews, *Philosophy of the Short Story*, p. 71.
56. Ernst Cassirer, *Language and Myth*, tr. Susanne Langer (New York 1947), p. 33.

Chapter One

1. The study of this process was the topic of my book *The Genesis of Arabic Narrative Discourse: A Study in the Sociology of Modern Arabic Literature* (London 1993).
2. For a detailed treatment of the 1930s crises in Egypt, see Muḥammad 'Alī Rif'at, *Mashākil Miṣr al-Iqtiṣādiyyah* (Cairo 1964), and C. Issawi, *Egypt, an Economic and Social Analysis* (Oxford 1970).
3. For an account of these attempts, see 'Abd al-Raḥmān al-Rāfi'ī, *Fī A'qāb al-Thawrah al-Miṣriyyah,* vol. 2, p. 176.
4. In this respect see Sir Samuel Hoare's reference to this point in *The Times*, 11 November 1935, and Mahmūd Y. Zayid, *Egypt's Struggle for Independence* (Beirut 1965), p. 153.
5. See 'Abd al-'Aẓīm Ramaḍān, *Taṭawwur al-Ḥaraka al-Waṭaniyyah fī Miṣr, 1937–1948* (Beirut 1973), p. 166.
6. For a detailed study of this event, see Muḥammad Anīs, *Ḥādith Arba'ah Fibrāyir* (Beirut, 1970), and 'A. Ramaḍān, *Taṭawwur al-Ḥarakah al-Waṭaniyyah fī Miṣr*, pp. 192–219.
7. For several interpretations, see 'A. al-Rāfi'ī, *Fī A'qāb al-Thawrah al-Miṣriyyah* (Cairo 1937—48), vol. 3, pp. 101, 108; 'A. Ramaḍān, *Taṭawwur al-Ḥarakah al-Waṭaniyyah fī Miṣr*, pp. 200—19, and Anīs, *Ḥādith Arba'a Fibrāyir.*
8. For a detailed account of this, see 'A. Ramaḍān, especially his study on Makram 'Ubayd's *Black Book, Taṭawwur al-Ḥarakah al-Waṭaniyyah fī Miṣr*, pp. 257—82.
9. For a detailed account of these events, see Alfred W. Sansom, *I Spied Spies*, and J. Aldridge, *Cairo: Biography of a City* (London 1969). Sansom says, 'Though it failed to develop into a full-scale revolution, this was the demonstration that forced the British to withdraw from Cairo and Alexandria', p. 239.
10. See Ṭāriq al-Bishrī, *Al-Ḥarakah al-Siyāsiyyah fī Miṣr* (Cairo 1972), pp. 5—75 and 'A. Ramaḍān, *Taṭawwur al-Ḥarakah al-Waṭaniyyah fī Miṣr*, pp. 350ff., and J. Berque, *Egypt, Imperialism and Revolution* (London 1972), pp. 559—615.
11. See al-Bishrī, *Al-Ḥarakah al-Siyāsiyyah fī Miṣr,* pp. 75–91.
12. See *Ibid.*, pp. 123—4.
13. For the inter-relationship between the political terror and the natural epidemic under Nuqrāshī, see Berque, *Egypt, Imperialism and Revolution,* the chapter entitled 'The Summons of Death', pp. 613—15.
14. He was assassinated by a member of the Muslim Brethren in the courtyard of the Ministry of Interior in December 1948.
15. Such as the various Communist groups, al-Talī'ah al-Wafdiyyah group, the student movement, and several intellectual gatherings.
16. For detailed study of the left-wing papers, see Rif'at al-Sa'īd, *al-Ṣaḥāfah al-Yasāriyyah fī Miṣr, 1925–1948* (Beirut 1974), and for the left-wing movements in general see his *al-Yasār al-Miṣrī* (Beirut 1972), and al-Bishrī, *Al-Ḥarakah al-Siyāsiyyah fī Miṣr,* pp. 154—66.

17. Such as the Muslim Brethren, Young Egypt, and the groups of Green and Blue Shirts.
18. P. J. Vatikiotis attributes most of the assassinations to the Muslim Brethren: see his *The Modern History of Egypt; From Muhammad Ali to Mubarak* (London 1985), pp. 365–68. Several leading politicians (Māhir, Amīn, 'Uthmān, Salīm Zakī, Nuqrāshī) were in fact assassinated and attempts on the lives of several others (the king and Naḥḥās) were aborted or foiled.
19. See al-Bishrī, *Al-Ḥarakah al-Siyāsiyyah fī Miṣr*, pp. 277–87.
20. *Ibid.*, p. 279.
21. *Ibid.*
22. See 'A. al-Rāfi'ī, *Fī A'qāb al-Thawrah*, vol. 3, p. 292.
23. Vatikiotis, *Modern History of Egypt*, p. 369.
24. The conflagration of 1952 is one of the most controversial events of the modern history of Egypt. For different views on this see al-Bishrī, *Al-Ḥarakah al-Siyāsiyyah fī Miṣr*, pp. 509–38, Muḥammad Anīs, *Ḥarīq al-Qāhirah* (Cairo 1972), Mahmud Hussein, *Class Conflict in Egypt* (New York 1973), pp. 82–7, Vatikiotis, *Modern History of Egypt*, p. 371, Peter Mansfield, *The British in Egypt*, p. 297, Aldridge, *Cairo*, pp. 240–2, and James P. Jankowski, *Egypt's Young Rebels* (Palo Alto, CA 1975), pp. 102–06.
25. The six months that followed the fire witnessed the formation of four unstable and short-lived governments.
26. For the details of this crisis, see Vatikiotis, *Modern History of Egypt*, pp. 383–6 and Peter Mansfield, *Nasser's Egypt* (London 1969), pp. 50–1.
27. For the details, see Vatikiotis, *Modern History of Egypt*, p. 392.
28. For example, up to 1961 about 250 compound rural units – a combination of school, health unit, agrarian unit, and social security office – were established out of the original plan, which aimed at building 865 units by that time.
29. All newspapers were nationalised and were subjected to governmental control during this process.
30. In 1963 there were 20,000, by 1964 40,000 and 70,000 by 1965. See Tom Little, *Modern Egypt* (London 1967), pp. 203–04.
31. Naturally the United States took sides with Saudi Arabia and the loyalists, and in 1964 Egyptian-American relations deteriorated and the United States cut off the aid Egypt used to receive through the PL480 food supplies and surplus wheat programme.
32. This was the period that witnessed a series of counter-revolutionary successes, i.e., the collapse of the Dominican revolution, the fall of Sukarno, Nkrumah, Mudibukita and the Left in Kenya, and the death of Nehru, etc.
33. For a detailed account of the events preceding the 1967 war and the process of luring the Egyptian regime into destruction, see Peter Mansfield, *Nasser's Egypt* (London 1969), pp. 112–13, and the memoirs of Maḥmūd al-Jayyār, Nasser's personal secretary, in *Ruz al-Y'ūsuf*, 12, 19, 26 Jan. 1976.
34. The population of Egypt only doubled during this period, rising from 14,218,000 in 1930 to 33,329,000 in 1970.
35. A number of laws played a decisive role in opening up education to the lower classes: e.g. in 1942 a free meal was provided for primary school children; in 1944 education in 'preparatory' schools was made free and in secondary education in 1950. In 1956 and 1961 university fees were reduced and finally abolished in 1962. There were a number of projects to encourage and give financial help to bright and talented students.
36. For a detailed account of this interaction, see Sabry Hafez, 'The Transformation

of Reality and the Arabic Novel's Aesthetic Response', *Bulletin of the School of Oriental and African Studies*, vol. 57, Part 1, 1994, pp. 93–112.

37. Jankowski, *Egypt's Young Rebels*, p. 3.
38. Berque, *Egypt, Imperialism and Revolution,* p. 457.
39. The 1930s was the period that witnessed the growth of fascist ideas across the world. In Egypt some sections of youth were deceived by the nationalist tones in this concept; apart from the establishment of Miṣr al-Fatah, several books on fascism and Nazism were published between 1934 and 1938. See Al-Sa'īd, *al-Yasār al-Miṣrī,* pp. 49–53.
40. These were the years of the rise and flourishing of the Muslim Brethren.
41. This was the period that witnessed the birth of many leftist cultural groups which formed the nucleus of the Communist movement. For further detail, see al-Bishrī, *Al-Ḥarakah al-Siyāsiyyah fī Miṣr,* pp. 123–4, and Al-Sa'īd, *al-Ṣaḥāfah al-Yasāriyyah fī Miṣr*, pp. 8–16.
42. For example, the number of girls at university level rose from 3,021 in 1951 to 19,063 in 1961 and then to 30,172 in 1965.
43. The general population rose between the above dates from 15,920,694 to 30,075,858.
44. See, Issawi, *Egypt in Revolution*, p. 204, and R. Mabro, *The Egyptian Economy* (Oxford 1974), p. 55.
45. See Mabro, *The Egyptian Economy*, p. 53.
46. Berque, *Egypt, Imperialism and Revolution,* p. 589.
47. 'It is hardly surprising to find that wages in Egyptian industry were among the lowest in the world, and that with the lag of money wage rates behind industrial prices, wages costs per unit of manufacturing output had fallen for over a decade. The falling share of wages in the gross value of industrial output between 1945 and 1950 also reflected declining labour costs. For the post war period at least Egyptian industry, unlike its counter-part in some developed countries, had experienced the very opposite of wage inflation.' Patrick O'Brien, *The Revolution in Egypt's Economic System* (Oxford 1966), p. 28.
48. Rif'at, *Mashākil Miṣr al-Iqtiṣādiyyah,* vol. 1, pp. 4–5.
49. Berque, *Egypt, Imperialism and Revolution,* p. 583.
50. For detailed information on this, see al-Bishrī, *Al-Ḥarakah al-Siyāsiyyah fī Miṣr,* pp. 208–11, 346–48, and Berque, *Egypt, Imperialism and Revolution,* pp. 662–3.
51. See ch. 1 of *The Genesis* for an account of an earlier interaction between journalism and fiction.
52. This idea was behind the writing of Ṭāhā Ḥusayn's outstanding book *Mustaqbal al-Thaqāfah fī Miṣr* (1938) and various other less important ones such as Maḥmūd al-Manj'ūrī's *Ittijāhāt al-'Aṣr al-Jadīd* (1937).
53. For a detailed account see Ibrāhim 'Abdū, *Taṭawwur al-Ṣiḥāfah al-Miṣriyyah: 1797–1951* (Cairo 1951), pp. 301–09.
54. See the Unesco survey on mass-media, *World Communications* (Unesco Press, 1975), pp. 53–4.
55. Although the forties witnessed the issue of the fine, and as yet unsurpassed, literary journal *al-Kātib al-Miṣrī,* the fifties and the sixties saw the appearance of some important, if not influential, cultural reviews, such as *al-Shahr, al-Majallah, al-Kātib,* and *al-Ṭalī'ah,* not to mention the short lived *al-Masraḥ, al-Fikr al-Mu'āṣir, al-Shi'r,* and *al-Qiṣṣah.*
56. Besides the fact that both declined to publish fictional works for many years,

al-Muqtaṭaf was critical of fiction and novels in general on the grounds that they spread immorality among the youth.

57. Even during the war when the acute paper shortage compelled the magazine to appear once every two months instead of monthly, *al-Hilāl* continued to do this. See January/February 1944, November 1945 and August 1948.
58. The magazines that developed a keen interest in fictional matters are many. To mention only a few: *al-Qaṣaṣ*, monthly 1930, Alexandria; *al-Jāmi'ah*, weekly, 1932, *Majallat al-'Ishrīn Qiṣṣah*, bi-weekly, 1932, *al-Risālah*, weekly, 1929, *al-Fuṣ'l*, bi-weekly, 1931, *al-Ma'rifah*, monthly, 1931, *Majallatī*, bi-weekly, 1934, *al-Kātib*, bi-weekly, 1937, *al-Thaqāfah*, weekly, 1939, and *al-Qiṣṣah*, bi-weekly, 1949.
59. Such as *al-Qaṣaṣ*, *al-Qiṣṣah*, *al-Riwāyah*, *Majallat al-'Ishrīn Qiṣṣa*, *Qiṣṣatī*, *Aḥsan al-Qiṣaṣ*, and *Qiṣaṣh al-Usb'ū'*.
60. For example, *Majallatī* started in 1934 without publishing any short stories. In February 1935 it began publishing one short story per issue, and by mid-1935 raised this to five or six.
61. *Al-Hilāl* began these as early as 1934 (see *al-Hilāl*, August 1934), then *Majallatī* and *al-Riwāyah* followed suit. One of the strange conditions in *Majallatī*'s competition was that the short story should be written in the first person; see *Majallatī*, the four issues of January and February 1936.
62. There were 473 entries for *al-Riwāyah*'s competition; *al-Riwāyah*, 15 August 1937.
63. The first prize in *Majallatī*'s competition was LE 50 and the prizes of *al-Hilāl* of 1945 were LE 50, LE 20, and three of LE 10.
64. That was the case when Maḥmūd Kāmil, short story writer and editor of the weekly *al-Jāmi'a* issued its bi-weekly sister issue *Majallat al-'Ishrīn Qiṣṣa* (1937–9) and also when Aḥmad Ḥasan al-Zayyāt, the editor of the weekly *al-Risāla*, issued its bi-weekly sister issue *al-Riwāyah* (1937–40).
65. *Al-Riwāyah* published 136 short stories in its first year, and *Majallat al-'Ishrīn Qiṣṣa* used to publish twenty short stories every fortnight, as its title indicates.
66. Apart from the periodicals mentioned above, nn. 64 and 65, there were also *al-Ghad* (1953), *al-Hadaf* (1954), *al-Risālah al Jadīdah* (1952), and *al-Adab* (1951).
67. To mention only a few, the Lebanese magazines that published Egyptian writing were: *al-Adīb*, *al-Adab*, *Adab*, *Hiwār*, *Shi'r*, and *Mawāqif*. There were also the Syrian *al-Ḥadīth*, *al-Nāqid* and *al-Ma'rifa*.
68. For further detail on left-wing journalism and its cultural role, see Al-Sa'īd, *al-Ṣaḥāfah al-Yasāriyyah fī Miṣr*, pp. 79–148, and apart from *al-Taṭawwur* and *al-Fajr al-Jadīd*, which he dealt with, there were also *al-Bashīr*, *al-Ghad* and *Kitābāt Miṣriyyah*.
69. Y. Ḥaqqī, *'Anṭar wa-Juliet*, p. 3.
70. For a detailed study, see Sha'bān 'Abd al-'Azīz Khalīfah, *Ḥarakat Nashr al-Kutub fī Miṣr: Dirāsah Taṭbīqiyyah* (Cairo 1974), p. 34.
71. *Ibid.*, p. 53.
72. *Ibid.*, p. 562.
73. This was the number of copies of the first edition of Maḥmūd Taymūr's introduction to the second edition of his collection of short stories *Mā Tarah al-'Uy'ūn* (al-Maṭba'ah al-Salafiyyah, 1927), p. 3.
74. See Khalīfah, *Ḥarakat Nashr al-Kutub fī Miṣr*, p. 47.
75. For further details see Laṭīf al-Zayyāt's unpublished Ph.D. thesis on this subject.
76. *Ibid.*, pp. 17—22.

77. Some of the editors of these magazines were themselves translators, e.g. Aḥmad al-Ṣawī Muḥammad of *Majallatī* and Aḥmad Ḥasan al-Zayyāt of *al-Risālah.*
78. The most famous example in this respect is that of Muḥammad Luṭfī Jum'ah, who published many fakes in the late thirties and early forties. He attributed some of them to real European authors, although for the majority he made up names. See e.g. his works in *al-Riwāyah* throughout 1938, No. 26, pp. 83–92, No. 27, pp. 137–50, No. 29, pp. 242–52, No. 30, pp. 312–15, No. 31, pp. 384–91, No. 32, pp. 430–6, No. 33, pp. 477–88, No. 34, pp. 530–40, No. 37, pp. 682–91, No. 38, pp. 738–48, No. 39, pp. 794–9, No. 40, pp. 859–69, No. 42, pp. 967–77. In a mocking and self-critical article (some years later) he admitted that he had faked all these works and waited in the expectation that someone would expose him, but to no avail.
79. See, e.g. *al-Hilāl,* July and Dec. 1936; Jan., Feb., June and July 1937; and *al-Majallah al-Jadīdah,* Jan., Feb., Mar. and Apr., 1934; and throughout 1935, 1936 and 1937.
80. See e.g. the cover of the November 1936 issue.
81. A few early examples include *Qiṣaṣ Ijtimā'iyyah,* translated by Muḥammad 'Abd Allāh 'Anān, 1932; *al-Adab al-Ḥadīth,* translated by Ibrāhīm al-Miṣrī, 1932; *Mukhtārāt min al-Qiṣaṣ al-Ingilīzī,* translated by Ibrāhīm 'Abd al-Qādir al-Māzinī, 1939; *al-Mar'ah al-Shā'irah,* translated by Naẓmi Khalīl, 1938; and *al-Bāb al-Dhahabī,* translated by Muḥammad Amīn Ḥass'ūnah, 1944.
82. Many of the Egyptian short story writers started their literary careers as translators, e.g. Najīb Maḥfūẓ's first published book *Miṣr al-Qadīmah* (1932) was a translation. He also admitted (see *al-Kātib,* Dec. 1962, and *al-Majallah,* Jan. 1963), that he started his career as a novelist by rewriting translated fiction. Maḥmūd al-Badawī started by translating short stories (see *al-Riwāyah,* June 1937 and *al-Risālah,* 11 Dec. 1935, 18 Dec. 1933, 19 Aug. 1936, and 12 Oct. 1936). Shukrī 'Ayyād translated Dostoevsky's novel *The Gambler* (1946) and many other short stories (see *al-Riwāyah,* 1 July 1937, 15 Aug. 1937, 1 Oct. 1937, 16 Oct. 1937, 1 Dec. 1937, 15 Jan. 1938, etc.). Idwār al-Kharrāṭ published several collections of translated short stories, e.g. *Qiṣaṣ R'māniyyah* (1959), *Qiṣaṣ 'Ālamiyyah* (1961), and *Qiṣaṣ Īṭāliyah* (1962). 'Abd al-Ghaffār Makkāwī published several translated short stories and Ghālib Halasā and Bahā Ṭāhir translated many short stories too.
83. *Al-Siyāsah al-Usbu'iyyah,* 28 June 1930.
84. *Ibid.*
85. *Al Siyāsah al-Usb'u'iyyah* on 12, 19, 26 July and 2, 9, 16, 23 Aug.1930.
86. Behind these two terms lies a long debate about the role and identity of Egypt. Was Egypt's role an isolated one, which had very little to do with the Islamic Orient in general, and in particular with what is known now as the Arab World; or was Egypt an integral part of this group of nations within or outside the framework of the Ottoman Empire?
87. See Muḥammad Zakī 'Abd al-Qādir's article in *al-Siyāsah al-Usb'u'iyyah,* 21 July 1930.
88. For a detailed account of this from the opposite viewpoint, see Muḥammad Muḥammad, Ḥusain, *al-Ittijāhāt al-Waṭaniyyah fi'l-Adab al-Mu'āṣir* (Cairo 1956), pp. 135–162.
89. This was the first round of the battle in the period under discussion. However, the question had been raised earlier with *Fi'l-Shi'r al-Jāhilī* in 1926 and even earlier with Nadīm's fictional episodes.

90. See Yaḥyā Ḥaqqī, *al-Majallah al-Jadīdah,* Aug.1931.
91. This period witnessed the rise and fall of many excellent critics, some of whom were before their time, e.g. Mu'āwiya Muḥammad N'ūr, *al-Siyāsah al-Usb'u'iyyah,* 3 Jan. and 22 Mar. 1930, *al-Hilāl,* Aug. 1931, and *Jarīdat Miṣr,* 15 Jan. 1932. Fakhrī Abu'l-Su'ūd, wrote regular articles in *al-Risālah* during the thirties and especially in 1935–7; Aḥmad Rāsim wrote articles in *Majallatī,* 1935; Maḥmūd al-Sharqāwī's studies were printed in *al-Majallah al-Jadīdah,* 1934, and *al-Risālah,* 1933–5 and Naẓmī Khālil's studies on romanticism.
92. For example, Miryat Ghālī's *Siyāsat al-Ghad* (1938), Muṣṭafā Maḥmūd Fahmī's *al-Ḥālah al-Ijtimā'iyyah fī Miṣr* (1940), Isḥāq M. al-Ḥusaynī's *'Awdat al-Safīnah* (1944), I. Bayy'ūmī Madkur and Miryat Ghālī's *al-Adāt al-Ḥuk'ūmiyyah* (1945), M. 'Abd al-Raḥīm 'Anbar's *Iṣlāḥ Adāt al-Ḥukm* (1945), M. Ghālī's *al-Iṣlāḥ al-Zirā'ī* (1945), Maḥmūd Kamīl's *al-'Amal li-Miṣr* (1945), Rāshid al-Barrāwī's *Naḥwa 'Alam Jadīd* (1945), Aḥmad Ṣadīq Sa'd's *Mushkilāt al-Fallāḥ* (1946), Ismā'īl Mazhar's *'Aṣr al-Ishtirākiyyah* (1947), R. al-Barrāwī's *al-Taṭawwur al-Iqtiṣādī fī Miṣr* (1948), and Aḥmad Ḥusayn's *al-Ishtirākiyyah allati Nad'ū Ilayhā* (1950).
93. In his books *Ḥāfiẓ wa Shawqī* (1933), *Ma'a Abi'l-'Ālā'* (1935), *Ma'a al-Mutanabī* (1936), *Min Ḥadīth al-Shi'r wa'l-Nathr* (1936), *Laḥaẓāt* (1942), etc.
94. In his books *Shu'arā Miṣr wa Bi'ātuhum al-Ijtimā'iyyah* (1937), *Sā'āt Bayn al-Kutub* (1937) and his numerous articles in periodicals.
95. Al-Māzinī's contribution can be found particularly in the periodicals of the period, especially *al-Hilāl.*
96. Nūr was a bright Sudanese critic who lived and worked in Cairo until his death at the age of thirty-two in 1941. His articles appeared in Cairo magazines and were recently collected in one volume *Dirāsāt fi'l-Adab wa'l-Naqd* (al-Kharṭūm 1970).
97. A knowledgeable critic who used to be a regular contributor to *al-Risālah* in the 1930s.
98. In his books *Abū Shādī al-Shā'ir* (1937) and *Tawfīq al-Ḥakīm* (1938), and his numerous articles in *al-Ḥadīth, al-Risālah, al-Muqtaṭaf, Adabī,* etc. For a full bibliography of his work, see G. H. A. Juynboll, 'Ismā'īl Aḥmad Adham (1911–1940) the Atheist', *Journal of Arabic Literature,* vol. 3, 1973, pp. 54–57.
99. In his books *Fi'l-Mīzān al-Jadīd* (1944), *al-Naqd al-Manhjī 'Ind al-'Arab* (1948), and *Fi'l-Adab wa'l-Naqd* (1949).
100. In his books *Kutub wa-Shakhṣiyyāt* (1946) and *al-Naqd al-Adabī* (1947).
101. In his studies on *al-Adab al-Ingilīzī* (1947) and his introduction to his translation of Shelley's *Prometheus Unbound* (1948), etc.
102. He was the influential critic of *al-Risālah* in the forties. See *al-Risālah* and his books *Namādhij Faniyyah fi'l-Adab wa'l-Naqd* (1951) and *Kalimāt fi'l-Adab* (1965).
103. M. M. Badawī, 'Commitment in Contemporary Arabic Literature', in *Cahiers d'histoire mondiale,* Unesco, vol. 14, no. 4, 1972, p. 866.
104. For the remaining few who questioned the validity of these new forms, see M. M. Ḥusain, *Al-Ittijāhāt al-Waṭaniyyah fi al-Adab al-Mu'āṣir* (Cairo 1956), pp. 329–34.
105. Amīn al-Kh'ūlī was the first to attack the concept of *l'art pour l'art; al-Adab li'l-Ḥayāh* was the slogan of his literary society al-Umanā', and the emblem of its literary journal, *al-Adab.*
106. See Chapter Four below.
107. For a detailed study of this poetic movement, see M. M. Badawī, *A Critical*

Introduction to Modern Arabic Poetry (Cambridge 1975), pp. 204—60, Nāzik al-Malā'ika, *Qaḍāyā al-Shi'r al-Mu'āṣir*, and Muḥammad al-Nuwayhī, *Qaḍiyyat al-Shi'r al-Jadīd.*

108. See Badawī, *Critical Introduction*, p. 873.
109. For an account of this suffering see the young writers' testimonies in the special issue of *'Hakadhā Yatakallam al-Udabā al-Shubbān'* of *al-Ṭalī'a,* Cairo, September 1969.
110. See Muḥammad Ḥāfiẓ Rajab's cry, *'Naḥ Jīl Bilā Asātidhah'*, in *al-Jumhuriyyah* newspaper 1962.
111. One of the obvious results of these critical discussions was the initiation of the series *Kitābāt Jadīda,* to publish the works of the younger generation of writers, by the Ministry of Culture.
112. This magazine is *Gallery 68.*
113. A novel by Najīb Maḥfūẓ.
114. A novel by Sun' Allāh Ibrāhīm.
115. A play by 'Abd al-Raḥmān al-Sharqāwī.

Chapter Two

1. For a detailed discussion of this question, see Q. D. Leavis, *Fiction and the Reading Public* (Oxford 1965), pp. 20—2, and the chapters entitled 'Author and Reader', pp. 33—80, and 'The Disintegration of the Reading Public', pp. 151—202.
2. Any glance through the dates of the publications and the reprints of the works of Lāshīn, Ḥaqqī, and al-Badawī, in comparison with those of the works of Maḥmūd Kāmil, Amīn Ghurāb, 'Abd al-Qudd'ūs could verify this argument; e.g. while many of Maḥmūd Kāmil's collections were reprinted twice in one year, it took Ḥaqqī thirty years to reprint his first collection.
3. Erich Auerbach, *Mimesis: The Representation of Reality in Western Literature* (Princeton 1953), p. 500.
4. Michel Zeraffa, *Fictions: The Novel and Social Reality* (London 1976), p. 138.
5. *Ibid.*, p. 139.
6. *Ibid.*
7. G. S. Fraser, *The Modern Writer and His World* (London 1972), p. 30.
8. Damian Grant, *Realism* (London 1970), p. 1.
9. Auerbach, *Mimesis*, p. 555.
10. Mario Praz, *The Romantic Agony* (London 1933), p. 21.
11. Mario Praz, *The Hero in Eclipse* (Oxford 1956), p. 38.
12. René Wellek, *Concepts of Criticism* (New Haven, CT 1963), p. 254.
13. *Ibid.*, p. 224.
14. *Correspondence,* II, 345, the quotation is taken from Grant, *Realism,* p. 17. 'what seems beautiful to me, what i would like, is a book about nothing, a book holding nothing, but the strength of it's own style, as the earth stays in the air without support ... if that was possible'
15. Wellek, *Concepts of Criticism*, p. 224.
16. This study will deal in detail with the conceptual approaches to reality in the Egyptian short story in the following chapter.
17. Raymond Williams, *The Long Revolution* (London 1965), pp. 300–01.
18. F. W. J. Hemmings, *The Age of Realism* (London 1974), p. 13.
19. The final chapter of this study deals with the experimental short story.
20. Hemmings, *The Age of Realism*, p. 36.

21. James M. Ritchie, *Periods in German Literature: A Symposium* (London 1976), 177.
22. René Wellek and Austin Warren, *Theory of Literature* (London 1963), p. 102.
23. See Frank Kermode, *The Sense of an Ending: Studies in the Theory of Fiction* (Oxford 1973), p. 144.
24. Lionel Trilling, *The Liberal Imagination: Essays on Literature and Society* (London 1964), p. 45.
25. Joseph Chiari, *Aesthetics of Modernism* (London 1970), p. 167.
26. Adolfo Sanchez Vazquez, *Art and Society: Essays in Marxist Aesthetics* (London 1973), p. 43.
27. Miriam Allot, *Novelists on the Novel* (London 1959), p. 69.
28. Vazquez, *Art and Society*, p. 39.
29. Chiari, *Aesthetics of Modernism*, p. 170.
30. *Ibid.*, p. 169.
31. Georg Lukács, *Studies in European Realism* (London 1972), p. 145.
32. Edwin H. Cady, *The Light of Common Day: Realism in American Fiction* (Bloomington 1971) p. 16, and for an elaborate definition of realism as a theory of common vision, see pp. 18—22.
33. *Ibid.*, p. 21.
34. Chiari, *Aesthetics of Modernism*, p. 64.
35. Published in Wellek, *Concepts of Criticism*, pp. 222—55.
36. *Ibid.*, p. 240.
37. Kenneth Burke, *The Philosophy of Literary Form* (Berkeley, CA 1973), p. 26.
38. Rene Wellek, *Concepts of Criticism*, p. 241.
39. Lukács, *Studies in European Realism*, p. 148.
40. Allot, *Novelists on the Novel*, p. 68.
41. Vazquez, *Art and Society*, pp. 31—2.
42. Kenneth Graham, *English Criticism of the Novel: 1865—1900* (Oxford 1965), p. 19.
43. *Ibid.*, p. 37.
44. Grant, *Realism*, p. 11.
45. Ernst Cassirer, *The Philosophy of Symbolic Forms* (New Haven CT 195), vol. 1, p.139.
46. Kermode, *The Sense of an Ending*, p. 140.
47. Cassirer, *Symbolic Forms*, p. 94.
48. Graham, *English Criticism of the Novel*, pp. 37–8.
49. Terry Eagleton, *Criticism and Ideology: A Study in Marxist Literary Theory* (London 1976), p. 59.
50. Christopher Caudwell, *Illusion and Reality*, 321.
51. Terry Eagleton, *Marxism and Literary Criticism* (London 1976), p. 69.
52. Wellek, *Concepts of Criticism*, p. 253.
53. *Ibid.*, p. 236, in his comment on Auerbach's *Mimesis*.
54. *Ibid.*, p. 253.
55. For details, see C. C. Walcutt, *Man's Changing Mask: Modes and Methods of Characterisation in Fiction* (Minneapolis 1966), pp. 5–19.
56. *Ibid.*, p.13.
57. Cady, *The Light of Common Day*, p. 8.
58. *Ibid.*
59. And also in the short story.
60. Cady, *The Light of Common Day*.

61. In fact, there are full-length books devoted to the work of some of these writers, in both Arabic and English.
62. For a study of the early works of Taymūr see chapter 5 of *The Genesis,* pp. 199–214.
63. The stories in his collection *Zāmir al-Ḥayy* are, but for one, rewritings of previous stories with some minor alterations and often with a change of title. His collection *Shabāb wa Ghāniyāt* contains rewritings of seven stories which appeared previously in earlier collections. The collection *Tamr Ḥinnah 'Ajab* contains rewritings of four earlier stories.
64. See his detailed discussion of this subject in his book *Bayn al-Maṭraqah wa'l-Sindān,* pp. 130–132.
65. *Al-Shaykh Jum'ah,* p. 12.
66. See his books *Dirāsāt fi'l Qiṣṣah wa'l-Masraḥ, Bayn al-Maṭraqa wa'l-Sindān,* and his introduction to his collection *Maktūb 'Alā al-Jabīn.*
67. See *Maktūb 'Alā al-Jabīn,* p. 11.
68. See *Dirāsāt fi'l-Qiṣṣah wa'l-Masraḥ,* p. 95.
69. See *Maktūb 'Alā al-Jabīn*, p.8.
70. See *Dirāsāt fi'l-Qiṣṣah wa'l-Masraḥ,* p. 146.
71. See *Ibid.*, pp. 152, 189.
72. *Maktūb 'Alā al-Jabīn,* pp. 69–84.
73. *Iḥsān li-llāh,* pp. 5–81.
74. *Ibid.*, pp. 103–09.
75. *Al-Bārūnah Umm Aḥmad,* pp. 113–18.
76. *Ḥikāyat Abū 'ūf,* pp. 7–21.
77. *Iḥsān li-llāh,* pp. 145–64.
78. *Kul 'Ām wa Antum bi-Khayr,* pp. 205–26.
79. *Ibid.*, pp. 191–203.
80. *Al-Bārūnah Umm Aḥmad,* pp. 7, 16.
81. *Tamr Ḥinnah 'Ajab,* pp. 97–125.
82. *Maktūb 'Alā al-Jabīn,* pp. 125–36.
83. *Iḥsān li-llāh,* pp. 201–13.
84. *Shabāb wa Ghāniyāt,* pp. 195–206. It is a rewriting of 'Mahzalat al-Mawt' in the earlier collection *'Amm Mitwallī,* pp. 84–116.
85. *Zāmir al-Ḥayy,* pp. 55–73. It is a rewriting of 'Ṣabiḥah' in the earlier collection *Abū 'Alī 'Āmil Artist,* pp. 30–43.
86. See 'al-'Ijl Waqa' in *Tamr Ḥinnah 'Ajab,* pp. 139–53, 'Ḥasan Aghā' in *al-Aṭlāl,* 149–156, and 'Man Minnā al-Waghd' in *Tamr Ḥinnah 'Ajab,* pp. 49–96.
87. *Al-Shaykh 'Afallah,* pp. 101–13.
88. *Khalf al-Lithām,* pp. 25–52.
89. *Al-Shaykh 'Afallah,* pp. 4–18.
90. *Ḥikāyat Abū 'ūf*, pp. 53–71.
91. *Al-Shaykh 'Afallah,* pp. 72–87.
92. *Anā al-Qātil,* pp. 5–19.
93. *Tamr Ḥinnah 'Ajab,* pp. 3–36.
94. *Ibid.*, pp. 37–48.
95. *Iḥsān li-llāh,* pp. 189–99.
96. *Al-Bārūnah Umm Aḥmad,* pp. 78–86.
97. See Muḥammad Taym'r's story 'Ṣuffarat al-'Īd' which was discussed in *The Genesis.*
98. *Tamr Ḥinnah 'Ajab,* pp. 163–78.
99. *Iḥsān li-llāh,* pp. 5–81.

100. *Shabāb wa Ghāniyāt*, pp. 5—145, which is in fact a rewriting of the title story in *al-Aṭlāl*, pp. 1—91.
101. *Tamr Ḥinnah 'Ajab*, pp. 49—96.
102. *Al-Shaykh 'Afallah,* pp. 123—34.
103. *Qalb Ghāniyah,* pp. 137—57.
104. *Kul 'Ām wa-Antum bi-Khayr,* pp. 5—28.
105. *Iḥsān li-llāh,* pp. 175—88.
106. *Khalf al-Lithām,* pp. 53—72.
107. *Ibid.*, p. 26.
108. *Ibid.*, p. 27.
109. *Kul 'Ām wa-Antum bi-Khayr,* pp. 55—102.
110. Those are 'Ta'mīn 'Alā al-Ḥayāh', pp. 25—52, "Indamā Tubṣir al-Qulūb', pp. 73—84, "Indamā Naḥyā Ma'a al-Aṭyāf', pp. 107—16, and 'Kayfa Ṭārat Minnī Oxford', pp. 17—130.
111. E.g. in *al-Aṭlāl* see 'al-Ṭifl wa'l-Muṣawwir', pp. 101—16, and 'Jarīmat Ḥubb', pp. 129—39, and in *Maktūb 'Alā al-Jabīn* see 'Dhāt Masā", pp. 195—211, and 'Ṣuḥbat al-Ward', pp. 213—26.
112. *Khalf al-Lithām,* pp. 93—106.
113. *Bint al-Shayṭān,* pp. 11—54.
114. *Tamr Ḥinnah 'Ajab,* pp. 155—62.
115. *Bint al-Shayṭān,* pp. 11—54.
116. *Al-Aṭlāl,* pp. 117—28 and also see its rewritten form entitled 'Fātāt al-Qiṭār' in *Zāmir al-Ḥayy,* pp. 74—97.
117. *Kul 'Ām wa-Antum bi-Khayr,* pp. 149—67.
118. *Zāmir al-Ḥayy,* pp. 32—54.
119. *Ihsān li-llāh,* pp. 103—19.
120. *Tamr Ḥinnah 'Ajab*, pp. 3–36.
121. *Al-Bārūnah Umm Aḥmad,* pp. 37—57.
122. Nazīh al-Ḥakīm, *Maḥmūd Tahmūr Rā'id al-Qiṣṣah al-'Arabiyyah,* p. 57.
123. *Qalb Ghāniyah,* pp. 137—57.
124. *Al-Aṭlāl,* pp. 129—39.
125. *Al-Bārūnah Umm Aḥmad,* pp. 69—77.
126. *Iḥsān li-llāh,* pp. 121—43.
127. *Kul 'Ām wa-Antum bi-Khayr,* pp. 103—17.
128. *Al-Shaykh 'Afllah,* pp. 123—34 and was rewritten under the title 'Nidā' al-Rūḥ' in *Tamr Ḥinnah 'Ajab,* pp. 235—48.
129. *Kul 'Ām wa-Antum bi-Khayr,* pp. 29—54.
130. *Qalb Ghāniyah,* pp. 71—91.
131. *Kul 'Ām wa-Antum bi-Khayr,* pp. 55—102.
132. *Al-Shaykh 'Afallah,* pp. 115—22.
133. *Maktūb 'Alā al-Jabīn,* pp. 187—94.
134. *Kul 'Ām wa-Antum bi-Khayr,* pp. 55—102.
135. *Al-Bārūnah Umm Aḥmad,* pp. 96—103.
136. *Maktūb 'Alā al-Jabīn,* pp. 159—76.
137. *Bint al-Shayṭān,* pp. 83—100.
138. *Kul 'Ām wa-Antum bi-Khayr,* pp. 169—89.
139. *Zāmir al-Ḥayy,* pp. 55—73.
140. *Shabāb wa-Ghāniyāt,* pp. 163—79.
141. *Anā al-Qātil,* pp. 23—44.
142. *Ibid.*, pp. 25—6.
143. *Al-Aṭlāl,* pp. 101—16.

144. *Zāmir al-Ḥayy,* pp. 98—113; the story is a rewriting of 'al-Yatīmah' in *al-Shaykh 'Afallah.* 19–32.
145. *Qalb Ghāniyah,* pp. 159—78.
146. *Tamr Ḥinnah 'Ajab,* pp. 219—33; the story is a rewriting of 'al-Tawba' in *al-Shaykh 'Afallah,* pp. 90—100.
147. *Maktūb 'Alā al-Jabīn,* pp. 213—26.
148. *Ibid.*, pp. 195—211.
149. *Al-Shaykh 'Afallah,* pp. 135—45.
150. *Maktūb 'Alā al-Jabīn,* pp. 177—86.
151. *Kul 'Ām wa-Antum bi-Khayr,* pp. 55—102.
152. *Al-Bārūnah Umm Aḥmad,* pp. 17—36.
153. *Ḥikāyat Abū 'ūf,* 3 pp. 5—51.
154. *Al-Aṭlāl,* pp. 93—9.
155. *Al-Shaykh 'Afallah,* pp. 72—87.
156. *Qalb Ghāniyah,* pp. 179—93.
157. *Bint al-Shayṭān,* pp. 111—15.
158. The story of a poor lonely *kibitka* driver who is sad and overwhelmed by the death of his son, and whose futile attempt to tell the story of his son's death to the passengers, who lend deaf ears and are only interested in reaching their destination quickly on this cold winter night, succeeds only in intensifying his grief. At the end of the night he collapses from grief, loneliness and exhaustion, and speaks to his horse about the tragic death of his son.
159. *Bint al-Shayṭān,* pp. 55—70.
160. *Ḥikāyat Abū 'ūf,* pp. 75—88.
161. *Al-Bārūnah Umm Aḥmad,* pp. 113—18.
162. *Anā al-Qātil,* pp. 177—89.
163. A glance through the critical articles published in the 1930s and 1940s in the leading literary reviews gives a rough idea of the scope and limits of this call.
164. *Iḥsān li-llāh,* pp. 165—74.
165. *Bint al-Shayṭān,* pp. 83—100.
166. *Khalf al-Lithām,* pp. 107—16.
167. *Al-Bārūnah Umm Aḥmad,* pp. 37—57.
168. *Zāmir al-Ḥayy,* pp. 32—54.
169. *Bint al-Shayṭān,* pp. 71—82.
170. *Ibid.*, pp. 120—50.
171. *Iḥsān li-llāh,* pp. 215—17.
172. *Al-Aṭlāl,* pp. 141, 148.
173. There are many of these stories in his work; in one collection, *Kul 'Ām wa-Antum bi-Khayr,* there are 'Hadhih al-Ḥaṣāh', 'Waraqat al-Naṣīb', and al-Ḥukm li-llah'.
174. In his collections, *Ahl al-Fann* (1934), *Qiṣaṣ Tawfīq al-Ḥakīm*, 3 vols (1949), and *Arinī al-Lah* (1953).
175. In many stories in his collections, *Usṭūrat Ḥubb* (1962), *Shāfi' wa-Nāfi'* (1965), and *al-Sāriq wa'l-Masrūq* (1967).
176. In his collection *al-Jum'ah al-Yatīmah* (1936), *Fatinat al-Shayṭān* (1940), *Hayākil fi'l-Rīf* (1953), and *'Alā Jisr al-Tur'ah* (1963).
177. In many stories of his collections *Kharīf Imra'ah* (1944), *Qulūb al-Nas* (1947), *Ka's al-Ḥayāh* (1947), and *Nuf's 'Āriyah* (1951).
178. Ḥaqqī commenced his literary career in *al-Fajr*, the organ of al-Madrasah al-Ḥadīthah, by publishing six of his short stories in 1926. When *al-Fajr* ceased publication at the beginning of 1927, Ḥaqqī published eight short stories in

al-Siyāsah al-Yawmiyyah that year. A list of these stories can be found in *Sab'ūn Sham'a fī Ḥayāt Yaḥyā Ḥaqqī,* pp. 262—3, except two of the *al-Fajr* stories. Those are 'Munīra' serialised from 22 July 1926 to 9 Sep. 1926 and 'al-Duktūr Shākir Afandī' serialised in *al-Fajr* from 25 Nov. 1926 to 13 Jan. 1927. Another list of these stories can be found in Muṣṭafā Ibrāhīm Ḥusayn's *Yaḥyā Ḥaqqī Mubdi'ā wa-Naqidā* (1970).

179. By publishing his important short story 'Ka'an' in *al-Masā* in the issues of 8 Jan. 1968, 15 Jan., 22 Jan., 29 Jan. and 5 Feb. 1968.
180. See e.g. the first essays in his book *Khuṭuwāt fi'l-Naqd* (1960).
181. *Al-Fajr,* 16 Sep. 1926.
182. *Al-Fajr,* 28 Oct. 1926.
183. *Al-Siyāsah al-Yawmiyyah,* 14 Jan. 1927.
184. *Al-Fajr,* 25 Nov. 1926 to 13 Jan. 1927.
185. *Al-Siyāsah al-Yawmiyyah,* 18 Feb. 1927.
186. *Ibid.,* 9 Sep. 1927.
187. *Al-Fajr,* 22 July 1926 to 9 Sep. 1926.
188. *Al-Siyāsah al-Yawmiyyah,* 26 Apr. 1927 and 29 Apr. 1927.
189. *Ibid.*, 10 Dec. 1926.
190. *Ibid.*, 22 Dec. 1926.
191. *Al-Fajr,* 15 July 1926.
192. However, many of these stories were later includeed in some volumes of his complete works.
193. In various leading periodicals of that time, e.g. *al-Siyāsah, al-Balāgh, Kawkab al-Sharq, al-Majallah al-Jadīdah,* and *al-Riwāyāt al-Muṣawwarah.*
194. This was his last collection, *al-Niqāb al-Ṭā'ir,* which contains four stories only.
195. *'Anṭar wa-Juliet,* p. 4.
196. See an interview with Ḥaqqī entitled 'Ta'amulātī fi'l-Ṭarīq sirr Quwwati' in *al-Jumhuriyyah,* a Cairene daily, on 20 Feb. 1960.
197. *Dimā' wa-Tīn,* pp. 83—104.
198. *Ibid.*, pp. 85—6.
199. *Ibid.*, p. 98.
200. *Umm al-'Awājiz,* pp. 54—9.
201. *'Anṭar wa-Juliet,* pp. 102—18.
202. *Dimā' wa-Tīn,* pp. 13—82.
203. *Ibid.*, pp. 46—47
204. *Ibid.*, p. 98.
205. See *Khuṭiwāt fi'l-Naqd,* pp. 196—208.
206. See Ḥaqqī's interview with Aḥmad 'Abbās Ṣāliḥ in *al-Jumhūriyyah* on 7 Apr. 1962.
207. *Ibid.*, pp. 17—26.
208. *Ibid.*, pp. 27—48.
209. *Ibid.*, p. 29.
210. *Ibid.*
211. *Ibid.*, pp. 49—62.
212. *Ibid.*, pp. 63—70.
213. An indication that the change concerns the head.
214. *Dimā' wa-Ṭīn*, p. 59.
215. *Ibid.*, pp. 71—82.
216. *Ibid.*, pp. 83—104 and *al-Majallah al-Jadīdah,* May 1931.
217. *Dimā' wa-Ṭīn*, pp. 105—42.

218. *Umm al-'Awājiz*, pp. 135–47.
219. For detailed discussion of those two forms, see Kenneth Burke, *Counter-Statement* (Berkeley, CA 1968), pp. 124–5.
220. M. H. Abrams, *A Glossary of Literary Terms* (New York 1971), pp. 81–2.
221. *Qindīl Umm Hāshim*, pp. 5–58.
222. 'Al-Būsṭajī' appeared first in *al-Majallah al-Jadīdah*, 8 May 1935.
223. In his autobiography, which appeared with the second edition of *Qindīl Umm Hāshim* (1975), Ḥaqqī says that the story was written in 1939–40, see pp. 43 and 59.
224. This was the heyday of this question; Ṭāhā Ḥusayn wrote his important book *Mustaqbal al-Thaqāfah fī Miṣr* (1938) at that time.
225. A. Yarmolinsky, *Letters of Anton Chekov* (New York 1973), p. 71.
226. For various critical assessments and interpretations of this story, see for example: Sayyid Quṭb, *Kutub wa-Shakhṣiyyāt*, pp. 190–201, 'Alī al-Rā'ī, *Dirāsāt fi'l-Riwāyah al-Miṣriyyah*, pp. 157–78, and M. M. Badawī 'The Lamp of Umm Hāshim, the Egyptian Intellectual between East and West', *Journal of Arabic Literature*, vol. I, pp. 145–61.
227. *Qindīl Umm Ḥāshim*, pp. 7–9.
228. *Ibid.*, p. 13.
229. *Ibid.*, p. 19–20.
230. Note the clear religious implications of her name.
231. *Qindīl Umm Hāshim*, p. 21.
232. Badawī, 'The Lamp of Umm Hāshim', p. 149.
233. Note the mythical terms in his description of Egypt throughout scene seven, *Qindīl Umm Hāshim*, p. 34.
234. For detailed discussion of the mythical elements in certain types of thinking, see Ernst Cassirer, *Language and Myth* (New York 1946), pp. 1–23.
235. Susanne K. Langer, in the translator's preface to Cassirer, *Language and Myth*, pp. ix-x.
236. *'Anṭar wa-Juliet*, pp. 35–47.
237. *Ibid.*, pp. 23–34.
238. *Qindīl Umm Hāshim*, 5 pp. 9–73.
239. *Ibid.*, pp. 74–86.
240. *Umm al-'Awājiz*, pp. 45–74.
241. *Ibid.*, pp. 66–74.
242. *'Anṭar wa-Juliet*, pp. 48–74.
243. *Ibid.*, pp. 92–101.
244. *Ibid.*, pp. 119–23.
245. *Umm al-'Awājiz*, pp. 99–103.
246. Fu'ād Duwwāra, *'Ashrat Udabā' Yuthaddathū'n*, pp. 99–124.
247. See Na'īm 'Aṭiyya's interpretation of this work in *Sab'ūn Sham'a fī Ḥayāt Yaḥyā Ḥaqqī*, ed. Yūsuf al-Shārūnī, pp. 140–65.
248. *Umm al-'Awājiz*, pp. 6–14.
249. *Ibid.*, pp. 29–44.
250. *Ibid.*, pp. 82–98.
251. *Ibid.*, pp. 15–28.
252. *Al-Ahrām*, 3 Feb. 1961.
253. *Al-Masā'*, 8, 15, 22, 29 January 1968 and 5 February 1968.
254. As in 'Kunnā Thalāthat Aytām' in *Qindīl Umm Hāshim*, pp. 74–86, 'Qiṣṣah fī Sijn', 'Iflās Khāṭibah' in *Umm al-'Awājiz*, pp. 45–53, 'Tanawwa'at al-Asbāb' in *Umm al-'Awajiz*, pp. 66–74, and 'Mūlid Bilā Ḥummuṣ'.

255. As in 'Qiṣṣah fī Sijn', 'Sūrah' in *Umm al-'Awājiz*, pp. 60—65, and 'al-Sulḥafāh Taṭīr'.
256. As in 'Abū Fūdah', 'Sūsū', 'al-Nisyān', 'al-Firāsh al-Shāghir', *al-Kātib,* April 1961, and 'al-Sarīr al-Nuḥās' in *'Anṭar wa-Juliet*, pp. 13—22.
257. *Qindīl Umm Hāshim,* pp. 59—73.
258. *'Anṭar wa-Juliet*, pp. 13—22.
259. *Al-Ahrām*, 31 Mar. 1961.
260. *Al-Kātib,* Apr. 1961.
261. The maturity and richness of this story make it subject to many different interpretations: see, e.g., the Oedipus complex interpretation in Muṣṭafā Ibrāhīm Ḥusayn's *Yaḥyā Ḥaqqī Mubdi'ā wa-Nāqidā,* 72 ff, and the socio-political interpretation of Na'īm 'Atiyya in his article 'al-Firāsh al-Shāghir: Dirāsah wa-Taḥlīl', *al-Thaqāfa,* January 1975, pp. 56—72.
262. Burke, *Counter-Statement,* pp. 153—4.
263. See Ḥaqqī's reply to the literary questionnaire on 'al-Adab al-Qaṣaṣī fī Miṣr, Mā Hiya Asbāb Rukūdih' conducted by Luṭfī 'Uthmān and published in *al-Majalla al-Jadīda,* Aug. 1931, pp. 1238—9.
264. Yaḥyā Ḥaqqī, 'al-Qiṣṣah Bayn Shiqqay al-Raḥā', *al-Majallah al-Jadīdah,* March 1931. This article shows not only his concern about artistic precision, but also his courage as a young writer in excoriating the didacticism and artistic redundancy of the work of well-established writers such as Ṭāhā Husayn.
265. See his collection *Ajwā'* (1956).
266. See his collections *Ka's al-Ḥayāh* (1947), *Nuf'ūs 'Āriyah* (1951), *Ṣirā' al-Rūḥ wa'l-Jasad* (1961), *'Ālam al-Gharā'iz wa'l-Aḥlām* (1962), and *al-Bāb al-Zahabī* (1963).
267. Al-Māzinī published many collections which contain many fictional sketches and some short stories: see *Ṣandūq al-Dunyā* (1929), *Khuyūt al-'Ankabūt* (1935), *Fi'l-Ṭarīq* (1937), *'A al-Māshī* (1937), and *Min al-Nāfidhah* (1949).
268. See his collection *Ajwā'* (1956) in which he tries to introduce new scenes as a means of justifying and validating the short story as a literary form.
269. In his collection *Ka's al-Ḥayāh* (1947), *Nufūs 'Āriyah* (1951), *Ṣirā' al-Rūḥ wa'l-Jasad* (1961), *'Ālam al-Gharā'iz wa'l-Aḥlām* (1962), and *al-Bāb al-Zahabī* (1963) in which he uses short stories as a means of psychoanalysing human character.
270. The battle between the old and the new, which was sparked off by the publication of *Fi'l-Shi'r al-Jāhilī,* continued on various levels until the early 1930s. Although the court ruling was in favour of Ṭāhā Ḥusain, he opted for suppressing the disputed sections of his book, and reissued it as *Fi al-'Adab al-Jāhili.*
271. Such as Ḥusayn Fawzī, who went to complete his postgraduate studies in France.
272. Such as *al-Majallah al-Jadīdah* (1929—4?), *al-Risālah* (1933—52), and *Majallatī* (1934—8). Although these magazines supported the new writings, they did not promote the short story in the manner of *al-Fajr.*
273. Al-Badawī's translations of Chekov appeared in *al-Risālah,* 11 Dec. 1933, pp. 38—40, 18 Dec. 1933, pp. 31—3, and 10 Aug. 1936, pp. 1310—2. He also translated Maupassant, *al-Risālah,* 17 Aug. 1936, pp. 1355—7, and Andreyev, *al-Risālah,* 12 Oct. 1936, pp. 1672—7.
274. For a full list of these collections, see the first part of the bibliography, Primary Sources: A Complete Bibliograpy of Collections of Egyptian Short Stories (1921–70).
275. In this study and in *The Genesis.*
276. Although Maḥfūẓ is now the most prominent figure in modern Arabic

literature, his early work in the field of the short story was far from coherent and mature. He started publishing short stories in 1934, in *al-Majallah al-Jadīdah,* and continued to do so until 1946 in various other magazines such as *al-Riwāyah, Majallatī, al-Risālah,* and *al-Thaqāfah.* Most of these stories, over seventy in number, are sentimental and incoherent, and many of them can be rated as cheap entertainment literature.

277. Maḥmūd Kāmil was one of the most productive short story writers in the thirties, and his work and wide influence will be discussed in the following chapter.

278. Ṣalāḥ Dhuhnī started publishing short stories in *al-Usbū'* in 1934 and his first collection, *Fi'l-Darajah al-Thāminah*, appeared in the following year. Despite his premature death in 1953 he wrote and published more than ten collections, a complete list of which can be found in the Appendix.

279. Yūsuf Ḥilmī started publishing in *Rūz al-Yūsuf* in 1934, and in 1936 his first and only collection *Min Ghawr al-Muḥīṭ* came out. In 1937 he established *al-Kātib,* a progressive magazine that promoted realistic writing, and in which he continued publishing his short stories. Although he wrote and published numerous short stories in *Ākhir Sā'ah* until 1946, he became more concerned with journalistic activities and did not publish further collections.

280. Yūsuf Jawhar started publishing in 1933 in *al-Risālah.* Although his stories continued to appear in *Majallatī, al-Kātib, Ākhir Sā'ah,* and *al-Thaqāfah* throughout the 1930s and 1940s, his first collection did not appear until 1955, after which he published few others.

281. Such as Ibrāhīm Ḥusayn al-'Aqqād (who published many stories in *al-Fuṣūl* and *al-Jāmi'ahh* between 1935—40), 'Izzat al-Sayyid Ibrāhīm (who published numerous stories in *al-Jāmi'ah, al-Fūnūn,* and *al-Usū'* between 1933—40), Muḥammad 'Alī Gharīb (who published many stories in *al-Usū', Ākhir Sā'ah, al-Risālah,* and others between 1933—48), and Muḥammad Aḥmad Shukrī (who published regularly in *al-Jāmi'ah* throughout 1934—5). There are also many other minor writers who published their work in periodicals, and even in book form throughout the 1930s and 1940s, such as Aḥmad Jalāl, Aḥmad al-Ṣāwī Muḥammad, Ḥasan Fatḥī Khalīl, Ḥilmī Murād, Dirīnī Khashabah, Ṣalāḥ Kāmil, 'Adil al-Jammāl, 'Abd al-Ḥalīm al-'Ushayrī, 'Abd al-'Azīz 'Umar Sāsī, 'Abd al-Mun'im al-Sibā'ī and Muḥammad Badr al-Dīn Khalīl.

282. See e.g. Muḥammad 'Alī Gharīb's favourable article on al-Badawī's early works in *al-Risālah,* 6 July 1936.

283. See e.g. Ḥilāl Aḥmad Shitāh, 'Fan al-Qiṣṣah fi'l-Adab al-Miṣrī al-Ḥadīth', *al-Risālah,* 24 and 31 Aug. 1936. In the second part of his article, Shitāh puts al-Badawī's work before that of Lāshīn.

284. Such as Rajā' al-Naqqāsh's article, 'al-Qaṣṣāṣ al-Shā'ir', *al-Shahr,* Jan. 1959, and Ghāli Shukrī's chapter on 'al-Mawt wa'l-Jins fī Adab al-Badawī' in his book *Azmat al-Jins fi'l-Qiṣṣah al-'Arabiyyah* (1962), pp. 141—62, and some brief and isolated reviews of one collection or another.

285. *Al-Raḥīl,* p. 24.

286. *Ḥāris al-Bustān*, pp. 151—61, the references to Chekhov are on pp. 151, 156.

287. *Al-'Arabah al-Akhīrah,* pp. 65—82, the reference to Chekhov is on p. 66.

288. *Al-Dhi'āb al-Jā'i'ah,* p. 143.

289. *Al-'Arabah al-Akhīrah*, 54–55.

290. *Ḥadath Dhāt Laylah,* p. 50. Freud is also mentioned in *al-Jamāl al-Ḥazīn*, p. 95.

291. *Ghurfah 'Alā al-Saṭḥ,* p. 61.

292. *Ḥāris al-Bustān,* p. 151.
293. *Al-'Arabah al-Akhīrah,* p. 70.
294. See e.g. his reference to Adler and Freud in *Ḥadath Dhāt Laylah,* p. 50 and that to Chekhov in *al-'Arabah al-Akhīrah,* p. 66.
295. As in 'Sa'āt al-Hawl' in *al-Dhi'āb al-Jā'i'ah,* pp. 11—17, 'Rajul 'Alā al-Ṭarīq' in *al-'Arabah al-Akhīrah,* 15–25, the title story of *al-A'raj fi'l-Mīnā,* pp. 5—16, and 'al-Zawraq' in *Laylah fi'l-Ṭarīq,* pp. 15—22.
296. As in 'Sukūn al-'Aṣifa' in *Funduq al-Danūb,* pp. 156—62, 'Qalb 'Adhrā'' in *al-Dhi'āb al-Jā'i'ah,* pp. 67—87, and 'Ḥāris al-Maḥaṭṭah' in *'Adhārā al-Layl,* pp. 21—8.
297. As in the first and third stories of the previous note, and 'Sayyida WaḥīḲda' in *al-A'raj fi'l-MḲnā',* pp. 30—8.
298. *Funduq al-Dānūb,* pp. 27—54.
299. *Al-A'raj fi'l-Mīnā',* pp. 136—51.
300. *Ḥadath Dhāt Laylah,* pp. 10—20.
301. *Al-A'raj fi'l-Mīnā',* pp. 5—16.
302. *Masā' al-Khamīs,* pp. 53—60.
303. *Laylah fi'l-Ṭarīq,* pp. 15—22.
304. *Funduq al-Dānūb,* pp. 143, 156.
305. *'Adhrā' wa-Waḥsh,* pp. 85—91.
306. His first story *al-Raḥīl* was about a trip to Europe in the 1930s, and since then he has had one or more stories on the same subject in almost every one of his collections: 'Fi Ivoriā' in *Rajul,* pp. 3–14, the title story of *Funduq al-Dānūb,* pp. 3—11, 'Fi'l-Ẓalām' in *al-Dhi'āb al-Jā'i'ah,* pp. 133—45, and so on.
307. Since his seventh collection, *al-A'raj fi'l-Mīnā',* the trip to Japan and the Far East seems to replace or to couple with that to Europe; see e.g. 'al-Ṣūra al-Nāqiṣa' in *Ibid.,* pp. 43—59. 'Laylah fī Bombay', pp. 19—26 and 'al-Ḥaqībah', pp. 115—24 in *al-Zallah al-Ūlā,* 'al-Tuffāḥah', pp. 129—36 and 'Jadwa fi'l-Ramād', pp. 147—62 in *Ghurfah 'Alā al-Saṭḥ,* and 'Taḥt al-Amṭār', pp. 54—63, 'al-Lu'lu'', pp. 106—16, and 'al-Tinnīn', pp. 126—43 in *Laylah fi'l-Ṭarīq,* and several others in the following collections.
308. See for example *al-Raḥīl,* and 'Dhirā' al-Baḥḥār' in *al-A'raj fi'l-Mīnā',* pp. 17—29.
309. See for example 'Fi Ivoria', *Rajul,* pp. 3—14, 'Sā'iq al-Qiṭār' in *Funduq al-Dānūb,* pp. 13—25, 'Fi'l-Qiṭār' in *al-Dhi'āb al-Jā'i'ah,* pp. 89—102, and 'Ḥāris al-Maḥaṭṭah', pp. 21—8, 'al-'Adhrā' wa'l-Layl', pp. 47—56, and 'al-Gharīq', pp. 109—14 in *'Adhārā al-Layl,* and many others.
310. As in 'Zuhūr Dhābilah' in *al-'Arabah al-Akhīrah,* pp. 43—55, 'Laylah fi'l-Ṣaḥrā'' in *'Adhārā al-Layl,* pp. 157—69, 'al-Arqām al-Nāṭiqah' in *Zawjat al-Ṣayyād,* pp. 83—8, and 'Fi al-Layl', in *al-Jamāl al-Ḥazīn,* pp. 72—7, and many others.
311. The stories that take place in Upper Egypt are too numerous to mention; e.g. 'Ṣawt al-Damm', pp. 55—80, 'al-Ḥubb al-Awwal', pp. 101—14, in *Funduq al-Dānūb,* 'al-Shaykh 'Umrān', pp. 27—41, and 'Zuhūr Dhābilah', pp. 43—55 in *al-'Arabah al-Akhīrah,* 'al-Dhahab', pp. 5—14, 'al-Ramād', pp. 42—6, and 'al-Ṭalqah al-Akhīrah', pp. 80—92 in *Laylah fi'l-Ṭarīq.*
312. See e.g. 'Sā'iq al-Qiṭār' in *Funduq al-Dānūb,* pp. 13—25, 'al-Amwāj', pp. 41—8, 'al-Ghūl', pp. 82—92, in *al-Zallah al-ūlā,* and 'al-Wasīṭ' in *Masā' al-Khamīs,* pp. 161—3.
313. See e.g. 'al-Lahab al-Aḥmar' in *Ḥadath Dhāt Laylah,* pp. 3—11, and 'al-'Izbah al-Jadīdah' in *'Adhārā al-Layl,* pp. 73—83.

314. Al-Badawī was born and brought up in a small village (al-Akrād) in the province of Asyūṭ in Upper Egypt.
315. See e.g. 'Ṣaqr al-Ṣaḥarā'' in *Masā' al-Khamīs,* pp. 38—43.
316. As in 'Laylah fi'l-Ṣaḥrā', 'al-Jawharah' in *'Adhrā' wa Waḥsh,* pp. 59—63, and 'Fi'l-Layl'.
317. *Ḥadath Dhāt Laylah,* pp. 35—40.
318. *'Adhārā al-Layl,* pp. 67—71.
319. *Al-Zallah al-Ūlā,* pp. 5—10.
320. *Funduq al-Dānūb,* pp. 95—9.
321. *Zawjat al-Ṣayyād,* pp. 19—23.
322. *Ibid.*, pp. 29—31.
323. *Ibid.*, pp. 49—51.
324. *Ibid.*, pp. 83—8.
325. *Al-Dhi'āb al-Jā'i'ah,* pp. 33—50.
326. *Ḥāris al-Bustān,* pp. 27—33.
327. *Al-'Arabah al-Akhīrah,* pp. 27—41.
328. *Al-Zallah al-Ūlā,* pp. 82—92.
329. *Laylah fi'l-Ṭarīq,* pp. 72—9.
330. *Zawjat al-Ṣayyād,* pp. 3—11.
331. *Al-A'raj fi'l-Mīnā',* pp. 77—81.
332. *Ibid.,* pp. 60—8.
333. *Al-Jamāl al-Ḥazīn,* pp. 67—71.
334. Such as 'Ṭarīq al-Fanā'' in *Funduq al-Dānūb,* 81—93, 'Rajul Marīd' in *al-Dhi'āb al-Jā'i'ah,* 27—32, 'Shakwā Ilā al-Samā'' in *'Adhārā al-Layl,* pp. 57—65.
335. *Al-'Arabah al-Akhīrah,* pp. 85—89.
336. See e.g. 'al-'Āṣifa' in *al-Zallah al-Ūlā,* pp. 82—92, 'al-Ṭalqa al-Akhīra', 'Raṣāṣah' in *al-Jamāl al-Ḥazīn,* pp. 97—105, and 'al-Rimāl' in *Ḥāris al-Bustān,* pp. 27—33.
337. The outlaws appear in many stories, e.g., 'al-Sirāj' in *al-'Arabah al-Akhīrah,* pp. 147—161, 'Laylah Rahībah' in *Ḥadath Dhāt Laylah,* pp. 29—34, 'Sūq al-Sabt' in *'Adhārā al-Layl,* pp. 91—8 and others.
338. See. e.g., 'Bansyūn Munīrva', 'Dūrūs Khuṣuṣiyya', 125–132, and 'al-Bashmuhandis', pp. 175—87 in *'Adhārā al-Layl,* 'al-A'raj fi'l-Mīnā'', and 'al-Miṣbaḥ' in *Ghurfah 'Alā al-Saṭḥ,* pp. 137—46.
339. As in 'Alḥān Rāqiṣah' in *Laylah fi'l-Ṭarīq,* pp. 64—71.
340. As in 'Ḥānat al-Maḥaṭṭah' in *al-A'raj fi'l-Mīnā',* pp. 136—51, 'al-Nāfidhah' in *'Adhrā' wa Waḥsh,* pp. 73—8, and the title story of *Ghurfah 'Alā al-Saṭḥ,* pp. 109—20.
341. *'Adhārā al-Layl,* pp. 139—49.
342. *Al-A'raj fi'l-Mīnā',* pp. 43—59.
343. *Ḥāris al-Bustān,* pp. 35—41.
344. *Al-Dhi'āb al-Jā'i'ah,* pp. 51—66.
345. *Al-'Arabah al-Akhīrah,* pp. 121—3.
346. *Ibid.,* pp. 125—35.
347. *Ḥadath Dhāt Laylah,* pp. 107—19.
348. *Ḥāris al-Bustān,* pp. 111—15.
349. *Ibid.,* pp. 73—80.
350. *Al-'Arabah al-Akhīrah,* pp. 137—46.
351. *Masā' al-Khamīs,* pp. 3—9.
352. See e.g. 'al-Shayṭān' in *'Adhrā' wa-Waḥsh,* pp. 17—27.
353. *Ḥadath Dhāt Laylah,* pp. 29—34.
354. *Al-Zallah al-Ūlā,* pp. 49—52.

355. *Adhrā' wa-Waḥsh*, pp. 111—17.
356. As in 'Min Ayyām al-Ṣibā' in *Funduq al-Dānūb*, pp. 115—17, 'al-Mijdāf' in *Ghurfah 'Ala al-Saṭḥ*, pp. 121–8, and 'Fi'l-Maḥaṭṭah' in *al-Jamāl al-Ḥazīn*, pp. 101—05.
357. As in 'Ṣawt al-Damm' in *Funduq al-Dānūb*, pp. 55—80, the title story of *al-Dhi'āb al-Jā'i'ah*, pp. 3—9, and 'al-Sirāj' in *al-'Arabah al-Akhīrah*, pp. 147—61.
358. *Funduq al-Dānūb*, pp. 55—80.
359. *Rajul*, pp. 15—36.
360. Ghālī Shukrī, in his *Azmat al-Jins*, pp. 141—62, argues that the blindness of the protagonist symbolises man's blindness before fate, but fails to see the significance of the various other symbols in constructing a fairly balanced work.
361. *Funduq al-Dānūb*, pp. 143—56.
362. *Al-Dhi'āb al-Jā'i'ah*, pp. 33—50.
363. Here the symbols of the wound and the fall into the well are very suggestive and carnally significant.
364. *Al-Zallah al-Ūlā*, pp. 5—10.
365. D. H. Lawrence, *Selected Literary Criticism* (London 1961), pp. 39, 46.
366. *Ibid.*, p. 53.
367. *Al-'Arabah al-Akhīrah*, pp. 15—25.
368. *Ibid.*, pp. 5—14.
369. To mention but a few, there are: 'al-Lahab al-Aḥmar', pp. 3—13, and 'Manzil al-Muqāmir', pp. 83—8, in *Ḥadath Dhāt Laylah*, and 'Ṣirā' Ma'a al-Sharr', pp. 35—41, 'Shakwa Ilā al-Samā'', pp. 57–65, 'al-Khinzīr', pp. 115—23, 'Ṣarkhah fi'l-Layl', pp. 133—8, and 'al-Bashmuhandis', pp. 175—87 in *'Adhārā al-Layl.*
370. *Ghurfah 'Alā al-Saṭḥ*, pp. 5—40.
371. *Ḥāris al-Bustān*, pp. 51—6.
372. *Masā' al-Khamīs*, pp. 26—37.
373. See e.g. 'al-Dawwāmah', in *al-A'raj fi'l-Mīnā'*, pp. 125—35, 'Jadhwah fi'l-Ramād', in *Ghurfah 'Alā al-Saṭḥ*, pp. 147—62, and 'Taḥt al-Amṭār' in *Laylah fi'l-Ṭarīq*, pp. 54—63.
374. As in 'Rajul 'Alā al-Ṭarīq'.
375. As in 'Fi'l-Qaryah'.
376. As in 'al-Rajul al-Sharīf' in *Adhrā' wa-Waḥsh*, pp. 85—91.
377. See e.g. 'al-Dars al-Awwal' in *al-'Arabah al-Akhīrah*, pp. 99—108, 'al-Ḥayā al-Bahīja', in *al-Jamāl al-Ḥazīn*, pp. 24—33, and the title story of *Masā' al-Khamīs*, pp. 16—25.
378. See e.g. 'Laylah Lan Ansāhā', in *al-'Arabah al-Akhīrah*, pp. 90—8, and 'Shakwā Ilā al-Samā'', in *'Adhāra al-Layl*, pp. 57—65.
379. *'Adhrā' wa-Waḥṣh*, pp. 45—54.
380. *Funduq al-Dānūb*, pp. 27—54.
381. See e.g. 'Jasad wa-Fannān', in *al-'Arabah al-Akhīrah*, pp. 109—20, 'al-Zallah al-ūlā', pp. 99—106, and 'al-'Arbūn', in *al-Zallah al-ūlā*, pp. 135—42, and 'al-Lu'lu'', in *Laylah fi'l-Ṭarīq*, pp. 106—16.
382. See e.g. *al-Raḥīl*, 'Ba'd al-'Urs', in *Funduq al-Dānūb*, pp. 131—42, and 'al-Jamāl al-Ḥazīn'.
383. See e.g. 'al-A'mā', 'Imra'at Aḥlamī', 'Ṭabīb al-Markaz', in *Ḥadath Dhāt Laylah*, pp. 41—51, and 'Rassāma', in *al-Jamāl al-Ḥazīn*.
384. As is the case in the title story of *al-'Arabah al-Akhīrah*, 'al-Layl wa'l-Rajul', the title of story of *Zawjat al-Ṣayyād*, pp. 3—11, 'Hadhih Hiya al-Ḥayāh', pp. 3—5, and 'al-Badīl', pp. 81—8 in *Ḥarīs al-Bustān*.

385. *'Adhrā' wa-Waḥsh,* pp. 100—10.
386. *Al-A'raj fi'l-Mīnā',* pp. 99 —109.
387. *Ḥarīs al-Bustān,* pp. 96—100.
388. As is the case with the heroine of 'al-Sirāj' in *al-'Arabah al-Akhīrah,* pp. 147—61.
389. As is the case with the heroines of 'al-Safīnah' in *'Adhārā al-Layl,* pp. 99—108, 'Imra'ah fi'l-Jānib al-Akhar', pp. 5—40, and 'al-Miṣbāḥ', pp. 137—46, in *Ghurfah 'Alā al-Saṭḥ.*
390. *Funduq al-Dānūb,* pp. 101—14.
391. *Ibid.*, pp. 3—11.
392. *Al-Dhi'āb al-Jā'i'ah,* pp. 67—78.
393. *'Adhārā al-Layl*, pp. 115—23.
394. *Zawjat al-Ṣayyād,* pp. 121—33.
395. *'Adhrā' wa-Waḥsh,* pp. 5—16.
396. *Al-'Arabah al-Akhīrah*, pp. 43—55.
397. *Al-Zallah al-Ūlā*, pp. 53—57.
398. *'Adhārā al-Layl,* pp. 73—83.
399. *Funduq al-Dānūb,* pp. 131—42.
400. *Al-A'raj fi'l-Mīnā',* pp. 152—6.
401. *Ḥadath Dhāt Laylah,* pp. 63—9.
402. *Al-'Arabah al-Akhīrah,* pp. 57—63.
403. *Ibid.*, pp. 83—4.
404. *Laylah fi'l-Ṭarīq,* pp. 45—54.
405. As in 'Jasad wa-Fannān' and 'Rūḥ al-Fannān' in *al-'Arabah al-Akhīrah,* pp. 125—35.
406. As in 'al-Zuhūr' in *Laylah fi'l-Ṭarīq,* pp. 72—9.
407. As in "Indama Tuḥibb al-Nisā" in *Ḥadath Dhāt Laylah,* pp. 77—82.
408. As in 'al-Jiyād al-Shahbā" in *Zawjat al-Ṣayyād,* pp. 39—48.
409. As in 'al-'Awda Min al-Sūq' in *al-Jamāl al-Ḥazīn,* pp. 22—3.
410. As in 'al-Mu'jizāt al-Sab" in *al-Zallah al-Ūlā,* pp. 27—31.
411. As in 'Jisr al-Ḥayā' in *Ghurfah 'Alā al-Saṭḥ,* pp. 65—78, and "Ālam al-Asrār' in *al-Jamāl al-Ḥazīn,* pp. 39—42.
412. *Ghurfah 'Alā al-Saṭḥ*, p. 67.
413. See for example the title story of *al-Dhi'āb al-Jā'i'ā,* pp. 3—9.
414. See e.g. the title stories of *Laylah fi'l-Ṭarīq,* pp. 47—53, and *Zawjat al-Ṣayyād,* pp. 3—11, and 'al-Samā' Tuṭill 'Alaynā', pp. 45—50, and 'al-Ḥabl', pp. 63—7, in *Ḥāris al-Bustān.*
415. See e.g. 'al-Nār' in *'Adhārā al-Layl,* pp. 29—34, 'Fi'l-Barriyyah' in *Laylah fi'l-Ṭarīq,* pp. 101–105, 'Jarīma', pp. 33—8, 'al-Aḥdab', 53—8, "Abir Sabīl', pp. 61—70, and 'al-Arqām al-Nāṭiqah' in *Zawjat al-Ṣayyād,* and many others.
416. *Al-Zallah al-Ūlā,* pp. 132—4.
417. *Funduq al-Dānūb,* pp. 156—62.
418. *Al-Dhi'āb al-Jā'i'ah,* pp. 11—17.
419. *Ḥadath Dhāt Laylah,* pp. 53—61.
420. *'Adhārā al-Layl,* pp. 47—56.
421. *Ibid.*, pp. 151—5.
422. *Ghurfah 'Alā al-Saṭḥ,* pp. 47—64.
423. Such as "Ind al-Buḥayrah', *Ibid.*, pp. 99—108, 'al-Ishāra' in *al-Jamāl al-Ḥazīn,* pp. 60—6, and 'al-Lawḥah' in *Ḥāris al-Bustān,* pp. 35—41.
424. Such as 'al-Ḥaqībah', pp. 115—24, and 'al-Mās', pp. 125—32, in *al-Zallah al-ūlā.*
425. See e.g. 'al-Dhi'āb al-Jā'i'ah', 'al-Thu'ban' in *al-A'raj fi'l-Mīnā',* pp. 77—81, 'al-

Dhi'b', in *al-Zallah al-Ūlā,* 49—52, 'Fi'l-Layl' in *al-Jamāl al-Ḥazīn*, and 'Waqfah 'Alā al-Darb', pp. 3—9, and 'Ṣaqr al-Ṣaḥrā'', pp. 38—43, in *Masā' al-Khamīs.*

426. *Al-Jamal al-Ḥazīn,* pp. 34—38, see also 'al-Layl wa'l-Waḥsh' in *al-Zallah al-Ūlā,* pp. 106—13, and the title story of *'Adhrā' wa-Waḥsh,* pp. 29—37.
427. Almost all his studies of failure are located in big cities; see 'Rajul Marīḍ', pp. 27—32, and 'al-Najm al-Ba'īd', pp. 103—15, in *al-Dhi'āb al-Jā'i'ah,* 'al-Kahrabī'ī' in *al-A'raj fi'l-Mīnā',* pp. 39—42, 'al-Zahab', pp. 5–14, and 'al-Rajul al-A'zab', pp. 30—40, in *Laylah fi'l-Ṭarīq,* and 'al-Manzil' in *Ḥāris al-Bustān,* pp. 57—62.
428. See e.g. 'Jisr al-Ḥayāh' and 'Tidhkār'.
429. *Ḥāris al-Bustān,* pp. 81—8.
430. See e.g. 'Ḥikāyah Min Tokyo', *Ibid.*, pp. 139—49 and many of the stories about the journey abroad.
431. This in itself is a significant achievement in a language so flowery and paronymous to the extent that exaggeration, especially at that time of its literary history, is widely considered to be one of its inherent characteristics.
432. Carlos Baker, *Hemingway: The Writer as Artist* (Princeton 1963), p. 117. Although he does not mention Hemingway among those who has influenced him, his technique bears a strong resemblance to that of the great American writer.
433. Such as 'al-Ramād' in *Laylah fi'l-Ṭarīq,* pp. 42—6, 'al-Amwāj' in *al-Zallah al-Ūlā,* pp. 41—8, 'al-Mijdāf' in *Ghurfah 'Alā al-Saṭḥ,* pp. 121—8, 'al-Jiyād al-Shahbā'', pp. 39—48, and 'Wajh al-Shams', pp. 71—81, in *Zawjat al-Ṣayyād,* and 'Taḥt al-Rīḥ' in *Ḥarīs al-Bustān,* pp. 51—6.
434. Baker, *Hemingway.*
435. *Ibid.*, p. 118.
436. Muḥammad Yusrī Aḥmad was a student at Cairo University's Faculty of Medicine in the forties and a prominent member of the city's literary society. He started publishing his short stories extensively in *al-Qiṣṣah* in 1949. In 1953 and 1954 his short stories became few and far between, and by 1955 he had stopped writing altogether, devoting all his time to medicine. Although he published more than twenty short stories in various magazines, he did not collect any of them in book form. His stories were marked by their apparent coherence and maturity, for he was one of the best writers among his young contemporaries.
437. This was 'Unshūdat al-Ghurabā', *al-Qiṣṣah,* 5 March 1950.
438. Muṣṭafā Maḥmūd began publishing his short stories in 1949 in *al-Nidā'* and *al-Qiṣṣah,* and continued to do so in *al-Maṣrī, al-Taḥrīr,* and *Rūz al-Yūsuf* in the early 1950s and in 1955 published his first collection, *Akl 'Aysh.*
439. Ṣalāḥ Ḥāfiẓ started publishing his stories in 1949 in *al-Nidā'* and *al-Qiṣṣah* also, and continued publishing in *al-Qiṣṣah* and *Rūz al-Yūsuf* in the early 1950s. He was more involved in politics, and as a result spent several years in prison. Thus his first collection, *Ayyām al-Qalaq,* did not come out until 1967.
440. Ibrāhīm Nājī, the famous poet, was also a minor short story writer. From 1933, his short stories continued to appear in numerous periodicals, and in the late 1940s he resumed writing short stories in *al-Qiṣṣah* after a brief interval. He published two collections.
441. Ṣūfī 'Abd Allāh started publishing her short stories in *al-Muṣawwar* in 1948 and continued to do so in various other magazines until her first collection, *Kulluhun 'Ayyūshah,* came out 1956. Subsequently she published six other collections.
442. Al-Khamīsī began his literary career as a poet in the mid-forties, then started publishing short stories in *al-Miṣrī* in 1947. His first collection, *al-A'māq*

(1951), was followed by seven other collections before he stopped writing short stories in 1962.

443. Al-Khūlī commenced his literary career in 1952 in *al-Miṣrī* and his first collection *Rijāl wa-Ḥadīd* appeared in 1955; he directed his efforts to politics, yet kept an eye on the short story and managed to publish another collection in 1966.
444. Aḥmad 'Abbās Ṣāliḥ began publishing his stories in *al-Qiṣṣah* in 1950, continued publishing in *al-Jumhuriyyah* and *Rūz al-Yūsuf* for a few years, then stopped and became a critic.
445. Aḥmad Rushdī Ṣāliḥ also started in *al-Qiṣṣah* in 1950, and published his first and only collection, *al-Zawjah al-Thāniyah*, in 1955, then turned to criticism.
446. Amīnah al-Sa'īd started with 'Abd Allāh in *al-Muṣawwar* in 1948, and published her first collection, *al-Hadaf al-Kabīr*, in 1958, then turned to journalism.
447. Such as Maḥmūd Ṣubḥī, who started publishing short stories in *al-Miṣrī* in 1950 and continued to do so until 1954. Although he published more than fifty stories, he did not collect any of them in book form. There is also Fu'ād Fahmī who started with 'Abd Allāh and al-Sa'īd in *al-Muṣawwar* in 1948 and continued to publish extensively in it until 1956, but he did not publish any collections.
448. His tenth collection, *Bayt Min Laḥm* (1971), falls beyond the scope of this study.
449. Here one thinks of various patterns of discourse preferred by certain well-known writers at the time, such as Yūsuf al-Sibā'ī – particularly in his short stories – Amīn Yūsuf Ghurāb, Birtī Bidār and Fu'ād al-Qaṣṣāṣ.
450. Because all the stories referred to here are from the same collection, only the title and the pages are given. 'Arkhaṣ Layālī', pp. 5—10.
451. 'Naẓrah', pp. 11—13.
452. 'Al-Shahādah', pp. 14—19.
453. 'Abū Sayyid', pp. 23—35.
454. "A al-Māshī', pp. 36—40.
455. "Alā Asyūṭ', pp. 20—2.
456. 'Al-Hajjānah', pp. 41—52.
457. 'Al-Ḥādith', pp. 53—61.
458. 'Rihān', pp. 62—5.
459. 'Al-Umniyah', pp. 78—81
460. 'Khamas Sā'āt', pp. 66—7.
461. 'Mishwār', pp. 119—31.
462. 'Maẓlūm', pp. 163—6.
463. *Arkhaṣ Layālī*, pp. 82—95.
464. A chronic disease caused by a parasite that lives in the blood and that is endemic in Egypt and other African countries.
465. 'Al-Murjayḥa', pp. 96—104.
466. 'Baṣrah', pp. 132—46.
467. 'Fi'l-Layl', pp. 167—80.
468. See e.g. in *Arkhaṣ Layālī* alone, the title story, pp. 5—10, 'Abū Sayyid', pp. 32—5, 'al-Ḥajjānah', pp. 41—52, 'al-Murjayḥah', pp. 96—104, 'Baṣrah', pp. 132—46, 'Fi'l-Layl', pp. 167—80, 'Khamas Sā'āt', pp. 66—77, 'al-Ma'ṭam', pp. 105—09, and 'Maẓlūm', pp. 163—6.
469. *Jumhūriyyat Faraḥāt*, pp. 9—27.
470. *Ḥādithat Sharaf*, pp. 84—112.
471. *Arkhaṣ Layālī*, pp. 119—31.

472. *Jumhūriyyat Faraḥāt*, pp. 34–47.
473. *Alaysa Kadhalik*, pp. 11–28.
474. *Ibid.*, pp. 71–95.
475. *Ibid.*, pp. 213–37.
476. *Al-Baṭal*, pp. 60–92.
477. *Ḥādithat Sharaf*, pp. 22–43.
478. *Ibid.*, pp. 44–57.
479. *Alyasa Kadhalik*, pp. 97–104.
480. *Ibid.*, pp. 105–133.
481. The name Muḥammad is a very common one, yet it implies a certain uniqueness, and reinforces his role, on the symbolic level, as the messenger of the cities of dream and salvation.
482. Such as 'Ḥādithat Sharaf', 'Laylat Ṣayf', 'Jumhūriyyat Faraḥāt', 'Baṣrah', and 'al-Yadd al-Kabīrah' in *Ḥādithat Sharaf*, pp. 58–72.
483. Such as 'Khamas Sā'āt', 'al-Murjayḥah', 'Mishwār', 'Dāwūd', 'Mārsh al-Ghurūb', 'Abu'l-Hawl', 'al-Jurḥ', and the title story of *al-Baṭal*, pp. 49–59.
484. *Alaysa Kadhalik*, pp. 47–53.
485. As in 'al-Nās', 'al-Ḥādith', pp. 53–61, 'Rub' Ḥawḍ', pp. 110–18, and 'al-Makanah', pp. 147–55 in *Arkhaṣ Layālī*, and 'al-Ḥālah al-Rābi'ah' in *Alaysa Kadhalik*, pp. 11–28.
486. As in 'Dāwūd', pp. 71–95, and 'al-Mustaḥīl', pp. 151–66 in *Alaysa Kadhalik*, and 'Taḥwīd al-'Arūsa', pp. 73–83, and 'Sirruh al-Bātī'', pp. 113–79, in *Ḥādithat Sharaf*.
487. Such as 'Abū Sayyid', pp. 23–35 and 'al-Ḥajjānah', pp. 41–52, along with the title story in *Arkhaṣ Layālī*, 'al-Ṭābūr', pp. 28–33, and the title story in *Jumhūriyyat Faraḥāt*, and 'Laylat Ṣayf' and 'Ḥādithat Sharaf'.
488. *Alaysa Kadhalik*, pp. 29–45.
489. Such as 'Laylat Ṣayf', 'Ḥādithat Sharaf', 'al-Yadd al-Kabīrah', and 'al-Maḥaṭṭah', in *Ḥādithat Sharaf*, pp. 5–22.
490. Such as 'Rihān', 'Arkhaṣ Layālī', 'Shughlānah' in *Arkhaṣ Layālī*, pp. 158, 162, and 'Mārsh al-Ghurūb'.
491. *Jumhūriyyat Faraḥāt*, pp. 34–47.
492. *Alaysa Kadhalik*, pp. 5–10.
493. *Ibid.*, pp. 135–49.
494. See e.g. the parents in 'Laylat Ṣayf', the villagers in 'Ḥādithat Sharaf', the medical people in 'Abu'l-Hawl', the officers in 'Jumhūriyyat Faraḥāt' and even when the obstacle is an individual, he is still an abstract one as in the case with the owner of the *Sūq* is 'al-Ṭābūr'.
495. *Ḥādithat Sharaf*, pp. 44–57.
496. *Ibid.*, pp. 78–83.
497. *Al-Baṭal*, pp. 24–48.
498. These are also the titles of two of his novels. He was aware from the outset of the uniqueness of the Egyptian/Arab/Islamic sense of sin and its difference from its Western, Christian counterpart.
499. Although dealing with Idrīs's work in a different genre (the novel), Hilary Kilpatrick's *The Modern Egyptian Novel* maintains that the double standard of morality inherent in the social convention is also Idrīs's personal stand vis-à-vis this question. See Hilary Kilpatrick, *The Modern Egyptian Novel: A Study in Social Cricitism* (London 1974), pp. 113–26.
500. *Alaysa Kadhalik*, 257–365.

501. Perhaps with the exception of Ibrāhīm 'Abd al-Qādir al-Māzinī's fictional world.
502. *Alaysa Kadhalik*, pp. 167—84.
503. See, e.g., 'Jumhūriyyat Faraḥāt', 'al-Ḥādith', 'al-Ḥālah al-Rābi'ah', 'Naẓrah', 'al-Tamrīn al-Awwal' and "A al-Māshī'.
504. A detailed account of these early changes can be found in the final chapter of this study.
505. After publishing five collections of more than fifty stories between 1954 and 1958, over the following twelve years he published only four more collections, with no more than thirty stories.
506. See e.g. 'Ḥālat Talabbus', pp. 7—17, 'Mu'āhadat Sīnā", pp. 27—34, 'al-Waraqah bi-'Asharah', pp. 41—50, 'Fawq Ḥudūd al-'Aql', pp. 51—64, 'Lughat al-Āy-Āy', 79—100, 'al-Lu'bah', pp. 101—09, 'Li'anna al-Qiyāmah lā Taqūm', pp. 11—123, and 'al-Awūrṭī', pp. 125—33.
507. See e.g. 'al-Zuwwār', pp. 19—26, 'Qiṣṣat Dhi al-Ṣawt al-Naḥīl', pp. 35—40, 'Ḥadhih al-Marrah', pp. 65—7—7, and 'Ṣāhib Miṣr', pp. 135—60.
508. See Shukrī Muḥammad 'Ayyād, *Tajārib fi'l-Adab wa'l-Naqd*, pp. 255—63.
509. *Al-'Askarī al-Aswad*, pp. 187—98.
510. This type of story reaches its peak thematically and artistically in his collection *Bayt Min Laḥm* (1971). See e.g. 'al-Riḥlah', pp. 73—80, 'al-Khid'ah', pp. 91—8, and 'Hiya', pp. 133—40.
511. *Ākhir al-Dunyā*, pp. 47—56.
512. *Ibid.*, pp. 27—46.
513. *Al-Naddāhah*, pp. 73—96.
514. A. E. Dyson, *The Crazy Fabric: Essays in Irony* (London 1966), p. 2.
515. Although Idrīs's talent was unanimously sanctioned at the beginning of his career, he was viewed in the sixties as a rebellious writer and did not have the establishment's seal of approval. He was denied the state prize in the short story, which was given to a much less important writer, Amīn Yūsuf Ghurāb. At the same time, many of his stories were translated into several European languages and many theses were written about his work at several European universities, London and Manchester among them, while there is not a single book on his work in Arabic.
516. Edwin Honig, *Dark Conceit, The Making of Allegory* (Oxford 1966), p. 30.
517. As is the case in 'Mu'jizat al-'Aṣr', 'Alif al-Aḥrār', the title story of *Al-Naddāhah*, 7–35, and 'al-Awūrṭī'.
518. *Bayt Min Laḥm*, pp. 99—118, but the story appeared in *al-Ahrām* in 1970.
519. As in 'Dustūr Yā Sayyidah' in *Al-Naddāhah*, pp. 125—47, 'al-Lu'bah', 'Ḥālat Talabbus', and 'Li'anna al-Qiyāmah Lā Taqūm' in *Lughat al-Āy-Āy*, pp. 111—23.
520. *Al-Naddāhah*, pp. 37—58.
521. *Al-'Askarī al-Aswad*, pp. 5—69.
522. A similar pair and identical technique can be found in 'Lughat al-Āy-Āy' and 'al-'Amaliyyah al-Kubrā' in *Al-Naddāhah*, pp. 103—24.
523. As in the case in 'Mashūq al-Hams', 'Snobism', 'Qiṣṣat Dhi al-Ṣawt al-Naḥīl' and 'al-Gharīb' in *Ākhir al-Dunyā*, pp. 92—157.
524. Such as 'Lughat al-Āy-Āy' and 'al-Martabah al-Muqa"arah', in *Al-Naddāhah*, pp. 69—71.
525. *Al-'Askarī al-Aswad*, pp. 159—84.
526. As in 'Li'anna al-Qiyāmah Lā Taqūm'.
527. As in the title story of *Ākhir al-Dunyā*, pp. 65—77.

528. As in 'Fawq Ḥud'd al-'Aql', in *Lughat al-Āy-Āy*, pp. 51—64.
529. As in 'Mu'jizat al-'Aṣr'.
530. In all the four collections of this stage there is not a single story in which the father is present, but there are several dealing with the effect of his death or absence.
531. Which appears also in 'al-Shaykh Shaykhah' in *Ākhir al-Dunyā,* pp. 14—26.
532. *Al-Naddāhah,* p. 22.
533. He is the king to whom Shahrazād tells the stories in *The Arabian Nights*; he has a desire to avenge himself upon woman and a love–hate relationship with her, thus he used to marry a virgin every night and kill her in the morning.
534. *Al-Naddāhah,* p. 24.
535. As in 'Mā Khafiya A'ẓam', pp. 59—68, and 'Dustūr Yā Sayyidah', pp. 125—47, in *Al-Naddāhah.*
536. Shukrī 'Ayyād, in his 'Min al-Baṭal Ilā al-Insān' maintains that most of Idrīs's stories in *Lughat al-Āy-Āy* are interesting experiments in form, *al-Jumhūriyyah,* 14 Oct. 1965, and *Tajārib fi'l-Adab wa'l-Naqd,* pp. 255—63.
537. And also in 'Mu'jizat al-'Aṣr', 'Alif al-Aḥrār', and 'al-'Amaliyyah al-Kubrā'.
538. See e.g. 'al-Lu'bah'. In this respect he is perhaps influenced by the French writer Michel Butor.
539. Such as 'Ḥālat Talabbus' and 'Hadhih al-Marrah'.
540. Such as 'Lughat al-Āy-Āy', 'Lu'bah', and 'Fawq Ḥudūd al-'Aql'.
541. See e.g. 'al-Lu'ba', 'al-Awūrṭī' and 'al-Nuqṭa', in *Al-Naddāhah,* pp. 97—101.
542. Walcutt, *Man's Changing Mask*, p. 16.
543. *Ibid.*
544. Catherine Cobham, 'The Importance of Yūsuf Idrīs' Short Stories in the Development of an Indigenous Egyptian Literary Tradition (Manchester 1974), p. 243.
545. *Ibid.*, p. 217.
546. Such as Ṣalāḥ Ḥāfiẓ, Muṣṭafā Maḥmūd and the others mentioned at the beginning of the section relating to him.
547. A detailed discussion of the composition and the work of the second group will follow in the next section dealing with the work of Abu'l-Ma'āṭī Abu'l-Najā.
548. Apart from Idrīs's individual talent, this was due to various factors connected with the social and political conditions of Egypt in the 1940s and with the many problems concerning the publication of creative writing at that period.
549. Aḥmad 'Abd al-Qādir al-Māzinī began to publish his short stories in *al-Hilāl,* 1939, and continued to do so throughout the 1940s and 1950 in *al-Hilāl* and *al-Radio.*
550. 'Abd al-Raḥmān Fahmī began publication in the early 1950s, first in *al-Thaqāfah, al-Miṣrī,* then *al-Jumhuriyyah* and *al-Shahr.* He also published three collections: *S'ūzī wa'l-Dhikrayāt* (1960), *al-Mulk Lak* (1962), and *al-'ūd wa'l-Zamān* (1969).
551. 'Abd al-Gaffār Makkāwī also started in the early 1950s in *al-Thaqāfah, al-Ādāb,* and *al-Shahr,* and published two collections, *Ibn al-Sulṭān* (1967), and *al-Sitt al-Ṭāhirah* (1967).
552. Sa'd al-Dīn Wahbah started also in the 1950s in *al-Taḥrīr, al-Risālah al-Jadīdah,* and *al-Shahr,* and published only one collection, *Arzāq* (1960).
553. Ḥilmī Murād, who started publishing in *al-Hilāl* in the late 1940s, then published his collection *'Indama Tuḥib al-Mar'ah* (1949). Nu'mān 'Āshūr also began in the late 1940s to publish his stories in *Rūz al-Yūsuf, al-Miṣrī* and

al-Taḥrīr, then published two collections, *Ḥawādīt 'Amm Faraj* (1959) and *Fawānīs* (1962). Muḥammad 'Afīfī in his collection *Anwār* (1946), Aḥmad 'Abd al-Ḥamīd al-Muḥāmī, who published many stories throughout the 1950s in *Majallat al-Idhā'ah al-Miṣriyyah,* Darwīsh al-Jamīl in his collection *Hakadhā Naṣīr* (1947), and Rashād Rushdī in his collection *'Arabat al-Ḥarīm* (1953).

554. Both Wahba and 'Ashūr focus on the theatre, Makkāwī concentrates on translation and philosophical and literary studies, and Fahmī on radio plays and programmes.
555. See e.g. *al-Riwāyah,* 1 July 1937, 15 Aug. 1937, and 1 Dec. 1937.
556. See e.g. *al-Riwāyah,* 1 Oct. 1937.
557. See e.g. *al-Riwāyah,* 16 Oct. 1937 where he publishes the first translation of *Riders to the Sea.*
558. See e.g. *al-Riwāyah,* 15 Jan. 1938.
559. See e.g. *al-Riwāyah,* 1 Feb. 1939.
560. See e.g. *al-Riwāyah,* 1 July 1939 where he translates and introduces this Spanish writer to the Egyptian reading public for the first time.
561. Such as Maḥmūd 'Abd al-Mun'im Murād, Maḥmūd al-Shinayṭī, and 'Abd al-Raḥmān al-Sharqāwī.
562. See e.g. *al-Jāmi'ah,* 27 May 1937, and *al-Riwāyah,* 15 March 1938.
563. At that time he published almost regularly in *al-Miṣrī,* then in *al-Kitāb, Rūz al-Yūsuf, al-Shahr,* and *al-Kātib.*
564. Such as Aḥmad al-Māzīnī, Ḥilmī Mūrad, and to some extent 'Abd al-Ghaffār Makkāwī, who is actually the most intellectual of the group.
565. See for example the stories 'Layla', pp. 81—90, 'al-Ghā'ib', pp. 101—06, 'al-Mi'addiyyah', pp. 117—27, and 'Ḥafnat Balaḥ', pp. 159–64, in *Mīlād Jadīd,* and 'Basmah', pp. 45—52, 'al-Balad', pp. 53—63, and 'al-Mustaḥimmah', pp. 109—16, in *Ṭarīq al-Jāmi'ah.*
566. Apart from being an eminent short story writer, 'Ayyād is Professor of Arabic Literature at the University of Cairo, where he obtained his Ph.D. in 1953.
567. *Mīlād Jadīd,* pp. 71—9.
568. *Ṭarīq al-Jāmi'ah,* pp. 71—81.
569. W. B. Yeats, 'J. M. Synge and the Ireland of his Time', in *Essays* (London 1924), p. 423.
570. Here lies some of the story's subtle political implication about the world inimical to anyone with a political, even patriotic, past, but favourable to the hypocrites, the conformists and the apathetic.
571. *Ṭarīq al-Jāmi'ah,* pp. 3—11.
572. See for example: 'Mīlād Jadīd', pp. 7—24, 'al-Kawālīnī', pp. 39—48, and 'Bayt min al-Qashsh', pp. 61—70, in *Mīlād Jadīd,* and 'Basmah', pp. 45—52, 'al-Balad', pp. 53—63, and 'Aḥlām' in *Ṭarīq al-Jāmi'ah.*
573. As in 'al-Mukāfa'ah', pp. 25—30, 'Fi'l-'Iyādah', pp. 31—8, and 'al-Mi'addiyyah', pp. 117—25, in *Mīlād Jadīd.*
574. As in 'al-Mukāfa'ah', and 'al-Balad', pp. 53—63, and 'al-Nās wa'l-'Uyūn', pp. 117—25, in *Ṭarīq al-Jāmi'ah.*
575. As in 'Bayt min al-Qashsh', pp. 71—9, 'al-Ghā'ib', pp. 101—06, and 'Jamāl', pp. 135—47, in *Mīlād Jadīd,* and 'Aḥlām' in *Ṭarīq al-Jāmi'ah,* pp. 83—93.
576. As in 'Ḥafnat Balaḥ' in *Mīlād Jadīd,* pp. 159—64, and 'al-Ḥujra al-Khalfiyya' in *Ṭarīq al-Jāmi'ah,* pp. 13—20.
577. Such as 'al-Mukāfa'ah', pp. 25—30, and 'Ḥafnat Balaḥ', pp. 169—64, in *Mīlād Jadīd,* and 'al-Ḥujrah al-Khalfiyyah' in *Ṭarīq al-Jāmi'ah,* pp. 13—20.
578. *Mīlād Jadīd,* pp. 39—48.

579. Apart from those discussed below, there are 'Ziyāra', pp. 49—59, 'Bayt min al-Qashsh', pp. 61—70, 'Shabāb', 'al-Ghā'ib', pp. 101—06, 'al-Nihāyah', pp. 107—16, and 'al-Qiṭṭ', pp. 165—74 in *Mīlād Jadīd,* and 'Ṣadīq Qadīm', pp. 37—43 and 'Shakhṣ Wāḥid', pp. 95—107, in *Ṭarīq al-Jāmi'ah.*
580. *Mīlād Jadīd,* pp. 7—24.
581. *Ṭarīq al-Jāmi'ah,* pp. 21—30.
582. *Mīlād Jādid,* pp. 149—57.
583. *Ibid.*, pp. 129—33.
584. *Ibid.*, pp. 135—47.
585. *Ṭarīq al-Jāmi'ah,* pp. 95—107.
586. Such as 'al-Mukāfa'ah', pp. 25—30, 'Fi'l-'Iyadah', pp. 31—8, and 'Ḥafnat Balaḥ', pp. 159—64, in *Mīlād Jadīd.*
587. *Mīlād Jadīd,* pp. 61—70.
588. *Ibid.*, pp. 81—90.
589. *Ibid.*, pp. 101—06.
590. *Ibid.*, pp. 107—16.
591. Such as 'al-Ḥujrah al-Khalfiyyah', pp. 13—20, 'al-Tha'r', 'Ṣadīq Qadīm', pp. 37—43, 'Basma', pp. 45—52, 'Ahlām' and 'al-Mustaḥimma', pp. 109—16, in *Ṭarīq al-Jāmi'ah.*
592. *Mīlād Jadīd,* pp. 91—100.
593. *Ṭarīq al-Jāmi'ah,* pp. 31—6.
594. *Ibid.*, pp. 64—70.
595. *Mīlād Jadīd,* pp. 159—64.
596. *Ibid.*, pp. 117—27.
597. *Ṭarīq al-Jāmi'ah,* pp. 83—93.
598. *Mīlād Jadīd,* pp. 165—74.
599. *Ṭarīq al-Jāmi'ah,* pp. 37—43.
600. It is sparked off by its hero, now a working man, introduced to a man by the name and with the mannerisms of the young boy of the family in the textbook, and through a series of flashbacks the story is narrated. By the end of the meeting the line between illusion and reality grows thin, and the hero asks the man if he went to France in 1935, and to his surprise, the answer is 'Yes'.
601. See for example 'Laylā', 'al-Kūmīdī', 'al-Tha'r', 'Bayt min al-Qashsh', and 'al-Mustaḥimmah'.
602. See e.g. 'al-Nihāyah', 'Dostoevsky wa'l-Sikkīr', and 'al-Qiṭṭ'.
603. See e.g. 'Laylā' and 'al-Kūmīdī'.
604. See e.g. 'Ṣadīq Qadīm', 'al-Mustaḥimmah', and 'Dostoevsky wa'l-Sikkīr'.
605. See e.g. 'al-Balad', 'al-Tha'r', and 'al-Nihāyah'.
606. See e.g. 'al-Kūmīdī' and 'Mīlād Jadīd'.
607. As in 'Ṭarīq al-Jāmi'ah', and 'al-Nihāyah'.
608. See e.g. 'Bayt min al-Qashsh' and 'al-Kūmīdī'.
609. As in 'Mīlād Jadīd', 'al-Qiṭṭ' and 'al-Ḥujrah al-Khalfiyyah'.
610. As in 'Ṣadīq Qadīm', 'al-Tha'r' and 'al-Sijn al-Kabīr'.
611. See e.g. 'al-Tha'r'.
612. 'Ayyād's M.A. thesis in 1948 was on *The Poetics* of Aristotle.
613. See e.g. *Mīlad Jādīd,* pp. 27, 61,109, and *Ṭarīq al-Jāmi'ah,* pp. 5, 23, etc.
614. As in the works of Muḥammad Taymūr, 'Īsā 'Ibayd, and Ṭāhir Lāshīn.
615. This is 'al-Rajul al-Marīḍ' in *al-Ḥajj Shalabī,* pp. 73—89.
616. *Ṭāriq al-Jāmi'ah,* pp. 117—25.
617. Although al-Ṭukhī is older than Idrīs, he started publishing only in 1956. His

collections are *Dāwūd al-Ṣaghīr* (1958), *Fi Ḍaw' al-Qamar* (1960), *al-Naml al-Aswad* (1963) and *Ibn al-'Alam* (1967).

618. Although Nash'at was born in the same year as Idrīs, he did not start publishing until 1956, when his first collection, *Masā' al-Khayr yā Gid'ān* (1956), appeared – it was difficult for his works, written solely in vernacular, to find a place in the periodicals. He remained faithful to his call of writing in 'āmmiyya despite severe opposition. His second and last collection, *Ḥilm Laylit Ta'ab*, appeared in 1962.
619. In 1953, Ḥusayn began publishing his works in various periodicals, then published two collections, *'Alāqah Basīṭah* (1963) and *Aṣl al-Sabab* (1967).
620. Fayyāḍ began in 1957, then published *'Aṭshān Yā Ṣabāya* (1961), *Wa-Ba'danā al-Ṭū'fān* (1968), *Aḥzān Ḥuzayrān* (1969), and *al-'Uyūn* (1972).
621. Munīb started in 1955, then published *al-Dīk al-Aḥmar* (1960), *Zā'ir al-Ṣabāḥ* (1964), and *Aḥzān al-Rabī'* (1967).
622. Mursī began, in 1956, publishing his works in periodicals, then published two collections, *al-Khawf* (1960), and *Khiṭāb Ilā Rajul Mayyit* (1967).
623. Zakī started in 1958, then published one collection, *Azmat Thiqah* (1965), before turning to cinema.
624. N'ūḥ started in 1956, published one collection, *Ṣabaḥiyyah Mubarakah* (1958), and then ceased writing.
625. Hāshim started in 1958, but his first and only collection, *al-Usṭurah,* did not come out until 1965.
626. Mūsā started, in 1953, younger than many of his colleagues, then published *al-Qamīs* (1958), *Ḥādith al-Nisf Mitr* (1962), *Ḥikāyāt* (1963), *Wajhā li-Zahr* (1966), and *Mashrū' Qatl Jārah* (1970).
627. 'Abd al-Raḥmān started in 1957, published *al-Baḥth 'an Majhūl* (1966) and then turned to television, plays and film.
628. Jād started as early in 1956, but his first and only collection, *al-Jidār,* did not appear until 1962.
629. Salīm started in 1956, then published *Lā Mafarr* (1960), and stopped writing for several years.
630. This list is long, yet there are still many other writers of this group who succeeded not only in publishing numerous works in periodicals but also in collecting them into book form. There are 'Abd al-Fattāḥ Rizq, who published *Bāb 14* (1960), and *'A al-Ribābah Yā Zaman* (1965); 'Abd al-Wahāb Dāwūd, who published *Nab' al-Ḥubb* (1963) and *al-Ḍaw'al-Aḥmar* (1968); Ṣalāḥ Ṭanṭāwi, who published *al-Nās wa'l-Ḥijārah* (1962) and *al-Naqsh 'Alā al-Ḥajar* (1966); 'Abd al-Mun'im Salīm, who published *Waraqat Tamghah* (1960) and *Mas'alat Karāmah* (1962); Fawziyya Muhrān, who published *Bayt al-Ṭalibāt* (1961); Muḥammad 'Abd al-'Azīz who published *Qiṣṣat Shajarah* (1964); Amīn Rayyān, who published *al-Mawqi'* (1967), and others.
631. Such as Abu'l-Najā, Fayyād, Mūsā, 'Abd al-Raḥmān and Jād.
632. Such as Nūḥ, Salīm, al-Ṭūkhī, Hāshim and Ḥusayn.
633. See the last section of the next chapter.
634. A detailed investigation of the second change in artistic sensibility is the subject of the final chapter of this study.
635. See *al-Risālah,* where he published many short stories between 1950 and 1953, e.g. in the issues of 5 June, 28 Aug., 16 Oct., 27 Nov. and 11 Dec. in 1950 and 19 March, 3 July and 3 Sept. in 1971.
636. The fact that it was a provincial institute, and that he remained there until he was twenty-one years old, may add weight to the argument.

637. Yet he read Maupassant's works in Muḥammad al-Sibā'i's translation before writing any of his published stories. His first published story, 'Khawfā min Abīh', exhibits striking Maupassant-like features. When he moved to Cairo to study at the university, he knew a group of friends – including 'Abd al-Jalīl Ḥasan and 'Abd al-Muḥsin Ṭaha Badr – who later became well-known critics; Ḥasan, especially, influenced his readings and introduced him to Chekhov and other Russian writers, who in turn had a tremendous impact on his work.
638. *Fatāh fi'l-Madīnah,* pp. 85—111.
639. *Ibid.*, pp. 25—40.
640. *Ibid.*, pp. 51—9.
641. *Ibid.*, pp. 41—50.
642. See e.g. 'al-Sibāq', pp. 25–44, and 'Nā'ib al-Ra'īs', pp. 111—21 in *al-Ibtisāmah al-Ghāmiḍah.*
643. *Al- Ibtisāmah al-Ghāmiḍah,* pp. 25—43.
644. *Ibid.*, pp. 87—98.
645. *Ibid.*, pp. 111—20.
646. *Ibid.*, pp. 3—11.
647. *Ibid.*, pp. 121—30.
648. *Ibid.*, pp. 45—57.
649. *Al-Nās wa'l-Ḥubb,* pp. 35—43.
650. *Al-Ibtisāmah al-Ghāmiḍah,* pp. 59—70.
651. If one judges by the sequence of narrative and the order of stories in the collection, 'Ḥādithat al-Wābūr' becomes the sequel to 'Qaryat Umm Muḥammad'; but if the historic course of events is the criterion, the order must be reversed.
652. *Al-Nās wa'l-Ḥubb.*
653. *Al-Nās wa'l-Ḥubb,* pp. 7—17.
654. *Ibid.*, pp. 45—57.
655. *Ibid.*, pp. 99—111.
656. *Fatāh fi'l-Madīnah,* pp. 60—84.
657. *Al-Ibtisāmah al-Ghāmiḍah,* pp. 71—86.
658. *Fatāh fi'l-Madīnah,* pp. 112—28.
659. *Al-Ibtisāmah al-Ghāmiḍah,* pp. 99—109.
660. *Ibid.,* pp. 131—43.
661. *Al-Nās wa'l-Ḥubb,* pp. 129—37.
662. Although there is evidence to suggest that the writer did not control the order of his stories in his first collection, and the publisher re-ordered them (see Anwar al-Mi'addawī's introduction to *Fatāh fi'l-Madīnah,* pp. 5—16), the order in the last two collections is clearly his own; for by then he was no longer a beginner and had established himself as a writer.
663. *Al-Nās wa'l-Ḥubb,* pp. 85—98.
664. See Anwar al-Mi'addawī's introduction to *Fatāh fi'l-Madīnah,* pp. 5—7.
665. See for example 'al-Ākharūn', *Ibid.,* pp. 51—9.
666. As is the case in most of the stories of his last collection, *al-Nās wa'l-Ḥubb,* however, the fact that it was published in Beirut might be responsible for the predominance of *fuṣḥā* in the dialogues of its stories.
667. See for example 'al-Sibāq', 'Nā'ib al-Ra'īs', 'al-Aslāk al-Shā'ika' in *al-Ibtisāmah al-Ghāmiḍah,* and 'al-'Ankabūt' and the title story of *al-Nās wa'l-Ḥubb.*
668. *Ibid.*
669. See e.g. most of his stories relating to conflict between the group and the

individual, particularly 'al-Ṭābūr', 'al-Ibtisāmah al-Ghāmiḍah', 'al-Aslāk al-Shā'ika', and 'al-'Ankabūt'.

Chapter Three

1. See Arthur O. Lovejoy, *Essays in the History of Ideas* (Baltimore, MA 1948), pp. 228–53. A similar argument can be found in Benedetto Croce, *Poetry*, III, ii: see Allan and Clark, *Literary Criticism: Pope to Croce* (Detroit 1962), p. 630.
2. See e.g. Mario Praz, *The Romantic Agony* (London 1933), and M. H. Abrams, *The Mirror and the Lamp* (Oxford 1953).
3. See René Wellek's papers 'The Concept of Romanticism in Literary History' and 'Romanticism Re-examined' in his collection *Concepts of Criticism* (New Haven, CT 1953), pp. 128–221.
4. See e.g. Ḥamdī Sakkūt, *The Egyptian Novel and its Main Trends* (Cairo 1971), pp. 11–45, Yūsuf 'Izz-l-Din, *al-Riwāyah fi'l-'Iraq* (Cairo 1973), pp. 153–203, and Nabīl Rāghib, *Fan al-Riwāyah 'ind Yūsuf al-Siba'ī* (Cairo 1973), pp. 194–235.
5. René Wellek and Austin Warren, *Theory of Literature* (London 1963), p. 265.
6. See Praz, *The Romantic Agony*, pp. 21–2.
7. Wellek and Warren, *Theory of Literature.*
8. Wellek, *Concepts of Criticism,* p. 196.
9. For a detailed study of romanticism in modern Arabic poetry in general and of these poets in particular, see M. M. Badawī, *A Critical Introduction to Modern Arabic Poetry* (Cambridge 1975), pp. 115–78.
10. See Chapter 3 of my *The Genesis of Arabic Narrative Discourse: A Study in the Sociology of Modern Arabic Literature* (London 1993), pp. 105–56.
11. Wellek, *Concepts of Criticism.*
12. *Ibid.*, p. 167.
13. Gabriel Josipovici, *The World and the Book: A Study in Modern Fiction* (London 1971), p. 180.
14. Northrop Frye, *Anatomy of Criticism: Four Essays* (Princeton, NJ 1957), p. 89, and for an elaborate discussion of the romantic views on symbolism and allegory see Edwin Honig, *Dark Conceit, The Making of Allegory* (Oxford 1966), pp. 39–50.
15. William Wordsworth, 'Poetry and Poetic Diction', in Edmund D. Jones, *English Critical Essays* (Oxford 1971), p. 7.
16. Charles Child Walcutt, *Man's Changing Mask: Modes and Methods of Characterisation in Fiction* (Minneapolis 1966), p. 7.
17. John Ruskin 'Of the Pathetic Fallacy', in Jones, *English Critical Essays,* p. 338.
18. See *Ibid.*, p. 326.
19. Mario Praz, *The Hero in Eclipse* (Oxford 1956), p. 45.
20. Wellek, *Concepts of Criticism*, p. 182.
21. Honig, *Dark Conceit*, p. 43.
22. *Ibid.*
23. Praz, *The Romantic Agony,* p. 32.
24. Wellek, *Concepts of* Criticism, p. 172.
25. *Ibid.*, p. 183.
26. Honig, *Dark Conceit*, p. 8.
27. Abrams, *The Mirror and the Lamp*, p. 102.
28. Wordsworth, 'Poetry and Poetic Diction', pp. 11–12.
29. Honig, *Dark Conceit*, p. 42.
30. Frank Kermode, *Romantic Image* (London 1957), p. 2.
31. Wellek, *Concepts of Criticism*, p. 161.

32. *Ibid.*, p. 179.
33. S. T. Coleridge, *Biographia Literaria* (London 1906), p. 166.
34. William Hazlitt, *Selected Essays,* p. 389.
35. Coleridge, *Biographia Literaria*, p. 160.
36. Frye, *Anatomy of Criticism*, p. 110.
37. Honig, *Dark Conceit*, p. 40.
38. James Gindin, *Harvest of a Quiet Eye: The Novel of Compassion* (Bloomington 1971), p. 16.
39. Frye, *Anatomy of Criticism*, pp. 96—7.
40. Gindin, *Harvest of a Quiet Eye*, p. 19.
41. Kermode, *Romantic Image*, 5.
42. F. W. J. Hemmings, *The Age of Realism* (London 1974), p. 37.
43. Frye, *Anatomy of Criticism*, p. 114.
44. Such as Tawfīq al-Ḥakīm, al-Māzinī, al-Miṣrī, *et al.*
45. A discussion of these themes and the older ones which remained from his early works can be found in section 3 of the previous chapter.
46. *Khalf al-Lithām*, pp. 5—24.
47. *Al-Aṭlāl,* pp. 117—28, it was rewritten as 'Fatah al-Qiṭār' in *Zāmir al-Ḥayy,* pp. 74—97.
48. *Khalf al-Lithām*, pp. 63—72.
49. *Al-Aṭlāl,* pp. 129—39.
50. *Al Shaykh 'Afallah,* pp. 123—34; it was rewritten as 'Nidā' al-Rūḥ' in *Tamr Ḥinnah 'Ajab*, pp. 235—48.
51. *Maktūb 'Alā al-Jabīn*, pp. 109—24.
52. *Ibid.*, pp. 137—58.
53. *Al-Shaykh 'Afallah,* pp. 34—69.
54. *Tamr Ḥinnah 'Ajab,* pp. 155—62.
55. *Maktūb 'Alā al-Jabīn,* pp. 187—94.
56. *Ibid.*, pp. 85—96.
57. *Kull 'Ām wa-Antum bi-Khayr,* pp. 129—48.
58. *Zāmir al-Ḥayy,* pp. 5—31.
59. *Al-Shaykh 'Afallah,* pp. 115—22.
60. Especially in its early version as the title story of *al-Shaykh 'Afallah*, pp. 4—18.
61. *Qalb Ghāniyah,* pp. 71—91.
62. *Ibid.*, p. 74.
63. *Ibid.*, p. 88.
64. *Ibid.*, p. 89.
65. *Ibid.*, p. 90.
66. *Al-Bārūnah Umm Aḥmad*, pp. 69—77.
67. *Qalb Ghāniyah,* pp. 137—57.
68. *Tamr Ḥinnah 'Ajab*, pp. 49—96.
69. As in 'Majnūn' in *Kull 'Ām...* pp. 55—102, and the title story of *Shabāb wa-Ghāniyat*, pp. 5—45.
70. See for example the title story of *Qalb Ghāniyah*, pp. 19—69, and 'Jarīmat Ḥubb'.
71. As in 'Zāmir al-Ḥayy' and 'Najiyyah Bint al-Fiqī' for example.
72. Maḥmūd Taymūr, *Dirāsāt fi'l-Qiṣṣah wa'l-Masraḥiyyah,* p. 13. Taymūr continues in the subsequent pages to develop a theory based on Coleridge's idea of primary and secondary imagination; see *Biographia Literaria,* XIII, pp. 153—67.
73. *Maktūb 'Alā al-Jabīn,* pp. 17—40.

74. *Ibid.*, pp. 125–36.
75. *Al-Bārūnah Umm Aḥmad*, pp. 7–16.
76. *Iḥsān Li'l-Lāh*, pp. 165–74.
77. *Tamr Ḥinnah 'Ajab*, pp. 97–125.
78. *Khalf al-Lithām*, pp. 131–5.
79. *Al-Aṭlāl*, pp. 101–16.
80. *Al-Shaykh 'Afallah*, pp. 19–32.
81. *Maktūb 'Ālā al-Jabīn*, pp. 213–26.
82. *Ibid.*, pp. 195–211.
83. *Qalb Ghāniyah*, pp. 115–36.
84. The romantic contradiction between the country and city can also be found in 'Muḥammad Afandī Ṣallī 'Ālā al-Nabī' in *Iḥsān Lil-Lah*, pp. 5–81, and 'Inā al-Sharīd' in *Tamr Ḥinnah 'Ajab*, pp. 199–218; while the nostalgia for the past is predominant in 'al-Ṭaqiyyah' in *al-Bārūnah Umm Aḥmad*, pp. 37–57.
85. *Qalb Ghāniyah*, pp. 93–113.
86. *Khalf al-Lithām*, pp. 107–16.
87. *Al-Shaykh 'Afallah*, pp. 147–57.
88. Such as the title story of *Bint al-Shayṭān*, pp. 11–54 and 'al-Ḥanash wa'l-'Aqrab' in *Ḥikāyat Abū 'ūf*, pp. 55–71.
89. See for example 'Kan fi Ghabir al-Zaman' in *Maktūb 'Alā al-Jabīn*, pp. 17–40, 'Zahrat al-Marqaṣ', pp. 83–101, and 'Ibnat Īzīs', pp. 165–74 in *Iḥsān lil-Lah* and 'Fī Ẓulmāt al-Layl'.
90. See for example 'Ḥasan Agha' in *al-Aṭlāl*, pp. 149–156, 'al-Sajīnah' in *Qalb Ghāniyah*, pp. 137–57, and 'Bambūsh' in *Maktūb 'Alā al-Jabīn*, pp. 97–108.
91. *Al-Shaykh 'Afallah*, pp. 101–13.
92. *Ibid.*, pp. 159–75.
93. See e.g. 'Bint al-Shayṭān', ''Indamā Naḥyā ma' al-Atyaf' and 'Ḥuriyyat al-Bahr'.
94. *Al-Shaykh 'Afallah*, pp. 90–100.
95. *Qalb Ghāniyah*, pp. 159–78.
96. *Tamr Ḥinnah 'Ajab*, pp. 199–218.
97. *Qalb Ghāniyah*, pp. 179–93.
98. *Maktūb 'Alā al-Jabīn*, pp. 227–32.
99. The manifesto was published on 28 June 1930 in *al-Siyāsah al-Usbū'iyyah*; the other signatories were Muḥammad Zakī 'Abd al-Qādir, Maḥmūd 'Izzat Mūsā, Muḥammad al-Asmar, Mu'awiya Muḥammad Nūr and Zakariyya 'Abdu. Although the manifesto was published only in 1930, some of the signatories, especially Nūr and 'Abd al-Qādir, aired many of its basic ideas in their articles in *al-Siyāsah al-Usbū'iyya*h throughout the preceding years. Yet when the manifesto was published it provoked wide response.
100. With the exception of al-Asmar and 'Abdu, the rest of the signatories tried their hand at the short story and published some of their work in *al-Siyāsah al-Usbū'iyyah* itself. After the closure of *al-Siyāsah al-Usbū'iyyah* few remained faithful to the genre.
101. Mūsā was among the most faithful to both the genre and the call to create a national literature. He gave considerable attention to short story writing, continuing, after the closure of *al-Siyāsa al-Usbū'iyya*, to publish his work in various magazines (such as *al-Jāmi'ah, al-Majallah al-Jadīdah, al-Fuṣūl, al-Usbū', al-Adab al-Ḥayy, Majallatī* and *al-Mihrajān*) throughout the 1930s and 1940s. Yet he failed to collect any of his numerous works in book form, and gave up writing altogether around 1949.

102. 'Abd al-Qādir started publishing his sketches of rustic scenes and characters in *al-Siyāsah al-Usbū'iyyah* in 1930 and continued afterwards in various other magazines, yet it took him a long time to develop his sketches into short stories, so his first collection, *Ṣuwar min al-Rīf,* did not come out until 1949.
103. Al-'Aqqād started publishing his stories in *al-Jāmi'ah* in the early 1930s, and published two collections: *Thawrah wa-Ḥanīn* (1939) and *Aḥlām al-Kharīf* (1941) before turning to radio plays.
104. Juhar stared in *al-Risālah* in the early 1930s, continued in various periodicals throughout the 1930s and 1940s, but did not publish his first collection, *Samirah Hanim*, until 1955, for he dedicated a great deal of his time and energy to writing films and screen-plays.
105. In his collection he advertised a forthcoming one, *al-Ḥubb 'ind Bā'i'i al-Lutariyya,* which he failed to publish before his premature death in the early 1950s.
106. The revolution and the war are a major strand in his novel *Ashbāl al-Thawrah* (1932).
107. He also translated articles on the beauty of ancient Egyptian antiquities, *al-Siyāsah al-Usbū'iyyah,* 26 July 1930.
108. *Al-Ward al-Abyaḍ*, pp. 56—92.
109. *Ibid.*, pp. 206—14.
110. *Ibid.*, pp. 94—110.
111. *Ibid.*, pp. 124—40.
112. *Ibid.*, pp. 188—94.
113. *Ibid.*, pp. 170—86.
114. *Ibid.*, pp. 112—22.
115. *Ibid.*, pp. 142—54.
116. *Ibid.*, pp. 156—68.
117. *Ibid.*, pp. 196—204.
118. *Ibid.*, pp. 216—24.
119. In his articles 'al-Nahḍah al-Qaṣaṣiyyah al-'Arabiyyah', *al-Siyāsah al-Usbū'iyyah,* 28 June 1930, and 'al-Thawrah al-Miṣriyyah: Atharuha fi'l-Ḥayāt al-Fikriyyah wa'l-Qaṣaṣiyyah', *al-Siyāsah al-Usbū'iyyah,* 6 June 1930, he blames sentimentality for the backwardness of his short stories.
120. For a detailed discussion see the following section (3) of this chapter.
121. Although mainly known as a poet, Nājī wrote and published many short stories. He began in *al-Jāmi'ah* in the 1930s and continued to publish his works in various periodicals, such as *Ḥakīm al-Bayt, al-Rāwī, Majallat*i, and *al-Qiṣṣah,* throughout the 1930s and 1940s. He collected many of these works into two collections (see the Appendix).
122. 'Abd Allāh is mainly a novelist, but he wrote short stories regularly from the mid-1940s until his death and published in various periodicals, such as *al-Kitāb, al-Riwāyah, Ruz al-Yūsuf, al-Muṣawwar, al-Risālah al-Jadīdah* and *al-Hilāl.* He also published many collections: see the Appendix.
123. Al-Qabbānī began to publish his stories in *al-Misriyyah* in the late 1940s and continued to do so in *al-Muṣawwar, al-Jumhūriyyah, al-Taḥrīr, al-Masā',* then turned to collections.
124. Like 'Abd Allāh, al-Siba'ī is mainly known as a novelist, but he started his career in the late 1930s as a short story writer, publishing in *al-Majallah al-Jadīdah, al-Kutla, Majallatī.* He continued to publish in the same journals throughout the 1940s and 1950s in *al-Hilāl, Ruz al-Yūsuf, al-Risālah al-Jadīdah,*

al-Hadaf, al-Būlīs and so on. His early works are more coherent than both his later ones and his novels; for a full list of his collections see the Appendix.

125. Al-Ḥabrūk's premature death did not allow him to develop his potential as a short story writer. His career began in the late 1940s in *Ruz al-Yūsuf,* and he continued to publish his works in *al-Jīl al-Jadīd, al-Idhā'ah al-Miṣriyyah, Ṣabāḥ al-Khayr* and others throughout the 1950s, and then collected most of them into two collections.
126. Sufi 'Abd Allāh started publishing her stories in *al-Muṣawwar* in the late 1940s and continued to do so in *al-Idhā'ah al-Miṣriyyah, al-Hilāl,* and *Ḥawwā'* throughout the 1950s. Although she continued to publish regularly and intensively since 1948, it took her almost ten years before starting to collect some of her works in book form.
127. There were some latecomers to the romantic genre: such as Sa'd Ḥāmid (1925—89), Ṣubḥī al-Jayyār (1927—80) and Tharwat Abāza (1927—98), whose collections are listed in the Appendix.
128. *Shahīrah,* pp. 7—80.
129. *Ibid.,* p. 10.
130. See e.g., 'al-Kursī al-Khālī' in *Rāhibah min al-Zamālik,* pp. 103—13, the title story of *Makhālib wa-Anyāb,* pp. 127—63, 'al-Wād al-Ḥilaywa' in *al-Mā' al-'Akir,* pp. 79—87, 'Ṭamṭam' in *Shahīrah,* pp. 87—100, the title story of *Majma' al-Shayāṭīn,* pp. 51—61, and 'Mawlid Mawwāl' in *al-Zaman al-Waghd,* pp. 20—5.
131. As in 'al-Taqrīr al-Awwal' in *Nisā' min Khazaf,* pp. 112—18, the title story of *Fī Qahwat al-Majādhīb,* pp. 5—13, and 'Fī Sūq al-Zalat' pp. 46—55, and 'al-Sitār al-Mumazzaq', pp. 92—100 of the same collection, 'Ḥubb' in *Shahīrah,* pp. 107—16, 'Thaghra fi'l-Jidār', 78–84, and 'Mu'jizat Kull Yawm', pp. 144—54 in *Majma' al-Shayāṭīn,* the title story of al-Zaman al-Waghd, pp. 3—19, and 'Qahwat al-Ṣabāḥ' in *al-Qamar al-Mashwī,* pp. 151—61.
132. As in the title story of *Majma' al-Shayāṭīn.*
133. As in 'Mawlid Mawwāl' in *al-Zaman al-Waghd,* pp. 20—5.
134. As in the title story of *Makhālib wa-Anyāb,* pp. 127—63.
135. As in 'al-Wād al-Ḥilaiwah' in *al-Mā' al-'Akir,* pp. 79—87, and 'Ṭamṭam' in *Shahīrah,* pp. 87—100.
136. As in 'Yawmiyyat Qalam' in *Rāhibah min al-Zamālik,* pp. 143—7.
137. As in 'Ḥubb' in *Shahīrah,* pp. 107—16, and "Urūq al-Wujūd' in *al-Qamar al-Mashwī,* pp. 71—6.
138. As in the title story of *al-Zaman al-Waghd,* pp. 3—19.
139. As in 'al-Kursī al-Khālī' in *Rāhibah min al-Zamālik,* pp. 103—13 which was rewritten later as 'Mīzān al-Ḥisāb' in *al-Qamar al-Mashwī,* pp. 133—42.
140. As in 'al-Rukn al-Mahjūr'in *Rāhibah min al-Zamālik.*
141. As in 'Thagra fi'l-Jidār' in *Majma' al-Shayāṭīn,* pp. 78—84, and 'Fann al-Mawt' in *al-Zaman al-Waghd,* pp. 113—28.
142. *Fī Qahwat al-Majādhīb,* pp. 56—62.
143. Such as the title stories of *Makhālib wa-Anyāb* and *al-Zaman al-Waghd,* and 'al-Wād al-Ḥilaywa' in *al-Mā' al-'Akir,* pp. 79—87.
144. *Al-Qamar al-Mashwī,* pp. 71—6.
145. *Shahīrah,* pp. 81—6.,
146. Such as 'Shahīrah' and 'Ṭamṭam' in *Shahīrah,* pp. 7—80 and 87—100, and 'Raqṣat al-Shams' in *Nisā' min Khazaf,* pp. 34—9.
147. As in the title story of *Fī Qahwat al-Majādhīb,* pp. 5—13.
148. See e.g. 'al-Wād al-Ḥilaiwa' in *al-Ma' al-'Akir,* pp. 79—87.

149. As in 'Ḥālat Nafs', in *Nisā' min Khazaf*, pp. 119—24, and 'Andalusiyyah' in *al-Zaman al-Waghd*, pp. 109—12.
150. See e.g. 'Qiddīsah min Bab al-Sha'ariyyah' in *Rāhibah min al-Zamālik*, pp. 7—27.
151. As in 'al-Wād al-Ḥilaiwa', and the title story of *Mama' al-Shayāṭīn*, pp. 51—61.
152. As in 'Mu'jizat Kull Yawm', *ibid.*, pp. 144—54, and 'al-Sitar al-Mumazaq' in *Fī Qahwat al-Majādhīb*, pp. 92—100.
153. As in 'Qiddīsah min Bāb al-Sha'ariyyah', in *Rāhibah min al-Samalik*, pp. 7—27.
154: *Rāhibah min al-Zamālik*, pp. 7—27.
155. Such as 'Ḥālat Nafs' in *Nisā' min Khazaf*, pp. 119—24, 'Ḥubb' in *Shahīrah*, pp. 107—16, and 'Naffūsah' in *Majma' al-Shayāṭīn*, pp. 5—13.
156. *Majma' al-Shayāṭīn*, pp. 5—13.
157. *Fī Qahwat al-Majādhīb*, pp. 34—42.
158. See e.g. 'Khuṭwah Mafqūdah' in *Rāhibah min al-Zamālik*, pp. 65—72.
159. As in 'al-Amīr Shīkhu' in *Makhālib wa-Anyab*, pp. 41—6.
160. As in 'al-Ajr wa'l-Thawāb', *ibid.*, pp. 51—61.
161. As in 'Darb Abū Liḥāf', *ibid.*, pp. 87—99, and 'Zihara' in *Majma' al-Shayāṭīn*, pp. 38—44.
162. *Nisā' min Khazaf*, pp. 20—31.
163. Such as 'Maẓlūma' in *al-Mā' al-'Akir*, pp. 25—32, and 'al-'Umr Kulluh' in *al-Zaman al-Waghd*, pp. 85—97.
164. *Fī Qahwat al-Majādhīb*, pp. 101—06.
165. As in 'Laylat al-'Urs al-Thāniya' in *Rāhibah min al-Zamālik*, pp. 57—64, and 'al-Rukh al-Mahjūr' in *al-Qamar al-Mashwī*, pp. 111—24.
166. *Nisā' min Khazaf*, pp. 86—93, then was rewritten as 'al-Ṭifl wa'l-Manbūdh' in *al-Zaman al-Waghd*, pp. 98—103.
167. See e.g. 'Bint min Sanah Khamisah' in *Majma' al-Shayāṭīn*, pp. 117—26, and 'Ṭarīq al-Qubūr' in *al-Mā' al-'Akir*, pp. 9—15.
168. See e.g. 'Mazlumah' in *al-Ma' al-'Akir*, pp. 25—32, and 'al-Jariyah', in *al-Zaman al-Waghd*, pp. 50—60.
169. As in the case of 'Ibn Anīsa', pp. 17—34, and "Asr 'Iways al-Dhahabī', pp. 43—8 in *al-Mā' al-'Akir*, and 'Bint al-Ḥalāl' in *Shahīrah*, pp. 123—32.
170. *Al-Mā' al-'Akir*, pp. 55—60.
171. *Al-Qamar al-Mashwī*, pp. 3—12.
172. This Byronic hero becomes in some of Makkāwī's work a recurrent type, see for example the title story of *Fī Qahwat al-Majādhīb*, 6—13 and 'Ṣāni' al-Mawt' in the same collection, pp. 74—80, and 'Ṭarīq al-Qubūr', pp. 9—15, 'Ibn Anīsa', pp. 17—24, and "Alā Baḥr Shibīn', pp. 89—103 in *al-Mā' al-'Akir*, the title story of *al-Zaman al-Waghd*, pp. 3—19, and 'al-Janāḥ al-Maksūr' in *al-Qamar al-Mashwī*, pp. 39—58.
173. As in 'al-Raqs fi'l-Ma'bad' in *Nisā' min Khazaf*, pp. 5—11, and 'al-Raghbah al-Maktūbah' in *Rāhibah min al-Zamālik*, pp. 39—48.
174. See e.g. 'al-Yanbū'' in *Rāhibah min al-Zamālik*, pp. 149—75.
175. As is the case in 'Jamā'at Inqādh al-Damāmah al-Musharradah' in *Rāhibah min al-Zamālik*, pp. 49—56.
176. See e.g. 'al-Raqs fi'l-Ma'bad', pp. 5—10, and 'Ḥādithat Khiyānah', pp. 79—83 in *Nisā' min Khazaf*, and 'Ḥikmat al-Majnūn' in *Rāhibah min al-Zamālik*, pp. 135—40.
177. As in 'Raqṣat al-Shams' in *Nisā' min Khazaf*, pp. 34—9.
178. 'Wahībah' in *Makhālib wa-Anyāb*, pp. 7—23.

179. As in 'Tawbat Nawāl' in *Fī Qahwat al-Majādhīb*, pp. 14–33, and 'Qarārīṭ Raḍwān al-Tis'ah' in *al-Mā' al-'Akir*, pp. 109–17.
180. See for example 'Rajulān fi Zinzānah' in *Majma' al-Shayāṭīn*, pp. 73–7 and 'Miṣriyyah' in *Shahīrah*, pp. 101–05.
181. See for example 'Ṣāni' al-Mawt' in *Fī Qahwat al-Majādhīb*, pp. 74–80.
182. Such as '7 September' in *Majma' al-Shayāṭīn*, pp. 62–72, and 'Andalusiyyah' in *al-Zaman al-Waghd*, pp. 109–12.
183. As is the case in 'Madad' in *Majma' al-Shayāṭīn*, pp. 45–50, and the title story of *Fī Qahwat al-Majādhīb*, pp. 5–13.
184. As in 'Ṣāfaḥt al-Mawt' in *Fī Qahwat al-Majādhīb*, pp. 107–12 and 'Asl al-Hikayah', in *Shahīrah*, pp. 133–9.
185. See e.g.'al-Ḥaṣīrah' in *Majma' al-Shayāṭīn*, pp. 14–21.
186. *Makhālib wa-Anyāb*, pp. 57–69, it also appeared in *al-Mā' al-'Akir*, pp. 69–78.
187. See e.g. 'al-Khinzīr' in *Nisā' min Khazaf*, pp. 77–8, 'al-Yanbū'' in *Rāhibah min al-Zamālik*, pp. 149–75, 'Ṣāfaḥt al-Mawt' in *Fī Qahwat al-Majādhīb*, pp. 107–12, and 'Nibayyin Zayn' in *Makhālib wa-Anyāb*, pp. 33–9.
188. See e.g. 'Fi'l-Mujtama'', pp. 43–5, and 'Fi Sūq al-Zalāṭ', pp. 46–55 in *Fī Qahwat al-Majādhīb* and 'Wahībah', pp. 7–23, and 'Maṣra' Ḥimār', pp. 79–85 in *Makhālib wa-Anyāb*.
189. 'Abd al-Raḥmān Abū 'Ūf, 'Ḥiwār Ma'a ... Sa'd Makkāwī', *Ruz al-Yūsuf*, 2 July 1973.
190. So when he speaks about his departure from romantic notions, he merely describes the artistic evolution of his work, and perhaps reflects the general impression about romanticism as a notorious charge. Apart from his flat out discordance with the label, he expresses most of his views of both the form and substance of his work in clear romantic terminology; see pp. 34–7 of the same interview, *ibid*.
191. See e.g. 'al-Raqṣ fi'l-Ma'bad', pp. 5–10, 'Cabaret', pp. 32–3, 'Raqṣat al-Shams', pp. 34–9, 'Āniyat al-'Iṭr', pp. 40–1, and 'Mashrū' Qublah', pp. 84–5 in *Nisā' min Khazaf*.
192. As is the case in 'al-Mutasha'biṭūn', pp. 26–36, 'al-'Umr Kullu', pp. 85–97, and "Izbit al-Shaykh al-Shadhili', pp. 139–52 in *al-Zaman al-Waghd*, and 'al-Janāḥ al-Maksur', pp. 39–58, and 'al-Rukn al-Mahjūr', pp. 111–24 in *al-Qamar al-Mashwī*, in addition to the title story of this collection, pp. 3–12.
193. In e.g. 'Maṣra' Ḥimār', *Makhālib wa-Anyāb*, pp. 79–85, the hero refers to the main action of the title story of *al-Mā' al-'Akir*, pp. 3–18 and to some of its characters.
194. There are many characters who appear in more than one story with reference to certain aspects of their personalities illustrated in the previous story/stories, see e.g. 'Fī Sūq al-Zalaṭ', pp. 46–55 and 'al-Sitār al-Mumazzaq', pp. 92–100 in *Fī Qahwat al-Majādhīb*, 'Maẓlūmah', pp. 25–32, "Alā Baḥr Shibīn', pp. 89–103, 'Qarārīṭ Raḍwān al-Tis'a', pp. 109–17 and the title story in *al-Mā' al-'Akir*.
195. Apart from Makkāwī's home village al-Dalātūn there is e.g. Birkit al-'Aymā' which appears in various *al-Mā' al-'Akir* stories and the theatre of Shahīrah Zuhdī, which appears in the title story of *Shahīrah* and in 'Fī Ṣabīl al-Fann' in *Makhālib wa-Anyāb*, pp. 71–8.
196. See the interview with Makkāwī, *Ruz al-Yūsuf*, 2 July 1973.
197. See e.g. 'al-Masākīn', pp. 56–62, and 'Ṣāni' al-Mawt', pp. 74–80 in *Fī Qahwat al-Majādhīb*, the title story of *Shahīrah*, and 'Bint min Sana Khamisa' in *Majma' al-Shayāṭīn*, pp. 117–26.

198. As is the case in the title stories of *al-Zaman al-Waghd,* pp. 3—19, and *al-Qamar al-Mashwī,* pp. 3—12, and 'Tawbat Nawal' in *Fī Qahwat al-Majādhīb,* pp. 14—33.
199. In the interview with him, Ruz al-Yūsuf, 2 July 1973, Makkāwī professes a clear conviction in the superhuman, in the super-individual in whom the gap between the essence and appearance vanishes.
200. See e.g. 'Wahībah', in *Makhālib wa-Anyab,* pp. 7—23, 'Fi Ṣiḥat Shalabī' in *Shahīrah,* pp. 141—7, and 'al-Mayyit wa'l-Ḥayy' in *al-Zaman al-Waghd,* pp. 37—49.
201. I. A. Richards, *Practical Criticism: A Study in Literary Judgment* (London 1929), pp. 258—9. There are of course many schools of thought that would disagree with this position.
202. R. Scholes and R. Kellogg, *The Nature of Narrative* (Oxford 1966), p. 83.
203. There are of course questions of taste and public preferences, as well as the need to educate the public and advance certain development in narrative, subjects that are worthy of lengthy investigation.
204. The publishing house is Dār al-Jāmi'ah li-l-Tab' wa'l-Nashr, which specialised in publishing novels and collections of short stories. However, Kāmil inherited much of this tradition, for he is the son of Muḥammad 'Alī Kāmil, the lawyer and owner of Dār al-Taraqqī li'l-Tab' wa'l-Nashr. Kāmil, the father, published Qāsim Amīn's famous book *Taḥrīr al-Mar'ah* (1899) and wrote its enthusiastic introduction. Dār al-Taraqqī also published Kāmil's first collection of short stories, *al-Mutamarridūn* (1931): a significant title which speaks for the generally enlightened milieu in which our author was brought up.
205. Although they are both from a middle-class background, Kāmil comes from a more comfortably off family; and unlike Ḥaqqī, he is of Egyptian descent.
206. See Maḥmūd Kāmil, *Yawmiyyāt Muḥām Misrī,* pp. 50—62.
207. For a detailed list of these collections, and of Kamil's other collections, see the Appendix.
208. The plays are *al-Wuḥūsh* (1926) and *Fāṭimah* (1929) and the novel is *Ḥayāt al-Ẓalām* (1934). He also published four translated plays and a book on drama, *al-Masraḥ al-Jadīd* (1933), in addition to a collection of literary essays, *Ṣayḥāt Jadīdah fi'l-Naqd wa'l-Fann wa'l-Adab* (1932).
209. Romantic and sentimental French literature constitute a great deal of his literary knowledge. His autobiographical work *Yawmiyyāt Muḥāmi Misrī,* demonstrates his exclusively French cultural background (pp. 53—8, 65, 82—3, 99, 102—09) and his poor command of English culture (see p. 75 where he refers to Samuel Johnson as the American thinker). He is also a great name dropper, for many of his stories are packed with references to French writers and their works; see e.g. 'Khaybat Ḥilm', pp. 8–20, 'al-Ḥanīn', pp. 123—35, and 'Zawjat al-Mu'allif', pp. 205—14 in *al-Mutamarridūn,* and 'Zawāj Zaynab Hānim', pp. 86—98, 'al-Ukdhūba', pp. 164—71, 'Gharām Mulawath', pp. 182—93, and 'Shabaḥ al-'Ashīqah', pp. 202—10 in *Awwal Yanāyir,* and 'Da'īnī Uḥibbuk', pp. 79—98, and 'al-Bayt al-Masmūm', pp. 99—144 in *Ḥuṭām Imra'ah.*
210. With the exception of 'al-Darajah al-Sādisah' the twenty stories of *al-Mutamarridūn* are peopled with middle- and upper-class characters. So are all the stories in *'Uyūn Ma'ṣūba, al-Rijāl Munāfiqūn, Ḥuṭām Imra'ah,* and *Fātayāt Mansiyyāt* and most of the stories of *Fi'l-Bayt wa'l-Shāri', Bā'i' al-Aḥlām, Awwal Yanāyir, al-Majnūnah,* and *al-Rabī' al-Āthim.*

211. See e.g. 'al-Ḥanīn' in *al-Mutamarridūn,* pp. 123—35, and the title story of *Awwal Yanāyir,* pp. 6—21, and 'Zawaj Zaynab Hānim', pp. 86—98, and 'Kibriyā' Imra'ah', pp. 122—30 in the same collection.
212. As is the case in 'al-Māl' in *al-Mutamarridūn,* pp. 233—43, the title story of *'Uyūn Ma'ṣūbah,* pp. 8—20, 'al-Qafaṣ al-Dhahabī' in *Awwal Yanāyir,* pp. 148—53 and 'Āmāl' in *al-Rijāl Munāfiqūn,* pp. 7—45.
213. See e.g. 'Khaybat Ḥilm' in *al-Mutamarridūn,* pp. 8—20, 'Imra'ah Ukhrā', pp. 42—9, 'Gharām Mafqūd', pp. 50—9, 'al-Laylah Laylatunā', pp. 60—3, and 'Shirrīra', pp. 95—134 in *'Uyūn Ma'ṣūbah.*
214. See e.g. 'Hiya al-Ghīrah', pp. 189—204, and 'al-Shakk al-Hā'il', pp. 224—34 in *al-Mutamarridūn,* the title story of *'Uyūn Ma'ṣūbah,* and 'Shabaḥ al-'Ashīqah' in *Awwal Yanāyir,* pp. 202—10.
215. As is the case in 'Ḥālat Junūn', pp. 22—32, and 'al-Rābiḥa', pp. 97—109 in *al-Mutamarridūn,* 'al-Ukdhūba' in *Awwal Yanāyir,* pp. 164—71, 'al-Liqā' al-Akhīr' in *'Uyūn Ma'ṣūbah,* and 'Baqiyyat Rajal', pp. 39—66, and 'al-'Umr al-Ḥālim', pp. 81—93 in *Fātayāt Mansiyyāt.*
216. See e.g. 'al-Ḥanīn', pp. 123—35, 'al-Kibriyā' al-Muḥaṭṭama', pp. 245—55 in *al-Mutamarridūn,* 'Zawaj Zaynab Hānim' in *Awwal Yanāyir,* pp. 86—98, and 'Anqāḍ Imra'ah' in *Fātayāt Mansiyyāt.*
217. As is the case in 'al-Rujūlah al-Kāmilah' in *al-Mutamarridūn,* pp. 165—76, 'Ba'd Layla' in *Awwal Yanāyir,* pp. 80—5, and 'Bukhur', and 'Muṭribah Mātat' in *Ḥuṭām Imra'ah,* pp. 53—78.
218. See e.g. 'al-Rasā'il al-Multahiba', pp. 111—21 and 'al-Rujūla al-Kāmila', pp. 165—76 in *al-Mutamarridūn,* 'Gharām Mulawwath' in *Awwal Yanāyir,* pp. 182—93, and 'Bukhūr', pp. 81—2, and 'Ra'dat al-Dhikrā', pp. 135—43 in *'Uyūn Ma'ṣūbah.*
219. Richards, *Practical Criticism*, p. 262.
220. See e.g. 'Ḥālat Junūn', pp. 22—32, and 'al-Ighrā'', pp. 156—63 in *al-Mutamarridūn,* 'al-Fāji'ah', pp. 100—10, and 'Shabaḥ al-'Ashīqah', pp. 202—10 in *Awwal Yanāyir.*
221. As is the case in 'Zawaj Zaynab Hānim', 'Thawrat Qalb', pp. 140—7, and 'Gharām Mulawwath', pp. 182—93 in *Awwal Yanāyir* and the title story of *Ḥuṭām Imra'ah,* pp. 5—52.
222. See e.g. 'Khaybat Ḥulm' in *al-Mutamarridūn,* pp. 8—20, most of the stories of *'Uyūn Ma'ṣūba*, and the title story of *al-Rijāl Munāfiqūn*, pp. 7—45.
223. As is the case in '25 December', pp. 22—38, and 'al-Mutaraddiyyah', pp. 172—80 in *Awwal Yanāyir*, 'Laylah Musammamah', pp. 47—82, and 'al-Maw'ūda', pp. 105—29 in *al-Rijāl Munāfiqūn.*
224. See e.g. 'al-Shahīd', pp. 59—74, 'al-Rābiḥah', pp. 97—109, and 'Hiya al-Ghīrah', pp. 189—204 in *al-Mutamarridūn*, and 'al-'Ayn Tabkī' in *Fātayāt Mansiyyāt*, pp. 7—37.
225. As is the case in 'al-Rujūlah al-Kāmilah', pp. 165—76, and 'al-Mal', pp. 233—43 in *al-Mutamarridūn*, and 'Ba'd al-Ḥādith' in Awwal Yanāyir, 50–56, and 'Shirrīrah' in *'Uyūn Ma'ṣūbah,* pp. 95—134.
226. See e.g. 'Ḥālat Junūn', pp. 22—32, and 'Rifqī Bey 'Anīd', pp. 45—57 in *al-Mutamarridūn,* and 'Imr'at al-Qadar', pp. 25—37, and 'Qāri'āt al-Hubb', pp. 38—41 in *'Uyūn Ma'ṣūbah.*
227. As is the case in 'al-Rasā'il al-Multahibah', pp. 111—21, 'al-Ḥanīn', pp. 123—35, and 'Mustaqbal Fāṭimah', pp. 147—54, in *al-Mutamarridūn,* and the title story of *Ḥuṭām Imra'ah,* pp. 5—52.
228. See e.g. 'Ḥālat Junūn', pp. 22—32, and 'al-Shaykh Khalīfa Yaqtul', pp. 137—45

in *al-Mutamarridūn*, '25 December' in *Awwal Yanāyir*, pp. 22—38, and 'Zallat al-Abad' in *Fātayāt Mansiyyāt*, pp. 67—80.

229. As is the case in 'al-Shahīd', pp. 59—74, 'al-Dimā'', pp. 87—96, and 'Ḥaḍrat al-Bāshmuhandis', pp. 177—88, in *al-Mutamarridūn*, 'al-Faḍīḥah', pp. 58—68, and 'al-Faji'ah', pp. 100—10 in *Awwal Yanāyir*, and 'al-Maw'ūdah' in *al-Rijāl Munāfiqūn*, 105—29.

230. Such as 'Khaybat Ḥilm', pp. 8—20, 'al-Shahīd', pp. 59—74, and 'al-Mal', pp. 233—43 in *al-Mutamarridūn*, the title story of *Awwal Yanāyir*, pp. 6—21, and 'Layla 'Āṣifa', pp. 130—48, and the title story of *al-Rijāl Munāfiqūn*, pp. 7—45.

231. See e.g. 'al-Fāji'a', pp. 100—10, 'Kibriyā' Imra'ah', pp. 122—30, and 'al-Qafaṣ al-Dhahabī', pp. 148—53 in *Awwal Yanāyir*, 'Gharām' in *'Uyūn Ma'ṣūbah*, pp. 64—80, and 'Da'īnī Uḥibbuk' in *Ḥuṭām Imra'ah*, pp. 79—98.

232. Such as 'Rifqī Bey 'Anīd', pp. 45—57, 'al-Shahīd', pp. 59—74, 'al-Dimā'', pp. 87—96, 'al-Ḥanīn', pp. 123—35, 'Mustaqbal Fāṭimah', pp. 147—54, and 'al-Shakk al-Hā'il', 224—32, in *al-Mutamarridūn*, and the title stories of *Ḥuṭām Imra'ah*, pp. 5—52, and *al-Rijāl Munāfiqūn*, pp. 7—45.

233. In this respect, Kāmil's father's support for women's emancipation may have influenced our author.

234. Such as 'Mustaqbal Fāṭimah' in *al-Mutamarridūn*, pp. 147—54, and 'Ṣawt Zaynab' in *Awwal Yanāyir*, pp. 132—9.

235. See e.g. 'al-Darajah al-Sādisah', pp. 34—43, and 'al-Kibriyā' al-Muḥaṭṭamah', pp. 245—55 in *al-Mutamarridūn*, and 'al-Faqr' in *Awwal Yanāyir*, pp. 40—8.

236. As is the case in 'al-Faqr' in *Awwal Yanāyir*, pp. 40—8, 'Āmāl' in *al-Rijāl Munāfiqūn*, pp. 84—104, and 'Dhikrā Gharām' in *al-Jāmi'ah*, 28 Feb. 1935.

237. See e.g. 'al-Dimā'', pp. 87—96, and 'al-Rujūlah al-Kāmilah', pp. 165—76in *al-Mutamarridūn*, and 'Kibriyā' Imra'ah' in *Awwal Yanāyir*, pp. 122—30. The interesting point in these stories is that Kāmil suggests that being poor brings out these moral and humane qualities in the character.

238. Such as 'al-Kibriyā' al-Muḥaṭṭamah' in *al-Mutamarridūn*, pp. 245—55 and 'Kibriyā' Imra'ah' in *Awwal Yanāyir*, pp. 122—30.

239. As is the case in 'al-Māl' in *al-Mutamarridūn*, pp. 233—43, and 'al-Faqr' in *Awwal Yanāyir*, pp. 40—8.

240. See e.g. 'al-Rujūlah al-Kāmilah' in *al-Mutamarridūn*, pp. 165—76, and 'al-Dasīsah' in *Awwal Yanāyir*, pp. 112—21.

241. As in 'Ṣawt Zaynab' in *Awwal Yanāyir*, pp. 132—9, the title story of *Ḥuṭām Imra'ah*, pp. 5—52, and 'Laylah Musammamah' in *al-Rijāl Munāfiqūn*, pp. 47—82.

242. As in the case in 'al-Dimā'', pp. 87—96 and 'Ḥaḍrat al-Bashmuhandis', pp. 177—88 in *al-Mutamarridūn*, the title story of 'Uyūn Ma'ṣūbah, pp. 8—20, and 'al-'Ayn Tabkī', in *Fātayāt Mansiyyāt*, pp. 7—37.

243. See e.g. 'al-Qātilah', pp. 75—85, 'al-Ḥanīn', pp. 123—35, and 'al-Ighrā'', pp. 155—63 in *al-Mutamarridūn*; 'al-Faqr', pp. 40—8, 'Ya Rayt Zamāni Marra', pp. 154—63 in *Awwal Yanāyir*, and 'Qublah Dhāt Laylah' in *al-Rijāl Munāfiqūn*, pp. 149—60.

244. Most of his love scenes take place in town, because of the association between love and refined cultural activities, often in cinemas, playhouses, opera houses and music halls. The rest are set in the urban domestic scenery, sports clubs and offices; see e.g. all the love stories in *al-Mutamarridūn* and *Awwal Yanāyir*.

245. As is the case in 'al-Ḥanīn' in *al-Mutamarridūn*, pp. 123—35 and 'al-Faḍīḥah' in *Awwal Yanāyir*, pp. 58—68.

246. See e.g. 'Ṣawt Zaynab' in *Awwal Yanāyir,* pp. 132—9.
247. As is the case in 'al-Ḥanīn', 'al-Shahīd', pp. 59—74, and 'al-Kibriyā' al-Muḥaṭṭama', pp. 245—55 in *al-Mutamarridūn*; 'al-Faḍīḥa' and 'Ṣawt Zaynab' in *Awwal Yanāyir*, and 'al-Bayt al-Masmūm' in *Ḥuṭām Imra'ah,* pp. 99—144.
248. Indeed, Kāmil seems to be a name-dropper by nature, and it is little surprising that his characters follow suit. In one short collection. *'Uyūn Ma'ṣūba,* there are more than twenty instances in which he mentions European memories, places, literary works, etc. See e.g. pp. 10, 14, 15, 35, 38—40, 52, 67, 76, 77, 85, 91—2, 95, 98, etc.
249. Such as 'al-Ḥanīn', pp. 123—35 and 'al-Ighrā'', pp. 155—63 in *al-Mutamarridūn.*
250. Such as 'al-Risā'il al-Multahibah' in *al-Mutamarridūn,* pp. 111—21; 'al-Tha'r al-Khā'ib' in *Awwal Yanāyir,* pp. 70—9; 'Da'inī Uḥibbuk' in *Ḥuṭām Imra'ah,* pp. 79—98; and 'al-Mutasharridah' in *Fātayāt Mansiyyāt,* pp. 121—36.
251. Such as 'Rifqī Bey 'Anīd', pp. 45—57, 'al-Shahīd', pp. 59—74, and 'Ḥādithat al-Marqaṣ', pp. 216-24, in *al-Mutamarridūn,* and the title stories of *Awwal Yanāyir,* pp. 6—21, and *al-Rijāl Munāfiqūn,* pp. 7—45.
252. See e.g. 'Zawjat al-Mu'allif' in *al-Mutamarridūn,* pp. 205—14; 'Shirrīrah', in *'Uyūn Ma'ṣūbah,* pp. 95—134; and the title story of *Ḥuṭām Imra'ah,* pp. 5—52.
253. Such as 'Ḥaḍrat al-Bashmuhandis', pp. 177—88 and 'al-Rujūlah al-Kāmilah', pp. 165—76 in *al-Mutamarridūn*; 'al-Tha'r al-Kha'ib' in *Awwal Yanāyir,* pp. 70—9; and 'Muṭribah Mātat' in *al-Rijāl Munāfiqūn,* pp. 53—78.
254. See e.g. his collection *al-Rijāl Munāfiqūn* where all the stories but two are in the form of a letter or letters; almost no collection is free from this form.
255. Apart from the fact that *adab al-rasā'il* is a traditional and popular form of writing, *Rasā'il al-gharām* was in great demand at that time. A semi-educated reader aspires to experience the joy of emotions and is unable to articulate his feelings; thus wants his writers to provide him with ready-made love letters to copy and mail to his sweetheart. Kāmil, who is interested in the wider reading public, used his stories to supply his reader not only with many examples of refined love letters, but also with the means to deliver them to the beloved in a closed society where girls have little or no privacy and where love is a furtive activity.
256. This is the major technique used in his only novel *Hayat al-Ẓalām* and in many short stories see e.g.; 'Zawāj Zaynab Hānim', pp. 68—98, and 'Thawrat Qalb', pp. 140—7 in *Awwal Yanāyir*, 'Laylah Musammamah' in *al-Rijāl Munāfiqūn*, 47—82; and 'Baqiyyat Rajul' in *Fātayāt Mansiyyāt,* pp. 39—66.
257. See e.g. 'Imra'at al-Qadar', pp. 25—7, 'Imra'ah Ukhrā', pp. 42—9, 'Gharām Mafqūd' pp. 50—9, and 'al-Liqā' al-Akhīr', pp. 83—94 in *'Uyūn Ma'ṣūbah,* and the title story of the same collection, pp. 8—20.
258. See e.g. *al-Mutamarridūn,* pp. 92, 144, 214, 243, 250.
259. See e.g. on *al-Mutamarridūn, al-Hilāl,* Jan. 1932, p. 458, *al-Balāgh,* 23 Jan. 1932, p. 3, and *al-Ṣabāḥ,* 29 Jan. 1932, p. 43; on *Fi'l-Bayt wa'l-Shāri', al-Jāmi'a,* 16 Mar. 1933, *al-Siyāsa,* 19 Mar. 1933, and *Ruz al-Yūsuf,* 3 Apr. 1933, p. 33, on *Awwal Yanāyir, al-Hilāl,* Feb. 1936, p. 474, and on *al-Majnūnah, al-Hilāl,* Nov. 1938, p. 15.
260. See e.g. *al-Hilāl,* Jan. 1932, p. 458, Feb. 1936, p. 474, and Nov. 1938, p. 115.
261. See e.g. *al-Hilāl* as above, and *al-Muqtataf,* Feb. 1932, p. 233.
262. Nu'mān 'Āshūr, *Ḥawādīt 'Amm Farj,* pp. 16—17.
263. 'Abd al-Raḥmān al-Sharqāwī, *al-Shawāri' al-Khalfiyyah*, pp. 207—08.
264. Especially in his first two collections *al-Rabī'* (1934) and *Madīḥah* (1936).

265. Al-'Aqqād was a regular contributor to Kāmil's magazines *al-Jāmi'a* and *Majallat al-'Ishrīn Qiṣṣah*. He almost stopped writing when Kāmil did so.
266. Such as 'Abd al-'Azīz Sāsī in his collection *Min al-A'māq* (1933), and 'Abd al-Samī' al-Miṣrī in his collection *Aḥlām al-Shabībah* (1940).
267. Al-Sibā'ī is clearly influenced by Kāmil's works; his collections of short stories which appeared, at regular intervals, throughout the 1940s reveal that most clearly.
268. Although Ṣidqī started publishing when Kāmil had stopped writing, at the beginning of the 1940s, Kāmil's influence on her work is apparent, especially on her themes and characterisation; for a complete list of her work see the Appendix.
269. Like al-Sibā'ī, al-Wirdānī is clearly influenced by Kāmil. He started publishing in the mid-1940s, but his first collection, *al-Madīnah al-Majnūnah*, did not come out until 1950. He almost stopped writing by 1960, but in the mid-1960s started collecting many of his old works in book form: see the Appendix.
270. Self-taught, Ghurāb started publishing in the early 1940s. His first collection, *al-Ḍabāb*, appeared in 1942 and after that he continued to publish regularly until his death. For a full list of his works see the Appendix.
271. Being the son of Fāṭimah al-Yūsuf, founder and owner of *Ruz al-Yūsuf*, publishing was easy for 'Abd al-Quddūs, so he began issuing his short stories in *Ruz al-Yūsuf* in 1938 and continued to publish in periodicals and in book form thereafter. Although he spent a great deal of his time on journalism and the novel, he published a considerable number of collections of short stories: see the Appendix.
272. Such as Shukrī 'Abdīn in his collections *Fātinat al-Ḥayy* (1953) and *Laylat al-Mawlid* (1953), and Birtī Bidār in his collection *Bā'i'at al-Dumū'* (1957).
273. For a detailed account of these debates see Mark Slonim, *Soviet Russian Literature, Writers and Problems 1917–67* (Oxford 1967), pp. 32—58 and 151—64; Alan Swingewood, *The Novel and Revolution*, pp. 68–111; and Jurgen Ruhle, *Literature and Revolution: A Critical Study of the Writer and Communism in the Twentieth Century* (London 1969), pp. 4—142.
274. However, the researcher subscribes to the views, expressed in detail in Swingewood's *The Novel and Revolution,* that socialist realism has little in common with true Marxian aesthetics, and presents a deviation from Lenin's *patiinost* in arts, for it becomes more or less an administrative means for the organisation and control of art and literature.
275. For a brief, but sufficient, account of this fundamental Marxist concept and its literary implication, see Raymond Williams, *Marxism and Literature* (Oxford 1977), pp. 45—82.
276. See K. Marx, *The Eighteenth Brumaire of Louis Napoleon, 1851—2*, for the original and detailed account of the concept.
277. The reflective function of art has been the core of the Marxist theory of literature. Lukács's important works developed it into a fine theory of typification, but the theory was further developed and deepened in the works of later Marxist critics, especially through L. Goldmann's concepts of 'mediation' and 'homology', W. Benjamin's 'correspondences' and 'dialectical images', A. Gramsci's 'hegemony', P. Macherey's 'literary production' and other concepts developed by the works of Marxist structuralists. However, all these are later developments, and many of them are reactions to the simplicity of the early version of socialist realism of the 1930s and 1940s.
278. Williams, *Marxism and Literature,* p. 102.

279. Swingewood, *The Novel and Revolution,* p. 99.
280. Georg Lukács, *The Meaning of Contemporary Realism* (London 1963), p. 96.
281. Anatoly Lunacharsky, *On Literature and Art* (Moscow 1973), p. 10.
282. Lukács, *The Meaning of Contemporary Realism*, pp. 98–9.
283. Swingewood, *The Novel and Revolution*, p. 73.
284. Slonim, *Soviet Russian Literature,* p. 156.
285. For discussion of the didactic goal of socialist art see Lunacharsky, *On Literature and Art,* pp. 9–70, and L. Trotsky, *The Age of Permanent Revolution: a Trotsky Anthology*, ed. Issac Deutscher (New York 1974), pp. 299–341.
286. Swingewood, *The Novel and Revolution*, pp. 80–1.
287. Ruhle, *Literature and Revolution*, p. 132.
288. Slonim, *Soviet Russian Literature,* p. 162.
289. Ruhle, *Literature and Revolution*, p. 138.
290. *Ibid.*, 140.
291. Raymond Williams, *Culture and Society* (London 1961), p. 265.
292. Adolfo Sanchez Vazquez, *Art and Society: Essays in Marxist Aesthetics* (London 1973), p. 34.
293. See Ruhle, *Literature and Revolution*, p. 138.
294. Such as Vazquez, *Art and* Society, and Lukacs, *The Meaning of Contemporary Realism*, pp. 127–30.
295. See Luncharsky, *On Literature and Art,* pp. 11–12.
296. Swingewood, *The Novel and Revolution*, p. 109.
297. *Ibid.*
298. Wellek and Warren, *Theory of Literature,* p. 109.
299. Swingewood, *The Novel and Revolution*, p. 100.
300. Ruhle, *Literature and Revolution*, p. 136.
301. Slonim, *Soviet Russian Literature,* 163.
302. Swingewood, *The Novel and Revolution*, p. 99.
303. Vazquez, *Art and Society*.
304. Such as Georg Lukács, A. S. Vazquez, Lucian Goldmann, and Pierre Macherey.
305. Kermode, *Romantic Image,* p. 11.
306. National, some of which are outlined in Chapter One, as well as international, for this was the heyday of socialism emerging triumphantly from the Second World War.
307. Al-Ḥijjāwī started publishing his short stories in the late 1940s in *al-Miṣri* and other periodicals. In the early 1950s he stopped writing short stories and turned to folkloric studies and the promotion of the art of the masses. Later on he collected some of his stories in his only collection *Nahr al-Banafsaj* (1956).
308. ʿAbd al-Ḥalīm started publishing his stories in the second half of the 1950s in *al-Shaʿb*, *al-Ghad*, and other periodicals. They were few and far between, and his only collection, *Azmat Kātib*, did not come out until 1965.
309. Al-Khamīsī tried his hand at many literary and artistic forms. His stories, which he started publishing intensively after 1947 in *al-Miṣrī* and other periodicals, are rich in their romantic and social romantic qualities, yet they are also abundant in realistic characteristics. However, most of his collections (six) appeared in the heyday of socialist romanticism, 1951–6. For a full list see the Appendix.
310. Like al-Ḥijjāwī, Ṣāliḥ's major activities were devoted to the study of Egyptian folkloric literature; indeed, his is the most important work in this field as yet. He also wrote and published short stories around the same period, and

collected some of them in his only collection, *al-Zawjah al-Thāniyyah* (1955). He stopped writing short stories in the mid-1950s.

311. Although al-Sa'danī started publishing his works in periodicals slightly later than the other writers, in the early 1950s, his first collection came out in 1956 and many of his works were clearly influenced by various tenets, themes and techniques of socialist romanticism.
312. The influence of socialist romanticism is evident in the works of many writers of Abū-l-Najā's lost generation. It is also evident in the works of many romantic writers (such as J. Ṣidqī, I. al-Ḥabrūk, and even in many of Makkāwī's works) and in the works of some realistic authors (such as Ṣalāḥ Ḥāfiẓ and Muṣṭafā Maḥmūd).
313. Apart from the apparent homogeneity of each collection, there is evidence to suggest that al-Sharqāwī was aware of this new concept of the collection. For he published many stories which he did not include in any of his collections, and some of the stories in the second collection were written long before the appearance of the first, but were retained for the second.
314. See e.g. 'Laylat al-Zifāf', pp. 21—30, and 'Ḥadath Dhāt Laylah', pp. 97—102 in *Arḍ al-Ma'rakah.*
315. As is the case in "Indama Yurīd al-Sha'b', pp. 31—40, 'Shu'ā' al-Fajr', pp. 41—52, and 'al-Baḥth 'an al-'Azā'', pp. 53—60 in *Arḍ al-Ma'rakah.*
316. See e.g. 'Ghulām fi'l-Muqāwamah', pp. 61—8, "Indama Tasūd al-Sakīnah', pp. 69—76, 'Fi'l-Aghlāl', pp. 78—88, and 'al-Thawrat lan Tamūt', pp. 89—96, *ibid.*
317. As is the case in 'Dukhūl al-Ẓāfirīn', pp. 131—8, and 'Tilk al-Ḥarb al-Muqaddasah', pp. 139—46, *ibid.*
318. See e.g. 'Fi'l-Sayf Ṣādū al-Ḥamām', pp. 147—52, 'Qaryah Mu'minah', pp. 153—60, 'Tāj al-Shawk', pp. 161—6, and the title story 'Arḍ al-Ma'rakah', pp. 167—74, *ibid.*
319. This is the case in most of the stories that portray a confrontation between the masses and their oppressors: see e.g. "Indama Yurīd al-Sha'b', pp. 31—40, 'Shu'ā' al-Fajr', pp. 41—52, 'Fi'l-Aghlāl', pp. 78—88, 'Ḥadath Dhāt Layl, pp. 97—102, 'Innahā Ayḍā Ma'rakah', pp. 103—12, and many others, *ibid.*
320. See e.g. 'al-Fa's', pp. 12—20, 'Miṣr li'l-Miṣriyyin', pp. 113—20, and 'al-Ra's al-Thāniyyah', pp. 121—30, *ibid.*
321. As is the case in 'Laylat al-Zifāf', pp. 21—30, 'Shu'ā' al-Fajr', pp. 41—52, and 'Ḥadath Dhāt Laylah', pp. 97—102, *ibid.*
322. See e.g. his analysis of the 'Urābī revolution in 'Dukhūl al-Ẓāfirīn' in *Arḍ al-Ma'rakah,* pp. 131—8.
323. As is the case in "Indama Tasūd al-Sakīnah', pp. 69—76, 'Miṣr li'l-Miṣriyyin', pp. 113—20, and 'Tāj al-Shawk', pp. 161—6, *ibid.*
324. By resorting to traditional Marxist analysis of social classes, and how their position on the class structure determines their actions.
325. See e.g. 'Shu'ā' al-Fajr', "Indama Yurid al-Sha'b', "Indama Tasūd al-Sakīnah', 'Fi'l-Aghlāl', 'al-Thawrah lan Tamūt', and 'al-Ra's al-Thāniyyah', *ibid.*
326. As in most of the stories mentioned in the previous note.
327. As is the case in "Indama Tasūd al-Sakīnah', pp. 69—76, *ibid.*
328. As is the case in 'al-Fa's', pp. 13—20, *ibid.*
329. As is the case in 'Ghulām fi'l-Muqāwamah', pp. 61—8, *ibid.*
330. See e.g. 'Ghulām fi'l-Muqāwamah', 'Fi'l-Aghlāl', and the title story 'Arḍ al-Ma'rakah', *ibid.*
331. As is the case in 'al-Baḥth 'An al-'Azā'', pp. 53—60 and the title story 'Arḍ al-Ma'rakah', pp. 167—74, *ibid.*

332. See e.g. 'Miṣr li'l-Miṣriyyin', pp. 113–20, and 'Fi'l-Sayf Ṣādū al-Ḥamām', pp. 147–52, *ibid.*
333. As is the case in 'Tilk al-Ḥarb al-Muqadasah', pp. 139–46 and 'Qaryah Mu'minah', pp. 153–60, *ibid.*
334. See e.g. 'Inahā Ayḍā Ma'rakah', pp. 103–12, *ibid*, and the two stories mentioned in the last note.
335. As is the case in "Indama Tasūd al-Sakīnah', pp. 69–76, 'al-Thawrah lan Tamūt', 89–96, and 'Tāj al-Shawk', pp. 161–6, *ibid.*
336. See e.g. 'al-Mu'jizah', pp. 37–50, 'al-'Aqrab', pp. 83–97, and 'Fi'l-Maṭar', pp. 151–60 in *Aḥlām Ṣaghīrah*. Indeed all the following examples are from this second collection.
337. As is the case in 'al-Khādim', pp. 107–19, and the title story 'Aḥlām Ṣaghīrah', pp. 9–18, *ibid.*
338. As is the case with the heroine of 'Fi'l-Maṭar', pp. 151–60, and most characters in 'al-'Aqrab', pp. 83–97, and 'al-Khādim', pp. 107–19, *ibid.*
339. As did the hero of 'al-'Aqrab', pp. 83–97, *ibid.*
340. See e.g. 'Ṭālibah', pp. 61–81, 'al-'Aqrab', and 'Ayyām al-Ru'b', pp. 121–33, *ibid.*
341. As is the case in 'Birkat al-Fīl', pp. 135–49, *ibid.*
342. See e.g. 'Ṭālibah', pp. 61–81, 'al-'Aqrab', 'Tajribah', pp. 99–105, and 'Birkat al-Fīl', pp. 135–49, *ibid.*
343. As is the case in the title story 'Aḥlām Ṣaghīrah', pp. 9–18, and 'al-'Aqrab', *ibid.*,
344. See the title story 'Aḥlām Ṣaghīrah', pp. 9–18, *ibid.*
345. 'al-Mu'jizah', pp. 37–50, *ibid.*
346. As is the case in 'al-Dars al-Awwal', pp. 51–60, 'Ṭālibah', pp. 61–81, and 'Tajribah', pp. 99–105, *ibid.*
347. See e.g. 'al-'Aqrab', pp. 83–98, 'al-Khādim', pp. 107–19, 'Ayyām al-Ru'b', 121–33, and 'Birkat al-Fīl', pp. 135–49, *ibid.*
348. As is the case in 'Tajribah', pp. 99–105, *ibid.*
349. As is the case in 'Ṭālibah', pp. 61–81, and 'Ayyām al-Ru'b', pp. 121–33, *ibid.*
350. As is the case in 'Laḥẓah', 19–36, *ibid.*
351. As is the case in 'al-Dars al-Awwal', pp. 51–60, *ibid.*
352. As is the case in 'al-Mu'jizah', pp. 37–50, *ibid.*
353. See e.g. 'al-'Aqrab', 'Tajribah' and 'al-Khādim', pp. 107–19, *ibid.*
354. As is the case in 'al-'Aqrab', 'Tajribah', and 'al-Khādim', pp. 107–19, *ibid.*
355. See e.g. 'al-'Aqrab', and 'Birkat al-Fīl', pp. 135–49, *ibid.*
356. See e.g. 'Ṭālibah', 'Ayyām al-Ru'b', and 'Birkat al-Fīl', *ibid.*
357. This is the case with the protagonists of both 'al-Khādim' and 'Birkat al-Fīl', *ibid.*
358. As is the case in 'Tajribah', 'al-Khādim', and 'Birkat al-Fīl', *ibid.*
359. See e.g. 'al-Mu'jizah', 'Ṭālibah', and 'Ayyām al-Ru'b', *ibid.*
360. As is the case in 'al-Dars al-Awwal', 'al-'Aqrab', 'Tajribah', and 'Ayyām al-Ru'b', *ibid.*
361. Lukács, *The Meaning of Contemporary Realism,* p. 118.
362. *Al-Anfār*, pp. 6–32.
363. Ṣidqī wrote most of his works during the 1950s, and although he published two collections in the 1960s, *Sharkh fī Jidār al-Khawf* (1967) and *Liqā' ma'a Rajul Majhūl* (1969), half these stories were written and published in various periodicals during the 1950s.
364. See e.g. 'Bukrah', pp. 66–70, and 'Bābā Daḥḥ', pp. 165–75 in *al-Anfār,* and 'Fi'l-Masbak', pp. 17–26, and 'Kullu Shughl', pp. 113–27 in *al-Aydi al-Khashinah.*

365. As is the case in 'Amīna', pp. 33—46, and 'al-Ḥimār', pp. 71—82, in al-Anfār, the title story of *al-Aydi al-Khashinah,* pp. 69—82, and 'Ḥajar 'Alā Saṭḥ al-Buḥayrah', in *Sharkh fī Jidār al-Khawf,* pp. 83—96.
366. See e.g. 'Taḥlum bi'l-Ḥubb', pp. 98—112, and "Awaḍayn', pp. 131—50 in *al-Anfār,* 'Mazzīkā', pp. 27—40 and 'al-Ḥikāyah', pp. 145—60, in *al-Aydi al-Khashinah,* 'Sittat Ashhur Sharaf' in *Sharkh fī Jidār al-Khawf,* pp. 123—35 and 'Ibnat Rajul Khā'in', in *Liqā' ma'a Rajul Majhūl,* pp. 92—153.
367. As is the case in most of the stories of *al-Anfār* and *al-Aydi al-Khashinah* in particular.
368. See e.g. 'Bukrah', pp. 66—70 and 'al-Wābūr al-Jadīd', pp. 83—97 in *al-Anfār* and 'Fi'l-Masbak', pp. 17—26, and 'Laḥẓat Sa'ādah', pp. 161—71, in *al-Aydi al-Khashinah.*
369. As is the case in 'Mazzīkā', pp. 27—46 and 'al-Baṭṭīkhah', pp. 47—53, in *al-Aydi al-Khashinah,* and 'al-Shāy bi-l-Ḥalīb', in *Sharkh fī Jidār al-Khawf,* pp. 43—60.
370. See e.g. 'Amīnah', pp. 33—46, 'Ḥayātunā lahā Rā'iḥah', pp. 52—65 and 'al-Baqarah', pp. 176—91 in *al-Anfār,* 'al-Fawānīs', pp. 5—15, in *al-Aydi al-Khashinah* and the title story of the same, pp. 69—82.
371. As is the case in 'Abū Jabal', pp. 131—51, and 'al-Khawf', pp. 220—7, in *al-Anfār,* and 'Ayy Khidmah', pp. 83—96 and 'Laḥẓat Sa'ādah', pp. 161—71 in *al-Aydi al-Khashinah.*
372. See e.g. 'al-Baqarah', pp. 176—91 in , and the title story of *al-Anfār,* pp. 192—206, 'al-Fawānīs', pp. 5—15, 'al-Baṭṭīkhah', pp. 44—53, and 'Laḥẓat Sa'ādah', in *al-Aydi al-Khashinah.*
373. As is the case in 'Fi'l-Utūbīs', pp. 47—51, and the title story of *al-Anfār,* pp. 192—206, 'Ayy Khidmah', in *al-Aydi al-Khashinah,* pp. 83—96, and 'al-Shāy bi'l-Ḥalīb', pp. 43—60, and 'Ḥajar 'Alā Saṭḥ al-Buḥayrah', pp. 83—96, in *Sharkh fī Jidār al-Khawf.*
374. See e.g. 'Bukrah', "Awaḍayn', and 'al-Baqarah', in *al-Anfār.*
375. As is the case in 'Amīnah' and 'Ḥayātunā lahā Rā'iḥah', pp. 52—62, in *al-Anfār* and the title story of *al-Aydi al-Khashinah,* and 'Abū Jabal', in *Liqā' ma'a Rajul Majhūl,* pp. 76—91.
376. See e.g. 'Bukrah' and 'al-Wābūr al-Jadīd' in *al-Anfār* and 'Fi'l-Masbak' in *al-Aydi al-Khashinah.*
377. As is the case in 'Bukrah', 'Bābā Daḥḥ' and 'Badlat al-'Īd', pp. 207—19, in *al-Anfār* and 'Saḥābah fi'l-Samā'', in *Sharkh fī Jidār al-Khawf,* pp. 97—121.
378. See e.g. the title story of *al-Aydi al-Khashinah.*
379. As is the case in 'al-Ḥimār', pp. 71—82, "Awaḍayn', and 'al-Baqarah', in *al-Anfār,* 'Bāb al-Khalq', pp. 55—68, and 'Mujarrad Thiqah', pp. 97—112, in 'al-Aydi al-Khashinah' and 'Sittat Ashhur Sharaf', in *Sharkh fī Jidār al-Khawf,* pp. 123—35.
380. See e.g. 'Taḥlum bi'l-Ḥubb, pp. 98—112 and 'al-Khawf', pp. 220—37, in *al-Anfār* and 'al-Shāy bi'l-Ḥalīb', in *Sharkh fī Jidār al-Khawf,* pp. 43—60.
381. As is the case in all the stories mentioned in the previous footnote and 'Sittat Asshur Sharaf' in *Sharkh fī Jidār al-Khawf,* pp. 123—35.
382. As is the case in most of the stories of his first two collections.
383. See e.g. 'al-Hudūm' in *al-Anfār,* pp. 238—55.
384. As is the case in 'al-Fawānīs', pp. 5—15, and'Bāb al-Khalq', pp. 55—68 in *al-Aydi al-Khashinah.*
385. See e.g. 'Ḥayātunā lahā Rā'iḥah' in *al-Anfār,* pp. 52—65, and 'Ibnat Rajul Khā'in', in *Liqā' ma'a Rajul Majhūl,* pp. 92—153.
386. As is the case in 'Amīnah', pp. 33—46, 'al-Nawm', pp. 113—30, in *al-Anfār,* the

title story of *al-Aydi al-Khashinah,* and 'Abū Jabal' in *Liqā' ma'a Rajul Majhūl,* pp. 76—91.

387. See e.g. "Awaḍayn' in *al-Anfār*, pp. 131—50 and 'Kullu Shughl', in *al-Aydi al-Khashinah,* pp. 113—27.
388. See e.g. 'Amīnah', pp. 33—46, 'Abū Jabal', pp. 151—64, and 'al-Hudūm', pp. 238—55, in *al-Anfār.*
389. As is the case in 'al-Nawm', pp. 113—30, 'Bābā Daḥḥ', pp. 165—75, in *al-Anfār,* and 'Ibnat Rajul Khā'in', in *Liqa' ma'a Rajul Majhūl,* pp. 92—153.
390. See e.g. 'al-Nawm' and 'al-Hudūm', in *al-Anfār* and 'Ibnat Rajul Khā'in', in *Liqā' ma'a Rajul Majhūl.*
391. As is the case in 'Amīna', 'Bukrah', 'al-Wābūr al-Jadīd' and "Awaḍayn' in *al-Anfār,* and "Alā Ṭūl' in *al-Aydi al-Khashinah,* pp. 129—44.
392. See e.g. 'al-Ḥimār', pp. 71—82, 'al-Nawm' and 'Bābā Daḥḥ' in *al-Anfār,* and 'Ibnat Rajul Khā'in' in *Liqa' ma'a Rajul Majhūl.*
393. As is the case in 'Taḥlum bi'l-Ḥubb', pp. 98—112, 'al-Baqarah', pp. 46—91, in *al-Anfār,* and 'Jarī'a Ḥabbitayn', pp. 154—78 in the title story of *Liqā' ma'a Rajul Majhūl,* pp. 4—50.
394. See e.g. 'Mujarrad Thiqah', pp. 97—112 and "Alā Ṭūl', pp. 129—144 in *al-Aydi al-Khashinah.*
395. Even al-'Ālim, who would normally tolerate and often encourage such optimistic endings, criticises Ṣidqī for his unjustifiable ending: see his introduction to *al-Anfār,* pp. 29—30.
396. See e.g. 'al-Nawm' in *al-Anfār* and 'Ibnat Rajul Khā'in' in *Liqā' ma'a Rajul Majhūl.*
397. As is the case in 'Amīnah', 'al-Wābūr al-Jadīd' and 'Bābā Daḥḥ' in *al-Anfār,* and 'Ibnat Rajul Khā'in' in *Liqā' ma'a Rajul Majhūl.*
398. See e.g. 'Fi'l-Utūbīs', pp. 47—51, and 'al-Ḥimār', pp. 71—82 in *al-Anfār;* 'Bāb al-Khalq' and 'Ayy Khidmah' in *al-Aydi al-Khashinah;* and 'Ḥajar 'Alā Saṭḥ al-Buḥayrah' in *Sharkh fī Jidār al-Khawf.*
399. For a detailed theoretical discussion on employing propaganda and agitation as a regulative principle see Lukács, *The Meaning of Contemporary Realism,* especially the section entitled 'Critical Realism and Socialist Realism', pp. 93—135.
400. Such as 'Amīnah', 'Ḥayātunā lahā Rā'iḥah', 'al-Wābūr al-Jadīd' and 'al-Baqarah' in *al-Anfār,* and 'Ḥajar 'Alā Saṭḥ al-Buḥayrah' in *Sharkh fī Jidār al-Khawf.*
401. See e.g. 'al-Baqara' in *al-Anfār,* 'Bāb al-Khalq' and 'Ayy Khidmah' in *al-Aydi al-Khashinah* and the title story of the same collection, and most of the stories of *Liqa' ma'a Rajul Majhūl.*
402. Lukács, *The Meaning of Contemporary Realism,* p. 119.
403. See his introduction to *al-Anfār,* pp. 6—7.

Chapter Four

1. Virginia Woolf, *Collected Essays* (London 1966), vol. 1, p. 321.
2. Malcolm Bradbury and James McFarlane (eds), 'The Name and Nature of Modernism', *Modernism* (London 1976), p. 51.
3. Harry Levin, *Refractions* (Oxford 1966), p. 271.
4. Bradbury and McFarlane, *Modernism,* p. 26.
5. Gabriel Josipovici, *The World and the Book: A Study in Modern Fiction* (London 1971), p. 194.
6. For the influence of European writers on what al-Shārūnī calls the writers of

absurd, see Yūsuf al-Shārūnī, 'al-Judhūr al-Tarīkhiyyah li-Adab al-Lāma'qūl', *al-Majallah,* November 1964.

7. The better known amongst these painters are Ramsīs Yūnān, Kāmil al-Tilmisānī and Fu'ād Kāmil.
8. Bradbury and McFarlane, *Modernism*, p. 48.
9. See *Plutoland,* pp. 11, 58. Most of the poems in the book are dated between 1938 and 1940, while the introduction singles out 1937 as the year in which he started thinking about his innovative experiment.
10. Leon Edel, *The Modern Psychological Novel* (New York 1964), p. 28.
11. *Ibid.*
12. *Ibid.*
13. Bernard Bergonzi, 'Thoughts on the Personality Explosion', in *idem* (ed.), *Innovations: Essays on Art and Ideas* (London 1968), p. 185.
14. C. Wright Mills, *Power Politics and People, the Collected Essays* (Oxford 1963) p. 293.
15. For a detailed study of this magazine, see R. al-Sa'īd, *al-Ṣaḥāfah al-Yasāriyyah fī Miṣr* (Beirut 1974), pp. 79—108.
16. See Yūnān's articles in *al-Majallah al-Jadīdah,* and most of the articles published in *al-Taṭawwur* especially those by Kāmil, al-Tilmisānī, 'Alī Kāmil, 'Iṣām al-Dīn Ḥifnī Nāṣif, Fayṣal Shabandar, and the creative work of George Ḥinayn, Albert Quṣayrī, and 'Abd al-'Azīz Ḥaykal.
17. *Al-Taṭawwur,* January 1940.
18. It published only five issues before being subject to censorship.
19. See in particular, Ḥaqqī's 'Ṣūrah', *al-Kātib al-Miṣrī*, January 1946 and 'Warā' al-Sitār', *ibid.*, July 1947, and Ḥasan Maḥmūd's 'Mughāmir', *ibid.*, March 1946, and Darwīsh al-Jamīl's 'Yajib Ann Na'īsh', *ibid.*, November 1946. See also the translation of Kafka's 'Ṭabīb al-Qaryah', *ibid.*, February 1944 and many poems by B. Fāris.
20. Among the members of that group were Yūsuf al-Shārūnī, Badr al-Dīb, 'Abbās Aḥmad, Aḥmad 'Abbās Ṣāliḥ and Fatḥī Ghānim.
21. *Al-Bashīr,* 2 October 1948.
22. For a detailed account of the works of this group see Yūsuf al-Shārūnī's articles and anthology on that topic, *al-Majallah,* November 1964 – February 1965.
23. The most well known of the Alexandrian writers of this period are Muḥammad Munīr Ramzī the poet, and Idwār al-Kharrāṭ whose work will be considered in a later part of this chapter.
24. Ihab Hassan, *Radical Innocence: Studies in Contemporary American Fiction* (New York 1961), p. 3.
25. Josipovici, *The World and the Book*, p. 193.
26. Edel, *The Modern Psychological Novel*, p. 27.
27. Josipovici, *The World and the Book*, p. 194.
28. Malcolm Bradbury, *Possibilities: Essays on the State of the Novel* (Oxford 1973), p. 19.
29. Bradbury and McFarlane, *Modernism*, 47.
30. *Ibid.*, p. 50.
31. *Ibid.*, p. 29.
32. John Fletcher and Malcolm Bradbury, 'The Introverted Novel', in *Modernism,* pp. 395—6.
33. It was established in January 1939, see *al-Taṭawwur*, January 1940, and R. al-Sa'īd, *al-Ṣaḥāfah al-Yasāriyyah fī Miṣr*, p. 86.

34. For a detailed study of the emergence and manifestation of symbolism in modern Arabic literature, see Anṭūn Ghaṭṭās Karam, *al-Ramziyyah fi'l-Shi'r al-'Arabī al-Ḥadīth* (Beirut 1949) and Salma Khadra Jayyusi, *Trends and Movements in Modern Arabic Poetry* (Leiden 1977), vol. 2, pp. 475–516.
35. See e.g. the numerous articles on symbolism and its masters in *al-Risālah* in 1938, the issues of 11, 18 and 25 April, 9, 23 and 30 May, 6, 13, and 20 June, and later in *al-Adīb* especially the issues of July, August and October 1942, November 1943, September, October and December 1944, January 1945, September, November and December 1946; see also *al-Thaqāfah* and *Majallatī* of the same period.
36. See in particular 'Qatal al-Ḥallāq Imra'atuh', *al-Taṭawwur*, January 1940, and 'Iḍṭirābāt fī Madrasat al-Shaḥḥādhīn', *al-Taṭawwur,* February 1940.
37. Jayyusi, *Trends and Movements in Modern Arabic Poetry,* pp. 510–11.
38. Bishr Fāris, *Mafriq al-Ṭarīq,* p. 5.
39. *Ibid.*, p. 6.
40. *Ibid.*, p. 7.
41. *Ibid.*, p. 8.
42. *Ibid.*, p. 9.
43. *Ibid.*, p. 10.
44. After the encouraging reception of his play, Fāris elucidated his ideas in three articles: 'Fi al-Madhhab al-Ramzi', *al-Risālah,* 25 April 1938, 'Hawl al-Ramziyyah', *al-Risālah,* 6 June 1938, and 'Hadith al-Ramziyyah', *al-Risālah,* 20 June 1938.
45. Jayyusi, *Trends and Movements in Modern Arabic Poetry,* p. 511.
46. Many of the outstanding writers praised it, see e.g. Zakī Ṭulaymāt, *al-Risālah,* 18 April 1938, Amīn al-Riḥānī and Mikhā'īl Nu'aymah, *al-Risālah,* 25 April 1938, and Ḥasan Kāmil al-Ṣayrafī, *al-Muqtaṭaf,* April 1938.
47. Josipovici, *The World and the Book*, p. 192.
48. He published several stories using the name Idwār Fāris in *al-Muqtaṭaf;* see e.g. 'Julnār', April 1927, 'al-Umūmah', July 1927, 'al-Qahqahah', February 1930.
49. *Sū' Tafāhum,* p. 9.
50. *Ibid.*, p. 10.
51. Luwīs 'Awaḍ, *Maqālat fi'l-Naqd wa'l-Adab,* p. 213.
52. *Ibid.*, pp. 214–16.
53. *Sū' Tafāhum,* pp. 13–22.
54. *Ibid.*, pp. 23–31.
55. *Ibid.*, pp. 75–82.
56. *Ibid.*, pp. 101–09.
57. *Ibid.*, pp. 49–74.
58. *Ibid.*, pp. 67–74.
59. Such as 'al-Safīnah', pp. 33–9, 'Qīthār Mughtarib', pp. 41–8; 'Kharīf', pp. 59–65, and 'Rajul', pp. 91–9 in *Sū' Tafāhum.*
60. *Ibid.*, pp. 114–24.
61. *Ibid.*, pp. 91–9.
62. *Ibid.*, p. 98.
63. *Ibid.*, p. 99.
64. Ralph Freedman, *The Lyrical Novel* (Princeton 1963), p. 8.
65. *Ibid.*, p. 2.
66. *Al-Muqtaṭaf,* January 1943.
67. W. K. Wimsat, *Hateful Contraries* (Kentucky 1965), pp. 51–2.

68. Published in the monthly supplement of *al-Fu'ād* entitled *Aḥsan ma Katabt*, November 1945.
69. Wimsatt, *Hateful Contraries*, p. 59.
70. Freedman, *The Lyrical Novel*, p. 21.
71. *Ibid.*
72. Hans Meyerhoff, *Time in Literature* (Berkeley 1960), p. 23.
73. *Ibid.*
74. Such as Badr al-Dīb, 'Abbās Aḥmad, Bahīj Naṣṣār, Aḥmad Mursī, and Yūsuf al-Shārūnī.
75. *Tajribat Ḥubb*, pp. 121–30.
76. *Sūr Ḥadīd Mudabbab*, pp. 35–42.
77. Heisenberg's uncertainty principle involves a whole body of modern philosophy of science which one need not go into in detail; it is important to emphasise its centrality to modernism in general, and the role of Maḥmūd Amīn al-'Ālim in making his group aware of its dynamics and significance.
78. *Ibid.*, pp. 15–23.
79. *Ibid.*, pp. 25–33.
80. *Ibid.*, pp. 71–8.
81. J. H. Matthews, *Surrealism and the Novel* (Michigan 1966), p. 10.
82. *Ibid.*
83. *Ibid.*
84. *Ibid.*, p. 8.
85. Bradbury, *Possibilities*, p. 85.
86. The 1950s witnessed the popularity of the monthly book series *Qiṣaṣ li'l-Jāmi'*, which later became *Kutub li'l-Jāmi'*, and the initiation of the successful series *al-Kitāb al-Dhahabī* which at one point sold 15,000–20,000 copies a month, and to which many writers owe their popularity and contact with the wider public.
87. One clear example in this respect is Y. Ḥaqqī who, by a stroke of luck, succeeded in publishing his first collection in 1944. Though he received reasonable critical acclaim at the time of its publication, he failed to publish many of the excellent stories that he had written and published in periodicals in the 1930s and 1940s in book form until 1955 when the favourable new atmosphere enabled him to issue two books in one year.
88. These were clearly influenced by Khalīl Jibrān and Ḥusayn 'Afīf, published in *al-Adīb* in the 1940s, and collected in a book entitled *al-Masā' al-Akhīr* (1963).
89. Although Egypt had several magazines at the time, some of the young writers of the 1940s had to publish their works in Lebanon. Al-Shārūnī, Badr al-Dīb, and Ghānim published their stories in *al-Adīb* in the early 1950s, and it soon became the beginning of the exodus of Egyptian writing which lasted throughout the 1950s and 1960s, and which was followed in the 1970s by the exodus of the writers themselves.
90. They are really only a collection and a half, for half of the latter collection consists of the rejects of the early days, stories that he wrote and published before the publication of his first collection and refused to include in it. However, al-Shārūnī was bent on redistributing the stories of his three collections in new combinations, so he created, particularly in the 1970s, the illusion of having more than three collections.
91. He studied philosophy at Cairo University, from which he graduated with a degree in philosophy in 1945.

92. See the interview with Nabīl Faraj in *al-Khawf wa'l-Shajā'ah: Dirāsāt fī Qiṣaṣ Yūsuf al-Shārūnī* (Cairo, 1972), pp. 52–8.
93. See e.g. *al-Ziḥām*, pp. 25, 42, 71.
94. See Nabīl Faraj's interview with al-Shārūnī, *al-Khawf wa'l-Shajā'ah,* p. 68.
95. See e.g. 'al-'Ushshāq al-Kahmsah', pp. 5–13, 'Qiddīs fī Ḥāratinā', pp. 24–30, 'Sariqah bi'l-Ṭābiq al-Sādis', pp. 31–50, 'Zayṭah Ṣāni' al-'Āhāt', 51–58, 'Masra' 'Abbās al-Ḥilw', pp. 59–68, and 'al-Wabā'', pp. 100–07 in *al-'Ushshāq al-Khamsah.*
96. Joseph Chiari, *The Aesthetics of Modernism* (London 1970), p. 94.
97. See e.g. 'Sariqah bi'l-Ṭābiq al-Sādis' pp. 31–50, 'al-Qayz', pp. 84–90, 'al-Ṭarīq', 91–9, and 'Difā' Muntaṣaf al-Layl', pp. 115–32 in *al-'Ushshāq al-Khamsah.*
98. Such as 'Difā' Muntaṣaf al-Layl' in *al-'Ushshāq al-Khamsah,* pp. 115–32, the title story of *Risālah Ilā Imra'ah,* pp. 46–59, and 'Lamaḥāt min Ḥayāt Mawjūd', pp. 25–45 and the title story, pp. 5–13, in *al-Ziḥām.*
99. As is the case in the title stories of *al-'Ushshāq al-Khamsah,* pp. 5–13 and *al-Ziḥām,* pp. 5–23.
100. See e.g. 'Sariq bil-Tariq al-Sadis', pp. 31–50, 'Difā' Muntaṣaf al-Layl', pp. 115–32, and 'Hadhayān', pp. 156–61 in *al-'Ushshāq al-Khamsah,* and 'Lamaḥāt min Ḥayāt Mawjūd' in *al-Ziḥām,* pp. 25–42.
101. As is the case in 'Zayṭah Sāni' al-'Āhāt', pp. 51–8, 'al-Ṭarīq', pp. 91–9, 'Difā' Muntaṣaf al-Layl', pp. 115–32 in *al-'Ushshāq al-Khamsah,* and the title story of *al-Ziḥām.*
102. Such as the heroes of 'Lamaḥāt min Ḥayāt Mawjūd' in *al-Ziḥām*, and 'Sariqah bi'l-Ṭābiq al-Sādis' and 'Difā' Muntaṣaf al-Layl' in *al-'Ushshāq al-Khamsah.*
103. As is the case in 'Sariqah bi'l-Ṭābiq al-Sādis' and 'Lamaḥāt min Ḥayāt Mawjūd'.
104. *Al-Ziḥām,* pp. 25–42.
105. Such as the heroes of 'Sariqah bi'l-Ṭābiq al-Sādis', pp. 31–50, 'al-Qayz', pp. 84–90, 'al-Ṭarīq', pp. 91–9, 'al-Wabā'', pp. 100–07, 'Difā' Muntaṣaf al-Layl', pp. 115–32, 'al-Ṭarīq Ilā al-Maṣaḥḥah', pp. 133–42 and 'Hadhayān', pp. 156–61 in *al-'Ushshāq al-Khamsah* and the title story of *al-Ziḥām.*
106. As is the case with the protagonist of 'Sariqah bi'l-Ṭābiq al-Sādis'.
107. Such as the heroes of 'Difā' Muntaṣaf al-Layl' and 'al-Ṭarīq Ilā al-Maṣaḥḥa'.
108. As are the protagonists of 'al-Laḥm wa'l-Sikkīn' pp. 67–82, and the title story of *al-Ziḥām,* pp. 5–30.
109. *Al-Ziḥām,* p. 25.
110. *Ibid.*
111. *Ibid.*
112. The Christian mythology is evident in many of al-Shārūnī's works, for he is a Christian, especially in 'Anīsah' in *al-'Ushshāq al-Khamsah,* pp. 69–77, 'Ra'sān fī'l-Ḥalāl' in *Risālah Ilā Imra'ah,* pp. 98–111 and 'al-Laḥm wa'l-Sikkīn' in *al-Ziḥām,* pp. 67–82.
113. The Christian idea of salvation through sacrifice is a latent and recurring theme in al-Shārūnī's work. It is the main theme of 'al-Laḥm wa'l-Sikkīn' in *al-Ziḥām,* pp. 67–82.
114. Such as 'al-Qayz', pp. 84–90, 'al-Ṭarīq', pp. 91–9, and 'al-Wabā'', pp. 100–07 in *al-'Ushshāq al-Khamsah* and the title story of *al-Ziḥām,* pp. 5–23.
115. See e.g. 'Zayṭah Ṣāni' al-'Āhāt', pp. 51–8, 'Masra' 'Abbās al-Hilw', pp. 59–68, 'Ṣiyāḥat al-Baṭal', pp. 143–55 in, and the title story of, *al-'Ushshāq al-Khamsah,* pp. 5–13.
116. As is the case in 'Maṣra' 'Abbās al-Hilw' and 'al- Wabā'', pp. 100–07 in *al-*

'Ushshāq al-Khamsah, 'al-Rajul wa'l-Mazra'ah', pp. 5—17, 'Ma'a Fā'iq al-Iḥtirām', pp. 112—27 and 'Nashrat al-Akhbār', pp. 128—37 in *Risālah Ilā Imra'ah.*

117. As is the case in the title story of *al-'Ushshāq al-Khamsah* and 'al-Laḥm wa'l-Sikkīn' in *al-Ziḥām,* pp. 67—82.

118. As is the case in the title stories of *al-'Ushshsāq al-Kahmsah* and *al-Ziḥām.*

119. As is the case in 'Zayṭah Ṣāni' al-'Āhāt', 'Masra' 'Abbās al-Hilw' and 'Difā' Muntaṣaf al-Layl' in *al-'Ushshāq al-Khamsah* and the title story of *Risālah Ilā Imra'ah,* pp. 46—59.

120. Such as 'al-'Īd', pp. 14—23, 'Sariqah bi'l-Ṭābiq al-Sādis', pp. 31—50, 'Masra' 'Abbās al-Hilw', pp. 59—68, 'Hadhayān', pp. 156—61, and 'Zawjī', pp. 169—74 in *al-'Ushshāq al-Khamsah,* 'al-Rajul wa'l-Mazra'ah', pp. 5—17, 'Ḥāris al-Marmā' pp. 33—45, and 'al-Nās Maqāmāt', pp. 66—82 in *Risālah Ilā Imra'ah.*

121. *Al-'Ushshāq al-Khamsah,* pp. 24—30.

122. *Ibid.*, pp. 51—8.

123. *Al-Ziḥām,* pp. 67—82.

124. Such as 'al-'Īd', pp. 14—23, 'Anīsah', pp. 69—77, 'al-Mu'dam al-Thāmin', pp. 78—83, and 'Zawjī', pp. 169—74 in *al-'Ushshāq al-Khamsah,* 'Ākhir al-'Unqūd', pp. 18—28, 'al-Lu'bah', pp. 29—32, and 'Qarār al-Ta'yīn', pp. 150—60 in *Risālah Ilā Imra'ah.*

125. Such as 'Difā' Muntaṣaf al-Layl' in *al-'Ushshāq al-Khamsah,* pp. 115—32, and 'Lamḥāt min Ḥayāt Mawjūd', pp. 25—42 in, and the title story of, *al-Ziḥām,* pp. 5—23.

126. Such as 'al-Rajul wa'l-Mazra'ah', pp. 5—17, 'Ākhir al-'Unqūd', pp. 18—27, 'Ḥāris al-Marmā', pp. 33—45, 'Ḥalawat al-Rūḥ', pp. 83—97, and 'Nashrat al-Akhbār', pp. 128—37 in *Risālah Ilā Imra'ah,* and 'al-Laḥm wa'l-Sikkīn'in *al-Ziḥām,* pp. 67—82.

127. 'al-Rajul wa'l-Mazra'ah' in *Risālah Ilā Imra'ah,* pp. 5—17.

128. 'Ākhir al-'Unqūd', *ibid.*, pp. 18—28.

129. 'al-Lu'bah', *ibid.*, pp. 29—32.

130. 'Ḥāris al-Marmā', *ibid.*, pp. 33—45.

131. 'Nāhid wa-Nabīl', pp. 60—5 and the title story 'Risālah Ilā Imra'ah', *ibid.*, pp. 46—59.

132. 'Al-Nās Maqāmāt', 66—82, and 'Ḥalawat al-Rūḥ', 83—97, *ibid.*

133. 'Ra'sān fi'l-Ḥalāl', *ibid.*, 98—111.

134. 'Nashrat al-Akhbār', *ibid.*, 128—37.

135. 'Bi-Ikhtiṣār', pp. 138—49, and 'Qarār al-Ta'yīn', 150—60, *ibid.*

136. *al-'Ushshāq al-Khamsah,* pp. 115—32.

137. This second collection was published in Beirut despite the triumph of modern sensibility in Egypt at the time. However, unlike his first collection, many of the stories that comprise this collection were published in Egyptian periodicals, particularly in *al-Majallah.*

138. Meyerhoff, *Time in Literature,* p. 35.

139. Such as 'al-Shaykh 'Īsa', pp. 21—39, 'Miḥaṭṭat al-Sikka al-Ḥadīd', pp. 41—52, 'Amām al-Baḥr', pp. 79—88, 'Qiṣṣat Mi'ād', pp. 89—103, 'Ṭalqat Nār', pp. 105—21, 'al-ūrkistrā', pp. 123—35, 'Abūnā Tūmā', pp. 137—51 and 'Ḥikāyah Ṣaghīrah fi'l-Layl', pp. 195—223 in *Ḥīṭān 'Āliyah.*

140. This phenomenon is apparent throughout his work, however; as an example, in the title story of *Ḥīṭān 'Āliyah* one finds 81 verbs in the past tense and 328 verbs in the present tense.

141. Such as the presence of the summer sun in 'Fī Ẓuhr Yawm Ḥarr', *Ḥīṭān 'Āliyah*, pp. 53—77.

142. These are 'al-Shaykh 'Īsa', pp. 21–39, 'Fī Ẓuhr Yawm Ḥārr', pp. 53–77, 'Ṭalqat Nār', pp. 105–21,'Abūnā Tūmā', pp. 137–51, and 'Ḥikāyah Ṣaghīrah fi'l-Layl', pp. 195–223 in *Ḥīṭān 'Aliya.*
143. *Ḥīṭān 'Āliyah,* pp. 53–77.
144. *Ibid.*, pp. 105–21.
145. *Ibid.*, pp. 137–51.
146. *Ibid.*, pp. 5–18.
147. Indeed most of the stories of this stage have nameless protagonists, such as: 'Muhattat al-Sikkah al-Ḥadīd', pp. 41–52, 'Amām al-Baḥr', pp. 79–88, 'Qiṣṣat Mi'ad', pp. 89–103, and 'Mughāmarah Gharāmiyyah', pp. 153–74, *ibid.*
148. *Ibid.*, pp. 123–35.
149. *Ibid.*, pp. 153–74.
150. *Ibid.*, pp. 175–93.
151. Such as 'Maḥaṭṭat al-Sikkah al-Ḥadīd', pp. 41–52, 'Amām al-Baḥr', pp. 79–88 and 'Qiṣṣat Mi'ād', pp. 89–103, *ibid.*
152. As is the case in 'Amām al-Baḥr', *ibid.*, pp. 79–88.
153. As is 'Qiṣṣat Mi'ād', *ibid.*, pp. 99–103.
154. *Ibid.*, pp. 41–52.
155. *Ibid.*, pp. 79–88.
156. When the first story of the collection, 'Taḥt al-Jāmi'', was published in *al-Majallah,* February 1963.
157. When the last story (the stories appear in the collection in chronological order) 'Fi'l-Shawāri'' was published in *al-Adab,* July 1970.
158. *Sā'āt al-Kibriyā',* pp. 32–45; the story was also published in *al-Majallah,* October 1967.
159. *Ibid.*, pp. 5–15 and *al-Majallah,* February 1963.
160. *Sā'āt al-Kibriyā',* pp. 45–55 and *al-Majallah,* August 1969.
161. *Sā'āt al-Kibriyā',* pp. 86–100 and *al-Adab,* July 1970.
162. The best example of this respect is Najīb Maḥfūẓ, who throughout the 1960s continued to publish novels laden with social and political criticism, not furtively or in limited editions, but in the official and most widely circulated paper in the country, *al-Ahram.*
163. Both al-Ḥakīm and Maḥfūẓ were awarded the highest literary prizes conferred by the state.
164. The author of this study is himself a member of the sixties generation, was an active participant in the literary movement in this decade, and hence speaks from first-hand experience. It is also appropriate to refer here to the cultural debate caused by Muḥammad Ḥāfiẓ Rajab's outcry 'Nahn Jīl bilā Asātidhah' in *al-Jumhūriyyah* in 1962/3. In September 1969 *al-Ṭalī'ah* published a special issue entitled 'Hakadhā Yatakallam al-Udabā' al-Shubbān' in which some twenty of the young writers aired their views. The issue contains some revealing documents and commentary which emphasises the gap, mistrust and hostility between the two generations. See particularly pp. 15, 18, 19, 20, 24, 29, 32, 36, 39, 40, 61–91. From 4 to 8 December 1969 a conference, 'Mu'tamar al-Udabā' al-Shubbān', was held in al-Zaqāzīq to discuss the subject. It turned into a heated and revealing occasion: see the comments of the press at the time and also Sabry Hafez, 'Ab'ād al-Ru'ya al-Shābba li'l-Wāqi' al-Adabī', *al-Majallah,* January 1970.
165. Richard Gilman, *The Confusion of Realms* (London 1970), p. 81.
166. Such as Muḥammad 'Abd al-Ḥalīm 'Abd Allāh, Tharwat Abāẓah, and 'Abd al-Ghaffār Makkāwī. It would be difficult to include in this list names like those

of Najīb Maḥfūẓ and Yūsuf Idrīs because writers of this calibre have a young spirit and do not stop developing their work with time.

167. Especially stories like 'Qiṣṣat Dhi al-Ṣawt al-Maḥīl', pp. 35—40, 'al-Lu'bah', pp. 101—09, 'al-Awurṭī', pp. 125—33, and 'Ṣāḥib Miṣr, pp. 135—60.
168. The cultural page of *al-Masā'*, the only evening daily in Egypt, is, in fact, the last page of this national newspaper. It is more or less a full page which, instead of being devoted to light news and gossip as is the case in most national dailies, had a cultural nature from the start. When al-Jamal had the editorship of this page at the beginning of 1960 he changed its nature, and instead of commissioning professional journalists to fill the page, he opened it to the creative and critical works of the young generation.
169. Apart from asking Ḥaqqī to contribute a weekly column in his page, al-Jamal used to recommend many young writers to Ḥaqqī; and Ḥaqqī in turn used to send many writers and works to al-Jamal when he could not find room for them in *al-Majallah* for one reason or another.
170. Malcolm Cowley, *A Second Flowering: Works and Days of the Lost Generation* (London 1973), p. 238.
171. As is the case in Ḥusayn Fawzī's book, *Sindibād Miṣrī* (1961) and Jamāl Ḥamdān's *Shakhṣiyyat Misr* (1968).
172. Frank Kermode, 'Modernisms', in Bergonzi (ed.), *Innovations*, p. 77.
173. Malcolm Cowley, *A Second Flowering*, p. 249.
174. Kermode, 'Modernisms', p. 88.
175. Bradbury, *Possibilities*, p. 90.
176. Hassan, *Radical Innocence* p. 5.
177. Freedman, *The Lyrical Novel*, p. 27.
178. Hassan, *Radical Innocence* p. 31.
179. James Gindin, *Harvest of a Quiet Eye: The Novel of Compassion* (Bloomington 1971), p. 16.
180. Georg Lukács, *The Meaning of Contemporary Realism* (London 1963), p. 21.
181. Josipovici, *The World and the Book*, p. 192.
182. Malcolm Bradbury, *What is a Novel?* (London 1969), p. 13.
183. Bradbury, *Possibilities*, p. 84.
184. Meyerhoff, *Time in Literature*, p. 1.
185. *Ibid.*, p. 2.
186. *Ibid.*, p. 23.
187. *Ibid.*
188. *Ibid.*, pp. 23, 24.
189. *Ibid.*, p. 85 and for a detailed discussion of these techniques see the whole of chapter three 'Time and the modern world', pp. 85—119.
190. Josipovici, *The World and the Book*, p. 192.
191. Bradbury, *Possibilities*, p. 82.
192. Freedman, *The Lyrical Novel*, p. 21.
193. *Ibid.*
194. Chiari, *The Aesthetics of Modernism*, p. 16.
195. Wright Mills, *Power Politics and People*, p. 297.
196. For a detailed study of this feature and other thematic and artistic characterisitics of the work of the sixties generation, see Ibrāhīm Fatḥī 'Malāmiḥ Mushtarakah fi'l-Intāj al-Qaṣaṣī al-Jadīd', *Gallery 68*, April 1969; Ghālib Halasā 'al-Adab al-Jadīd: Malamih wa-Ittijahat', *Gallery 68*, April 1969; and Sabry Hafez, 'al-Uqṣūṣah al-Miṣriyyah wa'l-Ḥadāthah', *Gallery 68*, October 1969.

197. Like each of the writers discussed below, Fayyāḍ deserves a detailed study, which should treat his works of the 1960s and 1970s as well as his earlier ones. Indeed, some articles devoted partially or entirely to his works have been published in Arabic; see e.g. Sabry Hafez, 'Mustaqbal al-Uqṣūṣah al-Miṣriyyah', *al-Majallah,* August and September 1966; *idem*, 'Naẓra fī Ba'ḍ Majmū'āt 68 al-Qaṣaṣīyyah', *al-Majallah,* March 1969; and Ghālib Halasā, 'al-Adab al-Jadīd: Malāmiḥ wa Ittijāhāt', *Gallery 68,* April 1969.
198. As is the case in 'al-Liṣṣ wa'l-Ḥāris', pp. 57—72 and 'Yahūdhā wa'l-Jazzār', pp. 73—96 in *'Aṭshān Yā Ṣabāyā,* and 'al-Gharīb', 51–89, 'Raghīf al-Batānūhi', pp. 112—27, in, and the title story of, *Wa-Ba'danā al-Ṭufān*, 3–49.
199. W. M. Frohock, *The Novel of Violence in America* (New Haven, CT 1976), pp. 6—7.
200. See e.g. 'Yahūdhā wa'l-Jazzār' in *'Aṭshān Yā Ṣabāyā,* pp. 73—96, and all the stories of *Wa-Ba'danā al-Ṭufān* without exception.
201. As is the case in 'al-Naddāhah', pp. 29—42; "Indamā Yalid al-Rijal', pp. 43—56; 'al-Liṣṣ wa'l-Ḥāris', pp. 57—72, 'Yahūdhā wa'l-Jazzār, 73–96, in, and the title story of, *'Aṭshān Yā Ṣabāyā,* pp. 5—28; and most of the stories of his second collection *Wa-Ba'danā al-Ṭufān.*
202. See e.g. "Indamā Yalid al-Rijal', pp. 43—56; "Alā al-Ḥudūd', pp. 97—132, and 'al-A'raj', pp. 133—58 in *'Aṭshān Yā Ṣabāyā;* and 'Janāḥ Istiqbāl al-Nisā", pp. 91—109, and 'Kull al-Mulūk Yamūtūn', pp. 129—72 in *Wa-Ba'danā al-Ṭufān.*
203. As is the case in 'al-Naddāhah', 'Yahūdhā wa'l-Jazzār', in, and the title story of, *'Aṭshān Yā Ṣabāyā.*
204. See all the stories of *Wa-Ba'danā al-Ṭufān* bar 'Raghīf al-Batānūhī', pp. 112—27.
205. For a detailed discussion of his work see the debate between him and many members of the older generation in *al-Jumhuriyyah* in 1962/3, and for treatments of his work see Sabry Hafez, 'Mustaqbal al-Uqṣūṣah al-Miṣriyyah', *al-Majallah,* August 1966, and *idem*, 'Ajinnat al-Ru'ā al-Jadīdah', *al-Ṭalī'ah,* October, 1972.
206. See his work in *al-Sha'ab, al-Masā', al-Qāhirhah,* and *al-Taḥrīr* in the 1950s and not included in either of his two collections.
207. As is often the case in a number of stories such as "Iẓām fi'l-Jurn', *al-Majallah,* February 1965; 'Asābi' al-Sha'r', *al-Qiṣṣah,* June 1965; and 'Marsh al-Huzn', pp. 17—28, 'al-Amṭār Talhū', pp. 51—63, and 'al-Abb Ḥānūt', pp. 77—84 in his second collection *al-Kurah wa-Ra's al-Rajul* (1967). Although this collection contains his more recent work it appeared before the publication of his first collection, *Ghuraba'* (1968), which contains his earlier work, the publication of which was delayed for administrative reasons, since it was due to appear in 1965/6.
208. Such as "Iẓām fi'l-Jurn', 'Ḥadīth Bā'i' Maksūr al-Qalb', and 'al-Abb Ḥānūt'.
209. Such as 'Jawlat Mīm al-Mumillah' and 'Ḥadīth Shā'ir Mahmūm', *Majallat Nādī al-Qiṣṣah,* June 1970.
210. Such as 'al-Fāris' in *Ghurabā',* and the title story of *al-Kurah wa-Ra's al-Rajul,* and 'Makhlūqāt Barrād al-Shāy al-Maghlī', *al-Majallah,* August 1966.
211. Such as 'Asabi' al-Sha'r', *al-Qiṣṣah,* June 1965, 'Marsh al-Huzn', 'al-Amṭār Talhū', 'al-Abb Ḥānūt', and 'al-Ṭuyūr al-Ṣaghīrah', pp. 105–5 in *al-Kurah wa-Ra's al-Rajul,* and "Iẓām fi'l-Jurn', *al-Majallah,* February 1965.
212. For a detailed study of Ṭāhir's work see Sabry Hafez 'Mustaqbal al-Uqṣūṣah al-Miṣriyyah', *al-Majallah,* September 1966, Kamāl Ramzī, 'al-Khuṭūbah', *al-*

Ādāb, September 1973, and Sabry Hafez, 'Bahā' Ṭāhir: 'Ālam al-Barā'a wa'l-Daynūnah', *al-Ādāb,* July/August 1975.

213. As is the case in 'al-Muẓāharah', *al-Katib,* March 1964, "Īd Mīlād', al-Masā', 14 July 1964, 'al-Abb', *Ṣabāḥ al-Khayr,* 26 November 1964, and 'al-Ṣawt wa'l-Ṣamt', *al-Kātib* March 1966, and 'Bi-Jiwār Asmāk Mulawwanah', *al-Masā',* 2 January 1970. Most of these stories, though not all of them, appeared in his collection *al-Khuṭūbah* (1972).

214. See e.g. 'al-Khuṭūbah', *Sabah al-Khahir,* 9 May 1968, 'al-Nafidah', *al-Akhbar,* 27 July 1969, 'Nahayat al-Hafl', *al-Majallah,* May 1970, and 'al-Lakmah', *al-Hilāl,* August 1970.

215. Such as 'al-Abb', pp. 29—36, 'al-Lakmah', pp. 63—70, 'Nahāyat al-Ḥafl', pp. 71—94, 'al-Muẓāharah', pp. 105—24 and 'Kūmbārs min Zamānina', pp. 133—54 in, and the title story of, *al-Khuṭūbah,* pp. 5—28, and 'al-Nāfidhah', *al-Akhbār,* 27 July 1970.

216. Frohock, *The Novel of Violence in America,* p. 17.

217. Although there are many critical studies on Qāsim's novel (to mention just a few, see H. Kilpatrick, *The Modern Egyptian Novel: A Study in Social Criticism* (London 1974), pp. 140—7, 'Abd al-Muḥsin Ṭāhā Badr, *al-Riwā'ī wa'l-Ard,* pp. 187—227, and Sabry Hafez 'Ayyām al-Insān al-Sab'ah', *al-Majallah,* September 1969), it is appropriate to refer here to some detailed studies on his short stories such as: 'Abd al-Raḥmān Abū 'ūf, 'al-Baḥth 'an Ṭarīq Jadīd li'l-Qiṣṣah al-Miṣriyyah al-Qaṣīrah', *al-Hilāl,* August 1969, Sabry Hafez, 'al-Uqṣūṣah al-Miṣriyyah wa'l-Ḥadāthah', *Gallery 68,* October 1969.

218. Such as 'al-Ṣafar', *al-Adab,* November 1965, 'al-Sundūq', *al-Adab,* April 1966, and 'Fī Dhalik al-Yawm', *al-Majallah,* August 1968.

219. Such as 'Ḥikāyat Ḥawl Ḥādith Ṣaghīr', *al-Majallah,* February 1968, 'al-Qaḍiyyah', *al-Majallah,* January 1969, 'Shajarat al-Ḥubb', *al-Hilāl,* August 1969, 'Taḥt al-Suqūf al-Sākhinah', *al-Majallah,* August 1969, and "An al-Banāt', *al-Hilāl,* August 1970.

220. As is the case in 'al-Qaḍiyyah', 'Shajarat al-Hubb' and "An al-Banāt'.

221. For a detailed study of Aṣlān's work see e.g. Idwār al-Kharrāṭ, 'I. Aṣlān wa-Qinā' al-Rafḍ', *Gallery 68,* February 1971; Ghālib Halasā, 'Qiṣaṣ I. Aṣlān', *Gallery 68,* February 1971; Khalīl Kalfat, 'I. Aṣlān fī Marḥalatih al-Jadīdah', *Gallery 68,* February 1971; 'Alī Ja'far al-'Allāq, 'Buḥayrat al-Masā'', *al-Ādāb,* December 1971; Radwa 'Ashur, 'Riḥlat al-Ta'ab fi'l-Bilād al-Gharībah', *al-Ṭalī'ah,* July 1972. His works were also discussed in 'Abd al-Raḥmān Abū 'ūf, 'al-Baḥth 'an Ṭarīq Jadīd li'l-Qiṣṣah al-Qaṣīrah':, *al-Hilāl,* August 1969 and Sabry Hafez, 'al-Uqṣūṣah al-Miṣriyyah wa'l-Ḥadāthah', *Gallery 68,* October 1969.

222. This is the image of the world portrayed in each story of Aṣlān's first collection, *Buḥayrat al-Masā'* (1971). Although the collection was published in 1971 all the stories were written and published in periodicals between 1965 and 1969. For detailed bibliographical information about the date and place of publication of each story see Khalīl Kalfat, 'I. Aṣlān fī Marḥaltih al-Jadīdah', *Gallery 68,* February 1971.

223. As is the case in most of the stories of his collection *Buḥayrat al-Masā',* as well as 'al-Ḍaw' fi'l-Khārij', *al-Masā'* 30 August 1968, 'al-Nawm fi'l-Dākhil', *al-Masā',* 23 October 1968, 'al-Baqā' fi'l-Bayt', *al-Masā',* 2 November 1968, and 'al-Rajul wa'l-Ashyā'', *al-Masā',* 7 November 1968.

224. See e.g. 'al-'Azif', 'al-Ṭawwāf', pp. 143—50, and the title story in *Buḥayrat al-Masā'.*

225. As is the case in 'al-Malhā al-Qadīm' and 'al-Lu'ab al-Ṣaghīrah', pp. 99—104, and the title story in *Buḥayrat al-Masā'.*
226. Such as 'Rā'iḥat al-Maṭar', pp. 43—56, 'al-Ṭāhārrur min al-'Aṭash', pp. 89—98, 'al-Musta'jir', pp. 113—20, and 'al-Jurḥ', pp. 135—42 in *Buḥayrat al-Masā',* and 'Bindūl min Nuḥās' in *al-Masā',* 12 October 1968.
227. See e.g. 'al-Malhā al-Qadīm', 'al-Baḥth 'an 'Unwān' and 'al-Tāḥārrur min al-'Aṭash' in *Buḥayrat al-Masā'.*
228. For a detailed study of al-Bisāṭī's work see Sabry Hafez, 'Mustaqbal al-Uqṣūṣah al-Miṣriyyah', *al-Majallah,* August 1966, Ghālib Halasā, 'al-Kibār wa'l-Ṣighār', *Gallery 68,* June 1968.
229. Such as 'Mishwār Qaṣīr', pp. 17—28, 'Nazwah', pp. 103—10, and 'al-Zaffah', pp. 143—58 in *al-Kibār wa'l-Ṣighār.*
230. Such as Ḥamdī Abu'l-Shaykh, Muḥammad Jād, al-Disūqī Fahmī, Bakr Rashwān, Maḥmūd Baqshīsh, 'Abbās Muḥammad 'Abbās, 'Ādil Ādam, Muṣṭafā Abu'l-Naṣr, Kamāl Mursī, Muḥammad Sālim, and Maḥmūd Diyāb.
231. Such as 'Nazwah', pp. 103—10 and 'al-Zaffah', pp. 143—58 in *al-Kibār wa'l-Ṣighār,* 'al-Muharrij', pp. 16—35, 'al-'Amm wa-Anā', pp. 36—53, and 'Mawkib al-Ḥuzn' in *Ḥadīth min al-Ṭābiq al-Thālith.*
232. *Al-Kibār wa'l-Ṣighār,* pp. 17—28.
233. Such as 'Qiṣṣat Rajul Mayyit', pp. 109—122, and the title story, pp. 54—63 in *Ḥadīth min al-Ṭābiq al-Thālith,* and 'Liqā'', *al-Qiṣṣah,* June 1965, 'Khafajah', *al-Masā',* 14 August 1965, and 'Abū Jabal', *al-Katib,* September 1965.
234. See e.g. 'al-Taḥaddī', pp. 4—15, 'Ibtisāmat al-Madīnah al-Ramādiyyah', pp. 64—73, 'Ḥikāyāt li-Rajul Fawq al-Saṭḥ' ,pp. 141—55, 'al-Janāza', pp. 156—67 and 'Nuzhat al-Zakāyib', pp. 175–187 in *Ḥadīth min al-Ṭābiq al-Thālith.*
235. As is the case in 'al-Taḥaddī', 'al-Muharrij', 'Lu'bat al-Muṭāradah', pp. 74—96, and 'al-'Alam', pp. 168—74 in *Ḥadīth min al-Ṭābiq al-Thālith.*
236. For a detailed study of 'Abd Allāh's work see Sabry Hafez, 'Mustaqbal al-Uqṣūṣah al-Miṣriyyah', *al-Majallah,* September and November 1966, and Idwār al-Kharrāṭ, 'al-Riḥlah ilā Ma-Warā' al-Waqi'iyyah', *al-Ṭalī'ah,* May 1972.
237. Such as 'Layl al-Shiṭā'', pp. 67—78, 'Ṭāḥunat al-Shaykh Mūsā', pp. 87—92, and 'Maḥbūb al-Shams' in his first collection, *Thalāth Shajarat Kabīrah Tuthmir Burtuqalā,* whose title story is one of his least successful works.
238. Such as 'Jabal al-Shay al-Akhdar', pp. 21—6, '35 al-Biltaji, 52 'Abd al-Khāliq Tharwat', pp. 33—42, 'Ḥiṣār Ṭirwādah', pp. 49—54, 'al-Thalāth Waraqāt', pp. 55—66, and 'Qābīl al-Sā'a al-Thāniyyah', pp. 79—86 in *Thalāth Shajarat Kabīrah*; 'Riḥlat al-Sanwāt al-Sab'' in *al-Ḥurriyyah,* 17 June 1966; and 'Fāntasyā al-'Unf al-Qabīḥ', *al-Hilāl,* August 1970.
239. Freedman, *The Lyrical Novel,* p. 9.
240. *Ibid.*
241. I. al-Kharrāṭ, 'al-Riḥlah ilā Mā-Warā' al-Waqi'iyyah', *al-Ṭalī'ah,* May 1972, pp. 188—94.
242. For a detailed study of al-Ghīṭānī's work see Sabry Hafez, 'Mustaqbal al-Uqṣūṣah al-Miṣriyyah', *al-Majallah,* October 1966, 'Abd al-Raḥmān Abu 'Uf, *al-Baḥth 'an Ṭarīq Jadīd lil-Qiṣṣah al-Qaṣīrah al-Miṣriyyah,* 117 ff, and Faruq 'Abd al-Qadir, 'al-Wajh wa'l-Qina'', *al-Ṭalī'ah,* June 1972.
243. As is the case in 'al-Qal'ah', *al-Adīb,* October 1964, 'Min al-Qāhirah ilā al-Zaqazīq', *al-Adīb,* November 1964, 'Akhbār Hāmmah', *al-Masā',* 25 March 1965, 'Aḥrāsh al-Madīnah', *al-Qiṣṣah,* June 1965, 'Risālat Fatāh min al-Shamāl', *al-Ādāb,* July 1965, and 'Khadījah', *al-Jumhūriyyah,* 5 June 1966.
244. These four stories are: the title story, pp. 5—21, 'al-Muqtabas min 'Awdat Ibn

Iyās', pp. 23—44, 'Hidāyat Ahl al-Wārā li-Ba'ḍ mimmā Jarā fi'l-Maqsharah', pp. 83—98, and 'Khashf al-Lithām 'an Ibn Sallām', pp. 99—110 in *Awrāq Shābb 'Āsh Mundh Alf 'Ām.*

245. Ihab Hassan, 'The Literature of Silence', in Bernard Bergonzi (ed.), *Innovations,* p. 93.

246. Such as 'Itḥāf al-Zamān', *al-Masā',* 28 March 1969, 'Dam'at al-Bākī', *al-Hilāl,* June 1969, 'Gharīb al-Ḥadīth', *al-Akhbār,* 6 July 1969, 'Akhbār Ḥarb al-Kafarah', *al-Hilāl,* August 1969, 'Bukā' al-Ḥazīn', *al-Masā',* 19 December 1969, 'al-Maghūl', *Ruz al-Yūsuf,* 21 January 1970, and 'Nāṭiq al-Zamān', *al-Majallah,* July 1970.

247. See e.g. 'al-Muqtabas ...' and 'Hidāyat Ahl al-Wārā ...' in *Awrāq Shābb 'Āsh Mundh Alf 'Ām,* and 'Itḥāf al-Zamān', 'Dam'at al-Bākā', 'Gharīb al-Ḥadīth' and 'Nāṭiq al-Zamān'.

248. Such as the title story of *Awrāq Shābb 'Āsh Mundh Alf 'Ām,* pp. 6—21, 'Dam'at al-Baki', 'Akhbar Harb al-Kararah' and 'al-Maghul'.

249. As is the case in 'Hidayat Ahl al-Wara ...', pp. 83—98, 'Kashf al-Litham', pp. 99—110 in *Awrāq Shābb 'Āsh Mundh Alf 'Ām,* and 'Ithaf al-Zaman', 'Gharib al-Hadith', and 'Buka' al-Hazin'.

250. T. S. Eliot, *To Criticise the Critic* (London 1965).

Bibliography

Since this book offers a survey of the modern Arabic short story in Egypt until 1970 and hopes to stimulate further studies in this field it deviates from the traditional bibliography, which confines itself to works cited or consulted. Instead, I have opted for two complementary bibliographies. The first, which covers the primary sources, does not list only the collections and works referred to in this study, but offers also a complete bibliography of all the collections of short stories that appeared in the period under discussion. This bibliography is concerned with historical accuracy rather than with the current availability of the books, so, against each collection, it gives the date of first publication, even if another edition is cited in the study. In the second bibliography, which is more like the normal bibliography of works cited and periodicals consulted, only those editions used or quoted in the study are given.

Primary Sources

A Complete Bibliography of the Collections of Egyptian Short Stories (1921–70)

This bibliography takes the pioneering works of Taymūr and 'Ubayd as its point of departure, then endeavours to scan the field as thoroughly as possible up to 1970.

It lists all the collections published by any writer up to 1970 and, for writers whose first collection appeared before then, it may include collections that appeared subsequently. The place of publication is Cairo unless otherwise stated; this is followed by the date of the first edition, and where this is not known, the standard abbreviation 'n.d.' is used. Dates in square brackets indicate the suggested date for an undated edition.

1. Abāẓa, Fikri
   al-Ḍāḥik al-Bāki (1948)
   al-Ḥubb Abū al'Ajā'ib (1960)
2. Abāẓa, Sharīf
   Fidā' (1963)
3. Abāẓa, Tharwat
   al-Ayyām al-Khaḍrā' (1960)

Dhikrayāt Ba'īdah (1964)
Hadhihi al-Lu'bah (1967)
Ḥīn Yamīl al-Mīzān (1970)
al-Sibāḥah fi al-Rimāl (Beirut, 1975)
4. 'Abd al-'Āl, Aḥmad Muḥammad
'Araq al-Jid'ān, n.d. [1967]
5. 'Abd al-'Azīz, Malak
al-Jawrab al-Maqṭū' (1962)
6. 'Abd al-'Azīz, Muḥammad
Quiṣṣat Shajarah (1964)
7. 'Abd al-Ḥalīm, Ibrāhīm
Azmat Kātib (1965)
8. 'Abd al-Ḥamīd, Muḥammad al-Khuḍari
Li-Ākhir Ramaq (1965)
al-Safar fi al-Layl (1970)
9. 'Abd al-Majīd, Muḥammad Fahmi
Ashwāk al-Ward, n.d. [1942]
10. 'Abd al-Qādir, Muḥammad Zaki
Ṣuwar min al-rīf (1949)
al-Ṣadafah al-'Adhrā' (1961)
al-Khayt al-Maqṭū' (1963)
Gharam 'Āṣif, n.d. [1964]
Namādhij min al-Nisā' (1965)
al-Dunyā Taghayyarat (1966)
Aqdām 'ala al-Ṭarīq (1967)
Qālat lah (1968)
11. 'Abd al-Quddūs, Iḥsān
Ṣāni' al-Ḥubb (1949)
Bā'i' al-Ḥubb (1959)
Sayyidat Ṣālūn (1952)
al-Naẓẓārah al-Sawdā' (1952)
Ayn 'Umri (1954)
al-Wisādah al-Khāliyah (1955)
Muntahā al-Ḥubb (1957)
al-Banāt wa-l-Ṣayf (Beirut 1957)
'Aqli wa-Qalbi (1959)
Shafatāh, n.d. [1961]
Lā Laysa Jasaduk (Beirut 1962)
Bint al-Sulṭān (1963)
Bi'r al-Ḥirmān (1963)
'Ulbah min al-Ṣafīḥ al-Ṣadi' (1967)
Sayyidah fi Khidmatak (1967)
al-Nisā' Lahunn Asnān Bayḍā' (1969)
al-Hazīmah Kān Ismuhā Fāṭimah (1975)
al-'Aẓra' wa-l-Sha'r al-Abyaḍ (1977)
12. 'Abd al-Raḥmān, Maḥfūẓ
al-Baḥth 'an al-Majhūl (1966)
13. 'Abd al-Tawwāb, Zaki
Fi Mawkib al-Shayṭān (1950)
Safīrat al-Shayṭān (1950)
14. 'Abdu, Ibrāhīm

al-Nās Maʿādin (1960)

15. ʿAbdu, Saʿīd
    al-Jumʿah al-Yatīmah (1936)
    Fātinat al-Shayṭān (1951)
    Hayākil fi al-Rīf (1953)
    ʿAla Jisr al-Turʿah (1963)
    Shurrabat al-Khurj (1972)
16. ʿAbdullah, ʿAbd al-Samīʿ
    ʿAṣāfīr, n.d. [1963]
    al-Silsilah (1972)
17. ʿAbdullah, Muḥammad ʿAbd al-Ḥalīm
    al-Nafidhah al-Gharbiyyah, n.d. [1953]
    al-Māḍī La Yaʿūd, n.d. [1956]
    Alwān min al-Saʿādah, n.d. [1958]
    Ashyāʾ lil-Dhikrā (1958)
    al-Ḍafīrah al-Sawdāʾ, n.d. [1963]
    Khuyūṭ al-Nūr, n.d. [1965]
    Ḥāffat al-Jarīmah, n.d. [1966]
    Usṭūrah min Kitāb al-Ḥubb, n.d. [1967]
18. ʿAbdullah, Ṣūfi
    Kulluhunn ʿAyyūshah (1956)
    Thaman al-Ḥubb, n.d. [1958]
    Baqāyā Rajul (1958)
    Madrasat al-Banāt, n.d. [1960]
    Niṣf Imraʾah (1962)
    Layāl Lahā Thaman, n.d. [1963]
    Muʿjizat al-Nīl (1964)
    Alf Mabrūk (1965)
    ʿArusah ʿala al-Raff (1966)
    al-Qafaṣ al-Aḥmar (1975)
    Shayʾ Aqwā minhā (1975)
    Nabḍah Taḥt al-Jalīd (1975)
19. ʿAbdullah, Yaḥya al-Ṭāhir
    Thalāth Shajarāt Kabīrah Tuthmir Burtugālā (1970)
    al-Duff wa-l-Ṣundūq (Baghdad, 1972)
    Anā wa-Hiya wa-Zuhūr al-ʿĀlam (1977)
    Ḥikāyāt lil-Amīr (1978)
20. ʿĀbidīn, Shukri
    Fātinat al-Ḥayy (1953)
    Laylat al-Mawlid (1953)
    al-Ṭifl al-Kabīr (1958)
21. Abū-Ḥadīd, Muḥammad Farīd
    Maʿa al-Zamān, n.d. [1945]
22. Abū-Kurrāt, Ibrāhīm al-Sayyid
    Ward wa-Shawk (1935)
    Al-Zafarāt (Būrsaʿīd, n.d.)
23. Abū-l-Najā, Muḥammad Abū-l-Maʿāṭi
    Fatāh fi al-Madīnah (Beirut, 1960)
    al-Ibtisāmah al-Ghāmiḍah, n.d. [1963]
    al-Nās wa-l-Ḥaqīqah (1974)

24. Abū-l-Naṣr, Muṣṭafā
Wāhidah Takfī (1965)
25. Abū-l-Shaikh, Ḥamdi
A'māq bayḍā' (1961)
26. Abū-l-Su'ūd, 'Abd al-Ḥafīẓ
Qaṣaṣ Azhari, n.d.
27. Abū-Ṭayilah, Muḥammad
Sirr al-Mar'ah al-Majhūlah (1955)
28. Abū-Zaid, Muḥammad 'Abd al-Ḥalīm
Kawthar (1960)
Hānim (1963)
29. 'Ādil, Aḥmad
Mawlid bilā 'Arūsah (1961)
al-Masīḥ fi al-Dukkān (1962)
30. 'Afifi, Muḥammad
Anwār (1946)
31. Aḥmad, Anwar
al-Lahab al-Muqaddas (1956)
32. Aḥmad, Ḥasan Rushdi
al-Arḍ, n.d. [1963]
33. 'Aish, Aḥmad Muḥammad
Ṣawt min al-Jannah (1963)
34. Al-'Alāyili, Jamīlah
al-Rā'iyah (Alexandria, 1941)
35. 'Ammār, Rizq
al-Ḥubb wa-l-Jidār al-Aswad (1967)
36. Al-'Aqqād, Ibrāhīm Ḥusain
Thawrah wa-Ḥanīn (1936)
Aḥlām al-Kharif (1941)
37. 'Āshūr, Nu'mān
Hawādīt 'Amm Faraj (1956)
Fawānīs, n.d. [1963]
Sibāq ma'a al-Ṣārūkh (1967)
Azmat Akhlāq (1976)
38. Al-'Askari, Ṣabri
Quyūd Muḥaṭṭamah (Damanhūr, 1954)
Da'wah ila al-Ḥubb (1976)
39. Aṣlān, Ibrāhīm
Buḥayrat al-Masā' (1971)
Yūsuf wa-l-Ridā' (1987)
40. Al-'Assāl, Najībah
Bayt al-Ṭā'ah, n.d.
al-Ghā'ibah, n.d. [1964]
al-Ḥaṣā wa-l-Jabal (1966)
Saṭr Maghlūṭ (1971)
41. Al-Aswāni, 'Abbās
al-Ḍāḥik al-Akhīr (1964)
42. 'Aṭā, Samīr Aḥmad
al-Shajarah wa-l-Rīḥ (1965)
43. 'Ayyād, Shukri Muḥammad
Milād Jadīd, n.d. [1958]

Ṭarīq al-Jāmi'ah, n.d. [1963]
Zawjati al-Raqīqah al-Jamilah (1976)
Rubā'iyyāt (1984)
Kahf al-Akhyār (1985)

44. Al-'Ayyūṭi, Muḥammad Yāsīn
Hasan al-Zujji (1970)

45. Al-'Azab, Maḥmūd Ḥasan
'Ūd al-Qaṣab (1967)

46. Al-Badawī, Maḥmūd
al-Raḥīl (1935)
Rajul (1936)
Funduq al-Dānūb (1941)
al-Dhi'āb al-Jā'i'Ah (1944)
al-'Arabah al-Akhīrah (1948)
Ḥadath Dhāt Laylah (1953)
'Adhārā al-Layl (1956)
al-A'raj fi al-Mīnā' (1958)
al-Zallah al-ūlā (1959)
Ghurfah 'Ala al-Saṭḥ (1960)
Laylah fi al-Ṭarīq (1962)
Zawjat al-Ṣayyād, n.d. [1962]
Ḥāris al-Bustān, n.d. [1963]
'Adhrā' wa-waḥsh (1963)
al-Jamāl al-Ḥazīn, n.d. [1963]
Masā' al-Khamīs (1966)
Ṣaqr al-Layl (1971)
al-'Adhrā' wa-l-Layl (1975)
al-Bāb al-Ākhar (1977)

47. Badrān, Samīr
Anā wa-l-Arḍ, n.d. [1964]

48. Bidār, Birti
Bā'i'at al-Dumū' (1957)

49. Bahjat, Muṣṭafa
Al-Lahw al-Khafi (1957)

50. Barakāt, Kāmil
Bidāyati (1937)

51. Al-Bindāri, Muḥammad Thābit
Fi Mawkib al-Shayṭān (1949)

52. Bint-l-Shāṭi'
Imra'ah Khāṭi'ah (1944)
Raj'at Fir'Awn (1948)
Sirr al-Shāṭi' (1952)
Ṣuwar min Ḥayātihinn (1959)

53. Al-Bisāṭi, Muḥammad
al-Kibār wa-l-Ṣighār (1964)
Ḥadīth min al-Ṭābiq al-Thālith (1970)
Aḥlām Rijāl Qiṣār al-'Umr (1979)
Hādhā Mā Kān (1988)
Munḥanā al-Nahr (1992)
Ḍaw' Ḍa'īf Lā Yakshif Shay'ā (1993)

54. Al-Dāli, Al-Sayyid

Nahāyat al-Ṭarīq (1946)
55. Dāwūd, 'Abd al-Wahāb
al-Ḍaw' al-Aḥmar, n.d. [1961]
Nab' al-Ḥubb (1964)
Warā'ana al-Baḥr (1971)
56. Dhuhni, Ṣalāḥ
Fi al-Darajah al-Thāminah (1935)
Min al-Māḍi (1936)
Ra'īs al-Taḥrīr (1938)
Ḍaḥikāt Iblīs (1941)
Dhāt Masā' (1944)
al-Ka's al-Sābi'Ah (1945)
Aqwā min al-Ḥubb (1948)
Ṣuwar min ūrūbbā (1949)
Jā' al-Kharīf (1953)
al-Ayyām al-Jamīlah (1954)
Saḥābat Ṣayf, n.d. [1959]
Yaqẓat Rūḥ (1964)
57. Al-Dīb, 'Alā'
al-Qāhirah (1964)
58. Diyāb, Maḥmūd
Khiṭāb min Qibli, n.d. [1962]
59. Fahmi, 'Abd al-Raḥmān
Sūẓi wa-l-Dhikrāyāt (1960)
al-Mulk lak, n.d. [1962]
al-'ūd wa-l-Zamān (1969)
Raḥalāt al-Sindibād al-Sab' (Beirut, 1971)
60. Fahmi, Sha'bān
Qiṣṣat Khaṭibayn (Alexandria, 1940)
Nidā' al-Ṣakhrah (Alexandria, 1941)
61. Fajr
Fi al-Mishmish (1939)
62. Faraḥ, Muḥammad
Qulūb Muḥaṭṭamah (1956)
63. Faraj, Alfrīd
Majmū'at Qiṣaṣ Qaṣīrah, n.d. [1968]
64. Fāris, Bishr
Sū' Tafāhum (1942)
65. Fatḥi, Aḥmad
al-Lāh wa-l-Shayṭān (1939)
66. Fatḥi, Ḥanīfa
al-Samā' Ayḍa Tabki (1966)
67. Fatḥi, Sihām
Aẓwāj wa-Zawjāt 'Araftuhum, n.d.
68. Fayyāḍ, Sulaymān
'Aṭshān Yā Ṣabāyā (1961)
Wa-Ba'danā al-Ṭūfān (1968)
Aḥẓān Ḥazīrān (Beirut, 1969)
al-'Uyūn (Beirut, 1972)
Zaman al-Ṣamt wa-l-Ḍabāb (Bierut, 1974)
al-Ṣūrah wa-l-Ẓill (Baghdad, 1976)

al-Sharnaqah (1993)

69. Fikri, Muḥammad
    'Amāliqah fi Zujājah (1966)
70. Ghallāb, Muḥammad
    Ḥanīn wa-'Awāṣif, n.d. [1963]
71. Ghānim, Fatḥi
    Tajribat Ḥubb (1958)
    Sūr Ḥadīd Mudabbab (1964)
72. Gharīb, Muḥammad 'Ali
    al-Baṭal al-Majhūl, n.d. [1963]
73. Al-Ghīṭānī, Jamāl
    Awrāq Shabb 'Āsh Mundh Alf 'Ām (1969)
    Arḍ ... Arḍ (1972)
    al-Ziwail (Baghdad, 1975)
    al-Ḥiṣār min Thalāth Jihāt (Damascus, 1975)
    Ḥikāyāt lil-Gharīb, n.d.
    Dhikr Mā Jarā (1978)
74. Ghunaim, Ghunaim Muḥammad
    Qiṣaṣ Fā'izah (1968)
75. Ghurāb, Amīn Yūsuf
    al-Ḍabāb (Damanhūr, n.d.) [1942]
    Hutāf al-Jamāhīr (1945)
    Nisā' fi Ḥayāti (1950)
    Arḍ al-Khaṭāyā (1951)
    Yawm al-Thulāthā' (1952)
    Tarīq al-Khaṭāyā (1953)
    Āthār 'Ala al-Shifāh (1953)
    Sāḥir al-Nisā' (1954)
    Imra'at al-'Aziz (1955)
    Qalb fi Lubnān (1956)
    Hādhā al-Naw' min al-Nisā' (1959)
    Nisā' al-Ākharīn (1962)
    Ashyā' Lā Tushtarā (1963)
    Imra'ah Ghayr Mafhūmah (1964)
    Yaḥduth fi al-Layl Faqaṭ (1970)
    Iklīl min al-'Ār (1974)
76. Ḥabīb, 'Abd al-Maqṣūd
    Baqāyā Dhikrāyāt, n.d. [1963]
    al-Liqā' (1966)
77. Ḥabīb, Kāmil Maḥmūd
    Qiṣaṣ min al-Ḥayāh (1958)
78. Al-Ḥabrūk, Ismā'īl
    Hāribah min al-Layl (1955)
    Imra'ah Bilā Muqābil (1958)
79. Ḥāfiẓ, 'Abbās
    Dumū' wa Ḍaḥikāt, (1949)
    'indamā Tuḥibb al-Mar'ah, (1951)
80. Ḥāfiẓ, Ṣalāḥ
    Ayyām al-Qalaq (1967)
    al-Walad al-Ladhi Ja'alanā Lā Nadfa' Nuqūdā (1967)

81. Al-Ḥakīm, Tawfīq
Ahl al-Fann, n.d. [1934]
'Ahd al-Shayṭān, n.d. [1938]
Qiṣaṣ Tawfīq al-Ḥakīm, 5 vols. (1939–49)
Laylat al-Zifāf, n.d. [1949]
Shajrat al-Ḥukm (1953)
Arini al-Lah, n.d. [1954]
'Awālim al-Faraḥ (1958)
Anā wa-l-Qānūn wa-l-Fann (1973)
82. Al-Ḥakīm, 'Uryān
Laylah fi al-Firdaws (1947)
83. Halasā, Ghālib
Wadī' wa-l-Qiddīsah Mīlādah (1968)
Zunūj wa-Badw wa-Fallāḥūn (Baghdad, 1977)
84. Ḥalīm, Asmā
Fi Sijn al-Nisā' (1958)
85. Al-Ḥamāmṣi, 'Abd al-'Āl
Lil-Katākīt Ajniḥah (1967)
Hādhā al-Ṣawt wa-Ākhrūn (1979)
Bi'r al-Aḥbāsh (1994)
86. Ḥamdi, 'izz-l-Dīn
Dumū' (1939)
87. Ḥamdi, Muṣṭafa Kamāl
al-Īmān (1954)
88. Ḥāmid, Sa'd
Arwāḥ Ḥa'irah (1945)
Ajsād lil-Bay', n.d. [1948]
Āmāl Ḍā'i'Ah (1953)
Tayyār al-Ḥayāh (1955)
Imra'ah Waḥīdah (1957)
Wajhān lil-Khaṭi'ah (1960)
Rimāl al-Shāṭi' (1961)
al-Shāṭi' al-Ākhar, n.d. [1962]
Aqṣar Ṭarīq, n.d. [1963]
Layl wa-Ḥanān (1966)
al-Rajul al-Ladhi Akrahuh (1975)
89. Ḥamrūsh, Aḥmad
Kumbārs, n.d. [1964]
90. Ḥaqqi, Maḥmūd Ṭāhir
Ghādiyāt Rā'iḥāt (1948)
Basamāt Sākhirah (1951)
91. Ḥaqqī, Yaḥyā
Qindīl Umm Hāshim (1944)
Dimā' wa-Ṭīn (1955)
Umm al-'Awājiz (1955)
'Antar wa-Juliet, n.d. [1961]
Sāriq al-Kuḥl (1985)
Al-Firāsh al-Shāghir (1986)
92. Ḥarīdi, Muḥammad
Ramād Ishtaddat bih al-Rīḥ (1966)
93. Ḥasan, Muḥammad Kāmil

al-Sābiḥah fī al-Nār (1957)
Sāriqat al-Rijāl (1958)
94. Ḥasan, Sa'id Muḥammad
Rabbunā Yustur (1965)
95. Hāshim, Fatḥi
al-Usṭūrah (1965)
96. Hāshim, Labībah
Ka's min al-Dumū' (1941)
97. Ḥassūnah, Muḥammad Amīn
al-Ward al-Abyaḍ (1933)
98. Ḥawwās, Ṭaha
al-Qārib al-Akhīr (1965)
99. Al-Ḥifnāwi, Hālah
Min Fam Rajul, n.d.
100. Al-Ḥijjāwai, Zakariyyā
Nahr al-Banafsaj (1956)
101. Ḥilmi, Su'ad
Da'ni li-Zawji (1967)
102. Ḥilmi, Yūsuf
Min Ghawr al-Muḥīṭ (1936)
103. Ḥimaidah, 'Abd al-Qādir
Raghm Kull Shay' (1963)
104. Ḥusain, Fahmi
'Alāqah Basīṭah, n.d.
Aṣl al-Sabab (1967)
105. Ḥusain, Ṭaha
al-Mu'Adhdhabūn fī al-Arḍ (1949)
106. Ibrāhīm, 'Abd al-Ḥalīm
Rā'iḥat Ḥayātina (1946)
107. Ibrāhīm, Farīd
Qulūb Muḥaṭṭamah
108. Ibrāhīm, 'izzat Muḥammad
Ḥārat al-Saqqāyīn (1960)
109. Ibrāhīm, 'izzat al-Sayyid
Waḥy al-Rimāl (1934)
110. Ibrāhim, Muḥammad 'Abd al-Fattāh
Qiṣaṣ al-Ḥayāh (1934)
Imra'ah fī Ḥayāt Rajul (1963)
111. 'Īd, Nāhid
Ashjān (1965)
112. Idrīs, Yūsuf
Arkhaṣ Layāli (1954)
Jumhūriyyat Faraḥāt (1956)
al-Baṭal (1957)
Alaysa Kadhālik (1957)
Ḥādithat Sharaf (Beirut, 1958)
Ākhir al-Dunyā (1961)
al-'Askari al-Aswad (1962)
Lughat al-Āy Āy (1965)
al-Naddāhah (1969)
Bayt min Laḥm (1971)

Anā Sulṭān Qānūn al-Wujūd (1976)
al-'Atab 'Ala al-Naẓar (1987)
113. 'Īsa, Maḥmūd
al-Nufūs al-Mu'Adhdhabah (1937)
114. 'Iwais, Sayyid
Nahāyat al-Mahzalah, n.d.
'Awdat al-Farāshah (1965)
115. Jād, Sayyid
al-Jidār (1962)
116. Jad-l-Rabb, Mu'Awwaḍ
al-Nās wa-l-Kilāb (1964)
117. Jalāl, Ibrāhīm
Majmū'At Qiṣaṣ (1960)
118. Al-Jamal, Muḥammad
al-'Uyūn al-Zujājiyyah (1965)
119. Jāmāti, Ḥabīb
Ibrāhīm fi al-Maydān (1934)
Ḍaḥāyā Mā Ahmalah al-Tārīkh, n.d. [1935]
Khafāyā al-Quṣūr (1936)
Aghrab Mā Ra'ayt (1949)
Buṭūlāt Arabiyyah, n.d. [1962]
Miṣr Maqbarat al-Fātiḥīn, n.d. [1962]
Bayn Judrān al-Quṣūr, n.d. [1963]
'Ala Ḍifāf al-Nīl, n.d. [1963]
Qayāṣirah wa-Salāṭīn, n.d. [1963]
Taḥt Samā' al-Maghrib (1964)
120. Al-Jamīl, Darwīsh
Hakadha Nasīr (1947)
121. Al-Jārim, Badr-l-Dīn 'Ali
Maw'id ma'a al-Dhikrā (1960)
122. Jawdat, Ṣāliḥ
Kullunā Khaṭāyā, n.d. [1958]
Fi Funduq al-Lah (1959)
Khā'ifah min al-Samā' (1962)
Asāṭīr wa-Ḥawādīt, n.d. [1963]
123. Al-Jayyār, Ṣubḥi
Yustur 'Ardak, n.d. [1961]*Sūq al-'Abīd* (1963)
124. Jirais, Yūsuf Iskandar
Tāj al-'Adhārā (1923)
Abūnā Sarjiyūs, n.d.
125. Jūhar, Yūsuf
al-Ḥayāh Qiṣaṣ (1951)
Samīrah Hānim (1955)
Nār wa-Ramād (1966)
Ummahāt lam Yalidn Abadā (1971)
Dumū' fi 'Uyūn Ḍāḥikah (1972)
Ibtisāmāt wa-Ḥayyah Raqṭa' (1973)
126. Al-Jūhari, Ra'ūf
al-Bukhūr al-Muḥtariq (1938)
127. Jum'A, Ṣāliḥ Ḥasan
Li-l-Shabāb Ajniḥah (1960)

128. Kamāl, Iḥsān
Sijn Amlukuh (1965)
Saṭr Maghlūt (1971)
129. Kāmil, Ḥasan 'Abd al-Mun'im
Wādi al-Nisyān (1936)
130. Kāmil, Maḥmūd
al-Mutamarridūn (1931)
Fi al-Bayt wa-l-Shāri' (1933)
8 Yūlū (1934)
Bā'i' al-Aḥlām (1935)
Awwal Yanāyir (1936)
Thalathūn Qiṣṣah (1936)
Ant wa-Anā (1937)
al-Majnūnah (1938)
al-Rabī' al-Āthim (1939)
Zawba'ah Taḥt Jumjumah (1941)
'Uyūn Ma'ṣūbah (1941)
al-Rijāl Munāfiqūn (1942)
Ḥuṭām Imra'ah (1942)
Lā'ibāt bil-Nār (1943)
Fatayāt Mansiyyāt (1946)
al-Qāfilah al-Ḍāllah (1946)
Ābār fi al-Ṣaḥrā' (1948)
al-Hāribūn min al-Mādi (1949)
Lawḥāt wa-Ẓilāl (1960)
Arwāh Bayn al-Suḥub (1962)
131. Kāmil, Ṣalāḥ-l-Dīn
Awrāq Mutanāthirah (1936)
132. Khaḍr, 'Abbās
al-Sitt 'Aliyyah (1960)
Madīḥah, n.d. [1962]
al-'Ajūz wa-l-Ḥubb (1976)
133. Khalīl, Ḥasan Fatḥi
Ighrā' (1960)
Qalb Kabīr, n.d. [1963]
134. Al-Khamīsi, 'Abd al-Raḥmān
al-A'māq, n.d. [1950]
Ṣayḥāt al-Sha'b (1952)
Qumṣān al-Damm (1953)
Lan Namūt (1953)
Riyāh al-Nīrān (1954)
Dimā' lā Tajiff (1956)
al-Bahlawān al-Mudhish Aḥmad Kishkish (1961)
Amīnah, n.d. [1962]
135. Al-Kharrāṭ, Idwār
Ḥīṭān 'Āliya, n.d. [1958]
Sā'āt al-Kibriyā' (Beirut, 1972)
Ikhtināqāt al-'ishq wa-l-Ṣabāḥ (1983)
Turābuhā Za'frān (1986)
Amwāj al-Layālī (1991)
Yā Banāt Iskindiriyyah (1993)

136. Al-Khaṭīb, Ibrāhim
Ṣuwar, n.d.
Mughāmarāt Ṣaghīrah, n.d.
137. Khayrat, 'Abdullah
Warā' al-Zujāj (1967)
Shams al-Ṣabāḥ al-Ba'īdah (1996)
138. Khazbak, Muḥammad
Nisā' fī al-Qaryah (1962)
139. Al-Khūli, Luṭfī
Rijāl wa-Ḥadīd, n.d. [1956]
Yāqūt Maṭḥūn (1966)
140. Khūrsīd, Fārūq
al-Kull Bāṭil (1961)
al-Qarṣān wa-l-Tinnīn (1971)
141. Khuzām, Māhir
Nihāyat al-Riḥlah, n.d.
142. Kīlāni, Kāmil
Mukhtār al-Qiṣaṣ (1929)
143. Al-Kīlāni, Najīb
Dumū' al-Amīr (1962)
144. Labīb, 'Azmi
Wujūh Jadīdah (1963)
145. Lāshīn, Maḥmūd Ṭāhir
Sukhriyat al-Nāy, n.d. [1926]
Yuḥkā Anna, n.d. [1929]
al-Niqāb al-Ṭā'ir (1940)
146. Lūqā, Naẓmi
Raqīq al-Arḍ (1951?)
al-Nās wa-l-Dunyā, n.d.
al-Muḥtariq Bayn al-Shakk wa-l-Yaqīn (1960)
147. Luṭfī, Aḥmad
al-Sabr Ṭayyib, n.d. [1962]
148. Luṭfī, Sa'id
'Aqd ma'a al-Shayṭān (1949)
149. Maḥfūẓ, Najīb
Hams al-Junūn, n.d. [1938]
Dunyā al-Lāh, n.d. [1963]
Bayt Sayyi' al-Sum'Ah, n.d. [1965]
Khammārat al-Qiṭṭ al-Aswad, n.d. [1968]
Taḥt al-Miẓallah, n.d. [1969]
Hikāyah Bilā Bidāyah wa-Lā Nihāyah, n.d. [1971]
Shahr al-'Asal, n.d. [1971]
al-Ḥubb Fawq Haḍabat al-Haram (1979)
al-Shayṭān Ya'iẓ (1980)
Ra'ayt Fīmā Yarā al-Nā'im (1982)
al-Tanẓīm al-Sirri (1984)
Ṣabāḥ al-Ward (1987)
al-Fajr al-Kādhib (1989)
Ṣadā al-Sinīn (1999)
Aḥlām Fatrat al-Naqāhah (2004)
150. Maḥjūb, Fāṭimah

Nīhāyat Shay' (1962)
151. Maḥmūd, Ḥasan
Ajwā' (1956)
152. Maḥmūd, Muṣṭafa
Akl 'Ais (1955)
'Anbar 7, n.d. [1958]
Qiṭ'At Sukkar (1959)
Shillat al-Uns, n.d. [1964]
Rā'iḥat al-Damm, n.d. [1967]
Qiṣaṣ Muṣṭafā Maḥmūd, n.d. [1971]
al-Ṭūfān (Beirut, 1976)
Nuqṭat al-Ghalayān (Beirut, 1977)
153. Makkāwī, 'Abd al-Ghaffār
Ibn al-Sulṭān (1967)
al-Sitt al-Ṭāhirah (1967)
154. Makkāwī, Sa'd
Nisā' min Khazaf (1948)
Fi Qahwat al-Majādhīb (1955)
Rāhibah min al-Zamālik (1955)
Makhālib wa-Anyāb (1956)
al-Mā' al-'Akir, n.d. [1957]
Shahīrah (1959)
Majma' al-Shayāṭīn (1959)
al-Zaman al-Waghd (1962)
Abwāb al-Layl (1964)
al-Qamar al-Mashwi (1967)
Rajul min Ṭīn (1970)
al-Raqṣ 'Ala al-'Ushb al-Akhḍar (1973?)
al-Fajr Yazūr al-Ḥadīqah (1975)
155. Mas'ūd, Maḥmūd
Rabīb al-Ḥurriyyah (1961)
156. Maẓhar, Ismā'īl
Ru'ya Hanā', n.d.
157. Al-Māzini, Ibrāhīm 'Abd al-Qādir
Ṣundūq al-Dunyā (1929)
Khuyūṭ al-'Ankabūt (1935)
Fi al-Ṭarīq (1937)
'A al-Māshi (1937)
Min al-Nāfidhah (1949)
Min al-Nāfidhah wa Ṣuwar min al-Ḥayāh (1960)
158. Miḥassib, Ḥasan
al-Kūkh (1964)
al-Taftīsh (1967)
159. Al-Minyāwi, Muḥammad Ibrāhīm
Nisā' wa-Rijāl (1950)
160. Miṣbāḥ, Ibrāhīm
al-Ayyām al-Ḥulwah (1966)
161. Misharrafah, Muṣṭafa
Hadhayān, n.d. [1967]
162. Al-Misīri, 'Abd al-Mu'ṭi
al-Ẓāmi'ūn (Damanhūr, 1938)

Aqāṣīṣ min al-Qahwah (Damanhūr, 1942)
Rūḥ wa-Jasad (Damanhūr, 1948)
Mishwār Ṭawīl (1964)
163. Al-Miṣri, 'Abd al-Majīd
Īmān (1952)
164. Al-Miṣri, 'Abd al-Samī'
Aḥlām al-Shabībah (Asyūṭ, 1949)
Ḥilm Laylah (1954)
Nahyāt al-Laḥn (1955)
al-Ighrīqiyyah al-Samrā' (1961)
165. Al-Miṣri, Ibrāhīm
al-Adab al-Ḥayy (1930)
al-Adab al-Ḥadīth (1932)
Kharīf Imra'ah (1944)
Qulūb al-Nās, n.d. [1947]
Ka's al-Ḥayāh (1947)
Nufūs 'Āriyah (1951)
al-Unthā al-Khālidah (1957)
al-Insān wa-l-Qadar (1959)
Ṣirā' al-Rūḥ wa-l-Jasad (1961)
Qalb 'Adhrā' (1962)
'Ālam al-Gharā'iz wa-l-Aḥlām (1962)
al-Bāb al-Dhahabi, n.d. [1963]
Ṣuwar min Insān (1965)
Ṣirā' ma'a al-Māḍi (1967)
al-Wajh wa-l-Qinā' (1971?)
166. Muḥammad, Muḥammad' Abd al-Fattāḥ
Arḍ al-Shayṭān (1950)
167. Muḥammad, Muḥammad Farīd
Nafs Ḥā'irah (Damanhūr, 1938)
168. Muḥammad, Muḥammad Kamāl
Ayyām min al-'Umr (1954)
al-Ḥayāh Imra'ah (1956)
al-Ayyām al-Ḍā'i'Ah (1958)
al-Iṣba' wa-l-Zinād (1965)
169. Muhrān, Fawziyyah
Bayt al-Ṭālibāt (1961)
170. Munīb, Fārūq
al-Dīk al-Aḥmar (1960)
Zā'ir al-Sabāḥ (1964)
Aḥzān al-Rabī' (1967)
Adam al-Ṣaghīr (1973)
171. Murād, Ḥilmi
'Indamā Tuḥibb al-Mar'ah (1949)
172. Mursi, Ṣāliḥ
al-Khawf, n.d. [1960]
Khiṭāb ilā Rajul Mayyit (1967)
173. Mūsā, Ṣabri
al-Qamīṣ (1958)
Ḥadith al-Nisf Mitr (1962)
Ḥikāyāt Ṣabri Mūsā (1963)

Wajhā li-Ẓahr (1966)
Mashrū' Qatl Jārah (1970)

174. Mūsā, Salāma
Iftaḥū lahā al-Bāb (1962)

175. Muṣṭafa, Tharwat
al-Dawr al-Khālid (1966)

176. Nāji, Ibrāhīm
Madīnat al-Aḥlām (1938)
Adrikni Yā Duktūr (1950)

177. Najīb, 'izz-l-Dīn
'Aish wa-Milḥ (1960)
Ayyām al-'izz (1962)
al-Muthallath al-Fayrūzi (1967)
Ughniyat al-Dumyah (Damascus, 1974)

178. Najīb, Victoria
Nawāfidh Maftūḥah, n.d. [1962]

179. Nash'at, Badr
Masā' al-Khair Yā Gid'ān (1956)
Ḥilm Laylat Ta'ab (1962)

180. Al-Nashshār, 'Ali Sāmi
al-Alḥān Al-Ṣāmitah (Alexandria, 1935)

181. Nūḥ, Aḥmad
Ṣabaḥiyyah Mubārakah, n.d. [1959]

182. Al-Qabbāni, Ḥusain
Yaqẓat al-Rūḥ (1947)
al-Sarāb (1957)
Qaṣr al-'Adhārā (1962)
Intaẓirīni Ghadā (1964)
al-Shu'ā' al-Ghārib (1964)
Huwa wa-l-Nisā' wa-l-Ḥubb (1975)
Gharāmiyyāt 'Ala al-Bilāj (1976)

183. Al-Qāḍi, Aḥmad Fatḥi
Ḥaqīqat al-Aḥlām (1960)

184. Al-Qalamāwi, Sahīr
Aḥādith Jaddati (1935)
Thumma Gharubat al-Shams (1949)
al-Shayāṭīn Talhū (1964)

185. Al-Qilish, Kamāl
al-Murāhiq (1965)

186. Al-Qirsh, Muḥammad
Zaynab wa-l-Rayyis Hamīdu (1966)

187. Qurrā'ah, Saniyyah
Udhkurūni (1940)

188. Rabī', Jamāl
Hamasāt al-Salām, n.d.
Qulūb Ṣā'imah, n.d. [1962]
al-Jazā' (1962)
Nidā'al-Ḥayāh (1965)

189. Rabī', Mawahib Ṣidqi
Innahu al-Qadar (Alexandria, 1965)

190. Raḍwān, Fatḥi

Usturat Ḥubb (1962)
Shāfi' wa-Nāfi' (1965)
al-Sāriq wa-l-Masrūq (1967)
191. Raḍwān, Kamāl-l-Dīn
Shāri' al-Tiyātru, n.d. [1960]
192. Rajab, Muḥammad Ḥāfiẓ
al-Kurah wa-Ra's al-Rajul (1967)
Ghurabā' (1968)
Makhlūqāt Barrād al-Shāy al-Maghli (1979)
Ḥamāṣah wa-Qahqahāt al-Ḥamīr al-Dhakiyyah (1992)
193. Al-Ramli, Fatḥi
Min Taḥt al-Anqāḍ, n.d.
Ibn al-Dāyrah, n.d. [1958]
194. Rāqim, Muḥammad 'Ali
Baqāyā Imra'ah (1960)
Alwān min al-Qalb wa-l-'Aql (1960)
195. Rayyān, Amīn
al-Mawqi' (1967)
196. Riyāḍ, Māhir
'Usfūrah min Būrsa'id (1957)
197. Rizq, 'Abd al-Fattāḥ
Bāb 14, n.d. [1960]
al-Ribābah Yā Zaman (1965)
Qiṣaṣ al-Damm wa-l-Raṣāṣ (1974)
198. Rushdi, Rashād
'Arabat al-Ḥarīm (1955)
199. Rustum, Durriyyah
al-Ḥā'irah, n.d. [1965]
Ahlā bil-'Adhāb, n.d.
Ghadā Ḥayāh Jadīdah, n.d.
200. Rustum, Maḥmūd Maḥmūd
Min Waḥi Qaryatinā (1958)
al-Wa'd wa-l-Maktūb, n.d. [1962]
201. Al-Ṣabiyy, Muḥammad Kāmil
Ḥayāh wa-Ḥayāh (Alexandria, 1942)
202. Ṣabri, Aḥmad
Ba'th al-Ālihah (1937)
203. Ṣabri, Yaḥya
Ashwāq (1952)
204. Sa'd, Aḥmad Ḥasan
al-Sikirtairah al-Ḥasnā' (1960)
205. Sa'd, Shawqi
Riḥlah ila al-Warā', n.d.
206. Al-Sa'dani, Maḥmūd
al-Samā'al-Sawdā', n.d. [1955]
Jannat Raḍwān (1956)
Bint Madāris (1960)
al-Afrīki (1965)
207. Al-Sa'dāwi, Nawāl
Ḥanān Qalīl (1962)

Ta'allamt al-Ḥubb (1964)
Laḥẓat Ṣidq (1965)
208. Al-Saḥḥār, 'Abd al-Ḥamīd Jūdah
Fi al-Waẓīfah, n.d. [1944]
Hamzāt al-Shayāṭīn, n.d. [1946]
Ṣadā al-Sinīn, n.d. [1953]
Imra'ah wa-Alḥān (1955)
Armalah min filastin (1959)
Laylah 'Āṣifah (1963)
209. Al-Sa'īd, Amīnah
al-Hadaf al-Kabīr (1958)
210. Ṣāliḥ, Aḥmad Rushdi
al-Zawjah al-Thāniyah (1955)
211. Sālim, 'Abd al-Ḥamīd
Ṣuwar (1928)
212. Salīm, 'Abd al-Mun'im
Waraqat Taamghah, n.d. [1960]
Mas'alat Karāmah (1962)
213. Sālim, Muḥammad
Ustādh fi al-Ḥārah (1961)
al-Baḥth 'An al-Sa'ādah (1964)
Afandi min la-Madīnah (1967)
214. Salīm, Ra'fat
Lā Mafarr (1960)
215. Sāsi, 'Abd al-'Azīz 'Umar
Min al-A'māq (Alexandria, 1933)
216. Al-Ṣāwi, Muḥammad
al-Judrān al-Arba'ah (Alexandria, 1964)
Nahr al-Nisyān (Alexandria, 1965)
al-Thawr wa-l-'Adhrā' (Alexandria, 1970)
217. Al-Shaikh, Aḥmad
Dā'irat al-Inḥinā' (1970)
218. Sha'lān, Muḥammad
Ḥikāyah min Shāri'inā, (1959)
219. Al-Sharīf, Aḥmad Hāshim
Wajh al-Madīnah (1965)
al-Aḥlām, al-Ṭuyūr, al-Karnafāl (1967)
220. Sharīf, Ṭāhir
Shumū' wa-Ẓilāl (1961)
221. Al-Sharqāwī, 'Abd al-Raḥmān
Arḍ al-Ma'rakah (1954)
Aḥlām Ṣaghīrah (1956)
222. Al-Sharqāwī, Ḍiyā'
Riḥlah fi Qiṭār Kull Yawm (1966)
Suqūṭ Rajul Jād (1969)
223. Al-Sharqāwi, Maḥmūd
A'āṣīr wa-Nasamāt (1968)
224. Al-Shārūnī, Yūsuf
al-'Ushshāq al-Khamsah (1954)
Risālah ilā Imra'ah (1960)
al-Ziḥām (Beirut, 1969)

Ḥalāwat al-Rūḥ (1971)
Ākhir al-'Unqūd (1973)
al-Umm wa-l-Waḥsh (1982)
al-Ḍaḥik ḥatā al-Bukā' (1997)
225. Al-Shāyib, Zuhair
al-Muṭāradūn (1970)
al-Maṣyadah (1974)
226. Al-Shinnāwi, Muḥammad
Ḥikāyāt min Baladna (1968)
227. Shitā, Hilāl
al-Shafaq al-Aḥmar (1937)
228. Al-Shumbuki, Ṭal'at
al-Ufuq al-Shāḥib (1962)
229. Al-Shūrbaji, Maḥmūd
Intiqām Qarawiyyah (1947)
230. Al-Sibā'i, 'Abd al-Mun'im
Ku'ūs al-Shaqā' (1955)
231. Al-Sibā'i, Muḥammad
al-Khādimah, n.d. [1957]
al-Faylasūf, n.d. [1957]
al-Samar, n.d. [1964]
232. Al-Sibā'i, Yūsuf
Nā'ib 'izrā'il, n.d. [1947]
Atyāf, n.d. [1947]
Ithnatā 'Ashrat Imra'ah, n.d. [1948]
Yā Ummah Ḍaḥikat, n.d. [1948]
Fi Mawkib al-Hawāh, n.d. [1949]
Khabāyā al-Ṣudūr, n.d. [1949]
Min al-'Ālam al-Majhūl, n.d. [1949]
Ithnā 'Ashr Rajulā, n.d. [1949]
Mabkā al-'Ushshāq, n.d. [1950]
Hadhih al-Nufūs, n.d. [1950]
Hadhā Huwa al-Ḥubb, n.d. [1951]
Ughniyāt, n.d. [1951]
Bayn Abū-l-Rīsh wa-Junaynat Nāmīsh [1951]
Ṣuwar Ṭibq al-Aṣl, n.d. [1951]
Summār al-Layāli, n.d. [1952]
Sitt Nisā'wa-Sittat Rijāl, n.d. [1952]
al-Shaikh Zu'rub wa-Ākharūn, n.d. [1952]
Nafḥah min al-Īmān, n.d. [1952]
Hamsah Ghābirah (1953)
Laylat Khamr (1954)
Layāl wa-Dumū', n.d. [1956]
al-Wiswās al-Khannās (1956)
233. Ṣidqī, Jādhibiyyah
Rabīb al-Ṭuyūr (1951)
Mamlakat al-Lah (1954)
Innah al-Ḥubb (1955)
Sattār Yā Layl (1956)
Wa-Bakā Qalbi (1957)
Shay' Ḥarām (1959)

Lailah Baiḍā (1960)
al-Layl Ṭawīl (1961)
al-Bint min Baḥari, n.d. [1962]
Ibn al-Nīl, n.d. [1963]
Ta'āla (1963)
Anta Qās (1966)
al-Dunyā wa-Anā (1972)
Bawabat al-Mutawalli (1975)
al-Baladi Yu'kal (1976)

234. Ṣidqī, Muḥammad
al-Anfār (1956)
al-Aydi al-Khashinah (1958)
Sharkh fi Jidār al-Khawf (1967)
Liqā' ma'a Rajul Majhūl (1969)

235. Al-Ṣīsi, Muḥammad Aḥmad Zaki
al-Miḥrāb al-Mawrūth (Alexandria, 1938)

236. Ṣubḥi, 'Aṭiyyah
Bākūrati (1936)

237. Sulaymān, 'Iṣām Muḥammad
al-Mar'ah lā Ḍamīr Lahā (1944)
al-Nisā' Khā'inat (1945)

238. Su'ūdi, Ḥusain
Asrār al-Hawānim (1926)
Asrār al-Dunyā (1927)

239. Al-Tābi'i, Muḥammad
Thalāth Qiṣaṣ (1951)
'indamā Nuḥibb (1964)
Alwān min al-Qiṣaṣ (1964)
Aḥbabt Qātilah (1966)
Ṣālat al-Nujūm (1970)

240. Ṭāhir, Bahā'
al-Khuṭūbah (1972)
Bi-lAms Ḥalumt Bik (1984)
Anā al-Malik Ji't (1985)
Dhahabt ilā Shallāl (1998)

241. Ṭanṭāwi, Ṣalāḥ
al-Nās wa-l-Ḥijārah (1962)
al-Naqsh 'Ala al-Ḥajar (1966)

242. Tawfīq, Ḥabīb
al-Rabī', n.d. [1934]
Madīḥah, n.d. [1936]
Fi Dinyā al-'Adam (1945)
Atyāf al-Fann (1948)

243. Taymūr, Maḥmūd
al-Shaikh Jum'Ah (1925)
'Amm Mitwalli (1925)
al-Shaikh Sayyid al-'Abīṭ (1926)
Rajab Afandi (1928)
al-Ḥajj Shalabi (1930)
Abū 'Ali 'Āmil Artist (1934)
al-Shaikh 'Afallah (1936)

al-Wathbah al-Ūlā (1937)
Qalb Ghāniyah (1937)
Fir'awn al-Ṣaghīr (1939)
Maktūb 'Ala al-Jabīn (1941)
Bint al-Shayṭān (1944)
Shafāh Ghalīẓah (1946)
Khalf al-Lithām (1948)
Iḥsān lil-Lah (1949)
Kull 'Ām wa-Antum Bikhayr (1950)
Shabāb wa-Ghāniyāt (1951)
Abū al-Shawārib (1953)
Zāmir al-Ḥayy (1953)
Abū 'Ali al-Fanān (1954)
Thā'irūn (1955)
Dinyā Jadīdah (1957)
Nabbūt al-Khafīr (1958)
Tamr Ḥinnah 'Ajab (1958)
Anā al-Qātil (1962)
Intiṣār al-Ḥayāh (1963)
al-Bārūnah Umm Aḥmad (1967)
Ḥikāyat Abū 'ūf (1969)
Qāl al-Rāwi (1970)
Bint al-Yawm (1971)

244. Taymūr, Muḥammad
Wamīḍ al-Rūḥ (1922)

245. Ṭūbyā, Majīd
Fūstūk Yaṣil ilā al-Qamar (1967?)
Khams Jarā'id lam Tuqra' (1970)
al-Ayyām al-Tāliyah (1972)

246. Al-Ṭūkhi, 'Abdullah
Dawūd al-Ṣaghīr (1958)
Fi Ḍaw' al-Qamar (1960)
al-Naml al-Aswad (1963)
Ibn al-'Ālam (1967)

247. Ṭūlān, 'Abd al-Majīd
Zahrat al-Rabi' (1945)

248. Al-Tūni, Muḥammad Shawkat
Fi Ẓilāl al-Dimū' (1929)

249. 'Ubayd, 'Īsā
Iḥsān Hānim (1921)
Thurayyā (1922)

250. 'Ubayd, Shiḥātah
Dars Mu'lim (1922)

251. Al-'Uryān, Muḥammad Sa'īd
Min Ḥawlinā (1945)

252. Wahba, Sa'd-l-Dīn
Arzāq, n.d. [1958]

253. Wākid, 'Abd al-Laṭīf
al-'Adhārā al-Khāṭi'āt (1965)
Raqiṣat al-Ṣaḥrā' (1966)

254. Waliyy-l-Dīn, Ismā'īl

Buqa' fi al-Shams (1968)
255. Waṣfi, Waṣfi Āl
Warā' al-Rijāl (1960)
'Adan Aw al-Jaḥīm, n.d. [1962]
256. Wāsif, Mīlād
Alḥān Qalb (1939)
257. Al-Wirdānī, Ibrāhīm
al-Madīnah al-Majnūnah (1950)
al-Layl (1953)
al-Madīnah, n.d.
al-Mu'allif wa-l-Nisā' (1965)
November al-Miṣri (1966)
Bil-Munāsabah Naḥn (1966)
al-Layāli al-Bayḍā' (1966)
al-Ghaḍab (1967)
258. Yūsuf, Nuqūlā
Dunyā al-Nās (Alexandria, 1950)
Mawākib al-Nās (Alexandria, 1952)
Humm wa-Hunn (Alexandria, 1962)
259. Zaki, Aḥmad Kamāl
Dhāt Yawm, n.d. [1962]
260. Zaki, Fatḥi
Azmat Thiqah (1966)
261. Zaki, Zamīl Fāḍil
Rabī' al-'Umr (1952)

Secondary Sources

1. Books in English and Other Languages

Abdel-Meguid, Abdel-Aziz, *The Modern Arabic Short Story: Its Emergence, Development and Form* (Cairo: Dar al-Ma'ārif, n.d.).

Abrams, M. H., *The Mirror and the Lamp* (Oxford: Oxford University Press, 1953).

—— *A Glossary of Literary Terms* (New York: Holts Rinehart and Winston, 1971).

Adams, Charles, *Islam and Modernisation in Egypt, A Study of the Modern Reform Movement Inaugurated by Muhammad Abdu* (Oxford: Oxford University Press, 1930).

Al-Biheiry, Kawthar A., *L'Influence de la literature française sur le roman Arabe* (Quebec: University of Quebec Press, 1980).

Aldridge, James, *Cairo: Biography of a City* (London: Macmillan, 1969).

Al-Khozai, Mohamed A., *The Development of Early Arabic Drama: 1847–1900* (London: Longman, 1984).

Allan, G. W. and Clark, H. H., *Literary Criticism: Pope to Croce* (Detroit: Wayne State University Press, 1962).

Allen, Roger, *The Arabic Novel: An Historical Introduction* (Manchester: Manchester University Press, 1982).

Allen, Walter, *Tradition and Dream* (London: Penguin, 1965).
—— *Some Aspects of the American Short Story* (Oxford: Oxford University Press, 1973).
Allot, Miriam, *Novelists on the Novel* (London: Routledge and Kegan Paul, 1959).
Al-Sayyid, Afaf Lutfi, *Egypt and Cromer: A Study in the Anglo-Egyptian Relations* (London: John Murry, 1968).
Anderson, Benedict, *Imagined Communities: Reflections on the Origin of Nationalism* (London: Verso, 1991).
Atiyah, Aziz S., *A History of Eastern Christianity* (London: Methuen, 1968).
Auerbach, Erich, *Mimesis: The Representation of Reality in Western Literature* (Princeton, NJ: Princeton University Press, 1953).
Aycock, Wendell M., ed., *The Teller and the Tale: Aspects of the Short Story* (Lubbock: Texas Tech Press, 1982).
Badawī, M. M., *A Critical Introduction to Modern Arabic Poetry* (Cambridge: Cambridge University Press, 1975).
—— *Early Arabic* Drama (Cambridge: Cambridge University Press, 1988).
—— *Modern Arabic Drama in Egypt* (Cambridge: Cambridge University Press, 1987).
—— *Modern Arabic Literature and the West* (London: Ithaca Press, 1985).
—— ed, *Cambridge History of Arabic Literature, Modern Arabic Literature* (Cambridge: Cambridge University Press, 1992).
Baker, Carlos, *Hemingway: The Writer as Artist* (Princeton, New Jersey, PUP, 1963).
Bakhtin, M. M., *The Dialogic Imagination: Four Essays*, ed. Michael Holquist, tr. Caryl Emerson and Michael Holquist (Austin: University of Texas Press, 1981).
—— *Problems of Dostoevsky's Poetics*, tr. Caryl Emerson (Manchester: Manchester University Press, 1984).
—— and Medvedev P. M. , *The Formal Method in Literary Scholarship: A Critical Introduction to Sociological Poetics* (Cambridge, MA: Harvard University Press, 1985).
—— and Volosinov V. N. , *Marxism and the Philosophy of Language*, tr. L. Matejka and I.R. Titunik (New York: Simenar Press, 1973).
Barthes, Roland, *S/Z*, tr. Richard Miller (New York: Hill and Wang, 1974).
—— *Image, Music, Text*, tr., Stephen Heath (New York: Hill and Wang, 1977).
Bates, H. E., *The Modern Short Story from 1809–1953* (London: Robert Hale, 1972)
Beachcroft, T. O., *The English Short Story I & II* (London: Longmans Green & Co. 1967).
—— *The Modest Art: A Survey of the Short Story in English* (Oxford: Oxford University Press, 1969).
Benjamin, Walter, *Illuminations*, tr. Harry Zohn (London: Fontana/Collins, 1973).

Bergonzi, Bernard, *The Situation of the Novel* (London: Penguin, 1972).
—— ed., *Innovations: Essays on Art and Ideas* (London: Macmillan, 1968).
Berque, Jacques, *Cultural Expression in Arab Society Today* (Austin: University of Texas Press, 1978).
—— *Egypt: Imperialism and Revolution,* tr. Jean Stewart (London: Faber and Faber, 1972).
—— 'The Establishment of the Colonial Economy', in William R. Polk and Richard L. Chambers, *Beginnings of Modernisation*.
Beyerl, Jan, *The Style of the Modern Arabic Short Story* (Prague: Charles University Press, 1971).
Boktor, Amir, *The Development and Expansion of Education in the United Arab Republic* (Cairo: AUC Press, 1963).
Bonheim, Helmut, *The Narrative Modes: Techniques of the Short Story* (Cambridge: D. S. Brewer, 1982).
Booth, Wayne C., *The Rhetoric of Fiction* (Chicago: University of Chicago Press, 1961).
Bottomore, T. B., *Elites and Society* (London: Penguin, 1973).
Bradbury, Malcolm and James McFarlane, eds, *Modernism* (London: Penguin, 1976).
—— *What is a Novel?* (London: Longman, 1969).
—— *Possibilities: Essays on the State of the Novel* (Oxford: Oxford University Press, 1973).
—— ed., *The Novel Today* (Manchester: Manchester University Press, 1977).
Brooks, Cleanth, *The Hidden God* (New Haven, CT: Yale University Press, 1963).
—— and Warren, Robert Penn, *Understanding Fiction* (New York: 1943).
Brugman, J., *An Introduction to the History of Modern Arabic Literature* (Lieden: Brill, 1984).
Bullata, Issa (ed), *Critical Perspectives on Modern Arabic Literature* (New York, Three Continents Press, 1980).
Burke, Kenneth, *Counter-Statement* (Berkeley: University of California Press, 1968).
—— *The Philosophy of Literary Form* (Berkeley: University of California Press, 1973).
Cady, Edwin H., *The Light of Common Day: Realism in American Fiction,* (Bloomington: Indiana University Press, 1971).
Calderwood, James and Toliver, Harold, *Perspectives on Fiction* (Oxford: Oxford University Press, 1968).
Cassirer, Ernst, *The Philosophy of Symbolic Forms,* 3 vols, tr. Ralf Manheim (New Haven, CT: Yale University Press, 1957)
—— *Language and Myth*, tr. Susanne K. Langer (New York: Dover, 1946).
Caudwell, Christopher, *Illusion and Reality: A Study of the Sources of Poetry*, (London: Lawrence and Wishart, 1937).
Chatman, Seymour (ed.), Literary Style: A Symposium (Oxford: Oxford

University Press, 1971).
—— *Story and Discourse* (Ithaca, NY: Cornell University Press, 1978).
Chiari, Joseph, *Aesthetics of Modernism*, (London: Vision Press, 1970).
Cobham, Catherine, 'The Importance of Yūsuf Idrīs' Short Stories in the Development of an Indigenous Egyptian Literary Tradition, Unpublished M. Phil. thesis, University of Manchester, 1974.
Coleridge, S. T., *Biographia Literaria* (London: J. M. Dent, 1906).
Cowley, Malcolm, *A Second Flowering: Works and Days of the Lost Generation*, (London: André Deutsch, 1973).
Croce, Benedetto, *Poetry*, III, ii, in Allen and Clark, *Literary Criticism: Pope to Croce*.
Culler, Jonathan, *The Pursuit of Signs: Semiotics, Literature, Deconstruction* (London: Routledge and Kegan Paul, 1981).
Daiches, David, *A Study of Literature for Readers and Critics* (London: André Deutsch, 1968)
—— *Critical Approaches to Literature* (London: Longman, 1956).
Dyson, A. E., *The Crazy Fabric: Essays in Irony* (London: Macmillan, 1966).
Eagleton, Terry, *Marxism and Literary Criticism* (London: Methuen, 1976).
—— *Criticism and Ideology: A Study in Marxist Literary Theory* (London: New Left Books, 1976).
—— *Walter Benjamin: or Towards a Revolutionary Criticism* (London: Verso, 1981).
Edel, Leon, *The Modern Psychological Novel* (New York: The Universal Library, 1964).
El-Enany, Rasheed, *Naguib Mahfouz: The Pursuit of Meaning* (London: Routledge, 1993).
Eliot, T. S., *To Criticise the Critic* (London: Faber, 1965).
Enright, D. J. and De Chickera, E., *English Critical Essays: 16th to 20th Century* (Oxford: Oxford University Press, 1962).
Ferguson, J. D. L., *Themes and Variations in the Short Story* (New York: Books for Libraries Press, 1972).
Fraser, G. S., *The Modern Writer and His World* (London: Penguin, 1972).
Freedman, Ralph, *The Lyrical Novel* (Princeton, NJ: Princeton University Press, 1963).
Friedman, Norman, *Form and Meaning in Fiction* (Athens, GA: University of Georgia Press, 1975).
Frohock, W. M., *The Novel of Violence in America* (New Haven, CT: Yale University Press, 1976).
Frow, John, *Marxism and Literary History* (Oxford: Basil Blackwell, 1986).
Frye, Northrop, *Anatomy of Criticism: Four Essays* (Princeton, NJ: Princeton University Press, 1957).
Genette, Gerard, *Figures*, vols. 1–3 (Paris: Édition du Seuil, 1966),
—— *Nouveau discours du récit* (Paris: Édition du Seuil, 1983).
—— *Narrative Discourse*, tr. Jane Lewin (Ithaca, NY: Cornell University

Press,1980)
—— *Narrative Discourse Revisited*, tr. Jane Lewin (Ithaca, NY: Cornell University Press, 1988).
—— *The Architext: An Introduction,* tr. Jane Lewin (Berkeley: University of California Press, 1992).
—— *Fiction and Diction,* tr. Catherine Porter (Ithaca, NY: Cornell University Press, 1993).
Gilman, Richard, *The Confusion of Realms* (London: Weidenfeld and Nicolson, 1970).
Gindin, James, *Harvest of a Quiet Eye: The Novel of Compassion* (Bloomington: University of Indiana Press, 1971).
Gioia, Dana and Gwynn, R. S., *The Art of the Short Story* (New York: Pearson Longman, 2006).
Girard, René, *Mensonge romantique et vérité romanesque* (Paris: Grasset, 1961); tr. Yvonne Freccero as *Deceit, Desire, and the Novel* (Baltimore, MA: Johns Hopkins University Press, 1965).
Goldmann, Lucien, *Le Dieu Câché* (Paris: Gallimard, 1956) ; tr. Philip Thody as *The Hidden God* (London: Routledge and Kegan Paul, 1964).
—— *Method in the Sociology of Literature*, tr. William Q. Boelhower (Oxford: Basil Blackwell, 1980).
—— *Pour une sociologie du roman* (Paris: Gallimard, 1964) ; tr. Alan Sheridan as *Towards a Sociology of the Novel* (London: Tavistock, 1975).
Gordon, Ian A., *Katherine Mansfield* (London: Longman, 1971).
Graham, Kenneth, *English Criticism of the Novel: 1865–1900* (Oxford: Clarendon Press, 1965).
Grant, Damian, *Realism* (London: Methuen, 1970).
Greenblatt, Stephen, 'Towards a Poetics of Culture', in *New Historicism*, ed. H. Aram Veseer (London: Routledge, 1989).
Grossvogel, David, *Limits of the Novel: Evolution of a Form from Chaucer to Robbe-Grillet* (Ithaca, NY: Cornell University Press, 1968).
Hafez, Sabry, *The Genesis of Arabic Narrative Discourse: A Study in the Sociology of Modern Arabic Literature* (London: Saqi, 1993).
—— 'The Transformation of Reality and the Arabic Novel's Aesthetic Response', *Bulletin of the School of Oriental and African Studies*, vol. 57, Part 1, 1994, pp. 93–112.
—— and Catherine Cobham, eds, *A Reader of Modern Arabic Short Stories* (London: al-Saqi, 1988).
Hall, Stuart and Paul DuGay, (eds), *Questions of Cultural Identity* (London: Sage, 1996).
Hanson, Clare, *Short Stories and Short Fictions: 1880–1980* (London: Macmillan, 1985).
Hale, Nancy, *The Realities of Fiction: An Author Talks about Writing* (London: Macmillan, 1963).
Hassan, Ihab, *Radical Innocence: Studies in Contemporary American Fiction* (New

York: Harper and Row, 1961).
Hassan, Ihab, 'The Literature of Silence', in *Innovations: Essays on Art and Ideas s*, ed. Bernard Bergonzi (London: Macmillan, 1968).
Hazlitt, William, *Selected Essays, ed. Geoffrey Keynes* (London: Nonesuch, 1946).
Head, Dominic, *The Modernist Short Story: A Study in Theory and Practice* (Cambridge: Cambridge University Press, 1992).
Hemmings, F. W. J., *The Age of Realism* (London: Penguin, 1974).
Hildick, Wallace, *Thirteen Types of Narrative* (London: Macmillan, 1968).
Hirsch, E. D., *Validity in Interpretation* (New Haven, CT: Yale University Press, 1967).
Hitti, Philip, *The Middle East in History* (Princeton, NJ: D. Van Nostrad, 1961).
Holt, J., ed., *Political and Social Change in Modern Egypt* (Oxford: Oxford University Press, 1965).
Honig, Edwin, *Dark Conceit, The Making of Allegory* (Oxford: Oxford University Press, 1966).
Hourani, Albert, *Arabic Thought in the Liberal Age, 1798–1939* (Oxford: Oxford University Press, 1970).
Hussein, Mahmud, *Class Conflict in Egypt: 1945—1970*, tr. Michel and Susanne Chirman (New York: Monthly Review Press, 1973).
Ingram, Forrest L., *Representative Short Story Cycles of the Twentieth Century* (The Hague: Mouton, 1971).
Issawi, Charles, *Egypt, an Economic and Social Analysis* (Oxford: Oxford University Press, 1970)
—— *Egypt in Revolution* (Oxford: Clarendon Press, 1974).
Jad, Ali, *Form and Technique in the Egyptian Novel 1912—1971* (London: Ithaca, 1983).
Jameson, Fredric, *The Political Unconscious: Narrative as a Socially Symbolic Act* (London: Methuen, 1981).
Jankowski, James P., *Egypt's Young Rebels: Young Egypt 1933—52* (Palo Alto, CA, Hoover Institute Press, 1975).
Jauss, Hans Robert, *Towards an Aesthetic of Reception,* tr. Timothy Bahti (Minneapolis: University of Minnesota Press, 1982).
Jayyusi, Salma Khadra, *Trends and Movements in Modern Arabic Poetry,* 2 vols (Leiden: E. J. Brill, 1977).
Jones, Edmund D., ed., *English Critical Essays: Nineteenth Century* (Oxford: Oxford University Press, 1971)
Josipovici, Gabriel, *The World and the Book: A Study in Modern Fiction* (London: Macmillan, 1971).
Kermode, Frank, *Romantic Image* (London: Routledge and Kegan Paul, 1957)
—— *The Sense of an Ending: Studies in the Theory of Fiction* (Oxford: Oxford University Press, 1973).
Kettle, Arnold, ed., *The Nineteenth-Century Novel, Critical Essays and Documents* (London: Heinemann Educational, 1972).

Kilpatrick, Hilary, *The Modern Egyptian Novel: A Study in Social Criticism* (London: Ithaca, 1974).

Landes, David S., *Bankers and Pashas: International Finance and Economic Imperialism in Egypt* (London: Macmillan, 1958).

Langer, Susanne K., in her preface to E. Cassirer, *Language and Myth*, pp. ix–x.

Lawrence, D. H., *Selected Literary Criticism*, ed. Anthony Beal (London: Mercury, 1961).

Leavis, Q. D., *Fiction and the Reading Public* (Oxford: Oxford University Press, 1965)

Levin, Harry, *Refractions* (Oxford: Oxford University Press, 1966).

Liddle, Robert, *A Treatise on the Novel* (London: Jonathan Cape, 1947).

Little, Tom, *Modern Egypt* (London: Weidenfeld and Nicolson, 1967).

Lodge, David, *Language of Fiction* (London: Routledge and Kegan Paul, 1966)

—— *The Modes of Modern Writing: Metaphor, Metonymy and the Typology of Modern Literature* (London: Edward Arnold, 1977).

Lohafer, Susan and Clarey, Jo Ellyn, *Short Story Theory at a Crossroad* (Baton Rouge: Louisiana State University Press, 1989).

Lovejoy, Arthur O., *Essays in the History of Ideas* (Baltimore, MA: Johns Hopkins University Press, 1948).

Lucas, F. L., *Style* (London: Cassell, 1955).

Lukács, Georg, *The Historical Novel*, tr. Hannah and Stanley Mitchell (London: Penguin, 1962)

—— *The Meaning of Contemporary Realism*, tr. John and Necke Mauder (London: Merlin Pres, 1963).

—— *Writer and Critic*, tr. A. Khan (London: Merlin Press, 1970).

—— *The Theory of the Novel*, tr. Anna Bostock (London: Merlin Press, 1971).

—— *Studies in European Realism* (London: Merlin Press, 1972).

Lunacharsky, Anatoly, *On Literature and Art* (Moscow: Progress, 1973).

Mabro, Robert, *The Egyptian Economy* (Oxford: Clarendon Press, 1974).

Macherey, Pierre, *A Theory of Literary Production*, tr. Geoffrey Wall (London: Routledge and Kegan Paul, 1978).

Mannheim, Karl, *Ideology and Utopia* (London: Routledge and Kegan Paul, 1960)

Mansfield, Peter, *The British in Egypt* (London: Weidenfeld and Nicolson, 1971).

—— *Nasser's Egypt* (London: Penguin, 1969).

Manzalaoui, Mahmoud, ed., *Arab Writing Today: The Short Story* (Cairo: American Research Center in Egypt, 1970).

—— *Arab Writing Today: Drama* (Cairo: American Research Center in Egypt, 1977).

Martin, Wallace, *Recent Theories of Narrative* (Ithaca, NY: Cornell University Press, 1986).

Marx, Karl, *The Eighteenth Brumaire of Louis Bonaparte* (London: Lawrence

and Wishart, 1954).
Matthews, Brander, *The Philosophy of the Short Story* (New York: Longman, Green and Co., 1901).
—— (ed), *The Short Story: Specimens Illustrating its Development* (New York: American Book Co., 1907).
Matthews, J. H., *Surrealism and the Novel* (Michigan: the University of Michigan Press, 1966).
Maugham, Somerset W., *Points of View* (London: Heinemann, 1958).
May, Charles E., ed., *Short Story Theories* (Athens: Ohio University Press, 1976.
—— *The New Short Story Theories* (Athens: Ohio University Press, 1994).
—— *The Short Story: The Reality of Artifice* (London: Routledge, 2002).
Mehrez, Samia, *Egyptian Writers between History and Fiction* (Cairo and New York: American University in Cairo Press, 1994).
Meyerhoff, Hans, *Time in Literature* (Berkeley: University of California Press, 1960).
Mirrielaes, E. R., *The Story Writer* (Boston: Little Brown, 1939).
Moussa-Mahmoud, Fatma, *The Arabic Novel in Egypt* (Cairo: General Egyptian Book Organisation, 1973).
Myszor, Frank, *The Modern Short Story* (Cambridge, Cambridge University Press, 2001).
O'Brien, Patrick, *The Revolution in Egypt's Economic System* (Oxford: Oxford University Press, 1966).
O'Connor, Frank, *The Lonely Voice: A Study of the Short Story* (Hoboken, New Jersey, Melville House Publishing, 2004).
O'Faolain, S., *The Short Story* (London: Collins, 1948).
Omran, Adel R., ed., *Egypt, Population Problems and Prospects* (Carolina Population Center, 1973).
Ostle, R. C., 'The City in Modern Arabic Literature', *BSOAS*, vol. 49, part 1, 1986, pp. 193–202.
—— ed., *Studies in Modern Arabic Literature* (Warminster: Aris and Philips, 1976).
—— ed., *Modern Literature in the Near and Middle East: 1850–1870* (London: Routledge, 1991).
Perkins, George, *Realistic American Short Fiction* (Illinois: State University of Illinois Press, 1972).
Polk, William Roe and Chambers, Richard L. (eds), *Beginnings of Modernization in the Middle East: The Nineteenth Century* (Chicago: University of Chicago Press, 1968).
Prawer, S. S., *Comparative Literary Studies* (London: Duckworth, 1973).
Praz, Mario, *The Romantic Agony* (London: Collins, 1933).
—— *The Hero in Eclipse* (Oxford: Oxford University Press, 1956).
Prendergast, Christopher, *The Triangle of Representation* (New York: Columbia University Press, 2000).

Propp, V., *Morphology of the Folktale*, tr. L. Scott and L. Wagner (Austin: University of Texas Press, 1968).
Reid, Ian, *The Short Story* (London: Methuen, 1977).
Richards, I. A., *Principles of Literary Criticism* (London: Routledge and Kegan Pual, 1924).
—— *Practical Criticism: A Study in Literary Judgment* (London: Routledge and Kegan Paul, 1929).
Richetti, John J., *Popular Fiction before Richardson: Narrative Patterns*, 1700–1739 (Oxford: Clarendon Press, 1967).
Ritchie, James M., ed., *Periods in German Literature: A Symposium* (London: Oswald Wolff, 1966).
Rodway, Allan, *The Truths of Fiction* (London: Chatto and Windus, 1970).
Ruhle, Jurgen, *Literature and Revolution: A Critical Study of the Writer and Communism in the Twentieth Century* (London: Pall Mall, 1969).
Ruskin, John, 'Of the Pathetic Fallacy', in *English Critical Essays: 16th to 20th Century*, ed. Enright D. J. and De Chickera, E. (Oxford: Oxford University Press, 1962).
Said, Edward, *Beginnings: Intention and Method* (New York: Columbia University Press, 1985)
—— *The World, the Text, and the Critic* (Cambridge, MA: Harvard University Press, 1983).
Sakkūt, Ḥamdī, *The Egyptian Novel and its Main Trends from 1913–52* (Cairo: AUC Press, 1971).
Sansom, Alfred W., *I Spied Spies* (London: Lawrence and Wishart, 1957).
Scholes, Robert, *Elements of Fiction* (Oxford: Oxford University Press, 1968).
Scholes, Robert, and Kellogg, Robert, *The Nature of Narrative* (Oxford: Oxford University Press, 1966).
Schūcking, Levin L., *The Sociology of Literary Taste* (London: Routledge and Kegan Paul, 1966).
Scott, Virgil, *Studies in the Short Story* (New York: Holt, Renehart and Wiston, 1968)
Shaheen, Mohammad, *The Modern Arabic Short Story: Shahrazad Returns* (London: Macmillan, 1989).
Shaw, Valerie, *The Short Story: A Critical Introduction* (London: Longman, 1983).
Slonim, Marc, *Soviet Russian Literature, Writers and Problems 1917–67* (Oxford: Oxford University Press, 1967).
Smith, A. J. and Mason, W. H. , *Short Story Study* (London: Edward Arnold, 1971).
Spearman, Diana, *The Novel and Society* (London: Routledge and Kegan Paul, 1966).
Swingewood, Alan, *The Novel and Revolution* (London: Macmilan, 1975).
—— *Sociological Poetics and Aesthetic Theory* (London: Macmillan, 1986).
Taha, Ibrahim, *The Palestinian Novel: A Communication Study* (London:

Routledge, 2002).
Tomiche, Nada, *Histoire de la littérature romanesque de l'Egypte moderne* (Paris, 1981).
Trilling, Lionel, *The Liberal Imagination: Essays on Literature and Society* (London: Secker and Warburg, 1964).
Trotsky, L., *The Age of Permanent Revolution: A Trotsky Anthology*, ed. Issac Deutscher (New York: Viking, 1964).
Vatikiotis, P. J., *The Modern History of Egypt; From Muhammad Ali to Mubarak* (London: Weidenfeld and Nicolson, 1985).
Vazquez, Adolfo Sanchez, *Art and Society: Essays in Marxist Aesthetics* (London: Merlin, 1973).
Walcutt, Charles Child, *Man's Changing Mask: Modes and Methods of Characterisation in Fiction* (Minneapolis: University of Minnesota Press, 1966).
Watt, Ian, *The Rise of the Novel* (London: Penguin, 1966).
Wayne Booth, *The Rhetoric of Fiction* (Chicago: University of Chicago Press, 1961).
Weedon, Chris, *Feminist Practice and Poststructuralist Theory* (Oxford: Basil Blackwell, 1987).
Wellek, René, *Concepts of Criticism* ed. Stephen G. Nicholas, (New Haven, CT: Yale University Press, 1963).
—— *The Attack on Literature* (Brighton: Harvester, 1982).
—— and Warren, Austin, *Theory of Literature* (London: Penguin, 1963).
West, Paul, *The Modern Novel*, 2 vols (London: Hutchinson University Library, 1967).
Wheelock, Keith, *Nasser's New Egypt, A Critical Analysis* (London: Stevens and Sons, 1960).
Whitbread, Thomas B., *Seven Contemporary Authors* (Austin: Texas, University of Texas Press, 1966).
Williams, Raymond, *Culture and Society* (London: Penguin, 1961).
—— *The Long Revolution* (London: Penguin, 1965).
—— *Marxism and Literature* (Oxford: Oxford University Press, 1977).
Wimsat, W. K., *Hateful Contraries* (Kentucky: University of Kentucky Press, 1965).
—— *The Verbal Icon: Studies in the Meaning of Poetry* (London: Methuen, 1970).
Wolff, Janet, *Aesthetics and the Sociology of Art* (London: George Allen and Unwin, 1983).
—— *The Social Production of Art* (London: Macmillan, 1982).
Woolf, Virginia, *Collected Essays*, ed. Leonard Woolf (London: Chatto and Windus, 1966).
Wordsworth, William, 'Poetry and Poetic Diction', in *English Critical Essays: 16th to 20th Century*, ed. Enright, D. J. and De Chickera, E, (Oxford: Oxford University Press, 1962).

Wright Mills, C., *Power, Politics, and People,* the Collected Essays, ed. Irving Louis Horowitz, (Oxford: Oxford University Press, 1963).

—— *The Sociological Imagination* (London: Penguin, 1970).

Yarmolinsky, Avrahm, *Letters of Anton Chekhov* (New York: Viking, 1973).

Yeats, W. B., *Essays* (London: Macmillan, 1924).

Zayid, Mahmūd Y., *Egypt's Struggle for Independence* (Beirut: Maktabat Khayyat, 1965).

Zeine, Zeine N., *Arab Turkish Relations and the Emergence of Arab Nationalism* (Beirut: Maktabat Khayyat, 1958).

Zeraffa, Michel, *Fictions: The Novel and Social Reality,* tr. Catherine Burns and Tom Burns (London: Penguin, 1976).

2. *Books in Arabic*

'Abd al-Malik, Anwar, *Nahḍat Miṣr* (Cairo: al-Hay'ah al-Miṣriyyah al-'Āmmah li-l-Kitāb, 1983).

'Abduh, Ibrāhim, *Taṭawwur al-Ṣiḥāfah al-Miṣriyyah: 1797–1951* (Cairo: Maktabat al-Ādāb, 1951).

Abū Sālim, Salaḥ al-Dīn, *Maḥmūd Taymūr: Al-Adīb al-Insān* (Cairo: Maṭba'at al-Istiqāmah, 1961).

Abū 'Ūf, 'Abd al-Raḥmān, *Al-Baḥth 'An Ṭarīq Jadīd Li-l-Qiṣṣah al-Qaṣīrah al-Miṣriyyah*, (Cairo: Al-Hay'ah al-Miṣriyyah al-'Āmmah Li-l-Nashr, 1971).

Al-Bishrī, Ṭāriq *Al-Ḥarakah al-Siyāsiyyah fī Miṣr* (Cairo: al-Hay'ah al-Miṣriyyah al-'Āmmah li-l-Kitāb, 1972).

Al-Disūqi, 'Abd al-'Azīz, *Tārīkh al-Ḥarakah al-Naqdiyyah* (Cairo: al-Hay'ah al-Miṣriyyah al-'Āmmah li-l-Kitāb, 1977).

Al-Fiqi, Ḥasan, *Al-Tarīkh al-Thaqāfī li-l-Ta'līm fi Miṣr* (Cairo: Dār al-Ma'ārif, 1971).

Al-Ḥakīm, Nazīh, *Maḥmūd Taymūr: Ra'id al-Qiṣṣah al-'Arabiyyah* (Cairo: Maṭba'at al-Nīl, 1944).

Al-Jundi, Anwar, *Qiṣṣat Maḥmūd Taymūr* (Cairo: Dār Iḥyā' al-Kutub al-'Arabiyyah, 1951).

Al-Malā'ika, Nāzik, *Qaḍāyā al-Shi'r al-Mu'āṣir*, (Beirut: Dār al-Ādāb, 1962).

Al-Manjūr, Maḥmūd *Ittijāhāt al-'Aṣr al-Jadīd* (Cairo: Maktabat al-Ādāb,1937).

Al-Maqdisi, Anīs, *al-Ittijāhāt al-Adabiyyah fi al-'Ālam al-'Arabi al-Ḥadīth* (Beirut, Dār al-'Ilm lil-Malāyīn, 1952).

Al-Mi'addāwi, Anwar, *Kalimāt Fi-l-Adab,* (Beirut: Al-Maktabah al-'Aṣriyyah, 1967).

Al-Nassāj, Sayyid Ḥāmid,*Taṭawwur Fann al-Qiṣṣah al-Qaṣīrah Fi Miṣr,* (Cairo: Dār al-Kātib al-'Arabi, 1968); *Dalīl Al-Qiṣṣah al-Miṣriyyah al-Qaṣīrah*, (Cairo: Al-Hay'ah al-Misriyyah Li-l-Kitāb, 1972).

Al-Nuwayhī, Muḥammad, *Qaḍiyyat al-Shi'r al-Jadīd* (Cairo: Dār al-Ma'rifah, 1964).

Al-Rāfi'i, 'Abd al-Raḥman, *Tārīkh al-Ḥarakah al-Qawmiyyah wa-Taṭawwur Niẓām al-Ḥukm fi Miṣr* (Cairo: Maṭba'at al-Nahḍah, 1929).

Fī A'qāb al-Thawrah al-Miṣriyyah, 3 Vols (Cairo: Maktabat al-Nahḍah al-Miṣriyyah, 1937–48).

Al-Rā'i, 'Ali, *Dirāsāt fi al-Riwāyah al-Miṣriyyah* (Cairo: al-Dar al-Miṣriyyah li-l-Ta'līf, 1965).

Al-Sa'īd, Rif'at, *al-Ṣaḥāfah al-Yasāriyyah fī Miṣr, 1925–1948* (Beirut: Dār al-Ṭalī'ah, 1974).

—— *al-Yasār al-Miṣri: 1925–40* (Beirut, Dār al-Ṭalī'ah, 1972).

Al-Sharīf, Maḥmūd bin, *Adab Maḥmūd Taymūr: Li-l-Ḥaqīqah wa-l-Tārīkh* (Cairo: Maṭba'at al-Kīlāni, n.d.).

Al-Shārūnī, Yūsuf, *Al-Qiṣṣah al-Qaṣīrah Naẓariyā wa-Taṭbīqiyā* (Cairo: Dār al-Hilāl, 1977).

—— (ed), *Sab'ūn Sham'a f Ḥayāt Yaḥyā Ḥaqqī,* (Cairo: al-Hay'ah al-Miṣriyyah al-'Āmmah Li-l-Kitāb, 1975).

—— 'al-Judhūr al-Tarīkhiyyah li-Adab al-Lāma'qūl', *al-Majallah,* November 1964.

Al-'Aqqād, 'Abbās Maḥmūd, *Murāja'āt fi al-Adāb wa-l-Funūn* (Cairo: al-Maṭba'ah al-Salafiyyah, 1925).

—— *Muḥammad Abduh* (Cairo: Maṭba'at Miṣr, 1962).

al-Zayyat, Latifah, *Harkat al-Tarjamah fi Misr: 1850—1950* unpublished Ph.D. thesis, Cairo University, 1959.

Anīs, Muḥammad, *Ḥādith Arba'ah Fibrāyir* (Beirut: Dār al-Fārābi, 1970).

—— *Ḥarīq al-Qāhira* (Cairo: 1972).

Anīs, Muḥammad and Al-Sayyid Rajab Ḥarrāz, *Thawrat Yūlū wa-Uṣūlhā al-Tārīkhiyyah* (Cairo: Dār al-Nahḍah al-'Arabiyyah, 1969).

'Awaḍ, Liwīs, *al-Mu'aththirāt al-Ajnabiyyah fi al-Adab al-'Arabi al-Ḥadīth* (Cairo: Dār al-Ma'rifah, 1963).

—— *Dirāsāt fi Adabinā al-Ḥadīth* (Cairo: Dār al-Ma'rifah, 1961).

—— *Maqālat fi'l-Naqd wa'l-Adab,* (Cairo: Maktabat al-Anglo, 1970).

'Ayyād, Shukri Muḥammad, *Al-Qiṣṣah al-Qaṣīrah Fi Miṣr: Dirāsah Fi Ta'ṣīl Fann Adabi* (Cairo: Ma'had al-Buḥūth wa-l-Dirāsāt al-'Arabiyyah, 1968).

—— *Tajārib fi al-Adab wa-l-Naqd* (Cairo: Dār al-Kātib al-'Arabi, 1967).

Badr, 'Abd al-Muḥsin Ṭaha, *Taṭawwur al-Riwāyah al-'Arabiyyah al-Ḥadīthah fi Miṣr* (Cairo: Dār al-Ma'ārif, 1963).

—— *al-Riwā'i wa'l-Arḍ,* (Cairo: al-Hay'ah al-Miṣriyyah al-'Āmmah Li-l-Kitāb, 1971).

Ḍayf, Shawqi, *Al-Adab al-'Arabi al-Mu'āṣir Fi Miṣr,* (Cairo: Dār al-Ma'ārif, 1961).

Duwwārah, Fu'ād, *'Ashrat udabā' Yutḥaddath'n,* (Cairo: Dār al-Hilāl, 1965).

Faraj, Nabīl, *al-Khawf wa'l-Shajā'ah: Dirāsāt fī Qiṣaṣ Yūsuf al-Shārūnī* (Cairo: 1972).

Fawzī, Ḥusayn, *Sindibād Miṣri* (Cairo: Dār al-Ma'ārif, 1961).

Ḥamdān, Jamāl, *Shakhṣiyyat Miṣr,* 4 vols. (Cairo: 'Ālam al-Kutub, 1968–80).

Ḥaqqī, Yaḥyā, *Fajr al-Qiṣṣah al-Miṣriyyah,* (Cairo: Dār al-Qalam, 1960).

—— *Khuṭuwāt Fi-l-Naqd,* (Cairo: Maktabat Dār al'Urūbah, 1962).

Haykal, Aḥmad, *al-Adab al-Qaṣaṣi wa-l-Masraḥi fī Miṣr: Min A'qāb Thawrat 1919 ilā Qiyām al-Ḥarb al-Kubrā al-Thāniyah* (Cairo: Dār al-Ma'ārif, 1970).

—— *Taṭawwur al-Adab al-Ḥadīth fī Miṣr* (Cairo: Dār al-Ma'ārif, 1974).

Haykal, Muḥammad Ḥusain, *Mudhakkirāt fī al-Siyāsah al-Miṣriyyah*, 2 vols (Cairo: Maktabt al-Nahḍah al-Miṣriyyah, 1951 and 1953).

Ḥusain, Muḥammad Muḥammad, *Al-Ittijāhāt al-Waṭaniyyah fī al-Adab al-Mu'āṣir*, 2 vols. (Cairo: Al-Maṭba'ah al-Numūdhajiyyah, 1956)

Ḥusain, Ṭaha, *Min Adabinā al-Mu'āṣir*, (Cairo: Al-Sharikah al-'Arabiyyah, 1959).

Ḥusayn, Muṣṭafā Ibrāhīm, *Yaḥyā Ḥaqqī Mubdi'ā wa-Nāqidā* (Cairo: Maktabat al-'Urūbah, 1969).

Ibrāhīm, 'Abd al-Ḥamīd, *Al-Qiṣṣah al-Miṣriyyah wa-Ṣūrat al-Mujtama' al-Ḥadīth*, (Cairo: Dār al-Ma'ārif, 1973).

Kāmil, Maḥmūd, *Yawmiyyāt Muḥāmi Miṣri: al-Jānib al-Insāni min Ḥayāt al-Maḥākim* (Cairo: Maktabat al-Anglo, 1944).

Karam, Anṭūn Ghaṭṭās, *al-Ramziyyah fī'l-Shi'r al-'Arabī al-Ḥadīth* (Beirut: Dār al-Makshūf, 1949).

Khalīfah, Sha'bān 'Abd al-'Azīz, *Ḥarakat Nashr al-Kutub fī Miṣr: Dirāsah Taṭbīqiyyah* (Cairo: Dār al-Thaqāfah, 1974).

Khiḍr, 'Abbās, *al-Qiṣṣah al-Qaṣīrah fī Miṣr: Mundh Nash'atih Ḥattā Sanat 1930* (Cairo: al-Dār al-Qawmiyyah, 1966).

—— *Muḥammad Taymūr: Ḥayātuh wa-Adabuh* (Cairo: al-Dār al-Qawmiyyah, 1966).

Kushayk, Muḥammad, *'Alāmāt al-Taḥdīth Fi-l-Qiṣṣah al-Miṣriyyah al-Qaṣīrah*, (Baghdād: Dār al-Shu'ūn al-Thaqāfiyyah, 1988).

Mikki, Al-Ṭāhir Aḥmad, *Al-Qiṣṣah al-Qaṣīrah*, (Cairo: Dār al-Ma'ārif, 1977).

Najm, Muḥammad Yūsuf, *Al-Qiṣṣah Fi-l-Adab al-'Arabi al-Ḥadīth*, (Cairo: Dār al-Nahḍah al-Miṣriyyah, 1952).

Quṭb, Sayyid, *Kutub wa-Shakhṣiyyāt* (Cairo: Maṭba'at al-Risālah, 1946).

Ramaḍān, 'Abd al-'Aẓīm Muḥammad, *Taṭawwur al-Ḥarakah al-Waṭaniyyah fī Miṣr: 1918–1936* (Cairo: Dār al-Katib al-'Arabi, 1968).

—— *Taṭawwur al-Ḥarakah al-Waṭaniyyah fī Miṣr, 1937–1948*, 2 vols. (Beirut: Dār al-Waṭan al-'Arabi, 1973).

Rifā'i, 'Abd al-'Azīz, *Thawrat Miṣr Sanat 1919* (Cairo: Dār al-Kātib al-'Arabi, 1966).

Rif'at, Muḥammad 'Alī, *Mashākil Miṣr al-Iqtiṣādiyyah* (Cairo: Nahḍat Miṣr, 1964).

Rāghib, Nabīl, *Fan al-Riwāyah 'ind Yūsuf al-Siba'ī* (Cairo: Dār al-Kātib al-'Arabi, 1973).

Sa'd, Aḥmad Ṣādiq, *Nash'at al-Takwīn al-Miṣri li-l-Ra'smāliyyah wa-Taṭawwuruh: Fi Ḍaw' al-Namṭ al-Āsyawi li-l-Intāj* (Beirut: Dār al-Ḥadāthah, n.d.).

—— *Tārīkh Miṣr al-Ijtimā'i al-Iqtiṣādi* (Beirut: Dŋār Ibn Khaldūn, 1979).

—— *Taḥawwul al-Takwīn al-Miṣri min al-Namaṭ al-Āsyawi ilā al-Namaṭ al-*

Ra'smāli (Beirut: Dār al-Ḥadāthah, 1981).
Shawkat, Maḥmūd Ḥāmid, *Al-Fann al-Qaṣaṣi Fi-l-Adab al-'Arabi al-Ḥadīth* (Cairo: Dār al-Fikr, 1963).
Shukrī, Ghālī, *Azmat al-Jins fi al-Qiṣṣah al-'Arabiyyah* (Beirut: Dār al-Ādāb, 1962).
Sulṭān, Jamīl, *Fann al-Qiṣṣah wa-l-Maqāmah* (Beirut: Dār al-Anwār, 1967).
Taymūr, Maḥmūd, *Nushū' al-Qiṣṣah wa-Taṭawwuruhā*, (Cairo: Al-Maṭba'ah al-Salafiyyah, 1936).
—— *Dirāsāt fi'l Qiṣṣah wa'l-Masraḥ*, (Cairo: Maktabat al-Ādāb, n.d.).
—— *'Iṭr wa-Dukhān* (Cairo: Maṭba'at Dār al-Hilāl, 1947).
—— *Shifā' al-Rūḥ* (Cairo: Maṭba'at Dār al-Kātib al-'Arabi, 1951).
—— *Bayn al-Maṭraqa wa'l-Sindān* (Cairo: Dār al-Kātib al-'Arabi, 1969).
Yūnis, 'Abd al-Ḥamīd, *Fann al-Qiṣṣah al-Qaṣīrah Fi Adabinā al-Ḥadīth* (Cairo: Dār al-Ma'rifah, 1973).
Zaydān, Jurji, *Tārīkh Ādāb al-Lughah al-'Arabiyyah*, 4 vols (Cairo: Maṭba'at al-Hilāl, 1914).

3. Periodicals

A. In English

Diacritics
English Institute Annual
Kenyon Review
Journal of Arabic Literature
The Times

B. In Arabic

Ākhir Sā'ah
al-Ādāb
al-Adab al-Ḥayy
al-Adīb
al-Būlīs
al-Fuṣūl
al-Hadaf
al-Hilāl
al-Idhā'ah al-Miṣriyyah
al-Jīl al-Jadīd
al-Jumhuriyyah
al-Jāmi'ah
al-Kitāb
al-Kutlah
al-Kātib
al-Kātibal-Miṣri
al-Majallah
al-Majallah al-Jadīdah

al-Masā'
al-Mihrajān
al-Misriyyah
al-Miṣri
al-Muṣawwar
al-Qiṣṣah
al-Qāhirhah
al-Radio
al-Risālah
al-Risālah al-Jadīdah
al-Rāwī
al-Riwāyah
al-Shahr
al-Sha'ab
al-Siyāsah al-Usbū'iyyah
al-Taḥrīr
al-Taṭawwur
al-Thaqāfah
al-Usbū'
Ḥakīm al-Bayt
Majallat al-Idhā'ah al-Miṣriyyah
Majallat al-'Ishrīn Qiṣṣah
Majallat Nādī al-Qiṣṣah
Majallatī
Rūz al-Yūsuf
Ṣabāḥ al-Khayr

Index

COPS ACROSS BORDERS

COPS ACROSS

Ethan A. Nadelmann

BORDERS

The Internationalization of U.S. Criminal Law Enforcement

The Pennsylvania State University Press
University Park, Pennsylvania

Library of Congress Cataloging-in-Publication Data

Nadelmann, Ethan Avram.
Cops across borders : the internationalization of U.S. criminal law enforcement / Ethan A. Nadelmann.
p. cm.
Includes bibliographical references and index.
ISBN 0-271-01094-0 (cloth : acid-free paper)
ISBN 0-271-01095-9 (paper : acid-free paper)
1. Transnational crime—History. 2. Law enforcement—United States—History. 3. Law enforcement—International cooperation—History. I. Title.
HV6252.N33 1993
363.2'0973—dc20 93–1305
CIP

Printed in the United States of America

Published by The Pennsylvania State University Press,
Suite C, Barbara Building, University Park, PA 16802-1003

It is the policy of The Pennsylvania State University Press to use acid-free paper for the first printing of all clothbound books. Publications on uncoated stock satisfy the minimum requirements of American National Standard for Information Sciences—Permanence of Paper for Printed Library Materials, ANSI Z39.48–1984.

To my mother,
Judith Wolpert Nadelmann
and
to the memory of my father,
Rabbi Ludwig Nadelmann
(1928–1986)

The laws of this country take no notice of crimes committed out of their jurisdiction. The most atrocious offender coming within their pale is received by them as an innocent man, and they have authorized no one to seize and deliver him. The evil of protecting malefactors of every dye is sensibly felt here as in other countries, but until a reformation of the criminal codes of most nations, to deliver fugitives from them would be to become their accomplice—the former, therefore, is viewed as the lesser evil.

—U.S. Secretary of State Thomas Jefferson
September 1793

Often more than 50 percent of my day is devoted to some matter relating to our international involvement in fighting drug trafficking, money laundering, international organized crime and business fraud, environmental depredations, terrorism or espionage.

—U.S. Attorney General Richard Thornburgh
August 8, 1989

Contents

Preface

This is a book about the internationalization of U.S. criminal law enforcement. It examines how and why U.S. law enforcement officials have extended their efforts beyond American borders, how they have dealt with the challenges confronting them, and why their efforts have proved more or less successful. These efforts date back to the nation's origins. They proliferated following World War II. And they have increased dramatically in frequency, scope, and intensity since the early 1970s. Police and prosecutors who rarely if ever pursued their investigations abroad or sought evidence from foreign jurisdictions now do so with increasing frequency. Federal regulatory agencies that traditionally perceived their responsibilities and turf entirely in domestic terms now focus increasing attention on transnational interactions. Diplomats who hardly gave a second thought to criminal matters now often find them high among their assigned priorities. And legislators on Capitol Hill who typically identified crime as a local concern now focus much more of their rhetoric and law-making on criminals beyond American borders. Never before have U.S. foreign policy and U.S. criminal justice been so deeply entangled.

This book represents the first significant engagement of two scholarly disciplines—U.S. foreign policy and criminal justice—that have had remarkably little to do with one another. The vast majority of criminal justice scholars have extended their attention no further than their nations' borders; the few exceptions are those who have analyzed and compared foreign criminal justice systems.[1] Among students of U.S.

1. See in particular the work of David Bayley: *Patterns of Policing: An International Comparative Perspective* (New Brunswick, N.J.: Rutgers University Press, 1985); *Forces of*

foreign policy, some have focused their attention on domestic influences, but almost no one has paid much attention to issues of crime and law enforcement. Even as scholarly analyses of U.S. international drug control policy have proliferated in recent years, few have focused on the criminal justice dimensions of that policy. Whatever arguments might once have justified this disengagement of the two disciplines can no longer be sustained. The interpenetration of foreign policy and criminal justice institutions and concerns have simply become too substantial to be ignored by scholars any longer.

People, products, money, information, ideas, and cultures transcend national borders today with an ease, and at a pace and volume, unprecedented in human history. At the same time, the United States and most other governments have assumed increasing responsibilities for enforcing food, drug, and consumer safety laws, policing the securities and commodities markets, protecting the environment, enforcing patent and copyright laws, collecting taxes, and protecting the general welfare of their citizens—all of which require increasing extraterritorial vigilance. This trend is not, to be sure, irreversible, but so long as it continues it will present a basic challenge to the state: how to control growing domains of transnational activities that either ignore or take advantage of national borders when the powers of the state remain powerfully circumscribed by the political, geographical, and legal limitations that attend notions of national sovereignty?

Among the principal responses of the United States and other governments to this challenge has been the internationalization of their criminal justice laws, policies, capabilities, and institutions. International criminal law enforcement can be understood as both the extraterritorial extension of criminal justice activities normally performed within a single jurisdiction and as the criminal justice dimension of foreign policy institutions and activities designed to protect and advance a state's national interests. It can be viewed, more broadly, as an essential component of states' unceasing efforts to control their borders and, by extension, their municipal realms. And it can be seen, more contempo-

Order: Policing Modern Japan (Berkeley and Los Angeles: University of California Press, 1991); "The Police and Political Change in Comparative Perspective," *Law and Society Review* 6 (1971), 91–112; and *The Police and Political Development in India* (Princeton: Princeton University Press, 1969). See also R. I. Mawby, *Comparative Policing Issues: The British and American System in International Perspective* (Boston: Unwin Hyman, 1990).

raneously, as part and parcel of the increasingly complex and multidimensional interdependence of states and societies today.

The broader relevance of this study stems primarily from its analysis of how municipal control systems respond to the demands of internationalization. Criminal justice systems in most countries evolve with little consideration of the need to interact with foreign systems. They may be influenced by foreign models, but they are almost entirely concerned with the control of municipal societies. The internationalization of crime and law enforcement thus places demands upon criminal justice systems to which they are generally ill suited to respond. Criminal justice systems are not, however, the only municipal control systems to have faced the challenges of internationalization. Therein lie the broader implications of this study.

The Evolution of This Study

When I began this study in 1983, my intent was to examine the evolution of U.S. international drug control policies. I conceived of the project as both an exercise in diplomatic history and a critical examination of the means employed to carry out those policies. I knew that the U.S. Drug Enforcement Administration (DEA), with its global operations and more than two hundred agents stationed abroad, would constitute part of the story, but I imagined my focus would be on the role played by the U.S. State Department.

As I pursued the study, however, my interest gradually shifted from the focus on diplomacy. To be sure, despite a number of fine studies of prewar U.S. drug control diplomacy,[2] no one had attempted (nor has yet attempted) a comprehensive analysis of subsequent developments in this area. But I remained reluctant to make that the focus of my research, for a number of reasons. It seemed to me that much of what was theoretically interesting about the nature and challenges of U.S. drug control diplomacy had apparently already been thoroughly analyzed by scholars of U.S. human rights diplomacy and other analogous dimen-

2. Arnold Taylor, *American Diplomacy and the Narcotics Traffic, 1900–1939* (Durham, N.C.: Duke University Press, 1969); William O. Walker III, *Drug Control in the Americas* (Albuquerque: University of New Mexico Press, 1981); and Peter D. Lowes, *The Genesis of International Narcotics Control* (Geneva: Librairie Droz, 1966).

sions of U.S. foreign policy.[3] I also increasingly realized that the "successes" and "failures" of U.S. international drug control efforts had relatively little impact on illicit drug abuse in the United States—a diplomatic analysis to show why was not needed.[4] But most important, while examining the activities of the DEA overseas, I stumbled onto a vein of inquiry so rich that it rapidly came to absorb all my attention. The more interesting questions, I discovered, concerned not how diplomats and other political authorities dealt with the international aspects of drug control but rather how law enforcement officials dealt with international matters.

My focus therefore shifted from examining the international drug control efforts of the United States as a subset of American foreign policy to examining them from the context of international law enforcement. The DEA became the focal point of an analysis that sought to shed light not just on the nature and challenges of international drug control but also on all criminal justice efforts evidencing an international dimension. The American drug enforcement agency, with its representatives in some sixty foreign cities around the world, was a unique phenomenon in the annals of both international relations and policing, but as I looked for and found both historical and contemporary analogues to the DEA, I realized that there was nothing particularly unique about the basic functions of the agency and the challenges confronting it. Historical parallels and antecedents abounded both within and without the United States, dating back to the origins of the American republic and beyond. The DEA's agents were not the only ones to travel overseas, to station representatives abroad, or even to operate undercover and recruit informants in foreign countries. The basic challenges of interacting with foreign law enforcement officials, deciphering foreign law enforcement systems, and generally operating in foreign political and legal environments beholden to very different criminal laws, procedures, and other norms were familiar not just to other police agents but also to the government attorneys charged with extradition and other mutual legal assistance tasks. I found, in short, a universe of governmental activity at the intersection of criminal justice and international

3. See, e.g., Lars Schoultz, *Human Rights and United States Policy Toward Latin America* (Princeton: Princeton University Press, 1981).

4. See my analyses in "International Drug Trafficking and U.S. Foreign Policy," *Washington Quarterly* 8 (1985), 87–104; and in "U.S. Drug Policy: A Bad Export," *Foreign Policy* 70 (1988), 83–108.

relations that had yet to be subjected to systematic scholarly examination.

My study of U.S. international law enforcement activities was further stimulated and complicated by the rapid expansion and transformation of those activities during the 1980s. This reassured me that the subject was indeed of increasing importance, but it also required persistent attention to new developments. As I scoured the scholarly literature during the mid-1980s for discussions of transnational crime and international law enforcement, I found strikingly little, so I set out to talk with those involved in international law enforcement activities. Between January 1984 and June 1990, I interviewed approximately three hundred individuals: DEA, FBI, IRS, Secret Service, and customs agents; U.S. marshals; CIA analysts; Justice, Treasury, and State Department officials; Congressional staff; Interpol employees; foreign police; and other government officials, as well as knowledgeable attorneys, journalists, and other experts. A majority of these interviews were conducted in 1984 and 1985 in Washington, D.C., Miami, and New York City, as well as during two international trips: the first in January 1985 to Jamaica, Panama, Ecuador, Peru, Chile, Argentina, and Bolivia; the second in May and June 1985 to France, Belgium, the Netherlands, Germany, Switzerland, Austria, Italy, and Great Britain. During part of this time, I was also employed as a consultant to the State Department's Bureau of International Narcotics Matters (INM) to write a report on U.S. and international efforts against drug-related money laundering activities.[5] Between 1986 and 1990, I conducted dozens of additional interviews in some of the same countries, as well as in Colombia, Mexico, and Spain. A small number of interviews were also conducted by phone. I interviewed resident DEA agents in all eighteen foreign countries visited and local law enforcement officials in most of them, supplementing my standard set of questions with others intended to elicit impressions and insights. In a few countries, I was permitted to sit in on agent conferences, observe interrogations, interview informants, and participate in surveillances of drug traffickers. I viewed my objective as finding out whatever was necessary to better understand the evolution, nature, and challenges of international law enforcement.

The interviews—most of which were conducted on a not-for-attribu-

5. A revised version of that report was later published as "Unlaundering Dirty Money Abroad: U.S. Foreign Policy and Financial Secrecy Jurisdictions," *University of Miami Inter-American Law Review* 18 (1986), 33–82.

tion basis—provided me with otherwise unavailable information and insights about the international and extraterritorial efforts of U.S. law enforcement officials. I learned how DEA agents had devised means of circumventing the civil law restrictions on undercover operations and the use and recruitment of informants in Europe and Latin America, how they had dealt with the obstacles presented by the virtually omnipresent police corruption in Latin America, and more generally how they compensated for the loss of their sovereign police powers on foreign territory. I learned how Justice Department officials had sought to improve their capacity to obtain evidence from abroad—in particular, financial documents from foreign financial secrecy jurisdictions—in a form admissible in American judicial proceedings. In the process, I also learned much about the nature of criminal justice and criminal investigation in foreign countries, as well as the ways in which foreign criminal justice systems had changed in response to American requests, pressures, and examples. And I gained a sense of how and why the internationalization of U.S. law enforcement had proceeded so quickly since the late 1960s.

My broader objectives, however, required that I examine not just the modern era of international law enforcement but also its historical parallels and antecedents. The international activities of the DEA, I came to realize, were part and parcel not just of U.S. international drug control diplomacy or of the domestic "war on drugs" but also of historical processes that can be traced back to Great Britain's diplomatic and naval campaigns against piracy and slavery, to the international secret police networks maintained by Metternich and the interior ministries of Russian czars and French emperors, and to the nineteenth-century efforts of U.S. customs and police agents to stem smuggling and banditry across the Canadian and Mexican borders. I initially intended these historical inquiries to serve primarily as contexts and correctives for my analysis of contemporary international law enforcement; to identify, as best as possible, the origins and evolution of international law enforcement, and to guard against the tendency to view contemporary developments as entirely new and unprecedented. But these inquiries eventually assumed a life and intellectual standing of their own, yielding a far deeper and more fundamental understanding of the nature and potential of international law enforcement endeavors, and their relationship to both political changes in the international system and technological innovations, than would have been possible had I examined only the contemporary era of international law enforcement. The results of these inquiries can be found in the more historical portions of the chapters that follow and in a forthcoming companion volume to this book tentatively entitled "Criminalization and Crime Control in International Society."

To Whom It May Concern: Questions and Audiences

This book is very much a hybrid designed to interest scholars and practitioners in many fields. Some distinguished colleagues have suggested that I address this book primarily to one audience, be it international relations, bureaucratic politics, criminal justice, international law, or some other well-defined scholarly discipline with its own favored questions, theories, and categories. I have chosen to pursue another tack: to identify and describe a heretofore unexamined domain of governmental activity, to ask a set of questions about the nature and challenges of that domain, and to offer a number of answers and hypotheses in response to those questions. In pursuing this tack, I have rifled through the scholarly literatures of diverse disciplines in search of models, analogies, and insights that might help me explain the internationalization of criminal law enforcement. I have assumed that this subject is sufficiently interesting and important in and of itself that you, the reader, have engaged this book primarily because you want to learn about this subject. But I suspect there is much in the analysis that follows to spark your thinking about subjects quite removed from this one.

This book resembles other studies of bureaucracies in that it analyzes the behavior of a particular set of agencies and officials, the tasks they perform, the challenges they confront, and the reasons they succeed or fail. It is exceptional, however, in analyzing these issues in an international rather than a domestic setting. This book resembles other studies, published principally in law journals, in its examination of issues related to extradition and mutual legal assistance. It differs from most, however, insofar as it analyzes these issues in historical perspective, focuses less on the legal issues and more on the behavior and perspectives of U.S. officials engaged in these areas, and relies on information derived from interviews with the officials themselves. This book resembles others in the field of comparative policing and criminal justice in that it compares the approaches and behavior of law enforcement officials in different countries. But it goes a step beyond these studies in its analysis of the interactions among systems and the ways in which criminal investigative norms and methods are influenced by those of other states.

This book also resembles many studies of U.S. foreign policy in its focus on how and why U.S. officials have pursued particular objectives abroad. It differs, however, in at least three respects: it examines an assortment of agencies and actors that have not previously been studied in the context of U.S. foreign policy; it focuses on the conduct of relatively low-level government officials, rather than high-level decision makers and bureaucrats; and it examines in relatively close and comparative detail the ways in which U.S. officials pursue their objectives on foreign territories. Implicit in my analysis is the assumption that much of what remains both interesting and unexplained about international relations can best be explained by multilayered analyses that integrate close examinations of domestic interests, processes, and norms with detailed analyses of international interactions.

Because this book is designed to interest scholars and practitioners in many fields, and because it addresses a set of questions that have not previously been addressed, readers may find some terms and concepts unfamiliar. I urge you, however, not to close your mind to them. Many readers, including some from the discipline of international relations, may wonder why I have resuscitated from the international relations literature of the early 1970s nearly forgotten concepts such as "transgovernmental relations" and "transnational organizations." I have done so not to pay homage to the passing fads of a discipline but rather because these concepts are peculiarly valuable for explaining much of what constitutes international law enforcement. Similarly, the notion of "harmonization" is much in vogue these days as economic and financial markets and systems become increasingly interdependent, and as governments attempt to coordinate their regulatory efforts. But I employ the notion—and define it as I do—principally because it is so valuable in describing and explaining a powerful current and objective in the evolution of international law enforcement. Many law enforcement agents, and some students of criminal justice and bureaucracy, will appreciate without further explanation what I mean by the "immobilization" of criminals. But it is also important that students of U.S. foreign policy recognize this as an increasingly important objective of foreign policy, and understand that it presents the U.S. government with challenges that are familiar in some respects and unique in others.

This book is relatively thick both in description and in analysis. Let me explain why. First, it offers not a new twist on a familiar subject but rather an introduction and series of twists on an entirely new subject (insofar as it has not heretofore been described or analyzed in any depth whatsoever). Second, it is designed, as I noted above, to interest not one scholarly or professional audience but many. I prefer that some readers skip and skim through the portions that interest them less, rather than leave those with a strong interest in the subject at hand frustrated. Third, the dominant cast of all the chapters but one (Chapter Five) is historical and evolutionary. This reflects my desire to develop the themes of continuity and change in the internationalization of U.S. law enforcement. And it is driven by my sense that any general propositions about the nature of international criminal law enforcement should meet the standards of historical scrutiny.

In choosing what to include and exclude, I had three objectives in mind: to offer a comprehensive examination of U.S. international law enforcement activities, to focus more intensively on dimensions that have not been analyzed elsewhere, and to provide new perspectives on subjects that have been examined by others. One reason why four of the six chapters that follow focus on police is because most of what has been written on U.S. international law enforcement is preoccupied with judicial decisions and law enforcement treaties. Chapter Two, which examines the internationalization of U.S. criminal law enforcement from 1789 to 1939, is included in part as a corrective to the tendency to see international criminal law enforcement as an entirely contemporary phenomenon. Chapter Three, which describes and analyzes the international activities of most federal law enforcement agencies since World War II, scopes out a domain of U.S. criminal justice and foreign policy that has not previously been identified as a distinct domain. Chapters Four and Five, which examine the operations of the DEA in Europe and Latin America, respectively, focus on the U.S. federal police agency that has been most intimately and extensively involved in international activities.

Where Chapters Two through Five describe and analyze a domain of U.S. foreign policy and criminal justice previously ignored by scholars, Chapters Six and Seven cut through familiar subjects in new ways. The collection of evidence and fugitives from abroad has been addressed in dozens of law review articles. What distinguishes Chapter Six from that literature is its focus on the negotiation of legal assistance treaties, my reliance on interviews with the Justice Department officials involved in the negotiations, and the relationships drawn between this domain of international law enforcement and others. What distinguishes Chapter Seven from other analyses of U.S. efforts to obtain fugitives from abroad is the historical nature of the analysis. Remarkably, no book-length history of the subject has been written since John Bassett Moore's classic treatise of 1891. Chapter Seven represents a modest first step toward filling that void.

Any claim to comprehensiveness demands an explanation of significant lacunae. Three related subjects are treated far too briefly in this book. The first is the role of U.S. law enforcement agencies in dealing with the transnational dimensions of espionage, terrorism, high-tech smuggling, and other criminal violations of national security laws. The second involves the complex and abundant relationships between U.S. intelligence agencies and law enforcement agencies. And the third concerns the law enforcement activities of the U.S. military investigative branches. The two first subjects—particularly the second—would have been extremely difficult to research and write about given the high degree of secrecy surrounding them. As for the third, my principal excuse is lack of time and resources. I am confident that few of the central themes in this book would be undermined or challenged by greater awareness of these subjects, but each raises important issues that I look forward to having others pursue.

Let me also explain what this book is not. First, it does not engage, at least directly, the long-standing debates among realists, neorealists, pluralists, liberals, and others in the academic discipline of international relations. I am quite satisfied to provide grist for the mill of each in the pages that follow. The realist model of the state as a unitary actor jibes nicely with reality when we focus our attention on the state as creator of laws—that is, as criminalizer. But alternative paradigms will find much support in my emphasis on the transgovernmental dimension of international law enforcement activities, in my references to the turf struggles among federal agencies, and in my discussion of the constraints on U.S. international law enforcement activities imposed by Congress and the judiciary. Realists can well point to the single-minded pursuit of U.S. law enforcement objectives abroad and to the relatively common reliance on coercive and unilateral measures by U.S. law enforcement agencies. But others can stress the high degree of consensus and mutual interest among states on many criminal justice matters, or point to the moralistic causes and consequences of injecting criminal justice objectives and concerns into U.S. foreign policy.

This book does, however, contribute to the debate over the impact of modernization on foreign policy and international politics. The technologically driven proliferation of transnational and transgovernmental interactions is changing the substance and processes of foreign policy as well as the meaning of power in international politics. Contemporary scholars are not the first to appreciate the consequences. "It has become a platitude," Ramsay Muir observed in 1932, "to say that the whole world is now interdependent." More systematic analysis of the consequences of modernization began in the late 1960s. Edward Morse, writing in 1970, observed that three sets of conditions had developed:

> First, the ideal and classical distinctions between foreign and domestic affairs have broken down, even though the myths associated with sovereignty and the state have not. Second, the distinction between "high policies" (those associated with security and the continued existence of the state) and "low policies" (those pertaining to the wealth and welfare of the citizens) has become less important as low policies have assumed an increasingly large role in any society. Third, although there have been significant developments in the instrumentalities of political control, the actual ability to control events either internal or external to modernized societies—even those that are Great Powers—has decreased with the growth of interdependence, and is likely to decrease further.[6]

Each of these observations is confirmed in the chapters that follow—although my analysis does indicate that there are some domains in which the ability of states to control particular events has increased.

Modernization also transformed the ways in which states pursued their objectives abroad. The postwar American "empire," Samuel Huntington pointed out, "was an empire of functions, not territory, . . . characterized not by the *acquisition* of new territory but by their *penetration*."[7] Wolfram Hanreider elaborated: "Access rather than ac-

6. Edward L. Morse, "The Transformation of Foreign Policies: Modernization, Interdependence, and Externalization," *World Politics* 22 (1970), 371–392.

7. Samuel Huntington, "Transnational Organizations in World Politics," *World Politics* 25 (1973), 343–344.

quisition, presence rather than rule, penetration rather than possession have become the important issues."[8] The power of states increasingly consists of their capacity to employ both municipal and international institutions and mechanisms to control transnational interactions. Where powerful states once relied on armies and navies to accomplish their objectives abroad, now police and other security officials play an increasingly important role. Spies and intelligence agencies provide an element of continuity with the past, but even they find themselves drawn into more frequent and multidimensional relationships with municipal agencies and issues.

Second, although this book addresses the question "Why have U.S. law enforcement agencies extended their efforts abroad?" that is not its sole or even principal objective. The question is not one that lends itself to broad theoretical generalizations or systematic evaluation of alternative hypotheses. The answers to the question are simply too many and too varied. One can point to the impact of technological developments, to expanding notions of jurisdiction, to municipal developments such as the creation of criminal investigative branches and the nationalization of crime control, to evolving attitudes regarding the degree to which Americans should assist foreign states in the enforcement of criminal laws, to rising levels of consensus and comity among governments in criminal justice matters, to changes in the domestic market for illicit imports, and much else. Most important, the answers to the question are so diverse because the criminal laws that U.S. agents seek to enforce both municipally and internationally are so diverse.

The criminal law identifies particular activities and labels them criminal. But all that criminal activities have in common is that they are the subject of criminal laws. Consider the variety of activities that are the subject of many U.S. international law enforcement actions: cocaine importing, insider trading, unsanctioned migration, espionage, terrorism, export of sophisticated technology to unapproved states, failure to declare purchases abroad worth more than $400, and failure to report that one has taken $10,000 or more in cash into or out of the country. Some of these activities have been treated as criminal for centuries, others not until quite recently. Just as governments employ administrative regulations to regulate domestic, transnational, and occasionally

8. Wolfram F. Hanreider, "Dissolving International Politics: Reflections on the Nation-State," *American Political Science Review* 72 (1978), 1276–1287.

extraterritorial interactions, so they employ criminal laws to bolster their regulatory efforts in a wide array of domains: trade, finance, migration, national security, the environment, public health, and much else. New criminal laws are enacted every year. Some are violated routinely, others barely at all. No single thesis comes close to explaining the internationalization of U.S. criminal law enforcement, for the same reason that no single thesis can persuasively explain the criminalization of some activities and not others.

Third, this book offers little in the way of policy prescriptions or normative judgments on U.S. involvement in international law enforcement matters. I did not perceive my task as one of telling government officials how to perform their tasks more effectively (although a number of DEA agents have told me that Chapters Four and Five should be assigned in their agency's training courses). Nor did I perceive a need or a responsibility to cast personal judgment upon the rightness and wrongness of U.S. police actions in foreign countries. More than enough commentators have already done so in the law journals and op-ed pages. I instead saw my responsibility as one of providing insights into the attitudes and methods of those who engage in international law enforcement activities.

One final prefatory note is warranted. I began this research enterprise with a strong dose of skepticism regarding the objectives, efficacy, and correctness of U.S. drug control policies. My research experience effectively confirmed my intellectual and ethical reservations. Even as I came to like and admire many drug enforcement agents and other officials, I also came to see both their efforts and the laws and policies they enforced as fundamentally misguided—for reasons that I have elaborated upon elsewhere.[9] Readers of this book, however, will find only scant references to these reservations. This study represents my effort to analyze the internationalization of U.S. criminal law enforcement as a historical, legal, and governmental process. I offer neither policy prescriptions nor normative judgments, but simply my best efforts at objective and scholarly analysis.

9. See the following articles by Ethan A. Nadelmann: "Drug Prohibition in the United States: Costs, Consequences, and Alternatives," *Science* 245 (Sept. 1, 1989), 939–947; "U.S. Drug Policy: A Bad Export," *Foreign Policy* 70 (1988), 1–39; and "The Case for Legalization," *Public Interest* 92 (1988), 3–31.

Acknowledgments

Any manuscript that begins as a Ph.D. dissertation, grows and divides into two books, and takes ten years to complete inevitably acquires an abundance of debts. I want therefore just to name the few dozens who have given the most in terms of their time, assistance, and support. I first must thank the many friends who read various chapters of the dissertation, offered their comments, and generously tolerated my obsessive bantering on this subject—in particular, John DiIulio, Aaron Friedberg, Jane Katz, Yuen Foong Khong, James Lindsay, Stephen Roof, and Nicholas Ziegler, as well as Vincent Auger, Manuel José Cepeda, Steven Cobrin, Jean-Marc Coicaud, Michael Daumer, Gregory Gause, Gustavo Gorriti, Jill Irvine, Mark Kleiman, Philip Kraft, Juan Lindau, Lloyd Lowy, Tony Malavenda, Arie Ofri, Peter Reynolds, Gabriel Schoenfeld, Michael Tiorano, Javier Trevino, and Matthew Zavitkovsky; my students David Medina, Adam Sexton, and Rhys Williams; my parents, Ludwig and Judith Nadelmann; my brothers, Jeremy and Daniel; and my sister, Deborah.

My dissertation advisors, Stanley Hoffmann, Philip Heymann, and Mark Moore, each played important roles in challenging and stimulating my thinking about various dimensions of this subject. I am most grateful to them not just for their advice but for their guidance and encouragement as well. I also must thank Robert Keohane, James Q. Wilson, Gary Marx, Peter Reuter, and especially Jorge Dominguez for their scholarly advice and comments on portions of the dissertation. Among those who have read various drafts of the manuscript since, I am particularly indebted to David Bayley, John DiIulio, Jameson Doig, Michael Doyle, Cyrille Fijnaut, Aaron Friedberg, Fred Greenstein, Peggy Hoover, Gary

Marx, Walter Murphy, Uwe Reinhardt, Mark Richard, and Sandy Thatcher, and I want to thank Michael Abbell, Christopher Blakesley, Heinrich Boge, Thomas Cash, Forrest Colburn, John Cusack, Wolfgang Danspeckgruber, Daniel Deudney, Albin Eser, Herbert Fuchs, Albrecht Funk, John Harris, Bob Hoogenboom, David Johnson, Yuen Foong Khong, Réne Lévy, John Langbein, Richard Martin, John Murphy, Richard Owens, Sebastian Scheerer, Richard Ullman, and Bruce Zagaris for their comments and advice on various chapters. Among the many able students who have worked as my research assistants, I am particularly indebted to Kristina Scott for her research and translations of German materials, Christine Zandvliet for her research and translations of Dutch materials, and David Jefferds, John Hickey, and Martin DeSantos for their overall commitment and resourcefulness. My thanks as well to my superb secretary, Sandy Paroly. I am grateful most of all to Donna Sherman, my partner in life from the time this project was conceived until its conclusion, and to our wonderful daughter, Lila.

A graduate student could hope for no finer place to write a dissertation than the Center for International Affairs at Harvard University. It provided a wonderful workplace and base of operations, as well as funding in the form of a NOMOS Fellowship and a John M. Olin Fellowship in International Security. My thanks in particular to Samuel Huntington, Chester Haskell, Michael Tiorano, Barbara Mitchell, and Janice Rand. I completed the manuscript as an assistant professor at the Woodrow Wilson School of Public and International Affairs and the Department of Politics at Princeton University. This too provided an excellent environment for research and writing, the benefits of association with Princeton's Center for International Studies and its Center for Domestic and Comparative Policy Studies, the dedicated and resourceful efforts of the Office of Interlibrary Services at Princeton's Firestone Library, as well as funding by the University Committee on Research in the Humanities and Social Sciences. My thanks in particular to Donald Stokes, Henry Bienen, James Trussell, Ingrid Reed, and Michael Stoner.

Other institutions also provided valuable financial support. A graduate student fellowship in international relations from the National Science Foundation provided funding during the genesis of this study. During the 1984–85 academic year, a graduate research fellowship (#84-IJ-CX-0065) from the National Institute of Justice provided further funding. Travel grants in 1985 from Harvard's Center for European Studies, the Program in European Society and Western Security, and the

Committee on Latin American and Iberian Studies enabled me to conduct the initial interviews in Europe and Latin America. An invitation from the United States Information Agency in March 1986 to speak at a conference hosted by the University of the Andes in Bogotá, Colombia, provided a quick research opportunity, as did invitations in March 1990 by the Centro de Estudios de Política Exterior in Madrid, Spain, and in October 1992 by the Dutch Police and Society Foundation in Amsterdam. Grants from the National Institute of Justice and the Deutsch Forschungsgemeinschaft proved essential in funding a June 1988 conference on international cooperation in law enforcement matters convened by Harvard Law School's Center for Criminal Justice, the Max-Planck-Instituts für ausländisches und internationales Strafrecht, and the Goethe Institute of Boston.

I am also grateful to the many U.S. government officials who assisted me in one way or another during the research phase of this dissertation. Some of the research was carried out while I was simultaneously preparing a report on drug-related international money laundering for the State Department's Bureau of International Narcotics Matters (INM). I must thank Jon Wiant, who opened the doors to the State Department; Robert Retka, who showed me the ropes; Mark Steinitz and Geoffrey Levitt, who provided me with their rich insights and became friends; and all of the people in INM for their hospitality during the months I worked out of their offices.

I interviewed more than three hundred individuals as part of the research. Some provided assistance and advice over and above the time and patience required to answer my questions. The most important and numerous of my interviews were with sixty-odd special agents and other officials of the Drug Enforcement Administration. I am indebted to Frank Monastero, Patrick Tarr, and Abe Azzam for opening the doors to their agency, and, for their help, assistance, and/or advice, to Bobby Nieves, Lee Rice, Jim Bramble, Richard Mangan, and Morton Goren in Washington; Gene Castillo and Jeff Hall in Latin America; and Bill Wolf, Greg Passic, Jerry Franciosa, and Dave Herrera in Europe. Other government officials who went out of their way to assist me included William Corcoran, John Harris, Alvin Lodish, Richard Owens, and Mark Richard in the Justice Department; Dick Stiener, Martin White, and Mary Jo Grotenrath, at the U.S. National Central Bureau of Interpol; Floyd Clarke and Ernest Porter, at the Federal Bureau of Investigation; Robert Liebscher, at the U.S. Marshals Service; the late

Seymour Bolten, at the Treasury Department; Lois Allder, at the Office of the Legal Adviser in the Department of State; and Eric Sterling, on the staff of the House Subcommittee on Crime. To all of them I express my gratitude.

Earlier versions of portions of this book have appeared in various journals. Portions of Chapter Five appeared in "The DEA in Latin America: Dealing with Institutionalized Corruption," *Journal of Interamerican Studies and World Affairs* 29 (Winter 1987–88), 1–40. Portions of Chapter Six appeared in "Negotiations in Criminal Law Assistance Treaties," *American Journal of Comparative Law* 33 (Summer 1985), 467–504. Much of Chapter Seven appeared in the *New York University Journal of International Law and Politics* 25 (1993). And small sections of a few of the chapters appeared in "The Role of the United States in the International Enforcement of Criminal Law," *Harvard International Law Journal* 31 (Winter 1990), 37–76.

Abbreviations

ACI	Administration of Criminal Investigation (Belgium)
ACND	Central Narcotics Department (Austria)
AFOSI	U.S. Air Force Office of Special Investigations, 1948–
AID	Agency for International Development
ATF	U.S. Bureau of Alcohol, Tobacco, and Firearms
BDAC	U.S. Bureau of Drug Abuse Control, 1965–1968
BKA	Bundeskriminalamt (German Federal Police)
BNDD	U.S. Bureau of Narcotics and Dangerous Drugs, 1968–1973
BSC	British Security Coordination
CA	country attaché
CCC	Customs Cooperation Council, 1953–
CCE	Continuing Criminal Enterprise Act, 1970
CENTAC	DEA's Central Tactical Unit program, 1973–1981
CFTC	Commodity Futures Trading Commission (U.S.), 1974–
CIA	U.S. Central Intelligence Agency, 1947–
CID	U.S. Army Criminal Investigative Division, 1918–
CNO	Central Narcotics Office (France)
CPA	U.S. Civil Police Administration, 1955–1962
CRI	Criminal Intelligence Service (Netherlands)
CTR	Currency Transaction Report
DEA	U.S. Drug Enforcement Administration, 1973–
EPIC	DEA's El Paso Intelligence Center
EXIS	ATF's Explosives Incident System
FBI	U.S. Federal Bureau of Investigation, 1909–
FBN	U.S. Federal Bureau of Narcotics, 1930–1968

FDA	U.S. Food and Drug Administration, 1927–
FIST	Fugitive Investigative Strike Team, U.S. Marshals Service, 1981–
HEW	U.S. Department of Health, Education, and Welfare
IACP	International Association of Chiefs of Police, 1893–
ICPC	International Criminal Police Commission, 1923–
IMAC	Swiss Federal Act on International Mutual Assistance in Criminal Matters, 1981
IMF	International Monetary Fund
INM	Bureau of International Narcotics Matters, U.S. State Department, 1978–1993
INS	U.S. Immigration and Naturalization Service
IOSCO	International Organization of Securities Commission
IRA	Irish Republican Army
IRS	U.S. Internal Revenue Service
ITAR	U.S. International Traffic in Arms program, BATF
LEGAT	FBI legal attaché
LKA	criminal investigative units in German states
L/LEI	U.S. Office of Law Enforcement and Intelligence, Office of the Legal Adviser, Department of State, 1979–
MLAT	mutual legal assistance treaty
MOU	memorandum of understanding
NACDL	National Association of Criminal Defense Lawyers (U.S.)
NADDIS	DEA's Narcotics and Dangerous Drug Information System
NATO	North Atlantic Treaty Organization, 1949–
NCB	National Central Bureau (Interpol)
NIS	U.S. Naval Investigative Service, 1966–
NYPD	New York Police Department
OCAM	Organization Communale Africaine et Malgache
ODALE	U.S. Office of Drug Abuse Law Enforcement, 1972–1973
OECD	Organization of Economic Cooperation and Development
OIA	U.S. Office of International Affairs, Criminal Division, Justice Department, 1979–
OLIA	Office of Liaison and International Affairs, FBI, 1987–
ONI	U.S. Office of Naval Intelligence, 1882–
ONNI	U.S. Office of National Narcotics Intelligence, 1972–1973
OPS	U.S. Office of Public Safety, 1962–1974
OSS	U.S. Office of Strategic Services, 1942–1945
PIP	Peruvian Investigative Police

PIS	U.S. Postal Inspection Service
RAC	resident-agent-in-charge
RICO	Racketeer Influenced and Corrupt Organizations Act, 1970
SA	special agent
SAC	special-agent-in-charge
SANU	Special Action Narcotics Unit (Colombia)
SCA	Servizio Centrale Antidroga (Italy)
SEC	U.S. Securities and Exchange Commission, 1934–
SEO	Special Enforcement Operation, DEA, 1981–
SIS	U.S. Special Intelligence Service, 1940–1945
SIU	Special Investigation Unit
SOG	Special Operations Group, U.S. Marshals Service, 1971–
TDY	temporary duty
TIAS	*Treaties and Other International Acts Series* (issued singly in pamphlets by the U.S. Department of State)
UMOPAR	Rural Mobile Patrol Unit (Bolivia), 1983–
USMS	U.S. Marshals Service, 1969–
USNCB	U.S. National Central Bureau (Interpol), 1962–
ZEPO	Central Police Office (Switzerland)

Chapter One

Introduction

The Internationalization of U.S. Criminal Law Enforcement

The internationalization of U.S. law enforcement cannot be explained entirely or even primarily in terms of the need to respond to a proliferation of transnational criminal activities. Rather, the principal impetuses underlying many of the more significant developments in the history of U.S. international criminal law enforcement were provided by federal statutes criminalizing activities that had not previously been regarded as criminal. Most contemporary efforts, for instance, are concerned with the enforcement of criminal laws that did not exist a century or even a few decades ago—not just drug prohibition laws, but also criminal laws directed at insider trading, money laundering, computer fraud, and the smuggling of sophisticated weaponry and other technology to blacklisted countries. The United States' imposition of immigration controls on Chinese migrants in the late nineteenth century and most other foreigners a few decades later similarly created a need for a substantial law enforcement effort. And the proliferation of federal statutes during the 1980s explicitly extending U.S. jurisdiction to terrorist and other violent acts against U.S. citizens abroad provided the legal basis for a substantial internationalization of the FBI's investigations. Conversely, the rendition of fugitive slaves constituted a central concern of U.S. international law enforcement efforts before the Civil War, and efforts to suppress the illicit traffic in alcoholic beverages preoccupied U.S. officials involved in international law enforcement matters between 1920 and 1933. Both ended with the abolition of the laws they were intended to enforce.

Given the initial impulses provided by Congressional and other legislative criminalizations, subsequent developments can be explained by a variety of factors. The United States' assumption of global economic and security responsibilities following World War II brought with it a host of international criminal law enforcement responsibilities ranging from the policing of hundreds of thousands of U.S. military personnel abroad to the creation of police training programs in dozens of less developed nations. Many increases in international law enforcement activity were motivated by perceived increases, both real and unreal, in particular types of transnational criminal activity. The explosion in transnational drug trafficking beginning in the 1960s, for instance, generated an international law enforcement response of unprecedented dimensions. The increase in transnational violations of U.S. securities laws that inevitably accompanied the dramatic internationalization of the securities markets during the 1980s similarly invited a response by the Justice Department and the Securities and Exchange Commission. Other international criminal law enforcement initiatives were motivated principally by domestic political considerations, such as when the Nixon administration extended its "war on drugs" to foreign countries during the early 1970s, and when the Reagan and Bush administrations did likewise during the 1980s. Additional incentives were provided by the proliferation of Congressional hearings addressing transnational drug trafficking and other criminal activities. The expansion of international criminal law enforcement capabilities in and of itself generated increasing activity and invited new laws. And in many cases, the principal motivations for developing a law enforcement agency's international capabilities could be traced to interagency rivalries and the desires of agency chiefs to claim more jurisdiction and responsibilities for their agencies.

The internationalization of U.S. law enforcement has involved an increasing number of federal agencies, activities, and resources. The Office of International Affairs (OIA) in the Justice Department's Criminal Division, and the Office of Law Enforcement and Intelligence (L/LEI) in the State Department's Legal Adviser's Office, both created in 1979, have assumed leading roles in coordinating extradition and other mutual legal assistance relations with foreign governments. In 1985, the Securities and Exchange Commission created its own special office devoted to handling international enforcement matters. And in 1987, the Justice Department initiated a policy of stationing its own attorneys abroad. Growing numbers of U.S. prosecutors now communicate with their foreign counterparts and travel abroad seeking cooperation and evidence in criminal cases. American judges confront an increasing number of cases in which evidence and witnesses must be obtained from abroad. And U.S. law enforcement agencies—most notably the Drug Enforcement Administration (DEA) but also the Federal Bureau of Investigation (FBI), the Internal Revenue Service (IRS), the Immigration and Naturalization Service (INS), the Secret Service, the U.S. Customs Service, the U.S. Marshals Service, the criminal investigative branches of the military services, and even state and city police departments—have dramatically increased their international responsibilities and activities. (See Appendix A.) Some of these activities have been assisted by the U.S. military and the intelligence agencies, and backed by the diplomatic efforts of the State Department, high-level Justice Department officials, and the White House. They also have come under increasingly frequent and intensive Congressional scrutiny as federal legislators have stepped up dramatically their legislative and rhetorical responses to transnational drug trafficking and other transnational criminal activity.

A few indications of the pace of the expansion can be found in the personnel statistics. Between 1967 and 1991, the number of U.S. drug enforcement agents stationed abroad rose from about 12 in eight foreign cities to about 300 in more than seventy foreign locations. (See Appendix B.) Between 1979 and 1990, the number of attorneys in the Criminal Division's Office of International Affairs rose from 4 to 40. During the same period, the U.S. national central bureau of Interpol, based in the Justice Department, increased its staff from 6 to 110, its budget from $125,000 to $6,000,000, and the number of law enforcement agencies represented from 1 to 16. The number of foreign police agencies with representatives in the United States also increased during this time, from no more than two or three to more than a dozen, and growing numbers of foreign law enforcement officials could be found in the United States on police business.

Other indications can be found in the caseload statistics. Between the early 1970s and 1990, for instance, the number of extradition requests to and from the United States each year increased from approximately 50 to 500. The number of requests for evidence and other forms of judicial assistance similarly increased, from less than 100 a year to well over 1,000. And the number of warrants for fugitives believed to be abroad rose from a few hundred to many thousands. Between 1976 and 1986, the annual caseload of the U.S. Interpol office rose from about 4,000 to 43,863, and the volume of message traffic from 14,365 to 101,859. These dramatic increases, I must stress, reflected a burgeoning of *both* transnational criminal activity *and* the capacity and desire of U.S. government agencies to handle international criminal law enforcement matters.

The Challenges of International Enforcement

The principal objective of most criminal law enforcement efforts, both domestic and international, is to "immobilize" criminals. Immobilization involves identifying individuals who engage in criminal activity, finding and arresting them, gathering the evidence necessary to indict and convict them, and finally imprisoning them; it also can, and increasingly does, include the identification, seizure, and forfeiture of the criminal's assets. For certain types of crimes, immobilization also requires seizing the criminal's contraband, be it stolen goods, drugs, weapons, counterfeit currency, computers, or anything else a criminal seeks to sell or buy illegally. As one DEA agent put it: "The bottom line is to get the dope off the street and put the cat in jail." Presumably, the more effective governments are at immobilizing criminals, the more successful they will be at deterring crime, disrupting criminal organizations, and diminishing the total level of criminal activity.

To successfully immobilize criminals, criminal justice systems typically require three things: information, evidence, and the body (i.e., the criminal). It is generally true that the more dispersed these things are, and the less they are to be found within the physical jurisdiction of the investigating government, the greater are the obstacles to successful law enforcement efforts. Law enforcement efforts within a single jurisdiction must contend with bureaucratic frictions, such as those within and among criminal justice agencies, and with legal frictions, such as those between citizens' civil liberties and the investigatory requirements of law enforcement agents. Additional frictions can arise among different jurisdictions even within one country; one need only consider the turf squabbles and other frictions that occasionally color the interactions of the FBI and other federal law enforcement agencies with local police agencies and with one another, or those that impede close cooperation between criminal justice officers of different states.

International law enforcement efforts must contend not just with the types of domestic frictions described above but also with those that stem from the need for sovereign states to interact. Whether one takes the perspective of the police officer, the prosecutor, the diplomat, or the theoretician of international politics, the fundamental "problem" of international law enforcement is the sovereign—that is, exclusive—power of governments within their own borders and virtually nowhere else. Stated otherwise, the effective jurisdiction of a state's law enforcement agents extends no further than the territory of that state (and the vessels and embassies that fly its flag). In practice, this means that although U.S. law may authorize American police to arrest and question people abroad, foreign laws do not bolster this authority; indeed, they often forbid any law enforcement activities by foreign agents. The same is true of the American prosecutor, whose subpoenas and other demands, if delivered abroad, are not backed by the police power of the state in which they are delivered. A state can claim extraterritorial effect for its criminal laws, but it is hard-pressed to directly enforce those laws beyond its borders. The sovereign power of states generally forecloses unilateral police action by one state in the territory of another. It requires that most international law enforcement efforts be in some sense bilateral, cooperative ventures. And it means that the popular image of the Interpol agent as a police officer with international arrest powers is entirely fictional.

The basic fact of state sovereignty is not the only obstacle to international law enforcement efforts. Sovereign states are distinguished not only by the territories they occupy but also by distinctive political, social, economic, and legal systems and cultures. No two are identical; the differences generate both opportunities for transnational criminals and frictions for international law enforcers. For the former, foreign territories and alien systems offer safe havens, lucrative smuggling opportunities, and legal shields and thickets to disguise their criminal enterprises. The latter, by contrast, typically find their police powers strictly circumscribed and their international efforts complicated by alien political and legal systems and inadequate transnational infrastructures. The challenge they confront is to nullify the advantages that criminals derive from operating across borders and to reduce, circumvent, or transcend the frictions that hamper international law enforcement.

The political frictions that complicate international law enforcement efforts are not substantially different in kind from the frictions that hamper other domains of international relations. Governments that are politically hostile tend to provide only the most limited forms of assistance in criminal justice matters, and may even applaud and abet criminal acts committed abroad, particularly if the act is in some respect political. Among closely allied states, conflicting political interests and viewpoints, often involving powerful domestic constituencies, may impede cooperation in law enforcement matters. And even in the absence of significant bilateral frictions, a state's pursuit of particular international law enforcement objectives is often constrained by the fact that criminal justice objectives are rarely alone, much less predominant, on its foreign policy agenda. No government has unlimited political capital available to seek all its objectives. Often the pursuit of one undermines the furtherance of another. Objectives tend to be rank-ordered, and different components of a government vie to give precedence to accomplishment of their specific objectives. This bureaucratic jockeying is a familiar dynamic of the foreign-policy-making process in most governments—one in which high-level criminal justice officials in the United States and other nations are increasingly involved and influential but hardly triumphant.

The frictions that do differ in kind from other domains of international relations are largely a consequence of asymmetries among criminal justice systems. The most basic of these involve differences in what states choose to criminalize. Most governments are reluctant to assist others in the enforcement of criminal laws that are not reciprocal. U.S. officials today, for instance, are handicapped in their efforts to investigate the extraterritorial dimensions of tax and securities law violations by the fact that many of these violations are not regarded as criminal by other states. The same was true of international drug enforcement efforts in decades past, of efforts by the United States and a few other states to enforce their prohibitions on the traffic in alcoholic beverages during the 1920s, and of Great Britain's efforts to suppress the international traffic in African slaves during the early decades of the nineteenth century. In a similar vein, authoritarian states are typically frustrated in their efforts to obtain assistance from nonauthoritarian regimes in enforcing criminal laws against nonviolent political activity; and law enforcement officials in theocratic states bemoan the lack of foreign assistance when it comes to the prosecution of heretical activities that are criminalized within their own nations but not elsewhere. Frictions result when states seek assistance but are rebuffed, when states employ unilateral law enforcement measures that infringe upon the sovereign prerogatives of other states, and when powerful states pressure weaker ones to conform.

Far more common, and often just as frustrating as the criminal law asymmetries, are the procedural, cultural, and institutional asymmetries that hamper law enforcement cooperation even among governments that share the same criminal laws and sincerely want to assist one another. U.S. law enforcement agents trying to operate abroad, for instance, are continually confounded by different methods of criminal investigation, alien bureaucracies, and unfamiliar cultural norms. Many drug enforcement techniques regarded as essential in the United States—including undercover operations, electronic surveillance by means other than telephone taps, and various methods of recruiting informants—have been forbidden or severely circumscribed elsewhere. Plea bargaining may be proscribed, police-prosecutor relations may differ markedly, interrogation practices may seem alien, and standards of propriety may not compare. U.S. prosecutors seeking evidence and fugitives from abroad must contend with unfamiliar procedures and different laws, some reflecting basic differences between the common law system of the United States and the civil law systems that dominate in much of the non-Anglophone world, others reflecting little more than national idiosyncracies. The frictions generated by these asymmetries create a drag on international law enforcement efforts; at the same time, efforts to circumvent and overcome these frictions, such as by acting unilaterally and by pressuring foreign states to accommodate their procedures and institutions to U.S. law enforcement needs, create frictions in their own right.

The Nature of International Enforcement

Governments and their law enforcement agencies have responded to these obstacles in a variety of ways, depending upon the degree to which their domestic societies are open or closed, the extent of the powers and resources accorded the police, the nature of the laws they are obliged to enforce, and the power of the criminals they confront. Most rely to some extent on unilateral measures both internally and externally. Governments keep track of foreigners within their borders; they mount police operations against those involved in the sale and purchase of goods exported and imported illegally; and they compile records of domestic transactions with an eye toward identifying those that are illicit. A few states, notably the United States, have also devised means of enforcing their laws extraterritorially by means of domestic legal processes, such as subpoenas issued to local branches and personnel of multinational corporations, and backed by court-ordered sanctions, requiring them to provide documents located abroad. Beyond a state's borders, its law enforcement agents retain some capacity for action on the high seas, where no nation is sovereign. Law enforcement officials working near their nations' borders have been known to cross into neighboring territories in "hot pursuit" of transnational bandits. Those based abroad may undertake unilateral law enforcement tasks in the context of joint investigations conducted in tandem with local police officials; or they may conduct their own investigations unilaterally, employing whatever discretion is required and operating in much the same fashion, and with just as few police powers, as private detectives. More dramatic measures, such as the unilateral abduction or murder of fugitives abroad, are not unknown; they are, however, relatively rare, more often conducted by agents of intelligence and security agencies than by criminal justice officials, and not always readily characterized as international law enforcement measures.

Abundant obstacles deter states from employing unilateral law enforcement measures beyond their borders. Most significant are the lack of sovereign powers and the illegality of such actions under both international law and the laws of the affected state. Also significant are the logistical difficulties, the desire to avoid generating tensions in foreign relations, the fear that one's unilateral actions will invite comparable initiatives by foreign agencies within one's own borders, and the general preference of most governments for cooperative measures over those likely to require or generate conflict. Unilateral extraterritorial measures are typically resorted to out of frustration with the inability or unwillingness of a foreign state to provide assistance, and with two objectives in mind: to obtain the information, evidence, or people required in a specific investigation; and, if the demanding state is sufficiently powerful, to pressure the uncooperative foreign state to be more forthcoming in the future.

It is not surprising that, given the severe limits on unilateral extraterritorial law enforcement activities, international law enforcement arrangements tend to be bilateral and generally cooperative. These are often episodic in nature, particularly where two states share relatively few law enforcement problems in common, or when police agencies with relatively little experience in international law enforcement matters become involved in an investigation requiring them to look beyond their borders. More frequent interactions, however, lead to patterns of relations that may point out recurring sources of conflict arising from political differences as well as tensions between different law enforcement systems, which in turn create pressures for more formal accommodations and the establishment of guidelines for future interactions. The results may include the stationing of police liaisons in one another's embassies, the creation of bilateral working groups of law enforcement officials, the negotiation of extradition and other legal assistance treaties, and the enactment and revision of domestic legislation to facilitate international cooperation against transnational crime. The net intention and effect of these arrangements, apart from the symbolic purposes occasionally served by them, is to facilitate the work of the police and prosecutors who pursue the routine law enforcement tasks involved in immobilizing transnational criminals.

Some areas of international law enforcement have invited not just bilateral but multilateral, and even global, arrangements, prompted in good part by the inadequacy of unilateral and bilateral law enforcement measures in the face of certain types of transnational criminal activity. These cannot compare with bilateral approaches in accommodating the mutual preferences and peculiarities of two different law enforcement systems; they are obliged instead to settle for the typically low level of accommodation required to win the adherence of a diversity of states. As a result, the symbolic incentives and functions of multilateral arrangements are generally greater than those of bilateral treaties. But multilateral arrangements also offer numerous advantages, not the least of which is that they may obviate the need to negotiate individual bilateral arrangements with large numbers of foreign governments. They can prove especially useful in facilitating law enforcement interactions between governments that are politically hostile, or that share relatively few law enforcement concerns in common; the communications facilities of Interpol, for instance, have proven of particular value in facilitating correspondence among police agencies in the less-developed world as well as among them and the police agencies in Europe and the United States with which they have relatively little contact. Some multilateral arrangements are designed to meet the particular law enforcement needs of multinational political alliances, such as CoCom, the postwar regime established by members of NATO and Japan to restrict the flow of sophisticated technology to Warsaw Pact countries. Others may reflect the common legal systems of countries linked by geographical proximity, similar political systems, and/or political alliances: the members of the Council of Europe, for instance, or the Soviet bloc states from the 1950s to 1989, or the majority of Latin American countries.

All multilateral law enforcement arrangements—be they regional police conferences, international police organizations such as Interpol, or the dozens of multilateral law enforcement conventions addressing either particular types of transnational activity or cooperative mechanisms such as extradition—are intended to help law enforcement agencies reduce, transcend, or circumvent the frictions generated by conflicting sovereignties, political tensions, and differences among law enforcement systems. They seek to attain consensus on the substance of each nation's criminal laws, to create commitments to cooperate, and to establish the guidelines and frameworks required to regularize and facilitate international cooperation among law enforcement systems. On a more fundamental level, these arrangements are motivated by the desire to make law enforcement systems more like one another, the guiding assumption being that like systems are better able to communicate and collaborate than unlike systems. The entire evolutionary process can well be described as one of *harmonization*, in which the notion incorporates three sorts of processes: that of *regularization* of relations among law enforcement officials of different states, that of *accommodation* among systems that retain their essential differences, and that of *homogenization* of systems toward a common norm.

Success and Failure

Why do some international law enforcement efforts succeed and others fail? The answers are many, but in the chapters that follow I advance two general propositions: that success or failure in particularly difficult cases is strongly influenced by the willingness of U.S. law enforcement officials to challenge the sovereign prerogatives of foreign states; and that success or failure over the long term depends upon the capacity of U.S. law enforcement officials to overcome the political and criminal justice obstacles to effective cooperation between the United States and foreign states. In other words, I contend that success in the first instance depends upon the willingness of U.S. officials to create, or risk generating, frictions with other states, and that success in the latter instance depends upon the capacity to reduce frictions by harmonizing criminal justice systems.

The principal criteria of success or failure in both instances are neither rates of transnational criminal activity committed or deterred nor proportions of smuggled goods seized, but rather whether transnational criminals are immobilized. The former criteria are both notoriously difficult to evaluate as well as influenced by many factors other than the quality and quantity of U.S. international criminal law enforcement efforts. One need only consider the dramatic range of estimates regarding the amount of heroin or the number of illegal immigrants that enter the United States each year; or the way in which law enforcement officials annually recite, without any evidence whatsoever, the mantra of seizing 10 percent of all drugs smuggled into the United States; or the varied factors that influence the type and amount of illicit drugs exported to the United States, and consumed therein, from one year to the next; or the sheer impossibility of establishing the number and magnitude of violations of U.S. securities, tax, and money laundering laws each year. Defining success or failure in terms of whether or not criminals are immobilized may seem a relatively trite indicator—not unlike "body counts" in counterinsurgency warfare—but it does represent both the actual objective of most international criminal law enforcement efforts and the most clearly defined and measurable one.

The Americanization of Foreign Systems

The internationalization of U.S. law enforcement during the twentieth century has shaped the evolution of criminal justice systems in dozens of other countries. No other government has pursued its international law enforcement agenda in as aggressive and penetrative a manner or devoted so much effort to promoting its own criminal justice norms to others. Foreign states have responded to the U.S. initiatives by signing extradition and other law enforcement treaties, by hosting U.S. law enforcement agents within their borders, and most significant, by adopting U.S. approaches to criminal law and policing. Beginning with the adoption of the United States' prohibitionist approach to drug control during the first decades of the twentieth century, foreign governments have followed in U.S. footsteps, adopting U.S.-style investigative techniques, creating specialized drug enforcement agencies, stationing law enforcement representatives abroad, and enacting conspiracy statutes, asset forfeiture laws, and checks and bans on drug-related money laundering. Since the 1970s, pressures to cooperate in U.S. drug trafficking investigations were largely responsible for instigating changes in the laws of Switzerland, the Bahamas, and other financial secrecy jurisdictions to authorize greater assistance to U.S. and other law enforcement authorities. And even apart from the area of drug control, the influence of the United States was readily apparent during the first decades of the twentieth century in shaping foreign and international approaches to white slavery, during the Cold War era with respect to export controls on weapons and sophisticated technology, and since the mid-1980s with respect to the regulation of securities markets, in particular the criminalization of insider trading. The result has been something of an "Americanization" of criminal justice systems throughout much of the world.

This argument obviously limits the extent to which generalizations about the nature of international criminal law enforcement can be derived from an examination of U.S. behavior. The ability and willingness of the United States to pursue its international criminal law enforcement agenda as aggressively as it has is relatively unique in the annals of international criminal law enforcement. Great Britain's global campaign against the slave traffic during the nineteenth century represents perhaps the only clear precedent. Similarly, the fact that the United States has dealt with the frictions between its own criminal justice norms and those of other states principally by inducing other states to change their norms and accommodate their systems to U.S. requirements, rather than vice versa, presents something of a special case. Nonetheless, there is much about the challenges U.S. officials have encountered in trying to immobilize transnational criminals, and the ways they have responded, that is typical of most states. The fact that U.S. law enforcement officials have on occasion acted more aggressively and unilaterally than officials of other states in obtaining information, evidence, and criminals from abroad does not mean U.S. officials have not struggled with the same types of issues and frictions encountered by others.

Objectives and Structure of This Book

The chapters that follow seek to elaborate on these themes in developing further the main objectives of this book. My principal objectives, pursued in each of the chapters, are to describe and explain the activities and issues that lie at the intersection of U.S. criminal justice and foreign policy. Chapters Two and Three examine the internationalization of U.S. policing, and particularly criminal investigation, from the origins of the nation's history until the early 1990s. The history of U.S. international criminal law enforcement efforts is one in which themes of both change and continuity are readily apparent. On the one hand, the complexity and scale of contemporary international criminal investigations have little in common with the ad hoc international police endeavors of a century ago. And one need only compare the concerns of nineteenth-century law enforcers with transnational bandits, filibusters, runaway slaves, and illegal slavers to the twentieth-century concerns with illicit drug smugglers, high-tech bandits, insider traders, and money launderers to understand how dramatically the substantive focus of U.S. international criminal law enforcement efforts have changed. On the other hand, the basic concerns with controlling the nation's borders, suppressing smuggling, and renditing criminal fugitives have remained constant. And the basic challenges presented by the need to deal with foreign sovereigns, conflicting political interests, and alien criminal law enforcement systems have persisted.

Chapters Four and Five analyze the efforts of the DEA to immobilize drug traffickers in Europe and Latin America. Chapter Four examines how DEA agents have dealt with the frictions generated by Europe's civil law traditions and general resistance to DEA-style investigative methods, and how European approaches to drug enforcement have gradually become "Americanized." Chapter Five examines the nature of drug-related corruption in Latin America and the efforts of DEA agents to immobilize drug traffickers notwithstanding that corruption. The next two chapters examine the efforts of U.S. officials, particularly those in the Justice Department and the State Department's Legal Adviser's Office, to obtain evidence and fugitives from abroad. Chapter Six focuses on the negotiation of mutual legal assistance treaties to facilitate the collection of evidence from foreign jurisdictions in a form admissable in U.S. courts. Chapter Seven analyzes both the evolution of U.S. extradition treaties and practice as well as the evolution of less formal means of recovering criminal fugitives from foreign territories.

Chapters Four and Five, the two DEA chapters, provide a link between the two chapters that precede them and the two that follow. Like Chapters Two and Three, the DEA chapters focus on the international activities of U.S. *police* officials and the nature of transgovernmental police work. But like Chapters Six and Seven, they examine in some detail how U.S. law enforcement officials have dealt with the challenges that arise in trying to extract information, evidence, and people from foreign jurisdictions. The latter four chapters contribute to my subsidiary objectives, which are to explain why some international law enforcement efforts prove more successful than others, to argue that the U.S. "war on drugs" has provided the crucial impetuses for many of the most substantial developments in the internationalization of U.S. criminal law enforcement since the late 1960s, and to provide evidence in support of the thesis that criminal justice systems throughout much of the world are evolving toward a more harmonious network of relationships strongly influenced by U.S. pressures, models, and examples.

Chapter Two

The Internationalization of U.S. Law Enforcement, 1789–1939

Origins and American Insularity

The emergence of the United States to the forefront of international law enforcement is a relatively recent phenomenon. It dates back, at best, to the close of World War II, when the U.S. government belatedly assumed a global role in a great variety of areas, of which law enforcement was one of the less significant. As for the worldwide presence of U.S. drug enforcement agents, that unprecedented—and still unparalleled—development dates only to the early 1970s. Before the 1940s, and especially before World War I, the notion of transnational cooperation between police was far more familiar to Europeans than to Americans. Yet it is also true that the origins of U.S. involvement in international law enforcement matters can be traced back to the first decades of the American republic.

The insularity of American law enforcement from developments outside its borders was generally consistent with the overall American disposition toward foreign affairs until well into the twentieth century. Separated by two oceans from all but two countries, and possessed of a relatively huge territory and population, the American preoccupation with itself was not entirely unwarranted. From the police officer's point of view, more than enough criminals remained at large somewhere within the United States to devote any resources to tracking down the relatively few who had fled to foreign lands. And given the scanty resources of the few federal law enforcement agencies, state and local police had their hands full merely trying to work with one another.

The United States' lag behind Europe in becoming more involved in the international dimensions of law enforcement also reflected different needs born of different political geographies. American fugitives on the run might flee no farther than across a state border. European fugitives fleeing an equivalent distance, on the other hand, would find themselves across a national border. For American police seeking assistance, the request would involve them in interstate but *intra*national dealings, as opposed to the international relations of their European counterparts. If an American fugitive did flee abroad, an American police officer giving chase was typically obliged to book passage on a steamer for far-off shores. European police, by contrast, needed to do little more than hop on a train or, after the turn of the century, get into a car. Only in the case of Canada, Mexico, and the few other foreign territories on the North American continent were American police not obliged to travel by sea vessel.

The federal political system in the United States posed some of the same advantages to criminals, and disadvantages to police cooperation, that national borders posed to European police. Unlike Europe, where before World War II centralized national police agencies were the norm in many countries, U.S. law enforcement was heavily dominated by state and municipal police agencies. Federal law enforcement agencies were slow to evolve, their funding and jurisdiction strictly limited by Congress and an American people wary of centralized police power. With the regulatory power of the federal government constitutionally limited to "interstate commerce," the growth of federal law enforcement agencies proceeded apace with the increase in national commerce and the judicial expansion of the notion of "interstate commerce."

So long as centralized federal law enforcement remained limited in the United States, most criminal investigations involving two or more states required the cooperation of police authorities powerless beyond their own borders. Federal authorities could transcend the jealousies and prerogatives of state sovereignty, constituting in effect a suprastate police force, but city and state officials possessed no such privileges. Even where officials from two different states proved willing to cooperate, their efforts were often hampered by the same sorts of political, legal, and institutional differences that have complicated international law enforcement efforts. Until the first decades of the twentieth century, centralized mechanisms for the collection and exchange of intelligence were nonexistent or at best skimpy. The basic problem of police officials not treating crimes committed in other jurisdictions with the same seriousness or concern as crimes committed within their own borders was omnipresent. Differences in criminal laws and procedures complicated cooperative efforts even where the will to cooperate existed. And more savvy and powerful fugitives often found havens from prosecution by cultivating relationships with local authorities in states where they had committed no crimes. With virtually no outside governmental scrutiny of any state's administration of its criminal justice system, highly irregular arrangements between criminals and law enforcement authorities were all too easy. Between the middle of the nineteenth century and the beginning of the twentieth, private detective agencies often represented the only effective option for those in need of competent criminal investigators capable of operating across and beyond state and national borders. Their clients included not just private interests but also state and local governments, the federal government, and foreign governments.

The lag in American involvement in international law enforcement could thus be explained in part by the fragmentation of American law enforcement. On the one hand, fugitives fleeing the arm of the law could find almost as reliable a refuge across a state border, and especially in distant American states, as they could in foreign countries. On the other hand, the absence of any powerful centralized law enforcement agency meant that the resources necessary for participation in international efforts were not readily available. A final consideration, which had little to do with the fragmentation of U.S. law enforcement, was the relative lag in the development of criminal investigative capabilities by American police forces. Nearly bereft of the professionalism that characterized many European police agencies, American police were more than likely to treat the departure of a criminal for foreign lands as the end of the case. With little interest in receiving foreign assistance, they can hardly have been expected to render much assistance in response to foreign requests.[1]

The principal exceptions to this insular disposition involved the border regions of the United States. Even today, with the rapid globalization of transnational crime and international law enforcement, the U.S. borders with Mexico and Canada remain the locus of most international law enforcement concerns and activities. The challenges confronted by law enforcement officials along the borders, and the tasks performed by them, include those associated with policing generally as well as many that are unique to border regions. It is not just that one can crawl, walk, run, drive, or even ride a horse, bicycle, or train across the United States' land borders with Mexico and Canada—all of which greatly ease the task of escaping, smuggling, migrating, or fomenting a revolution—but also that the frontier region is the only place where international law enforcement is often synonymous with local law enforcement. Nowhere else must local officials be so concerned about the state of law and order in a foreign country; nowhere else do state and local law enforcement officials play such a prominent role in international law enforcement matters, routinely liaising with foreign officials and crossing national boundaries; and nowhere else does one find such a diversity and concentration of federal law enforcement agencies.

Evolution and Change in U.S. Involvement

In tracing the origins and evolution of U.S. involvement in international law enforcement, we thus find that U.S. law enforcement authorities, particularly those along the land borders and in the major East Coast cities, were drawn into international law enforcement efforts by concerns not unlike those of the Europeans. Governments throughout the world were obliged to deal with the problems of transnational banditry, particularly in less-populated and less-developed frontier regions; the United States was no different, confronting outlaws first along the borders with Canada and Spanish Florida, and then with Mexico—although, unlike the Europeans, U.S. authorities also faced the maraud-

1. See Raymond B. Fosdick, *American Police Systems* (New York: Century Co., 1921), for a discussion of the sorry state of American law enforcement in the early twentieth century.

ing activities of Indian warriors. Like other governments, the United States occasionally attempted to recover fugitives who had fled abroad. But unlike most European states during the first half of the nineteenth century, it sought not just the return of criminal fugitives and military deserters, but escaped slaves as well. There were the two problems posed at sea by piracy and the illicit slave trade, both of which receded as the nineteenth century passed its midpoint. There was the need to protect the lives and interests of Americans abroad. Whenever the United States was at war, or otherwise troubled by foreign political intrigues and agitators, police agents were called upon to undertake the types of tasks that professional intelligence agencies and secret services would perform in later decades. And there was the need, which rarely required foreign travel, to respond to foreign requests to extradite fugitives from foreign justice, to keep tabs on political dissidents and agitators havened in the United States, and to enforce the U.S. neutrality laws by suppressing gun running and the plots of filibusters.

Finally, there was the very substantial concern with smuggling, not so much of forbidden goods as of goods on which customs duties were supposed to be paid. Since customs duties provided the majority of the federal government's revenues until the institution of the income tax in 1913 (excepting the years during and immediately following the Civil War, when an income tax was imposed to pay for war expenses), high priority was given to ensuring their payment. Customs agents, unlike other law enforcement agents, were primarily interested not in apprehending felons but in maximizing the collection of revenue. They therefore represented a sound economic investment in the eyes of legislators charged with appropriating funds. It is not surprising that the first significant U.S. involvement in international law enforcement arose with the delegation of Treasury agents and informants to investigate smuggling and other efforts to circumvent the revenue laws.

Although the historical analysis that follows focuses on the internationalization of police activities, it also demonstrates the porous boundaries of what may be defined as international law enforcement. On the one hand, U.S. law enforcement agents were occasionally called upon to perform chores that had little or nothing to do with the enforcement of U.S. criminal laws; their peculiar talents and skills rendered them particularly well suited for conducting espionage and counterespionage tasks for a government that had yet to develop a specialized agency for such purposes. On the other hand, police agents were neither the only nor even the principal agents of U.S. international law enforcement activities until well into the twentieth century. The U.S. Army and Navy performed law enforcement functions ranging from the suppression of piracy and slave trading to the tracking down of transnational bandits and revolutionaries and the suppression of Indian raids and revolts; the enactment of the Posse Comitatus Act in 1877 severely restricted but did not entirely end the military's involvement in domestic and international law enforcement matters. Much of the work of international law enforcement in foreign countries, including the collection of information, evidence, and fugitives, was performed by consular officials operating out of U.S. embassies. Government agencies often hired special agents to carry out the sorts of tasks that today would be performed by federal law enforcement agents. The most challenging transnational criminal investigations were routinely undertaken by private detective agencies. Fugitives in foreign lands were as likely to be pursued and apprehended by the employees of such agencies, or by freelance bounty hunters, as by officials of the U.S. government. Law enforcement raids across the Mexican border were as likely to include vigilante parties and undeputized posses as U.S. military units and officially sanctioned posses. And both government and private police agencies routinely relied upon the services of informants, including U.S. civilians, foreign nationals, and even Indian scouts, to facilitate their international activities.

No one theme can sufficiently explain the evolution of U.S. involvement in international law enforcement. Some of the most vigorous international law enforcement efforts before World War I were directly linked to the broader national security concerns of a relatively new and expanding nation contending with persistent challenges to its internal and external sovereignty from foreign states, irredentist and revolutionary movements, and aboriginal nations resisting their own dislocation and destruction. Most of these were resolved by the 1920s, although the potential for renewed political violence along the U.S.-Mexican border certainly remains. Similarly, the involvement of the U.S. military and other substantial contingents of personnel to deal with these and other transnational violations of American law seems a thing of the past—until one considers the 1983 amendment to the Posse Comitatus Act to allow the military once again to play a role in civilian law enforcement; the increased involvement of the military and National Guard units during the late 1980s in policing the border with Mexico and interdicting illicit drug shipments; and the 1989 military invasion of Panama to, among other things, arrest a foreign dictator who had been indicted on criminal charges in a U.S. court.

Other ebbs and flows in the internationalization of U.S. law enforcement reflected changing domestic political concerns, criminal laws, and police priorities within the United States. The efforts devoted to apprehending fugitive slaves who had fled across the border were little more than the international manifestations of domestic law enforcement concerns that ended with the Civil War. The same was true of the quite substantial energies devoted to curtailing the illicit import of alcohol into the United States during Prohibition. And the need to track down and immobilize transnational outlaws who robbed banks and trains, rustled cattle and generally wreaked havoc along the border with Mexico during the second half of the nineteenth century was merely the international dimension of a much broader domestic law enforcement effort directed at suppressing outlawry throughout the sparse territories and states of the West. As domestic laws and internal political and social conditions changed, thereby legalizing, eliminating, or undermining particular types of criminality, the need to contend with the transnational violations of these laws was likewise eliminated. Conversely, as criminal justice institutions came to play an increasingly important role in the domestic regulation of psychoactive drugs, so the need to investigate and suppress transnational violations of U.S. drug laws fundamentally altered the character, objectives, and scope of U.S. involvement in international law enforcement matters.

Certain aspects of international law enforcement, however, have remained relatively constant. The federal government's reliance on customs officials to investigate frauds against the customs laws dates back to the origins of the nation, as does its reliance on special agents with expertise in criminal investigation for espionage and counterespionage tasks. The peculiar day-to-day requirements of law enforcement officials alongside the border, particularly those in towns and cities a stone's throw from "twin" towns and cities in Canada or Mexico, have also changed relatively little. And even as the targets of most international law enforcement efforts have shifted from the fugitive slaves, Indians, and Mexican and American outlaws of the nineteenth century to the drug traffickers of recent decades, the basic mechanisms of rendition—extradition, deportation, and various less formal measures—have not fundamentally changed.

Apart from the changing substantive focus of U.S. international law enforcement efforts, the most significant procedural transformation since the nineteenth century has been the virtual monopolization of international law enforcement activities in the hands of government law enforcement agencies, primarily at the federal level. As federal police agencies proliferated and advanced dramatically in terms of personnel, resources, and jurisdiction during the twentieth century, they developed the capacity to more than fill the void that had existed during the previous century. And as the federal government sought to regularize its relations, both friendly and hostile, with foreign governments, its willingness to allow private citizens and even state and local governments to take international law enforcement matters into their own hands waned.

Treasury, Customs, Immigration, and Smuggling

Created in 1789, the U.S. Customs Service faced its first major challenge in 1807–8, when Congress passed the Embargo Act to protest British seizures of American vessels and sailors. The situation proved particularly acute along the Canadian border with New York and Vermont, where traders continued their trade despite its redefined status. Unable to cope with the tremendous volume of smuggling across the border, customs collector Jabez Penniman wrote to Treasury Secretary Gallatin requesting that he seek greater assistance from President Jefferson. Jefferson responded by authorizing the purchase of revenue cutters and the hiring of additional customs officers and by sending federal troops to police the border.[2] Their efforts, however, proved largely futile, as the smuggling continued even throughout the War of 1812 with Great Britain. Two years into the war, the British governor-general in Canada reported to the Foreign Office: "Two-thirds of the army in Canada are at this moment eating beef provided by American contractors, drawn principally from the States of Vermont and New York."[3] In retrospect, the Customs Service's experience with trying to enforce the Embargo Act was just the first of many futile efforts to enforce laws banning the flow of goods across U.S. borders.

Even today, but especially during its earlier years, most Customs

2. Don Whitehead, *Border Guard: The Story of the United States Customs Service* (New York: McGraw-Hill Book Co., 1963), 33–44.

3. Cited in ibid., 44.

efforts were directed not toward keeping goods out of the country but rather toward collecting a duty on their import. Early on, secretaries of the treasury and their customs collectors recognized the advantage of securing cooperation and information from abroad, whence most smuggling ventures were planned. One approach was to persuade foreign governments to cooperate against smuggling. In a letter of April 4, 1844, Treasury Secretary John Spencer urged Secretary of State John C. Calhoun to impress upon the Canadians the benefits and obligations of mutual cooperation in this area:

> The attention of this Department having been especially directed to the extensive system of smuggling heretofore existing on the Canadian Frontier, it has been suggested that among the most effective means of checking illicit traffic, would be an arrangement with the Governor of Canada, by which it would become the reciprocal duty of the officers of the Revenue on either side of the line to furnish immediate information of any known intentions to engage in unlawful trade. It is not doubted that the Canadian authorities would be ready to unite cordially with the Government of the United States in the measure proposed which, while it guarded the revenue on either side, would be calculated to promote friendly feelings between revenue officers of the respective governments, and to prevent the recurrence of incidents of an unpleasant character, such as recently took place in the seizure of the Canadian Steamboats, the Admiral and the America.[4]

The second approach involved sending or stationing agents outside the country's borders. These agents operated both overtly—liaising with foreign authorities—and covertly, even to the extent of keeping their identities secret from local officials. The employment of such agents both within and without the country represented the first systematic use of undercover techniques for law enforcement purposes by American authorities. During the first half of the nineteenth century, a number of

4. Quoted in U.S. Customs Service, *A History of Enforcement in the United States Customs Service, 1789–1875* (Washington, D.C.: Treasury Department, 1986), chap. 4, pp. 29–30; the unnamed author of the report is Michael N. Ingrisano Jr., former acting director of the Information Services Division, U.S. Customs Service. (Hereafter cited as *History of Customs Enforcement*, with chapter and page separated by a colon, as 4:29.)

these agents were assigned along the frontier with Canada. Evidence of the employment of one such agent, a N. Goodsell, was provided in a confidential letter from Treasury Secretary Ingram to the Collector at Genesee, New York, in 1829:

> Mr. N. Goodsell, who was employed by the late collector at Genesee, with the approbation of this Department as an Inspector of Customs, was confidentially charged by our late Secretary of the Treasury with the special duty of visiting the neighbouring parts of the British possessions for the purpose of discovering attempts which were understood to be on foot for introducing foreign merchandise into the U. States in violation of the revenue laws. . . . In consequence he has again been charged with the same confidential service; and will receive his instructions from, and make his reports directly to, this Department.[5]

Less than a year earlier, the customs collectors from the New York cities of Sacket Harbor, Genesee, and Oswego had met and discussed the possibility of stationing, not just sending, an undercover operative abroad. In a report on the meeting to Treasury Secretary Richard Rush, one of the attendees wrote:

> Among other things we agreed in the opinion that a suitable character ought to be employed in the City of Montreal to obtain information and to impart the name to the different collectors and for this purpose agreed to address your department. . . . By placing a suitable man at Montreal, and to render the arrangement more effectual, place another at Little York, whose sole employment should be to ascertain the names of all suspicious characters, the arrival and departures and destinations of Boats, the property on board, the Consignees of Cargoes and every aspect of information which in any degree can afford a clue to trace and detect the operators of smuggling and to impart the information weekly to each of the Colls which may be done from Montreal to Niagara by means of the mail and Steam Boat could in my estimation (considering the expense) be the most effectual means to enable us to enforce the laws.[6]

5. "Confidential" letter from Treasury Secretary Ingram to a collector, July 11, 1829, quoted in ibid., 4:8.
6. Ibid., 4:6.

No evidence has been uncovered indicating whether such a character was appointed. Further evidence that the practice continued, however, was provided in a letter from Treasury Secretary Chase to the customs collector at Lewiston, New York, in 1862:

> I have received your letter of the 26th ulto and hereby approve your nomination of Eben B. Shears at a compensation of $3 per day and William Wadsworth at $1.50 per day as Aids to the Revenue [a euphemism for secret agents], commencing July 1 to be nominally located at Lewiston but to reside in Canada, and travel from point to point as the interest of the revenue may require.[7]

Few sections of the United States proved more amenable to smuggling ventures than the region around Puget Sound, which developed rapidly during the latter half of the nineteenth century. Customs officials could expect relatively little assistance from either Canadian officials or American settlers along the border, neither of whom perceived much of an interest in enforcing U.S. tariffs on rum, sugar, wool, opium, and other goods as well as the new immigration laws directed at the Chinese.[8] Frustrated by the particular porousness of the border in that corner of the country, customs officials supplemented their more reactive border inspection and patrol functions with a variety of more proactive efforts. During the 1880s, Customs employed undercover female inspectors on passenger steamers to detect petty smugglers; it also rewarded Canadian informers by sharing cash derived from the sale of confiscated goods.[9] One particularly resourceful collector of customs, Herbert F. Beecher, hired private detectives to infiltrate smuggling rings in Canada and collect information about planned shipments.[10] He was more successful than most in immobilizing major smugglers and seizing their illicit shipments of opium and other goods, but most smugglers remained unfazed.

With the opening of the West, customs inspectors were needed to supervise the collection of revenue along the border with Mexico—and

7. Ibid., 4:18.
8. Roland L. De Lorme, "The United States Bureau of Customs and Smuggling on Puget Sound, 1851–1913," *Prologue* 5 (1973), 76–88.
9. Ibid., 81–82.
10. Ibid., 86.

special agents to detect revenue evaders. As early as 1845, immediately following Congress' vote to annex the independent republic of Texas, one John A. Parker was nominated as a "travelling agent for the Government to Texas or to Mexico."[11] A decade later, with the development of trade between the west and east coasts of the United States via the Isthmus of Panama, customs agents were assigned to special duty in the foreign transit point. In this case, their appointment was legislated by Congress. In "An Act to Extend the Warehousing System by Establishing Public Bonded Warehouses, and for Other Purposes," passed in March 1854, the treasury secretary was authorized

> to appoint special sworn agents as inspectors of the customs, to reside in said foreign territory when such goods may be landed or embarked, with power to superintend the landing and shipping of all goods passing coastwise between the ports of the United States on the Pacific and Atlantic, and whose duty it shall be, under such regulations and instructions as the Secretary of the Treasury may prescribe, to guard against the perpetration of any frauds upon the revenue.[12]

Confirmation that such an agent was in fact posted to Panama is in the Official Register of the United States for 1873, where a William Dill, customs agent in the Isthmus of Panama, is noted among the list of government employees.

In collecting information on smuggling, the Treasury Department and its Customs Service were not left solely to their own devices. U.S. embassies abroad, staffed at that time largely by members of the State Department, were charged with collecting whatever intelligence might be of use to their government. On occasion, the Customs Service was the beneficiary of such information. On March 6, 1805, for instance, Treasury Secretary Albert Gallatin forwarded to two customs collectors a confidential letter that contained an extract from a letter received from the U.S. Consul in Bordeaux, France:

> By the enclosed extract of a letter from the American Consul at Bordeaux, dated December 20, 1804, you will observe that the

11. *History of Customs Enforcement*, 4:10.
12. Act of Mar. 28, 1854, quoted in ibid., 3:9.

> masters of certain vessels trading between that place and your port and whose names are annexed to the extract, are suspected of being guilty of infractions of the Revenue laws. As this information, however, has been recd from the Consul under injunctions of secrecy you will be pleased to consider it as communicated in confidence by me to you.[13]

The military branches, most notably the Navy, also offered information based on encounters and observations made at sea. Before the Civil War, a good portion of such information dealt with the illicit slave trade. On one occasion in 1799, Treasury Secretary Oliver Wolcott wrote to the collector in Boston, Benjamin Lincoln, about information he had received from the Navy:

> Captain [Stephen] Decatur of the Navy has given information that during his late cruise near Cuba he met with the Brig "Dolphin" of Boston, William White, Master, with 140 to 150 slaves for sale procured on the coast of Africa.
>
> I request you to take the requisite measures to enforce the Law against the persons who have been concerned in this traffic.[14]

Unlike Canada, or Mexico for that matter, Europe presented greater obstacles to the collection of intelligence by U.S. customs agents for the simple reason that it was so far away. Investigations took longer, given the need to cross the Atlantic. Travel expenses were higher, communications were slower, and the opportunities to regularize relations with foreign counterparts were fewer. In 1848, Treasury Secretary Robert Walker sent two agents to England to learn how the British were using bonded warehouses, which were about to be instituted in the United States.[15] Beginning in 1870, when Congress for the first time gave the treasury secretary specific authority to appoint special agents exclusively for customs business, confirmation of the presence of Treasury agents can be found in the Official Register of the United States.[16] The first such agent was Frederick Augustus Starring, a graduate of Harvard and a major-general in the Civil War, listed as a special Treasury agent

13. Quoted in ibid., 3:17.
14. Quoted in ibid.
15. Telephone interview with Michael Ingrisano, June 20, 1986.
16. *History of Customs Enforcement*, 5:2.

stationed in Europe from 1869 to 1883. His successors, according to the Official Registers of 1883 and 1885, were George Tichenor and Amos Tingle, the latter of whom later became chief of the Special Agent Section of the Customs Service. By the turn of the century, Treasury agents were stationed in five European cities—Paris, London, Berlin, Cologne, and Saint Gall—with their headquarters in the French capital under the supervision of agent Major Williams.[17] Their efforts were supplemented by visits from U.S.-based agents working on specific cases of sufficient import to warrant transatlantic travel.

The Treasury agents in Europe, as well as those who traveled abroad on shorter visits, performed a variety of tasks. They investigated plots to smuggle both licit and illicit goods into the United States, they found ways to determine the actual value of imported goods that were undervalued by those declaring them,[18] they investigated corruption among the customs inspectors, and they generally sought to uncover all other varieties of fraud on the U.S. Treasury. In 1908, William H. Theobald, a Treasury agent who had shuttled back and forth between New York and Europe for a number of years, recounted some of his exploits and those of fellow agents in his memoirs.[19] Many of the cases on which he and other Treasury agents worked involved smugglers of diamonds and jewelry, no doubt because the unpaid duties on these were substantial enough to justify the expenses for his European jaunts.[20] Some of these criminals were no more than wealthy individuals seeking to evade paying all or part of the duty on purchases for themselves. Others, however, were sophisticated international criminals who trafficked in diamonds and other jewels. Some of these had the resources to hire their own private detectives to follow and intimidate government agents and potential witnesses alike.

Theobald and other agents relied in their investigations on informants and contacts among local police, the jewelry merchants, and their

17. William H. Theobald, *Defrauding the Government* (New York: Myrtle Publishing Co., 1908), 353.

18. According to one account, "in 1879 the special agents force struggled to establish the true market value of fine kid gloves from France and proved that velvets imported from Germany were being systematically undervalued" (see Miriam Ottenberg, *The Federal Investigators* [Englewood Cliffs, N.J.: Prentice-Hall, 1962], 291).

19. Theobald, *Defrauding the Government.*

20. Andrew Tully, *Treasury Agent: The Inside Story* (New York: Simon & Schuster, 1958), 118–126.

employees. They spied on suspicious Americans making large purchases at stores such as Tiffany in Paris.[21] In one case, they even succeeded in persuading a clerk in a jewelry shop to display a smuggler's purchases in the show window so they could be photographed as evidence.[22] Often the ultimate success of a case depended upon their ability to persuade witnesses to come to the United States and testify, because U.S. prosecutors could not compel foreigners to come to the United States for such purposes. In one case involving a notorious diamond smuggler, the prosecution in the United States was successful only because the Treasury agent had persuaded a jeweler in Holland and an abandoned mistress in England to come to the United States to testify.[23]

In 1937, the Treasury Department sent Al Scharff, an experienced agent who had worked along the Mexican border for twenty years, to Paris "to assist the Treasury attache in organizing a system to combat the flow of narcotic drugs from the Far East through Europe to the United States."[24] Regarded with suspicion by the French Sûreté, Scharff turned first to a Swede in charge of the Wells Fargo Express police in Paris to make the necessary introductions; when that proved unsuccessful, U.S. Ambassador William Bullitt provided the required political leverage to open doors. With forty-six men in key European cities, Scharff was able to investigate drug smuggling throughout the continent.[25] Informers and stool pigeons were hired. Sam Schwartz, an expert smuggler and undercover operative with vast knowledge of the international narcotics traffic, was brought to Europe from Shanghai and paid $1,000 a month to assist the Treasury agents in developing cases.[26] And Scharff personally liaised with drug enforcement chiefs around the continent, including the Gestapo's narcotics chief.[27]

The westward expansion of the United States during the nineteenth century substantially expanded the duties of the customs agency. In 1886, "mounted inspectors," later known as customs patrol inspectors, were posted along the Mexican border to deter and intercept the

21. Ibid., 231.
22. Ibid., 327.
23. See the chapters on the "Lasar Diamond Case" in ibid.
24. Garland Roark, *The Coin of Contraband* (Garden City, N.Y.: Doubleday & Co., 1964), 336.
25. Ibid., 343.
26. Ibid., 342.
27. Ibid., 344.

extensive smuggling ventures. The size of the force remained relatively modest for forty years, until Prohibition prompted both the creation of a second inspector force along the northern border and an overall increase in the number of inspectors from 111 in 1925 to 723 in 1930.[28] Most of the inspectors' efforts naturally focused on interdicting the smuggling of goods and animals—particularly cattle around the turn of the century, on which a stiff protective tariff had been imposed—into the United States, but they were also obliged to keep an eye on the outward flow of particular items, notably guns being exported to Mexican revolutionaries and government forces. Following the enactment of the Chinese Exclusion Act in 1882, they were also charged with curtailing the smuggling of Chinese into the United States via Mexico and Canada—a responsibility that overlapped substantially with the morally charged campaign to suppress the "white slave trade" in Chinese women and girls to American houses of prostitution.[29] This duty was partially taken over in 1904 by the Immigration Service, which hired a renowned customs inspector, Jefferson Milton, as its first "Chinese Inspector."[30] Following the enactment of far broader and more restrictive immigration legislation in the early 1920s, an Immigration Border Patrol was created in 1924 to stem the flow of Mexicans and other aliens into the United States.[31]

Any account of the Treasury Department's efforts to investigate and deter smuggling is complicated by the many bureaucratic shufflings and reorganizations in the department's history, the frequently changing titles of its agents, and the fact that so many law enforcement agencies have been under its umbrella.[32] Not all of the Treasury agents stationed

28. Arthur Millspaugh, *Crime Control by the National Government* (Washington, D.C.: The Brookings Institution, 1937), 68.

29. Carl E. Prince and Mollie Keller, *The U.S. Customs Service: A Bicentennial History* (Washington, D.C.: Government Printing Office, 1989), 171–194. See also the account of a scandal involving illicit Chinese migration that shook Nogales in 1901, in George E. Paulsen, "The Yellow Peril at Nogales: The Ordeal of Collector William M. Hoey," *Arizona and the West* 13 (1971), 113–128.

30. J. Evetts Haley, *Jeff Milton: A Good Man with a Gun* (Norman: University of Oklahoma Press, 1948), 340–355.

31. See John Myers Myers, *The Border Wardens* (Englewood Cliffs, N.J.: Prentice-Hall, 1971). See also the celebratory account by Mary Kidder Rak, *Border Patrol* (Boston: Houghton Mifflin, 1938), and the memoir of a Border Patrol agent, Clifford Alan Perkins, *Border Patrol: With the U.S. Immigration Service on the Mexican Boundary, 1910–1954* (El Paso: Texas Western Press, 1978).

32. See Laurence F. Schmeckebier, *The Customs Service: Its History, Activities, and*

abroad reported solely to the Customs Service, and not all customs representatives abroad could be described as special agents. That being said, the network of Treasury representatives and agents stationed abroad by the 1930s could well be described as a nascent transnational police organization. Dozens of agents could be found in Europe, as well as many more in cities from Shanghai to Mexico City. Some focused on drug trafficking, others on assorted frauds, but all were charged principally with investigating and curtailing smuggling and other violations of U.S. revenue laws.

Many of the successes of the Treasury and border control agents depended upon their ability to cultivate good relations with local officials, to operate covertly, and to develop effective informant networks. Although they frequently obtained assistance from foreign police agencies, they did not always restrict their activities to those countenanced by the formal rules of international diplomacy. Nowhere was this more so than along the border with Mexico. In many ways, these agents were the forefathers of the activist approach to international law enforcement employed in recent decades by the U.S. Drug Enforcement Administration.

Suppression of the African Slave Trade

Between independence and the Civil War, the issue of slavery periodically dominated American politics, played no small part in the foreign relations of the United States, and generated an abundance of activity in the realm of international law enforcement. The "Act to Prohibit the Importation of Slaves Into Any Port or Place Within the Jurisdiction of the United States" was signed by President Thomas Jefferson in March 1807 and went into force in 1808. The law was amended and reinforced thereafter, most notably by an 1820 act that equated the illicit slave trade with piracy and authorized the death penalty for violators. From 1808 until the abolition of slavery in 1863, however, the laws prohibiting the slave trade were enforced with less vigor than almost any others passed by Congress. The initial act was not accompanied by the author-

---

Organization (Washington, D.C.: The Brookings Institution, 1924); Tully, *Treasury Agent*; and Millspaugh, *Crime Control by the National Government*.

ization of any funds or mechanisms for its enforcement. The law was repeatedly denounced by Southern politicians, including John C. Calhoun, who announced his regret that the term "piracy" had ever been applied to the slave trade. It was consistently violated by entrepreneurs all along the eastern and southern seaboard. New York City was described by *The Times* of London in 1846 as the "greatest slave-trading mart in the world," where ships were outfitted and deals negotiated to obtain black Africans from western Africa and deliver them to markets in Brazil, Cuba, and the United States.[33] As for the occasional naval officers, U.S. marshals, and others who attempted to enforce the laws seriously, they risked condemnation by superior officials as well as the likely prospect of seeing those they arrested set free by sympathetic judges and juries.[34]

Nonetheless, there were periodic efforts to enforce the prohibition on the African slave trade. The Navy patrolled the Caribbean fairly vigorously in an effort to curtail the slave traffic from Cuba to the United States. A particular target of their efforts, however, was Captain Aury, a "buccaneer governor" whose piratical attacks on slave-trading vessels both violated the law and threatened established slave-trading interests in the United States.[35] In 1820 four naval vessels were sent to patrol the west coast of Africa, where they collaborated with the Royal Navy and succeeded in capturing a number of slavers, but were withdrawn in 1823. Following the signing of the Webster-Ashburton Treaty in 1842, another naval squadron comprised of four vessels was delegated to the African coast, where it remained until the Civil War. The U.S. naval commanders who captained the small African fleet were typically committed to their mission but handicapped by their reliance on sailing vessels rather than steamers, by the 1,000-mile distance between their base at the Cape Verde Islands and the African shores from which most slaving ventures departed, and by the lack of political, logistical, and moral support at home.[36] The persistent refusal by Congress to permit

33. Quoted in Robert Ralph Davis Jr., "James Buchanan and the Suppression of the Slave Trade, 1858–1861," *Pennsylvania History* 33 (1966), 446–459.

34. Warren S. Howard, *American Slavers and the Federal Law, 1837–1862* (Berkeley and Los Angeles: University of California Press, 1963); Paul Finkelman, ed., *The African Slave Trade and American Courts* (New York: Garland Publishing, 1988).

35. W. E. B. Du Bois, *The Suppression of the African Slave Trade to the United States of America, 1638–1870* (New York: Longmans, Green & Co., 1896), 113–114.

36. W. E. F. Ward, *The Royal Navy and the Slavers* (London: Allen & Unwin, 1969), 149–161.

the Royal Navy to search suspected slavers flying the American flag placed severe limits on Britain's ability to enforce other nations' laws vicariously. U.S. naval commanders compensated by developing joint cruising arrangements with the Royal Navy's African squadron, but the small number of U.S. vessels (which never exceeded six) precluded any sustained collaborations.[37]

U.S. officials made occasional efforts to recruit informants on the slave trade, but there is little indication that these ever amounted to much. U.S. agents in Africa provided some useful information, one item of which, however, was that the slave traders "were enabled by a regular system to gain intelligence of any cruizer being on the coast."[38] The most substantial crackdown on the African slave trade did not occur until the late 1850s, when the Buchanan administration supplemented the African squadron and sent four steamers to patrol the Cuban coast.[39] The result was a dramatic increase in the number of slavers apprehended. Secretary of the Interior Jacob Thompson also took the unusual step of sending an undercover agent, Benjamin Slocumb, throughout the South to obtain information on incoming slavers and their distribution systems.[40] These belated efforts, successful as they were, underscored how much might have been accomplished if the U.S. government had committed itself to suppressing the transatlantic slave trade earlier and more vigorously. In 1861, the American squadron was withdrawn from the African coast following the outbreak of the Civil War. The slave trade picked up briefly thereafter but was brought to a fairly swift end during the course of the war.

Fugitive Slaves and Foreign Territories

The institution of slavery depended upon the capacity of slave owners to deter their slaves from escaping and to recover and punish them when they did. Slave owners who lived in close proximity to free states, and to

37. Ibid. See also Christopher Lloyd, *The Navy and the Slave Trade* (New York: Longmans, Green, 1949), 176–183; and the memoir by a U.S. naval officer who was captain of a vessel in the African Squadron in 1850–51, Andrew H. Foote, *Africa and the American Flag* (New York: D. Appleton & Co., 1854).

38. Du Bois, *Suppression of the African Slave Trade*, 126.

39. Davis, "James Buchanan and the Suppression of the Slave Trade."

40. Howard, *American Slavers and the Federal Law*, 147–154.

foreign jurisdictions in which slavery was prohibited, clearly had greater cause for concern than those ensconced in the Deep South. They viewed the territorial expansion of the United States by purchase and conquest as beneficial both because it opened up new lands to slavery and because it provided buffers between slave jurisdictions in the United States and foreign refuges for fleeing slaves. When their slaves did escape to free states and foreign jurisdictions, they sought to recover them through both formal and informal procedures. The frustrations of slave owners in attempting to recover their escaped slaves from free states were addressed in a series of federal Fugitive Slave Acts. Similar frustrations stemming from the flight of slaves to foreign jurisdictions resulted in U.S. efforts to negotiate treaties requiring the rendition of fugitive slaves. Indeed, the many efforts devoted to recovering fugitive slaves from nearby British possessions, Florida, and Mexico generated more diplomatic activity and political controversy than all other international law enforcement activities by U.S. citizens and officials prior to the Civil War.

Florida

International disputes over runaway slaves predated the independence of the American colonies. English requests to Spanish authorities in Florida for the recovery of escaped slaves date back at least to 1688.[41] Although the Spaniards were not averse to slavery—and indeed continued to uphold the institution in Cuba until after the American Civil War—they perceived the flight of slaves to Florida as both harmful to their enemy, the English, and beneficial in strengthening their own colony.[42] In 1731, the Council for the Indies in Madrid decided to reverse its previous policy of either returning escaped slaves to the British or providing compensation; thereafter, escaped slaves were assured their freedom. A settlement known as Gracia Real de Santa Teresa de Mose was established for their benefit in 1739 near Saint Augustine, and a fort, Fort Mose, constructed for their protection. Proactive efforts to entice British slaves to Florida were also made. According to one historian, "Negro sergeants, with secret *rendezvous* in Carolina, were sent into that colony

41. "Dispatches of Spanish Officials Bearing on the Free Negro Settlement of Gracia Real De Santa Teresa de Mose, Florida," *Journal of Negro History* 9 (1924), 145.

42. Kenneth Wiggins Porter, "Negroes and the East Florida Annexation Plot, 1811–1813," *Journal of Negro History* 30 (1945), 11.

to instigate desertions from the plantations and, if possible, insurrection."[43] The result was a constant trickle of runaway slaves into Florida, which only slowed with the ceding of the territory to Britain under the Treaty of Paris of 1763.

The flow of runaway slaves to Florida picked up again in 1775, when the British rulers of Florida began encouraging slaves to flee their rebel masters, and continued after 1783, when the territory reverted to Spanish possession. Pleas from disgruntled Carolinan and Georgian slave owners led to small steps by the federal government to stem the problem of runaways. In 1788, Secretary of State John Jay sought assurances from the government in Madrid that slaves fleeing to Florida would be returned; the Spanish, themselves concerned with the flight of a number of murderers from Florida to the United States, replied favorably, but no agreement was formalized.[44] In 1791, an agreement was signed by James Seagrove, a commissioner of the United States, with the governor of East Florida, but there is no record that it was ever executed.[45] Throughout the remainder of the decade, U.S. officials, notably the governor of Georgia, and Spanish officials in Florida continued to complain about the mutual lack of cooperation in surrendering both free and slave fugitives, but initiatives to conclude an extradition agreement similar to that included in the Jay Treaty proved inconclusive.[46]

Complaints by American slave owners also led to the negotiation of treaties with the Creek Indians in 1790 and 1796 in which the Creeks agreed to deliver all runaway black slaves in their territory, including those in Florida.[47] The provision was rejected, however, by one faction of the Creek Confederacy, the Seminoles, who had acquired many black slaves of their own during the previous decades and had thoroughly integrated them into their societies under conditions approximating equality. By 1804, the Seminoles had largely seceded from the Creek Confederacy, alienated in good part by the split over the treatment of the black runaways. The escaped slaves, or freedmen, among them soon came to play a central role in the Seminoles' struggles against the Americans, first on behalf of the Spaniards' efforts to resist annexationist

43. Ibid.

44. John Bassett Moore, *A Treatise on Extradition and Interstate Rendition* (Boston: Boston Book Co., 1891), 84.

45. Ibid., 85–86.

46. Ibid., 87–89.

47. Joseph A. Opala, *A Brief History of the Seminole Freedman* (Austin: University of Texas, African and Afro-American Studies and Research Center, 1980), 2.

plots by the United States, and thereafter on behalf of the Seminoles' efforts to resist dispossession from their homes.[48]

"The persistent desire of the United States to possess the Floridas between 1801 and 1819," K. C. Babcock wrote in 1906, "amounted almost to a disease, corrupting the moral sense of each succeeding administration."[49] Apart from the conviction of manifest destiny and the compulsion to suppress the Indians who insisted on keeping their land and their independence, the strong desire to curtail the problem of fugitive slaves ranked high among the incentives of American annexationists. "The people of Georgia," Eugene Southall wrote in 1934, "were greatly excited at seeing those who had once been slaves in South Carolina and Georgia now living quietly and happily in Florida. . . . The subject of fugitive slaves in Florida was constantly on the calendar of the Georgia Legislature."[50] Following the failure of a plot sponsored by President Madison to annex East Florida in 1811–13, troops were sent to Florida. The first Seminole war began in late 1817 when the chief of the Mikasuki Seminoles, Kenhagee, rejected a demand by the head of the U.S. expeditionary force to allow his troops to enter the Seminole territory in search of fugitive slaves; it ended a year later with Andrew Jackson's conquest of the peninsula. Some of the Seminole blacks fled to Andros Island in the Bahamas, others fled to Guanabacoa on the northern coast of Cuba, and the remainder stayed with the Seminole Indians, playing a leading role in the second Seminole war from 1835 to 1842 and therafter being removed with them to Indian territory in what is now eastern Oklahoma; in 1850, many of the Seminole blacks relocated once again, to Mexico.[51]

Canada

The principal foreign haven for American slaves, however, was Canada. By 1842, an estimated 12,000 former slaves had found freedom north of the border.[52] Although the welcome was generally not as warm as that

48. J. Leitch Wright Jr., *Creeks and Seminoles* (Lincoln: University of Nebraska Press, 1986).

49. Kendrick Charles Babcock, *Rise of American Nationality* (1906), xiii, cited in Porter, "Negroes and the East Florida Plot," 9.

50. Eugene Portlette Southall, "Negroes in Florida Prior to the Civil War," *Journal of Negro History* 19 (1934), 81, 83.

51. Opala, *Seminole Freedman*, 8.

52. Roman J. Zorn, "Criminal Extradition Menaces the Canadian Haven for Fugitive Slaves, 1841–1861," *Canadian Historical Review* 38 (1957), 285.

extended by the Seminoles,[53] the British and Canadian authorities were deeply reluctant to deliver fugitive slaves back to the United States. The issue had first emerged in U.S.-British relations following the conclusion of the American War of Independence, and then again following the War of 1812, after both of which the U.S. government sought first the return of slaves who had fled to or been seized by the British and (when the British steadfastly refused to deliver those to whom freedom had been promised) compensation for their lost property. Indeed, the most common and vigorous protests voiced against Jay's treaty during the Congressional debate over ratification concerned his failure to obtain compensation for the slaves who had fallen into the hands of the British.[54] The matter was finally brought to a close in 1826, when the British government reluctantly agreed to pay $1,204,960.

More threatening to American slave owners was the continuing lure of freedom in Canada, as well as other British possessions, such as the Bahamas, for slaves brave enough or desperate enough to venture the trip. Southern Congressmen pressured successive administrations to negotiate a treaty with the British to ensure recovery of fugitive slaves, and in 1828 the House of Representatives adopted a resolution requesting the President to open negotiations with the British on the subject.[55] The British, however, steadfastly refused to "depart from the principle recognized by the British courts that every man is free who reaches British soil."[56] Disagreements over the issue were largely responsible for the inability of the two governments to conclude an extradition treaty during the 1820s and 1830s. The only other alternatives were the abduction of slaves from Canada by slave owners and their agents, which was legal under U.S. law but illegal under Canadian law, and the initiation of extradition requests alleging that the fugitive slaves had committed criminal offenses before or pursuant to their flight. Evidence that the former technique was resorted to with some frequency appeared

53. Jason H. Silverman, *Unwelcome Guests: Canada West's Response to American Fugitive Slaves, 1800–1865* (New York City: Associated Faculty Press, 1985); Jason H. Silverman, "The American Fugitive Slave in Canada: Myths and Realities," *Southern Studies* 19 (1980), 215–227.

54. Arnett G. Lindsay, "Diplomatic Relations Between the United States and Great Britain Bearing on the Return of Negro Slaves, 1783–1828," *Journal of Negro History* 5 (1920), 391–419; and "Interesting Notes on Great Britain and Canada with Respect to the Negro," *Journal of Negro History* 13 (1928), 185–192.

55. Moore, *Treatise on Extradition* (supra n. 44), 90–92.

56. Zorn, "Criminal Extradition Menaces the Canadian Haven," 284.

in an open letter from black residents of Canada to British officials in 1828 in which the they sought a land grant to establish a settlement that would "be the means of preventing the system of kidnapping which is now carried on through his Majesty's provinces by the Georgia and Virginia kidnappers from the southern states of America."[57] The petitioners described both the recent case of James Smith, who had been abducted and taken across the Niagara River but then escaped, as well as a less-fortunate fugitive who had been successfully abducted "by Kentucky or Virginia kidnappers" the previous year. A more notorious case occurred two years later, when a slave owner from Kentucky tracked a former slave by the name of Andrew to the Canadian home of a Charles Baby on the Detroit River. When Mr. Baby adamantly refused to sell the fugitive slave back to his former master, the latter hired some men in Detroit to apprehend his former slave; their effort ended unsuccessfully, however, when Andrew and Mr. Baby fought off the kidnappers.[58] Yet another abduction, this one successful, was recorded in 1836, when a slave catcher seized two fugitive slaves in Saint Catharines.[59]

The second alternative, extradition, was provided in February 1833 when the Parliament of Upper Canada passed an act authorizing the extradition of fugitive criminals. Four requests were submitted under that law, three of them from Kentucky. The first, that same year, was for a Thornton Blackburn, a slave who had fled to Canada from Detroit after being rescued by a mob that had blocked his forced return to Kentucky under the American fugitive slave law.[60] His extradition was refused on the grounds that he had committed no crime in making his escape. The second request was for a Solomon Moseby, who had taken his master's horse in making his escape to Canada, selling the animal before departing the United States.[61] Canadian officials approved his extradition, but he was freed when a mob accosted the guards attempting to transport him back across the Niagara River.[62] Although two men died in the attack on the guards, Mosely lived out the rest of his life in

57. "Documents," *Journal of Negro History* 15 (1930), 115–116.

58. William Renwick Riddell, "The Slave in Canada," *Journal of Negro History* 5 (1920), 342–343.

59. Silverman, *Unwelcome Guests*, 36.

60. Riddell, "Slave in Canada," 345–347.

61. Ibid., 347–350.

62. Janet Carnochan, "A Slave Rescue in Niagara Sixty Years Ago," *Niagara Historical Society* 2 (1897), 7–17.

freedom in England and Canada. The third request involved another slave, James Happy, who also had stolen his master's horse in making his escape but, unlike Mosely, had arranged before crossing into Canada for the horse to be returned to its owner.[63] The request was not forwarded by the governor of Kentucky until 1837; unlike the previous two cases, it was extensively considered by Canadian and British authorities, including the attorney general, the Executive Council, and the lieutenant governor of Upper Canada, as well as the secretary of state of the British colonies, British Foreign Secretary Lord Palmerston, and the law officers of the Crown. Although the moral issue of returning a freedman to slavery was noted and debated throughout the deliberations, the final denial of the extradition request was based primarily upon Happy's obvious lack of felonious intent with respect to the taking of the horse. The law officers' decision, which was intended to provide guidance in future cases, stated that "no distinction should . . . be made between the demand for Slaves or for Freemen," but the strict legal requirements they placed upon the extradition request, including both a strict dual criminality standard and the requirement that any extradition request be supported by evidence taken in Canada, was perceived as favoring the interests of the fugitive slave.[64]

The fourth extradition request, in 1841, was the only one that resulted in the return of a slave to his American owner.[65] In making his escape, the slave, Nelson Hacket, had taken not only his master's fastest horse but also a fine beaver overcoat, a gold watch, and a comfortable saddle. His owner, a widely respected businessman in Arkansas, tracked him to the Negro settlement at Chatham in Upper Canada, where he beat him severely and then took him into custody with the assistance of the local county sheriff. The Provisional Executive Council responded favorably to the extradition request from the Arkansas governor, in good part because Hacket had not confined himself to taking no more than he needed to escape. One historian observed that the new Canadian governor-general, Sir Charles Bagot, "was not unmoved by the thought of what Hackett's fate would be if he were surrendered. But he had been

63. Riddell, "Slave in Canada," 350–354; and Silverman, *Unwelcome Guests*, 38–42.

64. Riddell, "Slave in Canada," 350–354; Silverman, *Unwelcome Guests*, 38–42.

65. Roman J. Zorn, "An Arkansas Fugitive Slave Incident and Its International Repercussions," *Arkansas Historical Quarterly* 16 (1957), 139–149; Zorn, "Criminal Extradition Menaces the Canadian Haven," 284–288.

explicitly instructed when appointed to concentrate upon restoring good relations with the United States."[66] Cognizant of the differences between Hacket's case and that involving James Happy, as well as wary of having Canada perceived as "an asylum for the worst characters provided only that they had been slaves before arriving here," Bagot authorized the fugitive slave's surrender to the Arkansas authorities.[67]

Hacket's surrender generated widespread comment and activity among abolitionists in Canada, Britain, and the United States. It occurred, interestingly enough, just shortly after the conclusion of another fugitive slave case in the Bahamas, where the U.S. consul had requested the extradition of several slaves who had seized the American ship *Creole*, killing two men in the process, and forced the crew to sail to Nassau. With no extradition law comparable to Canada's in place, the local authorities rejected the request on both legal and humanitarian grounds and were supported overwhelmingly by political and legal authorities in Britain.[68]

During roughly the same time, negotiations between the United States and Britain over an extradition treaty—which had commenced in 1839 following the State Department's rejection of a British request for the extradition of several criminals who had fled across the Canadian border into Vermont—were merged into the broader negotiations between Lord Ashburton and Secretary of State Daniel Webster intended to remedy a broad array of tensions in relations between the two nations. U.S. incentives to conclude the treaty heightened in 1841, when a British court in the Bahamas refused to extradite to the United States the men who had seized the *Creole*.[69] Article 10 of the Webster-Ashburton Treaty signed the following year renewed the bilateral extradition relationship that had been initiated by the Jay Treaty of 1794 and expired in 1807; it made no mention, however, of the specific issue of fugitive slaves. The treaty negotiators were both concerned lest the irreconcilable differences between the two governments over the slavery issue sabotage the entire treaty. "For the first time," Alexander Murray wrote, "the British ministers had to defend their policy [toward American fugitive slaves]

66. Alexander L. Murray, "The Extradition of Fugitive Slaves from Canada: A Re-evaluation," *Canadian Historical Review* 43 (1962), 303.

67. Ibid., 304.

68. Ibid.

69. Howard Jones, "The Peculiar Institution and National Honor: The Case of the *Creole* Slave Revolt," *Civil War History* 21 (1975), 28–50.

against the morally indignant attacks of the abolitionists while trying to avoid embarrassing discussions with a pro-slavery American government."[70] Colonial officials were instructed to interpret Article 10 as narrowly as possible in responding to requests for the extradition of fugitive slaves.[71] In the first case to arise under the treaty—a U.S. request for the extradition of seven slaves who had escaped from Florida to Nassau, killing at least one individual in the process—the governor of the Bahamas relied on legal technicalities in refusing to deliver the fugitives.[72] The British government thereafter adhered rigidly to its narrow interpretation of the extradition clause in the face of vocal American protests and diplomatic pressures. Between 1847 and 1861, at least five occasions arose in which British and Canadian officials either refused to surrender a fugitive slave or severely punished junior officials who did.[73] The last of these, involving a fugitive named John Anderson who had killed his owner in escaping, generated enormous controversy on both sides of the Atlantic in 1860 when the provincial Court of Queen's Bench approved his surrender. Anderson was ultimately freed, however, when the Canadian Court of Common Pleas ruled that the magistrate's warrant had been technically defective.[74]

Mexico

The development of the fugitive slave issue with respect to Mexico combined virtually all of the features described with respect to Florida and Canada: frequent diplomatic overtures as well as repeated attempts to negotiate extradition treaties; private and state-sponsored expeditions across the border to recover runaway slaves; efforts by foreign citizens and officials to lure slaves across the border; steadfast refusal by the foreign government to return escaped slaves; discreet complicity by foreign officials near the border in the American initiatives to recover slaves; differences of opinion within the refuge nation regarding the desirability of inviting thousands of fugitive slaves into their territory; as

70. Murray, "Extradition of Fugitive Slaves from Canada," 312.
71. Zorn, "Criminal Extradition Menaces the Canadian Haven," 291.
72. Ibid.
73. Murray, "Extradition of Fugitive Slaves from Canada," 313–314.
74. Fred Landon, "The Anderson Fugitive Slave Case," *Journal of Negro History* 7 (1922), 233–242; Riddell, "Slave in Canada," 355–358; Zorn, "Criminal Extradition Menaces the Canadian Haven," 292–294. See also the extensive examination of the case in P. Brode, *The Odyssey of John Anderson* (Toronto: University of Toronto Press, 1989).

well as abundant links between the issue of fugitive slaves and annexationist plots, filibustering expeditions, conflicts with Indian tribes, and the variety of transnational criminal activities engaged in by free whites. The net results of all these developments between 1800 and 1862 were the escape of thousands of American slaves to Mexico and the recovery of only a small fraction of them by those who claimed ownership.[75]

Conflicts over the fugitive slave issue began immediately following the Louisiana Purchase in 1803, when the United States replaced France as Spain's neighbor on the Texas border. Within a year, tensions had arisen—not unlike those along the Florida border—over the flight of slaves from Louisiana to Mexico, reportedly at the encouragement of Spaniards.[76] Mexico's independence in 1821, her prohibition of the slave trade in 1824, and her abolition of slavery in 1829 ensured that the flight of fugitive slaves into Mexico would continue to generate bilateral tensions so long as slavery persisted in the United States.[77] Influenced in no small part by the British, many Mexicans perceived the prohibition of slavery not just as a humanitarian imperative but also as a weapon that could be useful in checking the growing influence of North Americans in Texas, many of whom had arrived with their slaves.[78] Competing pressures, however, led to the exemption of Texas from the abolition decree. In 1825, Secretary of State Henry Clay instructed the U.S. minister to Mexico to include in the proposed Treaty of Amity, Commerce, and Navigation with Mexico a provision for the "regular apprehension and surrender . . . of any fugitive slaves."[79] Although the treaty negotiators did insert such a clause, opposition to its inclusion by the Mexican Chamber of Deputies played an important role in delaying the ratification of a treaty until 1832 and resulted in the removal of the provision from the treaty.[80]

The number of slaves in Texas rose rapidly during the Texas republic's

75. The following account, unless otherwise noted, is largely from Rosalie Schwartz, *Across the Rio to Freedom: U.S. Negroes in Mexico*, Southwestern Studies Monograph No. 44 (El Paso: Texas Western Press, 1975).

76. Ibid., 5.

77. Lester G. Bugbee, "Slavery in Early Texas," *Political Science Quarterly* 13 (1898), 389–412, 648–668.

78. Alleine Howren, "Causes and Origin of the Decree of April 6, 1830," *Southwestern Historical Quarterly* 16 (1912–13), 387–390.

79. Schwartz, *Across the Rio to Freedom*, 9.

80. U.S.-Mexican extradition negotiations between 1826 and 1861 are briefly discussed in Moore, *Treatise on Extradition* (supra n. 44), 95–97.

period of independence between 1836 and 1845; so too did the number who sought refuge south of the Rio Grande, including two belonging to the president of Texas, Sam Houston. Slave owners advertised in newspapers for the return of their slaves, offering lucrative rewards, and hired agents to collect their escapees south of the border. Two Texas Rangers sent to Matamoros for this purpose, however, were arrested by Mexican officials on their arrival and sent home empty-handed.[81] Following the annexation of Texas by the United States and the conclusion of the war with Mexico that followed, slave owners in the new state continued their efforts to recover their lost slaves from Mexican territory. Pleas to Washington to negotiate an extradition treaty or otherwise secure favorable action by the Mexican government generated diplomatic activity, but all proposals were adamantly rejected by the Mexicans. They expressed their willingness to sign a treaty for the extradition of criminals alone, but the U.S. negotiator declined, "thinking a Treaty, which did not extend to all the subjects of extradition, unjust to Texas."[82] The Mexican viewpoint on the issue of fugitive slaves was firmly enshrined in Mexican law in 1857, when an article protecting fugitive Negro slaves from extradition was included in the new Mexican constitution.

Texan slave owners responded to the persistent Mexican intransigence on the issue by taking matters into their own hands and by attempting to reach accommodations with the variety of officials, generals, freebooters, and rebels operating south of the border. Particularly worrisome to the slave owners was the arrival in 1849–50 of the Seminole Indian chief Wild Cat in northern Mexico with a band of hundreds of Indian and Negro Seminoles.[83] Their presence, it was feared, would incite thousands of slaves throughout Texas to flee. Mobilized by the perceived threat, Texan slave owners created an association to provide rewards for the capture of fugitive slaves, offering greater amounts for those recovered from well south of the border.[84] They also persuaded the Texas governor, Peter Bell, to appoint a notorious filibuster and experienced "Negro-thief," Warren Adams, to recover as many slaves as possible from Mexico. Among his successes was the capture of John

81. Ronnie C. Tyler, "Fugitive Slaves in Mexico," *Journal of Negro History* 57 (1972), 2.

82. Schwartz, *Across the Rio to Freedom*, 50.

83. Kenneth W. Porter, "The Seminole in Mexico, 1850–1861," *Hispanic American Historical Review* 31 (1951), 1–36; Tyler, "Fugitive Slaves in Mexico," 5; Opala, *Seminole Freedman* (supra n. 47), 15.

84. Tyler, "Fugitive Slaves in Mexico," 5.

Horse, the acknowledged leader of the black Seminoles near Santa Rosa.[85]

When the head of one Mexican insurgency in 1851–53, Jose Carvajal, promised assistance to Texas slave owners in recovering their fugitives, many Texans supported his unsuccessful efforts to transform the northeastern Mexican state of Tamaulipas into the Sierra Madre Republic. In 1855, Texas slave owners contacted Mexican military officials in the Mexican states of Nuevo León and Coahuila to seek their assistance in slowing the flight of slaves across the border. Later that year, the governor of Texas, E. M. Pease, sent a company of Texas Rangers under the command of James Callahan across the border with the ostensible objective of suppressing the Lipan Indians who had been raiding American settlements. Abundant evidence suggested, however, that Callahan's additional—indeed, many suspected his principal—motive was the recovery of fugitive slaves.[86] The Texan expedition was repelled, however, by Indians as well as the Mexican military officials who the Texans had hoped would welcome them. With the Mexicans' rejection of yet another U.S. overture for extradition negotiations in 1857, the state of Texas enacted an "Act to Encourage the Reclamation of Slaves, Escaping Beyond the Limits of the Slave Territories of the United States," which provided that those returning runaway slaves to their owners would be rewarded from the state treasury.[87]

The American victory in the war with Mexico had not entirely sated the appetites of some American filibusters and others for Mexican territory. Some, such as Sam Houston, took advantage of the fugitive slave issue to muster support among slave owners for additional annexations. Others went so far as to demand the annexation of Cuba and the renewal of the Atlantic slave trade if Congress failed to provide Texas with the authority to negotiate an extradition treaty with Mexico. The outbreak of the Civil War in the United States, however, finally promised relief to Mexico from the demands of Texan slave owners and their advocates in the U.S. government. An extradition treaty that prohibited

85. Porter, "The Seminole in Mexico," 8. *Webster's Ninth New Collegiate Dictionary* defines "freebooter" as a pirate or plunderer, and "filibuster" as "an irregular military adventurer," specifically "an American engaged in fomenting insurrections in Latin America in the mid-nineteenth century." It is in those senses that the two terms are used in this book.

86. Ernest C. Shearer, "The Callahan Expedition," *Southwestern Historical Quarterly* 54 (1950–51), 438; Tyler, "Fugitive Slaves in Mexico," 8–9.

87. Tyler, "Fugitive Slaves in Mexico," 9–10.

the return of fugitive slaves was signed in 1861 and went into force the following year.[88] Confederate officials, however, continued to represent the interests of the slave owners. In late 1861, a Confederate captain led some fifty volunteers into Coahuila in pursuit of a fugitive slave.[89] A secret agreement between Texas slave owners and the new governor of Tamaulipas, Albino Lopez, providing for the exchange of fugitive slaves for Mexican peons who had fled north, momentarily raised the hopes of Texans, but efforts to conclude a formal agreement were doomed by the Mexican constitution. With the conclusion of the Civil War in 1865, this substantial irritant in U.S.-Mexican relations was finally eliminated.

Like the Canadians and British to the north, the Mexicans had mostly stood their ground in the face of aggressive U.S. efforts to reclaim fugitive slaves, choosing instead to forgo the advantages of appeasing the United States and regularizing bilateral law enforcement relations. Refusing either to countenance uninvited expeditions into its territory or to accede to the extradition of fugitive slaves, Mexico had provided at least as safe a haven for the enslaved blacks of the United States fleeing south as Canada had done for those heading north. Where the Canadians and British had often resorted to legalistic technicalities in rejecting American requests for the return of fugitive slaves, the Mexican response had been both more nationalistic and more moralistic—not least because American efforts to recover their slaves south of the border were so much bolder and more blatant. Moreover, the aggressiveness of the U.S. efforts reflected not just the very different tenor of the two neighborly relationships but also the fact that the Mexican haven, unlike the Canadian one, bordered on a slave state. Then as now, the different norms south of the border generated all sorts of transnational activities of particular concern to those living on the northern frontier.

The Case of the "Amistad"

The clash between slave owner efforts to recover their slaves from foreign jurisdictions, and federal efforts to suppress the extraterritorial dimensions of the slave trade, came to a head in the case of the schooner *Amistad*. In 1839, a number of black Africans on board a slaver en route from one Cuban port to another escaped from their chains, killed

88. The treaty is reproduced in Moore, *Treatise on Extradition* (supra n. 44), 1118–1121.
89. Tyler, "Fugitive Slaves in Mexico," 11.

the captain and mate, and took control of the schooner. Some weeks later, the *Amistad* was seized by a U.S. naval vessel off the coast of Montauk, Long Island, and the Africans were imprisoned. The Spanish government demanded the return of the Africans, who were variously described as the personal property of the Spaniards who had purchased them and as criminal fugitives. The case landed in the courts, where it ultimately climbed to the U.S. Supreme Court.[90] In an opinion delivered by Justice Joseph Story and supported by all but one justice, the Court set the Africans free.[91] The Africans could not be legally described as slaves, the Court ruled, because they had been kidnapped in Africa and imported into a Spanish colony in violation of the laws of Spain. Both the events leading up to the ruling, and the decision itself, generated substantial tensions between the governments of the United States and Spain, attracted strong interest from the British, and became a cause célèbre among both abolitionists and supporters of slavery in the United States and abroad.[92] Although the Supreme Court's decision provided little precedent for other blacks born into slavery, it represented a powerful declaration of the rights of black Africans to resist enslavement.

Earliest Law Enforcement Agencies

From the nation's origins until the Civil War, federal law enforcement in the United States was monopolized by three law enforcement agencies.[93] The Customs Service, as we have seen, was quick to rely on undercover agents and to send its operatives abroad. The second agency, whose origins also dated to colonial days, was the Postal Inspection Service. The person known as the forefather of contemporary postal inspectors was Benjamin Franklin, who, upon being appointed postmaster at Philadelphia in 1737, set out to inspect and improve the postal service. When Franklin was appointed postmaster general in 1775 by the Conti-

90. See the five documents relating to the case, including the lower court decision and the arguments by John Quincy Adams and Roger S. Baldwin before the Supreme Court, in Finkelman, ed., *African Slave Trade and American Courts* (supra n. 34), 145–408.

91. See *U.S. v. Amistad*, 15 Peters 518 (1841).

92. See the fine account of the episode in Howard Jones, *Mutiny on the Amistad* (New York: Oxford University Press, 1987).

93. See David R. Johnson, *American Law Enforcement: A History* (Arlington Heights, Ill.: Forum Press, 1981), 73–88.

nental Congress, he in turn appointed William Goddard "Surveyor of the Post." His agents, known first as "Goddard's Surveyors" and after 1800 as special agents, assumed responsibility for investigating theft of the mails.[94] In 1830 an Office of Instructions and Rail Depredations was created within the Post Office Department to organize its investigative functions. Its agents operated both openly and undercover; unlike comparable agents in most other countries, they had arrest powers.[95]

Plagued initially by charges of corruption and political involvement, the Inspection Service gained in effectiveness and prominence under the tenure of David Parker, who served as chief special agent for the United States Post Office from 1876 to 1883. Such was Parker's reputation that German postal authorities, who lacked any investigative service, turned to him for assistance in an investigation of employee theft of registered letters between Hamburg and Berlin.[96] A few decades later, another highly regarded agent, Bill Kenyon, was charged with setting up a secure postal sysem in South America to stem the theft of parcel post; in 1919, the same agent was sent to Spain, where he successfully investigated a series of thefts of funds sent by American tourists by registered mail to New York.[97] Despite these occasional contacts with foreign lands, however, the postal inspectors focused their efforts within the United States, and like the Secret Service they were often called upon to perform investigative and other law enforcement tasks having little to do with the mails—such as tracking down safecrackers, transporting gold bullion for the federal government, and protecting foreign dignitaries. The author of one celebratory account of the agency described their activities:

> They've been protecting the mails under one title or another since long before the nation was born. They hunted highwaymen on the lonely post roads of colonial times, rode west with the covered wagons, launched the "Pony Express," balked the nineteenth century brand of confidence men, warred on the "Black Hand" band of extortionists, fought it out with Prohibition era gangsters

94. On the origins of the Postal Service's special agents, see Millspaugh, *Crime Control* (supra n. 28), 62–64; Elinore Denniston, *America's Silent Investigators* (New York: Dodd, Mead & Co., 1964), 19–76; and E. J. Kahn, *Fraud* (New York: Harper & Row, 1954), 5–7.

95. See Wayne E. Fuller, *The American Mail: Enlarger of the Common Life* (Chicago: University of Chicago Press, 1972).

96. Denniston, *America's Silent Investigators*, 73–74.

97. Ibid., 95–96.

> raiding post offices and mail trains, and now unravel mail frauds as complex as the mind of man can devise.[98]

The U.S. Marshals Service, authorized by the Judiciary Act of 1789 to support the federal courts, was the closest thing to a general law enforcement agency before the development of the FBI. Although it fell under the direct control of the federal judges and district attorneys, Congress too assigned it a variety of responsibilities. The result was that the U.S. marshals became, as one historian has noted, the "handymen" of a number of government agencies in the first part of the nineteenth century.[99] Among their international chores was the collection and delivery of fugitives between the United States and other countries. Marshals also assisted U.S. consular courts in China, Japan, Siam, and the Ottoman Empire, the governments of which had acknowledged the extraterritorial jurisdiction of the United States and other foreign governments over their citizens. These marshals, wrote the historian for the U.S. Marshals Service, "were essentially the same as the marshals in the United States and its territories. They served the process of the consular courts, arrested those accused of crimes, kept custody of its prisoners, and executed the orders of the courts."[100]

With the Customs Service and the Postal Inspection Service largely relegated to specific tasks, and the U.S. marshals subject to the demands of a great variety of bosses, no law enforcement agency was in a position to develop sustained contacts with foreign law enforcement agencies to handle a variety of criminal matters. Indeed, Congress had repeatedly made clear that nothing resembling a generic national police agency be created. Such an organization, it was feared, would be the first step on the road to European-style police states. The cost of such fears, however, was the great advantage given to criminals by the lack of either domestic or international law enforcement coordination. Into this void stepped

98. Ottenberg, *Federal Investigators* (supra n. 18), 309–310.

99. Larry D. Ball, *The United States Marshals of New Mexico and Arizona Territories, 1846–1912* (Albuquerque: University of New Mexico Press, 1978), 4. For an overview of the evolution of the U.S. marshals, see chapter 1 of Ball's book or Rita W. Cooley, "The Office of United States Marshal," *Western Political Quarterly* 12 (1959), 123–140. Profiles of the first sixteen U.S. marshals are assembled in Frederick S. Calhoun, "The First Generation of United States Marshals," *The Pentacle* 5 (Summer 1985), 26–35 (part 1), and 6 (Winter 1986), 28–33 (part 2). (*The Pentacle* is the periodical of the U.S. Marshals Service.)

100. Frederick S. Calhoun, *The Lawmen: United States Marshals and Their Deputies, 1789–1989* (Washington, D.C.: Smithsonian Institution Press, 1990), 175–176.

private detective agencies (of which the Pinkerton Detective Agency became the largest and most famous) and a new federal police agency, the Secret Service.

One of the Pinkerton Agency's principal clients between 1870 and 1892 was the federal government of the United States. Before 1870, the U.S. Attorney General's Office had prohibited any funds allocated for federal court and law enforcement expenses from being used to pay detectives.[101] With the formation of the Justice Department in 1870, Congress recognized the need to allocate some funds for the detection and prosecution of violations of federal law. Popular sentiment prevented the establishment at that time of a law enforcement agency within the new department, so the attorney generals sought out alternative sources of investigators. The Pinkerton Agency provided many of these until 1892, when Congress, in the aftermath of its investigation of the Pinkertons' role in suppressing the Homestead strike, prohibited the hiring of private detectives to enforce federal law.[102] The Attorney General's Office, which had supervisory powers over the U.S. marshals given them by Congress in 1861, also made frequent use of the marshals. On occasion, they appointed their own "special detectives" or "special agents," sometimes designating them "general deputy marshals." And with increasing frequency they and other government agencies in need of investigative services called upon the Secret Service housed in the Treasury Department.[103]

The Secret Service was established in 1865 with the sole purpose of preventing and investigating cases of counterfeiting. Congress had not appropriated any money for that task until 1861. During the Civil War, the Union government relied on private investigators, such as the Pinkertons, to pursue such cases. But as the war drew to an end, Treasury Secretary Hugh McCulloch suggested the establishment of a specialized agency, and President Lincoln concurred. The first chief of the Secret Service was William P. Wood, who had established his reputation as a skilled criminal investigator during the Civil War, first tracking down contractors who were defrauding the government, then developing an expertise in counterfeiting cases.[104] The agency quickly established a

101. Homer Cummings and Carl McFarland, *Federal Justice: Chapters in the History of Justice and the Federal Executive* (New York: Macmillan Co., 1937), 371.

102. Ibid., 373; James D. Horan, *The Pinkertons: The Detective Dynasty That Made History* (New York: Crown Publishers, 1967), 350–358.

103. Cummings and McFarland, *Federal Justice*, 371.

104. Michael Dorman, *The Secret Service Story* (New York: Delacorte Press, 1967), 4–7.

good reputation for criminal investigation and soon found itself called upon to perform similar services for other branches of the government.

During its first three decades, the Secret Service established connections with European and other foreign law enforcement agencies. More so than with most crimes, governments tended to recognize the benefits of reciprocity in cooperating against counterfeiters of one another's currencies. The Secret Service thus focused on detecting criminal efforts to counterfeit not only U.S. currency but foreign currency as well. One notable investigation, in 1909, uncovered a scheme based in a small Kentucky town to flood Mexico with counterfeit 100 peso notes on the Banco Nacional de Mexico. Another counterfeit currency investigation, described by the Secret Service chief in 1910 as "the most important victory for the Government since the breaking up of the Lancaster-Philadelphia gang of counterfeiters in 1898," led to the arrests of leading members of the Italian "Black Hand."[105]

However, it was in political intelligence operations, not in counterfeiting cases, that the Secret Service extended itself farthest beyond American borders. During the 1880s the Secret Service cooperated with the newly created "Special Branch" of Scotland Yard's Criminal Investigative Division (CID) against Irish terrorists seeking independence for their country.[106] In 1898, with a dynamic new chief and the war with Spain rapidly approaching, the Secret Service was obliged to undertake espionage and counterespionage operations both within the United States and abroad. In one case, Secret Service agents operating undercover in Montreal successfully exposed the somewhat incompetent espionage efforts of the naval attaché of the Spanish legation, Lieutenant Ramon Carranza.[107] In a more dramatic operation, a Secret Service operative posing as a Mexican millionaire collected valuable information in Spain on the enemy's naval preparations.[108]

With the war over, the Secret Service returned to its more traditional law enforcement tasks. In mid-1902, the chief of the agency, John Wilkie, was asked to travel incognito to Europe to investigate a lace-smuggling case involving well-connected importers.[109] In another smug-

105. John E. Wilkie, *Annual Report of the Chief of the Secret Service Division for the Fiscal Year Ended June 30, 1910* (Washington, D.C.: Government Printing Office, 1910), 7.

106. Thomas A. Reppetto, *The Blue Parade* (New York: Free Press, 1978), 31.

107. Don Wilkie, as told to Mark Lee Luther, *American Secret Service Agent* (New York: Frederick A. Stokes Co., 1934), 16–23.

108. Ibid., 23–25.

109. Ibid., 27.

gling case involving complicity by a corrupt customs official, the Secret Service chief ventured to London and Lyons, where he successfully investigated the matter and persuaded the necessary witnesses to come to the United States to give testimony.[110] Although there were Treasury agents delegated to customs business in foreign locations, the Secret Service was far more likely to be called upon by other government departments when criminal investigative services at home or abroad were required. Until 1908, when Congress forbade the Justice Department to borrow any Secret Service operatives from Treasury (reportedly because the agents' investigations had led to the indictment and conviction of some of their members[111]), the Secret Service reigned as the leading federal law enforcement agency. And even thereafter it continued to assist other agencies in investigating violations of U.S. drug laws, neutrality laws, and so on.[112]

The Justice Department, established in 1870, was not authorized to create its own specialized law enforcement agency until 1908.[113] Thereafter, a disproportionate amount of responsibility continued to fall on the shoulders of the prosecutors. This state of affairs was described in the leading history of federal law enforcement's early days, co-authored in 1937 by the attorney general at the time, Homer Cummings:

> Prosecuting attorneys in the states and the district attorneys of the United States also came to be regarded as responsible for the detection of offenses against both civil and criminal law and for the collection of evidence to support proceedings in the courts—duties very seldom specified in the statutes. They came to exercise the functions of an "investigator" concurrently with the sheriff or police, as well as the function of a "magistrate" in determining who should be brought to trial, the function of a "solicitor" in preparing cases for trial, and that of an "advocate" in trying them

110. Ibid., 185–186.

111. Cummings and McFarland, *Federal Justice*, 375–378.

112. The "effective cooperation between Secret-Service operatives and Treasury special agents in customs investigations, . . . particularly in the suppression of the smuggling of and traffic in smoking opium," is noted in John E. Wilkie, *Annual Report, Chief of the Secret Service Division, Fiscal Year Ended June 30, 1912* (Washington, D.C.: Government Printing Office, 1912), 8. Cooperation "in the investigation and suppression of revolutionary movements in this country in violation of the neutrality laws" is noted in ibid., *Fiscal Year Ended June 30, 1909*, 8.

113. See Albert Langeluttig, *The Department of Justice of the United States* (Baltimore: Johns Hopkins University Press, 1927).

> and in arguing appeals. "This uniting of a general responsibility for enforcement of law and duty of criminal investigation with the function of carrying on prosecutions," reported the National Commission on Law Enforcement in 1931, "was appropriate enough in a simple colonial society of the eighteenth century."[114]

During its first decades, the Justice Department depended upon investigators borrowed from other agencies as well as upon a number of special agents whose status remained ambiguous. When Congress deprived the Justice Department of its principal source of investigators in 1908, the subsequent reaction from the executive branch obliged them to provide a substitute. In the face of increasing pressure and pleas from President Theodore Roosevelt, Attorney General Charles Bonaparte, and the district attorneys to allow the creation of a federal detective service, Congress relented and voted in 1908 to appropriate funds specifically for special agents in the Justice Department. The following year, Bonaparte's successor, Attorney General George C. Wickersham, christened the now officially sanctioned department of detectives (comprised initially of former Secret Service agents) the "Bureau of Investigation"[115] (the word "Federal" was added in 1935). Its jurisdiction included a hodgepodge of crimes, including bribery, antitrust and banking violations, customs, post office and internal revenue frauds, violations of the neutrality, peonage and bucket-shop laws, white slave cases, crimes on the high seas, murders on government reservations, and so on. Within a few years, the demands of reporting on Mexican revolutionary activity and enforcing the neutrality laws along the southwestern frontier would provide the Bureau with both a rationale for substantial growth and an opportunity to prove its worth. Yet until 1934, despite the wide variety of criminals they were expected to encounter, the Justice Department agents were not authorized to carry arms, serve warrants and subpoenas, or make seizures and arrests.[116] Their role during that first generation was viewed as purely investigative.

In 1916, one of the first books glorifying the work of the Bureau, *Uncle Sam, Detective,* appeared.[117] Although the author chose to create

114. Cummings and McFarland, *Federal Justice*, 367.

115. On the origins of the FBI, see ibid., 375–380; Harry and Bonaro Overstreet, *The FBI in Our Open Society* (New York: W. W. Norton, 1969), chap. 2; and Millspaugh, *Crime Control by the National Government* (supra n. 28), 73–78.

116. Cummings and McFarland, *Federal Justice*, 381.

117. William Atherton Dupuy, *Uncle Sam, Detective* (New York: McKinlay, Stone & Mackenzie, 1916).

a fictional composite of an agent, whom he named Billy Gard, as the main protagonist, each of the stories was founded on an actual investigation that Bureau agents had related to the author. It is interesting that three of the twelve stories found Special Agent Billy Gard abroad and actively engaged in undercover operations. In one he posed as a retired manufacturer on vacation in Kingston, Jamaica, while he investigated "a huge conspiracy for the smuggling of opium and Chinamen into the States." In another case, involving the illegal shipment of arms to Mexico during its revolution, Billy Gard stowed away aboard a ship while pursuing a Russian arms merchant and quite unexpectedly found himself first in the port of Odessa and then in Hamburg. And in yet another adventure, the special agent pursued a wilely fugitive wanted for customs fraud, first to Montreal and then to London and Paris. In Paris, he secured the cooperation of the local police, persuaded them to introduce an undercover agent into his surveillance operation, and then had her place a listening device (then known as a dictagraph) in the apartment where he correctly suspected the fugitive was hiding.

It is worth noting that the accounts of Bureau agent Billy Gard's activities differed little from those of the Secret Service and Treasury agents who traveled overseas. Agents from all three agencies operated relatively freely overseas, working undercover, developing informants, securing cooperation from the local police, and conducting their own surveillance when necessary. When necessary, they dabbled in political intelligence and operations as well. Al Scharff, who began his lengthy law enforcement career with the Bureau of Investigation in 1917 before transferring to the customs agency, was initially hired to locate and destroy a German wireless station on the coast of Sonora, Mexico.[118] Somewhat more surprising is that the focus of the Bureau agents and to a lesser extent the Secret Service agents, not just the Treasury agents, was on smuggling and enforcement of customs laws. The principal reason is that much of transnational crime is smuggling in one form or another. It also reflects the fact that foreign law enforcement agencies are reluctant, certainly in practice and often in principle, to devote resources to enforcing the customs laws of other governments. Customs violations are not the types of crimes that tend to inspire moral indignation. Often the specific laws violated have no parallels in the country whose assistance is sought. Indeed, the country may even derive financial

118. Roark, *Coin of Contraband* (supra n. 24), 16–42.

benefits from being the source of goods legally purchased but illegally smuggled into another country. Consequently, requests for foreign police assistance in enforcing one's customs laws are unlikely to be given the same priority that requests involving more serious crimes receive. If a government wants such matters investigated abroad, it is best to send its own agents to do so.

A final consideration has to do with the nature of the assistance American agents abroad requested from local police. Locating fugitives who have committed serious crimes is a service local police often are both willing and able to offer. The same is true of other aspects of an investigation initiated after a serious crime has been committed. For instance, foreign police have few inhibitions about offering assistance in identifying fingerprints, documents, weapons, and other evidentiary items that can help in identifying or prosecuting a criminal. However, when foreign police are asked to devote time and personnel to the *investigation* of an ongoing series of crimes or of a criminal organization, problems often arise, particularly if no crimes have been committed in their country. One of the principal developments in the evolution of international law enforcement in the past century has been the increasing willingness of foreign police to cooperate in the investigation of an ever-broadening array of crimes, including many that would not be prosecuted if committed in their own country. Enforcement of other government's customs laws, however, remains far more the exception than the rule. Only when the laws concern goods that are banned or strictly controlled in both countries is cooperation likely.

Throughout the nineteenth century and into the twentieth, the investigative dimension of international cooperation remained relatively undeveloped. In good part, this reflected no more than the fact that there were few serious crimes one could commit *from* a foreign country. Other than smuggling, primarily to evade revenue laws, and cross-border forays to commit common crimes, there were only so many crimes that could be perpetrated from abroad. This changed over the twentieth century primarily as a consequence of two developments. International consensuses calling for cooperation against transnational trafficking in goods such as drugs developed. And advances in telecommunications facilitated the commission of crimes in which the perpetrator had no need personally to cross an international border. Police increasingly needed to ask their counterparts abroad for assistance in investigating drug traffickers, money launderers, and financial charlatans. This in turn required that police work more closely with fellow investigators in foreign countries. The evolution of the transnational police community in recent decades is largely a consequence of these developments.

Law Enforcement for Hire

In 1845, a former member of the New York City police force, Gil Hays, opened "an office for the arrest of burglars and the prevention of pickpockets," which he called the "Independent Police."[119] During the next few years, former police officers in Saint Louis, Baltimore, and Philadelphia established similar agencies. In the mid-1850s, a number of investigators with no previous experience in policing also founded agencies. Calling themselves "private policemen," "preventive police," or "counterfeit police," these entrepreneurs engaged in a variety of investigative and law-related tasks, both honorable and unsavory.[120] The most famous of them was a Scottish immigrant to the United States, Allan Pinkerton. After proving himself as an amateur detective in Dundee, Illinois, he was hired as a special agent by the U.S. Post Office to investigate mail thefts. At about the same time, during the late 1840s, the newly organized Chicago Police Department hired him as its first and only detective—or "plain clothes man," as the specialization was called at first.[121] When shortly thereafter the railroad companies appealed to him to devote his skills to investigating the growing number of train robberies, Allan Pinkerton decided the time had come to open his own private detective agency.

Apart from his detective activities, Pinkerton continued to engage in another covert venture connected with an entirely different sort of railroad—the "underground railway," by which slaves were transported to freedom from their southern bondage.[122] As civil war approached, Allan Pinkerton was called upon by the federal government to organize an intelligence agency that would both spy in the South and engage in counterespionage in the North.[123] Utilizing many of the skills that are so

119. David R. Johnson, *Policing the Urban Underworld* (Philadelphia: Temple University Press, 1979), 60.

120. Ibid.

121. Richard Wilmer Rowan, *The Pinkertons: A Detective Dynasty* (Boston: Little, Brown & Co., 1931), 25.

122. Ibid., 23–24.

123. Ibid., 123–125.

easily transferred from criminal to political investigation, Pinkerton and some of his men went to work for the federal government, while the remainder kept the office running throughout the war.

Following the war, the Pinkerton agency expanded throughout the United States and around the world. Both within the United States and abroad, the agency enhanced its value and effectiveness by virtue of its ability to liaison with and between law enforcement agencies that were unable or unwilling to communicate with one another.[124] Pinkerton's sons, particularly William Pinkerton, also assumed leading roles in American police circles. They spoke out forcefully in favor of more professional police forces, adoption of modern investigative techniques, and more efficient interstate cooperation. They also were elected to high positions in American police associations, notably the International Association of Chiefs of Police.[125]

One of the Pinkertons' first multinational cases blossomed when they were hired by the Bank of England to track down the counterfeiters of its notes. In what was perhaps the most widespread criminal investigation of its time, half a dozen Pinkerton agents went to London, a few others joined the New York police in arresting one of the perpetrators as he disembarked in that city, and another agent tracked down the last of the fugitives in Havana.[126] In all aspects of the investigation outside the United Kingdom, it was the Pinkerton agency that played the lead role. Around the same time, the agency, and in particular Allan Pinkerton's son William, began its investigation of a brilliant thief named Adam Worth, who was to resist the clutches of both private and public detective agencies for virtually his entire career.[127] Traveling around Europe in pursuit of these and other international criminals, William Pinkerton developed the contacts and friendships with foreign police agencies that were to serve his agency in good stead in subsequent investigations.[128] Other agents were sent to Latin America, such as when Charles Siringo

124. James D. Horan, "The Pinkerton Detective Agency," in Allan Pinkerton, *Thirty Years a Detective* (1884; reprint, Montclair, N.J.: Patterson Smith Publishing Co., 1975), vi.

125. Frank Morn, *"The Eye that Never Sleeps": A History of the Pinkerton National Detective Agency* (Bloomington: Indiana University Press, 1982), 110–127.

126. Rowan, *The Pinkertons*, 281–289. The story is told from the perspective of one fugitive in George Bidwell, *Bidwell's Travels from Wall Street to London Prison* (Hartford, Conn.: Bidwell Publishing Co., 1897).

127. James D. Horan and Howard Swiggett, *The Pinkerton Story* (New York: G. P. Putnam's Sons, 1951), 161–200.

128. Horan, *The Pinkertons* (supra n. 102), 280–320.

was dispatched to Mexico City to locate a Wells Fargo robber who had stolen $10,000 during a train wreck in Colorado.[129] One historian of the detective agency described the evolution of the Pinkerton agency's international activities:

> In the late 1870s the operations of the Pinkertons became worldwide when they began hunting some of the most colorful, ingenious, and little-known international criminals of the Victorian Age who robbed express cars, banks, and brokerage houses of millions of dollars. The Bank of England and investment and jewelry firms in France and Belgium were among the criminals' victims. Here the Pinkertons filled the role of a paid national police force that cooperated with the principal police organizations of Europe. Letters from criminal divisions of Scotland Yard, the Sûreté, Turkish, and Cuban police, and our State Department showed they were sharing their knowledge of these colorful rogues in an informal, international pool of police information. The Pinkertons appeared to be a crude but effective Victorian Age Interpol.[130]

By the 1890s, Pinkerton's sons had opened branches in Europe.[131] So well known had the name "Pinkerton" become by then that many Europeans thought it was the title of the American criminal police.[132] But the agency's successes had also inspired a proliferation of competitors, including most notably a Saint Louis–based agency created by Thomas Furlong, who like Pinkerton had acquired his experience first as a spy for the Union Army and then headed the Missouri Pacific Railway's police, and the Burns National (later International) Detective Agency, created in 1909 by a former Secret Service agent, William J. Burns, whose fame and political contacts ultimately yielded him the directorship of the U.S. Bureau of Investigation from 1921 to 1924.[133] Burns's agency rapidly emerged as the Pinkertons' principal competitor, begin-

129. Ben E. Pingenot, *Siringo* (College Station: Texas A&M University Press, 1989), 17.

130. Horan, *The Pinkertons*, 254–255.

131. Horan, "Pinkerton Detective Agency," xviii.

132. Jürgen Thorwald, *The Century of the Detective*, trans. Richard and Clara Winston (New York: Harcourt, Brace & World, 1965), 91.

133. Thomas Furlong, *Fifty Years a Detective* (Saint Louis: C. E. Barnett, 1912); William R. Hunt, *Front-Page Detective: William J. Burns and the Detective Profession, 1880–1930* (Bowling Green, Ohio: Bowling Green State University Popular Press, 1990).

ning with its early success in winning away the more established agency's biggest single client, the American Banking Association, at a time when the Pinkerton agency had fallen into some disrepute, and eventually expanding its presence throughout the United States and abroad. It attracted substantial attention in 1920 when a Burns agent pursued a suspected bomber who had killed twenty-nine people on Wall Street all the way to Eastern Europe.[134]

The rising demand for the services of the private detective agencies arose from many corners.[135] Most prominent among these were America's industrialists, who hired the detective agencies to spy on labor organizers, compile blacklists of suspected agitators, disrupt efforts at unionization, and otherwise police their factories and other properties—all of which eventually proved harmful to the popular reputations so carefully cultivated by the leading private detective agencies. The agencies' clients, however, were far more diverse, sharing only in their capacity to pay the fees required. Major banks and other commercial institutions turned to the detective agencies to investigate significant frauds and thefts; foreign governments paid them to collect information on political émigrés and other perceived threats; and federal, state, and local governments in the United States turned to them wherever the services of government police agents were either lacking or under suspicion. All sorts of clients as well paid them to dig up dirt on political opponents, business competitors, prying journalists, and unfaithful spouses. Sometimes the detectives were hired only after police agencies had failed to provide satisfaction; on other occasions they complemented or substituted for public detective forces that had insufficient resources, sophistication, or incentive to conduct a difficult investigation for a wealthy client on their own. But most commonly they were called upon to perform the sorts of discreet detecting tasks that only private agencies could and would provide.

With their expenses paid, the Pinkertons and other private detectives did not shy away from traveling virtually anywhere in the world on behalf of an investigation or in pursuit of a fugitive. In his 1931 history of the agency, Richard Rowan described the challenges that confronted a detective, private or otherwise, on a global manhunt:

> Nowadays a fleeing rascal can hardly find a desert island which is not blanketed by governmental understandings. But before 1890,

134. Morn, *"Eye That Never Sleeps,"* 181.
135. See Hunt, *Front-Page Detective.*

> securing the person of a fugitive who had landed on foreign soil depended upon the luck and resolution of the pursuing detective, and the possible complaisance of local authorities. When the unbeatable Frank Froest of Scotland Yard cornered Jabez Balfour in the Argentine, he had no treaties to depend upon, and so got the notorious swindler aboard a car attached to a locomotive, which traveled at full speed to Buenos Aires, where, despite efforts to stop him, he managed to put Balfour on a ship bound for England. And Pinkerton agents, even though wanting government sanction, brought evil-doers from Asia, Africa and the South East Isles, with often an equally informal decisiveness.[136]

In 1886, the U.S. Supreme Court abetted such informal efforts when it held in *Ker v. Illinois* that a fugitive kidnapped from abroad could not claim any violation of the Constitution, laws, or treaties of the United States.[137] The incident leading to the decision arose when a Pinkerton agent, Henry Julian, was hired by the federal government to collect a larcenist, Frederick Ker, who had fled to Peru.[138] Although Julian possessed the necessary extradition papers—the two governments having negotiated an extradition treaty a decade earlier—he found there was no official to receive his extradition warrant because of a recent Chilean military occupation of Lima. Rather than return home empty-handed, Julian kidnapped the fugitive and, with the assistance of Chilean forces, forcibly placed him on a U.S. vessel headed back to the United States.[139] The Supreme Court not only affirmed the validity of such abductions but also suggested that in gaining custody of a fugitive almost any illegality abroad was permissible. Indeed, one implication for law enforcement authorities was that, even where an extradition treaty existed, it might be preferable to obtain custody of the fugitive informally because prosecution would not be limited by the terms of the treaty to the crimes for which he would have been formally extradited.

Even when Pinkerton agents were successful in locating fugitives abroad, they did not always succeed in bringing them home alive.

136. Rowan, *The Pinkertons*, 285.

137. 119 U.S. 436 (1886).

138. See Charles Fairman "*Ker v. Illinois* Revisited," *American Journal of International Law* 47 (1953), 678–686.

139. The background to the *Ker* case is in ibid. See also Michael Cardozo, "When Extradition Fails, Is Abduction the Solution?" *American Journal of International Law* 55 (1961), 127, for a discussion of this subject before more recent case law.

Between 1901 and 1907, the State Department was the recipient of protests by the Bolivian government about a number of murders and bank robberies committed by fugitive American outlaws. The perpetrators proved to be none other than Robert LeRoy Parker and Harry Longbaugh, otherwise known as Butch Cassidy and "the Sundance Kid," who had gained a certain notoriety during Cassidy's leadership of an outlaw gang known as the "Wild Bunch." The Pinkerton agency had pursued them within the United States at the behest of the American Bankers' Association, but the bankers had refused to continue footing the bill when the duo fled abroad. The State Department called on the Pinkerton agency, which sent detective Frank Dimaio to find the infamous duo in the jungles of Bolivia.[140] To the best knowledge of historians and moviegoers alike, find them he did—accompanied by a substantial detachment of the Bolivian military that brought their escapades to a violent end in 1907.[141]

In extending their operations overseas, Pinkerton and other private detective agencies had two advantages the federal agents lacked. They were already experienced in undertaking criminal investigations without the benefit of state authority, since even in their domestic investigations they were not entitled to carry any police badge. And as private rather than government investigators, they were far less likely than U.S. federal agents to be perceived as challenges to a foreign government's sovereign powers. Police around the world offered them their cooperation not out of any sense of international comity but because the Pinkerton agents were seen as fellow professionals pursuing the same ends. In the nascent transnational police subculture of the late nineteenth and early twentieth century, the Pinkertons provided the initial transatlantic link.

Border Troubles

Until just about the end of the nineteenth century, the notion of the "frontier" carried many meanings for Americans. It referred initially to the lands outside the jurisdiction of the United States, claimed by various

140. Horan, *The Pinkertons*, 383–387; Horan, "Pinkerton Detective Agency," xviii.

141. The fate of the two outlaws has never been definitively established. See Malcolm W. Browne, "On Trail of Two Outlaws, Team Finds Skeletons," *New York Times*, Jan. 17, 1992, A12.

European powers and inhabited by assorted Indian nations, that eventually would be purchased, seized, or otherwise acquired by the United States. Even following acquisition, the same territories retained the appellation "frontier," one that Americans defined as the absence of settled inhabitation by European immigrants to North America and their descendants. As the territorial reaches of the United States extended to the Pacific, Americans increasingly identified as their frontiers the U.S. borders with Canada and Mexico; for many, the notion also referred to the borderlands on either side of those geographically undistinguished political boundaries. For our purposes, the last of these definitions is the relevant one, although it is important to recall that the origins of U.S. involvement in transfrontier policing included Georgia's border with Spanish Florida, Louisiana's border with first a Mexican-owned Texas and then an independent Texas, as well as other borders that have since faded into memory.

In the United States as in Europe, the most abundant transnational law enforcement contacts have always been with one's neighbors—except in those relatively unusual cases (absent in the case of North America) when hostile states have proscribed and effectively suppressed most cross-border activities. Most of the responsibility for regulating transnational interactions has fallen to law enforcement officials in the immediate vicinity of the borders. Obliged to deal with smuggling and illicit migration, as well as the movement of criminals across borders either to commit crimes or to flee apprehension, law enforcement officials in border locales have typically tried to develop working relationships with their counterparts across the border; on many occasions too, albeit more frequently in the nineteenth century than in the twentieth, they have taken matters into their own hands, motivated as often as not by frustration with the lack of cooperation from officials across the border.

In the case of cities along the northern border of the United States, Canadian and American police tended to work out cooperative relationships, particularly after the tensions of the late 1700s and early 1800s had passed. As much as possible, one avoided complicating the relationship by involving the central government. Some formalities might be required in extradition proceedings, but typically both sides maintained a strong interest in keeping their relations informal. By contrast, law enforcement relations across the Mexican border have been far more haphazard. Mexican resentment over the seizure of their territory by

American force in the 1840s ebbed slowly and bitterly. Political relations between the two central governments have soured often and sometimes nastily, with concomitant disruptions in the law enforcement arena. The ineffectiveness and corruption of Mexican law enforcement agencies have frustrated American police officials and occasionally stirred them to take unilateral action. At the same time, if only because of their close proximity, law enforcement officials along the southern border, not unlike those to the north, have found ways to work together effectively. Far removed from their nation's capitals, they have cultivated informal links contingent upon ignoring considerations of sovereignty and international law. Even more so than with most transnational law enforcement relationships, the personal dimension has been central to the success or failure of U.S.-Mexican law enforcement efforts.

International law enforcement activities along the frontiers of the United States have consistently proven more abundant, more complex, and more politically significant than any others. The border has represented the point across which ordinary domestic law enforcement activities—the recovery of fugitive criminals and escaped slaves, the suppression of outlaw gangs and Indian marauders, the tracking down of cattle rustlers and train robbers, and even the order maintenance functions of urban and rural law enforcement officers in border towns—become internationalized. At the same time, it has represented the dividing line between two sovereign jurisdictions with distinct economic regulations, law enforcement systems, and political interests, constituencies, and upheavals. Criminals who have crossed this line have sometimes done so with indifference to its jurisdictional consequences; more often, however, they have regarded the easily crossed border as an advantage, one that has offered lucrative profits to smugglers, safe havens to bandits, fugitives, and freebooters, and economic opportunities to illegal migrants. Law enforcement officials, by contrast, have typically perceived the border as a serious impediment to their tasks. The border has symbolized the limits of their police powers, a line across which they have no control and are typically dependent on foreign authorities, and one they have crossed only at the risk of being arrested by foreign law enforcement officers and angering central governments on both sides of the border.

The first efforts to investigate and deter smuggling across the border with Canada have already been noted. U.S. customs officials alongside the northern and southwestern borders focused their efforts both on nonsmuggling customs frauds and on the smuggling of both licit and illicit goods: diamonds, watches, textiles, opium, booze, Chinese "coolies," garlic, and just about anything else that could be transported. Some of these smuggling activities, particularly across the Mexican border in the decades after the U.S.-Mexican War of 1846–48 and the 1853 Gadsden Purchase of southern Arizona, involved no more than the continuation of commercial relations that had been established before the relocation of the border; most, however, were stimulated by the desire to earn the more substantial profits associated with illicit commerce. The early efforts to collect fugitive slaves from their foreign havens have also been discussed. The pages that follow therefore focus on the other concerns and activities of U.S. law enforcement authorities alongside the border with Mexico between the Civil War and World War I. This was a period during which most of the concerns of contemporary law enforcement agencies were in evidence, as well as some that are no longer problematic and others that may well reemerge in the future.

The border during this time was also a place where the entire array of law enforcement and investigative authorities could be found: the U.S. military, including the cavalry, the intelligence divisions, National Guard units under federal control, and the special agents of the War Department; the State Department's consular officials in Mexican cities near the border, as well as the department's special agents; the assorted federal law enforcement agencies, including customs officials, U.S. marshals, the Secret Service, the Bureau of Investigation, the Postal Inspection Service, the U.S. attorneys, and immigration officials; the Ranger units and National Guards of the border states; the local sheriffs and police officials of counties, cities, and towns alongside the border; and the nongovernmental private detective agencies, undeputized posses and vigilante bands, and unorganized private citizens. This multitude of law enforcers combined, competed, and conflicted with one another, as well as with the array of federal, state, local, and private Mexican law enforcement authorities who operated across the border.

The single most important determinant of the ebbs and flows of law enforcement activity along the U.S.-Mexican border was the degree of political stability within Mexico. "The true function of the Rio Grande," two historians of the border have observed, "was to identify a region rather than to delineate a border. . . . So closely was south Texas linked to northern Mexico that a political upheaval in one was bound to have a major impact on the other."[142] The central years of the Porfirio Díaz regime in Mexico, beginning roughly in the early 1880s, when he consolidated his power, and ending a few years before his ouster in 1911, were years of relative tranquility along the border. Those before and after, during which fiercely contending forces vied for power both in Mexico City and the northern Mexican states, were far more tumultuous times for American law enforcers at the frontier.

The principal law enforcement concerns from the 1860s to the 1880s were smuggling and cattle rustling, both of which had evolved into very substantial organized criminal activities.[143] Raiding on both sides of the border by Indians—some of them native to the region, others recently transplanted to government reservations—was also of particular concern, as was cross-border raiding by assorted outlaw gangs, vigilantes, military soldiers and deserters, and hopeful filibusters and revolutionaries. Law and order on both sides of the border were generally sporadic, with political upheaval common in Mexico, the tensions of Reconstruction apparent in the southwest, and vast areas of territory with few people and almost no police protection on either frontier. Even where officials on either side of the border were willing to cooperate, such as in delivering fugitives, legal objections to the extradition of nationals stood in the way.[144] Much of the task of preserving law and order throughout the middle decades of the nineteenth century fell to the U.S. Army and Mexican armed forces.[145] Both Mexican and U.S. law enforcement officials routinely complained about lack of cooperation from counterparts across the border and occasionally accused one another of complicity in cross-border criminality. "Mexican officers and soldiers make regular raids into Texas, stealing, robbing and murdering," U.S. Attorney D. J. Baldwin wrote to the attorney general in 1872.[146] The most notorious was General Juan Nepomuceno Cortina, who was

142. Don M. Coerver and Linda B. Hall, *Texas and the Mexican Revolution: A Study in State and National Border Policy, 1910–1920* (San Antonio, Tex.: Trinity University Press, 1984), 6.

143. Robert D. Gregg, *The Influence of Border Troubles on Relations Between the United States and Mexico, 1876–1910* (Baltimore: Johns Hopkins University Press, 1937), 12–13.

144. Moore, *Treatise on Extradition* (supra n. 44), 164–167. See also *Foreign Relations of the United States 1878*, 534–540, 560–567; and *1879*, 734–741. See also Chapter Seven of the present book.

145. See Francis Paul Prucha, *The Sword of the Republic: The United States Army on the Frontier, 1783–1846* (New York: Macmillan Co., 1969).

146. Calhoun, *Lawmen* (supra n. 100), 188.

indicted by a federal grand jury in Brownsville that year for "holding a saturnalia of crime, violence and rapine upon the soil of Texas" though never arrested on either side of the border.[147] But American outlaws were also prominent along the frontier, particularly a notorious gang known as the Cowboys that raided both American and Mexican towns and homes within riding distance of Tombstone, Arizona, during the late 1870s and early 1880s.[148] So serious were their depredations that President Chester Arthur ultimately issued a proclamation against the Cowboys and declared the area in a state of rebellion, thereby circumventing the prohibitions on military involvement in civilian law enforcement imposed by the 1877 Posse Comitatus Act.[149] With respect to the Indians, the charges and recriminations were fierce and reciprocal. Mexicans charged that the U.S. authorities were insufficiently concerned with preventing both "wild" Indians and those on the reservations from staging raids into Mexico. Americans responded in kind, charging that Mexican troops were not only failing to suppress the Indians but even providing them with food and equipment and purchasing their booty.[150]

Writing late in 1877, just weeks after the border troubles had prompted Congressional attention, a correspondent of the *New York Times* placed the problem in perspective:

> The Canada border was very many years ago made use of by thieves and robbers, who would steal on one side of the line and take refuge on the other. Extradition treaties and the settlement of the country has made impossible the affairs of 50 years ago, when scarcely a week passed that the farmers in New York and Vermont were not called to unite in pursuit of thieves flying to Canada. The conditions on the Rio Grande are most favorable for plundering enterprises. There is an almost desert country, sparsely populated, the greater proportion of the inhabitants being adventurers who have drifted thither from the whole world, and who do no labor of any kind. There are scattered over a vast territory, at long distance apart, the "ranches" of such men as

147. Ibid.
148. Ibid., 189–196.
149. Ball, *U.S. Marshals*, 126.
150. Gregg, *Influence of Border Troubles*; Robert M. Utley, *Frontier Regulars: The United States Army and the Indian, 1866–1891* (New York: Macmillan Co., 1973), 353–377; Clarence C. Clendenen, *Blood on the Border: The United States Army and the Mexican Irregulars* (New York: Macmillan Co., 1969), 45–115.

> attempt the honest business of stock-raising. They are too far apart to unite for defense, and when a few armed robbers come upon them they can do nothing but submit to the mercy of the band, and endeavor to secure, if possible, their own lives. If the ranch robbed happens to be upon the Mexican side, which is not often, the robbers cross into Texas. More often, because the most tempting fields are upon the American side, the flight is into Mexico. The suppression of the raids and the capture and punishment of the thieves properly devolves upon the State of Texas. But the State is powerless, and partly for the reason that the fraternity of the raiders is so widespread that the processes of courts cannot be executed, nor can the criminals be convicted and punished. The situation, therefore, instead of involving two countries in hostilities, ought to unite them in earnest attempts to suppress crime and protect the honest, bona fide settlers along the border.[151]

The consolidation of power within Mexico in the hands of President Porfirio Díaz provided the opportunity to make good on the New York journalist's recommendations. The routine response of American law enforcers—be they cavalry, posses organized by U.S. marshals, or Texas Rangers—to transnational criminality before the 1880s had been to take matters into their own hands and pursue bandits into Mexico. "Suffice it to say," Robert Gregg wrote in his study of the border, "that the United States government, starting in 1836, more or less consistently for the next forty years held to the right of pursuit by United States forces of marauders fleeing into Mexico. . . . As a rule permission was asked for such crossings and when it was not forthcoming—as it never was in the explosive state of Mexican public opinion—crossings were carried out without permission."[152] These crossings were generally confined to the "Indian country" along the upper Rio Grande and the Arizona and New Mexico boundaries. But as the number and severity of both Indian and non-Indian raids from Mexico increased in 1877, political and military officials in Washington as well as along the border sought both to regularize and to extend past practices. On June 1, 1877, Secretary of War McCrary issued an order to General Sherman officially sanction-

151. "The Mexican Border Difficulty," *New York Times*, Dec. 14, 1877, 1.
152. Gregg, *Influence of Border Troubles*, 15.

ing the border crossings instigated by the military commander along the Texas border, General E. O. C. Ord. The result was a fierce nationalist backlash against the order in Mexico City, which was in contrast to the strikingly cooperative relationship established between General Ord and his Mexican counterpart, General Geronimo Trevino, who risked condemnation from the capital for his efforts to maintain a successful working relationship with the Americans. During the three years the order remained in effect, U.S. troops crossed the border more than a dozen times, only once came close to open hostilities with Mexican forces, and proved increasingly successful in suppressing the border banditry.

The second step the two nations took was to sign an agreement in 1882, after years of tense negotiations, authorizing the troops of either state to cross the border, albeit only in desert or unpopulated regions, "when they are in close pursuit of a band of savage Indians."[153] With the Díaz regime in firm control of Mexican territory, and desirous to both avoid conflicts with the United States and suppress threats to civil order in the northern states, the frontier region was far more peaceful by the mid-1880s than it had been for decades. Economic development, railroad construction, and substantial settlement in the frontier regions also helped to transform the uncivilized character of the frontier. The Cowboy gang's demise represented the passing of the last of the more substantial outlaw gangs operating across the border. And the frequency of Indian raids declined as many Indians were killed and others were relocated to reservations far from the border. By the mid-1880s the Comanche, Lipan, and Kickapoo bands that had raided settled populations on both sides of the border had been effectively suppressed. The last of the Indian raiders were almost all Apaches, who raided both sides of the Arizona and New Mexico borders and fought fiercely with American troops until well into the 1890s.[154] Led by Victorio and Nana during the late 1870s and early 1880s, then by Geronimo until 1886, and finally by "Kid" during the 1890s, the Apache bands, usually numbering no more than a hundred warriors, were at times pursued by as many as 2,000 cavalry and hundreds of Indian scouts.[155] Their final

153. Ibid., 152.

154. The struggles of the Apaches during the nineteenth century are recounted in Paul I. Wellman, *Death in the Desert: The Fifty Years' War for the Great Southwest* (New York: Macmillan Co., 1935).

155. Gregg, *Influence of Border Troubles*, 110–111.

demise ultimately owed as much to the efforts of Mexican forces as U.S. troops, both of whom pursued the Apaches within their territories and occasionally across the borders.[156]

Law enforcement activities directed at the suppression of the Indians fell largely to the cavalry. Suppression of non-Indian outlawry, however, was largely in the hands of nonmilitary state and federal agents, in part because the Posse Comitatus Act prohibited the military from playing a role absent a declared state of emergency. U.S. marshals were often leery of devoting too much energy to policing the border, in good part because the modest compensation they received for serving process did not cover the expense and trouble of tracking down outlaws;[157] it is not surprising that they were least keen about pursuing the American bandits who raided into Mexico but refrained from criminality north of the border. Among the more dedicated and courageous marshals was Crowley Dake, the U.S. marshal for Arizona from 1878 to 1882, who pursued the Cowboys throughout his tenure, ultimately proving successful when President Arthur's emergency declaration provided him with cavalry support.[158] In Texas, the Rangers, created at the outbreak of the Texas revolution in 1835, and in particular its Frontier Battalion, which operated from 1874 to 1881, assumed many of the responsibilities for tracking down Indians and assorted outlaws.[159] The marshals, like the cavalry, occasionally crossed the border in pursuit of their antagonists, both with and without permission from Mexican authorities, but their freedom of action was constrained to some extent by directives from Washington.[160] The Rangers, by contrast, had the freedom of a relatively single-minded unit with neither distant overseers nor broader foreign policy considerations to hamper them; they crossed the border often in pursuit of Indians and outlaws and acquired a reputation for shooting first and asking questions second. On occasion, they joined the cavalry and the marshals in policing both sides of the border.

156. Utley, *Frontier Regulars*, 367–409; John Gregory Bourke, *On the Border with Crook* (1891; reprint, Chicago: Rio Grande Press, 1962); James B. Gillett, *Six Years with the Texas Rangers, 1875 to 1881*, ed. M. M. Quaife (New Haven: Yale University Press, 1925). See also C. L. Sonnichsen, ed., *Geronimo and the End of the Apache Wars* (Lincoln: University of Nebraska Press, 1986), which includes interesting essays and a useful annotated bibliography on the end of the Apache wars.

157. Ball, *U.S. Marshals* (supra n. 99), 129; Calhoun, *Lawmen* (supra n. 100), 189.

158. Ball, *U.S. Marshals*, 109–133; Calhoun, *Lawmen*, 189–196.

159. Walter Prescott Webb, *The Texas Rangers: A Century of Frontier Defense* (Austin: University of Texas Press, 1935), 305–342.

160. Ball, *U.S. Marshals*, 112–114.

The American southwestern frontier has always been intimately linked to the political and economic currents of the nation to the south. The incidence and character of smuggling was as strongly influenced by Mexican regulations and the state of the economy as by U.S. regulations and economic conditions. The security of Americans north of the border often depended as much upon the state of law and order south of the border as in neighboring American locales. Similarly, political upheavals within Mexico inevitably affected those living across the frontier. Troops, rebels, violence, and bullets spilled easily over the border. Refugees, revolutionaries, filibusters and assorted other insurrectionists viewed the United States, and particularly Texas, as a natural refuge for those fleeing oppression, disorder, and armed forces and as an ideal base of operations for those *revoltosos* plotting an insurgency, revolution, or coup d'état. For all these Mexicans, the territory north of the border represented not just a relatively safe haven into which Mexican troops and agents were leery to enter but also a source of weapons, intelligence, personnel, and the political and financial support of sympathizers among both the substantial Mexican and Mexican-American communities and other Americans with political and economic interests in Mexico's governance. At the same time, not a few Mexicans viewed the United States with great hostility; they sought both revenge and reparations for the territorial seizures, capitalist exploitations, and general arrogance of the "gringos" to the north. Their activities and dispositions influenced, and were themselves shaped by, the swirls of intra-Mexican political turbulence.

The political turbulence generated betwen 1910 and 1920 by the Mexican revolution presented law enforcement authorities north of the border with a disparate set of challenges: ensuring both the territorial integrity of the United States and the security of Americans and others north of the border; enforcing the neutrality laws of the United States, which involved surveillance of Mexican activists, suppression of armed expeditions into Mexico, and curtailment of gun running; and protection of American lives and interests south of the border. In that decade, virtually every federal, state, and local agency present at the border and empowered to carry a weapon—and even some not so empowered—played a role in responding to these challenges. Conflicts among them were often severe, reflecting not merely ordinary turf squabbles but intense differences of opinion regarding which Mexican groups should be supported or suppressed, what the United States' interests in Mexico were, what restrictions should be placed on American law enforcement operations south of the border, and how to interpret and apply the neutrality and other laws of the United States. The sharpest disagreements were typically between federal authorities in Washington and state and local officials along the border, with the latter generally dismissive of Washington's broader foreign policy concerns and perceived detachment from the particular problems of the border. Relations with Mexican authorities accordingly varied, depending upon the particular interests and perspectives of the assorted U.S. agencies involved in the fray, all of which were further complicated between 1911 and 1915 by the recurring question of which Mexican forces were actually in control of Mexico City and Mexico's northern states and cities.

An additional factor shaping the various American responses to the Mexican Revolution was the radical cant and style of many of the revolutionaries. The socialist and anarchist rhetoric and writing of many of those involved in the struggle for power within Mexico struck a tone familiar to U.S. officials and citizens faced with their own revolutionary activists and organizations. It also invited concerns for American lives and interests in foreign countries not unlike those that have provided such an important impetus for the many U.S. military interventions and covert operations in Central America and the Caribbean throughout the twentieth century. When Mexican miners in the American-run mining town of Cananea, Mexico, began a violent strike in June 1906, in which a few American foremen were killed, the reaction of U.S. law enforcement authorities suggested elements both of the response to union strikes within the United States and the response to threats to U.S. economic interests abroad; indeed, the reaction may have been shaped by the fact that the organizers of the strike included not only the radical Mexican Liberal Party but also labor agitators and socialists from the United States, notably the Western Federation of Miners.

The first to respond to calls for help from company officials and the resident American consul was Captain Rynning of the Arizona Rangers, who organized a posse of 270 cowboys, miners, and merchants from Bisbee, Arizona, and headed to Naco to confer with Mexican officials.[161] Rynning was a former Rough Rider in Teddy Roosevelt's unit during the

161. The exploits of the Arizona Rangers, as related in the local newspapers of the period, are collected in Joseph Miller, ed., *The Arizona Rangers* (New York: Hastings House, 1972). See also W. Dirk Raat, *Revoltosos: Mexico's Rebels in the United States, 1903–1923* (College Station: Texas A&M University Press, 1981), 84.

Spanish-American War of 1898 who had already broken a number of strikes in Arizona. The Arizona Rangers, created in 1901 by the Territorial Legislature of Arizona and modeled after the Texas Rangers, had worked closely with the Arizona Cattle Growers' Association and been previously employed to protect the local interests of Colonel William C. Greene, the Arizonan rancher who owned the Cananea mine.[162] Exactly what transpired at the point of crossing the border has never been conclusively determined. According to one historian's version, the assistance of the Rangers was solicited by the governor of Sonora, Rafael Izabal.[163] According to a journalist, Carl Rathbun, who wrote an article, "Keeping the Peace Along the Mexican Border" for *Harper's Weekly* later that year, the governor and Captain Rynning conferred at the border:

> Rynning told the governor that the occasion was urgent, and offered himself and his men as volunteers. Knowing the captain's military experience and the reputation of the Rangers, Yzabal at once accepted and proceeded to instruct him as to the manner in which he should proceed. In order to avoid international complications the Americans were instructed to cross the line as an unorganized mob, and as soon as they were on Mexican soil they would be sworn in as Mexican volunteers by the governor, who held the requisite military authority.
>
> This was done at once, and the Americans were lined up and duly sworn, thus becoming temporarily Mexican troops. Perhaps it was a bit irregular, but necessity is not a nice observer of red tape. The captain was appointed a colonel, and seven of the Ranger force who accompanied him were also given commissions as officers of the new troops. The matter having thus been arranged, the larger part of the force at Naco then proceeded to Cananea.[164]

The hometown newspaper, the *Phoenix Republican*, reported a somewhat different version:

162. Raat, *Revoltosos*, 89.

163. Paul J. Vanderwood, *Disorder and Progress: Bandits, Police, and Mexican Development* (Lincoln: University of Nebraska Press, 1981), 147.

164. Carl M. Rathbun, "Keeping the Peace Along the Mexican Border" (1906), reprinted in Miller, ed., *Arizona Rangers*, 1–12.

> At the Mexican line Governor Yzabal of Sonora met Captain Rynning and forbade his entrance into Mexico, pointing out that permission could not possibly be given to an armed party of Americans to come into his country. Captain Rynning replied that they were not going in as a party but as individuals; that they were going on a peaceful mission to Cananea to protect and rescue Americans in peril and they were going on that train. Governor Yzabal made the best of the situation and went along. He afterwards lost his job when it was represented to President Diaz that he had permitted Captain Rynning to cross the line.[165]

As events transpired, the Cananea strike was ultimately suppressed not by Rynning's posse but by a unit of the Mexican Rurales under the direction of Colonel Emilio Kosterlitzky, a particularly effective commander known as the "Mad Russian," who patrolled the Mexican state of Sonora.[166] Despite the embarrassment and offense to the Mexicans created by the presence of the American posse, conflict was avoided as a result of the close relationship that had already evolved between Kosterlitzky and the Arizona Rangers. The principal cost of the entire episode was to the aging Porfirio Díaz regime, which was obliged to respond to charges that Mexican sovereignty had been violated by the U.S. intervention.[167] More significant is that the incident at Cananea foreshadowed many of the international dimensions of the brewing Mexican revolution.

The details of the Mexican revolution south of the border and of the activities of the *revoltosos* north of the border need not concern us here. Suffice it to say that the two were frequently and intimately linked and that law enforcement authorities within the United States were obliged to pay close attention to revolutionary activities on both sides of the border. The principal national security concern was that the violence and armed combatants of the Mexican revolution not spill over into American territory. This had been a minor concern during the late 1870s, when Díaz's troops had crossed into Texas in pursuit of rebel troops led by General Escobedo, the former war minister of the Lerdo government that Díaz had ousted; and again in 1880, when Mexican

165. Miller, *Arizona Rangers*, 124–125.

166. See Vanderwood, *Disorder and Progress*, for a fine discussion of the Rurales and Mexican banditry.

167. Ibid., 148–149.

troops in pursuit of suspected deserters fired shots across the border.[168] The greater intensity of the conflict near the border during the revolutionary period after 1910, however, generated far greater concerns. In April 1911, a rebel attack on the border town of Agua Prieta, in Sonora, resulted in two deaths and eleven injuries in the neighboring American town of Douglas, Arizona, and an attack on Ciudad Juárez the same month killed six and wounded fifteen in El Paso, Texas.[169] In March 1913, battles in Nogales, Sonora, inevitably crossed the street into Nogales, Arizona; in late 1914, Naco, Arizona, suffered dozens of casualties during a siege of Naco, Sonora.[170] Local authorities in El Paso could not help but keep their attentions on Ciudad Juárez, which changed hands seven times during the decade. The possibility of spillover into U.S. territory similarly preoccupied Mexican combatants, with many highly cautious of transgressing the border and quick to warn American officials of forthcoming hostilities, while a few deliberately invited such incidents to provoke American intervention. Efforts both by Mexican combatants and by U.S. authorities to avoid inflicting casualties within the United States were hampered by the fact that the revolution had become something of a spectator sport on the American side of the border, with military actions in border towns drawing large crowds.[171]

The responses of U.S. authorities included mobilizations of U.S. troops, the Ranger and National Guard units of the border states, local police, and civilian posses under the command of border sheriffs. Thousands of federal troops were massed along the border, as both a warning and a deterrent to Mexican crossings and in case threats to American lives and interests in Mexico required intervention; and President Taft agreed to federal financing of the Texas Rangers, which had been on the verge of being disbanded until the Mexican revolution broke out. But despite periodic scares of cross-border violence at El Paso, Brownsville, and other points, as well as repeated calls by the governor of Texas and other local officials for U.S. military intervention across the border, Presidents Taft and Wilson studiously avoided sending federal troops into Mexico absent deliberate attacks on American citizens.

168. Gregg, *Influence of Border Troubles* (supra n. 143), 59, 98.

169. Coerver and Hall, *Texas and the Mexican Revolution* (supra n. 142), 24–27.

170. Linda B. Hall and Don M. Coerver, *Revolution on the Border: The United States and Mexico, 1910–1920* (Albuquerque: University of New Mexico Press, 1988), 32–33.

171. Coerver and Hall, *Texas and the Mexican Revolution*, 24–26; Hall and Coerver, *Revolution on the Border*, 31.

As the Mexican revolution wore on, various factions increasingly looked at the United States not just as a haven but as an enemy. The first manifestation of this was a campaign of violence during 1915 and 1916 conducted by Mexicans and Mexican-Americans against Anglos north of the border. Known as the Plan of San Diego, the campaign derived its name from a document drawn up in the small southern Texas town of San Diego calling for a Mexican-American rebellion, the slaying of all Anglo males over the age of sixteen, and creation of an independent republic in the southwest.[172] The campaign drew its sustenance from the brewing anti-American and anti-Anglo sentiment that had simmered for decades on both sides of the border; it was discreetly organized and financed, however, by Venustiano Carranza, leader of the dominant faction in the Mexican revolution during the latter part of the decade, who attempted to manipulate the violence to pressure the Wilson administration to recognize his government. Although most of the dozens of raids carried out in U.S. territory under the banner of the Plan were initiated from Mexican territory, President Wilson resolutely refused to authorize any border crossings, even in hot pursuit. American interventions were limited to the covert intelligence missions of the Justice Department's special agents and a number of Japanese-Mexican informants, who confirmed reports that Carranza had supported the raids and that representatives of the German government had provided funding, hoping to provoke the Wilson administration into a distracting war with Mexico.[173] The raids generated much hysteria and fear among non-Mexicans north of the border, but only a few dozen casualties. The cavalry restricted their police actions to the U.S. side of the border. The principal victims of the Plan were the hundreds of Mexican Americans lynched and executed by the Texas Rangers and local vigilantes and the thousands forced to hide or flee across the border to safety.

The incident that finally prompted President Wilson to order a military expedition across the border was sponsored not by Carranza but by his bitter opponent, Pancho Villa, who had turned against the United

172. See James A. Sandos, "The Plan of San Diego: War and Diplomacy on the Texas Border, 1915–1916," *Arizona and the West* 14 (1972), 5–24; Charles C. Cumberland, "Border Raids in the Lower Rio Grande Valley, 1915," *Southwestern Historical Quarterly* 57 (1954), 285–311; and Charles H. Harris III and Louis R. Sadler, "The Plan of San Diego and the Mexican–United States War Crisis of 1916: A Reexamination," *Hispanic American Historical Review* 58 (1978), 381–408, reprinted in Charles H. Harris III and Louis R. Sadler, *The Border and the Revolution* (Las Cruces: New Mexico State University, 1988), 71–100.

173. Sandos, "Plan of San Diego," 19–24.

States with bitterness following Wilson's recognition of the Carranza regime in October 1915.[174] Villa's forces began their campaign against Americans with a massacre of American mining employees en route to Santa Ysabel, Chihuahua, in January 1916; on March 9, they attacked Columbus, New Mexico, killing seventeen Americans and burning and looting the town before being chased out by U.S. Army troops, who managed to killed dozens of the *villistas*. Wilson thereupon ordered General John "Black Jack" Pershing to lead a "punitive expedition" into Mexico in pursuit of Pancho Villa and his forces.[175] But Pershing's forces failed to apprehend Villa, and their very presence in Mexico induced Carranza to renew the Plan of San Diego raids on U.S. border towns. A Mexican attack on Glenn Springs, Texas, and nearby towns on May 5 resulted in a further escalation of hostilities between Carranza and the United States. Both governments drew up plans to invade the other and massed their troops in anticipation of large-scale hostilities. U.S. Army troops were at last authorized to cross the border in "hot pursuit" of raiders. Proclaiming "I am clear of red tape, and I know no Rio Grande," Major George Langhorne led his troops into Mexico in pursuit of the Glenn Springs raiders, with "no pause," he noted, "for orders or State Department negotiations."[176] On May 9, President Wilson federalized the National Guards of Texas, New Mexico, and Arizona; on June 18, he extended the order to all National Guard units in the United States. Neither government, however, was eager for war, with Wilson wary of the potential need for U.S. troops in Europe and Carranza concerned lest a military conflict with the United States result in his downfall.[177] By July, the crisis had passed and Carranza had ordered a halt to the Plan of San Diego raids. Pershing continued to pursue Villa and even secretly commissioned two Japanese-Mexican agents to assassinate Villa with poison tablets, but both overt and covert efforts failed

174. See Clarence C. Clendenen, *The United States and Pancho Villa: A Study in Unconventional Diplomacy* (Ithaca, N.Y.: Cornell University Press, 1961).

175. Frank E. Vandiver, *Black Jack: The Life and Times of John J. Pershing* (College Station: Texas A&M University Press, 1977), 2:595–668; Clendenen, *Blood on the Border* (supra n. 150), 248–284. The argument that Pershing's expedition was designed to serve broader foreign policy objectives of the Wilson administration is advanced in Michael L. Tate, "Pershing's Punitive Expedition: Pursuer of Bandits or Presidential Panacea?" *The Americas* 32 (1975–76), 46–71.

176. Coerver and Hall, *Texas and the Mexican Revolution* (supra n. 142), 100. See Ronnie C. Tyler, "The Little Punitive Expedition in the Big Bend," *Southwestern Historical Quarterly* 78 (1975), 271–291.

177. Coerver and Hall, *Texas and the Mexican Revolution*, 105.

to do away with the Mexican rebel.[178] In early 1917, with Villa's forces still at large in Mexico but no longer operational near the border, Pershing's units were withdrawn from Mexico.

The series of Mexican raids and military responses by the United States during 1916 were significant in a number of respects. Pershing's punitive expedition represented one of the largest, as well as one of the last, employments of U.S. military force to track down criminal fugitives who had fled abroad. Like the cross-border cavalry raids against Indians in earlier decades—but unlike the posse Captain Rynning led to Cananea, or the assorted military expeditions to Central America and the Caribbean during the early decades of the twentieth century, both of which were directed primarily at the protection of American interests abroad—Pershing's expedition had as its primary objective enforcement of U.S. laws. But it also represented the last significant deployment of either police or military force across a land border of the United States on behalf of national security objectives. The border did not quiet entirely until the mid-1920s; U.S. military units continued to cross the border in pursuit of raiders, and in June 1919 they intervened in Juárez when an attack on that city by a band of *villistas* resulted in casualties north of the border from stray bullets. The cross-border attack by the military units, which were comprised largely of black infantrymen and backed by a deadly artillery barrage not previously employed along the border, dealt a devastating and fatal blow to Villa's forces and ambitions.[179] The U.S. troops were all back in the United States within two days, however. There was neither the need nor the desire to replicate Pershing's expedition.

The Neutrality Network

Even as the Army and assorted posses responded to the more large-scale threats of disorder generated by the Mexican revolution, federal and state law enforcement agents were busily engaged investigating violations of U.S. neutrality laws. Nineteenth-century American history was

178. Charles H. Harris III and Louis R. Sadler, "Termination with Extreme Prejudice: The United States Versus Pancho Villa," in Harris and Sadler, *The Border and the Revolution*, 7–23.

179. Clendenen, *The U.S. and Pancho Villa*, 305–313.

rich with plots by both American filibusters and foreign revolutionaries to launch foreign military expeditions from U.S. soil. Neutrality laws dating back to 1794 forbade such activities, but the actual enforcement of the laws varied greatly, depending upon popular attitudes, the state of relations between the United States and the targeted nation, and the varied motives of whatever administration occupied the White House. The Latin American wars of independence against Spain during the first decades of the nineteenth century attracted much support within the United States. In 1837, approximately 1,000 Canadian revolutionaries known as the "Patriots" launched a military expedition from northern New York in an effort to spark a war for independence against Britain; it was quickly suppressed, however, by British troops and Canadian militia with the assistance of U.S. marshals.[180] During the 1850s, American filibusters plotted takeovers of Cuba, Mexico, Nicaragua, Ecuador, Guatemala, El Salvador, Costa Rica, Peru, and Honduras.[181] The most notorious of these, William Walker, succeeded in conquering Nicaragua and ruling it for a year. In 1866 and again in 1870, Irish Fenians invaded Canada from U.S. territory, seeking thereby to pressure Britain to free Ireland, but they too were quickly routed by Canadian troops north of the border and U.S. troops and marshals in New York and Vermont. By the end of the nineteenth century, filibusterism and most other violations of U.S. neutrality laws consisted primarily of gun running from the United States and the plotting of foreign revolutionaries and coup makers on U.S. soil. Such activities reached their height during the Mexican revolution.

The rise of opposition to the Díaz regime in Mexico after 1905 provided the occasion for the first significant neutrality law enforcement efforts since the first years of Díaz's reign. In March 1907, the Mexican ambassador to the United States, Enrique Creel, informed Secretary of State Elihu Root of the machinations of the Mexican Liberal Party and its leader, Ricardo Flores Magón, within the United States and requested that the U.S. government take action to enforce its neutrality laws. Root, who wanted to maintain the close relationship that had developed

180. Albert B. Corey, *The Crisis of 1830–1842 in Canadian-American Relations* (New Haven: Yale University Press, 1941); Wilson Porter Shortridge, "The Canadian-American Frontier During the Rebellion of 1837–1838," *Canadian Historical Review* 7 (1926), 13–26.

181. Charles H. Brown, *Agents of Manifest Destiny: The Lives and Times of the Filibusters* (Chapel Hill: University of North Carolina Press, 1980); Calhoun, *Lawmen* (supra n. 100), 67–72.

between the United States and the Díaz regime, asked Attorney General Charles Bonaparte to take the appropriate actions. Following an armed attack by *magonistas* from Del Rio, Texas, into Mexico in June 1908, the local U.S. attorney, customs collector, U.S. marshal, cavalry commander, and the U.S. consul stationed at Ciudad Porfirio Díaz, investigated the incident and recommended "that a special secret service be established to keep in touch with Mexican revolutionary movements and border conditions."[182]

The network of agents that developed thereafter to enforce the neutrality laws outlasted both the suppression of the *magonista* movement and the fall of the Díaz regime. It ultimately included agents representing every federal law enforcement agency: U.S. Customs, the Immigration Service, the Marshals Service, the Secret Service, the Postal Inspection Service, the State Department, the Army's Intelligence Division, and the newly created Bureau of Investigation, which assumed a leading role in investigating neutrality law violations.[183] Some of the arrangements were somewhat irregular. For instance, the ambitious and well-informed U.S. consul in Ciudad Porfirio Díaz, Luther T. Ellsworth, was appointed a "special representative" of the Justice Department in November 1909 to supervise the neutrality work.[184] The prohibition on lending Secret Service agents to other law enforcement agencies was circumvented by lending a top agent, Joe Priest, to the State Department and then placing him under Justice Department supervision. Texas law enforcement officials occasionally helped enforce the federal neutrality laws—albeit with much reserve, given the substantial support enjoyed by the *magonistas* and subsequent revolutionary groups among the local Mexican-American population. Far more significantly, the U.S. neutrality network worked closely with agents of the Mexican government, including not just resident consuls and Secret Service agents but also employees of the American private detective agencies hired by the Mexican government.

Given the abundant twists and turns of the Mexican revolution and U.S.-Mexican relations, it is not surprising that the process of enforcing

182. Dorothy Pierson Kerig, *Luther T. Ellsworth: U.S. Consul on the Border During the Mexican Revolution*, Southwestern Studies Monograph No. 47 (El Paso: Texas Western Press, 1975), 15–16.

183. Charles H. Harris III and Louis R. Sadler, "United States Government Archives and the Mexican Revolution," *New World: A Journal of Latin American Studies* 1 (1986), 108–116, reprinted in Harris and Sadler, *The Border and the Revolution*, 133–141.

184. Kerig, *Ellsworth*, 25.

the neutrality laws was both complex and laden with intrigue.[185] Informants and agents often worked for two or three agencies at once, including some that were at loggerheads with one another. Private investigators—in particular, those of the Furlong Detective Agency employed by the Díaz regime and the Thiel Detective Agency hired by the Madero regime—played a central role, tracking down and even arresting *revoltosos* and others targeted by their Mexican employers.[186] State and federal officials often clashed with one another and among themselves over differing interpretations of the neutrality laws and varying perceptions of which side to support in the Mexican revolution. And Mexican agents were afforded wide latitude in investigating the various revolutionary groups, often conducting the principal investigations and only calling upon the local U.S. authorities to make the necessary arrests. Hundreds of Mexican agents and informants could be found in El Paso and other centers of revolutionary intrigue, surveilling and infiltrating the antigovernment plotters and gun smuggling rings. At one point, in mid-1912, Mexican agents were even authorized to search passengers on streetcars leaving El Paso for Juárez across the border, but the practice was discontinued after a public outcry against the notion of foreign agents searching American citizens on U.S. territory.[187] Their substantial presence, frequent indiscretions, and occasional bunglings of joint investigations also angered some U.S. authorities, but the Americans' dependence upon the Mexican agents for intelligence and personnel ensured their continued presence.[188]

Notwithstanding the plethora of U.S. agents, Mexican secret service men, private detectives, and assorted double agents often working at cross-purposes with one another, the neutrality laws of the United States were enforced with some vigor. *Revoltosos* were followed, harassed, and arrested by agents of both governments; prosecuted in U.S. courts; deported or extradited to Mexico; and occasionally kidnapped in the United States and secretly brought across the border.[189] The results

185. See Mark T. Gilderhus, *Diplomacy and Revolution: U.S.–Mexican Relations Under Wilson and Carranza* (Tucson: University of Arizona Press, 1977).

186. Furlong, *Fifty Years a Detective* (supra n. 133), 137–148.

187. Charles H. Harris III and Louis R. Sadler, "The 'Underside' of the Mexican Revolution: El Paso, 1912," *The Americas: A Quarterly Review of Inter-American Cultural History* 39 (1982), 69–83, reprinted in Harris and Sadler, *The Border and the Revolution*, 53–70.

188. Kerig, *Ellsworth*, 50.

189. Raat, *Revoltosos* (supra n. 161), esp. 124–148.

included the arrest and conviction of Flores Magón and the effective suppression of the *magonista* movement.[190] Efforts against the next leading *revoltoso*, Francisco Madero, were complicated, however, by the substantial financial, legal, and political support engendered by the politically moderate Mexican activist and by his careful efforts to avoid any appearance of violating the neutrality laws.[191] After a federal warrant for Madero's arrest was issued in February 1911, the Texas governor, Oscar Colquitt, offered his assistance in arresting Madero and facilitating the efforts of Díaz's agents, but federal agents were much less eager to aid in repressing Madero's movement.

With the fall of the Díaz regime and Madero's accession to the presidency, federal, state, and local law enforcement agents in the United States worked with Madero's agents to suppress challenges to his regime. The first challenge, by General Bernardo Reyes, a prominent military and political figure in the Díaz regime, received powerful support from leading members of the Mexican-American community and Governor Colquitt, but it was quickly suppressed in the latter half of 1911 when a federal grand jury indicted Reyes and his supporters and U.S. law enforcement authorities followed up by confiscating the arms, ammunition, and horses that the *reyistas* had assembled to mount their counterrevolution.[192] Efforts during the following year by a former ally of Madero, Pascual Orozco, to organize a rebellion against the Mexican regime from U.S. territory were significantly undermined by the success of U.S. and Mexican government agents in stemming the flow of weapons across the border.[193] Following the fall of the Madero regime in 1913, U.S. authorities refrained from aiding the short-lived regime of Victoriano Huerta and played an important role in suppressing the revolutionary movements activated by Huerta and Pascual Orozco (and partially financed and supplied by the German government) after Huerta's overthrow in 1914. Agents of the Bureau of Investigation infiltrated, surveilled, and otherwise collected intelligence on their activities. U.S. attorneys and marshals along the border were directed by the Justice

190. Ibid., 149–168.

191. Coerver and Hall, *Texas and the Mexican Revolution* (supra n. 142), 17–20.

192. Charles H. Harris III and Louis R. Sadler, "The 1911 Reyes Conspiracy: The Texas Side," *Southwestern Historical Quarterly* 82 (1980), 325–348, reprinted in Harris and Sadler, *The Border and the Revolution*, 27–50; Vic Niemeyer, "Frustrated Invasion: The Revolutionary Attempt of General Bernardo Reyes from San Antonio in 1911," *Southwestern Historical Quarterly* 67 (1963), 213–225.

193. Harris and Sadler, "The 'Underside' of the Mexican Revolution," 53–67.

Department to watch for violations of the neutrality laws.[194] By late 1915, both Huerta and Orozco had been indicted and detained by federal authorities. Orozco died violently shortly thereafter, when he escaped from confinement but was chased down and killed by a posse of federal, state, and local authorities; Huerta died in custody in January 1916 from medical complications following an operation. During the following years, U.S. authorities continued with their efforts to curtail gun running by both supporters and opponents of the Carranza regime in Mexico City, but the principal impact of their efforts to enforce the neutrality laws was the undermining of violent opposition to the Carranza government.

By 1915, U.S. military and police forces in the Southwest were concerned with yet another threat: the efforts of the German government to cultivate ties first with Huerta and other revolutionaries and thereafter with the Carranza regime. The Germans sought to create whatever troubles they could along the southwestern border, to distract U.S. attention and military forces from the conflict in Europe, and to win the Mexican government's assistance in their war with the United States. The neutrality network that had developed in response to the Mexican revolution rapidly shifted its focus to the tasks of espionage and counterespionage against German activities in Mexico and north of the border. Intelligence agents of the Army, Navy, and State Department combined with the law enforcement agents of the Treasury Department and the Bureau of Investigation as well as British intelligence agents. Charged with maintaining the economic blacklist against German firms and fronts and with collecting political and military intelligence, the U.S. agents clashed frequently among themselves over turf and tactics but ultimately succeeded in countering and even penetrating many of the Germans' efforts at espionage and other political intrigue in Mexico.[195]

The Transnational Relations of City Police

So long as the federal police agencies remained underdeveloped, most overseas investigations of noncustoms criminal matters fell to municipal

194. Coerver and Hall, *Texas and the Mexican Revolution*, 112.

195. Friedrich Katz, *The Secret War in Mexico* (Chicago: University of Chicago Press, 1981), 433–441; Charles H. Harris III and Louis R. Sadler, "The Witzke Affair: German Intrigue on the Mexican Border, 1917–1918," *Military Review* 59 (1979), 36–50, reprinted in Harris and Sadler, *The Border and the Revolution*, 115–129.

police agencies. Most murderers, thiefs, rapists, and other common criminals violated not federal but state and municipal laws. From the middle of the nineteenth century until the first decades of the twentieth, the detective divisions of municipal police departments were likely to be as large and as sophisticated as anything the federal government had to offer. Its principal competitors and collaborators were the private detective agencies, which were themselves often composed of former police officials. Even as early as the first half of the nineteenth century a number of chief constables in leading American cities had acquired impressive reputations based upon their knowledge of the criminal world and their detecting skills. This was especially the case with New York's finest. During much of the first half of the nineteenth century, Jacob Hays, the High Constable of New York City, was consulted frequently by European police officials.[196] In 1818, he personally pursued a counterfeiting investigation to Canada, where he located "the principal manufactory" of the criminals.[197] And in 1851, New York City's police force was sufficiently well regarded that the British government invited it, along with other leading European police departments, to send representatives to the Great Exhibition in London.[198] The first public detective branches were created in Boston in 1846, then New York in 1857, Philadelphia in 1859, and Chicago in 1861.[199] Most were quickly struck by corruption scandals and disbanded temporarily, but the rising need for their services inevitably led to their reestablishment.[200] Not until 1880, however, when an uneducated but clever Irishman, Thomas Byrnes, was appointed police chief, was New York's detective division pulled together into something of an effective force. Combining old-fashioned methods with the development of photo identification files, Byrnes saw his detective force as the equal of the French Sûreté and Scotland Yard.[201] His tenure lasted sixteen years, until he was forced from his position by Teddy

196. Gerald Astor, *The New York Cops: An Informal History* (New York: Charles Scribner's Sons, 1971), 14.

197. Johnson, *Policing the Urban Underworld* (supra n. 119), 48.

198. Phillip Thurmond Smith, *Policing Victorian London: Political Policing, Order, and the London Metropolitan Police* (Westport, Conn.: Greenwood Press, 1985), 89–93.

199. Johnson, *Policing the Urban Underworld,* 65.

200. Craig D. Uchida, "The Development of the American Police: An Historical Overview," in Roger G. Dunham and Geoffrey P. Alpert, eds., *Critical Issues in Policing: Contemporary Readings* (Prospect Heights, Ill.: Waveland Press, 1989), 14–30.

201. Thorwald, *Century of the Detective* (supra n. 132), 95–98.

Roosevelt, then the activist chief police commissioner in New York. Although much of Byrne's historical reputation has focused on his heavy-handed methods against criminals and his accommodating approach to vice control,[202] he brought his detective force into the mainstream of international police interactions. His department assembled an extensive rogues' gallery, including pictures of European as well as American criminals, and exchanged information on criminals and fugitives with European police departments.[203] Indeed, as police chief of what was fast becoming the world's most cosmopolitan city, Byrnes had little choice but to keep tabs on itinerant criminals throughout the Americas and abroad.

By the beginning of the twentieth century, municipal police departments, not just in New York but also throughout much of the United States, were undergoing the same process of professionalization that had occurred decades earlier in Europe.[204] Much of the initial impetus was provided by the increasing professionalism of criminals in the areas of counterfeiting, burglary, fraud, and fencing.[205] Motivated also by European influences, but even more so by a wave of police corruption investigations around the country, police reform movements were contributing to an increasing sophistication in American criminal investigations.[206] One aspect of these developments was the increasing police consciousness of the need to interact with foreign counterparts. First, however, police departments needed to resolve the problems of interstate cooperation and develop some sense of a national police community. The first significant efforts in this regard were sponsored in 1871 by the commissioners and chief of the Saint Louis police. They organized a National Police Convention attended by more than one hundred delegates from twenty-one states and the District of Columbia. Criminal

202. Reppetto, *The Blue Parade* (supra n. 106), 52–68.

203. Thomas Byrnes, *Rogue's Gallery* (1887; reprint, Secaucus, N.J.: Castle, 1988).

204. Robert Fogelson, *Big-City Police* (Cambridge, Mass.: Harvard University Press, 1977), 93–166; Johnson, *American Law Enforcement* (supra n. 93), 105–122; Samuel Walker, *A Critical History of Police Reform: The Emergence of Professionalism* (Lexington, Mass.: Lexington Books, 1977), 33–106.

205. Larry K. Hartsfield, *The American Response to Professional Crime, 1870–1917* (Westport, Conn.: Greenwood Press, 1985); Johnson, *Policing the Urban Underworld*, 12–67.

206. See Reppetto, *The Blue Parade*; and Gene E. Carte and Elaine H. Carte, *Police Reform in the United States: The Era of August Vollmer* (Berkeley and Los Angeles: University of California Press, 1977), for a thorough discussion of these developments.

investigative techniques were discussed, criminal justice issues such as prostitution debated, and calls for greater cooperation and communication proclaimed.[207] Efforts thereafter to institutionalize police cooperation and form an association faltered, however, and no further steps were taken for more than two decades. In 1893, the National (later International) Association of Chiefs of Police was created and shortly thereafter began holding annual conferences. Three years later, a group of law enforcement officials from around the nation met in Chicago to discuss ways of improving interstate coordination in criminal investigations.[208] As American police officers gradually grew accustomed to looking beyond their municipal and state borders, the notion of dealing with foreign counterparts began to seem somewhat more realistic.

A principal factor contributing to American participation in the developing international police community was the dissemination of European developments in police science. For instance, during the 1890s, police experts around the world studied and promoted the new anthropometric method of criminal identification created by, and named after, Alphonse Bertillon.[209] The Chicago police department adopted the *bertillonage* system in 1890, and other American police departments followed suit after the Frenchman's book was translated into English in 1896.[210] Likewise, the fingerprint method was gradually gaining notice. In 1903 the International Association of Chiefs of Police (IACP) appointed a committee of three to examine the new methodology. One of the members, W. G. Baldwin of Baldwin Railroad Detectives, toured European police departments in 1904 and returned with favorable reports.[211] Another member, William Pinkerton, went to England the next year and "declared that Scotland Yard had reduced criminal investigation to a matter of bookkeeping."[212] At the 1905 World's Fair in Saint Louis, the IACP sponsored a display of the various systems of criminal identification in use around the world. Scotland Yard was

207. Walker, *Critical History of Police Reform*, 47.

208. Thorwald, *Century of the Detective* (supra n. 132), 93.

209. IACP, *Proceedings: 27th Convention* (Detroit, June 7–10, 1920), 83. See Henri Couchon, "Alphonse Bertillon: Criminalistics," in Philip John Stead, *Pioneers in Policing* (Montclair, N.J.: Patterson Smith, 1977), 121–147.

210. R. W. M'Claughry and John Bonfield, "Police Protection at the World's Fair," *North American Review* 156 (1893), 711–713.

211. Morn, *"The Eye That Never Sleeps"* (supra n. 125), 126.

212. Ibid.

persuaded to send a representative to demonstrate the "Henry Finger Print Method," which had been published five years earlier.[213] The IACP had also established a National Bureau of Criminal Identification to serve as a central repository of Bertillon cards of major criminals from around the country.[214] In the 1920s, this bureau was given over to the Justice Department. Eventually, its files and those from the federal penitentiary in Leavenworth were combined under the supervision of the FBI.

As with many techniques, fingerprinting took time to be accepted and used by American police, who were accustomed to more-familiar methods and who had already gone through the laborious process of being converted to the Bertillon method. In New York shortly after the turn of the century, the newly appointed police commissioner, William McAdoo, was eager that his department keep up with developments in Europe. Accordingly, in 1904 he sent a detective sergeant, Joseph A. Faurot, to London to learn what Scotland Yard was doing in the area of fingerprinting. Two years later, Faurot was able to prove the merits of the new identification technique to American skeptics. Back on foot patrol, he happened to arrest an Englishman who was lurking suspiciously in the Waldorf Astoria Hotel. Uncertain of his true identity, Faurot sent the suspect's fingerprints to Scotland Yard. The reply two weeks later confirmed that the Englishman was a professional hotel thief and fugitive from British justice.[215] Given prominent play in the New York newspapers, the incident helped persuade American police departments to develop fingerprint files on criminals. It also suggested the potentials of greater cooperation with foreign police departments.

At the 1905 annual convention of the IACP, Major Richard Sylvester, chief of the Washington, D.C., police and president of the association, delivered his annual report and address. The portion addressing international aspects of law enforcement, although excessively optimistic, reflected the sense of growing cooperation between police agencies around the world as well as within the United States:

> The International Association continues to grow in numbers and influence. . . . Police co-operation is more prompt and thorough

213. IACP, *Twelfth Annual Session*, May 22–25, 1905 (Washington, D.C.: IACP, 1905).
214. Ibid., 68–70.
215. Thorwald, *Century of the Detective* (supra n. 132), 98–99.

> throughout the world than ever before. There was a time when responses from authorities abroad were only obtained after the aid of the State Department had been invoked and procured, but such confidence has been established within a short time between the police authorities of our own and other lands that the delays, interferences and suspicions which once prevailed have generally disappeared. The interchange of domestic and foreign descriptive circulars has largely increased. We find the finger print of England and the finger print of United States filed within the police cabinets of the principal cities of these two great countries. The photographs and measurements of the criminals of Paris may be found in the galleries of the department in Washington, and vice versa. Our own cities have established an intercourse which operates as a preventive of crime, and which in the great majority of cases surely weaves a web about the criminal who is to be detected. The head of one police department enjoys personal as well as official acquaintance with that of another. The most recent applicances and modern methods of practice have been adopted. These are but a few of the advantages which have accrued through the maintenance of your association.[216]

Despite Sylvester's plaudits, the membership of the IACP was then, as now, composed almost entirely of American and a few Canadian police chiefs. Each year, invitations were sent to chiefs of police from around the world, and each year the great majority expressed their regrets at not being able to attend. Following World War I, which severely disrupted ties with European police departments, the establishment of Interpol undermined much of the need abroad for the U.S.-based association. But within the United States it continued to serve a valuable purpose by enhancing links between municipal police departments, advancing their professionalization, furthering a sense of police community and professional association, and heightening awareness of the international dimensions of law enforcement.

Although the sense that Americans could learn something from Europe in the area of policing had first emerged in the mid-nineteenth century, it was not until the first two decades of this century that serious study of the police systems across the Atlantic began. A number of the

216. IACP, *Twelfth Annual Session*, 16–17.

"studies" by police chiefs were little more than excuses for subsidized vacations to Europe, but many were seriously motivated by concern for the credibility and effectiveness of American police departments. One impetus was the desire to learn about new criminal investigative techniques—for instance, Faurot's fingerprinting expedition. Another impetus, prompted by the 1894 Lenox investigation into police corruption in New York, and similar investigations in other cities during the following decade, was the desire to learn why the European police agencies had been relatively successful in resisting corruption. Bureaucratic reorganization was one of the principal solutions being advocated in the United States. Accordingly, these studies focused on the organization of foreign police systems.

In 1902, Avery Andrews, a former police commissioner of New York appointed by Mayor Seth Low to recommend a scheme of reorganization for the New York Police Department (NYPD), visited Europe to study their police systems; his findings were published the next year in *The Cosmopolitan*.[217] Six years later, William McAdoo, no longer police commissioner of New York but still interested in police matters, studied the London police system and published his conclusions in *The Century Magazine*.[218] Perhaps the most comprehensive and influential study of Europe's police by an American was that of Raymond Fosdick, a young scholar who had spent a few years as a city investigator of corruption.[219] Funded by the police reform movement,[220] he spent the two years before the outbreak of the world war in Europe investigating police systems throughout the continent.[221] Some years later, in a similar study of municipal police departments in major American cities, Fosdick contrasted his findings in Europe with what he found to be the rather embarrassing situation in many American cities.[222] By this time, the study of European police administration by incoming police commissioners had become virtually a prerequisite for the job. As police historian Thomas Reppetto wrote concerning the appointment of Theodore Roosevelt's protégé, Arthur Woods, as New York's police commis-

217. See Avery D. Andrews, "The Police Systems of Europe," *The Cosmopolitan*, Mar. 1903, 495–504.

218. William McAdoo, "The London Police from a New York Point of View," *The Century Magazine*, Sept. 1909, 649–670.

219. Reppetto, *The Blue Parade* (supra n. 106), 77.

220. Fogelson, *Big-City Police* (supra n. 204), 62.

221. Raymond B. Fosdick, *European Police Systems* (New York: Century Co., 1916).

222. Fosdick, *American Police Systems* (supra n. 1).

sioner in 1914: "Though not exactly an administrative expert, he had made the ritual study of European police and moved in circles where the new science was being developed."[223] Yet another study was undertaken in 1926 by Sheldon Glueck, a graduate student at Harvard who later became one of the nation's leading criminologists. Commissioned by now former Commissioner Woods, who had retained his interest in comparative police studies, Glueck's report provided a succinct update of Fosdick's findings and recommendations.[224] Also significant was the convening of a National Conference on Criminal Law and Criminology at Northwestern University in 1909, one result of which was the establishment of a committee to translate the leading books of European criminology into English.[225]

Travel abroad by municipal police agents on criminal investigations appears to have been a relatively unusual occurrence. The principal exceptions involved the collection of fugitives from abroad, such as when two Saint Louis police officers traveled to New Zealand in 1885 to collect a much-desired fugitive.[226] The same appears to have been the case with respect to visits to the United States by foreign police officers—although cities such as New York certainly received a fair number of official and unofficial visits.[227] The principal opportunities for American and foreign police to interact arose at the world's fairs. In 1893, the Chicago Police Department prepared for the Exposition by collecting Bertillon cards from large city police departments throughout the United States, Canada, Mexico, and Europe and by inviting each department to send two members to the Exposition to surveil the crowds and exchange information and techniques with one another.[228]

Perhaps the most famous instance of an American detective pursuing an investigation overseas occurred in 1909. Rising concern in New York

223. Reppetto, *The Blue Parade*, 158. Woods did his study in 1907 following his appointment as head of the detective bureau.

224. The report was not published until 1974. See Sheldon Glueck, *Continental Police Practice in the Formative Years* (Springfield, Ill.: Charles C. Thomas, 1974).

225. Hartsfield, *American Response to Professional Crime* (supra n. 205), 184.

226. Furlong, *Fifty Years a Detective* (supra n. 133), 13.

227. The visit of a French police official, M. Casselari, is recounted in the memoir of the policeman Michael Fiaschetti (as told to Prosper Buranelli), *The Man They Couldn't Escape: The Adventures of Detective Fiaschetti of the Italian Squad* (London: Selwyn & Blount, 1928), 147–156 (also published under the title *You Gotta Be Rough* [Garden City, N.Y.: Doubleday, Doran, 1930]).

228. M'Claughry and Bonfield, "Police Protection at the World's Fair" (supra n. 210), 712–715.

over the spread of the notorious "Black Hand," as the Mafia was then called, had induced Commissioner of Police Theodore Bingham to set up a "Secret Service" specifically to deal with the Italian-born criminals. Bingham appointed as its chief Joe Petrosino, the highest-ranking Italian-American in the city's police force and already head of the department's Italian Squad. A legendary figure in Italy, where he was called the "Italian Sherlock Holmes," Petrosino was sent to Sicily.[229] His tasks were to determine which criminals had left Italy for the United States, to obtain copies of the penal certificates needed to deport members of the Black Hand from the United States, and to establish a network of agents capable of supplying the New York police authorities with similar information in the future. Petrosino began his mission in Rome, where he met with the Italian interior minister and obtained from him letters to the prefects in Sicily, Calabria, and Naples ordering them to assist the New York police agent in his investigation. Once in Sicily, Petrosino liaised with the local police and kept the U.S. consul in Palermo, William Henry Bishop, informed of his work. However, Petrosino operated primarily on his own, keeping secret his plan to set up a secret information network. He quickly obtained and forwarded to Bingham the records of several criminals, assuring him that more would follow soon. His mission came to a disastrous end when he was murdered in Palermo by unknown assailants; the local Mafia chieftan, Don Vito Cascio Ferro, claimed credit, but the available evidence suggested otherwise. Bishop attempted to undertake a thorough investigation of the assassination but was hindered both by the obstructionist efforts of Sicilian authorities and by a series of death threats, which restricted his movements.

In an attempt to salvage something of Petrosino's efforts, Bingham sent two additional detectives to Italy, including Petrosino's lieutenant on the Italian Squad, Anthony Vachris, and an Italian-speaking detective sergeant, John Crowley.[230] The two spent several months in Italy, where they succeeded in persuading the authorities in Rome—who preferred that the American detectives not travel to Sicily—to provide them with the penal certificates and photographs of hundreds of Italian ex-convicts

229. The following account is based largely upon Thomas Monroe Pitkin and Francesco Cordasco, *The Black Hand: A Chapter in Ethnic Crime* (Totowa, N.J.: Littlefield, Adams & Co., 1977); Arrigo Petacco, *Joe Petrosino*, trans. Charles Lam Markmann (New York: Macmillan Co., 1974; originally published in Italian in 1972); and George E. Pozzetta, "Another Look at the Petrosino Affair," *Italian Americana* 1 (1974), 81–92.

230. Pitkin and Cordasco, *Black Hand*, 121–137.

and to forward hundreds more thereafter. Optimistic expectations that their mission would succeed in ridding New York of hundreds of Black Hand members, however, were quickly dashed by the corrupt politics of New York. Acting at the apparent behest of Tammany Hall, Mayor George McClellan reportedly ordered that the fruits of Vachris's and Crowley's labors not be harvested. Although the city's secret service, with some help from the Italian Squad, shortly thereafter concluded a major drive against a prominent gang of Black Hand counterfeiters and extortionists, the NYPD's unusual initiative to strike a major blow against the mafiosi was effectively defused. Not until 1914, when the reform administration of Mayor John Purroy Mutchel appointed Arthur Woods as police commissioner, did the Black Hand once again need to fear the city's police enforcers.

In 1920, one of Petrosino's successors as chief of the Italian Squad, Michael Fiaschetti, embarked on a similar trip to Italy.[231] The purpose of the trip was to locate two fugitives accused of murder, to investigate the whereabouts of a backlog of other criminals who the police suspected had fled to Italy, and to identify the murderer of Petrosino. Working undercover in Rome and Naples, as well as in cooperation with the Italian police, Fiaschetti was able to penetrate the Camorra and accomplish most of his objectives. Two years later, in 1922, he was obliged to return to give testimony in the trial of one of the fugitives, who was being tried in Italy because as an Italian citizen he could not be extradited. With Mussolini's Fascists now in power, the threat from the Camorra was substantially diminished. The fugitive was convicted, and Fiaschetti was decorated by the Italian government for his work in the case.

Beyond the foreign exploits of Petrosino and Fiaschetti, the NYPD possessed one other claim to fame in the early annals of international law enforcement. Throughout the 1920s and into the 1930s, it attracted the beneficence of a wealthy businessman and police buff, Baron Collier,[232] whose particular interest was furthering the international coordi-

231. The following account is derived from the detective's autobiography; see Fiaschetti, *The Man They Couldn't Escape*, 253–284. See also Pitkin and Cordasco, *The Black Hand*, 214–215.

232. The story of Collier and the police is related more fully in Harry Söderman, *Policeman's Lot* (New York: Funk & Wagnalls, 1956), 270–271; and in Trevor Meldal-Johnsen and Vaughn Young, *The Interpol Connection: An Inquiry into the International Criminal Police Organization* (New York: Dial Press, 1979), 39–41.

nation of police efforts against crime.[233] Aided by the chief inspector of the police department and given the honorary title of Special Deputy Police Commissioner in Charge of Foreign Relations, Collier pursued his objective in a variety of forums. One of these was a group not unlike the IACP, founded in 1921, called the International Police Conference. Paying all of the expenses of its occasional conferences, Collier was able to attract police from around the world. To them he promoted the notion of a new organization, the International World Police, which would in his view supplement the efforts of the International Criminal Police Commission (ICPC, the organization later known as Interpol). He argued that his organization was necessary because neither the ICPC nor the Division of Identification in the Justice Department (formerly the IACP'S National Bureau of Identification) served as a clearinghouse for international police matters involving nonfederal police agencies. Most European police chiefs, however, felt that the ICPC was already sufficient to handle such matters. By the mid-1930s, all that remained of his grand scheme was an office on the first floor of the NYPD headquarters on Center Street with "International World Police" written on the door.[234]

Perhaps the only reason Collier's idea was given serious consideration by American police was that they considered the ICPC largely irrelevant to their needs at that time. Throughout the 1920s and 1930s, American police at both the federal and the municipal level were courted by the ICPC. The organizer of the first meeting, in 1923, invited the Washington, Chicago, and New York police departments to send delegates, but only the latter sent a representative.[235] During the following years, invitations were also sent to the Justice Department, and the United States was asked to become a full-fledged member of the organization. The federal government expressed little interest, however, responding that it had limited jurisdiction over many of the crimes that concerned the ICPC and that the United States would derive little benefit from becoming a member.[236] On occasion, the U.S. embassy in whatever country was hosting the ICPC conference would send its own delegate. In 1936, for instance, the vice-consul at the U.S. embassy in Belgrade

233. Baron Collier, "International World Police," *Journal of Criminal Law and Criminology*, Sept.–Oct. 1932.
234. Soderman, *Policeman's Lot*, 270–271.
235. Meldal-Johnsen and Young, *Interpol Connection*, 41.
236. Ibid., 44.

attended. In his report, he concluded that it "brought forth nothing that is not already known to the American police."[237] On the other hand, he argued, the ICPC helped to foster among the "chiefs of the various criminal police of the world"

> an esprit de corps in the commission and, at the same time, [enabled] them to discuss in a friendly but business like manner methods which may eventually be developed into a simple and uniform international system for combatting and controlling crime.[238]

In 1937, J. Edgar Hoover sent his assistant director, W. H. Drane Lester, as a delegate to the annual meeting being held in London. Lester's report to Hoover concluded that, although the United States would not benefit from membership as much as the Europeans, the opportunity to meet foreign counterparts and obtain information on criminals warranted joining the organization.[239] The following year, Hoover recommended to Congress that the United States become a member of the ICPC. Although the organization had already fallen under the domination of the Nazis, Congress agreed.

By the 1930s, significant transformations in the relationship between municipal police departments in the United States and both federal and foreign police agencies were already apparent. Federal police agencies had continued to gain in resources and jurisdiction, first as a result of federal enforcement of the Volstead Act, and thereafter as part and parcel of the Roosevelt administration's efforts to enhance federal involvement in most domains of governmental activity, including crime control. The rising profile of J. Edgar Hoover's FBI—with its reputation for professionalism in policing and its director's penchant for public relations—stood in stark contrast to the fading profile of big city police departments, many of which had been harshly criticized in 1931 by a national crime commission created by President Hoover and chaired by former Attorney General Wickersham.[240] On the other hand, many

237. Ibid., 48.

238. Ibid.

239. Ibid., 49–51.

240. See U.S. National Commission on Law Observance and Enforcement, *Lawlessness in Law Enforcement*, vol. 11; and Walker, *Critical History of Police Reform* (supra n. 204), 125–166.

police departments had sufficiently modernized their methods that some European police officials saw merit in studying their successes. In 1933, the chief constable of Glasgow, Percy Sillitoe, attended the IACP convention in Chicago, where he met with J. Edgar Hoover, and then set out to inspect police systems in Chicago, New York, Los Angeles, Berkeley, and Portland.[241] Impressed in particular with the NYPD's pioneering use of radio patrol cars, he brought one back to Great Britain and introduced it to British policing.

The FBN on the International Scene

The use of federal law enforcement agents to enforce federal narcotics laws dates back to before the twentieth century. Beginning in 1890, Congress levied increasingly heavy duties and restrictions on imported opium,[242] which were enforced primarily by Treasury agents assisting the Customs Service and occasionally by other agencies as well. Following two international conferences condemning the international narcotics traffic, Congress completely outlawed the over-the-counter sale of opiates and cocaine with the passage of the Harrison Narcotic Act in 1914. Drafted as a revenue law, its enforcement was delegated to a Narcotics Section in the Miscellaneous Division of the Bureau of Internal Revenue in the Treasury Department. During the 1920s, the gradually expanding narcotics enforcement unit bounced around the Treasury Department under the supervision of the Prohibition Unit. In 1930, with the death knells of Prohibition growing louder by the month, enforcement of the narcotics and alcohol laws was separated. The Bureau of Prohibition was shifted to the Justice Department, and a Federal Bureau of Narcotics (FBN) was created within the Treasury Department. There the latter remained until a major reorganization of the drug enforcement bureaucracy in 1968.

For the first thirty-two years of the FBN's existence, the agency was presided over by Commissioner Harry J. Anslinger.[243] As a Foreign

241. Sir Percy Sillitoe, *Cloak Without Dagger* (New York: Abelard-Schuman, 1955), 110; A. W. Cockerill, *Sir Percy Sillitoe* (London: W. H. Allen, 1975), 114–125. Sillitoe later served as director-general of MI5 from 1946 to 1953.

242. Millspaugh, *Crime Control* (supra n. 28), 79–80.

243. See John C. McWilliams, *The Protectors: Harry J. Anslinger and the Federal Bureau of Narcotics, 1930–1962* (Newark: University of Delaware Press, 1989).

Service officer during the 1920s, Anslinger had been assigned to the Bahamas, where he focused his efforts on stopping the smuggling of liquor into the United States. After he succeeded in persuading the British to establish landing certificates that would keep a record of all ship movements, the Treasury Department asked that Anslinger be detailed temporarily to its Prohibition Unit.[244] There he soon was appointed chief of the unit's Foreign Control Section, which had agents stationed in about ten foreign countries, before being elevated to assistant commissioner of Prohibition in 1929.[245] His successful investigation of a number of liquor smuggling cases, and his leading role in negotiating a smuggling information agreement among eighteen nations, contributed to his next promotion as head of the Prohibition Bureau's Narcotics Division.[246] When that division was legislated into a separate agency a few months later, Anslinger was appointed commissioner of narcotics. Given his background and perception of the problem, it is not surprising that Anslinger began his tenure by stressing the international dimension of the narcotics traffic. As the present Drug Enforcement Administration (DEA) noted in a history of its organization:

> Henceforth, Commissioner Anslinger announced in an order to his field forces, the federal narcotics effort would be concentrated on the sources of supply. The law that created the FBN authorized the commissioner to enforce the Harrison Act and to administer the regulatory requirements of the Narcotic Drugs Import and Export Act. . . . It also gave him authority to assign certain FBN officers at ports of entry. The main enforcement problem in his view was outside the United States, and in the years to come he would spend much of his time overseas. Meanwhile, in the absence of any adequate international instruments of control, he reached personal agreements with the heads of twenty counterpart agencies in foreign countries to exchange intelligence. As a result of the new international effort, seizures took a quantum leap

244. David F. Musto, *The American Disease: Origins of Narcotic Control* (New Haven: Yale University Press, 1973), 211.

245. The Foreign Control Division is discussed briefly in Laurence F. Schmeckebier, *The Bureau of Prohibition: Its History, Activities, and Organization* (Washington, D.C.: The Brookings Institution, 1929), 26–27, 156.

246. Douglas Clark Kinder, "Bureaucratic Cold Warrior: Harry J. Anslinger and Illicit Narcotics Traffic," *Pacific Historical Review* 50 (1981), 172–173.

> from 3,440 ounces of morphine in 1929 to 26,492 ounces in 1930.[247]

On the domestic front, Anslinger concentrated his energies on lobbying for stiffer and broader penalties for drug trafficking, building up his agency and protecting it from bureaucratic opponents, and going after the Mafia. Overseas, Anslinger became a leading figure in the international conferences and agencies concerned with narcotics, as well as the leading American diplomat on drug enforcement issues.[248] He also played a pioneering role in coordinating the collection and dissemination of intelligence on international drug trafficking. In 1931, Alan Block and John McWilliams have written, Anslinger "organized a secret panel of narcotics law enforcement officers from Canada, Great Britain, Germany, Switzerland, and France that functioned as a mini-Interpol, exchanging information on the movements of alleged international dope dealers. This 'Committee of One Hundred' functioned until 1939, when war in Europe disrupted global affairs."[249]

Anslinger had few inhibitions about sending his agents abroad on investigations, although they were required to seek his approval before going. Customs agents also continued to devote some of their time and resources to the drug traffic. Therein lay the roots of the bureaucratic tangles and occasionally cooperative ventures that have marked relations between the two agencies ever since. Mexico, then as now, presented perhaps the greatest challenge to U.S. drug control efforts because it was a drug supplier, transit country, and neighbor all wrapped in one. William O. Walker, in his history of inter-American drug control before World War II, notes:

> Based upon its record in the early 1930s, the government in Mexico City appeared willing to act with the United States to

247. "A Chronicle of Federal Drug Law Enforcement" (editorial), *Drug Enforcement* 7 (Dec. 1980), 26.

248. See Douglas Clark Kinder and William O. Walker III, "Stable Force in a Storm: Harry J. Anslinger and United States Narcotic Foreign Policy, 1930–1962," *Journal of American History* 72 (1986), 908–927, and three books co-authored by Harry Anslinger: with William F. Tompkins, *The Traffic in Narcotics* (New York: Funk & Wagnalls, 1953); with Will Oursler, *The Murderers* (New York: Farrar, Straus & Co., 1961); and with J. Dennis Gregory, *The Protectors* (New York: Farrar, Straus & Co., 1964).

249. Alan A. Block and John C. McWilliams, "On the Origins of American Counterintelligence: Building a Clandestine Network," *Journal of Policy History* 1 (1989), 357.

> stop smuggling. In 1930 the two countries concluded an informal agreement for the exchange of information on drugs. The following year officials sent a special agent to coordinate antidrug activity with Consul William Blocker in the Juarez–El Paso region. Mexico next requested that agents of both countries be permitted unrestricted border crossings there pursuant to their duties. The State Department and Bureau of Narcotics turned down the request, although United States agents would continue to cross into Mexico with Anslinger's express approval. By mid-1932 all the Mexicans had achieved was another informal arrangement for the exchange of information.[250]

Throughout the 1930s, a combination of drug enforcement agents, Treasury agents, customs officials from border stations, and U.S. consular officials continued to collect information on the smuggling of drugs across the border. Their work often was undertaken discreetly, even covertly, with the Mexican government being kept in the dark about many of the Americans' antismuggling activities. Indeed, even the consular officials were not always notifed of the agents' comings and goings.[251] Among the most active of the Treasury agents was the assisting supervisory customs agent at San Antonio, Texas—the previously mentioned Al Scharff—who cultivated close relations with Mexican officials and with the U.S. ambassador to Mexico, Josephus Daniels, but whose aggressive style alienated State Department officials wary of criminal controversies.[252] Scharff ran undercover operatives in Mexico, conducted his own investigations across the border, and played a significant role in Mexico's first major opium eradication campaign in 1938.[253]

Throughout the late 1930s and early 1940s, a major role in drug control diplomacy was played by H. S. Creighton, first in his capacity as the chief customs agent in San Antonio, Texas, and later as the Treasury Department's special representative in Mexico City. A passage from William Walker's history, dealing with talks in early 1941 between the Treasury agent and the Mexican official in charge of drug policy, is

250. William O. Walker III, *Drug Control in the Americas* (Albuquerque: University of New Mexico Press, 1981), 81.

251. Ibid., 82.

252. Roark, *Coin of Contraband* (supra n. 24); Walker, *Drug Control in the Americas*, 119.

253. Roark, *Coin of Contraband*, esp. 328–332, 356–359, 397.

indicative of the manner in which law enforcement operations were conducted:

> During the talks Creighton sought formal approval from the Avila Camacho administration for the continued presence of United States drug agents in Mexico. All prior agreements had been informal. Creighton's translator William K. Ailshie, vice consul at Mexico City, favored formalization because of the uneven record of drug control in Mexico. "The Federal Narcotics Service in Mexico City," he said, "does not have facilities to prevent the cultivation of poppy and marijuana plants throughout the Republic or the manufacture of opium derivatives, not to mention the illegal introduction of narcotics into Mexico, chiefly from Japan." The Mexicans soon agreed to formalization, but sought an official request from Washington. Herbert S. Bursley of the State Department attached a handwritten note to the report on the talks. It read: "I think it unfortunate that this question was aired. The situation regarding our people going to Mexico was OK." The United States therefore deemed a formal accord unwise, and Mexico did not insist upon one. Washington's reluctance did not greatly offend the Mexicans, for the government named Dr. Zaragoza Cuellar Garcia, new chief of the narcotics service, as correspondent with the United States for the exchange of narcotic information. His selection reinforced the informal arrangements first made in the 1930s.
>
> Throughout the year the United States continued the practice of sending agents into Mexico to investigate smuggling and other drug-related activities. Three special agents arrived at the height of anti-narcotic efforts in the fall. Discretion was in order. As [State Department official] George Morlock commented: "I said . . . that I thought Treasury should be very careful not to overrun Mexico with its agents."[254]

The most telling dimension to Walker's account of U.S. drug control diplomacy and enforcement in Mexico and Latin America during this period is the parallels it suggests with events a half-century later. Although the scale of operations has increased somewhat, as have the

254. Walker, *Drug Control in the Americas*, 164.

formalities associated with them, much remains the same: the problems of high- and low-level corruption, the economic incentives to engage in drug production and trafficking, the impossibility of adequately policing the border, the special role played by law enforcement agents stationed along the border, and the touchiness of both foreign governments and the U.S. embassy concerning the operations of freewheeling U.S. drug enforcement agents south of the border. Mexico's role has always been a special one, given the long land border and the magnitude of its illicit drug production, but in most other respects its situation has been mirrored elsewhere in Latin America.

During the 1930s, most opiates illegally consumed in the United States were smuggled from China.[255] In Shanghai, a Treasury agent named M. R. Nicholson kept tabs on smuggling of all sorts. John Pal, a former official of the Chinese Maritime Customs who stayed in Shanghai to make his fortune, referred to the agent in his memoirs. Recounting the story of some criminal escapade, Pal concluded by noting that one of the participants

> was shortly after this rounded up by U.S. Federal agent Nicholson as an escaped convict from the United States, wanted for a felony. Little "Nicky," one of the United States Treasury's smartest operators in the Far East, stood but 5 ft. 2 in. high and was therefore no muscleman in his job. All the same he brought Nemesis to bear upon numerous currency forgers and narcotic agents in the course of his stay. His was the tip which broke up a gang operating out of Shanghai around 1937–8 described by Harry Anslinger . . . in his *Saturday Evening Post* memoirs . . . and involving several deaths.[256]

255. See William O. Walker III, *Opium and Foreign Policy: The Anglo-American Search for Order in Asia, 1912–1954* (Chapel Hill: University of North Carolina Press, 1991); and Terry M. Parssinen and Kathryn S. Meyer, *Profit and Power: A History of International Narcotic Trafficking from the Eighteenth Century to the Present* (forthcoming).

256. John Pal, *Shanghai Saga* (London: Jarrolds, 1963), 161–162. The first part of Pal's book is a vivid description of the challenges facing a customs agent in cosmopolitan Shanghai. Nicholson's reports to Washington provide much of the source material for an excellent article on the opium traffic from China by Jonathan Marshall, "Opium and the Politics of Gangsterism in Nationalist China, 1927–1945," *Bulletin of Concerned Asia Scholars* 8 (July–September 1976), 19–48. Nicholson is also mentioned in Block and McWilliams, "On the Origins of American Counterintelligence," 358; and in Roark, *Coin of Contraband*, 330.

In Europe during the first years of Anslinger's tenure, narcotics matters were handled by the Treasury agents stationed in the major cities and by occasional trips by FBN agents. In 1936, it was decided to station three FBN agents in Europe. Francis X. Dilucia was based in Rome and focused on the heroin traffic out of Italy in which deported American mafiosi played a role. Charley Dyar and Quentin Violet both operated out of Paris, with the former specializing in northern Europe and the latter handling matters in the Balkans.[257] These three agents roved around Europe. "Jacks of all trades," in the words of one of their successors, "they did undercover, . . . they would energize and pull together different investigations, . . . and they would be the link in international cooperation, which was pretty good in any case."[258] Three years later, with war breaking out in Europe, they departed. A decade later, however, a new contingent of FBN agents would follow in their footsteps.

Conclusion

The internationalization of American law enforcement during the first 150 years of the nation's existence was in many respects quite modest, compared with either the European experience or the American experience to follow. It was not, however, insignificant. Along the land borders, particularly the border with Mexico, a striking array of private and public law enforcement officials, as well as a conspicuous number of foreign agents, investigated violations of both U.S. and foreign laws. And even apart from the land borders, evidence of U.S. involvement in international law enforcement endeavors could be found. Treasury agents investigated smuggling as part of their dual mandate to enhance federal revenue collection at the border and to keep out prohibited goods, animals, and people. Private detectives, notably those of the Pinkerton Agency, were commissioned not only by private individuals, corporations, and foreign governments but also by a federal government with few criminal investigative resources of its own to track down fugitives who had fled abroad and to investigate transnational criminal

257. Telephone interview with Jack Cusack, former regional director of the FBN in Europe, May 22, 1986.
258. Ibid.

activities. As municipal police departments developed their detective branches and investigative capabilities, they became part of an evolving transnational police community with a common interest in keeping track of known criminals and assisting one another in serious law enforcement matters. Along the borders, federal, state, and local police dealt with smugglers, bandits, and all sorts of other criminals who found advantage in operating on both sides of a border. And the assorted federal law enforcement agencies each engaged in international ventures related to their particular jurisdictions: the Secret Service to track down counterfeiters, the Federal Bureau of Narcotics to investigate drug smugglers, the Bureau of Investigation to search out white slave traders, con men, and assorted violators of the neutrality laws, the Border Patrol to stem illicit migration into the United States, and the U.S. marshals to assist the courts in arresting and transporting fugitives.

In comparing the internationalization of American law enforcement to the parallel process in Europe during the same period, three differences stand out. The first and most obvious was the relative detachment from the more intensive international interactions on the continent, in particular the international police conferences and the first decades of Interpol. Apart from the leading private detective agencies, and a few of the more innovative and forward-thinking public police agencies such as the NYPD, the U.S. Secret Service, and after 1930 the Federal Bureau of Narcotics, most American police officials devoted little thought to interactions beyond American borders. The second difference was the virtual absence of any extraterritorial law enforcement efforts against political émigrés. U.S. officials confronted little in the way of nationalist movements (although both the Mexican and the American Indian resistance to the territorial expansion of the United States might be categorized as such), and their concerns with anarchists, socialists, and other revolutionaries were almost entirely confined to the home front. Moreover, unlike Britain, the United States was the target of relatively few foreign pressures regarding the many political émigrés who sought refuge within its borders. Most foreign governments regarded the distant American continent as the most innocuous of havens for its enemies; indeed, the most persistent plaints—apart from those emanating from Mexico—arose from the British, who feared transnational Fenian activism. The third difference was most apparent along the Mexican border, where U.S. officials confronted transnational criminality of a sort long since absent within Europe and where they responded with an informality and disregard for neighborly sovereignty no longer permissible across the Atlantic. In late nineteenth-century Europe, no border stretched as far as that between Mexico and the United States, no frontier region retained a comparable openness and wildness, and no transnational tribes akin to the Comanches, Lipans, Kickapoos, or Apaches remained. By comparison, the roving gypsy bands that so concerned European police officials looked relatively tame.

A student of contemporary international law enforcement would observe that although the scope and magnitude of U.S. involvement in international law enforcement have expanded greatly, the fundamental obstacles, dilemmas, and nature of that involvement have not changed all that much. The very nature of the enterprise requires that law enforcement agents of one nation either depend on the resources of their foreign counterparts or else act unilaterally with a large measure of discretion. Like private detectives, they are largely deprived of the sovereign powers that normally accrue to the police agents of a state. They must rely on their own skills at cultivating personal relationships with foreign police, developing informant networks, and running undercover operations across or outside U.S. borders, and only occasionally on the diplomatic leverage of their government. They are rarely welcomed by the State Department's representatives abroad, and often viewed warily by local government officials, including many law enforcement agents. All this was true during the early years of U.S. involvement in international law enforcement, and all of it remains true today. The accretion of dozens of extradition and other law enforcement treaties, of internal agency guidelines for operating overseas, and of sophisticated telecommunications links among national police agencies have added new dimensions to the internationalization of law enforcement, but the basics of criminal investigation across and beyond national borders have remained more or less the same.

We examine the past, of course, not only because it helps to explain why the present is the way it is, but also because it suggests the possible way of the future. By 1939, the American involvement in international law enforcement was far less dependent upon navies and armies, posses and vigilante gangs, private police and bounty hunters, and even New York's finest, than ever before. Federal police agencies had assumed most of the tasks previously undertaken by this multitude of law enforcers, while those that could not readily be assumed proved no longer necessary. The American involvement in international law enforcement, like that of so many other nations, had been demilitarized, professionalized, and "policizied." This evolution was a function of changes in the nature of transnational criminality, of technological progessions in transnational intercourse, and of the increasingly high levels of international civil order, most notably on the high seas and along the United States' borders. But apart from its technological dimensions, the evolution was not an irreversible one. Even as the demands on law enforcers to suppress illicit slaving and recover fugitive slaves seemed unlikely to return, no comparable assurances could be offered regarding either the stability of the Mexican border or the passing of transnational criminal organizations susceptible only to the might of military forces. Changing markets and morals, and new laws and security interests, would transform the character of international law enforcement in ways both new and familiar.

Chapter Three

The Internationalization of U.S. Law Enforcement, 1940–1992

Expansion of International Efforts

That the scope of U.S. international law enforcement activities has expanded significantly since the close of World War II should come as little surprise. Indeed, the magnitude of that expansion pales beside the growth of other U.S. government activities abroad, ranging from intelligence, military, and economic ventures to diplomacy and foreign aid programs. All of these arose in good part from two developments: (1) the U.S. government's decision not to return to a policy of relative isolationism, as it had following World War I, but rather to assume leading roles in the struggle against communism and the invigoration of the capitalist world; and (2) the proliferation of transnational nongovernmental activities—financial, industrial, legal, environmental, and otherwise—in which the U.S. government perceived a political or regulatory interest.

Even absent this new internationalist perspective, however, two other developments would have obliged U.S. law enforcement officials to expand their international efforts. The more readily anticipated was the increase in transnational criminal activity that inevitably accompanied the dramatic growth in the volume of legitimate transnational intercourse. As transnational securities transactions, banking exchanges, commercial ventures, and credit card charges all increased dramatically, so too did the number of frauds associated with them. One need only assume that the criminal proportion of overall transnational economic activity has remained constant to conclude that the overall magnitude of transnational criminal activity must have increased dramatically. Less readily anticipated, from the perspectives of the 1940s and 1950s, was the remarkable growth in the illicit traffic in cannabis, cocaine, and heroin. Related to all these developments, moreover, was a persistent expansion in the reach of both the substantive criminal law and the claims of extraterritorial jurisdiction to cover an ever broader array of undesirable activities. Much of this was driven, as before, by domestic politics, but much of it was also initiated and driven—to a far greater extent than ever before—by the advocacy efforts of federal law enforcement officials.

The leadership role of the United States in the struggle against communism resulted in four significant developments in the domain of international law enforcement. First, police were needed to provide for law and order among the hundreds of thousands of U.S. military personnel stationed around the world, as well as between them and the host country populations. The criminal investigative dimension of this need was filled by the Army's Criminal Investigative Division (CID), the Naval Investigative Service (NIS), and the Air Force's Office of Special Investigations (AFOSI)—each of which has more agents stationed overseas than the Drug Enforcement Administration, which is the civilian agency with by far the greatest global presence. Second, a police training dimension was added to U.S. foreign assistance programs, motivated in part by the perceived need to bolster anticommunist governments and suppress communist insurgencies. Third, U.S. law enforcement agencies were charged with investigating violations of new laws prohibiting the export of weapons and sophisticated technology to pro-Soviet and other unfriendly governments. And fourth, espionage activities directed against the United States needed to be investigated, not just by the intelligence agencies but—because criminal prosecution of spies is the principal counterespionage weapon employed by democratic governments—by law enforcement agents as well.

Apart from the national security incentives, the most important factor contributing to the internationalization of both crime and law enforcement was the growing ease of transnational interactions as a consequence of developments in technology. Increasingly rapid and accessible jet travel permitted both criminals and police to travel easily and quickly almost anywhere in the world. Advances in telecommunications allowed criminals to conspire and commit crimes transnationally even as the same advances facilitated transnational exchange of information and coordination of joint investigations among law enforcement agents. Computers with international hookups presented new opportunities for criminals, both in defrauding legitimate actors and in setting up their own operations, but they also provided police with more efficient means of keeping track of transnational criminals, exchanging intelligence with foreign counterparts, and creating data bases on criminals and criminal activities. In all these respects, crime and law enforcement have been internationalized by technological developments in much the same way as other types of transnational commerce and governmental regulation.

Almost as significant were new laws that created new types of transnational crime. Some did so by criminalizing conduct that had not previously been criminalized. The Export Control Act of 1949 and subsequent legislation enhancing that act extended the reach of the criminal law to transnational activities that previously had been legal.[1] The crime of transnational money laundering did not exist until 1970 at the earliest, when Congress made it illegal to take $5,000 or more in or out of the United States without reporting that fact, and it attained independent standing only in 1986, when Congress criminalized the act of money laundering.[2] By 1990, enforcement of criminal laws directed at money laundering had become a major preoccupation of U.S. international law enforcement efforts. Other laws extended the reach of U.S. criminal jurisdiction abroad, such as by criminalizing terrorist and other offenses and conspiracies against U.S. citizens and interests that previously had fallen outside the purview of American courts.

Many of these developments followed naturally from the nationaliza-

1. Gernot Stenger, "The Development of American Export Control Legislation After World War II," *Wisconsin International Law Journal* 6 (1987), 1–42.

2. Ethan A. Nadelmann, "Unlaundering Dirty Money Abroad: U.S. Foreign Policy and Financial Secrecy Jurisdictions," *Inter-American Law Review* 18 (1986), 33–82.

tion of crime and crime control within the United States. The emergence of crime as a national issue, and of crime control as a federal responsibility, are best dated to 1964, when Senator Barry Goldwater focused attention on rising crime rates during his presidential campaign, and President Lyndon Johnson reluctantly responded by placing crime control on the federal agenda.[3] Both the nationalization of the crime issue and the federalization of crime control had received their first substantial impetuses during the 1930s, when the administration of Franklin Delano Roosevelt included crime control among the array of issues on his New Deal agenda.[4] Congressional interest in racketeering provided additional impetuses in following decades.[5] But by the 1960s, the inhibitions on federal intrusions into what had traditionally been perceived as domains of state jurisdiction had faded substantially. The Johnson administration laid the initial groundwork, after which the Nixon administration entered office committed to an aggressive federal involvement in crime control and a dramatic escalation in the "war on drugs."[6] The Ford and Carter administrations brought a diminution in the rhetoric as well as revelations of legal and illegal excesses by federal police agencies. But the Reagan and Bush administrations revived the crime issue and sponsored dramatic increases both in the reach of federal criminal laws and in the resources of federal criminal justice agencies. Despite modest reservations by its more liberal members, Congress endorsed most of these initiatives and occasionally supplemented them of its own accord.

The internationalization of crime and crime control represented extensions of these developments. Having declared a "war on drugs," the Nixon administration focused substantial attention and resources on the foreign sources of the heroin, cocaine, and most of the marijuana consumed in the United States. Indeed, the international dimension was attractive both because it offered a rare domain of criminal justice activity where the federal government could predominate over state and local agencies and because it provided an inviting political target for

3. Gerald Caplan, "Reflections on the Nationalization of Crime, 1964–1968," *Law and the Social Order* (Arizona State University Law Journal), 1973, 583–635.

4. See *Proceedings of the Attorney General's Conference on Crime*, Washington, D.C., Dec. 10–13, 1934, and the articles collected under the title, "Extending Federal Powers over Crime," in *Law and Contemporary Problems* 1 (1934), 399–508.

5. Craig M. Bradley, "Racketeering and the Federalization of Crime," *American Criminal Law Review* 22 (1984), 213–266.

6. Edward Jay Epstein, *Agency of Fear: Opiates and Political Power in America* (New York: G. P. Putnam's Sons, 1977).

those who preferred not to focus too much attention on the domestic causes for increasing illicit drug use. Similar motivations could be discerned in the international extensions of the antidrug campaign during the 1980s. The rapid growth of the federal law enforcement agencies—in particular, the Bureau of Narcotics and Dangerous Drugs and the DEA—also provided the institutional bases required to sustain a substantial international presence. As these agencies expanded their activities but found their investigations frustrated by both criminal ingenuity and restrictions on their investigative powers and capacities, they proposed and lobbied for new criminal legislation to improve their powers of detection and to increase the variety of legal stumbling blocks on which criminals and their accomplices might trip. The results were laws requiring information about financial transactions to be divulged, criminalizing involvement in the laundering of illicitly derived revenues, authorizing the forfeiture of assets associated with criminal activity, and otherwise seeking to complicate and uncover criminal endeavors.

For all of the U.S. law enforcement agencies, these developments have meant increases in interactions with foreign police, international travel, international investigations, and, for many of the agencies, foreign offices. Some U.S. police agents—notably those of the DEA and the military's criminal investigative units—have become intimately involved in the more operational aspects of criminal investigation abroad, typically in collaboration with foreign police officials. They have recruited and run informants, conducted physical and electronic surveillance, employed undercover operations, supervised controlled deliveries of illicit drugs and other illegal commodities, and so on. Many federal law enforcement agencies now station representatives overseas, and all are increasingly involved in developing and cultivating closer links with foreign counterparts. The internationalization of law enforcement, I should stress, has been very much a two-way street, even if most of the traffic still carry U.S. badges.

Three Models of Transnational Policing

Most international criminal law enforcement activities are aptly characterized as "transgovernmental relations"—a notion advanced by Robert Keohane and Joseph Nye Jr. to refer to "sets of direct interactions among sub-units of different governments that are not controlled or closely guided by the policies of the cabinets or chief executives of those governments."[7] High-level officials generally pay scant attention to the international activities of law enforcement agents or prosecutors—except when those activities assume political significance, attract media attention or otherwise threaten to disrupt other dimensions of a state's foreign relations. Criminal justice officials generally view international politics as a hindrance and seek to avoid involving high-level officials except when their intervention is required to gain leverage in transgovernmental interactions. In these respects, the police and prosecutors involved in international law enforcement, most of whom work for the Justice Department, have much in common with the lower-level officials in the Departments of Agriculture, Commerce, Energy, Labor, Transportation, and the Treasury charged with handling international matters. They all work for government agencies responsible primarily for domestic matters; they all are engaged in frequent interactions with foreign counterparts employed by comparable agencies; and they all seek to establish working relationships with those counterparts based upon shared expertise and divorced to some extent from considerations of high politics. International agreements negotiated at this level typically seek to depoliticize relations in a particular issue area, to set mutually acceptable standards for cooperation, and to establish channels for communication unburdened by the tensions generated by differing political and legal systems.

Three models are particularly useful in understanding the nature of transnational policing: the private detective, the liaison, and the transnational organization. The first sheds light on the more operational aspects of extraterritorial police activity. The second explains what most agents stationed abroad do; and the last applies most aptly to the military's criminal investigative units, the police advisory programs, and the DEA. The work that private detectives perform has much in common with the investigative work of publicly employed police investigators. The principal difference is that the former are obliged to pursue their vocation without benefit of any of the arrest and other powers conferred by a police shield. U.S. law enforcement agents abroad are in much the same position—with two caveats. On the one hand, the fact that they

7. Robert Keohane and Joseph Nye Jr., "Transgovernmental Relations and International Organizations," *World Politics* 27 (1974), 43.

represent and are employed by a foreign sovereign power often presents complications that to do not hamper private detectives. These may include not just local laws specifically proscribing foreign police agents from engaging in certain activities, but also the nationalist sensitivities and antagonisms that many police officials experience when confronted with foreign, and particularly U.S., police agents on their own turf. On the other hand, U.S. law enforcement agents benefit from both the spirit of international comity that often accompanies bilateral and multilateral law enforcement efforts and from the diplomatic pressures that their embassies and their government can exert when more congenial efforts fail to produce satisfaction.

Those caveats aside, the model of the private detective offers abundant clues to the nature of the U.S. law enforcement agent's tasks abroad, over and above those associated with the lack of sovereign police powers. Like the private detective, the police agent relies both on his own powers of investigation and on his contacts within government and without. His concerns are largely pragmatic ones, focused on the task at hand and relatively unconcerned with the broader ramifications or consequences of his activities. He is not particularly interested in changing local law enforcement systems, since his principal preoccupation is accomplishing the specific task requested by his client. Portions of his work—in particular, the rougher and more invasive forms of acquiring information—straddle the edge of what is legal under local law. Faced with the somewhat contradictory demands that he perform the functions of a police officer without having the powers normally associated with those functions, he relies on discretion in both senses of the word: he is circumspect yet flexible, cautiously undertaking whatever is within "the effective limits" of his power.[8]

The second model is that of the liaison, in the dual role of formal representative and informal "fixer." Like the assorted representatives of the many non–law enforcement agencies that increasingly crowd U.S. embassies, few of whom engage in detective-like activities, U.S. law enforcement agents stationed abroad are expected to act both as official representatives of their agencies and as "fixers" for the assorted requests and problems that come their way. U.S. agents abroad often find their days crowded with fielding inquiries from U.S.-based agents, transmit-

8. "Effective limits" should be distinguished from the narrower notion of legal limits. The term is taken from Kenneth Culp Davis, *Discretionary Justice* (Urbana: University of Illinois Press, 1971), 4.

ting requests for information and other assistance between local police agencies and U.S.-based law enforcement agencies, serving as hosts for fellow agents flown in on specific investigations, arranging reservations and programs for visiting politicians and high-level officials, dealing with the media, giving speeches, and attending assorted social functions.

The most comprehensive model—in that it sheds light not only on the nature of the agent's tasks but also on the objectives of his agency and the ramifications of its activities—is that of the transnational organization. Samuel Huntington distinguished the "transnational organization" from "international organizations" and defined it as "a relatively large, hierarchically organized, centrally directed bureaucracy [that] performs a set of relatively limited, specialized, and, in some sense, technical functions . . . across one or more international boundaries and, insofar as it is possible, in relative disregard of those boundaries."[9] His formulation highlighted the important similarities between governmental agencies such as the Central Intelligence Agency (CIA), the Army, and (although Huntington did not note it) the DEA, on the one hand, and nongovernmental organizations such as IBM, the Catholic Church, and the Pinkerton Detective Agency, on the other. Indeed, in some respects, the international activities of the DEA, and the obstacles encountered by it, are atypical of most government agencies and far more typical of multinational corporations. Like multinational corporations, the DEA's offices abroad become to some extent a part of the society they enter and must adapt their operations to local laws and customs. But as powerfully connected outsiders with substantial resources of their own, they are also occasionally able to effect changes in local laws and oblige adaptations in local customs to suit their needs. And like businessmen everywhere, DEA agents and their foreign counterparts are part of a transnational subculture based on common functions and objectives. What making a profit is to businessmen regardless of their nationality, so catching the criminal is to cops all over the world.

Huntington's formulation is peculiarly useful for our purposes, and for reasons not explicitly stated in his analysis. In pointing out the important similarities between governmental and nongovernmental transnational organizations, he laid his finger on one of the more important innovations of modern states in responding to the challenge

9. Samuel Huntington, "Transnational Organizations in World Politics," *World Politics* 25 (1973), 333.

of an increasingly complex and multidimensional interdependent world. On the one hand, the badge and gun of the police officer, and the criminal laws he or she enforces, continue to represent the ultimate symbols of a government's sovereignty. Governments understandably place a high priority on maintaining a monopoly over these symbols. Even the most compliant of governments is unwilling to tolerate the exercise of a foreign government's police powers within its territory; concessions to the right of police from neighboring states to enter one's territory in "hot pursuit" of fleeing criminals remain, for instance, very much the exception. The presence of foreign police may be accepted, but virtually never the legal authority that underpins them in their own country. On the other hand, the experience of the DEA demonstrates that it is possible for a state agency—and not just any state agency, but one specifically charged with performing the most sovereign of a state's functions—to operate and accomplish its objectives extraterritorially despite the limitations imposed by the sovereign prerogatives of foreign states. The key to the DEA's success lies in its adoption—albeit more by chance than by calculation—of the organizational model and operating principles associated with nongovernmental transnational organizations. "Only organizations that are disinterested in sovereignty," Huntington observed, "can transcend it."[10]

The Public Safety Program and Its Successors: Training Foreign Police

The U.S. experience with extending police assistance to foreign governments dates back to the first decades of the century, when U.S. Marines occupied Caribbean and Central American nations to promote internal security and U.S. interests.[11] Before departing, the occupation authorities did their utmost to ensure that native military and police forces were properly trained and disposed to maintain stability and safeguard U.S. interests. In Cuba, the first country to receive U.S. police assistance, the U.S. Marines created, trained, and equipped a constabulary following

10. Ibid., 368.
11. See Whitney T. Perkins, *Constraint of Empire: The United States and Caribbean Interventions* (Westport, Conn.: Greenwood Press, 1981).

the 1898 occupation, and retired New York City police officers helped organize the Havana police system.[12] The U.S. War Department established additional constabularies in Haiti in 1915, the Dominican Republic in 1916, and Panama in 1918, and the State Department arranged a private contract whereby a former U.S. officer in the Philippine Constabulary was hired to organize the Nicaragua Constabulary.[13] Governments other than the United States did likewise, albeit not quite on the same scale in Latin America and the Caribbean. During the mid- and late 1930s, the State Department and U.S. law enforcement and intelligence officials, as well as the British Secret Service and the German Gestapo, assisted Latin American police in their anticommunist efforts.[14] And during the 1940s the task of directing the reorganization of the Iranian national police force fell to a former superintendent of the New Jersey State Police, H. Norman Schwarzkopf.[15]

Following World War II, the U.S. experience with training new police forces in occupied countries, such as Japan and Germany, as well as in Greece and Turkey, set the stage for the expansion of police training to other parts of the world. Initially, the promotion of police and paramilitary training fell to the CIA, the Pentagon, and the Civil Police Administration (CPA) (a branch of the Agency for International Development's predecessor, the International Cooperation Administration). Created in 1955, the CPA was headed by Byron Engle, a former police officer from Kansas City who had played a leading role in restructuring the Japanese police during the postwar occupation and then joined the CIA in 1950 to train foreign police and intelligence agencies. Engle built a force of eighty police advisors, whom he stationed around the world. Training was provided in-country, at the Inter-American Police Academy in the Panama Canal Zone, and in the United States, with the International Association of Chiefs of Police playing a role in placing foreign police officials in police departments around the United States as well as at FBI headquarters.[16] The agency focused its efforts on developing the more technical capabilities of foreign police forces in such matters as admin-

12. Martha K. Huggins, "U.S.-Supported State Terror: A History of Police Training in Latin America," *Crime and Social Justice* 27/28 (1987), 149–171.

13. Ibid., 151.

14. Ibid., 152–153.

15. Roger Cohen and Claudio Gatti, *In the Eye of the Storm: The Life of General H. Norman Schwarzkopf* (New York: Farrar, Straus & Giroux, 1991), 47–56.

16. Huggins, "U.S.-Supported State Terror," 160.

istration, record keeping, and traffic control. This was viewed as an indirect means of enhancing crime control capabilities, promoting political stability, and ensuring the conditions necessary for economic growth. It also provided a cover for many of the CIA's operatives and activities related to more political dimensions of policing.[17]

The Office of Public Safety (OPS) was created by the Kennedy administration in 1962 with the intention of centralizing all police assistance to foreign countries.[18] Housed within the Agency for International Development (AID) and headed by Byron Engle, the OPS represented an expansion of the CPA's scope and mission. During its twelve-year existence, it provided aid to police agencies in approximately fifty Third World nations, spending more than $300 million on training, weaponry, and telecommunications and other equipment.[19] Hundreds of active and retired American police officers were sent to these countries, where they trained tens of thousands of police officials in administration, riot and traffic control, interrogation, surveillance, intelligence, and assorted other tasks. Thousands of mid- and high-level police officials from those countries came to Washington to study at the OPS-run International Police Academy, which had replaced the Panama-based police school. Because Great Britain and France had undertaken similar responsibilities in their former colonies, the OPS's efforts focused on other areas, primarily Latin America but also Southeast Asia, South Korea, and Ethiopia, Liberia, and Zaire.[20] The two largest recipients of OPS assistance were South Vietnam and Thailand. In Latin America the most substantial recipient was Brazil. In fiscal year 1968, the program attained its peak strength, with a budget of $55.1 million and a total of 458 advisors in thirty-four countries.[21]

17. Thomas Lobe, *United States National Security Policy and Aid to the Thailand Police* (Denver: Graduate School of International Studies, University of Denver, 1977), 4; Thomas Lobe, "U.S. Police Assistance for the Third World" (Ph.D. diss., University of Michigan, 1975); Huggins, "U.S.-Supported State Terror."

18. U. Alexis Johnson, "The Role of Police Forces in a Changing World," *Department of State Bulletin*, Sept. 13, 1971, 280–283.

19. For an official U.S. government perspective on the OPS, see the Congressional testimony of AID administrator John Hannah in *Foreign Assistance and Related Agencies Appropriations for 1974: Hearings Before the Subcommittee on Foreign Operations and Related Agencies of the House Committee on Appropriations*, 93d Cong., 1st Sess., Part 2, 181–194 (1973).

20. Ernest Lefever, "U.S. Public Safety Assistance: An Assessment" (1973), cited in Lobe, *U.S. National Security Policy and Aid to the Thailand Police*, 6.

21. Alan K. Yu, "U.S. Assistance for Foreign Police Forces," (Washington, D.C.: Congressional Research Service, 1989), 5.

Like all U.S. programs to train foreign police, the OPS confronted numerous dilemmas. The first was the problem of providing training to police in countries whose socioeconomic systems, political cultures, and law enforcement institutions varied dramatically from those in the United States.[22] There was value in teaching foreign police specific techniques, ranging from traffic and riot control to surveillance methods and administrative measures, that could be easily transferred or adapted to foreign environments. But the capacity of American police officers to apply what they had learned in the cities and suburbs of American cities to far-reaching police reform in less-developed countries was another matter. As one OPS advisor put it:

> Cement police just weren't able to advise rice paddy cops. For instance, a whole bunch of OPS advisors originated out of Walnut Creek, California, one of San Francisco's bedroom cities. When they were suppressing crime in Walnut Creek, that meant shoplifting, traffic violations, family squabbles, petty stealing, throwing beer bottles out of speeding cars, and some Friday night mooning. Are their experiences going to help poor countries?[23]

A second problem, well described by Martha Cottam and Otwin Marenin, was the tension between the two competing models of effective policing promoted by OPS officials:

> State Department officials and OPS advisors tended to argue for a civil police force subject to law, public demands, and legally instituted political authority. Civil, democratic police forces are visible, dispersed, and accessible; their members live among the people and conduct their work in the open. They use arms and force sparingly and concentrate on maintaining order, controlling crime, and providing services.
>
> In contrast, U.S. officials working for secret and military agencies tended to argue for a paramilitary, intelligence-oriented counterinsurgency police force. Such forces tend to be concen-

22. Otwin Marenin, "United States' Aid to African Police Forces: The Experience and Impact of the Public Safety Assistance Programme," *African Affairs* 85 (1986), 509–544; Thomas Lobe, "The Rise and Demise of the Office of Public Safety," *Armed Forces and Society* 9 (1983), 187–213.

23. Cited in Lobe, *U.S. National Security Policy and Aid to the Thailand Police*, 10.

> trated for easy command: they are armed, secretly or openly repressive, concerned with gathering intelligence, and subject to direct political control.[24]

Despite efforts to reconcile these two models, Cottam and Marenin observed, the paramilitary one ultimately prevailed.

A third problem was the OPS's real and perceived association with political policing in foreign countries. Much of the impetus for establishing the OPS as a separate entity had derived from the Kennedy administration's strong interest in counterinsurgency. The creation of Special Force units and more general counterinsurgency training within the military was one response. The OPS was another, reflecting the recognition that counterinsurgency efforts in many countries were conducted primarily by the police, rather than the military. Although often scorned by CIA agents abroad as just police trainers, OPS advisors in many countries developed close relationships with the CIA, provided occasional cover for intelligence operations, and pursued similar goals. Their success in accomplishing their more immediate political objectives depended in good part upon their ability to develop close relationships with local police. Wherever the host government was unpopular and/or repressive, the OPS's association with the police, who epitomized the regime's power and methods, proved harmful to their public image in both the United States and the host country.

A fourth problem, which would ultimately play a significant role in the demise of the OPS, was that of police torture.[25] Although the stated OPS policy was adamantly against such methods, although such practices were explicitly condemned in classes at the International Police Academy, and although many OPS advisors personally abhorred the use of torture, the OPS could not avoid being associated with such methods. Field telephones provided with OPS funding ended up being used to administer electric shocks during interrogations. Some OPS advisors acknowledged the impossibility of "teaching" foreign police not to resort to such methods, and some even condoned them. Reports periodically emerged of Americans thought to be OPS advisors being present at, and even conducting, interrogations involving physical torture. The bottom

24. Martha Cottam and Otwin Marenin, "Predicting the Past: Reagan Administration Assistance to Police Forces in Central America," *Justice Quarterly* 6 (1989), 598–599.

25. The information in this and the following paragraph is from A. J. Langguth, *Hidden Terrors* (New York: Pantheon Books, 1978).

line, however, was that many police agencies that had received training from OPS advisors regarded the torture of suspects as an efficient and legitimate means of interrogation. In some cases, moreover, police agencies that had not previously resorted to torture on a systematic basis began to do so at the same time that OPS officials arrived to advise them. Even where not directly implicated, the OPS was found guilty by association.

By the early 1970s, Congressional critics of the OPS were beginning to question whether the agency's political liabilities outweighed the benefits in foreign police efficiency. Senator James Abourezk in particular focused public attention on the agency's abuses and associations with police torture in the Third World. Disclosures that the CIA's Operation Phoenix in Vietnam, funded in part by OPS, had tortured and killed thousands of suspected Vietcong members, many of whom had been incarcerated in the notorious "tiger cages" at Con Son prison, proved especially damaging.[26] With no powerful constituency willing to expend political capital in its support, the OPS was gradually phased out, closing its doors in 1974. At the same time, the use of foreign assistance funds to provide overseas training, advice, or financial support for foreign police, prison, or other internal security forces was legally prohibited by Congress, although an exemption was inserted to preserve drug enforcement training programs.[27] The final blow to the OPS was delivered by the Greek movie director Costa Gavras in his 1973 movie, *State of Siege*. Based on the true story of the 1970 kidnapping and execution of an OPS advisor, Dan Mitrione, by the Tupamaro guerrilla organization in Uruguay, the movie dramatized and distorted the OPS advisor's involvement in political policing and torture.[28] Combining ugly truths with abundant rumors, Gavras's powerful movie contributed to the growing sentiment in Congress that the United States should avoid being tainted by too close an association with the instruments of repression in Latin America.[29]

26. See the unpublished memorandum by the Congressional Arms Control and Foreign Policy Caucus, "Police Aid to Central America: Yesterday's Lessons, Today's Choices" (1986), 4.

27. See Section 660 of the Foreign Assistance Act of 1961 (P.L. 87-195), as amended on Dec. 30, 1974.

28. See Langguth, *Hidden Terrors*.

29. The Public Safety Program has been the subject of extensive critical analysis by leftist research organizations, which have compiled reliable information on the abuses and irregularities that attended its efforts. See Michael T. Klare and Cynthia Aronson, *Supplying Repression: U.S. Support for Authoritarian Regimes Abroad* (Washington, D.C.: Institute for Policy Studies,

In 1971, a staff member of the Senate Foreign Relations Committee, Pat Holt, reported on the OPS program in one Central American country. His account provides a useful summary of the activities and dilemmas of the OPS program:

> From its beginning in 1957 through fiscal year 1971, the AID public safety program has accounted for $3,787,000 or a little more than one per cent of the total post–World War II aid to Guatemala. There are currently in Guatemala six public safety advisors.
>
> The public safety program in Guatemala has had an unusally high component of equipment. The police force in Guatemala City has been completely supplied with radio patrol cars and a radio communications net has been installed. Funds have also been provided for a National Police Academy, which is yet to be built. Other than this, the program has been mainly devoted to training—on-the-job in Guatemala, in the International Police Academy in Washington, in the Canal Zone, and in third countries (mainly Puerto Rico and Colombia).
>
> The program has obviously had an impact on the Guatemalan police—after all, the blue patrol cars are highly visible. The lesson plans for the training courses taught in Guatemala by the public safety advisors say all the right things about how to control mobs with minimum force, to respect the rights of suspects under interrogation, etc.
>
> But the police in Guatemala continue to be held in low public esteem. (I upset a university rector by arriving with a police escort—insisted on by the Embassy to insure I was not kidnapped. The rector said that the mere presence of police in the vicinity, even though the policeman was only waiting for me, made him nervous. And not without reason. A few days later, a professor of economics was kidnapped by government agents. On another day, I went to a university in a taxi by myself, and

---

1977; rev. ed. 1981); Center for Research on Criminal Justice, *The Iron Fist and the Velvet Glove: An Analysis of the U.S. Police* (Berkeley, Calif.: Center for Research on Criminal Justice, 1975), 87–102; Mike Klare, "Over There: Policing the Empire," in National Action/Research on the Military-Industrial Complex (NARMIC), *Police on the Homefront* (Philadelphia: NARMIC, 1971), 104–118; and Michael McClintock, *The American Connection*, vol. 2: *State Terror and Popular Resistance in Guatemala* (London: Zed Books, 1985).

> everything was perfectly peaceful.) The police are widely admitted to be corrupt (and with a take home pay of $82 a month, who is to cast the stone?) and are commonly held to be brutal.
>
> The argument in favor of the public safety program in Guatemala is that if we don't teach the cops to be good, who will? The argument against is that after 14 years, on all the evidence, the teaching hasn't been absorbed. Furthermore, the U.S. is politically identified with police terrorism.
>
> Related to all this is the fact that the Guatemalan police operate without any effective political or judicial restraints, and how they use the equipment and techniques which are given them through the public safety program is quite beyond U.S. control. They receive their political direction from very hard-line right-wingers who have been itching for a confrontation with students. The judiciary is intimidated—not by the police, but by the guerrillas who regularly secure the release of their comrades by threatening judges. This is one reason why the corpses of alleged guerrillas are being found on roadsides instead of the bodies of live guerrillas being produced in court.
>
> AID public safety advisors are not supposed to participate in police operations. Yet they have accompanied Guatemalan police on anti-hippie patrols. (A reportedly good grade of marijuana grows wild in parts of Guatemala, a fact which has brought on a modest influx of long-haired North American youth and which can be expected to bring more as the word spreads.) They have also worked with Guatemalan police in polygraph operations.
>
> On balance, it seems that AID public safety has cost the United States more in political terms than it has gained in improved Guatemalan police efficiency.[30]

Despite the demise of the OPS in 1974, many of its activities persisted under different agency umbrellas, where the advisors often found new employment. Some activities were simply transferred to other divisions of the AID. In 1973, Congress authorized the Law Enforcement Assistance Administration, established in 1968 to assist in state and local law enforcement development, to provide technical assistance to foreign

30. *Guatemala and the Dominican Republic: A Staff Memorandum Prepared for the Use of the Subcommittee on Western Hemisphere Affairs of the Senate Committee on Foreign Relations*, 92d Cong., 1st Sess. (1971).

governments in the areas of drug enforcement, skyjacking, and terrorism.[31] More foreign police were invited to attend training sessions at the FBI Academy in Quantico, Virginia. The State Department's international drug control program, which had grown rapidly during the early 1970s, provided a global umbrella for any activities that could be linked to drug enforcement. Quite a number of Public Safety advisors found positions with the State Department's narcotics assistance units in the major drug-producing countries.[32]

The principal successor to the OPS program was the federal drug enforcement agency, which was undergoing a dramatic international expansion (and bureaucratic reorganization) at the same time that the OPS was winding down its activities. As the number of U.S. drug enforcement agents stationed abroad rose from about 24 in 1969 to more than 200 in 1975, a number of OPS officers merely switched organizations. With their foreign experience and extensive contacts among local police forces, they were ideally placed to facilitate the drug enforcement agency's rapid international expansion. Although their mandate was now restricted to drug matters, they no longer operated under the restraints imposed by the OPS program. Indeed, they were expected to become directly involved in local drug enforcement investigations to a greater extent than they had in their capacity as OPS advisors. During the same six-year period, the number of foreign police officials trained by the DEA (but paid for by the State Department's narcotics assistance program) in both U.S. and in-country schools rose from zero to more than 2,000 a year before declining somewhat in the latter half of the 1970s.[33] Substantial numbers also received training from the U.S. Customs Service. Where once U.S. police assistance had focused on developing police capabilities in general and counterinsurgency capabilities in particular, it now focused almost entirely on drug enforcement agencies and tasks. A foreign police agency interested in

31. See Section 515(c) of the Crime Control Act of 1973, cited by an LEAA official in *Departments of State, Justice, Commerce, the Judiciary, and Related Agencies Appropriations for 1975: Hearings Before a Subcommittee of the House Committee on Appropriations*, 93d Cong., 2d Sess., Part 1 (1974).

32. See Comptroller General of the United States, *Stopping U.S. Assistance to Foreign Police and Prisons*, General Accounting Office Report to the Congress, Feb. 19, 1976, 20–27.

33. See *Departments of State, Justice, Commerce, the Judiciary, and Related Agencies Appropriations for 1977: Hearings Before a Subcommittee of the House Committee on Appropriations*, 94th Cong., 2d Sess., Part 4 (1976), 1073.

obtaining U.S. training and funds for equipment had little chance of success if it could not establish some connection with drug enforcement.

Beginning in 1983, the Reagan administration began urging Congress to permit the renewal of OPS-type training programs. In testimony before a Congressional subcommittee investigating torture, the assistant secretary of state for human rights and humanitarian affairs, Elliott Abrams, called for changes in Section 660, the 1974 amendment to the Foreign Assistance Act that had banned foreign police assistance. As had OPS advocates one and two decades previously, he argued:

> There are still a large number of police forces in the world where they simply don't understand that they can effectively do their work without indiscriminate violence and brutality. Perhaps if they learned a little bit more about modern professional police tactics, they would be more effective and more compassionate.[34]

Increasingly concerned about the activities of right-wing and left-wing death squads in Central America, Congress responded to the administration's appeals by authorizing a number of partial waivers to Section 660.[35] The first, in late 1983, authorized the creation of the Anti-Terrorism Assistance Program, coordinated by the State Department's Office of Counterterrorism Programs, to train foreign police (albeit only in the United States) in protecting aviation and other transportation systems, strategic installations, and VIPs from terrorist attacks, in managing bombs and explosives, and in responding to hostage and other crisis situations;[36] the budget for this program rose from $2.5 million in its first year to $10 million in fiscal year 1990. A second waiver, in 1984, authorized the International Criminal Investigative Training Assistance Program (ICITAP) as part of the State Department's Administration of Justice Program directed at instituting judicial reform projects in Latin America and the Caribbean.[37] In August 1985, two additional waivers were enacted: one to allow the Defense Department to provide military

34. Congressional testimony of Elliott Abrams, May 16, 1984, cited in an article critical of renewed police training by Holly Burkhalter and Alita Paine, "Our Overseas Cops," *The Nation*, Sept. 14, 1985, 197.

35. The information in this paragraph is from Yu, "U.S. Assistance for Foreign Police Forces"(supra n. 21).

36. Foreign Assistance Act of 1961, Part II, Chapter 8, Sections 571–576, codified at Section 572 of the act.

37. Ibid., Section 534.

training to national police programs in Costa Rica and a number of Eastern Caribbean nations, most of which claim no standing military forces;[38] and another, stimulated by the June 1985 guerrilla attack on an outdoor café in San Salvador that killed four off-duty U.S. Marines and nine others, to provide emergency police assistance to El Salvador and Honduras.[39]

The assistance to El Salvador, which also included a specific allotment to train a special police unit to investigate human rights cases, quickly drew most of the attention from human rights organizations, Congressional critics, and the media.[40] Many of the responsibilities previously undertaken by the OPS were assumed by the FBI. A selected group of Salvadoran police recruits were invited to attend an intensive criminal investigative training program by the FBI in Puerto Rico. Upon returning to El Salvador, they were assigned to investigate human rights abuses, including the June 1985 attack on the café.[41] The FBI also trained a police unit to provide protection for judges and witnesses in politically sensitive trials.[42] By 1989, the cumulative efforts of the FBI, the AID, the U.S. military, and the State Department had resulted in the creation of an El Salvador Commission on Investigations specifically to investigate politically motivated and other serious crimes, and a well-trained Special Investigative Unit (SIU) and forensic laboratory to conduct the investigations. A report on the Salvadoran investigative unit by the U.S. General Accounting Office in mid-1990 concluded that it had succeeded, despite substantial political interference, in "building a reputation as an impar-

38. Ibid., Section 660(c).

39. Ibid., Section 660(d).

40. Lindsey Gruson, "Salvador Divided over Aid to Police," *New York Times*, Oct. 22, 1987, A11. A fine historical and critical analysis of U.S. police assistance to El Salvador, which also addresses most of the broader issues raised by the OPS and the successor programs, is Stephanie Nichols Simonds, "United States Aid to Central American Police—A Policy Analysis: The Case of El Salvador, 1957–1988" (senior thesis, Princeton University, 1988). See also the report by Jim Lobe, Anne Manuel, and David Holliday, "Police Aid and Political Will: U.S. Policy in El Salvador and Honduras, 1962–1987" (Washington, D.C.: Washington Office on Latin America, Nov. 1987).

41. James LeMoyne, "Duarte Meets FBI on Raid Inquiry," *New York Times*, June 27, 1985.

42. These and other developments in U.S. police and judicial assistance to Latin America are discussed in a brief report by the Bureau of Public Affairs, U.S. State Department, *Hemispheric Cooperation in the Administration of Justice*, Special Report No. 145, Apr. 1986; and in an unpublished memorandum by the Congressional Arms Control and Foreign Policy Caucus, "Police Aid to Central America," which argued against a renewal of police training until *after* the "rule of law" has been established in Central America.

tial, professional, investigative unit"—albeit one that devoted less attention to human rights cases than was initally intended.[43]

Whether the police training programs in place by the early 1990s evolve into a program comparable to the OPS will depend as much upon the political climate as upon their capacity to avoid the pitfalls that contributed to the demise of the OPS. The OPS failed in part because it never successfully separated itself from the brutal techniques used by the foreign police with which its advisors were associated. In this respect, the emphasis placed in the mid-1980s on training foreign police to investigate human rights abuses and right-wing death squads provided somewhat of an antidote to memories of the OPS's bad associations. Equally important, however, was the significant change in the American political climate regarding foreign policy. In the early 1970s, the growing criticism of the OPS program reflected the strong desire to cleanse American hands of any identification with oppression overseas—one that contributed to the popular sentiment for withdrawing from Southeast Asia, to the emergence of human rights as a substantive foreign policy concern, and even to such low-profile measures as the 1974 "Mansfield Amendment" restricting DEA involvement in foreign police operations. Ultimately, a few too many reports of OPS advisors attending brutal interrogations obscured the fact that the vast majority of OPS advisors had avoided such situations and often opposed the use of torture. But the few accurate reports of such OPS improprieties, combined with a high degree of sensitivity to foreign misperceptions of the OPS, were sufficient in the political climate of the early 1970s to seal the agency's fate. During the 1980s, by contrast, the Reagan administration proved itself far more willing, and politically able, to dirty its hands abroad in support of U.S. foreign policy objectives regardless of the appearance created by such activities.

One of the paradoxes of foreign police training programs such as the OPS or the FBI's initiatives is that they are highly susceptible to public criticism precisely because they are the least secretive of such undertakings. Both the CIA and the U.S. military, for instance, have been involved in training foreign counterterrorist units in Central America. As the *New York Times* correspondent in El Salvador noted in mid-1985, these activities are far more suspect than the FBI's Central American efforts:

43. U.S. General Accounting Office, *Foreign Aid: Efforts to Improve the Judicial System in El Salvador*, GAO/NSIAD-90-81, May 1990.

American military advisors have also trained a special police antiterrorist team to be used in urban areas, according to a spokesman for the United States Embassy here. The spokesman said the training was legal because the antiterrorist unit, although drawn from the ranks of the police forces, had been placed under the direct command of the Chief of Staff of the army and was therefore a military unit, rather than a police unit.

The distinction appears somewhat dubious, since army officers command all police units here and since each police force also has battalions that are indistinguishable from regular army units and in fact are deployed in sweeps against rebel forces as part of army operations.

A great deal of confusion appears to surround the new American-trained antiterrorist unit. Both Salvadoran and American officials have refused to specify who belongs to the unit, how they were selected, how they were trained and where the unit is stationed.

. . . It is believed that the unit was used to break up a strike by public hospital workers three weeks ago. Although the unit is supposedly under the control of the army Chief of Staff, [President] Duarte said it was actually commanded in the operation by Col. Lopez Nuila, who is in charge of all police forces.

In their first foray during the hospital strike, the antiterrorist specialists mistakenly killed four plainclothes policemen who had infiltrated inside the hospital. They also tied up most of the strikers and left them lying on the floor. . . .

Mr. Duarte said today that he would create special antiterrorist units in all three police forces. One of the units was sworn in today at the Treasury police, a partially reorganized force that was once notorious for torturing and killing civilians.

The new commander of the Treasury police, Col. Rinaldo Golcher, said in an interview last year that he had stopped the killing by disbanding the unit's intelligence squad. He said at that time that the Treasury police would be used only for guarding the borders to stop smugglers. Today, however, Colonel Golcher said the unit was an essential part of the struggle against Marxist terrorists.[44]

44. LeMoyne, "Duarte Meets FBI on Raid Inquiry."

The basic dilemma of U.S. police assistance programs is to some extent a subset of the broader dilemma of incorporating human rights objectives into the conduct of U.S. foreign policy. The U.S. government has repeatedly demonstrated its influence in persuading foreign governments to pursue particular criminal investigations or to release particular individuals from prison. But it has proved much less effective in changing the ways foreign political and police systems conduct their affairs, apart from a few exceptions where it has intervened directly or expended substantial political and financial resources. It was thus hardly surprising that by the late 1980s many of the Central American police officials accused of torturing and killing political dissidents and participating in death squad activities were alumni of the U.S. training programs.[45] By and large, U.S. officials have had little choice but to work with and within existing foreign systems in pursuing objectives that involve internal changes in those systems. The dilemma they now face is the same one their predecessors faced in the 1950s and 1960s: whether the benefits to be gained from training foreign police justify the political and moral costs of "dirtying their hands" in the process.

The Military Investigative Divisions: Policing U.S. Soldiers Abroad

During the American Revolution, the War of 1812, and the Civil War, a provost corps, or military police, was created to maintain order among the American troops and then disbanded at the war's end. Given the development of civilian law enforcement at those times, it is not surprising that these military police forces did not include anything resembling a detective division. Only in late 1918, as the U.S. military faced the prospect of occupying large portions of Europe for a few years, did the need for such a force become apparent. Formally established shortly after the Armistice, the Army's Criminal Investigative Division (CID) in Europe soon totaled 67 officers and 767 agents. Within a few years, however, the occupation had ended, the Army had demobilized, and the CID was virtually disbanded. Two decades later, the CID once again expanded dramatically to meet the military policing needs of World War

45. Cottam and Marenin, "Predicting the Past" (supra n. 24), 607–616.

II. With the end of that war, however, the CID remained in place to police the U.S. troops left in allied and defeated nations alike. By the late 1980s, more than 1,000 special agents of the CID were stationed around the world to handle criminal matters involving U.S. troops.[46] Their jurisdiction covered the gamut of conceivable crimes, including murder and rape, illicit trafficking in arms, drugs, and stolen goods, terrorist activities, espionage, counterfeiting, and frauds of every sort.

By and large, the greater the U.S. military presence in a country, the more active the CID's involvement. In Vietnam, for instance, hundreds of CID agents worked a tremendous variety of criminal cases. The principal responsibility for investigating drug trafficking to and by U.S. soldiers, for instance, fell to them, although the civilian drug enforcement agency also had agents stationed there. The military police were largely responsible for cracking down on drug use by soldiers and on small-scale dealing. CID agents, however, investigated the more serious trafficking, some of it involving deals between American soldiers and powerful Vietnamese criminals. They ran undercover operations, conducted electronic surveillance, ran informants, made drug purchases, and so on. Some even were killed in the process.

The CID also has retained an important role in law enforcement in Germany and Japan, in part because of the special relationships that developed with local law enforcement agencies during the postwar occupation. When civilian U.S. drug enforcement agents began opening offices around Germany in the early 1970s, the biggest problem they encountered, in the view of one of the agents, was a turf conflict with the resident CID agents, known as Detachment A, who maintained close and long-standing relations with the German police. The turf problem arose in part from the fact that the CID agents were not confining their investigations to cases with a strong connection to the U.S. military presence but were also conducting joint operations with the local police against civilian criminals and even occasional unilateral operations. They also, recalled one DEA agent with some envy, were

> doing everything that DEA did and more. . . . They were very good. They did undercover work, including some deep undercover, . . . which DEA almost never does. . . . They had more

46. Miriam Ottenberg, *The Federal Investigators* (Englewood Cliffs, N.J.: Prentice-Hall, 1982), 48–94; Joel L. Leson, "The Fight Against Drugs in Europe," *Narc Officer* 7 (Mar. 1991), 39.

> money than DEA and more authority than DEA agents, . . . for instance to pay large sums of money to informants. They never wore uniforms and rarely reported to anyone or showed up on base. . . . They had safe houses around Germany and ran their informants out of them. . . . And they travelled all around Europe, to Lebanon and so on.

Eventually, the DEA's regional director in Europe, Jack Cusack, and the CID's provost-general worked out an agreement that partially resolved the turf conflict. In the early 1980s, however, when the DEA started closing some of the offices it had opened a decade earlier, the CID once again stepped in to fill the void.

The criminal investigative branches of the Navy and the Air Force have conducted themselves overseas in much the same fashion as the Army's CID. Like the FBI but unlike the Army's CID, the Naval Investigative Service (NIS) and the Air Force Office of Special Investigation (AFOSI) have handled not just criminal matters but counterespionage tasks as well. (In the Army the military intelligence division is responsible for counterintelligence tasks.) Until 1966, the Navy's criminal investigative needs were handled by the Office of Naval Intelligence (ONI). Created in 1882, the ONI expanded during wartime to handle security threats to naval installations and espionage in general.[47] Not until after World War II did the ONI take on responsibility for investigating crimes involving naval personnel. A bureaucratic reorganization in 1966 shifted that responsibility to a newly created agency, the NIS. Most of its agents, unlike those of the CID and the AFOSI, have been civilians, stationed not only within the United States and in U.S. bases abroad but also on U.S. aircraft carriers.[48]

The youngest of the military's criminal investigative divisions, the Air Force Office of Special Investigation dates its origins to 1948, when a Congressional investigation into procurement fraud led to the creation of a centralized criminal investigative division under the inspector general.[49] Its first two directors were recruited from the FBI, and the agency

47. See the two books by Jeffery M. Dorwart: *The Office of Naval Intelligence: The Birth of America's First Intelligence Agency, 1865–1918* (Annapolis: Naval Institute Press, 1979), and *Conflict of Duty: The U.S. Navy's Intelligence Dilemma, 1919–1945* (Annapolis: Naval Institute Press, 1983).

48. Blair M. Gluba, "Law Enforcement at Sea," *Police Chief* 55 (Nov. 1988), 85–86.

49. The story of the AFOSI's origins is told in two brief unpublished (and updated) papers provided to me by the official AFOSI historian, Edward C. Mishler, in 1987. One was written

initially modeled itself after that agency.[50] As its responsibilities evolved, slightly less than half of its efforts were devoted to varied criminal investigations against Air Force personnel and property, with the other half split between fraud investigations and counterintelligence activities directed at espionage, sabotage, and terrorism. Like the CID, both the NIS and the AFOSI operate worldwide, although most extensively in countries, such as the Philippines, that have hosted large Navy and Air Force bases. All three military detective agencies have developed close relationships with local police forces in host countries and with civilian U.S. law enforcement agencies—notably the DEA and Customs vis-à-vis drug trafficking, and the FBI and the CIA on terrorism and espionage—although relations have also been strained by turf struggles, personality conflicts, and nationalist sensitivities. Their agents have operated abroad in much the same style as U.S. drug enforcement agents, developing their own cases, conducting undercover operations and electronic surveillance, and recruiting and paying informants. However, unlike their civilian counterparts, who have no sovereign police powers when they are outside the United States, the military detectives have benefited from their sovereign authority at least within the confines of U.S. military bases.

The announcement of awards presented each year by the International Narcotic Enforcement Officers Association provides a revealing glimpse into the more successful overseas exploits of CID, AFOSI, and NIS agents.[51] In 1990, three of the seven Army covert drug agents based in Germany were recognized for their work with different state police agencies and the German customs unit. One was praised as "a fully operational member" of a German state drug enforcement unit, and another was described as "one of two [CID] agents to be sworn as a police officer by the German government in recognition of his activity in covert operations and testimony in foreign courts." The U.S. agents investigated not only drug trafficking but also terrorist activities, counterfeiting, and transnational arms smuggling. The new deputy com-

by his predecessor, Captain Kurt K. Kunze, and entitled "The Genesis of AFOSI." The other, with no author noted, is entitled "Brief History of the Air Force Office of Special Investigations."

50. "U.S. Air Force Office of Special Investigations," and Celeste Morga, "Exclusive Interview with Brigadier General Francis R. Dillon, Commander OSI," in *Narc Officer* 4 (Nov. 1988), 13, 15, 22, 23, 25.

51. "INEOA Names 1990 Award Recipients," *Narc Officer* 6 (Sept. 1990), 60–63.

mander for operations of the AFOSI's largest detachment—at Ramstein Air Base in Germany—was praised for having revitalized a "lethargic drug suppression team." In fifteen months he supervised the drug enforcement unit's production of more than 180 convictions in German and U.S. military courts-martial, directed "the first-ever undercover drug operation at a sensitive NATO command and control center," and coordinated joint operations with the CID involving the sharing of information, informants, funds, and undercover personnel. Another AFOSI agent, stationed in the Philippines, was recognized for the success of numerous ventures with Japanese police and the Philippines drug enforcement agency, one of which involved a subordinate AFOSI agent posing undercover as a member of the Yakuza. He also was credited for his involvement, together with NIS agents, in assisting the Philippines police in their marijuana eradication campaign. Two CID agents based in Panama were also recognized for their work—one as coordinator, the other as undercover operative—in infiltrating and collecting evidence on a cocaine smuggling ring involving Colombians, Panamanians, and U.S. military personnel.

Among all the U.S. law enforcement agencies, only the military agencies appeared poised for a significant contraction in their international presence and activities during the 1990s. The principal reason was the planned withdrawal of U.S. military forces from overseas posts as the Cold War ended, as the two large U.S. bases in the Philippines readied for closure in the wake of volcanic activity and a diplomatic impasse, and as public and Congressional sentiment in the United States appeared to favor a reduction in the military's budget. The relatively brief attention devoted here to the military's international law enforcement activities should be seen as a reflection both of the little that has been published about their activities and of my own decision to focus my research resources on the international activities of the civilian agencies—not as an indication of their relative significance in the annals of transnational policing. In contrast to all the civilian U.S. law enforcement agencies, the military agencies can rightfully claim to have mounted the most substantial presence abroad, to have investigated the greatest number of crimes, and to have worked most intimately with foreign law enforcement agencies. Much of the analysis that follows is equally applicable to the military agencies, but a more substantial analysis of their international activities is certainly warranted.

The FBN Abroad: Anslinger's "Briefcase Agents"

In its overseas capacity, the U.S. Drug Enforcement Administration plays a unique role in international politics. As a transnational organization, it is a hybrid of a national police agency and an international law enforcement organization. It represents the interests of one nation and its agents abroad are responsible to the ambassador, yet it has a mandate and a mission effectively authorized by international conventions and the United Nations. Like most agencies with representatives in U.S. embassies abroad, its principal role is one of liaison. But unlike virtually all other agencies except the CIA and the military's investigative divisions, its agents are "operational" in most of the countries where they are stationed—they cultivate and pay informants, conduct undercover operations, and become directly involved in the activities of their local counterparts. The DEA's principal objective, broadly stated, is to stem the flow of drugs to the United States, yet it has devoted considerable efforts to assisting foreign law enforcement agencies in countering drug trafficking that has little or no impact on the United States.

To pick up where I left off at the end of the previous chapter, the flow of narcotics from Europe and Asia to the United States came to a virtual halt during World War II as smuggling routes were dramatically disrupted by military hostilities. Iran, Mexico, and India replaced China, Yugoslavia, and Italy as the principal sources of illicit opiates, albeit on a much smaller scale.[52] Moreover, with the occupation of Japan and the territories it had previously occupied in Asia by British, Dutch, and U.S. troops, the government opium-smoking monopolies that had existed were liquidated by the returning colonial powers at the urging of U.S. officials.[53] This move temporarily prolonged the disruption of supplies initiated by the war. Working out of Japan, five FBN agents attached to General Douglas MacArthur's staff worked to dismantle the monopolies

52. FBN, *Traffic in Opium and Other Dangerous Drugs for the Year Ended December 31, 1943* (Washington, D.C.: Government Printing Office, 1944), 18–21.

53. See the report on the November 1943 conference convened in Washington to decide the future of opium policy in ibid., 1–3; Alfred R. Lindesmith, *The Addict and the Law* (Bloomington: Indiana University Press, 1965), 199–221; Arnold H. Taylor, *American Diplomacy and the Narcotics Traffic, 1900–1939: A Study in International Humanitarian Reform* (Durham, N.C.: Duke University Press, 1969), 279–280; and William O. Walker III, *Opium and Foreign Policy: The Anglo-American Search for Order in Asia, 1912–1954* (Chapel Hill: University of North Carolina Press, 1991), 153–158.

in Japan, Korea, and other Asian nations,[54] and another FBN agent was sent to occupied Germany to assist in reestablishing the drug control system.[55] There and elsewhere, their efforts were supplemented and aided by the criminal investigative branches attached to U.S. military forces around the world.

As affairs in Europe gradually settled down in the aftermath of the war, FBN Commissioner Harry Anslinger considered stationing his agents abroad once again.[56] In 1948, district supervisor Garland Williams was sent to Europe on a four-month exploratory survey trip. The following year, another district supervisor (and former agent of the Office of Strategic Services), George White, conducted a similar tour, albeit with a more operational dimension. In France, Italy, Germany, Turkey, Iran, and elsewhere, Williams and White made contact with local police, followed up leads developed in the United States, and conducted law enforcement operations in cooperation with local counterparts. In July 1950, a third agent, Charles Siragusa, who had worked under Williams and White in New York in the early 1940s and also served in the OSS, was sent to Europe for three months to pursue assorted leads. After visiting Istanbul, Beirut, and Athens, Siragusa rendezvoused in Rome with another agent, Benedict Pocoroba, who had been working on a specific case involving a deported American gangster, and with Henry Manfredi, an Army CID agent stationed in Trieste but with responsibility for Italy. Working with Italian and Yugoslavian police, the three succeeded in arresting a number of drug traffickers. After a winter visit to Washington, Siragusa returned to Europe for another brief tour, accompanied by agents Joe Amato and Martin Pera. Working both together and separately—with Amato covering Germany, Pera covering Turkey, and Siragusa covering Italy—the agents traveled widely, developing informants, making contacts with local police, conducting undercover operations, pursuing leads developed by agents in the United States, and so on.

54. "A Chronicle of Federal Drug Law Enforcement" (editorial), *Drug Enforcement* 7 (Dec. 1980), 37.

55. FBN, *Traffic in Opium and Other Dangerous Drugs for the Year Ended December 31, 1945* (Washington, D.C.: Government Printing Office, 1946), 4.

56. The following paragraphs are based on Charles Siragusa (as told to Robert Wiedrich), *The Trail of the Poppy* (Englewood Cliffs, N.J.: Prentice-Hall, 1966); Andrew Tully, *Treasury Agent: The Inside Story* (New York: Simon & Schuster, 1958), 104–111; Frederic Sondern Jr., *Brotherhood of Evil: The Mafia* (New York: Farrar, Straus & Cudahy, 1959), 123–166; and interviews with John Cusack, Oct. 23, 1984, and May 22, 1986.

By September 1951, Anslinger had obtained the consent of both the State Department and the Italian government to open a permanent FBN branch office in Rome. Siragusa, having served briefly as chief investigator for the Senate Rackets Committee in the interim, thus began his eight-year stint as chief of FBN operations in Europe. A few months later, he was joined by Jack Cusack, an experienced agent who would later rise to the highest levels of the DEA. In late 1952, agent Paul Knight joined them in Rome. Two years later, he opened a second FBN office—in Beirut. The three agents, joined from time to time by agents from the United States on temporary assignment in Europe, covered all of the continent as well as the Middle East. Eight years later, as Siragusa returned to the United States, the FBN's presence in Europe had barely expanded—to six agents all told.

Throughout the 1950s, FBN agents continued to operate elsewhere as well, albeit without the benefit of resident offices. They also worked together and competitively with the small number of U.S. customs agents stationed in foreign cities from Antwerp to Japan.[57] As before the war, drug trafficking activities in Mexico and Canada were dealt with by agents stationed along the borders who crossed over to conduct operations with Mexican and Canadian police and occasionally to operate and collect intelligence covertly on their own.[58] Where a case needed to be pursued or investigated overseas, Anslinger sent either the agent already working on the case or delegated one of his senior agents. George White, for instance, upon whom Anslinger relied to conduct many of the more difficult and sensitive foreign operations, worked not just in Europe but also Mexico, Canada, India, Iran, Iraq, Turkey, Ecuador, Peru, and Cuba.[59] Because the FBN agents already stationed in Europe were among the best, as well as experienced in operating outside U.S. borders, they also were charged with conducting investigations elsewhere.

In 1960, the FBN began the first of its two waves of expansion. With Jack Cusack now in charge of European operations, agent Andrew Tartaglino was delegated to open a Paris office, and Sal Vizzini began operations in Istanbul. In 1961, Anthony Pohl opened an office in

57. See Don Whitehead, *Border Guard: The Story of the United States Customs Service* (New York: McGraw-Hill, 1963).

58. Tully, *Treasury Agent*, 183–187.

59. Derek Agnew, *Undercover Agent—Narcotics* (London: Souvenir Press, 1959), 112–124.

Marseilles and Cusack participated in a global survey mission by the Treasury Department to consider where other Treasury agents should be stationed. In late 1962 and early 1963, FBN agents set up shop in Bangkok, Mexico City, and Monterrey, with the office in the former handling all of Asia and that in the Mexican capital handling all of Latin America. During the next few years, other offices were opened in Hong Kong, Singapore, Korea, and Manila. Fortunately for historians of this subject, the overseas exploits of these agents have been recounted in the autobiographies of FBN agents Siragusa and Vizzini[60] and in the celebratory accounts of FBN operations by such writers as Frederic Sondern, Derek Agnew, and Alvin Moscow.[61] To be sure, one must read these books with a certain amount of skepticism, given the literary license taken by all of the authors and their tendency to focus on incidents that reflected best on the agency. And Siragusa and Vizzini were rather unique characters, selected for their positions because they were especially adept at the skills required of an overseas narcotics agent. Yet amid all the bravado and semi-fictional dialogue, one can discern basic features of the FBN's activities abroad.

During the early years of the FBN overseas, Siragusa and the agents who reported to him operated with relatively few legal or organizational guidelines. This posed both advantages and disadvantages. On the one hand, U.S. embassies were unaccustomed to housing and assuming responsibility for gun-toting law enforcement agents who might end up shooting someone. Similarly, foreign governments often had legal and political objections to foreign law enforcement authorities operating within their borders. And foreign police could be quite sensitive about foreign counterparts presuming to tell them how to go about their business. Yet because the FBN presence abroad represented a rather new phenomenon, its agents also benefited from a lack of restrictions. With so few agents abroad, the FBN had little need to develop the detailed manuals that officially establish the constraints on DEA activities abroad today. U.S. law presented few restraints on the FBN's foreign activities. And most foreign governments had yet to establish any policies determining what such agents could or could not do. By and large, the FBN

60. Siragusa, *Trail of the Poppy*; Sal Vizzini (with Oscar Fraley and Marshall Smith), *Vizzini: The Secret Lives of America's Most Successful Undercover Agent* (New York: Arbor House, 1972).

61. Sondern, *Brotherhood of Evil*; Alvin Moscow, *The Merchants of Heroin* (New York: Dial Press, 1968); Agnew, *Undercover Agent.*

agents were obliged, and allowed, to work out their own methods of operating abroad.

During his eight years in Europe, Siragusa worked in twenty-nine countries.[62] Although based in Rome, his office was, in his own words, "mostly headquartered in my briefcase"[63]—or, as John Cusack put it, they were "briefcase agents."[64] Constantly on the go, they maintained contact with high-level police officials throughout Europe and the Middle East, developed informants, pressured local police and their governments to do more against drug trafficking, conducted operations both unilaterally and in league with local police, pursued leads from U.S.-based investigations, and generally performed whatever services they were called upon to provide. Siragusa, describing an undercover operation in Turkey, noted some of the features and limitations of their operations:

> In 1955 there were still only three of us assigned to Europe and the Middle East. We . . . functioned somewhat as roving ambassadors of the Federal Bureau of Narcotics. For the most part we kept in touch with a few good informers we had in Turkey by long-distance telephone, cable and the mails. As often as possible, one of us flew to Turkey to make personal contacts. We were spread thin.[65]

Even in the early 1960s, with offices in only four or five cities, the agents continued to travel extensively. Vizzini, although stationed in Istanbul, conducted investigations in Italy, France, Lebanon, Thailand, and elsewhere. As the number of offices proliferated, the need to constantly be on the road declined. Agents still continued to travel, however, not only to coordinate activities with U.S. drug agents in other countries but also to conduct the undercover aspects of investigations in other countries.

One feature of international police work that both Siragusa and Vizzini stressed in their memoirs was the receptiveness of foreign police to working together with the FBN. This, they noted, was in contrast to the attitudes of higher-level political officials. American drug agents

62. Siragusa, *Trail of the Poppy*, 169, 219.
63. Ibid., 4.
64. Interview with John Cusack, Oct. 23, 1984.
65. Siragusa, *Trail of the Poppy*, 144.

tapped into the transnational police subculture that had been developing for nearly a century. When this proved to be insufficient to overcome hostile or suspicious sentiments among political officials, FBN agents took advantage of American diplomatic power. As Siragusa noted:

> The police overseas almost always worked willingly with us. It was their superiors in the government who were sometimes unhappy that we had entered their countries. Most of the time, though, I found that a casual mention of the possibility of shutting off our foreign-aid programs, dropped in the proper quarters, brought grudging permission for our operations almost immediately.[66]

During the 1950s and 1960s, Interpol was especially valuable to FBN activities in Europe in a number of ways. Hoover had withdrawn the FBI from Interpol in 1950 when the Czechoslovakian government used the Interpol network to circulate wanted notices for political refugees.[67] Soon thereafter, the Treasury Department's law enforcement agencies—the FBN, the Secret Service, and Customs—stepped into the empty American shoes at Interpol. In 1951, Malachi Harney, assistant commissioner of the FBN, attended Interpol's annual meeting in Lisbon as an "unofficial observer" and served on the subcommittee on drugs.[68] Siragusa became a regular participant at the annual General Assembly meetings, which were attended by other Treasury representatives as well. Annual dues were also paid. In 1954, the assistant secretary of the treasury in charge of enforcement wrote: "To obtain and assure access to information from European police officials and an extra degree of collaboration and assistance by them to American Treasury agents carrying on Treasury business in Europe, it has been considered advisable to make certain payments to Interpol at a stipulated rate."[69] Siragusa, in his memoirs, commented on the value of Interpol in cutting through transgovernmental red tape. Refused permission at the Turkish-Syrian border to cross into the Arab country on an investigation, Siragusa pulled strings to persuade the border guard:

66. Ibid., 212.

67. Trevor Meldal-Johnsen and Vaughn Young, *The Interpol Connection: An Inquiry into the International Criminal Police Organization* (New York: Dial Press, 1979), 96.

68. Ibid., 98.

69. Quoted in ibid., 100.

> I asked that he telephone the Syrian Chief of Police in Damascus. I told him that I was an American policeman on very important business. I hinted to the guard that he might be in serious trouble if he did not follow my instructions. He came through for me. So did the phone call. With a top priority, I was soon talking to the chief in Damascus from a line in the border shack. It only took a reminder to the chief that we had met the year before at an Interpol meeting to get clearance. I promised to explain all when I saw him in Damascus.[70]

Beyond the information and contacts, the FBN derived another benefit from its association with Interpol. With the notion of foreign law enforcement agents, especially operationally oriented ones, stationed in one's country still somewhat unfamiliar, both the U.S. government and foreign governments preferred that their status remain somewhat ambiguous. Vizzini, for instance, was officially designated an Interpol representative when he opened the FBN office in the American consulate in Istanbul.[71] The FBN also derived some benefits from the Interpol title in that it helped obscure the fact that its agents were those of a foreign government whose principal objective was the stemming of crime affecting the United States. Said Myles Ambrose, a U.S. official who was involved with international law enforcement matters on and off from the 1950s to the 1970s:

> Operational agents from the Bureau of Narcotics abroad could claim and did claim to be Interpol agents to give their work a veneer of legitimacy. We didn't give a goddamn about Interpol early on. We wanted Interpol to legitimize our police operations overseas as we were the only country in the world that sends cops abroad operationally.[72]

Even without the Interpol network, the sense of comradery among police of different nations often has succeeded in inducing cooperation between governments with severe political differences. FBN agents often found themselves in the role of intermediaries encouraging police chiefs

70. Siragusa, *Trail of the Poppy*, 31.
71. Vizzini, *Vizzini: Secret Lives*, 98.
72. Quoted in Meldal-Johnsen and Young, *The Interpol Connection*, 101–102.

from hostile countries to work together.[73] In one major heroin case, Siragusa was able to persuade police from Turkey, Greece, and Syria to put aside their political differences long enough to cooperate in a joint investigation. In another, Siragusa and Army CID agent Henry Manfredi traveled to Belgrade and secured the assistance of Tito's police.[74] Of course, relations between police of politically hostile governments are not always so successful, but when they are it is a reflection of the strength of the transnational police subculture—the sense among policemen that they are united by a common task that has nothing to do with politics.

Another feature of the FBN's early activities overseas, which is no longer so prominent as it was then, was the assistance given to criminal investigations having nothing to do with drugs. Even today, DEA agents who come across information of use to other law enforcement agencies will in most cases pass it on. But by and large, they tend not to become involved in other agencies' investigations unless there is a drug angle to them. Siragusa's and Vizzini's memoirs, however, make frequent mention of performing tasks for fellow U.S. agencies, including the intelligence agencies. The area that most distracted the FBN agents in the early 1950s was the illicit diversion of strategic materials to the Soviet bloc. A few passages from Siragusa's book suggest both the extent of his involvement in this area and the nature of cooperation with other agencies, both American and European:

> We encountered some great operators in those days as my small staff in Rome devoted a full fifty percent of its time to the problem. Every piece of information obtained about the commercial cheats was passed on to a network of European cops we trusted. Among them was a police officer in Antwerp with whom I had worked on several narcotics cases. His beat was the waterfront, and for several years he furnished me with copies of the manifests of Soviet bloc ships that called in the Belgian seaport.[75]

After describing a joint operation with the Swiss police to expose the Romanian commercial attaché, Siragusa recalled how the FBN's involvement in this area came to an end:

73. Siragusa, *Trail of the Poppy*, 3–32.
74. Ibid., 90.
75. Ibid., 137.

> My agents and I had several other skirmishes with Soviet spies before the American Government woke up and assigned an excellent United States Air Force officer, Col. Edward Brown, to head a group charged with making sure that laws related to this illicit trade were properly enforced. Colonel Brown did a splendid job including the establishment of economic defense programs in American embassies throughout Western Europe.
>
> One of the last pieces of work I did for our Intelligence people began with a conversation with a U.S. naval attaché in Rome. He told me it was important that the West obtain samples of fuel oil used by Russian vessels. On my next flight to Lebanon on narcotics business, I enlisted the aid of a Lebanese customs official. He had previously been of great help in breaking up a dope-smuggling operation. A few days later he delivered to my hotel room a quantity of oil obtained surreptitiously from a Russian freighter docked in Beirut.[76]

Vizzini's memoirs are even more revealing regarding interagency cooperation abroad. At one point he notes: "It wasn't unusual for an undercover man from one federal agency to be loaned out to another on a special assignment. I had already done stints for Customs, the C.I.A. and the Justice Department, as well as Secret Service."[77] In one counterfeiting case, which grew out of a lead developed by one of Vizzini's informants in Bangkok, the FBN agent performed the undercover work while the Secret Service agent who had flown in from Honolulu acted as the "covering agent." The two agents also received assistance from the State Department's security officer at the embassy, whose responsibilities were to some degree related to those of the law enforcement agents.[78] In another case, Vizzini went undercover for the CIA in Beirut in an operation designed to destroy a cache of arms being delivered to a Soviet-backed group.[79] In Thailand, Vizzini turned to a U.S. intelligence agency when he needed demolitions to blow up a heroin lab in the Golden Triangle.[80] And in Istanbul, Vizzini and the Turkish narcotics squad he had trained were called upon by the chief of police to work

76. Ibid., 141–142.
77. Vizzini, *Vizzini: Secret Lives*, 255.
78. Ibid., 253–269.
79. Ibid., 175–193.
80. Ibid., 246.

cases ranging from rape to bank robbery.[81] Although the notion of interagency cooperation took hold during the 1980s with the proliferation of multiagency task forces, today's overseas DEA agent is less likely to become directly involved in other agencies' cases to the extent that Vizzini and Siragusa did. The jurisdictional lines have been drawn more sharply since then, and other agencies have developed their overseas capacities.

Another aspect of overseas drug enforcement that has declined since the 1960s is the involvement of U.S. agents in "firefights" (gun battles) with drug traffickers. Vizzini's memoirs in particular, but also Siragusa's, are full of accounts of the agents being shot at, shooting others, and generally being directly involved in the more violent aspects of foreign law enforcement. Without the formal power of arrest in any country outside the United States, and often with no formal authorization to carry a weapon, FBN agents frequently found themselves in very undiplomatic situations. Although direct involvement in law enforcement operations was not officially required and in fact was often forbidden, FBN agents had numerous incentives to become so involved. This was particularly the case outside Europe. Whether in Turkey, Mexico, Pakistan, Afghanistan, Thailand, or any of a dozen other countries, a raid on a drug trafficker's hideout or lab was fraught with danger, as it is today.

FBN agents often perceived a strong need to participate in potentially dangerous operations. To a certain extent, it seemed only fair that American agents assume some of the risk when they were asking local authorities to conduct dangerous law enforcement operations on their behalf. The presence of the FBN agents also ensured that the local law enforcement agents did what they had been asked to do, and increased the chances that they would do it right. Often, an element of machismo was also involved. Vizzini, for instance, recalled that when he went to Istanbul the officer in charge of the narcotics squad "never fully accepted me until we had our first shoot-out with opium smugglers in the interior."[82] Sometimes, of course, one ended up in a dangerous situation without looking for it or expecting it—and this still happens frequently today. A simple interview or surveillance, for instance, has the potential to take a violent turn. But what has changed to some degree, in part

81. Ibid., 204–209.
82. Ibid., 209.

because of Congressionally mandated restrictions on U.S. agent involvement in foreign law enforcement operations, is the frequency of scenarios in which U.S. drug enforcement agents are the first through the door of a drug trafficker's hideout with guns ablaze.

From the perspective of the U.S. government, the prospect of agents becoming involved in firefights and killing or being killed was upsetting for a couple of reasons. Concern for the lives of the agents was of course one consideration. But of no less concern was the potential public reaction in a foreign country to its citizens, no matter how criminal they might be, being killed by American police. FBN agents were thus placed in an awkward position. On the one hand, they were drawn into potentially dangerous operations by both the unofficial requisites of the job and the expectations of the local police with whom they worked. On the other hand, political figures and high-level legal authorities tended to be both ignorant of the actual nature of FBN operations within their country and sensitive to apparent infringements on national sovereignty, particularly those seized upon by the media. State Department officials tended to be highly cognizant of the same sorts of considerations because it was they who would be obliged to offer explanations in the event that FBN agents landed in a diplomatically awkward situation. From time to time, local authorities and FBN agents conspired to avoid diplomatic imbroglios after FBN agents had killed drug traffickers by having the locals claim that they had fired the fatal shots.[83] And, as with intelligence operations, one never knows of the assorted criminals who disappeared without anyone in the government or media asking what had happened.

The BNDD and the DEA: The Modern Era of International Drug Enforcement

Despite occasional proposals to merge the Federal Bureau of Narcotics with the FBI, which were always rejected by J. Edgar Hoover, the FBN remained an independent law enforcement agency within the Treasury

83. In his memoirs, Vizzini relates one such offer from the Turkish police, which he refused (*Vizzini: Secret Lives*, 211). A similar story, involving Mexican police, is recounted in a book by a former deputy director of the BNDD, John Finlator, *The Drugged Nation: A "Narc's" Story* (New York: Simon & Schuster, 1973), 141.

Department for almost four decades. Then, in the space of five years, the federal drug enforcement bureaucracy underwent two major reorganizations. The first occurred in 1968, when the FBN, which had been wracked by a series of corruption scandals involving its New York office, was transferred from the Treasury Department to the Justice Department. There it was merged with the Bureau of Drug Abuse Control (BDAC), which had been created in 1966 to regulate barbiturates, amphetamines, hallucinogens, and counterfeit drugs. Housed in the Food and Drug Administration (FDA) within the Department of Health, Education, and Welfare (HEW), the BDAC had come into frequent conflict with the Treasury Department's drug agency. With the consolidation of the two agencies under the Justice Department roof, the Bureau of Narcotics and Dangerous Drugs (BNDD) came into being.[84]

Five years later, a second reorganization sought to resolve the increasingly fierce turf battles between the BNDD, Customs' drug section, and two other drug enforcement agencies that had been formed in the interim: the Office of National Narcotics Intelligence (ONNI) and the Office of Drug Abuse Law Enforcement (ODALE). The proposed solution was the merger of all drug enforcement and intelligence in one organization within the Justice Department—the Drug Enforcement Administration.[85] An angry U.S. Customs agency saw 500 of its agents transferred to the DEA (although almost half soon resigned, with many returning to Customs)[86] and its overseas presence substantially curtailed. Among the thirty or so overseas Customs agents, a number merely switched hats, either merging with the resident BNDD office or opening a new DEA office.

In 1967, the last full year of the FBN's existence, the budget of the

84. The brief history of the BDAC and its conflicts with the FBN is in Finlator, *Drugged Nation*, 22–55.

85. "Reorganization Plan #2," as the merger was known, has been the subject of substantial analysis. One study, undertaken "to examine why reorganizations fail more often than they succeed," is Patricia Rachal's *Federal Narcotics Enforcement: Reorganization and Reform* (Boston: Auburn House, 1982). A second study, aimed at examining the difficulties in pursuing an international drug control policy, is Mark H. Moore's "Reorganization Plan #2 Reviewed: Problems in Implementing a Strategy to Reduce the Supply of Drugs to Illicit Markets in the United States," *Public Policy* 26 (1978), 229–262. A third study, with a far more novel approach, is Epstein's *Agency of Fear* (supra n. 6). Epstein draws a close link between Watergate and the reorganization, arguing that Nixon intended the DEA to be used as a clandestine political police force. His thesis is challenged by Rachal, *Federal Narcotics Enforcement*, 67–70.

86. Rachal, *Federal Narcotics Enforcement*, 136.

Treasury Department's drug agency was approximately $3 million. Roughly a dozen of its 300 agents were stationed in eight locations outside the United States. Six years and two bureaucratic reorganizations later, in the last full year of BNDD operations, the drug agency boasted a budget of $74 million and 1,446 total agents, of whom 124 were abroad in 47 offices in 33 countries. By 1976, just before a minor contraction in its size, the DEA's budget was just short of $200 million. Some 228 of its 2,117 agents were stationed overseas, in 68 offices in 43 countries. In less than a decade, a small overseas complement of American narcotics agents had grown into the first global law enforcement agency with operational capabilities. (See Appendix B.)

The drug enforcement agents, like the few dozens of overseas FBI and Customs agents, liaised with their counterparts overseas and collected intelligence of value to domestic investigations. But unlike the FBI and customs agents, they continued to participate in joint operations with local police, conducted undercover operations, and were generally more operationally oriented. In a few capitals, DEA agents restricted their activities to liaison with local officials, although an agent might be brought in from other countries or the United States if a fresh face was needed for an undercover operation.[87] As an intelligence network on international drug trafficking, the DEA was likewise unparalleled. Where once Interpol had been universally relied on for intelligence on transnational criminals and the transmission of requests to foreign law enforcement agencies, the DEA now was quicker and more effective at the same task where narcotics cases were concerned.

The dramatic expansion of the U.S. drug enforcement presence abroad was motivated in large part by the Nixon administration's declaration of a "war against drugs" and its desire to involve foreign governments in its campaign. The "Nixon doctrine," which called for foreign governments to assume responsibility for the national security tasks previously undertaken by U.S. forces, was extended to the drug war. But unlike the effort to "Vietnamize" the war in Southeast Asia, the political and diplomatic campaign to internationalize the war against drugs combined an expansion of the global presence of U.S. agents with efforts to develop the vicarious drug enforcement capabilities of foreign police agencies (see Chapters Four and Five). The U.S. drug enforcement agents sta-

87. References to the DEA hereinafter should be interpreted as referring to the post-FBN era of U.S. drug enforcement, not as distinct from the BNDD.

tioned overseas thus fulfilled a symbolic role, providing a visible manifestation of the U.S. government's commitment to *international* drug enforcement and its willingness to assist foreign police agencies. Their presence in U.S. embassies served as a constant reminder both to foreign governments and to U.S. ambassadors that drug enforcement was now a high-level foreign policy objective of the President and the Congress.

On a more practical level, the proliferation of overseas agents contributed to the central objective of the agency: immobilizing drug traffickers. The logic of stationing 100 or 200 agents overseas was much the same as the logic that motivated Anslinger to send Siragusa, Vizzini, and their cohorts abroad. Immobilizing drug traffickers meant obtaining the information necessary to identify and catch them, obtaining the evidence necessary to convict them, and of course apprehending the traffickers themselves. Because most illicit drugs originated from abroad, most of the information, evidence, and traffickers could be found there as well. Without agents stationed overseas, U.S.-based agents would either have to collect them on their own or rely on foreign police. The first option would require that agents travel long distances to countries where they might not know the language, the terrain, or anybody at all. The latter was problematic in that foreign police were unlikely to give a request from abroad high priority. If the request were for something relatively simple, such as a criminal record or an identification of a document or fingerprint, Interpol channels might suffice, so long as time was not important. But if something more complicated were required, such as a surveillance, interview, or undercover operation, it was highly unlikely that a foreign police agency would be either willing or able to comply. Having U.S. drug agents on the scene could therefore be highly advantageous. The agents would treat as a priority a request that local police might dismiss or delay in responding to. If the U.S. agents were unable to handle the matter personally, they at least would be in a far superior position to persuade the local police to comply. And if U.S.-based agents themselves needed to come over, overseas agents could serve as guides and liaisons with local officials.

The drug agents sent abroad were also expected to devote substantial efforts to building up and training foreign drug enforcement units to the point that they could function independent of U.S. assistance. This was true not just in Latin America, where many criminal investigative units were not specialized and were little concerned with narcotics, but also in Europe, where drugs were likewise a relatively small concern. The overseas drug agent was given the task of carving out drug enforcement units from local police forces and training them in the investigative techniques employed by the agency in the United States. In the 1970s, as already noted, the number of foreign police trained annually first by BNDD and then by the DEA jumped from zero to almost 2,000, thereby stepping at least partially into the vacated shoes of the Office of Public Safety. Unlike the OPS, the drug enforcement agency also provided specialized training for police agents from Europe and other countries with more sophisticated police forces.

Although a number of the original overseas FBN agents had attained high positions within the BNDD by the early 1970s, the opening of a new BNDD office overseas was still not an established process. One agent who opened the offices in Frankfurt and Munich recalled, "We went there stone cold. There was no game plan." Nonetheless, the BNDD agents who headed overseas to open the new offices were not stepping into entirely virgin territory. More often than not, other U.S. drug agents stationed in either the United States or in another foreign post had been there before and could help make the necessary introductions. In some cases, the agent delegated to open the office had previously been there himself on a temporary duty assignment.

Nor was the BNDD agent necessarily the first or the only American law enforcement agent in town. In the early 1970s, the FBI had some forty LEGATs (short for legal attachés) stationed in twenty foreign cities who maintained liaison relations with police agencies in dozens of countries. Customs also had a number of its attachés abroad, who handled both drug matters and a variety of others. If American military bases were nearby, agents of the criminal investigative divisions were sure to be around. And the Public Safety Program sponsored by the Agency for International Development (AID) still had a substantial number of its police advisors around the world engaged in training local police. Any of these agents was a potential source of contacts and introductions for the new drug agent. And even if left to his own devices, the drug agent could make his own introductions directly, via the embassy security officials, through Interpol channels, or any number of other ways.

In dozens of cases, BNDD agents newly arrived in a foreign city found that their greatest problems were not in making contacts with local police but in resolving turf conflicts with other U.S. agents resident in the country. The experience of the BNDD agent, described above, who arrived in Germany only to find that the local Army CID drug enforcement unit, Detachment A, was already well connected with local police and not about to share its contacts, was not atypical. Depending upon the country, the CID and other military investigative agencies had more agents, were better funded, operated under fewer restraints, and already had years of experience in conducting drug investigations in Europe. But the agency with which the BNDD had the most frequent turf problems was U.S. Customs, which had long retained some jurisdiction over international drug trafficking.[88] The conflict was exacerbated in March 1972, when Customs jurisdiction over drug cases was temporarily expanded, allowing them to expand their international presence from 16 to 29 agents.[89] Although Customs' principal contacts were with foreign customs agencies, turf struggles were both inevitable and bitter. In July 1973, the conflict was resolved in the BNDD's favor when the lion's share of jurisdiction over drug cases was given to the BNDD's successor, the Drug Enforcement Administration.

For foreign police agencies trying to develop working relationships with the American police, the intra-American turf struggles quickly became a source of anger and frustration. In France, for instance, where both Customs and the FBN had stationed agents for many years, a French police official expressed his frustration to American reporters in 1972:

> There is one thing about the American anti-drug effort that we of the French police cannot understand. . . . Why is it that the two American agencies fighting drugs here [BNDD and Customs] are always fighting each other? We can't understand this. Here in France, we work smoothly with our people in customs. But the U.S. customs and the U.S. BNDD here are just about not speaking to each other. We don't think that this helps the battle against drugs.[90]

The turf struggle with other U.S. agencies presented one not insurmountable problem for the BNDD as it expanded rapidly abroad.

88. See Rachal, *Federal Narcotics Enforcement* (supra n. 85), which deals at length with the BNDD-Customs turf conflicts.

89. Andrew Tully, *The Secret War Against Dope* (New York: Coward, McCann & Geoghegan, 1973), 29.

90. Gilbert Raguideau, quoted in *The Heroin Trail* (New York: Holt, Rinehart & Winston, 1973), 98 (previously a series of articles published in *Newsday*, Feb. 1 to Mar. 4, 1973).

Another obstacle was the uncertainty of local officials regarding what the U.S. agents should and should not be permitted to do. Some police resented the intrusion of BNDD agents, with their different techniques and priorities and their tendency to act as if they were still on U.S. soil. In most cases, a personable and competent agent, as most of the BNDD agents were, could overcome such resistance over time, appealing to the same value system that bound police throughout the world. Somewhat tougher were the higher-level officials in foreign governments, who demonstrated a greater sensitivity to any apparent infringements on national sovereignty. From time to time, the fact that U.S. drug enforcement agents were operating out of the American embassy would emerge in media exposés intended to embarrass the government and/or the United States. In the vast majority of cases, however, the agents were not required to leave the country; they merely adopted a lower profile until the storm had passed.

One problem that the BNDD agents confronted as they went overseas was largely of their own making. They had been delegated overseas not just to make cases and handle the foreign dimensions of cases originating in the United States but also to act as drug enforcement diplomats and advocates. They were expected to push for structural changes in drug enforcement wherever they were stationed, to lobby for tougher laws, to train local police in drug enforcement techniques, to sensitize local officials to U.S. concerns in this area, and so on. But, as one scholar serving a brief stint in the upper echelons of the DEA in 1974 observed:

> The agents from BNDD did not fully understand their roles as "policy planners" and "institution builders." They were trained to make criminal cases. Their natural inclination was reinforced by a formal evaluation system that placed heavy emphasis on case production. Thus, rather than play staff roles in the development and training of effective police forces, or effective liaison roles in making specific cases, the agents often tried to operate on their own, making cases in Morocco as they did in New York City. When language or political barriers frustrated individual case-making activities, the agent lapsed into homesickness.[91]

If the passage of time has not exactly eliminated these problems, it has at least ameliorated them. Turf struggles may be a perpetual irritation

91. Moore, "Reorganization Plan #2 Reviewed" (supra n. 85), 238–239.

wherever two agencies are charged with overlapping tasks; they clearly have not disappeared from the domain of U.S. drug enforcement. But the consolidation in 1973 of almost all drug enforcement responsibilities in the DEA, combined with the passage of time since then, has rendered the turf struggles a relatively small irritant in U.S. drug enforcement activities abroad. So too most DEA agents overseas now have a keener sense of the different nature of their responsibilities abroad, although the basic preoccupation with "making cases" has not changed. Indeed, many of the institution-building chores expected of them during the 1970s have now proven sufficiently successful that the DEA agents can once again focus their efforts on immobilizing traffickers.

The single most important factor determining how DEA agents operate overseas and how successful they are is largely resistant to change; it is the personality and capability of each agent stationed abroad. The numbers of agents have remained sufficiently few, and their situations sufficiently particularistic, that the individual agent's basic characteristics continue to play a major role in defining his or her function. Some are never able to adapt to the different demands of being an overseas agent. Some adapt to the extent of being able to pursue investigations in the foreign country. Others never adjust to the loss of their police powers that is the inevitable handicap of being an overseas agent. Some respond to the demands of diplomacy and foreign lobbying with striking ease. Others are unable to acquire a feel for the local culture and ways of doing things. If a foreign office is large enough, the agents may be able to accommodate themselves to the particular abilities and preferences of each agent by assigning each the tasks that come most naturally to him or her. In an office of one or two agents, however, no such option exists. By and large, most DEA agents stationed overseas prove highly adaptable to the local environment and the constraints and demands imposed upon them—at least that was my impression based upon interviews with DEA agents in eighteen foreign countries.

The likelihood that overseas agents will possess the particular skills and dispositions required abroad is increased by the tendency for most agents to serve in foreign posts more than once. In recent years, the DEA has discouraged its agents from remaining overseas for too long, fearing they might "go native." Stories are told of agents who stayed overseas for a decade and were no longer able to adjust once they returned to the United States. The present rule, which is only rarely waived, is that no agent remains abroad for more than six years. Quite often, however, an agent is brought home for a few years and then stationed overseas again, both because he possesses or has acquired the necessary skills, language and otherwise, and because he requests the transfer overseas. Only rarely, however, is an agent sent to a city where he had been previously posted.

One pattern in agent assignments that emerged during the 1970s and 1980s was the informal division of overseas agents into two groups: those who have served in Latin America, and those who have served in Europe and Asia. Within each group, an agent will typically serve in one country or two over a six-year period, return to the United States for two to six years, and then be sent abroad again. There are now at least a few dozen agents who have served in half a dozen different cities in Latin America or in a similar number of posts throughout Europe, Asia, and the Middle East—with one to two intervening assignments in the United States. It is highly unusual, however, for an agent to have served in both Latin America and a foreign post (other than Spain) in another continent; at least a few Hispanic American agents attributed this de facto policy to a subtle sense of racism in the higher echelons of the agency.

At a very minimum, the DEA agent stationed abroad has a liaison role. This involves developing and maintaining contacts with foreign government officials who are in a position to aid or hinder the agent in his task. Most of the officials are in the police agencies; others are in the customs agency, the military, the justice and interior ministries, or other agencies with related interests. The extensiveness of the agent's contacts will depend upon a number of factors, including the size and sophistication of the foreign government, the state of the government's relations with the United States, the degree of control exercised by the government over the DEA's operations, the priority given the drug issue by the U.S. embassy, the degree of latitude and support given the DEA by the U.S. ambassador, and, perhaps most important, the needs and resourcefulness of the agent. In some countries, the DEA's contacts are mostly with lower-level officials, and those with officials in the higher reaches of government are sporadic and largely formal. This is typically the case in many European countries. Elsewhere, the DEA agent may have instant access to officials at the highest level and may have developed professional and social relationships with top police officials, generals, cabinet-level ministers, and their top aides. In a few countries, most notably in Latin America but also in countries whose governments are not on good terms with the United States, the DEA agent's access may exceed that of both the ambassador and the CIA.

An important determinant of the level of a DEA agent's contacts is his position in the hierarchy of the specific office. The top DEA agent in a foreign country, known as the country attaché (CA), is usually responsible for most high-level contacts.[92] In countries where the DEA also has offices outside the capital, such as in Guayaquil, Guadalajara, Milan, or Marseilles, high-level local liaison is handled by the head of the office, known as the resident-agent-in-charge (RAC). The likelihood that lower-ranking agents, known both inside and outside the United States as special agents (SAs), will engage in high-level contacts depends in good part upon the size of the office and the country. The smaller either is, the greater the possibility that a special agent will also interact with high-level officials. In the smaller countries, located mostly although not entirely in the Caribbean and Central America, the country attaché's contacts will likely range from lower-level detectives to top police officials and cabinet-rank ministers and their deputies. In a large foreign country with a significant DEA presence, especially outside Europe, the country attaché's contacts will probably extend to the same high levels of government, but many of the lower-level contacts will be left to the other agents in the office. These high-level contacts assume much greater significance in much of Latin America, the Caribbean, and Asia, where law enforcement, politics, and corruption are far more intimately connected than is true in most of Europe and the United States today (see Chapter Five).

Within any foreign country, the country attaché is in charge of all DEA activities ranging from liaison to training to criminal investigations. The one exception, at least until the DEA was placed under the umbrella of the FBI in 1981, was the Central Tactical Unit program (CENTAC). Designed to target major drug trafficking organizations whose activities crossed multiple state and national borders, CENTAC investigations were coordinated not by any one special-agent-in-charge (SAC) or country attaché but by a special section in DEA headquarters. Over its eight-year life span, CENTAC conducted approximately two dozen investigations, almost all of which involved foreign countries. CENTAC's three heads all had served abroad as FBN agents in the 1950s and 1960s—first Anthony Pohl, the agent who opened the Marseilles office

92. The head of a *domestic* DEA office is referred to as the special-agent-in-charge (SAC).

in 1961, then Martin Pera, who had worked with Siragusa in Europe in the 1950s and supervised FBN operations in Europe from the Rome office during the early 1960s, and finally Dennis Dayle, who had covered the Middle East in the mid-1960s from the FBN office in Beirut.[93] The CENTAC agents included many of the DEA's best, drawn from headquarters as well as the field offices, as well as agents from the IRS, Customs, other federal, state, and city police agencies, and foreign police agents. Despite persistent opposition from the DEA's regional directors, many of whom bitterly resented the infringements on their authority by the centrally directed units, CENTAC thrived.[94] Using less than 3 percent of the DEA's resources, it accounted for more than 12 percent of the agency's arrests of high-level violators.[95]

CENTAC's dissolution in 1981 coincided with a significant reorganization in the internal structure of the DEA. Until that year, all DEA offices and operations had been supervised by regional offices. Until 1971, and then again from 1976 to 1981, there were three such offices overseas, in Paris, Bangkok, and Mexico City. During the intervening years, three additional DEA locations were expanded into regional offices, in Manila, Caracas, and Karachi. In 1981, the DEA eliminated the organizational plan in which all overseas offices reported to one of three overseas regional offices in favor of a centralized FBI-type organizational structure stressing functional rather than geographic lines of authority. Instead of reporting to regional offices, the foreign offices, as well as the domestic offices, all reported to a heroin, cocaine, or marijuana desk based at headquarters, depending upon the type of investigation. To some extent, the reorganization represented a vindication of CENTAC's centralized direction, with its lack of geographical limits on operations. The CENTAC concept was partially retained as well, with the CENTAC units now renamed "Special Enforcement

93. James Mills, *The Underground Empire: Where Crime and Governments Embrace* (Garden City, N.Y.: Doubleday, 1986), 66–70, 117–122.

94. CENTAC's bureaucratic struggles are discussed in James Q. Wilson, *The Investigators: Managing FBI and Narcotics Agents* (New York: Basic Books, 1978), 148–152; U.S. General Accounting Office (GAO), *The Drug Enforcement Administration's CENTAC Program—An Effective Approach to Investigating Major Traffickers That Needs to Be Expanded* (1980); and Mills, *Underground Empire*, 118–129.

95. The calculation, based on the years 1976–78, is in the GAO report on CENTAC (supra n. 94). The exploits of three CENTAC investigations were the subject of a best-selling book by James Mills, *The Underground Empire: Where Crime and Governments Embrace* (1986), which vividly describes the activities and dilemmas of the CENTAC agents.

Operations" (SEOs). Like CENTAC, the SEOs have tried to deemphasize the organizational preoccupation with maximizing the numbers of arrests and seizures and have focused instead on complex, long-term conspiracy investigations aimed at destroying major drug trafficking organizations. In part because they have been more numerous, the SEOs do not appear to have accomplished the dramatic successes attributed to CENTAC.

The FBI Abroad: LEGATs and International Criminal Investigations

Throughout much of the world, the one law enforcement agency most identified with the U.S. government is the Federal Bureau of Investigation. As the lead criminal investigative agency in the United States, this is hardly surprising, although the public image cultivated by J. Edgar Hoover, the FBI's longtime director, must be credited as well. On the other hand, since the early 1970s, the FBI's overseas presence has paled beside that of the drug enforcement agencies. In 1990, its overseas agents, known as legal attachés (LEGATs), numbered only 40 in 16 countries, up from 31 in 13 countries in 1985 but down from 41 in 20 countries in 1973. (See Appendix D.) In certain respects, the FBI's foreign offices have changed relatively little since the 1950s. It has remained among the least operational of all U.S. law enforcement agencies overseas. "We've always billed ourselves as a liaison organization," one LEGAT emphasized to me; "that's part of our international reputation." On the other hand, the FBI has, like most other U.S. police agencies, significantly enhanced its international presence since the mid-1980s. FBI agents travel abroad with increasing frequency to conduct international investigations, lead training programs, lend their expertise in forensic and other investigative techniques, and attend international law enforcement conferences. Since January 1987, all of the FBI's international activities have been coordinated by an Office of Liaison and International Affairs (OLIA).

When J. Edgar Hoover was appointed director of the Bureau of Investigation in 1924, he focused his efforts on professionalizing the agency, the reputation of which had recently reached its nadir. The prospect of agents such as Billy Gard globe-trotting to foreign lands to enforce U.S. laws could hardly have appealed to the new director, concerned as he was with maintaining a tight rein on his agents. The few agents who did travel outside the country were usually stationed in American cities along the borders with Canada and Mexico. In 1939, one of these, the special agent in charge in El Paso, became the first to be stationed abroad, when he was delegated to Mexico for intelligence purposes.[96]

The heyday of the FBI's international program paralleled the history of the CIA's predecessor, the Office of Strategic Services (OSS). In June 1940, President Franklin Roosevelt assigned all intelligence responsibilities for the western hemisphere to the FBI. Shortly thereafter, Hoover created a Special Intelligence Service (SIS) to undertake the major task of countering Axis activities in South and Central America. Within a few years, 360 agents were stationed throughout the region, particularly in Mexico, Argentina, and Brazil. Some operated undercover, others served openly as legal attachés in U.S. embassies and liaison officers with foreign police forces. Hoover and his agents worked closely with the British Security Coordination (BSC), the U.S.-based British intelligence agency directed by the "Man Called Intrepid," William Stephenson.[97] South American officials working covertly for the Nazis were exposed, as were the pro-Nazi activities of the large German communities throughout the continent. In Bolivia, SIS agents foiled a planned coup d'état by pro-Axis forces. In Chile, the U.S. agents contributed to the government's shift away from its initial support for Germany. Elsewhere, the agents used their influence with friendly governments to have pro-Axis elements jailed or deported. Local police were cultivated with money and invitations to the National Police Academy in Washington. Throughout the war, a network of FBI-trained police that would continue to aid the FBI's more mundane law enforcement efforts in peacetime was built up.

Toward the end of the war, Hoover vied with the OSS to have the SIS

96. Sanford J. Ungar, *FBI* (Boston: Little, Brown, 1975), 226.

97. The FBI's activities in Latin America are discussed in Stanley E. Hilton, *Hitler's Secret War in South America, 1939–1945* (Baton Rouge: Louisiana State University Press, 1981), 196–229; Leslie B. Rout Jr. and John F. Bratzel, *The Shadow War: German Espionage and American Counterespionage in Latin America During World War II* (Frederick, Md.: University Publications, 1986); and Silvia Galvis and Alberto Donadio, *Colombia Nazi* (Bogotá: Planeta, 1986), esp. 39–54. See also the brief discussions of the SIS in Ungar, *FBI*, 225, and in Richard Gil Powers, *Secrecy and Power: The Life of J. Edgar Hoover* (New York: Free Press, 1987), 251–253, 545.

serve as the nucleus of the postwar intelligence system. When he failed, many of the SIS agents based in Latin America went to work for the new CIA. A few remained where they had been stationed, in Latin America, London, and Ottawa, becoming the first of what would soon develop into a modest international network of LEGATs. Some were assigned to new locations where the OSS rather than the SIS had handled wartime intelligence activities. And a number were delegated, at General Douglas MacArthur's request, to assist the American occupation forces in Japan. Unlike the SIS agents, the LEGATs were charged not just with counter-espionage responsibilities but with investigating criminal matters as well. They also were ordered to refrain from engaging in the types of operational activities undertaken by the SIS during the war and by U.S. drug enforcement agents thereafter. Within a few years, the LEGATs became widely recognized as the official U.S. police liaisons to foreign governments and police agencies.

LEGATs are expected to handle all international matters that fall within the FBI's jurisdiction. This includes counterintelligence, criminal investigation (much of it involving white-collar crime and organized crime) and counterterrorism (which can involve both counterintelligence and criminal investigative tasks and contacts). With respect to the first, most of the LEGATs' contacts are with foreign intelligence agencies, of which there are typically two—one engaged in domestic intelligence, the other specializing in foreign matters. Because the FBI is responsible for counterintelligence in the United States and the CIA has jurisdiction over similar matters overseas, substantial overlap occurs between the two agencies. This is partially resolved by the FBI's focusing on the aspects of counterintelligence that have some link with domestic cases. In the counterterrorism area, the LEGAT usually needs to liaise with both of the local intelligence agencies as well as with the criminal investigative agencies and the CIA—a task that requires a fair degree of diplomatic skill, given the often fierce turf squabbles between the two intelligence agencies in each country as well as between them and the police agencies. Almost every LEGAT, for instance, can recall instances of being provided with information by a foreign intelligence agency only on condition that the LEGAT not share it with the other intelligence agency in the country.

In the criminal area, the LEGAT, like the U.S.-based FBI agent, oversees a hodgepodge of matters. He typically refrains from investigating criminal matters personally, confining his involvement to one of liaison between American and local law enforcement agencies and prosecutors. His role is that of a facilitator of requests to and from the United States for information, evidence, interrogations, searches, arrests, and extraditions. The requests may be transmitted in a variety of ways: informally by phone, wire, letter, or personal visit, or formally via Interpol, letters rogatory, or the procedures laid out in the few mutual legal assistance treaties to which the United States is a party. Although the LEGAT need not be involved in, or even know of, many of the requests, a resourceful agent can play a crucial role in cutting through red tape and hastening a response. He is likely to know personally a variety of local police officials, including the national police director, in whichever countries fall under his jurisdiction. He can use his informal contacts with local authorities to gain information or to prod them to respond quickly to a request from the United States. Where information is required in the form of evidence admissable in U.S. courts, U.S. prosecutors may request by letter rogatory or pursuant to a treaty that the LEGAT be permitted to conduct an interview, or attend an interrogation, or collect documents. The more extensive a LEGAT's connections with foreign law enforcement officials, the more effective the LEGAT is likely to be and, as one FBI agent put it, "the more business he is likely to generate." "In the Legats perhaps more than anywhere else in the FBI," Sanford Ungar wrote, "the special agent is a combination of investigator, bureaucrat, diplomat, gumshoe, gossip, and public relations man."[98]

Throughout the 1950s and 1960s, the LEGAT program was limited to approximately ten foreign offices, with each responsible for liaison with many other countries as well. Early in the Nixon administration, the program grew when Hoover persuaded the President of the advantages of expanding the LEGAT network, primarily for intelligence purposes. He reportedly argued that his agents could provide better intelligence than the CIA was producing, and that the growing number of Vietnam draft resisters, deserters, and black extremist fugitives overseas, as well as the increasing volume of terrorism, hijacking, drug trafficking, and other transnational criminal cases, required an expanded international presence.[99] Within a few years, the number of overseas offices had doubled—despite persistent opposition by the FBI's chief of intelligence, William Sullivan, who argued that the CIA could handle

98. Ungar, *FBI*, 224.
99. Ibid., 241–242.

most of the intelligence tasks and that the State Department could handle the criminal liaison functions.[100] In his view, Ottawa and Mexico City were the only foreign cities where LEGATs were required because of the large volume of criminals and spies crossing the borders. And even with respect to Mexico City, Sullivan opposed Hoover's instructions to the Mexico City LEGAT office authorizing its agents, unlike those in all other countries apart from Canada, to be operational.

Sullivan's objections were difficult to refute in the early 1970s when even the LEGATs themselves wondered what they were supposed to be doing in places like La Paz and Singapore. Some agents within the FBI also questioned the dedication of the agents abroad, cynically referring to what they called the "LEGAT shuffle." As one agent put it, "LEGATs have the reputation of never doing any work and giving everyone the runaround. As soon as they get overseas, they think they work for the State Department, and all they do is go to cocktail parties and play golf."[101] On the other hand, the LEGAT network has repeatedly proven its value in numerous international criminal investigations. Perhaps the most vivid description of what a dedicated LEGAT can accomplish is provided in *Labyrinth*, a book by Taylor Branch and Eugene M. Propper about the U.S. investigation of the 1976 Washington, D.C., murder of Orlando Letelier, the Chilean foreign minister during the Allende regime. Robert Scherrer, the LEGAT in Buenos Aires with responsibility for liaison in Chile as well, played a crucial role in the investigation, conducting a variety of tasks ranging from record searches to tactical advice on evidence-gathering to prying information out of the chiefs of the Chilean intelligence and police agencies. During his six-year stint in Argentina, Scherrer undertook a great variety of responsibilities, some of them at his own initiative. During the mid-1970s, he worked with the U.S. ambassador in Paraguay to dissuade the Paraguayan president, General Stroessner, from offering a haven to international fugitives, such as Robert Vesco and Meyer Lansky.[102] Within Argentina, he was able to make use of his contacts among the police to find out the fate of suspected leftists who had been "disappeared"; among those he assisted was Rabbi Morton Rosenthal, an American rabbi who specialized in

100. See William C. Sullivan, *The Bureau: My Thirty Years in Hoover's FBI* (New York: W. W. Norton, 1979), 39–41, 199–201, 241–242, 272–273.

101. Quoted in Taylor Branch and Eugene M. Propper, *Labyrinth* (New York: Viking Press, 1982), 328–329.

102. Ibid., 401.

locating Jewish citizens seized by rightist regimes in the southern part of the continent.[103]

Until Hoover's death in 1972, LEGATs were charged with handling all international dimensions of U.S. investigations. U.S.-based agents were not permitted to pursue their investigations overseas, no matter how important or complicated the case. Exceptions were made for FBI agents stationed in border cities, but even they were constrained by strict guidelines that limited the amount of time they could spend in Canada or Mexico.[104] A special exception was made in 1965, when sixteen agents were sent to the Dominican Republic in the wake of the military intervention to conduct security checks on potential members of the provisional government and collect intelligence on political developments.[105] The agency's restriction on foreign travel was predicated in part upon the assumption that LEGATs could handle any foreign matters that might arise. In fact, many cases arose in which it became clear that LEGATs, no matter how well they knew their country, could not substitute for a U.S.-based agent who had spent months investigating a particular case.

The case that ultimately prompted the FBI to change its policy on agents traveling overseas involved an international securities fraud investigation initiated by the New York City Police Department (which also broke with tradition in sending an agent overseas). In late 1972 the FBI's acting director, L. Patrick Gray, agreed to permit agent Richard Tamarro to accompany New York City detective Joseph Coffey on a trip to Germany, Luxembourg, and Austria to pursue their investigation.[106] By 1978, the policy against foreign travel had been relaxed enough that FBI agents investigating the Letelier killing were permitted to accompany a U.S. prosecutor on his trips to Venezuela and Chile despite the presence of LEGATs in those countries. Although the FBI still prefers to rely on its LEGATs to handle foreign matters, and it remains wary of sending lower-level agents overseas lest they create diplomatic imbroglios, foreign travel by FBI agents has become far less of an exceptional undertak-

103. Ibid., 400.

104. Ungar, *FBI* (supra n. 96), 226.

105. Athan G. Theoharis and John Stuart Cox, *The Boss: J. Edgar Hoover and the Great American Inquisition* (Philadelphia: Temple University Press, 1988), 396; W. Mark Felt and Ralph de Toledano, *The FBI Pyramid from the Inside* (New York: G. P. Putnam's Sons, 1979), 82–85.

106. Richard Hammer, *The Vatican Connection* (New York: Holt, Rinehart & Winston, 1982), 148, 272–277.

ing. By the late 1980s, a LEGAT in Paris recalled, he could expect to see a U.S.-based FBI agent passing through his office either on an investigation or en route to a conference about once a week. (Agents from other U.S. law enforcement agencies might also drop by, particularly if their agency lacked a representative in the embassy, but the LEGAT could often send them down the hall to the State Department's Regional Security Officer.) And even though most FBI agents must still secure approval from FBI headquarters to travel abroad, those stationed near the Canadian and Mexican borders routinely liaise with law enforcement authorities, crossing into foreign territory frequently and with no need to secure prior approval from headquarters. The same is true, albeit to a slightly lesser degree, of the agents stationed in Miami and Puerto Rico who cover the Caribbean islands.

The incentives and pressures on the FBI to shed most of its inhibitions regarding international involvements arose from a variety of sources. In 1982, the FBI was made the parent agency of the DEA and given joint jurisdiction over drug cases involving organized crime. The DEA's international drug enforcement activities were little affected by this development except in three locations: Italy, Canada, and to a lesser extent Switzerland. Largely because drug trafficking investigations in those countries tend to have some connection with "traditional" organized crime—that is, the Mafia—the FBI and the DEA agreed that the parent agency would retain its own lead in domestically initiated drug cases. In the early 1980s, FBI and DEA agents, working with the New York Police Department and federal prosecutors, began investigating a new generation of Sicilian mafiosi who had become involved in trafficking heroin to the United States. In what became known as the "Pizza Connection Case," FBI and DEA agents as well as Italian police engaged in a wide-ranging investigation that took them to Italy, Spain, Switzerland, Brazil, Canada, and the United States.[107] A U.S.-Italian Working Group on Organized Crime was created early in the investigation to promote closer cooperation and resolve disputes. FBI agents shed some of their traditional reluctance to operate more aggressively overseas; Italian police were drawn into surveillances in the United States. In early 1987, the case was successfully concluded in U.S. and Italian courts with

107. See Ralph Blumenthal, *Last Days of the Sicilians* (New York: Times Books, 1988); and Claire Sterling, *Octopus: The Long Reach of the International Sicilian Mafia* (New York: W. W. Norton, 1990).

the conviction of most of those involved in the drug trafficking operation.

Another incentive for the FBI to become more active overseas arose during the 1980s in response to the rising number of terrorist incidents and politically motivated murders involving American citizens. Until well into the 1970s, the FBI played a very limited role in investigating terrorist incidents abroad, even those directed at American citizens, because no federal laws were violated by such acts. In 1978, its extraterritorial activities, and the extraterritorial reach of U.S. law, expanded with the investigation of the death of Congressman Leo J. Ryan and a U.S. embassy official in Jonestown, Guyana, the subsequent prosecution of Larry Layton, and the federal court's assertion of jurisdiction over the crime.[108] In 1983, FBI forensics specialists were sent to Beirut to investigate the April bombing of the U.S. embassy and the October bombing of a U.S. marine facility.

The principal impetus for an expanded FBI role in investigating international terrorist incidents was provided by Congress, which in 1984 and 1986 enacted legislation that greatly broadened the United States' extraterritorial jurisdiction over terrorist acts.[109] Coordinating its efforts with the CIA and the State Department's Counterterrorism Office, as well as with foreign police agencies, FBI agents participated in investigations of more than fifty terrorist incidents outside U.S. borders between 1985 and the middle of 1989, including the repeated abductions of American citizens in Lebanon.[110] FBI agents traveled frequently to El

108. D. F. Martell, "FBI's Expanding Role in International Terrorism Investigations," *FBI Law Enforcement Bulletin* 56 (Oct. 1987), 28–32. See also *U.S. v. Layton*, 509 F.Supp. 212 (N.D. Cal. 1981), appeal dismissed, 645 F.2d 681 (9th Cir. 1981), cert. denied, 452 U.S. 972 (1981); and *The Assassination of Representative Leo J. Ryan and the Jonestown, Guyana Tragedy: Report of a Staff Investigative Group to the House Committee on Foreign Affairs*, 96th Cong., 1st Sess. (1979).

109. The Comprehensive Crime Control Act of 1984, for instance, included a new law, 18 U.S.C. 1203, which implements the International Convention Against the Taking of Hostages. The statute provides for U.S. federal jurisdiction over any hostage taken overseas in which the victim or the perpetrator is an American citizen, in which the United States is the target of the hostage-taker's demands, or in which the offender is found within the United States. The Omnibus Diplomatic Security and Antiterrorism Act of 1986, 18 U.S.C. 2331, broadened the extraterritorial jurisdiction of the United States to include any terrorist act in which an American citizen is killed or seriously injured.

110. See *Extraterritorial Jurisdiction over Terrorist Acts Abroad: Hearings Before the Subcommittee on Crime of the House Committee on the Judiciary*, 101st Cong., 1st Sess. (May–July, 1989), 5 (testimony of Oliver B. Revell), which refers to investigations of twenty-two incidents. See also *FBI Authority to Seize Suspects Abroad: Hearing Before the Subcommittee on Civil and Constitutional Rights of the House Committee on the Judiciary*, 101st

Salvador during the 1980s, for instance, where they trained local police and investigated the killings of Americans both by leftist guerrillas and by the government's security forces.[111] When four U.S. marines and nine others were killed in a San Salvador café in June 1985, FBI agents even met with the Salvadoran President, José Napoleón Duarte, to seek his assistance. A few months later, FBI Director William Webster announced that he had sent "two crack teams" of FBI agents to assist in the investigation of the hijacking of the Italian cruise ship *Achille Lauro*, in particular to gather forensic information on board the ship.[112] Agents also were sent to investigate the June 1985 hijackings of TWA Flight 847 while en route from Athens to Rome and of Royal Jordanian Airlines (Alia) Flight 402 in Beirut (which carried three American passengers), the November 1985 hijacking of Egypt Air Flight 648, the April 1986 bombing of TWA Flight 840, and the September 1986 bombing of Pan Am Flight 73 in Karachi.[113] The investigation of the Alia hijacking proved more successful than most when one of the hijackers, a Lebanese named Fawaz Younis, was lured out of his Lebanese haven in a sting operation code-named "Operation Goldenrod" and arrested in international waters off the Cypriot coast in September 1987.[114]

During the latter part of the 1980s, FBI agents joined with agents of the military's law enforcement agencies in investigating bombings at U.S. military bases in Spain, Italy, Greece, and the Philippines, as well as the assassinations of U.S. military personnel in Athens in June 1988 and Manila in April 1989 by the "17 November" organization and the Philippine New People's Army, respectively; they combined with Italian police in investigating the Japanese Red Army's attack on the U.S. embassy in Rome in June 1987; they participated in the investigation of the August 1988 airplane crash in Pakistan that killed President Mohammad Zia ul-Huq, many top Pakistani military officials, and the U.S. ambassador, Arnold Raphel (although only after Congressional criticism

Cong., 1st Sess. (Nov. 8, 1989), 48 (statement of Oliver B. Revell), which refers to "at least 50 separate investigations."

111. LeMoyne, "Duarte Meets F.B.I. on Raid Inquiry" (supra n. 41).

112. Peter T. Kilborn, "F.B.I. Chief: A U.S. Trial Far Off," *New York Times*, Oct. 13, 1985, 26; "FBI Sends Agents to Italy to Monitor Case," *Boston Globe*, Oct. 13, 1985, 28.

113. Martell, "FBI's Expanding Role" (supra n. 108), 30.

114. See G. Gregory Schuetz, "Apprehending Terrorists Overseas Under United States and International Law: A Case Study of the Fawaz Younis Arrest," *Harvard International Law Journal* 29 (1988), 499–531.

of the initial State Department decision to bar the FBI agents from Pakistan cleared the way ten months later);[115] and they investigated the May 1989 assassination of two Mormon missionaries in Bolivia by a group known as the "Fuerzos Armadas de Liberación Zarate Willco," which a year earlier had attempted to bomb the motorcade of Secretary of State George Shultz during a visit to La Paz. Throughout the decade, agents also investigated leads regarding the abduction of seventeen Americans in Lebanon during the 1980s. The most intensive international investigation by the FBI during the decade, however, involved the terrorist explosion of Pan Am Flight 103 over Lockerbie, Scotland, in December 1988. Dozens of FBI agents, including LEGATs as well as forensic experts and other agents based in the United States, combined with English, Scottish and German police in tracking down leads in over forty countries from Sweden and Malta to the Far East.[116]

By early 1987, the need to provide some coordination of the FBI's growing number of international activities had resulted in the creation of an Office of Liaison and International Affairs (OLIA) at FBI headquarters. By 1990, the OLIA's responsibilities included supervision of the rising number of LEGAT offices, the two agents stationed at the U.S. Interpol office, the three agents based at Interpol headquarters in Lyons (including the chief of Interpol's antiterrorism unit), and the stream of agents from headquarters and the field offices on TDY (temporary duty) assignments abroad. OLIA also was charged with supervising the growing number of foreign police representatives based in the United States, as well as most visits by foreign police officials. The tendency of many high-level foreign police officials to visit FBI headquarters when they come to the United States—be it to pursue an investigation, attend a conference, seek medical care, or visit a child at an American school—has helped ease the growing internationalization of the FBI's activities. Additional opportunities to develop close relationships with foreign law enforcement officials have emerged at the FBI's National Academy in Quantico, where 50–100 of the 800 students participating in the school's eleven-week command-level training program in recent years are from

115. Robert Pear, "FBI Allowed to Investigate Crash That Killed Zia," *New York Times*, June 25, 1989, 13; *Extraterritorial Jurisdiction over Terrorist Acts Abroad: Hearings* (supra n. 110).

116. Steven Emerson and Brian Duffy, *The Fall of Pan Am 103: Inside the Lockerbie Investigation* (New York: G. P. Putnam's Sons, 1990).

abroad; some efforts are made to maintain contact with its foreign alumni. Top-level FBI officials and the LEGATs in Europe have also attended, albeit officially with observer status, the periodic sessions of TREVI—the collaborative arrangement among European interior ministers and top law enforcement officials designed to improve cooperation against terrorism, drug trafficking, organized crime, and other threats to public security. Particularly influential in many of these foreign initiatives was Oliver "Buck" Revell, a top FBI official throughout the 1980s who served as a high-level advocate for internationalizing the FBI's outlook and operations.

The U.S. Customs Service: Dealing with High-Tech Smugglers, Money Launderers, and Contrabandistas

The one agency whose jurisdiction has most naturally encompassed transnational crime is the U.S. Customs Service. For much of the century, its overseas presence exceeded that of any other civilian law enforcement agency, until the Bureau of Narcotics and Dangerous Drugs (BNDD) surpassed it during the late 1960s. From 1930 to 1973, Customs vied first with the Federal Bureau of Narcotics and thereafter with the BNDD for greater jurisdiction over international drug trafficking cases, but the turf struggle was ultimately resolved to Customs' detriment when a major bureaucratic reorganization in 1973 led to the merger of its drug enforcement departments with the BNDD into the newly created Drug Enforcement Administration (DEA).[117] Thereafter, most of the overseas Customs agents transferred to the DEA; the remainder were either recalled or limited their investigations to what was left of Customs' overseas jurisdiction. The Customs Service retained some jurisdiction over drug cases by virtue of its border authority, but the follow-up investigation of leads resulting from seizures was delegated to the DEA. Periodic memoranda of understanding between the heads of Customs and the DEA were necessary thereafter to resolve lingering tensions between the two agencies.[118] Customs eventually acknowledged the

117. The best discussion of these developments is Rachal, *Federal Narcotics Enforcement* (supra n. 85).

118. One such memorandum of understanding, dated Dec. 11, 1975, is reproduced in *The*

DEA's lead in drug matters and, for the remainder of the decade, confined its few remaining overseas offices to enforcement of anti-dumping statutes and non-drug-related smuggling. By 1979, its presence abroad had been reduced to eight foreign offices.

With an eye constantly open to new overseas opportunities, however, the Customs Service was able in the early 1980s to take advantage of two developments to expand its jurisdiction and presence overseas. The first was the increasing concern over the smuggling of sophisticated technology to Soviet-bloc countries as well as to others, including close allies of the United States, who had been refused an export license for either security or competitive commercial reasons. The Customs Service had overseen this area since the beginning of the Cold War, but new opportunities emerged with the passage of the 1979 Export Administration Act, the Carter administration's growing interest in this issue following the Soviet invasion of Afghanistan, and the high priority subsequently given the issue by the Reagan administration. In late 1981, Customs launched Operation Exodus, a more systematic effort to investigate and curtail high-tech smuggling. At first, its agents were criticized for their lack of expertise in investigating and deterring this form of smuggling.[119] Within a few years, however, they had acquired a much more sophisticated knowledge of the illicit commerce, the principal criminals, and their methods—all of which differ substantially from the drug traffic. Although the FBI, the Bureau of Alcohol, Tobacco, and Firearms (ATF), the Commerce Department, and the intelligence agencies all retain some slice of jurisdiction in this area—one consequence of which was the fierce turf struggles during the early 1980s with the Commerce Department's Export Enforcement Office, which opened offices in Vienna, Bern, and Stockholm during the 1980s[120]—the Customs Service has remained the lead agency in most regards.[121] By the late 1980s, high-tech smuggling had emerged as the top priority of virtually all Customs attachés overseas, whose numbers have been gradually growing to pre-1973 levels.

Mexican Connection: Hearings Before the Subcommittee to Investigate Juvenile Delinquency of the Senate Committee on the Judiciary, 95th Cong., 2d Sess. (1978), 157–161.

119. August Bequai, *Technocrimes* (Lexington, Mass.: Lexington Books, 1987), 92–93.

120. U.S. Department of Commerce, Bureau of Export Administration, *Annual Report, FY 1989* (Washington, D.C.: Government Printing Office, 1990).

121. The principal account of Customs' efforts to stem the flow of high technology, and its turf struggles, is Linda Melvern, David Hebditch, and Nick Anning, *Techno-Bandits* (Boston: Houghton Mifflin, 1984).

The second development, the potential of which Customs was initially slow to recognize, was the enactment of the Bank Secrecy Act in 1970. The legislation was prompted by growing concern over the use of foreign financial secrecy jurisdictions to launder illegally earned money, and by the emerging realization that tracing the paper trail of laundered money could implicate the high-level drug traffickers and other criminals who received most of the profits.[122] One provision of the act, which required that individuals taking more than $5,000 in or out of the country file a Currency Transaction Report (CTR), provided Customs with a reentry into the area of narcotics investigation as well as other areas of criminal investigation. In the first interagency task force to focus on money laundering—Operation Greenback, in Miami—customs agents once again began to travel overseas in drug-related cases, although their focus was now on the movement of money rather than drugs. In late 1983, after overcoming DEA resistance, Customs opened an office in the Panama City embassy—its first in Latin America (excluding Mexico) since it lost its jurisdiction over drug cases a decade earlier. Although that office resembled others overseas in that its first priority was high-tech smuggling out of the Colón Free Trade Zone, its second priority was investigating drug-related money laundering through Panama's infamous banks.[123] Its efforts thereafter to expand its presence in Latin America were stymied, however, by resistance from the DEA. An attempt in 1986 to station an agent in Bogotá on more than a TDY basis failed, and no additional offices were opened in South America until 1990, when permission was granted to station an agent in Montevideo, one of the few Latin American capitals without a resident DEA agent. That office, however, represented U.S. Customs' twentieth foreign office—a far cry from the diminished presence of a decade before. (See Appendix A.) Also significant was the negotiation of an interagency agreement under which 1,000 customs agents were designated to investigate drug smuggling and money laundering—an accomplishment that the new commissioner of customs, Carol Hallett, described as her greatest achievement.[124]

122. See Chapter Six for a more thorough analysis of U.S. efforts to deal with international money laundering.

123. *U.S. Narcotics Control Programs Overseas, an Assessment: Report of a Staff Study Mission to Southeast Asia, South America, Central America, and the Caribbean, August 1984 to January 1985, to the House Committee on Foreign Affairs*, 99th Cong., 1st Sess. (1985), 33.

124. Robert D. Hershey Jr., "In the Customs Service, an Open Door at the Top," *New York Times*, Aug. 18, 1990, 9.

Apart from high-tech smuggling and money laundering, Customs' attachés have continued to investigate violations of antidumping laws, commercial fraud, arms and pornography smuggling, and other contraband activities. In one major investigation during the mid-1980s, known as "Operation Retread," customs agents conducted a worldwide investigation into the illicit diversion of U.S. military equipment to proscribed governments.[125] Their attachés have tended to be slightly more "operational" than the LEGATs in that they become directly involved in investigations, but with one or two exceptions (such as Germany) they have exercised greater restraint in their activities than most overseas DEA agents. Only toward the late 1980s did the Customs Service start shedding its inhibitions against acting more operationally overseas. In one case, Customs collaborated with British authorities in an investigation of a front company for the Iraqi government's arms-procurement network that involved undercover negotiations by a customs agent as well as a controlled delivery of detonator components.[126] But customs attachés still interact primarily with foreign customs agencies, which in most cases (Great Britain is an exception) lack the police powers and sophistication of the U.S. agency.

Customs' principal obstacle abroad—one that it shares with the Immigration and Naturalization Service—is that many of the violations of U.S. laws that concern it are not violations of local laws, or are violations only in egregious cases. Only toward the end of the 1980s, for instance, did a number of governments begin to criminalize money laundering. Similarly, most non-NATO countries demonstrated relatively little interest in regulating high-tech exports, and even the NATO members differed on important details of the export controls. And with regard to many other forms of contraband, often foreign governments do not prohibit the export of goods that cannot be imported legally into the United States. All of this contrasts with the laws that the DEA and the Secret Service are charged with enforcing, which are in effect throughout the world and backed by global conventions. Customs has tried to compensate for this disadvantage by vigorously developing bilateral relationships with dozens of foreign customs agencies—not least by offering a broad array of training and other assistance programs—and by playing a leading role in the Customs Cooperation Council (CCC)

125. See *Federal Licensing Procedures for Arms Exports: Hearing Before the Senate Committee on Governmental Affairs*, 100th Cong., 1st Sess. (1987), 48–49, 103–139.
126. *U.S. Customs, Update 1990*, 16–17.

and the assorted regional customs conferences.[127] Its efforts to cultivate a transnational community of customs officials akin to that which bonds drug enforcement agents across borders have yielded dividends, but the diversity of its mandate ensures that it will never attain the level of consensus that underlies U.S. efforts to suppress drug trafficking and counterfeiting.

The Secret Service: Contending with Counterfeiters

With more than half of all counterfeit U.S. dollars produced and circulated overseas, where they are found in roughly fifty countries each year, the Secret Service has been obliged to operate internationally since its origins.[128] The emergence of the U.S. dollar as a sort of international currency following World War II increased this need. The Secret Service has maintained an agent in Europe since 1947, when three Secret Service agents were sent to France to investigate a criminal ring engaged in counterfeiting U.S. dollars. Working undercover and in cooperation with the Sûreté, the agents succeeded in identifying and apprehending the counterfeiters.[129] With the problem of counterfeiting U.S. dollars widespread in Europe in the years after the war, an agent was assigned to operate out of the U.S. embassy in Paris and maintain contact with European law enforcement agencies. The one office sufficed until 1985 when an apparent rise in international activity in counterfeit dollars prompted an expansion of the Secret Service's international presence. With the Paris office overwhelmed by requests for assistance from Italian police, a second foreign office was opened in Milan in 1985 and then relocated to Rome in 1988. By the end of the 1980s, two agents had also been stationed in Bonn and London, from where they reported to the Paris office. Liaison with Asia was handled out of the Honolulu office and, beginning in 1987, a resident office in Bangkok; by the end of the decade, a Secret Service agent could also be found on a virtually constant TDY basis in the Philippines. Latin America and the Caribbean were

127. Ibid., 28–30.

128. In 1989, approximately $100 million in counterfeit U.S. currency was seized within the United States, and approximately $120 million abroad.

129. Michael Dorman, *The Secret Service Story* (New York: Delacorte Press, 1967), 74–79.

covered until 1986 by the San Juan, Puerto Rico, office; thereafter an international squad in the Miami office assumed responsibility for Latin America, Jamaica, and the Bahamas, with San Juan retaining responsibility for the remainder of the Caribbean islands. The principal focus of first the San Juan office and then the Miami office throughout the 1980s was Colombia, which has long been regarded as one of the principal sources of counterfeit dollars; plans to station an agent in Bogotá were seriously considered during the 1980s but ultimately abandoned in good part because of security considerations. Mexico, which in contrast to other areas of transnational crime has been the source of relatively little counterfeit currency, is covered by Secret Service offices stationed in U.S. cities near the border. Agents stationed in cities near the northern border handle liaison with the Canadians, whose counterfeit currency laboratory based in Ottawa works closely with the Secret Service's lab in Washington. Within the Honolulu, Miami, and San Juan offices, individual Secret Service agents are each charged with responsibility for liaising with foreign officials in particular countries.

Unlike many U.S. law enforcement agencies abroad, the Secret Service has not had to contend with the common problem of disinterest on the part of foreign law enforcement agencies. Because most counterfeit dollars are produced and circulated in foreign countries, most police agencies recognize the counterfeiting of U.S. dollars as not merely a violation of local laws but also a threat to domestic interests. The tendency of most counterfeiters to diversify into counterfeiting other currencies as well as passports and other official documents has also abetted the coincidence of interests between the Secret Service and their foreign counterparts. Virtually no non-U.S. counterfeit currency, however, is believed to be produced within the United States; as a result, few foreign police ever need to come to the United States on a counterfeiting investigation, and the involvement of Secret Service agents in investigations of foreign currency counterfeiting is largely limited to investigations abroad involving co-production of counterfeit dollars and foreign currencies.

The general disposition of Secret Service agents abroad is to maintain a low profile but to "be prepared," as one agent put it, "to be able to make themselves available to do whatever local agents need them to do." The most common task required of the overseas agents is to assist in the identification of counterfeit dollars, a process that generally involves checking a suspected note against the "circularized note" files at headquarters.[130] The array of activities performed by Secret Service agents stationed overseas, as well as by those sent on TDY visits, is quite as diverse as that of DEA agents. Secret Service agents have cooperated closely in foreign investigations, providing intelligence on suspected counterfeiters and their techniques, assisting in the recruitment, evaluation, and payment of informants,[131] performing undercover roles, testifying in court, providing affidavits, keeping tabs on retail paper producers, and offering technical and professional advice to foreign police agencies. The level of assistance provided by foreign police has varied, of course, depending upon the existence of counterfeit specialists within foreign police agencies, their level of competence, and their governments' willingness to extend assistance. An agent based in Europe during the early 1980s recalled that the German Bundeskriminalamt, Scotland Yard, and the French, Swiss, and Dutch police agencies each had fine counterfeit squads; the Belgian and Italian police agencies were generally less sophisticated, although both possessed a few highly qualified counterfeit experts. The same agent also recalled that in at least one case he had worked closely with the Hungarian police agency—an indication that counterfeiting, even more so than drug trafficking, is the sort of criminal activity that inspires law enforcement agencies to transcend political differences.

The Secret Service expects to expand its international presence in the future, albeit not dramatically. Although counterfeiting of U.S. dollars appears to have increased steadily over the years, it has remained, as one agent put it, "a nickel and dime business. . . . The Mafia knows the Feds are involved, they know the tracking [through the circularized note files] is superb, and they know there's not big money involved. . . . They're more drawn to forged bonds, which can be very big money," but which typically does not fall within the Secret Service's jurisdiction unless government bonds are involved. Another agent lamented the change in

130. All counterfeit dollars are "circularized"—a process that involves analyzing a note to identify its distinctive features, determining whether it is part of a previously identified counterfeit series, establishing a new file if it is not, and collating all available information about the movement of all notes within a particular counterfeit series. By the end of the 1980s, between 2,500 and 3,000 new notes were being identified each year. The United States is the only government that circularizes its own currency. The counterfeit division at Interpol headquarters provides this service for a number of national currencies.

131. The Secret Service's budget for informants pales in comparison with that of the DEA. Informants routinely are paid several hundred or several thousand dollars. A five-figure payment, according to one agent interviewed in 1990, "happens once in a decade."

the character of the counterfeiters: "They used to be skilled printers looking for a challenge or down on their luck; now there's many more drug traffickers involved, looking to rip off one another," and getting caught when they try to buy drugs from an undercover agent with counterfeit currency. The 1985 movie about a Secret Service investigation of counterfeiters, *To Live and Die in L.A.*, is also held accountable for inspiring many novices to try their hand at counterfeiting. "Up to 40 percent of counterfeiters," one agent claimed, "say they got the idea from the movie." By and large, counterfeiting is seen as a "dumb crime" offering criminals relatively low rates of return despite the high risks involved in putting the currency into circulation.

The rather prominent international profile of the Secret Service has stemmed from more than its international assistance in investigating counterfeit dollar cases. Apart from its responsibility in this area, as well as its jurisdiction over check forgery and various frauds against the government, which consume a relatively small proportion of international duties, the Secret Service has covered the globe on behalf of its other chief responsibility—protecting U.S. officials and other notable persons on their trips abroad. This task has involved extensive liaison with foreign officials but little in the way of criminal investigation apart from the collection and dissemination of intelligence on potential threats to their charges. The prominent role of counterfeiting investigation in the evolution of international policing may also account for some of the Secret Service's high profile internationally, one symbolized by the appointment of a Secret Service agent, Richard Stiener, as chief of the U.S. Interpol office in 1979, and by the 1985 election of the head of the Secret Service, John Simpson, to a four-year appointment as president of Interpol.

The U.S. Marshals Service: Apprehending Fugitives, Protecting Witnesses

The federal agency that has undergone the most dramatic expansion in overseas activities is the U.S. Marshals Service (USMS). In November 1979, the attorney general transferred some of the responsibility for apprehending federal fugitives from the FBI to the Marshals Service; this authority was augmented in August 1988, much to the annoyance of the

FBI.[132] The agency responded by setting up an international branch to coordinate the apprehension and recovery of fugitives who had fled abroad. Much of the marshals' international work involves no more than escorting fugitives who already have been captured by foreign police agencies back to the United States. But during the 1980s, the marshals began to play a more direct role in locating fugitives abroad, assisting foreign police in their apprehension, and devising sting operations to lure fugitives to the United States or into the hands of cooperative authorities overseas. In a major Florida-based Fugitive Investigative Strike Team (FIST) effort in 1985 to capture fugitives, U.S. marshals operated throughout the Caribbean, working with local police on the islands to return fugitives to U.S. territory.[133] In early 1985, a special unit of marshals joined an international team of investigators including Israelis and West Germans to determine the location of the Nazi war criminal, Josef Mengele. Their investigation ended apparently successfully with forensic and documentation experts confirming the Nazi doctor's death in Brazil.[134]

The most challenging of the marshals' work has involved international undercover operations, called "ruses" by the marshals, that target white-collar fugitives—including such famous swindlers as Robert Vesco, Marc Rich, and Takis Veliotis.[135] A small number of marshals, trained in the intricacies and fashions of international high finance, today operate globally, trying to trick the high-flying fugitives into making the deal that will allow U.S. authorities or the police of a friendly government to seize them. In one scheme, which ultimately faltered, the plan involved persuading the fugitive to board a helicopter thinking that he was being taken to a yacht when in fact the intended destination was a U.S. aircraft carrier patrolling the Mediterranean near Libya. In another case, involving an investigation of a former CIA agent, Edwin Wilson—who had become a major supplier of plastic explosives and other lethal equipment to the Qadaffi regime in Libya—an undercover U.S. marshal and an informant duped Wilson into leaving his Libyan haven to attend a

132. See *Departments of Commerce, Justice, and State, the Judiciary, and Related Agencies Appropriations for 1990: Hearings Before a Subcommittee of the House Committee on Appropriations*, 101st Cong., 1st Sess., Part 2 (1989), 1814–1816.

133. *The Pentacle* 5 (Summer 1985), 3–5.

134. Ibid., 17.

135. A. Craig Copetas, "White-Collar Manhunt," *New York Times Magazine*, June 8, 1986, 45.

meeting in the Dominican Republic, where police authorities had already agreed to seize him and put him on a plane to the United States.[136] A few months later, the prosector in the Wilson case, accompanied by the operational chief of the marshals, Howard Safir, and two other marshals, flew to Beirut in hopes of apprehending one of Wilson's accomplices, Frank Terpil. Arrangements had been made with the Phalangists to have the local police make the arrest. When the Lebanese police failed to seize the American fugitive, the prosecutor and the marshals began their own stakeout on the streets of Beirut, which ultimately proved unsuccessful.[137] And in yet another case, U.S. marshals played a leading role in persuading Honduran officials to put a notorious drug trafficker, Juan Matta Ballesteros, on a plane to the Dominican Republic, from which he was quickly transferred to the United States.

Apart from their involvement in collecting and delivering fugitives, the U.S. Marshals Service has shared its expertise in other matters with foreign law enforcement agencies. During the 1980s, police officials in a number of countries confronting threats by organized crime and terrorist groups became aware of the Marshal Service's Witness Protection Program; representatives from Canada, Britain, Australia, Italy, and Germany came to the United States to learn about the program, and in a few cases the U.S. program was even used to assist foreign criminal justice authorities in protecting vulnerable witnesses. By late 1989, both Australia and Germany were actively considering the creation of similar programs at the national level. In the area of court security, the Marshals Service has both assisted foreign criminal justice systems, such as El Salvador and Grenada following the U.S. invasion in 1983, and studied the court security systems of foreign countries, notably France and Italy, which have been obliged to protect their judicial officials and courtrooms from Arab terrorists and powerful organized crime gangs.[138] The Marshals Service's Special Operations Group (SOG), created in 1971 to respond to such emergency situations as civil disturbances, terrorist incidents, and the more difficult courtroom security and fugitive apprehension tasks, has trained foreign police in counterterrorist methods and played a role in coordinating the transport of particularly notorious fugitives to the United States; the two most prominent examples during the 1980s were the first drug traffickers extradited by Colombia in 1985,

136. Peter Maas, *Manhunt* (New York: Random House, 1986), 238, 255, 266–267.
137. Ibid., 286–287.
138. Howard Safir, "International Court Security," *The Pentacle* 7 (Summer 1987), 23–28.

and Panamanian dictator General Manuel Noriega, following the U.S. invasion of Panama in late 1989.

Unlike the DEA, Customs, and the FBI, with their numerous foreign representatives abroad, the Marshals Service has not been able to rely on representatives stationed abroad; the one exception is the U.S. marshal stationed at Interpol headquarters in France, who occasionally is called upon to handle fugitive investigations in Europe. By the late 1980s, two marshals were stationed in the Alien Fugitive Enforcement Unit at the U.S. national central bureau of Interpol, through which pass most international requests both to and from the United States for the apprehension of fugitives. Marshals also have cultivated contacts with the growing number of foreign police representatives stationed in the United States.[139] The international branch at the Marshals Service's headquarters has attempted to compensate for its lack of an international presence by taking advantage of the diverse contacts, and opportunities to establish contacts, available to the agency. It has relied on its various training programs, the occasional visits by foreign police to the United States, and the growing number of international police conferences to develop the sorts of personal contacts with foreign police that so often prove crucial to successful international investigations. Particularly useful has been the International Association of Chiefs of Police (IACP), a U.S.-based police association that undertook significant efforts during the 1980s to internationalize its membership. Much of the Marshals Service's success in developing its international contacts and reputation can be attributed to its chief of operations for much of the 1980s, Howard Safir, whose personal contacts with foreign police officials may well have exceeded those of any other U.S. law enforcement agent. Having developed an awareness of the importance of personal relationships with foreign law enforcement authorities during his service with the DEA, Safir traveled abroad frequently to pursue investigations, attend conferences, and participate in periodic meetings, such as the Italian-American Working Group on Organized Crime, and became prominently involved with the IACP, serving as the only U.S. vice-chairman of the IACP's Advisory Committee for International Policy.

139. As of 1990, the United States was host to police liaison officials from Australia, Canada, France, Germany, India, Israel, Japan, Korea, and the United Kingdom. Most were stationed in their governments' embassies in Washington, D.C., but a few were based in Los Angeles, Miami, and New York City.

The Bureau of Alcohol, Tobacco, and Firearms: Cracking Down

Foreign demands to crack down on the smuggling of firearms and explosives out of the United States during the early 1970s required the Bureau of Alcohol, Tobacco, and Firearms (ATF) to adopt a more international perspective. Although this issue fell primarily within the jurisdiction of the Customs Service and the FBI, ATF was called upon by both foreign police agencies and Congress because of its greater expertise in regulating domestic sales of weapons. The first to request its assistance was the Mexican government, which had enacted a tough gun control law in 1968 that generated a lucrative black market for imported firearms; it was particularly concerned about the flow of weapons into the hands of domestic insurgencies.[140] Additional requests followed from the British government, whose concerns focused—as they had for more than a century—on weapons acquisitions in the United States by and for the Irish Republican Army (IRA). ATF responded by creating a program it called ITAR (International Traffic in Arms) to concentrate on identifying and apprehending those involved in arms dealing destined for foreign markets. Although most of its energies were devoted to gun running across the Mexican border—a subject that attracted Congressional interest in 1977[141]—it also collaborated with foreign police in investigations of weapons-smuggling to the United Kingdom, Jamaica, Haiti, Canada, Japan, Lebanon, Colombia, Nicaragua, and Rhodesia.[142]

During the 1980s, Mexico remained a target of concern even as the number of ITAR investigations proliferated. Many of the requests from abroad involved no more than help in tracing seized weapons—the most notable of which involved the Italian government's request for assistance in tracing the Browning semi-automatic pistol seized from Mehmet Ali Agca, the Turk accused of shooting Pope John Paul II. In 1987, ATF responded to a Jamaican police request for assistance in tracing eight handguns; the subsequent investigation played a role in uncovering the

140. See the extensive discussion of ATF's relationship with Mexican officials during the mid-1970s in *Illicit Traffic in Weapons and Drugs Across the United States–Mexican Border: Hearing Before the Permanent Subcommittee on Investigations of the Senate Committee on Government Operations*, 95th Cong., 1st Sess. (1977), 55–87 (testimony of ATF Director Rex Davis).

141. Ibid.

142. See annual reports of the ATF for fiscal years 1974 (p. 12), 1975 (p. 8), 1976 (pp. 6–7), and 1978 (pp. 11–13).

extensive criminal activities of organized criminal groups called "Jamaican posses" in the United States.[143] By the late 1980s, ATF's international investigations were increasingly focused on gun running to Brazil, Colombia, the Dominican Republic, and the Philippines.[144] As during the 1970s, many of these involved gun running to antigovernment groups in foreign countries, but an increasing share of its international investigations, as well as most of the firearms reported to it from abroad for tracing, involved drug trafficking cases.

The Bureau of Alcohol, Tobacco, and Firearms has played a similar role in its efforts to curtail the illicit traffic in explosives. In the late 1970s and early 1980s, its agents participated in the investigation of former CIA agent Edwin Wilson.[145] At the request of the State Department and various foreign governments, ATF agents have trained foreign law enforcement personnel in explosives detection and handling. Foreign investigators have benefited from ATF's computerized data base known as EXIS (the Explosives Incident System), which includes information on common devices, components, trends, targets, and methods of operation in explosions—although a separate data base on foreign explosives incidents (known as I-EXIS) was created only in 1986. In 1987, ATF established liaison with bomb data centers in Canada, Germany, Australia, and Israel to exchange information on explosives incidents in those countries.[146] The agency has also attempted to introduce an element of standardization to the reporting of explosives incidents abroad by developing a format that can be circulated through Interpol channels.

Despite the expanding array of contacts with foreign law enforcement officials, as well as closer collaboration on international terrorism investigations with the FBI, the CIA, and the State Department's Counterterrorism Office, ATF had yet to assume a strong international presence by the end of the 1980s. The 258 firearms smuggling investigations completed by ATF during 1988 represented a substantial increase over its caseload a decade earlier but a small fraction of what

143. Wayne King, "A Bureau That Battled Bootleggers Is Tough Target for Budget-Cutters," *New York Times*, Feb. 1, 1988, A26.

144. *Treasury, Postal Service, and General Government Appropriations for Fiscal Year 1990: Hearings Before the Subcommittee on the Treasury, Postal Service, and General Government Appropriations, House Committee on Appropriations*, 100th Cong., 1st Sess., Part 1 (1989), 542–543, 751.

145. See Maas, *Manhunt* (supra n. 136).

146. *Treasury, Postal Service, and General Government Appropriations for Fiscal Year 1990*, 552.

other federal agencies were involved in. Persistent requests since the mid-1970s to station an attaché in Mexico City had failed to meet with success, although by 1990 ATF had informally opened an office in Bogotá.[147] International travel by agents had increased during the 1980s—most frequently to Colombia but also to Jamaica, Japan, and Mexico—as ATF became more involved in joint operations with the DEA and in its own international investigations. But operational activity by ATF agents abroad, such as engaging in undercover operations, recruiting and running informants, and accompanying foreign police on surveillances, is still rare. In the Edwin Wilson investigation, for instance, ATF agents operated undercover within the United States, but the principal reason for traveling abroad in that case, as in most others, was the need to conduct an interview.[148] Like most other federal U.S. law enforcement agencies, ATF's most frequent foreign contacts have been with law enforcement authorities in Canada and Mexico, and like the U.S. Marshals Service and other agencies with few or no foreign offices, ATF has been obliged to make the most of its participation in international gatherings and in the International Association of Chiefs of Police to establish ties with foreign counterparts. The basic reason for its relatively modest international presence has been the fact that the FBI, Customs, the DEA, and other agencies claim primary jurisdiction over most of the international dimensions of ATF's domestic jurisdiction. In 1979, for instance, the FBI had created a special squad to investigate illicit flows of weapons and money to the IRA.[149] ATF's director of enforcement summed up his agency's international role—as one of supporting the investigations of sister agencies—in Congressional testimony in March 1989. Responding to a question about ATF's involvement in counterterrorism investigations, he explained:

> For a long period of time we have supported the FBI domestically, and then in foreign law enforcement, as well as the Department of Defense and the CIA internationally in explosives and firearms. We have programs that are set up for the tracing of American arms that are recovered anywhere in the world so we can trace

147. *Connection Between Arms and Narcotics Trafficking: Hearing Before the House Committee on Foreign Affairs*, 101st Cong., 1st Sess. (1989), 11–12.

148. Maas, *Manhunt* (supra n. 136), 192.

149. James Adams, *The Financing of Terror* (New York: Simon & Schuster, 1986), 145–153.

> them back to the purchaser, and sometimes provide investigative leads. We also provide explosives training on tracing for recovered explosives that may turn up in other parts of the world. We track the types of devices being used by certain groups where we can prepare a list of components and sometimes provide a signatory mark identifying the group that has committed the crime. . . .
>
> We are very active in the terrorist area, although we function more in a support mode for our expertise on weapons and explosives rather than jurisdiction.[150]

The INS, the IRS, and the PIS

The principal law enforcement concerns of the seventeen Immigration and Naturalization Service (INS) offices abroad (see Appendix A)—most of which include at least one special agent—have been twofold: investigating and deterring efforts to smuggle illegal aliens into the United States, and ensuring that aliens with criminal records do not enter the United States. Reasoning, like the drug enforcement agency, "that it is easier and more cost efficient to intercept or prevent potential illegal aliens from entering the country before their actual arrival at our gates," the INS decided in 1985 to increase the criminal investigative responsibilities of its overseas agents.[151] The INS has increasingly concerned itself not just with violations of the immigration laws but also with any number of criminal activities in which the role of aliens has been conspicuous. Often, a violation of U.S. immigration laws, like a violation of tax laws, has provided the relatively innocuous hook with which to indict criminals guilty of far more serious crimes for which they cannot be prosecuted for one reason or another. In one case, for instance, a senior member of the Japanese organized crime group Yakuza was convicted of false statements in connection with obtaining a visa and entry into the United States.[152] The INS's most extensive foreign interactions, however, have involved Mexico and the long border separating the two countries.

150. *Treasury, Postal Service, and General Government Appropriations for Fiscal Year 1990*, 568 (testimony of Daniel Hartnett).
151. *INS Reporter*, Fall/Winter 1985–86, 13.
152. Ibid., 15.

The Postal Inspection Service (PIS), which claims to be the oldest of the federal law enforcement agencies, has stationed one agent, known as a postal inspector, at Interpol headquarters in France since 1983 and another in Wiesbaden, Germany, since 1993. Its jurisdiction includes mail fraud, mail theft, and pornography sent through the mail, as well as many of the insider trading cases.[153] In the latter area, it has worked closely with the Securities and Exchange Commission, which opened its own international enforcement section in 1985. The postal inspectors, who are given much greater latitude in their investigations than, for instance, FBI agents, are permitted to travel overseas, although the trip must first be cleared with top officials at headquarters. In fact, relatively few agents, perhaps a dozen or so, actually travel abroad each year. The reasons for doing so vary: someone may need to be interviewed; a request for evidence or an extradition may need to be accompanied by some personal diplomacy; and continuation of an undercover operation begun within the United States is always a possibility, although an infrequent one. One of the more notable international investigations by a postal inspector occurred in 1950, when an agent in Honolulu uncovered an extensive black market in U.S. postal money orders. His international investigation ultimately led to the uncovering of a number of counterfeiting rings in the Philippines and a money laundering operation involving Chinese communists working out of Hong Kong.[154] Agents are also sent overseas on occasion to liaise with foreign police, explain their agency's particular law enforcement interests, and seek assistance in accomplishing them. For instance, two postal inspectors were sent to Denmark, Sweden, and the Netherlands in the early 1980s to discuss the traffic in pornography from those countries to the United States.

The Internal Revenue Service (IRS) opened its first overseas office in 1938 in Manila, when the Philippines were still a possession of the United States, and its first foreign offices in 1939 in Paris and London.[155] It currently stations approximately the same number of representatives abroad as the FBI. Virtually all of them, however, are primarily concerned with providing tax assistance to Americans resident abroad.[156]

153. The activities of the PIS are briefly described in Arnold H. Lubasch, "Postal Inspectors' No-Frills Unit Handles Big Cases," *New York Times*, June 16, 1986, B5.

154. The story is in Ottenberg, *Federal Investigators* (supra n. 46), 318–332.

155. John C. Chommie, *The Internal Revenue Service* (New York: Praeger Publishers, 1970), 120.

156. Ibid., 117–136.

One or two have some background in criminal investigation, but it is highly unusual for an IRS representative in a U.S. embassy to become directly involved in investigating criminal violations of U.S. tax laws. The Intelligence Division, created in 1919 and renamed the Criminal Investigation Division in 1978, has never stationed agents abroad—although its agents occasionally have pursued their investigations to foreign territories.[157] Most governments are reluctant to offer assistance in a foreign government's criminal investigation of tax evaders within their borders. Only in Mexico and the Caribbean, where U.S. law enforcement agents admit to operating occasionally "as if they are in their own back yard," have IRS agents actively pursued criminal investigations. In a number of cases, IRS agents operating undercover have pursued their targets to various Caribbean tax havens, although arrests have always taken place in the United States. Nowhere has this been more true than in the Bahamas, which for many decades served as perhaps the principal tax haven and offshore money laundering center for American criminals of all sorts. In 1965, the Miami office of the IRS's Intelligence Division initiated an aggressive investigation, known as "Operation Tradewinds," into the uses of Bahamian banks to evade U.S. tax laws.[158] During the following ten years, until it was undermined by a newly appointed IRS commissioner—Donald Alexander, who strongly opposed most of the IRS's criminal investigative initiatives—IRS agents recruited informants, operated undercover, bought information from bank employees, and employed a wide array of other investigative techniques to gather information and evidence on the illicit uses of the banks.[159] The successes of that operation yielded another one, "Project Haven," which together provided the IRS with unprecedented intelligence on the means employed both by the banks and by those interested in their confidential services; the operations also provided something of a model for future investigations into Caribbean-based money laundering.

157. The history of the Intelligence Division's first fifty years is in Hank Messick, *Secret File* (New York: G. P. Putnam's Sons, 1969).

158. See Alan A. Block, *Masters of Paradise: Organized Crime and the Internal Revenue Service in the Bahamas* (New Brunswick, N.J.: Transaction Publishers, 1991).

159. The struggle between Commissioner Alexander and the Intelligence Division agents is discussed in ibid., 215–246; and in David Burnham, *A Law Unto Itself: Power, Politics, and the IRS* (New York: Random House, 1989), 103–107.

Big City and Border City Policing

Unlike the federal police agencies, whose international activities generally increased over time, the municipal police departments never institutionalized their international links. In New York, a police department policy was instituted, apparently in the 1920s, forbidding any police to travel abroad on official investigations. Not until 1972, fifty years after Fiaschetti's second trip to Italy, was this policy reversed. An NYPD detective, Joseph Coffey, conducting an electronic surveillance on an apparently low-level mafioso was surprised to find the criminal making plans to go to Munich. Given permission to continue the surveillance in Europe, Coffey liaised with the Munich police—and with the CIA, who provided the bugging devices—and ended up uncovering a criminal ring marketing hundreds of millions of dollars of stolen and forged securities. Those implicated included not only American mafiosi and an odd selection of international con men, but also high-level officials in the governments of Italy and the Vatican.[160]

Having broken the ice, a trickle of New York City police agents began to travel abroad on investigations. With most of the more sophisticated and far-reaching criminal investigations under the jurisdiction of federal agencies, the opportunities have hardly been abundant. Some have arisen in the course of joint federal-city investigations into organized crime and drug trafficking. In one case involving car-theft and other charges against the Gambino Mafia family in New York, two NYPD detectives traced a shipment of stolen cars from Port Newark, New Jersey, to Kuwait. In 1983, they traveled to the sheikdom and secured the cooperation of the national police in finding the cars.[161] Such cases, however, have hardly been typical of the police department's investigations. With fewer financial resources than the federal agencies, and with the ability to draw on the international resources of the DEA and the FBI as well as the Interpol network, the city police have typically handled most international investigations from within the boundaries of the five boroughs. Nonetheless, the fact that most criminal investigations in the United States are conducted by municipal police, combined with the fact that many criminal offenses still do not fall under federal jurisdiction, suggests that

160. The entire case, in which the FBI and a number of European law enforcement agencies ultimately became involved, is recounted in Hammer, *Vatican Connection* (supra n. 106).

161. Ronald Smothers, "Gambino Jury Following Paper Trail," *New York Times*, Nov. 24, 1985, 42.

city and state police agencies throughout the United States have become far more involved in transnational travel and communication than ever before.

The city and state police forces with the greatest experience in transnational policing are those who work near the borders with Mexico and Canada. Although posses no longer ride headlong across the border in pursuit of cattle rustlers and other criminals, the problems shared by the successors to Colonel Kosterlitzky and Captain Rynning have not changed all that much. Relations between police departments on either side of the U.S.-Canadian border tend to be very close and professional, not all that different in many cases than relations across municipal and state borders in the United States. Relations along the Mexican border are more varied, ranging from close and long-standing personal relationships that can cut through any red tape, to bitter antagonisms and suspicions stemming as often as not from corrupt and criminal behavior by the Mexican police. During the 1970s and 1980s, state and municipal police agencies near both borders—but most significantly along the Mexican border—took steps to regularize and formalize their cross-border relations, in part by creating specialized liaison units to handle cross-border matters. Indeed, not just border cities but also others within a few hours' driving distance from the border undertook similar steps. The Los Angeles Police Department, for instance, created a Foreign Prosecution Liaison Unit in 1984 when it realized that approximately 100 of its 237 murder warrants involved suspects who were Mexican nationals.[162] During the same time, but particularly after the mid-1980s, the federal law enforcement presence along the border increased dramatically, motivated primarily by the intensification of the war on drugs and secondarily by a renewed desire to crack down on illicit migration from Mexico.

In late 1976, the San Diego Police Department began an eighteen-month experiment to deal not with the customary problem of illegal immigration but with the increasing crimes directed against the *pollos*, as the migrants were called, during the nighttime crossings. Known as BARF, for Border Alien Robbery Force, the exploits and travails of its dozen-odd members were recounted by Joseph Wambaugh in *Lines and Shadows*. The BARF police worked undercover, dressing, talking, and

162. Daryl F. Gates and Keith E. Ross, "Foreign Prosecution Liaison Unit Helps Apprehend Suspects Across the Border," *Police Chief* 57 (Apr. 1990), 153–154.

walking like the *pollos* they had been delegated to protect. In conversations with the *pollos*, they heard numerous accounts of their being robbed, extorted, and even killed by Mexican police. Shortly after the squad began patrolling the border, they too were accosted by thieves and extortionists that turned out to be Mexican police. The results were encounters in which American and Mexican cops were drawing on one another, and in a few cases actually shooting at each other.

The San Diego Police Department, like other municipal police departments along the border, assigned a few officers to handle foreign liaison. In 1977, the principal responsibility for liaison with the Mexican police fell to two Mexican-Americans on the force named Manuel Smith and Ron Collins. In *Lines and Shadows*, Joseph Wambaugh described their duties:

> Both cops were of patrolman rank, Ron Collins having been a liaison officer longer but Manuel Smith generally thought of as the spokesman by virtue of his incredible connections south of the imaginary line. He had a cousin in the *judiciales* [the Mexican police] and another in the municipal police. Just watching him operate was a thing to behold. Manuel Smith couldn't even cross the border without having to pause and chat with the Mexican border guards, who normally only stopped cars heading south when they wanted to peddle some tickets to the police rodeo at the downtown bullring.
>
> And when he got to the headquarters of the *judiciales* it was as though Santa Claus had arrived. Tijuana cops had a thousand problems that needed solving up north. There were personal problems, relatives who needed assistance with documents, immigration problems, insurance problems, employment problems. There were professional needs, the endless information search by cops who had no access to computers. There was impounded property linked to persons who traveled south to do business, legal and otherwise. The Mexican authorities had to labor under a maddening information gap that Manuel Smith and Ron Collins could help them narrow through American sources.
>
> By the time he could even set foot inside state judicial police headquarters, Manuel Smith had a laundry list hanging out every pocket, and more to come when he got inside. An FBI agent coming to the same headquarters might cool his heels in the lobby

> for a whole afternoon, while Manuel Smith had ten *judiciales* falling all over themselves just to help him locate the son of some American cop who was last seen smoking pot laced with PCP and running naked through the Tijuana cemetery on a big frat weekender.[163]

In many respects, the liaison role played by Manuel Smith represents the most traditional, typical, and universal dimension of transnational police relations.[164] Relations among the law enforcement agents of neighboring countries, and especially among agents who are stationed close to the border, fall into a special category notable for its familiarity and informality. The friendlier the governments, and the greater the overall scale of cross-border commerce, travel, and general interaction, the more this is so. Under such conditions, mutually beneficial transnational understandings and operating procedures that are best comprehended within the context of the border environment emerge. These often may be unsanctioned by and even unknown to central government officials in the capital, but they are essential to the functioning of law enforcement where national laws and international politics retain the potential to create bureaucratic and legal nightmares. Sensitivities of national sovereignty may still get pricked from time to time, such as when agents "forget" which side of the border they are on or fall into personal or policy disputes. But by and large, cross-border law enforcement cooperation functions on a scale and level of familiarity unparalleled by more distant transnational law enforcement relationships. That is the case along the United States' borders with Canada and Mexico, and it is also true of friendly borders throughout the rest of the world. It is even true, albeit to a lesser extent, of U.S. law enforcement dealings with Bermuda and many Caribbean islands.

One other factor that accounts for the informality of relations between police on either side of a border is the jurisdictional and bureaucratic

163. Joseph Wambaugh, *Lines and Shadows* (New York: Bantam Books, 1984), 144–145.

164. For an interesting discussion by a political scientist of law enforcement relations across the U.S.-Mexican border, see Marshall Carter, "Law Enforcement and Federalism: Bordering on Trouble," *Policy Studies Journal* 7 (1979), 413–418; Marshall Carter, "Law, Order, and the Border: El Paso del Norte" (Paper presented at the annual meeting of the National Council on Geographic Education, Mexico City, Nov. 1979); and C. Richard Bath, H. Marshall Carter, and Thomas J. Price, "Dependence, Interdependence, or Detachment? Three Case Studies of International Relations Between El Paso, Texas, and Ciudad Juárez, Mexico" (Paper presented at the Third World Conference, Omaha, Nebraska, Oct. 1977).

distance between law enforcement agents in border locales and the central government. This is particularly the case in federally constituted nations such as the United States and Germany, but even in most nonfederated countries municipal and state police in border towns and cities often have little occasion or desire to deal with federal authorities other than those stationed in the vicinity. They tend to adapt to local law enforcement needs without much regard for the formalities and niceties of diplomacy and international law. From their perspective, dealing with counterparts across the border is regarded not as international relations but as police business. If investigating a case or seizing a fugitive means working the other side of the border, then one contacts one's counterparts across the border directly. If that is seen as being either unnecessary or potentially problematic, one goes it alone and "to hell with sovereignty." Unlike federal agents, who often operate in much the same fashion anyway, local agents need not worry quite so much about accounting for their cross-border operations to a national headquarters with a keener sense of correct international behavior than the local mayor or state police chief.

U.S. Involvement in Interpol: Assuming Leadership

Unlike other federal law enforcement agencies, the U.S. office of Interpol, known as the National Central Bureau (Interpol-USNCB), is not charged with the enforcement of any federal criminal laws. Its function is primarily one of facilitating communication between U.S. and foreign police agencies by providing a central office through which international messages can be both channeled and distributed. With some 20,000 federal, state, and local police agencies in the United States, foreign police are often at a loss as to whom to contact in providing and seeking information and other assistance. The same holds true of most police departments in the United States, many of which occasionally need to communicate with foreign police but have little idea how to do so efficiently if at all. As police departments have become more aware of the accessibility of the Interpol system and the identity of the National Central Bureau, the process of internationalization has begun to penetrate the provincialism of many local police forces.

The U.S. involvement in Interpol can be roughly divided into three phases. The first, from about 1950 to 1969, was more a case of noninvolvement by the United States. The FBI director, J. Edgar Hoover, generally shunned the international agency, preferred that U.S. police agencies rely on the LEGAT system to communicate internationally, and made small efforts to preclude other federal agencies from participating in Interpol. The Secret Service and the Federal Bureau of Narcotics nonetheless participated on an informal basis, and in 1958 the attorney general officially designated the Treasury Department—which oversaw both agencies—as the official U.S. representative to Interpol. The second phase began in 1969, when the USNCB, which had been officially created in 1962, was provided with an office and a staff of three. The scale of its operations throughout the 1970s remained limited, with the NCB handling an average of 300 cases a year. The most notable developments involved legal suits against Interpol by the Church of Scientology, attempted exposés of the agency's history and misdeeds, and Congressional inquiries into U.S. involvement in Interpol, none of which led to significant revelations. Their principal impact was to remind the USNCB forcefully of the need to screen all transmissions adequately to ensure that they were for legitimate criminal investigative purposes.[165]

The third phase, beginning in 1979, was ushered in with the appointment of a dynamic Secret Service agent, Richard Stiener, as chief of the USNCB. Stiener quickly resolved the controversies surrounding the NCB, reassuring those who had criticized the office that it was a valuable and nonsecretive member of the law enforcement community.[166] Stiener also embarked on an ambitious and successful campaign to increase dramatically the NCB's staff and budget, computerize its operations, involve the federal law enforcement agencies in its activities, publicize its existence and services to state police agencies, and enhance the USNCB's role and status at Interpol headquarters in France. Between 1979 and 1990, the NCB staff increased from 6 to 110, its budget rose from $125,000 to $6,000,000, and the number of law enforcement agencies represented at the NCB went from 1 to 16. Concerns that the bureau

165. See U.S. General Accounting Office, *United States Participation in Interpol, the International Criminal Police Organization*, GAO/ID-76-77, Dec. 27, 1976; and Diana Gulbinowicz, "The International Criminal Police Organization: A Case Study of Oversight of American Participation in an International Organization" (Ph.D. diss., City University of New York, 1978).

166. See Malcolm Anderson, *Policing the World: Interpol and the Politics of International Police Co-operation* (New York: Oxford University Press, 1989).

would be hampered by civil and criminal claims filed against it were allayed by President Reagan's designation of Interpol as a public international organization entitled to civil and criminal immunity under U.S. law.[167] In an international organization frequently criticized for its unwillingness to integrate advanced techonlogy, the USNCB devoted substantial efforts to computerizing its files and installing automated electronic communications systems. Its personnel gained access to most of the major computerized law enforcement records systems in the United States. And participation by state police agencies in Interpol increased significantly in response to the rising need for its services and the promotional efforts of Stiener and his staff. By 1990, most state police agencies were formally affiliated with the NCB, many had established their own Interpol liaison office, and one—the Illinois State Police—had stationed an agent in the NCB. Also significant was the full implementation of the U.S./Canadian Interface Project, a semi-automated link between U.S. and Canadian law enforcement information networks that allows police in each country to get information from other nations' networks.[168]

Not all U.S. law enforcement agencies depend on the NCB for their international communications. The FBI and the DEA, with their international networks of overseas agents, are the least dependent upon Interpol; indeed, other police agencies, both U.S. and foreign, have been known to turn to the DEA, and to a lesser extent the FBI, when Interpol channels have been too slow or unresponsive. Although both agencies do make use of Interpol's facilities, particularly in communicating with countries in which they are not represented, their representatives at the NCB tend to handle far more incoming than outgoing requests. For state and city police, on the other hand, as for police in most other countries around the world, the absence of ongoing relationships and liaison with police in other countries makes the Interpol network virtually indispensable in conducting transnational inquiries and tasks—although one survey of police chiefs in 1991 found that relatively few had ever found Interpol of assistance to their agencies.[169] The same is even more true of

167. See Executive Order No. 12,425, 48 Fed. Reg. 28,069 (1983), and the discussion in William R. Slomanson, "Civil Actions Against Interpol: A Field Compass," *Temple Law Review* 57 (1984), 553–600.

168. Department of Justice, *1990 Annual Report of the Attorney General of the United States*, 51.

169. Jerry Seper, "Police Chiefs Seek Interpol Curbs," *Washington Times*, Apr. 4, 1991, A4.

U.S. federal law enforcement agencies that station few if any representatives abroad and that can expect only limited assistance from overseas DEA agents and FBI LEGATs. Given Interpol's near-global membership, moreover, the NCB has often provided the only means of communicating with police agencies whose governments are not on friendly terms with the United States. During the 1980s, routine requests were exchanged with Soviet-bloc states and with Qadaffi's Libya.

Between 1976 and 1986, the annual caseload of the USNCB increased from approximately 4,000 to 43,863, and the volume of message traffic went from 14,365 to 101,859. Collection of such statistics was abandoned thereafter, but the numbers most certainly continued to increase. The requests range from checks on driver's licenses, auto registrations, addresses, phone numbers, and criminal record histories, to identification of photographs, fingerprints, and documents, requests for bank records, location and seizure of stolen property, and the arrest of fugitives. The dramatic increases in the NCB's caseload were a function not only of the rising demand for its services but also of its success in promoting its value to U.S. and foreign police agencies and of its "pivotal position in a criminal intelligence communications network" linking the international Interpol communications system with the on-line computerized systems of the FBI, the DEA, the INS, and the Treasury Department.[170]

U.S. participation in Interpol has contributed to the evolution of international law enforcement in at least three ways. In providing a link between the police agencies of most governments that is relatively quick and efficient, it has increased the capacity of city, state, and national law enforcement agencies to deal with the challenges posed by transnational crime. Interpol is primarily responsible for the increasing difficulty that fugitives face in finding a haven where they can remain undetected. When Interpol issues an international wanted notice, for instance, police agencies in more than 150 countries are put on notice—in theory if not always in practice—to arrest that person. The same is also true, albeit to a lesser extent, of stolen property.

Second, Interpol offers an international professional association for police. Its annual meetings in recent years have drawn delegates from more than 100 countries. Its regional conferences similarly play a role in bringing together police from nearby countries in a forum where they

170. Anderson, *Policing the World* (supra n. 166), 85.

are able to exchange information and opinions and establish the personal relationships that will help speed requests and cut through red tape thereafter. Interpol also acts as a channel for the dissemination of new police methods and investigative techniques. Its publication, translated into half a dozen languages, is the only police magazine circulated around the world. In many respects, Interpol is, as Secretary-General Raymond Kendall claimed, "the only existing organization which is structured to deal with the handling of international police information."[171]

The third contribution is the most recent. Interpol in recent years has become an increasingly effective means for the U.S. government to internationalize its law enforcement concerns. During the 1970s, the emphasis was placed on drug trafficking. During the 1980s, the U.S. government encouraged Interpol as an organization, and through Interpol other governments, to improve their international cooperation against terrorism and the financial aspects of drug trafficking. The first efforts to raise the issues of money laundering and forfeiture of drug-related assets were made by Customs agents in the late 1970s. During the 1980s, two Customs agents were stationed at Interpol headquarters in Saint Cloud, where they created a small financial intelligence section. By the end of the decade, Customs' efforts had been joined by the USNCB as well as upper echelons of the Treasury and Justice Departments, and foreign law enforcement agencies were increasingly receptive to pursuing similar and joint investigations. Much the same occurred with respect to counterterrorism efforts. Until the early 1980s, Interpol resisted cooperating in terrorist cases, fearing that its reputation as a strictly apolitical organization would be undermined. But significant U.S. pressures, combined with the recognition that Interpol's failure to reform in this area would relegate it to the sidelines of a crucial domain of international law enforcement, led to a change in policy. As the United States has come to play a more dominant role in the previously Europe-centered organization—the head of the U.S. Secret Service was elected Interpol president in 1985—its ability to internationalize its own law enforcement concerns and approaches has grown apace.

Even as the NCB emerged as a significant player in the internationalization of U.S. law enforcement, the charges leveled against it by the Church of Scientology and other critics persisted. These charges were

171. Philip Shenon, "Interpol, aka 'Strait-Laced Guys,' " *New York Times*, Oct. 5, 1985, 7.

publicized anew in early 1991, when the National Association of Chiefs of Police (not to be confused with the International Association of Chiefs of Police) sent a questionnaire regarding Interpol—and copies of a pamphlet produced by the Church of Scientology, entitled "Interpol: Private Group, Public Menace"—to directors of 14,000 U.S. police agencies throughout the United States.[172] Principal among these were accusations that the USNCB was cooperating with foreign NCBs, such as those in Panama and Mexico, directed by police officials who had been implicated in drug trafficking and other crimes. Others focused on the possibility that sensitive information could be provided to police officials in countries implicated in terrorist activities against U.S. citizens, such as Libya. The charges reflected the inevitable vulnerability of any global organization to charges of consorting with unseemly governments. But it also pointed to the frictions inherent in an international organization seeking both to maximize the speed, breadth, and intensity of police cooperation across borders and to minimize the possibility that its facilities might be taken advantage of by criminals.

Conclusion

The internationalization of U.S. law enforcement since the end of World War II cannot be explained by any one event or theory. To describe it as a response to either the internationalization of crime or the proliferation of transnational criminal activities would be only partially true, given the substantial impact of U.S. legislation in defining as crimes, both substantively and jurisdictionally, activities that were not the business of U.S. law enforcers just decades ago. Indeed, when we stretch our horizons backward to the early years of the American republic, we realize that most of what today engages U.S. international law enforcement efforts was then either inconceivable or legal. Eighteenth- and nineteenth-century law enforcers would have recognized the efforts of contemporary customs officials to collect the revenues, and of special agents to investigate transnational frauds and recover fugitives, and even

172. See Seper, "Police Chiefs Seek Interpol Curbs," and the response to the charges by the Church of Scientology in Darrell W. Mills, "A Clearer Picture of What Interpol Is and Does," *Washington Times*, Mar. 19, 1991, G2. See also unpublished commentaries available from the USNCB.

of FBI and ATF agents to enforce the neutrality laws, but they would have regarded as quite novel the contemporary efforts to restrict the transnational movements of people, money, cannabis, and derivatives of the coca and opium plants. Certainly much of the contemporary expansion can be explained by national security concerns; the more broadly we define the term, the more robust the explanation. Nonetheless, a national security thesis—even broadly construed—fails as well to capture much of what was described above, for the simple reason that so much of international law enforcement is concerned with the extraterritorial dimensions of common crimes familiar to the average citizen.

When we focus on the perspective of the United States not as creator of laws but as enforcer, one can say that all of the international efforts—with the partial exception of the police assistance programs—have been motivated by two basic objectives: the "immobilization" of criminals and the seizure of contraband. These objectives have required law enforcement agents to collect information, evidence, and criminals wherever they can be found, which increasingly has included foreign territories. The same objectives have also yielded an abundance of transgovernmental interactions ranging from discreet efforts to operate abroad unilaterally and in informal relationships with foreign police, to the institutionalization of foreign offices and liaison relationships. At the same time, U.S. police have played a central role in the evolution of a transnational police community, training tens of thousands of foreign police officials, advocating more intensive and systematic bilateral and multilateral cooperation, making its computerized data bases and other intelligence resources available to foreign investigators, and initiating new endeavors in both criminal procedures and criminal legislation.

The specifics of these efforts, however, have varied substantially from one agency to the next. Some extended their efforts abroad to investigate smuggling of one sort or another more effectively. This was especially true of Customs, the INS, ATF and the FBN, the BNDD, and the DEA. Some were drawn overseas by national security concerns: the military needed to police itself; the Office of Public Safety was designed in good part to aid anticommunist governments in maintaining public order; U.S. Customs was delegated to investigate the smuggling of high technology to hostile countries; and the FBI was directed to deal with espionage and terrorist acts against U.S. citizens and interests abroad. Most U.S. agencies were obliged to locate, apprehend, and attempt to recover fugitives from abroad. The DEA and the FBI have been particularly involved in such efforts, but no one agency as much as the U.S. Marshals Service in recent years.

The methods and styles of U.S. police operations abroad have changed in some respects but not in others. Posses no longer chase cattle rustlers over the border with Mexico, and military expeditions no longer pursue the likes of "Pancho" Villa—although the amendment to the Posse Comitatus Act and the paramilitarization of U.S. drug enforcement activities in Bolivia and Peru during the late 1980s pointed to a revival of large-scale law enforcement ventures. Respect for foreign sovereignty has climbed noticeably in the domain of international law enforcement, albeit not so much that the Bahamas' sovereignty is given the same deference as Canada's. To the extent that any trends can be discerned, two stand out. The first has been the overall increase in the scope and magnitude of U.S. police efforts abroad. The second has been the emergence of a transnational police community and subculture based upon common tasks and the common objective of "immobilizing" the criminal and powerfully shaped by the fact of U.S. involvement.

Chapter Four

The DEA in Europe: Dealing with Foreign Systems

Drug Enforcement in Comparative and International Perspective

"To get the dope off the street and put the cat in jail." That, as one agent from the Drug Enforcement Administration concisely put it, has remained the central objective of American drug enforcement agents since the beginning. Whether based in Miami, Marseilles, or Mexico City, be it 1939, 1969, or 1989, U.S. drug enforcement agents have concentrated their energies on immobilizing drug traffickers and seizing illicit drugs within or destined for American markets. Time and place have, of course, affected the nature of the agents' challenges and tasks, and a variety of political and bureaucratic considerations have often determined where the agents are stationed and the identities of their targets, both human and psychoactive. (See Appendix C.) Yet even as the assorted directives have flowed from above, the agents have kept their sights on the agency's central objective.

My objective in this chapter is to analyze, more deeply than in the preceding chapters, the relationship between the objectives and tasks of U.S. law enforcers and the foreign environments in which they have operated. The fact of operating extraterritorially dramatically transforms the nature of the DEA agent's work, which is why the task of an agent stationed in Frankfurt has more in common with that of an agent stationed in Lima or Bangkok than one located in Detroit or Los Angeles. Within the United States, the DEA agent is lawfully authorized to arrest those who he believes have violated federal drug laws. He is often expected to coordinate his efforts with state and municipal drug enforcement agents, but it is not a legal condition of his work. By contrast, the agent abroad retains no powers of arrest, and the requirement that he coordinate his efforts with local agents is ignored only rarely and at some risk. In many foreign countries, DEA agents are forbidden to carry firearms, and in some they are legally precluded from even conducting interviews and other investigatory inquiries on their own.

The relationship between the DEA agent abroad and host police agencies is thus one of substantial dependence. If the latter close their doors to him, there is relatively little he can accomplish. On the other hand, the resourceful agent is typically successful at creating a relationship of mutual dependence based upon his own access to intelligence, funds, and expertise desired by his hosts.

All three of the models of transnational policing advanced in the previous chapter provide insights into the nature of the DEA's tasks and challenges abroad. Like the private detective, the DEA agent pursues his investigations without benefit of any sovereign powers, relying on his investigative skills, contacts, and an abundance of discretion. In his capacity as liaison and "fixer," he handles an array of mundane and extraordinary matters. When we recall the disparate activities of Siragusa, Vizzini, and the other FBN and BNDD agents sent overseas in the 1950s, 1960s, and early 1970s, both models are clearly in evidence. When we focus on the DEA's country attachés in foreign capitals, especially those who either preside over relatively large offices or are precluded by local laws from acting in a more operational capacity, the liaison model readily applies. And when we consider the work engaged in by most DEA agents stationed abroad, as well as by most of those sent abroad on TDYs and individual cases, the model of the private detective rings true.

The most comprehensive model, however, is that of a transnational organization. Like a private corporation that retains most of its operations within the United States but earns a disproportionate share of its profits from its overseas activities, the U.S. drug enforcement agency has always retained a strong international orientation despite the small proportion of its personnel stationed abroad. Among all other federal law enforcement agencies, only U.S. Customs has shared a comparable perspective. Driven by both the international nature of drug trafficking and the strong international orientation of its first chief administrator, the Federal Bureau of Narcotics, and thereafter the Bureau of Narcotics and Dangerous Drugs and the Drug Enforcement Administration, always emphasized the inherently international nature of the task delegated to them. But while the central objective of the DEA in 1990 differed in no substantial way from that of the FBN in 1930, the ways in which the contemporary agency has pursued its objectives, as well as the consequences of its activities for foreign law enforcement systems, have differed substantially from those associated with the original drug enforcement agency. If we say that the FBN's international activities are similar to those of a small corporation with modest but highly profitable sales overseas, we can fairly say that the DEA's international operations can be analogized to those of leading multinational corporations such as IBM, General Motors, and MacDonald's. By and large, smaller organizations extract what they require without changing in any substantial way the environments in which they operate. By contrast, major multinational organizations powerfully influence both the foreign environments in which they operate and the ways in which comparable institutions pursue comparable objectives. That influence stems not just from the pressures they exert but also from the models they provide, the examples they suggest, and the concessions they expect as the costs of doing business together.

When we focus on the efforts of American drug enforcement agents in Europe between the late 1960s and the late 1980s, all three models are applicable, but that of the transnational organization is the most valuable. During that time, the central objective of the agency remained constant, as did most of the limitations on its agents' actions imposed by considerations of national sovereignty. By the mid-1970s, the agency's personnel in Europe had also reached the level it would more or less maintain thereafter. As for their quarry, the people who were doing the drug trafficking changed over time, as did many of their routes, their evasive tactics, and to a certain extent the drugs in which they trafficked, but the basic contours of their activities remained much the same. What did change, however, were the criminal justice environments in which the American drug enforcement agents pursued their objectives.

These changes were of three types. One was institutional. Until well into the 1960s, relatively few European police agencies had specialized drug enforcement squads, and virtually no prosecutors specialized in drug trafficking cases. By the late 1980s, most European police agencies, be they national, state, cantonal, or municipal, claimed such units and quite a few worked closely with specialized prosecutors.

A second change was operational. When U.S. drug enforcement agents arrived in Europe, they brought with them a variety of investigative techniques—including "buy and bust" tactics and more extensive undercover operations, "controlled delivery" of illicit drug consignments, various forms of nontelephonic electronic surveillance, and offers of reduced charges or immunity from prosecution to known drug dealers to "flip" them into becoming informants—that had been practiced in the United States for decades and approved by U.S. courts during Prohibition if not before.[1] Throughout most of continental Europe, however, virtually all of these techniques were viewed, even by police officials, as unnecessary, unacceptable, and often illegal.[2] Only the internal security agencies in certain countries resorted to such techniques with any frequency, and their activities were rarely subjected to any sort of judicial oversight. Nonetheless, during the following two decades most of these investigative tactics were adopted by European drug enforcement units, albeit at strikingly different rates and to very different degrees.

A third change was legal. Even as European drug enforcement agents adopted DEA-style techniques during the 1970s and 1980s, their legality remained highly questionable. Judges, and even prosecutors, were often kept in the dark as to the exact nature of the agents' investigations, and all sorts of charades were concocted in order to obscure the true nature of many of the drug enforcement operations. By the late 1980s, however, many of the DEA-style methods had been not only adopted by the local

1. Kenneth M. Murchison, "Prohibition and the Fourth Amendment: A New Look at Some Old Cases," *Journal of Criminal Law and Criminology* 73 (1982), 471–532.

2. References to Europe hereafter refer only to the western and central European nations on the continent, all of which adhere to the civil law tradition. The common law nations of Great Britain and Ireland, as well as the previously socialist law nations of Eastern Europe, are excluded from the discussion.

police but also authorized, and hence legalized, by local courts and legislatures.

All of these changes can be viewed as part and parcel of the harmonization of drug enforcement both within Europe and in relation to the United States. But how one evaluates these changes depends in good part upon one's perspective. From the perspective of the DEA, and more generally of the U.S. government, all of these changes were of consequence less in and of themselves than for what they contributed to the accomplishment of the DEA's central objective. This is not to say that the changes occurred only as incidental by-products of the DEA's efforts, or to suggest that the urge to proselytize or the satisfaction derived from seeing one's own approaches adopted by others were entirely absent. Quite the contrary, DEA agents consciously advocated and lobbied for the reforms and felt a sense of vindication when they were adopted by their hosts. Their principal motivation, however, was to improve the capacity of the DEA, and by extension European police agencies, to immobilize drug traffickers and seize illicit drugs destined for American markets. Underlying this motivation was the realization that the DEA's success abroad depended less upon its own freedom of action in foreign territories than upon its capacity to generate effective vicarious drug enforcement capabilities within foreign police agencies.

From the Europeans' perspective, however, the changes wrought in part by the efforts of the DEA were of significant consequence in and of themselves. This was particularly true of the changes in the laws, which occurred in many countries only after substantial political, legal, and professional debate about the nature of policing and the proper reaches and methods of the state. As in the United States, but in a far more compressed period of time, judicial, legislative, and executive authorities in Europe were obliged to address difficult legal issues regarding the distinction between legitimate undercover techniques and entrapment, the degree to which undercover agents could participate in criminal activities, the credibility of informants who had been offered financial or judicial compensation for their services, the need to shield informants' identities in court, and the proper limits on electronic surveillance. But unlike their American counterparts, European judges, administrators, and legislators also had to address more basic obstacles to the "Americanization" of their drug enforcement, including a deeply felt, and historically rooted, antipathy toward the notion of *agents provocateurs* and even undercover agents generally, the absence of any clear legal authority for police undercover operations, and the powerful influence of the "legality principle," or "rule of compulsory prosecution"—all of which greatly hindered the acceptance of undercover operations and controlled deliveries as well as the ability of criminal justice agents to recruit informants from among those arrested for illicit drug dealing or any other crime.

It is fair, I believe, to speak of the "Americanization" of European drug enforcement, provided the term is understood broadly and the substantial differences within Europe are acknowledged at the outset. The notion of "Americanization" applies most accurately to the changes demanded and incited by the Americans. With respect to some, evidence of the DEA's active hand is readily apparent and openly acknowledged by the Europeans: the creation of specialized drug enforcement units in major police agencies; the initial adoption of DEA-style undercover tactics and the subsequent training of European police in a variety of DEA-style techniques; the notion of "flipping" informants; and the enactment of legislation authorizing the forfeiture of drug traffickers' assets. But the notion of "Americanization" can also be understood more passively as including changes in European drug enforcement caused not only by American pressures, incitements, and training but also those changes shaped by the experience gained in working with U.S. drug enforcement agents, by the models and examples suggested by the DEA's own history and modus operandi, and by the popularization through fiction and nonfiction media of the American approach to drug enforcement.

There is, of course, an even more passive sense in which one can speak of the "Americanization" of European drug enforcement, one that suggests only an element of chronology, not one of causality. Many of the changes in European drug enforcement may well have had nothing whatsoever to do with the influences or examples of the Americans; rather, they may have reflected the simple lack of effective alternatives for dealing with the spread of illicit drug trafficking. That those changes appeared as an "Americanization" of European drug enforcement was simply a consequence of the Americans' chronological "advantage" both in confronting a drug trafficking boom some years before the Europeans, and in having first addressed many of the same difficult legal issues raised by drug enforcement tactics decades earlier during Prohibition—an experience in alcohol control eschewed by most European nations south of Scandinavia. On the other hand, the fact that some European countries, notably Germany, Austria, and Belgium, have followed closely in the footsteps of the Americans while others, such as France and Italy, have proven more resistant, suggests that the DEA's approach to drug enforcement was not the only option for dealing with the common problem of illicit drug trafficking.

The process of "Americanization" described in this chapter can well be contrasted with the very different "Americanization" of criminal justice and other governmental domains that preceded it.[3] Many of the curbs on police powers that have so frustrated DEA agents were initially imposed by U.S. occupying forces in the aftermath of World War II. U.S. policy makers initially regarded the centralization of police and other governmental power associated with the defeated fascist regimes as an evil to be avoided in the postwar era. But the onset of the Cold War, rising concern with Soviet espionage and communist agitation, and the growing threat of terrorism all provided incentives for U.S. policy makers to reverse stride and encourage the expansion of police powers in Europe as in America. Criminal justice norms and institutions were among the first to be shaped by the "national security state" mentality that emerged in tandem with the Cold War.

The evolution of European drug enforcement since the late 1960s has also been shaped by other influences.[4] Many of the tactics and laws initially devised to investigate and suppress such terrorist groups as the Red Brigade in Italy and the Baader-Meinhof in Germany provided the initial experience, legal authority, and practical models for subsequent responses to illicit drug trafficking and organized crime.[5] National approaches to drug enforcement within Europe have also been influenced by the initiatives taken by individual countries as well as by multilateral initiatives. The German BKA (Bundeskriminalamt), for instance, has promoted itself as a model for other European police agencies and assumed a leading role in inter-European police affairs. Multilateral law enforcement conventions, as well as multilateral arrangements such as Interpol, TREVI, the Council of Europe, and the Pompidou Group have played an increasingly important role.[6] The European Court of Human

3. I am indebted to Walter Murphy for this point.

4. See Ethan A. Nadelmann, *Criminalization and Crime Control in International Society* (New York: Oxford University Press, forthcoming); and Hans-Jörg Albrecht and Anton van Kalmthout, eds., *Drug Policies in Western Europe* (Freiburg: Max-Planck-Institut, 1989).

5. See, e.g., Leonard Weinberg and William Lee Eubank, *The Rise and Fall of Italian Terrorism* (Boulder, Colo.: Westview Press, 1987), 125–133.

6. Cyrille Fijnaut, "The Internationalization of Criminal Investigation in Western Eu-

Rights has exercised some influence by virtue of its decisions in a number of cases involving the use of informants and of electronic surveillance.[7] Regional arrangements, such as those among the Scandinavian and the Benelux nations respectively, have shaped the domestic law enforcement policies of the member countries. And more generally the prospects of open borders in 1992 have created pressures for greater conformity among European criminal justice systems.[8]

My focus on the adoption of U.S.-style methods in Europe should not obscure the extent to which European police have been able to take advantage of police powers that do not exist in the United States. In many European countries (but not all), police and prosecutors can legally detain criminal suspects for much longer than is permissible in the United States; access to counsel can be more delayed and restricted; telephone taps can be more easily obtained and kept in place longer; warrantless searches can be conducted more readily; evidence gathered illegally is rarely excluded from court; residents are required to carry special identity cards; and police are legally entitled to ask anyone to show them those cards. U.S. agents in Europe have been known to covet these powers, but they have also found that the Europeans' greater authority and discretion to question, detain, and search do not compensate for the restrictions on their ability to use the types of investigative methods that are regarded as so essential by U.S. agents. It is worth observing, however, that even as European drug enforcement has been becoming increasingly "Americanized," it is also possible to point to evidence of what one might call a "Europeanization" of American law enforcement—albeit one in which the hands of the Europeans are nowhere apparent. In a series of U.S. Supreme Court decisions beginning in the 1980s and continuing into the 1990s, many of the European police powers coveted by the few DEA agents familiar with them have been legalized in the United States. The scope of warrantless searches has been expanded, the exclusionary rule narrowed, the right to counsel circumscribed, and the allowable period of detention lengthened.[9] The

rope," in C.J.C.F. Fijnaut and R. H. Hermans, eds., *Police Cooperation in Europe* (Lochem: Van den Brink, 1987), 32–56; Paul Wilkinson, "European Police Cooperation," in John Roach and Jürgen Thomaneck, eds., *Police and Public Order in Europe* (London: Croom Helm, 1985).

7. Note, "Secret Surveillance and the European Convention on Human Rights," *Stanford Law Review* 33 (1981), 1113.

8. Clyde Haberman, "Europeans Fear '92 Economic Unity May Benefit Mafia," *New York Times*, July 23, 1989, 1.

9. This trend is critically analyzed in Steven Wisotsky, "Not Thinking Like a Lawyer:

cumulative consequences of developments in drug enforcement on both sides of the Atlantic since the 1970s have been a convergence toward similar and greater police powers.

The "Americanization" of European drug enforcement has also involved more than the changes in criminal investigative methods discussed in this chapter. Europeans have encountered many of the same sorts of illicit drug problems the Americans encountered, albeit more belatedly and somewhat less dramatically. They responded, as in the United States, by imposing increasingly severe criminal sanctions beginning in the late 1960s.[10] During the 1970s, the movement to decriminalize the sale of small amounts of cannabis and the possession of small amounts of "harder" drugs spread throughout much of Europe. During the 1980s, European legislatures renewed the trend toward broader and tougher sanctions, enacting stiffer penalties for illicit drug possession and distribution as well as laws designed to seize drug traffickers' assets, to identify and punish drug-related money laundering, and to better prosecute drug trafficking conspiracies.[11] More recently, rising frustration over the apparent lack of success of drug laws in stemming drug abuse, and growing concern over the spread of AIDS by illicit drug abusers, have sparked a renewal of calls for drug legalization, implementation of "harm reduction" measures, and generally greater reliance on public health approaches to the problems of illicit drug abuse.[12] Since the early 1970s, the Netherlands has developed and quietly defended its more public health-oriented policies, while Germany has taken the lead in advocating the more punitive criminal-justice-oriented approaches emanating from the United States.[13] Among the Scandinavian countries,

---

The Case of Drugs in the Courts," *Notre Dame Journal of Law, Ethics, and Public Policy* 5 (1991), 651–692.

10. See European Committee on Crime Problems, *Penal Aspects of Drug Abuse* (Strasbourg: Council of Europe, 1974); and Albrecht and Kalmthout, eds., *Drug Policies in Western Europe* (supra n. 4).

11. Alexander MacLeod, "Europe Plans Assault on Growing Drug Menace," *Christian Science Monitor*, Sept. 14, 1989, 1.

12. See, e.g., the interview with Hamburg Mayor Hennig Voscherau in *Spiegel*, July 17, 1989, 27–30; the interview with former German Health Minister Rita Süssmuth in *Frankfurter Allgemeine*, Nov. 7, 1988; "Burton Bollag, "To the Swiss and Dutch, Tolerance Is Anti-Drug," *New York Times*, Dec. 1, 1989, A4; and cover stories on drug legalization, in *L'Espresso*, Apr. 2, 1989, and *Cambiol* 6, October 2, 1989. See also Peter Cohen, "Building upon the Successes of Dutch Drug Policy," *International Journal on Drug Policy* 2 (1989), 22–24. More generally, see Albrecht and Kalmthout, eds., *Drug Policies in Western Europe*, 77–78 (Austria), 104–105 (Belgium), 127–128 (Denmark), 150–151 (France), 182–184 (Germany), 221–225 (Italy), 255–256 (Netherlands), 298–299 (Spain), and 373–378 (Switzerland).

13. See Sebastian Scheerer, "The New Dutch and German Drug Laws: Social and Political Conditions for Criminalization and Decriminalization," *Law and Society Review* 12 (1978),

Denmark's more lenient drug prohibition policies—in particular its toleration of the counterculture communities of Christiania and Frøstrup-Lejren—have similarly upset its neighbors.[14] Hard-liners throughout Europe were also hostile to Spain's revision of its drug laws in 1983, which introduced a Dutch-like distinction between "soft" and "hard" drugs and formalized the decriminalization of drug possession previously instituted by the courts.[15] In all these respects, one can find evidence of "Americanizing" pressures, examples, and precedents, be it in the influence of the American counterculture on European youth and culture during the 1960s and 1970s, the Europeans' adoption of methadone maintenance programs developed initially in the United States, the trend toward decriminalization of cannabis during the mid-1970s, or the more prevalent trend toward tougher and broader criminal sanctions since the 1960s. Indeed, some of the countries that have been the most outspoken in advocating "harm reduction" approaches to drug abuse and small-scale drug dealing have also been the quickest to adopt DEA-style approaches to investigating drug trafficking.

It is not surprising that evidence of any real "Europeanization" (in the active sense of the term) of American drug enforcement, or even of

---

585–606; Ineke Haen Marshall, Oscar Anjewierden, and Hans Van Atteveld, "Toward an 'Americanization' of Dutch Drug Policy?" *Justice Quarterly* 7 (1990), 391–420. Henk Jan van Vliet, "The Uneasy Decriminalization: A Perspective on Dutch Drug Policy," *Hofstra Law Review* 18 (1990), 717–750; E. D. Engelsman, "Dutch Policy on the Management of Drug-Related Problems," *British Journal of Addiction* 84 (1989), 211–218, and subsequent commentaries at pp. 989–997; David Downes, *Contrasts in Tolerance: Post-war Penal Policy in the Netherlands and England and Wales* (Oxford: Clarendon Press, 1988), 123–162; Govert F. van de Wijngaart, "A Social History of Drug Use in the Netherlands: Policy Outcomes and Implications," *Journal of Drug Issues* 18 (1988), 481–495; O. Anjewierden and J. M. A. van Atteveld, "Current Trends in Dutch Opium Legislation," in Albrecht and Kalmthout, eds., *Drug Policies in Western Europe* (supra n. 4), 235–258; A. M. van Kalmthout, "Characteristics of Drug Policy in the Netherlands," in Albrecht and Kalmthout, eds., *Drug Policies in Western Europe*, 259–291; and Frits Ruter, "The Pragmatic Dutch Approach to Drug Control: Does It Work?" reprinted in *Legalization of Illicit Drugs, Impact and Feasibility: Hearing Before the Select Senate Committee on Narcotics Abuse and Control*, 100th Cong., 2d Sess., Part 1 (1988), 517–538.

14. Flemming Balvig, "Crime and Criminal Policy in a Pragmatic Society: The Case of Denmark and Christiania, 1960–1975," *International Journal of the Sociology of Law* 10 (1982), 9–29; J. Jepsen, "Drug Policies in Denmark," in Albrecht and Kalmthout, eds., *Drug Policies in Western Europe*, 107–141, esp. 107–108.

15. See J. L. de la Cuesta, "The Present Spanish Drug Criminal Policy," and J. L. Díez-Ripollés, "Principles of a New Drug Policy in Western Europe from a Spanish Point of View," both in Albrecht and Kalmthout, eds., *Drug Policies in Western Europe*, 293–320 and 321–341.

American criminal justice generally, has been relatively scant. During the 1970s, a number of legal scholars on both sides of the Atlantic debated whether the American criminal justice system might learn something from Europe's "inquisitorial" legal system, but no apparent changes resulted. Alternative drug control policies in the United Kingdom—where doctors had retained the power to prescribe maintenance doses of heroin, injectable methadone, and other prohibited drugs for addicts—also stimulated debate, but no changes in U.S. policy.[16] Of potentially greater consequence was the rising sense among American drug policy experts toward the end of the 1980s and into the 1990s that the United States might have something to learn from European "harm reduction" policies directed at stemming the transmission of AIDS by and among illicit drug users, but even that injection of European influence had yet to penetrate official government policies in the United States.[17] All of these differences of opinion and policy both within Europe and between some European states and the United States have occasionally colored relations among drug enforcement officials, but they have had relatively little impact on the debates over the criminal investigative tactics discussed below.

Finding and Creating Foreign Partners

The cooperation which foreign governments and law enforcement agencies are willing and able to give the DEA varies dramatically from one country to the next. With governments that are more willing but less able, the DEA has sought as free a hand as possible in conducting its

16. See Edwin M. Schur, *Narcotic Addiction in Britain and America* (Bloomington: Indiana University Press, 1962); Alfred R. Lindesmith, *The Addict and the Law* (Bloomington: Indiana University Press, 1965); Horace Freeland Judson, *Heroin Addiction in Britain* (New York: Harcourt Brace Jovanovich, 1973); and Arnold S. Trebach, *The Heroin Solution* (New Haven: Yale University Press, 1982).

17. Pat O'Hare, Russell Newcombe, Alan Matthews, Ernst C. Buning, and Ernest Drucker, eds., *The Reduction of Drug Related Harm* (London: Routledge, 1991); Nick Heather, Alex Wodak, Ethan Nadelmann, and Pat O'Hare, eds., *Psychoactive Drugs and Harm Reduction: From Faith to Science* (London: Whurr Publishers, 1993). See also John Strang and Gerry V. Stimson, eds., *AIDS and Drug Misuse: The Challenge for Policy and Practice in the 1990s* (New York: Routledge, 1990); and Robert J. Battjes and Roy W. Pickens, eds., *Needle Sharing Among Intravenous Drug Abusers: National and International Perspectives* (Washington, D.C.: National Institute on Drug Abuse, 1988).

operations. With others, such as in Europe, who are more able to give assistance but less flexible in allowing the DEA a free hand, the DEA has sought greater cooperation in gathering intelligence, making seizures, and arresting and prosecuting traffickers. In both cases, however, the DEA has pursued a common subsidiary objective: the development of effective drug enforcement capabilities within local police agencies. Where such a capability already exists, the DEA has sought to augment it and increase its effectiveness by offering training, information, and other assistance. Where the capability has been lacking, the DEA has devoted its resources to creating specially trained units with whom it can work. Where such a capability has existed but is endangered, the DEA has tried to protect it from whatever political, budgetary, or other forces threatened it. Particularly in the last case, which is far more likely in less developed countries, the DEA's efforts have been supplemented by political pressures from Washington and the State Department.

The priority the DEA has placed on creating and maintaining effective drug enforcement capabilities within foreign countries stems from a number of factors. To begin with, any foreign drug enforcement force, even a relatively corrupted one, can assist the DEA in its mission—particularly if it is familiar with drug enforcement techniques. Moreover, the DEA has little choice but to depend on local law enforcement agencies for many of the functions it would carry out itself within the United States. Budgetary and personnel restrictions pose severe limits on DEA resources around the world. Two hundred agents abroad may be more than twice the total of all other civilian American law enforcement agents stationed overseas, but it is not much when a major investigation is under way. And even if the DEA had enough agents in a country, the laws of both the United States and the foreign country bar U.S. agents from conducting many of the tasks normally associated with law enforcement. For instance, no government other than the United States empowers U.S. agents to arrest people within its borders, or to conduct a search or seizure, to compel witnesses or suspects to talk to them, or to obtain the necessary search warrant. In many countries, they are not even allowed to carry a gun. Indeed, in some countries foreign prosecutors and law enforcement agents may be jailed for engaging in unauthorized activities as innocuous as questioning a resident compatriot or asking to see a hotel register.[18]

18. See, e.g., Claus Schellenberg, "The Proceedings Against Two French Customs Officials in Switzerland for Prohibited Acts in Favor of a Foreign State, Economic Intelligence Service and Violation of the Banking Law," *International Business Lawyer* 9 (1981), 139–140.

DEA agents abroad rely greatly on their ability to establish strong working relationships with foreign counterparts that can be isolated from political influences and accommodated to the often undiplomatic requirements of international law enforcement. These relationships, based upon both personal and professional links, are essential to cutting through red tape, bending rules and laws that can restrict an agent's flexibility, and even securing cooperation in matters on which higher levels of their respective governments do not see eye to eye. As one FBI LEGAT put it, reflecting the views of most law enforcement agents, cooperative efforts across borders tend to work "so long as issues are resolved among the agents themselves rather than decided by the policy-makers. When politics get involved, things stop working." This is not to say that foreign law enforcement agents will betray their country's interests out of friendship or police comradery. But it is to say that police tend to place a higher priority than most politicians on going after criminals, and a lower priority on political considerations and sensitivities of national sovereignty. The common sentiment that a cop is a cop no matter whose badge he or she wears, and that a criminal is a criminal no matter what his or her citizenship is or where the crime was committed, serves as a kind of transgovernmental value system overriding political conflicts between governments. It provides, in many ways, the oil and glue of international law enforcement.

Transgovernmental values aside, among the most difficult challenges to effective DEA liaison and cooperation overseas has been its need to avoid the bureaucratic minefields and turf struggles of foreign law enforcement agencies. In many countries, the tensions between law enforcement agencies with overlapping drug enforcement responsibilities are at least as severe as those between the DEA and other U.S. agencies.[19] In each country, the DEA's choice of which law enforcement agency to work with is determined by a variety of factors. In many cases, the choice is taken out of its hands by an interagency agreement, a memorandum of understanding, an oral agreement, or a government fiat specifying who the DEA must notify regarding its activities and who the DEA may and may not deal with. In other cases, the DEA can deal with whomever it chooses so long as it gives prior notice to some designated office. And in still other countries, the DEA has a free hand to deal with whomever it chooses.

19. This challenge is not unique to the DEA; the FBI often encounters similar problems abroad in its dealings with local law enforcement and intelligence agencies.

When given the choice of whom to work with, the DEA considers many factors. It may take advantage of one agency's expertise in one area, such as visual or electronic surveillance, and a different agency's expertise in another area, such as intelligence, undercover operations, interrogation, searches and seizures, arrests, or internal liaison. It may rely entirely on one agency because it is better trained in all tasks, or because there are established personal and political relationships with that agency, or because it is free of corruption or at least less corrupt than the alternatives. It may make an effort to work with all agencies, even where working with one would be just as effective, in order to maintain good relations all around. And it may forgo or limit its contacts with particular agencies by agreement with other U.S. agencies, such as U.S. Customs.

In Europe, where degrees of corruption are far less of a consideration, the DEA tends to work with whichever agency proves most helpful. DEA agents generally have found the drug enforcement units of the national, state, or municipal police more useful than those of the more paramilitary police agencies supervised in whole or in part by European defense ministries. In quite a number of countries, however, the DEA's options are controlled or supervised by a special unit set up to coordinate all national and international drug enforcement activities. In France, that unit is the Central Narcotics Office (CNO) (Office Central de Répression du Trafic Illicite de Stupéfiants) within the Criminal Investigative Department (Police Judiciaire) of the National Police, which during the mid-1980s included about 100 agents.[20] If DEA agents want to deal with any of the other police units, such as the Gendarmerie, the customs agency, the Air and Frontier Police (Service Central de la Police de l'Air et des Frontières), or Paris' municipal drug unit (the Brigade des Stupéfiants et du Proxenétisme), the agents must request permission from the head of the CNO. In Italy, an interagency unit, the Servizio Centrale Antidroga (SCA), has a say in whether the DEA will work with the State Police, the paramilitary Carabinieri, or the Treasury police (the Guardia di Finanza), each of which has its own drug enforcement units.[21] During

20. For an overview of the French police (though one that devotes little attention to the issues discussed here), see Philip John Stead, *The Police of France* (New York: Macmillan, 1983), and the briefer description in J. R. Jammes, "Some Aspects of the French Police," *Police Journal* 55 (1982), 113–124.

21. A brief but solid history of the Italian police is Richard O. Collin, "The Blunt Instruments: Italy and the Police," in Roach and Thomaneck, eds., *Police and Public Order in Europe*, 185–214. A classic study of the Italian police is Robert C. Fried, *The Italian Prefects:*

the mid-1980s, the DEA office in Milan worked most closely with the Guardia di Finanza, while the Rome office relied primarily on the other two agencies, working principally with the State Police in Rome but also with the Carabinieri in Naples. The preferences were less a reflection of the three police agencies' respective specializations than of the personalities involved.

In the Netherlands, the DEA is required to coordinate its activities with the National Criminal Intelligence Service (Centrale Recherche Informatiedienst, CRI) in the Ministry of Justice. The CRI acts as a coordinating and advisory body for both domestic and international criminal investigations, but its personnel are mostly nonoperational. Most of the DEA's dealings are with the municipal police forces (Gemeentepolitie), especially those in major cities, such as Amsterdam and Rotterdam.[22] Similarly, in Switzerland, a small, nonoperational central police office (ZEPO) coordinates the DEA's work with the canton police, who are responsible for almost all law enforcement operations. In Spain, the DEA works primarily with the drug enforcement agents of the National Police, coordinating its activities with the Central Narcotics Brigade, which like the Dutch CRI is largely nonoperational, and with the twelve drug enforcement brigades distributed around the country.[23] About 20 percent of the DEA's work involves the Guardia Civil, whose drug enforcement agents are distributed similarly to the way the National Police brigades are, and about 5 percent requires the cooperation of Spain's customs agency. One of the few countries that places no restrictions on whom the DEA may work with is Belgium. There the DEA may choose between the Judiciary Police (Police Judiciaire/Gerechtelijke Politie) and the Gendarmerie (Rijkswacht), neither of which has large drug units but both of which have jurisdiction over drug law violations and certain agents who specialize in drug enforcement. In cases with an inter-European angle, the DEA will likely work with the Gendarmerie because its liaison with other European law enforcement agencies is quite good. But in cases initiated by the DEA, or involving

---

A Study in Administrative Politics (New Haven: Yale University Press, 1963), although it does not address the criminal investigative matters discussed here.

22. An interesting analysis of Dutch policing is Maurice Punch, *Policing the Inner City: A Study of Amsterdam's Warmoesstraat* (London: Macmillan & Co., 1979). The CRI also publishes an annual report in English on the activities of its Narcotics Branch.

23. The organization of the Spanish police is briefly described in Robert Hudson, "Democracy and the Spanish Police Forces Since 1975," *Police Journal* 61 (1988), 53–62.

just Belgium, the DEA agents prefer to work with the Judiciary Police, who are generally more aggressive in recruiting informants and initiating proactive investigations—so aggressive, in fact, that their efforts periodically have resulted in public scandals not unlike those that occasionally flare up in American cities.

In West Germany, the DEA's principal partner has changed over time. When the BNDD first opened a number of offices around Germany in the early 1970s, the federal police agency (the Bundeskriminalamt, BKA), based in Wiesbaden, was largely nonoperational, similar in many ways to the CRI in Holland today. Like the Dutch service, it provided some coordination in criminal investigations, served as a central repository of criminal information, and acted as the national central bureau of Interpol. The vast majority of law enforcement investigations, including those with international dimensions, were conducted by the police forces of the individual German states (Länderpolizeien). On occasion, the BKA's few investigators might initiate a drug investigation of its own or participate in a state police investigation at the behest of the latter. Although the DEA maintained a liaison relationship with the BKA, most of its operations were done jointly with the state police agencies. During the 1970s, however, this decentralization of police power, which had originally been demanded by the occupying powers after the war, came under increasing pressure. The urgings of U.S. drug enforcement officials provided some of the impetus, but most of the incentive was provided by the dramatic increase in terrorist attacks sponsored by the Baader-Meinhof gang and the subsequent recognition of the need for better national coordination of complex criminal investigations. In 1973, new legislation gave the BKA original jurisdiction in cases involving counterfeiting, arms trafficking, and international drug trafficking.[24] Thereafter, the state police were required to clear any contacts with foreign law enforcement agencies, apart from routine cross-border communications, through the federal agency. Frustrated by the "provincialization" of the state police, the DEA cut back on its interactions with state police, closed its office in Munich in 1982, and began working much more closely with the BKA.

The BKA has grown rapidly since the 1970s, with its drug enforcement

24. See Reinhard Schweppe, *FBI und BKA* (Stuttgart: Ferdinand Enke Verlag, 1974), which argues that the BKA had been heavily influenced by the FBI and would continue to evolve in its footsteps as a consequence of the 1973 legislation. See also A. F. Carter, "The West German Bundeskriminalamt," *Police Journal* 49 (1976), 199–209.

responsibilities providing a substantial impetus for new initiatives both within Germany and abroad. By the mid-1980s, most of the Länderpolizeien had also jumped back into the drug enforcement fray. All of the Länderpolizeien created their own elite criminal investigative units (Landeskriminalamt, LKA), which are generally modeled after U.S. drug enforcement units and the BKA. The BKA typically takes the lead in most transnational and multi-Länder investigations, and it retains the power to preempt criminal investigations initiated by the LKAs. As in the United States, most drug enforcement is still performed by nonfederal police agencies, and evidence of a vigorous rivalry between the BKA and the LKAs abounds (as is also true in the United States of relations between the DEA and the FBI, on the one hand, and state and local agencies, on the other), but today most of the DEA's operations are coordinated with the federal agency, whose drug unit has emerged as the most innovative and aggressive in Europe.[25] The relationship has been a robust one, with complaints on both sides. The Germans, one DEA agent commented to me, "often fail to realize that international cooperation is a two-sided affair." Some tensions were also characteristic of any relationship between a mentor agency and its rapidly maturing protégé. But by and large, the DEA has viewed favorably the emergence of the BKA as a major force in its own right.

Although the DEA has been responsible for inspiring or instigating a number of the organizational changes in European drug enforcement forces, few agencies have been as influenced by the Americans as Austria's. As in Germany, the postwar occupiers and popular sentiment as well had resisted any return to a national police agency. Until the late 1970s, neither the Federal Police (Bundespolizei), whose units reported to the security director in the respective Länder, nor the Gendarmerie devoted virtually any personnel to drug enforcement. Following the opening of a DEA office in Vienna in 1974, an Austrian Central Narcotics Department (ACND) was established in the Federal Police headquarters. With only two agents available to cooperate with local police on drug cases, it was, in the words of one DEA agent, primarily a "paper-pushing agency responding to requests from Interpol." The first DEA attaché, Robert Waltz, is credited by Austrians with playing a central role in the development of Austria's drug enforcement capabili-

25. A fine overview of the German police is Jürgen Thomaneck, "Police and Public Order in the Federal Republic of Germany," in Roach and Thomaneck, eds., *Police and Public Order in Europe* (supra n. 6), 143–184.

ties.[26] By the early 1980s, the ACND had been transformed into the only operational police unit at the national level. Its agents were involved in most major drug investigations, although the Gendarmerie and local units of the Federal Police continued to work on drug cases as well. During the mid-1980s, resident DEA agents much preferred to work directly with the ACND and its longtime chief, Herbert Fuchs. The Federal Police units, one agent told me, "were just not that good. They're not well funded, not that imaginative, not that adaptable, and tend to do things very much by the book."

The requirement that the DEA notify or request permission from a central drug enforcement unit to work with a different agency does not mean that lines of authority are never crossed. Once resident DEA agents have established working relationships with their counterparts in local drug enforcement units, informal links tend to obscure formal lines of authority. Often local police resent interference from the central unit, not only in their dealings with the DEA but in their dealings with other foreign law enforcement agencies as well. This is especially so among police working along the border, who may have more in common with foreign counterparts across the border than with their fellow agents based at headquarters in the capital. In a number of countries, responsibility for informing the central drug enforcement unit of a cooperative investigation falls to the agency that initiated the lead. If that agency is the DEA—which often it is, given the DEA's generally superior intelligence network—the central unit is typically notified, albeit not always in advance. But if a local agency is the initiator, it may choose not to notify the central unit; the DEA tends to remain uninvolved in such decisions. Much also depends upon the individual personalities and the criminal justice cultures. In France and Austria, for instance, the lines of authority are relatively strict, in Italy a little less, in Holland even less so, and in Belgium they barely exist. In Germany, the DEA attaché described a situation not unlike that in many other countries: "Sometimes the LKAs come directly to us. They might ask us to work undercover. We tell them they're supposed to notify the BKA. But ultimately it's their responsibility."

The DEA's foreign partners also include local prosecutors, investigating magistrates, and judges, particularly those who specialize in drug

26. Herbert Fuchs, "DEA's Role in Austria" (unpublished manuscript by the director of the ACND, 1986).

cases. The extent and closeness of these relationships depends greatly on the nature of the relationship between local police and prosecutors. As in the United States, most police/prosecutor relationships are characterized by tensions involving differences in class and culture, professional perspectives, turf and tactics, but some transcend these differences and become quite intimate. DEA agents abroad tend to view their relationships with local prosecutors and other judicial officers through the same eyes as at home. They generally take their lead from the local police with whom they are working. The results are closer relationships in some countries than in others, very close relationships in particular situations, but generally cool and somewhat distant relationships in most cases.

Intelligence-Gathering and Informants

A fundamental aspect of making cases against drug traffickers is the collection of intelligence on their identities, organizations, methods, and activities. The DEA has distinguished three types of intelligence:

> The first is *tactical* intelligence which contributes directly and immediately to making a case. The collection requirements are usually defined by either the agent on the case or the intelligence analyst supporting him. . . . The second is *operational* intelligence, i.e., that which may contribute to a case against a specific violator, but does not necessarily fit into the case at the time. . . . Usually the purpose is to develop profiles of traffickers and do network analysis. The third type is *strategic* intelligence which is general information about drug sources and the external environment in which DEA operates. Strategic intelligence does not necessarily contribute to making any single case, but does influence the overall plan of operation. In general, it provides an overview of the narcotics threat and trend and of the magnitude and direction of the domestic supply. It enables U.S. policy makers to place political emphasis on foreign governments when required.[27]

27. "Drug Enforcement Administration Appropriation Summary Statement," in *Departments of State, Justice, and Commerce, the Judiciary, and Related Agencies Appropriations for 1977: Hearings Before a Subcommittee of the House Committee on Appropriations*, 94th Cong., 2d Sess., Part 4 (Department of Justice, 1976), 1065.

Intelligence on drug trafficking is gathered not only by DEA agents but also by most other U.S. law enforcement agencies, the military and intelligence agencies, and foreign law enforcement agencies. It is then processed through one or both of the DEA's two computerized intelligence support systems: the El Paso Intelligence Center (EPIC), which acts as a clearinghouse for operational and tactical drug enforcement information, and the Narcotics and Dangerous Drugs Information System (NADDIS), a "data base which consist[ed in 1976] of about 1,800,000 records on persons, businesses, ships, aircraft and certain airfields, [and] is the centralized index of all DEA investigative reports."[28] The DEA's intelligence analysts, of whom about two dozen are located overseas, assess and analyze the information, develop estimates, look for trends, and disseminate the processed intelligence to DEA offices, other U.S. law enforcement and intelligence agencies, and favored foreign drug enforcement agencies.

The DEA's capacity to collect intelligence overseas depends upon three factors: the intelligence capabilities of the local law enforcement agencies, the willingness of those agencies to share their intelligence with the DEA, and the DEA agent's freedom and ability to gather his or her own intelligence, such as by recruiting informants. Accordingly, the DEA agent seeks to maximize all three. With regard to the first, his or her efforts include encouraging local police to devote greater resources to intelligence collection and coordination, advocating the adoption of DEA-style methods for recruiting informants, and assisting the German BKA in developing its own NADDIS-type computer system. The second factor also varies greatly, depending not only upon personal and bureaucratic relationships but also, particularly in countries where corruption is more pervasive, upon the local agent's need to keep the DEA in the dark on some matters.

The DEA agents' ability to collect information on their own depends upon any number of factors, the most important of which is the agent's capacity to cultivate and recruit informants. Visual surveillance is among the simplest forms of information collection. Discreetly following a suspect or keeping an eye on an apartment is an activity in which virtually all agents engage. Somewhat more complicated, from the legal viewpoint, is questioning people who may have information—for in-

28. *Reauthorization of the Drug Enforcement Administration for Fiscal Year 1988: Hearing Before the Subcommittee on Crime of the House Committee on the Judiciary*, 100th Cong., 1st Sess. (1987), 88.

stance, talking to a relative or friend of a suspect, interviewing a possible witness to a crime, or obtaining information from hotel employees regarding their guests. But given the nature of drug trafficking, the importance of informants to drug enforcement cannot be overestimated. This is especially true in the many foreign countries where undercover operations and most types of electronic surveillance are strictly circumscribed or illegal, and where prosecutors are legally prohibited from offering immunity or a reduction in charges to criminals in return for their cooperation in an investigation. The value of informants often extends beyond the information they provide; many assist DEA activities in a more operational manner, either acting in an undercover role themselves or providing undercover DEA agents with the necessary contacts and entrees.

The DEA agent's process of recruiting informants abroad does not differ much from the process in the United States,[29] with the significant exception that the agent's capacity to coerce those involved in illicit drug dealing into becoming informants by first arresting them or threatening them with arrest is inevitably diminished by lack of arrest powers. The agent's ability to recruit informants in this fashion—which is the principal means of informant recruitment in the United States—thus depends entirely upon his or her relationship with local agents and their willingness and ability either to lend the necessary legal coercion to his efforts or engage in the same tactics themselves. Also crucial are the agent's personal abilities; some are better at recruiting informants from a particular milieu. The variety of motives that induce people to become informants is not determined by geography, although DEA agents have noticed that a higher proportion of the best informants in Europe are "walk-ins"—people who simply come into the police station or the DEA office in the U.S. embassy and volunteer to become informants. Money

29. For a more developed discussion of the recruitment and use of informants by the DEA and the FBI during the mid-1970s, see James Q. Wilson, *The Investigators*, chap. 3. The FBN's use of informants is discussed in "Informers in Federal Narcotics Prosecutions," *Columbia Journal of Law and Social Problems* 2 (1966), 47–74. See also Peter K. Manning, *The Narcs' Game: Organizational and Informational Limits on Drug Law Enforcement* (Cambridge, Mass.: M.I.T. Press, 1980), 47–49, 140–191; Mark Harrison Moore, *Buy and Bust* (Lexington, Mass.: Lexington Books, 1977), 121–185; Jay R. Williams and L. Lynn Guess, "The Informant: A Narcotics Dilemma," *Journal of Psychoactive Drugs* 13 (1981), 235–245; Michael F. Brown, "Criminal Informants: Some Observations on Use, Abuse, and Control," *Journal of Police Science and Administration* 13 (1985), 251–256; and Paul Fuqua, *Drug Abuse: Investigation and Control* (New York: McGraw-Hill, 1978), 171–179.

is usually a factor, although not necessarily the initial incentive. That may come from the fear of a participant in a drug deal who decides he wants out, the vengeance of a jilted lover, the self-interest of a business competitor or political opponent, the need for self-esteem, a sense of identity with police agents, or simply a sense of friendship with a law enforcement agent. Sometimes the motive is nothing more than a citizen's sense of obligation to report a crime he or she has witnessed. This sense of obligation, a number of DEA agents have noticed, seems more developed in parts of Europe than in much of the United States. They attribute it to the greater homogeneity of European populations, a greater respect for the law and the police, and, as one DEA agent in Holland put it, the greater tendency of people "to mind each other's business." It has also been argued that "the French system of the *correspondant honorable*—who works out of love, fear of blackmail, and for small favors—is not as fully developed in the United States."[30]

The law enforcement agent's relationship with a criminal informant is often a complex one replete with legal and ethical ambiguities. Agents have been known to supply seized drugs to their addict informants, to ignore their informants' continued involvement in criminal activities, and to intervene with other law enforcement authorities who had arrested their informants.[31] The relationship can be one marked by strong mutual dependencies. Agents rely on their informants for information and introductions, without which they are unable to do their jobs, and informants are dependent upon the agents not only for money and protection from the law but also, on occasion, for protection against other criminals who have discovered they are stool pigeons. More often than not, most aspects of the agent's relationship with an informant are not supervised closely, if at all, by superior officers, prosecutors, or judges. Although certain procedures are usually required when an informant is initially recruited—for instance, filling out an official form and meeting with a superior officer—the nature of the relationship is determined largely by the personal discretion of the drug agent and the personality of the informant.

In recruiting informants, DEA agents seek out anyone who may be in

30. Gary Marx, "Thoughts on a Neglected Category of Social Movement Participant: The Agent Provocateur and the Informant," *American Journal of Sociology* 80 (1974), 419.

31. For a vivid description of all these aspects of the agent-informant relationship, see Robert Daley, *Prince of the City* (London: Granada Publishing, 1979), 227–230, 237–238, 244–249.

a position to provide or discover useful information. Contacts are developed and potential informants sought out at all levels of society, ranging from the barrios and urban slums to the diplomatic receptions and elite social clubs. At one level, the agent must, in the words of one who was stationed in Latin America, "establish a working relationship with the scumbag community." Both inside and outside that community, the agent must make contacts with anyone in a position to see or overhear activity related to drug trafficking. Typical sources include bouncers, bartenders, prostitutes, hotel doormen, hotel clerks, and other hotel employees. At the airports, the DEA agent looks to recruit informants among the pilots, baggage handlers, stewardesses, security people, and other employees. Bank employees, taxi drivers, waitresses, and others who come into contact with many people, especially out-of-towners, on a daily basis may also prove valuable sources of information.

The DEA's policy with respect to informants varies from country to country. In some, especially in Latin America, it closely guards the identities of its informants, even from local counterparts. In others, it is obliged to share those identities with local police, and it does so. Likewise, the DEA's freedom to recruit informants varies substantially from one country to another.[32] In countries with financial secrecy laws, the DEA must be concerned with violating the law if it recruits informants from among bank employees. Recruiting informants among government officials can also be tricky, particularly in countries where corruption is rampant. Most DEA informants, however, are private citizens, and a substantial proportion have some relationship with ongoing criminal activity.

The extent to which the DEA shares its informants with local law enforcement agencies, and vice versa, depends upon a number of factors. When informants are recruited by the local agency, they may be shared with, or given to, the DEA because the American agency has funds to pay informants whereas most foreign law enforcement agencies, even in Europe, have relatively little or no money for such purposes. Indeed, the DEA's reputation in that regard is often a strong incentive for potential informants to seek out the DEA overseas, although the agency tends to

32. In Singapore, for instance, the DEA reportedly was prohibited from recruiting any citizens as informants. See *U.S. Narcotics Control Programs Overseas, An Assessment: Report of a Staff Study Mission to Southeast Asia, South America, Central America, and the Caribbean, August 1984 to January 1985, House Foreign Affairs Committee*, 99th Cong., 1st Sess. (1985), 9.

pay only in cases that have a clear connection to the American drug market. By 1990, the DEA and other U.S. law enforcement agencies were authorized by law to pay informants up to $250,000 a case if their assistance resulted in the seizure from a drug dealer of cash and other assets worth more than $1 million.[33] Throughout virtually all of Latin America, police themselves are paid so little that the idea of paying informants for information is often perceived as somewhat bizarre. In Europe, the traditional reluctance to pay informants is waning as greater priority is given to drug enforcement and as asset-forfeiture laws, often modeled after those passed in the United States, are implemented. At the same time, agencies that have long been accustomed to paying informants have tended to increase the size of their payments at a pace more than sufficient to cover the effects of inflation. Where once European police agents who sought to recruit informants were obliged to dig into their own pockets, now they are increasingly able to turn to their agencies for the money. In Europe, the most generous are the Germans. During the 1970s, payments of a few hundred dollars were common.[34] By the late 1980s, both the BKA and the Landespolizei in the wealthier states were able to pay their most valuable informants up to $100,000. The Dutch and the British also pay informants, but only after the drugs have been seized.[35] The Danes have no specific budget for paying informants, but they will compensate informants out of their general operating funds; the highest payments authorized as of 1990 amounted to between $1,000 and $1,500. The Spanish typically pay the equivalent of a few hundred dollars, although one exceptionally valuable informant in the late 1980s was paid $20,000—half by the Spanish police, half by the DEA. The French police have long maintained a discreet policy of paying informants, one that became public only in 1986.[36] Most pay-

33. Arnold H. Lubasch, "Drug Trial Shows the Rich Rewards of Informing," *New York Times*, Nov. 4, 1990, 47.

34. According to a 1977 BKA report, information leading to the confiscation of cannabis was valued at 45 DM per kilogram, with bonuses paid for special efforts. In one case, an undercover informant was paid 700 DM for a tip that led to the arrest of five Italian drug traffickers and confiscation of 13 kilos of marijuana. In another case, an informant received 1,700 DM for a tip that led to the arrest of four Turkish traffickers and the seizure of 26 kilos of cannabis. See "Dem Verbrechen an die Wurzel," *Spiegel*, May 5, 1977, 62–73.

35. Both the Dutch and the Irish police were reported to have access to funds to pay informants in James Leo Walsh, "Research Note: Cops and 'Stool Pigeons'—Professional Striving and Discretionary Justice in European Police Work," *Law and Society Review* 6 (1972), 299. The same has long been true in England. See John Coatman, *Police* (New York: Oxford University Press, 1959), 134.

36. Edwy Plenel, "Le ministre de la sécurité augmente la rémunération des informateurs," *Le Monde*, May 21, 1986, 12.

ments were quite modest, although a few informants during the 1980s received more than 100,000 francs for information on terrorist attacks and assassinations, and French police reportedly spent 500,000 francs for information on the terrorist bombing of the Goldenberg restaurant in 1982.[37] DEA agents in France during the same period reported that the French customs agency was able to pay drug-related informants more than the police were. Payment simply for information, or for the cultivation of informants, remains highly atypical in Europe. Many law enforcement agencies will also share their informants with the DEA as a matter of course whenever it believes that the DEA may be interested in the information for sale. Likewise, the DEA will often share its informants with local law enforcement agencies, particularly if the information provided bears on investigations within the country. As the money available to pay informants has increased all around, so too have the conflicts over their "ownership" both between European police agencies in the same country and between them and the DEA.

Although most DEA informants overseas are shared with local agencies, the DEA does shield the identities of some. Informants may approach the DEA because they do not trust the local law enforcement agency; they may think the local agency lacks either the interest or the resources to use the information they want to give, trade, or sell, or they may worry that the information will be accidentally revealed, thereby exposing the informant's identity. Even in Germany, with its highly professional police, one DEA agent complained: "The BKA doesn't understand the 'third agency rule'—that you're supposed to check with the provider of information before giving it to a third agency." There is also a chance that a corrupt law enforcement agent will resell the information to those willing to pay for it, or will otherwise use the information to his or her own advantage and the informant's detriment. Finally, an informant who wishes to sell information relating to government corruption in drug enforcement may not know who, if anyone, can be trusted with the information. In all these cases, the DEA's relatively clean reputation makes it an attractive purchaser of information. Unlike virtually all other foreign law enforcement agencies, moreover, the DEA can offer informants a well-established witness protection program and other resources to safeguard those whose lives are endangered.[38] A number of foreign informants initially recruited by foreign

37. Ibid.

38. See *Federal Witness Security Program and Protection of Foreign Nationals: Hearing Before the Government Information, Justice, and Agriculture Subcommittee of the House Committee on Government Operations*, 101st Cong., 2d Sess. (1990).

law enforcement agencies have ended up in this program; the most famous of these was Tomasso Buscetta, the highest-ranking member of the Sicilian Mafia ever to break the code of *omerta*, whose information and testimony played a central role in the mid-1980s "Pizza Connection" case against Mafia drug trafficking and money laundering.[39]

That most high-level drug informants around the world are recruited and paid by the DEA is not all that surprising given the agency's global presence. Among all national drug enforcement agencies, it has the largest budget, the greatest number of agents, the most sophisticated equipment, the most extensive files, and the political power of the United States government behind it. Wherever the DEA is represented, local drug enforcement agencies depend heavily upon its international network of agents and informants for the leads and other information needed to make cases within their borders. By the mid-1970s, the DEA had come to be regarded, by both foreign police and criminals, as a sort of operational Interpol with vast resources at its disposal. "If we want to know who lives in Kuala Lumpur, Bondstreet, No. X, on the third floor," former BKA Director Horst Herold stated in an interview, "we just ask the DEA Paris office and we get the information in a few hours."[40] Although the popular image of the DEA is surely overblown, it serves as both a deterrent to drug traffickers and as a drawing card for foreign law enforcement agencies and potential informants. And the fact that the DEA can provide or withhold abundant information provides perhaps the greatest incentive for foreign drug enforcement units to cooperate with DEA investigations.

European drug enforcement agents are no different from their American counterparts in being heavily dependent upon informants; they are, as one German police chief put it, "as indispensable as radio-patrol cars, guns, and the officers themselves."[41] Aside from their relatively limited budgets for paying informants and their comparatively provincial intelligence systems, European prosecutors and drug enforcement agents have been sorely handicapped by their legal inability to make the sorts

39. See Ralph Blumenthal, *Last Days of the Sicilians* (New York: Pocket Books, 1988); and Shana Alexander, *The Pizza Connection* (New York: Weidenfeld & Nicolson, 1988).

40. *Frankfurter Rundschau*, Oct. 12, 1979, 3, quoted by Sebastian Scheerer, "Drogen und Strafrecht" ("Drugs and Criminal Law"), in Jan van Dijk et al., eds., *Criminal Law in Action: An Overview of Current Issues in Western Societies* (Arnhem: Gouda Quint, 1986), 199–213.

41. "Drugs: Dicker Manny," *Spiegel*, July 7, 1981, 68–70, quoting the veteran chief of the Hamburg Criminal Investigation Department (Kripo-Chef) Hans Zühlsdorf.

of deals with informants that play such a central role in U.S. drug enforcement, by the ambiguous legal status of informants, and by strict limitations on the use of informants as undercover operatives. These obstacles have slowly been overcome by changes in European laws, judicial decisions, and police practices, but even today much of what is deemed acceptable and legal in U.S. drug enforcement remains not permissible in Europe.

The most valuable informants tend to be those who are directly involved in illicit drug dealing. In the United States, a common recruitment tactic, known as "flipping" an informant, involves arresting, or threatening to arrest, a person for his or her involvement in drug trafficking or other crimes and then offering that person a deal in return for cooperation in making cases against other traffickers, ideally those operating at a higher level of criminal activity. The nature of the deal depends in part upon when it is struck. It may involve not proceeding with the arrest, or arranging to have the charges reduced or dropped, or getting the sentence reduced. Once the arrest is processed, the cooperation of a prosecutor, and often a judge, may be necessary to approve a deal. Unlike the typical "plea bargain," in which a prosecutor and defense attorney agree to have the defendent plead guilty to a lesser charge in return for forgoing the right to a trial, the deal between the drug agent or prosecutor and the prospective informant involves greater consideration by both sides. An informant who makes such a deal is said to be "working off a beef." Informants may be given their freedom, or a promise of freedom, and be paid for whatever information and assistance they provide.

Although informants are valuable for the information they possess at the time they are flipped or otherwise recruited, their greatest value often stems from the services they provide after that point. Criminals who get immunity from prosecution in return for testimony against fellow conspirators and other criminals are among the more passive types of informants. Far more essential to drug and other proactive criminal investigations are informants who retain their freedom and continue to interact with others engaged in crime. Such informants may be left in place after recruitment so they can help build a case against already known criminals. Or they may become employees of sorts of the law enforcement agency, either retaining their real identity or assuming aliases and operating entirely in an undercover capacity. The use of informants in these ways raises some of the same issues that arise when law enforcement agents themselves operate undercover.

Outside the United States, the DEA agent's ability to flip informants is limited by the simple fact that the agent lacks the power to arrest anyone. But the DEA agent, as well as local police and prosecutors, has also been handicapped by the questionable legality of the flipping process in many civil law countries.[42] The principal obstacle has been the "legality principle," which requires that the police arrest and the prosecutors prosecute anyone known to have committed a crime. Also known as "the rule of compulsory prosecution," this restraint on police and prosecutorial discretion greatly hampered the introduction of DEA-style informant recruitment methods, especially in Germany,[43] Austria, and Italy.[44] But even in Belgium,[45]

42. The flipping process is relatively common in most common law countries. In Britain, informants are known as "grasses." Much has been written about the informants, referred to as "supergrasses," who operate undercover and provide the most valuable intelligence to the police. See Steven C. Greer, "Supergrasses and the Legal System in Britain and Northern Ireland," *Law Quarterly Review* 102 (1986), 198–249, and Paddy Hillyard and Janie Percy-Smith, "Converting Terrorists: The Use of Supergrasses in Northern Ireland," *Journal of Law and Society* 11 (1984), 335–355. The British police must obtain the grant of immunity for a "supergrass" from the director of public prosecutions. The use of "supergrasses" and the quality of their information has been the subject of substantial criticism. See, e.g., David Seymour, "What Good Have Supergrasses Done for Anyone but Themselves?" *LAG Bulletin*, Dec. 1982, 7–9; and Etienne Bloch, "The Struggle Against Terrorism in France and Northern Ireland: A French Jurist's Perspective" (Paper for the International Security Studies Program, Woodrow Wilson International Center for Scholars, Washington, D.C., January, 1987).

43. The German practice is discussed in Hans-Heinrich Jeschek, "The Discretionary Powers of the Prosecuting Attorney in West Germany," *American Journal of Comparative Law* 18 (1970), 508–517; Glenn Schram, "The Obligation to Prosecute in West Germany," *American Journal of Comparative Law* 17 (1969), 627–632; Mirjan R. Damaška, "The Reality of Prosecutorial Discretion: Comments on a German Monograph," *American Journal of Comparative Law* 29 (1981), 119–138; John H. Langbein, "Controlling Prosecutorial Discretion in Germany," *University of Chicago Law Review* 41 (1974), 439–467; and Joachim Herrmann, "The Rule of Compulsory Prosecution and the Sagente of Prosecutorial Discretion in Germany," *University of Chicago Law Review* 41 (1974), 468–505, reprinted with comments in Kenneth Culp Davis, ed., *Discretionary Justice in Europe and America* (Chicago: University of Illinois Press, 1976), 16–74.

44. The Italian attitude with respect to prosecutorial discretion is discussed in Guido Neppi Modono, "The Italian Versus the American Response to the Mafia: A Comparison Between Two Juridical Cultures" (Paper presented at the Center for European Studies, Harvard University, Apr. 27, 1987). See Lawrence J. Fassler, "The Italian Penal Procedure Code: An Adversarial System of Criminal Procedure in Continental Europe," *Columbia Journal of Transnational Law* 29 (1991), 245–278, for an analysis of revisions to the penal code in 1988–89.

45. A brief introduction to Belgian criminal procedure can be found in Marc Chatel, "Human Rights and Belgian Criminal Procedure at Pre-trial and Trial Level," in J. A. Andrews,

France,[46] the Netherlands,[47] and Denmark,[48] where the alternative "opportunity principle" (or "expediency principle") permitted the prosecutor to take the public interest into account in deciding whether to prosecute, "the ethic of compulsory prosecution nonetheless persist[ed],"[49] thereby hindering the flexibility of prosecutors and police to make deals with potential informants.[50]

Human Rights in Criminal Procedure: A Comparative Study (The Hague: Martinus Nijhoff, 1982), 188–201.

46. The French practice is well described in Edward A. Tomlinson, "Nonadversarial Justice: The French Experience," 42 *Maryland Law Review* 42 (1983), 131–195, esp. 146–147. A good description that devotes greater attention to the role of the police is Stead, *The Police of France*, 144–157. See also A. E. Anton, "L'instruction criminelle," *American Journal of Comparative Law* 9 (1960), 441–457; George W. Pugh, "Administration of Criminal Justice in France: An Introductory Analysis," *Louisiana Law Review* 23 (1962), 1–28; and Robert Vouin, "The Role of the Prosecutor in French Criminal Trials," *American Journal of Comparative Law* 18 (1970), 483–497.

47. The Dutch practice is described in Arthur Rosett, "Trial and Discretion in Dutch Criminal Justice," *UCLA Law Review* 19 (1972), 353–390; L. H. Leigh and J. E. Hall Williams, *The Management of the Prosecution Process in Denmark, Sweden, and the Netherlands* (Warwickshire: James Hall, 1981), 41–71; and A. C. 't Hart, "Criminal Law Policy in the Netherlands," in van Dijk et al., eds., *Criminal Law in Action* (supra n. 40), 73–99.

48. See Leigh and Williams, *Management of the Prosecution Process*, 9–23; and Ole Krarup, "The Free Town of Christiania and the Role of the Courts," *International Journal of the Sociology of Law* 10 (1982), 31–47.

49. Abraham Goldstein and Martin Marcus, "The Myth of Judicial Supervision in Three 'Inquisitorial' Systems: France, Italy, and Germany," *Yale Law Journal* 87 (1977), 240–283, quote from 269.

50. During the late 1970s and early 1980s, a number of legal scholars debated whether European prosecutors were as constrained in their exercise of discretion as the principle of compulsory prosecution suggested. The impetus for the debate was concern over the growth and abuse of the plea bargaining system in the United States, and curiosity as to whether certain aspects of Europe's "inquisitorial" system contained lessons for the American common law system. Although the debate proved somewhat inconclusive, it did stimulate greater inquiry into the actual functioning of Europe's criminal justice systems. In a controversial article entitled "The Myth of Judicial Supervision in Three 'Inquisitorial' Systems: France, Italy, and Germany," two scholars from Yale, Abraham Goldstein and Martin Marcus, argued that European criminal procedures were not dramatically different from American processes. Contrary to conventional wisdom, they argued, European judges did not exercise much greater control over criminal investigations and prosecutions; European police and prosecutors did exercise substantial discretion in their investigations and charging; and European prosecutors and defendants often participated in negotiations analogous to plea bargaining. Some critics, such as John Langbein and Lloyd Weinreb, charged that the pair had carried their analogizing too far. Neither set of scholars, however, investigated the extent to which prosecutors were parties, both explicitly and discreetly, to bargains with criminal suspects for information. Each acknowledged that such deals occurred, but they did not pursue the matter in detail. See Goldstein and Marcus, "Myth of Judicial Supervision"; John Langbein and Lloyd Weinreb, "Continental Criminal Procedure: 'Myth' and Reality," *Yale Law Journal* 87 (1978), 1549–

That being said, one of the most significant changes in European drug enforcement since the early 1970s has been the easing of the "legality principle" in drug-related cases. Where once police shied away from efforts to flip drug dealers, and prosecutors studiously avoided any suggestion that they make deals with drug traffickers, today police and prosecutors in most European countries openly acknowledge their involvement in such practices. What began as a discreet police tactic employed first by DEA agents working closely with local agents, and then by local agents operating without the clear sanction of the law, has evolved into a relatively common law enforcement practice explicitly authorized by European prosecutors, courts, and legislatures. In some European countries, the initial impulses in this direction were motivated by the need to extract information about terrorist groups from members who had been arrested by the police. But in quite a number of countries, the evolution was one in which the hand of the DEA—as proponent, example, tutor, and lobbyist—was also readily apparent.

Although the legality principle is supposed to constrain both prosecutors and police, its strictures have always applied more strictly to the former than to the latter. European prosecutors, however, tend to be more powerful vis-à-vis the police than is the case in the United States and Great Britain; in many countries, the hierarchical nature of this relationship is set out explicitly in codes of criminal procedure. As a consequence, the ability of European police to negotiate and make deals with criminal suspects for their cooperation has depended greatly upon the nature of police-prosecutor relations, both legal and personal. This has been true both in Germany, where the prosecutor is bound by the *Legalitätsprinzip*, and in France and the Netherlands, where the prosecutor's discretion is much greater.[51] In Europe, the point at which a

1569; and the rebuttal by Goldstein and Marcus, "Comment on 'Continental Criminal Procedure,'" *Yale Law Journal* 87 (1978), 1570. See also the assessment of this debate in Mark G. Gertz, "The Dynamics of Plea Bargaining in Three Countries," *Criminal Justice Review* 15 (1990), 48–63; and Dennis P. McLaughlin, "Dealing with Dealing: Plea Bargaining in the Federal Republic of Germany," in Gale A. Mattox and John H. Vaughan Jr., eds., *Germany Through American Eyes* (Boulder, Colo.: Westview Press, 1989), 129–143.

51. In Germany, the public prosecutor's leading role in directing criminal investigations is mandated by the Code of Criminal Procedure, notably paragraph 161, which requires the police to assist the prosecutor in conducting his investigation and to make available to him any relevant information. In France, in the words of Tomlinson ("Nonadversarial Justice: The French Experience" [supra n. 46], 146–147), "Prosecutorial supervision of the police is quite intensive by American standards. The Code of Criminal Procedure places the police's investigatory activity under the direction of the local prosecutor; and in actual practice, the French prosecutor works more closely with the police than does his American counterpart, particularly

prosecutor's involvement is legally required tends to come earlier than in the United States. In most European countries, as in the United States, the police may not conduct an electronic surveillance or search a residence without authorization from a prosecutor, investigating magistrate, or judge. But unlike their American counterparts, police in most European countries require a prosecutor's approval to conduct an undercover operation, pay an informant, and take a variety of other investigative steps. In some countries, prosecutors are required to be present at the interrogation of suspects once there is a reasonable suspicion that the suspect is guilty, although the question of when a suspect is sufficiently suspicious so that the police must stop interrogating is in practice left up to the police to decide.[52]

Police in every country, however, tend to avoid involving prosecutors in investigations until it is absolutely necessary. They also can be quite resourceful in devising ways to circumvent the requirements for prosecutorial supervision, and hence the strictures of the legality principle as well.[53] Informants may be compensated from sources other than a prosecutorial supervised fund. A search can be made without a warrant whenever police can reasonably claim that the police were looking for a weapon. The moment of arrest, when the prosecutor's powers relative to the police suddenly multiply, can be delayed by the police in any number of ways—for instance, "if a suspect can be made to feel that the heat is on," a DEA agent in France said, "he may try to cut a deal" before

---

during the early stages of an investigation. In addition, the Code requires the police to inform the prosecutor promptly of any offenses known to them and to forward to him the dossier they prepare during the course of their investigation. Members of the prosecutor's office normally arrive at the scene of a serious offense soon after the police." Relations between police and prosecutors in the Netherlands are analyzed in Leigh and Williams, *Management of the Prosecution Process*, 45–71; and in L. H. C. Hulsman, "The Dutch Criminal Justice System from a Comparative Legal Perspective," in D. C. Fokkema et al., eds., *Introduction to Dutch Law for Foreign Lawyers* (The Netherlands: Kluwer-Deventer, 1978), 300–313. The powers of Dutch prosecutors are contrasted with those of British prosecutors in Leigh and Williams, *Management of the Prosecution Process* (supra n. 47), and in Downes, *Contrasts in Tolerance* (supra n. 13), 13–18.

52. K. W. Lidstone and T. L. Early, "Questioning Freedom: Detention for Questioning in France, Scotland, and England," *International and Comparative Law Quarterly* 31 (1982), 488, 492.

53. David K. Linnan, "Police Discretion in a Continental European Administrative State: The Police of Baden-Württemberg in the Federal Republic of Germany," *Law and Contemporary Problems* 47 (1984), 200–203; Gunther Artz, "Responses to the Growth of Crime in the United States and West Germany: A Comparison of Changes in Criminal Law and Societal Attitudes," *Cornell International Law Journal* 12 (1979), 49, 54–55.

being arrested. To the extent the agent is bluffing, it is worth observing, he is not in violation of the legality principle. Quite often, prosecutors and judges are aware of the greater discretion exercised by the police; indeed, they often rely on the police to "screen" cases and work out their own informal arrangements with informants.[54] Especially in drug investigations and others in which there is no victim to file a complaint, police and prosecutors often have an implicit understanding that any deals with criminal informants will be worked out informally without involving the prosecutor's office. In countries in which prosecutors exercise a strong hand in supervising investigations, this may require a conscious effort on the part of the prosecutor not to examine or question too closely some otherwise unexplainable aspects of the police's investigation. Some prosecutors are concerned about this abdication of power to the police; in Germany, for instance, prosecutors and legal scholars have expressed great concern at the "police-izisation" of criminal procedure generated by the proliferation of proactive drug trafficking investigations in which police have naturally seized the initative, but their efforts to curtail this development have been frustrated by the slow pace of legal evolution in this area.[55]

Once a drug dealer has been arrested and taken to the police station, the drug enforcement agent's ability to "flip" the dealer depends upon when a prosecutor must be informed. In this respect, most European drug enforcement agents have an advantage over U.S.-based agents. In France, which is typical in this regard of many European countries, police may question suspects for twenty-four hours—and up to seventy-two hours in drug and terrorist cases—before bringing them before a prosecutor. Once a prosecutor is introduced into the picture, however, the agent's ability to flip the dealer diminishes greatly. At that point, about all that can be offered in return for cooperation is a chance at a reduced sentence. European police also have less flexibility than American police in protecting an informant who has been arrested by another officer.

54. The argument that the police play a major role in alleviating the pressures on prosecutors created by the legality principle is advanced in Damaška, "The Reality of Prosecutorial Discretion" (supra n. 43), 123–124.

55. Michael Füllkrug, "Neue Formen der Kriminalitätsbekämpfung und ihre Auswirkungen auf das Verhältnis von Staatsanwaltschaft und Polizei" ("New Forms of Crime Fighting and the Consequences for the Relationship Between the Public Prosecutor and the Police"), *Zeitschrift für Rechtspolitik* 17 (1984), 193–195.

The challenge for the European drug enforcement agent is thus to identify drug traffickers, persuade them that there is sufficient evidence to arrest, then flip them, and finally protect them as best the agent can, given that no assistance can be expected from the prosecutor's office. With all these constraints, it is no wonder that few European drug enforcement agents are able to build up the networks of informants that are the pride and necessity of the better American drug enforcement agents. DEA agents in Europe regard the German, Austrian, and Swiss police as increasingly aggressive and sophisticated in flipping informants, the Dutch a little less so, and the Italians and French as not particularly interested in adapting the DEA's methods.

Nonetheless, as public and law enforcement concerns over illicit drug trafficking rose during the 1980s, so too did the pressures to allow criminal justice officials greater latitude and power in investigating and prosecuting traffickers. And as police responded to the new challenge, and to the influence of the DEA, by informally developing their capacity to recruit informants, pressures built to legalize and regulate what the police were already doing anyway and to allow the prosecutors and the courts the authority to reduce or drop charges, or reduce sentences, in return for cooperation. In 1982, German law was revised and the courts were explicitly provided with the discretion to reward drug trafficker defendants with a reduced sentence, or even no punishment at all, in return for their cooperation in a successful investigation.[56] In Italy, similar laws were enacted in 1978, 1980, and 1982 to induce repentant (*pentiti*) terrorists to cooperate with counterterrorist investigations, but efforts to offer repentant drug dealers comparable inducements have met with greater resistance.[57] In Belgium and Germany, drug laws were revised at the urging of drug enforcement officials to allow defendants who cooperated to be granted immunity from prosecution for misdemeanors and a milder sentence for felonies. Unlike their American counterparts, however, prosecutors in both countries have generally shied away from making the most of these revisions, perhaps because

56. Section 31 of the Narcotics Law (*Betäubungsmittelgesetz*). See Hans-Jörg Albrecht, "Criminal Law and Drug Control: A Look at Western Europe," *International Journal of Comparative and Applied Criminal Justice* 10 (1986), 17, 37.

57. Weinberg and Eubank, *Rise and Fall of Italian Terrorism* (supra n. 5), 127–130. The Italian legislation (Law No. 304 of May 29, 1982) is briefly discussed in *Terrorism and Security: The Italian Experience*, 98th Cong., 2d Sess. (1984), S. Rpt. 246.

they retain an inkling of the civil law's historic antipathy toward such deal-making.[58] Nonetheless, in Germany the provision was extended in 1989 to those involved in terrorist acts. In most European countries, moreover, including a number that have not enacted any legislation regarding those who turn state's evidence, prosecutors can request that judges take into account a defendant's cooperation in deciding on the sentence.[59] Although judges are not obliged to accept prosecutors' recommendations, they typically are taken into account.

More difficult to legislate have been guidelines for the recruitment and management of informants by police.[60] As the use of informants has expanded significantly, the courts and criminal justice authorities have struggled with the difficulties of providing explicit legal authority and effective regulation.[61] In Germany, the legal basis for the authority of the police to use informants remains the subject of debate among criminal justice officials and scholars.[62] Periodic rulings by the German Supreme Court, the Bundesgerichtshof, have been perceived as vague and open to varied interpretations by law enforcement officials. Internal guidelines regulating the use of informants, as well as undercover operations, have been slow to develop.[63] Even within high-level police circles during the

58. E. Boutmans, "The Situation in Belgium," and Hans-Jörg Albrecht, "Drug Policy in the Federal Republic of Germany," both chapters in Albrecht and Kalmthout, eds., *Drug Policies in Western Europe* (supra n. 4), 89–105 and 175–194, esp. 95–96 and 184.

59. Jürgen Meyer, *Betäubungsmittelstrafrecht in Westeuropa: Eine rechtsvergleichende Untersuchung im Auftrag des Bundeskriminalamts* (Freiburg im Br.: Max-Planck-Instituts für Ausländisches und Internationales Strafrecht, 1987), 809–810.

60. The use of informants in undercover operations, which has presented the most difficult legal and policy issues, is discussed in the following section.

61. See "Abgetönte Scheibe, Verstellte Stimme: Hamburgs Innensenator Alfons Pawelczyk (SPD) über die V-Leute der Polizei" ("Tinted Glass, Disguised Voice: Hamburg's Senator for Internal Affairs Alfons Pawelczyk on Undercover Police Agents") *Spiegel*, May 3, 1982; Harald Körner, "Die Bekämpfung der organisierten Rauschgiftkriminalität durch V-Leute" (The Fight Against Organized Drug Criminality by Undercover Agents") in *Taschenbuch für Kriminalisten* 35 (1985), 29–113.

62. See, e.g., the discussion in Hans Ellinger, "Aktuelle Fragen des Betäubungsmittelrechts—Eine Tagung der Deutschen Richterakademie" ("Current Questions Regarding the Narcotics Law: A Conference of the German Judges' Academy"), in *Monatsschrift für Kriminologie und Strafrechtsreform* 67 (1984), 271–276; and Peter Marqua, "Rechtliche Grauzone? Ein Hearing der Grünen zur V-Mann-Problematik—zwischen faktischen Zwängen und juristischer Bewertung" ("Gray Legal Area? A Hearing of the Greens on Informants—Between Actual Restraints and Legal Assessment"), in *Deutsche Richterzeitung*, no. 4, (1985), 153.

63. The frustration of BKA drug enforcement officials with the slow pace of legal evolution to accommodate more effective investigative techniques is reflected in a four-part series on drug enforcement in *General Anzeiger*, Sept. 20–23, 1989.

late 1970s, discussion was muted and largely limited to exchanging experiences and debating the appropriateness of past actions;[64] only in 1982 did Hamburg become the first German state to establish guidelines for police working with informants.[65] These issues are gradually being resolved, albeit at varying paces and in different ways in the various German states. The Dutch reportedly have modernized their system for managing informants along DEA lines, identifying informants by numbers, appointing special agents to manage particular informants, and maintaining blacklists of undesirable informants. Other European countries have tended to lag behind the Dutch and the Germans in addressing these issues.

Most European courts have also struggled—as in the United States—over the degree to which the identity of informants, undercover agents, and other witnesses can be shielded in court. By the end of the 1980s, no consensus could be discerned, with some states absolutely prohibiting the introduction into court of information provided anonymously, others permitting it with relatively few restrictions, and a number debating the extent to which police officials could be allowed to report (as hearsay) what they had learned from their anonymous informants. In France, a police officer is not required to divulge the name of an informant in court. Switzerland and Italy are quite strict about prohibiting the introduction of such evidence provided by anonymous informants.[66] In the Netherlands, the use of anonymous witnesses attracted substantial controversy during the 1980s, with two advisory panels appointed by the Dutch judiciary association and the government concluding that evidence provided anonymously should not be excluded so long as the interests of the defendant were taken into account.[67] In Germany, the Bundesgerichtshof first addressed the question in 1952 and struggled with it repeatedly thereafter without coming to any final resolution. The trend during the 1980s favored permitting police to testify to information provided by an anonymous informant.[68] Only in

64. "Dem Verbrechen an die Wurzel" ("Attacking the Roots of Crime"), *Spiegel*, May 5, 1977, 62–73.

65. "Abgetönte Scheibe, Verstellte Stimme" (supra n. 61).

66. See A. Manna and E. Barone Ricciardelli, "The Limitations and Formalities of Criminal Law Provisions Concerning Narcotics: Considerations on Legislation in Italy," and H. Schultz, "Drugs and Drug Policies in Switzerland," both in Albrecht and Kalmthout, eds., *Drug Policies in Western Europe* (supra n. 4), 195–234 and 361–381, esp. 247, 366.

67. See Anjewierden and Atteveld, "Current Trends in Dutch Opium Legislation," (supra n. 13), 247–248, which refers to both reports.

68. Klaus Lüderssen, ed., *V-Leute: Die Falle im Rechtsstaat* (Frankfurt: Suhrkamp, 1985),

1991 was the issue largely resolved by federal legislation requiring informants to reveal their faces but allowing them to withhold other information about their identities if necessary for their personal security. In Denmark, a 1986 revision of the drug laws, stimulated in part by a controversial Supreme Court decision in late 1983, restricted the prosecution's use of anonymous informants; judges were authorized to exclude all nonrelevant individuals as well as the defendant from the courtroom and to swear the defense attorney not to reveal the informant's identity, but defendants retained their right to read the informant's testimony.[69] In both Denmark and Germany, as in the United States, restrictions on the ability of prosecutors to shield the identities of their informants in court have provided some of the stimulus for creating witness protection programs.

From the perspective of DEA agents working in Europe, the evolution in police practices, judicial rulings, and legislative enactments has proven helpful both directly and vicariously. What began as a discreet effort by European police agents to accommodate and adapt the DEA's methods of cultivating and running informants had evolved in much of Europe by the late 1980s into a legally sanctioned system of informant recruitment and maintenance that in many respects shared more in common with the American system than it did with the European system of the 1960s. Nonetheless, DEA agents have continued to find the legal inhibitions on flipping drug dealers, and the ambiguity of their informants' legal status, a source of substantial frustration in collecting intelligence and making cases. Making deals with drug dealers in return for their cooperation, and inducing criminals to testify against others in return for immunity from prosecution, still strike many Europeans as somewhat bizarre and risky means of attacking crime; indeed, these methods continue to be criticized in the United States, particularly after revelations about informants who implicated innocent individuals.[70] The process of recruiting

---

502–507, 514–516; Körner, "Die Bekämpfung" (supra n. 61), 73–106; Albrecht, "Drug Policy in the Federal Republic of Germany" (supra n. 58).

69. Sysette Vinding Kruse, "Drug Criminality from a Legal Point of View," in Per Stangeland, ed., *Drugs and Drug Control, Scandinavian Studies in Criminology*, vol. 8 (Oslo: Norwegian University Press, 1987), 34–52; J. Jepsen, "Drug Policies in Denmark" (supra n. 14), 115–116. See the Supreme Court decision of Dec. 2, 1983 (Ugeskrift for Retsvaesen 1984, 81 H) and Section 848(2) of the Code of Procedure, as formulated by Act No. 321 of June 4, 1986 ("Prohibition Against Anonymous Informants").

70. See, e.g., Mark Curriden, "No Honor Among Thieves," *ABA Journal* 75 (1989), 52–56.

informants in Europe will no doubt continue to follow in American footsteps, albeit gradually and in haphazard fashion.

Undercover Operations

Aside from the low priority given to drug enforcement by most foreign governments until recently, the greatest challenge facing U.S. drug enforcement agents as they expanded their international operations during the late 1960s and 1970s was the widespread and deeply felt resistance to using undercover investigative methods. From the beginning of the postwar era until the late 1960s, and in many countries until well into the 1980s, most Europeans, including many police, viewed the use of undercover tactics by law enforcement agents as anathema. The very notion instantly conjured up images of the despised *agent provocateur* employed by governments in previous decades and centuries to discredit dissident political groups.[71] So great was the antipathy toward this tactic that the use of infiltrators not to provoke but solely to gather information was also cast into disrepute. To the greatest extent possible, Europeans preferred that police not disguise their identity in investigating crime. Resistance to police reliance on informants and other nonpolice agents to conduct undercover tasks was felt only slightly less strongly.

One reaction of European legal systems to their bitter experience with *agents provocateurs* was their preference for a strict interpretation of the legality principle and their rejection of a legal notion that has become central to proactive law enforcement in the United States, that "[a]cts which would be criminal when done by a private citizen are justifiable and not criminal when done by a government agent in the reasonable exercise of law enforcement power."[72] In much of Europe, police could

71. See Paul Chevigny, *Cops and Rebels: A Study of Provocation* (New York: Pantheon Books, 1972), esp. chap. 10; and Walter Otto Weyrauch, "Gestapo Informants: Facts and Theory of Undercover Operations," *Columbia Journal of Transnational Law* 24 (1986), 553–596. Perhaps the finest description of the *agent provocateur* is Joseph Conrad, *The Secret Agent* (New York: Knopf, 1992).

72. Robert I. Blecker, "Beyond Undercover in America: Serpico to Abscam," *New York Law School Law Review* 28 (1984), 823, 855. The best overall discussion of undercover operations is Gary T. Marx, *Undercover: Police Surveillance in America* (Berkeley and Los Angeles: University of California Press, 1988). See also the essays collected in Gerald M. Caplan, ed., *ABSCAM Ethics: Moral Issues and Deception in Law Enforcement* (Cambridge, Mass.: Ballinger, 1983).

not even go through the motions of a criminal act. Undercover agents could not pretend to take or offer a bribe in order to catch a corrupt politician or public official; they could not play the role of a fence and purchase stolen goods in order to gather evidence against thieves; and they could not assume the guise of a drug trafficker interested in purchasing drugs. If agents performed any of these "crimes," they were as guilty as any criminal performing the same act for real. The same restrictions also applied, albeit not always as strictly, to informants and others acting at the behest of law enforcement agents.

Beyond the traditional association with *agents provocateurs,* the DEA also was obliged to overcome two other misperceptions. The first was the tendency of most Europeans to regard all undercover operations as an unacceptable form of entrapment. The second was the popular image of all undercover operations as "deep cover" operations—those in which an agent becomes deeply enmeshed in a criminal organization or milieu and is obliged to play the role of a criminal virtually twenty-four hours a day for months at a time.[73] The reality of most undercover operations, at least those engaged in by DEA agents, is something quite different. The DEA, like most other U.S. law enforcement agencies, occasionally runs deep cover undercover operations. The vast majority of undercover operations involving DEA agents, however, are part-time affairs in which the agent is able to return to office or home after meeting someone in an undercover capacity. Few DEA operations require an agent to remain undercover for more than a few days at a time.

Despite European antipathies and restrictions, throughout the 1950s and 1960s American drug enforcement agents employed by both the FBN and the Army's Criminal Investigative Division routinely operated undercover and ran undercover informants.[74] Relying on personal contacts and an abundance of extralegal discretion to skirt the legal prohibitions on their U.S.-style tactics, the few FBN agents stationed in Europe pursued their cases without trying too hard to change the local systems.

With the expansion of the U.S. drug enforcement presence in Europe during the early 1970s, however, the U.S. agents began actively encour-

73. A fine example of this type of operation is recounted in Joseph Pistone with Richard Woodley, *Donnie Brasco: My Undercover Life in the Mafia* (New York: New American Library, 1987).

74. See the memoirs of Charles Siragusa (*The Trail of the Poppy* [Englewood Cliffs, N.J.: Prentice-Hall, 1966]); and of Sal Vizzini (*Vizzini: The Secret Lives of America's Most Successful Undercover Agent* [New York: Arbor House, 1972]).

aging their European counterparts to integrate undercover techniques into their own drug enforcement investigations. They were motivated not just by the proven effectiveness of undercover operations but also by their agency's institutional bias in favor of the technique. Electronic surveillance was also important, but many European police agencies already had developed their expertise in this area independent of U.S. influences. DEA efforts initially focused on familiarizing European police with undercover tactics.[75] As they developed a constituency for undercover operations among the police, the DEA agents extended their advocacy efforts to higher levels of European law enforcement systems. They briefed prosecutors, judges, and legislators regarding their investigative techniques and the changes in the law necessary to accommodate them. In particular, they sought to persuade high-level European law enforcement officials either that undercover operations did not clash with local laws or that local laws should be changed or reinterpreted to sanction such tactics.

Throughout much of Europe in the early 1970s, the straightforward "buy and bust" tactic so fundamental to drug enforcement in the United States was regarded as either illegal or at best of questionable legality and rarely employed. An undercover agent who purchased drugs was, according to the dominant legalist interpretation, as guilty of violating the law as the illicit drug dealer from whom they were purchased. DEA agents working in Europe responded to this constraint by developing circuitous tactics on their own and by co-opting local police and prosecutors in their efforts. One approach involved a slight modification of the "buy and bust" technique, in which an undercover agent would set up an illicit transaction but not actually complete the purchase. For instance, agents might arrange with a trafficker to purchase some drugs, meet with the trafficker to inspect the drugs, and then either back out of the deal or excuse themselves for a moment—at which point the local police would introduce themselves and make the arrest. One problem with this approach was that it made it difficult to charge traffickers with anything more than possession because the agent, who was obliged to remain anonymous, could not offer evidence regarding the planned sale. In some countries, this limitation was partially remedied by creating a

75. Examples of DEA training lessons are provided by Mortimer D. Moriarty, "Undercover Negotiating: Dealing for Your Life," *Police Chief* 57 (Nov. 1990), 44–47; and Gary E. Wade, "Undercover Negotiating: Flashroll Management," *Police Chief* 57 (Nov. 1990), 48–49.

legal presumption that possession of a sufficiently large amount of drugs assumed the intent to sell them.

The receptivity of European prosecutors and judges to participating in these charades varied not just among countries but also among districts and even personalities. In Denmark, where undercover operations had been legally sanctioned but employed relatively infrequently for decades, DEA agents encountered little resistance—although the 1986 revision of the drug laws imposed greater judicial control over such tactics and prohibited the use of nonpolice agents and informants as undercover operatives.[76] In Italy, much depends upon the personal views of the investigating magistrate. Those who want to cooperate, one DEA agent observed, "usually know an agent or informant has played a part, and they let it go if they can, but you can't slap the judge in the face with the facts." In some countries, most notably the Netherlands, Germany, and (somewhat later) Spain, certain prosecutors became specialists in drug trafficking cases and quickly learned to accommodate the DEA's methods. This in effect required keeping two sets of files on a case. The unofficial one, which was not necessarily compiled in any formal sense, would describe the investigation exactly as it had taken place. The official one, to be delivered to the judge, would present the charade according to which an unidentified participant in the transaction—the undercover agent or informant—"failed to appear" or "escaped."[77] An arrest warrant might even be issued for that participant, although the name would likely be the alias used by the undercover agent or informant. If, however, the arrested trafficker were able to identify the undercover agent or informant by his or her real name, serious difficulties could result. On occasion, the police have been obliged to issue an arrest warrant for an undercover informant whose cover has been blown, although not without first warning the informant to leave the country.[78] When the accurately identified undercover operative is a law enforcement agent, it is highly unlikely that the informant will be charged. But on the rare occasions when an undercover agent is identi-

76. Section 754 (a-d) of the Code of Procedure, as formulated by Act No. 319 of June 4, 1986, discussed briefly in Jepsen, "Drug Policies in Denmark" (supra n. 14), 114–115.

77. Boutmans, "The Situation in Belgium" (supra n. 58), 95, briefly refers to a number of court cases in which this ruse was employed: C. A. Antwerp, Dec. 2, 1977, *Rechtkundig Weekblad,* 1978–79, 875; *Corr Tongeren*, Nov. 9, 1977, and July 13, 1977, *Limburgs Rechtsleven*, 1978, 47, and 1979, 215.

78. There are a few cases in which informants whose covers have been blown have been obliged to spend years in virtual exile from their countries.

fied, courts are prone to dismiss the case as in clear violation of the prohibition against *agent provocateur* operations.

This charade continues to be integral to undercover drug investigations in a few countries, notably France, but it became far less of a necessity during the 1980s. The first to do away with it were the Germans, who adopted DEA models of investigation more quickly, and with fewer inhibitions, than any other Europeans. During the early 1970s, DEA agents stationed in Germany actively lobbied for the acceptance and use of undercover techniques. At first they conducted most undercover operations themselves, and virtually acted as informants for the German police. With relations among German police and prosecutors generally closer then than they are now, DEA agents also proved successful in persuading the latter of the merits of undercover techniques. As their resistance dwindled, the DEA agents, often in league with local police, gave presentations on undercover operations to judges. By the mid-1970s, some of the judges had not only gotten to know the U.S. agents but also come to view the fact that they were involved in a case as an indication that it should be taken more seriously. DEA agents also testified in German courts, which was a departure from the usual agency policy of maintaining as low profile a presence as possible. Since their testimony could prove helpful in protecting the identities of German police informants, German police were all the more grateful for DEA involvement.

The DEA's undercover tactics were quickly adopted by the BKA and by the LKA in Bavaria and Hesse. During the 1980s, resistance in other parts of Germany dwindled as the tactics became increasingly familiar and as drug enforcement assumed greater importance in German policing. By the late 1980s, few German drug enforcement units depended any longer on DEA agents to perform undercover tasks. The few exceptions were mostly investigations requiring an American undercover role, or an agent capable of posing as an Italian or Latin American, as a number of the Italian-American and Hispanic-American agents could.

From the late 1960s to the late 1980s, prosecutors, courts, and legislators struggled to respond to the undercover initiatives of the police.[79] The Bundesgerichtshof ruled on the undercover issue numerous times without ever clarifying either the legal basis for undercover operations or the boundaries of permissible activity by an agent.[80] Debate over

79. See Lüderssen, *V-Leute* (supra n. 68); and Körner, "Die Bekämpfung" (supra n. 61).

80. The rulings of the Bundesgerichtshof include BGH 10.6.1975, BGH 15.4.1980, BGH

appropriate guidelines for undercover activities by police and informants was also a central issue of discussion at the periodic conferences of the interior and justice ministers of the German states.[81] In the fall of 1986, the ministers agreed to two sets of guidelines, one regulating the use of informants, the other regulating the employment of undercover police agents. But their lack of consensus was reflected in their appeal to the Ministries of Justice and the Interior to clarify the legal status of undercover agents and to create the legal basis for employing them. Only in 1991 were most of the legal issues resolved by federal legislation formally legalizing undercover operations but requiring that they be approved by a prosecutor and employed only when less-intrusive tactics appeared not feasible.[82]

In Austria, a similar process occurred, albeit on a much smaller scale and more belatedly than in Germany. Throughout the mid-1970s, the Austrian police relied on the DEA to perform all undercover tasks. In 1977, a new activist chief of Austria's Central Narcotics Department, Herbert Fuchs, encouraged the resident DEA agents to train Austrian police in U.S. drug enforcement techniques. Shortly thereafter, the chief judge of the Salzburg region was persuaded to reinterpret the prohibition on undercover tactics in drug investigations. By creating a legal presumption that a person caught in possession of a large amount of drugs was intending to sell them, the contrary presumption that the sale had been "provoked" by the undercover agent was negated. During the 1980s, more substantial legal support for undercover operations was provided by a "legal interpretation" contained in a parliamentary report and by a number of supreme court decisions.[83] Until well into the 1980s,

---

21.10.1980, BGH 6.2.1981, and BGH 23.5.1984. See the discussions in Körner, "Die Bekämpfung" (supra n. 61); Arthur Kreuzer, "Wenn der Spitzel lockt: Die Karlsruher Richter billigen fragewürdige Praktiken der Polizei" ("When the Informant Entraps: Judges of Karlsruhe Approve Questionable Police Practices"), *Zeit*, Jan. 29, 1982, 53; and in Albrecht, "Drug Policy in the Federal Republic of Germany" (supra n. 58), 184–185.

81. See Klaus Rogall, "Strafprozessuale Grundlagen und Legislative Probleme des Einsatzes Verdeckter Ermittler im Strafverfahren" ("Criminal Trial Elements and Legislative Problems of Using Undercover Agents in Criminal Proceedings"), *Juristen Zeitung* 42 (1987), 847–853.

82. See Section 110 of the 1991 Organized Crime Act.

83. See the discussion in Manfred Burgstaller, "Drogenstrafrecht in Oesterreich," in Jan van Dijk et al., eds., *Criminal Law in Action* (supra n. 40), 187, 189, 190. Burgstaller notes that the 1980 amendment has been challenged in the legal literature as conflicting with Section 25 of the Austrian Penal Code, which generally prohibits the police from committing a crime for the purpose of gathering information or implicating a criminal. For critical analyses of the legalization of undercover operations, see A. Pilgrim, "Die Kosten der Kriminalisierung des

however, police and prosecutors generally continued to write up their reports as they had before the change in the law—that is, omitting any explicit mention of the undercover agent or informant. Only toward the end of the decade did the reluctance to be explicit about the use of undercover tactics gradually fade.

The Austrian situation regarding undercover operations is typical of much of the rest of Europe as well. In most countries, it remains a matter of controversy, but the general movement is in favor of increased use of the tactic; the European Commission for Human Rights bolstered this trend in 1986 when it declared that the use of undercover agents could be reconciled with Articles 6 and 8 of the European Human Rights Convention.[84] In Switzerland, where police agents trained by the DEA and the BKA have utilized undercover techniques in drug and counterfeiting cases, both the 1975 drug law and a 1986 judicial opinion by the Federal Tribunal have supported their use.[85] Drug enforcement agents in Spain do work undercover but typically must rely on the types of charades described above.

In Italy, Spain, and France, there is still substantial resistance to employing law enforcement agents in undercover capacities. The resistance, it should be noted, stems not only from the reluctance of prosecutors and judges to approve the use of such tactics but also from the unfamiliarity of the police with employing them. Exceptions do, however, exist. For instance, one DEA agent spoke of working closely during the late 1970s with an agent of Corsican origins on the Parisian police force who excelled at posing as a drug trafficker. Another agent, based in Spain, observed that it was relatively unusual for Spanish police to engage in undercover operations but that a number of agents of the National Police drug branch based in Madrid were very good and aggressive at working undercover.

Drogenkonsums" ("The Costs of Criminalizing Drug Consumption"), in R. Mader and H. Strotzka, eds., *Drogenpolitik zwischen Therapie und Strafe* ("Drug Policy Between Therapy and Punishment") (Vienna, 1980), 117–148, discussed in J. Fehérváry, "Drug Policy in Austria," in Albrecht and Kalmthout, eds., *Drug Policies in Western Europe* (supra n. 4), 67–68. I have also relied upon information provided in a correspondence from Mag. Herbert Fuchs, Apr. 20, 1990.

84. Rogall, "Strafprozessuale Grundlagen" (supra n. 81).

85. See the brief discussion in Schultz, "Drugs and Drug Policies in Switzerland" (supra n. 66), which refers to Section 23(2) of the 1975 Drug Law and the Federal Tribunal decision reported at BGE 112 (1986) 1a, 21, c. 3 and 4, which held that undercover operations were legal even in cantons that had not explicitly authorized their use.

By and large, however, police in southern Europe specializing in drug trafficking investigations do not view undercover operations as integral to their job. The fact that the courts remain reluctant—despite the lobbying efforts of the DEA—to permit any extended forms of undercover operations no doubt contributes to this view. In both France and Italy, for instance, an undercover agent cannot actually purchase drugs but can only do a "knock-off"—that is, order the drugs and then seize them without paying. The principal difference between the Italian practice and the French and Spanish practice is that whereas the former are similarly leery of using informants in undercover roles, the latter have shown no such reserve.

In Belgium, U.S. drug enforcement agents of both the BNDD and the Army's Criminal Investigative Division began encouraging local police to recruit informants and work undercover during the late 1960s. Their efforts contributed to the creation of a special criminal intelligence unit, the Administration of Criminal Investigation (ACI) in the Ministry of Justice in 1971, which in turn prompted the Gendarmerie to establish their own criminal intelligence unit two years later. The ACI unit quickly integrated DEA-style tactics into their investigations but encountered resistance from prosecutors. Top Gendarmerie officials meanwhile resisted pressures by the DEA and the chief of the Gendarmerie drug unit, Captain François, to incorporate similar tactics into their investigations. Their resistance dwindled following a 1974 drug enforcement conference in which the U.S. ambassador praised François as a model law enforcement officer, and then increased when corruption in the drug enforcement unit, and a scandal involving Francois and an informant, were exposed to public view.[86]

During roughly the same time, the ACI was also shaken by a series of scandals. As a result, both drug enforcement units were dissolved and undercover work was gradually integrated into the regular criminal investigation branches of the Gendarmerie and the Police Judiciaire. As in Germany, the courts have struggled with defining the legal authority and limits of undercover operations, with the trend toward acknowledging the legitimacy of the basic technique.[87] During the 1980s, Police

86. Cyrille Fijnaut, *De Zaak François* ("The François Case") (Antwerp: Kluwer, 1983).

87. See esp. the June 1984 decision by the Tribunal Correctionnel, 24th Chamber of the State Court of Brussels, which acknowledged the legality of undercover operations and controlled deliveries, discussed in Körner, "Die Bekämpfung" (supra n. 61), 39. See also Boutmans, "The Situation in Belgium" (supra n. 58), 93–94, which notes a series of cases in which Belgian courts have struggled with the appropriate limits on undercover operations.

Judiciaire agents were more likely than agents of the Gendarmerie to work undercover, but their efforts similarly resulted in scandal when three top police officials in the drug enforcement brigade in Brussels were suspended by the minister of justice in 1990 for excesses related to the employment of undercover operations and informants.

In the Netherlands, the impetus for employing undercover operations was provided by the dramatic growth of the Chinese-dominated heroin trade in Amsterdam in the early 1970s. Totally unprepared for this development, the Dutch police turned to the DEA for assistance. DEA agents and their informants began working undercover, setting up drug busts and co-opting Dutch police into the legal charades required to square DEA methods with Dutch law. Some local police reacted uneasily. "One detective in the Drugs Squad," Maurice Punch noted in his analysis of Dutch policing, "was said to have had 'sleepless nights and sweaty palms' about the 'dicey' reports he had to write to cover certain operations and was relieved when he was transferred because in Dutch law the DEA men were as guilty as anyone else involved in a deal."[88] On occasion, Dutch courts responded to these developments by dismissing cases in which the evidence had been gathered by undercover agents and informants and in which the police refused to reveal the identity of their informants.[89]

By the late 1970s, however, Dutch police officials were increasingly interested in integrating undercover operations into their own investigations. The willingness of the courts to grant a degree of legitimacy to undercover operations eased the process.[90] Particularly notable was the 1979 *Tallon* case, involving a DEA undercover investigation that had begun in the United States and culminated in arrests on Dutch territory, in which a court acknowledged that not all undercover tactics constituted entrapment. During the mid-1980s, the police chief of Amsterdam, Kees Sietsma, investigated the possibility of formally integrating undercover operations into Dutch criminal investigations, in part by participating in a Canadian undercover training program, and decided in favor. He was opposed, however, by the police chief of Rotterdam.[91] Two

88. Maurice Punch, *Conduct Unbecoming: The Social Construction of Police Deviance and Control* (New York: Tavistock Publications, 1985), 46.

89. Ibid.

90. See Anjewierden and Atteveld, "Current Trends in Dutch Opium Legislation" (supra n. 13), 245–246, which refers to two supreme court decisions: HR Nov. 1, 1983, NJ 1984, 586; and HR Jan. 1984, NJ 1984, 405.

91. "Undercover Agents: gevaar en verleiding groter dan resultaten," *Elseviers Magazine*,

commissions set up to propose changes in the drug laws also debated whether and how undercover techniques should be employed.[92] In 1985, the Ministry of Justice formally authorized their use, and the Amsterdam police force quickly established its own undercover unit. Virtually all undercover operations were initially employed in drug trafficking investigations. By 1990, however, almost half involved other sorts of crimes.

During the 1980s, public controversy over undercover operations and foreign drug enforcement operations focused not on the DEA but on German drug enforcement efforts. In one case, German police were publicly embarrassed when Dutch television reporters posing as drug traffickers tricked German drug enforcement agents into conducting a unilateral law enforcement operation in Dutch territory and filmed them in the act. In other cases, tensions flared when German drug enforcement agents conducted undercover operations in the Netherlands, or used informants and private detectives to lure drug traffickers across the border, without notifying CRI officials in advance—although in a number of cases, local Dutch authorities consented to the operations but did not inform the CRI (the Dutch National Criminal Intelligence Service).

There is little question that European attitudes toward undercover operations have evolved greatly since the 1970s. At the one extreme are the BKA and some of the Landespolizei, who have followed increasingly in the DEA's footsteps. At the other extreme are the southern Europeans, who employ police agents in undercover operations relatively infrequently and who are still obliged to rely on charades to circumvent the legal restrictions. Between the two extremes, one can discern a number of common attitudes regarding use of the tactic.

As in the United States, European courts have struggled with where to draw the line between legitimate undercover techniques and those that qualify as entrapment; most continue to interpret entrapment far more broadly than do American courts. Even where undercover agents are able to purchase drugs legally, most countries still require that the seller be arrested at that time. The notion of an undercover agent making a series of undercover buys to establish one's credibility, to expand one's

May 11, 1985; Carel Brendel and Theo Gerritse, "De undercover-agenten van commissaris Sietsma," *Vrij Nederland*, May 11, 1985, 1.

92. See the discussion in "Politie, openbaar ministerie and bewijsverkrijging" ("Police, Public Prosecutors, and Obtaining Criminal Evidence"), *Handelingen der Nederlands Juristen-Vereninging* 112 (1982), 5–66.

contacts, and to work one's way up the hierarchy of a drug trafficking organization, has yet to be accepted widely in Europe.

One also finds persistent resistance to the straightforward "buy and bust" tactic so commonly employed by American drug enforcement agents. The notion, derived from the historical experience with *agents provocateurs*, that a police agent should not "provoke" a crime remains quite powerful. An agent may properly be introduced into a situation in which a drug transaction is going to take place anyway, but he or she may not create the situation. More penetrative techniques, such as deep undercover operations, are exceptionally rare, and no European police agencies have yet followed the DEA's lead in employing "reverse undercover," or "sell-and-bust," operations.[93] One also finds a common disposition that undercover techniques should only be used as a last resort, when more traditional and less intrusive tactics have failed or offer no promise of success, and that they should be employed only in investigations of relatively serious offenses. With some exceptions, informants are generally freer than law enforcement agents to stretch some of the guidelines defining appropriate behavior in the service of the law. Many European drug enforcement units continue to rely heavily on DEA agents and the informants recruited by them to perform undercover tasks in major investigations; they also welcome the "flashrolls" provided by the American agency, which can amount to as much as $5 million. And in most countries undercover agents are still used only or primarily in drug investigations. The general trend, however, is in the direction of expanded use of undercover operations throughout Europe. In short, the integration of undercover operations into European drug enforcement has progressed dramatically over the last two decades, but it has yet to approximate the extensive and aggressive use of undercover operations by U.S. drug enforcement agents.

Controlled Deliveries

The technique of controlled delivery, in which drug enforcement agents "let the drugs walk"—that is, allow a consignment of illicit drugs they

93. These operations are discussed by Captain Timothy A. Raezer, "Needed Weapons in the Army's War on Drugs: Electronic Surveillance and Informants," *Military Law Review* 116 (1987), 1–65.

have detected "to go forward under [their] control and surveillance . . . in order to secure evidence against the organizers of such illicit drug traffic"—is regarded by many drug enforcement agents as a particularly valuable tactic,[94] one that has been employed for decades.[95] During the 1970s, DEA agents and cooperative European agents continually found their efforts to investigate drug trafficking organizations hampered by the legality principle's requirement that the agents seize illicit drugs immediately upon identifying their location or coming into contact with them, and by customs regulations requiring that all imported goods be declared and cleared through customs. The result was that many investigations ended with the seizure of the drug consignment, or at best with the arrest of the "mules," or drug couriers, who often knew little about the organizations for which they worked. As with the evolution of undercover operations, DEA and European agents responded to the legal prohibition of a valuable investigative technique first by discreetly employing it anyway, then by persuading and pressuring prosecutors to sanction it, and ultimately by inducing judges and legislators to legalize it. Because so many controlled deliveries cross national borders, the control and legal status of this investigative technique have been addressed not just within the confines of individual European states but by the Council of Europe and various international associations and conferences of drug enforcement agents as well. Particularly influential was the inclusion in the United Nations Convention Against Illicit Traffic in Narcotic Drugs and Psychotropic Substances (1988) of provisions encouraging the use of controlled deliveries.[96]

In relying on controlled deliveries to investigate drug trafficking organizations, DEA agents first co-opted those local agents willing to bend the law for legitimate investigative goals. Prosecutors were kept in the dark, as were other law enforcement agents, particularly customs officials, who might not be inclined to cooperate with the drug agents;

94. P. D. Cutting, "The Technique of Controlled Delivery as a Weapon in Dealing with Illicit Traffic in Narcotic Drugs and Psychotropic Substances," *Bulletin on Narcotics* 35 (Oct.–Dec. 1983), 15–22.

95. The annual report of the FBN in 1931 discusses an investigation of an opium shipment from Istanbul destined for the United States via Amsterdam and Hamburg in which Dutch officials agreed to allow the opium to pass through its port so that the drug traffickers could be identified and arrested in Hamburg. See U.S. Treasury Department, *Traffic in Opium and Other Dangerous Drugs for the Year Ended December 31, 1931* (Washington, D.C.: Government Printing Office, 1932), 43.

96. See Art. 11 of the U.N. Convention.

the likelihood that customs officials would find the drugs crossing the border without a tip from the drug agents was slight. The same held true for foreign law enforcement and customs agents, who might seize the drugs either because they felt bound by the legality principle or customs regulations or because they wanted the credit for the seizure. Whoever was not essential to conducting the controlled delivery was simply not informed. According to the recollections of DEA agents who had worked in France and Italy, for instance, police would allow the drugs "to walk" if they had found out about the drug delivery from an informant or by monitoring an illegal wiretap. But if the tap had been legally authorized by a prosecutor, who would have access to the transcripts of any recorded conversations, the police would carry out their official duties and arrest the drug courier. Although prosecutors were highly unlikely actually to prosecute drug agents for conducting unauthorized controlled deliveries, the agents generally refrained from defying the prosecutors' authority.

Since the mid-1980s, however, prosecutors in almost every European country have begun to play at least some role in authorizing, supervising, or informally shielding controlled deliveries. This has involved first circumventing, then bending and ultimately redefining the legality principle to accommodate controlled deliveries. Initially prosecutors agreed to ignore or wink at the legal charades engaged in for their benefit by the police. It has since progressed to the point where prosecutors can legally authorize a controlled delivery, impose certain constraints on its conduct, and demand certain assurances from the police. They may require the police to guarantee that they will not lose the drugs once they walk; they may insist upon an assurance that the courier will be prosecuted in the destination country; they may prefer that the courier be flipped before proceeding with the controlled delivery; and they may prefer that the drugs be discreetly seized and that only a small portion of the drugs, combined with some innocuous white powder, be substituted for the original package in the controlled delivery. From the perspective of the police, the importance of the prosecutors' growing role stems less from their oversight functions than from their ability to authorize, and in effect legalize, an essential investigative technique. Controlled deliveries are now regarded as legal throughout most of Europe even if their changed status has yet to be codified in the assorted codes of criminal procedure.

Responsibility for reinterpreting the legality principle to allow controlled deliveries has fallen not just to the prosecutors and the courts but also to legislators, interior and justice ministers, and international working groups. The courts have responded by relaxing customs regulations and the requirements of the legality principle to allow broader use of controlled deliveries. Legislators under increasing pressure during the 1980s to enact tougher drug legislation have enacted laws explicitly authorizing the investigative technique. In Austria, efforts by DEA and local drug enforcement agents to employ controlled deliveries along the notorious "Balkan connection" raised the same sorts of legal disputes that had hampered the introduction of undercover operations.[97] When those were resolved favorably by the Austrian supreme court, debate focused on customs regulations requiring that all goods imported into Austria be declared and cleared; a 1985 amendment to the customs laws removed this obstacle and further allowed for the reexport of illicit drug shipments provided they remained under surveillance.[98] The practice is much the same in France, where controlled deliveries from Spain to the Netherlands are not unusual; magistrates will authorize a controlled delivery but insist that the police arrest the couriers and seize the drugs if they think there is a chance they will lose track of either. In Denmark, controlled deliveries have been regarded as entirely legal; Dutch and Danish police cooperate frequently, particularly on shipments passing through Denmark en route to Sweden. In Germany, the interior and justice ministers of the Länder appointed working groups to devise national guidelines for conducting controlled deliveries. In 1983 and 1986, for instance, the Northern Working Group on the Suppression of Drug Trafficking, which includes police representatives from the Netherlands and the Scandinavian countries, the German border control and customs agencies, and Hannover, Bremen, Hamburg, Berlin, and Kiel, conducted controlled delivery exercises—code-named Baltica 83 and Baltica 86—to test the capacity of the police to transfer surveillance across national borders.[99] Elsewhere, legal formalities continue to pose substantial problems. In Spain, for instance, a South American informant employed by the DEA on a controlled delivery from Bolivia to Spain in 1988 was arrested by Spanish customs because the DEA and

97. The disputes, which focused on Section 25 of the Austrian Code of Criminal Procedure, are briefly discussed in Fehérváry, "Drug Policy in Austria" (supra n. 83), 68.

98. The information is in correspondence from ACND chief Herbert Fuchs to the author, Apr. 20, 1990. See Art. 121 of the 1955 Austrian Customs Law as amended on May 10, 1985.

99. W. Tabarelli, "Baltica 86, an International Exercise on Controlled Deliveries," in Fijnaut and Hermans, *Police Cooperation in Europe* (supra n. 6), 79–84.

Spanish police had failed to notify the proper customs authorities; two years later, the unfortunate informant remained incarcerated in a Spanish jail. Throughout much of Europe, however, pressures to better coordinate controlled deliveries—generated in part by the elimination of border checks in 1992—are certain to lead to greater harmonization of the laws and guidelines regulating uses of the technique.

Wiretapping

Among the various investigative techniques best suited to drug trafficking investigations, wiretapping was the one with which most European police agencies were most familiar when American drug enforcement agents began fanning out through Europe in the 1960s and 1970s. Indeed, many relied on electronic surveillance with substantially greater frequency than was the case in the United States. As in the United States, however, the investigative technique generated substantial political and legal controversy. Some forms of electronic surveillance, such as pen registers (which reveal only the telephone number that one has dialed), are relatively less invasive as such techniques go. Wiretaps on telephones, and listening devices ("bugs") in people's homes, offices, and cars, are far more intrusive. Most governments authorize but strictly control the use of such devices by law enforcement authorities.[100] The principal exception is Belgium, which absolutely forbids their use, although information obtained abroad from a legal wiretap is admissible in Belgian courts.[101] Others routinely rely on them in conducting criminal investigations. In a few countries, the police make frequent use of illegal wiretaps. The broad exception to all restrictions on electronic surveillance is national security. In much of Europe, wiretapping by the intelligence agencies is subject to even less vigorous scrutiny and oversight than it is in the United States, although occasional media exposés, most notably in Germany and Britain, have generated intense debate about the use of such techniques and how they should be regulated.[102]

100. Council of Europe, Legal Documentation and Research Division, *Telephone Tapping and the Recording of Telecommunications in Some Council of Europe Member States*, Legislative Dossier No. 2 (Strasbourg, 1982).

101. Cass. May 24, 1983, Rechtskundig Weekblad 1984-9-84, 1701, cited in Boutmans, "The Situation in Belgium" (supra n. 58), 97.

102. See Note, "Secret Surveillance and the European Convention on Human Rights" (supra n. 7).

During the 1980s, wiretapping practices also came under scrutiny by the European Commission of Human Rights and the European Court of Human Rights.[103]

The country with the most ambiguous legal attitude toward wiretapping is France, in which an estimated 70,000 wiretaps were reportedly employed each year as of the late 1980s.[104] Wiretapping was not considered a punishable offense until 1970, when the French Parliament amended the privacy provisions of the penal code to make overhearing or intercepting private telephone conversations a *délit* (minor crime).[105] On the other hand, the practice has never been explicitly authorized by the French legislature, and the courts have yet to arrive at a consistent approach. The Criminal Court of the Seine in Paris, in a series of decisions dating back to the 1950s, consistently admitted wiretap evidence, even for minor crimes such as illegal bookmaking.[106] Appellate courts, conversely, rejected wiretapping as unreliable or "indelicate."[107] In the 1980 *Tournet* case, the Court of Cassation for the first time upheld the use of a wiretap, provided it had been authorized by the *juge d'instruction* (examining magistrate) in the course of a judicial investigation following the *inculpe* (formal accusation of a suspect).[108]

Even as the courts have debated the legality of wiretaps, the French police routinely have used wiretaps for purposes of gathering intelligence on criminal matters. As one student of the French system noted in the early 1980s:

> It is widely acknowledged in France that the police always have done a good deal of illegal wiretapping and have used the

103. See the *Malone Case*, E.C.H.R., Series A, No. 82, and the *Klass Case*, E.C.H.R., Series A, No. 28, 2 E.H.R.R. 214, discussed in John Andrews, "Telephone Tapping in the United Kingdom," *European Law Review* 10 (1985), 68–70; and in Istvan Pogany, "Telephone Tapping and the European Convention on Human Rights," *New Law Journal* 134 (1984), 175–177, 290, 300.

104. Meyer, *Betäubungsmittelstrafrecht in Westeuropa* (supra n. 59), 808.

105. The discussion of wiretapping in France is drawn largely from Walter Pakter, "Exclusionary Rules in France, Germany, and Italy," *Hastings International and Comparative Law Review* 9 (1985), 1; and Tomlinson, "The French Experience" (supra n. 46).

106. Pakter, "Exclusionary Rules," 37.

107. Ibid.

108. In 1985, the same court narrowed the discretion of the *juge d'instruction* somewhat, holding that he could only authorize a wiretap on probable cause justifying opening an investigation for a specific infraction, and that the tap must be under his control, without any artifice or compromise of the suspect's rights. See ibid., 38.

> information they obtain as leads for the subsequent acquisition of the same information in a legal fashion. The *procès verbal* [*written* report] presented in the court reflects only the second operation and is thus in proper legal form. The courts generally have shown little interest in probing into the sources for the second, apparently legal police operation. Their concern is primarily to preserve the legal formalities and not to regulate police behavior. The latter concern is collateral to a particular defendant's guilt or innocence, and the French courts have always been hostile to collateral issues because they deflect the official inquiry from its central task.[109]

As one DEA agent described the process, although the surveillance transcripts cannot be used as evidence, the information acquired from them is used, for instance, to obtain a legal search warrant from the *juge d'instruction*. In the formal request for the warrant, the source of the information is referred to as a confidential informant. Although more often than not the *juge d'instruction* knows better, he usually refrains from pressing for the informant's true identity. As for the DEA, any information garnered from an illegal French wire can also be used to obtain a warrant from an American judge. For instance, if a conversation intercepted by an illegal wiretap in Paris makes reference to a stash of drugs in an apartment in New York City, the DEA can obtain a legal warrant based upon that information (provided the DEA did not ask the French police to intercept an American's conversations). The rationale for this sanctioning of illegal police behavior abroad is that the U.S. courts have interpreted the exclusionary rule as primarily intended to deter illegal conduct by U.S. law enforcement agents within the United States and against U.S. citizens overseas.[110]

By the late 1980s, the wiretapping practices of the French police were

109. Tomlinson, "The French Experience," 177–178.

110. In 1990, the U.S. Supreme Court resolved a number of the lower court disputes over the applicability of the Fourth Amendment to the extraterritorial actions of U.S. law enforcement agents when it held that U.S. agents need not obtain a warrant from either a U.S. judge or a foreign judge to conduct a search directed against a foreign national in a foreign country. See *U.S. v. Verdugo-Urquidez*, 110 S.Ct. 1056, *International Legal Materials* 29 (1990), 441. The issue is discussed in Andreas F. Lowenfeld, "U.S. Law Enforcement Abroad: The Constitution and International Law," *American Journal of International Law* 83 (1989), 880–893; continued at *American Journal of International Law* 84 (1990), 444–493. The specific case is discussed in a note on the case by Ruth Wedgwood, *American Journal of International Law* 84 (1990), 747–755.

coming under increasing attack from both domestic and European critics.[111] In 1982, a study commission on wiretapping chaired by French Supreme Court Justice Robert Schmelck criticized the police practice of employing wiretaps without the authorization of *juges d'instruction* and before the formal initiation of a judicial inquiry. Its recommendations for placing all control of wiretaps in the hands of the judiciary, however, were largely ignored. In late 1988, a report issued by the European Commission of Human Rights criticized not just the police practices but also the failure of the French penal code to provide sufficient guarantees against arbitrary judgments involving wiretaps, which it regarded as violative of Article 8 of the European Convention on Human Rights. One year later, the French Supreme Court echoed the European Commission's conclusions in a decision involving a drug trafficking case.[112] The court ruled that the common police practice of installing a wiretap without a warrant from a *juge d'instruction*, and then "regularizing" the tap thereafter by obtaining post facto approval from a magistrate or *juge d'instruction*, violated both the European Convention of Human Rights and the French code of penal procedure. Whether this decision will in fact curtail the long-standing reliance of the French police on unauthorized wiretaps, however, remains to be seen. In 1991, the French government partially addressed the issue with new legislation authorizing nonjudicial "preventive" wiretapping in terrorism, organized crime, economic espionage, and national security investigations in which the police request had been countersigned by a responsible cabinet minister; the new law established a special commission to provide oversight over all such wiretaps.

In postwar Germany, wiretapping in criminal investigations was permitted on a fairly restricted basis after 1949. The first federal legislation formally authorizing the legal use of wiretapping by law enforcement and intelligence agencies was passed in 1968, the same year in which the U.S. Congress first enacted a federal wiretapping statute.[113] Since that

111. The following analysis is derived from Edwy Plenel, "Un arrêt de la Cour de cassation: Les écoutes téléphoniques non autorisées par un juge sont illégales" ("A Ruling of the Supreme Court of Justice: Wiretapping Not Authorized by a Judge Is Illegal"), *Le Monde*, Mar. 21, 1990, 14.

112. *Epoux Huvig contre France*, requête no. 11105/84 (Dec. 14, 1988), Judgment of November 24, 1989.

113. The U.S. wiretapping legislation, known as Title III of the Omnibus Crime Control and Safe Streets Act, is codified at 18 U.S.C. 2510–2520 (1970). The United States did not enact legislation covering wiretapping by the intelligence agencies until the Foreign Intelligence Surveillance Act of 1978, codified at 50 U.S.C. 1801–1811. The 1968 German law authorizing

time, the use of wiretapping by police has become a relatively routine matter. During the late 1970s, approximately 500 a year were granted. By comparison, in the United States the total numbers granted each year were only 100 to 200 more.[114] James Carr, a U.S. magistrate who investigated Germany's wiretapping procedures during the late 1970s, found that in at least three respects German procedures allowed a greater degree of intrusiveness than did the provisions of Title III in the United States: wiretaps in Germany were subject to less judicial supervision; they could be installed for three months, as opposed to one month in the United States; and there were no restrictions, like the American "minimization requirement," to limit the agents from taping conversations having nothing to do with the investigation at hand.[115] In a speech to the International Narcotics Enforcement Officers Association in 1988, the head of the BKA's drug enforcement branch, Jürgen Jeschke, discussed electronic surveillance in Germany:

> There are hardly any investigations today in which not at least one or even several telephone taps are put in place. It is not merely the high evidential value which plays a role. Telephone taps are to an increasing extent used as a tactical means, for example in addition to or during the surveillances and for the preparation of tactical measures. Contrary to the U.S., the legal threshold for telephone taps is lower in my country. They have to be ordered by a judge in principle, provided that certain requirements are fulfilled, but in very urgent cases a telephone tap may be ordered at short notice by the Public Prosecutor—limited to a period of three days, however. New transmission systems currently present big practical problems to us as far as the monitor-

---

the wiretapping was divided into two parts: the "G-10 Law" covering wiretapping by federal and state intelligence and internal security authorities; and Section 100a–101 of the Code of Criminal Procedure providing for police wiretapping. See the excellent discussions in James G. Carr, "Wiretapping in West Germany," *American Journal of Comparative Law* 29 (1981), 607–645; and Thomas Weigend, "Using the Results of Audio-Surveillance as Penal Evidence in the Federal Republic of Germany," *Stanford Journal of International Law* 24 (1987), 21–53.

114. See Carr, "Wiretapping in West Germany," 607–608, for the specific numbers, which count only law enforcement, not intelligence, wiretaps.

115. Ibid., 644. For an interesting discussion comparing German and British approaches to wiretapping, see Note, "Secret Surveillance and the European Convention on Human Rights" (supra n. 7), 1113.

> ing of telecommunications facilities is concerned. We have, for example, not yet found a way of tapping telefax machines.[116]

Elsewhere in Europe, police reliance on wiretaps is at least as common as it is in Germany and the United States. In Italy, where many more cases are developed by wiretaps than from informants or undercover operations, one FBI attaché noted that the police have "much broader wiretap authority. . . . They can just call the magistrate and get an oral OK. It's very informal and quick . . . compared to the U.S."[117] Much the same is true in Spain, where wiretapping was initally authorized by the 1980 "Antiterrorist Act." In Austria, Switzerland, Denmark, and the Netherlands, wiretaps are similarly considered relatively routine.[118] In Denmark, the number of court orders authorizing wiretaps increased from 30 in 1975 to about 330 in 1982 and to 700 in 1985, some 95 percent of which involved drug trafficking investigations.[119] In the Netherlands, a Justice Ministry official estimated in 1985 that between 100 and 200 wiretaps were installed each year, most of them in drug trafficking cases. In 1991, an Amsterdam police official pointed out that the principal limitation on wiretaps was financial and that only so many lines could be tapped at any one time—that number had increased from four to fifteen in 1983, and was set to double again by 1992. He estimated the total number of wiretapping cases in Amsterdam that year at about 250, of which about 80 percent involved drug trafficking investigations. As in the United States, a police request for permission to have a wiretap installed must be joined by a prosecutor and approved by a judge, but as is also the case in the United States, judges rarely if ever deny such requests. Similarly, evidence obtained by an unauthorized wiretap must be excluded from court.[120] The extent to which police

116. Jürgen Jeschke, "Drug Crime and Drug Enforcement in the Federal Republic of Germany," *Narc Officer* 4 (Dec. 1988), 33–35.

117. The legal status of wiretapping in Italy is discussed briefly in Pakter, "Exclusionary Rules" (supra n. 105), 48–50. Wiretaps can be authorized by a prosecutor or an investigating judge; see Arts. 226 and 339 of Italy's Code of Criminal Procedure.

118. Wiretapping in Austria is authorized by Article 10 of the Austrian Constitution and regulated by Arts. 149(a), 149(b), and 414. In Switzerland, it is controlled by Arts. 66 and 72 of the Federal Criminal Procedure Act as well as by the law of the cantons.

119. Jepsen, "Drug Policies in Denmark" (supra n. 14), 109. Wiretapping is authorized by Art. 72 of the Danish Constitution and regulated by Art. 787 of the Administration of Justice Act.

120. The Dutch wiretapping law can be found in articles 125g–h of the Code of Criminal Procedure. It is discussed in N. Keijzer and J. H. A. Steenbrink, "The Results of Electronic Eavesdropping as Evidence in Criminal Procedures," in P. H. M. Gerver, E. H. Hondius, and

resort to illegal wiretaps to gather criminal intelligence obviously varies from country to country. Given the relative ease with which legal wiretaps can be obtained, the principal reason to install an unauthorized tap is the absence of sufficient evidence to persuade a court to authorize a legal tap.

Most European countries have differed significantly from the United States in their treatment of forms of electronic surveillance other than telephone wiretaps. In much of Europe, it is the Postal Ministry that attaches the wiretap, typically by adding a secret extension line between a central post office telephone exchange and the police listening post.[121] The police tend not to get involved in the installation process, which may explain in part the reluctance of many states to legalize the placement of listening devices in homes and offices and the practice of wiring an undercover agent or informant for sound to gather incriminating information. By the late 1980s, both these practices were becoming increasingly common in Europe, although courts have remained reluctant to admit as evidence the information gained by such means. In Germany, for instance, undercover agents and informants may wear body wires for their own protection, but the information recorded cannot be used as evidence. Indeed, the entire practice of consensual wiretapping, in which only one party to a conversation knows that it is being recorded, has proven far more controversial in most European countries than in the United States, where it is the most frequently employed electronic surveillance technique and need not even be judicially approved.[122] By the late 1980s, however, European police investigators were pushing hard to legalize and integrate most of the electronic surveillance techniques employed in the United States, including not just body wires and "bugs" in vehicles and residences but also video cameras

---

G. J. W. Steenhoff, eds., *Netherlands Reports to the Twelfth International Congress of Comparative Law, Sydney-Melbourne 1986* (The Hague: T. M. C. Asser Institut, 1987), 309–316.

121. Carr, "Wiretapping in West Germany" (supra n. 113), 631.

122. The federal wiretapping statute passed by Congress in 1968 explicitly authorized consensual wiretapping; see 18 U.S.C. 2511(2)(c). The constitutionality of warrantless consent surveillance was upheld by the Supreme Court in *U.S. v. White*, 401 U.S. 745 (1971). See the discussion in James G. Carr, *The Law of Electronic Surveillance*, 2nd ed. (New York: Clark, Boardman, 1985), 3–55ff. It is interesting that although evidence obtained from an improperly executed wiretap cannot be excluded from a German trial, evidence gained from a consensual recording is inadmissible in court. The basis for this application of an exclusionary rule stems from the German constitutional right to the "free development of one's personality." See Craig M. Bradley, "The Exclusionary Rule in Germany," *Harvard Law Review* 96 (1983), 1032.

and parabolic microphones. As in the United States, police agencies were also working with private companies to develop new technologies to intercept communications by telefax, cellular phones, and other emerging means of telecommunication. All of these developments were in evidence, for instance, in the Netherlands, which only a decade earlier had shown relatively little enthusiasm for following down this path.

Given the persistent reluctance of many European police agencies—particularly in southern Europe—to engage in undercover operations, electronic surveillance has remained important to the investigation of drug trafficking even as growing numbers of drug traffickers have learned to exercise greater discretion in their use of telecommunications. Local police often oblige the DEA and other civilian and military law enforcement agencies by installing wiretaps requested by them and permitting their agents to jointly monitor the taps or read the transcripts.[123] The DEA, and the FBI, which traditionally has resorted to wiretapping more often and undercover operations less often than the U.S. drug enforcement agency, have permitted foreign police agents to do the same in the United States.[124] In the "Pizza Connection" investigation of Mafia drug trafficking and money laundering during the mid-1980s, U.S. and foreign law enforcement agents tapped phones in the United States, Brazil, Switzerland, Sicily, and Mexico.[125] Although that investigation was unusual in terms of its scope and notoriety, it reflected the trend toward increased cooperation among police agencies in conducting electronic surveillance. The same trend could also be discerned in the Council of Europe's consideration and adoption of a 1985 recommendation to facilitate inter-European cooperation in the interception of telecommunications.[126]

123. The use of electronic surveillance by the U.S. Army's Criminal Investigative Division (CID), virtually all of which is conducted overseas, is discussed in M. Wesley Clark, "Electronic Surveillance and Related Investigative Techniques," *Military Law Review* 128 (1990), 155–224.

124. Indeed, foreign agents are sometimes essential to decipher local dialects. Few European police, for instance, are able to understand the dialects of Caribbean and American blacks. Israeli, African, and Sicilian police have likewise assisted with wiretaps on their compatriots in the United States.

125. Alexander, *Pizza Connection* (supra n. 39), 154.

126. See Council of Europe, *Letters Rogatory for the Interception of Telecommunications (Recommendation No. R(85) 10 Adopted by the Committee of Ministers of the Council of Europe on 28 June 1985)* (Strasbourg, 1986).

Conclusion

The central paradox of international law enforcement is the need for law enforcement agents to perform outside their nation's borders a function that relies primarily on the sovereign powers of the state. Aside from simple liaison functions, much of what is expected of a DEA agent working abroad does not mesh neatly with the requirements of U.S., foreign, and international law. DEA agents accordingly rely on the exercise of substantial discretion in carrying out some of their tasks unilaterally or in informal cooperation with foreign counterparts. This was especially true before the late 1960s, when the few FBN agents overseas cultivated personal relationships with foreign police, took advantage of Interpol to obscure their national identity, and focused on the traditional tasks of criminal investigation. But with the expansion of the BNDD's international presence during the late 1960s and early 1970s, and the institutionalization of the DEA's global presence thereafter, U.S. drug enforcement agents devoted greater efforts to persuading foreign police to develop their own drug enforcement capabilities and to model them after the DEA's model. The "Americanization" of foreign drug enforcement came to be seen as a useful means of sharing the burden of international drug enforcement, improving the capacity of foreign criminal justice systems to assist U.S.-based investigations, and easing the DEA's ability to carry out its own investigative functions abroad. Stated otherwise, the transnational law enforcement organization recognized that the key to its success abroad lay not in expanding its own freedom of operation in foreign territories but in developing vicarious capabilities within and among foreign police agencies.

In developing their drug enforcement capabilities, most European criminal justice systems have been motivated less by the DEA than by their own need to respond to significant increases in domestic illicit drug trafficking. Indeed, it is reasonable to assume that even in the absence of an agency such as the DEA, European police would have developed their own drug enforcement capabilities and adopted many of the proactive investigative techniques identified with the DEA once the limitations of their customary methods of criminal investigation became apparent. But there can also be little doubt that the DEA has played a central role in hastening and shaping the evolution of European drug enforcement. The U.S. agency provided a substantial impetus for the initial creation of specialized drug enforcement units within European police agencies; it has provided much of the intelligence on local involvement in transnational drug trafficking needed to stimulate local concern and enable local police to target local drug traffickers; it has served as an advocate for the integration of undercover operations, controlled deliveries, and new means of recruiting informants into European drug enforcement; and it has provided a role model and mentor for European drug enforcement units. Not since the European powers trained colonial police forces has one nation's police agency exerted such a powerful international influence.

The integration of DEA-style methods into European drug enforcement has required metamorphoses not just in the modus operandi of European police but in the laws regulating their behavior as well. Changes in the laws of criminal procedure can be seen as responses both to changing public demands on the police and to changing police practices. Courts, legislators, and the authors of internal police guidelines tend to respond to perceived police excesses by restricting the power and discretion of the police, and to perceived inadequacies by expanding their power and discretion. In the latter case, the pressures often arise from the need to legalize and regulate what the police have already begun to do "extralegally" or illegally. The evolution of European drug enforcement since the early 1970s has been characterized by exactly this process. Where once most bargaining between European police and informants was both informal and illegal, today prosecutors in many countries can legally offer drug dealers who have been arrested the possibility of reduced charges or even immunity in return for their cooperation. Where once European police agents relied on their informants or DEA agents to perform undercover tasks illegally, today European drug enforcement agents are increasingly able to conduct legal undercover operations themselves. Where once police were obliged to reach into their own pockets to pay informants small amounts of money, today many police agencies in Europe can legally pay their best informants many thousands of dollars. And where once all sorts of charades were necessary to keep prosecutors and judges in the dark about the exact nature of drug trafficking investigations, today many of the techniques drug enforcement agents rely on are both legal and supervised by prosecutors. To be sure, no European criminal justice system has legalized all of the drug enforcement tactics that are legal in the United States, and many Europeans still cling to their traditional views of the legality principle and the ban on *agents provocateurs*, but the trend in most of Europe seems to favor continuing in American footsteps. European drug enforcement, and in certain respects European criminal procedure as well, are becoming increasingly "Americanized."

Throughout this chapter, I have portrayed this evolution as both a process and a consequence. From the perspective of U.S. drug enforcement agents, the "Americanization" of European drug enforcement has represented not an end in itself but rather a means of improving their own capacity to immobilize drug traffickers. Even as DEA agents have spoken with pride of the changes in European drug enforcement stimulated by their efforts and examples, they also have observed that the changes are of significance only insofar as they represented vicarious extensions of the DEA's own objectives and capabilities. Europeans, however, have viewed those same transformations as significant consequences in their own right. Harmonization, from their perspective, has involved not just regularization of relations with the U.S. drug enforcement agency but also accommodation and adaptation to American methods.

Chapter Five

The DEA in Latin America: Dealing with Institutionalized Corruption

The Most Troublesome Problem

Among the many obstacles that hamper U.S. drug enforcement objectives abroad, drug-related corruption of foreign government officials ranks as the most troublesome. It is present in virtually every country. Witness the testimony of DEA administrator John Lawn, as he is questioned by Senator John Kerry during hearings before a Senate subcommittee in July 1988:

> SENATOR JOHN KERRY: What do you think will happen to an honest law enforcement person who wants to do the job when the government is corrupt and it can simply transfer and fire him, move him out, put him on the night shift. What does it mean?
>
> DEA ADMINISTRATOR JOHN LAWN: It means, sir, that there is a serious problem with corruption in every single country.
> If I could take a moment, sir, to read something.

> SENATOR KERRY: Sure.
>
> MR. LAWN: This is an end of the tour report, one of our personnel leaving a country. His summary was this. "Police corruption is endemic in this country. The government pays extremely low salaries. Yet, it is not uncommon for police to drive luxury cars and own more than one multimillion dollar residence. Corruption is not limited to the police and is, in fact, widespread throughout the government. Furthermore, it is a way of life in that it has been going on for hundreds of years. Police bid for transfers to lucrative posts on the borders such as—where the winning bid may be as high as *x* number of dollars just to get the job so that the individuals will be in a position to accept corruption."
>
> I read that report at a meeting of country attachés representing 14 [Latin American] countries. I said would you, in hearing that commentary, tell me which country that described. All 14 country attachés told me it described accurately their particular country.[1]

In many of the less developed nations in Asia, Africa, Latin America, and the Caribbean, such institutionalized corruption is pervasive. Not just police officers and customs officials, but also judges, generals, cabinet ministers, and even presidents and prime ministers are implicated. Corruption in most of these countries is nothing new, although the temptations posed by the illicit drug traffic are unprecedented. Nor are U.S. officials unaccustomed to dealing with foreign corruption. Their experience dates back to the origins of American foreign relations. But the need to rely on foreign criminal justice systems to accomplish U.S. foreign policy objectives has posed challenges that are in some respects unique.

The central objective of the DEA in Latin America and the Caribbean, as in every other part of the world, is not to weed out corruption or reform foreign police agencies but to immobilize drug traffickers. In pursuing this objective south of the United States, DEA agents have encountered all of the same obstacles that have hampered their efforts in

1. Congressional testimony of DEA administrator John C. Lawn, in *Drugs, Law Enforcement, and Foreign Policy, the Cartel, Haiti, and Central America: Hearings Before the Subcommittee on Terrorism, Narcotics, and International Operations of the Senate Committee on Foreign Relations,* 100th Cong., 2d Sess., Part 4 (July 12, 1988), p. 124.

Europe: the legal and policy restrictions on flipping informants, conducting undercover operations, and conducting controlled deliveries of drugs; the institutional limitations of local police agencies with skimpy budgets and inadequate resources, irritating frictions with competing agencies, few if any specialized drug enforcement agents, and little if any money to pay informants; the occasional professional and nationalist resistance to working with the better paid and more sophisticated police agents of the United States; and, of course, the basic lack of sovereign police powers in foreign territories. As in Europe, many of these obstacles have dwindled substantially since the late 1960s, although the progress in Latin America and the Caribbean pales beside that in much of Europe. But the one problem that has posed the greatest obstacles, and required DEA agents to make the most of their diplomatic skills, personal charms, and association with the U.S. government, has been that of corruption. The nature of that problem, and the means by which DEA agents have dealt with it, are the subject of this chapter.

From the perspective of interstate relations, epitomized by dealings between the U.S. ambassador and high-level officials in the host government, diplomatic efforts aimed at reducing corruption can be particularly frustrating because they involve a form of transgovernmental penetration that traditional diplomacy is ill-suited to accomplish. In many respects, reforming drug-related corruption in foreign governments poses problems that are little different from those involved in trying to reduce human rights abuses. The U.S. government must contend with different criminal justice traditions and modi operandi, conflicting political interests, and insufficient power at the top of government to challenge vested interests at lower levels. In some cases, foreign heads of government would like to oblige U.S. demands but lack the capacity to do so. For instance, just as the civilian presidents of El Salvador and Guatemala typically lack the political power to punish senior military officials responsible for severe human rights abuses, so the presidents of Peru, Colombia, and Bolivia are not powerful enough to order the prosecution of every official known to have been corrupted by drug traffickers. Alternatively, foreign heads of government may have sufficient power to accommodate U.S. demands but lack the desire to do so. This apparently was the case during the 1980s with both the top-to-bottom corruption that permeated the military establishments in Panama and Paraguay and with the human rights abuses perpetrated by military dictatorships in Latin America and elsewhere throughout the century. Then again, the apparent power of a Stroessner, a Noriega, or a Pinochet certainly depended at least in part upon their willingness to tolerate behavior condemned by external observers. To the extent that was the case, U.S. pressures on those dictators to reform their corrupt agencies were no more likely to succeed than pressures on well-intentioned civilian leaders whose lack of power was more evident to outsiders.

Where U.S. efforts to deal with foreign drug-related corruption differ from those targeted at human rights abuses is in the existence of an agency—a transnational organization—specifically tasked to address that problem. The DEA, with its agents stationed in most Latin American countries, has offered a hands-on complement to the diplomatic efforts of State Department representatives and other high-level officials. DEA agents, with their greater access to and influence over the actual workings of foreign government agencies, are often in a stronger position to effect, at least to some degree, changes in government behavior. There is virtually no counterpart in the human rights area, or in almost any other area of international relations, with the possible exception of the CIA, and perhaps the U.S. military in a few countries. Because DEA agents work together with foreign police agencies, they are in a position to provide some degree of oversight and direction. Their influence is limited, however, because they lack any sovereign powers and are obliged to rely on foreign police as their vicarious surrogates. What influence they are able to exert derives from their connection to the U.S. government, their ability to reward and threaten local police in various ways, and their own powers of diplomacy and persuasion.

Even where DEA-backed efforts to reform corrupt agencies are successful, the reforms are seldom institutionalized in any meaningful way. Elite investigative units and anticorruption squads eventually are corrupted. Young and idealistic agents eventually mature into older, more cynical agents with more substantial material concerns. And legislative and media oversight of corrupt agencies can be maintained only for so long. When we analyze corruption from the perspective of international law enforcement, the notion of harmonization advanced in the preceding and following chapters loses much of its explanatory power. Given the extraordinary difficulties of institutionalizing anticorruption reforms, neither homogenization nor accommodation of criminal justice systems makes much sense. Only the notion of regularization—understood in its more personal as distinct from institutional sense—offers any analytical value. The keys to circumventing the obstacles of drug-related corruption ultimately boil down to personal relationships and political pressures.

Perspectives on Drug-Related Corruption

Drug-related corruption of governments in Latin America and the Caribbean can be viewed from a number of perspectives. First, it clearly is a consequence of the creation and failure of the global drug prohibition regime.[2] If the international markets for marijuana, cocaine, and heroin had never been criminalized, the need and opportunities for government officials to be corrupted by drug trafficking organizations would have been far less, akin perhaps to the corruption attendant to government regulation of the coffee markets in Latin American countries. Alternatively, if the global drug prohibition regime had proven successful in preventing the emergence of a tremendous consumer demand for those substances, drug corruption similarly would have been relatively insignificant. Drug-related corruption can thus be seen as a consequence of the tensions between the two demands emanating from the United States: the U.S. government's demand that Latin American and Caribbean governments criminalize the drug markets and enforce the laws aimed at their suppression; and the demand of American consumers for the psychoactive substances produced and exported by those countries. In the absence of either demand, drug-related corruption would be a fraction of what it is today.

Second, drug-related corruption can be seen as a necessary and perhaps inevitable corollary to the economic opportunities presented to Latin American and Caribbean countries by the illicit drug traffic. The foreign demand for illicit drugs has represented a principal source of foreign exchange and a significant proportion of the gross national product for many of them, as well as an important source of employment for hundreds of thousands of mostly poor people in Bolivia, Peru, and Colombia and tens of thousands in Mexico, Jamaica, Belize, and elsewhere. The notion of turning their backs on the substantial opportunities presented by the illicit traffic has made no more sense to them than

2. See Ethan A. Nadelmann, "Global Prohibition Regimes: The Evolution of Norms in International Society," *International Organization* 44 (1990), 479–526.

ignoring large discoveries of oil or gold would have. Indeed, given the relative paucity of legitimate sources of wealth and employment, the antidrug laws have been largely incapable of deterring people from taking advantage of the only significant economic opportunity available to them. From this perspective, drug-related corruption can be seen as the inevitable consequence of trying to repress a highly dynamic and economically significant market.

Corruption is typically associated with the impoverishment of countries, as government officials siphon off disproportionate shares of the public treasury and complicate the worthwhile endeavors of local and foreign enterprises. Drug-related corruption, however, presents exactly the opposite situation, since the lucrative economic opportunities created by wealthy foreign markets would be much less available if the drug laws were strictly enforced. This form of corruption thus offers support for the "revisionist" school of political scientists who argued during the 1970s that corruption could have beneficial consequences in developing polities.[3] But whereas the revisionists stressed the political benefits of corruption, the benefits of drug-related corruption have been almost entirely economic while the political consequences have been largely disastrous.[4] Viewed from this perspective, drug-related corruption is the most effective means available for reconciling the economic needs of developing countries with the international legal obligations imposed by the more powerful developed countries.

Third, drug-related corruption can be seen as merely an extension and expansion of preexisting corruption throughout much of Latin America and the Caribbean. Bribery of police, customs officials, and other government regulators to waive their enforcement of minor laws is the norm in many countries. So is the expectation that many politicians and high-level officials will seek to enrich themselves while in office. Viewed from this perspective, the bribes paid by drug traffickers to government officials are little different from the bribes paid by otherwise legitimate businesses to evade taxes, duties, and a variety of burdensome government regulations. But it is also possible in many countries to

3. These arguments are summarized and analyzed in Gabriel Ben-Dor, "Corruption, Institutionalization, and Political Development," *Comparative Political Studies* 7 (1974), 63–83.

4. See Ethan A. Nadelmann, "U.S. Drug Policy: A Bad Export," *Foreign Policy* 70 (1988), 83–108; and "Víctimas involuntarias: Consecuencias de las políticas de prohibición de drogas," *Debate Agrario* 7 (1989), 127–164.

avoid arrest and prosecution for major crimes, up to and including murder, by bribing and if need be threatening police, prosecutors, and judges. Victims of crime, moreover, often must pay the police and prosecutors to conduct their criminal investigations. In such environments, drug traffickers typically find it relatively easy to pay rather than be prosecuted for their crimes.

Fourth, the relatively high levels of drug-related corruption in Latin America and the Caribbean can be seen as a function of "overcriminalization."[5] Antony Simpson noted two of the consequences in his study of police corruption:

> The first consequence is an increase in that proportion of the population engaged in behavior which has been defined as criminal. This leads to a greater likelihood of confrontation between the police and the public which in turn produces a hostile environment for the individual officer. His role in society is made more difficult, and he is likely to become disillusioned and cynical as he is obliged to enforce laws which a large proportion of the population (including, possibly, the officer himself) considers to be neither just nor reasonable.
>
> A second consequence of the existence of an "overcriminalized" body of law is the likelihood of illegal institutions arising to meet demands which are not legitimized by the society. Faced with these popular but unlawful institutions, police may come to redefine their role from enforcers of the law to *regulators* of illegal markets. They certainly will be tempted to share the illicit and usually substantial profits from the activities they regulate.[6]

The opportunity for vice control agents to become corrupted is also increased by the fact that the criminal activity is not one that creates victims with an interest in complaining to the authorities. When a police officer accepts a bribe or even extorts a payment from a drug trafficker, there usually is no one to complain that the law has not been enforced as a consequence. Furthermore, the strong dependence of drug enforce-

5. See Sanford Kadish, "The Crisis of Overcriminalization," *Annals of the American Academy of Political and Social Science* 374 (1967), 157–170.

6. Antony E. Simpson, *The Literature of Police Corruption* (New York: John Jay Press, 1977), 94. These arguments are also developed in Bruce L. Benson, "An Institutional Explanation for Corruption of Criminal Justice Officials," *Cato Journal* 8 (1988), 139–163.

ment agents on informants, undercover operations, and other deceptive techniques presents uniquely corrupting opportunities, what Peter Manning and Lawrence Redlinger have called the "invitational edges of corruption."[7] Or, as one DEA agent put it to me, "Anyone involved in vice enforcement for too long becomes part of the subculture . . . and eventually evolves into a corrupt animal."

Fifth, the uniqueness of drug-related corruption in Latin America and the Caribbean must also be acknowledged. No other criminal activity comes close in terms of its magnitude, its lucrativeness, its capacity to corrupt the previously uncorruptible, its political consequences, and its impact on international relations. The bribes paid by drug traffickers are much greater, both in an absolute sense and in proportion to government salaries, than those paid by any other type of criminal. Moreover, unlike the sizable bribes paid by foreign corporations, which are available only to a select group of high-level officials, drug traffickers' bribes are available to all who can place themselves in the right place at the right time. They are most available, however, to employees of the criminal justice system from the lowly police officer and prison guard to the judge and cabinet minister. Such is the magnitude of the drug traffic in many countries that not just individuals but entire agencies have been corrupted.

The drug-related corruption also derives its specialness from the tremendous power of some of the drug trafficking organizations. As one DEA agent well acquainted with drug corruption in Latin America reflected, "Almost everyone has their price, and the drug trafficker can usually pay it." Most criminals corrupt government officials with money and other valuables. Drug traffickers typically do the same, but they also have been effective in corrupting with threats as well as money. Often, both inducements are used. Officials are warned to accept the money "or else." The choice, as some traffickers have put, is to take the *plata o plomo*—the silver or the lead (bullet). This power has been the ultimate corrupter of government institutions, because even the most honest officials are hard-pressed to resist such pressures. At the same time, the increasing brazenness of the drug traffickers in intimidating government

7. Peter K. Manning and Lawrence John Redlinger, "Invitational Edges of Corruption: Some Consequences of Narcotic Law Enforcement," in Paul E. Rock, ed., *Drugs and Politics* (New Brunswick, N.J.: Transaction Books, 1977). See also Gary T. Marx, *Undercover: Police Surveillance in America* (Berkeley and Los Angeles: University of California Press, 1988).

officials has represented the principal instigator of government action to suppress the drug traffic.

Sixth, drug-related corruption in Latin America and the Caribbean can be viewed as an obstacle to the international drug enforcement efforts of the U.S. government. There would, of course, still be a substantial flow of illicit drugs from and through the region even if government corruption in Latin America and the Caribbean were comparable to that found in the United States and Western Europe. The economics of the market, the characteristics of the commodity, and the nature of the activity all ensure this. But the intensity and pervasiveness of drug-related corruption in Latin America has certainly played an important role in undermining U.S. efforts to immobilize drug traffickers.

Different forms and degrees of corruption obviously present different problems and different opportunities to be circumvented or reformed. Much of what is presented below is characteristic of other drug-producing and transit regions outside Latin America and the Caribbean, including the Golden Crescent in southwestern Asia, the Golden Triangle in southeastern Asia, most of Africa, and even parts of the Mediterranean region. The only difference is that the cocaine boom since the late 1970s has had a proportionately greater impact on some Latin American and Caribbean countries than any other form of drug trafficking elsewhere.

It is worth noting that corruption in Latin America, despite its breadth and depth, has been the subject of strikingly little analysis by scholars (although journalists have produced an increasingly impressive body of work). The same is true of police corruption in all of the less developed world (except India). When Arnold Heidenheimer assembled fifty of the leading writings on political corruption into one volume in 1970, not a single one was devoted solely or even primarily to either corruption in Latin America or police corruption in the less-developed world.[8] A subsequent edition, published in 1989, included two articles on political corruption in Latin America, but the bibliography to the volume listed fewer publications on Latin America than on any other multinational continent, and virtually nothing still on police corruption in less-developed nations.[9] When Antony Simpson published an excellent and

8. Arnold J. Heidenheimer, ed., *Political Corruption: Readings in Comparative Analysis* (New York: Holt, Rinehart & Winston, 1970).

9. Arnold J. Heidenheimer, Michael Johnston, and Victor T. LeVine, eds., *Political Corruption: A Handbook* (New Brunswick, N.J.: Transaction Publishers, 1989).

exhaustive bibliographical review of the literature on police corruption in 1977, there was virtually nothing that could be included on the less-developed world except for the work of David Bayley and a few others on India.[10] What follows is in part an effort to develop the link between these two bodies of literature.[11]

Virtually all studies of government corruption and anticorruption efforts view their subject within the context of a self-contained unit, be it a city, a country, or a multinational region. Outsiders are not deemed to have an interest in such matters, and in fact they rarely exercise any influence even when they are affected. Many factors no doubt account for the irrelevance of outsiders, ranging from their sense that corrupt ways are an accepted mode of interaction with the local government, to a feeling of helplessness about any outsider being able to effect any changes, to an assessment that attempting to remedy the corruption is not worth the effort, to a belief that local corruption is not any outsider's business and that outside interference would be neither warranted nor welcome. There are, of course, a few exceptions. One, which does not fall totally within the outsider/insider distinction, is the investigation of local corruption in the United States by federal authorities, especially the FBI.[12] The other is the burst of attention and Congressional action that greeted reports of bribes by American multinational companies to foreign officials in the late 1970s.[13] Even in that case, however, the

10. Simpson, *Literature of Police Corruption*, 94. On India, see David H. Bayley, *The Police and Political Development in India* (Princeton: Princeton University Press, 1969). The chapter on corruption is reprinted in Lawrence Sherman, ed., *Police Corruption: A Sociological Perspective* (Garden City, N.Y.: Anchor Books, 1974). It is worth noting that I have found nothing to suggest that more extensive materials on this subject can be found in any language other than English.

11. One of the few scholars to devote attention to both police corruption and political corruption in developing polities, albeit the American one, was V. O. Key Jr. in his *Techniques of Political Graft in the United States* (Chicago: University of Chicago Libraries, 1936), and "Police Graft," *American Journal of Sociology* 40 (1935), 624.

12. Charles F. C. Ruff, "Federal Prosecution of Local Corruption: A Case Study in the Making of Law Enforcement Policy," *Georgetown Law Journal* 65 (1977), 1171–1228, excerpted in Heidenheimer, Johnston, and LeVine, eds., *Political Corruption* (supra n. 9), 627–637.

13. W. Michael Reisman, *Folded Lies: Bribery, Crusades, and Reforms* (New York: Free Press, 1979); Neil H. Jacoby, Peter Nehemkis, and Richard Eells, *Bribery and Extortion in World Business: A Study of Corporate Political Payments Abroad* (New York: Macmillan Co., 1977); Yerachmiel Kugel and Gladys X. Gruenberg, *International Payoffs: Dilemma for Business* (Lexington, Mass.: Lexington Press, 1977); Victor T. LeVine, "Transnational Aspects of Political Corruption," in Heidenheimer, Johnston, and LeVine, eds., *Political Corruption*,

reaction was prompted not by outrage at corruption in foreign governments but by the purportedly unethical practices of American businessmen. One might imagine that a third exception would involve efforts by the United States, multinational banks, and international organizations such as the World Bank and the International Monetary Fund (IMF) to pressure indebted governments to reduce the corruption that siphons off so much of foreign loans and aid.[14] Yet to my knowledge none of these exceptions has received more than a smattering of scholarly attention.

Government corruption, and in particular police corruption, are not easily amenable to precise definition.[15] For instance, lawyers and political scientists differ in their understanding of the term. The former tend to begin by looking at the letter of the law. Corruption, from their perspective, is government conduct that violates a legal obligation. Political scientists, on the other hand, are more concerned with examining the phenomenon in its political or societal context. It is the *norms*, not the law, that determine whether conduct is corrupt. Corruption, from this perspective, "is behavior of public officials which deviates from accepted norms in order to serve private ends."[16] In Latin America, where the divergence between *the law* and *accepted norms* is often strikingly broad, defining corruption is a particularly ambiguous task. As Alan Riding has written, with specific reference to Mexico:

> The problem starts with the very word "corruption," which inserts the custom into a moral context that many Mexicans do not recognize: for them, economic crimes do not carry the same weight as human or spiritual offenses. What the Protestant ethic might consider corruption emerged as a practical way of bridging the gap between idealistic legislation and the management of day-to-day living. Rigid laws have always been adopted, but they were promulgated in an environment where they could not be applied. Corruption was therefore an aberration of the law, but not of society. And in a traditional Mexico, it provided a parallel system of operating rules. If corruption has become a political problem

---

685–700; and Michael Rosenthal, "An American Attempt to Control International Corruption," in Heidenheimer, Johnston, and LeVine, eds., *Political Corruption*, 701–715.

14. This problem is discussed in James S. Henry, "Where the Money Went," *New Republic*, Apr. 14, 1986, 20–23.

15. See Heidenheimer, Johnston, and LeVine, eds., *Political Corruption*, 3–66, 165–172.

16. Samuel P. Huntington, *Political Order in Changing Societies* (New Haven: Yale University Press, 1968), 59.

> today, it is because Mexico's new "Westernized" middle classes now measure it with alien yardsticks. But even they focus only on government corruption, unwilling to look for its deeper roots in society itself.[17]

A second reason why corruption in many Latin American countries has become such a political problem and resists definition is that external forces, not just domestic political forces, are vitally and indignantly interested in it. The fundamental reason for this external interest, which emanates principally from the United States, is that corruption is widely perceived as being principally responsible for the failure of states to curtail the flow of drugs to the United States. In examining drug corruption in Latin America, one's analysis is thus further complicated by the clash between two standards of ethical governmental behavior—that of the local government and that of the U.S. government. This clash is not entirely unfamiliar. During the 1960s and early 1970s, it created disputes among the political scientists who debated the significance of corruption in their analyses of political development in less-developed countries.[18] Shortly thereafter, the same clash generated substantial controversy and even foreign policy repercussions when payments by U.S.-based multinational companies to foreign politicians were exposed in the American media and Congress responded with the Foreign Corrupt Practices Act. But whereas many Americans viewed the multinationals' bribes with a fair degree of indifference, readily accepting the notion that other nations employed different standards, few were prepared to view drug-related corruption in the same light. Drug trafficker payoffs to police tended to be considered not in the context of meager government salaries but as government corruption, pure and simple. As a consequence, the label of "corruption" was attached to economic transactions that were viewed by many Latin Americans and Caribbeans as normative rather than corrupt behavior. It was not that the notion of corruption did not exist in these countries, just that it was interpreted according to different standards.

Of course, much of the corruption that baffles U.S. drug enforcement policies in Latin America can hardly be described by any other label.

17. Alan Riding, *Distant Neighbors: A Portrait of the Mexicans* (New York: Alfred A. Knopf, 1985), 113.

18. See the articles collected in Heidenheimer, ed., *Political Corruption* (supra n. 8), and Heidenheimer, Johnston, and LeVine, eds., *Political Corruption* (supra n. 9).

There is, for instance, a clear distinction in the eyes of both North and South Americans between a clerk who accepts a "tip" to expedite the processing of some routine government function and a police officer or judge who takes a substantial bribe in return for throwing out a case against a major drug trafficker. In the latter case, few would question that the official is corrupt. Since most drug enforcement corruption is relatively clear-cut, defining it poses less of a problem than defining corruption in general. Government corruption will therefore be defined here as complicity by a government official in criminal activity in return for some benefit, typically a material one. This definition is equally applicable to both North and South American contexts. What varies, however, is the extensiveness and pervasiveness of the corruption in the southern context.

To be sure, the United States has had its own fair share of corruption at all levels of government. From the White House to the municipal police officer, corruption has rarely been absent from the administration of criminal justice and government in general in the United States. In New York, for instance, the cycle of police corruption, investigatory commission, reform, and corruption once again has run its course every twenty years for the last hundred years.[19] During the late 1960s, an investigation into corruption among the FBN agents in New York City led to the discharge of more than fifty agents and the indictment of more than a dozen for selling drugs and taking bribes.[20] During the 1980s, virtually every federal police agency saw at least a few of its agents prosecuted on charges of drug-related corruption.[21] Yet by comparison with many municipal police departments, the federal police agencies

19. See Commission to Investigate Allegations of Police Corruption and the City's Anti-Corruption Procedures, *Commission Report*, published as *The Knapp Commission Report on Police Corruption* (New York: George Braziller, 1973), 5. Corruption in the New York City Police Department is also the subject of Peter Maas, *Serpico* (New York: Bantam Books, 1973), and Leonard Shecter with William Philips, *On the Pad* (New York: G. P. Putnam's Sons, 1973). Corruption can infect not just police agencies but also all aspects of the criminal justice system. See Robert Daley, *Prince of the City* (New York: Granada, 1978); and Todd S. Purdum, "Drugs Seen as an Increasing Threat to Police Integrity," *New York Times*, Nov. 12, 1988, 29.

20. John Finlator, *The Drugged Nation: A "Narc's" Story* (New York: Simon & Schuster, 1973), 65–67.

21. Richard L. Berke, "Corruption in Drug Agency Called Crippler of Inquiries and Morale," *New York Times*, Dec. 17, 1989, A1. A year-long investigation into corruption in the U.S. Customs Service, for instance, resulted in sixteen criminal prosecutions of customs inspectors in a dozen cities. See "Customs Inquiry Finds Drug Bribes," *New York Times*, June 18, 1987, A18.

have proven relatively free of corruption. New York City has not been alone, nor even the worst, in terms of corruption in its criminal justice system—witness the exposés of police corruption in Miami, Los Angeles, and even rural Georgia during the mid-1980s.[22] Throughout the United States, police, prosecutors, judges, and other government officials in the criminal justice systems and other branches of government have repeatedly demonstrated their susceptibility to corrupting influences.[23] The police have proven most vulnerable in their enforcement of the vice laws, in particular the drug laws.[24] In many cities, drug corruption has emerged as the pinnacle of police corruption, enriching law enforcement agents more than any other vice activity and inviting the most heinous forms of criminal complicity. Even more damaging to the nation, however, was the corruption at all levels of government that contributed greatly to the savings and loan crisis in the United States during the 1980s. Latin Americans who respond defensively to U.S.-fingerpointing at corruption in the southern hemisphere have accurately observed that corruption to the north often appears less pervasive because it is more "white collar," better insinuated into the political establishment, better obscured by the legal establishment, and not so vulnerable to the prying oversight of outsiders.

Yet despite the abundance of corruption in the United States, four checks prevent it from descending to the levels of corruption found in much of Latin America. The first is the potential of the media and investigatory commissions to expose the corruption periodically, to cleanse the police departments, and to institute reforms that impede the renewal of corrupt practices. Typically, this occurs in Latin America only with a radical change in the form of government, such as a military takeover. In most countries, the media are cowed from probing too deeply, or the civilian authorities are too weak to impose fundamental reforms despite revelations in the media. Where brave journalists occa-

22. The corruption of Southern sheriffs by drug traffickers is described in Fred Grimm, "Moonshiners' Network in Dixie Adapts Easily to Cocaine Trading," *Miami Herald*, Dec. 11, 1985, 8A. The corruption of the Miami Police Department is described in Paul Eddy, Hugo Sabogal, and Sara Walden, *The Cocaine Wars* (New York: W. W. Norton & Co., 1988). Corruption in New York City is described in Crystal Nix, "Drug Influx a Strain on the Beat," *New York Times*, Sept. 26, 1986, B1.

23. See Philip Shenon, "Enemy Within: Drug Money is Corrupting the Enforcers," *New York Times*, Apr. 11, 1988, A1; John Dillin, "Drug War Takes Its Toll on Integrity of U.S. Law Enforcers," *Christian Science Monitor*, May 31, 1990, 1.

24. John Dombrink, "The Touchables: Vice and Police Corruption in the 1980s," *Law and Contemporary Problems* 51 (1988), 201–232.

sionally have banded together to investigate and expose corruption in high places, they often have seen their presses destroyed, their newspapers censored, and their lives threatened.[25] Even when civilian leaders are able to discharge corrupt officials, they have little chance of deterring their replacements from taking advantage of the same opportunities that enriched their predecessors.

The second check is the role played by the federal government. Even despite the crimes of the Watergate period and the occasional scandals in the federal government and law enforcement agencies, the U.S. government has maintained a higher standard of integrity than most municipal and state governments. Both in presenting criminals with a powerful and largely incorruptible opponent, and in investigating corrupt activities by state and municipal authorities, its prosecutors and law enforcement agencies have strengthened the norms and power of legitimate government and the legal system. In much of Latin America, on the other hand, national government agencies have often been little more than magnified versions of corrupted municipal governments. The same is true of many, if not most, national police agencies.

The third, related check is the relative independence of the federal judiciary from political influence, intimidation, and bribery. From the mid-1930s to the mid-1980s, few federal judges were prosecuted for corruption, only one was impeached, and only one was killed by criminals.[26] These numbers increased during the late 1980s but still totaled barely 1 percent of the federal judiciary. Constant investigations and prosecutions of high-level officials in each administration have demonstrated that few if any Americans remain above the criminal law for long. In much of Latin America, on the other hand, judges are

25. Journalists writing about drug trafficking and drug-related corruption in Mexico and Colombia have been especially in danger. See "Dying by the Sword in Mexico," *Newsweek*, July 28, 1986, 15, which focuses on the murder of Ernesto Flores, the publisher of *El Popular* in the border town of Matamoros, after he published numerous reports of drug trafficking and government corruption. In Panama, the opposition newspaper, *La Prensa*, was the target of violence and censorship for its critical reporting of corruption in the Noriega regime. The same was true during the 1980s of *ABC Color* in Paraguay. During the mid-1970s, the most vigorous reporter of government corruption in Colombia was *Alternativa*, a magazine published by a number of young journalists who braved various intimidations and challenged the more traditional forces in the government and the media. In Peru, Gustavo Gorriti, a courageous investigative reporter for the leading news magazine, *Caretas*, reported extensively on drug-related corruption in police agencies, the military, and political circles during the mid-1980s.

26. A somewhat different perspective on the American judiciary is Charles R. Ashman, *The Finest Judges Money Can Buy* (Los Angeles: Nash Publishing, 1973), but even that book focuses primarily on the corruption of state, as opposed to federal, judges.

ordered and threatened by powerful officials and private individuals to pervert the law. In Colombia, the drug traffickers so intimidated the Supreme Court during the 1980s that the justices twisted the law in an effort to absolve themselves of any responsibility over cases involving the extradition of drug traffickers. Elsewhere, judges dare not find against a powerful government official accused of corruption or other crimes. The cowing of the judiciary in Latin America thus eliminates a crucial check on government corruption. At the same time, it undermines the cases the police do make and reduces whatever incentive they may have to resist being corrupted.

A fourth check, if it can be called that, is that most law enforcement agents in the United States are paid a livable salary so that, at least in theory, their economic survival is not dependent upon accepting bribes. Most judges, especially at the federal level, may make significantly less than they would as lawyers in private practice, but they too are able to maintain a respectable standard of living. This is clearly not the case in most of Latin America, where salaries are insufficient to permit economic survival and where the acceptance of bribes is tacitly understood to be an essential economic perquisite of a law enforcement agent's job.[27] Most judges are also poorly paid, which reflects not just the tradition of low government salaries but also the fact that lower court positions are held in lesser esteem and filled by relatively young and inexperienced lawyers (as is the tradition in most civil law countries).[28] The relatively low pay of criminal justice officials, combined with the opportunities presented to them by virtue of their positions, seems to be the single most important reason for the high level of corruption in Latin American criminal justice systems.

Mordida Typologies: Drug Corruption in Latin America

That corruption varies in kind, degree, and effect goes without saying. The challenge for scholars is to impose some order on this subject

27. Mary Williams Walsh, "Many Mexican Police Supplement Low Pay with 'Tips' and 'Fines,' " *Wall Street Journal*, Nov. 21, 1986, 1.

28. John Henry Merryman, *The Civil Law Tradition*, 2nd ed. (Stanford, Calif.: Stanford University Press, 1985), 34–38.

without distorting the complicated reality. Students of police corruption have been particularly imaginative in this respect, generating typologies that focus on different aspects of corruption. The Knapp Commission, which investigated police corruption in New York City in 1971, categorized corrupt police officers into two groups: the "grass-eaters" and the "meat-eaters." The former took bribes only when the opportunity arose; the latter actively sought out opportunities.[29] They and others also distinguished between "clean" and "dirty" graft, the latter being tied to illicit activities generally considered more odious, such as drug trafficking.[30] One of the leading scholars in this area, Lawrence Sherman, has also constructed a "typology of corrupt police departments." Focusing on three features, "the *pervasiveness* of corruption, its *organization*, and the *source* of bribes," Sherman distinguished between the least corrupt departments, which he designated "Rotten Apples and Rotten Pockets," those with "Pervasive Unorganized Corruption," and those with "Pervasive Organized Corruption."[31] What follows are my own adaptations of these typologies, one for individual corruption, one for organizational corruption, and one for moral corruption, each of which can be laid out along a continuum from least to most corrupt. Although the typologies apply to all law enforcement corruption in Latin America, I have constructed them with drug corruption particularly in mind. *Mordida*, it should be noted, is the Mexican term for a payoff. Translated literally, it means "a bite."

The typology of individual corruption distinguishes corrupt officials by their degree of complicity in criminal activity. The least corrupt is best described as a *passive cooperator*, the moderately corrupt is typically a *facilitator*, and the most corrupt is the *initiator*. At one end of this continuum is the honest police officer who cooperates only because his or her family has been threatened. At the other end is the drug dealing police chief, general, or dictator. The compensation which each receives for corrupt activity may vary both in frequency and in amount. He or she may receive a retainer or be paid only when an occasion arises. The amount may be as little as a few dollars or as much as hundreds of thousands of dollars. Although there tends to be a correlation between the size of the bribe and the official's rank, there is no substitute for

29. *Knapp Commission Report*, 65.

30. "Narcotics and the Police in New York," in ibid., 91–115, reprinted in Sherman, ed., *Police Corruption* (supra n. 10), 129–152.

31. Introduction to Sherman, ed., *Police Corruption*, 6–12.

being in the right place at the right time to extract the maximum possible bribe. Not a few lowly officials have put away the equivalent of a lifetime's savings for neglecting their official duties for just a moment. At the same time, many drug traffickers have supplemented and even replaced their bribe offers with threats to harm the official and his family if he fails to cooperate. In Colombia, for instance, where threats and murders are frequently used to eliminate official meddling, bribes are reportedly lower than in other countries, where drug traffickers and officials treat one another in a more civilized manner.

Passive cooperators are typically those who are paid to look the other way. Rather than being paid to do something, they are paid to do nothing. Passive cooperators may either be offered a bribe or demand (i.e., extort) one. Law enforcement agents can become passive cooperators in a number of ways: they can stumble across information or a transaction and be offered or demand a bribe merely for not acting as their official capacity requires; they can be offered or demand a bribe in advance to not investigate a case; they can be offered or demand a retainer from a known drug trafficker for not interfering in the dealer's business; or they can simply be intimidated by threats to refrain from interfering in drug trafficking. This last form of corruption, although it is the least assailable from an ethical perspective, is the most threatening to a society and government because it represents a shift in the balance of power between criminal elements and the legitimate government in favor of the former. This is particularly so when the intimidated officials occupy high levels of the government.

The *facilitator's* participation in drug trafficking can assume many forms. Perhaps the most common is the sale of information: the time and place of police raids; the identity of informants; the fact that the trafficker is under surveillance; the radio frequencies used by police to communicate with one another; and any other information that can help the drug trafficker avoid seizure of his drugs and his own apprehension, arrest, and/or prosecution. Other facilitators may become far more involved with drug traffickers, sometimes to the extent of actually becoming their partners. They may provide transportation; they may assist with security, either in person or by providing uniforms and equipment; and they may offer protection from interference by other law enforcement agents, both honest and corrupt. The relationships between facilitators and drug traffickers can vary greatly depending on their relative power, the degree to which either is beholden to the other, and the existence of any nonfinancial components to the relationship. For instance, facilitators may be willing to aid a drug trafficker so long as they are not caught red-handed or caught by an agent or agency more powerful than the facilitators or their agencies. If that event occurs, the facilitator may disavow any knowledge of the trafficker and the illegal activities.

Initiators are often the most elusive of drug traffickers because they are able to disguise and shield their activities by virtue of their position. Many initiators become involved by selling what they seize from drug traffickers. For instance, an agent may arrest a trafficker with 5 kilograms of cocaine, keep 2 kilograms to resell, and deliver the remainder to the authorities. Another agent may keep all 5 kilograms and silence the ripped-off trafficker by threatening or killing him or her. Two other types of initiators are both connected to high levels of the government. One type (who lies outside the bounds of this typology) is the diplomat or other official (or the official's friend or relative) who acts as a courier, taking advantage of diplomatic immunity or special status to minimize or avoid searches at the border. The other type is the high-level military or police official who controls all drug trafficking in the district and receives a large share of the profits. Those who control and share less of the profits fall more readily into the category of facilitators.

A second typology that is useful in examining corruption from a comparative perspective distinguishes the organizational networks of corrupt officials by size, sophistication and hierarchical structure. At one end of this continuum is corruption that may be deemed *sporadic*. In the middle are two forms of what may be termed *systemic corruption*. And at the other end is what may be called *institutionalized corruption*.

Sporadic corruption is characterized by the absence of a broad pattern of corruption. It involves individuals or small groups of officials who take bribes but who do not share either their payoffs or knowledge of their activities with others in the government. Although sporadic corruption may occur in countries where the more organized forms of corruption also exist, it is more likely to occur in societies in which corruption is not viewed as a natural feature of government and law enforcement.

There are two types of systemic corruption, which conform to Sherman's "pervasive unorganized" and "pervasive organized" corruption. The first is typified by a society in which corruption is pervasive but poorly organized. In such a society, corruption may be rampant, but one cannot safely assume that everyone is corrupt. Although most police and judges may accept bribes, those who are honest can perform their duties without being harassed by others within the government. Given the right connections and/or enough money, drug traffickers who encounter such officials can eventually circumvent them by relying on other corrupt officials to set things right. The second type of systemic corruption is characterized by hierarchical payoff systems in which lower-level officials turn over most of what they collect in bribes to their superiors, who in turn must give most of their share to their superiors. Money may also flow in the reverse direction because most large-scale traffickers will cut their deals directly with the high-level officials. Those officials then direct their underlings to ignore or aid the drug trafficker's activities. The wiser and more generous high-level officials will distribute some of their intake down the ladder to keep their underlings both happy and loyal. Lower-level officials who engage in sporadic corruption despite the existence of this type of systemic corruption must beware because their "freelancing" may be regarded by their superiors as impermissible skimming of their own profits.

Individual countries may each have a number of such "payoff cones" within their borders. Often, one such cone will exist in each subdivision of the country, such as a province, police district or military district. Problems arise when two cones overlap or share the same district. In such cases, the head military officer and the head police commander, for instance, may compete for traffickers' payoffs and seek to undermine the deals the other makes with traffickers.

When all "payoff cones" fall within the umbrella of a centralized national "payoff cone," or when only one "payoff cone" exists for the entire country, the nation may be said to have *institutionalized* corruption. In such a system, the president or other effective authority in the country controls virtually all corrupt arrangements of any magnitude, particularly within the military and the police. This control typically includes knowledge of such transactions, veto power over them, and perhaps a direct or indirect cut in them. The official may personally arrange deals with drug traffickers, delegate that responsibility to a trusted assistant, or give approval to arrangements worked out independently by high-level officers. Although this official may not personally take a cut of each bribe, he or she will aim to distribute the opportunities for earning corrupt dollars as a form of patronage. The official may also exercise substantial influence over the judicial system, ensuring that its decisions do not endanger or expose his or her arrangements. When the payoff cone is dependent largely on drug-related money, the regime may fairly be characterized as a "formal narcocracy."[32]

The Pinnacle of Corruption

Classifying countries according to the above typology is a tricky process. Countries tend to shift from one category to another over time as regimes and political systems change and as crackdowns on drug trafficking alter payoff patterns. Different cities and regions within the same country may fall into different categories. And in some cities and regions, two categories may coexist simultaneously. Moreover, it is often impossible for an outsider to discern the true nature of a corrupt system because so much of the evidence is kept secret by those who participate in it.

At the same time, both typologies are useful in that they allow one to understand better the variations and gradations in both individual and organized corruption. Institutionalized corruption, for instance, is most likely to be found wherever an antidemocratic strongman has consolidated his position and is able to remain in power for more than a few years—consider Paraguay under General Alfredo Stroessner, Panama under General Manuel Antonio Noriega, Nicaragua under General Anastasio Somoza, Haiti under the Duvaliers, the Dominican Republic under Rafael Leónidas Trujillo, Cuba during Fulgencio Batista, and a host of others.[33] Although each was obliged to worry about challenges from below, and none was entirely free to eliminate potential rivals or threats, each exercised dominant control over all payoff cones of significance in his country for at least part of his reign. Individual colonels and generals may have established their own cones in the districts under their supervision, but all fell under the umbrella of the dictator's national cone.

Although each of these dictators accumulated much of their fortunes

32. The notion of formal and informal narcocracies is developed in Anthony Henman, "Cocaine Futures," in Anthony Henman, Roger Lewis, and Tim Malyon, *Big Deal: The Politics of the Illicit Drugs Business* (London: Pluto Press, 1985), 118–189.

33. See Laurence Whitehead, "On Presidential Graft: The Latin American Evidence," in Michael Clarke, ed., *Corruption: Causes, Consequences, and Control* (London: Frances Pinter, 1983).

by taking a share of legitimate activities and simply stealing from their national treasuries, almost all certainly profited from involvement in illegitimate transnational commerce, most notably drug trafficking. During the 1950s, Fulgencio Batista established close ties with such American mobsters as Meyer Lansky and the Mafia boss in Tampa, Santo Trafficante.[34] In return for cash payments to the Cuban dictator, the American criminals were provided with lucrative casino concessions as well as substantial freedom in the conduct of their other criminal activities. With Batista's ouster in January 1959, the Mafia sought a new gambling haven in the Caribbean and approached Haiti. According to one account:

> François ("Papa Doc") Duvalier entertained Joseph Stassi, a member of the Carlo Gambino family of Cosa Nostra, at the Presidential Palace. Later, a gambling concession was issued to Vito Filippone, a Bonnano family man. In 1964 and 1965, Cosa Nostra men pushed two series of Haitian lottery tickets in this country.[35]

While in the Dominican Republic,

> [Rafael Trujillo] bought machine guns and other small arms from Joseph ("Bayonne Joe") Zicarelli, a Capo in the Bonanno family, after the U.S. had shut him off from military aid. Later, Zicarelli arranged for the assassination of Andres Requena, an anti-Trujillo exile living in New York, and for the kidnapping and delivery to Santo Domingo of Jésus de Galindez, another political enemy of the dictator.[36]

In the case of Somoza, one trafficker middleman reportedly negotiated personally with the president in the late 1960s for unencumbered use of three Nicaraguan airports and several Pacific ports for his clients. Thereafter, he told one source:

34. Lansky's relationship with Batista and other Cuban leaders is discussed in Dennis Eisenberg, Uri Dan, and Eli Landau, *Meyer Lansky: Mogul of the Mob* (New York: Paddington Press, 1979).

35. Ralph Salerno and John S. Tompkins, *The Crime Confederation* (Garden City, N.Y.: Doubleday, 1969), 386–387.

36. Ibid., 388.

> My own dealings with the Somoza government amounted to giving them a total of more than $13.5 million over a period of about ten years. All was paid in cash to Anastasio or [his brother] Luis, or other family members. Now and then I would give money to one or more of the generals in his government in order to keep them happy, because you never can tell in a country like Nicaragua; you have to make sure that everyone is taken care of. The President also had many cousins. They all needed assistance from time to time, and three of them manned the airports in the highlands. We made our deals man to man, I always paid in cash, and it was always understood that Somoza's relatives would receive appropriate payoffs commensurate with their positions within the government.[37]

Among all Latin American countries, Stroessner's Paraguay stood out for the blatant involvement of its officials in the contraband trade, including drug trafficking. With the exception of one incident in the early 1970s, when the Nixon administration vigorously insisted on the extradition of an infamous drug trafficker, Auguste Ricord, the Paraguayan leader and his cronies managed their illicit transnational enterprises with little foreign interference.[38] One account, typical of many of the reports that have emerged from Paraguay over the years, described the situation in 1971:

> Since the early sixties the contraband traffic has replaced the public sector as the major source of finance for the purchase of equipment by the Paraguayan armed forces. Arms for the armoured divisions, which were previously paid for by siphoning funds from the state alcohol monopoly (APAL), are now financed out of the profits from the traffic in contraband cigarettes, which is controlled by the chief of the *Caballarria*—General Andrés Rodríguez. Traffic in scotch whiskey has likewise replaced funds from the state water board (CORPOSANA) in the case of Stroessner's own crack *Regimiento Escolta*. And the traffic in heroin has replaced the customs department as the major financial support

37. Andrew Starrhill Vallejo, quoted in Wayne Greehaw, *Flying High: Inside Big-Time Drug Smuggling* (New York: Dodd, Mead & Co., 1984), 43–44.

38. For a full account of the Ricord episode, see Evert Clark and Nicholas Horrock, *Contrabandista!* (New York: Praeger, 1973), 177–231.

> for the counter-insurgency Regimiento group—R114—whose chief, General Patricio Colmán, is one of the organizers of the heroin smuggling. General Rodríguez handles re-export by air with old DC-4's belonging to the government, and also his own private fleet of Cessnas. River borne contraband is handled by Rear-Admiral Hugo González.[39]

The severance of the French and Latin American heroin connections the following year temporarily took Paraguay out of the drug trade. Within a few years, however, the developing cocaine boom had opened up new opportunities. In January 1985, another flap in U.S. relations with Paraguay arose when President Stroessner refused to destroy a large shipment of ether and other chemicals, which had been imported into Paraguay to process cocaine. Information soon emerged that General Andrés Rodríguez—a former backer of Ricord and reportedly the second most powerful person in the country—was deeply involved in the transaction.[40] By the mid-1980s, with Stroessner aging, the precise balance of power between the president and his generals and colonels, and the intricacies of the payoff relationships, could no longer be assumed to favor Stroessner. When he was ousted in a coup led by General Rodríguez in 1988, it appeared that that the payoff system was sufficiently well institutionalized that it would survive his passing.[41]

In the case of Panama, claims of official involvement in drug trafficking date back at least to the early 1970s. Top officials, including Joaquim Him Gonzales, a well-connected figure in Panama who held the position of chief of air traffic control and deputy inspector general of civil aviation, and Moises Torrijos, the brother of President Omar Torrijos Herrera, who also served as Panama's ambassador to Spain, were both indicted by U.S. prosecutors on drug trafficking charges.[42] Suspicions

39. *Latin America Newsletter*, Nov. 19, 1971, cited in Whitehead, "On Presidential Graft," 153. The official involvement in the contraband trade is also described in Paul H. Lewis, *Paraguay Under Stroessner* (Chapel Hill: University of North Carolina Press, 1980), 135–137; Catherine Lamour and Michel R. Lamberti, *The International Connection: Opium from Growers to Pushers*, trans. Peter and Betty Ross (New York: Pantheon Books, 1974), 52–53; Jack Anderson, "Drug Traffic in Paraguay," *Washington Post*, May 24, 1972, B15.

40. "The Guaraní Connection," *Latin America Regional Reports Southern Cone*, Aug. 2, 1985.

41. Tina Rosenberg, "Smuggler's Paradise," *New Republic*, June 8, 1987, 14–16.

42. Lamour and Lamberti, *International Connection*, 53–56; Evert and Horrock, *Contrabandista!* 193–203.

also centered on Foreign Minister Juan Tack, on Manuel Antonio Noriega, then the chief of the military's intelligence unit, G-2, and even on President Torrijos personally—although a special investigation by the Senate Intelligence Committee, discussed in a closed-door session of the U.S. Senate, revealed no conclusive evidence that Omar Torrijos was involved in or otherwise sanctioning official involvement in drug trafficking.[43] In all of these cases, official Panamanian involvement in the drug traffic was played up by U.S. opponents of the Panama Canal Treaty, most notably Senator Robert Dole.[44]

With the death of General Torrijos in 1981 and the emergence of Noriega as Panama's de facto ruler, the 15,000-person Panama Defense Force evolved into "a kind of Mafia that makes millions from kickbacks and drug dealing."[45] American drug enforcement agents had suspected Noriega of involvement in drug trafficking since his days as chief of intelligence under Torrijos. Indeed, in 1972 Noriega's name had been included on a list of major traffickers drawn up by a special unit within the Bureau of Narcotics and Dangerous Drugs, made up largely of former CIA agents, that considered assassinating leading drug traffickers around the world, although reportedly the plan was vetoed by top BNDD officials.[46] General Torrijos was personally informed of Noriega's involvement in drug trafficking by the head of the BNDD, John Ingersoll, but no action was taken by the Panamanian leader. More than a decade later, little had changed. In 1985, new information emerged linking Noriega with a major Peruvian drug trafficker, Reynaldo Rodríguez López. In June 1986, the investigative reporter, Seymour Hersh, provided an extensive exposé of Noriega's, and the Panamanian military's,

43. See the account by the former U.S. ambassador to Panama, William J. Jorden, *Panama Odyssey* (Austin: University of Texas Press, 1984), 523–524. See also *New York Times*, Feb. 17, 1978, 2; and Feb. 22, 1978, 1.

44. Jorden, *Panama Odyssey*.

45. James LeMoyne, "Elements in Ouster of Panama Chief: Beheading and a Power Duel," *New York Times*, Oct. 2, 1985, A12.

46. The plan to set up an assassination unit within the DEA was investigated in 1975 by a special team appointed by the attorney general. The final report, named for its principal author, was "The DeFeo Report." Although classified, information about the report and the report itself were leaked to journalists. See Richard Wieland, "Secret Report Reveals Panama Death Plot," in *Freedom*, June 1978 (published by the Church of Scientology). E. J. Epstein also refers to the assassination plans, although without naming Noriega as a target, in *Agency of Fear: Opiates and Political Power in America* (New York: G. P. Putnam's Sons, 1977), 141–146. See also Seymour M. Hersh, "U.S. Aides in '72 Weighed Killing Officer Who Now Leads Panama," *New York Times*, June 13, 1986, A1.

involvement in drug and arms trafficking and money laundering activities.[47] Two years later, he was indicted on drug trafficking charges in a U.S. court, and in late 1989 he was arrested by U.S. agents in Panama City following the U.S. military invasion mounted to oust him from power.

In each of these cases, a dictator with firm control over the country's military forces was able to exercise a strong influence over most large-scale corruption within the country. Payoffs were extracted from legitimate foreign and local businesses; government contracts were awarded to one's family and friends and oneself; and special arrangements were negotiated with transnational criminals. That such leaders typically developed close relationships with American mafiosi, Colombian drug traffickers, and other transnational criminals was no doubt a reflection of their common methods, common mind-sets, and kindred spirits recognizing common interests. As Stanislav Andreski pointed out in his analysis of Latin American and Caribbean "kleptocracy," the "levying of tribute by the pretorians . . . is simple and exactly analogous to that used by the Mafia in Sicily or by Al Capone in Chicago, the only difference being that here the gangsters are recognized as the official government."[48] Sharing both a gangster mentality and an overriding interest in acquiring illegitimate revenue, dictators and transnational criminals have represented a natural match.

Corruption All Around

Most Latin American and Caribbean governments tend to be characterized by systemic but disorganized corruption. Indeed, one of the basic characteristics of civilian regimes in the region is the presence of disorganized corruption, although military regimes in which no one general is dominant also may fit this description. Within each country, corruption in certain localities may fit into either the sporadic or the payoff cone model. Relations between corrupt officials vary from close cooper-

47. Seymour M. Hersh, "Panama Strongman Said to Trade in Drugs, Arms, and Illicit Money," *New York Times*, June 12, 1986, A1.

48. Stanislav Andreski, *Parasitism and Subversion: The Case of Latin America* (New York: Pantheon Books, 1966), 66.

ation in profiting from drug traffickers to intense infighting to attract the drug traffickers' bribes and business. Perhaps nowhere are relations so complex as in Mexico. Throughout the 1970s and 1980s, federal, state, and local police alternately competed and cooperated with one another and with assorted prosecutors, judges, military units, political officials, and agents of the security services in extracting bribes from drug traffickers, actively participating in drug trafficking operations, and cracking down on drug trafficking. Even though top-level officials in Mexico City reportedly exercised substantial influence over career, policy, and operational decisions with implications for drug enforcement and drug-related corruption, substantial power was exercised more or less independently by regional commanders and political bosses.

To the extent that Mexican corruption can be described as unique, that is largely a reflection of Mexico's greater size and its proximity to the United States.[49] Otherwise, the above description is equally valid for most other Latin American and Caribbean countries, provided adjustments are made for scale. To be sure, every country has its small share of mostly or entirely honest government officials. The growth of the international drug traffic, however, has reduced that share by increasing the size of the temptations to unprecedented levels and by supplementing the temptations with threats. Especially in the more impoverished countries, the lure of drug dollars has virtually overwhelmed preexisting resistance to corruption. In the Bahamas, for instance, numerous high-level officials, including Prime Minister Lynden Pindling and a number of his cabinet ministers, were accused during the 1980s of accepting bribes from a variety of American and Colombian drug traffickers, including the notorious Colombian drug trafficker, Carlos Lehder.[50] Elsewhere in the Caribbean, top officials in Haiti,[51] Trinidad and To-

49. The evolution of drug-related corruption in Mexico from 1960 to 1990 is described well by Peter A. Lupsha, "Drug Lords and Narco-Corruption: The Players Change but the Game Continues," *Crime, Law, and Social Change* 16 (1991), 41–58.

50. See the excellent six-part series on drug trafficking and corruption in the Bahamas by Carl Hiaasen and Jim McGee, "A Nation for Sale," *Miami Herald*, Sept. 23–28, 1984; and Joel Brinkley, "Drugs and Corruption Color Vote in Bahamas," *New York Times*, June 14, 1987, A1.

51. In Haiti, suspicions centered on Ernest Bennett, father-in-law of former President Jean-Claude Duvalier, who reportedly became known as the "Godfather" because of his role in assisting Colombian drug traffickers using Haiti as a transshipment point. See Don Bohning, "Duvalier Father-in-Law Linked to Colombian Cocaine Traffic," *Miami Herald*, June 13, 1986, 1A.

bago,[52] the Turks and Caicos islands,[53] and the British Virgin Islands[54] were all implicated during the mid-1980s in illegal dealings with drug traffickers.

In many of these countries, corruption had either been relatively absent or at low levels commensurate with the economic activity on the islands. When American and Colombian drug traffickers were drawn to the islands by the need to transport their drugs and launder their funds, however, the nature of corruption on the islands was dramatically altered. Some government officials suddenly were provided with the opportunity to become wealthy beyond their wildest dreams. But at the same time, outsiders such as the DEA developed an interest in how they had acquired their new, and often conspicuous, fortunes. By the late 1980s, none of the island nations had figured out how to deal with the tensions between the drug traffickers' temptations and the DEA's unfortunate interest in the recipients of those temptations.

Virtually no government in Latin America and the Caribbean has been untouched by the lure of drug dollars. The important variations between countries are in the extent to which government was corrupted before the advent of drug dollars, and in the degree to which drug-related corruption has changed the nature and scale of overall corruption. Government in Bolivia, for instance, has long been notoriously corrupt, but the lure of cocaine dollars virtually eliminated whatever limits had previously existed. The apex, or nadir, was reached when a cocaine trafficking junta led by a General Luis García Meza seized control of the government in 1980 and maintained itself in power for a year and a half. Although U.S. pressures eventually forced the regime from power, and although the subsequent civilian leaders, Hernan Siles Zuazo and Víctor

52. In April 1984, Prime Minister George Chambers appointed a Commission of Enquiry to investigate drug-related corruption. Its report, released in January 1987 by Chambers's successor, Prime Minister A. N. R. Robinson, implicated two of Chambers's cabinet ministers, two magistrates, and fifty-three police officers, including senior officials and hotel operators, with drug trafficking in Trinidad and Tobago. See *Latin American Monitor—Caribbean*, Mar. 1987, 393; and *Caribbean Insight*, Mar. 1987, 13.

53. In March 1985, Chief Minister Norman Saunders, Minister of Commerce and Development Stafford Missick, and another legislator were arrested in a DEA undercover operation in Miami after accepting bribes to provide safe transit for cocaine shipments. See Liz Balmaseda, "Drug Net Snares Island Ministers," *Miami Herald*, Mar. 6, 1985, 1A; and Jon Nordheimer, "U.S. Arrests Atlantic Islands' Leader in Drug Plot," *New York Times*, Mar. 6, 1985, A1.

54. New elections were called after revelations that Chief Minister Cyril Romney held a majority share in a company under investigation by British police and the DEA for suspected money laundering. See *Latin American Monitor—Caribbean*, Sept. 1986, 329.

Paz Estenssoro, were regarded as relatively honest, drug-related corruption has continued to permeate the military, the criminal justice system, the legislature, and reportedly even the cabinet. The transition from García Meza's regime to the relatively impotent civilian regimes that followed thus represented no more than a switch from a formal narcocracy to an informal narcocracy. Neither the economy's dependence on the cocaine trade nor the debilitating consequences of the pervasive drug-related corruption changed in any significant way.

In Colombia, where traditions of official rectitude are somewhat stronger, drug traffickers nonetheless succeeded during the 1970s and 1980s in corrupting all levels of government, including a significant share of the legislature and cabinet-level ministers. In 1978, for instance, President Alfonso Lopez Michelsen was told by top U.S. drug enforcement officials that some thirty high-level officials, including two cabinet ministers and five federal judges, had been corrupted by drug traffickers.[55] No action was taken, however, by the Colombian leader. Even the Colombian military, which has remained a powerful and relatively corruption-free organization, could not resist the inducements offered by the drug traffickers. In 1978, martial law was declared in the Guajira peninsula, where most Colombian marijuana is grown, and the military took over drug enforcement responsibilities from the national police. Two years later, the military was removed after drug traffickers had succeeded in corrupting most high-level military officials in the region.[56] During the 1980s, the drug traffickers grew even more powerful, investing in the legitimate economy, buying protection from all branches and levels of government, and bribing, intimidating, and killing those who challenged them.

Peru's situation is of a similar magnitude but slightly different character than Colombia's. Its military also has remained largely indifferent to drug trafficking, fearing its corrupting effects and preferring to concentrate their energies on combatting the two leftist insurgencies: Sendero Luminoso (Shining Path) and the Túpac Amaru Revolutionary Movement. During the mid-1980s, its customs agency was regarded as

55. The U.S. delegation included the DEA administrator Peter Bensinger and the chief drug officials in the White House and State Department, Peter Bourne and Mathea Falco. Interview with Peter Bourne, November 1, 1984. This incident was also the subject of a CBS "60 Minutes" story entitled "The Cocaine Memorandum," April 2, 1978.

56. Peter Lupsha, "Drug Trafficking: Mexico and Colombia in Comparative Perspective," *Journal of International Affairs* 35 (1981), 95–115.

entirely corrupt and the other law enforcement agencies—the Peruvian Investigative Police (PIP) and the Guardia Civil—as mostly so. The same was true of the various intelligence agencies.[57] The judiciary has remained underpaid, overworked, virtually inoperative, and riddled with corruption.[58] In late 1985, the new president, Alan García Perez, launched a "moralization" campaign against the extensive corruption that had been uncovered throughout the government.[59] Suspicious connections between a major drug trafficker, Reynaldo Rodríguez López, and top officials in the interior ministry were investigated. Dozens of police generals suspected of collusion with the drug traffickers were dismissed, as were many others of lower rank,[60] but many of those dismissed simply went to work full-time for the traffickers. By the time García left office in 1990, the names and faces of the corrupt officials benefiting from the traffickers' largesse had changed, but not the essential patterns of corruption.

Although Bolivia, Colombia, and Peru have been the leading producers of illicit cocaine for the international market, the corruption attendant to the traffic has reached to high and low levels of virtually every government in the region. The extent of specifically drug-related corruption depends primarily on the availability of opportunities, which is in turn dependent on the impact of law enforcement efforts in other countries and the routes preferred by the traffickers. For instance, the Colombian government's periodic crackdowns on the drug trade since mid-1984 have diverted substantial portions of the traffic to neighboring countries such as Brazil,[61] Venezuela,[62]

57. Corruption in the Peruvian police is noted in James Mills, *The Underground Empire: Where Crime and Governments Embrace* (Garden City, N.Y.: Doubleday, 1986), 879.

58. That was the conclusion of an extensive investigation by the West German Friedrich Naumann Foundation. "Report condemns Peru's Judiciary," *Latin America Weekly Report*, Feb. 22, 1985, 6.

59. See Jeffrey L. Klaiber, "Reform Politics in Peru: Alan Garcia's Crusade Against Corruption," *Corruption and Reform* 2 (1987), 149–168.

60. Alan Riding, "Peru Joins Attack on Cocaine Trade," *New York Times*, Sept. 1, 1985, A1. See the exposé, "Las amistades de don Reynaldo," *Caretas* (Peru), Aug. 12, 1985, 12–20; and "Caso Gigante," *Caretas*, July 30, 1985, 40–46.

61. See the following three articles by Alan Riding: "Brazil Tries to Stop Spread of Cocaine Trafficking," *New York Times*, Mar. 14, 1985, A6; "Brazil Acting to Halt New Trafficking in Cocaine," *New York Times*, June 7, 1987, 19; and "Brazil Now a Vital Crossroad for Latin Cocaine Traffickers," *New York Times*, Aug. 28, 1988, 1. See also James Brooke, "Brazil's Amazon Basin Becomes Cocaine Highway," *New York Times*, Apr. 14, 1991, 14.

62. Merrill Collett, "Venezuela Gaining Notoriety as Pipeline for Illegal Drugs," *Miami*

Panama,[63] and Ecuador,[64] creating new opportunities for their law enforcement and other officials. As the European market for cocaine has grown, Uruguay and Argentina have become increasingly important transit countries for Bolivian and Peruvian cocaine shipped east—with the northern Argentine province of Salta gaining special notoriety in recent years.[65] Similarly, Central American police and military officials have occasionally seized opportunities to provide transit services, such as airstrips and docking locations, for the drug traffickers.[66] Some have also offered their countries as refuges to assorted traffickers willing to pay their hosts handsomely. Even as the national and ethnic identities of the traffickers changed from the Corsican and Italian heroin traffickers of the 1960s to the Colombian, Peruvian, and North American cocaine and marijuana dealers of the 1970s and 1980s, the patterns remained the same.

In Ecuador, which is fortuitously situated between Peru and Colombia, DEA agents described the corruption as pervasive from top to bottom during the mid-1980s. According to one agent who had been stationed there for more than five years:

> The whole country is a dog and pony show. . . . If you have money, you don't spend time in jail. You buy the cops, or the judges, the evidence disappears . . . you escape from jail. . . . The leading trafficker in Ecuador . . . has tons of relatives, not one of whom has ever spent more than a week in jail. . . . The chief of the prison is always being thrown in jail for letting criminals

Herald, Dec. 21, 1986, 34A; Alan Riding, "Cocaine Finds a New Route in Venezuela," *New York Times*, June 18, 1987, A15; Alan Riding, "Colombian Drugs and Rebels Upset Venezuela," *New York Times*, Jan. 20, 1988, A9.

63. *Drugs, Law Enforcement, and Foreign Policy—Panama: Hearings Before the Subcommittee on Terrorism, Narcotics, and International Operations of the Senate Committee on Foreign Relations*, 100th Cong., 2d Sess., Part 2, Feb. 8–11, 1988.

64. Richard L. Berke, "Drug Cartels, Squeezed, Are Turning to Ecuador," *New York Times*, Mar. 25, 1990, A22.

65. Shirley Christian, "Drug Traffic Rises Sharply in Argentina," *New York Times*, Apr. 28, 1988, A5.

66. Drug-related activities in Honduras are discussed in Wilson Ring, "U.S. Looks at Honduras as Drug Transfer Point," *Washington Post*, Dec. 7, 1987, A27; James LeMoyne, "Military Officers in Honduras Are Linked to the Drug Trade," *New York Times*, Feb. 12, 1988, A1; Mark B. Rosenberg, "Narcos and Politicos: The Politics of Drug Trafficking in Honduras," *Journal of Interamerican Studies and World Affairs* 30 (Summer–Fall 1988), 143–166; and Mort Rosenblum, "Hidden Agendas," *Vanity Fair* 53 (Mar. 1990), 102–106, 114–120.

> escape; then he becomes the head again. . . . And traffickers "escape" from jail with all their furniture.

Such descriptions of drug-related corruption were repeated to me in one form or another by DEA agents who had served in most Latin American and Caribbean countries. For every country there were stories of customs and drug enforcement agencies corrupted from top to bottom, of ludicrously porous prisons, of prosecutors and judges taking bribes and even actively seeking them out, of legislators, regional governors, and cabinet ministers linked to powerful drug traffickers, and of military officers providing protection to drug traffickers. There were exceptions, of course—occasional honest officials, relatively uncorrupted police agencies and military branches, upstanding cabinet ministers, and so on. But overall the atmosphere of corruption pervades most governments throughout the region.

The most corruption-free governments—those fitting the model of sporadic corruption—emerge during the years immediately following the ouster of a democratic regime by a military coup d'état.[67] Both Chile immediately following Allende, and Argentina following the ouster of Isabel Perón, fit into this category. A number of factors probably account for this. Coup leaders typically justify their actions by promising to eliminate the rampant corruption of the previous regime.[68] This is not to say that coups are primarily motivated by revulsion at civilian corruption, just that the military does have a stake in minimizing corruption to gain popular support and legitimize itself. A second factor, which also accounts for the greater preponderance of corruption among police services than within the military, is the professionalism of the military services. Trained in prestigious military academies, and inculcated with

67. The term "corruption-free" refers only to the absence of the type of corruption discussed in this chapter—that is, complicity in criminal activity in return for a material benefit. The lawless killing of civilians suspected of leftist activities by Latin American militaries after they overthrow a civilian government constitutes a very different form of corruption, one that typically is at its worst immediately following a coup d'état. The latter form of corruption is analyzed in Arnold A. Rogow and Harold D. Lasswell, *Power, Corruption, and Rectitude* (Englewood Cliffs, N.J.: Prentice-Hall, 1963).

68. Eric Nordlinger, in *Soldiers in Politics: Military Coups and Governments* (Englewood Cliffs, N.J.: Prentice-Hall, 1977), 85–88, 92–93, notes that charges of corruption are intrinsic to the political rhetoric of coups but that the corruption itself is not a strong motivating factor for the coup. Rather, the corruption helps to set the stage for the coup by reducing the respect of the military and the public for the civilian regime and by undermining the regime's legitimacy.

notions of honor and order, military officers are often predisposed against engaging in corrupt activities, particularly the more shady varieties such as drug trafficking. A third factor is that most new regimes, including democratic ones, enter power with a relatively clean reputation, which lingers for a while. Typically, the initial period of rule is marked by a sense of idealism and fervor for good government, which creates a hostile environment for corrupt activities. Equally important, the new power holders and those who wish to secure favors from them have yet to make contact, establish trust in one another, and get down to business.

Despite the sense of professionalism instilled in the academies, military regimes are little better than their democratic counterparts in resisting the temptations that corrupt those who hold power. The longer they remain in power, the more this is so. And when their power persists to the point of becoming institutionalized, their corruption can exceed that of the most corrupt democratic regimes. Without a free press or relatively independent judiciary, there is almost no check on corruption, no matter how blatant, outside the internal politics of the regime itself. To an outside observer, the corruption in a democratic regime may appear greater because it is more broadly distributed given the nature of the regime. But the depth and virulence of the corruption in an aging military regime are difficult to replicate even in the most decadent of democracies. More than three decades of Stroessner's rule in Paraguay attested to this. Argentina shortly before the return of civilian rule also was marked by a dramatic upswing in corruption from the earlier years when the military had concentrated its energies on repressing the left and their suspected allies. In Chile, one of Pinochet's first gestures to the United States following his seizure of power was the delivery of a number of drug traffickers, including Chilean citizens, to the U.S. government. Ten years later, one of the two national police agencies, the Investigaciones, was regarded as perhaps the leading drug trafficking organization in the country.

The Relative Immorality of Drug-Related Corruption

In addition to the typology/continua of individual and organizational corruption, a third typology/continuum is useful in analyzing the nature of corruption, particularly with regard to drug trafficking. That is the typology/continuum of moral corruption.[69] What makes it both interesting and difficult to examine is that in many ways it bears little relationship to the other two typology/continua. In other words, the corrupt *initiator* and the *institutionalized* system of corruption are not necessarily the most immoral. Rather, the best indicator of the "corruption" or immorality of a corrupt individual or system is not the extent of participation in corrupt deeds but the nature of the activity in which the corrupt individual or system acquiesces or participates. The more heinous the crime, the more immoral is the corruption that aids it. Evaluating the moral corruption of crimes and corrupt deeds is, however, a highly subjective process in which assessments vary greatly depending on the religious, cultural, ideological, and other values of an individual community or society at any one time.

Of all the apolitical crimes, with the possible exception of white-collar crimes such as insider trading, vice crimes are the most prone to widely varying moral judgments. Unlike most other acts that fall within the purview of the criminal law, vice crimes do not involve the government in punishing individuals for the harm they cause to one another or the state. Instead, they are activities involving only consenting parties that are criminalized by the government to reflect its, and often the majority's, sense of moral disapproval. To a certain extent, the criminalization of such acts also stems from a belief in human nature's susceptibility to the temptations of vice, and from the fear that such acts would proliferate if they were not illegal. Enforcing such laws becomes problematic not only because there often are no complaining parties to notify the police of the act's occurrence, but also because the consensus that underlies most criminal laws tends to dissipate in the absence of a victim. The greater the disparity between the severity of laws governing vice crimes and the tolerance or indifference of those charged with enforcing vice laws, the greater the likelihood of corruption.

Of all the vice crimes, drug trafficking has probably attracted the most varied moral judgments in Latin America and the Caribbean in recent decades. The harshest judgments are usually reflected in the criminal laws. Popular attitudes in most countries tend not to be as severe, and significant minorities in many are highly skeptical of the laws against

69. This theme is addressed in four articles by John G. Peters and Susan Welch, Michael Johnston, Kenneth M. Gibbons, and Laurence Whitehead reproduced in Heidenheimer, Johnston, and LeVine, eds., *Political Corruption* (supra n. 9), 719–800.

drugs and drug trafficking. Thus, although drug trafficking is often treated in both the penal law and political rhetoric as the equivalent of crimes such as murder and kidnapping, there are countless criminals and government officials whose ethical codes would allow them to profit from the former but not the latter. In the words of one DEA agent, most Latin American police "don't look at the trafficker as just a crook. Rather, they see him as a businessman who happens to deal in drugs, with certain contacts, interests and protectors." They deal with him accordingly, and the DEA agent often has little choice but to deal with the trafficker's counterparts within the constraints of that context. The widespread sense in Latin America that drug trafficking is qualitatively and morally almost indistinguishable from trafficking in other forms of contraband plays an important role in undermining American efforts to generate the moral outrage that might facilitate cooperation.

The location of drug enforcement corruption in the typology/continuum of moral corruption is thus a highly subjective matter. The consensus emerges only with respect to the subsidiary crimes and corruptions that often accompany corruption in drug enforcement. Killing in and of itself is not necessarily seen as all that reprehensible because violence is often the sole means of protection and contract enforcement in an illicit market. The murder of innocent people and honest officials, however, does not fall within the gray area of moral judgments. Typically, it is only when drug traffickers and the officials whom they corrupt sink to that level of behavior that the public and the government perceive a need to crack down on drug trafficking and corruption.

Clearly each society is characterized by certain expectations regarding what types and degrees of corruption in law enforcement are tolerable. Such expectations are shaped by traditional modes of interaction between a government and its citizens, by changes in regimes and the values they stress, and by fluctuations in the economy. At the same time, when one examines the course of corruption in drug enforcement in Latin America from the 1970s to the 1980s, one can discern a tendency for it to increase along each of the three continua described above. In some countries, the tendency characterizes the entire nation; elsewhere, it is true only of certain regions or cities. Each society, however, seems to have a breaking point at which its tolerance for corruption ceases. The breaking point may be occasioned by a particularly outlandish act, such as the killing of Colombia's justice minister in April 1984, or by total capitulation to corruption, which characterized the Bolivian regime of General Luis García Meza in 1980–81, or by the findings of a commission of inquiry like that which investigated Bahamian involvement in drug trafficking in 1983–84, or by a combination of media exposés and a change in regime, such as occurred in Peru in 1985 with the election of Alan García to the presidency. Following the breaking point, corruption subsides as the most egregious violators are dismissed and as others who are corrupt wait for the wave of moral fervor to recede. But so long as the drugs retain both their illegal status and their foreign markets, the renewal of the cycle of escalating corruption is inevitable.

The DEA's Unique Challenge: Dealing with Foreign Corruption

How have DEA agents dealt with the obstacles posed by drug-related corruption in Latin America and the Caribbean? The following analysis differs from virtually all other studies of corruption and reform in two respects. First, it focuses on the role played by an outsider, one that lacks any sovereign powers, in trying to influence the nature and impact of government corruption. Second, it is primarily concerned with how corrupt agencies are induced to perform their designated tasks despite that corruption, not with how they are reformed. The question addressed below is thus one involving a hitherto unstudied aspect of foreign policy behavior: When Government A seeks cooperation from Government B in pursuing Policy Objective A′ but is hindered by corruption in Government B, what are the options available to it? More specifically, when the U.S. government seeks cooperation from Latin American and Caribbean governments in apprehending, arresting, prosecuting, and punishing drug traffickers, but is hindered by corruption in those governments, what are the options available to it? Even more specifically, how does the DEA pursue its objective of immobilizing drug traffickers abroad despite pervasive corruption in foreign governments?

The DEA's capacity to deal with foreign corruption in any country is influenced most strongly by the type of organizational corruption characteristic of that country. Even in countries in which drug-related corruption is integrated into institutionalized corruption, however, DEA agents have options beyond packing their bags and leaving. The diplomatic leverage of the U.S. government, combined with the international consensus of sorts among governments that drug trafficking is both illegal and evil, ensure that no government can blatantly turn its back on U.S. requests for cooperation without incurring some costs. Even where a government has thoroughly succumbed to the influences of drug traffickers, skilled agents can still rely on their own diplomatic skills and appeals to the transnational value system of police. And no matter how deeply rooted the corruption, the fact remains that almost no one is totally corrupt. Even those who have virtually no moral limits on their corruption still will lack on occasion the opportunities to be corrupted. It may be because they have failed to make the necessary contact, or because the spotlight is on them when the opportunity arises. Whatever the case, it means that at times they may have no option left but to cooperate with the DEA agent.

In most Latin American countries, the DEA agent encounters drug-related corruption at every level of government, from the street cop and airport customs official, to the police chief, the military general, and the cabinet minister. The breadth of the corruption tends to reflect two factors. The first is the number of government agencies involved in drug enforcement. The fewer the agencies, the less dispersed the corruption, since there is little need or incentive for drug traffickers to bribe officials whose jurisdiction does not include them. The second is the pervasiveness of drug trafficking in the country. The more pervasive it is, the greater the opportunity for officials who have nothing to do with drug enforcement to profit by becoming corrupt facilitators and initiators. Thus, in Mexico, Bolivia, Colombia, Peru, Belize, Jamaica, Ecuador, the Bahamas, much of the Caribbean, and most of Central America, drug-related corruption has infected many levels and departments of government from top to bottom. Elsewhere, particularly in countries that have played a relatively minor transit role, the opportunities to profit from drug-related corruption often have been limited to top government officials and those involved in law enforcement.

Customs officials in most countries have generally been regarded as the most corruptible, perhaps because of their long experience in "regulating" all forms of contraband smuggling. The military, which has stayed out of drug enforcement activities in most Latin American countries, has had the greatest success in preserving a reputation for clean hands in this area, although there are conspicuous exceptions. In Mexico, for instance, military officers and police officials have competed for the largesse of drug traffickers. In Colombia, the military was unable to resist the corrupting influences of the drug traffickers when it briefly assumed principal responsibility for marijuana eradication in the Guajira in 1979–80. According to some reports, the general in charge of the effort retired shortly after the military was withdrawn, having become a wealthy man during his months in the Guajira. Indeed, the fear of drug traffickers' corrupting powers has been a major consideration of both military and civilian chiefs in choosing to keep the military out of drug enforcement. Military officers also have found that opportunities to profit from the drug trade exist even when the military is not charged with drug enforcement responsibilities. Among the police services, the agencies and units specializing in drug enforcement have tended to acquire the most notorious reputations for corruption. The exceptions are a number of elite units with which DEA has worked very closely—about which more below. Drug-related corruption also tends to be more pervasive in outlying areas as opposed to the capitals. Far from the prying eyes of superiors and DEA agents, police and military *comandantes* typically feel far more at ease working out their profitable relationships with drug traffickers. Not surprisingly, many regard a transfer to headquarters in the capital as a serious financial setback.

Finding Someone You Can Trust

In most Latin American countries, DEA agents have a great degree of freedom—much more so than in most of Europe—in choosing which agencies and agents they will work with.[70] This provides some degree of flexibility in their efforts to circumvent corruption, although the degree of corruption is not the only factor the DEA considers in choosing with whom to work. Often DEA agents prefer to work with a corrupt agency or agent instead of an honest one because of significant differences in their abilities. As one DEA agent who had worked throughout much of Latin America said of the Mexican Federal Police: "Sure the *Federales* are corrupt, but when a *Federale* is doing his job, there's no better cop anywhere." In Bolivia, the U.S. embassy pressured the Siles Zuazo

70. A conspicuous exception during the mid-1980s was Panama, where the resident DEA and Customs agents were required to clear virtually everything they did through a high-level official who reported directly to General Noriega.

government to appoint as head of the government's Narcotics Coordination Committee someone they knew to be corrupt because the alternative was an honest but ineffective official. The corrupt appointee, on the other hand, was a smart, ambitious politician who could get things done—even if he would accept and even solicit bribes in some cases. The U.S. embassy hoped that it could work around his corruption while it used him to get the antidrug programs under way. Then, once the programs had become somewhat institutionalized, the embassy would get him fired and replaced by a more honest official—at least that was the plan.

In international law enforcement efforts, there is little substitute for the cultivation of good personal and working relationships based on trust, even with those who are corrupt. With scarce personnel and resources in any country outside the United States, the DEA country team abroad has little choice but to rely on local agents for most investigative tasks. When the agent with whom the DEA agent works is always on the lookout for corrupt sources of money, the DEA agent has little choice but to appeal to one of an agent's three basic instincts: friendship, the pride and professionalism of a fellow police officer, and fear. Although all three, and particularly the first two, are often linked, the first seems to be the most important.

Most DEA agents in Latin America seek to develop special relationships with a few local agents. These relationships are characterized by different forms of trust. Of these agents, a DEA agent might say: "I'd trust him with my life," or "He's one hundred percent honest," or "I know he'll always be straight with me," or "He's a great cop," or "I tell him about everything we're doing here." Many DEA agents consider the development of these relationships the most essential aspect to effective functioning abroad, especially in a corrupt environment. There are a number of reasons for this: the legal, political, and practical constraints on unilateral DEA actions abroad; the discretionary nature of law enforcement, which makes it impossible to operate effectively "by the book"; the vulnerability of the agent to violence or otherwise being set up; the need for a free flow of information; and the need to recognize the variety of obstacles that might render DEA efforts against certain traffickers futile. To some extent, there is also a requisite element of mutuality to such relationships based on both friendship and professional courtesy. As one agent stationed in the Caribbean said: "It's just like in the U.S. If the guy finds out you're holding back information from him, he'll stop helping. He'll 'do' you, tell you to go through formal channels. Then you may as well forget about it. So you try to be up front and sincere."

The fact that a DEA agent trusts a local agent does not necessarily indicate that he never accepts a bribe. But it does tend to mean that the DEA agent can trust him totally on whatever matters they work on together. Indeed, given the corrupt environment and low pay of most police in Latin America, DEA agents typically assume that almost all police—with the exception of a few well-paid, honest high-level officials and an occasional person of exceptional principle in the lower ranks—will find illicit sources of money somehow. What the agents count on, however, is that to the extent the local agent is corrupt, he or she will not let it undermine their relationship. These local agents won't take bribes in a case they are working on with a DEA agent. If the local agent is being paid by a particular trafficker, he or she will find a way to let the DEA agent know there is no point in wasting time pursuing that target. And regardless of whom local agents may be taking money from, they will not let the DEA agent get hurt.

In the rare cases where a DEA agent cultivates a relationship with a local agent who is both intelligent and honest, he often must make special efforts to maintain the relationship. One effort is financial, in the form of supplements to the local agent's salary. Another is more political and requires that the DEA agent develop a good sense for the internal politics of the domestic law enforcement agency. With some agencies, DEA agents can use their influence to lobby for promotions, salary raises, and other perquisites, such as trips to the United States to testify in a case or to attend a DEA training session. In more corrupt organizations, however, too-favorable comments from the DEA can represent, as one DEA agent put it, a "kiss of death" for the local agent because they indicate that the agent is not playing by the de facto rules of his agency. Such an agent can find himself transferred to an exceptionally undesirable position. One DEA agent described the situation in Peru, which is not atypical, as follows:

> Sure there are honest cops, not at the top but among the majors and colonels. But they get screened. One major who had made some big drug cases was sent for two years to a post on the Peruvian border with Brazil—a horrible jungle area. When he

> came back to Lima, he wasn't doing narcotics anymore. And he'll probably never get promoted again.

Depending upon the influence of the DEA and the American embassy with the local government, the DEA can offer some protection to those who help them, in effect shielding them from their superiors. But in the long run, the DEA and cooperative agents must hope for a change in the regime or the organization if they are to outlast the superiors they have antagonized.

Since there are so few police whom DEA agents can trust entirely, and since many law enforcement operations involve at least a few agents, the DEA has little choice but to work with corrupt agencies and agents. This is particularly so when agencies do not have overlapping or competing jurisdictions. The modes of operation that DEA agents develop under such conditions vary dramatically, depending upon the degrees of organizational and individual corruption, the susceptibility of the government to pressures from both traffickers and the United States, and the freedom and willingness of agents to increase the extent of their operational activities. Much also may depend upon the relationship between the DEA office in the embassy and the ambassador, whose willingness to back the resident DEA agents when they get into trouble, and to use his or her influence on behalf of DEA objectives, can be crucial to the success of DEA activities.

One of the most successful measures employed by the DEA has been the creation of elite drug enforcement units composed of local police. Resident DEA agents have taken an active hand in creating these units, often training them, handpicking their chiefs and overseeing their hiring, and generally working closely with them in all aspects of their operations. Some of these units have been independent agencies, others part of an established police agency. In some cases, they have been funded in good part by the DEA and the State Department, with all of their training and much of their nonlethal equipment provided at U.S. expense. Because these units typically have represented a threat to established institutions and interests, both the DEA and the U.S. ambassador often have been obliged to use their influence to guard against interference by corrupt officials and others.

During the mid-1980s, the elite units generally fell into two categories: the paramilitary units known as Mobile Rural Patrol Units (UMOPAR) in both Peru and Bolivia, and as Special Action Narcotics Units (SANU) in Colombia (although the formal names tended to change every few years) that were primarily involved in raiding and destroying coca bushes and refineries in the outlying areas; and the elite criminal investigative divisions, usually within the national police agencies, with whom the DEA worked drug cases. In Colombia and, to a lesser extent, Bolivia, the investigative units maintained relatively good reputations for staying mostly clean of drug-related corruption. In Bolivia, the unit was closely supervised by the DEA and sheltered from those seeking to undermine it by the political influence of the ambassador. In Colombia, the unit had the first pick of new police recruits, and its agents were rotated to other units after a while to avoid their developing overly close relations with traffickers. In Argentina, the DEA began to carve out a small narcotics unit in the customs agency. And in other countries, the DEA carved out less-formal groups or divisions, often headed by an intermediate-rank official whom the DEA agents respected for his or her honesty and ability.

The ability of the DEA to maintain such units both free of corruption and operationally effective depends upon the political will of the United States and the host government, as well as upon key personalities within and above those units. The DEA's experience with the creation of Denactie in Ecuador provides a warning. There the DEA office succeeded in having a trusted friend of one its agents, a European-born Ecuadoran, appointed as head of the new agency. After a brief run of success, however, the agency was unable to resist the political pressures that arose when it arrested two traffickers who turned out to be the children of two high-level officials, including one of the most powerful generals in the country. After refusing a bribe and then being threatened, the agency chief resigned. Thereafter, Denactie proved unable to resist not only corrupting influences but also political pressures from higher-ups and a competing drug enforcement division in the national police.

Somewhat different problems plagued the Bolivian UMOPAR unit, known as the Leopards. The first serious problem was apparently unrelated to the drug traffic. Shortly after the 300-member strike force was created, funded, and trained by the United States, U.S. officials were deeply embarrassed when the unit led a coup against the Siles Zuazo government, kidnapping the president in the process.[71] After the U.S. ambassador intervened, the coup was defeated with little violence and

71. Marlise Simons, "Bolivian Plot Embarrasses the U.S.," *New York Times*, July 17, 1984.

UMOPAR's commanders were replaced. A second problem that arose in both Bolivia and Peru stemmed from the military's resentment about the emergence of an independent paramilitary force consisting of police officers. In Bolivia, the military seized a foreign gift of expensive guns intended for the Leopards and confined the unit to its barracks by declaring the Chaparé, where much of the coca is grown, a military zone.[72] In Peru, military operations against the Maoist Shining Path guerrilla movement led to the suspension of antidrug operations in the coca-growing region around Tingo María.[73] Although both UMOPAR units survived and continued to operate, the antagonisms and jealousies of the military and other police units persisted.

A third problem was the underfunding of the elite units by local governments. The DEA and the State Department's Narcotics Assistance Units were unwilling to assume the entire burden for funding the drug enforcement units, believing that foreign governments should share the responsibility. The governments, however, proved far from generous in funding these units. Bolivia's UMOPAR troops, for instance, went for months without receiving their salaries, money for rations, medical supplies, and other essentials.[74] In Ecuador, agents in the Denactie unit were better paid than most other Ecuadoran police but otherwise provided with virtually no money for weapons, transportation, gasoline, or almost anything else. Its chief was obliged to appeal to foreign weapons manufacturers and local citizens for contributions to keep his unit operating.

The general problem of lack of funding contributed to a fourth problem: the tendency for even the elite units to become corrupted as well. In virtually all of the countries where the DEA and the State Department have assisted in the creation of such units, drug-related corruption has extended to the very highest levels of government, up to and including the interior and defense ministers, top military and police officials, and their aides. No amount of diplomatic pressure and liaison has been sufficient to isolate the elite units from the corruption all around them. Ed Merwin, who served as the chief U.S. government adviser to UMOPAR in Bolivia from 1984 to 1986, described in an interview the corruption he had encountered:

72. "Caged 'Leopards' of the Drug War," *New York Times*, Sept. 12, 1984, A16.

73. Marlise Simons, "Peruvian Rebels Halt U.S. Drive Against Cocaine," *New York Times*, Aug. 13, 1984, A1.

74. David Kline, "How to Lose the Coke War," *Atlantic Monthly*, May 1987, 22–27.

Q: You had eight different commanders?
A: Eight. It was mostly because they either got too blatant about accepting bribes or, in the case of the only really good tactical field commander we had, he refused to take a bribe and he got fired by his boss, who had offered him the bribe.
Q: So the drug dealers were buying off [former director of the Narcotics Police] Colonel Guido López while you were there, as far as you know?
A: I was under that impression.
Q: How solid is the information?
A: Very solid.
Q: Can you reveal the source of it?
A: No, not really. . . . The U.S. is a very technological society and we have a lot of capabilities. That's something that the Bolivians never quite understood. Every time they talked on the telephone, we knew about it, you know.
Q: Is [the current director of the Narcotics Police] on the take?
A: I don't even know who he is right now. . . . If this one isn't, his predecessors all were.
Q: All of them?
A: To my knowledge, all of them.
Q: In what ways?
A: New cars. Send your kids to the States to go to school. One of the former Leopard commanders who was dishonest—he was bad when we got him and he got worse—I understand that he now has a really nice ranch. Has a new BMW. Wears very nice clothes. All of the national directors [of the Narcotics Police], very natty dressers. Some of them had amazingly good taste.
Q: And the rest of the enforcement structure in Bolivia . . . how corrupted was that structure?
A: I have to tell you I think that a hundred percent of the Bolivian enforcement structure was corrupted.
Q: Bought by the cocaine traffickers?
A: Yeah.[75]

Yet even given all of these problems, the elite drug enforcement units have been indispensable to the DEA's efforts to immobilize drug traffick-

75. Ibid., 24.

ers in Latin America. They often offer the only opportunity to accomplish anything at all. Especially with units that have an esprit de corps, DEA agents have been able to conduct fairly sophisticated operations against major drug traffickers. These operations have been most successful when their objective has been to do no more than seize a trafficker and spirit him or her out of the country as quickly as possible. More typical, however, are the successful operations that have been undermined by the capacity of the drug traffickers to corrupt others in the criminal justice system who have the power to undo what the elite units had accomplished.

The question of rotation of police in and out of drug enforcement units, and in and out of regions where drug trafficking is pervasive, is also a complicated one. On the one hand, rotation is regarded as an important check on the potential for police and other government officials to be corrupted. In Mexico, for instance, where the military was heavily involved in both drug enforcement and drug-related corruption during the mid-1980s, the de la Madrid government responded to U.S. pressures in early 1987 by deploying a unit of 5,000:

> The Mars Task Force, named after the Roman god of war, roams the Sierra Madre in 35-man units, searching for the marijuana and poppy plantings that seem to be omnipresent in the region and destroying them.
>
> Brig. Gen. Adrián Almazán Alarcón, commander of the task force, said his soldiers, volunteers from various army units, undergo a rigorous training and drug education program. They are then sent into the mountains for six months, and food and other supplies are airlifted to them every two weeks.
>
> He said the men are under orders not to go into hamlets or to socialize with the local people; even contact with their own families is discouraged. At the end of their tour of duty in the Mars Task Force, the men are returned to their former units.
>
> General Almazán added that his own assignment is temporary. He said that in a few weeks after having served six months, he and his entire staff will take on new commands elsewhere and that their replacements will also serve for six months.
>
> General Reta [regional commander of the Mexican armed forces] said the strict rotation and discipline policies are intended to prevent troops from "acquiring the habits of the populace."

> Other Mexican and foreign sources were more blunt: They said the task force is so organized in hopes of reducing the potential for corruption that has crippled previous drug eradication campaigns.[76]

On the other hand, rotation presents serious problems. It makes impossible the creation of an institutional memory within the drug enforcement units. It undermines the DEA's efforts to create a trained corps of drug enforcement agents in the police force. And it requires resident DEA agents to build new relationships with local police every year. In Argentina, for instance, the resident DEA agent expressed his frustration with the annual rotation of the federal police every December. The operating assumption of the agency was that its agents were not specialists but generalists, who should be exposed to all areas of policing as they are transferred and promoted. Argentine police trained by the DEA in drug enforcement methods were no exception, so that every year the narcotics unit of the Federal Police was transferred practically en masse to other units. The DEA agents were thus obliged to form new relationships every year with a new crop of drug enforcement agents. Occasionally, they were able to request that a particularly skilled agent continue to work with them, but only at the cost of creating tensions and jealousies with other police officials.

In Peru, the DEA country attaché expressed even greater frustration with the annual rotations, known as *cambios*. Police in all of the agencies, including the top officials, were transferred every year with few exceptions. During the mid-1980s, 300 to 400 Peruvian police were being trained by the DEA each year but then being transferred to other units. In an effort to retain trained personnel to work with for a longer period, the DEA office refused in 1984 to send any Peruvian police to the much-desired training course in the United States. It also demanded that agents trained by the DEA remain in the drug enforcement units for at least two years and that the DEA choose which agents would be sent to training programs. In the DEA's view, the *cambio* had not significantly reduced the susceptibility of police to corruption. Rather, most police officials transferred to the drug unit regarded the move as an opportunity to earn more illicit revenue than they could in other units. As the DEA

76. Larry Rohter, "Mexico Battles Drugs Anew, Says War Is Far from Over," *New York Times*, June 15, 1987, A1, A10.

agents saw it, the increased risk of corruption presented by two years in the drug unit, as opposed to one, was outweighed by the benefit of being able to work with better-trained agents and particularly by the opportunity to retain the few good agents who also happened to be more honest and dedicated.

The Ins and Outs of Working Around Corruption

Instilling fear may not secure eager cooperation, but at least it will limit the degree to which joint operations are undermined. As one DEA country attaché stated regarding his approach toward corrupt officials: "I just tell them I don't care how they make their money as long as they don't screw me on drug cases. If they do, I tell them, I'll nail 'em to the wall; I'll get them arrested or kicked out of their job. And I can do it."

The capacity of DEA agents to maintain their credibility and fulfill their threats depends upon the existence of higher-ups in the government, typically in the Ministry of the Interior, to whom the agents can appeal. Although even the higher-ups are not necessarily honest, they may be more sensitive to considerations of professionalism, the "image" of the police force, and the government's international reputation. And if they are not getting paid off by the same trafficker as their underling, or getting a cut, they may have little to lose by complying with the DEA's wishes.

The DEA agent's capacity to threaten directly and to carry through on the threat also is dependent on the rank and connections of the corrupt official. The most vulnerable is obviously the lower-level agent, who can be influenced by any DEA agent. The next is the middle ranking official, on whom the country attaché can either apply direct influence or seek support from his superiors. Less vulnerable are those who occupy high-level positions. Dealing with such officials can become a far more politically sensitive matter. The DEA agent, even the country attaché, is unlikely to try to threaten or intimidate them directly. Rather, the agent or the ambassador may approach a higher-level official (assuming that one is available) to ask that something be done. Finally, there are officials, such as interior ministers and senior generals, whose power is such that they can be regarded as essentially untouchable by the United States. To these may be added the relatives and close friends of the most powerful officials. In such cases, the ambassador must often decide whether seeking the assistance of the head of government is worth the potential political backlash that may result. On occasion, a senior-level official from Washington, such as the DEA administrator, the assistant secretary of state for international narcotics matters, or the chief White House aide on drug matters, may bring up sensitive cases when he or she meets with top officials either in Washington or in the foreign country. As for the occasional country in which the president himself is suspected of being involved in drug trafficking, U.S. government officials must rely on less direct methods of expressing their dissatisfaction—such as leaks to the media.

The susceptibility of the highest-level officials to American pressure in this area is tied closely to their overall dependence on the United States and the leverage the U.S. government has and is willing to exercise. With few exceptions, the U.S. government has rarely accorded the drug control objective such priority that it has been willing to sacrifice all other objectives. This has been true not just of Mexico, where the tremendous importance of other U.S. interests is obvious, but even in relatively small countries such as Bolivia, Paraguay, and the Bahamas, whose leaders were strongly suspected of complicity with drug traffickers. Only in Bolivia was the U.S. government able and willing to exert significant pressure to have the García Meza regime deposed—and even there it required more than a year of overt and covert pressures. Nor have cabinet-level ministers been much more vulnerable to pressures from the U.S. government. U.S. ambassadors in a number of countries have found that even after presenting foreign leaders with indisputable evidence of drug-related corruption by their cabinet ministers, those ministers have remained in office. Foreign leaders have responded with expressions of curiosity, sympathy, and even anger, but rarely by dismissing their political cohorts and almost never by throwing them in jail.

When informed by U.S. officials about drug-related corruption in their governments, foreign leaders often have responded by asking to see the evidence. More often than not, the U.S. officials have declined to provide it, claiming the need to protect their sources. Consider the following incident in 1985, as reported in the *New York Times*:

> The scene was familiar, both to John Gavin, then the U.S. Ambassador to Mexico, and to the Mexican officials he was meeting, including President Miguel de la Madrid.

> United States officials had put together information implicating a Mexican Government official in drug trafficking, and . . . Mr. Gavin wanted to tell Mr. de la Madrid about the case, as he had done with others before it.
>
> But this time the case involved the son of the Defense Minister, who directs a significant part of Mexico's drug-eradication program.
>
> Asked how the Mexican officials reacted to his information, Mr. Gavin imitated them with a shrug and a grimace of mock concern.
>
> In that case and several others, Mr. Gavin said with frustration, "they would say to to me: 'Show me the proof. Show me the proof.' "
>
> "But as they knew," he said, "to show the proof would be the death warrant for my sources."[77]

Another source U.S. officials have not felt comfortable revealing, for very different reasons, are the telephone, electronic, and satellite intercepts provided by the CIA and especially the National Security Agency. Indeed, that probably has constituted the principal source of U.S. information on high-level drug-related corruption in foreign governments.[78] Often it is so highly classified that even the DEA is not privy to it. Nor is information derived from such sources usable for purposes of prosecution. The availability of such information has thrust U.S. ambassadors and others in the frustrating position of knowing about drug-related corruption but not being able to provide the evidence to U.S. prosecutors or foreign leaders.

It is only in the smallest countries that the United States can fully throw its weight around, and even there its options are limited. In the Bahamas, for instance, an abundance of information indicated that a number of cabinet ministers, up to and including Prime Minister Sir Lynden O. Pindling, were receiving payoffs from drug traffickers. Direct U.S. pressures met with little response. Only when the information was

77. Joel Brinkley, "Mexico and the Narcotics Traffic: Growing Strain in U.S. Relations," *New York Times*, Oct. 20, 1986, A1.

78. See Kline, "How to Lose the Coke War." Seymour Hersh, in his exposé of Panamanian General Noriega's involvement in drug trafficking, similarly notes that much of the information U.S. government officials gave him was "gleaned from National Security Agency intercepts." See Hersh, "Panama Strongman" (supra n. 47). See also James Bamford, *The Puzzle Palace* (New York: Penguin Books, 1982), 325–336.

leaked to the U.S. media, causing an uproar in the Bahamas and providing ample ammunition for his political opponents, was Pindling pressured to appoint a commission of inquiry to investigate the corruption charges. Pindling survived the uproar, but a number of his ministers were obliged to resign.[79] Three years later, however, as charges of drug-related corruption dominated pre-election campaigning, Pindling indicated that if he won it was "very possible" that he would reappoint one of the ministers who had been obliged to resign.[80]

For DEA agents abroad, high-level corruption in foreign governments is particularly frustrating in part because it directly undermines their basic instinct of going after not just the biggest traffickers but also the people who are most in the public eye, such as celebrities and politicians. Most agents who spend no more than a few years abroad are reluctant to abandon this operating principle and to accept politically motivated constraints on their operations. This can, of course, lead to frictions with State Department officials in the embassy whose institutional and occupational predispositions make them shy away from viewing foreign officials as criminals. High-level corruption in foreign governments in effect imposes specific limits on which cases DEA agents can pursue. In many countries, for instance, they never know when an investigation will lead to the door of an official who is, for all intents and purposes, untouchable.

In some instances, corruption has been so pervasive and institutionalized that the DEA's capacity to function effectively has been almost totally undermined. In the case of the García Meza regime, the U.S. government went public with its protests and withdrew both its ambassador and the DEA presence, although undercover DEA agents continued to operate within Bolivia.[81] Agents within the DEA are divided as to the merits of such a policy. Some believe that it is always better to maintain the agency's presence in a country, no matter how widespread and high-level the corruption, because it at least represents something of a deterrent to drug traffickers and can be useful for gathering intelli-

79. See *Report of the Commission of Inquiry (Appointed to Inquire into the Illegal Use of the Bahamas for the Transshipment of Dangerous Drugs Destined for the United States of America, November 1983–December 1984)* (Bahamas, 1984); and Hiaasen and McGee, "A Nation for Sale" (supra n. 50).

80. Joel Brinkley, "Drugs and Corruption Color Vote in Bahamas," *New York Times*, June 14, 1987, 1.

81. Jonathan Kandell, "The Great Bolivian Cocaine Scam," *Penthouse* 14 (1982), 73–74, 164–170.

gence. Others feel that there is a point at which it is no longer worth the cost of maintaining the overseas office, and where the symbolic value of withdrawing the office and announcing the reason for doing so is ultimately more valuable.

The typical decision in such cases is to maintain the DEA presence provided that a minimum of cooperation is forthcoming and that high-level involvement in the drug trafficking is not too blatant. As one DEA agent who worked in Paraguay and Panama said:

> You can't dwell on drug involvement at the highest levels. There's nothing you can do about it. If you do, you'd just get depressed. What you can do is play on their weaknesses, for instance, their desire for a better international image. And you try to show them why they have an interest in helping you out.

In such situations, DEA agents abroad recognize two limits on their activities. They do not target the most powerful officials, even though agents may gather intelligence on their involvement in drug trafficking. And DEA agencies don't bother trying to get the richer and more powerful traffickers prosecuted within the country. What they can do is secure cooperation in gathering intelligence, arresting drug couriers, seizing vessels and airplanes transporting drugs, seizing shipments of ether and other chemicals used to refine coca into cocaine, collecting evidence for prosecutions in the United States, and getting a few high-level drug traffickers deported or extradited to the United States.

DEA agents who tacitly accept this arrangement are of course open to the criticism of having acquiesced in the most virulent forms of drug trafficking in return for cooperation in getting the "small fry." The criticism is most acute when trafficking in the country is dominated by a few powerful "untouchables" within and outside the government. The DEA's willingness to work with rather than against such people can be perceived as succumbing to the organizational temptation to build up the number of seizures and arrests while allowing the biggest violators to go about their business unimpeded. In fact, such a strategy can be viewed as a boon to the untouchable traffickers because it helps to eliminate competition and increase their control of the traffic at the same time that the corrupt officials are publicly lauded for what limited assistance they offer.[82] The DEA's response is typically threefold: that

82. This argument has similarities to Mark Kleiman's analysis of domestic drug enforce-

pursuing such a limited strategy is better than the alternative, that is, closing the office in the country; that given the constraints imposed by the State Department they in effect have no choice; and that they are just waiting for the time when the "untouchables" become vulnerable.

One price the State Department and, to a lesser extent, the DEA have paid in pursuing such a policy is that they must publicly endorse the drug enforcement efforts of corrupt officials both in Congress and within the countries. For instance, when the leading opposition newspaper in Panama, *La Prensa*, published a report linking General Noriega to a notorious Peruvian drug trafficker, the progovernment newspaper was able to respond the following day with a disclaimer from the resident DEA agent. Following other charges, Panama's embassy sent out copies of a letter from the DEA administrator to Noriega thanking the general for his cooperation against drug traffickers.[83] In Congressional testimony, high-level DEA officials have similarly lauded the token efforts of the Bolivian, Colombian, Peruvian, Jamaican, and other foreign governments, while mostly avoiding any direct criticism of corruption at the highest levels. They have repeatedly cited their frequent drug seizures, courier arrests, and crop destruction forays as evidence of increasing cooperation, portraying such steps in the most optimistic light possible.

At the same time, it would not be entirely accurate to accuse the DEA, and even the State Department, of pursuing a policy of accommodation in every case. In some countries, the DEA has simply acknowledged the futility of getting anything accomplished by a resident agent and closed the country office. That reportedly was the action taken in Paraguay, where the local police had to steer clear of interfering in the drug trafficking activities of the military who run the country. The opposite tack was pursued in the Bahamas for a brief period. There the two resident DEA agents, a Miami-based FBI agent, and the embassy's chargé d'affaires (who was in charge pending the arrival of a new ambassador) pursued an aggressive law enforcement policy that thoroughly antago-

---

ment, in which he argues that "under conditions of increased enforcement, those traffickers most willing and able to use violence and corruption to avoid punishment—the ones who most resemble 'organized crime'—will gain competitive advantages over their rivals." See Mark A. R. Kleiman, "Allocating Federal Drug Enforcement Resources: The Case of Marijuana" (Ph.D. diss., Harvard University, 1985).

83. Copies of the DEA administrators' letters to Noriega are reproduced in *Drugs, Law Enforcement, and Foreign Policy—Panama: Hearings Before the Subcommittee on Terrorism, Narcotics, and International Operations of the Senate Committee on Foreign Relations,* 100th Cong., 2d Sess., Part 2, (Feb. 8–11, 1988), 391–398.

nized the Pindling government. The activism in this case no doubt reflected a number of factors: the personalities of the agents, the presence of a State Department official interested in giving drug enforcement top priority, the vast influence of the United States over the Bahamas, and the fact that the Bahamas were regarded as the principal transit point for cocaine on its way from the Colombian coast to the southern part of the United States.

In the Bahamian case, however, pressures for a more conciliatory policy eventually won out. According to some reports, the DEA decided, or was told, not to reveal evidence it had obtained that strongly suggested drug payoffs had been given to Prime Minister Pindling. When the Bahamian Commission of Inquiry subpoenaed the U.S. agents who had dealt with the Bahamas, the DEA responded by sending the Miami special-agent-in-charge, who played down the tensions that had arisen. Pindling responded by agreeing to substantially increased cooperation, including an extensive U.S.-Bahamian joint interdiction effort codenamed Operation BAT and the commencement of negotiations on a treaty to improve cooperation in criminal prosecutions.[84]

In countries (most typically democracies) in which extensive personnel changes occur following elections and changes in the government, the levels of corruption and the DEA's capacity to work with corrupt officials follow a cyclical pattern. The worst corruption typically emerges toward the end of a political administration, be it a civilian or military regime, when officials actively pursue any and all opportunities to enrich themselves before leaving office. One agent discussed the typical evolution of a DEA agent's relationship with a *comandante* of the Mexican Federal Judicial Police during the *sexenio*:

> When a new *Federale* arrives in town, for instance at the beginning of a new presidential term, he has a couple of incentives to cooperate with the DEA. First, he needs DEA most then. Usually his predecessor will leave nothing but an empty filing cabinet—if that. So he must rely on DEA to find out who is who and what is what. Second, he has an interest in making a statement, cracking down hard soon after his arrival to show who's in charge. Thus, during the first year or so, DEA will tend to get excellent cooperation from him.

84. Joel Brinkley, "In Fighting Drug Traffic, Attitude Wins the Aid," *New York Times*, Oct. 7, 1986, A28.

Sometime during the first year, the traffickers will try to cut deals with the commandante to buy protection. So the commandante starts receiving offers: a car, an apartment, a house, women, free dining and travel, and so on. Eventually, he decides which offers he will accept. Then he and the chosen traffickers will reach a special understanding, usually involving a retainer. The traffickers understand that if they do anything stupid, the police will have to act. But there is also an understanding that he will not pursue them too hard. He will stall and find ways to avoid cooperating with other authorities, such as the DEA, who have targeted the traffickers. There are many subtle aspects to this, but eventually the DEA agent will get the message. At that point, there is often little he can do.

During the next three years, the DEA agent will often get great cooperation in any operations not involving one of the commandante's special relationships. It is important to understand that unlike most Latin American police, a Mexican *Federale* is a great cop, when he's being a cop. They can also be pretty rough, but they know how to get the job done.

The last year or two, however, cooperation can really go down hill. Everyone is trying to make a killing before he leaves office. As the end of the term nears, the chances for any cooperation get very slim. By that point, there is almost nothing the DEA can do.

Probably seventy five percent of DEA-*Federale* relationships fit this model. The other twenty five percent don't because of bad relations. The two don't hit it off, the *Federale* is insecure, he's greedy, he's anti-U.S., any number of things.

Is this "corruption"? By U.S. standards, sure—although the U.S. has lots of corruption itself. But in Latin America, that's just the way the system works. Every cop goes along with it or he's out.[85]

One option available to the DEA agent, although it may entail risks to his relationship, involves deceiving the local agent. For instance, the DEA agent may persuade the local agent to arrest a trafficker who, unknown to the local agent, has high-level protection from someone superior to the local agent or outside his or her jurisdiction. When the

85. This is a nonverbatim quote that has been reconstructed from my notes.

heat comes down on the local agent, the DEA agent may blame the informant or create some other excuse. Obviously, the willingness of a DEA agent to utilize such techniques depends upon his or her assessment of the risks to the local agent and the quality of the relationship between the two.

Another tactic to circumvent corrupt officials to which DEA agents often resort is withholding information until the very last minute of an operation. Since most traffickers of any substance have contacts within the police who are paid to provide them with information and warnings of impending raids, the DEA is often frustrated by leaks before major operations. Throughout the 1980s, police raids aimed at arresting such major traffickers as the Bolivian Roberto Suárez Gómez and the Colombians Pablo Escobar Gaviria and Carlos Lehder Rivas arrived at their destinations only to find the houses empty and the refineries shut down. To minimize the potential for such leaks, the DEA agent often tries to withhold the identity of a target of a planned raid until the local agents involved are no longer in a position to notify the target. Typically, a trusted senior local agent will be provided with the information, since often DEA has no choice, but on occasion no one will be told until after the operation has commenced. Only when all the agents are already in the car or helicopter en route to the target will the ultimate destination be revealed to the driver or pilot.

Because most countries in Latin America have at least two agencies that play overlapping roles in drug enforcement, the DEA can often work with the one that is less corrupt. In 1984–85, for instance, the DEA office in Peru had reduced its reliance on the increasingly corrupt Peruvian Investigative Police (PIP) in favor of the somewhat less corrupt Guardia Civil, although it retained its links with a few PIP officers who had proven relatively cooperative. In Chile during the same period, drug-related corruption in the Investigaciones had become so extensive that the DEA office had refused to work with them and was relying solely on the Caribineros. Although some agencies seem to have long-standing biases for or against extensive corruption, variations do occur over time, particularly following large-scale overhauls or the appointment of new officials at the top of the agency. In a few countries, the DEA may work with one agency in one city and another agency elsewhere. For instance, in Ecuador the two agencies involved in drug enforcement, Denactie and Interpol (no relation to the international Interpol), were far from immune from corrupting influences. They also were fierce competitors, with the drug section of Interpol, the national police agency under the Minister of Interior, resentful of the upstart Denactie, which had been created in the Justice Ministry at the DEA's urging with the hope that it would become an elite police force. Each was headed by both honest and corrupt officials during the 1980s, and the DEA's working relationships varied accordingly. At one point, when corruption was within tolerable but troublesome limits in both agencies, the Quito DEA office worked only with Interpol and the Guayaquil office only with Denactie. The split reflected both personal relationships and different degrees of corruption among the local agents.

A DEA agent also can exact some leverage from the fact that most foreign law enforcement agencies are highly dependent upon the DEA for leads and other information. Such access is important for making the arrests and seizures an agency needs to justify itself bureaucratically and politically. It also is useful for less-legitimate purposes, such as maintaining some control over the illicit drug market for corrupt purposes. The DEA's intelligence, used corruptly, can provide opportunities to extort money from drug traffickers and to seize drugs that will be resold rather than turned in as evidence for prosecution. When the local DEA office ostracizes an agency that is deemed too corrupt to work with in preference for working solely with a competitor agency, the former consequently loses a valuable creator of both legitimate and illegitimate opportunities.

One factor that has particularly complicated the DEA's efforts in Latin America has been the intense competition between law enforcement agencies. This has especially been so when the DEA has chosen to work solely with one agency to the exclusion of another. In such cases, relations between the two have become quite nasty, with the more corrupt unit trying to undermine its competitor by arresting its informants and agents, spreading rumors and planting evidence implicating them in drug trafficking, and even threatening, wounding, and killing the competitor agency's informants and agents. From the DEA's perspective, such virulent competition is particularly problematic when the target is an agency with whom it has developed a good working relationship. On the other hand, the DEA has occasionally benefited from such competition when corrupt agents and traffickers under their protection have been arrested by a competitor agency.

Elsewhere, DEA agents have encountered problems where the arresting unit in a police agency has undermined the intelligence unit with which the DEA agents have been working. In both Bolivia and Argentina during the mid-1980s, for instance, the DEA developed very good relationships with select units in the national police that had the capacity to develop and undertake sustained drug investigations. These units, however, were considered primarily as intelligence units and thus lacked the authority to make arrests in drug cases. As an investigation neared completion, the unit was obliged to call in the drug enforcement unit of the national police agency to make the arrest. In both countries, the drug units demonstrated exceptional capacities for corruption. On numerous occasions, DEA agents and the police unit collaborating with them saw cases developed over many months destroyed shortly after arrest because the target had succeeded in bribing the drug unit to eliminate the evidence or otherwise undermine the case. Although the DEA tried to circumvent corruption in the narcotics units and pressured them to cooperate, its efforts met with scant success. The uncorrupted police units, moreover, typically refrained from reporting their fellow officers' corruption because of their loyalty to the national police agency.

Even where the DEA has created or identified a relatively corruption-free agency with which it can work, the ultimate objective of putting the high-level traffickers in jail for any length of time has remained elusive. Any high-level trafficker who is so careless or unfortunate as to get arrested in the first place still has multiple opportunities to gain freedom. He or she can bribe other police agencies who may have become involved, or the *fiscal* (prosecutor), or the judge, or, as a last resort, the prison warden. In the absence of overwhelming political and/or public pressure to punish the trafficker, it is a rare criminal of any means who will not be able to avoid a lengthy stay in jail. In exceptional cases, pressures emanating from the U.S. government and occasionally from the local media and politicians have managed to keep a major trafficker in prison for a longer period of time. As for the officials who are implicated in drug-related corruption and obliged to resign, they almost never spend any time at all in prison. More often than not, they are simply transferred to another district or agency. Some quietly leave office and maintain a low presence until the storm has passed.

The inability of the DEA, and the U.S. government in general, to follow through on cases after the arrest stage has represented the greatest failing of the DEA's transnational efforts to deal with drug-related corruption in Latin America. Often all DEA efforts to circumvent police corruption have come to naught as soon as higher-level judicial officials have entered the picture. As in Europe, the extent of the DEA's contact with *fiscals* usually depends on how closely *fiscals* in the country work with the police. In Mexico, for instance, where police and *fiscals* often work fairly closely, DEA agents have tended to become familiar with them. Elsewhere in Latin America, the relationship has often been far more distant and formal, in good part because of the strong class divisions that separate them. But even where local police and *fiscals* work closely together, DEA agents often are reluctant to pursue cases through the courts for another reason. As one New York City police officer said regarding the frustration of seeing criminals whom one had arrested go free a short while later: "What happens in the courts is somebody else's business—we teach that in the academy—and if cops allowed themselves to be frustrated, they'd be doing nothing in the streets."[86] Many DEA agents abroad find it difficult to alter the police mind-set in which their role is largely over once the criminal is arrested. And even where they do adapt, the options for dealing with corruption among prosecutors and judges are far more limited than they are with respect to the police.

Corruption in the higher reaches of law enforcement systems is particularly debilitating, not just because it renders futile the successful investigations and arrests of uncorrupted police officials but also because it undermines their morale and weakens whatever incentive they may have had to remain honest. When police believe that any wealthy or powerful criminal they arrest will be able to gain freedom by bribing a prosecutor or judge, the incentive to pocket the bribe personally can become both logical and irresistible. When the DEA does succeed in obliging its counterparts to resist drug-related corruption, the chief impact is often to shift the financial benefit from police agent to judge. Only in cases that generate either extensive publicity or U.S. pressure must the judge beware of crossing the DEA.

Obviously, levels of judicial corruption vary widely from country to country, from court to court, and even from year to year. In Ecuador during the mid-1980s, judges reportedly competed, and even bid, to hear drug-related cases because those presented the most lucrative opportunities. In Argentina, the judge who rejected a U.S. extradition request for the former Bolivian interior minister, Luis Arce Gómez, was

86. Jane Gross, "In the Trenches of a War Against Drugs," *New York Times*, Jan. 8, 1986, B4.

rumored to have received half a million dollars for his decision. Similarly, corruption of the judiciary has been rampant in Mexico, Bolivia, and Peru, although many honest judges can still be found in those countries. In Colombia, where traffickers are known to shoot before offering a bribe and where the tradition of judicial rectitude is stronger, many judges resist placement in districts where drug cases abound. So great is the drug traffickers' power to intimidate in Colombia that even the Colombian supreme court has caved in to their threats. After upholding the validity of an extradition treaty between the United States and Colombia that authorized the extradition of Colombian citizens, the supreme court saw half its members murdered in a 1985 attack by the guerrilla group M-19 that many believe was organized at the behest of the drug traffickers. During the following two years, another justice was murdered and two chief justices in succession resigned when the threats became too fierce.[87] The result was a persistent effort during the 1980s by a majority of the supreme court to abdicate any responsibility over cases involving the drug traffickers.[88]

The abundant possibilities of securing one's cooperation by corrupt means are supplemented by the significant potential that legitimate legal procedures offer. Most police in less-developed countries are even less likely than their U.S. counterparts to abide by all the procedural requirements of the law, such as obtaining a proper warrant, in carrying out their operations. In all these countries, as in the United States, high-priced and sophisticated legal counsel are available to take every advantage of technicalities and loopholes in the law to protect their client. In some countries, of course, a drug trafficker may still have to pay a judge to go by the book, but the legal route is frequently an important option for the trafficker with the means to pay his or her way through it.

Most DEA efforts abroad seek to immobilize drug traffickers by having them arrested, prosecuted, and incarcerated in Latin American prisons. But the most effective tactics have involved getting major traf-

87. Supreme Court President Fernando Uribe Restrepo resigned in March 1986 after four months in office. His successor, Nemesio Camacho Rodriguez, resigned in January 1987. See *Miami Herald*, Jan. 22, 1987, 4A.

88. In early 1987, the Colombian supreme court invalidated the extradition treaty on a technicality. When the defect was corrected, the court was no longer empowered to rule on extradition requests. In March 1987, it declared unconstitutional the state-of-siege measures enacted by the Barco government that gave the military special powers to judge civilians arrested in drug trafficking cases. See "Colombia Resurrects Extradition Treaty," *Miami Herald*, Dec. 16, 1986, 15A; and *Latin American Monitor—Andean Group*, Apr. 1987, 405.

fickers into U.S. courts by formal extradition procedures, less formal deportation orders, and informal rendition tactics. These are analyzed in detail in Chapter Seven. Suffice it to say at this point that no method of immobilization has stimulated more innovation by U.S. agents than the informal rendition of fugitives from abroad. Both drug traffickers and law enforcers know that once a drug trafficker is on a plane to the United States the possibilities of buying or intimidating one's way to freedom are nil.

Conclusion

Corruption is not the only obstacle to immobilizing major drug traffickers in Latin America and the Caribbean; indeed, some DEA agents would say that the underfinancing and poor training of police throughout Latin America constitute equally severe obstacles. Nor is corruption solely or even principally responsible for the continuing flow of illicit drugs to the United States and Europe. Even if corruption in Latin America and the Caribbean were far less severe, drug traffickers would continue to thrive just as they do in Europe and the United States. Nonetheless, drug-related corruption has substantially hindered the DEA's efforts to immobilize major drug traffickers in Latin America and the Caribbean.

With no more than a hundred agents stationed throughout all of Latin America and the Caribbean, and entirely bereft of any extraterritorial police powers, the DEA has been hard-pressed in pursuing its objective. Yet as we have seen, DEA agents have devised means of working above and around the corruption that infests criminal justice agencies throughout the region. They have pleaded, cajoled, threatened, and tricked their local counterparts into cooperating with them. Relying both on the diplomatic leverage exercised by the U.S. ambassador, and on the transnational police subculture that unites police the world over, DEA agents have succeeded in immobilizing many top traffickers who thought they had purchased their safety. Indeed, by 1990 virtually every one of the most notorious drug traffickers of the previous decade was either dead or in prison. In many cases, DEA agents have gone well beyond the privileges accorded them as representatives of a foreign police agency. Their diplomatic efforts, if their activities in the region can be called that, have most closely resembled those of the CIA and various nongovernmental transnational organizations in their pursuit of a common mission around the world and in their persistent but discreet disregard of sovereign prerogatives.

The intensity and pervasiveness of drug-related corruption can be explained in many ways: as a consequence of the creation and failure of the global drug prohibition regime; as an extension and magnification of preexisting patterns and traditions of governmental behavior throughout Latin America and the Caribbean; as a natural response of economically impoverished peoples and regions to an immensely lucrative economic opportunity; as a function of "overcriminalization"; and as a consequence of what the criminologist Donald Cressey called "multiple moralities."[89] Unlike other obstacles that hinder U.S. international law enforcement efforts in this region and elsewhere, the frictions generated by drug-related corruption are likely to prove far more resilient. Governments can change their laws to better accord with U.S. preferences and modi operandi, and foreign law enforcement agencies can adapt U.S. approaches to criminal investigation, but there is little the U.S. government can do to undermine the temptations presented by drug trafficker bribes and threats. Among all the obstacles to the long-term harmonization of criminal justice systems, governmental corruption represents the most resilient.

It thus is difficult to foresee an end to the drug-related corruption that pervades Latin American and Caribbean governments so long as the international market for marijuana, cocaine, and heroin remain both lucrative and illegal. In a few cases, such as Mexico in the mid-1970s, successful drug eradication programs succeeded in destroying most of the illicit crops for a number of years, thereby limiting the availability of corrupting opportunities. But within a few years, the same officials responsible for the successful programs succumbed to the temptations proffered by the drug traffickers. Throughout virtually all of Latin America and the Caribbean, no government has succeeded in devising a means of institutionalizing checks against corruption. Resources are lacking to pay government employees enough so that they will not feel dependent upon accepting bribes to maintain a decent standard of living. Governmental elites are often too few in number for officials to deal

89. Donald R. Cressey, "Why Managers Engage in Fraud," in *White Collar Crime: Hearings Before the Senate Committee on the Judiciary*, 99th Cong., 2d Sess. (1986), 112–140.

with corruption by arresting one another. Legitimate economic opportunities are typically too limited to condemn with conviction those who seize the opportunity to profit from the drug traffic. And black markets are too pervasive, and often too essential to local economies, to contemplate any radical change in popular perceptions of legitimate versus illegitimate economic activity. The cumulative impact of U.S. economic assistance programs, witness protection programs, and other aid to Latin American and Caribbean criminal justice agencies pales beside the power of the incentives associated with drug-related corruption.

Most DEA agents who have spent time in Latin America and the Caribbean recognize the contextual limitations on what they can accomplish. But in many respects that does not matter, for their task is relatively straightforward: to immobilize drug traffickers. The fact that all their efforts have almost entirely failed to curtail the flow of illicit drugs to the United States pales beside the fact that they have essentially succeeded in their basic objective. The drug-related corruption that they encounter each day is regarded not as something to be reformed but as a challenge to be circumvented, circumscribed, transcended and occasionally used to their advantage. The process of dealing with it day in and day out is exceptionally frustrating. Some agents are overcome with a profound sense of cynicism, and others occasionally ponder the existentialist question of what it's all about anyway. But for most, the chase is the challenge—one in which they eventually prevail.

Chapter Six

International Evidence-Gathering

The Challenges

Obtaining evidence from abroad—in a form admissible in American judicial proceedings—is as essential to the success of criminal prosecutions as collecting intelligence and obtaining the offender. It is also the most dependent upon legal formalities and affords the least latitude for the sorts of informal measures and understandings upon which police normally rely in their international dealings. The obstacles are varied. Differences between national law enforcement systems—in particular, between the adversarial, common law system of the United States and the inquisitorial, civil law system found in much of Europe and Latin America—generate confusions, misunderstandings, and tensions that even the most cooperatively inclined of officials find difficult to circumvent. Foreign courts are unfamiliar with the constitutional safeguards and evidentiary rules of U.S. law, and U.S. courts regard foreign legal processes as equally strange. Prosecutors and judges may lack the legal authority to obtain evidence on behalf of foreign judicial proceedings. Local laws may bar foreign law enforcement authorities from engaging in even the most limited judicial tasks. Justice ministries may lack any officials charged with oversight of international requests for evidence. Long-standing laws and traditions may require elaborate procedures for the transnational collection and transmission of evidence. And, most seriously, financial and corporate secrecy laws as well as blocking statutes designed specifically to limit the availability of information to inquiring parties may impede prosecutors' efforts to secure essential documents.

The demands of American prosecutors for evidence located abroad have risen dramatically since the 1960s. The reasons are varied. Traditional transnational criminal activities such as drug trafficking, terrorism, tax evasion, and assorted frauds have proliferated. Congress has both criminalized and asserted extraterritorial jurisdiction over an ever-widening array of transnational activities and granted U.S. law enforcement agencies greater extraterritorial powers. The internationalization of the securities and commodities markets has required the Securities and Exchange Commission (SEC) and the Commodity Futures Trading Commission (CFTC) to expand the scope of their regulatory efforts overseas. And all of the federal law enforcement agencies have become far more aggressive in targeting, investigating, and prosecuting transnational activities. Where once the need to collect bank or corporate records from overseas, or to locate and interview witnesses abroad, was sufficient to deter an investigator or prosecutor from pursuing an investigation or prosecution, today law enforcement authorities have a growing number of increasingly effective mechanisms to secure such evidence.

The pace of developments in the area of international evidence-gathering is such that any analysis becomes rapidly dated. New treaties and other international agreements are being negotiated by the Justice Department, the Treasury Department, the SEC, and the CFTC each year. New legislation is being enacted by Congress in one session after another. Growing numbers of federal and even state prosecutors are looking and traveling abroad in search of evidence, and the more innovative among them are devising new and increasingly effective means of obtaining that evidence. Federal courts are deciding dozens of relevant cases annually, and generally validating the prosecutors' innovations. New offices charged with responsibility for international law enforcement are popping up throughout the federal law enforcement bureaucracy. Foreign states are similarly enacting new laws and regulations—sometimes of their own initiative, sometimes in response to U.S. examples, actions and pressures—with great import for U.S. evidence-gathering efforts. And international meetings, conventions, and organizations are introducing resolutions, promoting and adopting model legislation, and otherwise attempting to facilitate international cooperation in the transmission of evidence.

All of these efforts can be seen as part and parcel of a global campaign—inspired originally by the United States but increasingly involving multinational initiatives—to better immobilize transnational criminals by obtaining the evidence required not just to indict and convict them in courts of law but also to freeze, seize, and forfeit their assets. As with other domains of international law enforcement, the broader story is one of trying both to transcend the basic obstacles created by notions of national sovereignty and to alleviate the frictions that occur when different law enforcement systems are obliged to interact; one in which the United States has made modest accommodations to foreign legal systems, and foreign authorities have made much greater accommodations to U.S. demands; one in which cooperative efforts have mixed with more coercive inducements; and one involving not just bilateral treaties and other arrangements but also unilateral measures and multilateral undertakings. On one level, the mutual legal assistance treaty (MLAT) negotiations analyzed below can be seen as quite fascinating exercises in comparative law in which U.S. and foreign government negotiators struggled to reconcile different legal systems and thereby reduce the frictions that had impeded international evidence-gathering efforts. On another level, however, many of the MLATs must be understood in the context of the bilateral conflicts generated by U.S. efforts to obtain evidence unilaterally, efforts designed both to obtain evidence in individual investigations and prosecutions and to pressure foreign governments more generally to be more accommodating to U.S. law enforcement needs. Indeed, the principal incentive for many foreign governments to negotiate MLATs with the United States was, and remains, the desire to curtail the resort by U.S. prosecutors, police agents, and courts to unilateral, extraterritorial means of collecting evidence from abroad. (See Appendix E for a list of MLATs signed by the United States between 1973 and 1992.)

The principal targets of U.S. extraterritorial evidence-gathering efforts have been multinational banks and other corporations. The increasing power, resources, and scope of multinational corporations during the twentieth century has been perceived variously as a challenge to the sovereign powers of all states and as a development favoring the interests of more-powerful states at the expense of less-powerful states.[1] The history of international law enforcement in recent decades lends strong support to the latter view. Multinational corporations have provided, most notably for the United States, a vicarious means of extending the state's sovereign powers extraterritorially.[2] Not just American multinational corporations, but foreign ones as well, have found that their affiliates and other contacts within the United States render all their operations outside the United States susceptible to court orders and sanctions imposed by U.S. courts as well as other requirements of U.S. law. Foreign companies have found themselves subject to American antitrust laws and export control laws; foreign banks have been ordered to hand over to U.S. criminal justice authorities financial documents stored in branches outside the United States, often in the face of financial secrecy laws and blocking statutes to the contrary. These extraterritorial extensions of jurisdiction have not been available to most states; the United States' capacity to make the most of these options has reflected not just the fact that almost all major multinational firms maintain affiliates and other contacts in the United States, but also the fact that those contacts are sufficiently important that foreign firms are willing to tolerate the extraterritorial assertions of the United States as a necessary cost of doing business. The broader point, however, is that even as the proliferation of transnational interactions has challenged the state's control of its territory, the same process has also provided opportunities for expanding its jurisdictional reach.

This chapter provides abundant evidence of the *harmonization* of criminal justice systems along lines suggested and dictated by the United States. The MLATs, with their emphasis on reconciling the needs,

1. Raymond Vernon, *Sovereignty at Bay* (New York: Basic Books, 1971).

2. This point is touched upon in Richard Cooper, "Economic Interdependence and Foreign Policy in the Seventies," *World Politics* 24 (1972), 169–170; and in Louis T. Wells Jr., "The Multinational Business Enterprise," in Robert O. Keohane and Joseph S. Nye Jr., eds., *Transnational Relations and World Politics* (Cambridge, Mass.: Harvard University Press, 1972), 111. It is consistent, moreover, with the basic thrust of Robert Gilpin's thesis that "the multinational corporation is actually a stimulant to the further extension of state power in the economic realm." See Robert Gilpin, "The Politics of Transnational Economic Relations," in ibid., 69.

procedures, and customs of different legal systems, epitomize the notion of *accommodation*. The promotion of model legislation and the enactment of legislation by many governments criminalizing activities such as insider trading and money laundering provide ample evidence of the *homogenization* of criminal norms. The proliferation of transgovernmental links among prosecutors and Justice Ministry officials of different nations, as well as the creation of governmental offices specializing in international law enforcement matters, exemplifies the *regularization* of international law enforcement. My principal objective in this chapter is to explain how U.S. law enforcement officials have accomplished this harmonization. But the analysis also advances two of the principal arguments of this book: that the U.S. "war on drugs" has provided the crucial impetuses for many of the most substantial developments in the internationalization of U.S. criminal law enforcement since the late 1960s, and that criminal justice systems throughout much of the world are evolving toward a more harmonious network of relationships strongly influenced by U.S. pressures, models, and examples.

I should, in all fairness, include a word of warning to the reader at this point. This chapter, to a greater extent than any other, addresses fairly technical issues in U.S. and foreign laws. Unlike most law review articles, it focuses its attentions on the perceptions and behavior of government officials involved in efforts to collect evidence abroad and to reduce the tensions that have hampered such efforts in the past. More attention is also devoted to the political and criminal justice contexts of these efforts. But it is impossible to explain the internationalization of evidence-gathering without reference to U.S. and foreign statutes and legal procedures. New federal statutes and legal innovations devised by prosecutors and approved by U.S. courts have significantly enhanced the capacity of prosecutors to obtain evidence from abroad. At the same time, many of the constraints that continue to complicate international evidence-gathering efforts and to hinder the admissibility in U.S. courts of the evidence that is obtained stem from the strictures imposed by the U.S. Constitution and the Federal Rules of Evidence. In short, the internationalization of law enforcement cannot be fully understood without some reference to the legal and somewhat technical issues addressed in this chapter.[3]

3. Readers interested in a *more* technical and comprehensive treatment of these issues should consult Michael Abbell and Bruno A. Ristau, *International Judicial Assistance* (Washington, D.C.: International Law Institute, 1990), vol. 3.

The analogy to interstate law enforcement cooperation within the United States and other federally constituted nations is useful for understanding both the objectives and the limitations of evidence-gathering efforts across borders. The interstate compacts and uniform acts to which most American states subscribe share much in common with the more multilateral efforts of national governments to facilitate international cooperation in criminal justice matters. Indeed, domestic uniform acts have provided models for the U.S. negotiators of international law enforcement treaties, and the treaties have been described as the natural extensions of those acts. Similarly, judicial decisions regarding the cross-border collection of evidence within the United States have provided legal analogues for addressing issues of international evidence gathering. We will see in the next chapter that the same analogies have also influenced the development of law and practice regarding the rendition of fugitives. There are, of course, substantial limitations to the federalist analogy. Absent is any supranational entity akin to the federal government. National legal systems are far more heterogeneous than the legal systems of the American states, with the partial exception of Louisiana's. And differences in languages and customs are far more pronounced in the international realm. But the fundamental objectives and challenges of collecting evidence from "foreign" jurisdictions do not differ substantially from the federal to the international system.

Letters Rogatory: The Origins of International Evidence-Gathering

Both the MLAT negotiations and many of the other initiatives intended to facilitate the collection of evidence from abroad can be understood as responses to the inadequacy of pre-existing methods. The principal means of requesting evidence from foreign authorities even today is by "letters rogatory"—written requests from a court in one state to a foreign court requesting the provision of evidence or some other form of assistance needed in a judicial proceeding. Law enforcement officials typically resort to letters rogatory when Interpol and other international police channels are unable to produce the requested evidence, typically because a court's authority is required to obtain the evidence. Governments vary dramatically, however, in the degree to which they require that requests for law enforcement assistance be transmitted by letters rogatory. Where some are willing, for instance, to obtain documents, conduct an interview, identify an unlisted telephone number, or undertake a joint undercover operation in response to a request forwarded via Interpol or a police liaison, others require that the request be transmitted by letter rogatory. Many U.S. requests, particularly those directed to financial secrecy jurisdictions such as Switzerland, Luxembourg, Liechtenstein, and the Caribbean islands, seek bank documents; some are for corporate documents, such as shipping bills; some request that a foreign court compel a suspect or witness to provide testimony; others seek permission for a U.S. law enforcement official or defense attorney to interview a suspect or witness, accompany a local official on such a requested interview, or attend and participate in a foreign judicial proceeding. During the 1980s, the Justice Department began to use letters rogatory to request that foreign governments freeze the assets of suspected criminals.

Letters rogatory remain the principal means of obtaining evidence from abroad and can be relatively effective when dealing with foreign authorities who are familiar with both the letters rogatory process and U.S. evidentiary requirements. They have proven ill-suited, however, to the increasingly complex and voluminous needs of modern international law enforcement efforts.[4] MLATs, and the legislation typically required to implement them, were intended and designed to remedy many of the limitations of letters rogatory. Whereas letters rogatory are executed solely as a matter of comity, MLATs obligate the requested country to provide evidence and other forms of assistance. Whereas letters rogatory are typically transmitted circuitously, passing through assorted layers of justice ministries and diplomatic channels on their way from one court to another, MLAT requests bypass both U.S. courts and all diplomatic channels, thereby drastically shortening the time required to secure foreign assistance. Unlike letters rogatory, MLATs can establish a procedural framework for ensuring that the evidence obtained will be admissible in U.S. courts; they also can require that requests under the treaty, as well as the responses to those requests, be kept confidential. And, most important, MLATs (and the accompanying implementing legislation) provide a powerful means of penetrating the financial secrecy laws that have so often frustrated U.S. criminal investigators.[5]

4. Harry Leroy Jones, "International Judicial Assistance: Procedural Chaos and a Program for Reform," *Yale Law Journal* 62 (1953), 515–562, esp. 554.

5. See "Prepared Statement of Mark M. Richard," in U.S. Senate, *Mutual Legal Assis-*

In 1927, fifty years before the first MLAT negotiated by the United States, with Switzerland, went into force, a Committee of Experts for the Progressive Codification of International Law, which had been appointed by the Assembly of the League of Nations, asked member nations to consider whether it was possible "to establish by means of general convention provisions concerning the communication of judicial and extra-judicial acts in penal matters and letters rogatory in penal matters."[6] Eighteen countries responded favorably to the codification proposal; Great Britain and four other members of the Commonwealth expressed their preference for bilateral agreements rather than a general convention, and one—the United States—dissented without offering any alternative.[7] In its view, no agreement was possible in light of state jurisdiction over criminal procedure and the restraints imposed by the Sixth Amendment of the U.S. Constitution.[8] The rare foreign judicial authority persistent enough to seek evidence in the United States by means of letter rogatory was more than likely to find the request ignored or rejected. Although Congress had enacted legislation in 1855 authorizing U.S. courts to execute foreign letters rogatory, the statute was inadvertently but severely restricted thereafter by later legislation and by the reluctance of U.S. courts to facilitate foreign judicial requests.[9] Foreign requests were more likely to receive a favorable response in many state courts than in federal court.

In the aftermath of World War II, however, the new American consciousness of the global responsibilities of the United States began to penetrate the domain of international law enforcement. The process was facilitated by the increasing homogenization of state criminal procedures as the U.S. Supreme Court incorporated much of the Bill of Rights into the Fourteenth Amendment and as interstate compacts and uniform criminal codes proliferated. In 1948, Congress responded to the new

---

tance Treaty Concerning the Cayman Islands, 101st Cong., 1st Sess., Exec. Rept. No. 101-8 (1989), 95–96.

6. Jones, "International Judicial Assistance," 554.

7. Ibid., 557.

8. Ibid., 554, 557.

9. Walter B. Stahr, "Discovery Under 28 U.S.C. 1782 for Foreign and International Proceedings," *Virginia Journal of International Law* 30 (1990), 597–641. The 1855 legislation can be found at 10 Stat. 630 (1855). Examples of a U.S. court's belief that it was not empowered to execute a letter rogatory in a criminal case include *In re Letters Rogatory from Examining Magistrate of Tribunal of Versailles*, 26 F.Supp. 852 (D.Md. 1939), and *In re Letters Rogatory of Republic of Colombia*, 4 F.Supp. 165 (S.D.N.Y. 1933).

conditions, albeit somewhat meagerly, with legislation (thereafter referred to as Section 1782) authorizing an expansion of American judicial assistance to foreign states.[10] Many of the limitations of this legislation—including the failure to provide for compulsory process in obtaining evidence, and the requirements that the foreign proceeding be before a court and that only U.S. procedure be permitted in the taking of testimony—were ameliorated in 1964 when Congress enacted a substantially revised version of Section 1782.[11] Even so, U.S. courts continued to interpret the amendments—which had substituted the word "tribunal" for "court" in order to broaden the availability of U.S. assistance to include administrative and quasi-judicial proceedings[12]—so narrowly as to bar assistance to foreign law enforcement authorities not recognizable as "tribunals" in the eyes of the court.[13] In the absence of legal challenges by defendants, however, U.S. authorities were more often than not willing to extend foreign judicial authorities fairly broad latitude in collecting evidence in the United States.

When U.S. prosecutors and police looked abroad for evidence, they encountered many of the same types of obstacles, as well as even higher

10. Act of June 25, 1948, ch. 646, 62 Stat. 949 (codified at 28 U.S.C. Sec. 1782 (1976); amended to encompass criminal proceedings as well, in Act of May 24, 1949, ch. 139, 63 Stat. 103). See also *In re Letter Rogatory from the Justice Court, Dist. of Montreal, Canada*, 523 F.2d 562, 564–565 (6th Cir. 1975), the appendix of which contains the texts of the various historical congressional acts relating to letters rogatory from abroad. See too the discussion of these laws in Jones, "International Judicial Assistance" (supra n. 4), 541–542; and in R. Doak Bishop, "International Litigation in Texas: Obtaining Evidence in Foreign Countries," *Houston Law Review* 19 (1982), 361–426, esp. 416.

11. Brian Eric Bomstein and Julie M. Levitt, "Much Ado About 1782: A Look at Recent Problems with Discovery in the United States for Use in Foreign Litigation Under 28 U.S.C. 1782," *Inter-American Law Review* 20 (1989), 429–472; and Stahr, "Discovery Under 28 U.S.C. 1782" (supra n. 9), 604.

12. H.R. Rept. 1052, 88th Cong., 1st Sess. 9 (1963); S. Rept. 1580, 88th Cong., 2d Sess. 1, reprinted in 1964 U.S. Code Cong. & Ad. News 3782, 3788. See also Bruce I. McDaniel, "What Is Foreign Tribunal Within 28 U.S.C. Section 1782 (as amended in 1964) . . . ," *ALR Fed.* 46 (1980), 956–960; Morris H. Deutsch, "Judicial Assistance: Obtaining Evidence in the United States, Under 28 U.S.C. Section 1782, for Use in a Foreign or International Tribunal," *Boston College International and Comparative Law Review* 5 (1982), 175–193; Comment, "International Judicial Assistance," *Texas International Law Journal* 12 (1977), 106; Comment, "International Judicial Assistance," *Texas International Law Journal* 9 (1974), 108.

13. *In re Letters Rogatory Issued by the Director of Inspection of the Government of India*, 385 F.2d 1017 (2d Cir. 1967); *In re Letters of Request to Examine Witnesses from the Court of Queen's Bench for Manitoba, Canada*, 59 F.R.D. 625 (N.D. Cal. 1973), aff'd per curiam, 488 F.2d 511 (9th Cir. 1973); and, rejecting a request from Colombia, *Fonseca v. Blumenthal*, 620 F.2d 322 (2d Cir. 1980). See the discussion in "Much Ado About 1782," 437–444.

levels of sensitivity to the performance of U.S. judicial functions on foreign territory. Even more problematic were inadequacies in U.S. law regarding collection of evidence from abroad. Not until 1926, in the aftermath of the Teapot Dome scandal, did Congress pass legislation on the subject.[14] The Walsh Act provided federal courts with the authority to issue letters rogatory to foreign courts requesting them to compel U.S. citizens and domiciliaries to "appear and testify" before them, and to issue subpoenas to compel U.S. citizens or domiciliaries in foreign countries to appear in the United States as witnesses in federal criminal trials.[15] In 1936, Congress enacted legislation providing for the admissibility of foreign business records in federal criminal trials.[16] Neither of these statutes, however, was all that useful to federal prosecutors. Few foreign laws obliged their courts to employ their powers on behalf of foreign law enforcement authorities, much less to accommodate foreign judicial procedures. Foreign courts were prone to reject requests emanating from grand juries and various regulatory agencies that had no counterparts in their own countries. Some were reluctant to obtain any evidence for foreign criminal proceedings or to permit U.S. officials any leeway in collecting evidence. As in the United States, justice ministries abroad lacked any officials specifically charged with responding to letters rogatory. U.S. prosecutors seeking evidence from abroad consequently found themselves in much the same situation as American attorneys seeking evidence in private suits, obliged to hire foreign counsel to pursue their requests. Even when foreign courts were willing to provide evidence, the chances were good that it would be provided in a form inadmissible in U.S. courts. Civil law judges typically did not take kindly to altering their customary procedures to accommodate U.S. constitutional and evidentiary needs, such as the right of confrontation by defendants and the demand for verbatim transcripts of testimony. U.S. prosecutors mostly had little choice but to rely on the good will and flexibility of foreign judges. The only other alternative involved persuading individuals living abroad to come to the United States to testify in court.[17] More often than not, the mere prospect of trying to collect

14. See Abbell and Ristau, *International Judicial Assistance* (supra n. 3), 3:14.

15. Act of July 3, 1926, Ch. 762, Sec. 1, 44 Stat. 835 (1926). See Abbell and Ristau, *International Judicial Assistance*, 3:15, 145–147.

16. Act of June 20, 1936, Ch. 640, Sec. 2–8, 49 Stat. 1561. See Abbell and Ristau, *International Judicial Assistance*, 3:15.

17. The memoirs and biographies of U.S. law enforcement officials active in international law enforcement matters consistently refer to such suasive efforts. See Don Wilkie, as told to

evidence from a foreign state was sufficient to deter an American prosecutor from even pursuing a case in which crucial evidence could only be found abroad.

Section 1782 and its subsequent amendments did, however, represent part of a broader movement during the 1960s and 1970s to reconcile the differences between legal systems by standardizing or equating judicial procedures. These included the negotiation of three Hague conventions to which the United States became a party: the convention abolishing the requirement of legalization for foreign public documents;[18] the convention on the service abroad of judicial and extrajudicial documents in civil or commercial matters;[19] and the convention on the taking of evidence abroad in civil or commercial matters[20]—all of which, however, largely excluded criminal matters from their consideration. The movement also included the negotiation between 1976 and 1979 of approximately twenty-four "executive agreements" for international judicial assistance following the revelations that American companies (most notably the airplane manufacturers, Boeing, Lockheed, and McDonnell-Douglas) had paid bribes to foreign officials.[21] The hectic negotiation of these agreements set the stage to some degree for the negotiation of the far broader mutual legal assistance treaties. Other precedents for international cooperation against crime were being encouraged by the United States' promotion of multilateral treaties against terrorism[22] and

---

Mark Lee Luther, *American Secret Service Agent* (New York: Frederick A. Stokes Co., 1934), 202–203; Garland Roark, *The Coin of Contraband* (Garden City, N.Y.: Doubleday, 1964), 364; William H. Theobald, *Defrauding the Government* (New York: Myrtle Publishing Co., 1908), 172.

18. Done at the Hague, Oct. 5, 1961; entered into force for the U.S. Oct. 15, 1981; TIAS 10072; 527 UNTS 189.

19. Done at the Hague, Nov. 15, 1965; entered into force for the U.S. Feb. 10, 1969; 20 UST 361; TIAS 6638; 658 UNTS 163.

20. Done at the Hague, Mar. 18, 1970; entered into force for the U.S. Oct. 7, 1972; 23 UST 2555; TIAS 7444. See Sharon DeVine and Christine M. Olsen, "Taking Evidence Outside of the United States," *Boston University Law Review* 55 (1975), 368–386.

21. These treaties are listed and discussed in an article by the former director of the Justice Department's Office of Foreign Litigation, Bruno Ristau, "International Cooperation in Penal Matters: The 'Lockheed Agreements,' " in *Transnational Aspects of Criminal Procedure*, 1983 Michigan Yearbook of International Legal Studies (New York: Clark Boardman, 1983), 85–104.

22. Convention to Prevent and Punish the Acts of Terrorism Taking the Form of Crimes Against Persons and Related Extortion That Are of International Assistance (done at Washington Feb. 2, 1971; entered into force for the United States Oct. 20, 1976; 27 UST 3949; TIAS 8413). Also, Convention on the Prevention and Punishment of Crimes Against Internationally

hijacking.[23] Also important were amendments to Rule 15 of the Federal Rules of Criminal Procedure permitting federal prosecutors to take depositions from witnesses who refused or were unable to appear in court. The first amendment, in 1970, was limited to organized crime cases.[24] The second, in 1975, extended the new prosecutorial power to all federal criminal trials, thereby eliminating a substantial obstacle to federal prosecutions dependent upon evidence from abroad.[25]

Breaking the Ice the Hard Way: Treaty with Switzerland

By the late 1960s, U.S. law enforcement officials were increasingly exasperated by the widening gap between criminals' abilities to hide transactions and assets abroad and their own abilities to detect and investigate what was going on. Organized crime, it was feared, was growing ever richer and more powerful, at least in part because of the protection afforded by foreign financial secrecy jurisdictions such as Switzerland.[26] But efforts by U.S. criminal investigators to obtain evidence from these jurisdictions were blocked time and time again by the refusal of foreign banks and government officials to cooperate with American criminal investigations.

During 1967–68, officials in the State, Justice, and Treasury Departments, and the Securities and Exchange Commission, agreed to seek an accord with the Swiss. This was not the first attempt to persuade the Swiss to negotiate a mutual legal assistance treaty; previous efforts had failed in 1922, 1925, and 1938, and again in 1963.[27] The two govern-

---

Protected Persons Including Diplomatic Agents (done at New York Dec. 14, 1973; entered into force for the U.S. Feb. 20, 1977; 28 UST 1975; TIAS 8532).

23. The three antihijacking treaties, which entered into force for the U.S. between 1969 and 1973, are (1) at 20 UST 2941; TIAS 6768; 704 UNTS 219; (2) at 22 UST 1641; TIAS 7192; and (3) at 24 UST 564; TIAS 7570.

24. Pub. L. 91-452, Title VI, Sec. 601, 84 Stat. 934 (1970), 18 U.S.C. 3503.

25. See Abbell and Ristau, *International Judicial Assistance*, 3:15. See also Michael J. Burke, "*United States v. Salim*: A Harbinger for Federal Prosecutions Using Depositions Taken Abroad," *Catholic University Law Review* 39 (1990), 895–943.

26. See Nicholas Faith, *Safety in Numbers: The Mysterious World of Swiss Banking* (New York: Viking Press, 1982).

27. Lionel Frei and Stefan Treschel, "Origins and Applications of the United States–Switzerland Treaty on Mutual Assistance in Criminal Matters," *Harvard International Law Journal* 31 (1990), 77–97, esp. 78–79.

ments had also struggled since World War II over the efforts of the United States and other Allied powers to uncover Nazi assets hidden in Swiss banks, as well as the efforts of German companies, in particular a holding company associated with I. G. Farben's international operations, Interhandel, to recover its seized assets from the U.S. government.[28] By the late 1960s, however, the U.S. government was far more concerned with the Mafia's uses of Swiss banks than the Nazis' uses.

Although other financial secrecy jurisdictions were known to accommodate organized criminals, Switzerland was chosen as the first subject of negotiations for a number of reasons. First, U.S. law enforcement officials perceived Switzerland as the toughest case and believed that an agreement with Swiss authorities would provide an especially effective precedent. Second, the Swiss represented a significant problem in two respects: they had erected substantial legal barriers against supplying information to foreign investigators, and their bank and government officials, unlike those in many other bank secrecy jurisdictions, were professional and generally uncorruptible, thus narrowing the informal and illegal options otherwise often available to American investigators in other financial secrecy jurisdictions.[29] Third, the Americans perceived in the Swiss certain advantages that would facilitate an agreement. While Swiss laws strictly limited the divulsion of information to foreigners, they nonetheless allowed for broad disclosure to Swiss investigators. This differed from the laws in some other financial secrecy jurisdictions, such as Panama, which prohibited disclosure even to their own judicial officials. The Americans reasoned that if Swiss law could be changed to allow Swiss judicial authorities to collect evidence at the request of the United States, then many of the previous obstacles could be overcome. The Americans also counted on the strong sense of law and order for which the Swiss had earned a reputation. The Swiss were known to have

28. See Elliot A. Stultz, "Swiss Bank Secrecy and United States Efforts to Obtain Information from Swiss Banks," *Vanderbilt Journal of Transnational Law* 21 (1988), 63–125, esp. 81–91; see also Faith, *Safety in Numbers*, chaps. 2 and 4.

29. The Swiss were not entirely immune to illicit approaches. During the mid-1970s, French customs officials investigating exchange control violations succeeded in buying a list of French clients of the Swiss bank corporation from an informant, in violation of Swiss law. However, a similar effort in 1980 backfired when two French customs officials were arrested in Basel, prosecuted for economic espionage, and convicted. See Faith, *Safety in Numbers*, 338–342; and Claus Schellenberg, "The Proceedings Against Two French Customs Officials in Switzerland for Prohibited Acts in Favor of a Foreign State, Economic Intelligence Service, and Violation of the Banking Law," *International Business Lawyer* 9 (1981), 139–140.

been embarrassed by the publicity in the United States associating Swiss banking institutions with organized crime. At the very least, the Swiss perceived a need to appear to be cooperative with American initiatives against organized crime. Finally, the Americans were conscious of Swiss priorities in their conduct of foreign relations. As a small, prosperous, and historically neutral country, Switzerland had concentrated in its foreign affairs on staying out of trouble and making as few enemies as possible. Clearly, there were limits to which the Swiss could turn their backs on a serious American proposal.

In 1967, Fred Vincent, the assistant attorney general in charge of the Criminal Division, visited Switzerland to discuss the need for increased cooperation. The Swiss officials responded by suggesting that the two countries negotiate a mutual legal assistance treaty. Unlike the Americans, the Swiss were already party to one such treaty, the European Convention on Mutual Assistance in Criminal Matters, done at Strasbourg on April 20, 1959.[30] Although that treaty was to provide substantial guidance during the negotiations, it had not provided the Swiss with any experience in negotiating with a common law country. There was, to the best knowledge of both sides, no precedent for a mutual legal assistance treaty between a civil law state and a common law state. Pressures to begin formal negotiations increased substantially in December 1968, when the influential U.S. Attorney in Manhattan, Robert Morgenthau, harshly criticized the Swiss at a hearing of the House Committee on Banking and Currency. Negotiations began in earnest in April 1969, when Swiss and U.S. officials met in Washington to discuss organized crime, narcotics trafficking, and SEC violations, and "to define the means by which private Swiss facilities were used by Americans to further or conceal illegal activities."[31] Under continuing pressure from Congress, the Swiss government consented to extended and relatively open-ended negotiations.

Unlike most other negotiations in the criminal law area, the MLAT

30. European Treaty Series No. 30; a protocol added in 1978 is at European Treaty Series No. 99.

31. *Foreign Bank Secrecy and Bank Records: Hearings on H.R. 15073 Before the Committee on Banking and Currency, House of Representatives*, 91st Cong., 1st and 2d Sess. (1969–1970), 15 (statement of Assistant U.S. Attorney General Will Wilson). See the Treaty Between the United States of America and the Swiss Confederation on Mutual Assistance in Criminal Matters, signed May 25, 1973; 27 UST 2019; TIAS 8302 (effective Jan. 23, 1977). Both the text and a section-by-section analysis of the treaty appear in U.S. Senate Exec. F, 94th Cong., 2d Sess. (1976). See also U.S. Senate Exec. Rept. 94-29, 94th Cong., 2d Sess. (1976).

talks included relatively high-level officials on both sides, up to and including the respective ambassadors. The demands were relatively one-sided insofar as both parties expected most of the requests for evidence to emanate from the United States. It is not surprising that the internal Swiss consultative process proved to be far more involved and politically sensitive than the American, in part because articles in the Swiss press periodically heightened suspicions regarding the negotiations and American intentions. Many banking and business leaders were concerned that any compromise of Swiss financial secrecy laws would encourage investors to seek more secure havens for their funds elsewhere.[32] By late 1971, as the treaty began to take shape, the Swiss negotiators reached out to leaders in the banking and business communities whose support was deemed essential to ensure acceptance of the treaty by the Swiss cantons and ratification by the Swiss Federal Council. Banking and business leaders were invited to participate in the negotiations and to meet individually with the U.S. negotiators. Eventually, the educational and consensus-building process proved effective in assuaging the fears of the banking-business community and winning support for the treaty in the cantons and the national government.

The American objectives in the MLAT negotiations with the Swiss, and in most subsequent negotiations with other governments, were twofold. They wanted the Swiss to be more forthcoming in providing evidence requested by U.S. authorities, and they wanted to ensure that the evidence would be provided in a form that would be admissible in U.S. courts. These objectives would later be supplemented by more ambitious objectives, requiring the Swiss not merely to accommodate U.S. evidentiary demands but also to adopt the assumptions and objectives of U.S. law enforcement officials as their own. In the early 1970s, however, the American negotiators had no choice but to set their sights on the more limited objectives. Indeed, even they had only a hazy notion of where these first steps would lead two decades later.

The principal source of conflict in the negotiations was over the extent to which Americans would be allowed to pierce the veil of secrecy that shrouded Swiss bank transactions. The principal American objective required the Swiss to pierce the veil of secrecy created by Article 47 of the Swiss Banking Code and Article 273 of the Swiss Penal Code.[33] That

32. The opposition of the Swiss banking community to the proposed treaty is discussed in *New York Times*, Aug. 12, 1972, 29.

33. See esp. Mario Kronauer, "Information Given for Tax Purposes from Switzerland to

veil, the Swiss were quick to point out to the Americans, had been created in 1934 primarily to prevent the Nazi government from identifying and seizing the assets of Jewish depositors in Swiss banks. Indeed, some Swiss pointed out, the tradition of secrecy had originated some two centuries before, when Swiss co-religionists of persecuted minorities elsewhere had been obliged to protect their assets against the inquiries of acquisitive governments.

The veil consisted principally of two laws: Article 47 of the Swiss Banking Code (as amended in 1970), which provided that any officer or employee of a bank or any auditor or any officer or employee of the Banking Commission who violated the duty of secrecy, or anyone who induced or attempted to induce such a person to violate that duty, could be punished with up to six months imprisonment and fined up to 50,000 francs;[34] and the economic espionage provision of the Swiss Penal Code, Article 273, which made it a crime to "elicit a manufacturing or business secret in order to make it available to any foreign official agency or to a foreign organization or private enterprise" either directly or through an agent, and to make such secrets available to such foreign authorities or organizations.[35]

The two foremost concerns of the Swiss were to protect the identities of "innocent parties" (i.e., persons who appeared not to be connected in any way with the offense for which assistance was requested) and to prevent the Americans from using any evidence for tax purposes. With regard to the first concern, the Swiss practice had been to excise the names of innocent parties from documents requested by letters rogatory. This posed two problems for the Americans: it rendered the documents inadmissible in American courts (although not in Swiss courts), and it disrupted efforts to trace the transactions of criminals seeking to hide

---

Foreign Countries Especially to the United States for the Prevention of Fraud or the Like in Relation to Certain American Taxes," *Tax Law Review* 30 (1974), 47–99; Walter Meier, "Banking Secrecy in Swiss and International Taxation," *International Lawyer* 7 (1973), 16–45; and M. Magdalena Schoch, "What Is a Secret Swiss Bank Account?" in *Hearings on Foreign Bank Secrecy and Bank Records* (supra n. 31), 363–368. See also Kurt Mueller, "The Swiss Banking Secret," *International and Comparative Law Quarterly* 18 (1969), 360–377; and Note, "Secret Swiss Bank Accounts: Uses, Abuses, and Attempts at Control," *Fordham Law Review* 39 (1971), 500.

34. The article did not apply to federal and cantonal provisions concerning the duty to testify and the duty to present information to an official. See the translation of Art. 47 in Meier, "Banking Secrecy," 18.

35. Schoch, "What Is a Secret Swiss Bank Account?" 364.

their assets. The American negotiators were able to make only limited headway on this issue, conceding to the Swiss a provision by which each government reserved the right "to balance the interests of [the innocent party] . . . with the need and the importance of the criminal investigation or proceeding in the requesting State [i.e., the United States]."[36] The Swiss further reserved the right to exclude American representatives in situations (involving the execution of American requests) where banking or manufacturing secrets would be disclosed[37] and insisted on a provision in which the Americans agreed to seek a protective order limiting access to documents provided by the Swiss which disclosed the identity of innocent parties.[38] Finally, the treaty included a reserve clause permitting each state to refuse assistance to the extent that "the requested State considers that the execution of the request is likely to prejudice its sovereignty, security or similar essential interests."[39]

The second concern of the Swiss—that information provided by them not be used to prosecute tax and other fiscal offenses—remained the principal bone of contention in the last two years of the negotiations and was only resolved with a vague formulation just days before the treaty was signed. The Swiss insisted that any requests for assistance in tax matters come under the bilateral Income Tax Convention of May 24, 1951[40]—a treaty that was notably lacking in the eyes of U.S. tax and law enforcement authorities.[41] The MLAT negotiators ultimately arrived at "a compromise between the Swiss concept of specialty of use which, in effect, holds that information furnished pursuant to a request for assistance may only be used for the specific purpose for which it was furnished, and the view of the United States that properly obtained information or evidence should be usable for any purpose by the requesting State."[42] The compromise allowed the United States to use

36. See the technical analysis of the Swiss MLAT, U.S. Senate Exec. Doc. F (supra n. 31), 48.

37. See Art. 12 of the Swiss MLAT.

38. Ibid., Art. 15. An accompanying letter set forth the parties' understanding with respect to which this provision was limited by the Supreme Court's interpretations of the public trial provision of the Sixth Amendment.

39. Ibid., Art. 3.

40. Convention for the Avoidance of Double Taxation with Respect to Taxes on Income (signed at Washington May 24, 1951; entered into force Sept. 27, 1951; 2 UST 1751; TIAS 2316; 127 UNTS 227).

41. See Kronauer, "Information Given for Tax Purposes" (supra n. 33).

42. See the technical analysis of the Swiss MLAT, U.S. Senate Exec. Doc. F, 41–42.

the information in other cases so long as it notified the Swiss in advance, and so long as Swiss assistance could be given in those cases (i.e., not including cases involving fiscal offenses).[43]

Insofar as much of the impetus for the treaty negotiations had derived from the mutual concern over the advantage taken by organized crime of Swiss banking secrecy laws to hide their ill-begotten proceeds, the Swiss agreed to waive the limitations on cooperation in investigations involving organized crime figures. Indeed, the Swiss believed that the U.S. negotiators would refuse to sign any treaty that did not waive the dual criminality requirement to allow assistance in tax and other fiscal offenses involving organized crime figures.[44] The Swiss regarded the American practice—employed most famously in the prosecution of Al Capone—of prosecuting organized figures for income tax evasion when admissible evidence of more serious crimes could not be obtained as somewhat strange and distasteful.[45] They nonetheless agreed to make the furnishing of assistance obligatory in organized crime cases even where the alleged offenses neither met the dual criminality test nor were included in the Schedule. The Swiss insisted, however, on stringent criteria where assistance was requested to investigate income tax violations. Wary of American "fishing expeditions" and a flood of requests from prosecutors seeking information on the lower-echelon "runners" and "bagmen" of organized crime, the Swiss demanded that requests be limited to cases in which the evidence requested was absolutely essential to incarcerating "upper-echelon" figures for substantial periods of time. The American negotiators ultimately acceded to this formulation in the hope that the prophylactic effect of the treaty itself, combined with a few cases, would cause organized crime figures to move their funds from Switzerland.[46]

Persuading the Swiss to let down the veil of their secrecy laws represented only part of the American challenge in the negotiations. The

43. An additional compromise, designed to reconcile conflicting positions regarding the future use of a witness's testimony (in the requested state) in any later criminal proceeding (in the requesting state) against that witness, provided that such testimony was admissible only if the witness had been advised at the time of his or her appearance of his or her right under the treaty to refuse testimony on the basis of possible self-incrimination or any other privilege available in either state.

44. Frei and Treschel, "Origins and Applications of the Swiss MLAT" (supra n. 27), 83.

45. Ibid., 80. See *Capone v. U.S.*, 56 F.2d 927 (1932); John Kobler, *Capone: The Life and World of Al Capone* (New York: Fawcett Crest, 1971).

46. See Swiss MLAT, Arts. 6, 7, 8.

Americans also needed to familiarize the Swiss with American legal requirements and to create guidelines so that evidence provided by Swiss judicial officers under Swiss law would be delivered in a form that would be admissible in U.S. courts and without undue delay. Swiss law strictly forbade the performance of judicial functions by foreign officials on Swiss territory; exceptions were not even permitted for the most innocuous tasks.[47] Although U.S. law similarly prohibited foreign judicial functions on American territory,[48] the statute had not been strictly enforced. The Swiss, by contrast, had surprised a number of foreign government officials with the stringency of their application. Both French and Dutch government attorneys, for instance, had landed in jail for doing no more than deposing their own nationals located in Switzerland.[49] American law enforcement authorities were thus particularly dependent upon Swiss officials for the performance of all judicial tasks, but Swiss officials—in particular, those at the cantonal level responsible for conducting most law enforcement tasks—were unlikely to be familiar with the evidentiary and constitutional requirements of U.S. law.

The substantial differences between the nature of judicial proceedings in the two countries had been responsible for many of the misunderstandings that hindered the letters rogatory process. For instance, whereas the judge in a common law system typically plays a quite limited role in obtaining evidence, relying on the adversary process to perform this function, the civil law judge "conducts every aspect of the proceeding and questions all witnesses himself":

> All proceedings following the institution of the suit are considered as parts of the "trial," which may be conducted as a series of evidentiary hearings. The trial is not viewed as a separate, isolated event apart from the rest of the suit. In many civil-law nations,

47. According to Art. 271 of the Swiss Penal Code, "Whoever, on Swiss territory, without being authorized so to do, takes on behalf of a foreign government any action which is solely within the province of a [Swiss] government authority or a [Swiss] government official, whoever does anything to encourage such action, . . . shall be punished by imprisonment, in serious cases in the penitentiary" (Jones, "International Judicial Assistance" (supra n. 4), 520). Switzerland was not the only state with such a restriction on the taking of evidence by foreigners. Denmark, Iran, Liechtenstein, Luxembourg, Venezuela and Zambia were also among the countries that regarded such actions as an infringement of their national sovereignty. See DeVine and Olsen, "Taking Evidence Outside of the United States" (supra n. 20), 374.

48. See 18 U.S.C. 951.

49. Schellenberg, "Proceedings Against Two French Customs Officials" (supra n. 29).

> witnesses are not placed under oath before they testify, and cross-examination is virtually unknown. Evidence taken by the judge automatically becomes part of the record in the case, even though no verbatim transcript of the proceedings is made. Instead, the judge summarizes the testimony, which may be subscribed by the witness later. Furthermore, many countries regard it as improper for the lawyers to talk with the witnesses before they testify.[50]

Many of the MLAT's provisions were designed to authorize the two very different systems to accommodate each other's requirements. One provision, for instance, stated that assistance could be granted in "investigations or court proceedings in respect of offenses the punishment of which falls or would fall within the jurisdiction of the judicial authorities of the requesting State or a state or canton thereof." The intention of this wording was threefold: to avoid falling prey to litigation over the inclusiveness of a narrower term, such as the "tribunal" in the modified Section 1782; to make clear to civil law judges that grand jury proceedings and investigations by regulatory agencies, notably the SEC, warranted cooperation to the same degree as requests at more-advanced stages of a criminal investigation; and to meet the general requirements of dual criminality. The Swiss regarded the phrasing as a significant concession on their part, arguing that traditional continental European concepts restricted assistance to requests emanating from judicial authorities, not administrative agencies such as the SEC.[51]

Other portions of the treaty were similarly devoted to reconciling the differences between civil law and common law procedures. Most of these were relatively uncontroversial once both sides understood the concepts underlying the other's procedural requirements. Various provisions accordingly provided for the authentication of documents, the taking of evidence under oath, the protection of constitutional privileges such as that against self-incrimination, and the presence and participation of foreign officials, defendants, and other representatives in the judicial proceeding—measures all designed to incorporate as much as

50. Bishop, "International Litigation in Texas" (supra n. 10), 363–364; see also Rudolph B. Schlesinger, *Comparative Law*, 4th ed. (Mineola, N.Y.: Foundation Press, 1980), 398. A fine description of European courts by an American writer is Sybille Bedford's *The Faces of Justice: A Traveller's Report* (New York: Simon & Schuster, 1961).

51. Frei and Treschel, "Origins and Applications of the Swiss MLAT" (supra n. 27), 80–83.

possible U.S. procedures into Swiss judicial actions taken at the behest of U.S. prosecutors. On the one hand, government prosecutors were aided in their efforts to gain relevant and admissible evidence. On the other hand, defendants' Sixth Amendment rights of confrontation were ensured, as were Swiss and American rights against self-incrimination. Special provisions provided for the retention of defendants and witnesses in custody when necessary, as well as for the safe conduct of witnesses who might be liable to prosecution in the court's jurisdiction. The Swiss refused, however, to include in the treaty a provision permitting U.S. law enforcement officials to conduct informal interviews in Switzerland.[52]

One article of the treaty addressed the problems that had arisen in the past as a result of differences in defining substantive crimes. Rigid and nonimaginative interpretations of the "dual criminality" requirement had resulted in the rejection of many letters rogatory requests on the grounds that the crime alleged in the request was not recognizable in the penal code of the requested state. U.S. authorities had encountered frequent frustrations as a consequence of the wording of many federal criminal statutes, which refer to the federal government's power over interstate commerce in order to bring an offense under federal jurisdiction. Violations of mail fraud and wire fraud statutes, for instance, are often incomprehensible to foreign judges. More than one foreign judge had been known to deny a U.S. request for judicial assistance on the grounds that it was not illegal in his country to use the telephone.[53] The negotiators sought to resolve this difficulty by attaching a "Schedule for Which Compulsory Measures Are Available" to the treaty and by requiring that judges look at the substance rather than the characterization of the crime alleged in the request. More difficult to resolve were Swiss doubts as to whether U.S. crimes such as money laundering and insider trading, neither of which were immediately recognizable in Swiss law, met the dual criminality requirement. Persistent disputes over this issue were ultimately addressed by the Swiss supreme court, Swiss legislation, and further agreements between the two governments.

The MLAT, accompanied by six exchanges of interpretive letters, was signed in 1973. An additional exchange of letters was required in late

52. Ibid., 92.

53. Lawrence Chamblee, "International Legal Assistance in Criminal Cases," in John M. Fedders, Joel Harris, Roger M. Olsen, and Bruno A. Ristau, eds., *Transnational Litigation: Practical Approaches to Conflicts and Accommodations* (Washington, D.C.: American Bar Association National Institute, 1984), 1:188.

1975 as a result of a misunderstanding regarding variations in cantonal law. Both governments ratified the treaty in 1976, which went into force in January 1977, almost a decade after the subject of negotiations had first been broached. Mobilized in part by the MLAT negotiations, in 1981 the Swiss Federal Assembly enacted a Federal Act on International Mutual Assistance in Criminal Matters (IMAC), which codified and expanded many of the provisions in the MLAT with the United States and the European Convention, offering, for instance, broader cooperation in tax fraud cases.[54]

Much to the dismay of the Justice Department, however, the Swiss debate over the implementing legislation had provided a second opportunity for banking and business interests to undermine the negotiators' concessions to the Americans. Combined with preexisting law, the IMAC provided both targets of an investigation as well as "innocent third parties" repeated opportunity to challenge Swiss compliance with U.S. requests for bank records and other confidential documents.[55] The treaty also failed to resolve fully the obstacles generated by variations in cantonal procedural law. And even where the treaty authorized Swiss courts to accommodate American evidentiary requirements, the reluctance of Swiss *juges d'instruction* to vary their customary procedures continued to present difficulties not unlike those that antedated the treaty.

U.S. prosecutors also found particularly irksome two treaty provisions of particular advantage to suspects of an investigation. One, in conjunction with Swiss domestic law, required that "[u]pon receipt of a request for assistance, the requested State shall notify . . . any person from

54. The Swiss Federal Act is briefly summarized in Lionel Frei, "International Mutual Assistance in Criminal Matters: The Swiss Federal Act," *Commonwealth Law Bulletin* 8 (1982), 794. The Swiss IMAC, which entered into force Jan. 1, 1983, was preceded by an Austrian IMAC and followed by a German IMAC. The Austrian Federal Law of Dec. 4, 1979, "Concerning Extradition and Mutual Assistance in Criminal Matters," is translated and analyzed in Edith Palmer, *The Austrian Law on Extradition and Mutual Assistance in Criminal Matters* (Washington, D.C.: Library of Congress Law Library, 1983). The German IMAC, enacted Dec. 23, 1982, can be found in English translation in *International Legal Materials* 22 (1983), 945–982.

55. A subject could file an objection with the Swiss Justice Department and then appeal a negative ruling first to the Swiss Federal Tribunal, then to the Consultative Commission specially created by the Swiss implementing legislation, and finally to the Swiss Federal Council, the composition of which resembles that of the American cabinet. An "innocent third party" was likewise entitled to pursue the same procedure.

whom a statement or testimony or documents, records, or articles of evidence are sought;"[56] the consequence was to forewarn suspects of the fact that they were under investigation (at an earlier stage of the investigation than was required under the Federal Rules of Criminal Procedure), thereby allowing them greater opportunity to shift their funds and otherwise obscure the evidentiary trail. The other troublesome provision required that a request for assistance include not only "the subject matter and nature of the investigation or proceeding" but also "*a description of the essential acts alleged or sought to be ascertained*";[57] the result was to notify the suspect of the prosecution's theory at a relatively early stage in the investigation—in the United States, the defendant often does not discover that theory until the indictment—and to "stick" the prosecution with a potentially untested theory vulnerable to attack and questioning in the Swiss courts.[58]

The most significant sources of tension, however, arose as a result of U.S. frustrations in attempting to obtain evidence in insider trading and tax fraud investigations, and Swiss anger at the Americans' resort to unilateral measures involving U.S. court orders compelling suspects and Swiss banks to provide evidence in violation of Swiss secrecy laws.[59] The rapid internationalization of the securities markets during the late 1970s required a comparable internationalization of the SEC's regulatory efforts. The agency's initiatives, however, engendered tensions with a number of governments that were unwilling to cooperate because their

56. Swiss MLAT, Art. 36(a).

57. Ibid., Art. 29(1)(a).

58. Many of these obstacles became apparent when U.S. prosecutors sought to obtain evidence in the *Interconex* case, one of the most significant investigations requiring Swiss assistance shortly after the MLAT went into force. See *U.S. v. Carver*, Crim. No. 81-00342 (D.C. 1981), aff'd sub nom. *U.S. v. Lemire*, 720 F.2d 1327 (D.C. Cir. 1983). "Interconex" was the name of one of the parties. The *Interconex* case is analyzed in Richard S. Shine, "Transnational Litigation in Criminal Matters: A Case Study of the *Interconex* Prosecution," in Fedders et al., *Transnational Litigation* (supra n. 53), 533. See also the testimony of D. Lowell Jensen, former assistant attorney general in charge of the Criminal Division, in *Crime and Secrecy: The Use of Offshore Banks and Companies, Hearings Before the Permanent Subcommittee on Investigations of the Senate Committee on Governmental Affairs*, 98th Cong., 1st Sess., S. Hrg. 98-151 (1983), 3–14, 210–233. Although the U.S. prosecutors regarded the issues in the *Interconex* case as not particularly complex, they were unable to obtain an indictment until just a few days before the running of the statute of limitations.

59. Lionel Frei, "Overcoming Bank Secrecy: Assistance in Tax Matters in Switzerland on Behalf of Foreign Criminal Authorities," *New York Law School International and Comparative Law Review* 9 (1988), 107–129.

laws did not treat insider trading and other violations of U.S. securities laws as criminal activities.[60] Pressures between the United States and Switzerland mounted in 1981 when the Swiss Federal Tribunal rejected a request from the SEC (via the Justice Department) for assistance in an investigation of insider trading involving the Kuwait Petroleum Corporation's takeover of Sante Fe International Corporation, asserting that the failure to meet the requirement of dual criminality precluded assistance.[61] Subsequent negotiations led to the signing of a Memorandum of Understanding (MOU) to facilitate the SEC's access to information relevant to investigations of violations of American insider trading laws.[62] The MOU included two provisions: an "exchange of opinions" in which the parties agreed that insider trading would under certain conditions constitute fraud, disclosure of business secrets, or other crimes that would pass the test of dual criminality and warrant compulsory assistance; and a description of a proposed private agreement,

60. See John M. Fedders, Frederick B. Wade, Michael D. Mann, and Matthew Beizer, "Waiver by Conduct: A Possible Response to the Internationalization of the Securities Markets," *Journal of Comparative Business and Capital Market Law* 6 (1984), 1–54, and "Response to Fedders' 'Waiver by Conduct,' " *Journal of Comparative Business and Capital Market Law* 6 (1984), 307–354; John J. Ryan IV, "International Enforcement of Insider Trading: The Grand Jury Process, Court Compulsion, and the United States–Switzerland Treaty on Mutual Assistance in Criminal Matters," *American Criminal Law Review* 26 (1988), 247; and Michael D. Mann and Joseph G. Mari, "Developments in International Securities Law Enforcement" (Paper, International Securities Markets, Practicing Law Institute, March 1990).

61. *SEC v. Certain Unknown Purchasers of the Common Stock of and Call Options for the Common Stock of Sante Fe International Corporation*, 81 Civ. 6553 (WC) (S.D.N.Y. Oct. 26, 1981). The opinion of the Swiss Federal Tribunal in the Santa Fe case has been translated into English and summarized in *International Legal Materials* 22 (1983), 785.

62. See Memorandum of Understanding, Aug. 31, 1982, United States–Switzerland, reprinted in *International Legal Materials* 22 (1983), 1. See also the discussion (and text) of the 1982 memorandum in Peter C. Honegger Jr., "Demystification of the Swiss Banking Secrecy and Illumination of the United States–Swiss Memorandum of Understanding," *North Carolina Journal of International Law and Comparative Regulation* 9 (1983), 1–49; Recent Developments, "International Agreements: United States–Switzerland Investigation of Insider Trading Through Swiss Banks," *Harvard International Law Journal* 23 (1983), 437–443; Lionel Frei, "The Service of Process and the Taking of Evidence on Behalf of U.S. Proceedings: The Problem of Granting Assistance," *Wirtschaft und Recht* 35:2/3 (1983), 196–210; JoAnn M. Navickas, "Swiss Banks and Insider Trading in the United States," *International Tax and Business Lawyer* 2 (1984), 159–191; and Beth A. Rushford, "The Effect of Swiss Bank Secrecy on the Enforcement of Insider Trading Regulations and the Memorandum of Understanding Between the United States and Switzerland," *Boston College International and Comparative Law Review* 7 (1984), 541–570. See also Ellen R. Levin, "The Conflict Between United States Securities Laws on Insider Trading and Swiss Bank Secrecy Laws," *Northwestern Journal of International Law and Business* 7 (1985), 318–350.

known as Convention XVI, among members of the Swiss Bankers' Association designed to facilitate cooperation with the SEC in cases involving tender offers or other acquisitions even when the SEC was unable to meet the dual criminality test.[63] The MOU had the intended impact of improving cooperation in U.S. investigations of securities violations. Continuing frustrations, however, inspired the SEC's enforcement division to propose the notion of "waiver by conduct," according to which investors who utilized a foreign bank or brokerage firm to buy or sell securities in a U.S. market would thereby waive their right to keep their identity secret from the SEC and to withhold their foreign bank accounts and trading secrets.[64] In the face of heated opposition, including a reported warning by the Swiss government to the SEC "to abandon the proposal or risk jeopardizing U.S.-Swiss agreements on law enforcement," the SEC ultimately abandoned the proposal.[65] In late 1987, however, the Swiss Parliament did oblige the SEC when it voted, after years of debate, to criminalize insider trading, thereby allowing U.S. authorities to obtain assistance under the MLAT.[66] No longer were Swiss authorities obliged to determine whether a particular charge of insider trading in the United States would have constituted a violation of Swiss law as well.

Perhaps no U.S. action during the 1980s so angered the Swiss as the Justice Department's efforts to penetrate Switzerland's secrecy laws unilaterally by issuing subpoenas *duces tecum* to the U.S.-based branches and subsidiaries of foreign corporations. (The use of these tactics is discussed in greater depth below in the context of the U.S. negotiations with the Cayman Islands.) Two cases in particular generated serious tensions. The first arose

63. See the brief discussion of the memorandum of understanding in the prepared statement by John Fedders, director of the SEC's Division of Enforcement, to the Senate Permanent Subcommittee on Investigations, in *Crime and Secrecy: Hearings* (supra n. 58), 326–327.

64. Fedders et al., "Waiver by Conduct."

65. Ingersoll, "SEC Proposal to Override Foreign Laws on Bank Secrecy Draws Wide Criticism," *Wall Street Journal*, Feb. 11, 1985, 13; "Response to Fedders' 'Waiver by Conduct.' "

66. A fine history of U.S.-Swiss relations regarding the bank secrecy issue (which includes a discussion and copy of the 1987 memorandum as well as the text of the insider trading law) is Stultz, "Swiss Bank Secrecy and United States Efforts" (supra n. 28), 63. The domestic Swiss opposition to the law, which described it as "a foreign body in the Swiss legal system," is discussed in Pierre de Charmant, "Switzerland," *International Lawyer* 21 (1987), 1212–1219. The evolution of the Swiss insider trading law is discussed in Peter Schibli, "Insider Trading: A New Criminal Bill in Switzerland Called 'Lex Americana,' " *International Enforcement Law Reporter* 3 (1987), 234–240. The law is described in H. R. Steiner, "Switzerland," *International Business Lawyer* 17 (1989), 138–142.

in an SEC investigation of insider trading involving a tender offer by the Canadian corporation, Seagrams, for all the outstanding shares of St. Joe Minerals Corporation.[67] When a Swiss bank, Banca Della Svizzera Italiana, refused to disclose a customer's identity in response to a discovery motion by the SEC delivered to the bank's New York office, arguing that to do so would subject it to civil and criminal liability in Switzerland, the SEC obtained a court order compelling the bank to disclose the requested information.[68] Even before the court order was issued, however, the bank capitulated, having obtained a waiver of the Swiss secrecy provision from its customers. The second, and far more serious, case involved the largest tax evasion case in American history. In an attempt to compel a highly successful commodities trader named Mark Rich and his associates to deliver documents to the United States, U.S. prosecutors had subpoenas issued to Marc Rich and the U.S. subsidiary of his Swiss-based company.[69] The two-year struggle that ensued between 1982 and 1984 became a principal source of tension in the two countries' relations, with the Swiss deeply resentful of the Justice Department's "heavy-handed tactics" and wary lest precedents be set for future evidence-gathering efforts.[70] By contrast, the Americans saw little reason not to make use of whatever evidence-gathering mechanisms they possessed, given the scale and profitability of Marc Rich's criminal activities. The case was finally settled in late 1984 when the Swiss-based corporation bearing Marc Rich's name paid $200 million in fines, including $21 million in contempt-of-court fines that had accumulated at the rate of $50,000 a day for failing to comply with the subpoena. The Swiss refused, however, to extradite Marc Rich and his principal associate, who had fled to Switzerland to avoid arrest by U.S. authorities.

One outgrowth of the Marc Rich conflict was the negotiation of a second MOU between the two governments, signed in 1987. In a concession to the Swiss, the agreement stipulated that every effort would be made to use the

67. See Andreas F. Lowenfeld, "Bank Secrecy and Insider Trading: The Banca della Svizzera Italiana Case," *Review of Securities Regulation* 15 (1982), 942–945.

68. *SEC v. Banca Della Svizzera Italiana*, 92 F.R.D. 111 (S.D.N.Y. 1981).

69. *In re Grand Jury Subpoena Directed to Marc Rich & Co., A.G.*, 707 F.2d 663 (2d Cir.), cert. denied, 463 U.S. 1215 (1983); *In re Grand Jury Subpoena Duces Tecum*, 731 F.2d 1032 (2d Cir.); *In re Marc Rich & Co., A.G.*, 736 F.2d 864 (2d Cir. 1984), 739 F.2d 834 (2d Cir. 1984).

70. Ingo Walter, *Secret Money: The Shadowy World of Tax Evasion, Capital Flight, and Fraud* (London: Allen & Unwin, 1985), 53–58; Sarah M. Barish, "International Paper Chase: Federal Grand Jury Subpoena Duces Tecum in Conflict with Swiss Nondisclosure Law," *Brooklyn Journal of International Law* 11 (1985), 149–169.

MLAT before resorting to unilateral measures, that the appropriate authorities would consult with one another in order to avoid or minimize jurisdictional conflicts, and that efforts would be made to prevent any unnecessary disclosure of the judicial assistance provided. In return, the Swiss promised to streamline the implementation process, the length of which had occasioned substantial American frustration, and to maximize their assistance in investigations of drug traffickers, money launderers, and other sorts of organized criminals.[71]

The principal Swiss frustration with U.S. assistance concerned the freezing and forfeiting of assets, which had been authorized in the Swiss legislation implementing the MLAT. Swiss officials were generally disappointed during the 1980s at the lack of reciprocity in this area. They noted that although Switzerland had frozen assets in response to U.S. requests, U.S. officials had failed to reciprocate, apparently because they lacked the authority to do so with the same dispatch that Swiss officials possess.[72] They also complained that whereas they had seized and forfeited criminal proceeds to the victims of crimes outside Switzerland,[73] the United States had failed to reciprocate. The Anti-Drug Abuse Act of 1986 sought to address some of these concerns by incorporating provisions authorizing the U.S. government to seize and forfeit the proceeds (or substitute assets) of drug traffickers charged with violating foreign drug laws and to share any forfeited proceeds with governments that assisted in the seizure or forfeiture.[74] In August 1989, the Justice Department accordingly announced that it would give $1 million each to Switzerland and Canada for their help in the investigation and prosecution of the Panama-based Banco de Occidente.[75]

By the end of the 1980s, many of the kinks in the treaty and the obstacles created by the implementing legislation had been successfully corrected or circumvented. The MOUs and new Swiss legislation were partially responsible, as were rulings by the Swiss Federal Tribunal and U.S. federal courts rejecting most challenges to the MLAT and international judicial assistance generally.[76] The growing cooperation of the Swiss banking community,

71. Somewhat to the dismay of the Justice Department, the provisions of the MLAT providing for expanded assistance in organized crime investigations had proven too restrictive to accommodate most U.S. requests.

72. Frei and Treschel, "Origins and Applications of the Swiss MLAT" (supra n. 27), 90–91.

73. See, e.g., "Government Obtains Bribe Money from Swiss Bank Accounts," *International Enforcement Law Reporter* 5 (1989), 287–288.

74. 18 U.S.C. 981(a)(1)(B) and 981(i) (1986).

75. Michael Isikoff, "U.S. to Pay 2 Nations $1 Million for Drug-Case Aid," *Washington Post*, Aug. 15, 1989, A14; *International Enforcement Law Reporter* 5 (1989), 283–285.

76. U.S. federal courts have rejected most challenges to the Swiss MLAT on the grounds

reflected in its adoption in October 1987 of stricter rules with respect to receiving foreign funds, provided an important complement to the government's actions.[77] Also important, however, was the growing familiarity of both Swiss and U.S. judicial authorities with the treaty's provisions and procedures. By 1983, six years after the MLAT entered into force, the Justice Department had made 202 requests under the treaty and the Swiss 65.[78] By 1990, the two central authorities were processing an estimated 100 requests a year, including a rising number involving the seizure and forfeiture of illegally derived funds deposited in Swiss banks. The Federal Tribunal's decisions, moreover, were a result of the willingness of officials in the Swiss Justice Department to faithfully pursue U.S. requests that had been challenged in Swiss courts throughout the lengthy appeals process.

The importance of Swiss assistance to U.S. criminal investigations was already apparent by the early 1980s. In January 1983, Justice Department officials estimated that the evidence obtained under the MLAT had contributed to 145 federal and state convictions, including those of the notorious Italian financier Michele Sindona, for fraud in connection with the collapse of the Franklin National Bank, and of an organized crime figure, Anthony Giacolone, for a $3 million embezzlement of Citibank.[79] By the end of the 1980s, the Swiss government's cooperation in international efforts to identify and freeze the assets of fallen dictators such as the Philippines' Ferdinand Marcos,[80] Haiti's Jean-Claude Duvalier,[81] Paraguay's Alfredo

---

that the treaty provides no standing to private parties. See *U.S. v. Johnpoll*, 739 F.2d 702 (2d Cir.), cert. denied, 469 U.S. 1075 (1984); *U.S. v. Davis*, 767 F.2d 1025 (2d Cir. 1985); and, rejecting a challenge to a freeze of assets by the Swiss government pursuant to an MLAT request, *Barr v. U.S. Department of Justice*, 819 F.2d 25 (2d Cir. 1987). In a series of Swiss judicial decisions involving challenges by third parties to U.S. requests for documents, the Federal Tribunal ruled that their identities could be disclosed if they were in any way connected with the subject of the investigation. The court also was liberal in its interpretation of the dual criminality requirement. See Frei and Treschel, "Origins and Applications of the Swiss MLAT" (supra n. 27), 84–88.

77. See the reports by Peter Schibli in *International Enforcement Law Reporter* 3 (1987), 154–58, and (1988), 148–150.

78. James I. K. Knapp, "Mutual Legal Assistance Treaties as a Way to Pierce Bank Secrecy," *Case Western Reserve Journal of International Law* 20 (1988), 405, 414.

79. Ibid., 414.

80. Pieter J. Hoets and Sara G. Zwart, "Swiss Bank Secrecy and the Marcos Affair," *New York Law School International and Comparative Law Review* 9 (1988), 75–105; Peter Norman, "Hasty Swiss Freeze on Marcos Millions Raises Questions on Banking Secrecy," *Wall Street Journal*, Apr. 4, 1986, 25; Olivier Dunant, "Switzerland," *International Lawyer* 22 (1988), 854, 856–860; the periodic reports in *International Enforcement Law Reporter*, 2:370, 3:79–81, 4:69–70, 5:366–367, 431–432, 463 (1986–89).

81. Clemens Kochinke, "Judicial Assistance Requests: The Duvalier and Marcos Cases, Two Approaches Toward Switzerland," *International Enforcement Law Reporter* 2 (1986), 370.

Stroessner, Romania's Nicolae Ceauşescu, and Panama's Manuel Noriega;[82] its substantial assistance in the Iran Contra investigation;[83] and its willingness to provide documents in the various investigations of Wall Street shenanigans,[84] and export control violations involving the Soviet Union[85] and North Korea,[86] stood in stark contrast to its response to similar efforts in earlier years.[87] Also significant was the Swiss Parliament's vote in late 1989 to criminalize money laundering, in effect criminalizing a wide variety of banking functions that had previously been regarded as virtually part and parcel of a banker's profession in a financial secrecy jurisdiction.[88] By all accounts, the Swiss have emerged as among the world's leaders in matters of international law enforcement.

Lessons, Spin-offs, and the Second Generation of MLATs

The negotiation of the Swiss treaty provided valuable experience in anticipating future pitfalls and objectives in other treaty negotiations. Also, the treaty went into effect as demands for international judicial

82. "Ex-Despots Can't Bank on the Swiss," *Los Angeles Times*, Jan. 31, 1990, A1.

83. Note, "Swiss Bank Secrecy and United States Efforts" (supra n. 28), 64–65; Philip Shenon, "Swiss Bank Records in Iran-Contra Case Are Released to U.S.," *New York Times*, Nov. 4, 1987, A1; Taylor, "Iran-Contra Counsel Walsh Is Upheld on His Authority, Access to Swiss Data," *Wall Street Journal*, Aug. 21, 1987, 38; Peter Schibli, "Swiss Supreme Court Rules Geneva Bank Accounts in the Irangate Affair Must Be Opened to U.S. Investigators," *International Enforcement Law Reporter* 3 (1987), 283–284.

84. Nathaniel Nash, "Swiss Help in Insider Case," *New York Times*, May 15, 1986, D1.

85. Bruce Zagaris and Clemens Kochinke, "Swiss Supreme Court Grants Request in the USSR Computer Case," *Taxes International* 56 (1984), 81.

86. Clemens Kochinke, "Swiss Supreme Court Defines Cooperation in Export Control Cases," *International Enforcement Law Reporter* 4 (1988), 12–13.

87. The Swiss had previously rejected, for instance, Ethiopian and Iranian requests to obtain the assets of Emperor Haile Selassi and the Shah. See John Tagliabue, "The Swiss Stop Keeping Secrets," *New York Times*, June 1, 1986, sec. 3, p. 4; but see Mark Schapiro, "Swiss Banks Still Sell Secrecy," *The Nation*, Sept. 6, 1986, 177–180. See also Paolo Bernasconi, "Swiss Bank Secrecy: Recent Developments in International Mutual Assistance in Criminal Matters," *International Enforcement Law Reporter* 5 (1989), 362–367.

88. Art. 305 of the Swiss Penal Code, as amended effective Aug. 1, 1990, makes it a crime to hinder an investigation of the origins, discovery, or confiscation of assets that an individual knows, or must assume, stem from criminal activity. See Nathalie Kohler, "Swiss Money Laundering Bill: Debates and Adoption by One of the Chambers of the Swiss Parliament," *International Enforcement Law Reporter* 5 (1989), 437–440, and the periodic reports in ibid., 5:121, 244–245; 6:96.

assistance and some coordination of U.S. international judicial responsibilities were increasing dramatically. The Swiss MLAT had included a provision requiring each government to establish a central authority for the processing of requests pursuant to the treaty. In 1979, Philip Heymann, the assistant attorney general in charge of the Criminal Division in the Department of Justice, created an Office of International Affairs (OIA). This office soon assumed responsibility for coordinating the Justice Department's international law enforcement concerns, handling extradition and judicial assistance matters and taking the lead in negotiating extradition treaties, MLATs, prisoner transfer treaties, and a variety of other law enforcement agreements.[89] By 1990, the size of the office had increased from the four attorneys present at its inception to more than forty attorneys; one attorney was stationed in Rome, additional offices in Mexico City and Hong Kong had been authorized, and plans were under way to expand the OIA's presence in Europe.

At about the same time the OIA was created, an Office of Law Enforcement and Intelligence (LEI) was created within the Legal Adviser's Office in the State Department. The two offices quickly worked out a relatively cooperative relationship, with attorneys from both participating in treaty negotiations.[90] What tensions resulted were principally a reflection of the differing concerns and expertise of the respective offices. Whereas the State Department attorneys were more attuned to the political aspects of judicial assistance and treaty negotiations, as reflected by their greater involvement in more political issues such as U.S. counterterrorist policy, the OIA attorneys were strongly influenced by their prosecutorial backgrounds and their day-to-day experience in dealing with foreign judicial requests and personnel. These differences occasionally resulted in a mutual skepticism, with the State Department negotiators bemoaning OIA's insensitivity to diplomatic considerations, and the OIA lawyers doubting their counterparts' awareness of the requirements of criminal law and procedure. The OIA lawyers also chafed somewhat at the State Department's involvement in MLAT negotiations, particularly because one of the principal reasons for negotiating the treaties was to eliminate the time-consuming diplomatic

89. The OIA was officially designated by the attorney general as the Central Authority referred to in all MLATs. See 28 C.F.R. 0.64-1, and Justice Department Directive 81, 44 FR 18661, Mar. 29, 1979, as amended at 45 FR 6541, Jan. 29, 1980; 48 FR 54595, Dec. 6, 1983.

90. Whereas MLATs typically specify that the attorney general is the responsible authority, in the area of extradition the secretary of state has retained the principal statutory authority.

channels through which letters rogatory were required to pass. When all was said and done, however, the OIA attorneys generally welcomed the involvement of their State Department counterparts for a number of reasons: their presence at treaty negotiation sessions was an indication to the foreign counterpart that the U.S. government attached diplomatic significance to the negotiations; they provided diplomatic leverage and expertise when the negotiations become somewhat acrimonious (as in the early stages of the negotiations with the Swiss); and, as one OIA attorney recounted cynically, their involvement prevented the State Department from later disavowing any agreements negotiated by the OIA lawyers.

Several lessons were gained from the negotiation of the Swiss treaty and the ensuing attempts to utilize its provisions. The first was never again to let the negotiations become so drawn out and complex. To some extent, the negotiators' lack of experience in negotiating MLATs was a source of delay. And Switzerland's extraordinary concern with bank secrecy, its strong tradition of legality, and its prickly sense of national sovereignty created time-consuming obstacles too. When confronted with similar concerns in future MLAT negotiations, American negotiators would strive to complete the negotiations quickly and to avoid the length, complexity, and tortured clauses of the Swiss treaty. As the OIA lawyers became involved in negotiating other treaties, they soon realized that the process would be facilitated if their foreign counterparts included at least one representative with experience in criminal prosecution. Such an individual was deemed necessary to explain the concepts underlying the other nation's criminal law and procedure, to communicate the practical requirements of its criminal justice system, and to establish a relationship with the American negotiators that would aid in the treaty's implementation. Accordingly, the OIA lawyers requested of each government that such an individual be included on the negotiating team. They also included, and expected to be included on the other's team, individuals with expertise in any areas (such as drug enforcement, securities regulation, or tax administration) that might be a subject of the negotiations.

As the OIA's attorneys became more familiar with the potential and limitations of the Swiss MLAT, in particular the length of the appeals process authorized by the Swiss implementing legislation, they also realized the need to amend U.S. law to better accommodate the admissibility of evidence supplied by foreign authorities. At their behest, Congress included five provisions in the Comprehensive Crime Control Act of 1984 specifically designed to assist the foreign evidence gathering process: 18 U.S.C. 3505, which allows a foreign business record (or copy) to be admitted into evidence without requiring a deposition of the custodian of the records;[91] 18 U.S.C. 3506, which requires a national or resident of the United States who files a formal opposition in a foreign court to an official U.S. request for evidence to serve a copy of that pleading on the United States;[92] 18 U.S.C. 3507, which specifically authorizes U.S. courts to appoint a special master to attend and preside over depositions conducted abroad and to advise foreign courts on U.S. law; 18 U.S.C. 3292, which permits a court to suspend the running of the statute of limitations in cases in which the indictment has been delayed by the need to obtain foreign evidence;[93] and 18 U.S.C. 3161(h), which allows exclusions from the running of the Speedy Trial Act in cases delayed by the need to obtain evidence abroad.[94]

One positive spin-off of the Swiss treaty was that it generated substantial interest in foreign justice ministries around the world. In many countries, particularly those with tough bank secrecy laws, governments were none too eager to allow greater access to snooping American prosecutors; indeed, some, reportedly including Austria, Luxembourg and Liechtenstein, took advantage of the changes in Switzerland to promote themselves as safer financial security jurisdictions. But in others, particularly elsewhere in Europe, government prosecutors began expressing interest in the Swiss treaty with the Americans. At the same time, the attorneys in the OIA and the LEI were involved in negotiating new extradition treaties around the world to replace the increasingly

91. The constitutionality of the statute was upheld by a federal court in 1987 in response to a challenge by a defendant who contended that it violated the confrontation clause of the Sixth Amendment. See *U.S. v. Miller*, 830 F.2d 1073 (9th Cir. 1987).

92. The Swiss have objected to this statute, contending that it circumvents the treaty process and violates Swiss law by requiring an individual, the identity of whom may be the subject of a U.S. request under the MLAT, to disclose his or her identity by affirming the existence of an account or deposit. See Frei and Treschel, "Origins and Applications of the Swiss MLAT" (supra n. 27), 89–90.

93. In 1987, a federal court rejected various challenges to the statute. See *U.S. v. Miller*, 830 F.2d 1073 (9th Cir. 1987).

94. See U.S. Department of Justice, *Handbook on the Comprehensive Crime Control Act of 1984*, Chap. 12, Part K (Foreign Evidence), 176–180; and the Congressional hearing on the provisions, *Foreign Evidence Rules Amendment: Hearing on H.R. 5406 Before the Subcommittee on Criminal Justice of the House Committee on the Judiciary*, 98th Cong., 2d Sess. (1984).

outdated existing ones. At these negotiations, questions were being raised about the increasing need for judicial assistance in criminal investigations and proceedings short of extradition.

The incentives for entering into MLAT negotiations with foreign governments varied substantially. In the case of Turkey, the treaty was demanded as a precondition for other treaty negotiations requested by the United States. The Turkish government had been incensed by the incident and publicity leading up to the filming and distribution of the movie *Midnight Express*, which was based on the account of an American who had been imprisoned in Turkey for attempting to smuggle hashish. Its request that the U.S. government intervene to stop the distribution of the film was, quite naturally, rejected—albeit for reasons not readily comprehensible to the Turks. At the same time, in response to pressures by families of Americans held in Turkish prisons, the U.S. government suggested to the Turkish government that they negotiate a prisoner transfer treaty similar to one the United States had already negotiated with Mexico. The Turks responded indignantly not only that the Americans had failed to do anything about the film, but also that negotiation of such a treaty would only embarrass them by giving credence to the movie's portrayal of the Turkish judicial and penal systems. They suggested, instead, that such a treaty be included in a three-part treaty package including extradition and mutual legal assistance treaties as well. The Americans agreed.

The MLAT negotiations with Colombia, by contrast, arose in response to the need to prosecute Colombian drug traffickers and counterfeiters more effectively. Those with Italy emerged in response to growing concern over the role of the Italian Mafia in the heroin traffic from southwestern Asia and a number of major extradition cases involving legal ambiguities and diplomatic sensitivities, notably that of the Italian financier Michele Sindona.[95] The MLAT with the Dutch reflected both mutual concern over drug trafficking and other transnational criminal activity, as well as the desire to head off potential conflicts involving U.S. efforts to obtain bank records located in the Netherlands Antilles. Similarly, efforts to negotiate an MLAT with the German government were motivated by the abundance of international law enforcement issues involving the two states, as well as the desire to avoid conflict over

95. See *Sindona v. Grant*, 619 F.2d 167 (2d Cir. 1980), and the discussion in *New York Times*, Mar. 22, 1980, 25; see also Nick Tosches, *Power on Earth* (New York: Arbor House, 1986).

unilateral efforts by U.S. prosecutors to secure documents from Germany. And the MLAT negotiations with Morocco may well have been motivated primarily by the need for some official agreement for U.S. Attorney General William French Smith to sign when he visited the kingdom.

The MLAT negotiations with the Swiss, as well as the subsequent talks and MOUs, had provided the American negotiators with useful precedents for reconciling the requirements of the U.S. common law system with foreign civil law systems and for penetrating foreign secrecy laws. In MLAT negotiations with other governments, the U.S. negotiators sought to build on this experience by designing treaties that were simpler and more effective both in obtaining evidence and in avoiding future squabbles. They experimented with more open-ended phrases and formulations intended to broaden the availability of evidence and minimize the likelihood that courts of either nation would impede the provision of legal assistance. Model MLATs were drafted and provided to potential negotiating partners to facilitate subsequent negotiations. And each treaty negotiation was viewed as an opportunity to experiment with a potentially more effective innovation.

The MLAT negotiations with the Turks were quick and relatively simple, even though they were combined with negotiation of the extradition and prisoner transfer treaties. There was no great concern with organized crime or bank secrecy, and the negotiations focused on the technical legal problems of reconciling the two rather different legal systems. The Americans' principal concern was to avoid the tortured compromises of the Swiss treaty and to create a fresh precedent for future negotiations by negotiating quickly a MLAT that would be short, simple, and straightforward. They succeeded easily in attaining all these objectives. The treaty was signed on June 7, 1979.[96] In a dramatic contrast with the flow of requests under the Swiss MLAT, by early 1988 the Turks had made ninety-eight requests in a variety of matters ranging from serious felonies to minor offenses while the United States had forwarded only one.[97]

The MLAT negotiations with the Colombians were taken far more

96. The "Treaty with the Republic of Turkey on Extradition and Mutual Assistance in Criminal Matters" was signed in Ankara and entered into force on Jan. 1, 1981 (32 UST 3111; TIAS 9891). The prisoner transfer treaty (officially the "Treaty on the Enforcement of Penal Judgments") was signed and entered into force on the same days (32 UST 3187; TIAS 9892).

97. Knapp, "Mutual Legal Assistance Treaties" (supra n. 78), 416.

seriously by the Americans. The U.S. ambassador to Colombia, Diego Asencio, played a fairly active behind-the-scenes role in the negotiations, as did a special assistant to President Turbay, Dr. Alvaro Perez Vives. Consideration was initially given to combining the MLAT and the extradition treaty in a single document, as had been done with Turkey, but the notion was rejected because of concern over how the Colombian Congress would respond to the MLAT. It was believed that the extradition treaty would have a better chance of being approved if its consideration were not complicated by the inclusion of a novel and controversial treaty. The Colombians lacked any experience in negotiating an MLAT and were wary of agreeing to anything that might be perceived as an infringement of their national sovereignty.[98]

As in other MLAT negotiations, the U.S. negotiators sought to facilitate the flow of information and admissible evidence to the United States.[99] They also were interested, however, in enhancing the Colombians' capacity to collect whatever evidence they required to prosecute drug traffickers in their own courts. Because neither party was particularly interested in narrowing the range of cases in which evidence could be provided, the negotiating sessions focused largely on reconciling the needs of the very different legal systems. Special provisions were inserted to make evidence provided by the other government admissible in the courts of the receiving country. In a significant departure from the Swiss treaty, the requirement of "dual criminality" was eliminated and the obligation to provide assistance was extended to civil and administrative investigations and proceedings. As in the Turkish MLAT, but unlike the Swiss MLAT, law enforcement officials were authorized to release government records to the same extent that they would be available to

98. The Organization of American States had briefly considered a proposal for a multilateral MLAT, but the proposal had never gotten off the ground. However, the Colombians were not novices in the area of judicial assistance. They claimed extensive experience in the use of letters rogatory and were party to two judicial assistance agreements with the United States. One was the multilateral Inter-American Convention on Taking Evidence Abroad, signed on Jan. 13, 1975; the other was the bilateral Executive Agreement with Colombia on Mutual Assistance in the Lockheed Investigation, signed on Apr. 22, 1976; entered into force Apr. 22, 1976; 27 UST 1059, TIAS 8244; extended by TIAS 9809 in the Textron Investigation and by TIAS 9860 in the Bethlehem Steel Investigation.

99. The treaty, accompanied by the Presidential message transmitting it to the Senate, is reproduced in U.S. Senate Treaty Doc. 97-11, 97th Cong., 1st Sess. (1981). Much of the following analysis of the treaty is taken from U.S. Senate Exec. Rept. 97-35, 97th Cong., 1st Sess. (1981), which includes a summary of the major provisions as well as a section-by-section analysis.

domestic authorities, with some limitations. Likewise, officials were formally authorized to grant foreign requests for searches and seizures, provided the request met the evidentiary standard of the requested state.

Among the more significant innovations of the Colombian MLAT was a provision designed to overcome domestic legal restrictions on disclosures by tax authorities. Its purpose was less to open up foreign bank accounts to U.S. investigations than to resolve some doubts, and perhaps bureaucratic resentments, on the part of the IRS. Under Title 26 U.S.C. 6103(k)(4), the IRS was authorized to disclose information in its possession to foreign authorities under any "convention relating to the exchange of tax information" subject "to the terms and conditions of such convention." However, since the Tax Reform Act of 1976 had imposed stringent standards on the disclosure of information, many officials at the IRS had adopted what many Justice Department officials regarded as an exceptionally restrictive view of the tax disclosure provision. In the case of the Colombian treaty, the "IRS had [expressed] some doubts whether it could make such disclosures under general mutual assistance treaties, in which another government official, the Attorney General, serves as the Central Authority designated to transmit the requested information to the foreign country."[100] The language of the treaty was accordingly designed to permit the IRS to disclose information to the attorney general "solely for communication to Colombian authorities." The "doubts," it would appear, arose in part from the IRS's sensitivity to the apparent infringement by the Justice Department on its jurisdictional authority.

The treaty was signed in August 1980 and ratified by the U.S. Senate in January 1982. In Colombia, however, the MLAT made little headway in the ratification process. Advocates of the extradition treaty were initially wary lest debate over the MLAT complicate the difficult task of securing approval for the extradition treaty. Shortly after the extradition treaty was ratified, President Julio Turbay Ayala was succeeded by Belisario Betancur, who initially showed little enthusiasm for promoting a treaty that jibed poorly with his nationalist rhetoric. Following the murder of Justice Minister Rodrigo Lara Bonilla by drug traffickers in April 1984, however, the Betancur government reversed course and launched a crackdown against the drug traffickers that included closer law enforcement cooperation with the United States. By that point,

100. See the technical analysis of the MLAT, U.S. Senate Exec. Rept. 97-35, 17.

however, few Colombians in either the Congress or the administration were interested in an additional struggle over the MLAT ratification process. By the end of the decade, the MLAT had become, to all intents and purposes, a dead letter in both the Colombian Congress and U.S.-Colombian relations. Indeed, in April 1988, the Justice Department official charged with overseeing most international law enforcement matters informed Congress that the Justice Department was "in no rush to see Colombia ratify our mutual legal assistance treaty," given the possibility that evidence provided to Colombia might end up in the hands of the traffickers.[101]

The attorneys in the OIA were eager to negotiate a treaty with the Dutch. The extradition treaty with the Netherlands was out of date, and as with other countries it was deemed beneficial to negotiate both treaties simultaneously. The Americans sensed that the Dutch were interested in 'getting results" and would negotiate accordingly, and they hoped that a treaty with the Dutch would provide a beneficial model for future agreements with European governments. Moreover, both the Justice Department and the IRS were eager to penetrate the financial secrecy laws of the Netherlands Antilles and to reduce or eliminate the special status of the Netherlands Antilles as an offshore banking haven. That status had been granted in 1963 to allow U.S. businesses to obtain low-interest financing so they would not suffer competitively from European access to similar funds.[102] By 1981, however, the Dutch islands had become both "the largest tax haven recipient of U.S. source income reported to the IRS" and "the tax treaty country most widely used by U.S. and foreign persons seeking to evade U.S. taxation."[103] The benefits

101. Testimony of Mark Richard, in U.S. Senate, *MLAT . . . Caymans* (supra n. 5), 69.

102. See the Protocol modifying and supplementing extension to the Netherlands Antilles of the convention for avoidance of double taxation and prevention of fiscal evasion with respect to income and certain other taxes, Apr. 29, 1948, signed at the Hague Oct. 23, 1963, entered into force Sept. 28, 1964; 15 UST 1900; TIAS 5665; 521 UNTS 377. The treaty allows American corporations to issue Eurobonds to foreign investors and to exempt from the American withholding tax the interest paid to them.

103. The negotiations and the problem are discussed at length in *Tax Evasion Through the Netherlands Antilles and Other Tax Haven Countries: Hearings Before the Commerce, Consumer, and Monetary Affairs Subcommittee of the House Committee on Government Operations*, 98th Cong., 1st Sess. (1983). See in particular the committee staff memorandum on the subject (568–572), which summarizes the American perspective and position, and the statement of the Netherlands Antilles government (798–810). Much of the following discussion is drawn from those documents. An excellent analysis of the tax haven phenomenon and the problems it presents for the United States can be found in Richard A. Gordon, *Tax Havens and Their Use by United States Taxpayers: An Overview*, a special report submitted to the

of the 1963 treaty, supplemented by the country's minimal level of taxation on financial transactions, and domestic laws requiring strict bank secrecy and permitting the use of anonymous "bearer share" corporations and financial accounts, had led the assistant secretary of the treasury for enforcement to characterize the Antilles as "one of the four countries having the most 'iron clad secrecy.' "[104]

Many of the issues that needed to be resolved were similar to those in the Colombian negotiations and were in fact resolved similarly in most cases.[105] The principal difference reflected the concern over the Netherlands Antilles, which accordingly attracted substantial interest and involvement by the IRS. Some of their concerns were similar to those noted with respect to the Colombian treaty—that is, that information provided by the IRS not be used for nontax purposes and that the Department of Justice not infringe on their jurisdictional turf. But the IRS was also involved in simultaneous efforts to renegotiate the U.S. tax convention with the Netherlands Antilles. IRS officials naturally preferred that as much authority as possible be provided for in the tax convention, under which the secretary of the treasury was designated the "competent authority." After some debate in the higher levels of the Treasury Department, however, a policy decision that supported the inclusion of tax matters in MLATs was reached. One implication of this decision was that the IRS thereby acknowledged that a foreign prosecutor was entitled to the same access as an American prosecutor in obtaining tax information for nontax-related criminal investigations under 26 U.S.C. 6103(i). The negotiators accordingly inserted a clause in the diplomatic note accompanying the MLAT to "make . . . it clear that [the] treaty is a 'convention relating to the exchange of tax information' within the meaning of 26 U.S.C. 6103(k)(4), under which the disclosure of tax information is authorized."[106] Much to the dismay of the Americans, however, the representatives of the Netherlands Antilles at the negotiations insisted on reserving the right to refuse requests for

---

commissioner of internal revenue, the assistant attorney general (Tax Division), and the assistant secretary of the treasury (Tax Policy) in Jan. 1981.

104. *Tax Evasion: Hearings* (supra n. 103), 569.

105. The treaty, accompanied by the Presidential message transmitting it to the Senate, is reproduced in U.S. Senate Treaty Doc. 97-16, 97th Cong., 1st Sess. (1981); it can also be found at TIAS 10734. Much of the following analysis of the treaty is taken from U.S. Senate Exec. Rept. 97-36, 97th Cong., 1st Sess. (1981), which includes a summary of the major provisions as well as a section-by-section analysis.

106. See the technical analysis of the Dutch MLAT, U.S. Senate Exec. Rept. 97-36, 6.

assistance in fiscal offenses until the tax convention had been renegotiated.[107] Unable to budge the negotiators from the Netherlands Antilles on this matter, or to persuade the Dutch government to use its influence on this issue, the Americans assented to the reservation.[108]

The renegotiation of the tax convention, it should be noted, was part of a broader effort initiated by the Treasury Department and the Tax Division of the Justice Department during the late 1970s to increase international cooperation in prosecution of tax violations. Most of the thirty-odd tax conventions to which the United States was a party were oriented primarily toward cooperation in civil cases and only a few allowed for disclosure in fraud investigations. To a certain extent, this reflected the traditional mind-set of finance ministries, whose principal concern was not criminal prosecution of tax evaders but rather assessment and collection of revenues. But as U.S. law enforcement authorities became increasingly interested in prosecuting drug traffickers and other organized criminals on tax evasion charges, IRS officials realized that the tax conventions would need to be revised to authorize cooperation in criminal prosecutions.[109]

Another issue that generated debate in both the extradition and MLAT negotiations involved the necessity of including a "political offense" exception in the treaties. The inclusion or exclusion of this grounds for refusing assistance was frequently a sensitive issue in extradition and MLAT negotiations; indeed, both the United States and many foreign states were wary of negotiating law enforcement treaties with governments viewed as likely to use or misuse their judicial systems to punish or harass political opponents. When obliged to negotiate such treaties with nondemocratic governments because of broader concerns such as drug trafficking, U.S. negotiators typically insisted on including the "political offense" exception clause. They saw little need, however, to

107. See the statement of the Netherlands Antilles government in *Tax Evasion: Hearings* (supra n. 103), 808.

108. The final word belonged to Congress. As part of the Deficit Reduction Act of 1984, Congress repealed the 30 percent withholding tax on interest earned by foreigners, thereby making it possible for American corporations to sell Eurobonds directly to foreign investors without setting up subsidiaries in the Antilles. The effect on the economy of the Netherlands Antilles, their minister plenipotentiary in the Washington, D.C., predicted in 1984, would be "devastating." See Oppenheimer, "U.S. Taking Lid Off Tax Havens' Secrets," *Miami Herald*, Oct. 8, 1984, Business Section, 1, 10.

109. Among the first to be renegotiated to include criminal provisions were those with Cyprus (TIAS 10965), Jamaica (TIAS 10206), Australia (TIAS 10773), and New Zealand (TIAS 10772).

include the clause in treaties with Western Europeans, particularly in MLATs. Some European negotiators, however, including the Dutch, were less convinced that the clause should be excluded; they were influenced by their own perceptions of the conflicts between civil rights activists and law enforcement officials in the American South during the 1960s, and by cases such as that involving the "Chicago 7." The American negotiators took umbrage at any suggestion that violations of U.S. laws, or prosecutions of criminal offenses, could be politically motivated or justified; they agreed, however, that insofar as extradition was deemed the most extreme form of international assistance in criminal cases, a "political offense" exception might be warranted in such treaties. They saw no need, however, for its inclusion in the MLAT. When the Dutch insisted, the Americans relented, but the negotiators agreed that "the 'political offense' grounds for refusing assistance . . . should not be invoked as readily as in extradition." They further noted their "appreciat[ion] that the United States adheres to the narrower 'British view' of political offenses, while the Netherlands adheres to the broader 'Swiss view.' "[110]

The MLAT was signed in June 1981 and went into force in September 1983.[111] By the late 1980s, the OIA was forwarding approximately twenty-five requests a year to the Dutch, approximately half of which were for information in the Antilles, and receiving about a dozen requests a year from Dutch authorities.[112]

The MLAT with Italy was notable primarily because of two novel provisions: an "international subpoena," whereby one state could request another to *compel* a person to appear and testify in the requesting state; and a provision authorizing the immobilization of assets in the requested state and their forfeiture to the requesting state. In the MLAT negotiations, the Italians agreed to virtually all of the provisions in the Americans' model treaty, including the elimination of any requirement of dual criminality.[113] Unlike the previous treaties, a provision was

110. See the technical analysis of the Dutch MLAT, U.S. Senate Exec. Rept. 97-36, 11.

111. Further analysis of the MLAT, with particular attention to the implications for the Netherlands Antilles, can be found in J. M. Saleh, "International Judicial Assistance Techniques in the Light of Modern International Need," *Tijdschrift voor Antilaans Recht-Justicia*, 1987, 110–126.

112. Knapp, "Mutual Legal Assistance Treaties" (supra n. 78), 416.

113. The treaty, accompanied by the Presidential message transmitting it to the Senate, is reproduced in U.S. Senate Treaty Doc. 98-25, 98th Cong., 2d Sess. (1984). A section-by-section analysis of the treaty appears in U.S. Senate Exec. Rept. 98-36, 98th Cong., 2d Sess. The two governments were not entirely inexperienced in the negotiation of mutual legal

included allowing the *requesting* state to "request that the application for assistance, the contents of the request and its supporting documents, and the granting of such assistance be kept confidential," thereby facilitating the use of the MLAT in grand jury investigations.[114] The first of the two major innovations provided that "[i]n emergency situations, the Requested State shall have authority to immobilize assets found in that state which are subject to forfeiture" and to order the forfeiture of those assets to the Requesting State. As with some of the forfeiture provisions in the Racketeer Influenced and Corrupt Organizations Act (RICO) and other antidrug trafficking statutes, this provision reflected the spreading belief in law enforcement circles that the most effective way to deter and punish drug traffickers was to immobilize their assets. Unlike the Swiss treaty, the proceeds were forfeited to the prosecuting country, not the seizing country.

The inclusion of the "international subpoena" provision in the treaty was regarded by many of the attorneys involved in international legal assistance as a potentially "revolutionary" development in mutual legal assistance, one that would pave the way for the same provision in a multilateral convention on mutual legal assistance.[115] Before the Italian treaty, all MLATs had required the consent of a witness requested to testify in a requesting state (whether he was in custody or not). The negotiators of the Italian treaty eliminated the requirement of consent and agreed that the requested state would compel a witness to go to the

---

assistance agreements. In 1976, they had signed a treaty to facilitate cooperation in investigating the Lockheed Aircraft Corporation matter (27 UST 3437; TIAS 8374). The MLAT, as well as the extradition treaty, is analyzed in Paolo Mengozzi, "A View from Italy on Judicial Cooperation Between Italy and the United States: The 1982 Mutual Assistance Treaty and the 1983 Extradition Treaty," *NYU Journal of International Law and Politics* 18 (1986), 813–831.

114. See Art. 8(2) of the Italian MLAT. Like the Swiss MLAT, the Italian treaty also allowed the *requested* state to require that the evidence and information provided be kept confidential, thereby making it easier for U.S. officials to provide Italy with tax information and information obtained during a grand jury investigation. The Italian treaty, like the Dutch, was also characterized as a "convention relating to the exchange of tax information" within the meaning of 26 U.S.C. 6103(k)(4). The provision of tax information to the Italian authorities remained contingent upon their request meeting the requirements of 26 U.S.C. 6103(h) and/or 6103(i). The grand jury information could be obtained pursuant to a court-ordered disclosure under Rule 6(e)(3)(C)(i), Federal Rules of Criminal Procedure. See the technical analysis of the Italian MLAT, U.S. Senate Exec. Rept. 98-36, 6.

115. The international subpoena is analyzed at length in Kenneth I. Juster, "International Legal Assistance in Criminal Law Enforcement" (Paper on file at the John F. Kennedy School of Government, Harvard University, April 1980).

requesting state so long as it had "no reasonable basis to deny the request" and insofar as "the person could be compelled to appear and testify in similar circumstances in the Requested State."

In anticipation of a skeptical Congressional response to their novel concept, the negotiators devoted a good part of the treaty analysis which they submitted to the Foreign Relations Committee to preempting potential criticisms of it.[116] They argued that the term "international subpoena" was a misnomer insofar as the state in which the subpoenaed witness resided served as an intermediary and evaluator of the request. Moreover, "since the requested country is to employ the procedures it uses in domestic cases when it compels a witness to appear and testify in the requesting country, witnesses in the United States, whose appearance and testimony in Italy is sought pursuant to the Treaty, will be able to move the court to quash the subpoena if compliance would be unreasonable or oppressive."[117] More important, they suggested, the notion was little more than an international extension of the Uniform Act to Secure the Attendance of Witnesses from Without a State in Criminal Proceedings—the intrastate compact, to which every state but one is a party, allowing each state to obtain compulsory appearance and testimony in its legal proceedings of witnesses located in other states.[118] Given the speed of modern jet transportation, the negotiators argued, the inconvenience of being ordered to go to Italy was little greater than that of being required to make a transcontinental flight to another state. Finally, they noted, persons compelled to appear in response to an international subpoena were further protected by another treaty provision, which (unlike the Uniform Act) afforded them immunity with respect to any truthful testimony given in the requesting country.[119]

The treaty with Italy was signed in November 1982 and went into force—after delays involving not the "international subpoena" but rather the forfeiture provisions—in November 1985. Within just two years, the MLAT had proven its value in facilitating both Italian and U.S. prosecutions of the Sicilian Mafia, including those implicated in the

116. See the technical analysis of the Italian MLAT, 6.

117. *Amsler v. U.S.*, 381 F.2d 37, 51 (9th Cir. 1967). Cf. Rule 17(c), Federal Rules of Criminal Procedure, U.S. Senate Exec. Rept. 98-36, 10.

118. 11 U.L.A. 1.

119. Theresa M. Catino, "Italian and American Cooperative Efforts to Reduce Heroin Trafficking: A Role Model for the United States and Drug-Supplying Foreign Nations," *Dickinson Journal of International Law* 8 (1990), 415–440.

"Pizza Connection" case in New York and the large-scale prosecution of hundreds of mafiosi in Sicily; the Italian requests, which numbered about twice as many as the U.S. requests, were largely for taking depositions and serving documents on witnesses.[120]

The sixth treaty to be signed, with the kingdom of Morocco, was the first with a nondemocratic government.[121] Both parties regarded the negotiations in part as a trial run for future negotiations on an extradition treaty. But the Moroccans' refusal to include a "political offense" clause in the MLAT reduced the Americans' interest in proceeding to the next step. As with the previous MLAT negotiations, the preliminary talks and early parts of the negotiating sessions were devoted to explaining domestic legal concepts and their consequences. Moroccan criminal law had been inherited largely from the French Napoleonic Code system and had assimilated some aspects of Islamic law as well. The Moroccan negotiators thus required much the same sorts of explanations as the Americans' previous partners in MLAT negotiations: why the Americans preferred not to rely on the traditional letters rogatory process; why arrest warrants were signed by clerks, and other requests for assistance by prosecutors, rather than by judges; what the rights of confrontation and cross-examination were and why they needed to be accommodated even in foreign judicial proceedings despite the inconveniences they entailed; why verbatim transcripts of judicial proceedings were necessary; why other parties might be required to be present at judicial proceedings; and so on.

Given the mutual concern over drug trafficking through Morocco, the treaty included an article on forfeiture that provided for "[t]he goods and assets held by any person punishable under laws relating to criminal narcotics matters . . . [to] be seized" and held until the requesting state had completed its judicial proceedings. Unlike the provision in the Italian MLAT, which specifically authorized the forfeited proceeds to be delivered to the Requesting State, the provision in the Moroccan MLAT was modeled after a practice that had developed under (but had not been specified in) the MLAT with the Swiss. It was anticipated that this provision would permit each government to seize and ultimately forfeit

120. Knapp, "Mutual Legal Assistance Treaties" (supra n. 78), 416–417.

121. The treaty, accompanied by the Presidential message transmitting it to the Senate, is reproduced in U.S. Senate Treaty Doc. 98-24, 98th Cong., 2d Sess. (1984). A section-by-section analysis of the treaty appears in U.S. Senate Exec. Rept. 98-35, 98th Cong., 2d Sess. (1984).

drug trafficker assets within its borders pursuant to a prosecution of the trafficker in the other state.

The principal difference between the Moroccan MLAT and others negotiated by the United States was the exclusion of any provisions for transferring witnesses or defendants in custody from one state to the other to give testimony. The Moroccan delegation claimed that their domestic law did not allow for the possibility of incarcerating an individual who had not committed a violation of Moroccan law. They also insisted that such provisions were more appropriate to an extradition or prisoner transfer treaty. Although the Americans suspected that Moroccan opposition stemmed primarily from an anticipation of bureaucratic complications in gaining assent to such a novel provision, they had little choice but to concede the provision.

More generally, the Moroccan treaty differed from the previously negotiated MLATs in terms of its relative lack of specificity. Many of the routine provisions describing the preferred procedures for gathering evidence or taking testimony so that it would be admissible in U.S. courts were either simplified or eliminated in the Moroccan treaty. Also absent were the self-executing provisions that had created a narrow exception to the hearsay rule by providing for foreign officials to certify the chain of custody of seized objects and the authenticity of government documents. The willingness of the U.S. negotiators to forgo these provisions probably reflected both their anticipation that they would make relatively little use of the treaty, as well as the apparent need to complete the negotiations quickly in anticipation of Attorney General Smith's planned visit to the kingdom. In any event, the MLAT between the two countries was signed in October 1983 during the U.S. attorney general's visit. The United States ratified it the following year, but the Moroccans had yet to do likewise as of 1993.

Extraterritoriality in the Caribbean: British Dependencies Past and Present

Even as U.S. officials were gradually succeeding in breaching the walls of secrecy surrounding Switzerland's banks, nations and dependencies throughout the Caribbean were enacting and tightening their own secrecy statutes and lenient tax laws. The Bahamas and a variety of British dependencies, notably the Cayman Islands but also including the Turks and Caicos, Anguilla, Montserrat, and the British Virgin Islands, were attracting billions in U.S. dollars from Americans and others drawn to the nearby, English-speaking islands. Panama was proving equally successful in attracting billions from Latin America and beyond. And the Netherlands Antilles remained an attractive haven as well. The financial secrecy jurisdictions offered legitimate tax havens to U.S. corporations as well as a protective shield for those trying to illegally avoid taxes or to hide and launder criminally derived funds. More often than not, requests for assistance by way of letters rogatory failed to produce satisfaction.

U.S. law enforcement officials responded to the situation in the Caribbean with a range of unilateral tactics designed both to obtain evidence in particular investigations and to pressure local governments into negotiating judicial assistance agreements. Undercover tactics were employed, bribes were paid to local government and bank officials, and subpoenas were directed to foreign banks and bankers with contacts in the United States. These led, not surprisingly, to substantial tensions between the U.S. government and those in the Caribbean. They also angered the British government, which represented many of the island dependencies, and the Canadian government, which found its sovereignty challenged by U.S. assertions of extraterritoriality directed at the Caribbean branches of Canadian banks. The unilateral tactics and other pressures did result, however, in the negotiation of MLATs and similar agreements with Canada and most of the Caribbean governments by the end of the 1980s.

The Cayman Islands

In 1976, the *Field* case, involving an official of a Cayman bank visiting the United States who received a grand jury subpoena compelling him to give testimony before a U.S. grand jury, persuaded the Cayman government to tighten its financial secrecy laws and increase the sanctions for unauthorized disclosure.[122] U.S. prosecutors, however, responded with an array of additional techniques for extracting documents from the Cayman Islands and other havens. They obtained the support of federal courts for the issuance of letters rogatory to Cayman courts.[123]

122. The use of the subpoena was upheld in *U.S. v. Field*, 532 F.2d 404 (5th Cir. 1976); cert. denied, 429 U.S. 940 (1976).

123. *U.S. v. Carver* (unpublished), aff'd sub nom., *U.S. v. Lemire*, 720 F.2d 1327 (D.C. Cir. 1983).

But when the Cayman courts rejected such requests, U.S. prosecutors resorted to more unilateral measures. The most controversial of these arose when a grand jury investigating tax and drug law violations issued a subpoena *duces tecum* in September 1981 to the Miami branch of the Canadian Bank of Nova Scotia for records maintained in the bank's Bahamian branch;[124] subsequent subpoenas issued in March 1983 sought additional documents in the bank's Bahamian branch as well as its branches in the Cayman Islands and Antigua.[125] When the bank refused to comply, claiming that to do so would place it in violation of the islands' bank secrecy laws, the U.S. courts levied daily fines of $25,000 on the bank. Although the *Bank of Nova Scotia* case was not the first in which U.S. attorneys had resorted to the technique thereafter identified with the case—indeed, the resort to compulsory process to compel U.S. corporations to provide documents located in their foreign branches dated back decades—it was the first in which they had responded to resistance in providing the evidence by obtaining sanctions from a court.

Unable to resolve the dispute through law enforcement channels, the Caymans' case was taken up by the British, who conduct the Caymans' foreign affairs, and by the Canadians, whose banks were those principally affected. The motivations of the British, beyond their legal obligation to represent the Caymans, included their concern for the economy of their former colony, their general objection both to U.S. assertions of extraterritoriality and to the notion of an American court presuming to "balance" U.S. interests with those of another state, and their attachment to the principle of financial confidentiality (often referred to as the *Tournier* principle).[126] The Canadians' motivations overlapped to a certain extent with those of the British; they also were upset not only by the threats to their politically influential banks but also by the unilateral nature of the American actions despite Canada's excellent record of

124. *U.S. v. Bank of Nova Scotia*, 691 F.2d 1384 (11th Cir. 1982), cert. denied, 462 U.S. 1119 (1983) (often referred to as *Bank of Nova Scotia I*).

125. *In re Grand Jury Proceedings, U.S. v. Bank of Nova Scotia*, 740 F.2d 817 (11th Cir. 1984), cert. denied, 469 U.S. 1106 (1985) (often referred to as *Bank of Nova Scotia II*).

126. The leading English case of *Tournier v. National Provincial and Union Bank* states that there is a duty of confidentiality between bankers and their customers. See the Library of Congress study by S. F. Clarke, "Bank Secrecy Jurisdictions in the English-Speaking Caribbean and Atlantic Regions," in *Crime and Secrecy: The Use of Offshore Banks and Companies, Staff Study by the Permanent Subcommittee on Investigations of the Senate Committee on Governmental Affairs*, 98th Cong., 1st Sess., S.Rpt. 98-21 (1983), 181–185.

cooperation in all other law enforcement matters. As for the Caymanians, their basic objective was to preserve, by whatever means possible, their lucrative reputation as a reliable financial secrecy jurisdiction.[127]

In an initial effort to resolve the dispute, the governments of the United States, the United Kingdom, and the Cayman Islands entered into a gentleman's agreement in October 1982 to cooperate in criminal investigations, such as of drug trafficking, where the mutuality-of-offense requirement was met.[128] The agreement, however, failed either to enhance Caymanian cooperation or to prevent U.S. prosecutors from obtaining grand jury subpoenas; indeed, no bank records had been delivered by the end of 1983.[129] One year later, the issue finally came to a head after the Cayman Grand Court twice enjoined the Bank of Nova Scotia from releasing documents held in the Caymans in response to a U.S. court order. Under pressure from the Bank of Nova Scotia, which was incurring substantial fines as a result of its failure to comply with the subpoena (a failure caused in part by the bank's negligence in locating even those documents it had been authorized by the Bahamian attorney general to deliver), the British intervened and obliged the Caymanian governor to order that the documents be disclosed.

The tensions generated by this and other disputes over extraterritoriality led to a November 1983 meeting between the American undersecretary of state, Kenneth Dam, and the British minister for foreign and commonwealth affairs, Malcolm Rifkind, one outcome of which was the establishment of a number of working groups to address particular disputes. One of these was charged specifically with the task of examining the problems created by criminal uses of the Caribbean secrecy jurisdictions. At about the same time, and in response to other international tensions generated by the flurry of *Bank of Nova Scotia* type of subpoenas obtained by prosecutors in the wake of that case, the Justice Department ordered that all subpoenas to institutions in the United

127. The perspective of the British and the Caymanians is well presented in their *amici curiae* brief to the U.S. Supreme Court in the *Bank of Nova Scotia* case, No. 84-329 (October term, 1984).

128. The letters clarifying each government's interpretation of the agreement can be found at Fedders et al., *Transnational Litigation* (supra n. 53), 737–743.

129. Disagreement over the extent and significance of the agreement was ultimately resolved by the Eleventh Circuit Court of Appeals in *Bank of Nova Scotia II*, which deemed the agreement "not a binding, enforceable agreement but rather an experimental and tentative alternative for the production of documents." See *U.S. v. Bank of Nova Scotia*, 740 F.2d 817, 829 (11th Cir. 1984).

States for records located abroad be cleared through the Office of International Affairs. The need for the order, which became known as "the Jensen memorandum" (after Associate Attorney General D. Lowell Jensen), was readily apparent.[130] It reflected the recognition that federal and other prosecutors, in their quest for evidence, would utilize whichever means seemed most effective and expedient, regardless of their broader consequences. Apart from the infrequently read U.S. Attorney's Manual, which required that prosecutors check with the Justice Department before taking any action that might have an impact on foreign relations, most prosecutors perceived few if any constraints on their resort to subpoenas to obtain evidence. As a result, OIA attorneys had been unpleasantly surprised and embarrassed on a number of occasions during 1982 and 1983 by angry phone calls from their foreign counterparts, particularly in London and Ottawa, complaining about the issuance of *Bank of Nova Scotia* subpoenas without any prior efforts to obtain the desired evidence through more conciliatory, bilateral channels. The Jensen memorandum, by requiring that all international requests be channeled through the OIA, thus allowed the Justice Department to gain greater control over the foreign policy of evidence-gathering. It provided OIA attorneys with an opportunity to inform prosecutors of more effective and less abrasive techniques for gathering evidence, some of which involved the OIA's own informal and expedited arrangements with foreign counterparts. And it allowed them as well as higher-level Justice Department officials to better manage their relations with both cooperative and less-cooperative foreign justice ministries. Although the Jensen memorandum did not apply to civil subpoenas and administrative summons issued by the SEC and other regulatory agencies, it effectively canalized through the OIA all criminal investigative requests for evidence located abroad.

Another outcome of the Dam-Rifkind meeting was the initiation of negotiations in early 1984 between U.S. and British officials on a legal assistance agreement with the Cayman Islands. Unlike the other MLATs negotiated by the United States, this one was limited, at the request of the British, to cooperation in narcotics cases and predicated on the provisions against drug trafficking in the multilateral Single Convention on Narcotic Drugs.[131] American law enforcement agencies were divided

130. The memorandum is reproduced in the appendix of Paul B. Bschorr, " 'Waiver by Conduct': Another View," *Journal of Comparative Business and Capital Market Law* 6 (1984), 307–318, esp. 313–315.

131. The Single Convention on Narcotic Drugs, 1961. Done at New York Mar. 30, 1961;

as to the advisability of negotiating a legal assistance treaty limited solely to drug investigations, but it was decided to accept the British condition. Under some pressure from the British, Caymanian officials accepted the necessity for an agreement but expressed their concern that the agreement not provide a means for U.S. law enforcement agencies, notably the IRS, to engage in "fishing expeditions."[132] The U.S. delegation was eager to minimize the amount of information that would have to be provided in support of a request for evidence; they were deeply concerned that the targets of some of the investigations involving Cayman banks, who included the more powerful Colombian drug traffickers, not be provided an opportunity to undermine U.S. investigations by means of either legal recourse or illicit intimidation and bribery. The mutual concerns were resolved by an agreement that the U.S. attorney general would personally certify that each request was for a drug-related prosecution. The second principal concern of the British and Cayman negotiators was to limit the use of subpoenas *duces tecum* by U.S. prosecutors. In what constituted their principal concession, the Americans "swallowed hard," as one Justice Department official put it, and agreed to waive their prerogative of obtaining a subpoena *duces tecum* and to confine their requests in drug related cases (but not in others) to the procedures specified in the agreement.

The agreement was signed by the British and U.S. governments on July 26, 1984, and went into effect on August 29, when the Caymanian implementing legislation took effect.[133] Unlike the MLAT with the Swiss, the Cayman agreement specified that any American request be kept confidential by both the Cayman attorney general and the provider of

entered into force Dec. 13, 1964; for the U.S. June 24, 1967; 18 UST 1407; TIAS 6298; 520 UNTS 204.

132. They were, however, willing to permit information they provided to be used to prosecute drug traffickers on Title 26 charges.

133. Exchange of Letters Between the Government of the United Kingdom of Great Britain and Northern Ireland and the Government of the United States of America Concerning the Cayman Islands and Matters Connected with, Arising from, Related to, or Resulting from Any Narcotics Activity Referred to in the Single Convention on Narcotic Drugs, 1961, as Amended by the Protocol Amending the Single Convention on Narcotic Drugs, 1972. The agreement can be found in *International Legal Materials* 24 (1985), 1110. The Caymanian implementing legislation is reproduced in ibid., 937. Because the agreement was an executive agreement rather than a full-fledged MLAT, Senate ratification was not required. Some of the events and cases noted above are also discussed in Comment, "Piercing Offshore Bank Secrecy Laws Used to Launder Illegal Narcotics Profits: The Cayman Islands Example," *Texas International Law Journal* 20 (1985), 133.

the documents; it waived the standard MLAT requirement that a request be accompanied by supporting documents, requiring only the U.S. attorney general's certificate. And the Cayman implementing legislation omitted the types of procedural hurdles that had so hampered the Swiss MLAT. For all these reasons, as well as the fact that requests could be sent only one way, many U.S. officials were reluctant to trade in the executive agreement for a full-fledged MLAT with the Caymans.

The Cayman agreement stipulated, however, that the signatories enter into MLAT negotiations before the end of 1985. On July 3, 1986, a full-fledged MLAT was signed by representatives of the U.S., British, and Cayman governments.[134] It was the first between the United States and a Caribbean financial secrecy jurisdiction, as well as the first MLAT of any kind signed by the British, who traditionally had avoided involvement in such arrangements—including the European Convention on Mutual Assistance—because of doubts that their strict rules of evidence could be accommodated to foreign judicial proceedings on their behalf.[135] From the U.S. perspective, the principal disadvantage of the MLAT (insisted upon by the British/Cayman delegation) was that the attorney general's certification could no longer substitute for the need to provide supporting documents spelling out the alleged offense. Justice Department officials had found, both in implementing the Swiss MLAT and in continuing to execute letters rogatory, that the need to provide supporting documents spelling out the alleged offense represented a substantial deterrent to U.S. prosecutors seeking evidence from abroad. Their concern was that the information provided in the request might be released—because of legal process, carelessness, corruption, or whatever—thus jeopardizing the success of the investigation and/or the source of the information. Although the U.S. delegation was disappointed about losing the novel certification provision in the Cayman agreement, they were partially reassured by the high level of trust developed in mutually

134. The treaty, accompanied by the Presidential message transmitting it to the Senate, is reproduced in U.S. Senate Treaty Doc. 100-8, 100th Cong., 1st Sess. (1988), and in *International Legal Materials* 26 (1987), 537. A section-by-section analysis of the treaty, as well as additional analysis of the treaty in response to Senate inquiries, appears in U.S. Senate Exec. Rept. 101-08, 101st Cong., 1st Sess. (1989), 8–50, 122–129, 140–145. See also Ilene Katz Kobert and Jonathan D. Yellin, "The United States Treaty with the United Kingdom Concerning the Cayman Islands and Mutual Legal Assistance in Criminal Matters: The End of Another Tax Haven," *Inter-American Law Review* 19 (1988), 663–697.

135. Michael Havers, "Legal Cooperation: A Matter of Necessity," *International Lawyer* 21 (1987), 185–193, esp. 192.

implementing the first agreement, by the inclusion of confidentiality clauses in the MLAT, and by the fact that in the future fewer requests would entail the sorts of risks involved in investigating the financial activities of Colombian drug traffickers.

The MLAT did, however, offer numerous advantages over the previous agreement. Not only was it not limited to drug-related cases, but the British and Cayman negotiators even agreed to cooperate in cases (such as insider trading and violations of the Foreign Corrupt Practices Act) in which the mutuality of offense requirement was not met. Tax offenses were explicitly excluded from the scope of the treaty, but the British agreed that evidence provided by Caymanian authorities could be used to prosecute fraud in connection with tax shelters and tax evasion or filing false statements with respect to illegally obtained income. Another advantage of the MLAT was that it included far broader types of assistance than were authorized in the executive agreement, including not just the production and authentication of documents but also the taking of testimony, serving documents, locating persons, transferring persons in custody for testimonial purposes, executing requests for searches and seizures, and assistance in freezing and forfeiting criminally obtained assets.[136]

Among the most important issues debated by the MLAT negotiators was the continued resort by U.S. prosecutors to subpoenas and other unilateral means of extraterritorially asserting U.S. jurisdiction. U.S. prosecutors had continued to employ *Bank of Nova Scotia* subpoenas in nondrug related investigations, particularly those involving tax shelter frauds, although they had tried to minimize their resort to such methods and to consult with their counterparts in the Cayman Islands before proceeding. The 1984 agreement had also not precluded an alternative technique devised by U.S. prosecutors to obtain evidence from foreign financial secrecy jurisdictions. Known as a "*Ghidoni* waiver" (after the first prominent court decision upholding its use), the technique involved obtaining a court order compelling the target of a grand jury investigation to authorize foreign banks to disclose the records sought in the subpoena.[137] Although intended to allow banks to comply with U.S.

136. U.S. Senate, *MLAT . . . Caymans* (supra n. 5), 125–128.

137. *U.S. v. Ghidoni*, 732 F.2d 814 (11th Cir. 1984), cert. denied, 469 U.S. 932 (1984) (involving a grand jury subpoena issued to the Miami branch of the Bank of Nova Scotia commanding it to produce documents located in its Cayman Islands branch). The "*Ghidoni* waiver" is critically analyzed in Harvey M. Silets and Susan W. Brenner, " 'Compelled Consent': An Oxymoron with Sinister Consequences for Citizens Who Patronize Foreign

subpoenas without violating foreign secrecy laws, the "compelled consent" technique had been rejected by the Grand Court of the Cayman Islands in 1984.[138] U.S. prosecutors, however, had largely ignored the ruling by the Cayman court, and most U.S. courts had upheld the use of the technique against constitutional challenges, notably the claim that it violated defendants' Fifth Amendment rights against self-incrimination.[139] During the MLAT negotiations, the British and Cayman delegates pressured the U.S. negotiators on this issue. The resultant compromise forbade U.S. authorities from seeking a *Bank of Nova Scotia* subpoena or *Ghidoni* waiver until after the assistance had been requested under the treaty and Cayman authorities had had ample opportunity to comply.[140] The U.S. negotiators refused, however, to apply the same conditions to the issuance of subpoenas or material person warrants for persons temporarily in the United States (i.e., the type of subpoena employed in the *Field* case) or to the issuance of administrative summons by the IRS, the SEC, or the CFTC unless the investigation concerned a "criminal offense" under the treaty.[141] They claimed that such a concession would constitute an undesirably broad restriction on each party's territorial sovereignty. Still wary of American "fishing expeditions," the Cayman and British negotiators also insisted on a provision, not included in other MLATs negotiated by the United States, requiring each request to contain "reasonable grounds" to believe both that the specific crime had been committed and that the information requested could be found in the territory of the requested state.[142] Although wary of

Banking Institutions," *Case Western Reserve Journal of International Law* 20 (1988), 435–508.

138. Chief Judge Summerfield stated: "On the face of it, the consent given in Ghidoni's case is consent given under compulsion and does not amount to consent for the purposes of our law." *In re an Application by ABC, Ltd. Under the Confidential Relationships (Preservation) (Amendment) Law, 1979*, Judgment of July 24, 1984, Grand Court, Cayman Islands, July 24, 1984 (Cause No. 269), discussed in Ellen C. Atwater, "Compelled Waiver of Bank Secrecy in the Cayman Islands: Solution to International Tax Evasion or Threat to Sovereignty of Nations?" *Fordham International Law Journal* 9 (1986), 680–733, esp. 703–705.

139. See *U.S. v. Ghidoni*. The *Ghidoni* waiver was upheld in *U.S. v. Davis*, 767 F.2d 1025 (2d Cir. 1985), *In re U.S. Grand Jury Proceedings (Cid)*, 767 F.2d 1131 (5th Cir. 1985), and *In re Grand Jury Subpoena*, 826 F.2d 1166 (2d Cir. 1987), but invalidated in *In re Grand Jury Proceedings (Ranauro)*, 814 F.2d 791 (1st Cir. 1987). The Supreme Court ultimately resolved the dispute in favor of the *Ghidoni* waiver in *Doe v. U.S.*, 108 S.Ct. 2341, 487 U.S. 201 (1988).

140. See Art. 17 of the Cayman MLAT.

141. See the technical analysis of the treaty in U.S. Senate, *MLAT . . . Caymans* (supra n. 5), 45–46.

142. See Art. 3(2)(c) of the Cayman MLAT.

tinkering with new language, the U.S. negotiators conceded the wording, confident that it would not prove onerous in practice.[143]

Among Caymanians, debate over the treaty and the implementing legislation was heated, as had been the case following the signing of the 1984 agreement. In an election held a few months after the agreement went into effect, the accord with the United States was a major campaign issue. Many of those in the government were ousted from office. Some observers suspected that the signing of the agreement was responsible and that the old government was perceived as having gone soft and caved in to the pressure exerted by the Americans and the British.[144] Despite the fallout from the 1984 agreement, and despite heated debate over the new MLAT, the Cayman legislature passed the necessary implementing legislation only weeks after the treaty was signed. Ratification by the U.S. Senate, however, was delayed as a result of unanticipated objections discussed below. The MLAT ultimately took effect late in 1989.

As anticipated, the executive agreement with the Caymans proved highly successful in obtaining evidence. By mid-1986, according to a British count, 39 requests had been transmitted,[145] and most had been processed quite rapidly by the Cayman authorities. By October 1, 1987, according to an American count, 51 initial requests and 40 follow-up requests had been transmitted; the evidence provided had contributed to the conviction of 95 drug traffickers, including approximately 30 for violation of the federal "drug kingpin" statute, and proven highly useful in asset forfeiture proceedings as well.[146] And by the time the MLAT entered into force, U.S. officials had used the executive agreement to transmit an estimated 200 requests. It was anticipated that the high level of assistance would continue under the MLAT.

The paramount question, in the eyes of the Caymanians and all other financial secrecy jurisdictions as well, was what impact the agreement would have on the Caymans' bank industry. Some bankers suggested that an outflow of funds to Panama and other financial secrecy jurisdictions followed the signing of the initial agreement. Others indicated that

143. See the technical analysis of the treaty in U.S. Senate, *MLAT . . . Caymans* (supra n. 5), 123.

144. Conflicting reports also suggested either that the police chief of the Caymans had been forced out of office for appearing too forthcoming with the Americans, or that he had merely retired in due course.

145. Havers, "Legal Cooperation," (supra n. 135).

146. Knapp, "Mutual Legal Assistance Treaties" (supra n. 78), 417. The "drug kingpin" statute is 18 U.S.C. 848, otherwise known as the Continuing Criminal Enterprise Statute.

the outflow has been negligible, that drug money had never constituted more than a small proportion of the funds sent to the Caymans, and that in fact the benefit to the Caymans' reputation as a result of the agreement has attracted business—just as the Swiss had claimed following the signing of their MLAT. Indeed, after the executive agreement the number of banks opening branches in the Cayman Islands continued to climb. Just days before the MLAT was signed, an article appeared in the *Miami Herald* on the Cayman banking industry. Its title: "Caymans Grow as 'Geneva of the Caribbean.' "[147]

Both the agreement and the treaty with the Caymans were expected to serve as models for future agreements with other financial secrecy jurisdictions, notably Britain's other dependencies in the Caribbean. The first to follow was the Turks and Caicos, whose banking assets were believed to be second only to the Caymans among the British financial secrecy jurisdictions in the Caribbean. The negotiators may also have been influenced by the islands' reputation for involvement in drug smuggling, a notoriety highlighted by the arrest of the Turks and Caicos Islands' chief minister and two other high-ranking officials in a DEA undercover operation in Miami in March 1985.[148] In September 1986, following an official inquiry into corruption that resulted in the dissolution of the Islands' governing Executive Council by the British governor-general, American and British negotiators signed an agreement that was virtually identical to the 1984 Cayman agreement.[149] Similar agreements were concluded and went into force the following year with Anguilla,[150] the British Virgin Islands,[151] and Montserrat.[152] By 1990, the total number of requests transmitted under all four of the agreements num-

147. James Russell, "Caymans Grow as Geneva of the Caribbean," *Miami Herald*, June 22, 1986, 1F.

148. Jon Nordheimer, "U.S. Arrests Atlantic Islands' Leader in Drug Plot," *New York Times*, Mar. 6, 1985, A1; Liz Balmaseda, "Drug Net Snares Island Ministers," *Miami Herald*, Mar. 6, 1985, A1; Mary Thornton, "Caribbean Prime Minister Arrested in Miami on Drug Charges," *Washington Post*, Mar. 6, 1985, A16. The reaction to the arrest in the Turks and Caicos was split, with many people angered by the arrest and the fact that the resident British governor had cooperated with the DEA. See Geoffrey Tomb, "Drug Arrests Divide Poverty-Stricken Turks and Caicos," *Miami Herald*, Mar. 12, 1985, 14A; Mary Thornton, "Drug Arrests Raise Islands' Tension," *Washington Post*, Mar. 11, 1985; and Joseph B. Treaster, "In Old Pirate Haunt, Daunting News of Drug Trade," *New York Times*, Mar. 13, 1985, 2.

149. Philip Shenon, "Pact Gives U.S. Access to Data in Drug Haven," *New York Times*, Sept. 19, 1986, B2.

150. Exchange of letters at Washington, Mar. 11, 1987; entered into force Mar. 27, 1987.

151. Exchange of letters at London, Apr. 14, 1987; entered into force Aug. 12, 1987.

152. Exchange of letters at Washington, May 14, 1987; entered into force June 1, 1987.

bered no more than two dozen, but British and U.S. officials were nonetheless preparing to extend the Cayman MLAT to the four dependencies in much the same fashion as they had the executive agreements.

Canada

Even as U.S. negotiators were hammering out the initial agreement with British and Caymanian officials, negotiations of comparable importance were under way with the Canadians; indeed, the Canadian MLAT was the first to address the dispute over *Bank of Nova Scotia* subpoenas.[153] It was not, however, the first time that the two governments had squared off on the issue of U.S. assertions of extraterritoriality. Canada had been among the nations most affected by U.S. efforts to extraterritorialize its laws after World War II. Conflicts over U.S. antitrust laws dated back to a 1947 investigation of Canadian paper and pulp companies, one result of which had been Ontario's first blocking statute. Further conflicts had arisen in response to U.S. antitrust charges against Canadian and other uranium producers during the early 1970s, as well as to U.S. efforts to apply its export control laws to Canadian trade with Cuba and Canadian involvement in the construction of the Siberian pipeline—all of which had led to both provincial and federal blocking statutes in Canada as well as frequent high-level negotiations and three memoranda of understanding designed to find a satisfactory compromise.[154] The rise in tensions over the *Bank of Nova Scotia* case during the early 1980s contributed to enactment of Canada's most sweeping blocking statute to date.[155] At the same time, the flood of subpoenas directed at Canadian bank branches in the Caribbean and other financial secrecy jurisdictions prompted the formation in 1983 of a U.S.-Canadian Subpoena Working Group composed of law enforcement and diplomatic officials from both

153. The treaty, accompanied by the Presidential message transmitting it to the Senate, is reproduced in U.S. Senate Treaty Doc. 100-14, 100th Cong., 2d Sess. (1988), and in *International Legal Materials* 24 (1985), 1092–1099. A section-by-section analysis of the treaty appears in U.S. Senate Exec. Rept. 101-10, 101st Cong., 1st Sess. (1989).

154. The blocking statutes and the 1969 MOU are reproduced in A. V. Lowe, *Extraterritorial Jurisdiction* (Cambridge: Grotius Publications, 1983). See also Sharon A. Williams and J.-G. Castel, *Canadian Criminal Law: International and Transnational Aspects* (Toronto: Buttersworth, 1981).

155. Catherine Botticelli, "Recent Canadian Blocking Legislation: A Vehicle to Foster Extraterritorial Discovery Cooperation Between the United States and Canada?" *Fordham International Law Journal* 10 (1987), 671–688.

nations. Among its conclusions was the recommendation that an MLAT be negotiated to formalize and facilitate the extensive law enforcement relations between the neighboring states.[156]

The MLAT negotiations were the first for Canada, as well as the first between the United States and a fellow common law state—albeit one with quite different criminal procedures. The two delegations began with the mutual understanding that the MLAT would provide for broad and wide-ranging cooperation. The principal obstacle to U.S. requests for assistance arose not from any penchant for secrecy in Canada's laws but rather from Canadian court decisions that had severely restricted the provision of assistance to U.S. prosecutors at the preindictment phase of grand jury proceedings.[157] The Canadians agreed to rectify the problem by inserting the appropriate language both in the treaty and in the implementing legislation.[158] They also agreed to waive any requirement of dual criminality, thereby authorizing assistance in U.S. investigations of money laundering and other activities that had not yet been criminalized in Canada.

The only significant disagreements over principle in the negotiations involved the *Bank of Nova Scotia* subpoenas and other U.S. assertions of extraterritorial jurisdiction, an irritation that the Canadians had come to perceive—in the words of one of the MLAT negotiators—as "a hardy perennial in U.S.-Canadian relations." The U.S. negotiators responded to the Canadians' desire for more cooperative bilateral mechanisms of

156. A summary of some of the Canadian views by one of the Canadian MLAT negotiators, Jonathan Fried, can be found in Serge April and Jonathan Fried, "Compelling Discovery and Disclosure in Transnational Litigation: A Canadian View," *NYU Journal of International Law and Politics* 16 (1984), 961. See also J.-G. Castel, "Compelling Disclosure by a Non-Party Litigant in Violation of Foreign Bank Secrecy Laws: Recent Developments in Canada–United States Relations," *Canadian Yearbook of International Law* 23 (1985), 261–284. For an overview of the extraterritoriality issue from the Canadian perspective, see William C. Graham, "Reflections on United States Legal Imperialism: Canadian Sovereignty in the Context of North American Economic Integration," *International Journal* 40 (1985), 478–509.

157. Canadian courts had interpreted Section 43 of Canada's Evidence Act as forbidding the use of compulsory process in behalf of foreign authorities unless the court were satisfied that the evidence produced would be used at trial and that it was not sought solely for the purpose of furthering an investigation. See in particular *Re United States of America and Executive Securities Corporation* (1977) 77 D.L.R. (3d) 157 (O.H.C.). See also the technical analysis of the treaty in U.S. Senate Exec. Rept. 101-10, 9, 34.

158. The same language also nullified the similar limitation that U.S. courts had placed on providing assistance under Section 1782 to foreign administrative agencies. See *Fonseca v. Blumenthal*, 620 F.2d 322 (2d Cir. 1980) and *In Re Letters Rogatory Issued by the Director of Inspection of the Government of India*, 305 F.2d 1016 (2d Cir. 1967).

evidence-gathering by agreeing to a "first resort" provision requiring both parties to seek assistance initially via the treaty and to consult thereafter in the event that the treaty mechanisms failed to provide the requested evidence. The formulation was to provide a model for the Cayman MLAT, which incorporated and expanded on the Canadian provision, and for the MLAT with the Bahamas. (It failed, however, to accommodate German officials, who were equally concerned about the United States' resort to subpoenas and other unilateral measures. Indeed, the relatively rapid negotiation of the Canadian MLAT, which required little more than a year, contrasted starkly with the German MLAT negotiations, which had begun during the early 1980s and then been stalled for the remainder of the decade primarily over differences regarding treaty restrictions on the United States' resort to unilateral measures.)

The remainder of the treaty provisions were relatively broad and noncontentious, reflecting both the United States' growing experience in negotiating and utilizing MLATs and the tradition of cooperative law enforcement relations between the two nations. No mention of political offenses or comparable limitations on assistance was included in the treaty. The negotiators specifically agreed that assistance *would* be granted for fiscal offenses.[159] As with most of the other MLATs apart from those with the Cayman Islands and the Bahamas, the treaty was recognized as a tax convention permitting the IRS to provide assistance. No restriction was placed on the use of information or evidence once it had become public in the requesting state. The "proceeds of crime" provision was broader and more open-ended than in previous MLATs, authorizing cooperation in "the forfeiture of the proceeds of crime, restitution to the victims of crime, and the collection of fines imposed as a sentence in a criminal prosecution." Its effect was to modify the longstanding rule of international law, articulated by Chief Justice John Marshall in the *Antelope* case, that "the courts of no country execute the penal laws of another."[160] Other concerns, such as the need to protect the identity of informants and the desire that individuals requested to appear in the requesting state be notified of outstanding warrants or other judicial orders, were addressed either with particular treaty language or with understandings formalized in the technical analysis ac-

159. See the technical analysis of the Canadian MLAT, U.S. Senate Exec. Rept. 101-10, 36.
160. 23 U.S. (10 Wheat.) 66, 123 (1825).

companying the treaty. In March 1985, President Ronald Reagan and the Canadian prime minister signed the completed MLAT in Quebec City.

Bahamas

Perhaps the most acrimonious MLAT negotiations were those with the Bahamians. As with the Cayman Islands, abundant evidence pointed to the advantage taken of the Bahamas' financial secrecy laws by drug traffickers and other criminals to launder and hide the proceeds of their activities.[161] But unlike the Caymans, the archipelago had also emerged as a major transshipment point for marijuana and cocaine in transit from Colombia to the United States. Until late 1984, the Bahamian government proved at least as uncooperative as that of the Caymans in refusing to provide assistance to American investigations;[162] the Justice Department in turn pursued a confrontational approach in its efforts to obtain information and evidence, utilizing *Bank of Nova Scotia* subpoenas and other judicial mechanisms to collect evidence, as well as a variety of informal, unilateral police measures. Periodic efforts to improve cooperation, and specifically to commence MLAT negotiations, were hampered by evidence of high-level corruption in the Bahamas, tensions over U.S. law enforcement operations in the Bahamas, and exposés of both in the U.S. Congress and media.[163] During late 1983, matters came to a head when DEA and FBI agents were declared persona non grata and when reports of high-level involvement in drug trafficking obliged Prime Minister Pindling to set up an independent Commission of Inquiry.[164]

161. *Crime and Secrecy: Staff Study* (supra n. 126), 54–62; Richard H. Blum, *Offshore Haven Banks, Trusts, and Companies: The Business of Crime in the Euromarket* (New York: Praeger, 1984), 133–146.

162. Reginald Stuart, "U.S.-Bahamian Relations Are Straining Under Drug Investigations," *New York Times*, Sept. 28, 1983, A21.

163. Law enforcement officials in both countries claimed they had broached the subject of MLAT negotiations as early as 1980 and been rebuffed by the other. The account of the director of the OIA, Philip White, is provided in his testimony to the Task Force on International Narcotics Control, in *U.S. Narcotics Interdiction Programs in the Bahamas: Hearings Before the Committee on Foreign Affairs, House of Representatives*, 98th Cong., 1st Sess. (1983), 184–193. The Bahamian perspective is provided in *Narcotics Review in the Caribbean: Hearing Before the Committee on Foreign Affairs, U.S. House of Representatives*, 100th Cong., 2d Sess. (1988), 54–56, 79–87.

164. One explosive exposé was delivered by NBC Nightly News on Sept. 5, 1983. It cited American officials who claimed that major drug traffickers, reportedly including the infamous

By late 1984, both governments had begun to reverse direction and restore their relationship. U.S. law enforcement agents were invited back, and joint drug enforcement operations were initiated. At about the same time, the Commission of Inquiry completed its report.[165] Among its recommendations were that an MLAT be negotiated and "that problems connected with the revenue laws of the United States . . . be set aside when negotiating an agreement to trace drug related funds."[166] MLAT negotiations accordingly commenced in January 1985 and were completed in mid-1987, a period during which relations between the two governments continued to wax and wane.[167] The negotiation sessions themselves were strongly influenced by the forceful and somewhat combative personalities of the two heads of delegation: Paul Adderley, a close associate of Prime Minister Pindling who served as both attorney general and foreign minister of the Bahamas during much of the negotiations; and Carol Hallett, a political appointee to the U.S. ambassadorship in the Bahamas who was later appointed commissioner of U.S. Customs by the Bush administration.[168] With both Adderley and Hallett closely attuned to, and responsible for, most other law enforcement and diplomatic issues between the two nations, the tenor and timing of the MLAT negotiations were rather more affected by external political considerations than any other MLAT negotiations.[169]

The Bahamians were also influenced initially by the Canadians. The fact that Canada had negotiated an MLAT with the United States in

---

fugitive Robert Vesco, were paying off Bahamian officials, including the prime minister. A second NBC Nightly News report, on Feb. 22, 1984, cited a DEA report in which Prime Minister Pindling was reported to have taken bribes from a Colombian trafficker.

165. Many of the commission's findings were detailed in a thorough report on corruption in the Bahamas that appeared in the *Miami Herald* in late 1984. See the six-part series entitled "A Nation for Sale," Sept. 23–28, 1984.

166. Report of the Commission of Inquiry (Appointed to Inquire into the Illegal Use of the Bahamas for the Transshipment of Dangerous Drugs Destined for the United States of America, Nov. 1983–Dec. 1984), Bahamas (Dec. 1984), 285. The commission also noted (353–356) that the United States had failed to respond to earlier proposals by Attorney General Paul Adderley to enter into negotiations.

167. The trend toward favorable relations is stressed in Joel Brinkley, "In Fighting Drug Traffic, Attitude Wins the Aid," *New York Times*, Oct. 7, 1986, A28.

168. Robert D. Hershey, "In the Customs Service, an Open Door at the Top," *New York Times*, Aug. 18, 1990, 9.

169. The treaty, accompanied by the Presidential message transmitting it to the Senate, is reproduced in U.S. Senate Treaty Doc. 100-17, 100th Cong., 2d Sess. (1988), and in *International Legal Materials* 24 (1985), 1092. A section-by-section analysis of the treaty appears in U.S. Senate Exec. Rept. 101-12, 101st Cong., 1st Sess. (1989).

which the issues of extraterritoriality and bank secrecy were addressed provided a precedent that the Bahamian government found useful in justifying its decision to commence MLAT negotiations with the United States. The text of the Canadian treaty also proved useful as the first model of a comprehensive MLAT between the United States and a common law nation concerned with financial secrecy. The Canadian government, moreover, was eager to avoid a repeat of the sorts of tensions and embarrassments generated by the *Bank of Nova Scotia* case; its diplomatic representatives accordingly let Bahamian officials know that they would favor their entering into MLAT negotiations with the United States. By the time those negotiations got seriously under way, however, the U.S. MLAT with the Cayman Islands had replaced the Canadian MLAT as the principal model for the Bahamian negotiations—although the Bahamian delegation also drew on draft uniform legislation regarding mutual legal assistance among the members of the Commonwealth.

Much discussion was devoted to the scope of offenses for which assistance would be required under the treaty. The Bahamians, like the Caymanians, insisted on excluding run-of-the-mill tax evasion investigations and refused to ensure cooperation in civil or administrative proceedings, such as those initiated by the SEC and the CFTC, but they agreed to cooperate in investigations of tax fraud as well as anything connected to drug trafficking, including tax and money laundering offenses.[170] The Bahamian delegation also resisted the extensive listing of criminal offenses for which assistance would be required that had been included in the Cayman MLAT, insisting on a briefer listing, albeit one that was worded to include most of the offenses inserted in the Cayman MLAT. As in the Canadian and Cayman negotiations, the U.S. negotiators were anxious that the treaty and implementing legislation

170. Among the more notable requests for assistance processed during the negotiations was one that involved the SEC's investigation of illicit transactions by Dennis Levine. Having failed in a previous investigation to obtain documents via Bahamian courts, the SEC successfully appealed to Attorney General Paul Adderley to issue the necessary written opinion to permit Bank Leu International to hand over the requested documents without violating the Bahamas' secrecy laws. Although the Bahamian government subsequently issued a press release limiting the precedential value of its assistance in the Levine case, its willingness to cooperate in the Levine investigation provided a further indication of the Bahamian government's changing attitude toward U.S. criminal investigations. See the defendant's account of the case in Dennis B. Levine with William Hoffer, *Inside Out: An Insider's Account of Wall Street* (New York: G. P. Putnam's Sons, 1991).

specify that cooperation be forthcoming in grand jury investigations and forfeiture proceedings;[171] the Bahamians in turn noted that a U.S. court had interpreted Section 1782 so as to preclude U.S. assistance in response to a request from the Bahamian Commission of Inquiry.[172] Both delegations agreed that the MLAT would address the concerns of the other.

The Bahamians also insisted upon additional restrictions that had been included in some previous MLATs. Whereas the Canadian MLAT stipulated that any information provided pursuant to the treaty that was publicly revealed in a court proceeding could thereafter be used with no restrictions, the Bahamians preferred to follow the Caymanian MLAT in imposing continued restrictions on the use of such information.[173] They also copied the Caymanian MLAT's anti-"fishing expedition" clause requiring that a U.S. request contain "reasonable grounds" to believe both that the specific crime had been committed and that the information requested could be found in the territory of the requested state. Concerned that U.S. requests for location of persons and service of documents not overburden the Bahamas' relatively limited law enforcement resources, the Bahamian delegation asked for and received concessions by the U.S. delegation on this score. They also insisted upon a provision derived from the Commonwealth Scheme precluding assistance in cases involving prosecution or punishment on account of a suspect's race, religion, nationality, or political opinions.[174] Their particular concern, the Bahamians noted, involved racially motivated requests.[175] With respect to the single most important issue in the view of the Bahamians—the resort by U.S. prosecutors to *Bank of Nova Scotia* subpoenas and

171. A 1978 British court decision had cast doubt on the ability of a court to execute a request from a U.S. grand jury. *Rio Tinto Zinc Corp. v. Westinghouse Electric Corp.* (1978) 1 All E.R. 434, per Lord Diplock (H.L.), discussed in the technical analysis of the treaty, U.S. Senate Exec. Rept. 101-12, 15.

172. *In the Matter of the Request for Judicial Assistance from the Supreme Court of the Commonwealth of the Bahamas*, Misc. No. 84-0113 (D.D.C., application denied June 5, 1984).

173. See Art. 8 of the MLAT.

174. See Art. 3(1)(d) of the MLAT.

175. U.S. Senate, *MLAT . . . Caymans* (supra n. 5), 138. The attitudes of the Bahamian negotiators on this score may have been reflected in an outburst by Bahamian Attorney General Adderley during the heat of the 1987 election campaign in which the U.S. government made known its preference for the opposition. U.S. officials, Adderley reportedly stated, "are too big, too white and too American to listen to us poor black fools down here in the Bahamas. . . . They're presumptuous and bloody arrogant." See Joel Brinkley, "Drugs and Corruption Color Vote in Bahamas," *New York Times*, June 14, 1987, 1.

other unilateral measures—the negotiators agreed to follow the Canadian MLAT in requiring first resort to the treaty process but permitting alternative measures where the MLAT process failed to provide satisfaction.[176] Unlike the Caymanians, however, the Bahamian delegation was not particularly concerned about the use of *Ghidoni* waivers, nor had their courts ruled on the legitimacy of the tactic under Bahamian law.

The treaty was signed by the Bahamas on June 12, 1987, just days before Prime Minister Pindling won reelection to a sixth term in a highly acrimonious campaign involving accusations of corruption hurled by the challenger and a successful manipulation of anti-U.S. sentiment by the prime minister.[177] In an unusual break from precedent, U.S. officials decided to delay their signature, preferring both to await the election returns and to get a glimpse of the proposed legislation implementing the MLAT. The Americans were concerned for a number of reasons. Bahamian law, as in most common law nations apart from the United States, regards treaties as inferior to domestic constitutions and laws unless implemented by appropriate domestic legislation. "In the eyes of a local judge," one OIA attorney indicated, the treaty would represent "little more than an interesting piece of paper" without the necessary implementing legislation. The Bahamians had reinforced this point by insisting on a provision in the MLAT requiring that "all requests . . . be executed in accordance with and subject to the limitations imposed by the laws of the Requested State." Although the legal systems of both Canada and the Cayman Islands presented similar concerns, the turbulent course of U.S.-Bahamian relations gave the Americans greater cause for concern. They feared in particular a replication of the problems occasioned by the Swiss implementing legislation a decade before. Shortly after the Bahamian government signed the MLAT, however, it reassured the U.S. delegation by providing them with a draft of the proposed implementing legislation. Although concerned about a few of the provisions contained in the draft,[178] the U.S. delegation expressed its satisfaction, and Ambassador Hallett signed the MLAT in August 1987.

Despite the hostilities generated during the campaign, the signing of the MLAT foreshadowed an impressive effort during 1988 by the Bahamian government to accommodate the U.S. drug enforcement effort; it

176. See Art. 18(2) of the MLAT.

177. Joseph B. Treaster, "Anti-U.S. Mood Was Key Bahamas Issue," *New York Times*, June 21, 1987, 3.

178. See U.S. Senate, *MLAT . . . Caymans*, 136–137.

included not just the passage of legislation implementing the MLAT in March 1988, but also additional legislation increasing mandatory minimum sentences for drug trafficking offenses, enacting asset forfeiture laws like those in the United States, and requiring mandatory drug testing of police and military personnel.[179] The government also established special drug courts, created an internal corruption unit in its police agency, began training police to form a drug enforcement unit, and extended far broader cooperation to DEA and other law enforcement agents than had previously been the case.[180] Although U.S. officials continued to express skepticism regarding the Bahamians' actual implementation of their new drug control measures, and to regard "the Bahamas as one of the toughest relationships to regularize," by the end of the 1980s the level of cooperation between the two governments stood in stark contrast to the hostile relations early in the decade.[181]

More MLATs and Problems in the U.S. Congress

Among the three remaining MLATs negotiated by the United States by 1988—with Belgium, Thailand, and Mexico—the first two encountered few legal or political obstacles.

Belgium

The MLAT with Belgium, which had not previously negotiated such a treaty with a common law state, was in most respects an updated version of the Dutch MLAT, although lacking the issues involving the Netherlands Antilles.[182] Like the Dutch MLAT negotiations, those with the

179. U.S. General Accounting Office, *Drug Control: Anti-Drug Efforts in the Bahamas* (March 1990), 29–35.

180. Ibid.

181. The continued skepticism is reflected in the report on the Bahamas in *Drugs, Law Enforcement, and Foreign Policy: A Report Prepared by the Subcommittee on Terrorism, Narcotics, and International Operations of the Senate Committee on Foreign Relations*, 100th Cong., 2d Sess. (Dec. 1988), S. Rrt. 100-165, 14–24.

182. The treaty, accompanied by the Presidential message transmitting it to the Senate, is reproduced in U.S. Senate Treaty Doc. 100-16, 100th Cong., 2d Sess. (1988). A section-by-section analysis of the treaty appears in U.S. Senate Exec. Rept. 101-11, 101st Cong., 1st Sess. (1989).

Belgians were linked to extradition treaty negotiations. They too were seen as "an opportunity to negotiate, in a rather short period, an MLAT with a European country that is a major commercial and financial center, and in doing so, to set the stage for MLAT negotiations with neighboring countries with legal systems quite similar to those of Belgium."[183] The MLAT included the same provisions designed to facilitate interaction between the common law and civil law judicial systems and to qualify the treaty as a tax convention under U.S. law. Like the Dutch MLAT, it also waived the requirement of dual criminality except with respect to requests requiring searches and seizures, in which case the alleged offense had to be punishable in both states by more than one year in prison.[184] But the Belgian MLAT was also tailored to accommodate broader types and levels of cooperation. Whereas the Dutch treaty required cooperation in "criminal investigations and proceedings," the Belgian MLAT referred to "all matters relating to the investigation, prosecution and suppression of offenses," thereby making clear that a much broader array of proceedings could be accommodated by the treaty. Fewer restrictions were placed on the use of information provided under the treaty and on the obligation to keep the information confidential. Broad cooperation in seizing and forfeiting the proceeds of crime and in ensuring restitution for victims was included—although the treaty omitted the clause included in other MLATs requiring assistance in the collection of fines imposed as a sentence in a criminal prosecution. The political offense exception to providing assistance was narrowed with the caveat that it should not apply to any offense not regarded as a political offense under other international agreements signed by both states. During the negotiations, the Belgian delegation assured the Americans that cooperation would be forthcoming in investigations of illicit arms shipments, sabotage, treason, and espionage involving states unfriendly to both the United States and Belgium, but that they were less certain about extending cooperation in cases such as the Iran Contra investigation.[185] The treaty was signed in January 1988 but had not yet been put into force by the end of the decade.

183. See statement of Mark Richard (supra n. 5), 205.

184. See Art. 7 of the MLAT. See Art. 6 in the Dutch MLAT, as well as the diplomatic note accompanying the treaty.

185. See the technical analysis of the MLAT, U.S. Senate Exec. Rept. 101-11, 14–15.

Thailand

The MLAT negotiations with the Thais, which followed the completion of extradition treaty negotiations, similarly proved relatively straightforward.[186] The Justice Department was eager both for a new extradition treaty and for an MLAT with Thailand in light of its prominent role in the flow of heroin (and to a lesser extent marijuana) to the United States and the important role it played as a meeting place and financial center for East Asian drug traffickers.[187] The Thais, who had recently negotiated an MLAT with the French, and who were already hosts to the largest DEA contingent outside the United States, agreed to fairly broad levels of cooperation. Their extensive experience in working with the resident DEA agents, and in responding to requests for evidence and other assistance transmitted from the United States via those agents, prepared them for negotiations with the United States. Absent from the treaty were the extended caveats regarding assistance in penetrating financial secrecy laws and restrictions on the use of unilateral measures. No requirement of dual criminality was imposed on requests for assistance, thereby permitting Thai assistance in drug conspiracy cases despite the lack of an exact counterpart in Thai law, and authorizing U.S. assistance in violations of Thai currency control laws for which dual criminality might not be found in U.S. law. The provision authorizing cooperation in the seizure and forfeiture of criminal assets was broadly worded, anticipating cooperation in restitution, the collection of fines, and the transfer of forfeited assets to the other state. An appendix to the treaty—also appended to the MLATs with the Bahamas and the Cayman Islands—included three certification forms designed by the United States to facilitate the admissibility of evidence provided by the Thais.

The few peculiarities of the Thai treaty included a provision, modeled after one in the Thai-French MLAT, requiring each state to consider a request from the other to initiate criminal proceedings in a particular case.[188] Although the provision made more sense in the context of

186. The treaty, accompanied by the Presidential message transmitting it to the Senate, is reproduced in U.S. Senate Treaty Doc. 100-18, 100th Cong., 2d Sess. (1988). A section-by-section analysis of the treaty appears in U.S. Senate Exec. Rept. 101-13, 101st Cong., 1st Sess. (1989).

187. See the prepared statement of Mary V. Mochary, in U.S. Senate, *MLAT . . . Caymans* (supra n. 5), 91–92.

188. See Art. 14 of the MLAT.

requests between civil law states with personal jurisdiction over their citizens' criminal activities abroad, the U.S. negotiators consented to its inclusion in the treaty because it did not impose any mandatory requirements.[189] The U.S. delegation also agreed to a unique provision specifying that any non-American served with a legal document in Thailand requiring him or her to appear in the United States would not be punished for failing to comply.[190] The Thais were concerned that Thai citizens might be compelled to travel to the United States in response to such a subpoena—a possibility that they regarded as a potential extraterritorial violation of their sovereignty. Because U.S. law typically did not provide for such sanctions, however, the U.S. negotiators raised no objection. The treaty was signed in Bangkok in March 1986 during a visit by Attorney General Meese; it entered into force on June 10, 1993. To a greater extent than in most other countries, the process of obtaining evidence and other assistance for use in the United States continued to rely heavily and quite successfully on the resident DEA offices.

Mexico

The MLAT negotiations with Mexico, like those with the Bahamas, were pursued in the context of acrimonious relations over drug trafficking, with legislative and executive officials in the United States castigating the Mexican government for its lack of cooperation in drug trafficking investigations, and Mexican officials incensed by the U.S. charges, particularly those involving alleged corruption in the Mexican government. Nonetheless, the MLAT ultimately signed by the two states resembled those negotiated with the Thais, the Canadians, and the Belgians more than it did the MLATs with the Caribbean islands.[191] No requirement of dual criminality was included, thereby allowing cooperation even in the investigation of tax offenses. Broad levels of cooperation were afforded in a variety of proceedings and with respect to the seizure and forfeiture of criminal assets. The Americans were reassured

189. The U.S. delegation also noted that the general language in most MLATs authorizing cooperation in matters not specified in the treaty rendered such a provision unnecessary.

190. See Art. 10(4) of the MLAT.

191. The treaty, accompanied by the Presidential message transmitting it to the Senate, is reproduced in U.S. Senate Treaty Doc. 100-13, 100th Cong., 2d Sess. (1988), and in *International Legal Materials* 27 (1988), 443. A section-by-section analysis of the treaty appears in U.S. Senate Exec. Rept. 101-9, 101st Cong., 1st Sess. (1989).

that Mexico's bank secrecy laws would not present serious obstacles to the provision of evidence, and that Mexican authorities would not object to the employment of *Ghidoni* waivers by U.S. prosecutors. The principal concession to Mexican sensitivity with respect to U.S. claims of extraterritorial jurisdiction was the inclusion of a provision asserting that the treaty did not create any new jurisdiction or operational authority by either state to undertake actions in the territory of the other.[192] The principal peculiarity of the treaty, albeit not one reflected in the provisions of the treaty, was the Mexicans' insistence that the taking of testimony requested by U.S. authorities could be compelled under Mexican law only if the alleged offense appeared to fall within Mexican jurisdiction. The Mexican delegation assured the U.S. negotiators that there was little chance of amending Mexican law to ameliorate this limitation. The Americans therefore consented, deriving some solace from the fact that the reach of Mexican jurisdiction far exceeded that of the United States, relying not just on the territorial and protective principles common in U.S. law but also on the nationality and passive personality notions of jurisdiction.[193] The treaty was signed and ratified by the Mexican government in December 1987. It thereby became the first MLAT with the United States to be ratified by a Latin American government.

Trouble in the U.S. Congress

The MLATS with Canada, Mexico, the Bahamas, the Cayman Islands, Belgium, and Thailand were submitted to the U.S. Senate for consideration in early 1988. State and Justice Department officials hoped and anticipated that the ratification process would involve no more than the pro forma reviews required for the previous generation of MLATs. But they quickly encountered a powerful series of obstacles from an eclectic array of critics, including Senator Jesse Helms, the American Civil Liberties Union, the criminal defense bar, and the first director of the OIA, Michael Abbell, who subsequently had become a criminal defense attorney.[194] In his statement submitted to the Foreign Relations Commit-

192. See the technical analysis of the MLAT, U.S. Senate Exec. Rept. 101-9, 12.

193. Ibid., 20–22.

194. The evolution of the MLAT ratification process, and of the debate over the treaties, is discussed in *International Enforcement Law Reporter* 3:345–351 (1987); 4:44–48, 131–136, 160–164, 197–200, 303–304, 350–352, 420–421 (1988); 5:146–148, 186–188, 258–259, 385–386 (1989). See also Bruze Zagaris, "Developments in International Judicial Assistance

tee, Abbell provided a technical critique of the MLATs from the perspective of the defense attorney, a viewpoint that had not been given much heed in previous hearings.[195] He criticized the Mexican and Thai treaties for "effectively amend[ing] the Federal Rules of Evidence . . . in an unacceptable manner; the Mexican treaty alone for failing to specifically authorize the presence of defendants and their attorneys at foreign judicial proceedings; the Canadian and Mexican treaties' omission of safe conduct provisions for those requested to appear and provide testimony under the treaties; the Belgian treaty's lack of restrictions on the use and disclosure of information and evidence provided under the treaty; and, most significant, all of the treaties for precluding their use on behalf of defendants in criminal cases."[196] It was neither fair nor consistent with the compulsory process clause of the Sixth Amendment, Abbell contended, to require defendants to continue to rely on letters rogatory when prosecutors had available the advantages of an MLAT.[197] Abbell bolstered his claims by obtaining the support of the National Association of Criminal Defense Lawyers (NACDL), the American Civil Liberties Union, and the American Bar Association.

Justice Department officials reacted angrily, and with some degree of

---

and Related Matters," *Denver Journal of International Law and Policy* 18 (1990), 339, 335–337.

195. One criticism leveled at the Justice Department in the hearings was its failure to make the treaties and the accompanying technical analyses publicly available until just shortly before the Congressional hearings. See the statement of Bruce Zagaris in U.S. Senate, *MLAT . . . Caymans* (supra n. 5).

196. See the prepared statements of Michael Abbell to the Senate Foreign Relations Committee, May 6, 1988, and June 14, 1988. The Thai and Bahamian MLATs provided that the treaties were intended solely for assistance between the criminal law enforcement authorities of the contracting states and are "not intended or designed to provide such assistance to private parties." The four other MLATs specified that the treaties "shall not give rise to a right on the part of a private party to obtain, suppress, or exclude any evidence, or to impede the execution of a request."

197. The notion of excluding private parties from access to MLATs had not been contained in the first MLATs negotiated by the United States—with Switzerland, Turkey, and the Netherlands—but had been included in the Colombian MLAT, in good part because it provided for assistance not just in criminal matters but in civil and administrative investigations and proceedings as well. The Moroccan MLAT specified that it was "established solely for mutual assistance between the law enforcement authorities of the Contracting States," and the Italian MLAT stated that it was "intended solely for mutual assistance between authorities of the Contracting States." However, neither made specific mention of private parties. Abbell argued that whereas the exclusion of private parties had been justified in the Colombian MLAT, given its inclusion of civil and administrative proceedings, it was not warranted in the six MLATs under consideration, which were restricted to assistance in criminal matters.

bitterness, to the criticisms by their former colleague, perceiving them as a thinly veiled attempt to scuttle all of the MLATs. In their testimony, they dismissed all of Abbell's criticisms. With respect to his claim that defendants be provided with access to the MLATs, Justice Department officials argued that "the treaties are frankly intended to be law enforcement tools" and further justified the exclusion of defendants on the grounds that the government, unlike defendants, bore the burden of proving guilt beyond a reasonable doubt. They asserted that the decision to preclude use of the treaties on behalf of defendants reflected the wishes not just of the U.S. negotiators but of both delegations in all of the MLAT negotiations. Indeed, the U.S. negotiators were deeply concerned that any reservations attached by the Senate in support of Abbell's claims would, at the very least, require additional and difficult treaty negotiations and, at the worst, cause the treaty partners to reject the treaties entirely.[198]

Far more troubling to the Justice Department than Abbell's criticisms, however, was the opposition of Senator Helms. Helms reiterated many of Abbell's criticisms—indeed, his staff had initiated the involvement of Abbell and other legal critics of the MLATs in the Senate ratification process—and insisted that he would oppose the Senate's ratification of the MLATs unless a reservation was attached to each specifying that nothing in the MLAT "requires or authorizes legislation or other action by the United States prohibited by the U.S. Constitution as interpreted by the United States." The reservation was identical to the Lugar-Helms reservation to the Genocide Convention that had been approved by Congress in February 1986. Senator Helms perceived the reservation as effectively creating a check on the power of the executive branch to impose its own interpretations on U.S. treaties. Justice Department officials argued that the reservation was unnecessary both because nothing in the MLATs could be construed as unconstitutional and because U.S. courts had always held that the Constitution supersedes treaties. They were deeply concerned that appending such a reservation would bolster the constitutional challenges to the MLATs raised by defendants, necessitate further clarifying negotiations with the treaty partners, invite some of the partners to append their own reservations, and generally aggravate relations with them.[199]

198. U.S. Senate, *MLAT . . . Caymans* (supra n. 5), 272–275.
199. Ibid., 265–272.

Both Senator Helms and Senator Murkowski also expressed concerns about the absence of dual criminality requirements in the MLATs—a clause that the U.S. negotiators had viewed as primarily beneficial to U.S. prosecutors given the broader scope of U.S. criminal law relative to most other treaty partners, but that also invited foreign requests for assistance in matters not regarded as criminal in the United States. Senator Murkowski, for instance, inquired during the hearing about the possibility that Canadian law enforcement authorities might seek assistance under the MLAT in criminal investigations regarding acid rain or other areas of contention between the two nations.[200] Senator Helms noted his concern that some foreign governments might use the treaties to obtain assistance in investigating capital flight from their countries.[201] He also articulated a concern typically voiced by the United States' treaty partners: that U.S. officials might be subjected to foreign "fishing expeditions" and otherwise flooded with requests. Many foreign governments, he noted, requested far more assistance from the United States under the MLATs or by letters rogatory than did U.S. officials from abroad (although he failed to note that the flow of requests with foreign financial secrecy jurisdictions was disproportionately in favor of the United States).

Senator Helms's principal motivation for opposing the MLATs, however, was apparently his general concern with drug-related corruption in the Bahamas and Mexico and his specific concern that the MLATs with those countries would be taken advantage of by corrupt officials. Having recently convened his own hearings with the specific intention of publicly castigating the Mexican government for its lack of cooperation in the American war on drugs, the senator reiterated the ample evidence of governmental corruption south of the border and in the Bahamas. The Justice and State Department officials testifying in favor of the treaty assured the senator that, despite persistent problems in law enforcement relations with the two governments, both had provided extensive cooperation in U.S. investigations, that the treaties would inevitably facilitate cooperative efforts, that U.S. officials were highly sensitive to potential misuses of the MLATs, and that any suspicious requests could be rejected. Not reassured, Senator Helms insisted that the two treaties be approved only on condition that reservations providing assurances

200. Ibid., 74–76.
201. Ibid., 174.

that no corrupt officials would be provided with assistance under the MLATs be attached.

Helms's objections met with overwhelming opposition by his colleagues on the Foreign Relations Committee. Senator John Kerry, who had assumed responsibility for marshaling the MLATs through the hearings, articulated the arguments favoring approval and rejecting the proposed reservations. He was joined by Senator Lugar, who explained why he did not favor burdening the MLATs with the same reservation appended to the Genocide Convention. Although the committee voted in favor of the treaties without appending any reservations by a vote of 17 to 2, the North Carolina legislator succeeded in preventing full Senate approval in 1988. Following an additional set of hearings in 1989, at which no critics of the treaties testified but during which Senator Helms repeated his objections, the Foreign Relations Committee once again rejected the senator's reservations and voted 17 to 2 to recommend that the Senate give its consent. Helms persisted, however, with the result that the MLATs were approved by the Senate in late 1989 with reservations reflecting the senator's objections—albeit in compromise language watered down to accommodate the concerns of the Justice and State Departments.[202] On January 2, 1990, President Bush signed the instruments of ratification for all six MLATs.

As the U.S. MLAT negotiators anticipated, their negotiating partners did not take kindly to the reservations. The Canadians expressed mild irritation but let it be known that they viewed the reservations as an American domestic matter of no concern to Canada. With the Canadian implementing legislation already in place, the MLAT entered into force on January 24, 1990. The Bahamian, Mexican, and Cayman/British delegations, however, were less prepared to write off the U.S. reservations with the Canadians' dispatch. Each proceeded to append its own reservations to the treaties containing comparable language regarding their own constitutions. With the British not particularly interested in complicating issues, the Cayman treaty entered into force on March 19, 1990. Bahamian and Mexican officials, however, who were specifically targeted by the reservations regarding corrupt officials, were incensed.

202. The reservations did not directly address any of Abbell's criticisms, in particular the issue of defendant access to the MLATs. Justice Department officials indicated, however, that they would respond to a court order requiring them to make use of an MLAT to obtain evidence sought by a defendant—as in fact had previously occurred with respect to a request by Michel Sindona for evidence under the Swiss MLAT.

Both perceived the Helms-inspired action as an ungrateful response to the fairly extensive assistance that their governments had provided to U.S. law enforcement officials. They also were not disposed to accept the assurances of the U.S. delegations that the reservations would have no impact on the actual implementation of the MLATs. After adding their own reservations to the treaties, both governments ratified the revised MLATs. The MLAT with the Bahamas entered into force on July 18, 1990, and the MLAT with Mexico on May 3, 1991.

Broader Developments: Drugs, Money, Securities, and Taxes

As the end of the 1980s approached, U.S. Justice Department officials persisted in their efforts to negotiate MLATs with dozens of other governments. U.S. officials had signed more-limited mutual legal assistance agreements with Haiti on August 15, 1986, and with Nigeria on November 2, 1987, both of which had emerged as significant drug transit countries during the 1980s. The Nigerian agreement was followed by a full-fledged MLAT in September 1989. An MLAT with Jamaica was also completed in July 1989. These were followed by MLATs with Spain in November 1990, Argentina in December 1990, Panama in April 1991, and Uruguay in May 1991. As this book went to press in mid-1993, only the MLAT with Argentina had entered into force. (See Appendix E.) Also high on the Justice Department's priority list in the early 1990s were Germany, which had been involved in sporadic MLAT negotiations with the United States since the early 1980s; Britain, whose officials desired to resolve a wide range of concerns about U.S. extraterritorial assertions; and Hong Kong, whose financial secrecy laws had attracted a broad array of transnational criminal activities ranging from securities and tax frauds to drug-related money laundering.

Even as the rising number of MLATs were easing the collection of evidence from abroad for prosecutors, federal judges were making it easier for evidence collected in other ways to be admitted in their courts. The U.S. Constitution and the Federal Rules of Evidence, with their strong preference for live testimony in criminal trials, had long presented U.S. prosecutors with substantial obstacles in their efforts to depose witnesses abroad who would not or could not come to the United States.

Indeed, prosecutors had been forbidden to take domestic depositions in criminal cases until 1970, when Congress responded to the problem of Mafia intimidation of witnesses by authorizing government depositions in organized crime cases.[203] Five years later, the authorization was extended to all other criminal cases. And as the need to obtain evidence from abroad increased dramatically during the 1980s, judges responded both by encouraging attorneys to employ videotapes and other new technological developments to simulate live depositions and preserve testimony, and by interpreting the constitutional and evidentiary requirements less strictly.[204] In the most far-reaching of the many cases to arise during the 1980s, *United States v. Salim*, a federal judge conducting a jury trial allowed as evidence a deposition conducted in France according to French procedures at which neither the defendant nor his defense attorney was permitted to be present.[205] Upheld on appeal, the case provided a clear indication of the increasing willingness of U.S. courts to make accommodations for the difficulties involved in obtaining evidence abroad.

During the 1970s and 1980s, many U.S. courts were also required to rule on the admissibility of evidence collected abroad by U.S. and foreign police agents. The Supreme Court had held in 1957 that American citizens abroad were entitled to most of the constitutional safeguards to which they were entitled within the United States.[206] Lower courts thereafter were confronted with numerous cases in which defendants argued that evidence collected abroad by law enforcement agents was not admissible in court because it had not been obtained in accordance with U.S. constitutional requirements. Most courts held that the protec-

203. Gordon Mehler, "Use of Foreign Depositions in Federal Criminal Trials," *New York Law Journal*, Oct. 3, 1988, 2, 6.

204. See *U.S. v. Kehm*, 799 F.2d 354 (7th Cir. 1986) (admitting transcript of deposition taken in the Bahamas); *U.S. v. Johnpoll*, 739 F.2d 702 (2d Cir.), cert. denied, 469 U.S. 1075 (1984) (admitting transcript of deposition taken in Switzerland); *U.S. v. Sindona*, 636 F.2d 792 (2d Cir. 1980) cert. denied, 451 U.S. 912 (1981) (deposition taken in Italy and attended by lead defense counsel admissible); *U.S. v. Sines*, 761 F.2d 1434 (9th Cir. 1985) (admitting government deposition taken in Thailand in a heroin trafficking case); *U.S. v. King*, 552 F.2d 833 (9th Cir. 1976), cert. denied, 430 U.S. 966 (1977) (admitting government deposition taken in Japan in a heroin trafficking case); and *U.S. v. Trout*, 633 F.Supp. 150 (N.D. Cal. 1985) (granting defendant's motion to depose witnesses in Brazil in a cocaine trafficking case).

205. *U.S. v. Salim*, 664 F.Supp. 682 (1987); 855 F.2d 944 (2d Cir. 1988). See Burke, "*United States v. Salim*: A Harbinger" (supra n. 25), as well as the account by the federal prosecutor in the case: Mehler, "Use of Foreign Depositions in Federal Criminal Trials."

206. *Reid v. Covert*, 354 U.S. 1 (1957).

tions of the Fourth Amendment and the exclusionary rule applied to evidence gathered overseas by U.S. agents acting unilaterally or in a "joint venture" with foreign officials[207] but not to evidence collected by foreign police acting on their own unless their actions were such as to "shock the conscience" of the court.[208] Much of the debate accordingly focused on whether evidence collected by foreign police at the behest of U.S. officials, or based on information supplied by them, constituted a "joint venture."[209] In 1990, the Supreme Court addressed the related issue of whether the Fourth Amendment protected not just U.S. citizens but also foreign nationals from extraterritorial actions involving U.S. officials—and ruled that it did not. There was no need, Chief Justice Rehnquist wrote, for U.S. law enforcement agents to obtain a warrant to conduct a search abroad when the target was a foreign national who lacked any "substantial connection" to the United States.[210] A Supreme Court decision to the contrary, many federal law enforcement officials had feared, would have significantly hampered the increasingly aggressive U.S. international drug enforcement campaign.

By the end of the 1980s, many other governments were following in the footsteps of the United States, and some were proceeding a step ahead. A Commonwealth Scheme for Mutual Assistance in Criminal Matters had been negotiated by senior officials from twenty-nine countries in London in early 1986 and endorsed some months later at a law ministers' meeting in Harare.[211] By 1990, the Canadian government had

207. *Powell v. Zuckert*, 366 F.2d 634 (D.C. Cir. 1966).

208. *Rosado v. Civiletti*, 621 F.2d 1179 (2d Cir. 1980), cert. denied, 449 U.S. 856.

209. See the analyses from the late 1970s and early 1980s by Keith Raffel, "Searches and Seizures Abroad in the Federal Courts," *Maryland Law Review* 38 (1979), 689–732; Stephen A. Saltzburg, "The Reach of the Bill of Rights Beyond the *Terra Firma* of the United States," *Virginia Journal of International Law* 20 (1980), 741–776; Steven M. Kaplan, "The Applicability of the Exclusionary Rule in Federal Court to Evidence Seized and Confessions Obtained in Foreign Countries," *Columbia Journal of Transnational Law* 16 (1977), 495–520; Roszell Dulany Hunter IV, "The Extraterritorial Application of the Constitution: Unalienable Rights?" *Virginia Law Review* 72 (1986), 649–676; and Steven H. Theisen, "Evidence Seized in Foreign Searches: When Does the Fourth Amendment Exclusionary Rule Apply?" *William and Mary Law Review* 25 (1983), 161–187.

210. *U.S. v. Verdugo-Urquidez*, 110 S.Ct. 1056, *International Legal Materials* 29 (1990), 441. The fact that the target was already incarcerated in the United States in anticipation of his prosecution for violation of U.S. laws did not, in the view of the Court, constitute a "substantial connection." The lower court decision, which held to the contrary, can be found at 856 F.2d 1214 (9th Cir. 1988). See the analysis of the Supreme Court decision in Mark Gibney, "Policing the World: The Long Reach of U.S. Law and the Short Arm of the Constitution," *Connecticut Journal of International Law* 6 (1990), 103–126.

211. David McClean, "Mutual Assistance in Criminal Matters: The Commonwealth Initiative," *International and Comparative Law Quarterly* 37 (1988), 177–190.

signed additional MLATs with Australia, France, Mexico, the United Kingdom, and the Bahamas; entered into negotiations with the Swiss and the Dutch; and enacted its own Mutual Legal Assistance Act. The Australian government had enacted similar legislation in 1987 and was also engaged in negotiating MLATs with a growing number of countries. Britain had finally signed the European Convention on Mutual Assistance, persuaded in part by the U.S. example that legal assistance arrangements between civil law nations and its own common law system could be worked out. It had also concluded a series of bilateral agreements with the United States and other governments providing for enhanced cooperation in drug enforcement matters; and in late 1989 it had introduced the legislation required to implement its proliferating mutual legal assistance arrangements.[212] Governments of financial secrecy jurisdictions such as Switzerland, Luxembourg, Austria, and Hong Kong had also initiated their own rounds of MLAT negotiations.

Of even greater significance were developments in four areas—drug enforcement, efforts directed at money laundering, securities and commodities regulation, and tax administration—in each of which U.S. initiatives undertaken unilaterally, bilaterally and multilaterally were complemented by the domestic and multilateral initiatives of other nations. Throughout the 1980s, the most powerful impetus to advances in international law enforcement was the rising global concern over illicit drug trafficking. Few governments did not expand and stiffen their penalties for drug trafficking and related activities. During the second half of the decade, U.S. influences began to be felt in the area of asset seizure and forfeiture. Governments throughout the world adopted legislation permitting the seizure and forfeiture of drug trafficker assets;[213] regional organizations, notably in Europe, committed themselves to broader cooperation; and international organizations such as Interpol and the United Nations' drug control organs promoted model legislation and international cooperation. By far the most significant development was the negotiation of the United Nations Convention Against Illicit Traffic in Narcotic Drugs and Psychotropic Substances, which mandated extensive cooperation in all law enforcement tasks directed at interna-

212. William C. Gilmore, "International Action Against Drug Trafficking: Trends in United Kingdom Law and Practice," *International Lawyer* 24 (1990), 365, 391.

213. See Jürgen Meyer, *Gewinnabschopfung bei Betaubungsmitteldelikten* (Weisbaden: Bundeskriminalamt, 1989), 31–59, which contains a comparative analysis, in English, of European and U.S. laws regarding the confiscation of proceeds derived from illicit drug trafficking.

tional drug trafficking, including extradition, mutual legal assistance, and the forfeiture and seizure of assets.[214] The U.N. convention was widely seen as providing both added legitimacy and legal authority for many of the international law enforcement measures designed to investigate and prosecute drug trafficking. It entered into force in November 1990.

The heightened focus on money laundering was largely a function of the rising sensitivity among drug enforcement officials to the financial dimensions of drug trafficking. By the end of the 1980s, the notion that "going after the money" was the most effective way to immobilize drug traffickers had become the conventional wisdom among government investigators and legislators in the United States, Canada, much of Europe, and a number of other countries. It was perceived as essential both to identifying and prosecuting the higher-level drug traffickers who rarely if ever came into contact with their illicit goods, and to tracing, seizing, and forfeiting their assets.[215] At the same time, the belief spread that individuals who assisted drug traffickers in laundering the proceeds of their activities merited harsh criminal sanctions as well.

U.S. legislation directed at money laundering had begun with the enactment of the Bank Secrecy Act in 1970, although the law's requirements that banks report cash transactions of $10,000 or more and that individuals transporting $5,000 or more in cash across the border submit currency reports were not seriously enforced until the mid-1980s. In 1986, however, Congress specifically criminalized the act of laundering drug-related proceeds. On the international front, the Justice Department assured foreign governments that the extraterritorial potential of the law would be substantially restricted.[216] It encouraged foreign governments, however, to enact parallel legislation and to cooperate in U.S. investigations and prosecutions of drug-related money laundering

214. U.N. Doc. E/Conf. 82/15 Dec. 19, 1988; *International Legal Materials* 28 (1989), 493. See David P. Stewart, "Internationalizing the War on Drugs: The U.N. Convention Against Illicit Traffic in Narcotic Drugs and Psychotropic Substances," *Denver Journal of International Law and Policy* 18 (1990), 387–404.

215. Ethan A. Nadelmann, "Unlaundering Dirty Money Abroad: U.S. Foreign Policy and Financial Secrecy Jurisdictions," *University of Miami Inter-American Law Review* 18 (1986), 33–82.

216. The assurance is contained in a letter of April 16, 1987, from Deputy Attorney General James Knapp to the British embassy, discussed in Bruce Zagaris, "Justice Letter Clarifies Extraterritorial Application of Money Laundering Act," *International Enforcement Law Reporter* 3 (1987), 221–223.

by waiving bank secrecy laws in drug trafficking investigations. In an indication of the growing importance of cooperation in this area, the G-7 summits in 1988 and 1989 addressed the subjects of money laundering and asset seizure and forfeiture. A Financial Action Task Force created at the latter meeting included not just the G-7 governments of the United States, Japan, Britain, France, Canada, Italy, and West Germany, but also the governments of Australia, Austria, Belgium, Luxembourg, the Netherlands, Spain, Sweden, and Switzerland. In its first report in early 1990, the task force urged governments to ratify the U.N. convention and to enact domestic legislation broadening the definition of money laundering and requiring financial institutions to screen and maintain records of customers and their transactions. The task force was subsequently expanded to include representatives of Denmark, Finland, Greece, Hong Kong, Ireland, New Zealand, Norway, Portugal, Turkey, and the Gulf Cooperation Council. By the end of the decade, Britain, France, Spain, Switzerland, and Luxembourg had all criminalized money laundering; the European Community Commission and the Council of Europe's Pompidou Group had assumed active roles in promoting legislation and cooperation against money laundering; the Bank for International Settlements in Basel, Switzerland, had prepared a "code of conduct" for banks regarding suspicious transactions; Interpol was actively promoting model legislation criminalizing money laundering; and even the principality of Liechtenstein, which many had perceived as taking advantage of Switzerland's declining reputation for secrecy, had effected an agreement with its banks regarding suspicious transactions and committed itself to criminalizing money laundering in the near future. In a development of potentially great significance, the Council of Europe adopted a new Convention on Anti-Money Laundering and the Search, Seizure, and Confiscation of Proceeds of Crime in November 1990 and invited the governments of Canada, Australia, the United States, and Eastern Europe to join.[217] Prominent both at the forefront of these developments and behind the scenes in task force meetings and negotiations were U.S. officials.

The dramatic internationalization of the securities and commodities markets since the 1970s had created a concomitant need to internationalize the regulation of those markets. This too was an area in which U.S.

217. *International Legal Materials* 30 (1991), 148. See Jeffrey Lowell Quillen, "The International Attack on Money Laundering: European Initiatives," *Duke Journal of Comparative and International Law* 1 (1991), 213–240.

officials, particularly SEC officials, took the lead.[218] As in other domains of international law enforcement, the SEC's experience during the early 1980s with seeking evidence by means of unilateral compulsory processes such as subpoenas and administrative summons had taught its officials both the extent and the limits of such measures. At the same time, the agency's extensive experience in working with Swiss officials had provided a sense of the potential of more cooperative initiatives. Following in the footsteps of the Justice Department, the SEC created its own Office of International Affairs in its Division of Enforcement in 1985. It rapidly began to negotiate, first, memoranda of understanding with its counterparts in Britain,[219] Japan,[220] Brazil, and the Canadian provinces of Ontario, Quebec, and British Columbia,[221] and thereafter, in 1989, more formal agreements with France[222] and the

218. More complete analyses are provided in Ronald E. Bornstein and N. Elaine Dugger, "International Regulation of Insider Trading," *Columbia Business Law Review* 2 (1987), 375–417; Mann and Mari, "Developments in International Securities Law Enforcement" (supra n. 60); Edward F. Greene, Alan B. Cohen, and Linda S. Matlack, "Problems of Enforcement in the Multinational Securities Market," *University of Pennsylvania Journal of International Business Law* 9 (1987), 325–373; Harvey L. Pitt, David B. Hardison, and Karen L. Shapiro, "Problems of Enforcement in the Multinational Securities Market," *University of Pennsylvania Journal of International Business Law* 9 (1987), 375–452; Michael A. Gerstenzang, "Insider Trading and the Internationalization of the Securities Markets," *Columbia Journal of Transnational Law* 27 (1989), 409–441; Harvey L. Pitt and Karen L. Shapiro, "Securities Regulation by Enforcement: A Look Ahead at the Next Decade," *Yale Journal of Regulation* 7 (1990), 149; and Paul G. Mahoney, "Securities Regulation by Enforcement: An International Perspective," *Yale Journal of Regulation* 7 (1990), 305–320.

219. The Memorandum of Understanding on Exchange of Information Between the United States Securities and Exchange Commission and the United Kingdom Department of Trade and Industry in Matters Relating to Securities and Between the United States Commodity Futures Trading Commission and the United Kingdom Department of Trade and Industry in Matters Relating to Futures, September 23, 1986, is in *International Legal Materials* 25 (1986), 1431. See Elizabeth E. Barlow, "Enforcing Securities Regulations Through Bilateral Agreements with the United Kingdom and Japan: An Interim Measure or a Solution?" *Texas International Law Journal* 23 (1988), 251–268; and Gerald A. Polcari, "A Comparative Analysis of Insider Trading Laws: The United States, the United Kingdom, and Japan: The Current International Agreements on Securities Regulation," *Suffolk Transnational Law Journal* 13 (1990), 167–199.

220. The Memorandum of the United States Securities and Exchange Commission and the Securities Bureau of the Japanese Ministry of Finance on the Sharing of Information, May 23, 1986, is in *International Legal Materials* 25 (1986), 1429. See the discussion in Barlow, "Enforcing Securities Regulations," and in Polcari, "Comparative Analysis."

221. Mark Roppel, "Extraterritorial Application of Securities Laws Between the United States and Canada," *Gonzaga Law Review* 24 (1988–89), 391–414.

222. Robert Bordeaux-Groult, "Problems of Enforcement and Cooperation in the Multi-

Netherlands.[223] It promoted resolutions on cooperation through the International Organization of Securities Commissions (IOSCO); it secured domestic legislation in Congress specifically authorizing and facilitating cooperation with foreign agencies;[224] and it encouraged foreign governments to develop and strengthen their own securities commissions and to criminalize such activities as insider trading. By 1989, the SEC's efforts, combined with the rising sensitivity elsewhere to the need for more-intensive securities regulation, had resulted in new laws criminalizing insider trading and creating more powerful regulatory agencies throughout much of Europe as well as Canada, Japan, and Hong Kong; the Council of Europe adopting a Convention on Insider Trading;[225] and the European Community being apparently well on its way to criminalizing insider trading in all member states by 1992.[226] Similar developments, many of them promoted by the CFTC, were simultaneously under way in the regulation of commodities trading, albeit with a lower profile.[227]

By far the most difficult area in which to create a consensus on

national Securities Market: A French Perspective," *University of Pennsylvania Journal of International Business Law* 9 (1987), 453–465.

223. Mark S. Klock, "A Comparative Analysis of Recent Accords Which Facilitate Transnational SEC Investigations of Insider Trading," *Maryland Journal of International Law and Trade* 11 (1987), 243–266; Pamela Jimenez, "International Securities Enforcement Cooperation Act and Memoranda of Understanding," *Harvard International Law Journal* 31 (1990), 295–311.

224. Theodore A. Levine and W. Hardy Callcott, "The SEC and Foreign Policy: The International Securities Enforcement Cooperation Act of 1988," *Securities Regulation Law Journal* 17 (1989), 115–150. See also *Globalization of Securities Markets: Hearing Before the Subcommittee on Telecommunications and Finance of the Committee on Energy and Commerce, House of Representatives*, 100th Cong., 1st Sess. (1987); *Insider Trading: Hearings on H.R. 4945 Before the Subcommittee on Telecommunications and Finance of the Committee on Energy and Commerce, House of Representatives*, 100th Cong., 2d Sess. (1988); and *International Securities Enforcement: Hearing on H.R. 1396 Before the Subcommittee on Telecommunications and Finance of the Committee on Energy and Commerce, House of Representatives*, 101st Cong., 1st Sess. (1989).

225. The text of the convention can be found in European Treaty Series No. 130 and in *International Legal Materials* 29 (1990), 309. See John P. Lowry, "The International Approach to Insider Trading: The Council of Europe's Convention," *Journal of Business Law*, Nov. 1990, 460–468.

226. P. L. Davies, "The European Community's Directive on Insider Dealing: From Company Law to Securities Markets Regulation?" *Oxford Journal of Legal Studies* 11 (1991), 92–105.

227. Peter G. McGonagle, "Serving Subpoenas Abroad Pursuant to the Future Trading Act of 1986," *Fordham International Law Journal* 10 (1987), 710–732.

international law enforcement matters concerned the administration of tax collection and the investigation of tax evasion and fraud. Yet even in this domain, substantial progress was recorded during the 1980s.[228] Some of the advances were a result of U.S. pressures—applied both bilaterally and by means of unilateral compulsory measures to obtain evidence—on its MLAT partners to provide cooperation in investigations of drug-related tax evasion and tax shelter frauds. Other advances were a result of IRS efforts to negotiate and renegotiate its international tax conventions to expand assistance not just in the administration of taxes but in the investigation of tax offenses as well. The Caribbean Basin Initiative and other legislation by Congress provided incentives for foreign governments to broaden their cooperation in U.S. tax investigations. The most significant development of the 1980s, however, was the completion of a Convention on Mutual Administrative Assistance in Tax Matters in January 1988 by the Council of Europe and the Organization of Economic Cooperation and Development (OECD).[229] Despite substantial controversy in Europe over the convention and the European Community's efforts to harmonize its members' tax policies, the United States signed the convention (with reservations) in June 1989. Although international cooperation in the enforcement of tax laws continued to lag behind other areas of international law enforcement, with numerous governments resisting on what they claimed were matters of principle, evidence of progress was tangible and clearly visible.

Amid the multiagency rush to expand and improve their international law enforcement capabilities during the 1980s, relatively little in the way of domestic opposition had emerged within the United States. Even as bankers and stock traders abroad had fiercely opposed their governments' concessions to U.S. law enforcement authorities, American businessmen had been relatively quiescent—with the possible exception of their vocal opposition to the SEC's "waiver by conduct" proposal. Fears that overly restrictive regulation of money movements and securities transactions might chase away foreign investors had generally been

228. John Turro, "The 'War on Drugs' Is Causing U.S. to Increase Investigations of Tax Evasion Through Tax Havens," *Tax Notes International* 2 (1990), 807–811.

229. The text can be found in European Treaty Series No. 127 and in *International Legal Materials* 28 (1988), 1160–1175. The treaty is analyzed in Karen Brown, "Allowing Tax Laws to Cross Borders to Defeat International Tax Avoidance: The Convention on Mutual Administrative Assistance in Tax Matters," *Brooklyn Journal of International Law* 15 (1989), 59–108; and in "Recent Developments," *Harvard International Law Journal* 30 (1989), 514–523.

counterbalanced by confidence in the overall attractiveness of investing in Americans banks and securities. Throughout the 1980s, moreover, foreign governments had directed relatively few requests for documents held by banks within the United States.

By the end of the decade, however, concern was emerging among sectors of the U.S. business community with respect to the impact of U.S. laws and treaties on foreign flight capital invested in the United States. In many respects, the United States had long represented the principal financial secrecy jurisdiction in the world, attracting hundreds of billions of dollars in investments by foreign citizens evading their own nations' tax and exchange control laws. Unlike the United States, which placed no prohibitions on the outflow of dollars from the United States, dozens of governments, both in the less-developed world and in Europe, restricted the outflow of their currencies. Before the late 1980s, U.S. officials had provided relatively little assistance to foreign governments investigating violations of their exchange control laws, and they had not been particularly cooperative with respect to the efforts of Latin American governments and others in the less-developed world to enforce their tax laws. Various developments in the late 1980s, however, suggested shifts in U.S. policy. With the criminalization of money laundering in 1986, many of the techniques legitimate businesses abroad use to invest in the United States and avoid their own nation's controls came under suspicion because they were often indistinguishable from the techniques drug traffickers use to launder their illegally derived funds.[230] At the same time, new tax conventions, notably the one signed with Mexico, were viewed with apprehension by foreign businessmen because of broadly worded provisions authorizing cooperation in investigations of tax offenses. Moreover, U.S. courts were increasingly receptive to requests for assistance from foreign law enforcement authorities, interpreting Section 1782 less restrictively than courts in the past.[231] The result of these developments, many in the American financial community feared, would be to chase foreign flight capital to countries that offered more secure confidentiality than the United States.

230. Jeff Gerth, "U.S. Seeks Tougher Line on Flight Capital," *New York Times*, Feb. 12, 1990, D1.

231. See, e.g., *In Re Request for Assistance from Ministry of Legal Affairs of Trinidad and Tobago*, 848 F.2d 1151 (11th Cir. 1988); Deirdre Fanning, "Fishing Expedition," *Forbes*, Oct. 31, 1988, 110; and "Much Ado About 1782" (supra n. 11).

Conclusion

Until well into the 1970s, the U.S. Justice Department and American prosecutors viewed the collection of evidence from abroad as a cumbersome and often unproductive process to be pursued only in the most important cases. The letters rogatory process was both slow and uncertain to produce documents in a form admissible in American courts. Few prosecutors were familiar with the requirements of foreign legal systems. Neither the Justice Department nor any other federal department had an office with expertise in collecting evidence from abroad. U.S. courts tended to look upon both letters rogatory from abroad and the evidence provided by foreign officials with jaundiced eyes, making few concessions to the irregularities of international evidence collection. Overseas, foreign law enforcement officials had few incentives to treat letters rogatory from the United States expeditiously. Judges and magistrates in civil law countries were unlikely to make allowances to the evidentiary requirements of U.S. law. And financial and corporate secrecy laws in Switzerland, the Caribbean, and other financial secrecy jurisdictions ensured that most requests for documents would meet with unsatisfactory responses.

As the demands of international law enforcement increased rapidly during the 1970s, so did the recognition that the United States' international evidence-gathering capabilities were grossly underdeveloped and needed to be improved. The MLAT with the Swiss provided the crucial opening, and the subsequent conflicts, negotiations, and agreements presented a series of opportunities for reducing the frictions and obstacles that had impeded the effective transmission of evidence to U.S. prosecutors. In the Caribbean, U.S. law enforcement officials encountered obstacles not unlike those in Switzerland, but in an environment that allowed them somewhat greater leeway to innovate, act unilaterally, and apply greater pressures. In Italy, U.S. law enforcement officials found accommodating allies eager to break new ground in forging ever-closer law enforcement relations. And the MLAT with the Canadians presented an opportunity to regularize law enforcement relations with a close friend and neighbor that had become increasingly annoyed by the extraterritorial infringements on its jurisdiction.

Ever since the end of World War II, the U.S. government had been criticized harshly by its closest allies for its aggressive assertions of extraterritorial jurisdiction in such areas as antitrust and export controls. Many had taken the step of enacting blocking statutes expressly forbidding local compliance with extraterritorial orders emanating from the United States. These hostile reactions, however, exercised little influence on U.S. officials seeking evidence in criminal investigations involving organized crime generally and illicit drug trafficking particularly. Indeed, it was precisely the focus on these domains of transnational criminality that provided the foot in the door for U.S. efforts to change the norms of international judicial assistance. Governments might differ on issues of antitrust and export controls, but the norms of international society no longer tolerated dissent on the issue of illicit drug trafficking. Neither the principle of financial secrecy nor the economic interests of states in maintaining their status as financial secrecy jurisdictions could stand in the way of the global campaign against illicit drug trafficking. Foreign governments thus acquiesced to U.S. demands for evidence in illicit drug trafficking investigations and thereby established a precedent for providing judicial assistance in cases that have nothing to do with drugs.

Viewed from the perspective of U.S. law enforcement officials, the evolution in international evidence-gathering capabilities since the 1970s can be equated with the development of an ever more powerful and efficient vacuum cleaner. The unilateral tactics devised during the early 1980s, such as the *Bank of Nova Scotia* subpoenas and the *Ghidoni* waivers, have proven useful both in obtaining evidence in specific cases and in inducing foreign governments to sign MLATs with the United States and otherwise improve their commitment and ability to provide assistance in criminal investigations. Those tactics remain in the arsenal of U.S. prosecutors and continue to be used effectively. The growing number of MLATs have provided relatively efficient bilateral arrangements for securing evidence from abroad. Changes in U.S. law both by the Congress and by the federal courts have facilitated the admissibility of evidence collected abroad. The creation of specialized offices in the Justice Department, the State Department, and the SEC with expertise in international law enforcement matters has provided a repository of information, assistance, and contacts that is valuable to prosecutors throughout the United States. Those offices have also made possible a coherent foreign policy of evidence collection and transmission. And the creation of comparable offices in foreign justice ministries has provided U.S. officials with reliable transgovernmental partners who share their language and their objectives.

All of these developments can be described as part and parcel of the regularization of international judicial assistance between the U.S. government and a growing number of foreign governments. But it is important to recognize that what began during the 1970s as a U.S. effort to persuade foreign governments to accommodate the evidentiary needs of its judicial system evolved during the 1980s into a far broader and more ambitious effort to bring foreign laws into greater accordance with U.S. laws. Foreign states began to criminalize money laundering and insider trading and to enact domestic laws authorizing the seizure and forfeiture of assets derived from illicit drug trafficking and other criminal activities. The U.S. government was not, of course, solely responsible for these developments. Just as the Council of Europe had developed its own multilateral MLAT and other international law enforcement arrangements decades before U.S. officials opted to do likewise, so the Council of Europe, some of its member states, and other multilateral organizations began during the 1980s to pursue their own initiatives in international judicial assistance. Particularly significant were the Council of Europe's new conventions on tax assistance, insider trading, and the detection, seizure, and forfeiture of criminal assets, as well as the European Community's efforts to better supervise securities transactions. Increasingly, efforts to improve international cooperation in judicial assistance involved not just mutual accommodation but also homogenization of legal systems.

Although the number of MLATs negotiated by U.S. officials by 1990 represented barely 15 percent of the number of U.S. extradition treaties, the MLAT partners represented a substantial diversity of governments from around the world—Europe, Asia, Africa, Latin America, the Caribbean, and Canada—and were proliferating rapidly. These bilateral law enforcement tentacles were supplemented by the 1988 U.N. antidrug trafficking convention, with its abundant provisions directed at enhancing international law enforcement cooperation. The cumulative result was an ever more inclusive net of national, bilateral, and multilateral criminal justice controls designed to deter, detect, and prosecute drug trafficking conspiracies, money laundering schemes, violations of securities laws, and other transnational criminal activities.

Chapter Seven

International Rendition of Fugitives

Issues, Methods, and Scope

The ultimate objective of most criminal investigations, both domestic and international, is to "immobilize" people who have violated the laws. When U.S. law enforcement officials want to "immobilize" a criminal who has fled to another country or who is living abroad and refuses to come to the United States to face trial, they have a number of options. They can request that the government of that country formally surrender the fugitive to the United States pursuant to its extradition laws or an extradition treaty with the United States. They can request that the foreign government make the fugitive available to U.S. authorities by less formal means, such as by employing more expeditious deportation procedures or otherwise kicking him out of the country. They can ask the foreign government to prosecute the fugitive in its own courts. Or they can attempt to gain custody over the fugitive by other methods, such as abduction or trickery. U.S. officials have employed each of these methods since early in the nation's history, and with increasing frequency since the 1970s.

This chapter, unlike the preceding chapters, focuses not only on the extraterritorial law enforcement efforts of the U.S. government but also on its responses to foreign government requests for assistance in law enforcement matters. The reasons are threefold. First, because unlike the domains of transnational police activity and evidence-gathering, in which the U.S. government has assumed a highly proactive and even aggressive profile, the domain of extradition is one in which the U.S. government has been the recipient of almost as many requests as it has sent; second, because the norm of reciprocity has loomed larger in the history of U.S. extradition than in other areas of international law enforcement; and third, because most of the controversies generated by U.S. involvement in extradition cases have involved foreign requests for the extradition of fugitives from the United States rather than vice versa. I should stress that none of these reasons apply to types of fugitive rendition other than formal surrender by means of extradition, but they provide ample justification for devoting some attention to the reactive side of U.S. involvement in international law enforcement matters.

U.S. efforts to obtain custody of fugitives from abroad are hindered principally by consideration of the sovereignty, laws, and political reactions of foreign states. By contrast, neither Congress nor the courts have created any significant legal obstacles to securing fugitives from abroad akin to those that so complicate the international collection of evidence. Nor have the restrictions on fugitive rendition imposed by international law played a prominent role since the first decades of the nation's history. U.S. officials generally have regarded extradition by treaty or the laws of foreign states as the preferred means of obtaining fugitives from abroad.[1] It has long been viewed as the accepted means of securing fugitives; it comports with the laws of the United States, the requested state, and international society; its procedures are detailed in written laws and treaties; and it typically allows for both judicial evaluation and executive oversight of all requests.

The option of extradition, however, is not always available. There may be no treaty between the United States and the foreign government, and

1. All U.S. extradition treaties in force (in 1993) are listed by country in Appendix F. Also see the annual editions of *Treaties in Force* published by the U.S. Department of State. The texts of the treaties are collected in Michael Abbell and Bruno A. Ristau, *International Judicial Assistance* (Washington, D.C.: International Law Institute, 1990), vol. 5.

even if there is a treaty, the foreign government may be reluctant, for any number of domestic and international political reasons, to honor its commitments under the treaty. The treaty may fail to cover either the particular crime or the particular fugitive sought, or it may create other obstacles to extradition or to the delivery of the fugitive on terms desired by the U.S. government. And even when a foreign government is willing and able to extradite a fugitive according to its laws or a treaty, U.S. officials may prefer to obtain custody of the fugitive by more expeditious means.

The basic dilemmas of U.S. extradition—which date back to the origins of the nation's history—reflect two limitations imposed by U.S. laws and one generated by the laws of most foreign states. The U.S. government, unlike most other governments, lacks the legal authority either to extradite anyone in the absence of an extradition treaty or to prosecute anyone for acts committed abroad that violate foreign laws but not U.S. laws. Neither of these limitations is required by the U.S. Constitution, but they do reflect legal traditions deeply embedded in American jurisprudence. The result has been to make of the United States a safe haven in which fugitives from foreign justice know they are immune from prosecution so long as the United States and the government of the country in which they committed their crimes are not bound by an extradition treaty. Most foreign governments, especially those shaped by civil law traditions, are bound by a very different limitation, one that the United States does not share. Their laws, and in some cases their constitutions, prohibit the extradition of their citizens to other states. The fact that they are able to prosecute their citizens for crimes committed abroad partially compensates for this limitation, although this compensation has often been more evident in rhetoric and principle than in practice. There is no compensation, however, for the limitations imposed by U.S. law. Much of the history of U.S. rendition of fugitives can be understood in terms of U.S. and foreign government efforts to compensate for these limitations without disavowing them.[2]

Tension between the executive and judicial branches of government is virtually inherent to the extradition process both in the United States

2. A fine discussion of the incompatibilities, both real and imagined, between European and U.S. criminal justice systems and extradition norms is in Christopher L. Blakesley and Otto Lagodny, "Finding Harmony Amidst Disagreement over Extradition, Jurisdiction, the Role of Human Rights, and Issues of Extraterritoriality Under International Criminal Law," *Vanderbilt Journal of Transnational Law* 24 (1991), 1–73.

and in most other nations. It stems primarily from the fact that the approval of both branches of government is typically required to allow the extradition of a fugitive to a foreign country and secondarily from the fact that a fugitive who is delivered to the United States eventually has an opportunity to assert certain rights before a court of law. On the one hand, extradition falls within the province of the secretary of state—even though it has been handled principally by attorneys in the Justice Department's Office of International Affairs since 1979—and has traditionally been viewed as a component of foreign relations. On the other hand, extradition, unlike other domains of international relations, is concerned with individual human beings not as representatives of a state but as residents of the United States entitled to the rights accorded by its laws and Constitution. It thus entails judicial proceedings whenever a fugitive insists on challenging the extradition order of the executive branch. It presents the possibility that the will of the executive branch may be thwarted by a court's ruling that extradition is not permitted. And it provides a forum in which individuals may demand and obtain standing to assert their rights—limited though they may be—under a treaty.

The tensions between the two branches of government are best reflected in the evolving language of U.S. extradition treaties. On the one hand, these treaties have represented enablers and facilitators of rendition, providing both the requisite legal authority for the U.S. government to satisfy foreign rendition requests, and the guidelines for carrying out the process. On the other hand, they have played an important role as limiters of the rendition process, imposing constraints on the executive's freedom both to deliver fugitives to foreign governments and to prosecute those extradited to the United States as it might wish. Those constraints have reflected not only the explicit language of the treaties and U.S. and foreign extradition laws, but also the interpretations and (it is fair to say) the misinterpretations of the language by U.S. and foreign courts as well as U.S. and foreign executive branch officials. In some cases, the ambiguity of the treaty language has lent itself to misinterpretation by subsequent interpreters. In others, however, the misinterpretations have fairly been attributed to ignorance of and indifference to the negotiators' intentions, as well as willful disregard of the evident meaning of the language.

The evolution of U.S. extradition law and treaties has been largely one of expanding the scope of rendition between the United States and foreign states. In each case of an extradition relationship between the U.S. government and a foreign government, a treaty was first required to establish the legal basis for fugitive rendition. Subsequent laws and treaties, including both supplementary revisions and new replacements, were thereafter required to correct for the limiting interpretations imposed by courts and occasional executive branch officials, to incorporate new types of criminality created by legislation in each nation, and to reflect the desires of both parties to afford one another broader cooperation than before. U.S. treaty negotiators thus sought to narrow the many conditions on which extradition could not be granted, to shift responsibility for making crucial determinations of fact from the judicial branch to the executive branch, and to draft language that would be sufficiently open-ended to accommodate foreseeable changes in each nation's laws. Particularly significant in this evolutionary process was the gradual shift from the rather explicit and formalistic notions of reciprocity that characterized U.S. extradition treaty language and practice during the nineteenth century to a more substantive and instrumental notion of reciprocity by the middle of the twentieth century.

The two trends of ever-increasing numbers of fugitives to extradite and ever more encompassing and accommodating extradition treaties did not, however, result in any substantial increase in extraditions until the 1970s. Between 1842 and 1890, the U.S. government requested the extradition of 549 fugitives, of which 206 were delivered to the United States, and foreign governments requested the extradition of 604 fugitives from the United States, of which 237 were delivered.[3] During the 1880s, the number of extradition requests by and to the U.S. government averaged about 40 a year[4]—a rate that was not exceeded until the 1970s. By the late 1970s, however, the number had risen to about 150,[5] and in 1982, it totaled 350.[6] And by the late 1980s, the U.S. government was

3. John Bassett Moore, *Treatise on Extradition and Interstate Rendition*, 2 vols. (Boston: Boston Book Co., 1891), 2:1060–1065. These and all other statistics on extradition must be viewed warily because they may include renditions to the United States other than formal extradition pursuant to a treaty. Moore's *Treatise on Extradition* contains the texts of all extradition treaties signed by the United States before 1891.

4. John Bassett Moore, *Report on Extradition* (Washington, D.C.: Government Printing Office, 1890), 167–229, cited in Abbell and Ristau, *International Judicial Assistance*, 4:11.

5. The annual totals for 1979, 1980, and 1981, broken down by country, are provided in *Extradition Reform Act of 1981: Hearings on H.R. 5227 Before the Subcommittee on Crime of the House Committee on the Judiciary*, 97th Cong., 2d Sess., Serial No. 72 (1983), 308–312.

6. David Lauter, "There's No Place to Hide: Extraditions Have Tripled, and It's Only the Beginning," *National Law Journal*, Nov. 26, 1984, 1.

receiving more than 200 requests a year and sending out more than 300.[7]

The single most important reason for the dramatic increase in the number of extraditions, as well as the even greater growth in the numbers of requests for evidence in criminal cases, was the creation of the Office of International Affairs (OIA) in the Justice Department in 1979. Established "for the purpose of centralizing and giving greater emphasis and visibility to [the Justice Department's] prosecutorial service functions in the international arena," the OIA quickly emerged as a repository of information, experience, and advice on most international law enforcement matters.[8] Although a sister Office of Law Enforcement and Intelligence (L/LEI) was created in the State Department's Legal Adviser's Office at about the same time, the attorneys in the OIA assumed principal responsibility for processing fugitive rendition requests to and from the United States. They began to renegotiate the United States' more dated extradition treaties; they provided assistance to federal prosecutors seeking the rendition of fugitives from abroad; they assumed an active role in supporting and representing foreign extradition requests to the United States; and they took over responsibility for processing all extradition requests from state prosecutors to foreign governments.[9] Federal and state prosecutors no longer had to process their requests through unfamiliar and often indifferent State Department channels, and foreign governments no longer were obliged to hire local counsel in the United States to file and press their extradition requests. And whereas the State Department's attorneys had often viewed extradition requests through the somewhat confining lenses of international law, diplomatic protocol, and traditional notions of reciprocity, the OIA attorneys, with their prosecutorial backgrounds, proved less distracted by such considerations and more focused on immobilizing fugitives by whatever means were likely to work. By the late 1980s, the OIA's existence and capabilities were widely known among law enforcement officials within and without the United States, a fact that in and of itself generated ever-increasing numbers of extradition requests.

The OIA's successes were dependent on comparable institutional

7. The U.S. Marshals Service, responsible for collecting fugitives from abroad, reported that it carried out 240 extraditions in FY 1989 and 230 in FY 1990. See the annual reports of the attorney general for 1989 (p. 39) and 1990 (p. 50).

8. Abbell and Ristau, *International Judicial Assistance*, 4:16–17.

9. Ibid.

developments abroad. The fact that similar specialized offices had already been created in many foreign justice ministries, and that others were soon to follow, provided the OIA with the essential partners it required to conduct its transgovernmental affairs. Equally significant was the development during the 1980s of Interpol's international capabilities and the U.S. National Central Bureau of Interpol in the Justice Department. Even as formal extradition procedures continued to require the attentions of courts and prosecutors, the challenges of locating and arresting fugitives fell principally on the shoulders of police officials. Interpol's facilities, and in particular its standardized system of notices, provided them with a rapid and reliable system of keeping tabs on the movements of criminal suspects. The circulation of a "red notice" provided an efficient means of informing foreign police that a fugitive should be arrested when found and provisionally detained until the formal extradition request could be forwarded—although in practice many governments, including that of the United States, have treated a "red notice" only as a notice to locate a fugitive and have refused to make an arrest until the extradition request has been received.[10] Although officials in the OIA and the U.S. Interpol office clashed during the late 1980s over who would control the processing of "red notice" requests, the system itself provided an essential channel for expedited communications among police apart from the extradition process.

The persistent enhancement of the U.S. government's capacity to extradite fugitives to and from abroad might have been expected to reduce its dependence upon other means of international rendition. In fact, quite the opposite was the case. The enhancement of the U.S. government's extradition capacity may have been persistent, but it also was slow. Treaties took time to negotiate, and the number of officials in the Departments of State and Justice with the necessary expertise to undertake the process was small. The demand for fugitive rendition, by contrast, increased at a more rapid pace, particularly following World War II, and it accelerated dramatically with the internationalization of drug enforcement in the 1970s and 1980s. U.S. law enforcement agents, prosecutors, and the Justice Department responded by developing and employing an array of tactics to apprehend fugitives from foreign territories. One result was the regularization of what had become known as irregular rendition.

10. Michael Fooner, *Interpol: Issues in World Crime and International Criminal Justice* (New York: Plenum Press, 1989), 138–147.

The Evolution of U.S. Extradition

American attitudes regarding the apprehension of fugitives who have fled abroad have evolved substantially since the nation's origins. Until well into the nineteenth century, Americans gave little thought to issues of extradition. Criminals were far more likely to flee across state borders or into less-settled regions of North America than to foreign countries, and those who did flee abroad were typically seen as good riddance. Indeed, the request and delivery of criminal fugitives from one state to another was called "extradition" until the end of the nineteenth century, when John Bassett Moore's comprehensive and authoritative *Treatise on Extradition and Interstate Rendition* drew a sharp distinction between international and intranational renditions.[11] Some attention was devoted to crimes committed at sea and by sailors at port. But the concerns with cross-border banditry and vagabondage that motivated many of the first extradition treaties in Europe were relatively insignificant in the United States. Most Americans were wary about entering into extradition treaties that would require reciprocal responsibilities, so strong were their perceptions of the United States as a haven from the oppressions of foreign governments. The principal exceptions, discussed in Chapter Two, reflected the efforts of slave owners to recover their human chattel from foreign havens by unilateral action, diplomatic undertakings, and pressures on the U.S. government to negotiate treaties with Spain, Mexico, and Great Britain. Unilateral action to obtain other types of fugitives was generally regarded as unwarranted and unwise.

Apart from an extradition provision in the Jay Treaty of 1794 with Britain,[12] which expired in 1807, no extradition agreement was signed by the U.S. government until the inclusion of an extradition provision in the Webster-Ashburton Treaty of 1842 with Britain. On rare occasions, U.S. officials asked foreign governments to hand over certain fugitives despite the absence of an extradition treaty and the inability of the U.S.

11. See Moore, *Treatise on Extradition* (supra n. 3). See also John Bassett Moore, "The Difficulties of Extradition," *Publications of the American Academy of Political Science* 1 (July 1911), reprinted in *The Collected Papers of John Bassett Moore* (New Haven: Yale University Press, 1944), 3:314–322, esp. 320.

12. Art. 27 of the Treaty of Amity, Commerce, and Navigation, United States–Great Britain, 8 Stat. 116, TS No. 105 (signed at London, Nov. 19, 1794; submitted to the Senate, June 8, 1795; resolution of advice and consent voted by Senate on condition, June 24, 1795; ratified by United States, Aug. 14, 1795; ratifications exchanged at London, Oct. 28, 1795; proclaimed on Feb. 29, 1796); TS 105, 12 Bevans 13, 8 Stat. 116, 18 Stat. 269.

government to reciprocate. On other occasions, foreign governments simply took the initiative in delivering fugitives—many of them mutineers on American ships—to the United States even in the absence of any request.[13] No more than a few dozen, however, were delivered in such a manner during the first half of the nineteenth century. The number handed over by U.S. officials to foreign governments during the same time probably amounted to no more than half a dozen, although very informal renditions by U.S. officials near the borders with Canada and other foreign territories might well have gone uncounted. One was extradited pursuant to the Jay Treaty. A few were delivered pursuant to a New York State extradition statute enacted in 1822 and subsequently ruled unconstitutional in 1872.[14] And a few others may well have been handed over by U.S. officials unfamiliar with the laws and policies that forbade any delivery of fugitives to foreign authorities. The very novelty of extradition generated substantial suspicion among Americans, and some state courts intervened by habeas corpus to negate federal court decisions authorizing the extradition of fugitives.

The most notable extradition case during this period—one that preoccupied Congress for two months in early 1799—was that of Jonathan Robbins, alias Nash, whom British authorities had charged with murder on board a British man-of-war on the high seas.[15] So powerful was the popular opposition to extraditing Robbins—who claimed, falsely, that he was an American citizen who had been impressed upon a British ship—that President John Adams's decision to deliver him to the British was subsequently viewed as a significant factor in Adams's failure to be reelected. The President's decision was opposed by both Attorney General Charles Lee and Secretary of State Timothy Pickering, who argued that the treaty did not apply to crimes committed on the high seas.[16] Others focused their criticism on the absence of any federal legislation regulating the extradition process or providing for any judicial review of the British charge. But Adams's decision was supported by John Mar-

13. Moore, *Treatise on Extradition*, 45–49.

14. The early extradition laws of U.S. states and territories are discussed in ibid., 53–78. Moore's analysis led him to conclude that no state extradition law other than that of New York was ever used to extradite a fugitive. The New York statute was ruled unconstitutional by the New York Court of Appeals in *People v. Curtis*, 50 N.Y. 321 (1872).

15. Moore, *Treatise on Extradition*, 90, 136, 550–51, 1039. See also the fine analysis of the *Robbins* case and its broader significance in Ruth Wedgwood, "The Revolutionary Martyrdom of Jonathan Robbins," *Yale Law Journal* 100 (1990), 229–368.

16. Moore, *Treatise on Extradition*, 136.

shall, a prominent congressman soon to be appointed secretary of state and thereafter Chief Justice of the Supreme Court, who argued persuasively that it was the duty of the President to fulfill the treaty obligations in the absence of any directive by Congress.[17] The controversy surrounding the case, John Bassett Moore wrote a century later, "served to retard rather than promote the progress of extradition."[18]

The formal origins of U.S. extradition can best be dated to the 1840s, when the U.S. government signed its first full-fledged extradition treaty and Congress enacted its first federal extradition statute.[19] The 1848 statute specified the procedures to follow in extradition proceedings, but it did not authorize extradition in the absence of a treaty. The new law thus codified what most U.S. officials had long assumed—that the U.S. government could not extradite anyone in the absence of a treaty specifically authorizing extradition. Combined with the strongly enshrined notion that no one could be prosecuted in U.S. courts for violations of foreign laws, it presented the U.S. government with the choice of negotiating an abundance of extradition treaties or continuing to present the United States as a haven for foreign criminals.

During the following decades, the U.S. government rapidly emerged as a world leader in the negotiation of bilateral extradition treaties. Between the enactment of the 1848 extradition law and the start of World War I, U.S. officials negotiated thirty-three extradition treaties. Only France, which by 1870 had extradition treaties in force with twenty-eight governments, as well as other sorts of extradition arrangements with dozens of others, claimed more.[20] U.S. courts, moreover, produced a jurisprudence of extradition that was cited and referred to throughout the world. "In the matter of extradition," Sir Edward Clarke wrote in his 1874 treatise, "the American law was, until 1870, better than that of any other country in the world; and the decisions of the American judges are the best existing expositions of the duty of extradition, in its relations at once to the judicial rights of nations and the general interests of the civilisation of the world."[21] Most of the issues

17. Wedgwood, "The Revolutionary Martyrdom of Jonathan Robbins," 333–353; Francis Wharton, *Digest of International Law of the United States* (Washington, D.C.: Government Printing Office, 1886), 2:803–804.

18. Moore, *Treatise on Extradition*, 1059.

19. U.S. extradition law is codified at 18 U.S.C. 3181 and 3184, enacted in 1848 and largely unchanged since then. See Moore, *Treatise on Extradition*, passim.

20. I. A. Shearer, *Extradition in International Law* (Dobbs Ferry, N.Y.: Oceana Publications, 1971), 16–19.

21. Quoted in ibid., 16.

that continue to dominate extradition negotiations today were first addressed during that time.

The initial extradition treaties negotiated by U.S. officials included a hodgepodge of governments, mostly but not entirely in Europe: France in 1843, the Hawaiian Islands in 1849, Switzerland in 1850, Prussia, Bavaria, and Hanover between 1853 and 1855, the Two Sicilies in 1855, and Austria-Hungary in 1856.[22] During the next forty years, eighteen new treaties were signed with a variety of governments in Europe and Latin America, as well as with Japan and the Ottoman Porte.[23] The last treaty signed, with Russia in 1893, generated substantial opposition within the United States among those opposed to the czar.[24] Like the extradition provision in the Webster-Ashburton Treaty, a number of these—with the Dominican Republic, the Hawaiian Islands, Haiti, the Orange Free State, Switzerland, the Two Sicilies, and Venezuela—were small sections of more comprehensive treaties. As extradition norms developed, as particular controversies required more formal and anticipatory resolutions, and as new governments replaced old, many treaties were either supplemented or replaced by entirely new treaties. Between 1900 and 1914, U.S. negotiators concluded fourteen new treaties, ten of them with governments in Latin America, as well as fifteen supplementary and replacement treaties.[25] During the 1920s, U.S. efforts focused on signing new treaties with eight Eastern European governments.[26] Between 1932 and 1943, six new treaties were signed—with Greece, Albania, Iraq, Liechtenstein, Liberia, and Monaco—but most efforts focused on concluding nineteen supplementary treaties as well as three replacement treaties, principally to expand the list of extraditable offenses.[27] Treaty negotiations ground to a virtual halt thereafter until 1970. Only one new treaty was signed—with Israel in 1963—as well as a few supplementary and replacement treaties, with South Africa, Sweden, Belgium, and Brazil, although the last (signed in 1961) was signifi-

22. These and all other extradition treaties signed by the U.S. government before 1890 are reproduced in Moore, *Treatise on Extradition*, 1059–1187.

23. The treaties are listed in Abbell and Ristau, *International Judicial Assistance* (supra n. 1), 4:6.

24. See the commentary of John Bassett Moore (who favored ratification of the treaty) in "The Russian Extradition Treaty," *The Forum* 15 (1893), 629–646, reprinted in *Collected Papers of John Bassett Moore* (supra n. 11), 1:256–273.

25. The treaties are listed in Abbell and Ristau, *International Judicial Assistance*, 4:7–8.

26. Ibid., 8.

27. Ibid., 9–10.

cant in that Brazil had become a notorious haven for fugitives from American justice since the abrogation of the previous treaty in 1913.[28] The pace of negotiations picked up dramatically during the 1970s, motivated both by the general need to modernize the United States' increasingly dated extradition treaties and by the particular demands generated by the dramatic internationalization of U.S. drug enforcement efforts. Between 1970 and 1990, U.S. negotiators concluded more than two dozen replacement and supplementary treaties.[29] The most significant treaty, in at least one respect, was that signed with Great Britain on December 22, 1931. Although the two governments eventually replaced that treaty with a more modern one in 1971, the 1931 treaty was retained by most of the colonies of the British Empire when they gained their independence. As a result, more than thirty of the roughly one hundred U.S. extradition treaties formally in force by the 1980s were represented by the same document.[30]

The large number of bilateral extradition treaties negotiated by the U.S. government could be explained not just by its inability to extradite anyone in the absence of a treaty but also by its reluctance to join multilateral extradition conventions. A substantial number of these had emerged by the 1980s:[31] the European Convention on Extradition,[32] the Benelux Extradition Convention,[33] the Arab League Extradition Agree-

28. See Alona E. Evans, "The New Extradition Treaties of the United States," *American Journal of International Law* 59 (1965), 351–362.

29. The treaties are listed in Abbell and Ristau, *International Judicial Assistance*, 4:9. See also *Worldwide Review of Status of U.S. Extradition Treaties and Mutual Legal Assistance Treaties: Hearing Before the House Committee on Foreign Affairs*, 100th Cong., 1st Sess. (1987), 17–25.

30. See Appendix F, in which the countries represented by the 1931 treaty are noted with the superscript "c." See also Abbell and Ristau, *International Judicial Assistance*, 5:A-146.

31. See U.N. Division of Narcotic Drugs, *Extradition for Drug-Related Offenses* (New York: United Nations, 1985), 17–19. The principal author of the report is Robert Linke.

32. European Treaty Series (ETS), No. 24 (Dec. 13, 1957). See also the additional protocol of Oct. 15, 1975, at ETS No. 86 and the protocol of Mar. 17, 1978, at ETS 98. See the discussion of these treaties in Dominique Poncet and Paul Gully-Hart, "The European Model," in M. Cherif Bassiouni, ed., *International Criminal Law*, vol. 2, *Procedure* (Dobbs Ferry, N.Y.: Transnational Publishers, 1986), 461–503 (the texts of the treaty and protocols are reprinted at 505–522).

33. The Benelux Extradition Convention, which also covers mutual assistance in criminal matters, was signed by Belgium, Luxembourg, and the Netherlands on June 27, 1962, and entered into force in 1967. It is modeled on the European convention but contains provisions authorizing even closer cooperation among the three Benelux states. See B. de Schutter, "International Criminal Law in Evolution: Mutual Assistance in Criminal Matters Between the Benelux Countries," *Netherlands Journal of International Law* 114 (1967), 382. See the text at 616 UNTS 8893 and at *Benelux Publicatieblad* (1960–62), 22.

ment,[34] the 1981 Inter-American Convention on Extradition[35] and its predecessor the Montevideo Convention,[36] and the Convention on Judicial Cooperation of the Organization Communale Africaine et Malgache (OCAM).[37] In addition, the Nordic Treaty members[38] and the members of the Commonwealth[39] had each agreed during the 1960s on schemes to enact reciprocal extradition legislation, and the Soviet bloc countries had worked out their own comprehensive scheme, including mutual assistance in criminal matters, based on separate but nearly identical bilateral treaties with one another.[40]

U.S. officials generally demonstrated little interest in the multilateral conventions, although the United States' accession in 1985 to the Council of Europe's Convention for the Transfer of Prisoners suggested a growing interest in the benefits of such treaties.[41] A U.S. delegate had signed the Inter-American Treaty for the Extradition of Criminals and for Protection Against Anarchism in Mexico City in 1902, but it had never been put into force for the United States.[42] The United States has yet to sign the Inter-American Convention on Extradition adopted by the Organization of American States in 1981, nor has it made much use of the 1933 Montevideo Convention, of which it is a member.[43] Only when the the supreme court of Colombia declared the 1979 extradition treaty between the United States and Colombia invalid did U.S. officials attempt to employ—albeit to little effect—the somewhat forgotten convention of an earlier era. U.S. officials also reacted warily to efforts

34. The Arab League Extradition Agreement was approved by the Council of the League of Arab States on Sept. 14, 1952; an English translation is in *British and Foreign State Papers* 159, p. 606, and in League of Arab States, *Collection of Treaties and Agreements*, No. 95 (1978). It is briefly discussed in Shearer, *Extradition in International Law*, (supra n. 20), 52–53.

35. OAS Treaty Series No. 60 (OEA/Ser. A/36 [SEPF]).

36. 49 Stat. 3111; TS 882; 3 Bevans 152; 165 LNTS 45. Signatories of this convention are listed in Appendix F marked with a superscript "b."

37. The agreement was signed on Sept. 12, 1961.

38. The Nordic Treaty of July 1, 1962, can be found at 434 UNTS 145.

39. The Scheme Relating to the Rendition of Fugitive Offenders Within the Commonwealth, signed in 1966, can be found at HMSO, London, Cmnd. 3008.

40. See the discussion of the Soviet bloc system in Lech Gardocki, "The Socialist System," in Bassiouni, ed., *International Criminal Law*, 2:133–149; and Karin Schmid, "Extradition and International Judicial and Administrative Assistance in Penal Matters in East European States," *Law in Eastern Europe* 34 (1987), 167–182.

41. Convention on the Transfer of Sentenced Prisoners, TIAS 10824. See also U.S. Senate Treaty Doc. 98-23 (1984).

42. See *American Journal of International Law* 29 (Supp.) (1935), 278–282.

43. 49 Stat. 3111; TS 882; 3 Bevans 152; 165 LNTS 45.

initiated by the Council of Europe in the late 1980s to negotiate a new European extradition convention, fearing that it would undermine the accomplishments of the United States' bilateral treaties with member states. The long-standing American resistance to multilateral extradition conventions can be explained in part by the relative complexity of the U.S. legal system, with its common law traditions, federal distribution of jurisdiction, and highly intricate rules of evidence, none of which has been particularly well suited to multilateral extradition arrangements with the majority of foreign states in which civil law traditions dominate. But much of the resistance can also be attributed to the tendency of multilateral arrangements to settle on the minimum common denominators of cooperation. Bilateral treaties, by contrast, provide an opportunity to push each negotiating partner to include the provisions that are of greatest interest and advantage to the United States. The only exceptions to this aversion for multilateral extradition treaties (all of which date back no further than 1970) have been the multilateral conventions directed at hijacking and other crimes involving aircraft, terrorism, crimes against diplomats, hostage taking, and illicit drug trafficking, each of which contains provisions regarding extradition.[44]

The years since 1970 can best be characterized as the modern era of U.S. extradition treaty negotiations. U.S. negotiators have sought to maximize the number of offenses for which a treaty partner will extradite; to narrow as much as possible the "political offense" exception, especially in negotiations with close allies; to accommodate the extraterritorial reach of U.S. and foreign criminal laws and jurisdictional notions; to persuade foreign governments to extradite their nationals, or else ensure vicarious prosecution at the request of the U.S. government; to reconcile U.S. capital punishment laws with the insistence of foreign governments that fugitives delivered by them not be executed; and, more generally, to clear up confusions and eliminate needless obstacles that had hobbled extradition relations under the older treaties. Multilateral conventions—such as the 1972 Protocol to the 1961 Single Convention on Narcotic Drugs and the 1988 United Nations Convention Against Illicit Traffic in Narcotic Drugs and Psychotropic Substances—have filled in some of the gaps in the older treaties, most notably the omission of

44. See *Treaties in Force* (supra n. 1), and Abbell and Ristau, *International Judicial Assistance* (supra n. 1), 5:A-1075–1114.

drug law violations as grounds for extradition, but they have proven too limited in scope to negate the general need for new extradition treaties.[45] During the early 1980s, the treaty negotiations were supplemented by efforts in Congress, stimulated in good part by State and Justice Department officials, to modernize the extradition laws, which had last been substantially revised in 1882. The judiciary committees responded favorably, but political opposition involving the "political offense" exception scuttled the attempt to overhaul the extradition statute.[46]

Dual Criminality and Extraditable Offenses

A chronological examination of U.S. extradition treaties reveals both the trend toward ever-increasing breadth and inclusiveness and the persistent need to eliminate and clarify ambiguities in the language of old treaties that had resulted in both U.S. and foreign courts, and executive branch officials, rejecting extradition requests. Beginning with the Jay Treaty's provision for the extradition of fugitives accused of murder and forgery, the list of extraditable offenses grew ever longer thereafter until it was simply replaced during the 1980s by a fairly open-ended "dual criminality" provision authorizing extradition for any crime punishable in both countries by imprisonment for at least one year. In 1845, just two years after the United States had signed with France its first full-fledged extradition treaty—which listed murder, attempted murder, rape, forgery, arson, and embezzlement by public officers as extraditable crimes—the two governments appended a supplementary treaty that added robbery and burglary to the list of such crimes (and carefully defined both terms). In 1858, a further supplement included counterfeiting and embezzlement by private persons. Beginning in the 1880s, treaty negotiators made sure to include embezzlement and other types of fraud, and also became more particular in listing specific types

45. See the discussion in U.N. Division of Narcotic Drugs, *Extradition for Drug-Related Offenses* (supra n. 31), 4–12.

46. See *Reform of the Extradition Laws of the United States: Hearings Before the Subcommittee on Crime of the House Committee on the Judiciary*, 98th Cong., 1st Sess., on H.R. 2643 (1983); *Extradition Reform Act of 1981: Hearings* (supra n. 5); and *Extradition Act of 1984: Report (98-998) submitted by the House Committee on the Judiciary*, 98th Cong., 2d Sess., on H.R. 3347 (1984).

of murder, forgery, counterfeiting, and other crimes previously included only as generic categories.[47] Bigamy and abortion were also added to the lists in the early 1880s. And a few treaties included crimes that were not repeated in any other—the treaty with Mexico, for instance, made specific mention of mutilation.[48] The additions to the lists continued throughout the twentieth century. During the worldwide economic depression of the 1930s, bankruptcy offenses were included in newly negotiated treaties. By 1980, the "Schedule of Offenses" appended to a new extradition treaty with the Netherlands included not only the familiar crimes listed one hundred years before but also antitrust violations, illicit currency transfers, tax evasion, hijacking of airplanes, governmental corruption, violations of securities and commodities laws, obstruction of justice, and criminal offenses involving firearms, incendiary devices, and nuclear materials.[49]

The reliance on lists of extraditable crimes in the treaties meant that new initiatives in criminalization were difficult to incorporate into preexisting treaties without going through the process of negotiating, ratifying, and effecting supplementary treaties. The governments of the United States and Canada, for instance, were obliged to negotiate one supplementary treaty after another in order to keep pace with changes in one another's laws and judicial rulings, notably those involving securities law violations and other frauds.[50] During the early 1970s, U.S. law enforcement officials found many of their efforts to extradite drug traffickers from Latin America and elsewhere stymied by the fact that thirty-six of their treaties, including most of those with Latin American governments, made no mention of drug law violations, having been negotiated mostly before World War I. The lacuna was partially ameliorated by including a provision in the multilateral 1972 Protocol to the 1961 Single Convention on Narcotic Drugs that provided the legal basis

47. John Bassett Moore, "Extradition" (1893), reprinted in *The Collected Papers of John Bassett Moore* (supra n. 1), 1:274–285.

48. Art. 3 of the 1861 extradition treaty between Mexico and the United States, concluded Dec. 11, 1861; ratifications exchanged at Mexico, May 20, 1862; proclaimed June 20, 1862.

49. See the appendix to the Treaty of Extradition Between the United States of America and the Kingdom of the Netherlands, signed at the Hague on June 24, 1980; entered into force Sept. 15, 1983 (TIAS 10733). See also U.S. Senate Treaty Doc. 97-7 (1981), TS 209, Bevans 817, 12 Stat. 1199.

50. See William H. Timbers and Irving M. Pollack, "Extradition from Canada to the United States for Securities Fraud: Frustration of the National Policies of Both Countries," *Fordham Law Review* 24 (1955), 301–325.

for signatory governments to incorporate drug law violations into their preexisting extradition treaties.[51] But many governments were slow to ratify the convention, and some were uncertain whether the language in the Protocol provided sufficient authority to extradite. Meanwhile, the negotiation of new bilateral treaties required the time and resources of a very small number of officials with experience in extradition matters.

Even with respect to those treaties that either supplemented or replaced their lists of extraditable crimes with liberal "dual criminality" provisions, the U.S. government encountered additional problems. Many foreign courts had long been confused by the language of federal criminal statutes, which provided for federal jurisdiction based on an individual's use of the mails, telephone, wire service, or other forms of interstate commerce to commit a crime. U.S. requests for extradition under the old treaties occasionally had been stymied when foreign courts ruled that it was not against their domestic law for someone to use a telephone or write a letter. As the federal government's role in law enforcement grew dramatically, and as federal rather than state prosecutors began to account for a majority of U.S. extradition requests, foreign confusions on this point became increasingly frustrating. Many foreign courts also looked suspiciously on extradition requests involving violations of two federal statutes created in 1970 to deal with drug trafficking and organized crime: the Racketeer Influenced and Corrupt Organizations Act (RICO) and the Continuing Criminal Enterprise (CCE) statute.[52] Similar skepticism greeted U.S. efforts during the 1980s to prosecute drug traffickers for violating U.S. tax laws and other statutes directed at drug-related money laundering. And at least a few foreign governments were wary of the increasingly extraterritorial drift of U.S. criminal statutes, which contrasted so starkly with U.S. jurisdictional notions before World War II. U.S. extradition treaty negotiators responded to all these developments and problems by combining liberal

51. TIAS 8118; 976 UNTS 3. See Nelson G. Gross and G. Jonathan Greenwald, "The 1972 Narcotics Protocol," *Contemporary Drug Problems* 2 (1973), 119–163.

52. Steven A. Bernholz, Martin J. Bernholz, and G. Nicholas Herman, "Problems of Double Criminality: International Extradition in CCE and RICO Cases," *Trial*, Jan. 1985, 59–63; idem, "International Extradition in Drug Cases," *North Carolina Journal of International Law and Commercial Regulation* 10 (1985), 353–382; Barbara Sicalides, "RICO, CCE, and International Extradition," *Temple Law Review* 62 (1989), 1281–1316; Michael J. Dinga, "Extradition of RICO Defendants to the United States Under Recent U.S. Extradition Treaties," *Boston University International Law Journal* 7 (1989), 329–354.

dual criminality provisions with specific clauses designed to avoid the distractions of different terminology and jurisdictional bases.

The Principle of Specialty

The principle of specialty, which requires that a fugitive not be tried for an offense other than that for which he or she was extradited, was one that complicated the first decades of U.S. extradition relations and that continues to arise in a substantial proportion of prosecutions subsequent to extradition.[53] The first dozen treaties concluded by the U.S. government contained no explicit limitation of this sort, but subsequent treaties, beginning with the Italian treaty of 1868, did incorporate the specialty principle. During the 1870s, extradition relations between the governments of Britain and the United States foundered on this issue. The extradition clauses in the 1842 Webster-Ashburton Treaty had made no reference to limitations on trial, but the British Extradition Act of 1870, which represented the culmination of Britain's first systematic consideration of extradition law and policy, incorporated the principle of specialty into British law. When Secretary of State Fish refused in 1876 to provide the British government with the assurances it requested on this issue, the latter responded by rejecting—albeit only temporarily—a number of extradition requests from the United States.[54] In 1886, the U.S. Supreme Court addressed the issue in *United States v. Rauscher* and came down firmly in favor of the British position.[55] Extradition treaties negotiated thereafter typically included both language reflecting the specialty principle as well as clauses providing for exceptions to the principle. By the 1980s, the exceptions to the principle allowed the requesting government substantially greater latitude in prosecuting offenders for crimes other than those for which they had specifically been extradited.[56] The *Rauscher* decision was also notable for its suggestion—developed thereafter in the lower courts—that a fugitive could raise the

53. The early history of the specialty principle in U.S. extradition law and practice is discussed in Moore, *Treatise on Extradition* (supra n. 3), 194–280.

54. Ibid., 196–240.

55. 119 U.S. 407 (1886).

56. Abbell and Ristau, *International Judicial Assistance* (supra n. 1), 4:76–80.

specialty principle as a defense even in the absence of a formal protest by the government that had extradited him to the United States.[57]

Extraterritorial Jurisdiction

Another issue that restricted the capacity of the U.S. government to respond favorably to foreign extradition requests was its reluctance to acknowledge the more expansive jurisdictional notions of civil law nations. In the 1873 case of a Prussian citizen, Carl Vogt (alias Stupp), the Prussian government requested his extradition by the United States so that he could be tried for certain heinous crimes committed in Belgium. (A request the previous year from the Belgian government for Vogt's extradition had been rejected—in the case that ruled New York's extradition statute unconstitutional—due to the absence of an extradition treaty between the United States and Belgium.[58]) Among the seventeen extradition treaties then in force, all but one referred to crimes committed "within the jurisdiction" of the requesting state by individuals "found within the territory" of the other. In keeping with their civil law traditions, most foreign governments defined the first term as including crimes committed by their citizens in other territories, and a few went so far as to extend their jurisdictional claims to extraterritorial crimes in which only the victims were their citizens. U.S. jurisprudence, by contrast, eschewed any claim to jurisdiction based on the nationality of either the criminals or the victims and largely limited its jurisdictional claims to acts committed within its own territorial boundaries. Few crimes committed abroad by Americans, with the exception of treason and international crimes such as piracy and slave-trading, were regarded as violations of U.S. laws. The Prussian extradition request was nonetheless approved by Judge Blatchford, but the Department of State then

57. See Jonathan George, "Toward a More Principled Approach to the Principle of Specialty," *Cornell International Law Journal* 12 (1979), 309–327. See *U.S. v. Levy*, 905 F.2d 326 (10th Cir. 1990), cert. denied 111 S.Ct. 759 (1991), and *U.S. v. Cuevas*, 847 F.2d 1417 (9th Cir. 1988), cert. denied, 489 U.S. 1012, 109 S.Ct. 1122 (1989). The standing of the defendant to assert the principle of specialty is questioned in *Demjanjuk v. Petrovsky*, 776 F.2d 571, cert. denied, 475 U.S. 1016 (1986).

58. *People v. Curtis*, 50 N.Y. 321, Nov. 19, 1872; discussed in Moore, *Treatise on Extradition*, 70.

submitted the question of jurisdiction to Attorney General George Williams, who held that the reference to jurisdiction in the treaty meant territorial jurisdiction.[59] The extradition request was thus rejected, Vogt was set free, and an extradition treaty was signed with Belgium the following year.[60]

This lack of complementarity in jurisdictional notions continued to hamper extradition relations for another century. Only in the 1960s did U.S. negotiators begin to address this problem. Much of the incentive arose from the enactment of new federal laws that extended U.S. criminal jurisdiction to acts committed entirely outside the United States that were deemed to have an undesirable effect within the United States. Based primarily on the principle of "objective territorial jurisdiction" or the "effects" doctrine, and secondarily on the "protective" principle of jurisdiction, these new laws (of which the Comprehensive Drug Abuse Prevention and Control Act of 1970 was by far the most significant) were the subject of an increasing number of U.S. extradition requests. Beginning in the 1960s, all new U.S. extradition treaties authorized extradition for offenses committed outside the territory of the requesting government if the U.S. government would have jurisdiction over such offenses in similar circumstances.[61] In the late 1970s, U.S. negotiators went a step further and included treaty provisions authorizing extradition in cases such as *In re Stupp*, where the foreign government's request involved a crime committed by a citizen outside its territory.[62] And by the mid-1980s, new U.S. extradition treaties virtually eliminated the obstacles posed by differing jurisdictional notions, providing for extradition so long as the dual criminality requirement had been met.[63] As the

59. Moore, *Treatise on Extradition*, 134–135; *In re Stupp*, 11 Blatchford 124, 23 Fed. Cas. 281 (S.D.N.Y. 1873), 14 Op. 281, Williams, 1873; For. Rel., 1873, 80–85, 301.

60. The treaty is reproduced in Moore, *Treatise on Extradition*, 1080–1087. Vogt's extradition to Belgium was subsequently upheld by Judge Blatchford. See *In re Stupp*, 12 Blatchford 501, 23 Fed. Cas. 296 (S.D.N.Y. 1875). The same issue emerged in extradition treaty negotiations with the Russian government in 1874. Secretary of State Fish's refusal to acknowledge the extraterritorial claims of foreign states in that instance is reproduced in Wharton, *Digest of International Law* (supra n. 17), 2:800.

61. Abbell and Ristau, *International Judicial Assistance*, 4:64–65. See, e.g., the 1963 extradition treaty with Sweden, Art. 4, TIAS 5496; the 1964 treaty with Israel, Art. 3, TIAS 5476; the 1964 treaty with Brazil, Art. 4, TIAS 5691; and the 1976 treaty with Australia, Art. 4, TIAS 8234.

62. Ibid., 65–66. See, e.g., the 1980 treaty with Japan, Art. 4, TIAS 9625.

63. Ibid., 66. See, e.g., the 1984 treaty with Italy, Art. 3, TIAS 10837, and the 1984 treaty with Ireland, Art. 3, TIAS 10813.

problems generated by the lack of complementarity and reciprocity in jurisdictional claims faded, conflicts involving mutual claims of jurisdiction appeared increasingly likely.[64]

Capital Punishment

Another issue that emerged during the nineteenth century and that has continued to complicate extradition relations throughout the twentieth involves the death penalty. Governments that have abolished the death penalty in their own countries generally refuse to extradite fugitives to the United States and other nations that retain capital punishment unless assurances are provided that the death penalty will not be employed. This issue first emerged in U.S. extradition relations during the nineteenth century. It became a source of conflict with the Italian government during the first decades of this century, when the latter refused to extradite Italian-American members of the Black Hand who had been condemned in the United States to death in the electric chair.[65] And it reemerged during the late 1980s as a major impediment to U.S. extradition efforts. The U.S. government has preferred not to include any waiver of capital punishment in its treaties. The compromise that emerged early in the twentieth century was to include a provision in extradition treaties formally acknowledging the right of a requested state not to extradite a fugitive unless the U.S. government promised to forgo the death penalty.[66] What has complicated matters on this issue, as on many other extradition issues, is the sovereign power of states within the United States to enforce their own criminal laws in the absence of an explicit federal law or treaty to the contrary. In 1985, the Canadian government agreed to extradite Tony Ng, who was wanted for his involvement in the murders of thirteen people in a Chinese gambling club in Seattle, only after Washington State officials promised not to seek the death penalty.[67] In late 1989, however, the same government consented to extradite

64. See Blakesley and Lagodny, "Finding Harmony Amidst Disagreement" (supra n. 2).

65. Thomas Monroe Pitkin and Francesco Cordasco, *The Black Hand: A Chapter in Ethnic Crime* (Totowa, N.J.: Littlefield, Adams & Co., 1977), 215.

66. See J. S. Reeves, "Extradition Treaties and the Death Penalty," *American Journal of International Law* 18 (1924), 298–300.

67. John F. Burns, "With Death at Issue, Can Canada Wash Its Hands?" *New York Times*, Nov. 1, 1988, A4.

Charles Ng (no relation to Tony), who had been charged with the abduction and murder of a dozen people, to California despite the refusal of state officials to forgo the death penalty.[68] The government reportedly had received 100,000 letters insisting that Ng be extradited.[69] In another case in 1989 with greater implications for U.S. extradition efforts, the European Court of Human Rights held that the British government could not extradite a German national, Jens Soering, to the United States to face charges of murder in a Virginia court without a promise from U.S. or Virginian authorities that the death penalty would not be sought or imposed.[70] In the court's judgment, the prospect of the relatively young man spending many years on death row in a state prison with a reputation for interprisoner violence violated the provision in the European Convention on Human Rights prohibiting torture or inhuman or degrading treatment or punishment. The British government responded to the decision by extraditing Soering to the United States only on charges for which he could not receive the death penalty. Some months later, the supreme court of the Netherlands refused to approve the extradition of an American serviceman, Sergeant Charles Short, accused of killing his Turkish wife and trying to dispose of her remains, in the absence of an assurance from U.S. authorities that he would not be tried for a capital offense. Relying heavily on the *Soering* decision and the European Convention on Human Rights, the court stated that international human rights obligations overrode the obligation to extradite. Following a commitment by U.S. officials not to prosecute Short for a capital offense, the Dutch government delivered the American soldier, who had been based with a U.S. unit at the Dutch Soesterberg Air Force Base, to U.S. authorities.[71] The two cases, combined with the

68. Bruce Zagaris, "Canada Extradites Ng Without Seeking Death Penalty Assurances," *International Enforcement Law Reporter* 5 (1989), 420–422.

69. This and other extradition cases involving the death penalty are discussed in Andrea Sachs, "A Fate Better Than Death," *Time*, Mar. 4, 1991, 52.

70. *Soering v. United Kingdom* (161 Eur. Ct. H.R., ser. AO (1989)). See the discussion of the case in John Quigley and S. Adele Shank, "Death Row as a Violation of Human Rights: Is It Illegal to Extradite to Virginia?" *Virginia Journal of International Law* 30 (1989), 241–271; "*Soering v. United Kingdom*: Whether the Continued Use of the Death Penalty in the United States Contradicts International Thinking," *New England Journal on Criminal and Civil Confinement* 16 (1990), 339–368; Wilson Finnie, "Extradition and the Death Penalty," *The Scots Law Times*, Feb. 16, 1990, 53–57; Stephan Breitenmoser and Gunter E. Wilms, "Human Rights v. Extradition: The *Soering* Case," *Michigan Journal of International Law* 11 (1990), 845–886; and John Andrews and Ann Sherlock, "Extradition, Death Row, and the Convention," *European Law Review* 15 (1990), 87–92.

71. The *Short* case and related developments are discussed in *International Enforcement Law Reporter* 7 (1991), 313–315.

abolition of capital punishment in virtually all of Europe as well as in many other countries, suggested that capital offenses might well be the only area of extradition law and practice in which U.S. efforts to extradite fugitives were finding themselves more rather than less constrained than before.[72]

The "Political Offense" Exception

No extradition issue has attracted as much attention and controversy as the "political offense" exception, a clause included in all U.S. extradition treaties as well as in most other extradition treaties currently in force that circumscribes extradition in cases involving politically motivated crimes and prosecutions.[73] The notion of a "political offense" exception to extradition had arisen during the 1830s in Europe when popular opinion in France and Belgium rebelled at the notion of extraditing political refugees who had committed violent acts to the governments against which those acts had been directed.[74] In 1833, the French government began to include the clause in its new extradition treaties and to supplement its older treaties accordingly. A "political offense" exception clause was thus included in the first full-fledged extradition treaty signed by the United States—the 1843 treaty with France.[75] The extradition provision included in the Webster-Ashburton Treaty approved the previous year had not included such a clause, but the message of President Tyler submitting the treaty to the Senate had.[76] With a few

72. A similar conflict arose when the U.S. government asked Italian authorities to extradite Anthony Sciacca, an Italian citizen who had been accused of murder in New York when he was seventeen years old. Italian courts rejected the extradition request on the grounds that Sciacca would be treated as an adult under New York law and thus face a sentence of up to life in prison, while under Italian law he would be treated as a juvenile and probably accorded a lenient sentence. When subsequent efforts to have Sciacca vicariously prosecuted in Italian courts faltered because of a statute of limitations, the district attorney of Queens, John Santucci, flew to Italy with Justice Department officials to attempt to find a solution. See Joseph P. Fried, "Santucci to Go to Italy in Battle over a Slaying," *New York Times*, July 14, 1990, 24.

73. There is an extensive and continually growing legal literature on this question. See esp. Christine Van den Wijngaert, *The Political Offence Exception to Extradition* (London: Kluwer, 1980).

74. Lora L. Deere, "Political Offenses in the Law and Practice of Extradition," *American Journal of International Law* 27 (1933), 247–270.

75. The extradition treaty with France was concluded on Nov. 9, 1843; ratifications exchanged at Washington, Apr. 12, 1844; proclaimed Apr. 13, 1844; TS 89, 7 Bevans 830, 8 Stat. 580.

76. Ibid., 214, 305.

exceptions, notably the extradition treaty with Prussia and other German states, all subsequent U.S. extradition treaties made reference to the "political offense" exception. During the 1850s, a controversy between the governments of Belgium and France involving the latter's request for the extradition of two Frenchmen who had attempted to blow up a train carrying Napoleon III yielded a new provision, known as the *attentat* clause, that excluded attempted assassinations of heads of state and their families from the "political offense" exception.[77] The clause quickly became a fixture of many extradition treaties. It was first included in the United States' extradition treaty with Belgium in 1882, just shortly after the assassination of President Garfield, and became a standard provision during the twentieth century.

The first case in which an extradition request was rejected on account of the "political offense" exception occurred in 1837, when Governor Marcy of New York refused—pursuant to New York's 1822 extradition statute—to extradite a Canadian, William Lyon McKenzie, who had led a minor insurrection against Governor Head in Toronto. The crime McKenzie had committed, Marcy pointed out, was in effect treason and thus not susceptible to extradition.[78] Between 1880 and 1920, requests from Mexico City for the extradition of revolutionaries were often turned down on much the same grounds—although in 1896 the Supreme Court approved the extradition of bandits operating along the border who had claimed they were part of a revolutionary movement but failed to show that their motives were primarily political.[79] In 1894, an extradition request from the government of Salvador for the delivery of General Antonio Ezeta—who had helped overthrow a previous regime and then been ousted from office himself—as well as four of his followers, was rejected by a U.S. magistrate. He relied heavily on a British case decided three years earlier, *In re Castione*, in which Judge Denman had refused to extradite the leader of an uprising in a Swiss canton on the grounds that crimes committed in the course of, or incident to, a revolution or uprising were political and hence nonextraditable.[80] This formulation, known as the "incidence test," emerged in

77. Deere, "Political Offenses in the Law and Practice of Extradition," 252–253; Moore, *Treatise on Extradition*, 308–311.

78. Moore, *Treatise on Extradition*, 313–315.

79. *Ornelas v. Ruiz*, 161 U.S. 502 (1896).

80. See *In re Ezeta*, 62 F. 972 (N.D. 1894); *In re Castione*, [1891] 1 Q.B. 149. See also the discussion in John Bassett Moore, "The Case of the Salvadorean Refugees," *American Law Review* 29 (1895), 1–20; and Barbara Ann Banoff and Christopher H. Pyle, " 'To Surrender

subsequent decades as the central determinant of whether a crime fell within the "political offense" exception.

The extradition cases that aroused the greatest public interest in the United States typically involved revolutionaries whose movements claimed substantial popular support in the United States. During the first decade of the twentieth century, requests from the czarist government for the extradition of two Russian revolutionaries accused of murder and other crimes were approved by U.S. commissioners but then rejected by the secretary of state in the wake of vocal public opposition.[81] The most controversial cases, however, involved Irish revolutionaries fighting British rule in Ireland. Beginning with the Lynchehaun case in 1903, U.S. refusals to extradite Irish revolutionaries who had committed violent acts have generated substantial tensions between the governments of Britain and the United States. Between 1979 and 1986, U.S. courts rejected four extradition requests from Britain for IRA members—in *McMullen*,[82] *Mackin*,[83] *Quinn*,[84] and *Doherty*[85]—who had been charged or convicted of murder and other violent crimes directed at British soldiers and other officials. The Reagan administration, which preferred to favor Britain's requests, responded in a variety of ways. Each case was appealed to higher courts, with the result that Quinn was extradited in 1986. Congressional bills narrowing the "political offense" exception were backed by the White House,[86] and a supplementary extradition treaty was negotiated with Britain, dramatically limiting the political offense exception.[87] Both encountered substantial opposition in the

---

Political Offenders': The Political Offense Exception to Extradition in United States Law," *New York University Journal of International Law and Politics* 16 (1984), 169–210.

81. Deere, "Political Offenses in the Law and Practice of Extradition," 267; Green Haywood Hackworth, *Digest of International Law* (Washington, D.C.: Government Printing Office, 1942), 4:49–50. See the debate over the political offense exception among J. Reuben Clark Jr., Frederic R. Coudert, and Julian W. Mack in *Proceedings of the American Society of International Law 1909*, 95–165.

82. The magistrate's denial of extradition can be found at No. 3-78-1099 (N.D. Cal. May 11, 1979), reprinted in *Congressional Record* S9146 (daily ed. July 16, 1986), 132.

83. 668 F.2d 122 (2d Cir. 1981).

84. 783 F.2d 776 (9th Cir. 1986), cert. denied 479 U.S. 882 (1986).

85. 786 F.2d 491 (2d Cir. 1986).

86. The proposed legislation is analyzed in M. Cherif Bassiouni, "Extradition Reform Legislation in the United States: 1981–1983," *Akron Law Review* 17 (1984), 495–574.

87. Supplementary Treaty to the Extradition Treaty of June 8, 1972, signed at Washington June 25, 1985, entered into force Dec. 23, 1986. See the text in U.S. Senate Treaty Doc. 99-8 (1985) and the analysis of the treaty in U.S. Senate Exec. Rept. 99-17 (1986). See also Terri Lee Wagner, "Expediting Extraditing: The United States–United Kingdom Supplemental Extradition Treaty of 1986," *Loyola of Los Angeles International and Comparative Law*

Congress and elsewhere.[88] The proposed extradition reform bill failed to make it through the Congress primarily because of this issue, and the first supplementary treaty submitted to the Senate required minor revisions before the Senate would approve it.[89] Similar treaty supplements were subsequently signed, however, with Germany,[90] Canada,[91] and Australia.[92] U.S. treaty negotiators had already begun, during the late 1970s, to include a clause explicitly authorizing the executive rather than the judicial branch to evaluate the motivations of the requesting state and, in a few cases, a clause to determine the applicability of the political offense exception[93]—but they were obliged to forgo the first clause in subsequent treaties as a result of the controversy in Congress. Determined to appease the British government, Justice Department officials instituted deportation proceedings against the three other IRA fugitives[94] and renewed their attempts to extradite McMullen and Doherty under the supplementary treaty.[95]

The IRA cases, however, represented more an aberration than a

---

Journal 10 (1988), 135–162; and Kathleen A. Basso, "The 1985 U.S.-U.K. Supplementary Extradition Treaty: A Superfluous Effort?" *Boston College International and Comparative Law Review* 12 (1989), 301–333.

88. See the fine discussion in Committee on Immigration and Nationality Law, "Report Recommending Reform of the Law of International Extradition," *Record of the Association of the Bar of the City of New York* 41 (1986), 587–614.

89. Steven V. Roberts, "Pact with Britain on Extraditions Backed by Senate," *New York Times*, July 18, 1986, A1.

90. *Supplementary Extradition Treaty with the Federal Republic of Germany*, U.S. Senate Treaty Doc. 100-6 (1987).

91. *Protocol Amending the Extradition Treaty with Canada*, U.S. Senate Treaty Doc. 101-17 (1990). See David K. Shipler, "U.S. and Canada Close Extradition Gap," *New York Times*, Jan. 12, 1988, A3.

92. *Protocol Amending the Treaty on Extradition Between the United States of America and Australia of May 14, 1974*; U.S. Senate Treaty Doc. 102-23 (1992).

93. See, e.g., the 1980 treaty with the Netherlands, TIAS 10733, U.S. Senate Treaty Doc. 97-7. The first clause can also be found in the 1983 treaty with Jamaica, U.S. Senate Treaty Doc. 98-18, and in the 1983 treaty with Ireland, TIAS 10813, U.S. Senate Treaty Doc. 98-19. The second clause is also in the 1978 treaty with Mexico, 31 UST 5059, TIAS 9656, and in the 1979 treaty with Colombia, U.S. Senate Treaty Doc. 9-8.

94. Desmond Mackin was deported to Ireland, with his permission, at the end of 1981. Litigation generated by efforts to deport Doherty to Ireland ultimately led to the Supreme Court. See *INS v. Doherty*, 112 S.Ct. 719 (1992). See also Michael J. Bowe, "Deportation as De Facto Extradition: The Matter of Joseph Doherty," *New York Law School Journal of International and Comparative Law* 11 (1990), 263–296. Efforts to deport McMullen are discussed in *In re McMullen*, 769 F.Supp. 1278 (S.D.N.Y. 1991).

95. Ronald Sullivan, "U.S. Court Blocks IRA Extradition," *New York Times*, Jan. 13, 1992, A7.

pattern of judicial intervention in extradition cases involving the "political offense" exception. In two cases involving attacks by Palestinian Arabs that had resulted in the deaths of Israeli civilians—the first in Tiberias, the second in the West Bank—federal courts rejected the defendants' attempts to invoke the exception.[96] U.S. courts also have hewed fairly close to the "rule of non-inquiry," according to which any inquiries into a foreign government's motives in making an extradition request as well as into the fairness of its judicial proceedings are reserved to the executive branch.[97] One exception to this rule arose in the latter of the Palestinian cases, *Ahmad v. Widen*, in which Judge Weinstein held a hearing to determine whether Ahmad would be accorded due process if extradited to Israel (and concluded that he would).[98]

The courts have similarly refrained from giving any sanctuary to Nazi war criminals who thought they had found a safe refuge in the United States. The one exception occurred in 1959, when a California federal court rejected a request from the government of Yugoslavia for the extradition of Andrija Artukovic, the former interior minister of the independent state of Croatia during World War II.[99] His alleged crimes, which included control over concentration camps and the murders of thousands of civilians, were viewed by the court as "political offenses" for which extradition could not be granted. Until well into the 1970s, moreover, the Immigration and Naturalization Service devoted few efforts to identifying and deporting Nazi war criminals. During the late 1970s, however, the chair of the House Judiciary Committee's Subcom-

96. See *Eain v. Wilkes*, 641 F.2d 504 (7th Cir. 1981), cert. denied, 454 U.S. 894 (1981), in which the defendant was accused of setting a bomb that exploded in an Israeli marketplace, killing two young boys and maiming or otherwise injuring more than thirty others. See also *Ahmad v. Wigen*, 910 F.2d 1063 (2d Cir. 1990), involving an attack on an Israeli civilian bus in the West Bank that resulted in the death of the bus driver. In the latter case, as in *Quinn*, the assertion of the "political offense" exception was acknowledged as a bar to extradition in the first judicial hearing, *In re Extradition of Atta*, No. 87-0551-M (E.D.N.Y. June 17, 1988) (Westlaw 1988 WL 66866), but then rejected in subsequent hearings. See the discussion in Sheryl A. Petkunas, "The United States, Israel, and Their Extradition Dilemma," *Michigan Journal of International Law* 12 (1990), 204–228.

97. The "rule of non-inquiry" is discussed in Michael P. Scharf, "Foreign Courts on Trial: Why U.S. Courts Should Avoid Applying the Inquiry Provision of the Supplementary U.S.-U.K. Extradition Treaty," *Stanford Journal of International Law* (1989), 257–288, and in Abraham Abramovsky, "The Political Offense Exception and the Extradition Process: The Enhancement of the Role of the U.S. Judiciary," *Hastings International and Comparative Law Review* 13 (1989), 1–24.

98. *Ahmad v. Wigen*, 726 F.Supp. 389 (E.D.N.Y. 1989).

99. *U.S. ex rel. Karadzole v. Artukovic*, 170 F.Supp. 383 (S.D. Cal. 1959).

mittee on Immigration, Elizabeth Holtzman, pushed through legislation requiring the Justice Department to assume responsibility for Nazi war crime cases.[100] Attorney General Griffen Bell responded in 1979 by creating an Office of Special Investigations (OSI) dedicated to finding Nazi war criminals and arranging for them to be extradited or deported to face charges in foreign courts.[101] Its efforts were aided by the widespread repudiation of the 1959 *Artukovic* decision by most commentators and all federal courts.[102] By 1991, the OSI's investigations had resulted in seventy-five extraditions and deportations,[103] including the 1986 extradition of Artukovic to Yugoslavia, where he died before his sentenced execution; the 1983 extradition of Hermine Braunsteiner-Ryan, a former SS member and Majdank concentration camp guard, to West Germany, where she was sentenced to life imprisonment for multiple murders; the 1984 deportation of Feodor Fedorenko, a Ukranian guard in the Treblinka concentration camp, to the Soviet Union, where he was executed for his crimes; the 1987 deportation of Karl Linnas, an Estonian who supervised the killing of Jews in the concentration camps at Tartu, to the Soviet Union, where he died while awaiting action on an appeal for a pardon;[104] and the 1986 extradition of John Demjanjuk, a Ukranian who had gained a reputation as "Ivan the Terrible" while serving as an SS guard at the Treblinka and Sobibor death camps, to Israel, where he was sentenced to death for his crimes.[105]

The transformation in the U.S. government's view of the "political offense" exception could also be seen in the evolving response to hijackers fleeing communist states. In 1950, the U.S. government had rejected, on "political offense" grounds, a request from the Czechoslo-

100. See Rena Hozore Reiss, "The Extradition of John Demjanjuk: War Crimes, Universality Jurisdiction, and the Political Offense Doctrine," *Cornell International Law Journal* 20 (1987), 281–315.

101. See Alan A. Ryan Jr., *Quiet Neighbors: Prosecuting Nazi War Criminals in America* (New York: Harcourt Brace Jovanovich, 1984).

102. See *Eain v. Wilkes*, 641 F.2d 504 (7th Cir. 1981), cert. denied 454 U.S. 894 (1981).

103. Jennifer Combs, "Time Running Out for Nazi War Criminals," *Reuter Library Report*, Sept. 4, 1991.

104. Damon J. Borrelli, "The Legacy of Nuremburg: Disguised Extradition and Karl Linnas," *Suffolk Transnational Law Journal* 11 (1987), 277–286.

105. These and other cases are listed in Michael Hedges, "U.S. Nazi Hunters Railroaded 'War Criminal,' Experts Say," *Washington Times*, Sept. 24, 1990, A1. The Demjanjuk case is analyzed in Reiss, "The Extradition of Demjanjuk" (supra n. 100); and in Steven Lubet and Jan Stern Reed, "Extradition of Nazis from the United States to Israel: A Survey of Issues in Transnational Criminal Law," *Stanford Journal of International Law* 23 (1986), 1–65.

vakian government for the extradition of eight Czech citizens who had hijacked a Czechoslovak Airlines plane to the U.S. Occupation Zone in Germany.[106] In 1951, another request involving a Czechoslovak train that had been hijacked to the U.S. zone was similarly rejected.[107] By the early 1970s, however, sentiments had shifted as the Cold War mellowed somewhat and as a rash of airplane hijackings prompted two multilateral conventions—signed in the Hague in 1970 and Montreal in 1971—directed at airplane bombing and hijacking, as well as an agreement between Cuba and the United States to cooperate in suppressing further incidents.[108] Most U.S. extradition treaties signed after 1978 accordingly included clauses that explicitly precluded violators of the multilateral conventions from asserting the "political offense" exception in their defense.[109]

The vast majority of extradition cases involving the political offense exception have involved requests to the United States. Among the few exceptions was a U.S. request to the Mexican government for the extradition of William Morales, a leader of the Puerto Rican independence group known as the Armed Forces of National Liberation (FALN) who had escaped from custody in the United States. Morales had been implicated in more than fifty terrorist attacks in the United States, including a 1975 bombing of an airplane in New York that killed four people and wounded sixty, and had been sentenced to up to ninety-nine years in prison. In 1988, the Mexican government chose to release Morales, who had been incarcerated in Mexico in 1983 following a shootout in which a Mexican policeman had been killed, and allow him to go to Cuba. The State Department responded to the Mexican government's invocation of the "political offense" exception by recalling its ambassador in protest. The Mexican decision, which bypassed any judicial evaluation, was motivated, many believed, by the government's desire to stir up nationalist sentiments in advance of the upcoming election.[110]

106. Marjorie M. Whiteman, *Digest of International Law* (Washington, D.C.: Government Printing Office, 1968).

107. Ibid., 811–813.

108. See Alona E. Evans, "The Apprehension and Prosecution of Offenders: Some Current Problems," and "Aircraft and Aviation Facilities," in Alona E. Evans and John F. Murphy, eds., *Legal Aspects of International Terrorism* (Lexington, Mass.: Lexington Books, 1978).

109. Abbell and Ristau, *International Judicial Assistance* (supra n. 1), 4:110–111.

110. Larry Rohter, "Mexicans Reject Criticism from U.S.," *New York Times*, July 1, 1988, A3; Elaine Sciolino, "U.S. Recalls Mexico Envoy over Militant's Release," *New York Times*, June 29, 1988, A3.

In many respects, the shift in U.S. perspectives on the "political offense" exception reflected less a rejection of the notion than a fairly explicit politicization of its application. Whereas it initially had been interpreted quite broadly by both the courts and the State Department to require denials of extradition requests even from governments with which the U.S. government was on friendly terms, by the 1980s the State Department and other executive branch departments increasingly insisted that the "political offense" exception could not provide a defense against an extradition request from a government that was both friendly and democratic. They also appeared increasingly willing to act favorably on extradition requests from governments not known for the rectitude or due process of their judicial institutions. Their efforts—in litigation, treaty negotiations, and proposed legislation—to minimize the role of the courts in deciding the applicability of the exception reflected this desire to transform the notion from one of principle to one of political expedience. The tension between the two perspectives was, of course, nothing new. But what had changed—in this domain of extradition as in others—was the perspective of the State Department. Where once it had routinely rejected extradition requests even for fugitives who had committed quite heinous crimes in the name of their revolutions, it increasingly perceived its role as representative of foreign government requests and defender of the foreign policy interests of the U.S. government.[111] It was determined, as never before, to interpret the "political offense" exception solely in terms of its bilateral relationship with the requesting government. Consideration would still be given to the question of whether the fugitive could expect a fair trial, but little if any regard would be given to motives for acts of violence.[112]

The Extradition and Non-extradition of Nationals

The source of greatest frustration in U.S. efforts to prosecute foreign violators of its laws in American courts has been the refusal of most governments to extradite their own citizens.[113] The legal traditions of

111. John G. Kester, "Some Myths of United States Extradition Law," *Georgetown Law Journal* 76 (1988), 1441–1493, esp. 1476–1489.

112. See the comments by Yoram Dinstein in "Major Contemporary Issues in Extradition Law," *Proceedings of the 84th Annual Meeting of the American Society of International Law, 1990*, 389–407, esp. 404.

113. See the excellent, if somewhat dated, analysis of this issue by Robert W. Rafuse, *The*

most civil law countries, as well as some common law countries, regard the nonextradition of their citizens as an important principle deeply ingrained in their legal traditions. They justify the principle on various grounds, including the state's obligation to protect its citizens, lack of confidence in the fairness of foreign judicial proceedings, the many disadvantages defendants confront in trying to defend themselves in a foreign country before a strange legal system, as well as the additional disadvantages posed by imprisonment in a foreign jail where family and friends may be distant and the chances of rehabilitation are significantly diminished.[114] By contrast, the legal traditions of the United States and most other common law nations reject the exception for nationals as an illegitimate relic of nationalist sentiments and argue that justice is most fully and conveniently served by trying defendants where they committed their crimes. Victims, witnesses, and evidence are most likely and easily found in the vicinity of the *locus delicti*, and common law rules of evidence present obstacles to the collection and admission of evidence from foreign countries that civil law prosecutors and judges do not confront. Yet despite the strong arguments against excepting nationals from extradition, the principle of nonextradition has evolved since the nineteenth century from a mere rule of custom to an emotionally charged conviction.

Historically, the U.S. government, like many other governments of common law countries, has been willing both in practice and principle to extradite its nationals abroad for crimes committed elsewhere. The first U.S. extradition agreements—with Great Britain, France, Hawaii, and Switzerland—made no exception for nationals, although the French government steadfastly refused to extradite its citizens, and the Swiss did so only once before insisting that the treaty be renegotiated. American insistence that nationals not be excepted from extradition was singularly responsible for delaying the conclusion of the first extradition treaties with Prussia, Belgium, and the Netherlands[115]—and it explained much of the U.S. hesitance to conclude extradition treaties with most Latin

Extradition of Nationals, Illinois Studies in the Social Sciences, No. 24 (Urbana: University of Illinois Press, 1939).

114. Shearer, *Extradition in International Law* (supra n. 20), 98, 118–125.

115. Moore, *Treatise on Extradition* (supra n. 3), 159–162. See also the extended defense of the extradition of nationals in the 1890 correspondence from Secretary of State Blaine to the Italian minister, Baron Falva, reprinted in John Bassett Moore, *Digest of International Law* (Washington, D.C.: Government Printing Office, 1906), 4:290–298.

American countries until the turn of the century. U.S. officials ultimately conceded the point, however, and agreed to a provision in their treaties with civil law and other similarly minded governments that allowed each party to refuse to extradite its nationals. Within the United States, the principal reservations against extraditing U.S. citizens were of two sorts. The first, debated since the origins of U.S. extradition practice, was the question of whether the U.S. government could and should extradite its citizens to governments that were unable or unwilling to reciprocate. The stress placed on formalistic notions of reciprocity in extradition relations during the nineteenth century generally favored nonextradition of U.S. citizens to such countries, although exceptions were made in numerous cases. In 1913, the Supreme Court repudiated the emphasis on reciprocity when it held, in *Charlton v. Kelly*, that the Italian government's failure to extradite its own citizens to the United States under a treaty that made no exception for nationals did not prevent the U.S. government from extraditing its own citizens.[116]

The second reservation emerged during the latter part of the nineteenth century in response to debate over the meaning of a provision included in many U.S. extradition treaties providing that "neither of the contracting parties shall be bound to deliver up its own citizens or subjects under the stipulations of this convention."[117] A supplementary clause, first included in the 1886 extradition treaty with Japan, appended the words "but they shall have the power to deliver them up if in their discretion it be deemed proper to do so." Debate focused on whether the unappended provision, which had been designed to accommodate the wishes of governments unable or unwilling to extradite their nationals, prevented the U.S. government from extraditing its own citizens. Between 1874 and 1891, Secretaries of State Fish, Frelinghuysen, Bayard, and Blaine each adopted the view that the extradition treaty with Mexico, which contained only the unappended provision, precluded the extradition of nationals.[118] Frelinghuysen and Bayard each refused to

116. *Charlton v. Kelly*, 229 U.S. 447 (1913). See also "The Charlton Extradition Case," *American Journal of International Law* 5 (1911), 182–192.

117. Rafuse, *Extradition of Nationals*, 31.

118. James Wilford Garner, "Non-Extradition of American Citizens: The Neidecker Case," *American Journal of International Law* 30 (1936), 480–486. Frelinghuysen, Garner notes, subsequently expressed "serious doubt as to the correctness of his interpretation [and] gave instructions that, if [the fugitive] were re-arrested, the President would not object to his extradition, or that of other American citizens, on the grounds of citizenship, provided they were informed that they were entitled to a hearing before the Supreme Court upon the question of his power under the treaty to surrender them."

deliver an American to Mexico, while Fish and Blaine refused to ask the Mexican government to extradite a Mexican citizen for crimes committed in the United States. That interpretation was also adopted in 1891 by a Texas federal court in *Ex parte McCabe*,[119] even though the supreme court of Mexico had held to the contrary in 1879.[120] The State Department responded to the *McCabe* decision by including the supplementary clause in six new treaties signed between 1896 and 1905, including a renegotiated treaty with Mexico.[121] Far more treaties, however, were signed without the appended phrase.[122]

In 1936, the Supreme Court resolved lingering disputes regarding this issue when it ruled, in *Valentine v. U.S. ex rel. Neidecker*, that the unappended provision (in the extradition treaty with France) did not permit the extradition of nationals.[123] The decision was heavily criticized on the grounds that the U.S. treaty negotiators had not intended the provision to forbid the extradition of U.S. citizens given the inability of the U.S. government to prosecute its citizens for violations of foreign laws—and that if the negotiators had so intended, they would have stated it explicitly.[124] The result of the decision, the critics pointed out, would be to create a nonreciprocal relationship in which foreign citizens of civil law nations could be prosecuted in their nation's courts for crimes committed in the United States but American citizens would be immune from prosecution for whatever crimes they committed abroad. Nonetheless, the "*Valentine* infirmity," as some Justice Department officials called it,[125] became law, with the result that many American fugitives from foreign justice found safe havens at home in the United States. In subsequent treaty negotiations, U.S. officials made sure to include both

119. 46 Fed. 363 (1891).

120. 1 Vallarta, *Cuestiones Constitucionales*, 1879, 35, and *Foreign Relations of the United States, 1878–1879*, 564ff., discussed in Garner, "Non-Extradition of American Citizens."

121. The other treaties were with Argentina (1896), 31 Stat. 1883, TS 6, Bevans 67; Orange Free State (1896), 26 Stat. 1508, TS 139, 12 Bevans 211; Guatemala (1902), 33 Stat. 2147, TS 425, 8 Bevans 482; Nicaragua (1905), 35 Stat. 1869, TS 462, 10 Bevans 356; and Uruguay (1905), 35 Stat. 2028, TS 501, 12 Bevans 979.

122. The treaties are listed in Rafuse, *Extradition of Nationals*, 31. See also Arthur K. Kuhn, "Extradition from the United States of American Citizens Under Existing Treaties," *American Journal of International Law* 31 (1937), 476–480. I have not been able to uncover the reasons for the omission of the appended phrase.

123. *Valentine v. U.S. ex rel. Neidecker*, 299 U.S. 5 (1936).

124. See Garner, "Non-Extradition of American Citizens," and Kuhn, "Extradition from the United States. . . ."

125. Author's interviews with treaty negotiators in the OIA, Criminal Division, Department of Justice, Washington, D.C.

the appended provision first used in the treaty with Japan as well as a new provision authorizing each party (but in fact the other government) to prosecute the fugitive in its own courts if it refused to extradite on account of the fugitive's citizenship. Each of the extradition reform bills considered by Congress in the early 1980s included a provision designed to correct the "*Valentine* infirmity," but none were enacted into law for reasons unrelated to this issue.[126] In November 1990, Congress at last corrected the problem with an extradition reform law—first suggested by critics of the *Valentine* decision in 1937—directed at this issue alone.[127]

Any global trend in attitudes toward the nonextradition of nationals is difficult to discern. The view that nationals should not be excepted from extradition had been adopted by the Institute of International Law in 1880 as well as by the influential Draft Convention on Extradition produced by the Harvard Research Project on International Law in 1935.[128] Most common law countries continue to extradite their citizens willingly, although Israel reversed stride in 1978 when it amended its penal code to expand Israeli jurisdiction over extraterritorial offenses and forbid the extradition of its citizens.[129] Among the Commonwealth nations, Cyprus stands out as one of the few exceptions. Within Western Europe, Germany, France, and Switzerland are among the majority that absolutely refuse to extradite their nationals while Italy—which had angered U.S. officials in the late nineteenth century by refusing to extradite its citizens under the bilateral treaty—is the most conspicuous among the minority that now do so.[130] In most cases, the custom of nonextradition of nationals dates at least to the early 1800s, although few countries enacted it into law or their constitutions until late in the nineteenth century or early in the twentieth. In Switzerland's case, the legislation was prompted by the widespread criticism that attended the

126. Ibid. The extradition reform bills are analyzed in M. Cherif Bassiouni, "Extradition Reform Legislation in the United States: 1981–1983" (supra n. 86), 495–574.

127. See 18 U.S.C. 3196, Pub. L. 101-623, Sec. 11(a), Nov. 21, 1990, 104 Stat. 3356. The suggestion was advanced in Kuhn, "Extradition from the United States. . . ." (supra n. 118).

128. See *American Journal of International Law* 29 (1935), Supp., 123–136, 236–238, 300–301.

129. C. Shachor-Landau, "Extra-territorial Penal Jurisdiction and Extradition," *International and Comparative Law Quarterly* 29 (1980), 274–295.

130. Shearer, *Extradition in International Law* (supra n. 20), 102–110. The change of heart on the part of the Italian government was confirmed in an exchange of notes with the U.S. government in 1946; TIAS 1699, 9 Bevans 192, 61 Stat. 3687. See Whiteman, *Digest of International Law* (supra n. 106), 6:872–873.

extradition of a Swiss citizen to the United States in 1890 under the terms of a bilateral 1850 extradition treaty that did not except nationals.[131] In France, the rule of nonextradition of nationals dates back to the 1840s, but it was not included in the 1843 extradition treaty with the United States and not incorporated into domestic legislation until 1927, when France enacted its first extradition law.[132] The Netherlands, by contrast, signed an extradition treaty with the United States in 1980 that authorizes the extradition of nationals provided both countries are also bound by a prisoner transfer treaty.[133] That condition was met as of 1985, when the United States became a party to the European Convention on the Transfer of Sentenced Prisoners.[134] Presumably, the Dutch negotiators regarded the lack of any means to have a Dutch offender serve his or her sentence in the Netherlands as the most important remaining justification for the nonextradition of nationals rule. The possibility exists that this feature of the U.S.-Netherlands extradition treaty will provide a model for other nations that so far have adhered strictly to the principle of nonextradition of nationals. The Europeans have compensated for their inability to extradite their citizens by improving their capacity for successful vicarious prosecution and by negotiating, under the auspices of the Council of Europe, a multilateral convention on transfer of criminal proceedings.[135]

In extradition negotiations with Latin American governments, U.S. officials have urged flexibility on this issue, stressing the importance of prosecuting drug traffickers wherever possible. Most governments, however, have refused to concede on the issue of extraditing their citizens, insisting that they will comply instead with U.S. requests to prosecute fugitives in their own courts. Among the few exceptions was the government of Colombia, which signed a new extradition treaty with the United States in 1979 that provided for the extradition of nationals.[136] This was neither the first nor the only Colombian extradition treaty to

131. Rafuse, *Extradition of Nationals*, 120–122; Moore, *Digest of International Law* (supra n. 115), 4:298–300.

132. Ibid., 75–92.

133. The treaty, signed at the Hague on June 24, 1980, entered into force Sept. 15, 1983 (TIAS 10733).

134. Done at Strasbourg Mar. 21, 1983 (TIAS 10824).

135. Julian Schutte, "Transfer of Criminal Proceedings: The European System," in Bassiouni, ed., *International Criminal Law* (supra n. 32), 2:319–335.

136. See the fascinating account in Guy Gugliotta and Jeff Leen, *Kings of Cocaine* (New York: Simon & Schuster, 1989).

approve such exchanges, but it did represent somewhat of an exception to Colombia's extradition traditions.[137] The treaty was ratified by the Colombian government and formally entered into force in 1982,[138] but it was not used to extradite a Colombian to the United States until 1984, when President Belisario Betancur activated the treaty in response to the assassination of his justice minister, Rodrigo Lara Bonilla, by Colombia's increasingly powerful and brazen drug traffickers. During the following two years, more than a dozen Colombians were extradited to the United States, as well as three Americans to Colombia. Throughout this period, the leading drug traffickers, calling themselves "The Extraditables," mounted an increasingly effective campaign of public relations, bribery, intimidation, and murder to shift public and official opinion against the treaty. Their first priority, they declared, was the recission of the extradition treaty with the United States, and in particular the provision permitting their own extradition.[139] Most Colombians recognized that their own judicial system was not capable of bringing the traffickers to justice and that only the U.S. judicial system could successfully prosecute and imprison the traffickers. Even so, many Colombians agreed in principle with the traffickers' criticism of the treaty. Under substantial pressure by the U.S. government, the administration of President Virgilio Barco refused to back away from the treaty. In December 1986, however, the Colombian supreme court, in what many perceived as a capitulation not to the traffickers' legal arguments but to their violence and threats, declared the treaty no longer valid because of a petty and arguably irrelevant technicality.[140] Barco thereupon took steps suggested by the court's opinion to correct the technical problems and was able to extradite one of the most famous traffickers, Carlos Lehder, when he was arrested by Colombian police in February 1987.[141] But in June 1987, the court once again declared the treaty invalid, thereby blocking any future extraditions to the United States.[142]

137. See, e.g., Art. 4 of the extradition treaty between Colombia and Chile, signed Nov. 16, 1914, ratified Aug. 4, 1928, which states that "extradition of their own nationals is not compulsory" (LNTS 82 at 244).

138. Signed at Washington Sept. 14, 1979; entered into force Mar. 4, 1982 (the treaty appears to have never received a TIAS number).

139. Gugliotta and Leen, *Kings of Cocaine*, 241–250.

140. See the fine discussion of these events in Bruce M. Bagley, "Colombia and the War on Drugs," *Foreign Affairs* 67 (Fall 1988), 70–92.

141. Gugliotta and Leen, *Kings of Cocaine*, 241–250. See also *U.S. v. Lehder Rivas*, 668 F.Supp. 1623 (M.D. Fla. 1987).

142. The Colombian supreme court's decision, translated into English, is reproduced at

In August 1989, President Barco responded to the assassination of the leading presidential candidate in the upcoming election, Senator Luis Carlos Galán, by invoking his state-of-siege powers under the constitution and renewing the summary extradition of Colombian traffickers without judicial review.[143] Much to the surprise of many observers, on October 4, the Colombian supreme court upheld the president's emergency action. During the following year, more than two dozen Colombian traffickers and money launderers—though none on the "most wanted list"—were extradited to the United States, with the Colombian president and supreme court continuing to stand by the extradition process.[144] Numerous public opinion polls, however, indicated that many Colombians had wearied of the war against the "extraditables" and wanted to seek alternative solutions.[145] When President Barco was succeeded in July 1990 by César Gaviria Trujillo, the new president quickly extradited a few more traffickers but decreed simultaneously that any major drug traffickers who surrendered to the government would not be extradited. His offer was taken up by the leading drug traffickers of Medellín, who had been responsible for most of the violence, and President George Bush indicated that he was prepared to give President Gaviria's strategy a chance to prove itself.[146] In 1991, the option of extraditing Colombian citizens to foreign countries was effectively eliminated when Colombia adopted a new constitution that explicitly prohibited any future extraditions of its citizens.[147] In Bolivia, meanwhile, the Colombian policy of offering immunity from extradition

---

International Legal Materials 27 (1988), 492–511. See Mark Andrew Sherman, "United States International Drug Control Policy, Extradition, and the Rule of Law in Colombia," *Nova Law Review* 15 (1991), 661–702.

143. Andres Oppenheimer, "Colombia Offers to Extradite Cocaine Trafficker," *Miami Herald*, Aug. 23, 1989, 8A; *Latin American Regional Reports: Andean Group*, Oct. 5, 1989, 1–5; Bruce Michael Bagley, "Dateline Drug Wars: Colombia: The Wrong Strategy," *Foreign Policy* 77 (1989–90), 154–171.

144. Eugene Robinson, "Colombia Says Extraditions to Continue," *Washington Post*, Oct. 25, 1989, A38; "Colombian Drug Suspect Extradited," *Washington Post*, Oct. 25, 1989, A20.

145. Joseph B. Treaster, "Colombians, Weary of the Strain, Are Losing Heart in the Drug War," *New York Times*, Oct. 2, 1989, A1; Michael Getler and Eugene Robinson, "Colombia's War on Drugs Zeroes in on Just Two Men," *Washington Post*, Oct. 29, 1989, A1.

146. Rensselaer W. Lee III, "Colombia's Cocaine Syndicates," in Alfred W. McCoy and Alan A. Block, eds., *War on Drugs: Studies in the Failure of U.S. Narcotics Policy* (Boulder, Colo.: Westview Press, 1992), 93–124.

147. See Sherman, "United States International Drug Control Policy" (supra n. 142). See also Mark Andrew Sherman, "Colombian Constitutional Assembly Endorses Ban of Extradition of Nationals," *International Enforcement Law Reporter* 7 (1991), 174–178.

to traffickers who surrendered was adopted by the Paz Zamora government.[148]

Most governments that refuse to extradite their nationals, however, are willing, at least in principle, to prosecute them for crimes committed elsewhere, provided the violation of foreign law would also be considered a violation of domestic law if committed within their borders. Unlike the United States, most civil law countries are able to adhere to the principle of *aut dedere, aut iudicare* because they interpret the nationality principle underlying their criminal jurisdiction far more broadly than the United States does—as extending to virtually all crimes committed by their citizens abroad that would also constitute a violation of domestic laws if committed at home. In a number of countries, the notion of vicarious administration of justice even extends to trying foreign citizens for certain crimes committed in their homeland or another foreign territory. In one mid-1980s case, for instance, German authorities agreed to prosecute a Hungarian national for crimes committed in Hungary once it became evident that German law did not permit him to be extradited.[149] By contrast, U.S. law only authorizes the prosecution of Americans or foreign citizens for crimes committed abroad that violate either multilateral conventions or the proliferating statutes that specifically criminalize extraterritorial acts perceived as harmful to U.S. citizens or interests.[150]

The more recent extradition treaties between the United States and governments that refuse to extradite their nationals include provisions making prosecution mandatory when extradition is denied on grounds of nationality. But the principle of *aut dedere, aut iudicare* tends to lose much of its force in practice, which explains in part why the U.S. government refused to incorporate the notion into its extradition treaties until well into the twentieth century.[151] Governments that refuse to

148. Michael Isikoff, "Bolivia Offers No-Extradition Deal to Traffickers," *Washington Post*, July 19, 1991, A13; "Questions About Surrender Policy: Politicians and Media Suspect More Than Meets the Eye," *Latin America Weekly Report*, Aug. 8, 1991, 4.

149. Reported by Paul Wilkitzki, director of office of international criminal law enforcement matters, Federal Ministry of Justice, Bonn, Germany, at the Harvard Law School Conference on International Cooperation in Criminal Matters, Cambridge, Massachusetts, June 16–18, 1988.

150. Christopher L. Blakesley, "A Conceptual Framework for Extradition and Jurisdiction over Extraterritorial Crimes," *Utah Law Review* 4 (1984), 685.

151. See the 1924 correspondence from Secretary of State Hughes to the French ambassador regarding this issue in Hackworth, *Digest of International Law* (supra n. 81), 4:58–59.

extradite their nationals often assign lower priority to requests for vicarious prosecution than they do to either domestic prosecutions or extradition requests for nonnationals. Requesting governments similarly lose interest in many such cases, no doubt in part because the personal and bureaucratic incentives of the prosecutor do not favor pursuing vigorously such vicarious prosecutions. Significant obstacles also arise from the difficulties involved in trying an individual for a crime committed in another country. The investigating judge must travel abroad to prepare the case according to his own country's judicial procedures, witnesses must be persuaded to travel to another country, and so on. Consequently, most requests to prosecute offenders for crimes committed abroad prove unsuccessful.[152] The principal exceptions are cases in which high-level U.S. officials express a strong and repeated interest in seeing the fugitive prosecuted.

No government has so frustrated U.S. law enforcement authorities with its refusal to extradite its nationals as the government of Mexico. Despite the renegotiation of the extradition treaty folllowing the *McCabe* case, the Mexican government fairly consistently refused to extradite its citizens to the United States[153]—although it did respond favorably, if irregularly, to U.S. requests for prosecution of the fugitives in Mexico. The U.S. response to Mexican requests for the extradition of U.S. citizens was mixed. In 1960, the State Department's legal adviser was able to point to at least nine cases in which American citizens had been extradited to Mexico, but more often than not, Mexican requests were rejected on grounds of lack of reciprocity despite the inability of the U.S. government to prosecute the offenders in American courts.[154] In 1976, the U.S. government responded to the continuing Mexican policy and the growing number of Mexican fugitives wanted on drug trafficking charges by creating Operation JANUS, a systematic effort to encourage and assist Mexican criminal justice officials in vicariously prosecuting Mexican drug traffickers for violations of U.S. drug laws.[155] Strongly

152. Wilkitzki comments at Harvard Law School Conference, 1988 (supra n. 149).

153. Moore, *Digest of International Law* (supra n. 115), 4:301–304; Hackworth, *Digest of International Law* (supra n. 81), 4:59–62.

154. Hackworth, *Digest of International Law*, 4:59–62; and Note, "Executive Discretion in Extradition," *Columbia Law Review* 62 (1962), 1313–1329, esp. 1322.

155. The program is briefly described in *Departments of State, Justice, Commerce, the Judiciary, and Related Agencies Appropriations for 1979: Hearings Before a Subcommittee of the House Committee on Appropriations*, 95th Cong., 2d Sess., Part 6 (1978), 969. See also James Mills, *The Underground Empire* (Garden City, N.Y.: Doubleday, 1986), 390, 1088.

backed at first by the Mexican attorney general, the operation initially appeared successful, but it was phased out within a few years, having largely failed to bring Mexican violators of U.S. laws to justice in Mexican courts.[156] Although the Mexican government continued to prosecute Mexican violators of U.S. drug laws in its courts, particularly when pressured strongly by U.S. officials, persistent U.S. frustrations in this regard ultimately contributed to more direct action by U.S. law enforcement agents, about which more below.

Alternatives to Extradition

The history of U.S. rendition of fugitives from abroad by means other than those provided for in extradition treaties dates back even further than that of extradition. When extradition treaties have been either unavailable or inadequate to accomplish the rendition of a fugitive, U.S. officials often have relied on foreign extradition and deportation laws as well as the occasional willingness of foreign officials to deliver fugitives to the United States by less formal means not explicitly sanctioned by their laws. U.S. law enforcement officials also have become increasingly involved in orchestrating and even managing the apprehension of fugitives from abroad. They have provided foreign authorities with the tactical intelligence needed to find and arrest fugitives on their territory. They have worked directly with foreign agents in apprehending fugitives abroad and arranging their transport to the United States, often via third countries. They have employed various ruses, both unilaterally and in cooperation with foreign police, to lure fugitives to the United States (where a sealed indictment awaits them) or to other countries from which their rendition can be more readily arranged, or into international waters where they can be seized and returned to U.S. territory. And they have relied on private agents, including informants, private detectives, bail bondsmen, and bounty hunters, to accomplish many of the same

156. *Worldwide Review of U.S. Extradition Treaties and MLATs: Hearings* (supra n. 29), 67–69. In 1985, the DEA reported that only seven defendants, none of whom was a major violator, had been prosecuted in Mexico on the basis of evidence and witnesses from the United States provided by the DEA. See *International Narcotic Control: Hearing Before the Subcommittee on Foreign Assistance and Related Programs of the Senate Committee on Appropriations*, 99th Cong., 1st Sess., S. Hrg. 99-90 (1985), 189.

tasks. These methods have acquired many names: "irregular rendition," "de facto extradition," "informal expulsion," and even "extradition Mexican-style," in deference to the long-standing arrangement by which fugitives are "pushed over the border" by Mexican police into the hands of U.S. law enforcement agents. Some Justice Department officials have claimed that the most common term, "irregular rendition," is largely a misnomer because rendition of fugitives by means other than an extradition treaty is neither illegal nor unusual. Nonetheless, the phrase has prevailed ever since John Bassett Moore so named the practice in his classic 1891 treatise on extradition.

U.S. government options for delivering fugitives to foreign governments have been relatively limited in comparison. Apart from one infamous incident in 1864—when U.S. officials summarily delivered to Spanish authorities in Cuba an army officer, Don José Augustin Arguelles, who had illegally sold a seized cargo of slaves in the United States[157]—the U.S. government has refrained from delivering fugitives to foreign governments without first allowing them to appeal the rendition in court. Without an extradition treaty, the only alternatives available to the U.S. government in responding to an extradition request have involved exclusion and deportation proceedings—the former with respect to fugitives apprehended as they attempt to enter the United States, the latter when fugitives are arrested within U.S. territory. Although both procedures are designed principally for purposes of immigration control, each has been relied upon to expel fugitives and other criminals both at the request of foreign governments and, far more frequently, at the initiative of the U.S. government. Such tactics have been used since the early 1900s to expel Italian-born mafiosi and, more recently, Nazi war criminals, IRA fugitives, and Latin American and Caribbean drug dealers.

U.S. courts have imposed virtually no restrictions on how U.S. officials obtain custody over fugitives. Under the Supreme Court's long-standing *Ker-Frisbie* rule, it is even legal under U.S. law to abduct fugitives from a foreign country[158]—although U.S. agents risk being charged with violations of foreign laws against kidnapping if they do so without the consent of host country officials. Courts have imposed only two restric-

157. Moore, *Treatise on Extradition* (supra n. 3), 33–35.

158. See *Ker v. Illinois*, 119 U.S. 436, 7 S.Ct. 225, 30 L.Ed. 421 (1886), and *Frisbie v. Collins*, 342 U.S. 519, 72 S.Ct. 509, 96 L.Ed. 541 (1952), which held that a court need not examine how a defendant had been brought within its jurisdiction.

tions on the rendition of fugitives by means other than extradition treaties. The first, imposed by a New York federal court in 1974 (in *U.S. v. Toscanino*) and rendered largely ineffectual since then, is that jurisdiction cannot be legally obtained by an abduction involving "the infliction . . . of grossly cruel and inhumane treatment by or at the direction of American officials or agents."[159] The second restriction, imposed by a federal judge in California in 1990 but rejected by the Supreme Court in 1992, is that any defendant apprehended abroad from a country with which the United States has an extradition treaty must be released if the foreign government formally protests the violation of the treaty.[160] This issue is discussed in greater depth below.

Most irregular renditions have involved Canada and Mexico, whose long borders with the United States have presented temptations both to fleeing fugitives and to those interested in obtaining custody over them. Until well into the twentieth century, few fugitives were deemed sufficiently important to invest substantial resources in procuring them by means other than extradition. The few exceptions were those who had attained some substantial notoriety. One unusual case, in that it involved a foreign territory where the U.S. government exercised extraterritorial rights, was the 1866 rendition from Alexandria, Egypt, of John Surratt, accused of participation in the assassination of President Lincoln.[161] In a 1934 effort to gain custody of Samuel Insull, a major Chicago financier who had engineered a substantial fraud and then fled abroad, the State Department first tried to extradite him from Greece, then pressured the Greek government to deport him following a court's rejection of the extradition request, and ultimately persuaded Turkish police to seize the fugitive aboard a Greek vessel in Turkish territorial waters.[162] And in

159. See *U.S. v. Toscanino*, 500 F.2d 267 (2d Cir. 1974); and *U.S. ex rel. Lujan v. Gengler*, 510 F.2d 62 (2d Cir.) cert. denied, 421 U.S. 1001, 95 S.Ct. 2400, 44 L.Ed.2d 668 (1975). The quotation is taken from *U.S. v. Orsini*, 424 F.Supp. 229, 231 (E.D.N.Y. 1976). The *Toscanino* case involved an Italian drug trafficker, Francisco Toscanino, who was seized by a special Uruguayan police unit operating under the direction of a U.S. drug enforcement agent. Toscanino was then driven over the border to Brazil, where he was kept for three weeks while the Brazilian police interrogated him under torture. He was then put on a commercial airline flight to the United States, where he was indicted and prosecuted. Although dozens of defendants have since pointed to the *Toscanino* case in an effort to invalidate their abduction, none has succeeded in showing a sufficiently direct and heinous involvement by U.S. officials to invoke the *Toscanino* exception.

160. *U.S. v. Alvarez-Machain* 112 S.Ct. 857 (1992).

161. Moore, *Treatise on Extradition*, 104–105.

162. See *Foreign Relations of the United States 1934*, 2:566–583; and Charles Cheney

1951, the FBI worked with Mexican security agents to arrest and deliver to the United States Morton Sobell, who had been charged with conspiring with the Rosenbergs to commit espionage against the United States.[163]

Before the 1970s, most irregular renditions were initiated by federal, state, and local police working near the borders. The few exceptions involving more distant nations were typically engineered by private detectives and bounty hunters. But the growing desire, beginning in the early 1970s, to collect dozens of drug traffickers from Latin America—in particular the Corsican criminals who had created the Southern Cone dimension of the heroin trafficking scheme known as the French Connection—provided the impetus for a more coordinated and systematic rendition effort initiated by the Bureau of Narcotics and Dangerous Drugs. Efforts to extradite many of these traffickers by more formal means were seriously hampered by the inadequacies of the extradition treaties, which mostly dated back to the turn of the century and thus contained no references to drug law violations or to extraterritorial violations of U.S. laws. In some cases, the fact that a Latin American government had signed the 1972 Protocol to the Single Convention on Narcotic Drugs rectified the omission. Even so, the challenges of processing the extradition requests through Latin American courts unfamiliar with U.S. legal notions as well as past judicial and executive officials susceptible to the bribes and intimidations of the drug traffickers proved daunting.

The U.S. response to these limitations was labeled "Operation Springboard." During the early 1970s, U.S. drug enforcement agents worked closely with specially created police units in Latin America to apprehend and expel almost five dozen major drug traffickers to the United States without resort to formal extradition procedures.[164] The willingness of the governments to cooperate was facilitated by the fact that most of the targets were not citizens of their countries. In the aftermath of the coup in Chile against President Allende, however, General Pinochet demonstrated his gratefulness to the United States by summarily deporting to

---

Hyde, "The Extradition Case of Samul Insull Sr. in Relation to Greece," *American Journal of International Law* 28 (1934), 307–312.

163. *U.S. v. Sobell*, 142 F.Supp. 515 (2d Cir. 1956).

164. See Robert Solomon, "The Development and Politics of the Latin American Heroin Market," *Journal of Drug Issues* 9 (1979), 363–364.

the United States about twenty Chileans whom the DEA had identified as major cocaine traffickers.[165] The expulsion, labeled Operation Grab-Bag, was significant for two reasons: it virtually eliminated Chile as a major refiner and exporter of cocaine, and it pointed out the hazards of resorting to such methods, when one of those expelled by the government turned out to be a case of mistaken identity.[166]

One fugitive rendition that appeared irregular despite its reliance on an extradition treaty and judicial proceedings involved a 1971 request to Paraguay for the extradition of a leading Corsican drug trafficker, Auguste Ricord. Although U.S. officials ultimately succeeded in bringing the trafficker to justice in a federal court in New York, the trip north was delayed for more than a year by a combination of legal obstacles and intra-Paraguayan political wrangles. The initial U.S. request was rejected by a Paraguayan district court on the grounds that the 1913 extradition treaty did not include drug law violations among the list of extraditable offenses, that Ricord had never entered the United States, and that the "dual criminality" requirement was not met because Paraguayan law included no counterpart to the U.S. statutes under which Ricord was charged.[167] With little confidence that the appellate court would reverse the lower court, the Nixon administration applied a heavy dose of diplomatic pressure. When the U.S. ambassador, Ray Ylitalo, failed to persuade the Paraguayan president, Alfredo Stroessner, of the importance of handing over Ricord, he was replaced. Shortly thereafter, President Nixon sent Nelson Gross, the senior narcotics official in the State Department, to Paraguay to threaten a cutoff in the $11 million of

165. Art. 24 of the Chilean constitution gives the government broad powers to expel Chilean citizens. The Pinochet government used those powers frequently to expel opponents of the regime. But the same article also provided the U.S. government with grounds to request that the Pinochet government expel two former high-level intelligence agents who had been implicated in the 1976 murder of President Allende's foreign minister, Orlando Letelier, in Washington. A previous effort to have the agents extradited was rejected by the Chilean supreme court in 1979. See Shirley Christian, "Chile Indicates It Won't Turn over Two to the U.S. in Letelier Case," *New York Times*, June 15, 1987, A10.

166. Pete Axthelm with Anthony Marro, "The Drug Vigilantes," *Newsweek*, Aug. 16, 1976, reprinted in *The Global Connection: Heroin Entrepreneurs: Hearings Before the Subcommittee to Investigate Juvenile Delinquency of the Senate Committee on the Judiciary*, 94th Cong., 2d Sess. (Vol. 1, 1976), 70–72.

167. John Patrick Collins, "Traffic in the Traffickers: Extradition and the Controlled Substances Import and Export Act of 1970," *Yale Law Journal* 83 (1974), 706–744, esp. 706–707.

annual U.S. aid and U.S. support for loans from the World Bank and the Inter-American Development Bank.[168] Stroessner protested that the matter was up to the courts and sent Gross to meet with both the solicitor general and the Chief Justice of the Supreme Court.[169]

Stroessner's real concerns, however, appeared to involve a power struggle between Ricord's protectors and those who preferred to see him extradited. On Ricord's side were three powerful figures who had first made their fortune smuggling whiskey and cigarettes in the early 1960s but who had expanded into drug smuggling with Ricord's assistance: General Andrés Rodríguez, whose power was reported to be second only to that of Stroessner (and who would eventually assume the presidency himself following a nonviolent coup in early 1989), General Patrício Colmán, "one of Stroessner's oldest and dearest friends"; and Pastor Coronel, the chief of the secret police.[170] On the other side were Interior Minister Sabino Montanaro and the chief of police, General Francisco Brítez, neither of whom had ever been linked to the drug traffic.[171] Although Stroessner had not been personally tied to Ricord, few doubted that the president was aware of Ricord's connections and high-level involvement in drug trafficking. His reluctance to hand the trafficker over to the United States was attributed to either loyalty to or fear of Colmán, Rodríguez, and Coronel. A week after Gross's visit, Colmán suddenly became ill and died shortly thereafter. Just before he died, the Paraguayan court of appeals unanimously granted the extradition request. A few weeks later, the supreme court also gave its approval, and Ricord soon after found himself in New York.[172] The courts' decisions, many believed, reflected more the interventions by powerful Paraguayan officials who preferred not to anger the United States government on

168. In a recent foreign aid act passed by Congress, the president had been authorized to cut off aid to any government that refused to cooperate against international drug trafficking.

169. See Evert Clark and Nicholas Horrock, *Contrabandista!* (New York: Praeger Publishers, 1973), 177–231, for an extensive description of the U.S. effort to extradite Ricord.

170. Paul Lewis, *Paraguay Under Stroessner* (Chapel Hill: University of North Carolina Press, 1980), 135–137.

171. Ibid.

172. The events preceding the extradition attracted substantial media attention. See, e.g., *Newsweek*, Jan. 24, 1972, 24–26; *Time*, Aug. 28, 1972, 24; *Latin America*, June 9, 1972, 188, and Aug. 25, 1972, 269. During this period, Jack Anderson devoted a number of columns to berating official Paraguayan involvement in drug trafficking. See *Washington Post*, Apr. 22, 1972, F11; Apr. 30, 1972, M1; May 24, 1972, B15; July 26, 1972, B15.

this issue, and less any substantive disagreements with the lower court's reasoning.

Operation Springboard and the other irregular renditions of the 1970s attracted substantial commentary in the law journals but not much excitement elsewhere. They did suggest, however, a change in American attitudes regarding the issue. For perhaps the first time, federal police officials, occasionally joined by federal prosecutors, began to devote substantial time and energy to concocting schemes to get foreign drug traffickers into U.S. courts. Their efforts were encouraged and facilitated not just by the *Ker-Frisbie* doctrine, with its virtually carte blanche invitation to engage in such operations, but by the newly established presence of U.S. drug enforcement agents in dozens of foreign countries and by clear indications of political support from the White House. Where federal law enforcement officials had previously assumed that extradition represented more or less the only possibility of obtaining custody of a fugitive from abroad, they began instead to consider a wide range of options apart from the procedures set down in the extradition treaties. This change in attitude quickly became conventional wisdom within the DEA, and thereafter took hold in the FBI and the U.S. Marshals Service, both of which were increasingly involved in the apprehension of fugitives from abroad.

Virtually all of these renditions, it should be stressed, were conducted in cooperation with law enforcement officials in the countries from which the fugitives were being deported or abducted. With rare exceptions, U.S. officials have never acted entirely unilaterally in abducting fugitives from foreign countries without the permission of host government officials. Abductions such as the 1960 kidnapping of the Nazi war criminal Adolf Eichmann from Argentina to face trial in Israel were viewed warily by U.S. officials. But the regularization of irregular rendition during the 1970s revealed the ambiguities inherent in conducting such operations, particularly when they appeared to flout foreign laws or targeted criminals with powerful protectors. Many renditions required that DEA and other U.S. law enforcement agents work closely with foreign police and military officials and at the same time keep secret their rendition plans from other officials who might disapprove either because they disagreed with the tactics or because they had been corrupted by the targeted fugitive. The fact that high-level foreign officials often disagreed regarding such renditions meant that it could be difficult to discern afterward whether "the government" had approved or disapproved of the operation. And the desire of many top police and military officials in foreign countries to retain a measure of plausible deniability and avoid assuming official responsibility for the renditions only heightened the degree of ambiguity. In many cases, moreover, the State Department and its representatives abroad were "cut out of the loop" by U.S. law enforcement officials who feared that their more diplomatic colleagues would undermine or veto renditions that might generate political problems.

These ambiguities became significant, from the perspectives of U.S. law and diplomacy, only when the renditions were met with public and diplomatic protests after the fact. A U.S. drug enforcement agent who had been prominently involved in Operation Springboard told me that the Uruguayan interior minister had approved the BNDD's irregular rendition plan only on condition that his consent would not be publicly revealed if anything went wrong. Indeed, he told the agent, he would be among the first to publicly condemn the entire operation if any backlash resulted. In other cases, U.S. law enforcement officials were given permission by top foreign officials to proceed with their operations and told that a formal—but otherwise meaningless—protest might thereafter be filed by their government. In the case of Operation Springboard, dozens of irregular renditions were accomplished with relatively few legal or diplomatic problems, apart from the brief concerns raised by the *Toscanino* decision. The same tactics continued to be used thereafter, often with even greater creativity and aggressiveness, but sometimes with greater problems as well.

Most irregular renditions involve cooperative endeavors by U.S. and local police agents to seize a fugitive and get him or her on a plane out of the country as fast as possible. The precise tactics, however, vary substantially. In some cases, U.S. agents have arranged for fugitives to be arrested during trips to foreign countries or even when their flights have stopped briefly in another country en route to the fugitive's destination. For instance, in 1975, DEA agents arranged for Dominique Orsini, a drug trafficker based in Argentina, to be arrested by Senegalese police and thereafter deported to the United States, when the flight on which he was traveling from Buenos Aires to Nice stopped briefly in Dakar.[173] Many irregular rendition schemes have required U.S. law enforcement agents to lure fugitives from their foreign havens to other

173. *U.S. v. Orsini*, 424 F.Supp. 229 (E.D.N.Y. 1976).

countries in which cooperative law enforcement officials would then arrest them and extradite or deport them to the United States. In a fairly typical case, in 1977, a DEA agent based in Venezuela tricked a drug trafficker into flying to Panama, where he was arrested and interrogated by the Panamanian police before being deported to the United States.[174] Similarly, in 1973 Julio Lujan, an Argentine pilot charged with heroin trafficking, was lured from Argentina to Bolivia by a DEA informant, where he was then seized by local police working for the DEA and put on a plane to the United States without ever being charged or extradited under Bolivian law.[175] And in 1982, a former CIA agent, Edwin Wilson, who had been charged with selling weapons to the Qaddafi regime in Libya, was lured by an undercover informant from his Libyan haven to the Dominican Republic, where he was seized by local police and put on a plane to the United States.[176] Each of these cases was typical of many others, not only in the tactics employed but also in their reliance on local police in Bolivia, Panama, and the Dominican Republic—in each of which DEA and other U.S. agents have often been able to work out informal rendition arrangements based on money, friendship, and professional understandings.

A variation of this tactic has been to lure a fugitive onto a sea vessel and then arrest him in international waters. In 1983, DEA and FBI agents operating out of Miami planned to do just that to a Bahamian cabinet minister, Kendal Nottage, who was strongly suspected of laundering money for drug traffickers; the operation was vetoed, however, by the local U.S. ambassador because he feared its consequences for other aspects of the U.S.-Bahamian relationship.[177] More successful was an undercover operation in September 1987 by the FBI, the DEA, and the CIA that lured Fawaz Younis, a Lebanese Shiite suspected in the June 1985 hijacking of a Jordanian airliner, from his Lebanese haven onto a yacht in the Mediterranean, where he was arrested in international waters.[178] Similarly, in early 1991, FBI agents lured two suspected money

174. *Di Lorenzo v. U.S.*, 496 F.Supp. 79 (S.D.N.Y. 1980).

175. *U.S. ex rel. Lujan v. Gengler*, 510 F.2d 62 (2d Cir.) cert. denied, 421 U.S. 1001.

176. The abduction is discussed in *U.S. v. Wilson*, 565 F.Supp. 1416 (1983). See also Peter Maas, *Manhunt* (New York: Random House, 1986), 254–268.

177. Reginald Stuart, "U.S.-Bahamian Relations Are Straining Under Drug Investigations," *New York Times*, Sept. 28, 1983, A21.

178. *U.S. v. Yunis*, 681 F.Supp. 909 (D.D.C. 1988) rev'd, 859 F.2d 953 (D.C. Cir. 1988). *Washington Post*, Sept. 18, 1987, A1; *Washington Post*, Sept. 19, 1987, A18. See the discussion in D. Cameron Findlay, "Abducting Terrorists Overseas for Trial in the United States: Issues of International and Domestic Law," *Texas International Law Journal* 23 (1988), 1–53; G.

launderers from Colombia to a private yacht off the Caribbean coast, where they were then arrested, transferred to a Coast Guard cutter, and sent to Los Angeles to await trial.[179]

Another common tactic has been to lure fugitives directly into U.S. territory, where a sealed indictment may await them. In one 1971 case, for instance, the corrupt and well-connected Panamanian chief of air traffic control, Joaquim Him Gonzales, was invited to a softball game in the Canal Zone, where he was arrested by U.S. police and soon after flown to the United States.[180] His irregular rendition, which the resident BNDD agents had planned without notifying the U.S. ambassador, briefly generated serious tensions in U.S. relations with the Torrijos regime. In March 1985, undercover DEA agents arrested the chief minister of the Turks and Caicos as well as one of his cabinet ministers in Miami after they agreed to ensure safe passage for cocaine and marijuana transiting their islands in return for a $20,000 payment.[181] A few weeks later, another DEA undercover operation lured a former Belizean cabinet minister to Miami and arrested him for conspiracy to import marijuana into the United States.[182] And in 1986, undercover DEA agents in Miami arrested Etienne Bourenveen, commander of the Suriname army and reportedly the second most powerful man in the country, when he agreed to provide protection for shipments of drugs and ether through his country.[183]

During the late 1980s, the Justice Department and U.S. law enforcement agencies adopted a far more aggressive attitude regarding irregular rendition. The reasons were numerous. A lingering reluctance to risk

Gregory Schuetz, "Apprehending Terrorists Overseas Under United States and International Law: A Case Study of the Fawaz Younis Arrest," *Harvard International Law Journal* 29 (1988), 499–531; and Abraham Abramovsky, "Extraterritorial Jurisdiction: The United States' Unwarranted Attempt to Alter International Law in *United States v. Yunis*," *Yale Journal of International Law* 15 (1990), 121–161.

179. David Johnston, "FBI Arrests 2 Drug Suspects on High Seas," *New York Times*, Feb. 22, 1991, A16; and *Money Laundering Alert* 2 (1991), 2.

180. See Clark and Horrock, *Contrabandista!* (supra n. 169), 193–198; and John Dinges, *Our Man in Panama* (New York: Random House, 1990), 53–58.

181. Jon Nordheimer, "U.S. Arrests Atlantic Islands' Leader in Drug Plot," *New York Times*, Mar. 6, 1985, A1; Liz Balmaseda, "Drug Net Snares Island Ministers," *Miami Herald*, Mar. 6, 1985, 1A.

182. Jon Nordheimer, "U.S. Accuses Ex-Minister from Belize in Plot to Import Marijuana," *New York Times*, Apr. 9, 1985, A15.

183. Brian Duffy, "Chief of Suriname Army Denies He Smuggled Drugs," *Miami Herald*, Apr. 5, 1986, 3A; and "Suriname Official Held in Drug Case," *New York Times*, Mar. 27, 1986, B13.

offending foreign governments by conducting quasi-unilateral law enforcement operations abroad—reflected in a legal opinion issued by the Justice Department's Office of Legal Counsel during the last year of the Carter administration—had faded considerably.[184] The boom in the international cocaine market, combined with the rapidly growing U.S. drug enforcement campaign mounted by the White House and Congress, meant that law enforcement officials had both the additional incentives and the necessary resources to pursue an ever growing number of drug traffickers abroad. Moreover, Congress had eased the way in 1985 and 1986 by carving out exceptions to the 1976 Mansfield Amendment that had prohibited U.S. law enforcement agents abroad from participating in arrests of drug traffickers.[185] Similarly, many officials in both branches of government were determined to take more aggressive action against Middle Easterners and others involved in hostage takings, airplane hijackings, assassinations, bombings, and other terrorist acts directed at U.S. citizens and interests abroad. The increasingly proactive stance of the FBI, the U.S. Marshals Service, and the CIA, as well as new federal legislation extending U.S. jurisdiction to terrorist acts committed abroad, were both reflections of this new attitude. Even though officials in the Justice Department and the State Department's Legal Adviser's Office had succeeded in renegotiating a number of outdated extradition treaties, irregular rendition options typically promised to be faster and less cumbersome, as well as less susceptible to circumvention by targeted fugitives. The fact that extradition requests had to be processed through the fairly small and incredibly busy Office of International Affairs in the Justice Department also provided something of an incentive to develop alternative measures. U.S. courts, meanwhile, had repeatedly held that the existence of an extradition treaty between the United States and another government did not bar the use of other means to obtain custody over a criminal located abroad.[186]

The changing perspective was formalized in 1989 in a legal opinion

184. The legal opinion is reproduced in Margaret Colgate Love, ed., *Opinions of the Office of the Legal Counsel of the U.S. Department of Justice* 4B (1980), 543–557, and in *FBI Authority to Seize Suspects Abroad: Hearing Before the Subcommittee on Civil and Constitutional Rights of the House Committee on the Judiciary*, 101st Cong., 1st Sess., Serial No. 134 (1989), 75–90.

185. The evolution of the Mansfield amendment is reviewed in Andrew B. Campbell, "The *Ker-Frisbie* Doctrine: A Jurisdictional Weapon in the War on Drugs," *Vanderbilt Journal of Transnational Law* 23 (1990), 385–433, esp. 422–428.

186. See, e.g., *U.S. v. Reed*, 639 F.2d 896 (2d Cir. 1981).

produced by William Barr, the assistant attorney general in charge of the Office of Legal Counsel, who would subsequently succeed Richard Thornburgh as attorney general, that explicitly repudiated the 1980 opinion.[187] Whereas the first opinion had determined that customary international law imposed absolute restrictions on the authority of the U.S. government to take extraterritorial action, and thus barred U.S. law enforcement agencies from conducting extraterritorial arrests contrary to customary international law norms, the 1989 opinion stated that the President and the FBI did in fact possess such authority under the Constitution. In testimony before Congress, both Barr and the State Department's legal adviser, Abraham Sofaer, tempered the significance of the opinion by emphasizing that it reflected neither a substantial change in actual policy nor any statement of intention to ignore the many political and practical constraints on conducting unilateral arrests on foreign soil.[188]

The single most important catalyst for the new policy was the abduction, torture, and murder of Enrique Camarena, a DEA agent stationed in Guadalajara (as well as a Mexican contract pilot employed by the DEA), by Mexican drug traffickers and corrupt police officials in 1985. When U.S. efforts to investigate the incident faced not just resistance on the part of Mexican authorities but also substantial evidence that top Mexican officials had been involved in both the abduction and the subsequent cover-up, DEA and Justice Department officials reacted with fury. Determined to send a powerful message that "no one could kill a DEA agent and get away with it," the drug enforcement agency combined with federal prosecutors and Justice Department officials in an all-out effort to track down those involved in Camarena's murder and to ensure that they were brought to trial. Most of the major Mexican drug traffickers were ultimately arrested by Mexican police and tried and convicted in Mexican courts in the wake of powerful pressures from the U.S. government. One of the most notorious, Rafael Caro Quintero, was arrested in Costa Rica in a joint operation mounted by resident DEA agents and local police and then expeditiously deported, with the

187. The legal opinion—which the attorney general refused to make public, or even to turn over to Congress until the House Judiciary Committee subpoenaed a copy—is summarized in Michael Isikoff, "U.S. 'Power' on Abductions Detailed," *Washington Post*, Aug. 14, 1991, A14, and in William Barr's testimony to Congress. See *FBI Authority to Seize Suspects Abroad: Hearing* (supra n. 184), 2–21, 59–71.

188. *FBI Authority: Hearings.*

approval of the Costa Rican president, to Mexico (since he had not yet been indicted in the United States).[189] A number of those involved in the Camarena abduction, however, were brought by one means or another into the United States to face criminal charges.

The most important of the traffickers involved in the Camarena abduction to be recovered by U.S. officials was Juan Ramón Matta Ballesteros—a Honduran citizen who had worked closely with the Colombian drug traffickers, acting as their liaison with Mexican traffickers based in Guadalajara, and who had emerged as one of Honduras' leading philanthropists. Efforts to extradite Matta from Honduras had been precluded both by Matta's influence with powerful Honduran officials and by Honduras' prohibition on extraditing its citizens. So agents of the DEA and the U.S. Marshals Service worked quickly and discreetly with selected Honduran officials to devise a plan whereby Matta would be quickly arrested and flown out of the country and thus deprived of any opportunity either to appeal to the courts or to contact his powerful protectors within the government. In April 1988, Matta was arrested at his home in Tegucigalpa by Honduran military officials, forced into a van driven by a U.S. marshal, taken to the airport, and flown to the United States.[190] The rendition was hardly the first from a Central American nation to be pulled off in such a manner, but it was the first of such a major figure. When news of the abduction became public the following day, a Honduran mob, incensed at the apparent affront to Honduran sovereignty and perhaps incited as well by drug trafficker funding, attacked the U.S. embassy and succeeded in setting part of it on fire.[191] Despite protests from a few Honduran congressmen, no formal protest was made by the Honduran president, foreign ministry, or congress.[192]

More significant, from the perspectives of U.S. law and policy, were the renditions of two Mexican fugitives, Rene Martin Verdugo-Urquidez and Dr. Humberto Alvarez-Machain, in January 1986 and April 1990, respectively. Both were apprehended and deported to the United States

189. Elaine Shannon, *Desperados: Latin American Drug Lords, U.S. Lawmen, and the War America Can't Win* (New York: Viking, 1988), 245–257.

190. *Matta-Ballesteros*, 697 F.Supp. 1040 (S.D. Ill. 1988), aff'd 896 F.2d 255 (7th Cir. 1990).

191. See Mark B. Rosenberg, "Narcos and Politicos: The Politics of Drug Trafficking in Honduras," *Journal of Interamerican Studies and World Affairs* 30 (Summer-Fall 1988), 143–166; and *Matta-Ballesteros ex rel. Stolas v. Henman*, 896 F.2d 255 (7th Cir. 1990).

192. *Matta-Ballesteros*, 697 F.Supp. 1040, 1044.

by Mexican police at the behest of the DEA, which paid rewards for their renditions. What distinguished these two renditions from most of the dozens that had preceded them were the formal protests by the Mexican government that followed. In the first case, Mexico lodged what it termed "a formal complaint regarding the kidnapping of" Verdugo by agents of the U.S. government and asked that the "U.S. judicial authorities" be informed of its position.[193] The latter case—which involved a fairly prominent Mexican gynecologist and occurred just a few months after the Mexican government had been embarrassed by the airing of an NBC mini-series based upon the Camarena murder and the ensuing investigation—occasioned a much stronger response.[194] The Mexican embassy presented three diplomatic notes to the State Department between April and July 1990. The first requested a detailed report on U.S. involvement in the abduction. The second stated the Mexican government's view that the abduction constituted a violation of the extradition treaty and demanded Alvarez-Machain's return to Mexico. And the third requested the provisional arrest and extradition of both the informant and the DEA agent who had played a role in the abduction.[195] Even more significant, a federal judge in California, Edward Rafeedie, ruled in both cases that the Mexican government's protest provided the defendants with standing to invoke the violation of the extradition treaty as grounds for their repatriation to Mexico.[196] The fact that the Mexican government had formally protested the violation of the treaty, the court ruled, distinguished these two cases from *Ker v. Illinois* and other cases of irregular rendition. Judge Rafeedie's rulings were upheld by the Court of Appeals for the Ninth Circuit[197] but rejected by a 6 to 3 majority of the Supreme Court in June 1992.[198] Neither the formal Mexican government protest nor the fact that the abduction had been engineered by U.S. agents, Chief Justice Rehnquist wrote, were sufficient to distinguish the Alvarez-Machain case from *Ker v. Illinois*.

193. *International Legal Materials* 30 (1991), 1197ff.

194. The miniseries, entitled "Drug Wars: The Camarena Story," aired on NBC on Jan. 7, 8, and 9, 1990. It was based on Shannon, *Desperados* (supra n. 189). See also Larry Rohter, "Mexicans React Furiously to an NBC Drug Series," *New York Times*, Jan. 18, 1990, A13.

195. See *U.S. v. Caro-Quintero*, 745 F.Supp. 599 (C.D. Cal. 1990), aff'd 946 F.2d 1466 (9th Cir. 1991).

196. Ibid.

197. *U.S. v. Verdugo-Urquidez*, 939 F.2d 1341 (9th Cir. 1991); *U.S. v. Alvarez-Machain*, 946 F.2d 1466 (9th Cir. 1991).

198. *U.S. v. Alvarez-Machain*, 112 S.Ct. 857 (1992).

Without any provision in the extradition treaty explicitly prohibiting abductions, the defendant lacked any right under U.S. law to invoke the treaty in his defense. The ruling was met with howls of official protest in Mexico and elsewhere, to which the Bush adminstration quickly responded with assurances that it had no intention of either increasing or institutionalizing the practice of extraterritorial abductions. Six months later, in December 1992, the Justice Department was deeply embarrassed when Judge Rafeedie acquitted Alvarez-Machain on all charges and rebuked the prosecution for presenting a case based on flimsy evidence.[199] The Mexican Attorney General's Office responded by renewing its call for the extradition of the two DEA agents who reportedly had orchestrated the abduction.[200]

The two abduction cases were not the first in which a foreign government had lodged a formal protest or requested the extradition of those involved in the rendition. In the case of Britain and Canada, such protests dated back to the first part of the nineteenth century, and in the case of Mexico to the 1880s.[201] The U.S. government had also had numerous occasions to protest abductions from its territory by agents of Britain, Canada, Mexico, and Spain[202]—as well as the 1952 abduction by Soviet agents of Dr. Walter Linse from the U.S. sector of Berlin to the Soviet sector. Some cases had involved unilateral actions, such as the 1841 seizure by a British military detachment of a fugitive from his home in Albury, Vermont,[203] or a variety of incidents in which Texan sheriffs and posses crossed into Mexico to recover a fugitive. Others bore a greater resemblance to the cases of Verdugo and Alvarez-Machain in that they involved unofficial cooperation between police officials and/or private detectives of both nations. In most of these, the protests had led to the release of the person seized, although in a few cases the protesting government had indicated that an apology would be sufficient. And in a

199. Lou Cannon, "U.S. Judge Acquits Mexican in DEA Agent's '85 Killing," *Washington Post*, Dec. 15, 1992, A1; and Seth Mydans, "Judge Clears Mexican in Agent's Killing," *New York Times*, Dec. 15, 1992, A20.

200. Tod Robberson, "Mexico Seeks DEA Agents on Charges of Kidnapping," *Washington Post*, Dec. 16, 1992, A10.

201. Moore, *Treatise on Extradition* (supra n. 3), 281–302; Moore, *Digest of International Law* (supra n. 115), 4:328–332; Hackworth, *Digest of International Law* (supra n. 81), 224–228.

202. Moore, *Treatise on Extradition*, 281–302; Moore, *Digest of International Law*, 4:328–332; Hackworth, *Digest of International Law*, 224–228.

203. Moore, *Treatise on Extradition*, 282–283.

few instances involving abductions by bounty hunters and other nongovernment agents, the abductors had been prosecuted or extradited at the request of the protesting government.

U.S.-Mexican relations regarding the rendition of fugitives, however, have always diverged from the norms of extradition practice between the United States and most other nations. In 1905–6, the U.S. government responded to the abduction from Mexico of a Mexican fugitive, Antonio Martinez, by another Mexican citizen, Antonio Felix, by extraditing the latter to Mexico to face charges of kidnapping but rejecting a Mexican government request that Martinez be returned to Mexico.[204] In 1934, another incident occurred that bore a strong resemblance to the Verdugo and Alvarez-Machain abductions. Luis Lopez, a bond defaulter charged with violating the Harrison Narcotic Act, had been abducted in Mexico by a U.S. informant and some Mexican soldiers and delivered at the border to Edward Villareal, a constable of Webb County, Texas, who had orchestrated the rendition in order to claim the reward of $750. The Mexican government responded by protesting the violation of its jurisdiction and the failure to make use of the extradition treaty, asking that Lopez be returned to Mexico and charging Villareal and the informant, Tom Hernandez, with the crime of kidnapping and requesting their extradition. The extradition request was pursued by the Justice Department and approved by a federal district court and court of appeals, but subsequently rejected by the secretary of state. Lopez was tried and convicted. In contrast with the Verdugo and Alvarez-Machain cases, the district court judge ruled that he lacked jurisdiction to determine whether the irregularity of Lopez's abduction or the protest by the Mexican government required his release. When the Mexican embassy pursued the matter, the attorney general refused to order Lopez's release, noting that although Lopez's rendition had been irregular, his trial and imprisonment had been lawful.[205] In an interesting twist, however, the State Department suggested that Lopez might be returned if the Mexican government dropped its extradition request for Hernandez.[206]

204. *Foreign Relations of the United States, 1906*, 2:1121–1122.

205. *Ex parte Lopez*, 6 F.Supp. 342 (S.D. Texas 1934), *Villareal v. Hammond*, 74 F.2d 503 (5th Cir. 1934); and Hackworth, *Digest of International Law* (supra n. 81), 4:224–225.

206. Department of State Ms. File No. 211.12 Hernandez, Tomas/135, referred to in Alona E. Evans, "Acquisition of Custody over the International Fugitive Offender: Alternatives to Extradition: A Survey of United States Practice," *British Yearbook of International Law* 40 (1966), 77–104 (see 89).

In contrast to the abductions from Mexico, an abduction of an American fugitive from his home in Canada by a bail bondsman and a professional bounty hunter in 1981 led to a very different result. The fugitive, a Florida land developer named Sidney Jaffe, who had violated Florida's Land Sales Act, was tried and convicted in a Florida court and sentenced to thirty years in prison as well as an additional five for jumping bail. The Canadian government protested forcefully and demanded both that Jaffe be released and that the two abductors be extradited. The Justice Department responded by seeking Jaffe's release, which was first rejected by Florida authorities but then allowed when his sentence for illegal land sales was overturned. Federal prosecutors also pursued the extradition request, which was approved by a federal judge, and the bail bondsman and the bounty hunter were delivered to Canada.[207] When the governments of Canada and the United States signed a protocol revising their extradition treaty in 1988, a note was attached explicitly reassuring the Canadians of U.S. cooperation in preventing and punishing any future abductions by bounty hunters.[208] The willingness of the U.S. government to respond so favorably to Canadian protests reflected the fact that the abductors had not been official government agents and the recognition that such tactics should not be permitted with respect to Canadian territory.[209]

One infamous fugitive who eluded U.S. rendition efforts throughout the 1980s was Luis Arce Gómez, who had served in 1980–81 as the interior minister of the short-lived Bolivian military junta under General Luis García Meza and gained a reputation as the "minister of cocaine."[210] Efforts to extradite him from Argentina, where he had fled following the junta's downfall, proved unsuccessful. When Arce Gómez returned to Bolivia during the mid-1980s, he had reason to believe that he was safe from U.S. extradition efforts, given the Bolivian government's ban on extraditing nationals. In December 1989, however, he was arrested by the U.S.-trained paramilitary drug enforcement unit, UMOPAR, and placed immediately on a plane to the United States.[211] This

207. See *Kear v. Hilton*, 699 F.2d 181 (4th Cir. 1983). See also Wade A. Buser, "The *Jaffe* Case and the Use of International Kidnapping as an Alternative to Extradition," *Georgia Journal of International and Comparative Law* 14 (1984), 357–376.

208. *Protocol Amending the Extradition Treaty with Canada*, U.S. Senate Treaty Doc. 101-17, 101st Cong., 2d Sess. (1990).

209. The history of irregular renditions between Canada and the United States is briefly reviewed in C. V. Coles, "Extradition Treaties Abound but Unlawful Seizures Continue," *International Perspectives*, Mar.–Apr. 1975, 40–44.

210. "Ex-Bolivian Minister Held on Drug Charges," *New York Times*, Dec. 14, 1989, A27.

211. "Extradition Causes Institutional Crisis: Judge Accuses President of Assault on Judicial

rendition differed from most other comparable efforts in three respects: the fugitive was not only a Bolivian citizen but also a former cabinet minister; the deportation was personally approved by the president, Jamie Paz Zamora; and the incident almost led to the downfall of the government. The Bolivian ambassador in Washington publicly stated that Arce Gómez had been deported "because of the scant confidence the government has in Bolivia's judicial system"—which led the chief justice of Bolivia's supreme court to accuse Paz Zamora of engaging in illegitimate action. That was followed by the initiation of impeachment proceedings against the president by an opposition deputy in the Bolivian Congress on grounds that Paz Zamora had violated the constitution with his deportation order.[212] The Bolivian president survived the attacks, however, and Arce Gómez was prosecuted and convicted in Fort Lauderdale.[213] In October 1990, Arce Gómez's special assistant, Herland Echeverría, met the same fate when he was seized by Bolivian police and immediately flown to the United States.[214]

The increasingly proactive stance of the U.S. government was motivated, I have suggested, by concern with terrorists as well as drug traffickers. The 1987 sting operation that netted Fawaz Younis in the Mediterranean represented the first extraterritorial arrest of a suspected terrorist by U.S. law enforcement agents, although it followed the October 1985 incident in which U.S. fighters intercepted a plane carrying the hijackers of the *Achille Lauro* and forced it down in Italy.[215] Both operations occurred in the midst of a fairly extensive debate within the National Security Council and other agencies of the executive branch over proposals for arresting terrorists abroad.[216] Although William Barr's legal opinion indicated that the Republican administration was ready to take such proposals seriously, both his comments and those of

Power," *Latin America Regional Reports: Andean Group*, Feb. 1, 1990, 3; and "Colonel Luis Arce Departs at Dawn: Extradition on Drugs Charges Triggers Row with Judiciary," *Latin America Weekly Report*, Jan. 18, 1990, 2.

212. "Judiciary Triggers Conflict of Powers: Behind Impeachment Row, a Clear Political Agenda," *Latin America Weekly Report*, Dec. 6, 1990, 4.

213. "Escalating Conflicts of Power in Bolivia," *Latin America Regional Reports: Andean Group*, Dec. 20, 1990, 4, and "Cocaine Minister Guilty," in ibid., Jan. 31, 1991, 8.

214. "Alleged Bolivian Drug Trafficker Sent to U.S. for Trial," *Reuter Library Report*, Oct. 26, 1990.

215. See the legal analysis of the incident in Jordan J. Paust, "Extradition and United States Prosecution of the *Achille Lauro* Hostage-Takers: Navigating the Hazards," *Vanderbilt Journal of Transnational Law* 20 (1987), 235–257.

216. Stephen Engelberg, "U.S. Is Said to Weigh Abducting Terrorists Abroad for Trials Here," *New York Times*, Jan. 19, 1986, 1.

Abraham Sofaer suggested that there were abundant reasons not to act hastily. The rendition of Younis represented an ideal operation precisely because it refrained from infringing directly on any other government's sovereignty.

The focus on extraterritorial arrests of terrorists represented, moreover, only one dimension of a much broader antiterrorist campaign promoted by the U.S. government that included everything from more intensive exchange of information among police and intelligence agencies, and pressures on foreign governments to enact tougher counterterrorism policies, to the bombing of Libyan territory by U.S. warplanes. Where other governments—notably those of Greece and France—seemed to dread the prospect of prosecuting Middle Eastern terrorists in their courts,[217] U.S. officials proudly proclaimed their desire to see such offenders prosecuted in American courts. When German police arrested Mohammed Ali Hamadei—a Lebanese who had been accused of participating in the hijacking of TWA Flight 847 to Beirut and the killing of a U.S. Navy diver on board—at the Frankfurt airport in early 1987, the U.S. government applied substantial (albeit ultimately fruitless) pressure on the German government to extradite him to the United States.[218] The Greek government was subjected to even stronger pressures when its police acted on a tip from U.S. law enforcement officials and arrested Mohammed Rashid, a Palestinian accused of planting a bomb in a Pan Am jet flying between Tokyo and Honolulu in 1982. The U.S. request for Rashid's extradition was approved by the Greek supreme court but then rejected by Prime Minister Constantine Mitsotakis. In the subsequent trial in Athens, which ended in Rashid's conviction on charges of premeditated murder, the prosecutors relied largely on evidence provided by the U.S. government, including the testimony of three FBI agents and a former accomplice of Rashid who had entered the U.S. witness protection program.[219] And in May 1987, U.S. officials obliged

217. The reluctance of many European governments to extradite Middle Eastern terrorists is discussed in Malcolm Anderson, *Policing the World: Interpol and the Politics of International Police Co-operation* (Oxford: Clarendon Press, 1989), 133–140; Juliet Lodge, "The European Community and Terrorism: From Principles to Concerted Action," in Juliet Lodge, ed., *The Threat of Terrorism* (Brighton, Sussex: Wheatsheaf Books, 1988), 229–264; and Richard Bernstein, "The Terror: Why France? Why Now?" *New York Times Magazine*, Oct. 19, 1986, 31ff.

218. David M. Kennedy, Torsten Stein, and Alfred P. Rubin, "The Extradition of Mohammed Hamadei," *Harvard International Law Journal* 31 (1990), 5–35.

219. William D. Montalbano, "Palestinian Guilty of Bombing U.S. Jet," *Los Angeles Times*, Jan. 9, 1992, A4.

the Israeli government by arranging for a Palestinian-American, Mahmoud El-Abed Ahmad, whom the Israelis had charged with participating in an attack on a civilian bus in the West Bank, to be deported from Venezuela to the United States and then extradited to Israel.[220]

Any analysis of irregular rendition of fugitives by the U.S. government cannot conclude without noting the arrest of General Manuel Noriega following the invasion of Panama in December 1989 by more than 25,000 U.S. troops. The White House justified the invasion, coined "Operation Just Cause," as an act of self-defense in response to a "pattern of aggression" by the Noriega government that included the general's declaration of war and the murder of a U.S. officer the previous weekend. In his speech to the nation, President Bush declared that the invasion had been intended "to safeguard the lives of Americans, to defend democracy in Panama, to combat drug trafficking, and to protect the integrity of the Panama Canal Treaty." The overriding objective, however, appeared to be the removal of Noriega (and his henchmen in the Panamanian Defense Forces) as the de facto leader of Panama by either capturing or killing him. When Noriega finally surrendered after ten days of hiding in the Nunciature, he was taken into custody not by U.S. soldiers—indeed, General Maxwell Thurman deliberately refused to allow him to make a military surrender—but by agents of the U.S. Marshals Service, who flew him to Howard Air Force Base.[221] There he was handed over to waiting DEA agents, who accompanied him on a flight to Miami to face charges on an indictment for drug trafficking and conspiracy charges handed down twenty-three months earlier.

The invasion was widely criticized as a violation of international law and the principle of nonintervention by foreign governments, in resolutions passed by the Organization of American States and the U.N. General Assembly, and by most international law scholars.[222] Much

220. The absence of an extradition treaty between Venezuela and Israel precluded Ahmad's direct extradition to Israel. See the analysis of the U.S. role in Andreas F. Lowenfeld, "Ahmad: Profile of an Extradition Case," *New York University Journal of International Law and Politics* 23 (1991), 723–749; and Robert E. Ryals, "*Ahmad v. Wigen* Extradition: Weapon Against International Terrorism or Violation of Due Process?" *George Mason University Civil Rights Law Journal* (1991), 133–148.

221. Margaret E. Scanlon, *The Noriega Years: U.S.-Panamanian Relations, 1981–1990* (Boulder, Colo.: Lynne Rienner Publishers, 1991), 207.

222. See Neil Lewis, "Scholars Say Arrest of Noriega Has Little Justification in Law," *New York Times*, Jan. 10, 1990, A12; and the three essays by Ved P. Nanda, Tom J. Farer, and Anthony D'Amato in "Agora: U.S. Forces in Panama: Defenders, Aggressors, or Human Rights Activists?" *American Journal of International Law* 84 (1990), 494–524.

criticism also focused on the fact that the brief conflict had left 10,000 to 20,000 civilian Panamanians homeless and at least several hundred dead. The Bush administration, however, had taken steps during the preceding months to provide the domestic legal authority and justification for an intervention such as Just Cause. The Barr opinion had alleviated one set of obstacles. Following a failed coup attempt against Noriega in October 1989, the office of the Army judge advocate general had drafted a new ruling that "significantly" expanded the scope of legal military operations against terrorists, drug traffickers, and other fugitives abroad.[223] And in November, the Justice Department's Office of Legal Counsel had produced another legal opinion that reinterpreted the Posse Comitatus statute to authorize arrests of fugitives abroad by U.S. military personnel.[224] Viewed in retrospect, the three legal opinions appeared to be not merely fortuitously timed but also a discreet foreshadowing of the invasion to come.

It is possible, in certain respects, to characterize the rendition of Noriega in terms of some of the renditions and other law enforcement actions, both successful and unsuccessful, that preceded it. General Pershing's pursuit of Pancho Villa into Mexican territory in 1917 provided the precedent of a military intervention into a foreign territory in order to apprehend a foreign political leader who had violated U.S. laws—although that case involved a relatively small military force pursuing a revolutionary who lacked any control over the central government. The undercover operation that culminated in the arrest of the chief minister of the Turks and Caicos in Miami in 1985 provided something of a precedent for the arrest of a foreign head of state to face drug trafficking charges in the United States—although that action took place on U.S. territory. The bombing of Libya in 1986 provided a rough precedent for responding to extraterritorial violations of U.S. law by a foreign leader with military force in an operation involving the deaths of substantial numbers of foreign civilians—although that attack did not appear to seek the apprehension of a foreign leader to face criminal charges in an American court. And the prosecution of German and Japanese officials following their apprehension or surrender at the end of World War II offered a precedent for trying foreign leaders on

223. Scanlon, *Noriega Years*, 193.

224. Ibid.; Isikoff, "U.S. 'Power' on Abductions Detailed" (supra n. 187). See also Jessica W. Julian, "Noriega: The Capture of a State Leader and Its Implications on Domestic Law," *Air Force Law Review* 34 (1991), 153–190.

criminal charges subsequent to a military conquest—although the tribunals at Nuremberg and Tokyo were not concerned with violations of a single nation's criminal laws. There was, in short, no close precedent for the manner and circumstances in which Noriega was apprehended and brought to trial in the United States.

Conclusion

The process of immobilizing criminals is both driven and bounded by law. Unlike waging war, it focuses on individuals not as representatives of foreign governments but as individuals *qua* individuals who are singularly and entirely responsible for their actions. It thus precludes the sacrifice of innocents in pursuit of any greater objective—hence the sense of discomfort among those who see the U.S. invasion of Panama as motivated primarily by the desire to apprehend a notorious criminal fugitive. Unlike covert operations, moreover, which occasionally seek to "immobilize" individuals by killing them, the immobilization efforts of law enforcement agents seek to bring fugitives before a court of law.

Nonetheless, what most distinguishes the international rendition of fugitives from other types of international law enforcement action and most domestic criminal justice activities is the tremendous extent to which it is unbounded by legal constraints. Both Congress and the courts have afforded the executive branch extensive latitude in bringing criminal fugitives before American courts. Like all other treaties, extradition treaties are regarded as the law of the land, but they also are viewed correctly as political, intergovernmental compacts that afford defendants few if any legal rights. The existence of a treaty is not viewed—under the laws of the United States and most other nations—as a prohibition against resorting to measures outside the treaty. And the absence of an extradition treaty does not preclude a wide array of other types of rendition tactics. The constraints on international fugitive rendition are primarily political and practical in nature, not legal, and the principal legal constraints involve foreign rather than domestic laws.

The principal intrusions of law on the international rendition process affect not the collection of fugitives but their delivery. Although the U.S. government has employed its powers of deportation and exclusion with increasing facility and frequency to deliver fugitives to foreign governments, its powers of extradition still remain largely dependent upon the existence of an extradition treaty. That requirement resulted in the negotiation of dozens of extradition treaties during the nineteenth century, and it accounts for the fact that the United States is now a party to more than 100 bilateral extradition treaties. Those treaties have provided the essential source of authority to comply with foreign government requests for fugitives, but the language and judicial interpretations of their clauses also have constrained the capacity of the Departments of State and Justice to accommodate foreign requests as much as they would have liked.

The evolution of U.S. extradition treaties and practice can best be understood as one of ever more encompassing treaty language and ever more accommodative institutions and procedures. Where once American views regarding extradition were shaped principally by perceptions of the United States as a haven for those fleeing the injustices of foreign political and criminal justice systems, contemporary Americans regard it as an essential component of U.S. and international efforts to suppress crime. And where once extradition treaties were negotiated with a keen sense of their intended limits, today they are increasingly designed to be highly open-ended. Legal obstacles that had hampered extradition relations for many decades—including substantive provisions, such as the political offense exception, and more legalistic hindrances, such as the "*Valentine* infirmity," the inevitably limited "Schedule of Offenses," and rigid notions of reciprocity—have been reduced or eliminated. Similarly, institutional handicaps, notably the relative lack of government officials or any government office with expertise in extradition matters, have evaporated with the creation and expansion of the OIA in the Justice Department's Criminal Division and the LEI in the State Department's Legal Adviser's Office.

The evolution of U.S. government involvement in the international rendition of fugitives has much in common with the evolution of U.S. involvement in international evidence-gathering efforts. Until well into the twentieth century, both types of international law enforcement action were seriously hampered by much the same obstacles: skepticism of foreign systems and requests; the cumbersome requirements of transmitting requests for assistance through slow and often neglectful diplomatic bureaucracies; the dominance of State Department officials who often had insufficient knowledge of criminal procedure and criminal justice systems; a general reluctance on the part of prosecutors, courts, and legislators to accommodate the peculiar requirements of international (as distinct from municipal) law enforcement, notably those involving foreign civil law systems; and the absence of any specialized office in the government with expertise in international law enforcement matters. Beginning in the 1970s, both domains of international law enforcement witnessed dramatic progress both in the numbers of requests forwarded and received and in the capacity of U.S. and foreign officials to provide and obtain what they needed. In both cases, the principal demands and conflicts were generated far more by U.S. initiatives than by those of foreign governments. U.S. officials devoted substantial efforts to negotiating ever more encompassing extradition and mutual legal assistance treaties. These and other officials developed and perfected a variety of more proactive and aggressive measures intended to obtain fugitives or evidence in specific cases and to pressure foreign governments to be more accommodating in the future. And in the vast majority of cases, these tactics were simultaneously or subsequently approved by most federal courts and reflected in the influential *Third Restatement of the Foreign Relations Law of the United States*. The evolution of U.S. international fugitive rendition capabilities, like the evolution of evidence-gathering capabilities, could well be compared to the development of an ever more powerful and efficient vacuum cleaner.

There are, however, significant differences as well between the evolution of U.S. rendition of fugitives and that of U.S. collection of evidence. The history of the former is both far more substantial and far more laden with controversy. Relatively free of the many constitutional, evidentiary, and other legal requirements that complicate international evidence-gathering efforts, U.S. rendition efforts have benefited from their capacity for informal action. On the other hand, the option of entirely unilateral action involving extraterritorial infringements on foreign sovereignty has been severely circumscribed. With relatively few exceptions, entirely unilateral actions by U.S. agents have limited themselves to luring fugitives from their havens into U.S., foreign, or international territories where they could be seized. By contrast, although U.S. evidence-gathering efforts have generally refrained from unilateral actions to collect evidence physically abroad, the contemporary history of those efforts is replete with *Bank of Nova Scotia* subpoenas, *Ghidoni* waivers, and other tactics viewed by foreign governments as unjustifiable infringements on their sovereignty. Unlike the more aggressive U.S. rendition efforts, moreover, which have been confined largely to Latin

America, unilateral evidence-gathering efforts have been directed at a great variety of nations, including many advanced industrialized nations.

In emphasizing the extent to which the U.S. government has enhanced its capacity to obtain fugitives from abroad, I have not meant to suggest that a substantial majority of fugitives are in fact apprehended and brought to justice in U.S. courts. Powerful legal notions such as the "political offense" exception and the prohibition on extraditing nationals continue to block rendition efforts directed at terrorists and drug traffickers respectively. Fears of retaliation by terrorist organizations and their discreet government sponsors, as well as powerful drug trafficking and other criminal organizations, have frequently persuaded foreign governments to reject extradition requests from the United States and other governments. And the time, expense, and hassle of locating, arresting, and extraditing fugitives who have fled abroad have ensured that most U.S. rendition efforts are limited to the more notorious criminals. Many thousands of fugitives wanted on criminal charges in the United States remain relatively free and safe in their foreign havens. Yet the fact remains that the number of fugitive renditions processed each year has increased more than tenfold since the 1970s.

It is also important to stress that many of the more irregular renditions of fugitives from abroad have been criticized extensively and severely by legal scholars both within and without the United States.[225] They have pointed out that *Ker v. Illinois*, the 1886 Supreme Court decision that gave a stamp of approval to irregular rendition, "was decided before it was so clear to us that arbitrary arrest is a fundamental wrong."[226] But the chief criticisms have focused on the violations of international law in cases such as the seizure of Noriega or the Mexican doctor involved in the Camarena killing. Imagine, the critics have suggested, how Americans would respond to abductions by agents of foreign governments of fugitives from U.S. territory. Their point is well taken, for even as the U.S. government has demonstrated a substantial willingness to accommodate foreign rendition requests, whether by extradition or deporta-

225. The more prominent and prolific critics include Abraham Abramovsky, M. Cherif Bassiouni, Lea Brilmayer, Richard Falk, Louis Henkin, Andreas Lowenfeld, Ved Nanda, and Ruth Wedgwood. See the references to their works cited in various footnotes here. A useful discussion among a number of international law scholars, including Henkin and Wedgwood, conducted shortly after the invasion of Panama, is in *Proceedings of the 84th Annual Meeting of the American Society of International Law, 1990*, 236–256.

226. Comment of Ruth Wedgwood, in *Proceedings, American Society of International Law, 1990*, 241.

tion, even in the absence of reciprocal capabilities, it has not been confronted with the sorts of aggressive and quasi-unilateral actions employed with increasing frequency by U.S. agents. Early in 1990, Robert Friedlander, the minority counsel of the Senate Foreign Relations Committee, observed with respect to international criminal law enforcement matters that "it seems to be the *practice* of the United States to do what it wants to do; it has long been so and probably will continue to be so."[227] It may well be that only when the United States finds itself on the receiving end of such practices will the government's tactics change.

Themes of regularization, accommodation, and homogenization pervade the evolution of U.S. rendition efforts. Although U.S. officials have devoted some efforts to persuading foreign governments to adopt U.S. approaches to extradition, most efforts have focused on seeking pragmatic approaches to fugitive rendition and making the most of the potential of foreign systems to complement the U.S. system. Rigid notions of reciprocity, for instance, have yielded to more pragmatic notions of fugitive immobilization motivated by the need to accommodate the legal and political constraints on foreign governments. Evidence of the regularization of fugitive rendition abounds: the creation of the OIA, the development of Interpol's "wanted notice" system, the enhancement of the capacity of the DEA, the FBI, and the U.S. Marshals Service to arrange fugitive renditions from abroad, and the inevitable familiarization with fugitive rendition procedures, both formal and informal, that has accompanied the great increase in the numbers of fugitives being collected and delivered each year. And the proliferation of criminal statutes directed at money laundering, insider trading, and other "white-collar" crimes has created an increasingly homogeneous, and hence receptive, international environment for U.S. fugitive rendition efforts. As in other domains of international law enforcement, the distinguishing features of U.S. rendition efforts have been their aggressiveness and their scope.

227. Ibid., 254.

Chapter Eight

The Transformation of U.S. International Law Enforcement

There has always been a criminal justice dimension to U.S. foreign policy and an international dimension to American criminal justice. The first secretaries of state forwarded and responded to requests for the rendition of fugitives. Customs agents crossed U.S. borders to collect intelligence on smuggling ventures destined for the United States. Federal and state officials as well as private citizens tracked down black men and women who had fled into foreign territories to escape their enslavement in the United States. Military and police officials patrolled the borders and occasionally pursued bandits across U.S. borders. U.S. naval forces and coast guard cutters searched for pirates and slavers in the Caribbean and the Atlantic. U.S. consular officials abroad collected intelligence on matters of potential interest to municipal law enforcers. And top police officials in New York City and other metropolitan centers kept in touch with fellow officers in foreign capitals.

By the end of the nineteenth century and the beginning of the twentieth, law enforcers no longer concerned themselves with fugitive slaves, slavers, and pirates. Transnational banditry across the Canadian border was no longer a concern either. But the southwestern border with Mexico had emerged as a hotbed of criminal and law enforcement activity. Military units, Rangers, local sheriffs, and citizen posses had their hands full with cattle rustlers, horse thiefs and bandits of all sorts, Indian bands resisting pacification, and Mexican revolutionaries plotting and hiding on U.S. territory. Smuggling persisted across both borders as well as along U.S. shores. The Chinese Exclusion Acts of 1882 and 1904 required enforcement, as did the Smoking Opium Exclusion Act of 1909. Prohibition during the 1920s introduced a wave of smuggling unlike anything the country had witnessed before. Treasury agents stationed around the world investigated violations of U.S. prohibition and tariff laws, and special agents were sent on missions to conduct operations of particular import. The delegation of hundreds of thousands of troops during World War I created a need for military investigative units abroad. Agents of the Secret Service and the Bureau of Investigation were called upon to perform espionage and counterespionage activities both inside and outside the United States. By the end of the 1930s, the first FBN and FBI agents could be found in foreign posts.

The modern era of international criminal law enforcement emerged in three stages following World War II. During the late 1940s and 1950s, hundreds of military criminal investigative agents were assigned to foreign posts to police the hundreds of thousands of U.S. military personnel stationed abroad. The assumption of global security responsibilities invited creation of a substantial police training program. The Customs Service reasserted its presence overseas, the FBI opened twenty offices, the Federal Bureau of Narcotics gradually expanded its presence, and the Secret Service opened an office in Paris. The second stage began during the 1960s, with the emergence of crime as a national political issue and the rapid nationalization of law enforcement within the United States. It took off in the early 1970s, with President Nixon's declaration of a "war on drugs" and the internationalization of U.S. drug enforcement activities. The Bureau of Narcotics and Dangerous Drugs and its successor agency, the Drug Enforcement Administration, rapidly emerged as the first (nonimperial) transnational police organization in world history.

The third stage of the modern era began during the late 1970s and blossomed during the 1980s. The Justice Department, the State Department, and the Securities and Exchange Commission each created offices to handle international criminal law enforcement matters. These grew rapidly in size and responsibility, as did the U.S. national central bureau of Interpol. More than a dozen mutual legal assistance treaties (MLATs) were negotiated and signed, as well as a host of agreements to improve cooperation in drug and securities law enforcement. All of the federal police agencies expanded their extraterritorial presence and activities. Foreign police agencies began to station their own attachés in Washington, D.C., and other U.S. cities. U.S. military forces reassumed international criminal law enforcement responsibilities for the first time since the antislaver patrols of the pre–Civil War era. Police training programs were reinstituted on a significant scale. Dozens of federal criminal statutes were modified and enacted to cover extraterritorial offenses against U.S. citizens and other interests abroad. Prosecutors devised, and federal judges approved, a variety of innovative techniques to compel foreign banks and corporations to provide evidence located abroad. And the U.S. attorney general revealed that he often spent more than 50 percent of his day dealing with international criminal law enforcement matters.

A prime example of the blossoming of U.S. international criminal law enforcement could be found in Italy. During the 1980s, the two governments signed and put into force both an updated extradition treaty and an innovative mutual legal assistance treaty, both of which were quickly put to use by U.S. and Italian law enforcement officials. An Italian-American Working Group on Organized Crime was created, and its sessions were frequently attended by the U.S. attorney general and top officials of the FBI and other federal law enforcement agencies. By the late 1980s, the law enforcement group within the U.S. embassy included representatives of the DEA, the FBI, the Secret Service, Customs, the IRS, the INS, the Naval Investigative Service, the Army Criminal Investigative Division, the Air Force Office of Special Investigations, and the first federal prosecutor stationed abroad, Richard Martin.[1] An Italian Office of International Affairs grew rapidly, and its chief, initially hostile to many U.S. initiatives, evolved into a vigorous proponent of closer law enforcement relations with the United States. The Italian Parliament enacted new legislation bringing its own drug laws and regulation of

1. Richard Martin was the lead prosecutor in the "Pizza Connection" case from 1985 to 1987. During his tenure in Rome (1987–90), his various titles included Special Representative of the U.S. Attorney General, Department of Justice Attaché, and Senior Counsel for International Law Enforcement.

financial and securities transactions more in line with U.S. norms.[2] And Italian criminal investigative methods increasingly resembled those employed by the DEA and other U.S. police agencies.

There is, clearly, no one explanation for the internationalization of U.S. criminal law enforcement. The perennial concerns with controlling the nation's borders, suppressing smuggling, collecting revenues, and renditing criminal fugitives have remained constant even as the energies, personnel, resources, and international agreements devoted to these tasks have multiplied. What have changed, however, are many of the criminal laws requiring extraterritorial enforcement efforts. Police and prosecutors today no longer need worry about fugitive slaves, illicit slavers, rum runners, and cross-border Apache raids. But unlike their counterparts a hundred years ago, they have their hands full with illicit heroin and cocaine smugglers, securities law violators, high-tech smugglers, money launderers, and tax offenders. As we contemplate the future of U.S. involvement in international criminal law enforcement matters, we do well to keep in mind the potential for current laws to be repealed, for new criminal laws to emerge, and for enforcement priorities to change. New laws justify the creation of new international law enforcement capabilities, which in turn invite additional laws and other new initiatives. Changing perceptions of U.S. national security interests, as well as changing markets and morals, have radically transformed the nature and objectives of U.S. international law enforcement efforts in the past and are certain to do so in the future.

That being said, I must stress the dominant role that drug enforcement has played in the evolution of U.S. international law enforcement since the late 1960s. The "war on drugs" proclaimed by the Nixon administration in 1969, and renewed on an even more ambitious scale during the 1980s, provided the crucial impetuses for a host of actions and agreements that otherwise would never have occurred. It was not just the transformation of a relatively small federal police agency into a substantial transnational police organization with agents stationed in more than sixty foreign cities. Over and above that significant development, the "war on drugs" provided a reason for other federal police agencies, including the FBI and Customs, to extend their efforts abroad. It accounted for roughly 70 percent of the 16,300 fugitives sought by the

2. Lawrence J. Fassler, "The Italian Penal Procedure Code: An Adversarial System of Criminal Procedure in Continental Europe," *Columbia Journal of Transnational Law* 29 (1991), 245–278.

U.S. Marshals Service in 1993. It led to the modification of the Posse Comitatus Act to allow U.S. military forces to play a role in civilian law enforcement. It provided the impetus for creation of paramilitary enforcement groups composed of U.S. military and police officials to target drug trafficker facilities in South America. It prompted the negotiation and renegotiation of dozens of extradition treaties as well as a number of mutual legal assistance treaties. It accounted for much of the business pursued by the Justice Department's Office of International Affairs. It led to a new role for the CIA and other intelligence agencies in criminal law enforcement matters.[3] It helped stimulate the negotiation of a number of global drug enforcement conventions, including a 1988 U.N. convention that dramatically increased the level of international law enforcement cooperation expected of governments. It exercised a profound influence on the nature of criminal investigation in dozens of foreign countries. It compelled dozens of foreign governments to change their financial and corporate secrecy laws. It provided a central justification for the military invasion of Panama. And it offered a powerful foot in the door with which to weaken domestic and foreign resistance to a range of other international criminal law enforcement endeavors. In short, there can be no question that but for the U.S. "war on drugs" the extent of U.S. involvement in international law enforcement matters would be far less developed than it is today.

My principal aim throughout much of this book has been to explain *how* U.S. law enforcement agents have responded to the challenges of internationalization—in particular, the need to collect from abroad the information, evidence, and bodies required to "immobilize" transnational criminals. The principal obstacles, I noted, are of three sorts: the loss of sovereign police powers outside U.S. borders; the foreign, international, and domestic political frictions that inevitably hamper most domains of foreign policy; and the frictions generated by the need to interact with alien law enforcement systems. My analysis accordingly focused on explaining how U.S. law enforcers have dealt with these obstacles.

The dominant theme in the evolution of U.S. international law enforcement is one of progress toward an ever more powerful capacity to immobilize transnational criminals. Extradition and mutual legal assis-

3. See William J. Broad, "Charting Drug Trade from the Skies," *New York Times*, Oct. 14, 1989, 6; and Jeff Gerth, "C.I.A. Shedding Its Reluctance to Aid in Fight Against Drugs," *New York Times*, Mar. 25, 1990, A1.

tance treaties have proliferated and become more and more inclusive. Prosecutors have devised an increasing array of techniques for acquiring evidence from abroad. Growing numbers of agencies and people have developed expertise in handling international law enforcement matters. The number of U.S. agents stationed abroad has steadily increased. Congress and the federal courts have consistently reduced and eliminated domestic legal obstacles to effective international law enforcement action and enhanced the legal powers of U.S. law enforcement officials. And foreign governments and law enforcement agencies have mostly worked at common purposes with U.S. officials to reduce the frictions that emanate from their own criminal justice systems. By contrast, the obstacles generated by Congress, U.S. courts, and foreign governments have been relatively few and brief. It is fair to say that U.S. international law enforcement capabilities have advanced three steps forward for every step backward. They are now more powerful and more streamlined than ever before.

The internationalization of U.S. law enforcement has proceeded in tandem with the internationalization and harmonization of foreign law enforcement systems. The evolutionary process has been both dynamic and interactive, involving efforts by U.S. law enforcers and foreign counterparts to regularize relations, to accommodate domestic systems to the requirements of foreign systems, and to homogenize criminal justice norms across borders. Most of these efforts have occurred at the transgovernmental level, where low- and middle-level officials, primarily in the Justice Department but also in smaller numbers in the Departments of State and Treasury and the intelligence agencies, have established relations with foreign counterparts. Many U.S. law enforcers involved in international law enforcement matters on a regular basis now perceive themselves both as representatives of the U.S. government and as members of a transnational subculture based on common functions and objectives. Indeed, it is this transnational identity—based on the notion that a cop is a cop, and a criminal is a criminal, no matter what their respective nationalities—that provides the oil and glue of contemporary international law enforcement. Where once U.S. law enforcers barely perceived a commonality of identity with foreign police and prosecutors, they now represent quite active and conscious developers of this transnational subculture.

U.S. law enforcers generally see the internationalization of criminal justice as relatively free of costs or trade-offs. The negotiation of extradition treaties has not required U.S. agents to forgo less-formal means of rendition. The negotiation of mutual legal assistance treaties have required relatively few concessions in terms of abstaining from *Bank of Nova Scotia* subpoenas, *Ghidoni* waivers, and other unilateral means of compelling the production of evidence. And the fairly operational activities of U.S. agents in foreign countries only rarely have led to demands that foreign police agents be permitted to do likewise in the United States.

There are three explanations for the relative absence of costs or trade-offs. The first is simply that many apparent concessions by the U.S. government have not been perceived as such by most law enforcement officials and other citizens. Unlike citizens of most civil law countries and many others as well, Americans have long been accustomed to the notion that U.S. citizens should be extradited to foreign countries for crimes committed abroad. Unlike citizens of countries that have experienced humiliating occupations and dominations by foreign powers, Americans have rarely been bothered by the presence of foreign law enforcement officials on U.S. territory. Most Americans regard undercover operations, wiretapping, the employment of informants, and the practice of recruiting informants with financial and legal rewards as natural components of criminal investigation. They tend not to view financial and corporate secrecy with the same deference as many foreign citizens. And they generally view criminal laws and the criminal justice system as appropriate methods for curtailing and suppressing a great variety of undesirable activities. As a consequence, U.S. officials rarely feel compelled to say no to foreign requests for law enforcement assistance from other advanced industrial democracies, and only occasionally are obliged to reject requests from other countries.

The second explanation is that the harmonization of national criminal justice systems during this century, and particularly since the 1960s, has been powerfully shaped by the United States. Unlike the last decades of the nineteenth century and the first decades of the twentieth, when U.S. law enforcement officials looked to Europe for lessons in police methods and organization, the modern era of international law enforcement is one in which U.S. criminal justice priorities and U.S. models of criminalization and criminal investigation have been exported abroad. Foreign governments have responded to U.S. pressures, inducements, and examples by enacting new criminal laws regarding drug trafficking, money laundering, insider trading, and organized crime and by changing financial and corporate secrecy laws as well as their codes of criminal procedure to better accommodate U.S. requests for assistance. Foreign police have adapted U.S. investigative techniques, and foreign courts and legislatures have followed up with the requisite legal authorizations. And foreign governments have devoted substantial police and even military resources to curtailing illicit drug production and trafficking. By contrast, the demands of foreign law enforcement systems have required remarkably few responses by Congress or accommodations by U.S. courts, prosecutors, and police. The threefold processes of regularization, accommodation, and homogenization by which states transcend the frictions of international law enforcement have hardly been equal or reciprocal. By and large, the United States has provided the models, and other governments have done the accommodating. It thus would be quite fair, in describing the evolution of drug enforcement and many other domains of law enforcement around the world since the 1960s, to substitute the word "Americanization" for "harmonization."

The third explanation is that Americans have not yet had to deal with the sorts of pressures and interventions that the U.S. government imposes on others. The U.S. government has little reason to fear the consequences of rejecting an extradition request from a foreign government. Only a small number of fugitives from foreign justice have been abducted from U.S. territory, and almost all of those occurred before World War I. The extensive presence of Mexican agents north of the border during the Mexican revolution has not been repeated by the Mexican or any other government since. U.S. corporations and banks only rarely have to deal with the sorts of sanctions levied by U.S. courts that want to obtain documents located abroad. And the United States generally has not been subjected to anything resembling the pressures it has exerted in promoting the war on drugs to foreign governments. Foreign governments that prohibit the sale of alcohol, or the importation of firearms, or the export of capital, or the pollution of the environment in ways that remain legal in the United States, lack the power to require the United States to submit to their own criminal norms. Should that balance of power shift, or should foreign governments impatient with U.S. criminal procedures decide to act more unilaterally on U.S. territory, the attitudes of American citizens and the U.S. government regarding international law enforcement may well undergo a striking change.

The fact that U.S. law enforcers still regard most dimensions of the internationalization process as cost-free does not mean that others share their perspective. It is important to keep in mind that the internationalization of law enforcement since the 1960s has coincided with a fairly persistent expansion of criminal justice systems in the United States and abroad, as well as quite extensive enhancements in the powers of law enforcement officials. Apart from a brief period during the mid-1970s, when Congress circumscribed the powers of federal law enforcement officials within and without the United States, both Congress and the courts have preferred to broaden the latitude and powers of law enforcement officials. Civil libertarians, criminal defense lawyers, and many others who oppose new extensions of police powers have decried the apparent evisceration of the "political offense" exception, the Supreme Court's refusal to apply Fourth Amendment standards to extraterritorial searches by U.S. law enforcement agents and its legitimation of extraterritorial abductions, the insistence of the State and Justice Departments on extraditing U.S. citizens to foreign countries that do not recognize American standards of due process, and the efforts of extradition and mutual legal assistance treaty negotiators to monopolize the benefits of the treaties for prosecutors. Banking and corporate interests both in the United States and abroad have regarded with concern the growing regulation of transnational money movements, the increasing criminalization of violations of those regulations, and the apparent willingness of U.S. law enforcement officials to provide information on capital flight to foreign governments that restrict exports of capital. In many foreign countries, the adoption of DEA-style investigative techniques has been viewed warily by citizens who recall the outrages perpetrated by *agents provocateurs* and secret police earlier in the century. DEA agents know that many drug trafficking suspects arrested in foreign countries on the basis of information provided by the DEA are tortured by local police. And critics of drug prohibition within and without the United States insist that current policies are no more successful, and even more costly and counterproductive, than the alcohol prohibition policies of the 1920s.

It is extremely difficult to gauge the impact of U.S. international law enforcement efforts on levels of crime. Law enforcement agencies can provide fairly reliable statistics on drug seizures and drug trafficker arrests, but they can only guess at the number of drug shipments and traffickers that are not detected. No one knows how many times U.S. securities and money laundering laws are violated each year, whether in the United States or abroad. Estimates of the number of illegal immigrants entering the United States vary dramatically as well. New laws transform activities that were once legal into criminal activities, thereby suddenly and often quite dramatically increasing the total amount of transnational crime. And some international law enforcement initiatives backfire, as when successes in immobilizing amateur criminals benefit more professional and organized criminals, or when successes in suppressing marijuana trafficking end up stimulating cocaine trafficking.

The internationalization of U.S. law enforcement can be judged a success, however, in at least one important respect. By and large, the odds that U.S. law enforcers will succeed in immobilizing a particular transnational criminal they have targeted have increased substantially since the 1960s. The number of havens in which transnational criminals can elude apprehension have diminished substantially. Foreign financial secrecy jurisdictions no longer provide quite the same protection for criminal assets and money movements. And the resources and expertise committed to U.S. international law enforcement efforts have increased to the point that they can sustain expensive and complex multinational criminal investigations for as long as it takes to immobilize a wanted transnational criminal. By 1991, virtually all of the most notorious Latin American drug traffickers sought by U.S. officials during the 1980s were either dead or incarcerated in U.S. and foreign prisons. Although transnational criminals continue to take advantage of the frictions generated by conflicting sovereignties, political interests, and law enforcement systems, the streamlining and enhancement of U.S. international law enforcement has succeeded in narrowing the criminals' advantage.

International law enforcement endeavors are generally bilateral and cooperative in nature, reflecting states' recognition of mutual interests in crime control as well as principles of reciprocity and comity. Among the features that distinguish U.S. international law enforcement behavior from that of most other states, however, are the relatively high number of endeavors in which U.S. officials act unilaterally and coercively. No other government has acted so aggressively in collecting evidence from foreign jurisdictions, apprehending fugitives from abroad, indicting foreign officials in its own courts,[4] targeting foreign government corruption, and persuading foreign governments to change their criminal justice norms to better accord with its own. Nor has any other government

4. Jean E. Engelmayer, "Foreign Policy by Indictment: Using Legal Tools Against Foreign Officials Involved in Drug Trafficking," *Criminal Justice Ethics*, Summer/Fall 1989, 3–31.

devoted comparable diplomatic resources to pursuing its international law enforcement agenda during the past few decades. The U.S. government has, more than any other government, proven willing and able to intrude on the prerogatives of foreign sovereigns, to challenge foreign political sensibilities, and to circumvent and override foreign legal norms.

This aggressiveness has been successful in two respects. First, it has, in individual cases, resulted in the immobilization of transnational criminals who would otherwise have eluded immobilization. One need only recall the ways in which August Ricord, Joaquim Him, Edwin Wilson, Carlos Lehder, Juan Matta Ballesteros, Humberto Alvarez Machain, Fawaz Younis, Luis Arce Gómez, and Manuel Noriega were delivered to U.S. custody to appreciate the effectiveness of aggressive action. Much the same could be said of the ways in which financial documents and other evidence were obtained by resorting to *Bank of Nova Scotia* subpoenas, *Ghidoni* waivers, and other coercive mechanisms devised by U.S. prosecutors and backed by U.S. courts. Aggressive actions in most of these cases produced angry reactions by foreign governments and societies, including diplomatic protests, enactment of blocking statutes, and expulsions of U.S. law enforcement agents—but they accomplished their central objectives.

Second, U.S. aggressiveness has proved successful in pressuring foreign governments to be more forthcoming in the future. Combined with public and private pressures by Congress, the White House, and other top U.S. officials, these aggressive actions have helped persuade foreign governments to change their own laws, create law enforcement working groups and other cooperative arrangements with U.S. law enforcers, enter into extradition and mutual legal assistance treaty negotiations desired by U.S. officials, and generally play a more active role in vicariously representing U.S. criminal justice interests. The success of U.S. international law enforcement efforts has thus depended upon the willingness and ability of the U.S. government to offend foreign sovereignties and sensibilities in particular cases, as well as on the capacity to avoid future frictions and improve cooperation by harmonizing U.S. and foreign criminal justice systems over the long term.

The relative success of the U.S. government in pursuing its international law enforcement agenda can be attributed to at least three factors. The first, and most obvious, is the overall power of the United States and its government. Foreign governments know that the costs of defying the

United States may be substantial, particularly if they represent relatively vulnerable, less-developed, countries. Foreign banks and corporations know that defiance of U.S. court orders for documents may result in their de facto exclusion from American territory and markets. And transnational criminals know that the U.S. government is sufficiently powerful and wealthy to sustain a global police presence as well as far-reaching and long-term criminal investigations.

The second factor is the elevation of criminal justice officials, concerns, and objectives to the upper echelons of U.S. foreign policy formulation and implementation—a phenomenon that can be explained largely by the persistent prominence of "law and order" themes in American national politics since the late 1960s. The first significant elevation occurred during the Nixon administration, when White House officials insisted that the State Department and the CIA take international drug enforcement objectives seriously. During the 1980s, drug enforcement ranked among the top three concerns of U.S. ambassadors in well over a dozen countries and engaged growing numbers of officials in the military, the intelligence agencies, and the White House. It provided the occasion for two Andean Summit meetings of President Bush and Latin American leaders. And it emerged, together with terrorism and money laundering, on the agendas of the G-7 meetings and other notable gatherings of world leaders. Congressional committees charged with oversight of foreign affairs took an active interest in international drug control matters and other crime control issues. Attorney generals of the United States were increasingly drawn into foreign policy deliberations as well as international negotiations and travel. The net result was to empower—both intragovernmentally and transgovernmentally—police, prosecutors, and other officials involved in international criminal law enforcement.

The third factor is the ever-present but increasingly strident and pervasive sense of moralism associated with criminal justice efforts both domestically and internationally. Within the federal bureaucracy of the United States, the number of government officials willing to oppose an international law enforcement initiative that might be costly to other U.S. foreign policy objectives has diminished in recent decades, particularly as anti-Soviet and anticommunist objectives have lost their place at the pinnacle of the U.S. foreign policy agenda. Where once officials in the White House and the State Department felt secure in pushing criminal justice issues onto the back burners, they now know that they risk public embarrassment by Congress and the media if they are accused of treating criminal justice objectives with insufficient regard. One result is that indictments of transnational criminals initiated by lower-level prosecutors are increasingly likely to proceed unimpeded by higher-level officials even if they threaten to disrupt relations with foreign governments.[5] Similarly, foreign governments are increasingly wary of arousing the ire of the U.S. Congress and the American public by appearing to be insensitive to U.S. criminal justice concerns. Where once anticommunism represented the principal moral imperative of U.S. foreign policy, drug enforcement and other criminal justice objectives have emerged as the new moral imperatives.

It is both easy and quite accurate to describe the internationalization of U.S. law enforcement as a natural and inevitable response to the internationalization of crime. As the flow of people, goods, money, and just about everything else across U.S. borders has increased dramatically in recent decades, so too have the criminal violations associated with those transnational movements. The dramatic internationalization of the financial, securities, and commodities markets since the 1970s—to take the most prominent examples—inevitably was accompanied by a proliferation of transnational frauds on those markets. But the internationalization of U.S. law enforcement must also be understood as a consequence of criminalizations of previously licit transnational activities as well as extensions of U.S. jurisdiction to offenses committed abroad. The FBI derives much of the justification for its expanding role overseas from Congressional legislation during the mid-1980s that brought terrorist offenses against U.S. citizens and interests abroad under U.S. federal law. U.S. Customs similarly was able to justify its international expansion during the 1980s as a response to the criminalization of transnational money movements and the expansion of export controls on technologically advanced products. And even the invasion of Panama and arrest of Noriega were justified primarily by Noriega's extraterritorial violations of U.S. drug laws.

There has, in short, been something of a fusion (or perhaps re-fusion would be more accurate) of U.S. criminal justice and U.S. national security concerns. These two concerns overlapped at sea during the first decades of the nation's history, when naval patrols sought to suppress

5. See Philip Shenon, "The Justice Department Takes on Diplomatic Tasks Pursuing Foreign Targets," *New York Times*, Aug. 28, 1988, E5.

piracy, and along the U.S. borders until World War I, where posses, law enforcers, and military units confronted challenges to frontier stability. With the quieting of the borders, the two sets of concerns were more or less disentangled. During the decades following World War II, espionage and high-tech smuggling represented virtually the only issues implicating both concerns. During the 1980s, extraterritorial terrorism, traditionally a national security concern, was added to the criminal justice agenda by Congressional statutes, and drug trafficking, traditionally a criminal justice concern, was placed on the national security agenda by the White House, Congress, and, in a formal sense, a National Security Directive.[6] During the mid-1980s, both the U.S. military and the intelligence agencies reoriented their priorities, often reluctantly, to devote greater attention to drug trafficking, money laundering, and other criminal activities they previously had largely ignored. By the early 1990s, this reorientation had progressed substantially, driven both by the emergence of advocates within the military and intelligence bureaucracies and by the general search for new agendas and objectives to fill the void left by the collapse of the Soviet Union and the international communist threat. A fusion of criminal justice and national security concerns could also be perceived along the border with Mexico, where substantial efforts were under way to enhance the presence and role of the Border Patrol, federal law enforcement agencies, and even the U.S. military.

The fusion of the two sets of concerns could be explained in part by the inherent malleability of definitions of national security. Defining transnational drug trafficking as a national security threat jibed neatly with the rhetoric of the "war on drugs" during the 1980s. One can well imagine, in this vein, the depiction of illicit migration into the United States as a national security threat of the future. But the fusion also reflected the more general domestication of U.S. foreign policy during the 1980s and into the 1990s—by which I mean both the injection of traditionally domestic concerns and norms into the formulation and implementation of U.S. foreign policy, and a diminished capability and desire to continue assuming the traditional military and economic costs of global hegemony. Indeed, the internationalization of U.S. law enforcement during the 1980s can well be viewed as a form of hegemony on the cheap. The Cold War vision of the United States as the world's policeman

6. President Reagan signed National Security Decision Directive No. 221, entitled *Narcotics and National Security*, in April 1986.

has yielded to a new post–Cold War vision, one that more closely aligns the ordinary citizen's notion of policing with U.S. involvement in international politics. This vision is dramatically less expensive than the former one, even if it increasingly invites the use of military force to deal with extraterritorial violations of U.S. laws.

There is every reason to believe that the internationalization of U.S. law enforcement will continue apace into the foreseeable future. The international tentacles of U.S. criminal justice will become more numerous and diverse and extend further. The channels will become more streamlined and efficient. Multilateral treaties, conventions, and institutions will proliferate and strengthen. Other nation's law enforcement systems will increasingly reflect U.S. examples and norms, thereby enhancing their vicarious enforcement of U.S. laws. U.S. diplomats, soldiers, and intelligence officials will find more and more of their responsibilities determined by U.S. criminal laws. International crime control issues will increasingly be redefined as national security issues. And national security issues will increasingly be dealt with by police and prosecutors.

All these developments are part and parcel of the increasingly complex and multidimensional interdependence of states and societies. All governments today face the challenge of controlling growing domains of transnational activities that either ignore or take advantage of national borders, even as their own powers remain powerfully circumscribed by the political, geographical, and legal limitations that attend notions of national sovereignty. The internationalization of law enforcement represents one of the more substantial responses to this challenge by the U.S. government and by most others as well. States have expanded the reach of their criminal laws over transnational and extraterritorial transactions and affairs, and criminal justice systems have improved their capacity to enforce these laws both unilaterally and in cooperation with one another. No one has done more in this regard than the United States government. Both its global police presence and its activist approach to transnational criminality dwarf those of any other government. The United States has consistently taken the lead in promoting both criminal prohibitions and criminal justice cooperation among nations. It has succeeded in making its own criminal justice norms and concerns those of most other states as well. And it has demonstrated a unique willingness to act decisively and unilaterally in responding to transnational crimes of all sorts. In this arena, more than most others, the United States retains the title of global hegemon.

Appendixes

Appendix A: Foreign Offices of U.S. Federal Law Enforcement Agencies, 1992–1993

	DEA	FBI	Customs	Secret Service	INS	Commerce
North America						
Belize, Belize City	x					
Canada, Ottawa	x	x	x			
Montreal	x					
Costa Rica, San José	x					
El Salvador, San Salvador	x					
Guatemala, Guatemala City	x					
Honduras, Tegucigalpa	x					
Mexico, Mexico City	x	x	x		x	
Guadalajara	x				x	
Hermosillo	x		x			
Mazatlán	x					
Mérida	x		x			
Monterrey	x		x		x	
Tijuana					x	
Panama, Panama City	x	x	x		x	
Caribbean						
Bahamas, Nassau	x					
Freeport	x					
Barbados, Bridgetown	x	x				
Dominican Republic, Santo Domingo	x		x			
Haiti, Port-au-Prince	x					
Jamaica, Kingston	x					
Netherlands Antilles, Curaçao	x					
South America						
Argentina, Buenos Aires	x					
Bolivia, La Paz	x					
Cochabamba	x					
Santa Cruz	x					
Brazil, Brasília	x					
Chile, Santiago	x					
Colombia, Bogotá	x	x				
Barranquilla	x					

Appendix A Continued

	DEA	FBI	Customs	Secret Service	INS	Commerce
South America (cont'd)						
Ecuador, Quito	x					
Guayaquil	x					
Paraguay, Asunción	x					
Peru, Lima	x					
Uruguay, Montevideo	x	x	x			
Venezuela, Caracas	x	x	x			
Maracaibo	x					
Europe						
Austria, Vienna	x		x		x	x
Belgium, Brussels	x	x	x			
Cyprus, Nicosia	x					
Denmark, Copenhagen	x					
France, Paris	x	x	x	x		
Marseilles	x					
Germany, Bonn	x	x	x	x		
Frankfurt	x				x	
Greece, Athens	x	x			x	
Italy, Rome	x	x	x	x	x	
Milan	x		x			
Netherlands, The Hague	x		x			
Spain, Madrid	x	x				
Sweden, Stockholm						x
Switzerland, Bern	x	x				x
Turkey, Ankara	x					
Istanbul	x					
United Kingdom, London	x	x	x	x	x	
Africa						
Egypt, Cairo	x					
Kenya, Nairobi					x	
Nigeria, Lagos	x					
Asia						
Hong Kong	x	x	x		x	
India, New Delhi	x				x	
Bombay	x					
Japan, Tokyo	x	x	x			
Korea, Seoul	x		x		x	
Malaysia, Kuala Lumpur	x					
Myanmar (Burma), Rangoon	x					
Pakistan, Islamabad	x					
Karachi	x					

Appendix A Continued

	DEA	FBI	Customs	Secret Service	INS	Commerce
Asia (cont'd)						
Lahore	x					
Peshawar	x					
Philippines, Manila	x	x		TDY	x	
Singapore	x		x		x	
Thailand, Bangkok	x	x	x	x	x	
Chiang Mai	x					
Songkhla	x					
Udon	x					
Australia						
Australia, Canberra	x	x				
Total foreign offices	73	20	22	5	17	3
Total countries	50	20	18	5	14	3

SOURCES: Public affairs offices of each of the federal law enforcement agencies in early 1993.
NOTE: Not listed in the table are the Postal Inspection Service, which stationed a special agent in Wiesbaden, Germany, in 1993, and the Department of Justice, which has stationed an attaché (counsel, not special agent) in Rome since 1987.

Appendix B: BNDD and DEA Offices and Personnel Abroad (Authorized), 1969–1993

	1969	1970	1971	1972	1973	1974	1975	1976	1977	1983	1990	1993
Foreign regional offices	3	3	3	6	6	6	6	6	3			
Foreign district offices	12	17	20	39	41	52	64	62	63	61	68	73
Total authorized personnel	34	70	91	186	203	293	401	417	325	285	358	416
Agents	26	47	61	115	124	174	222	228	162	188	240	293
Other (professional, clerical & foreign nationals)	8	23	30	71	79	119	179	189	163	97	118	123

SOURCE: DEA Office of Public Affairs; annual editions of *Hearings Before the Subcommittee on Departments of State, Justice, Commerce, the Judiciary, and Related Agencies, Committee on Appropriations, U.S. House of Representatives.*

Appendix C: DEA Offices Abroad (Authorized), 1975 and 1993

	1975	1993
North America		
Belize, Belize City		x
Canada, Ottawa	x	x
Montreal	x	x
Vancouver	x	
Toronto	x	
Costa Rica, San José	x	x
El Salvador, San Salvador		x
Guatemala, Guatemala City	x	x
Honduras, Tegucigalpa		x
Mexico, Mexico City	x	x
Acapulco	x	
Guadalajara	x	x
Hermosillo	x	x
Mazatlán	x	x
Mérida	x	x
Monterrey	x	x
Veracruz	x	
Panama, Panama City	x	x
Caribbean		
Bahamas, Nassau		x
Freeport		x
Barbados, Bridgetown		x
Dominican Republic, Santo Domingo		x
Haiti, Port-au-Prince		x
Jamaica, Kingston	x	x
Netherlands Antilles, Curaçao		x
South America		
Argentina, Buenos Aires	x	x
Bolivia, La Paz	x	x
Cochabamba		x
Santa Cruz		x
Brazil, Brasília	x	x
Rio de Janeiro	x	
São Paulo	x	
Chile, Santiago	x	x
Colombia, Bogotá	x	x
Barranquilla		x
Cali	x	
Ecuador, Quito	x	x
Guayaquil	x	x
Paraguay, Asunción	x	x

Appendix C Continued

	1975	1993
South America (cont'd)		
Peru, Lima	x	x
Uruguay, Montevideo	x	x
Venezuela, Caracas	x	x
Maracaibo		x
Europe		
Austria, Vienna	x	x
Belgium, Brussels	x	x
Cyprus, Nicosia		x
Denmark, Copenhagen	x	x
France, Paris	x	x
Marseilles	x	x
Nice	x	
Germany, Bonn	x	x
Frankfurt	x	x
Hamburg	x	
Munich	x	
Greece, Athens		x
Italy, Rome	x	x
Genoa	x	
Milan	x	x
Netherlands, The Hague	x	x
Spain, Madrid	x	x
Barcelona	x	
Switzerland, Bern	x	
Turkey, Ankara	x	x
Adana	x	
Istanbul	x	x
Izmir	x	
United Kingdom, London	x	x
Africa		
Egypt, Cairo		x
Morocco, Rabat	x	
Nigeria, Lagos		x
East Asia/Pacific		
Hong Kong	x	x
India, New Delhi	x	x
Bombay		x
Indonesia, Jakarta	x	
Japan, Tokyo	x	x
Okinawa	x	

Appendix C Continued

	1975	1993
East Asia/Pacific (cont'd)		
Korea, Seoul	x	x
Laos, Vientiane	x	
Malaysia, Kuala Lumpur	x	x
Myanmar (Burma), Rangoon		x
Philippines, Manila	x	x
Singapore	x	x
Taiwan, Taipei	x	
Thailand, Bangkok	x	x
Chiang Mai	x	x
Songkhla	x	x
Udon		x
Vietnam, Saigon	x	
Southwest Asia/Near East		
Afghanistan, Kabul	x	
Iran, Tehran	x	
Lebanon, Beirut	x	
Pakistan, Islamabad	x	x
Karachi	x	x
Lahore		x
Peshawar		x
Australia		
Australia, Canberra		x

SOURCES: DEA Office of Public Affairs; annual editions of *Hearings Before the Subcommittee on Departments of State, Justice, Commerce, the Judiciary, and Related Agencies, Committee on Appropriations, U.S. House of Representatives.*

Appendix D: FBI Foreign Liaison Posts, 1965–1993

	1965	1973	1978	1985	1990	1993
North America						
Canada, Ottawa	x	x	x	x	x	x
Mexico, Mexico City	x	x	x	x	x	x
Nicaragua, Managua		x				
Panama, Panama City				x	x	x
Caribbean						
Barbados, Bridgetown					x	x
South America						
Argentina, Buenos Aires	x	x	x			
Bolivia, La Paz		x				
Brazil, Brasília		x				
Rio de Janeiro	x					
Colombia, Bogotá				x	x	x
Uruguay, Montevideo				x	x	x
Venezuela, Caracas		x	x			x
Asia						
Hong Kong		x	x	x	x	x
Japan, Tokyo	x	x	x	x	x	x
Philippines, Manila	x	x	x		x	x
Singapore		x				
Thailand, Bangkok						x
Europe						
Belgium, Brussels					x	x
Denmark, Copenhagen		x				
France, Paris	x	x	x	x	x	x
Germany, Bonn	x	x	x	x	x	x
Greece, Athens						x
Italy, Rome	x	x	x	x	x	x
Spain, Madrid		x	x			x
Switzerland, Bern	x	x	x	x	x	x
United Kingdom, London	x	x	x	x	x	x
Middle East						
Israel, Tel Aviv		x				
Lebanon, Beirut		x				
Australia						
Canberra				x	x	x
Total posts	11	20	13	13	16	20

SOURCE: FBI Office of Public Affairs; annual editions of *Hearings Before the Subcommittee on Departments of State, Justice, Commerce, the Judiciary, and Related Agencies, Committee on Appropriations, U.S. House of Representatives.*

Appendix E: Mutual Legal Assistance Treaties Signed by the United States, 1973–1992

Country	Signed	Entered into Force	Citations
Argentina	Dec. 4, 1990	Feb. 9, 1993	Treaty Doc. 102-18 Ex. Rpt. 102-33
Bahamas	June 12, 1987 Aug. 18, 1987	July 18, 1990	Treaty Doc. 100-17 Ex. Rpt. 100-3 Ex. Rpt. 101-12
Belgium	Jan. 28, 1988		Treaty Doc. 100-16 Ex. Rpt. 100-29 Ex. Rpt. 101-11
Canada	Mar. 18, 1985	Jan. 24, 1990	Treaty Doc. 100-14 Ex. Rpt. 100-28 Ex. Rpt. 101-10 24 *ILM* 1092
Colombia	Aug. 20, 1980		Treaty Doc. 97-11 Ex. Rpt. 97-35
Italy	Nov. 9, 1982	Nov. 13, 1985	Sen. Ex. 98-25 Ex. Rpt. 98-36
Jamaica	July 7, 1989		Treaty Doc. 102-16 Ex. Rpt. 102-32
Mexico	Dec. 9, 1987	May 3, 1991	Treaty Doc. 100-13 Ex. Rpt. 100-27 Ex. Rpt. 101-9 24 *ILM* 447
Morocco	Oct. 17, 1983		Sen. Ex. 98-24 Ex. Rpt. 98-35
Netherlands	June 12, 1981	Sept. 15, 1983	TIAS 10734 Treaty Doc. 97-16 Ex. Rpt. 97-36
Nigeria	Sept. 13, 1989		Treaty Doc. 102-26
Panama	Apr. 11, 1991		Treaty Doc. 102-15
Spain	Nov. 20, 1990	June 30, 1993	Treaty Doc. 102-21 Ex. Rpt. 102-35
Switzerland	May 25, 1973	Jan. 23, 1977	TIAS 8302 20 UST 2019 Ex. Rpt. 94-29 Ex. Rpt. F (1976)

Appendix E Continued

Country	Signed	Entered into Force	Citations
Thailand	Mar. 19, 1986	June 10, 1993	Treaty Doc. 100-18 Ex. Rpt. 100-31 Ex. Rpt. 101-13
Turkey	June 7, 1979	Jan. 1, 1981	TIAS 9891 Exec. AA (1979)
United Kingdom (Cayman Isl.)	July 3, 1986	Mar. 19, 1990	Treaty Doc. 100-8 Ex. Rpt. 100-26 Ex. Rpt. 101-8 26 *ILM* 536
Uruguay	May 6, 1991		Treaty Doc. 102-16 Ex. Rpt. 102-34

SOURCE: Office of the Legal Adviser, U.S. Department of State.
NOTES: "Sen. Ex." (Senate Executive Print), "Ex. Rpt." (Executive Report), and "Treaty Doc." (Treaty Document) refer to documents published by the U.S. Senate. "TIAS" refers to *Treaties and Other International Acts Series*, issued singly in pamphlets by the Department of State. "UST" refers to *United States Treaties and Other International Agreements*. "*ILM*" refers to *International Legal Materials*.

Appendix F: Countries with Which the United States Has Extradition Treaties in Force (May 1, 1993)

Country	Signed	Entered into Force	Official Citation
Albania	Mar. 1, 1933	Nov. 14, 1935	49 Stat. 3313 TS 902 5 Bevans 22 53166 LNTS 195
Antigua & Barbuda[a]	June 8, 1972	Jan. 21, 1977	28 UST 227 TIAS 8468
Argentina[b]	Jan. 21, 1972	Sept. 15, 1972	23 UST 3501 TIAS 7510
Australia	May 14, 1974	May 8, 1976	27 UST 957 TIAS 8234
Protocol	Sept. 4, 1990	Dec. 21, 1992	Treaty Doc. 101-23 Ex. Rpt. 102-30
Austria	Jan. 31, 1930	Sept. 11, 1930	46 Stat. 2710 TS 822 5 Bevans 358 106 LNTS 379
Suppl.	May 19, 1934	Sept. 5, 1934	49 Stat. 2710 TS 873 5 Bevans 378 153 LNTS 247
Bahamas[c]	Dec. 22, 1931	June 24, 1935	47 Stat. 2122 TS 849 12 Bevans 482 163 LNTS 59
Exch. of Notes	Mar. 7, June 19, Aug. 17, 1978	Aug. 17, 1978	30 UST 187 TIAS 9185 1150 UNTS 99
Barbados[c]	Dec. 22, 1931	June 24, 1935	47 Stat. 2122 TS 849 12 Bevans 482 163 LNTS 59

Appendix F Continued

Country	Signed	Entered into Force	Official Citation
Belgium	Oct. 26, 1901	July 14, 1902	32 Stat. 1894 TS 409 5 Bevans 566 164 LNTS 205
1st Suppl.	June 20, 1935	Nov. 7, 1935	49 Stat. 3276 TS 900 5 Bevans 566 164 LNTS 205
2nd Suppl.	Nov. 14, 1963	Dec. 25, 1964	15 UST 2252 TIAS 5715 522 UNTS 237
Belize[a]	June 8, 1972	Jan. 21, 1977	28 UST 227 TIAS 8468
Bolivia	Apr. 21, 1900	Jan. 22, 1902	32 Stat. 1857 TS 399 5 Bevans 735
Brazil	Jan. 13, 1961	Dec. 17, 1964	15 UST 2093 TIAS 5691 532 UNTS 177
Add. Protocol	June 18, 1962	Dec. 17, 1964	15 UST 2112 TIAS 5691 532 UNTS 198
Bulgaria	Mar. 19, 1924	June 24, 1924	43 Stat. 1886 TS 687 5 Bevans 1086 26 LNTS 27
Suppl.	June 8, 1934	Aug. 15, 1935	49 Stat. 3250 TS 894 5 Bevans 1103 161 LNTS 409
Burma[c]	Dec. 22, 1931	Nov. 1, 1941	47 Stat. 2122 TS 849 5 Bevans 482 163 LNTS 59

Appendix F Continued

Country	Signed	Entered into Force	Official Citation
Canada	Dec. 3, 1971	Mar. 22, 1976	27 UST 983 TIAS 8237
Protocol	Jan. 11, 1988	Nov. 26, 1991	Treaty Doc. 101-17 Ex. Rpt. 102-2 27 *ILM* 422
Exch. of Notes	June 28, 1974 July 9, 1974	Mar. 22, 1976	27 UST 983 TIAS 8273
Chile[b]	Apr. 17, 1900	June 26, 1902	32 Stat. 1850 TS 407 6 Bevans 543
Colombia[b]	Sept. 14, 1979	Mar. 4, 1982	Treaty Doc. 97-8 Ex. Rpt. 97-34
Congo	Jan. 6, 1909	July 27, 1911	37 Stat. 1526 TS 561 7 Bevans 872
1st Suppl.	Jan. 15, 1929	May 19, 1929	46 Stat. 2276 TS 787 7 Bevans 972 92 LNTS 259
2nd Suppl.	Apr. 23, 1936	Sept. 24, 1936	50 Stat. 1117 TS 909 7 Bevans 995 172 LNTS 197
Costa Rica	Dec. 4, 1982	Oct. 11, 1991	Treaty Doc. 98-17 Ex. Rpt. 98-30
Croatia	Oct. 25, 1901	June 12, 1902	32 Stat. 1890 TS 406 12 Bevans 1238
Cuba	Apr. 6, 1904	Mar. 2, 1905	33 Stat. 2265 TS 440 6 Bevans 1128
Add. Protocol	Jan. 14, 1926	June 18, 1926	44 Stat. 2392 TS 737 6 Bevans 1136 61 LNTS 363

Appendix F Continued

Country	Signed	Entered into Force	Official Citation
Cyprus[c]	Dec. 22, 1931	June 24, 1935	47 Stat. 2122 TS 849 12 Bevans 482 163 LNTS 59
Czech Republic	July 2, 1925	March 29, 1926	44 Stat. 2367 TS 734 6 Bevans 1247 50 LNTS 143
Suppl.	Apr. 29, 1935	Aug. 28, 1935	49 Stat. 3253 TS 895 6 Bevans 1283 162 LNTS 83
Denmark	June 22, 1972	July 31, 1974	25 UST 1293 TIAS 7864
Dominica[a]	June 8, 1972	Jan. 21, 1977	28 UST 227 TIAS 8468
Dominican Republic[b]	June 19, 1909	Aug. 2, 1910	36 Stat. 2468 TS 550 7 Bevans 200
Ecuador[b]	June 28, 1872	Nov. 12, 1873	18 Stat. 199 TS 79 7 Bevans 321
Suppl.	Sept. 22, 1939	May 29, 1941	55 Stat. 1196 TS 972 7 Bevans 346
Egypt	Aug. 11, 1874	Apr. 22, 1875	19 Stat. 572 TS 270 10 Bevans 642
El Salvador[b]	Apr. 18, 1911	July 10, 1911	37 Stat. 1516 TS 560 7 Bevans 507
Estonia	Nov. 8, 1923	Nov. 15, 1924	43 Stat. 1849 TS 703 7 Bevans 602 43 LNTS 277

Appendix F Continued

Country	Signed	Entered into Force	Official Citation
Fiji[c]	Dec. 22, 1931	June 24, 1935	47 Stat. 2122 TS 849 12 Bevans 482 163 LNTS 59
Exch. of Notes	July 14, 1972 Aug. 17, 1973	Aug. 17, 1973	24 UST 1965 TIAS 7707
Finland	June 11, 1976	May 11, 1980	31 UST 944 TIAS 9626 1203 UNTS 165
France	Jan. 6, 1909	July 27, 1911	37 Stat. 1526 TS 561 7 Bevans 872
Suppl.	Feb. 12, 1970	Apr. 3, 1971	22 UST 407 TIAS 7075 791 UNTS 273
Gambia[c]	Dec. 22, 1931	June 24, 1935	47 Stat. 2122 TS 849 12 Bevans 482 163 LNTS 59
Germany	June 20, 1978	Aug. 29, 1980	32 UST 1485 TIAS 9785 1220 UNTS 269
Suppl.	Oct. 21, 1986	Mar. 11, 1993	Treaty Doc. 100- Ex. Rpt. 102-28
Ghana[c]	Dec. 22, 1931	June 24, 1935	47 Stat. 2122 TS 849 12 Bevans 482 163 LNTS 59
Greece	May 6, 1931	Nov. 1, 1932	47 Stat. 2185 TS 855 8 Bevans 353 138 LNTS 293
Protocol	Sept. 2, 1937	Sept. 2, 1937	51 Stat. 357 EAS 114 8 Bevans 366 185 LNTS 408

Appendix F Continued

Country	Signed	Entered into Force	Official Citation
Grenada[c]	Dec. 22, 1931	June 24, 1935	47 Stat. 2122 TS 849 12 Bevans 482 163 LNTS 59
Guatamala[b]	Feb. 27, 1903	Aug. 15, 1903	33 Stat. 2147 TS 425 8 Bevans 482
Suppl.	Feb. 20, 1940	Mar. 13, 1941	55 Stat. 1097 TS 963 8 Bevans 528
Guyana[c]	Dec. 22, 1931	June 24, 1935	47 Stat. 2122 TS 849 12 Bevans 482 163 LNTS 59
Haiti	Aug. 9, 1904	June 28, 1905	34 Stat. 2858 TS 447 8 Bevans 653
Honduras[b]	Jan. 15, 1909	July 10, 1912	37 Stat. 1616 TS 569 8 Bevans 892
Suppl.	Feb. 21, 1927	June 5, 1928	45 Stat. 2489 TS 761 8 Bevans 903 85 LNTS 491
Hungary	July 3, 1856	Dec. 13, 1856	11 Stat. 691 TS 9 5 Bevans 211
Iceland	Jan. 6, 1902	Apr. 16, 1902	32 Stat. 1096 TS 405 7 Bevans 38
Suppl.	Nov. 6, 1905	Feb. 19, 1906	34 Stat. 2887 TS 449 7 Bevans 43
India[c]	Dec. 22, 1931	Mar. 9, 1942	47 Stat. 2122 TS 849 12 Bevans 482 163 LNTS 59

Appendix F Continued

Country	Signed	Entered into Force	Official Citation
Iraq	June 7, 1934	Apr. 23, 1936	49 Stat. 3380 TS 907 9 Bevans 1 170 LNTS 267
Ireland	July 13, 1983	Dec. 15, 1984	TIAS 10813
Israel	Dec. 10, 1962	Dec. 5, 1963	14 UST 1707 TIAS 5476 484 UNTS 283
Exch. of Notes	Apr. 4 & 11, 1967		18 UST 382 TIAS 6246
Italy	Oct. 13, 1983	Sept. 24, 1984	TIAS 10837
Jamaica	June 14, 1983	July 7, 1991	Treaty Doc. 98-18 Ex. Rpt. 98-31
Japan	Mar. 3, 1978	Mar. 26, 1980	31 UST 892 TIAS 9625 1203 UNTS 225
Kenya[c]	Dec. 22, 1931	June 24, 1935	47 Stat. 2122 TS 849 12 Bevans 482 163 LNTS 59
Exch. of Notes	May 14, 1965 Aug. 19, 1965	Aug. 19, 1965	16 UST 1866 TIAS 5916 574 UNTS 153
Kiribati[a]	June 8, 1972	Jan. 21, 1977	28 UST 227 TIAS 8468
Latvia	Oct. 16, 1923	Mar. 1, 1924	43 Stat. 1738 TS 677 9 Bevans 515 27 LNTS 371
Suppl.	Oct. 10, 1934	Mar. 29, 1935	49 Stat. 3131 TS 884 9 Bevans 554 158 LNTS 263

Appendix F Continued

Country	Signed	Entered into Force	Official Citation
Lesotho[c]	Dec. 22, 1931	June 24, 1935	47 Stat. 2122 TS 849 12 Bevans 482 163 LNTS 59
Liberia	Nov. 1, 1937	Nov. 21, 1939	54 Stat. 1733 TS 955 9 Bevans 589 201 LNTS 151
Liechtenstein	May 20, 1936	June 28, 1937	50 Stat. 1337 TS 915 9 Bevans 683 157 LNTS 491
Lithuania	April 9, 1924	Aug. 23, 1924	43 Stat. 1835 TS 699 9 Bevans 655 51 LNTS 191
Luxembourg	Oct. 29, 1883	Aug. 13, 1884	23 Stat. 808 TS 196 9 Bevans 694
Suppl.	Apr. 24, 1935	Mar. 3, 1936	49 Stat. 3355 TS 904 9 Bevans 707 168 LNTS 129
Macedonia	Oct. 25, 1901	June 12, 1902	32 Stat. 1890 TS 406 12 Bevans 1238
Malawi[c]	Dec. 22, 1931	June 24, 1925	47 Stat. 2122 TS 849 12 Bevans 482 163 LNTS 59
Exch. of Notes	Dec. 17, 1966 Jan. 6, 1967 April 4, 1967	April 4, 1967	18 UST 1822 TIAS 6328 692 UNTS 191
Malaysia[c]	Dec. 22, 1931	July 31, 1939	47 Stat. 2122 TS 849 12 Bevans 482 163 LNTS 59

Appendix F Continued

Country	Signed	Entered into Force	Official Citation
Malta[c]	Dec. 22, 1931	June 24, 1935	47 Stat. 2122 TS 849 12 Bevans 482 163 LNTS 59
Mauritius[c]	Dec. 22, 1931	June 24, 1935	47 Stat. 2122 TS 849 12 Bevans 482 163 LNTS 59
Mexico[b]	May 4, 1978	Jan. 25, 1980	31 UST 5059 TIAS 9656
Monaco	Feb. 15, 1939	Mar. 28, 1940	54 Stat. 1780 TS 959 9 Bevans 1272 202 LNTS 61
Nauru[c]	Dec. 22, 1931	Aug. 30, 1935	47 Stat. 2122 TS 849 12 Bevans 482 163 LNTS 59
Netherlands[d]	June 24, 1980	Sept. 15, 1983	TIAS 10733
New Zealand	Jan. 12, 1970	Dec. 8, 1970	22 UST 1 TIAS 7035 791 UNTS 253
Nicaragua[b]	Mar. 1, 1905	July 14, 1907	35 Stat. 1869 TS 462 10 Bevans 356
Nigeria[c]	Dec. 22, 1931	June 24, 1935	47 Stat. 2122 TS 849 12 Bevans 482 163 LNTS 59
Norway	June 9, 1977	Mar. 7, 1980	31 UST 5619 TIAS 9679 1220 UNTS 221
Pakistan[c]	Dec. 22, 1931	Mar. 9, 1942	47 Stat. 2122 TS 849 12 Bevans 482 163 LNTS 59

Appendix F Continued

Country	Signed	Entered into Force	Official Citation
Panama[b]	May 25, 1904	May 8, 1905	34 Stat. 2851 TS 849 10 Bevans 673
Papua New Guinea[c]	Dec. 22, 1931	Aug. 30, 1935	47 Stat. 2122 TS 849 12 Bevans 482 163 LNTS 59
Paraguay	May 24, 1973	May 7, 1974	25 UST 967 TIAS 7838
Peru	Nov. 28, 1899	Feb. 22, 1901	31 Stat. 1921 TS 288 10 Bevans 1074
Poland	Nov. 22, 1927	July, 1929	46 Stat. 2282 TS 789 11 Bevans 206 92 LNTS 101
Suppl.	Apr. 5, 1935	June 5, 1936	49 Stat. 3394 TS 789 11 Bevans 265 170 LNTS 287
Portugal	May 7, 1908	Nov. 14, 1908	35 Stat. 2071 TS 512 11 Bevans 314
Romania	July 23, 1924	Apr. 7, 1925	44 Stat. 2020 TS 713 11 Bevans 391
Suppl.	Nov. 10, 1936	July 27, 1937	50 Stat. 1349 TS 916 11 Bevans 423 181 LNTS 177
Saint Kitts & Nevis[a]	June 8, 1972	Jan. 21, 1977	28 UST 227 TIAS 8468
St. Lucia[a]	June 8, 1972	Jan. 21, 1977	28 UST 227 TIAS 8468
St. Vincent & the Grenadines[a]	June 8, 1972	Jan. 21, 1977	28 UST 227 TIAS 8468

Appendix F Continued

Country	Signed	Entered into Force	Official Citation
San Marino	Jan. 10, 1906	July 8, 1908	35 Stat. 1971 TS 495 11 Bevans 440
Suppl.	Oct. 10, 1934	June 28, 1935	49 Stat. 3198 TS 891 11 Bevans 446 161 LNTS 149
Seychelles[c]	Dec. 22, 1931	June 24, 1935	47 Stat. 2122 TS 849 12 Bevans 482 163 LNTS 59
Sierra Leone[c]	Dec. 22, 1931	June 24, 1935	47 Stat. 2122 TS 849 12 Bevans 482 163 LNTS 59
Singapore[c]	Dec. 22, 1931	June 24, 1935	47 Stat. 2122 TS 849 12 Bevans 482 163 LNTS 59
Exch. of Notes	Apr. 23, 1969 June 10, 1969	June 10, 1969	20 UST 2764 TIAS 6744 723 UNTS 201
Slovak Republic	July 2, 1925	Mar. 29, 1926	44 Stat. 2367 TS 734 6 Bevans 1247 50 LNTS 143
Suppl.	Apr. 29, 1935	Aug. 28, 1935	49 Stat. 3253 TS 895 6 Bevans 1283 162 LNTS 83
Slovenia	Oct. 25, 1901	June 12, 1902	32 Stat. 1890 TS 406 12 Bevans 1238
Solomon Islands[a]	June 8, 1972	Jan. 21, 1977	28 UST 277 TIAS 8468
South Africa	Dec. 18, 1947	Apr. 30, 1951	2 UST 884 TIAS 2243 148 UNTS 85

Appendix F Continued

Country	Signed	Entered into Force	Official Citation
Spain	May 29, 1970	June 16, 1971	22 UST 737 TIAS 7136 796 UNTS 245
Suppl.	Jan. 25, 1975	June 2, 1978	29 UST 2283 TIAS 8938
2nd Suppl.	Feb. 9, 1988	July 2, 1993	Treaty Doc. 102-24 Ex. Rpt. 102-31
Sri Lanka[c]	Dec. 22, 1931	June 24, 1935	47 Stat. 2122 TS 849 12 Bevans 482 163 LNTS 59
Surinam	June 2, 1887	July 11, 1889	26 Stat. 1481 TS 256 10 Bevans 47
Extension	Jan. 18, 1904	Aug. 28, 1904	33 Stat. 2257 TS 436 10 Bevans 53
Swaziland[c]	Dec. 22, 1931	June 24, 1935	47 Stat. 2122 TS 849 12 Bevans 482 163 LNTS 59
Exch. of Notes	May 13, 1970 July 28, 1970	July 28, 1970	21 UST 1930 TIAS 6934 756 UNTS 103
Sweden	Oct. 24, 1961	Dec. 3, 1963	14 UST 1845 TIAS 5496 494 UNTS 141
Suppl.	Mar. 14, 1983	Sept. 24, 1984	TIAS 10812
Switzerland	May 14, 1900	Mar. 29, 1901	31 Stat. 1928 TS 354 11 Bevans 904
1st Suppl.	Jan. 10, 1935	May 16, 1935	49 Stat. 3192 TS 889 11 Bevans 924 159 LNTS 243
2nd Suppl.	Jan. 31, 1940	Apr. 8, 1941	55 Stat. 1140 TS 969 11 Bevans 938

Appendix F Continued

Country	Signed	Entered into Force	Official Citation
Tanzania[c]	Dec. 22, 1931	June 24, 1935	47 Stat. 2122 TS 969 12 Bevans 482 163 LNTS 59
Exch. of Notes	Nov. 30, 1965 Dec. 6, 1965	Dec. 6, 1965	16 UST 2066 TIAS 5946
Thailand	Dec. 14, 1983	May 17, 1991	Treaty Doc. 98-16 Ex. Rpt. 98-29
Tonga[c]	Dec. 22, 1931	June 24, 1935	47 Stat. 2122 TS 849 12 Bevans 482 163 LNTS 59
Exch. of Notes	Mar. 14, 1977 Apr. 13, 1977	Apr. 13, 1977	28 UST 5290 TIAS 8628 1087 UNTS 289
Trinidad & Tobago[c]	Dec. 22, 1931	June 24, 1935	47 Stat. 2122 TS 849 12 Bevans 482 163 LNTS 59
Turkey	June 7, 1979	Jan. 1, 1981	32 UST 3111 TIAS 9891
Tuvalu[a]	June 8, 1972	Jan. 21, 1977	28 UST 227 TIAS 8468
United Kingdom[a]	June 8, 1972	Jan. 21, 1977	28 UST 227 TIAS 8468 1049 UNTS 167
Suppl.	June 25, 1985	Dec. 23, 1986	Treaty Doc. 99-8 Ex. Rpt. 99-17
Uruguay	Apr. 6, 1973	Apr. 11, 1984	TIAS 10850
Venezuela	Jan. 19 & 21, 1922	Apr. 14, 1923	43 Stat. 1698 T.S. 675 12 Bevans 1128 49 LNTS 435
Yugoslavia	Oct. 25, 1901	June 12, 1902	32 Stat. 1890 T.S. 406 12 Bevans 1238

Appendix F Continued

Country	Signed	Entered into Force	Official Citation
Zambia[c]	Dec. 22, 1931	June 24, 1935	47 Stat. 2122 T.S. 849 12 Bevans 482 163 LNTS 59

SOURCE: U.S. Department of State, *Treaties in Force* (Washington, D.C.: Government Printing Office, 1992); Michael Abbell and Bruno A. Ristau, *International Judicial Assistance* (Washington, D.C.: International Law Institute, 1990), vol. 5, appendix A-135 to A-145; Office of the Legal Adviser, U.S. Department of State.

NOTES: "Ex. Rpt." (Executive Report) and "Treaty Doc." (Treaty Document) refer to documents published by the U.S. Senate. "TIAS" refers to *Treaties and Other International Acts Series*, issued singly in pamphlets by the Department of State. "UST" refers to *United States Treaties and Other International Agreements*. "*ILM*" refers to *International Legal Materials*. Other abbreviations used are as follows: "Stat." = United States Statutes at Large; "TS" = Treaty Series, issued singly in pamphlets by the Department of State (until replaced in 1945 by the TIAS); "EAS" = Executive Agreement Series, issued singly in pamphlets by the Department of State (until replaced in 1945 by the TIAS); "Bevans" = Treaties and Other International Agreements of the United States of America 1776–1949, compiled under the direction of Charles I. Bevans; "LNTS" = League of Nations Treaty Series; "UNTS" = United Nations Treaty Series.

[a]Extradition relations governed by 1972 Treaty with United Kingdom (28 UST 277; TIAS 8468).

[b]Also a signitory of the multilateral 1933 Convention on Extradition adopted by the Seventh International Conference of American States (the Montevideo Extradition Treaty), signed Dec. 26, 1933, entered into force Jan. 25, 1935. 49 Stat. 3111; TS 882; 3 Bevans 152; 165 LNTS 45.

[c]Extradition relations governed by 1931 Treaty with United Kingdom (47 Stat. 2122; TS 849).

[d]Applicable to Aruba and the Netherland Antilles.

[e]Applicable to all U.K. territories, Channel Isl., Isle of Man, Bermuda, British Indian Ocean Territory, British Virgin Isl., Cayman Isl., Falkland Isl. and dependencies, Gibraltar, Hong Kong, Montserrat, Pitcairn, Henderson, Ducie and Oeno Isl., Anguilla, St. Helena and dependencies, Sovereign Base Areas of Akrotiri and Dhekelia in the Island of Cyprus, and Turks and Caicos Isl.

Index